Lecture Notes in Computer Science 13178

More information about this subseries at https://link.springer.com/bookseries/7410

Goichiro Hanaoka · Junji Shikata ·
Yohei Watanabe (Eds.)

Public-Key Cryptography – PKC 2022

25th IACR International Conference
on Practice and Theory of Public-Key Cryptography
Virtual Event, March 8–11, 2022
Proceedings, Part II

Springer

Editors
Goichiro Hanaoka
National Institute of Advanced Industrial Science and Technology (AIST)
Tokyo, Japan

Junji Shikata
Yokohama National University
Yokohama, Japan

Yohei Watanabe
The University of Electro-Communications
Tokyo, Japan

ISSN 0302-9743 ISSN 1611-3349 (electronic)
Lecture Notes in Computer Science
ISBN 978-3-030-97130-4 ISBN 978-3-030-97131-1 (eBook)
https://doi.org/10.1007/978-3-030-97131-1

LNCS Sublibrary: SL4 – Security and Cryptology

This Springer imprint is published by the registered company Springer Nature Switzerland AG
The registered company address is: Gewerbestrasse 11, 6330 Cham, Switzerland

Preface

The 25th IACR International Conference on Practice and Theory of Public-Key Cryptography (PKC 2022) was held virtually during March 8–11, 2022. (Initially, the conference was scheduled to be held in Yokohama, Japan, but unfortunately, due to the prolonged global outbreak of COVID-19, it was finally decided to hold the conference virtually.) This conference is organized annually by the International Association of Cryptologic Research (IACR), and is the main IACR-sponsored conference with an explicit focus on public-key cryptography. The proceedings are comprised of two volumes and include the 39 papers that were selected by the Program Committee. (Initially, 40 papers were accepted, but one of them was later withdrawn by the authors.)

A total of 137 submissions were received for consideration for this year's program. Submissions were assigned to at least three reviewers, while submissions by Program Committee members received at least five reviews. The review period was divided into two stage. The first stage was reserved for individual reviewing and lasted four weeks. It was followed by the second stage, which lasted about five weeks, in which the Program Committee members engaged in discussion. On a number of occasions, authors were contacted regarding reviewer questions and provided clarifications. One of the papers was conditionally accepted and received a final additional round of reviewing. The reviewing and paper selection process was a difficult task and I am deeply grateful to the members of the Program Committee for their hard and thorough work. Additionally, my deep gratitude is extended to the 145 external reviewers who assisted the Program Committee. PKC 2022 was the first PKC to use HotCRP in the peer review process. I would like to express my sincere thanks to Kevin McCurley for his support in using HotCRP.

Two invited talks were given at PKC 2022. The first invited talk, entitled "The First 25 Years of the PKC Annual Conference", was delivered by Yuliang Zheng, who is the chair of the PKC steering committee. Since PKC 2022 was the 25th PKC, this invited talk was a review of the history of the past quarter century. The second invited talk, entitled "The Beginning of the End: The First NIST PQC Standards", was delivered by Dustin Moody. In this invited talk, he presented the latest status of NIST Post-Quantum Cryptography Standardization. I would like to express my deepest gratitude to both invited speakers for accepting the invitation and contributing to the program this year as well as all the authors who submitted their work. I would like to also thank co-editors of these two volumes, Junji Shikata and Yohei Watanabe, who served as general co-chairs this year. I would also like to express my appreciation to the PKC 2022 local organizing committee members (Keita Emura, Ryuya Hayashi, Takahiro Matsuda, Takayuki Nagane, Yusuke Naito, Kazumasa Shinagawa, Jacob Schuldt, Naoto Yanai, and Kazuki Yoneyama) for their dedication and cooperation. Finally, I am deeply grateful to our industry sponsors, listed on the conference's website, who provided generous financial support.

March 2022 Goichiro Hanaoka

Organization

General Chair

Junji Shikata	Yokohama National University, Japan
Yohei Watanabe	University of Electro-Communications, Japan

Program Committee Chair

Goichiro Hanaoka	AIST, Japan

Steering Committee

Masayuki Abe	NTT, Japan
Jung Hee Cheon	Seoul National University, South Korea
Yvo Desmedt	University of Texas at Dallas, USA
Juan Garay	Texas A&M University, USA
Goichiro Hanaoka	AIST, Japan
Aggelos Kiayias	University of Edinburgh, UK
Tanja Lange	Eindhoven University of Technology, Netherlands
David Pointcheval	ENS, France
Moti Yung	Google and Columbia University, USA
Yuliang Zheng (Chair)	University of Alabama at Birmingham, USA

Program Committee

Prabhanjan Ananth	University of California, Santa Barbara, USA
Daniel Apon	NIST, USA
Christian Badertscher	IOHK, Switzerland
Manuel Barbosa	University of Porto and INESC TEC, Portugal
Carsten Baum	Aarhus University, Denmark
Jonathan Bootle	IBM Research Zurich, Switzerland
Chris Brzuska	Aalto University, Finland
Liqun Chen	University of Surrey, UK
Ilaria Chillotti	ZAMA, France
Craig Costello	Microsoft Research, USA
Geoffroy Couteau	Paris Diderot University, France
Bernardo David	IT University of Copenhagen, Denmark
Nico Döttling	CISPA, Germany

Thomas Espitau	NTT, Japan
Sebastian Faust	TU Darmstadt, Germany
Dario Fiore	IMDEA Software Institute, Spain
Pierre-Alain Fouque	ENS, France
Pierrick Gaudry	CNRS, Nancy, France
Junqing Gong	East China Normal University, China
Rishab Goyal	MIT, USA
Goichiro Hanaoka	AIST, Japan
Shuichi Katsumata	AIST, Japan
Elena Kirshanova	Immanuel Kant Baltic Federal University, Russia, and Ruhr-Universität Bochum, Germany
Fuyuki Kitagawa	NTT, Japan
Ilan Komargodski	Hebrew University of Jerusalem, Israel, and NTT Research, USA
Tanja Lange	Technische Universiteit Eindhoven, The Netherlands
Changmin Lee	KIAS, South Korea
Benoit Libert	CNRS and ENS de Lyon, France
Feng-Hao Liu	Florida Atlantic University, USA
Giulio Malavolta	Max Planck Institute for Security and Privacy, Germany
Alexander May	Ruhr-Universität Bochum, Germany
Jiaxin Pan	NTNU, Norway
Alice Pellet-Mary	CNRS and University of Bordeaux, France
Christophe Petit	Université libre de Bruxelles, Belgium
Bertram Poettering	IBM Research Zurich, Switzerland
Jacob Schuldt	AIST, Japan
Luisa Siniscalchi	Aarhus University, Denmark
Yongsoo Song	Seoul National University, South Korea
Akshayaram Srinivasan	Tata Institute of Fundamental Research, India
Igors Stepanovs	ETH Zürich, Switzerland
Atsushi Takayasu	University of Tokyo, Japan
Qiang Tang	University of Sydney, Australia
Serge Vaudenay	EPFL, Switzerland
Benjamin Wesolowski	Institut de Mathématiques de Bordeaux, France
David Wu	University of Texas at Austin, USA
Keita Xagawa	NTT, Japan
Bo-Yin Yang	Academia Sinica, Taiwan
Yu Yu	Shanghai Jiao Tong University, China
Mark Zhandry	Princeton University and NTT Research, USA

Additional Reviewers

Nuttapong Attrapadung
Subhadeep Banik
Razvan Barbulescu
James Bartusek
Andrea Basso
Balthazar Bauer
Daniel J. Bernstein
Pedro Branco
Yanlin Chen
Arka Rai Choudhuri
Sherman S. M. Chow
Daniel Collins
Sandro Coretti
Maria Corte-Real Santos
Ben Curtis
Jan Czajkowski
Poulami Das
Thomas Decru
Rafael Del Pino
Amit Deo
Jelle Don
Jesko Dujmovic
Julien Duman
Reo Eriguchi
Andreas Erwig
Daniel Escudero
Andre Esser
Hanwen Feng
Matthias Fitzi
Cody Freitag
Hiroki Furue
Rachit Garg
Romain Gay
Nicholas Genise
Lorenzo Gentile
Satrajit Ghosh
Aarushi Goel
Aditya Gulati
Keisuke Hara
Dominik Hartmann
Keitaro Hashimoto
Kathrin Hoevelmanns
Loïs Hughenin-Dumittan
Yasuhiko Ikematsu
Ilia Iliashenko
Ryoma Ito
Joseph Jaeger
Aayush Jain
Sam Jaques
Yao Jiang
Fatih Kaleoglu
Harish Karthikeyan
Hamidreza Khoshakhlagh
Jiseung Kim
Duhyeong Kim
Susumu Kiyoshima
Dimitris Kolonelos
Yashvanth Kondi
Anders Konring
David Kretzler
Mikhail Kudinov
Sabrina Kunzweiler
Péter Kutas
Qiqi Lai
Changmin Lee
Jiangtao Li
Yanan Li
Xiao Liang
Mingyu Liang
Jacob Lichtinger
Damien Ligier
Xiangyu Liu
Jiahui Liu
Zhen Liu
Patrick Longa
George Lu
Yuan Lu
Ji Luo
Lin Lyu
Monosij Maitra
Takahiro Matsuda
Pierre Meyer
Carl Miller
Niklas Miller
Hart Montgomery
Pedro Moreno-Sánchez

Fabrice Mouhartem
Alexander Munch-Hansen
Michael Naehrig
Ryo Nishimaki
Anca Nitulescu
Semyon Novoselov
Julian Nowakowski
Kazuma Ohara
Jean-Baptiste Orfila
Maximilian Orlt
Pascal Paillier
Lorenz Panny
Alain Passelègue
Ray Perlner
Thomas Peters
Sihang Pu
Chen Qian
Tian Qiu
Willy Quach
Anais Querol
Divya Ravi
Michael Reichle
Siavash Riahi
Angela Robinson
Yusuke Sakai
Shingo Sato
Lars Schlieper
Yu-Ching Shen
Sina Shiehian
Tjerand Silde
Daniel Slamanig
Daniel Smith-Tone
Yongha Son
Fang Song
Nick Spooner
Shifeng Sun
Abdullah Talayhan
Bénédikt Tran
Ida Tucker
Bogdan Ursu
Prashant Vasudevan
Michael Walter
Yuyu Wang
Han Wang
Zhedong Wang
Florian Weber
Charlotte Weitkaemper
Yunhua Wen
Stella Wohning
David Wu
Shota Yamada
Takashi Yamakawa
Yusuke Yoshida
Greg Zaverucha
Runzhi Zeng
Xiao Zhang
Yongjun Zhao

Contents – Part II

Contents – Part I

Cryptanalysis

MPC and Secret Sharing

Cryptographic Protocols

Tools

SNARKs and NIZKs

Key Exchange

Post-quantum Asynchronous Deniable Key Exchange and the Signal Handshake

Jacqueline Brendel[1(✉)], Rune Fiedler[1], Felix Günther[2], Christian Janson[1], and Douglas Stebila[3]

[1] Technische Universität Darmstadt, Darmstadt, Germany
{jacqueline.brendel,rune.fiedler,christian.janson}@cryptoplexity.de, mail@felixguenther.info
[2] ETH Zürich, Zurich, Switzerland
[3] University of Waterloo, Waterloo, Canada
dstebila@uwaterloo.ca

Abstract. The key exchange protocol that establishes initial shared secrets in the handshake of the Signal end-to-end encrypted messaging protocol has several important characteristics: (1) it runs asynchronously (without both parties needing to be simultaneously online), (2) it provides implicit mutual authentication while retaining deniability (transcripts cannot be used to prove either party participated in the protocol), and (3) it retains security even if some keys are compromised (forward secrecy and beyond). All of these properties emerge from clever use of the highly flexible Diffie–Hellman protocol.

While quantum-resistant key encapsulation mechanisms (KEMs) can replace Diffie–Hellman key exchange in some settings, there is no replacement for the Signal handshake solely from KEMs that achieves all three aforementioned properties, in part due to the inherent asymmetry of KEM operations. In this paper, we show how to construct asynchronous deniable key exchange by combining KEMs and designated verifier signature (DVS) schemes, matching the characteristics of Signal. There are several candidates for post-quantum DVS schemes, either direct constructions or via ring signatures. This yields a template for an efficient post-quantum realization of the Signal handshake with the same asynchronicity and security properties as the original Signal protocol.

Keywords: Authenticated key exchange · Deniability · Asynchronous · Signal protocol · Post-quantum · Designated verifier signatures

1 Introduction

The Signal protocol [66,67], designed by Marlinspike and Perrin, has enabled mass adoption of end-to-end encrypted messaging in consumer applications such as WhatsApp, Signal, Facebook Messenger, Skype, and more. From a cryptographic perspective, the Signal protocol consists of an initial handshake and key

G. Hanaoka et al. (Eds.): PKC 2022, LNCS 13178, pp. 3–34, 2022.
https://doi.org/10.1007/978-3-030-97131-1_1

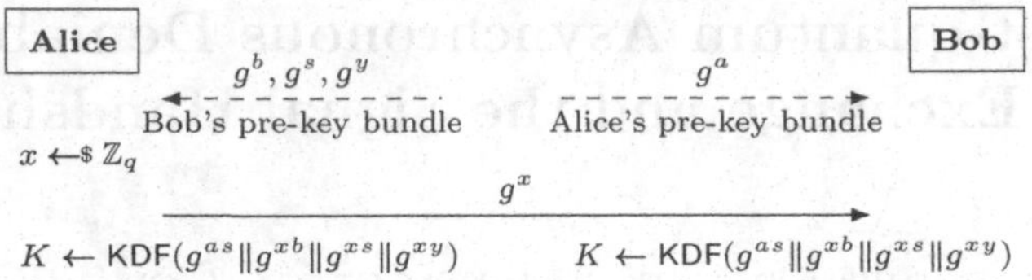

Fig. 1. Simplified version of Signal's X3DH handshake. Long-term keys a and b; semi-static key s; ephemeral keys x and y.

exchange (called "X3DH" [67], a simplified version of which is shown in Fig. 1), asymmetric and symmetric key exchange "ratchets" that establish new keys for every new chat message sent (called the "double ratchet" algorithm [66]), and symmetric authenticated encryption for application data. Each of these components contributes to Signal's interesting and useful security features:

- *Implicit mutual authentication in the handshake*: The session key K established in the handshake can only be computed by the intended peer. This comes from the terms involving the long-term secret keys a and b in Fig. 1.
- *Forward secrecy in the handshake*: The session key K established in the handshake remains secret even if long-term keys are later compromised. This comes from the terms involving the ephemeral keys x and y in Fig. 1.
- *Offline deniability of the handshake*: A judge seeing a transcript of an honest communication session cannot be convinced that a particular party was actually involved in the session. This comes from the use of Diffie–Hellman for authentication rather than signatures; all of the DH shared secrets input to the key derivation function in Fig. 1 could have been computed unilaterally either by Alice or by Bob (e.g., both Alice and Bob can compute g^{as}, using a and s respectively). We provide a new formalization of deniability reflecting the specification of Signal more closely. We discuss the differences between the deniability notions in Sect. 3 and in more detail in the full version. While a formal proof that X3DH fulfills our new notion is not known to the authors, we expect it to hold without any additional assumptions. See [81] for a detailed analysis of the deniability of X3DH with respect to the deniability notion of [29].
- *Asynchronicity*: The two communicating parties need never be online simultaneously, and can leave packets at an untrusted relay server until the other party comes back online. The handshake is made asynchronous by allowing each party to upload a *pre-key bundle* to an untrusted server in advance, consisting of long-term, medium-term, and ephemeral public keys, and an initiator can start sending text messages before their peer comes online. The restrictions on communication flow in an asynchronous protocol are weaker than those of non-interactive key exchange [41].
- *Forward secrecy and post-compromise security* [22] *in long-lived conversations*: Keys are updated using a new DH key exchange with each chat message via the asymmetric ratchet, enabling secrecy of past and future messages after a compromise.

1.1 Making Signal Post-quantum

Since the Diffie–Hellman problem upon which much of Signal relies is not secure against quantum adversaries, it is important to have a post-quantum alternative available.

The symmetric ratchet and authenticated encryption components of Signal are built on symmetric primitives, and thus are not in immediate danger from quantum algorithms. The asymmetric ratchet was phrased by Marlinspike and Perrin [66] and analyzed by Cohn-Gordon, Cremers, Dowling, Garratt, and Stebila [21] in terms of Diffie–Hellman. Alwen, Coretti, and Dodis [1] generalized it into a primitive called continuous key agreement that can be built from KEMs, yielding post-quantum security. Hence, our focus in the rest of this paper is on the handshake.

The post-quantum primitives to be standardized by the United States National Institute of Standards and Technology (NIST) post-quantum standardization project are signatures and key encapsulation mechanisms (KEMs), so these would be most preferable to employ. It is certainly possible to generically construct an authenticated key exchange protocol from signatures and KEMs, but it is not possible to use *only* KEMs and signatures in a generic way to create a post-quantum replacement for Signal with all of the properties listed above. Suppose one tried to use KEMs instead of Diffie–Hellman in Fig. 1. Recall that, to use a KEM for key exchange, one party uses the key generation algorithm to create a public-key/secret-key pair and transmits the public key to their peer; the peer encapsulates against that public key, producing a ciphertext and a shared secret, then transmits the ciphertext, which the first party decapsulates using their secret key to compute the shared secret. In the Signal handshake, one could try using KEM public keys to replace the Diffie–Hellman shares in Alice and Bob's pre-key bundles. We can still obtain ephemeral key exchange (by having Alice encapsulate against Bob's ephemeral public key) and implicit Bob-to-Alice authentication (by having Alice encapsulate against Bob's long-term public key). However, we cannot obtain Alice-to-Bob authentication using KEMs without adding an extra flow: Bob cannot produce a ciphertext for Alice to decapsulate without knowing Alice's public key first, so he cannot asynchronously produce a pre-key bundle for Alice to immediately use. This highlights the difference between DH and KEMs: in DH, both parties' shares are objects of the same type and can be generated independently, but in generic KEMs, public keys and ciphertexts are in principle objects of differing types and a ciphertext is generated with respect to a given public key. To obtain Alice-to-Bob authentication without adding an extra communication round, Alice could of course produce a signature for Bob to verify, but this undermines deniability.

The problem, in a nutshell, is to create an *asynchronous deniable authenticated key exchange protocol* that can be instantiated in the post-quantum setting, preferably with an efficient construction based on standardized primitives or at least cryptographic assumptions used in standardized primitives.

1.2 Options for PQ Asynchronous DAKE

There are several examples of authenticated key exchange protocols built generically from KEMs which have the potential for deniability [11,12,27,42,75] but do not have the desired asynchronicity property for reasons similar to the discussion above.

One post-quantum option that avoids the problem with KEMs described above is to use CSIDH [20], a primitive based on supersingular isogenies that yields a commutative group action which enables non-interactive key exchange. CSIDH could be used to achieve implicit Alice-to-Bob authentication while maintaining asynchronicity and deniability; indeed several key exchange protocols from CSIDH have been proposed [26,52]. Unfortunately, there are several reasons CSIDH may not be a fully satisfactory solution: it is much more computationally expensive than most other forms of post-quantum cryptography, and there is ongoing debate about the security of its concrete parameters [10,69].

Most other post-quantum assumptions used in KEMs, including SIDH [50] and learning-with-errors (LWE) [72], are insecure against key reuse attacks without additional protection such as the Fujisaki–Okamoto transform [43] that leaves them unable to be used for non-interactive key exchange (since the ciphertext must be generated with respect to a given public key). There have been several attempts at SIDH-based non-interactive key exchange which have ended up being insecure [2,31,32,36], and one attempt relying on an additional novel assumption [9] the security of which is unknown.

Brendel, Fischlin, Günther, Janson, and Stebila [15] previously considered the question of building a post-quantum version of the Signal handshake, highlighting many of these problems. They proposed decomposing the three operations of a KEM into a 4-operation "split KEM", and showed how a Signal-like handshake could be built from a split KEM meeting a suitably strong security notion. They showed how CSIDH and LWE could be used to build split KEMs meeting a weaker security notion, but these constructions did not achieve the strong security notion required for their Signal-like handshake, effectively leaving the overall problem unsolved.

Unger and Goldberg [79,80] also consider deniable authenticated key exchange (DAKE) protocols for secure messaging. Their protocol permits the optional use of a PQ KEM for ephemeral key exchange to achieve forward secrecy against future-quantum adversaries. To achieve deniability, they employ ring signatures with classical security and further rely on dual receiver encryption, which does not yet appear to have a PQ instantiation in the literature. Observe that their formalization of deniability is given in the UC model.

The recent work by Hashimoto, Katsumata, Kwiatkowski, and Prest [46] is closest to ours. Their core protocol is meant to replace the Signal handshake based on (post-quantum) KEMs and signatures. It achieves security against exposure of long-term keys and session state and a weaker deniability level. Unlike Signal (and our proposed protocol), it does however not provide security against randomness exposure and lacks support for semi-static keys to mitigate the exhaustion of ephemeral pre-keys. Hashimoto et al. provide an imple-

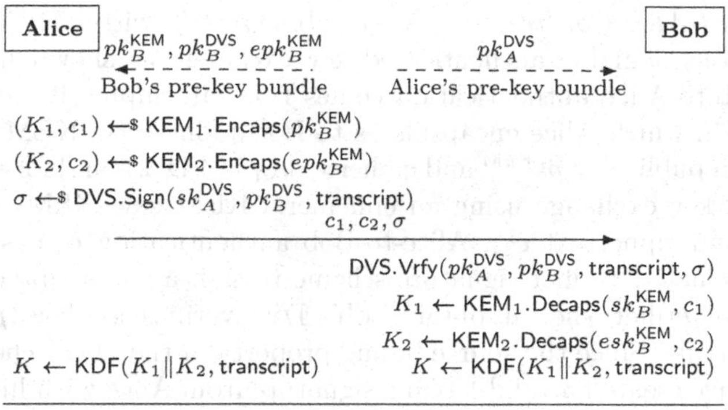

Fig. 2. Our core asynchronous asynchronous DAKE protocol, combining static and ephemeral key encapsulation schemes KEM_1 and KEM_2, and a designated verifier signature DVS.

mentation for their weakly-deniable protocol and further discuss two additional variants achieving stronger deniability. The second protocol achieves deniability against semi-honest adversaries based on ring signatures, while their third protocol additionally uses non-interactive zero-knowledge arguments and strong knowledge-type assumptions for plaintext-aware [4] KEMs to achieve deniability against malicious adversaries.

Dobson and Galbraith [30] recently proposed using SIDH key exchange to replace the DH key exchange in the (slightly modified) X3DH protocol. Even though SIDH is in general insecure against adaptive attacks, Dobson and Galbraith show that carefully adding a zero-knowledge proof enables them to prove that the long-term SIDH public keys are generated honestly. In order to prove deniability, they require strong knowledge-type assumptions following [81].

1.3 Our Contributions

We show how to construct an asynchronous deniable authenticated key exchange protocol generically from designated verifier signature schemes and key encapsulation mechanisms.

Introduced by Jakobsson, Sako, and Impagliazzo [49], a *designated verifier signature (DVS) scheme* allows a signer to convince a chosen recipient, called the designated verifier, of the authenticity of a message, but in such a way that the designated verifier cannot convince any other party of the authenticity. In a DVS scheme, both the signer and the verifier have a public-key/secret-key pair; signing requires both the signer's secret key and the verifier's public key, and verification uses both parties' public keys. To achieve the non-transferability property (called "source hiding"), a DVS scheme is accompanied by an additional simulation algorithm with which the designated verifier can, using its own secret key, construct a signature indistinguishable from one generated by the signer.

Asynchronous DAKE Construction. We combine a DVS with a KEM to achieve an asynchronous deniable authenticated key exchange as shown in Fig. 2. As expected, Bob-to-Alice authentication comes from an implicitly authenticated key exchange in which Alice encapsulates to Bob's long-term KEM key (KEM_1 with long-term public key pk_B^{KEM} and ciphertext c_1 in Fig. 2), and forward secrecy comes from a key exchange using an ephemeral KEM key (KEM_2 with public key epk_B^{KEM} and ciphertext c_2). Alice-to-Bob authentication comes from Alice using the designated verifier signature scheme to sign a transcript with Bob as the designated verifier; she can obtain Bob's DVS verification key (pk_B^{DVS}) from his pre-key bundle. Since the source hiding property of the DVS scheme enables Bob to also have created a valid-looking signature from Alice with himself as the designated verifier, the transcript of the key exchange protocol could have been constructed by either Alice or Bob, yielding the desired deniability property.

Deniability. We model the informal deniability requirement from the Signal specification [67, §4.4] through a new deniability notion (for asynchronous DAKE) capturing the following scenario: Alice wants to convince a judge that a certain conversation took place between her and Bob. Hence, Alice gives the corresponding transcript to the judge. The judge may coerce Alice and Bob to give up their secret keys (e.g., by law). Under these circumstances, the judge should not be able to tell if this transcript stems from a real conversation or if Alice faked the transcript on her own without Bob's interaction. On the one hand, our new notion is weaker than the definition of [29] in the sense that we limit Alice to stick to the protocol description (i.e., be semi-honest) and allow the use of a secret key for faking a transcript. On the other hand, our new notion is stronger in the sense that we allow the judge to know *all* secret keys. On a more technical note, we provide a game-based definition while [29] uses the simulation paradigm. In a nutshell, a strength of our notion is that it provides deniability against powerful judges that can compromise secret keys of users. A consequence of our new, incomparable deniability definition is that we can achieve it without strong knowledge assumptions needed for X3DH [81] and in the work of Hashimoto et al. [46,47]; we conjecture both protocols can likewise be shown to be deniable wrt. our definition without such assumptions.

Post-quantum Designated Verifier Signatures. To achieve our goal of post-quantum asynchronous DAKE, we thus need a post-quantum designated verifier signature scheme. While there is a long line of research on DVS schemes from pre-quantum assumptions (including [16,25,49,55,59,74,77,84]), comparatively little is available in the literature on post-quantum DVS schemes. An isogeny-based DVS scheme was proposed in [78] but is insecure due to key reuse attacks identified in [44]. There are several lattice-based DVS schemes which may fit the bill [57,68,82,83,87], but these have not received much scrutiny in the mainstream cryptographic literature; we summarize this literature in Sect. 2.1. These lattice-based DVS schemes are direct constructions not based on any NIST candidates, so they would require their own thorough analysis.

DVS from Ring Signatures. Rather than constructing DVS schemes directly, it is possible to use a *ring signature scheme* [73] as a designated verifier signature scheme. In a ring signature scheme, one signer can sign a message intended to verify under a *ring* of public keys, only one of which is theirs; yet no one should be able to determine which signer produced such a signature. Following ideas sketched in [6, 73], we show in Sect. 2.2 how to use a 2-user ring signature scheme to build a DVS scheme: the ring used by the signer consists of the public keys of themselves and the one designated verifier. There are several candidates for post-quantum ring signatures whose properties we discuss in Sect. 2.2.

In a concurrent update to their work, Hashimoto et al. have shown the reverse, i.e., constructing a ring signature scheme from a DVS scheme [47] (which is the full version of [46]). Hence, in the 2-user case ring signatures and DVS are equivalent under the security notions put forward in this paper.

Given this equivalence, observe that our core asynchronous DAKE protocol (Fig. 2) is indeed similar to the second construction of [46]. While our construction sends the DVS signature as is, their construction employs a ring signature that is masked with the output of a PRF evaluation.

Application to the Signal Handshake. We present a version of the Signal X3DH handshake which we call SPQR—Signal in a Post-Quantum Regime—based on our asynchronous DAKE design that uses KEMs and a designed verifier signature scheme. We show that the SPQR handshake achieves strong ("maximal-exposure") session key security in a variant of the security model of [21] covering compromises of long- and medium-term keys and ephemeral randomness, as well as deniability.

Outline of the Paper. Section 2 focuses on the security properties of designated verifier schemes and how to construct these in a post-quantum setting, including existing direct constructions as well as via ring signatures; the full version of this paper [14] gives a discussion of our failed attempts at constructing DVS from chameleon hash functions in an earlier version of this work. In Sect. 3 we present a security model for key exchange that captures session key indistinguishability with implicit mutual authentication and weak forward secrecy, as well as offline deniability. In Sect. 4 we show that our core asynchronous deniable authenticated key exchange protocol from Fig. 2 fulfills these security notions; in particular, offline deniability is based on the source hiding property of the DVS scheme. In Sect. 5 we introduce a complete post-quantum version of the Signal handshake that extends our core protocol to include additional components present in the Signal handshake (e.g., semi-static keys); we provide a security model and proof of session key indistinguishability and deniability for the full protocol in the full version [14]. In Sect. 6, we conclude with a discussion of the results and some limitations.

1.4 Notation

To sample an element x uniformly at random from a set $\mathcal{S}$ (or a distribution on an underlying set) we write $x \leftarrow_{\$} \mathcal{S}$. For deterministic algorithms A we denote by $y \leftarrow \mathsf{A}(x)$ the execution of A on input x with output y. Similarly, $y \leftarrow_{\$} \mathsf{A}(x)$ denotes the probabilistic execution of A, and $y \leftarrow \mathsf{A}(x; r)$ the deterministic execution of a probabilistic algorithm A with its random coins fixed to r. Adversaries are typically denoted by $\mathcal{A}$ and we write $\mathcal{A}^{\text{ORACLE}}$ to indicate that $\mathcal{A}$ has access to the oracle ORACLE. Adversaries can have local quantum computation power but their oracle access and outputs are still classical. For an integer n, we denote by $[n]$ the set $\{1, \ldots, n\}$. Double square brackets $[\![\cdot]\!]$ that enclose a boolean statement return the bit 1 if the statement is true, and 0 otherwise.

2 Designated Verifier Signatures

Designated verifier signature (DVS) schemes were introduced by Jakobsson, Sako, and Impagliazzo [49]. Their goal is for a signer to convince a chosen recipient (the "designated verifier") that a message is authentic but in such a way that the designated verifier cannot convince any other party of the authenticity of the message[1]. This property is typically modeled by requiring that the designated verifier can efficiently simulate signatures that are indistinguishable from signatures produced by the signer.

Definition 1. *A* designated verifier signature scheme *(DVS) is a tuple of algorithms* $\mathsf{DVS} = (\mathsf{SKGen}, \mathsf{VKGen}, \mathsf{Sign}, \mathsf{Vrfy}, \mathsf{Sim})$ *along with a message space* $\mathcal{M}$*.*

- $\mathsf{SKGen}() \rightarrow_{\$} (pk_S, sk_S)$*: A probabilistic key generation algorithm that outputs a public-/secret-key pair for the signer.*
- $\mathsf{VKGen}() \rightarrow_{\$} (pk_D, sk_D)$*: A probabilistic key generation algorithm that outputs a public-/secret-key pair for the verifier.*
- $\mathsf{Sign}(sk_S, pk_D, m) \rightarrow_{\$} \sigma$*: A probabilistic signing algorithm that uses a signer secret key* sk_S *to produce a signature* σ *for a message* $m \in \mathcal{M}$ *for a designated verifier with public key* pk_D*.*
- $\mathsf{Vrfy}(pk_S, pk_D, m, \sigma) \rightarrow \mathsf{true}/\mathsf{false}$*: A deterministic verification algorithm that checks a message* m *and signature* σ *against a signer public key* pk_S *and verifier public key* pk_D*.*
- $\mathsf{Sim}(pk_S, sk_D, m) \rightarrow_{\$} \sigma$*: A probabilistic signature simulation algorithm that uses the verifier's secret key* sk_D *to produce a signature* σ *on message* m *for signer public key* pk_S*.*

A DVS scheme DVS *is* correct*, if, for any honestly generated key pairs* $(pk_S, sk_S), (pk_D, sk_D)$ *and every message* $m \in \mathcal{M}$*, it holds that* $\Pr[\mathsf{Vrfy}(pk_S, pk_D, m, \mathsf{Sign}(sk_S, pk_D, m)) = \mathsf{true}] = 1$.

We follow Laguillaumie and Vergnaud [55] in defining separate key generation algorithms for signers and designated verifiers; in some cases these two algorithms may be identical.

[1] In contrast, a *strong* DVS scheme allows only the designated verifier to verify a signature by requiring the verifier's secret key as input to the verification algorithm.

$\mathcal{G}^{\mathsf{uf}}_{\mathsf{DVS}}(\mathcal{A})$:

$Q \leftarrow \emptyset$
$\mathcal{L} \leftarrow \emptyset$
$(pk_S, sk_S) \leftarrow_\$ \mathsf{DVS.SKGen}()$
$(pk_D, sk_D) \leftarrow_\$ \mathsf{DVS.VKGen}()$
for $i \in [n]$
  $(pk_i, sk_i) \leftarrow_\$ \mathsf{DVS.VKGen}()$
  $\mathcal{L} \leftarrow \mathcal{L} \cup \{(pk_i, sk_i)\}$
$(m^*, \sigma^*) \leftarrow_\$ \mathcal{A}^{\mathrm{SIGN}}(pk_S, pk_D, \mathcal{L})$
$d \leftarrow \mathsf{DVS.Vrfy}(pk_S, pk_D, m^*, \sigma^*)$
return $[\![d = \mathsf{true} \wedge m^* \notin Q]\!]$

$\mathrm{SIGN}(pk, m)$:

if $pk = pk_D$
  $Q \leftarrow Q \cup \{m\}$
else if $(pk, \cdot) \notin \mathcal{L}$
  return $\perp$
$\sigma \leftarrow_\$ \mathsf{DVS.Sign}(sk_S, pk, m)$
return σ

$\mathcal{G}^{\mathsf{srchid}}_{\mathsf{DVS}}(\mathcal{A})$:

$(pk_S, sk_S) \leftarrow_\$ \mathsf{DVS.SKGen}()$
$(pk_D, sk_D) \leftarrow_\$ \mathsf{DVS.VKGen}()$
$b \leftarrow_\$ \{0, 1\}$
$b' \leftarrow_\$ \mathcal{A}^{\mathrm{CHALL}}(pk_S, sk_S, pk_D, sk_D)$
return $[\![b' = b]\!]$

$\mathrm{CHALL}(m)$:

if $b = 0$
  $\sigma \leftarrow_\$ \mathsf{DVS.Sign}(sk_S, pk_D, m)$
else
  $\sigma \leftarrow_\$ \mathsf{DVS.Sim}(pk_S, sk_D, m)$
return σ

Fig. 3. Unforgeability (top) and source hiding (bottom) of a designated verifier signature scheme DVS.

A long line of research has scrutinized the security of DVS schemes in different settings, e.g. strong DVS schemes, including [16,25,49,55,59,74,77,84]. For the purpose of this paper, it suffices to define the security notions of *unforgeability* and *source hiding*. Unforgeability for DVS schemes is similar to that for standard signature schemes, providing the adversary with a signing oracle and asking it to forge a signature on a (fresh) message of its choice. Prior work restricts the signing oracle to the challenge designated verifier key. In contrast, and to account for settings where a signer's key is used with many other users' verifier keys (cf. Sect. 4), we allow the adversary to pick the designated verifier key to be used in the signing oracle from a set of additional, honestly generated key pairs.

Definition 2. *A designated verifier signature scheme* DVS *is* (t, ϵ, n, Q_S)-unforgeable *if, for any adversary* $\mathcal{A}$ *with running time at most* t*, having access to* n *additional DVS verifier key pairs beyond the challenge keys, and making at most* Q_S *queries to the* SIGN *oracle, we have that* $\mathsf{Adv}^{\mathsf{uf}}_{\mathsf{DVS}}(\mathcal{A}) = \Pr\left[\mathcal{G}^{\mathsf{uf}}_{\mathsf{DVS}}(\mathcal{A}) = 1\right] \leq \epsilon$*, where* $\mathcal{G}^{\mathsf{uf}}_{\mathsf{DVS}}(\mathcal{A})$ *is as in Fig. 3.*

The second property we consider is called source hiding [55], demanding that it should be infeasible for an adversary to determine whether a given signature has been generated by the signer (using Sign) or by the designated verifier (using Sim), even if the adversary learns the secret keys of both parties.

Definition 3. *A designated verifier signature scheme* DVS *is* (t, ϵ, Q_{Ch})-source hiding *if, for any adversary* $\mathcal{A}$ *with running time at most* t *and making at most* Q_{Ch} *to the* CHALL *oracle, we have that* $\mathsf{Adv}^{\mathsf{srchid}}_{\mathsf{DVS}}(\mathcal{A}) = \left|\Pr\left[\mathcal{G}^{\mathsf{srchid}}_{\mathsf{DVS}}(\mathcal{A}) = 1\right] - \frac{1}{2}\right| \leq \epsilon$*, where* $\mathcal{G}^{\mathsf{srchid}}_{\mathsf{DVS}}(\mathcal{A})$ *is defined in Fig. 3.*

The property of source hiding also appears under different terms in the literature such as the designated verifier property [49,74], non-transferability [77], source deniable [40], untransferability [16], and recently off-the-record [25]. While all these definitions share the intuition that the sender can blame another party (in particular, the designated receiver) as the originator of a signature, they vary in the adversary capabilities, i.e., whether the adversary is unbounded or whether it gets access to the secret keys.

2.1 Post-quantum DVS Schemes: Prior Work

For this work, we are interested in DVS constructions that promise post-quantum security. Despite the long line of research on DVS schemes, there are only a few candidate post-quantum constructions available in the literature; furthermore, most of those have not received much scrutiny in the mainstream cryptographic literature. In the following, we summarize prior direct constructions before turning to generic constructions from ring signatures in Sect. 2.2.

An isogeny-based strong DVS scheme was proposed by Sun, Tian, and Wang [78] which turned out to be insecure due to key reuse attacks identified by Galbraith, Petit, Shani, and Ti [44].

Wang, Hu, and Wang [82] construct a strong DVS scheme directly from lattice assumptions (LWE and SIS) by combining the Bonsai tree lattice trapdoor of [19] with the GPV lattice-based signature scheme [45]; a subsequent paper of theirs [83] extends this to the identity-based setting.

Noh and Jeong [68] improve on [82,83] by giving direct constructions from lattices that can be proven without relying on random oracles; they do so by replacing the random oracle with a chameleon hash function.

Li, Liu, and Yang [57] construct a universal DVS scheme directly from ideal lattice assumptions (ring-SIS) by combining a ring version of the GPV signature scheme [64] with a ring chameleon hash function [35] and adding a Fiat–Shamir-with-aborts technique [62,63].

Zhang, Liu, Tang, and Tian [87] also give a universal DVS constructed directly from SIS by adapting the Lyubashevsky signature scheme [63].

2.2 Building Post-quantum DVS Schemes from Ring Signatures

We now turn to building DVS schemes generically from ring signatures, show which properties are required to obtain a post-quantum-secure instantiation and evaluate several ring signature candidates. Our constructions draws from the idea sketched in [6,73], with syntax and security closely following the exposition of Bender, Katz, and Morselli [6].

Definition 4. *A* ring signature scheme *is a tuple of algorithms* $\mathsf{Ring} = (\mathsf{KGen}, \mathsf{Sign}, \mathsf{Vrfy})$ *along with a message space* $\mathcal{M}$*.*

- $\mathsf{KGen}() \stackrel{\$}{\rightarrow} (pk, sk)$*: A probabilistic key generation algorithm that outputs a public-/secret-key pair.*

- $\mathsf{Sign}(sk_s, m, \mathsf{R}) \xrightarrow{\$} \sigma$: *A probabilistic signing algorithm that uses a secret key* sk_s *to produce a signature* σ *for a message* $m \in \mathcal{M}$ *w.r.t. to a list of distinct public keys* R, *where* (pk_s, sk_s) *is an honestly generated key pair and* $pk_s \in \mathsf{R}$.
- $\mathsf{Vrfy}(\mathsf{R}, m, \sigma) \to \mathsf{true/false}$: *A deterministic verification algorithm that checks a message* m *and signature* σ *against a ring* R.

A 2-user ring signature *is a ring signature fixed to rings of size 2. A ring signature scheme* Ring *is* correct, *if, for honestly generated key pairs* $\{(pk_i, sk_i)\}_{i=1}^n$, *any* $s \in [n]$, *and any message* $m \in \mathcal{M}$, *it holds that* $\Pr[\mathsf{Vrfy}(\{pk_i\}_{i=1}^n, m, \mathsf{Sign}(sk_s, m, \{(pk_i)\}_{i=1}^n)) = \mathsf{true}] = 1$.

The unforgeability and anonymity property we require for ring signatures are subtly different from prior literature. Like in the unforgeability notion w.r.t. insider corruption defined in [6], we consider an unforgeability adversary with access to a corruption oracle CORR. However, our unforgeability adversary is limited to rings consisting of honestly generated public keys for both its final forgery as well as the queries to the signing oracle (like the unforgeability against chosen-subring attacks defined in [6]). It is easy to see that unforgeability w.r.t. insider corruption implies our unforgeability notion. Herranz [48] informally discusses a similar notion.

Definition 5. *A ring signature scheme* Ring *is* $(t, \epsilon, n, Q_S, Q_{Co})$-unforgeable w.r.t. honest-ring insider corruption *if, for any adversary* $\mathcal{A}$ *with running time at most* t, *having access to* n *public keys, and making at most* Q_S *queries to the* SIGN *oracle and* Q_{Co} *queries to the* CORR *oracle, we have that* $\mathsf{Adv}^{\mathsf{uf}}_{\mathsf{Ring}}(\mathcal{A}) = \Pr\left[\mathcal{G}^{\mathsf{uf}}_{\mathsf{Ring}}(\mathcal{A}) = 1\right] \leq \epsilon$, *where* $\mathcal{G}^{\mathsf{uf}}_{\mathsf{Ring}}(\mathcal{A})$ *is as in Fig. 4.*

We consider an anonymity notion based on anonymity against full key exposure [6]. The first difference is that we directly give all secret keys to the adversary instead of providing a signing and a corruption oracle to the adversary, where the latter in [6] returns the key generation randomness. The other difference is that we parameterize the game in the number of queries Q_{Ch} allowed to the challenge oracle. As a result, anonymity against full key exposure implies our anonymity notion with $Q_{Ch} = 1$. Similarly, the anonymity notions of [60] and [39], where the attacker has access to a key generation oracle, imply our anonymity notion with $Q_{Ch} = 1$.

Definition 6. *A ring signature scheme* Ring *is* (t, ϵ, n, Q_{Ch})-anonymous against key exposure *if, for any adversary* $\mathcal{A}$ *with running time at most* t, *having access to* n *key pairs, and making at most* Q_{Ch} *queries to the* CHALL *oracle, we have that* $\mathsf{Adv}^{\mathsf{anon}}_{\mathsf{Ring}}(\mathcal{A}) = \Pr\left[\mathcal{G}^{\mathsf{anon}}_{\mathsf{Ring}}(\mathcal{A}) = 1\right] \leq \epsilon$, *where* $\mathcal{G}^{\mathsf{anon}}_{\mathsf{Ring}}(\mathcal{A})$ *is as in Fig 4.*

It is easy to see that one can transform any $(t, \epsilon, n, 1)$-anonymous (as per Definition 6) ring signature scheme into a $(t, \epsilon \cdot Q_{Ch}, n, Q_{Ch})$-anonymous scheme via a hybrid argument.

$\mathcal{G}_{\mathsf{Ring}}^{\mathsf{uf}}(\mathcal{A})$:

1 $Q_S \leftarrow \emptyset$
2 $Q_{Co} \leftarrow \emptyset$
3 $\mathcal{L} \leftarrow \emptyset$
4 for $i \in [n]$
5    $(pk_i, sk_i) \leftarrow_\$ \mathsf{Ring.KGen}()$
6    $\mathcal{L} \leftarrow \mathcal{L} \cup \{pk_i\}$
7 $(\mathsf{R}^*, m^*, \sigma^*) \leftarrow_\$ \mathcal{A}^{\mathrm{SIGN,CORR}}(\mathcal{L})$
8 $d_1 \leftarrow \mathsf{Ring.Vrfy}(\mathsf{R}^*, m^*, \sigma^*)$
9 $d_2 \leftarrow [\![(m^*, \mathsf{R}^*) \notin Q_S]\!]$
10 $d_3 \leftarrow [\![\mathsf{R}^* \subseteq \mathcal{L} \backslash Q_{Co}]\!]$
11 return $[\![d_1 \wedge d_2 \wedge d_3]\!]$

$\mathrm{SIGN}(s, m, \mathsf{R})$:

12 if $pk_s \notin \mathsf{R} \vee s \notin [n]$ //sign wrt. honest key
13   return $\bot$
14 if $\mathsf{R} \not\subseteq \mathcal{L}$ //sign wrt. honest ring
15   return $\bot$
16 $Q_S \leftarrow Q_S \cup \{(m, \mathsf{R})\}$
17 $\sigma \leftarrow_\$ \mathsf{Ring.Sign}(sk_S, m, \mathsf{R})$
18 return σ

$\mathrm{CORR}(i)$:

19 $Q_{Co} \leftarrow Q_{Co} \cup \{pk_i\}$
20 return sk_i

$\mathcal{G}_{\mathsf{Ring}}^{\mathsf{anon}}(\mathcal{A})$:

1 $\mathcal{L} \leftarrow \emptyset$
2 for $i \in [n]$
3    $(pk_i, sk_i) \leftarrow \mathsf{Ring.KGen}()$
4    $\mathcal{L} \leftarrow \mathcal{L} \cup \{(pk_i, sk_i)\}$
5 $b \leftarrow_\$ \{0, 1\}$
6 $b' \leftarrow_\$ \mathcal{A}^{\mathrm{CHALL}}(\mathcal{L})$
7 return $[\![b' = b]\!]$

$\mathrm{CHALL}(m, i_0, i_1, \mathsf{R})$:

8 if $\{pk_{i_0}, pk_{i_1}\} \not\subseteq \mathsf{R}$ //challenge signers in ring
9   return $\bot$
10 if $\{i_0, i_1\} \not\subseteq [n]$ //sign with honest keys only
11   return $\bot$
12 $\sigma \leftarrow_\$ \mathsf{Ring.Sign}(sk_{i_b}, m, \mathsf{R})$
13 return σ

Fig. 4. Unforgeability w.r.t. honest-ring insider corruption (top) and anonymity against key exposure (bottom) of a ring signature scheme Ring. The latter game is specialized for the ring size 2.

The Construction. Our construction, denoted RingDVS, is a straightforward adaption of a 2-user ring signature Ring to the DVS setting as detailed in Fig. 5. The security of the resulting DVS scheme hinges on the unforgeability and anonymity of the ring signature as per Definitions 5 and 6.

Theorem 1 (Unforgeability of RingDVS). *If Ring is a $(t, \epsilon, n+2, Q_S, Q_{Co})$-unforgeable w.r.t. honest-ring insider corruption 2-user ring signature scheme, then RingDVS defined in Fig. 5 is (t', ϵ, n, Q_S)-existentially unforgeable under chosen message attacks, with $t' \approx t$.*

Proof. We reduce the existential unforgeability of RingDVS to the unforgeability w.r.t. honest-ring insider corruption of Ring.

Initialization of $\mathcal{A}$. The adversary $\mathcal{B}$ against unforgeability of the ring signature receives as input a list $\mathcal{L}$ of honestly generated public keys $\{pk_i\}_{i=1}^{n+2}$. Next, $\mathcal{B}$ corrupts all keys except the first two via its CORR oracle. It sets the first two public keys as challenge keys for $\mathcal{A}$ as $pk_S \leftarrow pk_1$ and $pk_D \leftarrow pk_2$. (Observe that we choose these two indices wlog. for easier bookkeeping.) The reduction then initializes the adversary $\mathcal{A}$ against unforgeability of the DVS on input $(pk_S, pk_D, \{(pk_i, sk_i)\}_{i=3}^{n+2})$.

$\underline{\mathsf{RingDVS.SKGen}():}$

$(pk_S, sk_S) \leftarrow\!\$\ \mathsf{Ring.KGen}()$
return (pk_S, sk_S)

$\underline{\mathsf{RingDVS.VKGen}():}$

$(pk_D, sk_D) \leftarrow\!\$\ \mathsf{Ring.KGen}()$
return (pk_D, sk_D)

$\underline{\mathsf{RingDVS.Sign}(sk_S, pk_D, m):}$

return $\mathsf{Ring.Sign}(sk_S, m, \{pk_S, pk_D\})$

$\underline{\mathsf{RingDVS.Sim}(pk_S, sk_D, m):}$

return $\mathsf{Ring.Sign}(sk_D, m, \{pk_S, pk_D\})$

$\underline{\mathsf{RingDVS.Vrfy}(pk_S, pk_D, m, \sigma):}$

return $\mathsf{Ring.Vrfy}(\{pk_S, pk_D\}, m, \sigma)$

Fig. 5. Designated-verifier signature scheme $\mathsf{RingDVS} = \mathsf{RingDVS}[\mathsf{Ring}]$ constructed from a 2-user ring signature scheme Ring.

Queries to Sign. Queries of $\mathcal{A}$ to the SIGN oracle are of the form (pk, m). If pk is not one of the honestly generated keys that the reduction gave to $\mathcal{A}$, return $\perp$. For each query, $\mathcal{B}$ queries its own signing oracle on $(1, m, \{pk_1, pk\})$ and returns the answer directly to $\mathcal{A}$. If $pk = pk_2$, record m in Q.

Existential Forgery. At some point, $\mathcal{A}$ outputs a DVS forgery (m^*, σ^*) wrt. pk_S and pk_D. The reduction outputs $(m^*, \sigma^*, pk_1, pk_2)$ as its own forgery.

The reduction soundly simulates the unforgeability game against $\mathsf{RingDVS}$. It simulates the signing oracle truthfully by using its own signing oracle.

If $\mathcal{A}$ outputs a valid DVS forgery wrt. sender key $pk_S = pk_1$ and verifier key $pk_D = pk_2$, the output of $\mathcal{B}$ is a valid ring forgery wrt. the ring $\{pk_1, pk_2\}$ by construction of $\mathsf{RingDVS}$. Furthermore, since $m \notin Q$, $\mathcal{A}$ has not queried its SIGN oracle on m and pk_D. Thus, the message-ring pair $(m, \{pk_1, pk_2\})$ was not queried by $\mathcal{B}$ to its oracle either. Lastly, the forgery is wrt. the keys $\{pk_1, pk_2\}$, which $\mathcal{B}$ did not corrupt. Hence, all winning conditions for the ring unforgeability game are met.

The running time t of $\mathcal{B}$ is dominated by the running time t' of $\mathcal{A}$ and we write $t \approx t'$; simulating the signing oracle and querying the corruption oracle n times are not expensive. If $\mathcal{A}$ outputs a successful DVS forgery with probability ϵ, then $\mathcal{B}$ is able to produce a valid ring forgery with the same probability. □

Theorem 2 (Source hiding of $\mathsf{RingDVS}$). *If* Ring *is a* (t, ϵ, n, Q_{Ch})*-anonymous against key exposure 2-user ring signature for* $n \geq 2$, *then* $\mathsf{RingDVS}$ *as shown in Fig. 5 is* (t', ϵ, Q_{Ch})*-source hiding, with* $t' \approx t$.

Proof. We reduce the source hiding of $\mathsf{RingDVS}$ to the anonymity against key exposure of Ring.

Initialization of $\mathcal{A}$. The adversary $\mathcal{B}$ against anonymity of the ring signature receives as input a list of honestly generated key pairs $\{(pk_i, sk_i)\}_{i=1}^{n}$. It sets the first two public keys as challenge keys for $\mathcal{A}$ as $pk_S \leftarrow pk_1$ and $pk_D \leftarrow pk_2$. The reduction then initializes the source hiding adversary $\mathcal{A}$ on input (sk_S, pk_S, sk_D, pk_D).

Queries to Chall. $\mathcal{A}$'s queries to the CHALL oracle are of the form m. For each of the Q_{Ch} queries, $\mathcal{B}$ forwards the query to its own CHALL oracle as $(m, 1, 2, \{pk_1, pk_2\})$ and returns the answer it gets directly to $\mathcal{A}$.

Output. When $\mathcal{A}$ outputs its guess b', the reduction outputs b'.

The reduction soundly simulates the source hiding game against RingDVS for $\mathcal{A}$. The runtime of $\mathcal{B}$ is essentially the runtime of $\mathcal{A}$ plus the runtime to forward the challenge queries and responses and we write $t \approx t'$.

Adversary $\mathcal{A}$ distinguishing between outputs of RingDVS.Sign and RingDVS.Sim amounts to distinguishing between Ring signatures under the two signing keys sk_1 and sk_2 in the ring $\{pk_1, pk_2\}$. Hence, $\mathcal{B}$ inherits $\mathcal{A}$'s winning probability ϵ. □

Implications and the Inverse Direction. Our construction above establishes that DVS schemes with the security properties needed for this work (i.e., unforgeability and source hiding) can be generically constructed from 2-user ring signatures that provide unforgeability w.r.t. honest-ring insider corruption and anonymity against key exposure. We note that the latter security properties are weaker than those put forward by Bender, Katz, and Morselli [6].

Hashimoto et al. have recently shown in the full version of their work [47] that it is indeed possible to construct also the reverse direction (in contrast to an earlier statement of ours). For their construction each ring member has a signer key pair and a designated verifier key pair. In the signing procedure, depending on the lexicographical order of the signer public keys either DVS.Sign or DVS.Sim is executed generating a ring signature. Verification follows analogously.

Post-quantum Ring Signature Candidates. Several post-quantum ring signature schemes were suggested in the literature. In the following, we list a selection of schemes having concrete instantiations and report on the signature sizes and other practical parameters provided in the corresponding works to illustrate their practicality. All schemes except Raptor (listed first) come with security proofs for unforgeability and anonymity definitions that imply our notions.

Lu, Au, and Zhang [61] introduce Raptor, which uses a chameleon hash function based on the NIST finalist FALCON [71], producing signatures of size approximately 5 KB for a 2-user ring. However, they argue that the best-known attack is inefficient instead of proving unforgeability and anonymity.

Yuen, Esgin, Liu, Au, and Ding [85] propose DualRing-LB (which is a lattice-based instantiation of their generic construction DualRing) with a signature size of 4.4 KB for rings of size 2. They prove anonymity (against full key exposure) of their scheme under a slightly different notion, where only the first-stage attacker has access to a signing oracle and only the second-stage attacker gets the randomness used in creating all keys (i.e., access to the secret keys).

The following two schemes use zero-knowledge proofs based on symmetric primitives, akin to the NIST alternate candidate Picnic [86]: Derler, Ramacher, and Slamanig [28] provide a scheme using NIZK proofs and accumulators. For their smallest reported ring size 2^5, signatures can have a size of 719 KB. Katz, Kolesnikov, and Wang [51] use NIZKPoK with the MPC-in-the-head paradigm. For their smallest ring size 2^7, signing takes 2 s and produces signatures of size 285 KB.

In terms of lattice-based constructions, a series of works [37–39] by Esgin et al. provide constructions relying on the hardness of M-LWE and M-SIS. The most recent candidate has a signature size of 18 KB for a 2-user ring. A construction by Lyubashevsky, Nguyen, and Seiler [65] relies on (variants of) M-LWE and M-SIS and their smallest signature for rings of size 2^5 is 16 KB. Beullens, Katsumata, and Pintore [7] introduce Falafl that also relies on M-LWE and M-SIS and produces signatures of size 29 KB in less than 100 ms.

Sheikhi-Garjan, Kiliç, and Cenk [76] recently presented an isogeny-based ring signature in which signing and verifying scale in the product nq of the ring size n and isogeny security parameter q.

3 Security Model for Asynchronous Deniable Key Exchange

From a formal perspective, an asynchronous authenticated key exchange protocol is just a traditional authenticated key exchange protocol with a specific type of message flow. In particular, asynchronicity allows one party to post pre-key bundles containing long-term and possibly ephemeral public keys, provided that they can be constructed without knowing the intended partner. We will formalize security for this setting based on a Bellare–Rogaway-type model [3] with implicit authentication and (weak) forward secrecy using post-specified peers [18, 53]. The model presented in this section is simplified to deal with basic Bellare–Rogaway-type security with only long-term keys; in the full version [14] we present a more granular model that accommodates the complex characteristics found in the Signal protocol handshake, including semi-static keys and stronger security against maximal exposure.

Parties and Sessions. Let $\mathcal{P}$ be the set of n_p parties, each of whom has a long-term public-key/secret-key pair generated by an algorithm KGenLT. Each party may run multiple instances of the protocol simultaneously or sequentially, each of which is called a session. The ith session at party P is denoted π_P^i. For each session, the party maintains the following collection of session-specific information:

- $\mathsf{oid} \in \mathcal{P}$: The identity of the session owner.
- $\mathsf{pid} \in \mathcal{P} \cup \{\star\}$: The identity of the intended peer, which may initially be unknown (indicated by $\star$).
- $\mathsf{role} \in \{\mathsf{initiator}, \mathsf{responder}\}$: The role of the party.
- $\mathsf{st_{exec}} \in \{\bot, \mathsf{running}, \mathsf{accepted}, \mathsf{rejected}\}$: The status of this session's execution.
- $\mathsf{sid} \in \{0, 1\}^* \cup \{\bot\}$: A session identifier defining partnering.
- $\mathsf{cid} \in \{0, 1\}^* \cup \{\bot\}$: A contributive identifier, defining a preliminary form of partnering (often as a substring or prefix of the session identifier) for the case the session is not yet bound to an authenticated peer [34].
- $\mathsf{K} \in \mathcal{K}_{\mathsf{KE}} \cup \{\bot\}$: The session key established in this session.
- Any additional protocol-specific data used during execution.

Protocol Specification. A 2-party key exchange protocol consists of the following algorithms:

- $\mathsf{KGenLT}() \xrightarrow{\$} (pk, sk)$: A probabilistic long-term key generation algorithm that outputs a public-key/secret-key pair.
- $\mathsf{Run}(sk, \boldsymbol{pk}, \pi, m) \xrightarrow{\$} (\pi', m')$: A probabilistic session execution algorithm that takes as input a party's long-term secret key sk, a list of long-term public keys for all honest parties $\boldsymbol{pk}$, a session state π, and an incoming message m, and outputs an updated session state π' and a (possibly empty) outgoing message m'. To set up the session sending the first message, Run is called with a distinguished message $m = \mathsf{create}$.

In a deniable key exchange protocol, we will demand the existence of an additional algorithm:

- $\mathsf{Fake}(pk_U, sk_V) \xrightarrow{\$} (\mathsf{K}, \mathsf{T})$: A probabilistic transcript simulation algorithm that takes as input one party's public key and the other party's secret key and generates a session key K and a transcript T of a protocol interaction between them.

Asynchronous Key Exchange. In principle, a key exchange protocol can have an arbitrary number of message flows, which correspond to multiple calls to Run for a single session. In normal execution of an asynchronous authenticated key exchange protocol, the following three calls to Run occur: 1) a call to Run at the responder (Bob)[2] with $m = \mathsf{create}$, which sets up the responder session and outputs the responder's pre-key bundle, including an ephemeral public key; 2) a call to Run at the initiator with the responder's pre-key bundle (long-term public and ephemeral public keys) which generates a session key and outputs a key exchange message; and 3) a call to Run at the responder with the initiator's long-term public key and key exchange message which generates a session key and has no output message.

Partnering. Two sessions π_U^i and π_V^j are said to be *partners* if they agree on the session identifier ($\pi_U^i.\mathsf{sid} = \pi_V^j.\mathsf{sid}$). An honest partner session is a partner session that is honest, i.e., not under adversarial control.

Session Key Indistinguishability. The first security property we want of an authenticated key exchange protocol is indistinguishability of session keys. At the start of the security experiment, long-term public-key/secret-key pairs are generated for all n_p honest parties and the public keys $\boldsymbol{pk}$ are provided to the adversary, as well as a random challenge bit b_{test} fixed for the duration of the experiment. The adversary is then able to interact with honest parties via the following queries:

---

[2] Note that we call Bob the *responder* in our model despite Bob outputting the first, asynchronous key exchange message. Based on the high-level protocol interaction, we deem it more natural to call Alice, who decides to *initiate* a Signal session with Bob, the initiator (in contrast to, e.g., [21,79,80]).

- SEND(U, i, m): Sends message m to session π_U^i, which corresponds to executing $\mathsf{Run}(sk_U, \boldsymbol{pk}, \pi_U^i, m)$, saving the updated session state π' as π_U^i, and returning the outgoing message m' to the adversary.
- CORRUPTLTKEY(U): Returns party U's long-term secret key sk_U to the adversary.
- REVEALSESSKEY(U, i): If session π_U^i has accepted, return its session key $\pi_U^i.\mathsf{K}$ to the adversary.
- TEST(U, i): If the TEST query has been called before or session π_U^i has not accepted, then return $\perp$. Otherwise, if $b_{\mathsf{test}} = 0$, return $\pi_U^i.\mathsf{K}$, otherwise return an element of $\mathcal{K}_{\mathsf{KE}}$ chosen uniformly at random. Record $\pi^* \leftarrow \pi_U^i$.

The test session $\pi^* = \pi_{U^*}^{i^*}$ is called *fresh* if the following all hold:

1. REVEALSESSKEY(U^*, i^*) was never called.
2. REVEALSESSKEY(V, j) was never called for any V, j such that $\pi^*.\mathsf{sid} = \pi_V^j.\mathsf{sid}$.
3. Either
   (a) there exists an honest partner session π_{p}^* ($\pi_{\mathsf{p}}^*.\mathsf{sid} = \pi^*.\mathsf{sid}$ if π^* is a responder, and $\pi_{\mathsf{p}}^*.\mathsf{cid} = \pi^*.\mathsf{cid}$ if π^* is an initiator), covering weak forward secrecy, or
   (b) CORRUPTLTKEY$(\pi^*.\mathsf{oid})$ and CORRUPTLTKEY$(\pi^*.\mathsf{pid})$ were never called, covering implicit authentication.

At the end of the experiment, the adversary outputs a bit b'. The adversary is said to win if $b' = b_{\mathsf{test}}$ and the test session π^* is fresh. Formally, if the test session is fresh, the experiment outputs 1 if $b' = b_{\mathsf{test}}$ and 0 otherwise; if the test session is not fresh, then the experiment outputs a random bit. The adversary's advantage in the key indistinguishability game is the absolute value of the difference between $\frac{1}{2}$ and the probability that the experiment outputs 1.

Deniability. The second security property we want is deniability. At the start of this experiment, long-term public-key/secret-key pairs are generated for all n_p honest parties and the public *and* secret keys are provided to the adversary. A random challenge bit b is fixed for the duration of the experiment. The adversary is given repeated access to a CHALL oracle which takes as input two party identifiers U and V. If b is 0, then CHALL will generate an honest transcript of an interaction between U and V using the Run algorithm and each party's secret keys. If b is 1, then CHALL will generate a simulated transcript of an interaction between U and V using the Fake algorithm. At the end of the experiment, the adversary outputs a guess b' of b. The experiment outputs 1 if $b' = b$ and 0 otherwise. The adversary's advantage in the deniability game is the absolute value of the difference between $\frac{1}{2}$ and the probability the experiment outputs 1.

There are several prior works giving definitions of offline deniability for key exchange [23,24,29,79,80]. Our definition differs from previous ones threefold: Firstly, the challenge oracle executes Run on behalf of the framing party, i.e., we consider semi-honest adversaries only. Secondly, the Fake algorithm (corresponding to the simulator in simulation-based definitions) has access to the receiver's secret key. Thirdly, the adversary (the judge in simulation-based settings) has access to all secret keys. This restricts the deniability to semi-honest adversaries and 1-out-of-2 (one needs a secret key of either party to create a transcript) but lifts us to the so-called big brother setting. The strong point of this deniability notion is that you get some deniability guarantees even against strong judges, who know all secret keys. This models the informal deniability requirement from the Signal specification [67, §4.4]. See the full version [14] for a more detailed discussion.

4 Security of the Core Protocol

We now show that our core protocol Π from Fig. 2 achieves the security properties defined in Sect. 3. Key indistinguishability of Π depends on the IND-CCA security of the two KEMs, the unforgeability of the DVS, and the security of the KDF; deniability of Π depends on the source hiding of the DVS. Both proofs are in the standard model.

To formally capture Π in the security model of Sect. 3, we need to specify a few more details:

- Alice takes the initiator role, Bob the responder role.
- The transcript in Fig. 2 corresponds to the session identifier and consists of the parties' identities and long-term public keys, the responder's ephemeral public key, and the KEM ciphertexts; the contributive identifier corresponds to the pre-key bundle part of the transcript, received by Alice from Bob:

$$\mathsf{transcript} = \mathsf{sid} = (A, B, pk_A^{\mathsf{DVS}}, pk_B^{\mathsf{KEM}}, pk_B^{\mathsf{DVS}}, epk_B^{\mathsf{KEM}}, c_1, c_2),$$
$$\mathsf{cid} = (B, pk_B^{\mathsf{KEM}}, pk_B^{\mathsf{DVS}}, epk_B^{\mathsf{KEM}}).$$

  Note that the session identifier does not include the DVS signature itself to avoid that the latter needs to be non-malleable (akin to strong unforgeability of regular signatures) [58].

4.1 Key Indistinguishability

Theorem 3 (Key indistinguishability of Π). *Let* DVS *be a* $(t, \epsilon_{\mathsf{DVS}}, n_p, Q_S)$*-unforgeable DVS scheme,* KEM_1 *be a* $(t, \epsilon_{\mathsf{KEM}_1}, n_s)$*-*IND-CCA*-secure KEM,* KEM_2 *be a* $(t, \epsilon_{\mathsf{KEM}_2}, 1)$*-*IND-CCA*-secure KEM, and* KDF *be a* $(t, \epsilon_{\mathsf{KDF}}, n_s)$*-*PRF*-secure key derivation function when keyed through either of the key components* K_1 *and* K_2*. Then the asynchronous DAKE protocol* Π *from Fig. 2 provides key indistinguishability (as defined in Sect. 3) in that the advantage* ϵ' *of any adversary* $\mathcal{A}$ *running in time* $t' \approx t$ *is upper bounded as*

$$\epsilon' \leq n_s \cdot \begin{pmatrix} n_s \cdot (\epsilon_{\mathsf{KEM}_2} + \epsilon_{\mathsf{KDF}}) \\ + n_p \cdot (\epsilon_{\mathsf{KEM}_1} + \epsilon_{\mathsf{KDF}}) \\ + n_p^2 \cdot (\epsilon_{\mathsf{DVS}} + n_s \cdot (\epsilon_{\mathsf{KEM}_2} + \epsilon_{\mathsf{KDF}})) \end{pmatrix},$$

where $n_s \leq Q_{Snd}$ *is the maximum number of sessions (upper bounded by the number* Q_{Snd} *of* SEND *queries) and* n_p *the number of parties.*

Proof. We proceed via a sequence of game hops starting from the key indistinguishability game for an adversary $\mathcal{A}$. We bound the difference between each hop until we reach a game where the adversary's advantage is 0.

Game 0. The initial key indistinguishability game, denoted $\mathcal{G}_0$, letting $\epsilon' := \mathsf{Adv}^{\mathcal{G}_0}_{\mathsf{ADAKE}}(\mathcal{A}) = |\Pr[\mathcal{G}_0 = 1] - \frac{1}{2}|$.

Game 1 (Guess test session π^*). We first guess the tested session π^* and "invalidate" the game by overwriting the adversary's bit guess with 0 if the adversary calls TEST on a different session. Guessing among the n_s many sessions (where n_s is at most the number Q_{Snd} of calls to the SEND oracle), $\mathsf{Adv}^{\mathcal{G}_0}_{\mathsf{ADAKE}}(\mathcal{A}) \leq n_s \cdot \mathsf{Adv}^{\mathcal{G}_1}_{\mathsf{ADAKE}}(\mathcal{A})$.

For the remaining proof, we distinguish the following three cases for the test session being fresh:

A. There exists an honest partner session π^*_{p} ($\pi^*_{\mathsf{p}}.\mathsf{sid} = \pi^*.\mathsf{sid}$ if π^* is a responder, and $\pi^*_{\mathsf{p}}.\mathsf{cid} = \pi^*.\mathsf{cid}$ if π^* is an initiator).
B. The tested session is an initiator ("Alice") session and CORRUPTLTKEY($\pi^*.\mathsf{pid}$) was never called.[3]
C. The tested session is a responder ("Bob") session and neither CORRUPTLTKEY($\pi^*.\mathsf{oid}$) nor CORRUPTLTKEY($\pi^*.\mathsf{pid}$) was ever called.[4]

Treating theses cases as events in $\mathcal{G}_1$, and writing $\mathcal{G}_1[X]$ to indicate that event X occurs, by the union bound we have:

$$\mathsf{Adv}^{\mathcal{G}_1}_{\mathsf{ADAKE}}(\mathcal{A}) \leq \mathsf{Adv}^{\mathcal{G}_1[\mathrm{A}]}_{\mathsf{ADAKE}}(\mathcal{A}) + \mathsf{Adv}^{\mathcal{G}_1[\mathrm{B}]}_{\mathsf{ADAKE}}(\mathcal{A}) + \mathsf{Adv}^{\mathcal{G}_1[\mathrm{C}]}_{\mathsf{ADAKE}}(\mathcal{A}).$$

Case A (Honest partner). In the first proof case, there exists a session π^*_{p} that agrees with the tested session π^* on the responder's ephemeral KEM public key epk^{KEM} used. We will leverage this to embed a challenge into the ephemeral KEM ciphertext c_2.

Game A.1 (Guess partnered session). We first guess a session π^*_{p} which is partnered via sid (if π^* is a responder) or cid (if π^* is an initiator) to the test session π^*, and let the adversary lose if the guess is incorrect. By this case's prerequisites, (at least) one partner session exists and is guessed with probability at least $1/n_s$, hence $\mathsf{Adv}^{\mathcal{G}_1[\mathrm{A}]}_{\mathsf{ADAKE}}(\mathcal{A}) \leq n_s \cdot \mathsf{Adv}^{\mathcal{G}_{A.1}}_{\mathsf{ADAKE}}(\mathcal{A})$.

Game A.2 (Ephemeral KEM). We now replace the KEM key K_2 with a random key $\widetilde{K_2}$ in π^* and also in π^*_{p} (unless the latter is a responder and receives a different ciphertext c_2 than sent by π^*).

[3] This is slightly stronger than what freshness condition 3 (b) demands. In the security result for our full SPQR protocol (see Sect. 5), this is captured more precisely.

[4] In our full SPQR protocol (see Sect. 5), we will strengthen this case by having Bob use *semi-static* DVS keys. This limits the time window for a key-compromise impersonation (KCI) attack [8] against Bob, as in the Signal handshake [67, §4.6].

We bound the difference introduced by this step through a reduction to the IND-CCA security of the KEM_2 scheme, which simulates $\mathcal{G}_{A.1}$ truthfully except for the following changes and runs in time $t \approx t'$. It embeds the obtained challenge public key pk into the ephemeral KEM public key epk of the responder session among π^* and π^*_{p}, the challenge ciphertext c^* as c_2 of the initiator session (among π^* and π^*_{p}), and the challenge (real-or-random) key K^*_{b}) as K_2 into both π^* and π^*_{p}. If π^* is an initiator session, it uses its DECAPS oracle (at most once, i.e., $Q_D \leq 1$) to decrypt a potentially different ciphertext $c'_2 \neq c_2 = c^*$ received by π^*_{p}. Depending on the IND-CCA KEM challenge bit, the reduction perfectly simulates $\mathcal{G}_{A.1}$ or $\mathcal{G}_{A.2}$, hence $\mathsf{Adv}^{\mathcal{G}_{A.1}}_{\mathsf{ADAKE}}(\mathcal{A}) \leq \epsilon_{\mathsf{KEM}_2} + \mathsf{Adv}^{\mathcal{G}_{A.2}}_{\mathsf{ADAKE}}(\mathcal{A})$.

Game A.3 (KDF). We finally replace the key derivation function KDF in both π^* and π^*_{p} (in the latter only if it uses $\widetilde{K_2}$) with a random function, in particular replacing the session key K of π^* with a randomly sampled key $\widetilde{K}$.

We bound the introduced advantage difference via a reduction to the pseudorandomness of the key derivation function KDF, treated as a PRF keyed through the second key component K_2 and taking $(K_1, \mathsf{transcript})$ as label. The reduction runs in time $t \approx t'$ and simulates Game $\mathcal{G}_{A.2}$ truthfully, except that it does not sample $\widetilde{K_2}$ itself but instead uses its oracle PRFCHALLENGE to compute the session key values derived from $\widetilde{K_2}$. It calls its oracle at most twice, once for π^* and possibly once for π^*_{p} on a different label, hence $Q_{PRF} \leq n_s$. Depending on whether its oracle output is the true KDF evaluation or that of a random function, the reduction perfectly simulates $\mathcal{G}_{A.2}$ or $\mathcal{G}_{A.3}$, thus $\mathsf{Adv}^{\mathcal{G}_{A.2}}_{\mathsf{ADAKE}}(\mathcal{A}) \leq \epsilon_{\mathsf{KDF}} + \mathsf{Adv}^{\mathcal{G}_{A.3}}_{\mathsf{ADAKE}}(\mathcal{A})$.

In Game $\mathcal{G}_{A.3}$, the challenge key K_{test} for π^* is a uniformly random key, independent of b_{test}. Furthermore, by the first two freshness conditions, $\mathcal{A}$ cannot reveal K_{test} via a REVEALSESSKEY query on π^* or any partnered session who might hold the same key. Thus, in $\mathcal{G}_{A.3}$, $\mathcal{A}$ cannot do better than guessing, leaving it with advantage $\mathsf{Adv}^{\mathcal{G}_{A.3}}_{\mathsf{ADAKE}}(\mathcal{A}) = 0$.

Case B (Initiator tested, peer uncorrupted). In the second proof case, we have that the tested initiator session π^* has an uncorrupted intended peer. We will leverage this to embed a challenge into the static KEM ciphertext c_1.

Game B.1 (Guess responder identity). We first guess the test session's intended peer, $V = \pi^*.\mathsf{pid}$, among the n_p many parties in the game and let the adversary lose if we guess incorrectly. This reduces the adversary's advantage by a factor at most n_p: $\mathsf{Adv}^{\mathcal{G}_1[\mathrm{B}]}_{\mathsf{ADAKE}}(\mathcal{A}) \leq n_p \cdot \mathsf{Adv}^{\mathcal{G}_{B.1}}_{\mathsf{ADAKE}}(\mathcal{A})$.

Game B.2 (Static KEM). We can now replace the KEM key K_1 in π^* (and any responder session of V receiving the same ciphertext c_1) with a random key $\widetilde{K_1}$.

We bound the advantage difference introduced by this step through a reduction to the IND-CCA security of the KEM_1 scheme. The reduction runs in time $t \approx t'$ and simulates $\mathcal{G}_{B.1}$ truthfully, but embeds the obtained challenge public key pk as V's public KEM key pk^{KEM}_V at the outset of the game. It further embeds the challenge ciphertext c^* as c_1 sent by π^* and the challenge (real-or-random) key K_b^*) as K_1 into π^* (and any responder session of V receiving c^*). The reduction uses the DECAPS oracle to decapsulate any ciphertexts $c_1 \neq c^*$ received by sessions of V (calling the oracle at most n_s times), and never has to respond to CORRUPTLTKEY(V) queries as otherwise π^* would not be fresh. Depending on the IND-CCA KEM challenge bit, the reduction perfectly simulates $\mathcal{G}_{B.1}$ or $\mathcal{G}_{B.2}$, hence $\mathsf{Adv}_{\mathsf{ADAKE}}^{\mathcal{G}_{B.1}}(\mathcal{A}) \leq \epsilon_{\mathsf{KEM}_1} + \mathsf{Adv}_{\mathsf{ADAKE}}^{\mathcal{G}_{B.2}}(\mathcal{A})$.

Game B.3 (KDF). We finally replace the key derivation function KDF in π^* (and any other session using $\widetilde{K_1}$) with a random function, in particular replacing the session key K of π^* with a randomly sampled key $\widetilde{K}$.

Analogous to Game $\mathcal{G}_{A.3}$, we can bound the introduced advantage difference by the pseudorandomness of KDF when keyed through the first key component K_1 and taking (K_2, transcript) as label. The challenge static KEM key $\widetilde{K_1}$ may possibly be decapsulated in many responder sessions of V, who use distinct transcript labels unless they are partnered with π^*; the PRF reduction, running in time $t \approx t'$, may hence make up to n_s queries to its PRFCHALLENGE oracle. Simulating either of the two games in the reduction, we get $\mathsf{Adv}_{\mathsf{ADAKE}}^{\mathcal{G}_{B.2}}(\mathcal{A}) \leq \epsilon_{\mathsf{KDF}} + \mathsf{Adv}_{\mathsf{ADAKE}}^{\mathcal{G}_{B.3}}(\mathcal{A})$.

Here, the challenge key K_{test} for π^* is uniformly random and independent, as only partnered sessions will use the same transcript label to derive their session keys, but for π^* to be fresh those cannot be revealed. Thus $\mathsf{Adv}_{\mathsf{ADAKE}}^{\mathcal{G}_{B.3}}(\mathcal{A}) = 0$.

Case C (Responder tested, both parties uncorrupted). In the final proof case, we know that the tested responder session π^* has an uncorrupted intended peer. We will leverage this to ensure that there is a partnered initiator session (which signed the transcript) and then embed a challenge into the ephemeral KEM ciphertext c_2 between these two sessions.

Game C.1 (Guess initiator and responder identities). We first guess the (responder) test session's owner $V = \pi^*.\mathsf{oid}$ and intended (initiator) peer $U = \pi^*.\mathsf{pid}$ among the n_p many parties in the game and "invalidate" the game (overwriting $\mathcal{A}$'s bit guess by 0) if we guess incorrectly. Guessing both parties induces a quadratic loss in n_p: $\mathsf{Adv}_{\mathsf{ADAKE}}^{\mathcal{G}_1[\mathrm{C}]}(\mathcal{A}) \leq n_p^2 \cdot \mathsf{Adv}_{\mathsf{ADAKE}}^{\mathcal{G}_{C.1}}(\mathcal{A})$.

Game C.2 (Signature unforgeability). We now "invalidate" the game (overwriting $\mathcal{A}$'s bit guess by 0) if the test session π^* accepts a DVS signature σ on a transcript that no session of U has issued.

We bound this event by a reduction against the existential unforgeability of DVS, running in time $t \approx t'$ and simulating $\mathcal{G}_{C.1}$ with the following modification: Instead of generating parties' DVS keys itself, the reduction embeds the unforgeability game's challenge public keys as $pk_U = pk_S$ and $pk_V = pk_D$, and assigns the additional DVS public-secret key pairs from the unforgeability game's list $\mathcal{L}$ to the remaining parties. (Note that the reduction obtains the secret keys for the latter keys, allowing it to fully simulate those parties.) The reduction uses its signing oracle to compute signatures under $pk_U = pk_S$ (and for any peer public key pk). As U and V remain uncorrupted in this proof case, the reduction never has to answer a CORRUPTLTKEY(U) or CORRUPTLTKEY(V) query. In the case that π^* receives a valid DVS transcript-signature pair (transcript, σ) that no session of U sent (and hence transcript was not queried to the DVS SIGN oracle), the reduction outputs this pair as its forgery and wins. Therefore, $\mathsf{Adv}^{\mathcal{G}_{C.1}}_{\mathsf{ADAKE}}(\mathcal{A}) \leq \epsilon_{\mathsf{DVS}} + \mathsf{Adv}^{\mathcal{G}_{C.2}}_{\mathsf{ADAKE}}(\mathcal{A})$.

Game C.3 (Guess partnered session). As of $\mathcal{G}_{C.2}$, we know that π^* receives a DVS signature on a transcript value transcript $= \pi^*.\mathsf{sid}$ sent by some session of U. We now guess this (sid-partnered) session π^*_{p} (among the n_s many sessions) and, invalidating the game (overwriting $\mathcal{A}$'s bit guess by 0) upon wrong guess, get $\mathsf{Adv}^{\mathcal{G}_{C.2}}_{\mathsf{ADAKE}}(\mathcal{A}) \leq n_s \cdot \mathsf{Adv}^{\mathcal{G}_{C.3}}_{\mathsf{ADAKE}}(\mathcal{A})$.

Game C.4 (Ephemeral KEM). We next replace the KEM key K_2 with a random key $\widetilde{K_2}$ in π^* and π^*_{p}.

As in Game $\mathcal{G}_{A.2}$, we bound the introduced advantage difference by the IND-CCA security of the KEM_2 scheme. The reduction runs in time $t \approx t'$, embeds the challenge pk and c^* into π^*'s ephemeral KEM public key, resp. π^*_{p}'s c_2 ciphertext, and uses the challenge key K^*_b in place of K_2 in both sessions. It does not need to use its DECAPS oracle (i.e., $Q_D = 0$), since pk is not used in another session and we are at this point guaranteed that π^* receives π^*_{p}'s ephemeral ciphertext. (So in fact we only need IND-CPA security of KEM_2 here.) The reduction simulates the difference between $\mathcal{G}_{C.3}$ and $\mathcal{G}_{C.4}$, so $\mathsf{Adv}^{\mathcal{G}_{C.3}}_{\mathsf{ADAKE}}(\mathcal{A}) \leq \epsilon_{\mathsf{KEM}_2} + \mathsf{Adv}^{\mathcal{G}_{C.4}}_{\mathsf{ADAKE}}(\mathcal{A})$.

Game C.5 (KDF). In the final game hop, we replace KDF in both π^* and π^*_{p} with a random function, replacing the session key K of π^* with a randomly sampled key $\widetilde{K}$.

As in Game $\mathcal{G}_{A.3}$, this is bounded by the pseudorandomness of KDF with key K_2 and label (K_1, transcript). Due to π^* and π^*_{p} agreeing on the transcript input to KDF, the corresponding reduction only makes one query, $Q_{PRF} = 1 \leq n_s$, running in time $t \approx t'$. Simulating the game difference through this reduction, we get $\mathsf{Adv}^{\mathcal{G}_{C.4}}_{\mathsf{ADAKE}}(\mathcal{A}) \leq \epsilon_{\mathsf{KDF}} + \mathsf{Adv}^{\mathcal{G}_{C.5}}_{\mathsf{ADAKE}}(\mathcal{A})$.

This completes the last proof case, as the challenge key K_{test} for π^* is now uniformly random and independent (beyond partnered sessions), leaving $\mathcal{A}$ with advantage $\mathsf{Adv}^{\mathcal{G}_{C.5}}_{\mathsf{ADAKE}}(\mathcal{A}) = 0$. □

4.2 Deniability

Observe that we use a different deniability notion compared to prior works as discussed in Sect. 3. A more thorough discussion of the different deniability notions can be found in the full version [14]. In consequence, we can forgo the strong knowledge assumptions that both [46,81] used to prove deniability of X3DH and their own construction, respectively. We conjecture that either construction can likewise be shown to be deniable wrt. our definition without strong knowledge assumptions.

Theorem 4 (Deniability of Π). *Let* $\mathsf{DVS} = (\mathsf{SKGen}, \mathsf{VKGen}, \mathsf{Sign}, \mathsf{Vrfy}, \mathsf{Sim})$ *be a* $(t, \epsilon_{\mathsf{srchid}}, Q_{Ch})$*-source hiding DVS scheme. Then the asynchronous DAKE protocol* Π *from Fig. 2 provides deniability (as defined in Sect. 3) in that the advantage* ϵ' *of any adversary* $\mathcal{A}$ *running in time* $t' \approx t$ *and making up to* Q_{Ch} *challenge queries is upper bounded as* $\epsilon' \leq n_p^2 \cdot \epsilon_{\mathsf{srchid}}$*, where* n_p *is the number of parties.*

Proof. The proof follows by a standard hybrid argument. Let $\mathcal{A}$ be a successful adversary against deniability of Π, then we can construct a reduction $\mathcal{B}$ against the source hiding property of DVS. Observe that $\mathcal{B}$ computes for each of the n_p parties a long-term key pair. It randomly guesses the identifiers of two parties $\mathsf{iid}^*, \mathsf{rid}^* \in [n_p]$ for which $\mathcal{A}$ can distinguish between Run and Fake. Let a number $i \in [n_p^2]$ uniquely denote two independent values iid, rid in a query (e.g., encoded as $(\mathsf{iid} - 1) \cdot n_p + \mathsf{rid}$) and let $i^* \in [n_p^2]$ denote the specific guess $\mathsf{iid}^*, \mathsf{rid}^*$ of $\mathcal{B}$. For party iid^*, $\mathcal{B}$ replaces the sampled long-term key with its challenge key pair (pk_S, sk_S) and similarly it replaces for party rid^* with (pk_D, sk_D).

In case $\mathcal{A}$ makes a query i for $1 \leq i < i^*$, then $\mathcal{B}$ answers as if $b = 0$, i.e., it runs DVS.Sign. For all $i^* < i \leq n_p^2$, if $\mathcal{A}$ makes a query, then $\mathcal{B}$ answers as if $b = 1$, i.e., it runs DVS.Sim. If $\mathcal{A}$ queries $i = i^*$, then $\mathcal{B}$ passes it to its own oracle. In all cases $\mathcal{B}$ returns the transcript and the session key K to $\mathcal{A}$. Finally, when $\mathcal{A}$ returns its guess bit b', $\mathcal{B}$ returns b' as its guess.

Observe that $\mathcal{B}$ faithfully simulates the deniability game for $\mathcal{A}$. Moreover, the runtime of $\mathcal{B}$ is essentially the runtime of $\mathcal{A}$ plus the runtime to generate the keys and answer the oracle queries.

Now we analyze the winning probability of $\mathcal{A}$ against deniability. For this, we define the hybrids $H_0, \ldots, H_{n_p^2}$ with H_i being the hybrid that answers all challenge queries for indices $1, \ldots, i$ with Run and the challenge queries for indices $i+1, \ldots, n_p^2$ with Fake. The extreme hybrids are $H_{n_p^2}$, which answers all the challenge queries with Run, and H_0, which answers all queries with Fake. Observe that H_{i-1} and H_i only differ in an execution of Run or Fake. Hence, the probability of distinguishing between H_{i-1} and H_i is bounded by $\epsilon_{\mathsf{srchid}}$. Since there are n_p^2 many hybrids, we overall obtain that $\mathcal{A}$'s probability of winning the deniability game is bounded by $\epsilon' \leq n_p^2 \cdot \epsilon_{\mathsf{srchid}}$. □

5 Signal in a Post-quantum Regime

We now extend our core protocol Π from Fig. 2 to capture all the characteristics of the Signal handshake. The core protocol already captures implicit mutual authentication, forward secrecy, offline deniability, and asynchronicity. Signal's X3DH has a few more subtle aspects and security features to consider, which we address in our extended asynchronous DAKE protocol: SPQR (Signal in a Post-Quantum Regime), depicted in Fig. 6.

Semi-static Keys. In Signal, asynchronicity is facilitated by a central, untrusted server which stores the users' pre-key bundles. To enable multiple users to asynchronously contact some responder user, say Bob, the latter uploads multiple

KGenLT():
$(pk^{\mathsf{KEM}}, sk^{\mathsf{KEM}}) \leftarrow\$ \mathsf{KEM}_1.\mathsf{KGen}()$
$(pk^{\mathsf{DVS}}, sk^{\mathsf{DVS}}) \leftarrow\$ \mathsf{DVS.SKGen}()$
$tk \leftarrow\$ \mathsf{tPRF.KGen}()$
$pk \leftarrow (pk^{\mathsf{KEM}}, pk^{\mathsf{DVS}})$
$sk \leftarrow (sk^{\mathsf{KEM}}, sk^{\mathsf{DVS}}, tk)$
return (pk, sk)

KGenSS():
$(sspk^{\mathsf{KEM}}, sssk^{\mathsf{KEM}}) \leftarrow\$ \mathsf{KEM}_2.\mathsf{KGen}()$
$(sspk^{\mathsf{DVS}}, sssk^{\mathsf{DVS}}) \leftarrow\$ \mathsf{DVS.VKGen}()$
$sspk \leftarrow (sspk^{\mathsf{KEM}}, sspk^{\mathsf{DVS}})$
$sssk \leftarrow (sssk^{\mathsf{KEM}}, sssk^{\mathsf{DVS}})$
return $(sspk, sssk)$

KGenEP():
return $(epk, esk) \leftarrow\$ \mathsf{KEM}_3.\mathsf{KGen}()$

Alice | **Signal Server** | **Bob**

Initiator Registration
$(pk_A, sk_A) \leftarrow\$ \mathsf{KGenLT}()$

Responder Registration
$(pk_B, sk_B) \leftarrow\$ \mathsf{KGenLT}()$
$(sspk_B, sssk_B) \leftarrow\$ \mathsf{KGenSS}()$

Responder Ephemeral Key Generation
$(epk_B, esk_B) \leftarrow\$ \mathsf{KGenEP}()$

Send Pre-Key Bundle to Initiator
$\longleftarrow B, pk_B, sspk_B, epk_B$

define: $cid := (B, pk_B, sspk_B, epk_B)$
define: $sid := (A, B, pk_A, pk_B, sspk_B, epk_B, n, c_1, c_2, c_3)$

Initiator Key Agreement and Protocol Message
$(sk_A^{\mathsf{KEM}}, sk_A^{\mathsf{DVS}}, tk_A) \leftarrow sk_A$
$(pk_B^{\mathsf{KEM}}, pk_B^{\mathsf{DVS}}) \leftarrow pk_B$
$(sspk_B^{\mathsf{KEM}}, sspk_B^{\mathsf{DVS}}) \leftarrow sspk_B$
$(n, r) \leftarrow\$ \{0,1\}^\lambda \times \mathcal{R}_{\mathsf{tPRF}}$
$r_1 \| r_2 \| r_3 \| r_4 \leftarrow \mathsf{tPRF}(tk_A, r)$
$(K_1, c_1) \leftarrow \mathsf{KEM}_1.\mathsf{Encaps}(pk_B^{\mathsf{KEM}}; r_1)$
$(K_2, c_2) \leftarrow \mathsf{KEM}_2.\mathsf{Encaps}(sspk_B^{\mathsf{KEM}}; r_2)$
if $epk_B \neq \bot$
  $(K_3, c_3) \leftarrow \mathsf{KEM}_3.\mathsf{Encaps}(epk_B; r_3)$
else $(K_3, c_3) \leftarrow (\varepsilon, \varepsilon)$
$\mathsf{ms} \leftarrow K_1 \| K_2 \| K_3$
$\sigma \leftarrow \mathsf{DVS.Sign}(sk_A^{\mathsf{DVS}}, sspk_B^{\mathsf{DVS}}, sid; r_4)$
$K \leftarrow \mathsf{KDF}(\mathsf{ms}, sid)$
$m \leftarrow (A, pk_A, n, c_1, c_2, c_3, \sigma)$
return $(K, sid, \mathsf{accepted}, m)$

Responder Key Agreement (on input m)
$(sk_B^{\mathsf{KEM}}, sk_B^{\mathsf{DVS}}, tk_B) \leftarrow sk_B$
$(sssk_B^{\mathsf{KEM}}, sssk_B^{\mathsf{DVS}}) \leftarrow sssk_B$
$(pk_A^{\mathsf{KEM}}, pk_A^{\mathsf{DVS}}) \leftarrow pk_A$
$(sspk_B^{\mathsf{KEM}}, sspk_B^{\mathsf{DVS}}) \leftarrow sspk_B$
if $\mathsf{DVS.Vrfy}(pk_A^{\mathsf{DVS}}, sspk_B^{\mathsf{DVS}}, sid, \sigma) = \mathsf{false}$
  return $(\bot, \bot, \mathsf{rejected}, \bot)$
$K_1 \leftarrow \mathsf{KEM}_1.\mathsf{Decaps}(sk_B^{\mathsf{KEM}}, c_1)$
$K_2 \leftarrow \mathsf{KEM}_2.\mathsf{Decaps}(sssk_B^{\mathsf{KEM}}, c_2)$
if $esk_B \neq \bot$
  $K_3 \leftarrow \mathsf{KEM}_3.\mathsf{Decaps}(esk_B, c_3)$
else $(K_3, c_3) \leftarrow (\varepsilon, \varepsilon)$
$\mathsf{ms} \leftarrow K_1 \| K_2 \| K_3$
$K \leftarrow \mathsf{KDF}(\mathsf{ms}, sid)$
return $(K, sid, \mathsf{accepted}, \varepsilon)$

$m = (A, pk_A, n, c_1, c_2, c_3, \sigma) \longrightarrow$

Responder Fake transcript
run *Responder Ephemeral Key Generation*, and *Initiator Key Agreement* with a modified randomness sampling and DVS generation:
$(K_1, c_1) \leftarrow\$ \mathsf{KEM}_1.\mathsf{Encaps}(pk_B^{\mathsf{KEM}})$
$(K_2, c_2) \leftarrow\$ \mathsf{KEM}_2.\mathsf{Encaps}(sspk_B^{\mathsf{KEM}})$
if $epk_B \neq \bot$ $(K_3, c_3) \leftarrow\$ \mathsf{KEM}_3.\mathsf{Encaps}(epk_B)$
else $(K_3, c_3) \leftarrow (\varepsilon, \varepsilon)$
$\sigma \leftarrow\$ \mathsf{DVS.Sim}(sssk_B^{\mathsf{DVS}}, pk_A^{\mathsf{DVS}}, sid)$
$K \leftarrow \mathsf{KDF}(\mathsf{ms}, sid)$
return $(K, m = (B, pk_B, sspk_B, epk_B, A, pk_A, n, c_1, c_2, c_3, \sigma))$

Fig. 6. The SPQR protocol (top: key generation, middle: protocol flow, bottom: fake transcript generation), combining static, semi-static and ephemeral key encapsulation schemes KEM_1, KEM_2, and KEM_3, a designated verifier signature DVS, and a twisted pseudorandom function tPRF.

ephemeral public pre-keys to the Signal server, of which one is handed to any initiator session that wants to contact Bob (along with the other pre-key bundle elements) and then deleted from the Signal server.

Bob will periodically upload new ephemeral pre-keys; however, if Bob has been offline for a long time, those pre-keys may run out. Therefore, the Signal protocol also includes a *semi-static* key in user pre-key bundles, and always includes key derivations based on that semi-static key. If the Signal server runs out of ephemeral pre-keys, the corresponding key share is not derived and left out; in that case the semi-static key share still provides delayed forward secrecy [13]. We capture this similarly in SPQR by encapsulating a key-ciphertext pair (K_3, c_3) against Bob's ephemeral KEM public key epk_B only if the latter is present.

Maximal-Exposure Security. Signal aims for very strong security guarantees, considering beyond long-term and session key compromise and also compromise of semi-static and ephemeral keys (via the randomness of sessions) [17,21,56]. We model this in an accordingly strong key exchange model and prove that SPQR achieves equivalent security in the post-quantum setting as Signal does in the classical setting in the full version [14]. In particular, we show that session keys remain secret, as long as any of the (Alice–Bob) secret combinations ephemeral–ephemeral, ephemeral–semi-static, ephemeral–long-term, and long-term–semi-static are uncompromised. Secrecy from the first three is straightforwardly achieved via encapsulations against the corresponding ephemeral, semi-static, and long-term KEM keys of Bob. To achieve secrecy from the last one (i.e., when all initiator randomness is compromised), beyond relying on the DVS scheme for initiator authentication, we apply a NAXOS-like [56] trick to extract randomness from Alice's long-term secrets via a twisted PRF [42,54]. Twisted PRFs can be generically instantiated from regular PRFs (see full version [14]) and yield output indistinguishable from random as long as a session's long-term secret *or* randomness is uncompromised.

Our formal security results establishing key indistinguishability and deniability for SPQR are as follows; see the full version [14] for the game-based formalizations of key indistinguishability and deniability as well as for the full proof details expanding beyond the core ideas from Sect. 4.

Theorem 5 (Key indistinguishability of SPQR). *Let* DVS *be a* $(t, \epsilon_{\mathsf{DVS}}, n_p \cdot n_{ss}, Q_S)$*-unforgeable DVS scheme.*

Let KEM_1 *be a* $(t, \epsilon_{\mathsf{KEM}_1}, n_s)$*–*IND-CCA*-secure KEM,* KEM_2 *be a* $(t, \epsilon_{\mathsf{KEM}_2}, n_s)$*–*IND-CCA*-secure KEM,* KEM_3 *be a* $(t, \epsilon_{\mathsf{KEM}_3}, 1)$*–*IND-CCA*-secure KEM with randomness space* $\mathcal{R}_{\mathsf{KEM}_3}$*, and* δ_{corr} *be the maximal correctness error among* KEM_1*,* KEM_2*, and* KEM_3*.*

Let KDF *be a* $(t, \epsilon_{\mathsf{KDF}}, n_s)$*–*PRF*-secure key derivation function when keyed through any key component* K_1*,* K_2*,* K_3*, and* tPRF *a* $(t, \epsilon_{\mathsf{tPRF}}, n_s)$*-secure twisted pseudorandom function with label space* $\mathcal{R}_{\mathsf{tPRF}}$*.*

Then the SPQR *protocol with randomness space* $\mathcal{R}_{\mathsf{KE}} = \{0,1\}^\lambda \times \mathcal{R}_{\mathsf{tPRF}} \times \mathcal{R}_{\mathsf{KEM}_3}$ *as shown in Fig. 6 provides* $(t', \epsilon', (Q_{Snd}, Q_{CorrLT}, Q_{CorrSS}, Q_{RevR}, Q_{RevSK}))$*–key indistinguishability (formalized in the full version) for* $t \approx t'$ *and*

$$\epsilon' \leq \frac{n_s^2}{2^\lambda} + \frac{n_s^2}{2^{|\mathcal{R}_{\mathsf{tPRF}}|}} + \frac{n_s^2}{2^{|\mathcal{R}_{\mathsf{KEM}_3}|}} + 3n_s \cdot \delta_{\mathsf{corr}} + n_s \cdot n_p^2 \cdot \begin{pmatrix} n_{ss} \cdot (\epsilon_{\mathsf{DVS}} + 2n_s \cdot (\epsilon_{\mathsf{tPRF}} + \epsilon_{\mathsf{KEM}_2} + \epsilon_{\mathsf{KDF}})) \\ + n_s \cdot (2\epsilon_{\mathsf{tPRF}} + \epsilon_{\mathsf{KEM}_1} + \epsilon_{\mathsf{KEM}_3} + 2\epsilon_{\mathsf{KDF}}) \end{pmatrix},$$

where $n_s \leq Q_{Snd}$ *is the maximum number of sessions (upper bounded by the number* Q_{Snd} *of* SEND *queries),* n_p *the number of parties, and* n_{ss} *the number of semi-static keys per party.*

Theorem 6 (Deniability of SPQR). *If* DVS *is a* $(t, \epsilon_{\mathsf{srchid}}, Q_{Ch})$*-source hiding designated verifier signature and* tPRF *is a* $(t, \epsilon_{\mathsf{tPRF}}, Q_{Ch})$*-pseudorandom function, then the* SPQR *protocol as shown in Fig. 6 is* (t', ϵ', Q'_{Ch})*-deniable, where* $t' \approx t$*,* $\epsilon' \leq n_p^2 n_{ss} \cdot \epsilon_{\mathsf{srchid}} + n_p Q_{Ch} \cdot \epsilon_{\mathsf{tPRF}}$*, where* n_p *is the number of parties and* n_{ss} *the number of semi-static keys per party, and* $Q'_{Ch} = Q_{Ch}$*.*

6 Discussion and Limitations

Our protocols demonstrate that designated verifier signatures are helpful for constructing practical AKE protocols with constraints on the message flow (asynchronicity) and with specialized security properties (deniability).

The key ingredient in our approach for achieving post-quantum asynchronous DAKE is a post-quantum designated verifier signature scheme. While there are several lattice-based DVS schemes in the literature as described in Sect. 2.1, we believe that their security merits further scrutiny before adoption. In the meantime, we propose instantiations via 2-user ring signatures, for which we discussed post-quantum candidates in Sect. 2.2.

We believe SPQR is a good start as a PQ replacement for the Signal X3DH handshake, but in any real-world protocol deployment there are many subtleties, some of which we now highlight.

The way Signal is used in practice has the semi-static keys signed under the long-term key. In SPQR the long-term key is not suitable for this purpose, so an additional long-term signing key might have to be introduced solely for the purposes of signing the other keys; note this could be done without undermining deniability. This characteristic was likewise not considered in the provable security analysis of Signal of [21].

SPQR is solely a replacement for the initial handshake (X3DH). A fully post-quantum Signal would require quantum-resistance in the ratcheting and message encryption; fortunately there are several generic treatments of ratcheting [1,5,70].

As Signal does not use certificates or a PKI, long-term public keys must be manually authenticated out-of-band, and that remains the case with SPQR.

Our analysis of SPQR considers randomness exposure, but not malicious randomness. The latter has been captured for ratcheting [1], but not yet in the initial handshake. Our security analysis shows that SPQR, as an authenticated key exchange protocol, has offline deniability. As discussed in the full version, we think that our deniability notion is the best one can hope for if the adversary has access to the secret keys. We leave formally proving this as future work.

Cryptographic deniability should be treated with caution. How cryptographers understand deniability may be different from how a judge in a legal system understands it [79]. Additionally, there are stronger notions of deniability [33] that SPQR (and the Signal handshake) does not achieve, such as if one party maliciously generates messages or colludes in real-time with the judge. One should further confirm deniability at all protocol levels, and that deniability of individual components composes appropriately. Despite all these subtleties, steps toward deniability are helpful, as Unger and Goldberg write [79]: "we should strive to design deniable protocols to avoid unintentionally incriminating users."

Acknowledgements. We thank Shuichi Katsumata and the anonymous reviewers of PKC 2022 for the helpful comments. Furthermore, we also thank anonymous reviewers who pointed out a flaw in our DVS constructions in an earlier version of this paper.

R.F. was supported by the German Federal Ministry of Education and Research and the Hessian Ministry of Higher Education, Research, Science and the Arts within their joint support of the National Research Center for Applied Cybersecurity ATHENE. F.G. was supported in part by German Research Foundation (DFG) Research Fellowship grant GU 1859/1-1. C.J. was (partially) funded by the Deutsche Forschungsgemeinschaft (DFG) – SFB 1119 – 236615297. D.S. was supported by Natural Sciences and Engineering Research Council of Canada (NSERC) Discovery grant RGPIN-2016-05146.

References

1. Alwen, J., Coretti, S., Dodis, Y.: The double ratchet: security notions, proofs, and modularization for the signal protocol. In: Ishai, Y., Rijmen, V. (eds.) EUROCRYPT 2019. LNCS, vol. 11476, pp. 129–158. Springer, Cham (2019). https://doi.org/10.1007/978-3-030-17653-2_5
2. Azarderakhsh, R., Jao, D., Leonardi, C.: Post-quantum static-static key agreement using multiple protocol instances. In: Adams, C., Camenisch, J. (eds.) SAC 2017. LNCS, vol. 10719, pp. 45–63. Springer, Cham (2018). https://doi.org/10.1007/978-3-319-72565-9_3
3. Bellare, M., Rogaway, P.: Entity authentication and key distribution. In: Stinson, D.R. (ed.) CRYPTO 1993. LNCS, vol. 773, pp. 232–249. Springer, Heidelberg (1994). https://doi.org/10.1007/3-540-48329-2_21
4. Bellare, M., Rogaway, P.: Optimal asymmetric encryption. In: De Santis, A. (ed.) EUROCRYPT 1994. LNCS, vol. 950, pp. 92–111. Springer, Heidelberg (1995). https://doi.org/10.1007/BFb0053428
5. Bellare, M., Singh, A.C., Jaeger, J., Nyayapati, M., Stepanovs, I.: Ratcheted encryption and key exchange: the security of messaging. In: Katz, J., Shacham, H. (eds.) CRYPTO 2017. LNCS, vol. 10403, pp. 619–650. Springer, Cham (2017). https://doi.org/10.1007/978-3-319-63697-9_21

6. Bender, A., Katz, J., Morselli, R.: Ring signatures: stronger definitions, and constructions without random oracles. J. Cryptol. **22**(1), 114–138 (2009)
7. Beullens, W., Katsumata, S., Pintore, F.: Calamari and Falafl: logarithmic (linkable) ring signatures from isogenies and lattices. In: Moriai, S., Wang, H. (eds.) ASIACRYPT 2020. LNCS, vol. 12492, pp. 464–492. Springer, Cham (2020). https://doi.org/10.1007/978-3-030-64834-3_16
8. Blake-Wilson, S., Johnson, D., Menezes, A.: Key agreement protocols and their security analysis. In: Darnell, M. (ed.) Cryptography and Coding 1997. LNCS, vol. 1355, pp. 30–45. Springer, Heidelberg (1997). https://doi.org/10.1007/BFb0024447
9. Boneh, D., et al.: Multiparty non-interactive key exchange and more from isogenies on elliptic curves. J. Math. Cryptol. **14**(1), 5–14 (2020)
10. Bonnetain, X., Schrottenloher, A.: Quantum security analysis of CSIDH. In: Canteaut, A., Ishai, Y. (eds.) EUROCRYPT 2020. LNCS, vol. 12106, pp. 493–522. Springer, Cham (2020). https://doi.org/10.1007/978-3-030-45724-2_17
11. Bos, J., et al.: CRYSTALS - Kyber: a CCA-secure module-lattice-based KEM. In: 2018 IEEE European Symposium on Security and Privacy, EuroS&P 2018, pp. 353–367 (2018). https://cryptojedi.org/papers/#kyber
12. Boyd, C., Cliff, Y., Nieto, J.M.G., Paterson, K.G.: One-round key exchange in the standard model. IJACT **1**, 181–199 (2009)
13. Boyd, C., Gellert, K.: A modern view on forward security. Comput. J. **64**(4), 639–652 (2020)
14. Brendel, J., Fiedler, R., Günther, F., Janson, C., Stebila, D.: Post-quantum asynchronous deniable key exchange and the Signal handshake. Cryptology ePrint Archive, Report 2021/769 (2021). https://eprint.iacr.org/2021/769
15. Brendel, J., Fischlin, M., Günther, F., Janson, C., Stebila, D.: Towards post-quantum security for signal's X3DH handshake. In: 27th Conference on Selected Areas in Cryptography (SAC) (2020)
16. Cai, J., et al.: ID-based strong designated verifier signature over $\mathcal{R}$-SIS assumption. Secur. Commun. Netw. **2019**, 9678095:1-9678095:8 (2019)
17. Canetti, R., Krawczyk, H.: Analysis of key-exchange protocols and their use for building secure channels. In: Pfitzmann, B. (ed.) EUROCRYPT 2001. LNCS, vol. 2045, pp. 453–474. Springer, Heidelberg (2001). https://doi.org/10.1007/3-540-44987-6_28
18. Canetti, R., Krawczyk, H.: Security analysis of IKE's signature-based key-exchange protocol. In: Yung, M. (ed.) CRYPTO 2002. LNCS, vol. 2442, pp. 143–161. Springer, Heidelberg (2002). https://doi.org/10.1007/3-540-45708-9_10
19. Cash, D., Hofheinz, D., Kiltz, E., Peikert, C.: Bonsai trees, or how to delegate a lattice basis. J. Cryptol. **25**(4), 601–639 (2012)
20. Castryck, W., Lange, T., Martindale, C., Panny, L., Renes, J.: CSIDH: an efficient post-quantum commutative group action. In: Peyrin, T., Galbraith, S. (eds.) ASIACRYPT 2018. LNCS, vol. 11274, pp. 395–427. Springer, Cham (2018). https://doi.org/10.1007/978-3-030-03332-3_15
21. Cohn-Gordon, K., Cremers, C.J.F., Dowling, B., Garratt, L., Stebila, D.: A formal security analysis of the Signal messaging protocol. In: IEEE European Symposium on Security and Privacy, EuroS&P 2017, pp. 451–466 (2017)
22. Cohn-Gordon, K., Cremers, C.J.F., Garratt, L.: On post-compromise security. In: CSF 2016 Computer Security Foundations Symposium, pp. 164–178 (2016)
23. Cremers, C., Feltz, M.: One-round strongly secure key exchange with perfect forward secrecy and deniability. Cryptology ePrint Archive, Report 2011/300 (2011). https://eprint.iacr.org/2011/300

24. Dagdelen, Ö., Fischlin, M., Gagliardoni, T., Marson, G.A., Mittelbach, A., Onete, C.: A cryptographic analysis of OPACITY. In: Crampton, J., Jajodia, S., Mayes, K. (eds.) ESORICS 2013. LNCS, vol. 8134, pp. 345–362. Springer, Heidelberg (2013). https://doi.org/10.1007/978-3-642-40203-6_20
25. Damgård, I., Haagh, H., Mercer, R., Nitulescu, A., Orlandi, C., Yakoubov, S.: Stronger security and constructions of multi-designated verifier signatures. In: Pass, R., Pietrzak, K. (eds.) TCC 2020. LNCS, vol. 12551, pp. 229–260. Springer, Cham (2020). https://doi.org/10.1007/978-3-030-64378-2_9
26. de Kock, B., Gjøsteen, K., Veroni, M.: Practical isogeny-based key-exchange with optimal tightness. In: Dunkelman, O., Jacobson, Jr., M.J., O'Flynn, C. (eds.) SAC 2020. LNCS, vol. 12804, pp. 451–479. Springer, Cham (2021). https://doi.org/10.1007/978-3-030-81652-0_18
27. de Saint Guilhem, C., Smart, N.P., Warinschi, B.: Generic forward-secure key agreement without signatures. In: Nguyen, P., Zhou, J. (eds.) Information Security. ISC 2017. LNCS, vol. 10599, pp. 114–133. Springer, Cham (2017). https://doi.org/10.1007/978-3-319-69659-1_7
28. Derler, D., Ramacher, S., Slamanig, D.: Post-quantum zero-knowledge proofs for accumulators with applications to ring signatures from symmetric-key primitives. In: Lange, T., Steinwandt, R. (eds.) PQCrypto 2018. LNCS, vol. 10786, pp. 419–440. Springer, Cham (2018). https://doi.org/10.1007/978-3-319-79063-3_20
29. Di Raimondo, M., Gennaro, R., Krawczyk, H.: Deniable authentication and key exchange. In: ACM CCS 2006, pp. 400–409 (2006)
30. Dobson, S., Galbraith, S.D.: Post-quantum signal key agreement with SIDH. Cryptology ePrint Archive, Report 2021/1187 (2021). https://eprint.iacr.org/2021/1187
31. Dobson, S., Galbraith, S.D., LeGrow, J.T., Ti, Y.B., Zobernig, L.: An adaptive attack on 2-SIDH. Int. J. Comput. Math. Comput. Syst. Theor. **5**(4), 282–299 (2020)
32. Dobson, S., Li, T., Zobernig, L.: A note on a static SIDH protocol. Cryptology ePrint Archive, Report 2019/1244 (2019). https://eprint.iacr.org/2019/1244
33. Dodis, Y., Katz, J., Smith, A., Walfish, S.: Composability and on-line deniability of authentication. In: Reingold, O. (ed.) TCC 2009. LNCS, vol. 5444, pp. 146–162. Springer, Heidelberg (2009). https://doi.org/10.1007/978-3-642-00457-5_10
34. Dowling, B., Fischlin, M., Günther, F., Stebila, D.: A cryptographic analysis of the TLS 1.3 handshake protocol candidates. In: ACM CCS 2015, pp. 1197–1210 (2015)
35. Ducas, L., Micciancio, D.: Improved short lattice signatures in the standard model. In: Garay, J.A., Gennaro, R. (eds.) CRYPTO 2014. LNCS, vol. 8616, pp. 335–352. Springer, Heidelberg (2014). https://doi.org/10.1007/978-3-662-44371-2_19
36. Duits, I.: The post-quantum Signal protocol: Secure chat in a quantum world. Master's thesis, University of Twente (2019)
37. Esgin, M.F., Steinfeld, R., Liu, J.K., Liu, D.: Lattice-based zero-knowledge proofs: new techniques for shorter and faster constructions and applications. In: Boldyreva, A., Micciancio, D. (eds.) CRYPTO 2019. LNCS, vol. 11692, pp. 115–146. Springer, Cham (2019). https://doi.org/10.1007/978-3-030-26948-7_5
38. Esgin, M.F., Steinfeld, R., Sakzad, A., Liu, J.K., Liu, D.: Short lattice-based one-out-of-many proofs and applications to ring signatures. In: Deng, R.H., Gauthier-Umaña, V., Ochoa, M., Yung, M. (eds.) ACNS 2019. LNCS, vol. 11464, pp. 67–88. Springer, Cham (2019). https://doi.org/10.1007/978-3-030-21568-2_4
39. Esgin, M.F., Zhao, R.K., Steinfeld, R., Liu, J.K., Liu, D.: MatRiCT: efficient, scalable and post-quantum blockchain confidential transactions protocol. In: ACM CCS 2019, pp. 567–584 (2019)

40. Fischlin, M., Mazaheri, S.: Notions of deniable message authentication. In: Proceedings of the 14th ACM Workshop on Privacy in the Electronic Society, WPES 2015, Denver, Colorado, USA, 12 October 2015, pp. 55–64 (2015)
41. Freire, E.S.V., Hofheinz, D., Kiltz, E., Paterson, K.G.: Non-interactive key exchange. In: Kurosawa, K., Hanaoka, G. (eds.) PKC 2013. LNCS, vol. 7778, pp. 254–271. Springer, Heidelberg (2013). https://doi.org/10.1007/978-3-642-36362-7_17
42. Fujioka, A., Suzuki, K., Xagawa, K., Yoneyama, K.: Strongly secure authenticated key exchange from factoring, codes, and lattices. In: Fischlin, M., Buchmann, J., Manulis, M. (eds.) PKC 2012. LNCS, vol. 7293, pp. 467–484. Springer, Heidelberg (2012). https://doi.org/10.1007/978-3-642-30057-8_28
43. Fujisaki, E., Okamoto, T.: Secure integration of asymmetric and symmetric encryption schemes. In: Wiener, M. (ed.) CRYPTO 1999. LNCS, vol. 1666, pp. 537–554. Springer, Heidelberg (1999). https://doi.org/10.1007/3-540-48405-1_34
44. Galbraith, S.D., Petit, C., Shani, B., Ti, Y.B.: On the security of supersingular isogeny cryptosystems. In: Cheon, J.H., Takagi, T. (eds.) ASIACRYPT 2016. LNCS, vol. 10031, pp. 63–91. Springer, Heidelberg (2016). https://doi.org/10.1007/978-3-662-53887-6_3
45. Gentry, C., Peikert, C., Vaikuntanathan, V.: Trapdoors for hard lattices and new cryptographic constructions. In: 40th ACM STOC, pp. 197–206 (2008)
46. Hashimoto, K., Katsumata, S., Kwiatkowski, K., Prest, T.: An efficient and generic construction for signal's handshake (X3DH): post-quantum, state leakage secure, and deniable. In: Garay, J.A. (ed.) PKC 2021. LNCS, vol. 12711, pp. 410–440. Springer, Cham (2021). https://doi.org/10.1007/978-3-030-75248-4_15
47. Hashimoto, K., Katsumata, S., Kwiatkowski, K., Prest, T.: An efficient and generic construction for signal's handshake (X3DH): post-quantum, state leakage secure, and deniable. Cryptology ePrint Archive, Report 2021/564 (2021). https://eprint.iacr.org/2021/616
48. Herranz, J.: Some digital signature schemes with collective signers. Ph.D. thesis, Universitat Politècnica de Catalunya, Barcelona (2005)
49. Jakobsson, M., Sako, K., Impagliazzo, R.: Designated verifier proofs and their applications. In: Maurer, U. (ed.) EUROCRYPT 1996. LNCS, vol. 1070, pp. 143–154. Springer, Heidelberg (1996). https://doi.org/10.1007/3-540-68339-9_13
50. Jao, D., De Feo, L.: Towards quantum-resistant cryptosystems from supersingular elliptic curve isogenies. In: Yang, B.-Y. (ed.) PQCrypto 2011. LNCS, vol. 7071, pp. 19–34. Springer, Heidelberg (2011). https://doi.org/10.1007/978-3-642-25405-5_2
51. Katz, J., Kolesnikov, V., Wang, X.: Improved non-interactive zero knowledge with applications to post-quantum signatures. In: ACM CCS 2018, pp. 525–537 (2018)
52. Kawashima, T., Takashima, K., Aikawa, Y., Takagi, T.: An efficient authenticated key exchange from random self-reducibility on CSIDH. In: Hong, D. (ed.) ICISC 2020. LNCS, vol. 12593, pp. 58–84. Springer, Cham (2021). https://doi.org/10.1007/978-3-030-68890-5_4
53. Krawczyk, H.: HMQV: a high-performance secure Diffie-Hellman protocol. In: Shoup, V. (ed.) CRYPTO 2005. LNCS, vol. 3621, pp. 546–566. Springer, Heidelberg (2005). https://doi.org/10.1007/11535218_33
54. Kurosawa, K., Furukawa, J.: 2-pass key exchange protocols from CPA-secure KEM. In: Benaloh, J. (ed.) CT-RSA 2014. LNCS, vol. 8366, pp. 385–401. Springer, Cham (2014). https://doi.org/10.1007/978-3-319-04852-9_20

55. Laguillaumie, F., Vergnaud, D.: Designated verifier signatures: anonymity and efficient construction from *any* bilinear map. In: Blundo, C., Cimato, S. (eds.) SCN 2004. LNCS, vol. 3352, pp. 105–119. Springer, Heidelberg (2005). https://doi.org/10.1007/978-3-540-30598-9_8
56. LaMacchia, B., Lauter, K., Mityagin, A.: Stronger security of authenticated key exchange. In: Susilo, W., Liu, J.K., Mu, Y. (eds.) ProvSec 2007. LNCS, vol. 4784, pp. 1–16. Springer, Heidelberg (2007). https://doi.org/10.1007/978-3-540-75670-5_1
57. Li, B., Liu, Y., Yang, S.: Lattice-based universal designated verifier signatures. In: 2018 IEEE 15th International Conference on e-Business Engineering (ICEBE), pp. 329–334 (2018)
58. Li, Y., Schäge, S.: No-match attacks and robust partnering definitions: defining trivial attacks for security protocols is not trivial. In: ACM CCS 2017, pp. 1343–1360 (2017)
59. Li, Y., Susilo, W., Mu, Y., Pei, D.: Designated verifier signature: definition, framework and new constructions. In: Indulska, J., Ma, J., Yang, L.T., Ungerer, T., Cao, J. (eds.) UIC 2007. LNCS, vol. 4611, pp. 1191–1200. Springer, Heidelberg (2007). https://doi.org/10.1007/978-3-540-73549-6_116
60. Libert, B., Ling, S., Nguyen, K., Wang, H.: Zero-knowledge arguments for lattice-based accumulators: logarithmic-size ring signatures and group signatures without trapdoors. In: Fischlin, M., Coron, J.-S. (eds.) EUROCRYPT 2016. LNCS, vol. 9666, pp. 1–31. Springer, Heidelberg (2016). https://doi.org/10.1007/978-3-662-49896-5_1
61. Lu, X., Au, M.H., Zhang, Z.: Raptor: a practical lattice-based (linkable) ring signature. In: Deng, R.H., Gauthier-Umaña, V., Ochoa, M., Yung, M. (eds.) ACNS 2019. LNCS, vol. 11464, pp. 110–130. Springer, Cham (2019). https://doi.org/10.1007/978-3-030-21568-2_6
62. Lyubashevsky, V.: Fiat-Shamir with aborts: applications to lattice and factoring-based signatures. In: Matsui, M. (ed.) ASIACRYPT 2009. LNCS, vol. 5912, pp. 598–616. Springer, Heidelberg (2009). https://doi.org/10.1007/978-3-642-10366-7_35
63. Lyubashevsky, V.: Lattice signatures without trapdoors. In: Pointcheval, D., Johansson, T. (eds.) EUROCRYPT 2012. LNCS, vol. 7237, pp. 738–755. Springer, Heidelberg (2012). https://doi.org/10.1007/978-3-642-29011-4_43
64. Lyubashevsky, V., Neven, G.: One-shot verifiable encryption from lattices. In: Coron, J.-S., Nielsen, J.B. (eds.) EUROCRYPT 2017. LNCS, vol. 10210, pp. 293–323. Springer, Cham (2017). https://doi.org/10.1007/978-3-319-56620-7_11
65. Lyubashevsky, V., Nguyen, N.K., Seiler, G.: SMILE: set membership from ideal lattices with applications to ring signatures and confidential transactions. Cryptology ePrint Archive, Report 2021/564 (2021). https://eprint.iacr.org/2021/564
66. Marlinspike, M., Perrin, T.: The double ratchet algorithm (November 2016)
67. Marlinspike, M., Perrin, T.: The X3DH key agreement protocol (November 2016)
68. Noh, G., Jeong, I.R.: Strong designated verifier signature scheme from lattices in the standard model. Secur. Commun. Netw. **9**, 6202–6214 (2017)
69. Peikert, C.: He gives C-Sieves on the CSIDH. In: Canteaut, A., Ishai, Y. (eds.) EUROCRYPT 2020. LNCS, vol. 12106, pp. 463–492. Springer, Cham (2020). https://doi.org/10.1007/978-3-030-45724-2_16
70. Poettering, B., Rösler, P.: Towards bidirectional ratcheted key exchange. In: Shacham, H., Boldyreva, A. (eds.) CRYPTO 2018. LNCS, vol. 10991, pp. 3–32. Springer, Cham (2018). https://doi.org/10.1007/978-3-319-96884-1_1

71. Prest, T.: FALCON. Technical report, National Institute of Standards and Technology (2020). https://csrc.nist.gov/projects/post-quantum-cryptography/round-3-submissions
72. Regev, O.: On lattices, learning with errors, random linear codes, and cryptography. In: 37th ACM STOC, pp. 84–93 (2005)
73. Rivest, R.L., Shamir, A., Tauman, Y.: How to leak a secret. In: Boyd, C. (ed.) ASIACRYPT 2001. LNCS, vol. 2248, pp. 552–565. Springer, Heidelberg (2001). https://doi.org/10.1007/3-540-45682-1_32
74. Saeednia, S., Kremer, S., Markowitch, O.: An efficient strong designated verifier signature scheme. In: Lim, J.-I., Lee, D.-H. (eds.) ICISC 2003. LNCS, vol. 2971, pp. 40–54. Springer, Heidelberg (2004). https://doi.org/10.1007/978-3-540-24691-6_4
75. Schwabe, P., Stebila, D., Wiggers, T.: Post-quantum TLS without handshake signatures. In: ACM CCS 2020, pp. 1461–1480 (2020)
76. Sheikhi-Garjan, M., Kiliç, N.G.O., Cenk, M.: A supersingular isogeny-based ring signature. Cryptology ePrint Archive, Report 2021/1318 (2021). https://eprint.iacr.org/2021/1318
77. Steinfeld, R., Bull, L., Wang, H., Pieprzyk, J.: Universal designated-verifier signatures. In: Laih, C.-S. (ed.) ASIACRYPT 2003. LNCS, vol. 2894, pp. 523–542. Springer, Heidelberg (2003). https://doi.org/10.1007/978-3-540-40061-5_33
78. Sun, X., Tian, H., Wang, Y.: Toward quantum-resistant strong designated verifier signature from isogenies. In 4th International Conference on Intelligent Networking and Collaborative Systems, pp. 292–296 (2012)
79. Unger, N., Goldberg, I.: Deniable key exchanges for secure messaging. In: ACM CCS 2015, pp. 1211–1223 (2015)
80. Unger, N., Goldberg, I.: Improved strongly deniable authenticated key exchanges for secure messaging. PoPETs **2018**(1), 21–66 (2018)
81. Vatandas, N., Gennaro, R., Ithurburn, B., Krawczyk, H.: On the cryptographic deniability of the signal protocol. In: Conti, M., Zhou, J., Casalicchio, E., Spognardi, A. (eds.) ACNS 2020. LNCS, vol. 12147, pp. 188–209. Springer, Cham (2020). https://doi.org/10.1007/978-3-030-57878-7_10
82. Wang, F., Hu, Y., Wang, B.: Lattice-based strong designate verifier signature and its applications. Malays. J. Comput. Sci. **25**, 11–22 (2012)
83. Wang, F., Hu, Y., Wang, B.: Identity-based strong designate verifier signature over lattices. J. China Univ. Post Telecommun. **21**, 52–60 (2014)
84. Yang, B., Yu, Y., Sun, Y.: A novel construction of SDVS with secure disavowability. Clust. Comput. **16**(4), 807–815 (2013). https://doi.org/10.1007/s10586-013-0254-y
85. Yuen, T.H., Esgin, M.F., Liu, J.K., Au, M.H., Ding, Z.: *DualRing*: generic construction of ring signatures with efficient instantiations. In: Malkin, T., Peikert, C. (eds.) CRYPTO 2021. LNCS, vol. 12825, pp. 251–281. Springer, Cham (2021). https://doi.org/10.1007/978-3-030-84242-0_10
86. Zaverucha, G., et al.: Picnic. Technical report, National Institute of Standards and Technology (2020). https://csrc.nist.gov/projects/post-quantum-cryptography/round-3-submissions
87. Zhang, Y., Liu, Q., Tang, C., Tian, H.: A lattice-based designated verifier signature for cloud computing. Int. J. High Perform. Comput. Netw. **8**, 135–143 (2015)

Post-quantum Anonymous One-Sided Authenticated Key Exchange Without Random Oracles

Ren Ishibashi(✉) and Kazuki Yoneyama

Ibaraki University, 4-12-1, Nakanarusawacho, Hitachi-shi, Ibaraki 316-8511, Japan
{21nm706r,kazuki.yoneyama.sec}@vc.ibaraki.ac.jp

Abstract. Authenticated Key Exchange (AKE) is a cryptographic protocol to share a common session key among multiple parties. Usually, PKI-based AKE schemes are designed to guarantee secrecy of the session key and mutual authentication. However, in practice, there are many cases where mutual authentication is undesirable such as in anonymous networks like Tor and Riffle, or difficult to achieve due to the certificate management at the user level such as the Internet. Goldberg et al. formulated a model of anonymous one-sided AKE which guarantees the anonymity of the client by allowing only the client to authenticate the server, and proposed a concrete scheme. However, existing anonymous one-sided AKE schemes are only known to be secure in the random oracle model. In this paper, we propose generic constructions of anonymous one-sided AKE in the random oracle model and in the standard model, respectively. Our constructions allow us to construct the first post-quantum anonymous one-sided AKE scheme from isogenies in the standard model.

Keywords: authenticated key exchange · one-sided secure · anonymity · post-quantum · isogenies

1 Introduction

Authenticated Key Exchange (AKE) is a cryptographic protocol to share a common session key among multiple parties through an unauthenticated channel such as the Internet. In ordinary PKI-based AKE, each party locally keeps its own static secret key (SSK) and issues a static public key (SPK) corresponding to the SSK. The validity of the SPK is guaranteed by a certificate issued by the certification authority. In a key exchange session, each party generates an ephemeral secret key (ESK) and sends an ephemeral public key (EPK) corresponding to the ESK to the other party. The session key is derived from these keys and the key derivation function. Ordinary AKE is intended for session key secrecy and mutual authentication, and provable security is formulated by security models such as CK model [8] and eCK model [34].

G. Hanaoka et al. (Eds.): PKC 2022, LNCS 13178, pp. 35–65, 2022.
https://doi.org/10.1007/978-3-030-97131-1_2

On the other hand, there are situations that the mutual authentication is undesirable such as anonymous networks like Tor [14] and Riffle [33]. In addition, in HTTPS transactions, it is common for an unauthenticated client to communicate with an authenticated server. In these cases, it is desirable for the client to be anonymous, and the mutual authentication is not necessary. The ordinary security models of AKE cannot cover such one-sided authentication and anonymity.

Anonymous one-sided AKE (OS-AKE) is a cryptographic protocol which guarantees the anonymity of the client with the one-sided authentication. In OS-AKE, there are a client and a server, and only the server locally keeps a SSK and publishes a certified SPK. In a key exchange session, both the client and the server generate ESK and EPK to share a common session key. Since the client does not have any static secret, OS-AKE is AKE without authentication to the client. Also, in OS-AKE, it is required that the client and the server can generate ESK/EPK in offline (i.e., before starting a session). Goldberg et al. [24] formulated a security model for OS-AKE (GSU model). The GSU model captures the anonymity of clients and exposure resilience for non-trivial leakage patterns, and they proposed a concrete scheme satisfying their model.

One of main objectives of this paper is to construct post-quantum OS-AKE because known OS-AKE schemes in the GSU model are not (fully) post-quantum.

1.1 Related Work

One-Sided AKE. The notion of one-sided AKE has been studied in many literatures. For example, to capture the security of SSL/TLS, various flavors of security models [12,13,15,23,29,31,32,38] are introduced. In these models, the application to the setting of anonymous networks is not considered and the anonymity is not focused.

Anonymous AKE. The notion of anonymous AKE has been studied in contexts of the symmetric key (including password) setting [1,3,35,44] or the group setting [10,42]. These models cannot be simply applied to (asymmetric key-based client-server) one-sided AKE.

OS-AKE. There are three existing OS-AKE schemes secure in the GSU model or its variant: ntor [24] by Goldberg et al., Ace [6] by Backes et al., and HybridOR [22] by Ghosh and Kate. These schemes are based on Diffie-Hellman (DH) problems, and HybridOR is also based on lattices. There are three problems in these schemes. First, these schemes are proved in the random oracle model. Random oracles do not exist, and cannot always be instantiated by real hash functions. Indeed, Canetti et al. [7] show that there are primitives which are secure in the random oracle model but insecure if random oracles are instantiated by real hash functions. Second, Ace and HybridOR are not proved to be secure in the original GSU model. The security of these schemes is guaranteed under an weaker freshness setting [6] than the original one. Finally, though these schemes use MAC for explicit authentication, implicit authentication is enough to satisfy the GSU model. Thus, removing such a MAC can make OS-AKE schemes be more simple and efficient. For more details of the security of existing schemes, please see Sect. 4.

Isogeny-Based AKE. Recently, many post-quantum AKE schemes are proposed from isogenies. Isogeny-based AKE schemes are classified into two settings: SIDH-based [26] and CSIDH-based [9]. There are several SIDH-based AKE schemes [19,21,36] from specific SIDH-related assumptions. Also, some generic constructions [17,25,43] of AKE can be instantiated from SIDH-based KEM. On the other hand, CSIDH-based AKE schemes [20,27,28] are also proposed. However, there is no known isogeny-based OS-AKE scheme.

1.2 Our Contribution

In this paper, we achieve the first post-quantum OS-AKE scheme without random oracles. Specifically, we propose a generic construction (GC-Std) for OS-AKE secure in the GSU model in the standard model from an IND-CCA secure KEM and an IND-CPA secure KEM with public-key-independent-ciphertext (PKIC-KEM) [45]. PKIC-KEM allows that a ciphertext can be generated independently from the public key, and a KEM session key can be generated with the ciphertext, the public key and randomness in generating the ciphertext. By instantiating GC-Std with CSIDH-based KEM schemes, we can obtain CSIDH-based anonymous OS-AKE in the standard model. Moreover, we also propose a generic construction (GC-RO) for OS-AKE secure in the GSU model in the random oracle model from an OW-CCA secure KEM and an OW-CPA secure PKIC-KEM.

Compared with existing DH-based OS-AKE schemes [6,24], an instantiation of GC-Std with DH-based KEM is secure in the standard model though existing schemes are secure in the random oracle model. For the DH-based instantiations, please see Sect. 6.

Also, the existing (partially) post-quantum OS-AKE scheme [22] is secure in the weaker model than the GSU model, and its post-quantum security is guaranteed only in a partial adversarial scenario. On the other hand, an instantiation of our generic constructions with isogeny-based KEM schemes guarantees the security in the original GSU model and is fully post-quantum for any adversarial scenario. For the isogeny-based instantiations, please see Sect. 7.

1.3 Key Technique

We start from the FSXY generic construction [18] of AKE (with the mutual authentication) from KEM (see Fig. 3). Since a difference between AKE and OS-AKE is static keys for clients, it seems that the FSXY construction removing static keys for clients works as OS-AKE. However, there are several problems in such a strategy. The eCK security model [34] and CK+ security model [18,30] for AKE allow leakage of the ESK of the target session, and the TPRF trick [18] and the NAXOS trick [34] are known as techniques to guarantee security against such leakage. However, since the client does not have the SSK in OS-AKE such tricks cannot be used in the client side. Hence, we need another solution to prove the security.

We focus on the definition of session freshness in the GSU model. Since the secrecy of the session key is trivially broken if all secret values of the client are revealed, the adversary cannot reveal at least a secret value of the client. Thus, if there is only one ESK used at the client side, there is no need to consider leakage at the client side. However, the FSXY construction uses two types of KEMs, and two randomness are necessary as ESKs. Our solution is to generate two types of randomness from an ESK with a pseudo-random function (PRF), and generate the ciphertext of each KEM from these output values of the PRF as randomness. Then, by erasing the two randomness used to generate the ciphertexts after sending the ciphertexts, the client only keeps single ESK. Therefore, the number of secret values used in our scheme is one on the client side (ESK) and two on the server side (ESK, SSK), and thus we only need to consider the case where (1) the SSK on the server side is revealed and (2) the ESK on the server side is revealed.

There is another problem to be solved. In the GSU model, both the client and the server need to be able to generate EPKs offline (i.e., before starting a session). However, in the FSXY construction, the server cannot generate a ciphertext of KEM in advance because it depends on the session-specifically generated public key sent from the client. We solve this problem by using PKIC-KEM. Since, in PKIC-KEM, the ciphertext can be generated independently from the public key, the server can generate the ciphertext offline. Finally, for reducing the computational cost of the client, we reverse procedures of the client and the server to generate such a ciphertext (i.e., the client generates the ciphertext of PKIC-KEM). For more details, please see Sect. 5.1.

2 Security Model for OS-AKE

In this section, we introduce the GSU security model [24] by Goldberg et al. Their model consists of the definitions of OS-AKE security and OS-anonymity, which cover the secrecy of session keys in one-sided authentication and the anonymity of clients, respectively.

As the notation, $x \in_R X$ denotes that the element x is sampled uniformly random from the set X.

2.1 System Model and Adversarial Capacity

Parties, Key Pairs, and Certificates. Parties are modeled as probabilistic polynomial-time Turing machines. Each party is activated by receiving an initialization message, and returns a message defined by the protocol.

A key pair that each party keeps is denoted in the form (x, X), where x is the secret value and X is the public value. The key pair includes, for example, the private key and public key in public key cryptography, and the ciphertext and the randomness used for encryption. There are two types of key pairs: ephemeral key pairs that are used in a specific session and static key pairs that are used through all sessions.

Each server owns a certificate $cert_X = (ID_S, X)$ that combines a public value X and a identifier ID_S as SPK, and uses it for the server authentication. When a party owns the secret value x corresponding to the public value X, the party is said to be the owner of the public value X.

Protocol and Sessions. Each execution of the protocol is called a session, and each session has a session identifier *sid* assigned to the party, where each *sid* must be unique within the party. Each session is associated with a session state containing intermediate values, and the session state of *sid* by party U_P is denoted by $M^P_{state}[sid]$. If a session *sid* is executed within a party, the party is called the owner of *sid*. Also, if the owner of a session completes the session by computing the session key *sk*, the session is called a completed session.

Session Execution. When the session *sid* in which party U_P is the owner is completed, the ephemeral key pair (x, X) used in the session is deleted, and U_P outputs $\perp$ or $(sk, pid, \vec{v})$ as the output $M^P_{out}[sid]$ of the session, where *sk* is the session key in the keyspace $\mathcal{SK}$, *pid* is the peer's identifier or anonymous symbol "⊛", Each vector $\vec{v_i}$ in $\vec{v} = (\vec{v_0}, \vec{v_1}, ...)$ is a vector of the public values of the static and the ephemeral keys used in the session. For example, $\vec{v_1}$ is a set of values consisting of the public values sent by party U_1. By including the public values used as part of the output, each session can be uniquely determined. If necessary, we use the notation $M^P_{out}[sid].sk$ to denote the session key of session *sid*. Other output values are denoted in the same way.

Adversary. Let *params* be a public parameter. The adversary $\mathcal{A}$ is modeled as a probabilistic polynomial-time Turing machine, which takes *params* as input and has oracle access to parties $P_1, \ldots, P_n$. $\mathcal{A}$ controls all communication between users including session activation. $\mathcal{A}$ can interfere in party U_P to execute a specific action using the following adversary's queries.

- Send$(params, pid) \rightarrow (sid, msg)$: Let a party activate a session. The party activates a new session and returns a message according to the protocol. The input value *params* is defined by the protocol and includes the following. (1) the protocol to be executed, (2) the certificate used by the party to authenticate itself if the party is a server, (3) the certificate used by the peer *pid* in the session. The *pid* is the identifier of the intended peer establishing the session. When the session is intended to be with an unauthenticated anonymous peer, the *pid* is a special symbol "⊛".

- $\mathsf{Send}(sid, msg) \to msg'$: The party executes the session sid with msg and returns the message msg' according to the protocol.
- $\mathsf{RevealNext} \to X$: $\mathcal{A}$ obtains a public value that is precomputed offline. The party generates a new key pair (x, X), records it as unused, and returns the public value X.
- $\mathsf{Partner}(X) \to x$: $\mathcal{A}$ obtains the secret value x corresponding to the public value X used in the session. If the key pair (x, X) is recorded in the party's memory, it returns the secret value x.
- $\mathsf{SessionKeyReveal}(sid) \to sk$: $\mathcal{A}$ obtains the session key of sid. It returns the session key $M^P_{out}[sid].sk$ of sid if the session is completed.

In addition, $\mathcal{A}$ can generate public keys and certificates using the following query.

- $\mathsf{EstablishCertificate}(ID_i, X)$: $\mathcal{A}$ registers a certificate containing the public value X of an unused identifier ID_i to all parties. $\mathcal{A}$ becomes the owner of the certificate as ID_i. If a party is registered by this query, we call the party *dishonest*, otherwise we call it *honest*.

Where necessary to avoid ambiguity, we use the superscript to indicate the party to whom the query is posed, such as $\mathsf{Send}^{P_i}(sid, msg)$.

Partnering. Unless a value X is the input of a Send query or the output of a RevealNext query to party P_i, and has not issued a Partner query to P_i, then the adversary $\mathcal{A}$ is called a partner of X. If a party generates a key pair (x, X) by a query from $\mathcal{A}$ or by executing a session, we call the party a partner of X. Also, If different public values X and X' are corresponding to the same secret value x, then if $\mathcal{A}$ is a partner of X, then $\mathcal{A}$ is also considered to be a partner of X'.

Correctness. If a two-party key exchange protocol Π satisfies the following conditions, Π is said to be *correct*.

- The adversary $\mathcal{A}$ relays all messages in the protocol running between the two parties without any modification.
- If a party is activated with a Send query with $pid \neq \circledast$, it will have the correct certificate for pid.
- Both parties output the same session key sk and the same vector $\vec{v}$.
- The value pid in the output of each party matches the pid in the Send query that was used to activate the party.

2.2 One-Sided AKE Security

For defining OS-AKE security, we need the notion of freshness.

Definition 1 (Freshness). *If the following conditions are satisfied, the session sid by party P_i is said to be OS-AKE fresh.*

1. *For each vector* $\vec{v_j}$ *in* $M_{out}^{P_i}$, *there is at least one public value* X *in* $\vec{v_j}$ *such that* $\mathcal{A}$ *is not a partner, where* $j \geq 1$.
2. $\mathcal{A}$ *does not issue a* SessionKeyReveal(sid) *query to any party* P_j, *where* P_j *is the owner of the certificate of* $M_{out}^{P_i}[sid].pid$ *such that it is* $M_{out}^{P_i}[sid].\vec{v} = M_{out}^{P_j}[sid].\vec{v}$.

The goal of the adversary $\mathcal{A}$ in the OS-AKE security game is to distinguish between the true session key and a random key. Initially, $\mathcal{A}$ is given a set of honest parties, and makes any sequence of the queries described above. During the experiment, $\mathcal{A}$ makes the following query.

- Test$(i, sid^*) \rightarrow \mathcal{SK}$: Here, sid^* must be OS-AKE fresh. If $M_{out}^{P_i}[sid^*].sk = \perp$ or $M_{out}^{P_i}[sid^*].pid = \circledast$, an error symbol is returned. Otherwise, it chooses $b \in_R \{0, 1\}$. If $b = 0$, then it returns $M_{out}^{P_i}[sid^*].sk$. Otherwise, it returns a random element of $\mathcal{SK}$. This query can be issued only once.

Since OS-AKE provides the one-sided authentication, the test session sid^* is only for the session of client-side that performs the authentication to the server. The adversary $\mathcal{A}$ obtains either the session key of sid^* or a random key with probability 1/2 respectively. After issuing the Test query, the game continues until $\mathcal{A}$ outputs b' as a result of guessing whether the received key is random or not. If sid^* is OS-AKE fresh by the end and the guess of $\mathcal{A}$ is correct (i.e., $b = b'$), then it defines $\mathcal{A}$ wins the game.

Definition 2 (One-sided AKE security). *The advantage of the adversary* $\mathcal{A}$ *in the above game with the OS-AKE protocol* Π *is defined as follows.*

$$Adv_{\Pi,\kappa}^{OS-AKE}(\mathcal{A}) = \Pr[b = b'] - 1/2$$

Let κ *be a security parameter. For all probabilistic polynomial-time adversaries* $\mathcal{A}$, Π *is one-sided AKE-secure if* $Adv_{\Pi,\kappa}^{OS-AKE}$ *is negligible in* κ.

Remark 1. Due to the RevealNext query, this model requires offline generation of ephemeral keys. Hence, the secret values may be stored in different locations for each generation. For example, a static key is stored in the database, an ephemeral key used for offline generation is stored in the storage, and another ephemeral key used for online generation is stored in the cache. In order to cover such a case, the leakage of each secret value is considered in OS-AKE fresh (Definition 1).

Remark 2. As described in the second condition of the Definition 1, the target session to be tested is the session in which sid matches between the two parties and the server's SSK can be revealed. Thus, the model captures weak forward secrecy which the adversary who does not modify the messages in the target session cannot break the security even if SSK is revealed. It also captures the adversarial arbitrary key registrant because of the EstablishCertificate query, which allow the adversary to establish a new party with registering an arbitrary certified keys. Furthermore, it also captures the known-key security because of the SessionKeyReveal query, which no information about the session key of the target session is revealed if other session keys are revealed.

2.3 One-Sided Anonymity

The goal of the adversary $\mathcal{A}$ in the OS-anonymity game is to distinguish which of the two clients is participating in the session. Here, instead of $\mathcal{A}$ querying directly to the target party, the challenger $\mathcal{C}$ relays its communication. $\mathcal{A}$ gives the indices i_0 and i_1 of the parties it is the target to identify to $\mathcal{C}$. $\mathcal{C}$ chooses $i^* \in_R \{i_0, i_1\}$ randomly and relays the message between $\mathcal{A}$ and P_{i^*}. $\mathcal{A}$ guesses i^*.

In the game, in addition to the normal queries, $\mathcal{A}$ can issue the following special queries to $\mathcal{C}$. The first two queries are for the activation and the communication of the target session.

- $\mathsf{Start}^{\mathcal{C}}(i_0, i_1, params, pid) \rightarrow msg'$: If $i_0 = i_1$, an error symbol is returned. Otherwise, it sets $i^* \in_R \{i_0, i_1\}$, and it poses $\mathsf{Send}^{P_{i^*}}(params, pid) \rightarrow (sid^*, msg')$. Then it returns msg'. This query can be issued only once.
- $\mathsf{Send}^{\mathcal{C}}(msg) \rightarrow msg'$: It poses $\mathsf{Send}^{P_{i^*}}(sid^*, msg) \rightarrow msg'$ and returns msg'.

The other queries that $\mathcal{A}$ can query to $\mathcal{C}$ are to leak information about the target session sid^*.

- $\mathsf{RevealNext}^{\mathcal{C}} \rightarrow X$: It queries $\mathsf{RevealNext}^{P_{i^*}}$ and returns the public value, under restriction that the returned public value is not used in any session other than the target session, and the public value generated by the adversary's direct queries to $\mathsf{RevealNext}^{P_{i^*}}$ is not used in the target session.
- $\mathsf{SessionKeyReveal}^{\mathcal{C}}() \rightarrow sk$: It poses $\mathsf{SessionKeyReveal}^{P_{i^*}}(sid^*)$ and returns the session key sk.
- $\mathsf{Partner}^{\mathcal{C}} \rightarrow x$: It poses $\mathsf{Partner}^{P_{i^*}}(X)$ and returns the secret value x, where X is the value returned by the $\mathsf{Send}^{\mathcal{C}}$ query.

Definition 3 (One-sided anonymity). *Let κ be a security parameter and $n \geq 1$. For all probabilistic polynomial-time adversaries $\mathcal{A}$, the protocol Π is one-sided anonymous if the advantage $Adv^{OS-anon}_{\Pi,\kappa}(\mathcal{A}) = \Pr[i^* = i'] - 1/2$ of $\mathcal{A}$ wins the following game is negligible in κ.*

- $\mathsf{Expt}^{OS-anon}_{\Pi,\kappa,n}(\mathcal{A})$:
  - Initialize $params$ and parties $P_1, \ldots, P_n$.
  - Sets $i' \leftarrow \mathcal{A}^{P_1,\ldots,P_n,\mathcal{C}}(params)$.
  - Suppose that $\mathcal{A}$ poses a $\mathsf{Start}^{\mathcal{C}}(i_0, i_1, params, pid)$ query and the challenger $\mathcal{C}$ chooses i^*. If $i^* = i'$ and the query of $\mathcal{A}$ satisfies the following restrictions, then $\mathcal{A}$ wins the game.
    * There is no $\mathsf{SessionKeyReveal}(sid^*)$ query to P_{i_0} nor P_{i_1}.
    * There is no $\mathsf{Partner}(X)$ query to P_{i_0} nor P_{i_1} for any public value X returned by $\mathcal{C}$.
    * There is no $\mathsf{Send}(sid^*, \cdot)$ query to P_{i_0} nor P_{i_1}.
    * Both P_{i_0} and P_{i_1} had the same certificate for pid during the run of the protocol for sid^*.

The restrictions in Definition 3 are to prevent $\mathcal{A}$ from knowing P_{i^*} trivially by obtaining information about the target session. For example, if $i^* = i_0$, then the $\mathsf{SessionKeyReveal}^{P_{i_0}}(sid^*)$ query returns the true session key, and the $\mathsf{SessionKeyReveal}^{P_{i_1}}(sid^*)$ query returns $\perp$ because P_{i_1} is not participating in sid^*. Therefore, $\mathcal{A}$ can determine $i^* = i_0$ trivially. Thus, the main restrictions in the OS-anonymity game are that queries for P_{i_0} and P_{i_1} must be posed through the challenger $\mathcal{C}$, and the public values used in the target session must not be used in any other session.

3 Building Blocks

3.1 Key Encapsulation Mechanism (KEM)

In this section, we shows the definition for KEM.

Definition 4 (KEM). *KEM consist of algorithms* (KeyGen, EnCap, DeCap) *as follows.*

- $(ek, dk) \leftarrow \mathsf{KeyGen}(1^\kappa; r_g)$*: The key generation algorithm takes* 1^κ *and* $r_g \in \mathcal{RS}_G$ *as input and outputs a key pair of public and private key* (ek, dk)*, where* κ *is a security parameter and* $\mathcal{RS}_G$ *is the randomness space of the key generation algorithm.*
- $(K, C) \leftarrow \mathsf{EnCap}(ek; r_e)$*: The encapsulation algorithm takes the public key* ek *and* $r_e \in \mathcal{RS}_E$ *as input and outputs the session key* $K \in \mathcal{KS}$ *and the ciphertext* $C \in \mathcal{CS}$*, where* $\mathcal{RS}_E$ *is the randomness space of the encapsulation algorithm,* $\mathcal{KS}$ *is the session key space, and* $\mathcal{CS}$ *is the ciphertext space.*
- $K \leftarrow \mathsf{DeCap}(dk, C)$*: The decapsulation algorithm takes the secret key* dk *and the ciphertext* $C \in \mathcal{CS}$ *as input and outputs the session key* $K \in \mathcal{KS}$*.*

Here, for any $\kappa \in \mathbb{N}$, any public and private key $(ek, dk) \leftarrow \mathsf{KeyGen}(1^\kappa; r_g)$, and any session key and ciphertext $(K, C) \leftarrow \mathsf{EnCap}(ek; r_e)$, it is satisfied that $K \leftarrow \mathsf{DeCap}(dk, C)$.

The definition of security for KEM is as follows.

Definition 5 (IND-CCA security for KEM). *For any probabilistic polynomial time adversary* $\mathcal{A} = (\mathcal{A}_1, \mathcal{A}_2)$*, the KEM scheme is IND-CCA secure if the advantage* $Adv^{ind-cca}_{KEM,\kappa} = |\Pr[(ek, dk) \leftarrow \mathsf{KeyGen}(1^\kappa; r_g); state \leftarrow \mathcal{A}_1^{\mathcal{O}}(ek); b \leftarrow_R \{0,1\}; (K_0^*, C_0^*) \leftarrow \mathsf{EnCap}(ek; r_e); K_1^* \in_R \mathcal{KS}; b' \leftarrow \mathcal{A}_2^{\mathcal{O}}(ek, (K_b^*, C_0^*), state); b' = b] - 1/2|$ *is negligible in* κ*, where* $\mathcal{O}$ *is the decryption oracle.*

Definition 6 (OW-CCA security for KEM). *For any probabilistic polynomial time adversary* $\mathcal{A} = (\mathcal{A}_1, \mathcal{A}_2)$*, the KEM scheme is OW-CCA secure if the advantage* $Adv^{ow-cca}_{KEM,\kappa} = |\Pr[(ek, dk) \leftarrow \mathsf{KeyGen}(1^\kappa; r_g); state \leftarrow \mathcal{A}_1^{\mathcal{O}}(ek); (K^*, C^*) \leftarrow \mathsf{EnCap}(ek; r_e); K'^* \leftarrow \mathcal{A}_2^{\mathcal{O}}(ek, C^*, state); K'^* = K^*]|$ *is negligible in* κ*, where* $\mathcal{O}$ *is the decryption oracle.*

A KEM scheme is a κ-min-entropy KEM if for any secret key, the distribution $\mathcal{D}_{\mathcal{KS}}$ for K defined by $(K, C) \leftarrow \mathsf{EnCap}(ek; r_e)$, the distribution $\mathcal{D}_{pub}$ for public information, and a randomness $r_e \in \mathcal{R}_E$, it holds that $H_\infty(\mathcal{D}_{\mathcal{KS}}|\mathcal{D}_{pub}) \geq \kappa$. Here, H_∞ denotes the min-entropy function.

3.2 PKIC-KEM

In this section, we show the definition of PKIC-KEM [45] that can generate the ciphertext independently to the public key.

Definition 7 (PKIC-KEM). *PKIC-KEM consist of algorithms* $(\mathsf{wKeyGen}, \mathsf{wEnCapC}, \mathsf{wEnCapK}, \mathsf{wDeCap})$ *as follows.*

- $(ek, dk) \leftarrow \mathsf{wKeyGen}(1^\kappa; r_g)$*: The key generation algorithm takes* 1^κ *and* $r_g \in \mathcal{RS}_G$ *as input and outputs a key pair of public and private key* (ek, dk)*, where* κ *is a security parameter and* $\mathcal{RS}_G$ *is the randomness space of the key generation algorithm.*
- $C \leftarrow \mathsf{wEnCapC}(r_e)$*: The ciphertext generation algorithm takes* $r_e \in \mathcal{RS}_E$ *as input and outputs a ciphertext* $C \in \mathcal{CS}$*, where* $\mathcal{RS}_E$ *is the randomness space of the encapsulation algorithm and* $\mathcal{CS}$ *is the ciphertext space.*
- $K \leftarrow \mathsf{wEnCapK}(ek, C, r_e)$*: The encapsulation algorithm takes the public key* ek*, the ciphertext* $C \in \mathcal{CS}$ *and a randomness* $r_e \in \mathcal{RS}_E$ *as input, and outputs the session key* $K \in \mathcal{KS}$*, where* $\mathcal{KS}$ *is the session key space.*
- $K \leftarrow \mathsf{DeCap}(dk, C)$*: The decapsulation algorithm takes the secret key* dk *and the ciphertext* $C \in \mathcal{CS}$ *as input and outputs the session key* $K \in \mathcal{KS}$*.*

For any $\kappa \in \mathbb{N}$, any public and private key $(ek, dk) \leftarrow \mathsf{wKeyGen}(1^\kappa; r_g)$, and any ciphertext $C \leftarrow \mathsf{wEnCapC}(r_e)$, it is satisfied that $K \leftarrow \mathsf{wEnCapK}(ek, C, r_e)$ and $K \leftarrow \mathsf{wDeCap}(dk, C)$.

The definition of security for PKIC-KEM is as follows.

Definition 8 (IND-CPA security for PKIC-KEM). *For any probabilistic polynomial time adversary* $\mathcal{A} = (\mathcal{A}_1, \mathcal{A}_2)$*, the PKIC-KEM scheme is IND-CPA secure if the advantage* $Adv^{ind-cpa}_{PKIC-KEM,\kappa} = |\Pr[(ek, dk) \leftarrow \mathsf{wKeyGen}(1^\kappa; r_g); state \leftarrow \mathcal{A}_1(ek); b \leftarrow_R \{0, 1\}; C_0^* \leftarrow \mathsf{wEnCapC}(r_e); K_0^* \leftarrow \mathsf{wEnCapK}(ek, C_0^*, r_e); K_1^* \in_R \mathcal{KS}; b' \leftarrow \mathcal{A}_2(ek, (K_b^*, C_0^*), state); b' = b] - 1/2|$ *is negligible in* κ*.*

Definition 9 (OW-CPA security for PKIC-KEM). *For any probabilistic polynomial time adversary* $\mathcal{A} = (\mathcal{A}_1, \mathcal{A}_2)$*, the PKIC-KEM scheme is OW-CPA secure if the advantage* $Adv^{ow-cpa}_{PKIC-KEM,\kappa} = |\Pr[(ek, dk) \leftarrow \mathsf{wKeyGen}(1^\kappa; r_g); state \leftarrow \mathcal{A}_1(ek); C^* \leftarrow \mathsf{wEnCapC}(r_e); K^* \leftarrow \mathsf{wEnCapK}(ek, C^*, r_e); K'^* \leftarrow \mathcal{A}_2(ek, C^*, state); K'^* = K^*]|$ *is negligible in* κ*.*

Also, the κ-min-entropy of PKIC-KEM can be defined in the same way as KEM.

Public parameter : H, g, G
Static secret key for U_S **:** $SSK_S := b, SPK_S := g^b$

Party U_C (Client)		Party U_S (Server)
$x_1, x_2 \leftarrow_R G$	$\xrightarrow{g^{x_1}, g^{x_2}}$	$y \leftarrow_R G$
	$\xleftarrow{g^y}$	
$SK \leftarrow \mathsf{H}((g^b)^{x_1} \cdot (g^y)^{x_2}, g^{x_1}, g^{x_2}, g^y, g^b, \mathsf{Ace})$		$SK \leftarrow \mathsf{H}((g^{x_1})^b \cdot (g^{x_2})^y, g^{x_1}, g^{x_2}, g^y, g^b, \mathsf{Ace})$

Fig. 1. Overview of Ace

Public parameter : $\mathsf{H}_1, \mathsf{H}_2, g, p, t, \mathcal{X}$
Static secret key for U_S **:** $SSK_S := s, SPK_S := a, g^s$

Party U_C (Client)		Party U_S (Server)
$(r_C, e_C) \leftarrow_R \mathcal{X}; x \leftarrow_R \mathbb{Z}_p^*$;		
$p_C \leftarrow ar_C + te_C$	$\xrightarrow{p_C, g^x}$	$(r_S, e_S, e_S') \leftarrow_R \mathcal{X}$
		$p_S \leftarrow ar_S + te_S$
$k_{1C} \leftarrow p_S r_C + te_C'$	$\xleftarrow{p_S, \alpha}$	$k_{1S} \leftarrow p_C r_S + te_S'$; $\alpha \leftarrow h^R(k_{1S})$;
$k_1 = f^R(k_{1C}, \alpha)$; $k_2 = (g^s)^x$		$k_1 = f^R(k_{1S}, \alpha)$; $k_2 = (g^x)^s$;
$SK \leftarrow \mathsf{H}_1(k_1, p_C, p_S) \oplus \mathsf{H}_2(k_2, g^x, g^s)$		$SK \leftarrow \mathsf{H}_1(k_1, p_C, p_S) \oplus \mathsf{H}_2(k_2, g^x, g^s)$

Fig. 2. Overview of HybridOR

3.3 Pseudo-Random Function

We show the definition of Pseudo-Random Function (PRF). Let κ be a security parameter and $\mathbf{F} = \{\mathsf{F}_\kappa : Dom_\kappa \times \mathcal{FS}_\kappa \to Rng_\kappa\}_\kappa$ be a function family with a family of domains $\{Dom_\kappa\}_\kappa$, a family of key spaces $\{\mathcal{FS}_\kappa\}_\kappa$ and a family of ranges $\{Rng_\kappa\}_\kappa$.

Definition 10 (Pseudo-Random Function). *We say that function family* $\mathbf{F} = \{\mathsf{F}_\kappa\}_\kappa$ *is a PRF family if for any probabilistic polynomial time distinguisher* $\mathcal{D}$, $Adv^{PRF} = |\Pr[1 \leftarrow \mathcal{D}^{\mathsf{F}_\kappa(\cdot,k)}] - \Pr[1 \leftarrow \mathcal{D}^{\mathsf{RF}_\kappa(\cdot)}]| \leq negl$, *where* $\mathsf{RF}_\kappa : Dom_\kappa \to Rng_\kappa$ *is a truly random function.*

3.4 Key-Derivation Function

Let κ be a security parameter and $\mathsf{KDF} : Salt \times Dom \to Rng$ be a function with finite domain Dom, finite range Rng, and a space of non-secret random salt $Salt$.

Definition 11 (Key-Derivation Function). *We say that function* KDF *is a KDF if the following condition holds for a security parameter* κ. *For any probabilistic polynomial time adversary* $\mathcal{A}$ *and any distribution* $\mathcal{D}_{Dom}$ *over* Dom *with* $H_\infty(\mathcal{D}_{Dom}) \geq \kappa$, $|\Pr[y \in_R Rng, s \in_R Salt; 1 \leftarrow \mathcal{A}(s, y)] - \Pr[x \in_R Dom; s \in_R Salt; y \leftarrow \mathsf{KDF}(s, x); 1 \leftarrow \mathcal{A}(s, y)]| \leq negl$.

4 Security of Ace and HybridOR in GSU Model

In this section, we revisit the security of existing OS-AKE schemes. While ntor [24] is proved in the GSU model, other two schemes Ace [6] and HybridOR [22] are proved in an weaker model. Specifically, the security of Ace and HybridOR are proved under an weaker freshness setting [6] than the original one. The weak freshness is called the double value freshness, and it requires that if the client and the server has two secret values (I_1, I_2) and (J_1, J_2) respectively, then the adversary cannot reveal (I_1, J_2) or (I_2, J_1). In the OS-AKE freshness in the GSU model, the adversary is allowed to reveal such secret values. Hence, the model that Ace and HybridOR are proved is weaker than the GSU model. Here, we show the definition of the double value freshness.

Definition 12 (Double value freshness [6]). *We say that a session is double value OS-AKE fresh if it is OS-AKE fresh and the following condition does not hold.*

If $\vec{v_i}$ is (I_1, I_2) and $\vec{v_j}$ is (J_1, J_2), $\mathcal{A}$ is not a partner of (I_1, J_2) nor (I_2, J_1).

We show that Ace is not secure in the GSU model. An overview of Ace is shown in Fig. 1, where G is the exponent group and H is a random oracle. It uses two ESKs x_1 and x_2 on the client side, and a SSK b and an ESK y on the server side. By the OS-AKE freshness definition of the GSU model, the adversary can reveal (x_2, b) or (x_1, y). For example, If (x_2, b) is revealed, the adversary can compute the session key as follows.

1. Obtain (x_2, b) by Partner queries.
2. Obtain the EPKs (g^{x_1}, g^{x_2}, g^y) from the communication channel.
3. Compute the session key $SK \leftarrow \mathsf{H}((g^{x_1})^b \cdot (g^y)^{x_2}, g^{x_1}, g^{x_2}, g^y, g^b, \mathsf{Ace})$.

Next, we show that HybridOR is not secure in the GSU model. An overview of HybridOR is shown in Fig. 2, where $f^R(\cdot)$ is a robust extractor, $h^R(\cdot)$ is a randomized algorithm used to generate the signal value α, $\mathcal{X}$ is the error distribution of the ring-LWE problem, and H_1 and H_2 are random oracles. It uses two ESKs (r_C, e_C) and x on the client side, and a SSK s and an ESK (e_S, e'_S) on the server side. By the OS-AKE freshness definition of the GSU model, the adversary can reveal $((r_C, e_C), s)$ or $(x, (r_S, e'_S))$. For example, If $((r_C, e_C), s)$ is revealed, the adversary can compute the session key as follows.

1. Obtain $((r_C, e_C), s)$ by Partner queries..
2. Obtain the EPKs (g^x, p_C, p_S, α) from the communication channel.
3. Compute the session key as follows.
   (a) $k_{1C} \leftarrow p_S r_C + t e_C$
   (b) $k_1 = f^R(k_{1C}, \alpha)$
   (c) $k_2 = (g^x)^s$
   (d) $SK \leftarrow \mathsf{H}_1(k_1, p_C, p_S) \oplus \mathsf{H}_2(k_2, g^x, g^s)$

Therefore, Ace and HybridOR are insecure in the GSU model.

Remark 3. By applying our technique of using a single randomness to produce two randomness via PRFs to these schemes, we can obtain secure schemes in the GSU model.

Public parameter $params$ **:** $\mathsf{F}, \mathsf{F}', \mathsf{PRF}, \mathsf{KDF}, s$

Static secret key for U_S **:** $SSK_S := (dk_S, \sigma_S \in \mathcal{FS}, \sigma'_S \in \{0,1\}^\kappa), SPK_S := ek_S$

Party U_C (Client)		Party U_S (Server)
$r_C \in_R \mathcal{RS}; r_{TC} \in_R \mathcal{RS}'$		
$(C_C, K_C) \leftarrow \mathsf{EnCap}(ek_S; r_C)$		
$(ek_T, dk_T) \leftarrow \mathsf{wKeyGen}(1^\kappa; r_{TC})$	$\xrightarrow{C_C, ek_T}$	
		$r_S \in_R \{0,1\}^\kappa; r'_S \in_R \mathcal{FS}$
		$r_{ST} \leftarrow \mathsf{F}(\sigma_S, r_S) \oplus \mathsf{F}'(r'_S, \sigma'_S)$
	$\xleftarrow{C_T}$	$(C_T, K_T) \leftarrow \mathsf{wEnCap}(ek_T; r_{ST})$
$K_T \leftarrow \mathsf{wDeCap}(C_T, dk_T)$		$K_C \leftarrow \mathsf{DeCap}(dk_S, C_C)$
$K'_C \leftarrow \mathsf{KDF}(s, K_C);\ K'_T \leftarrow \mathsf{KDF}(s, K_T)$		$K'_C \leftarrow \mathsf{KDF}(s, K_C);\ K'_T \leftarrow \mathsf{KDF}(s, K_T)$
$sid := (ID_S, (C_C, ek_T), C_T)$		$sid := (ID_S, (C_C, ek_T), C_T)$
$SK = \mathsf{PRF}(sid, K'_C) \oplus \mathsf{PRF}(sid, K'_T)$		$SK = \mathsf{PRF}(sid, K'_C) \oplus \mathsf{PRF}(sid, K'_T)$
$M^C_{out}[sid]$		$M^S_{out}[sid]$
$:= (SK, ID_S, (C_C, ek_T), (C_T, ek_S))$		$:= (SK, \circledast, (C_C, ek_T), (C_T, ek_S))$

Fig. 3. FSXY-based OS-AKE scheme

5 Our Generic Constructions

In this section, we propose two generic constructions of OS-AKE from KEM in the standard model (GC-Std) and the random oracle model (GC-RO). GC-Std is based on IND-CCA secure KEM and IND-CPA secure PKIC-KEM, and GC-RO is based on OW-CCA secure KEM and OW-CPA secure PKIC-KEM. Our constructions are secure in the GSU model. The protocols of GC-Std and GC-RO are shown in Fig. 4 and 5, respectively.

5.1 Construction Idea

As discussed in Sect. 1.3, our generic construction are based on the FSXY construction [18] which is CK+ secure AKE scheme. Since a client does not have any static keys in OS-AKE, we show a naive FSXY-based OS-AKE protocol in Fig. 3 by simply removing static keys and related computations of the client, where $(\mathsf{KeyGen}, \mathsf{EnCap}, \mathsf{DeCap})$ is an IND-CCA secure KEM and $(\mathsf{wKeyGen}, \mathsf{wEnCap}, \mathsf{wDeCap})$ is an IND-CPA secure KEM. The CK+ security model allows leakage of the ephemeral key of the test session, and the TPRF trick is used to guarantee security against such a leakage such that $r_{ST} \leftarrow \mathsf{F}(r_S, \sigma_S) \oplus \mathsf{F}'(\sigma'_S, r'_S)$. Naturally, OS-AKE provides the one-sided authentication and clients that need to guarantee anonymity cannot have the static key pairs, and thus the TPRF trick is not available on the client side. Furthermore, though all ESKs (r_C, r_{TC}) are revealed at once by a query to the client in the CK+ model and the freshness definition prohibits leakage of ESKs if there is no SSK, the Partner query in the GSU model reveals the secret value x for the public value X and the OS-AKE freshness definition allows leakage of one of ESKs. For example, the session key can be computed if the adversary reveals an

ESK r_{TC} of the client and the SSK dk_S of the server (such a leakage is allowed in the GSU model) because the adversary can compute dk_T from r_{TC} and then can decrypt both C_C and C_T. Therefore, it is not trivial to construct OS-AKE secure scheme from the FSXY construction.

Also, in the GSU model, for RevealNext queries, the ephemeral keys used by both parties in each session must be able to be generated offline in advance. On the other hand, in the FSXY-based construction, the server needs to generate the EPK after receiving the client's message, and thus the IND-CPA secure KEM is not sufficient for OS-AKE.

For the problem on leakage in the client side, we propose a technique such that two types of randomness are generated from a single ESK. According to the definition of OS-AKE freshness, if there is only one ESK used at the client side, there is no need to consider leakage at the client side. However, the FSXY-based construction requires the generation of a ciphertext of a session-specific public key of IND-CCA KEM and IND-CPA KEM at the client side, thus two types of randomness are required. We generate two types of randomness from a single ESK through a PRF, and generate the ciphertext of each KEM from these randomness. Concretely, we construct the PRF F to obtain two outputs from one randomness by using a PRF F' and two PRFs F_0', F_1' having each range is each randomness space of KEMs. Then, two randomness $(r_0||r_1) \leftarrow \mathsf{F}(ID_S, r)$ is computed as $(r_0||r_1) = (\mathsf{F}_0'(ID_S, \mathsf{F}'(0, r))||\mathsf{F}_1'(ID_S, \mathsf{F}'(1, r)))$. In this way, two types of randomness are generated from one randomness. Here, if only F' is used in this technique, the OS-AKE security cannot be reduced to the CCA security or the CPA security. For example, in a game of the reduction to the CCA security, $r_1'^*$ is masked first, but the simulator needs to simultaneously input the correct value of r_C^* into F' to generate r_0'. This case cannot be simulated correctly because the simulator does not have r_C^*. Therefore, the output of F' is passed through F_0' and F_1' to be enabled for these reductions. We prove that our constructions are still secure under such a randomness generation in Sect. 5.2. Then, by erasing the two randomness used to generate the ciphertext and the session-specific public key after sending client's message, the target of the Partner query can be one ESK that was generated first. Therefore, the number of secret values can be one on the client side (ESK) and two on the server side (ESK, SSK).

Next, for the problem on the offline generation of EPKs, we use an IND-CPA secure PKIC-KEM instead of IND-CPA secure KEM. Since the PKIC-KEM can generate ciphertexts independently of the public key, it is possible to generate the EPK for each session before starting the session. Specifically, the server can generate C_T before starting session by using wEnCapC algorithm of PKIC-KEM.

Finally, we reverse procedures of the client and the server to generate the public key ek_T and the ciphertext C_T of PKIC-KEM. If the client generates ek_T and the server generates C_T as the FSXY construction, the client must compute wKeyGen again before decrypting C_T because the client must erase dk_T after sending client's message. Since the computational cost for the client is increased by wKeyGen, and it is not efficient, we reverse the procedures. If the client generates C_T and the server generates ek_T, then the client does not need to compute wKeyGen again.

Public parameter $params$: $\mathsf{F}', \mathsf{F}'_0, \mathsf{F}'_1, \mathsf{PRF}, \mathsf{KDF}, s$

Static secret key for U_S : $SSK_S := dk_S, SPK_S := ek_S, cert_{ek_S} = (ID_S, ek_S)$

Party U_C (Client)		Party U_S (Server)
verify ek_S using $cert_{ek_S}$ $r_C \in_R \mathcal{FS}$ $r'_0 \leftarrow \mathsf{F}'(0, r_C))$ $r'_1 \leftarrow \mathsf{F}'(1, r_C))$ $r_0 \leftarrow \mathsf{F}'_0(ID_S, r'_0)$ $r_1 \leftarrow \mathsf{F}'_1(ID_S, r'_1)$ $(C_1, K_1) \leftarrow \mathsf{EnCap}(ek_S; r_1)$ $C_0 \leftarrow \mathsf{wEnCapC}(r_0)$ erase (r'_0, r'_1, r_0, r_1)		$r_S \in_R \mathcal{RS}_G^{cpa}$ $(ek_T, dk_T) \leftarrow \mathsf{wKeyGen}(r_S)$ erase r_S
	$\xrightarrow{C_0, C_1, ID_S}$	
	$\xleftarrow{ek_T}$	
$r'_0 \leftarrow \mathsf{F}'(0, r_C))$ $r_0 \leftarrow \mathsf{F}'_0(ID_S, r'_0)$ $K_0 \leftarrow \mathsf{wEnCapK}(ek_T, C_0; r_0)$ $K'_1 \leftarrow \mathsf{KDF}(s, K_1)$; $K'_0 \leftarrow \mathsf{KDF}(s, K_0)$ $sid := (ID_S, C_0, C_1, ek_T)$ $SK = \mathsf{PRF}(sid, K'_1) \oplus \mathsf{PRF}(sid, K'_0)$ erase (r_C, r'_0, r_0) $M_{out}^C[sid]$ $:= (SK, ID_S, (C_0, C_1), (ek_T, ek_S))$		$K_1 \leftarrow \mathsf{DeCap}(dk_S, C_1)$ $K_0 \leftarrow \mathsf{wDeCap}(dk_T, C_0)$ $K'_1 \leftarrow \mathsf{KDF}(s, K_1)$; $K'_0 \leftarrow \mathsf{KDF}(s, K_0)$ $sid := (ID_S, C_0, C_1, ek_T)$ $SK = \mathsf{PRF}(sid, K'_1) \oplus \mathsf{PRF}(sid, K'_0)$ erase dk_T $M_{out}^S[sid]$ $:= (SK, \circledast, (C_0, C_1), (ek_T, ek_S))$

Fig. 4. Generic construction in the standard model (GC-Std)

In the proof of the proposed construction, by the definition of freshness, the ESK on the client side is not revealed, and thus we need to consider the case where (1) the SSK on the server side is revealed and (2) the ESK on the server side is revealed. In (1), since the ESK at the server side is not compromised, the adversary cannot compute K_0 which is the session key of the IND-CPA secure PKIC-KEM. Similarly, in (2), since the SSK at the server side is not compromised, the adversary cannot compute K_1 which is the session key of the IND-CCA secure KEM. Thus, the proposed construction satisfies the OS-AKE security. Moreover, since the ESK used by the client side in each session is only one randomness independent to the client's ID, no information about the client can be obtained from the ciphertext. Hence, the proposed construction satisfies the OS-anonymity.

5.2 OS-AKE in Standard Model

The protocol in the standard model consists of an IND-CCA secure KEM (KeyGen, EnCap, DeCap) and an IND-CPA secure PKIC-KEM (wKeyGen, wEnCapC, wEnCapK, wDeCap) as follows.

Protocol

Public Parameters: Let κ be a security parameter, $\mathsf{F}' : \{0,1\}^\kappa \times \mathcal{FS} \to \mathcal{FS}$, $\mathsf{F}_0' : \{0,1\}^\kappa \times \mathcal{FS} \to \mathcal{RS}_E^{cpa}$, $\mathsf{F}_1' : \{0,1\}^\kappa \times \mathcal{FS} \to \mathcal{RS}_E^{cca}$, and $\mathsf{PRF} : \{0,1\}^* \times \mathcal{FS} \to \{0,1\}^\kappa$ be pseudo-random functions. Also, let $\mathsf{KDF} : Salt \times \mathcal{KS} \to \mathcal{FS}$ be a key derivation function and it chooses $s \in_R Salt$, where $\mathcal{RS}_E^{cpa}$ and $\mathcal{RS}_G^{cpa}$ are randomness spaces of the encapsulation algorithm and the key generation algorithm of IND-CPA secure PKIC-KEM, $\mathcal{RS}_E^{cca}$ and $\mathcal{RS}_G^{cca}$ are randomness spaces of the encapsulation algorithm and the key generation algorithm of IND-CCA secure KEM, $\mathcal{FS}$ is a key space of the pseudo-random functions ($|\mathcal{FS}| = \kappa$), $\mathcal{KS}$ is a session key space of KEM, and $Salt$ is a salt space of the key derivation functions. These are provided as part of the public parameters.

Secret and Public Keys: Party U_S selects a randomness $r \in_R \mathcal{RS}_G^{cca}$, computes $(ek_S, dk_S) \leftarrow \mathsf{KeyGen}(1^\kappa; r)$ and sets $cert_{ek_S} = (ID_S, ek_S)$ as a certificate for U_S. The static key pair for party U_S is (ek_S, dk_S).

Key Exchange: Let U_S which has a static key pair (ek_S, dk_S) be a server, and U_C be a client. When U_C is initialized as a client, it obtains the certificate $cert_{ek_S} = (ID_S, ek_S)$ of U_S.

1. U_C verifies the server using $cert_{ek_S} = (ID_S, ek_S)$. U_C chooses an unused ephemeral key pair $((C_0, C_1), r_C)$ or chooses a ephemeral secret key $r_C \in_R \mathcal{FS}$ and sets $r_0' \leftarrow \mathsf{F}'(0, r_C))$, $r_1' \leftarrow \mathsf{F}'(1, r_C))$, $r_0 \leftarrow \mathsf{F}_0'(ID_S, r_0')$, and $r_1 \leftarrow \mathsf{F}_1'(ID_S, r_1')$. Also, U_C computes $(C_1, K_1) \leftarrow \mathsf{EnCap}(ek_S; r_1)$, $C_0 \leftarrow \mathsf{wEnCapC}(r_0)$, and erases (r_0, r_1). Then, U_C sends (C_0, C_1, ID_S) to U_S.
2. Upon receiving (C_0, C_1, ID_S), U_S chooses an unused ephemeral key pair (ek_T, dk_T) or chooses a randomness $r_S \in_R \mathcal{RS}_G^{cpa}$ and computes $(ek_T, dk_T) \leftarrow \mathsf{wKeyGen}(r_S)$ to generate a key pair, and sends ek_T to U_C. Also, U_S computes $K_1 \leftarrow \mathsf{DeCap}(dk_S, C_1)$, $K_0 \leftarrow \mathsf{wDeCap}(dk_T, C_0)$, $K_1' \leftarrow \mathsf{KDF}(s, K_1)$, and $K_0' \leftarrow \mathsf{KDF}(s, K_0)$. U_S sets $sid = (ID_S, C_0, C_1, ek_T)$ and computes the session key $SK = \mathsf{PRF}(sid, K_1') \oplus \mathsf{PRF}(sid, K_0')$. Then, U_S erases (r_S, dk_T) and outputs $(SK, \circledast, (C_0, C_1), (ek_T, ek_S))$.
3. Upon receiving ek_T, U_C sets $r_0' \leftarrow \mathsf{F}'(0, r_C))$, $r_0 \leftarrow \mathsf{F}_0'(ID_S, r_0')$, computes $K_0 \leftarrow \mathsf{wEnCapK}(ek_T, C_0, r_0)$, $K_1' \leftarrow \mathsf{KDF}(s, K_1)$, and $K_0' \leftarrow \mathsf{KDF}(s, K_0)$. U_C sets $sid = (ID_S, C_0, C_1, ek_T)$ and computes the session key $SK = \mathsf{PRF}(sid, K_1') \oplus \mathsf{PRF}(sid, K_0')$. Then, U_C erases (r_C, r_0, r_1) and outputs $(SK, ID_S, (C_0, C_1), (ek_T, ek_S))$.

Remark 4. Existing OS-AKE schemes contain the explicit authentication of the server with the key confirmation by MAC. As discussed in Sect. 1.1, the implicit authentication is sufficient to satisfy the security in the GSU model. It is trivial to be able to add the explicit authentication to our construction by the same key confirmation step.

Security. We show the security of the proposed scheme in the standard model. An intuition of the proof is shown in Sect. 5.1.

Theorem 1. *If* (KeyGen, EnCap, DeCap) *is an IND CCA secure and* κ*-min-entropy KEM,* (wKeyGen, wEnCapC, wEnCapK, wDeCap) *is an IND-CPA and* κ*-min-entropy PKIC-KEM,* F', F'_0, F'_1, *and* PRF *are pseudo-random functions, and* KDF *is a key derivation function, GC-Std is OS-AKE secure.*

Proof. *Suc* denotes the event that $\mathcal{A}$ wins. We consider the following events that cover all cases of the behavior of $\mathcal{A}$.

-E_1: The ESK dk_T^* of the server is revealed.
-E_2: The SSK dk_S^* of the server is revealed.

Let κ be a security parameter. In the OS-AKE security game, sid^* is a session ID of the target session, and the maximum number of parties is n and the maximum ℓ sessions are activated. Let the adversary $\mathcal{A}$ be a probabilistic polynomial-time adversary in κ, and construct the IND-CCA or IND-CPA adversary $\mathcal{S}$ and a distinguisher $\mathcal{D}$ from $\mathcal{A}$ that performs the OS-AKE game.

To finish the proof, we investigate events $E_i \wedge Suc$ $(i = 1, 2)$ that cover all cases of event *Suc*. Due to the page limitation, we give the proof of event $E_1 \wedge Suc$, and the proof of the other event is given in the full version.

Event $E_1 \wedge Suc$*:* We change the interface of oracle queries and the computation of the session key. These instances are gradually changed over eight hybrid experiments, depending on specific subcases. In the last hybrid experiment, the session key in the test session does not contain information of the bit b. Thus, the adversary clearly only outputs a random guess. We denote these hybrid experiments by $\mathbf{H}_0, \ldots, \mathbf{H}_7$, and the advantage of the adversary $\mathcal{A}$ when participating in experiment $\mathbf{H}_\mathbf{i}$ by $Adv(\mathcal{A}, \mathbf{H}_\mathbf{i})$.

Hybrid Experiment $\mathbf{H}_0$: This experiment denotes the real experiment for OS-AKE security and in this experiment the environment for $\mathcal{A}$ is as defined in the protocol. Thus, $Adv(\mathcal{A}, \mathbf{H}_0)$ is the same as the advantage of the real experiment.

Hybrid Experiment $\mathbf{H}_1$: This experiment aborts when a session ID is matched with multiple sessions.

By the randomness of KEM, the probability of outputting the same ciphertext from different randomness in each session is negligible. Thus, $|Adv(\mathcal{A}, \mathbf{H}_1) - Adv(\mathcal{A}, \mathbf{H}_0)| < negl$.

Hybrid Experiment $\mathbf{H}_2$: This experiment chooses a party U_S^* and a party U_C^*, an integer $i^* \in [1, \ell]$ in advance, and fixes parties and the session for the Test query. If $\mathcal{A}$ queries a session other than the i^*-th of client U_C^* (partner is U_S^*) in Test query, it aborts the experiment.

The probability that the guess of the test session is correct is $1/n^2\ell$, thus $Adv(\mathcal{A}, \mathbf{H}_2) \geq 1/n^2\ell \cdot Adv(\mathcal{A}, \mathbf{H}_1)$.

Hybrid Experiment $\mathbf{H_3}$: This experiment changes the way of the computation of $r_0'^*$ and $r_1'^*$ in the i^*-th session of U_C^* (partner is U_S^*). Instead of $r_0'^* \leftarrow \mathsf{F}'(0, r_C^*)$ and $r_1'^* \leftarrow \mathsf{F}'(1, r_C^*)$, it is changed as $r_0'^* \in_R \mathcal{FS}$ and $r_1'^* \in_R \mathcal{FS}$.

We construct a distinguisher $\mathcal{D}_0$ that distinguishes if F^* is either a pseudo-random function F' or a random function RF from $\mathcal{A}$ in $\mathbf{H_2}$ or $\mathbf{H_3}$. $\mathcal{D}_0$ performs the following steps.

[setup]

$\mathcal{D}_0$ is given a pseudo-random function $\mathsf{F}' : \{0,1\}^\kappa \times \mathcal{FS} \rightarrow \mathcal{FS}$. Then, $\mathcal{D}_0$ chooses pseudo-random functions $\mathsf{F}_0' : \{0,1\}^\kappa \times \mathcal{FS} \rightarrow \mathcal{RS}_E^{cpa}$, $\mathsf{F}_1' : \{0,1\}^\kappa \times \mathcal{FS} \rightarrow \mathcal{RS}_E^{cca}$, $\mathsf{PRF} : \{0,1\}^* \times \mathcal{FS} \rightarrow \{0,1\}^\kappa$, a key derivation function $\mathsf{KDF} : Salt \times \mathcal{KS} \rightarrow \mathcal{FS}$, and $s \in_R Salt$.

$\mathcal{D}_0$ generates (ek_i, dk_i) for each server U_i including (ek_S^*, dk_S^*) of U_S^* according to the protocol, publishes ek_i, and sets $cert_{ek_i} = (ID_i, ek_i)$ as a certificate for each server U_i. $\mathcal{D}_0$ poses 0 and 1 to the oracle F^*, receives $r_1'^*$ and $r_0'^*$ as a challenge, and computes $r_0^* \leftarrow \mathsf{F}_0'(ID_S, r_0'^*)$, $r_1^* \leftarrow \mathsf{F}_1'(ID_S, r_1'^*)$, $(C_1^*, K_1^*) \leftarrow \mathsf{EnCap}(ek_S^*; r_1^*)$, and $C_0^* \leftarrow \mathsf{wEnCapC}(r_0^*)$ for the i^*-th session of U_C^*.

[simulation]

$\mathcal{D}_0$ keeps the list L_{SK} that contains queries and answers of SessionKeyReveal. $\mathcal{D}_0$ simulates oracle queries by $\mathcal{A}$ as follows.

1. $\mathsf{Send}(params, pid)$: If the session is the i^*-th session of U_C^*, then $\mathcal{D}_0$ sets $K_1 = K_1^*$, returns (C_0^*, C_1^*, ID_S^*), and records $(\Pi, ID = pid, (C_0^*, C_1^*), (*, *), *, K_1)$ in L_{SK}. Otherwise, $\mathcal{D}_0$ chooses $((C_0, C_1), r_C)$ from the unused key pairs and returns it, or computes $((C_0, C_1), r_C)$ according to the protocol and returns it, and records $(\Pi, ID = pid, (C_0, C_1), (*, *), *, K_1)$ in L_{SK}.
2. $\mathsf{Send}(sid, msg = (C_0, C_1, id))$: If $msg = (C_0^*, C_1^*, ID_S^*)$, then $\mathcal{D}_0$ sets $K_1 = K_1^*$, chooses (ek_T^*, dk_T^*) from the unused key pairs and returns it, or generates (ek_T^*, dk_T^*) according to the protocol and return it, computes SK, and records $(\Pi, ID = id, (C_0^*, C_1^*), (ek_T^*, ek_S^*), K_0, K_1)$ and SK as a completed session in L_{SK}. Otherwise, $\mathcal{D}_0$ chooses (ek_T, dk_T) from the unused key pairs and returns it, or generates ek_T according to the protocol and returns it, computes SK, and records $(\Pi, ID = id, (C_0, C_1), (ek_T, ek_S), K_0, K_1)$ and SK as a completed session in L_{SK}.
3. $\mathsf{Send}(sid, msg = ek_T)$: If the session is the i^*-th session of U_C^*, $\mathcal{D}_0$ computes $K_0^* \leftarrow \mathsf{wEnCapK}(ek_T, C_0^*, r_0^*)$, sets $K_0 = K_0^*$, computes SK according to the protocol, and records $(\Pi, ID = id, (C_0^*, C_1^*), (ek_T, ek_S), K_0, K_1)$ and SK as a completed session in L_{SK}. Otherwise, $\mathcal{D}_0$ computes SK according to the protocol and records $(\Pi, ID = id, (C_0, C_1), (ek_T, ek_S), K_0, K_1)$ and SK as a completed session in L_{SK}.
4. $\mathsf{SessionKeyReveal}(sid)$:
   (a) If sid is not completed, then $\mathcal{D}_0$ returns error.
   (b) Otherwise, $\mathcal{D}_0$ returns SK as recorded in L_{SK}.
5. $\mathsf{Partner}(X)$: $\mathcal{D}_0$ returns the secret value x of the public value X as defined.
6. $\mathsf{RevealNext}()$: $\mathcal{D}_0$ generates a key pair (ESK,EPK), keeps it as unused, and returns the EPK to $\mathcal{A}$ as defined.

7. $\mathsf{EstablishCertificate}(ID_i, X)$: $\mathcal{D}_0$ registers the public key of ID_i as X according to the protocol, and marks U_i as a dishonest party.
8. $\mathsf{Test}(sid)$: $\mathcal{D}_0$ returns as defined.
9. $\mathcal{A}$ outputs a guess $b' \in \{0,1\}$. If $\mathcal{A}$ outputs $b' = 0$, then $\mathcal{D}_0$ outputs that $\mathsf{F}^* = \mathsf{F}'$, otherwise $\mathcal{D}_0$ outputs that $\mathsf{F}^* = \mathsf{RF}$.

[Analysis]

For $\mathcal{A}$, the simulation by $\mathcal{D}_0$ is the same as the experiment $\mathbf{H_2}$ if $\mathsf{F}^* = \mathsf{F}'$. Otherwise, the simulation by $\mathcal{D}_0$ is the same as the experiment $\mathbf{H_3}$. Thus, since the advantage of $\mathcal{D}_0$ is negligible due to the security of the PRF, $|Adv(\mathcal{A}, \mathbf{H_3}) - Adv(\mathcal{A}, \mathbf{H_2})| \le negl$.

Hybrid Experiment $\mathbf{H_4}$: This experiment changes the way of the computation of r_1^* in the i^*-th session of U_C^* (partner is U_S^*). Instead of $r_1^* \leftarrow \mathsf{F}_1'(ID_S^*, r_1')$, it is changed as $r_1^* \in_R \mathcal{RS}_E^{cca}$.

We construct a distinguisher $\mathcal{D}_1$ that distinguishes if F^* is either a pseudo-random function F_1' or a random function RF from $\mathcal{A}$ in $\mathbf{H_3}$ or $\mathbf{H_4}$. $\mathcal{D}_1$ performs the following steps.

[setup]

$\mathcal{D}_1$ is given a pseudo-random function $\mathsf{F}_1' : \{0,1\}^\kappa \times \mathcal{FS} \rightarrow \mathcal{RS}_E^{cca}$. Then, $\mathcal{D}_1$ chooses pseudo-random functions $\mathsf{F}' : \{0,1\}^\kappa \times \mathcal{FS} \rightarrow \mathcal{FS}$, $\mathsf{F}_0' : \{0,1\}^\kappa \times \mathcal{FS} \rightarrow \mathcal{RS}_E^{cpa}$, $\mathsf{PRF} : \{0,1\}^* \times \mathcal{FS} \rightarrow \{0,1\}^\kappa$, a key derivation function $\mathsf{KDF} : Salt \times \mathcal{KS} \rightarrow \mathcal{FS}$, and $s \in_R Salt$.

$\mathcal{D}_1$ generates (ek_i, dk_i) for each server U_i including (ek_S^*, dk_S^*) of U_S^* according to the protocol, publishes ek_i, and sets $cert_{ek_i} = (ID_i, ek_i)$ as a certificate for each server U_i. $\mathcal{D}_1$ poses ID_S to the oracle F^*, receives r_1^* as a challenge, and computes $(C_1^*, K_1^*) \leftarrow \mathsf{EnCap}(ek_S^*; r_1^*)$, and $C_0^* \leftarrow \mathsf{wEnCapC}(r_0^*)$ by using $r_0'^* \in_R FS$ according to the protocol for the i^*-th session of U_C^*.

[simulation]

$\mathcal{D}_1$ keeps the list L_{SK} that contains queries and answers of $\mathsf{SessionKeyReveal}$. $\mathcal{D}_1$ simulates oracle queries by $\mathcal{A}$ as follows.

1. $\mathsf{Send}(params, pid)$: If the session is the i^*-th session of U_C^*, then $\mathcal{D}_1$ sets $K_1 = K_1^*$, returns (C_0^*, C_1^*, ID_S^*), and records $(\Pi, ID = pid, (C_0^*, C_1^*), (*, *), *, K_1)$ in L_{SK}. Otherwise, $\mathcal{D}_1$ chooses $((C_0, C_1), r_C)$ from the unused key pairs and returns it, or computes $((C_0, C_1), r_C)$ according to the protocol and returns it, and records $(\Pi, ID = pid, (C_0, C_1), (*, *), *, K_1)$ in L_{SK}.
2. $\mathsf{Send}(sid, msg = (C_0, C_1, id))$: If $msg = (C_0^*, C_1^*, ID_S^*)$, then $\mathcal{D}_1$ sets $K_1 = K_1^*$, chooses (ek_T^*, dk_T^*) from the unused key pairs and returns it, or generates (ek_T^*, dk_T^*) according to the protocol and return it, computes SK, and records $(\Pi, ID = id, (C_0^*, C_1^*), (ek_T^*, ek_S^*), K_0, K_1)$ and SK as a completed session in L_{SK}. Otherwise, $\mathcal{D}_1$ chooses (ek_T, dk_T) from the unused key pairs and returns it, or generates ek_T according to the protocol and returns it, computes SK, and records $(\Pi, ID = id, (C_0, C_1), (ek_T, ek_S), K_0, K_1)$ and SK as a completed session in L_{SK}.

3. $\mathsf{Send}(sid, msg = ek_T)$: If the session is the i^*-th session of U_C^*, $\mathcal{D}_1$ computes $K_0^* \leftarrow \mathsf{wEnCapK}(ek_T^*, C_0^*, r_0^*)$, sets $K_0 = K_0^*$, computes SK according to the protocol, and records $(\Pi, ID = id, (C_0^*, C_1^*), (ek_T, ek_S), K_0, K_1)$ and SK as a completed session in L_{SK}. Otherwise, $\mathcal{D}_1$ computes SK according to the protocol and records $(\Pi, ID = id, (C_0, C_1), (ek_T, ek_S), K_0, K_1)$ and SK as a completed session in L_{SK}.
4. $\mathsf{SessionKeyReveal}(sid)$:
   (a) If sid is not completed, then $\mathcal{D}_1$ returns error.
   (b) Otherwise, $\mathcal{D}_1$ returns SK as recorded in L_{SK}.
5. $\mathsf{Partner}(X)$: $\mathcal{D}_1$ returns the secret value x of the public value X as defined.
6. $\mathsf{RevealNext}()$: $\mathcal{D}_1$ generates a key pair (ESK,EPK), keeps it as unused, and returns the EPK to $\mathcal{A}$ as defined.
7. $\mathsf{EstablishCertificate}(ID_i, X)$: $\mathcal{D}_1$ registers the public key of ID_i as X according to the protocol, and marks U_i as a dishonest party.
8. $\mathsf{Test}(sid)$: $\mathcal{D}_1$ returns as defined.
9. $\mathcal{A}$ outputs a guess $b' \in \{0,1\}$. If $\mathcal{A}$ outputs $b' = 0$, then $\mathcal{D}_1$ outputs that $\mathsf{F}^* = \mathsf{F}'_1$, otherwise $\mathcal{D}_1$ outputs that $\mathsf{F}^* = \mathsf{RF}$.

[Analysis]

For $\mathcal{A}$, the simulation by $\mathcal{D}_1$ is the same as the experiment $\mathbf{H_3}$ if $\mathsf{F}^* = \mathsf{F}'_1$. Otherwise, the simulation by $\mathcal{D}_1$ is the same as the experiment $\mathbf{H_4}$. Thus, since the advantage of $\mathcal{D}_1$ is negligible due to the security of the PRF, $|Adv(\mathcal{A}, \mathbf{H_4}) - Adv(\mathcal{A}, \mathbf{H_3})| \leq negl$.

Hybrid Experiment $\mathbf{H_5}$: This experiment changes the way of computation of K_1^* on the client side in the i^*-th session of U_C^*. Instead of computing $(C^*, K_1^*) \leftarrow \mathsf{EnCap}(ek_S^*, r_1^*)$, it is changed as $K_1^* \in_R \mathcal{KS}_{cca}$.

We construct an IND-CCA adversary $\mathcal{S}$ from $\mathcal{A}$ in $\mathbf{H_4}$ or $\mathbf{H_5}$. The $\mathcal{S}$ performs the following steps.

[init]

$\mathcal{S}$ receives ek_S^* from the challenger as a challenge.

[setup]

$\mathcal{S}$ chooses pseudo-random functions $\mathsf{F}' : \{0,1\}^\kappa \times \mathcal{FS} \to \mathcal{FS}$, $\mathsf{F}'_0 : \{0,1\}^\kappa \times \mathcal{FS} \to \mathcal{RS}_E^{cpa}$, $\mathsf{F}'_1 : \{0,1\}^\kappa \times \mathcal{FS} \to \mathcal{RS}_E^{cca}$, $\mathsf{PRF} : \{0,1\}^* \times \mathcal{FS} \to \{0,1\}^\kappa$, a key derivation function $\mathsf{KDF} : Salt \times \mathcal{KS} \to \mathcal{FS}$, and $s \in_R Salt$.

$\mathcal{S}$ receives (K_b^*, C_1^*) as a challenge and sets $C_1 = C_1^*$ for the i^*-th session of U_C^*. Also, $\mathcal{S}$ generates (ek_i, dk_i) for each server U_i other than U_S, publishes ek_i, and sets $cert_{ek_i} = (ID_i, ek_i)$ as a certificate for each server U_i.

[simulation]

$\mathcal{S}$ keeps the list L_{SK} that contains queries and answers of $\mathsf{SessionKeyReveal}$. $\mathcal{S}$ simulates oracle queries by $\mathcal{A}$ as follows.

1. $\mathsf{Send}(params, pid)$: If the session is the i^*-th session of U_C^*, then $\mathcal{S}$ computes $C_0^* \leftarrow \mathsf{wEnCapC}(r_0^*)$ where $r_0^* \in_R \mathcal{RS}_E^{cpa}$, sets $K_1 = K_b^*$, $C_1 = C_1^*$, and $C_0 = C_0^*$, returns (C_0, C_1, ID_S^*), and records $(\Pi, ID = pid, (C_0, C_1), (*, *), *, K_1)$

in L_{SK}. Otherwise, $\mathcal{S}$ chooses $((C_0, C_1), r_C)$ from the unused key pairs and returns (C_0, C_1), or computes $((C_0, C_1), r_C)$ according to the protocol and returns (C_0, C_1), and records $(\Pi, ID = pid, (C_0, C_1), (*, *), *, K_1)$ in L_{SK}.

2. $\mathsf{Send}(sid, msg = (C_0, C_1, id))$: If $id = ID_S^*$ and $C_1 \neq C_1^*$, $\mathcal{S}$ poses C_1 to the decryption oracle to obtain K_1, chooses (ek_T, dk_T) from the unused key pairs and returns ek_T, or generates (ek_T, dk_T) and returns ek_T, computes SK, and records $(\Pi, ID = id, (C_0, C_1), (ek_T, ek_S), K_0, K_1)$ and SK as a completed session in L_{SK}. Also, else if $id = ID_S^*$ and $C_1 = C_1^*$, $\mathcal{S}$ sets $K_1 = K_b^*$, chooses (ek_T^*, dk_T^*) from the unused key pairs and returns it, or generates (ek_T^*, dk_T^*) according to the protocol and returns it, computes SK, and records $(\Pi, ID = id, (C_0, C_1), (ek_T^*, ek_S^*), K_0, K_1)$ and SK as a completed session in L_{SK}. Otherwise, $\mathcal{S}$ chooses (ek_T, dk_T) from the unused key pairs and returns it, or generates (ek_T, dk_T) according to the protocol and returns it, computes SK, and records $(\Pi, ID = id, (C_0, C_1), (ek_T, ek_S), K_0, K_1)$ and SK as a completed session in L_{SK}.
3. $\mathsf{Send}(sid, msg = ek_T)$: $\mathcal{S}$ computes SK according to the protocol and records $(\Pi, ID = id, (C_0, C_1), (ek_T, ek_S), K_0, K_1)$ and SK as a completed session in L_{SK}.
4. $\mathsf{SessionKeyReveal}(sid)$:
   (a) If sid is not completed, then $\mathcal{S}$ returns error.
   (b) Otherwise, $\mathcal{S}$ returns SK as recorded in L_{SK}.
5. $\mathsf{Partner}(X)$: $\mathcal{S}$ returns the secret value x of the public value X as defined.
6. $\mathsf{RevealNext}()$: $\mathcal{S}$ generates a key pair (ESK,EPK), keeps it as unused, and returns the EPK to $\mathcal{A}$ as defined.
7. $\mathsf{EstablishCertificate}(ID_i, X)$: $\mathcal{S}$ registers the public key of ID_i as X according to the protocol, and marks U_i as a dishonest party.
8. $\mathsf{Test}(sid)$: $\mathcal{S}$ returns as defined.
9. $\mathcal{A}$ outputs a guess $b' \in \{0, 1\}$. If $\mathcal{A}$ outputs b', then $\mathcal{S}$ outputs b'.

[Analysis]

For $\mathcal{A}$, the simulation by $\mathcal{S}$ is same the as the experiment $\mathbf{H_4}$ if the challenge is (C_1^*, K_0^*). Otherwise, the simulation by $\mathcal{S}$ is same the as the experiment $\mathbf{H_5}$. Thus, since the advantage of $\mathcal{S}$ is negligible due to the security of the IND-CCA secure KEM, $|Adv(\mathcal{A}, \mathbf{H_5}) - Adv(\mathcal{A}, \mathbf{H_4})| \leq negl$.

Hybrid Experiment $\mathbf{H_6}$: This experiment changes the way of the computation of the $K_1^{'*}$ in the i^*-th session of U_C^*. Instead of computing $K_1^{'*} \leftarrow \mathsf{KDF}(s, K_1^*)$, it is changed as choosing $K_1^{'*} \in_R \mathcal{FS}$.

Since K_1^* is randomly chosen in $\mathbf{H_5}$, it has sufficient min-entropy because the KEM is κ-min-entropy KEM. Thus, by the definition of the KDF, $|Adv(\mathcal{A}, \mathbf{H_6}) - Adv(\mathcal{A}, \mathbf{H_5})| \leq negl$.

Hybrid Experiment $\mathbf{H_7}$: This experiment changes the way of the computation of SK in the i^*-th session of U_C^*. Instead of computing $SK = \mathsf{PRF}(sid, K_1) \oplus \mathsf{PRF}(sid, K_0)$, it is changed as $SK = x \oplus \mathsf{PRF}(sid, K_0)$, where $x \in_R \{0, 1\}^\kappa$.

We construct a distinguisher $\mathcal{D}_2$ that distinguishes if F^* is either a pseudo-random function PRF or a random function RF from $\mathcal{A}$ in $\mathbf{H_6}$ or $\mathbf{H_7}$. $\mathcal{D}_2$ performs the following steps.

[setup]

$\mathcal{D}_2$ is given a pseudo-random function $\mathsf{PRF} : \{0,1\}^* \times \mathcal{FS} \rightarrow \{0,1\}^\kappa$. Then, $\mathcal{D}_2$ chooses pseudo-random functions $\mathsf{F}' : \{0,1\}^\kappa \times \mathcal{FS} \rightarrow \mathcal{FS}$, $\mathsf{F}'_0 : \{0,1\}^\kappa \times \mathcal{FS} \rightarrow \mathcal{RS}_E^{cpa}$, $\mathsf{F}'_1 : \{0,1\}^\kappa \times \mathcal{FS} \rightarrow \mathcal{RS}_E^{cca}$, $\mathsf{PRF} : \{0,1\}^* \times \mathcal{FS} \rightarrow \{0,1\}^\kappa$, a key derivation function $\mathsf{KDF} : Salt \times \mathcal{KS} \rightarrow \mathcal{FS}$, and $s \in_R Salt$.

$\mathcal{D}_2$ generates (ek_i, dk_i) for each server U_i including (ek_S^*, dk_S^*) of U_S^* according to the protocol, publishes ek_i, and sets $cert_{ek_i} = (ID_i, ek_i)$ as a certificate for each server U_i.

[simulation]

$\mathcal{D}_2$ keeps the list L_{SK} that contains queries and answers of $\mathsf{SessionKeyReveal}$. $\mathcal{D}_2$ simulates oracle queries by $\mathcal{A}$ as follows.

1. $\mathsf{Send}(params, pid)$: If the session is the i^*-th session of U_C^*, then $\mathcal{D}_2$ computes $(C_1^*, K_1^*) \leftarrow \mathsf{EnCap}(ek_S^*; r_1^*)$ and $C_0^* \leftarrow \mathsf{wEnCapC}(r_0^*)$, where $r_0^* \leftarrow \mathsf{F}'_0(ID_S^*, r_0'^*)$ and $r_1^* \in_R \mathcal{RS}_E^{cca}$, returns (C_0^*, C_1^*, ID_S^*), and records $(\Pi, ID = id, (C_0^*, C_1^*), (*, *), *, K_1^*)$ in L_{SK}. Otherwise, $\mathcal{D}_2$ chooses $((C_0, C_1), r_C)$ from the unused key pairs and returns (C_0, C_1), or computes $((C_0, C_1), r_C)$ according to the protocol and returns (C_0, C_1), and records $(\Pi, ID = id, (C_0, C_1), (*, *), *, K_1^*)$ in L_{SK}.
2. $\mathsf{Send}(sid, msg = (C_0, C_1, id))$: If $msg = (C_0^*, C_1^*, ID_S^*)$, then $\mathcal{D}_2$ chooses (ek_T^*, dk_T^*) from the unused key pairs and returns it, or generates (ek_T^*, dk_T^*) according to the protocol and returns it. Also, $\mathcal{D}_2$ sets sid according to the protocol, poses it to the oracle (PRF or RF), obtains $x \in \{0,1\}^\kappa$, computes $SK^* = x \oplus \mathsf{PRF}(sid, K_0)$, and records $(\Pi, ID = id, (C_0^*, C_1^*), (ek_T^*, ek_S^*))$ and SK^* as a completed session in L_{SK}. Otherwise, $\mathcal{D}_2$ chooses (ek_T, dk_T) from the unused key pairs and returns ek_T, or generates (ek_T, dk_T) according to the protocol and returns ek_T. Also, $\mathcal{D}_2$ computes SK and records $(\Pi, ID = id, (C_0, C_1), (ek_T, ek_S))$ and SK as a completed session in L_{SK}.
3. $\mathsf{Send}(sid, msg = ek_T)$: If the session is the i^*-th session of U_C^*, then $\mathcal{D}_2$ sets sid according to the protocol, poses it to the oracle (PRF or RF), obtains $x \in \{0,1\}^\kappa$, computes $SK^* = x \oplus \mathsf{PRF}(sid, k_0)$, and records $(\Pi, ID = id, (C_0, C_1), (ek_T, ek_S))$ and SK^* as a completed session in L_{SK}. Otherwise, $\mathcal{D}_2$ computes SK according to the protocol and records $(\Pi, ID = id, (C_0, C_1), (ek_T, ek_S))$ and SK as a completed session in L_{SK}.
4. $\mathsf{SessionKeyReveal}(sid)$:
   (a) If sid is not completed, then $\mathcal{D}_2$ returns error.
   (b) Otherwise, $\mathcal{D}_2$ returns SK as recorded in L_{SK}.
5. $\mathsf{Partner}(X)$: $\mathcal{D}_2$ returns the secret value x of the public value X as defined.
6. $\mathsf{RevealNext}()$: $\mathcal{D}_2$ generates a key pair (ESK,EPK), keeps it as unused, and returns the EPK to $\mathcal{A}$ as defined.
7. $\mathsf{EstablishCertificate}(ID_i, X)$: $\mathcal{D}_2$ registers the public key of ID_i as X according to the protocol, and marks U_i as a dishonest party.
8. $\mathsf{Test}(sid)$: $\mathcal{D}_2$ returns as defined.
9. $\mathcal{A}$ outputs a guess $b' \in \{0,1\}$. If $\mathcal{A}$ outputs b', then $\mathcal{D}_2$ outputs b'.

[Analysis]

For $\mathcal{A}$, the simulation by $\mathcal{D}_2$ is the same as the experiment $\mathbf{H_6}$ if $\mathsf{F}^* = \mathsf{PRF}$. Otherwise, the simulation by $\mathcal{D}_2$ is the same as the experiment $\mathbf{H_7}$. Thus, since the advantage of $\mathcal{D}_2$ is negligible due to the security of PRF, $|Adv(\mathcal{A}, \mathbf{H_7}) - Adv(\mathcal{A}, \mathbf{H_6})| \leq negl$.

In $\mathbf{H_7}$, the session key in the test session is perfectly randomized. This gives $\mathcal{A}$ no information from the Test query, therefore $Adv(\mathcal{A}, \mathbf{H_7}) = 0$ and $\Pr[E_1 \wedge Sec] = negl$.

□

Theorem 2. *In the standard model, GC-Std is one-sided anonymous.*

Proof. We proceed by introducing another experiment, in which cannot win more than random guessing. In this new experiment, the choice of i^* is independent of the behavior of the rest of the system. Then, we show that no adversary can distinguish this new experiment from the original experiment, thereby showing the OS-anonymity of the protocol.

$\mathsf{Expt}_{GC-Std}^{OS-anon'}(\mathcal{A})$ is the same experiment as $\mathsf{Expt}_{GC-Std}^{OS-anon}(\mathcal{A})$ except for the following oracle used by the challenger $\mathcal{C}$.

- $\mathsf{Start}'(i_0, i_1, params, pid = ID_S^*) \rightarrow msg'$:
  1. If $i_0 = i_1$, then abort.
  2. Set $i^* \leftarrow_R \{i_0, i_1\}$.
  3. Set $ID^* \leftarrow ID_S^*$.
  4. Choose $((C_0^*, C_1^*), r_C^*)$ from the unused key pairs and returns (C_0^*, C_1^*, ID^*).
- $\mathsf{Send}'(sid, msg = ek_T^*)$:
  1. Compute $r_0'^* \leftarrow \mathsf{F}'(0, r_C^*))$ and $r_0^* \leftarrow \mathsf{F}_0'(ID_S, r_0'^*)$
  2. Compute $K_0^* \leftarrow \mathsf{wEnCapK}(ek_T^*, C_0^*, r_0^*)$.
  3. Compute SK according to the protocol.
- $\mathsf{SessionKeyReveal}'() \rightarrow SK$: If the test session is a completed session, return SK.
- $\mathsf{Partner}'(C^*) \rightarrow r_C^*$: Return the secret value r_C^* corresponding to C^*.
- $\mathsf{RevealNext}' \rightarrow X$: Return the future public value X and record it as unused.

Since all messages computed in $\mathsf{Expt}_{GC-Std}^{OS-anon'}(\mathcal{A})$ are independent of the choice of i^*, the adversary $\mathcal{A}$ has no advantage, thus the probability that $\mathcal{A}$ wins the game is as follows.

$$\Pr[\mathsf{Expt}_{GC-Std}^{OS-anon'}(\mathcal{A}) = win] = 1/2 \qquad (1)$$

Also, the distribution of messages returned by the challenger in $\mathsf{Expt}_{GC-Std}^{OS-anon'}(\mathcal{A})$ is the same as that returned in $\mathsf{Expt}_{GC-Std}^{OS-anon}(\mathcal{A})$. Furthermore, messages from all parties except P_{i_0} and P_{i_1} are unchanged. For messages from P_{i_0} and P_{i_1} in $\mathsf{Expt}_{GC-Std}^{OS-anon'}(\mathcal{A})$, all queries return messages of the same distribution as in $\mathsf{Expt}_{GC-Std}^{OS-anon}(\mathcal{A})$.

Public parameter $params$: $\mathsf{H}_0, \mathsf{H}_1, \mathsf{H}$

Static secret key for U_S : $SSK_S := dk_S, SPK_S := ek_S, cert_{ek_S} = (ID_S, ek_S)$

Party U_C (Client)		Party U_S (Server)
verify ek_S using $cert_{ek_S}$		
$r_C \in_R \{0,1\}^\kappa$		
$r_0 \leftarrow \mathsf{H}_0(r_C)$		
$r_1 \leftarrow \mathsf{H}_1(r_C)$		
$(C_1, K_1) \leftarrow \mathsf{EnCap}(ek_S; r_1)$		$r_S \in_R \mathcal{RS}_G^{cpa}$
$C_0 \leftarrow \mathsf{wEnCapC}(r_0)$		$(ek_T, dk_T) \leftarrow \mathsf{wKeyGen}(r_S)$
erase (r_0, r_1)		erase r_S
	$\xrightarrow{C_0, C_1, ID_S}$	
	$\xleftarrow{ek_T}$	
$r_0 \leftarrow \mathsf{H}_0(r_C)$		$K_1 \leftarrow \mathsf{DeCap}(dk_S, C_1)$
$K_0 \leftarrow \mathsf{wEnCapK}(ek_T, C_0, r_0)$		$K_0 \leftarrow \mathsf{wDeCap}(dk_T, C_0)$
$sid := (ID_S, C_0, C_1, ek_T)$		$sid := (ID_S, C_0, C_1, ek_T)$
$SK = \mathsf{H}(sid, K_0, K_1)$		$SK = \mathsf{H}(sid, K_0, K_1)$
erase (r_C, r_0)		erase dk_T
$M_{out}^C[sid]$		$M_{out}^S[sid]$
$:= (SK, ID_S, (C_0, C_1), (ek_T, ek_S))$		$:= (SK, \circledast, (C_0, C_1), (ek_T, ek_S))$

Fig. 5. Generic construction in the random oracle model (GC-RO)

Here, queries that reveal information about whether P_{i_0} or P_{i_1} participated in the test session are prohibited by the definition. For example, $\mathcal{A}$ is prohibited from using a $\mathsf{SessionKeyReveal}(sid)$ query to P_{i_0} to find out if P_{i_0} has the session key for the target session.

Thus, $\mathcal{A}$ cannot distinguish between the two games.

$$\Pr[\mathsf{Expt}_{GC-Std}^{OS-anon'}(\mathcal{A}) = win] = \Pr[\mathsf{Expt}_{GC-Std}^{OS-anon}(\mathcal{A}) = win] \quad (2)$$

From Eqs. (1) and (2), the scheme has one-sided anonymity. □

5.3 OS-AKE in Random Oracle Model

The protocol in the random oracle model consists of an OW-CCA secure KEM $(\mathsf{KeyGen}, \mathsf{EnCap}, \mathsf{DeCap})$ and an OW-CPA secure PKIC-KEM $(\mathsf{wKeyGen}, \mathsf{wEnCapC}, \mathsf{wEnCapK}, \mathsf{wDeCap})$ as follows.

Protocol

Public Parameters: Let κ be a security parameter, and $\mathsf{H}_0 : \{0,1\}^* \rightarrow \mathcal{RS}_E^{cpa}$, $\mathsf{H}_1 : \{0,1\}^* \rightarrow \mathcal{RS}_E^{cca}$, $\mathsf{H} : \{0,1\}^* \rightarrow \{0,1\}^\kappa$ be hash functions, where $\mathcal{RS}_E^{cpa}$ and $\mathcal{RS}_G^{cpa}$ are randomness spaces of the encapsulation algorithm and the key generation algorithm of OW-CPA secure PKIC-KEM, $\mathcal{RS}_E^{cca}$ and $\mathcal{RS}_G^{cca}$ are randomness spaces of the encapsulation algorithm and the key generation algorithm of OW-CCA secure KEM. These are provided as part of the public parameters.

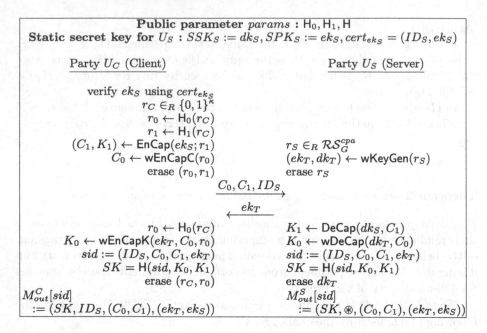

Secret and Public Keys: Party U_S selects a randomness $r \in_R \mathcal{RS}_G^{cca}$, computes $(ek_S, dk_S) \leftarrow \mathsf{KeyGen}(1^\kappa; r)$ and sets $cert_{ek_S} = (ID_S, ek_S)$ as a certificate for U_S. The static key pair for party U_S is (ek_S, dk_S).

Key Exchange: Let U_S which has a static key pair (ek_S, dk_S) be a server, and U_C be a client. When U_C is initialized as a client, it obtains the certificate $cert_{ek_S} = (ID_S, ek_S)$ of U_S.

1. U_C verifies the server using $cert_{ek_S} = (ID_S, ek_S)$. U_C chooses an unused key pair $((C_0, C_1), r_C)$ or chooses a ephemeral secret key $r_C \in_R \{0,1\}^\kappa$ and sets $r_0 \leftarrow \mathsf{H}_0(r_C)$, and $r_1 \leftarrow \mathsf{H}_1(r_C)$. Also, U_C computes $(C_1, K_1) \leftarrow \mathsf{EnCap}(ek_S; r_1)$, and $C_0 \leftarrow \mathsf{wEnCapC}(r_0)$, and deletes (r_0, r_1). Then, U_C sends (C_0, C_1, ID_S) to U_S.
2. Upon receiving (C_0, C_1, ID_S), U_S chooses an unused ephemeral key pair (ek_T, dk_T), or chooses a randomness $r_S \in_R \mathcal{RS}_G^{cpa}$ and computes $(ek_T, dk_T) \leftarrow \mathsf{wKeyGen}(r_S)$, and sends ek_T to U_C. Thus, U_S computes $K_1 \leftarrow \mathsf{DeCap}(dk_S, C_1)$ and $K_0 \leftarrow \mathsf{wDeCap}(dk_T, C_0)$, sets $sid = (ID_S, (C_0, C_1), ek_T)$, and computes the session key $SK = \mathsf{H}(sid, K_0, K_1)$. U_S erases (r_S, dk_T) and outputs $(SK, \circledast, (C_0, C_1), (ek_T, ek_S))$.
3. Upon receiving ek_T, U_C sets $r_0 \leftarrow \mathsf{H}_0(r_C)$ and computes $K_0 \leftarrow \mathsf{wEnCapK}(ek_T, C_0, r_0)$. Also, U_C sets $sid = (ID_S, (C_0, C_1), ek_T)$ and computes the session key $SK = \mathsf{H}(sid, K_0, K_1)$. Then, U_C erases (r_C, r_0), and outputs $(SK, ID_S, (C_0, C_1), (ek_T, ek_S))$.

Security. We show the security of the proposed scheme in the random oracle model. An intuition of the proof is shown in Sect. 5.1.

Theorem 3. *If* $(\mathsf{KeyGen}, \mathsf{EnCap}, \mathsf{DeCap})$ *is an OW-CCA secure KEM,* $(\mathsf{wKeyGen}, \mathsf{wEnCapC}, \mathsf{wEnCapK}, \mathsf{wDeCap})$ *is an OW-CPA secure PKIC-KEM, and* $\mathsf{H}_0, \mathsf{H}_1, \mathsf{H}$ *are random oracles, GC-RO is OS-AKE secure.*

Theorem 4. *In the random oracle model, GC-RO scheme is one-sided anonymous.*

We show the proof of Theorem 3 and 4 in the full version.

6 Instantiations Based on DH Problems

A comparison of the efficiency among our instantiations and existing schemes is shown in Table 1.

Table 1. Comparison among existing DH-based schemes and our instantiations

Protocol	Model	Resource	Assumption	Exp. (client)		Exp. (server)		Communication complexity
				Off-line	On-line	Off-line	On-line	
ntor [24]	GSU	RO	gap DH	1	2	1	1.33	$\|ID\| + 2\|G\|$
Ace [6]	weak GSU	RO	gap DH	2	1.08	1	1.08	$\|ID\| + 3\|G\|$
Ours1 [6.1]	GSU	RO	CDH	3	1	1	3	$\|ID\| + 3\|G\| + \kappa$
Ours2 [6.2]	GSU	Std	DDH	5.08	1	1	3.16	$\|ID\| + 5\|G\|$

For exponentiation costs, we apply the parallel computation technique [39] for two exponentiations using the same base, which costs 1.33 exponentiations for κ, and Avanzi's algorithm [4] for multi-exponentiations in the elliptic curve setting, which costs 1.08 exponentiations for κ. $|ID|$ is the length of server's ID and $|G|$ is the size of a group element.

6.1 Random Oracle Model

We can obtain an OS-AKE scheme in the random oracle model by instantiating GC-RO using the PSEC-KEM [40] which is an OW-CCA secure KEM, and the ElGamal KEM which is an OW-CPA secure PKIC-KEM. It is shown that the ElGamal KEM can be PKIC-KEM [45], and the PSEC-KEM and the ElGamal KEM are obviously κ-min-entropy KEM. Since these KEM schemes are based on the computational DH (CDH) assumption, the instantiation is also secure under the CDH assumption though ntor and Ace rely on the gap DH assumption. Also, the online computational cost of a client is smaller than existing schemes.

6.2 Standard Model

We can obtain an OS-AKE scheme in the standard model by instantiating GC-Std using CS3 [11] which is an IND-CCA secure KEM, and the ElGamal KEM which is an IND-CPA secure PKIC-KEM. CS3 is obviously κ-min-entropy KEM. Since these KEM schemes are based on the decisional DH (DDH) assumption, the instantiation is also secure under the DDH assumption. This scheme is the first DH-based anonymous OS-AKE scheme in the standard model. Moreover, the online computational cost of a client is smaller than existing schemes even in the standard model.

7 Instantiations Based on Isogeny Problems

7.1 Random Oracle Model

SIDH-Based. We can obtain a SIDH-based OS-AKE scheme in the random oracle model by instantiating GC-RO using the SIKE-KEM [5] which is an IND-CCA secure KEM, and an OW-CPA PKIC-KEM which is obtained by a transformation of SIKE-PKE [5]. In order to transform the SIKE-PKE to PKIC-KEM, we remove the generation of the ciphertext $C_1 = F(j) \oplus m$ (i.e., masking of plaintext m) in the encapsulation algorithm and the decryption procedure $m = F(j) \oplus C_1$ in the decryption algorithm, and use $j = \mathsf{isoex}_2(pk_3, sk_2)$ as the session key of PKIC-KEM. Such a PKIC-KEM based on SIKE-PKE is shown in Fig. 6. SIKE-KEM and PKIC-KEM in Fig. 6 are obviously κ-min-entropy KEM.

Public parameter : $\mathcal{K}_3, \mathcal{K}_2$, isogen$_3$, isogen$_2$, isoex$_2$, isoex$_3$			
wKeyGen(1^κ)	wEnCapC	wEnCapK(pk_3, C_0, sk_2)	wDeCap(sk_3, C_0)
$sk_3 \in_R \mathcal{K}_3$	$sk_2 \in_R K2$	$j = \mathsf{isoex}_2(pk_3, sk_2)$	$j = \mathsf{isoex}_3(C_0, sk_3)$
$pk_3 = \mathsf{isogen}_3(sk_3)$	$C_0 = \mathsf{isogen}_2(sk_2)$	$K = j$	$K = j$
return: (pk_3, sk_3)	**return:** C_0	**return:** K	**return:** K

Fig. 6. PKIC-KEM scheme based on SIKE-PKE [5]

Public parameter : $X, G, E_0 \in G, H$			
wKeyGen(1^κ)	wEnCapC	wEnCapK($pk, C, \mathfrak{r}$)	wDeCap(sk, C)
$\mathfrak{s} \in_R G$	$\mathfrak{r} \in_R G$	$S = [\mathfrak{r}] * pk$	$S = [sk] * C$
$sk = \mathfrak{s}$	$C = [\mathfrak{r}] * E_0$	$K = H(S)$	$K = H(S)$
$pk = [\mathfrak{s}] * E_0$	**return:** C	**return:** K	**return:** K
return :(pk, sk)			

Fig. 7. Hashed CSIDH-KEM scheme

Note that PKIC-KEM in Fig. 6 is regarded as a SIDH version of the ElGamal KEM and it is pointed that it is OW-CPA secure under the supersingular decisional DH (SSDDH) assumption [37]. Since SIKE-KEM is based on the supersingular computational DH (SSCDH) assumption, the instantiation is secure under the SSDDH assumption.

CSIDH-Based. We can obtain a CSIDH-based OS-AKE scheme in the random oracle model by instantiating GC-RO using the CSIDH-PSEC-KEM [46] which is an IND-CCA secure KEM, and CSIDH-KEM [9] which is an OW-CPA secure KEM. Note that CSIDH-KEM can be used as PKIC-KEM in the same way as Fig. 6. CSIDH-PSEC-KEM and CSIDH-KEM are obviously κ-min-entropy KEM. Note that CSIDH-KEM is pointed that it is OW-CPA secure under the commutative supersingular decisional DH (CSSDDH) assumption [37]. Since CSIDH-PSEC-KEM is based on the commutative supersingular computational DH (CSSCDH) assumption, the instantiation is secure under the CSSDDH assumption.

7.2 Standard Model

We can obtain a CSIDH-based OS-AKE scheme in the standard model by instantiating GC-Std using the KEM from smooth projective hashing [2] which is an IND-CCA secure KEM based on the hash proof system under the existence of weak pseudorandom effective group action (wPR-EGA) (a generalization of CSIDH assumptions), and a hashed CSIDH-KEM. The hashed CSIDH-KEM is a variant of CSIDH-KEM such that the session key is computed as the output of the entropy-smoothing hash function H on inputting the result of the group action of the randomness and the public key ($K = H([\mathfrak{r}] * pk)$) or the secret key and the ciphertext ($K = H([\mathfrak{s}] * C)$). We can use the hashed CSIDH-KEM as PKIC-KEM as Fig. 6. The protocol of hashed CSIDH-KEM is shown in Fig. 7. As the same as the hashed ElGamal KEM [41], it is pointed that the hashed CSIDH-KEM is IND-CPA secure under the CSSDDH assumption [37]. This instantiation is the first post-quantum anonymous OS-AKE scheme in the standard model under the wPR-EGA and the CSSDDH assumption.

Also, very recently, a KEM scheme called SimS [16] was proposed as a CSIDH-based IND-CCA secure KEM in the standard model. By using SimS as the instantiation of IND-CCA secure KEM, we can also construct the OS-AKE scheme from a knowledge of exponent-type assumption and the CSSDDH assumption.

References

1. Abdalla, M., Izabachène, M., Pointcheval, D.: Anonymous and transparent gateway-based password-authenticated key exchange. In: Franklin, M.K., Hui, L.C.K., Wong, D.S. (eds.) CANS 2008. LNCS, vol. 5339, pp. 133–148. Springer, Heidelberg (2008). https://doi.org/10.1007/978-3-540-89641-8_10
2. Alamati, N., De Feo, L., Montgomery, H., Patranabis, S.: Cryptographic group actions and applications. In: Moriai, S., Wang, H. (eds.) ASIACRYPT 2020. LNCS, vol. 12492, pp. 411–439. Springer, Cham (2020). https://doi.org/10.1007/978-3-030-64834-3_14
3. Alwen, J., Hirt, M., Maurer, U., Patra, A., Raykov, P.: Anonymous authentication with shared secrets. In: Aranha, D.F., Menezes, A. (eds.) LATINCRYPT 2014. LNCS, vol. 8895, pp. 219–236. Springer, Cham (2015). https://doi.org/10.1007/978-3-319-16295-9_12
4. Avanzi, R.M.: The complexity of certain multi-exponentiation techniques in cryptography. J. Cryptol. **18**(4), 357–373 (2005). https://doi.org/10.1007/s00145-004-0229-5
5. Azarderakhsh, R., et al.: Supersingular isogeny key encapsulation. NIST Post-Quantum Cryptography Standardization (2020)
6. Backes, M., Kate, A., Mohammadi, E.: Ace: an efficient key-exchange protocol for onion routing. In: 11th ACM WPES, pp. 55–64 (2012)
7. Canetti, R., Goldreich, O., Halevi, S.: The Random Oracle methodology, revisited. J. ACM **51**, 557–594 (2004)
8. Canetti, R., Krawczyk, H.: Analysis of key-exchange protocols and their use for building secure channels. In: Pfitzmann, B. (ed.) EUROCRYPT 2001. LNCS, vol. 2045, pp. 453–474. Springer, Heidelberg (2001). https://doi.org/10.1007/3-540-44987-6_28
9. Castryck, W., Lange, T., Martindale, C., Panny, L., Renes, J.: CSIDH: an efficient post-quantum commutative group action. In: Peyrin, T., Galbraith, S. (eds.) ASIACRYPT 2018. LNCS, vol. 11274, pp. 395–427. Springer, Cham (2018). https://doi.org/10.1007/978-3-030-03332-3_15
10. Chow, S.S.M., Choo, K.-K.R.: Strongly-secure identity-based key agreement and anonymous extension. In: Garay, J.A., Lenstra, A.K., Mambo, M., Peralta, R. (eds.) ISC 2007. LNCS, vol. 4779, pp. 203–220. Springer, Heidelberg (2007). https://doi.org/10.1007/978-3-540-75496-1_14
11. Cramer, R., Shoup, V.: Design and analysis of practical public-key encryption schemes secure against adaptive chosen ciphertext attack. SIAM J. Comput. **33**, 167–226 (2003)

12. Dagdelen, Ö., Fischlin, M., Gagliardoni, T., Marson, G.A., Mittelbach, A., Onete, C.: A cryptographic analysis of OPACITY. In: Crampton, J., Jajodia, S., Mayes, K. (eds.) ESORICS 2013. LNCS, vol. 8134, pp. 345–362. Springer, Heidelberg (2013). https://doi.org/10.1007/978-3-642-40203-6_20
13. Diemert, D., Jager, T.: On the tight security of TLS 1.3: theoretically sound cryptographic parameters for real-world deployments. J. Cryptol. **34**(3), 1–57 (2021). https://doi.org/10.1007/s00145-021-09388-x
14. Dingledine, R., Mathewson, N., Syverson, P.: Tor: the second-generation onion router. In: 13th USENIX Security Symposium, pp. 303–320 (2004)
15. Dodis, Y., Fiore, D.: Unilaterally-authenticated key exchange. In: Kiayias, A. (ed.) FC 2017. LNCS, vol. 10322, pp. 542–560. Springer, Cham (2017). https://doi.org/10.1007/978-3-319-70972-7_31
16. Fouotsa, T.B., Petit, C.: SimS: a simplification of SiGamal. In: Cheon, J.H., Tillich, J.-P. (eds.) PQCrypto 2021 2021. LNCS, vol. 12841, pp. 277–295. Springer, Cham (2021). https://doi.org/10.1007/978-3-030-81293-5_15
17. Fujioka, A., Suzuki, K., Xagawa, K., Yoneyama, K.: Practical and post-quantum authenticated key exchange from one-way secure key encapsulation mechanism. In: AsiaCCS 2013, pp. 83–94 (2013)
18. Fujioka, A., Suzuki, K., Xagawa, K., Yoneyama, K.: Strongly secure authenticated key exchange from factoring, codes, and lattices. Des. Codes Crypt. **76**(3), 469–504 (2015). https://doi.org/10.1007/s10623-014-9972-2
19. Fujioka, A., Takashima, K., Terada, S., Yoneyama, K.: Supersingular isogeny Diffie–Hellman authenticated key exchange. In: Lee, K. (ed.) ICISC 2018. LNCS, vol. 11396, pp. 177–195. Springer, Cham (2019). https://doi.org/10.1007/978-3-030-12146-4_12
20. Fujioka, A., Takashima, K., Yoneyama, K.: One-round authenticated group key exchange from isogenies. In: Steinfeld, R., Yuen, T.H. (eds.) ProvSec 2019. LNCS, vol. 11821, pp. 330–338. Springer, Cham (2019). https://doi.org/10.1007/978-3-030-31919-9_20
21. Galbraith, S.D.: Authenticated key exchange for SIDH. IACR Cryptology ePrint Archive, Report 2018/266 (2018)
22. Ghosh, S., Kate, A.: Post-quantum forward-secure onion routing. In: Malkin, T., Kolesnikov, V., Lewko, A.B., Polychronakis, M. (eds.) ACNS 2015. LNCS, vol. 9092, pp. 263–286. Springer, Cham (2015). https://doi.org/10.1007/978-3-319-28166-7_13
23. Giesen, F., Kohlar, F., Stebila, D.: On the security of TLS renegotiation. In: ACM CCS 2013, pp. 387–398 (2013)
24. Goldberg, I., Stebila, D., Ustaoglu, B.: Anonymity and one-way authentication in key exchange protocols. Des. Codes Cryptogr. **67**, 245–269 (2013). https://doi.org/10.1007/s10623-011-9604-z
25. de Saint Guilhem, C., Smart, N.P., Warinschi, B.: Generic forward-secure key agreement without signatures. In: Nguyen, P., Zhou, J. (eds.) Information Security, ISC 2017. LNCS, vol. 10599, pp. 114–133. Springer, Cham (2017). https://doi.org/10.1007/978-3-319-69659-1_7
26. Jao, D., De Feo, L.: Towards quantum resistant cryptosystems from supersingular elliptic curve isogenies. In: Yang, B.-Y. (ed.) PQCrypto 2011. LNCS, vol. 7071, pp. 19–34. Springer, Heidelberg (2011). https://doi.org/10.1007/978-3-642-25405-5_2
27. Kawashima, T., Takashima, K., Aikawa, Y., Takagi, T.: An efficient authenticated key exchange from random self-reducibility on CSIDH. In: Hong, D. (ed.) ICISC 2020. LNCS, vol. 12593, pp. 58–84. Springer, Cham (2021). https://doi.org/10.1007/978-3-030-68890-5_4

28. de Kock, B., Gjøsteen, K., Veroni, M.: Practical isogeny-based key-exchange with optimal tightness. In: Dunkelman, O., Jacobson, Jr., M.J., O'Flynn, C. (eds.) SAC 2020. LNCS, vol. 12804, pp. 451–479. Springer, Cham (2021). https://doi.org/10.1007/978-3-030-81652-0_18
29. Kohlar, F., Schäge, S., Schwenk, J.: On the security of TLS-DH and TLS-RSA in the standard model. IACR Cryptology ePrint Archive, Report 2013/367 (2013)
30. Krawczyk, H.: HMQV: a high-performance secure Diffie-Hellman protocol. In: Shoup, V. (ed.) CRYPTO 2005. LNCS, vol. 3621, pp. 546–566. Springer, Heidelberg (2005). https://doi.org/10.1007/11535218_33
31. Krawczyk, H., Paterson, K.G., Wee, H.: On the security of the TLS protocol: a systematic analysis. In: Canetti, R., Garay, J.A. (eds.) CRYPTO 2013. LNCS, vol. 8042, pp. 429–448. Springer, Heidelberg (2013). https://doi.org/10.1007/978-3-642-40041-4_24
32. Krawczyk, H., Wee, H.: The OPTLS protocol and TLS 1.3. In: EuroS&P 2016, pp. 81–96 (2016)
33. Kwon, A., Lazar, D., Devadas, S., Ford, B.: Riffle: an efficient communication system with strong anonymity. In: 16th PETS, pp. 115–134 (2016)
34. LaMacchia, B., Lauter, K., Mityagin, A.: Stronger security of authenticated key exchange. In: Susilo, W., Liu, J.K., Mu, Y. (eds.) ProvSec 2007. LNCS, vol. 4784, pp. 1–16. Springer, Heidelberg (2007). https://doi.org/10.1007/978-3-540-75670-5_1
35. Lee, M.-F., Smart, N.P., Warinschi, B., Watson, G.J.: Anonymity guarantees of the UMTS/LTE authentication and connection protocol. Int. J. Inf. Secur. **13**(6), 513–527 (2014). https://doi.org/10.1007/s10207-014-0231-3
36. Longa, P.: A note on post-quantum authenticated key exchange from supersingular isogenies. IACR Cryptology ePrint Archive, Report 2018/267 (2018)
37. Moriya, T., Onuki, H., Takagi, T.: SiGamal: a supersingular isogeny-based PKE and its application to a PRF. In: Moriai, S., Wang, H. (eds.) ASIACRYPT 2020. LNCS, vol. 12492, pp. 551–580. Springer, Cham (2020). https://doi.org/10.1007/978-3-030-64834-3_19
38. Morrissey, P., Smart, N.P., Warinschi, B.: A modular security analysis of the TLS handshake protocol. In: Pieprzyk, J. (ed.) ASIACRYPT 2008. LNCS, vol. 5350, pp. 55–73. Springer, Heidelberg (2008). https://doi.org/10.1007/978-3-540-89255-7_5
39. M'Raíhi, D., Naccache, D.: Batch exponentiation: a fast DLP-based signature generation strategy. In: ACM CCS 1996, pp. 58–61 (1996)
40. Shoup, V.: A proposal for an ISO standard for public key encryption. IACR Cryptology ePrint Archive, Report 2001/112 (2001)
41. Shoup, V.: Sequences of games: a tool for taming complexity in security proofs. IACR Cryptology ePrint Archive, Report 2004/332 (2004)
42. Walker, J., Li, J.: Key exchange with anonymous authentication using DAA-SIGMA protocol. In: Chen, L., Yung, M. (eds.) INTRUST 2010. LNCS, vol. 6802, pp. 108–127. Springer, Heidelberg (2011). https://doi.org/10.1007/978-3-642-25283-9_8
43. Xu, X., Xue, H., Wang, K., Au, M.H., Tian, S.: Strongly secure authenticated key exchange from supersingular isogenies. In: Galbraith, S.D., Moriai, S. (eds.) ASIACRYPT 2019. LNCS, vol. 11921, pp. 278–308. Springer, Cham (2019). https://doi.org/10.1007/978-3-030-34578-5_11

44. Yang, X., Jiang, H., Hou, M., Zheng, Z., Xu, Q., Choo, K.-K.R.: A provably-secure two-factor authenticated key exchange protocol with stronger anonymity. In: Au, M.H., et al. (eds.) NSS 2018. LNCS, vol. 11058, pp. 111–124. Springer, Cham (2018). https://doi.org/10.1007/978-3-030-02744-5_8
45. Yoneyama, K.: One-round authenticated key exchange with strong forward secrecy in the standard model against constrained adversary. In: Hanaoka, G., Yamauchi, T. (eds.) IWSEC 2012. LNCS, vol. 7631, pp. 69–86. Springer, Heidelberg (2012). https://doi.org/10.1007/978-3-642-34117-5_5
46. Yoneyama, K.: Post-quantum variants of ISO/IEC standards: compact chosen ciphertext secure key encapsulation mechanism from isogenies. IEICE Trans. Fundam. Electron. Commun. Comput. Sci. **104–A**, 69–78 (2021)

Theory

Lockable Obfuscation from Circularly Insecure Fully Homomorphic Encryption

Kamil Klucznik[1,2](✉)

[1] CISPA Helmholtz Center for Information Security, Saarbrücken, Germany
kamil.klucznik@cispa.saarland
[2] Stanford University, Stanford, USA
kamil.klucznik@stanford.edu

Abstract. In a lockable obfuscation scheme, a party called the obfuscator takes as input a circuit C, a lock value y, and a message m, and outputs an obfuscated circuit. Given the obfuscated circuit, an evaluator can run it on an input x and learn the message if $C(x) = y$. For security, we require that the obfuscation reveals no information on the circuit as long as the lock y has high entropy even given the circuit C.

The only known constructions of lockable obfuscation schemes require indistinguishability obfuscation ($i\mathcal{O}$) or the learning with errors (LWE) assumption. Furthermore, in terms of technique, all known constructions, excluding $i\mathcal{O}$-based, are build from provably secure variations of graph-induced multilinear maps.

We show a generic construction of a lockable obfuscation scheme built from a (leveled) fully homomorphic encryption scheme that is circularly insecure. Specifically, we need a fully homomorphic encryption scheme that is secure under chosen-plaintext attack (IND-CPA) but for which there is an efficient cycle tester that can detect encrypted key cycles. Our finding sheds new light on how to construct lockable obfuscation schemes and shows why cycle tester constructions were helpful in the design of lockable obfuscation schemes. One of the many use cases for lockable obfuscation schemes are constructions for IND-CPA secure but circularly insecure encryption schemes. Our work shows that there is a connection in both ways between circular insecure encryption and lockable obfuscation.

1 Introduction

In program obfuscation, we want to compile a circuit C to an obscure form $\widehat{C}$ while preserving the functionality of the input circuit. For security, we require that $\widehat{C}$ reveal no information on C, except what is trivially known from inspecting the input/output relations. We refer to this strong security property as virtual black-box (VBB) security. Unfortunately, Barak et al. [BGI+01,BGI+12] showed that it is impossible to achieve virtual black-box security for general functionalities. On the other hand, it turns out that it is possible to realize VBB security for some relaxed classes of functions. One such relatively expressive class consists of compute-and-compare programs, for which Goyal, Koppula,

G. Hanaoka et al. (Eds.): PKC 2022, LNCS 13178, pp. 69–98null, 2022.
https://doi.org/10.1007/978-3-030-97131-1_3

and Waters [GKW17a] and independently Wichs and Zirdelis [WZ17] construct obfuscators under the learning with errors assumption. Additionally, Wichs and Zirdelis [WZ17] show a simple construction assuming indistinguishability obfuscation [BGI+01,BGI+12]. In short, we call obfuscation for such classes lockable obfuscation as in [GKW17a].

While the functionality of lockable obfuscation is limited to evasive functions, both works [GKW17a,WZ17] show numerous applications. For example, we can compile encryption schemes to their anonymous versions that hide the recipients public key, identity, or attributes, or construct a private sketch [DS05] from a non-private one [DRS04,DORS08]. Importantly, lockable obfuscation implies obfuscators for other important classes of functionalities like point functions [Can97,LPS04,Wee05] or conjunctions [BR13,BVWW16,BKM+18, BW19,BLMZ19].

Both works [GKW17a,WZ17], constructed lockable obfuscation from a variant of the graph induced multilinear maps of Gentry, Gorbunov, and Halevi [GGH15] also known as GGH15 directed encodings. Chen, Vaikuntanathan, and Wee [CVW18b] gave an extension of GGH15 encodings from permutation branching programs to read-once matrix branching program, and along the way, showed a lockable obfuscator for that class of functions. Recently, Goyal et al. [GKVW20] extended the construction from [GKW17a], to offer perfect correctness.

While all current constructions [GKW17a,WZ17,CVW18b,GKVW20] can be proven secure assuming the hardness of the learning with errors (LWE) problem [Reg05] with subexponential modulus-to-noise ratio, all lockable obfuscators, excluding the $i\mathcal{O}$ based, build upon on a variant of the GGH15 encodings technique [GGH15]. Despite recent advancements in constructing $i\mathcal{O}$ [LT17,AJL+19,Agr19,JLMS19,BHJ+19,JLS20,GJLS20,LPST16, BDGM20a,GP20,BDGM20b,WW20], the existing constructions are heavy and require circular or subexponential security of the underlying primitives. We note that even if $i\mathcal{O}$ is realizable from standard assumptions in the near future, lockable obfuscation may actually be the tool of choice in many applications for efficiency reasons or simplicity of the constructions. Nevertheless, to us, the current state of affairs is unsatisfactory. Notably, while the GGH15-based constructions themselves are elegant, the used techniques do not reveal any general design pattern from weaker primitives. Furthermore, current techniques are insufficient to instantiate lockable obfuscation from other assumptions. For instance, it is not clear how to realize lockable obfuscation from the ring version of LWE [LPR10], approximate greatest common divisor [HG01] or NTRU-style [HPS98] assumptions, in a way that exploits the underlying structure of the problems to get more efficient constructions.

1.1 Contribution

In this paper, we show generic constructions for lockable obfuscation, assuming the existence of a symmetric encryption scheme and a (leveled) fully homomorphic encryption (FHE) scheme that is indistinguishable under chosen-plaintext attack (IND-CPA). Additionally, we assume that the FHE is circularly insecure, in the sense that it is feasible to detect encrypted key cycles or encryptions of key-dependent plaintexts. We give a thorough study of our main idea and show multiple variations and extensions of our lockable obfuscation schemes.

Base Generic Constructions. Our basic construction assumes that the symmetric key encryption scheme is IND-CPA secure. We show that when we consider cryptosystems with weak keys or, in other words, leakage resilient symmetric encryption, then we can achieve lockable obfuscation where the lock value has high HILL pseudo-entropy [HILL99,HLR07] or is unpredictable given the circuit. An important observation is that when the fully homomorphic encryption scheme is itself leakage resilient for a class of leakage, then we can build the obfuscation scheme only from the FHE scheme. In particular, for the class of uniformly distributed lock values, we need to assume only the existence of the circularly insecure FHE.

Then we show a slight modification that may be of interest for concrete efficiency that assumes that the symmetric key encryption has pseudorandom ciphertexts. That is, the ciphertexts are indistinguishable from pseudorandom given an adaptive encryption oracle. We will call both schemes the base schemes.

Based on the analysis of the base schemes, we note that in the case where the FHE scheme is key-dependent message insecure, i.e., there exists a cycle tester for a key cycle of length one, then we can implement the symmetric encryption scheme as a one time pad.

Extensions. We show how to extend both schemes to lockable obfuscation with multi-bit messages. We note that there are generic methods to build such extensions. In particular, [GKW17a, WZ17] use a method that requires providing an obfuscated program for every bit of the message. Our method is conceptually different and exploits the homomorphism of the underlying FHE scheme to decode an encrypted message. Crucially, we do not need to publish an obfuscated circuit for every single bit of the message.

Finally, we observe that our technique to encode and decode a message in our lockable obfuscator can be used to launch a key recovery attack. Consequently, we show that FHE schemes that are circularly insecure and are capable of binary decomposing an encrypted message are naturally susceptible to key recovery attacks. We note, however, that the result does not influence the security of our lockable obfuscation.

Implications. As our constructions are generic and as we showcase several versions targeting different settings for lockable obfuscation, we believe that the results give us a better understanding of the primitive. Importantly we believe that the overall design paradigm is very simple and can even be used as a classroom example for lockable obfuscation. An important consequence of our work is that we showcase the usefulness of IND-CPA secure but circularly insecure encryption. Furthermore, our results, together with [GKW17a, WZ17], show a two-way connection of such encryption with lockable obfuscation. In summary, the works [GKW17a, WZ17] show that given a lockable obfuscation scheme and an IND-CPA secure encryption scheme, we can build an IND-CPA secure encryption scheme equipped with a cycle tester. We note that the encryption scheme may be a fully homomorphic encryption scheme. For completeness we give the construction in [Klu21, Appendix A]. In this paper, we show that we can build a lockable obfuscation scheme given a (leveled) fully homomorphic encryption scheme with an efficient cycle tester. We believe that our results explain why GGH15 multilinear maps or similar cascading cancellations techniques [KW16, GKW17c] devised to build cycle testers proved to be so useful to build lockable obfuscation.

Finally, in this paper, we focus solely on the generic construction, its variations, and its extensions. While our result opens the gate to lockable obfuscation schemes, secure under assumptions other than LWE, and may perhaps even admit concretely efficient instantiations, we leave concrete constructions of such to future work.

1.2 Overview of Our Techniques

In the following section, we informally discuss our results and techniques.

Our Main Idea. Let us remind again that in lockable obfuscation, a party can evaluate an obfuscation $\widehat{C}$ of the circuit C on an input x, and learn a message msg if $C(x) = \mathsf{lock}$, where lock is a lock value. We require that $\widehat{C}$ reveals no information on C, assuming that lock has large min-entropy even if the adversary (the evaluator) would be given C and some auxiliary information aux. Let us, for now, focus on the simplified case, where msg is always 1. In other words, if $C(x) = \mathsf{lock}$, then the lockable obfuscator returns 1, and $\perp$ otherwise. Intuitively, we can think of a lockable obfuscation $\widehat{C}$ as an encryption of C that we can evaluate and then test whether $C(x) = \mathsf{lock}$ or not. Note that the concept is very similar to zero testable homomorphic encryption and multilinear maps. However, in the case of lockable obfuscation, we allow testing an element of high min-entropy in contrast to testing zeros.

Encrypting the Circuit and Testing Ciphertexts. To encrypt a circuit, we can use a fully homomorphic encryption (FHE) scheme. That is an encryption scheme in which we can evaluate any polynomial-size circuit over encrypted data. We can also use a somewhat/leveled homomorphic encryption scheme where the circuit's depth is upper-bounded. Still, for simplicity, we refer to the scheme as fully homomorphic. As usual, we require that the fully homomorphic encryption scheme is indistinguishable under chosen plaintext attacks (IND-CPA). Hence an encryption of the circuit is indistinguishable from an encryption of zero and, in particular, reveals no information on the circuit. But to realize the testing part of the obfuscation seems to be rather difficult. This is because, at first glance, the IND-CPA property seems to stand in the way of testing anything about the plaintexts. However, we observe that actually, there already exist encryption schemes that are provably IND-CPA secure but allow to test whether a ciphertext encrypts its secret key or not. A long line of works [Rot13, BHW15, KRW15,

KW16, AP16, GKW17c, GKW17b, GKW17a, WZ17] showed separations between IND-CPA secure encryption and circular secure encryption. Roughly speaking, an encryption scheme is said to be n-circular secure if a vector of encryptions $\mathtt{Enc}(\mathsf{sk}_1, \mathsf{sk}_2), \ldots, \mathtt{Enc}(\mathsf{sk}_n, \mathsf{sk}_1)$ is indistinguishable from encryptions of zero. Previous works were primarily concerned with whether IND-CPA secure encryption is also circular secure. Fortunately, for our work, the answer is negative. That is, there are provably IND-CPA secure encryption schemes that are not circular secure, and in some drastic cases allow to recover the secret key if given a key cycle. We exploit such distinguishing or key recovery attacks to test whether the evaluated obfuscation of C equals the lock or not. In particular, we use the concept of cycle testers first formalized by Bishop, Hohenberger, and Waters [BHW15]. For instance, the folklore[1] circularly insecure encryption does satisfy our needs, as we need cycle testers that work correctly when given a FHE ciphertext that is not necessarily a fresh ciphertext. We note that previous work considered only cycle testers for fresh encryptions. For simplicity, we focus on the special case of 1-cycles in this section, and show a generalized construction in Sect. 3.

The Lockable Obfuscation. At first, it seems that our job is done. We set lock to the secret key sk of the FHE scheme equipped with a cycle tester, encrypt the circuit C, and we have a lockable obfuscation of C. There is but one more problem to overcome. Namely, we need to be able to choose the lock independently from the FHE parameters. Let SKE be a symmetric key encryption scheme. In the final obfuscation scheme, we give an encryption of the FHE secret key using the lock as a secret key for SKE. Concretely, we compute $\overline{\mathsf{ct}}^{(\mathsf{lock})} \leftarrow \mathsf{SKE}.\mathtt{Enc}(\mathsf{lock}, \mathsf{sk})$, $\mathsf{ct}^{(\mathsf{lock})} \leftarrow \mathsf{FHE}.\mathtt{Enc}(\mathsf{sk}, \overline{\mathsf{ct}}^{(\mathsf{lock})})$ and $\mathsf{ct} \leftarrow \mathsf{FHE}.\mathtt{Enc}(\mathsf{sk}, C)$. Then we set the obfuscated circuit as $\widehat{C} = (\mathsf{ct}^{(\mathsf{lock})}, \mathsf{ct})$. To evaluate on x, we homomorphically evaluate the universal circuit U_x that takes a circuit f and outputs $f(x)$. Specifically, we evaluate U_x on ct, obtaining as a result $\mathsf{ct}^{(C)}$ such that $\mathsf{FHE}.\mathtt{Dec}(\mathsf{sk}, \mathsf{ct}^{(C)}) = C(x)$ with high probability. Then we homomorphically evaluate the SKE decryption circuit on $\mathsf{ct}^{(\mathsf{lock})}$ using the plaintext in $\mathsf{ct}^{(C)}$ as the secret key. Precisely, we compute $\mathsf{ct}^{(\mathsf{Test})} \leftarrow \mathsf{FHE}.\mathtt{Eval}([\mathsf{ct}^{(C)}, \mathsf{ct}^{(\mathsf{lock})}], \mathsf{SKE}.\mathtt{Dec}(.,.))$. If $C(x) = \mathsf{lock}$, then $\mathsf{SKE}.\mathtt{Dec}(\mathsf{lock}, \overline{\mathsf{ct}}^{(\mathsf{lock})}) = \mathsf{sk}$ and $\mathsf{FHE}.\mathtt{Dec}(\mathsf{sk}, \mathsf{ct}^{(\mathsf{Test})}) = \mathsf{sk}$. In other words, $\mathsf{ct}^{(\mathsf{Test})}$ encrypts its secret key what we can test with a cycle tester. Otherwise, with overwhelming probability, we end up with an FHE encryption of something different from the FHE secret key.

Proving Security. To prove security, we need to construct a simulator and show that the real obfuscation is computationally indistinguishable from a simulated obfuscation. The simulator gets as input only the dimensions of the circuit and the security parameter and outputs FHE encryptions of zero of the same quantity

[1] The folklore counterexample for 1-cycles is an augmented construction of any IND-CPA secure encryption. In short, we append $y \leftarrow F(\mathsf{sk})$ to the public key, where F is a one-way function. Encryption of a message m is as in the original encryption scheme, except we return m if $F(m) = y$.

and with the same parameters as in the real obfuscation algorithm. Now we give a hybrid argument showing that a real obfuscation is indistinguishable from a simulated one.

Hybrid 0: This is the real obfuscation algorithm.

Hybrid 1: Instead of $\overline{\mathsf{ct}}^{(\mathsf{lock})} \leftarrow \mathsf{SKE.Enc}(\mathsf{lock}, \mathsf{sk})$, we compute $\mathsf{SKE.Enc}(\mathsf{lock}, 0)$. Indistinguishability of the hybrids follows from IND-CPA security of the SKE scheme.

Hybrid 2: Instead of $\mathsf{ct}^{(\mathsf{lock})} \leftarrow \mathsf{FHE.Enc}(\mathsf{sk}, \overline{\mathsf{ct}}^{(\mathsf{lock})})$, we compute $\mathsf{FHE.Enc}(\mathsf{sk}, 0)$. Indistinguishability of the hybrids follows from the IND-CPA security of the FHE scheme. Note that from Hybrid 1, $\overline{\mathsf{ct}}^{(\mathsf{lock})}$ is independent of any parameter of the FHE scheme. In particular, $\overline{\mathsf{ct}}^{(\mathsf{lock})}$ does not depend on sk anymore. Hence we can use IND-CPA of the FHE scheme, even if the adversary would know/chose lock.

Hybrid 3: Instead of $\mathsf{ct} \leftarrow \mathsf{FHE.Enc}(\mathsf{sk}, C)$, we compute $\mathsf{FHE.Enc}(\mathsf{sk}, 0)$. Indistinguishability of the hybrids follows again from the IND-CPA security of the FHE scheme.

Finally, after Hybrid 3, we end up with an obfuscation that is equivalent to a simulated one.

Lock Ciphertext in the Plain. Note that for the simulator to work, we need to encrypt the ciphertext $\overline{\mathsf{ct}}^{(\mathsf{lock})}$ with the FHE key. In many concrete instantiations, this requirement may pose a significant problem for concrete efficiency, and especially the size of the obfuscated circuit. Technically, if $\overline{\mathsf{ct}}^{(\mathsf{lock})}$ would be given in the clear, then the simulator still needs to know the lock value, and IND-CPA security is insufficient to get rid of lock. To overcome the problem, we need to assume that ciphertexts of the SKE scheme are indistinguishable from uniformly random strings. We also need to redefine the simulator, to choose $\overline{\mathsf{ct}}^{(\mathsf{lock})}$ uniformly at random. Then, in Hybrid 1, we choose $\overline{\mathsf{ct}}^{(\mathsf{lock})}$ uniformly at random, and we set Hybrid 3 in place of Hybrid 2. That is, after we change the obfuscation to choose $\overline{\mathsf{ct}}^{(\mathsf{lock})}$ uniformly in Hybrid 1, we compute $\mathsf{FHE.Enc}(\mathsf{sk}, 0)$ instead of $\mathsf{FHE.Enc}(\mathsf{sk}, C)$ in Hybrid 2.

Extending the Message Space. Finally, we show an extension of both the above obfuscation methods to the general case, where the obfuscation returns a message $\mathsf{msg} \in \{0,1\}^{\ell_{\mathsf{msg}}}$, instead of just indicating whether $C(x) = \mathsf{lock}$ or not.

Previous Approaches. Similarly, as in previous work [GKW17a, WZ17], we could encode the message by building an obfuscation for each bit of the message. To encode a 1-bit, the obfuscation is as given by the specification. To encode a 0-bit, the obfuscation is created as in a simulation. There are some additional problems with the above solution that we can resolve using pseudorandom generators as in [GKW17a, WZ17]. The obvious problem with this repetition approach is efficiency, as every single bit of the message requires publishing and evaluating an obfuscated circuit. Additionally, Goyal, Kopppula, and Waters [GKW17a] show an extension that is specific to their lockable obfuscation construction. In particular, it is not a generic construction. We show how to exploit the homomorphism of the FHE scheme in the presence of a cycle tester to encode a large message. Consequently, we obtain a generic construction that does not require publishing an obfuscated program for every bit in the circuit. Furthermore, the evaluator only need to perform a small constant number of homomorphic operation per bit of the message, in contrast to evaluating an entire obfuscated circuit.

Decoding Messages via Homomorphism and Cycle Testing. The main observation is as follows. Suppose that along with the obfuscated circuit, we publish $\mathsf{FHE.Enc}(\mathsf{msg}_i)$, where msg_i is the ith bit of the message msg. Then assuming the FHE scheme is multiplicatively homomorphic, we have with high probability

$$\mathsf{FHE.Dec}\big(\mathsf{sk}, \mathsf{FHE.Enc}(\mathsf{sk}, \mathsf{sk}) \cdot \mathsf{FHE.Enc}(\mathsf{sk}, \mathsf{msg}_i)\big) = \mathsf{msg}_i \cdot \mathsf{sk}.$$

Now, it is easy to see that if $\mathsf{msg}_i = 0$, then we have an encryption of zero, and the cycle tester will output that the ciphertext does not encode the FHE secret key. Otherwise, if $\mathsf{msg}_i = 1$, then the cycle tester will output 1 with high probability. This way, we can restore all bits of msg. Security follows immediately from our base lockable obfuscators' security and IND-CPA security of the FHE scheme.

Key Recovery Attack. The way we test the message as described above gave us a simple idea of constructing a key recovery attack against a fully homomorphic encryption scheme that has a cycle tester. The attack requires an encrypted secret key (or key cycle) and assumes the FHE scheme is capable of binary decomposing an encrypted message. Fully homomorphic encryption schemes with a binary plaintext space satisfy the later requirement immediately. Then it is easy to see that we can use the decoding technique from the previous paragraph to decode the secret keys from the key cycle.

A consequence of this observation is that a party capable of evaluating a lockable obfuscation to output a message may also be able to decrypt the obfuscated circuit. Note that this does not contradict the security notion for lockable obfuscation. However, we note that our lockable obfuscation schemes, together with the key recovery attack, tightly exemplify the security guarantees that a lockable obfuscator may offer. For instance, in constructions based on the GGH15 directed encodings technique [GGH15], it is not immediately clear whether one can easily decrypt the circuit upon successful evaluation.

1.3 Related Work and Applications

As mentioned in the introduction, all current constructions [GKW17a, WZ17, CVW18b, GKVW20] rely on the GGH15 directed encoding technique [GGH15], or indistinguishability obfuscation[2] [BGI+01, BGI+12] to build lockable obfuscation. The original works [GKW17a, WZ17] showed the first applications of lockable obfuscation. Both works show how to use lockable obfuscation to build one-sided predicate encryption assuming, additionally, attribute-based encryption, or anonymous broadcast encryption from non-anonymous broadcast encryption. A similar technique can be used to build indistinguishability obfuscation for evasive functions assuming, additionally, witness encryption. Finally, we can also compile a public key or identity-based encryption to their anonymous counterparts where ciphertexts do not reveal the receiver's public key or its identity. An important use for lockable obfuscation is to show separations between IND-CPA security and circular security. Additionally, Goyal, Koppula, and Waters [GKW17a] show random oracle uninstantiability results. Wichs and Zirdelis [WZ17], show how to use lockable obfuscation to obfuscate affine functions and conjunctions. It is worth noting that there is only a handful of conjunction obfuscator constructions. In particular, Brakerski and Rothblum [BR13] show such obfuscators from multilinear maps, Brakerski et al. [BVWW16] assume entropic LWE. Bishop et al. [BKM+18] followed by Beullens and Wee [BW19] show conjunction obfuscators in the generic group model or from new knowledge assumptions. Recently, Bartusek et al. [BLMZ19], building upon [BKM+18], showed conjunction obfuscators for exponential alphabets in the generic group model and for binary alphabets from learning parity with noise. Notably, lockable obfuscation gives the only conjunction obfuscator for exponential alphabets from standard LWE with subexponential modulus-to-noise ratio. Our work shows the first way of building such schemes generically. Furthermore, lockable obfuscation trivially implies point function and hyperplane obfuscation [Can97, LPS04, Wee05, CD08, DKL09, GKPV10, CRV10, YZ16, BS16, KY18]. Finally, [WZ17] show how to build private secure sketches [DS05] from lockable obfuscation and non-private secure sketches [DRS04, DORS08].

As discussed, the core of our technique relies on IND-CPA secure encryption that is breakable/testable in the presence of a key cycle. We explicitly use the terminology of cycle testers introduced by Bishop, Hohenberger, and Waters [BHW15]. The first separations for IND-CPA secure and circular secure encryption are due to Haitner and Holenstein [HH09] who show that there is no black-box reduction from circular secure encryption to one-way functions, or any cryptographic assumption if the adversary can obtain encryption of an arbitrarily chosen function of the secret key. Acar et al. [ABBC10] and later Cash, Green and Hohenberger [CGH12] construct encryption schemes that are testable in the presence of a key cycle of the length of 2. Rothblum [Rot13] showed encryption schemes that allow to recover the secret key given a key cycle for bit encryption. Koppula, Ramchen, and Waters [KRW15] show a IND-CPA secure encryption scheme that allows testing n-length cycles assuming indistinguishability obfuscation. Later Koppula and Waters [KW16], and independently

[2] Specifically, Wichs and Zirdelis show a lockable obfuscator from null-$i\mathcal{O}$, that is, $i\mathcal{O}$ for evasive functions. However, the only known realization requires lockable obfuscation and witness encryption which we know how to build from $i\mathcal{O}$ or multilinear maps that imply $i\mathcal{O}$.

Alamati and Peikert [AP16] achieve a similar result from LWE and ring-LWE. Goyal, Koppula, and Waters [GKW17b] showed 1-circular insecure bit encryption from $i\mathcal{O}$. Finally, [GKW17a, WZ17] used lockable obfuscation to construct cycle testers for bit encryption of unbounded cycle length.

We note that the idea of exploiting circular insecure encryption to build useful cryptographic algorithms is borrowed from a very recent paper by Kluczniak [Klu20], who shows a witness encryption scheme from a variant of fully homomorphic encryption with a cycle tester.

Other Applications. Chen et al. [CVW+18a] used lockable obfuscation to build traitor tracing schemes. Badrinarayanan et al. [BKSW18] showed separations for encryption secure under chosen ciphertext attack and Functional Encryption compatible encryption using lockable obfuscation. Chen et al. [CVW+18a] use lockable obfuscation to build mixed functional encryption [GKW18]. Lockable obfuscation was also used by Bitansky, Khurana, and Paneth [BKP19] to construct zero-knowledge arguments with low round complexity. Recently Ananth and La Placa [AL20], and Bitansky and Shmueli [BS20] constructed constant-round post-quantum secure zero-knowledge arguments using lockable obfuscation.

2 Preliminaries

Notation. We denote as $[i]_{i=1}^{n}$ the vector $[1, 2 \ldots, n]$. For brevity, we denote as $[n]$ the vector $[i]_{i=1}^{n}$ and as $[n, m]$ the vector $[n, n+1, \ldots, m]$. We sample a variable a from a distribution S as $a \leftarrow_{\mathsf{D}} S$. We sample a variable a from the uniform distribution over S as $a \leftarrow_{\mathsf{R}} S$. By default, we sample from the uniform distribution unless said otherwise. We denote as $x \leftarrow \mathsf{A}^{\mathcal{O}(.)}(y)$ an execution of the algorithm A on input y that gets access to an oracle $\mathcal{O}$ and treats it as its subroutine. In general, we mark unassigned variables when calling an algorithm with a ".".

We denote any positive polynomial as $\mathsf{poly}(.)$. Finally, we denote as $\mathsf{negl}(.)$ any negligible function. That is, for any positive polynomial $\mathsf{poly}(.)$ there exists $c \in \mathbb{N}$ such that for all $\lambda \geq c$ we have $|\mathsf{negl}(\lambda)| \leq \frac{1}{\mathsf{poly}(\lambda)}$.

Entropy. The min-entropy of a random variable A is defined as $\mathbf{H}_\infty(A) = -\log(\max_a \Pr[A = a])$. Let $\mathbf{E}$ denote the expectation of a random variable. The average conditional min-entropy of a random variable X conditioned on a possibly correlated variable Y is defined as

$$\widetilde{\mathbf{H}}_\infty(X|Y) = -\log\left(\mathbf{E}_{y \leftarrow Y}\left[2^{-\mathbf{H}_\infty(X|Y=y)}\right]\right).$$

Definition 1 (Conditional (HILL) Pseudo-Entropy [HILL99, HLR07]**).** *Let λ be a security parameter. Let $X = \{X_\lambda\}$, $Y = \{Y_\lambda\}$ be ensembles of jointly distributed random variables. We define the conditional pseudo-entropy of X conditioned on Y to be at least $\alpha(\lambda)$, denoted $\mathbf{H}_{\mathsf{HILL}}(X|Y) \geq \alpha(\lambda)$ if there exist some*

$X' = \{X'_\lambda\}$ *possibly jointly distributed with* Y *such that* $\widetilde{\mathbf{H}}_\infty(X'_\lambda|Y_\lambda) \geq \alpha(\lambda)$, *and for all* **PPT** *adversaries we have*

$$\big|\Pr[\mathsf{A}(X,Y)=1] - \Pr[\mathsf{A}(X',Y)=0]\big| = \mathsf{negl}(\lambda).$$

Symmetric Encryption. Below we give a generalized definition of symmetric key encryption. Our correctness definition states explicitly that decryption with a wrong key should result in an incorrect message with high probability. We define indistinguishability under chosen-plaintext attack and pseudorandom ciphertexts of symmetric-key ciphers. We define the security properties for secret keys sampled from a given class of distributions. Later we recall popular classes of distributions from the literature, but we stress that our results are shown generically, without relying on any particular class.

Definition 2 (Symmetric Key Encryption). *An encryption scheme* $\mathsf{SKE} = (\mathtt{Enc}, \mathtt{Dec})$ *consists of an encryption algorithm* $\mathtt{Enc}$ *and decryption algorithm* $\mathtt{Dec}$ *with the following syntax.*

$\mathtt{Enc}(\lambda, \overline{\mathsf{sk}}, \mathsf{msg})$: *Takes as input a security parameter* λ, *a secret key* $\overline{\mathsf{sk}} \in \{0,1\}^{\ell_{\mathsf{sk}}}$ *and a message* $\mathsf{msg} \in \{0,1\}^{\ell_{\mathsf{msg}}}$ *where* $\ell_{\mathsf{sk}}, \ell_{\mathsf{msg}} = \mathsf{poly}(\lambda)$, *and outputs a ciphertext* $\overline{\mathsf{ct}} \in \{0,1\}^{\ell_{\mathsf{ct}}}$ *where* $\ell_{\mathsf{ct}} = \mathsf{poly}(\lambda)$.

$\mathtt{Dec}(\overline{\mathsf{sk}}, \overline{\mathsf{ct}})$: *This deterministic algorithm takes as input a secret key* $\overline{\mathsf{sk}} \in \{0,1\}^{\ell_{\mathsf{sk}}}$ *and a ciphertext* $\overline{\mathsf{ct}} \in \{0,1\}^{\ell_{\mathsf{ct}}}$, *and outputs* $\mathsf{msg} \in \{0,1\}^{\ell_{\mathsf{msg}}}$.

Correctness: *We say that* $\mathsf{SKE} = (\mathtt{Enc}, \mathtt{Dec})$ *is correct, if for all security parameters* $\lambda \in \mathbb{N}$, $\overline{\mathsf{sk}} \in \{0,1\}^{\ell_{\mathsf{sk}}}$ *and* $\mathsf{msg} \in \{0,1\}^{\ell_{\mathsf{msg}}}$, *where* $\ell_{\mathsf{sk}}, \ell_{\mathsf{msg}} = \mathsf{poly}(\lambda)$ *we have*

$$\mathtt{Dec}(\overline{\mathsf{sk}}, \mathtt{Enc}(\lambda, \overline{\mathsf{sk}}, \mathsf{msg})) = \mathsf{msg},$$

and for all $\overline{\mathsf{sk}}' \in \{0,1\}^{\ell_{\mathsf{sk}}}$ *such that* $\overline{\mathsf{sk}}' \neq \overline{\mathsf{sk}}$ *we have*

$$\Pr\left[\mathtt{Dec}(\overline{\mathsf{sk}}', \mathtt{Enc}(\lambda, \overline{\mathsf{sk}}, \mathsf{msg})) = \mathsf{msg}\right] = \mathsf{Err}^{\mathsf{corr}}_{\mathsf{SKE}}(\lambda),$$

where $\mathsf{Err}^{\mathsf{corr}}_{\mathsf{SKE}}(\lambda) = \mathsf{negl}(\lambda)$.

$\mathcal{D}$**-Indistinguishability Under Chosen Plaintext Attack:** *Let* $\lambda \in \mathbb{N}$ *be a security parameter and* $\mathsf{A} = (\mathsf{A}_0, \mathsf{A}_1)$ *be a* **PPT** *adversary. Let* $\mathcal{D}$ *be a class of distribution ensembles* $\{D_k\}_{k\in\mathbb{N}}$ *that sample* $(\overline{\mathsf{sk}}, \mathsf{aux}) \leftarrow_{\mathsf{D}} D_k$ *with* $\overline{\mathsf{sk}} \in \{0,1\}^{\ell_{\mathsf{sk}}}$ *where* $\ell_{\mathsf{sk}} = \mathsf{poly}(k)$. *We define the advantage of the adversary* A *against a* $\mathsf{SKE} = (\mathtt{Enc}, \mathtt{Dec})$ *encryption scheme in the* $\mathcal{D}$-$\mathsf{IND\text{-}CPA}$ *game as*

$$\mathsf{Adv}^{\mathsf{IND\text{-}CPA}}_{\mathsf{A},\mathsf{SKE}}(\lambda) = \Pr\left[\mathsf{A}_1(\overline{\mathsf{ct}}_b, \mathsf{st}) = b : \begin{array}{c} (\overline{\mathsf{sk}}, \mathsf{aux}) \leftarrow_{\mathsf{D}} D_\lambda, \\ (\mathsf{st}, \mathsf{msg}_0, \mathsf{msg}_1) \leftarrow \mathsf{A}_0^{\mathcal{O}(\overline{\mathsf{sk}},.)}(\lambda, \mathsf{aux}), \\ b \leftarrow_{\mathsf{R}} \{0,1\}, \\ \overline{\mathsf{ct}}_b \leftarrow \mathtt{Enc}(\lambda, \overline{\mathsf{sk}}, \mathsf{msg}_b) \end{array}\right],$$

where the oracle $\mathcal{O}$ *on input a message* msg *outputs* $\overline{\mathsf{ct}} \leftarrow \mathtt{Enc}(\lambda, \overline{\mathsf{sk}}, \mathsf{msg})$.
We say that $\mathsf{SKE} = (\mathtt{Enc}, \mathtt{Dec})$ *is* $\mathcal{D}$-IND-CPA-*secure if for all* **PPT** *adversaries* $\mathsf{A} = (\mathsf{A}_0, \mathsf{A}_1)$ *we have* $\mathsf{Adv}^{\mathcal{D}\text{-IND-CPA}}_{\mathsf{A},\mathsf{SKE}}(\lambda) = \mathsf{negl}(\lambda)$.
We say that a cryptosystem $\mathsf{SKE} = (\mathtt{Enc}, \mathtt{Dec})$ *is* $\mathcal{D}$*-semantically secure if the above holds but* A *has no access to the oracle* $\mathcal{O}$.

$\mathcal{D}$-Pseudorandom Ciphertexts: *Let* $\lambda \in \mathbb{N}$ *be a security parameter and* $\mathsf{A} = (\mathsf{A}_0, \mathsf{A}_1)$ *be a* **PPT** *adversary. Let* $\mathcal{D}$ *be a class of distribution ensembles* $\{D_k\}_{k\in\mathbb{N}}$ *that sample* $(\overline{\mathsf{sk}}, \mathsf{aux}) \leftarrow_{\mathsf{D}} D_k$ *with* $\overline{\mathsf{sk}} \in \{0,1\}^{\ell_{\mathsf{sk}}}$ *where* $\ell_{\mathsf{sk}} = \mathsf{poly}(k)$. *We define the advantage of* A *against a* $\mathsf{SKE} = (\mathtt{Enc}, \mathtt{Dec})$ *encryption scheme in the pseudorandom ciphertexts game as*

$$\mathsf{Adv}^{\mathsf{RandCt}}_{\mathsf{A},\mathsf{SKE}}(\lambda) = \Pr\left[\mathsf{A}_1(\overline{\mathsf{ct}}_b, \mathsf{st}) = b : \begin{array}{r} (\overline{\mathsf{sk}}, \mathsf{aux}) \leftarrow_{\mathsf{D}} D_\lambda, \\ (\mathsf{st}, \mathsf{msg}) \leftarrow \mathsf{A}_0^{\mathcal{O}(\overline{\mathsf{sk}},\cdot)}(\lambda, \mathsf{aux}), \\ b \leftarrow_{\mathsf{R}} \{0,1\}, \\ \overline{\mathsf{ct}}_0 \leftarrow \mathtt{Enc}(\lambda, \overline{\mathsf{sk}}, \mathsf{msg}), \overline{\mathsf{ct}}_1 \leftarrow_{\mathsf{R}} \{0,1\}^{\ell_{\mathsf{ct}}} \end{array}\right],$$

where the oracle $\mathcal{O}$ *on input a message* msg *outputs* $\overline{\mathsf{ct}} \leftarrow \mathtt{Enc}(\lambda, \overline{\mathsf{sk}}, \mathsf{msg})$.
We say that $\mathsf{SKE} = (\mathtt{Enc}, \mathtt{Dec})$ *has* $\mathcal{D}$*-pseudorandom ciphertexts if for all* **PPT** *adversaries* $\mathsf{A} = (\mathsf{A}_0, \mathsf{A}_1)$ *we have* $\mathsf{Adv}^{\mathcal{D}\text{-RandCt}}_{\mathsf{A},\mathsf{SKE}}(\lambda) = \mathsf{negl}(\lambda)$.
Analogously to semantic security, we say that a cryptosystem $\mathsf{SKE} = (\mathtt{Enc}, \mathtt{Dec})$ *has weakly* $\mathcal{D}$*-pseudorandom ciphertexts if the above holds but* A *has no access to the oracle* $\mathcal{O}$.

Classes of Distributions. Let us recall popular classes of distributions. The following classes were also considered by Wichs, and Zirdelis [WZ17] for their lockable obfuscation scheme.

Uniform: The variable x is chosen uniformly at random. This is the standard definition of IND-CPA.

Unpredictable: Informally, it is hard to predict x given aux. Formally, a class $\mathcal{D}$ is unpredictable if for all **PPT** adversaries A, security parameters $\lambda \in \mathbb{N}$, and distribution ensembles $\{D_k\}_{k\in\mathbb{N}} \in \mathcal{D}$ we have

$$\Pr[x \leftarrow \mathsf{A}(\mathsf{aux}) : (x, \mathsf{aux}) \leftarrow_{\mathsf{D}} D_\lambda] = \mathsf{negl}(\lambda).$$

Pseudo-Entropy: For a function $\alpha(\lambda)$ in the security parameter λ the class of α-pseudo-entropy distributions consists of ensembles $\{D_k\}_{k\in\mathbb{N}}$ such that $(x, \mathsf{aux}) \leftarrow_{\mathsf{D}} D_\lambda$ satisfies $\mathbf{H}_{\mathsf{HILL}}(x|\mathsf{aux}) \geq \alpha(\lambda)$.

Symmetric or public-key encryption schemes secure for the class of unpredictable distribution can be constructed from learning parity with noise [DKL09], decisional Diffie-Hellman and learning with errors [DGK+10] assumptions and from point function obfuscators satisfying some special properties [CKVW10]. For the class of pseudo-entropy distributions we know constructions from learning with errors [AGV09, GKPV10] hash proof systems [NS09, ADN+10], assumptions in bilinear groups [DHLW10], computational Diffie-Hellman and subgroup indistinguishability assumptions [BG10, BLSV18]. It is worth mentioning that we might realize leakage resilient encryption from pseudorandom functions with weak seeds [Pie09, AKPW13] and encryption schemes with semantic security and weakly pseudorandom ciphertexts from leakage resilient pseudorandom generators [DP08, Zha16].

Fully Homomorphic Encryption. We recall the definition of fully homomorphic encryption [RAD+78, Gen09]. In the definition, the Setup algorithm takes as input a depth of the circuit reflecting leveled/somewhat homomorphic schemes capable of evaluating the circuit of the given depth. We note, however, that our results apply to unbounded fully homomorphic encryption schemes as well. For brevity, we will omit "leveled/somewhat" and refer to the schemes as fully homomorphic. Additionally, we note that usually, we define a public key or an evaluation key in fully homomorphic encryption schemes. In this paper, we do not use such keys explicitly. Therefore, we assume that such a public/evaluation key is part of the secret key or ciphertext.

Definition 3 (Fully Homomorphic Encryption). *A fully homomorphic encryption* FHE *consists of algorithms* (Setup, Enc, Eval, Dec) *with the following syntax.*

$\mathtt{Setup}(\lambda, \delta)$: *This* **PPT** *algorithm takes as input a security parameter* λ *and bound on the circuit depth* δ. *The algorithm outputs a secret key* sk. *Sometimes we omit the circuit depth in the input when it is not needed in the given context.*

$\mathtt{Enc}(\mathsf{sk}, \mathsf{msg})$: *This* **PPT** *algorithm takes as input a secret key* sk, *and a message* msg, *and returns a ciphertext* ct.

$\mathtt{Eval}([\mathsf{ct}_i]_{i=1}^{\kappa}, C)$: *Given as input a set of ciphertexts* $[\mathsf{ct}_i]_{i=1}^{\kappa}$, *and a circuit* C, *the algorithm outputs a ciphertext* ct.

$\mathtt{Dec}(\mathsf{sk}, \mathsf{ct})$: *This deterministic algorithm given a secret key* sk *and a ciphertext* ct, *outputs a message* msg.

Correctness: *We say that* $\mathsf{FHE} = (\mathtt{Setup}, \mathtt{Enc}, \mathtt{Eval}, \mathtt{Dec})$ *is correct, if for all security parameters* $\lambda \in \mathbb{N}$, *circuits* $C : \mathcal{M}^{\kappa} \mapsto \mathcal{M}$ *over the message space* $\mathcal{M}$ *of depth* $\delta = \mathsf{poly}(\lambda)$, *and messages* $[\mathsf{msg}_i \in \mathcal{M}]_{i=1}^{\kappa}$ *we have*

$$\Pr\left[\mathtt{Dec}(\mathsf{sk}, \mathsf{ct}_{\mathsf{out}}) = C([\mathsf{msg}_i]_{i=1}^{\kappa}) : \begin{array}{c} \mathsf{sk} \leftarrow \mathtt{Setup}(\lambda, \delta), \\ [\mathsf{ct}_i \leftarrow \mathtt{Enc}(\mathsf{sk}, \mathsf{msg}_i)]_{i=1}^{\kappa} \\ \mathsf{ct}_{\mathsf{out}} \leftarrow \mathtt{Eval}([\mathsf{ct}_i]_{i=1}^{\kappa}, C) \end{array}\right] = 1 - \mathsf{Err}_{\mathtt{Eval}}^{\mathsf{corr}}(\lambda),$$

where $\mathsf{Err}_{\mathtt{Eval}}^{\mathsf{corr}}(\lambda) = \mathsf{negl}(\lambda)$. *We call* $\mathsf{Err}_{\mathtt{Eval}}^{\mathsf{corr}}(\lambda)$ *the correctness error.*

The distribution of evaluated ciphertexts and fresh ciphertexts may differ. In our correctness analysis, we need conveniently denote to what message a given ciphertext decrypts. Therefore, we denote as $\mathsf{ct}_{\mathsf{out}} \approx \mathtt{Enc}(\mathsf{sk}, \mathsf{msg})$ the fact that $\mathtt{Dec}(\mathsf{sk}, \mathsf{ct}_{\mathsf{out}}) = \mathsf{msg}$ with some correctness error $\mathsf{Err}_{\mathtt{Eval}}^{\mathsf{corr}}(\lambda)$.

Efficiency: We require that $\texttt{Setup}$, $\texttt{Enc}$ and $\texttt{Dec}$ run in $\mathsf{poly}(\lambda, \delta)$ time, and $\texttt{Eval}$ runs in $\mathsf{poly}(\lambda, |C|)$ time.

Indistinguishability Under Chosen Plaintext Attack: We define indistinguishability under chosen plaintext attack as in Definition 2, with the exception that the $\texttt{Setup}$ algorithm generates the secret key. Furthermore, we note that, while it is possible to define fully homomorphic encryption with weak keys, it does not play a special role in our paper. Therefore, we consider the secret keys' distribution to be uniform (the $\texttt{Setup}$ algorithm works on a uniformly random seed), and we use IND-CPA as the acronym instead of $\mathcal{D}$-IND-CPA.

We use the concept of cycle testers introduced by Bishop, Hohenberger, and Waters [BHW15]. However, we use the definition by Kluczniak [Klu20], as it is easier to use for our purposes[3]. We give the construction from [GKW17a] of a fully homomorphic encryption with a cycle tester in [Klu21, Appendix A]. Furthermore, we note that the the scheme can be instantiated from LWE with subexponential modulus-to-noise ratio.

Definition 4 (Cycle Testing). *We define an additional algorithm* $\texttt{Test}$ *with the following syntax.*

$\texttt{Test}([\mathsf{ct}_{i,j}]_{i=1,j=1}^{n,m})$: *The algorithm on input a vector of ciphertexts* $[\mathsf{ct}_{i,j}]_{i=1,j=1}^{n,m}$ *outputs a bit* $b \in \{0,1\}$.

Efficiency: *We require that* $\texttt{Test}$ *runs in time* $\mathsf{poly}(\lambda)$.

Correctness: *Let* $\mathsf{FHE} = (\texttt{Setup}, \texttt{Enc}, \texttt{Eval}, \texttt{Dec}, \texttt{Test})$ *be a fully homomorphic encryption scheme with an n-cycle tester* $\texttt{Test}$ *for functions* $\mathsf{F}_j : \mathcal{S} \mapsto \mathcal{M}$, *where* $\mathcal{M}$ *is the message space and* $\mathcal{S}$ *is the secret key space and* $j \in [m]$. *We say that the cycle tester is correct if for all security parameters* $\lambda \in \mathbb{N}$, *and all executions* $\left[\mathsf{sk}_i \leftarrow \texttt{Setup}(\lambda)\right]_{i=1}^{n}$, *we have* $\mathsf{Err}_{\texttt{Test}}^{\mathsf{corr}}(\lambda) = \mathsf{negl}(\lambda)$, *where*

$$\Pr\left[\texttt{Test}([\mathsf{ct}_{i,j}]_{i=1,j=1}^{n,m}) \neq 1\right] \leq \mathsf{Err}_{\texttt{Test}}^{\mathsf{corr}}(\lambda)$$

given that $[\mathsf{F}_j(\mathsf{sk}_{(i \bmod n)+1})]_{i=1,j=1}^{n,m} = [\mathsf{Dec}(\mathsf{sk}_i, \mathsf{ct}_{i,j})]_{i=1,j=1}^{n,m}$, *and*

$$\Pr\left[\texttt{Test}([\mathsf{ct}_{i,j}]_{i=1,j=1}^{n,m}) \neq 0\right] \leq \mathsf{Err}_{\texttt{Test}}^{\mathsf{corr}}(\lambda)$$

given that $[\mathsf{F}_j(\mathsf{sk}_{(i \bmod n)+1})]_{i=1,j=1}^{n,m} \neq [\mathsf{Dec}(\mathsf{sk}_i, \mathsf{ct}_{i,j})]_{i=1,j=1}^{n,m}$.

[3] As pointed by Kluczniak [Klu20], the definition by Bishop, Hohenberger, and Waters [BHW15] does not make a distinction between a cycle tester and an encryption scheme with an efficient zero tester.

Lockable Obfuscation. Now we recall lockable obfuscation introduced by Goyal, Koppula, and Waters [GKW17a], and independently by Wichs and Zirdelis [WZ17].

Definition 5 (Lockable Obfuscation). *A lockable obfuscation scheme* $\mathsf{LObf} = (\mathtt{Obf}, \mathtt{Eval})$ *consists of an obfuscation algorithm* $\mathtt{Obf}$ *and an evaluation algorithm* $\mathtt{Eval}$ *with the following syntax.*

$\mathtt{Obf}(\lambda, C, \mathsf{lock}, \mathsf{msg})$: *This algorithm takes as input a security parameter* $\lambda \in \mathbb{N}$, *a circuit* $C : \{0,1\}^\kappa \mapsto \{0,1\}^\eta$, *a lock string* $\mathsf{lock} \in \{0,1\}^\eta$, *and a message* $\mathsf{msg} \in \{0,1\}^{\ell_{\mathsf{msg}}}$. *The algorithm outputs an obfuscated circuit* $\widehat{C}$.

$\mathtt{Eval}(\widehat{C}, x)$: *This deterministic algorithm takes as input an obfuscated circuit* $\widehat{C}$ *and input* $x \in \{0,1\}^\kappa$, *and outputs* msg *or* $\perp$.

Efficiency: *We say that the lockable obfuscation scheme is polynomially efficient, if* $\mathtt{Obf}$ *and* $\mathtt{Eval}$ *run in time* $\mathsf{poly}(\lambda, |C|)$.

Correctness: *We say that a lockable obfuscator* $\mathsf{LObf} = (\mathtt{Obf}, \mathtt{Eval})$ *is correct if for all* $\lambda \in \mathbb{N}$, $C : \{0,1\}^\kappa \mapsto \{0,1\}^\eta$, $\mathsf{msg} \in \{0,1\}^{\ell_{\mathsf{msg}}}$, $\mathsf{lock} \in \{0,1\}^\eta$, *and* $x \in \{0,1\}^\kappa$, *given that* $\widehat{C} \leftarrow \mathtt{Obf}(\lambda, C, \mathsf{lock}, \mathsf{msg})$ *and* $C(x) = \mathsf{lock}$, *we have*

$$\Pr[\mathtt{Eval}(\widehat{C}, x) \neq \mathsf{msg}] \leq \mathsf{Err}^{\mathsf{corr}}_{\mathsf{LObf}.\mathtt{Eval}}(\lambda),$$

and given that $C(x) \neq \mathsf{lock}$ *we have that*

$$\Pr[\mathtt{Eval}(\widehat{C}, x) \neq \perp] \leq \mathsf{Err}^{\mathsf{corr}}_{\mathsf{LObf}.\mathtt{Eval}}(\lambda),$$

where $\mathsf{Err}^{\mathsf{corr}}_{\mathsf{LObf}.\mathtt{Eval}}(\lambda) = \mathsf{negl}(\lambda)$ *and the probability is over random coins of the obfuscation algorithm* $\mathtt{Obf}$.

We consider also a limited version, where the lockable obfuscation has the message set to $\mathsf{msg} = 1$ for $C(x) = \mathsf{lock}$ and outputs 0 instead of $\perp$. In particular, our first construction given in Sect. 3 follows the limited functionality. Later in Sect. 4.2, we show how to extend the scheme to handle any polynomial-size messages.

Distributional Virtual Black-Box ($\mathcal{D}$-DVBB) Security: *Let* $\mathcal{C}_k = \{C_{\kappa,\eta,\upsilon}\}$ *be the set of all circuits with* κ *input variables,* η *output variables and size* υ, *where* $\kappa, \eta, \upsilon = \mathsf{poly}(k)$. *Let* $\mathcal{D}$ *be a class of distribution ensembles* $\{D_k\}_{k\in\mathbb{N}}$ *that sample* $(\mathsf{lock}, \mathsf{aux}) \leftarrow_{\mathsf{D}} D_k$ *with* $\mathsf{lock} \in \{0,1\}^\eta$.
We say that the lockable obfuscation is distributional virtual black-box secure for the distribution class $\mathcal{D}$ *if for all* **PPT** *adversaries* $\mathsf{A} = (\mathsf{A}_1, \mathsf{A}_2)$, *there exists a* **PPT** *simulator* $\mathtt{Sim}$, *such that* $\mathsf{Adv}^{\mathcal{D}\text{-DVBB}}_{\mathsf{A},\mathsf{LObf}}(\lambda) = \mathsf{negl}(\lambda)$, *where*

$$\mathsf{Adv}^{\mathcal{D}\text{-DVBB}}_{\mathsf{A},\mathsf{LObf}}(\lambda) = \left| \Pr\left[\mathsf{A}_2(\widehat{C}_b, \mathsf{st}) = b : \begin{array}{c} (\mathsf{lock}, \mathsf{aux}) \leftarrow_{\mathsf{D}} D_\lambda, \\ b \leftarrow_{\mathsf{R}} \{0,1\}, \\ (C, \mathsf{msg}, \mathsf{st}) \leftarrow \mathsf{A}_1(\lambda, \mathsf{aux}), \\ \mathsf{msg} \in \{0,1\}^{\ell_{\mathsf{msg}}}, C \in \mathcal{C}_\lambda \\ \widehat{C}_0 \leftarrow \mathtt{Obf}(\lambda, C, \mathsf{lock}, \mathsf{msg}), \\ \widehat{C}_1 \leftarrow \mathtt{Sim}(\lambda, \kappa, \eta, \upsilon, \ell_{\mathsf{msg}}) \end{array} \right] - \frac{1}{2} \right|,$$

We call $\mathsf{Adv}^{\mathcal{D}\text{-DVBB}}_{\mathsf{A},\mathsf{LObf}}(\lambda)$ *the advantage of the adversary* A *against* DVBB *security.*

3 Lockable Obfuscation from Circular Insecure FHE

In this section, we show the basic construction of lockable obfuscation from fully homomorphic encryption with an efficient cycle tester. The lockable obfuscation returns a single bit that is set to 1 when the outcome of the obfuscated function is equal to the lock, and $\perp$ otherwise.

Construction 1 (Our Lockable Obfuscation Construction). *Let* $\mathsf{FHE} = (\mathtt{Setup}, \mathtt{Enc}, \mathtt{Dec}, \mathtt{Test})$ *be a fully homomorphic encryption scheme with a cycle tester detecting* n*-length key cycles for* F_j *where* $j \in [m]$. *Let* $\mathsf{SKE} = (\mathtt{Enc}, \mathtt{Dec})$ *be a symmetric encryption scheme with secret key space* $\{0,1\}^\eta$ *and message space* $\{0,1\}^{\ell_{\mathsf{sk}}}$. *Denote as* $U_x(.)$ *the universal circuit that on input a circuit* $C : \{0,1\}^\kappa \mapsto \{0,1\}^\eta$, *outputs* $C(x)$, *where* $x \in \{0,1\}^\kappa$. *Let* $\delta \in \mathbb{N}$ *be the depth of the circuit* $\mathsf{SKE.Dec}(U_x(.),.)$. *We define the lockable obfuscation* $\mathsf{LObf} = (\mathtt{Obf}, \mathtt{Eval})$ *as follows.*

$\mathtt{Obf}(\lambda, C, \mathsf{lock})$: *Takes as input a security parameter* λ, *a circuit* $C : \{0,1\}^\kappa \mapsto \{0,1\}^\eta$, *and a lock string* $\mathsf{lock} \in \{0,1\}^\eta$.

1. *For* $i \in [n]$ *do*
   - *Run* $\mathsf{sk}_i \leftarrow \mathsf{FHE}.\mathtt{Setup}(\lambda, \delta)$.
   - *Run* $\mathsf{ct}_i \leftarrow \mathsf{FHE}.\mathtt{Enc}(\mathsf{sk}_i, C)$.
   - *For* $j \in [m]$ *do*
     - *Run* $\overline{\mathsf{ct}}^{(\mathsf{lock})}_{i,j} \leftarrow \mathsf{SKE}.\mathtt{Enc}\big(\lambda, \mathsf{lock}, \mathsf{F}_j(\mathsf{sk}_{(i \bmod n)+1})\big)$.
     - *Run* $\mathsf{ct}^{(\mathsf{lock})}_{i,j} \leftarrow \mathsf{FHE}.\mathtt{Enc}(\mathsf{sk}_i, \overline{\mathsf{ct}}^{(\mathsf{lock})}_{i,j})$.
2. *Return* $\widehat{C} \leftarrow \big([\mathsf{ct}_i]_{i=1}^n, [\mathsf{ct}^{(\mathsf{lock})}_{i,j}]_{i=1,j=1}^{n,m}\big)$.

$\mathtt{Eval}(\widehat{C}, x)$: *Takes as input an obfuscated circuit* $\widehat{C} = \big([\mathsf{ct}_i]_{i=1}^n, [\mathsf{ct}^{(\mathsf{lock})}_{i,j}]_{i=1,j=1}^{n,m}\big)$, *and an input* $x \in \{0,1\}^\kappa$.

1. *For* $i \in [n]$ *do*
   - *Compute* $\mathsf{ct}^{(C)}_i \leftarrow \mathsf{FHE}.\mathtt{Eval}(\mathsf{ct}_i, U_x)$.
   - *For* $j \in [m]$ *compute*

$$\mathsf{ct}^{(\mathsf{Test})}_{i,j} \leftarrow \mathsf{FHE}.\mathtt{Eval}\big([\mathsf{ct}^{(C)}_i, \mathsf{ct}^{(\mathsf{lock})}_{i,j}], \mathsf{SKE}.\mathtt{Dec}(.,.)\big).$$

2. *If* $\mathsf{FHE}.\mathtt{Test}([\mathsf{ct}^{(\mathsf{Test})}_{i,j}]_{i=1,j=1}^{n,m}) = 1$, *then output* 1, *and output* $\perp$ *otherwise.*

Theorem 1 (Correctness). *For all* λ, $C : \{0,1\}^\kappa \mapsto \{0,1\}^\eta$, *all* $\mathsf{lock} \in \{0,1\}^\eta$, LObf *as given by Construction 1 is a polynomially efficient and correct lockable obfuscation with correctness error*

$$\mathsf{Err}^{\mathsf{corr}}_{\mathsf{LObf}}(\lambda) \leq n \cdot m \cdot \mathsf{Err}^{\mathsf{corr}}_{\mathsf{FHE}.\mathtt{Eval}}(\lambda, \delta) + \mathsf{Err}^{\mathsf{corr}}_{\mathsf{SKE}}(\lambda) + \mathsf{Err}^{\mathsf{corr}}_{\mathsf{FHE}.\mathtt{Test}}(\lambda).$$

Proof. Polynomial efficiency follows directly from the efficiency of the underlying encryption schemes. Thus we focus on analyzing the correctness. From correctness of the FHE scheme we have $\mathsf{ct}_i^{(C)} = \mathsf{FHE.Eval}(\mathsf{ct}_i, U_x) \approx \mathsf{FHE.Enc}(\mathsf{sk}_i, C(x))$ and

$$\begin{aligned}\mathsf{ct}_{i,j}^{(\mathsf{Test})} &= \mathsf{FHE.Eval}\big([\mathsf{ct}_i^{(C)}, \mathsf{ct}_{i,j}^{(\mathsf{lock})}], \mathsf{SKE.Dec}(.,.)\big)\\ &\approx \mathsf{FHE.Enc}\big(\mathsf{sk}_i, \mathsf{SKE.Dec}(C(x), \overline{\mathsf{ct}}_{i,j}^{(\mathsf{lock})})\big)\end{aligned}$$

with probability of failure bounded by $\mathsf{Err}^{\mathsf{corr}}_{\mathsf{FHE.Eval}}(\lambda, \delta)$ for each $i \in [n]$ and $j \in [m]$.

If $C(x) = \mathsf{lock}$ we have $\mathsf{ct}_{i,j}^{(\mathsf{Test})} \approx \mathsf{FHE.Enc}\big(\mathsf{sk}_i, \mathsf{F}_j(\mathsf{sk}_{(i \bmod n)+1})\big)$. Then we have $\mathsf{Test}([\mathsf{ct}_{i,j}^{(\mathsf{Test})}]_{i=1,j=1}^{n,m}) = 1$ with probability failure bounded by $\mathsf{Err}^{\mathsf{corr}}_{\mathsf{FHE.Test}}(\lambda)$.

If $C(x) \neq \mathsf{lock}$, then we have $\mathsf{ct}_{i,j}^{(\mathsf{Test})} \approx \mathsf{FHE.Enc}(\mathsf{sk}_i, \widetilde{\mathsf{msg}}_{i,j})$, where the plaintext is $\widetilde{\mathsf{msg}}_{i,j} = \mathsf{SKE.Dec}(C(x), \overline{\mathsf{ct}}_{i,j}^{(\mathsf{lock})})$. From correctness of the SKE scheme we have that there exists $i \in [n]$ and all $j \in [m]$ such that $\widetilde{\mathsf{msg}}_{i,j} \neq \mathsf{F}_j(\mathsf{sk}_{(i \bmod n)+1})$ with probability at least $1 - \mathsf{Err}^{\mathsf{corr}}_{\mathsf{SKE}}(\lambda)$. Therefore, the ciphertexts $\mathsf{ct}_{i,j}^{(\mathsf{Test})}$ does not encode a proper cycle. Consequently, we have $\mathsf{Test}([\mathsf{ct}_{i,j}^{(\mathsf{Test})}]_{i=1,j=1}^{n,m}) = 0$ with probability of failure bounded by $\mathsf{Err}^{\mathsf{corr}}_{\mathsf{FHE.Test}}(\lambda)$.

To summarize we have the probability of failure of the lockable obfuscation $\mathsf{Err}^{\mathsf{corr}}_{\mathsf{LObf}}(\lambda) \leq n \cdot m \cdot \mathsf{Err}^{\mathsf{corr}}_{\mathsf{FHE.Eval}}(\lambda) + \mathsf{Err}^{\mathsf{corr}}_{\mathsf{SKE}}(\lambda) + \mathsf{Err}^{\mathsf{corr}}_{\mathsf{FHE.Test}}(\lambda)$.

Theorem 2 (Security). *Let $\mathcal{D}$ be a class of distribution ensembles $\{D_\lambda\}_{\lambda \in \mathbb{N}}$ that sample $(\mathsf{lock}, C) \leftarrow_{\mathsf{D}} D_\lambda$, with $C : \{0,1\}^\kappa \mapsto \{0,1\}^\eta$, $\mathsf{lock} \in \{0,1\}^\eta$ and $\kappa, \eta = \mathsf{poly}(\lambda)$. Let* SKE *be a* $\mathcal{D}$-IND-CPA *secure symmetric key encryption scheme, and* FHE *be a* IND-CPA *secure fully homomorphic encryption scheme. Then,* LObf *given by Construction 1, is* $\mathcal{D}$-DVBB *secure.*

Proof. Let us first describe the simulator. The simulator $\mathtt{Sim}$ takes as input λ, κ, η, v and ℓ_{msg}. Then $\mathtt{Sim}$ runs $\mathsf{sk}_i \leftarrow \mathsf{FHE.Setup}(\lambda, \delta)$ as in the real scheme, and computes $\widehat{C} \leftarrow \big([\mathsf{ct}_i]_{i=1}^n, [\mathsf{ct}_{i,j}^{(\mathsf{lock})}]_{i=1,j=1}^{n,m}\big)$, where $\mathsf{ct}_i \leftarrow \mathsf{FHE.Enc}(\mathsf{sk}_i, 0)$ and $\mathsf{ct}_{i,j}^{(\mathsf{lock})} \leftarrow \mathsf{FHE.Enc}(\mathsf{sk}_i, 0)$, for all $i \in [n]$ and $j \in [m]$.

Via the following hybrid argument, we show that a simulated program is computationally indistinguishable from an obfuscated program. We denote as $\mathcal{H}_j$ the event that an adversary guesses the bit b in Hybrid j.

Hybrid 0**:** This is the DVBB game with the bit $b = 0$. That is we compute $\widehat{C}_b \leftarrow \mathtt{Obf}(\lambda, C, \mathsf{lock}, \mathsf{msg})$. We have $\mathsf{Adv}^{\mathsf{DVBB}}_{\mathsf{A,LObf}} = |\Pr[\mathcal{H}_0] - \frac{1}{2}|$.

Hybrid $(i-1) \cdot m + j$**:** For $i \in [n]$ and $j \in [m]$ we compute the ciphertext $\overline{\mathsf{ct}}_{i,j}^{(\mathsf{lock})} \leftarrow \mathsf{SKE.Enc}(\lambda, \mathsf{lock}, 0)$ instead of the ciphertext $\overline{\mathsf{ct}}_{i,j}^{(\mathsf{lock})} \leftarrow \mathsf{SKE.Enc}\big(\lambda, \mathsf{lock}, \mathsf{F}_j(\mathsf{sk}_{(i \bmod n)+1})\big)$.

Claim. If an adversary A distinguishes between Hybrid $(i-1)\cdot m+j$ and Hybrid $(i-1)\cdot m+j-1$, then there exists a distinguisher D, that uses A to break $\mathcal{D}$-$\mathsf{IND\text{-}CPA}$ security of SKE. We have

$$\left|\Pr[\mathcal{H}_{(i-1)\cdot m+j}] - \Pr[\mathcal{H}_{(i-1)\cdot m+j-1}]\right| = \mathsf{Adv}^{\mathcal{D}\text{-}\mathsf{IND\text{-}CPA}}_{\mathsf{D},\mathsf{SKE}}(\lambda).$$

Proof. First, the solver generates all secret keys of the FHE scheme. For $i' \in [n]$ and $j' \in [m]$ such that $(i'-1)\cdot m+j' < (i-1)\cdot m+j$ the solver queries the $\mathcal{O}$ for $\overline{\mathsf{ct}}^{(\mathsf{lock})}_{i',j'} \leftarrow \mathcal{O}(\mathsf{lock},0)$. For $(i'-1)\cdot m+j' > (i-1)\cdot m+j$, the solver queries $\overline{\mathsf{ct}}^{(\mathsf{lock})}_{i',j'} \leftarrow \mathcal{O}(\mathsf{lock},\mathsf{F}_{j'}(\mathsf{sk}_{(i' \bmod n)+1})$. Finally, the solver submits $\mathsf{msg}_0 = \mathsf{F}_j(\mathsf{sk}_{(i \bmod n)+1})$ and $\mathsf{msg}_1 = 0$ as the challenge, and obtains $\overline{\mathsf{ct}}^{(\mathsf{lock})}_{i,j}$. The rest of the obfuscated program is computed as given by the specification. Then if the adversary outputs that it is Hybrid $(i-1)\cdot m+j-1$, then the solver answers that the encrypted message is msg_0. Otherwise, the solver answers that the message is msg_1.

Hybrid $n\cdot m+(i-1)\cdot m+j$: For $i \in [n]$ and $j \in [m]$ we compute $\mathsf{ct}^{(\mathsf{lock})}_{i,j} \leftarrow \mathsf{FHE.Enc}(\mathsf{sk}_i, 0)$ instead of $\mathsf{ct}^{(\mathsf{lock})}_{i,j} \leftarrow \mathsf{FHE.Enc}(\mathsf{sk}_i, \overline{\mathsf{ct}}^{(\mathsf{lock})}_{i,j})$.

Claim. If an adversary A distinguishes between Hybrid $n\cdot m+(i-1)\cdot m+j$ and Hybrid $n\cdot m+(i-1)\cdot m+j-1$, then there exists a distinguisher D, that uses A to break $\mathsf{IND\text{-}CPA}$ security of FHE.

We have

$$\left|\Pr[\mathcal{H}_{n\cdot m+(i-1)\cdot m+j}] - \Pr[\mathcal{H}_{n\cdot m+(i-1)\cdot m+j-1}]\right| = \mathsf{Adv}^{\mathsf{IND\text{-}CPA}}_{\mathsf{D},\mathsf{FHE}}(\lambda).$$

Proof. First, the solver generates all secret keys of the FHE scheme except sk_i. For all $i' \in [n]$ such that $i' \neq i$ and all $j' \in [m]$, the solver generates $\mathsf{ct}^{(\mathsf{lock})}_{i',j}$ and $\mathsf{ct}_{i'}$ as in the previous hybrid. To obtain ct_i the solver queries $\mathcal{O}(sk_i, .)$ on input C. To obtain $\mathsf{ct}^{(\mathsf{lock})}_{i,j'}$ the solver submits 0 for all $j' < j$, and $\overline{\mathsf{ct}}^{(\mathsf{lock})}_{i,j'}$ for $j' > j$. Finally, to obtain $\mathsf{ct}^{(\mathsf{lock})}_{i,j}$ the solver sets the challenge query as $\mathsf{msg}_0 = \overline{\mathsf{ct}}^{(\mathsf{lock})}_{i,j'}$ and $\mathsf{msg}_1 = 0$.

If the adversary outputs that it is Hybrid $n\cdot m+(i-1)\cdot m+j-1$, then the solver answers that the encrypted message is msg_0. Otherwise, the solver answers that the message is msg_1.

Hybrid $2\cdot n\cdot m+i$: For $i \in [n]$ we compute $\mathsf{ct}_i \leftarrow \mathsf{FHE.Enc}(\mathsf{sk}_i, 0)$ instead of $\mathsf{ct}_i \leftarrow \mathsf{FHE.Enc}(\mathsf{sk}_i, C)$.

Claim. If an adversary A distinguishes between Hybrid $2\cdot n\cdot m+i$ and Hybrid $2\cdot n\cdot m+i-1$, then there exists a distinguisher D, that uses A to break $\mathsf{IND\text{-}CPA}$ security of FHE.

We have

$$\left|\Pr[\mathcal{H}_{2\cdot n\cdot m+i}] - \Pr[\mathcal{H}_{2\cdot n\cdot m+i-1}]\right| = \mathsf{Adv}^{\mathsf{IND\text{-}CPA}}_{\mathsf{D},\mathsf{FHE}}(\lambda).$$

Proof. The proof is a standard reduction to IND-CPA of the FHE scheme analogous to the proof of Hybrids $n \cdot m + (i-1) \cdot m + j$ for $i \in [n]$ and $j \in [m]$.

In Hybrid $2 \cdot n \cdot m + n$ the obfuscated program is equivalent to a simulated program. In particular all encryptions that constitute the obfuscated program are encryptions of 0. To summarize, we have that the advantage to distinguish between Hybrid 0 and Hybrid $2 \cdot n \cdot m + n$ is $\mathsf{Adv}^{\mathsf{DVBB}}_{\mathsf{A,LObf}} \leq n \cdot m \cdot \mathsf{Adv}^{\mathcal{D}\text{-}\mathsf{IND\text{-}CPA}}_{\mathsf{D,SKE}}(\lambda) + (n \cdot m + n) \cdot \mathsf{Adv}^{\mathsf{IND\text{-}CPA}}_{\mathsf{D,FHE}}(\lambda)$.

4 Extensions and Variants of the Lockable Obfuscation Scheme

In this section, we show a variant of the lockable obfuscation scheme and an extension that allows the obfuscator to output polynomial-size messages.

4.1 Lock Ciphertext in the Plain

We show a slight modification of Construction 1, where instead of encrypting the lock ciphertexts $[\overline{\mathsf{ct}}^{(\mathsf{lock})}_{i,j}]^{n,m}_{i=1,j=1}$, with the FHE encyption algorithm, we include these ciphertexts into the obfuscated program. However, for the security proof to work, we need to assume that SKE has pseudorandom ciphertexts. To not restate the construction from Sect. 3, we only give the changes.

Construction 2 (Lock Ciphertexts in the Plain). *Let* LObf *be as in Construction 1, except we do not compute* $\mathsf{ct}^{(\mathsf{lock})}_{i,j}$*, and* `Obf` *returns the obfuscated circuit* $\widehat{C} = ([(\mathsf{ct}_i]^n_{i=1}, [\overline{\mathsf{ct}}^{(\mathsf{lock})}_{i,j}]^{n,m}_{i=1,j=1})$*. Furthermore, in the* `Eval` *algorithm we compute* $\mathsf{ct}^{(\mathsf{Test})}_{i,j} \leftarrow \mathsf{FHE.Eval}(\mathsf{ct}^{(C)}_i, \mathsf{SKE.Dec}(., \overline{\mathsf{ct}}^{(\mathsf{lock})}_{i,j}))$.

Theorem 3 (Correctness). *For all* λ, $C : \{0,1\}^\kappa \mapsto \{0,1\}^\eta$*, all* $\mathsf{lock} \in \{0,1\}^\eta$*,* LObf *as given by Construction 2 is a polynomially efficient and correct lockable obfuscation with correctness error*

$$\mathsf{Err}^{\mathsf{corr}}_{\mathsf{LObf}}(\lambda) \leq n \cdot m \cdot \mathsf{Err}^{\mathsf{corr}}_{\mathsf{FHE.Eval}}(\lambda, \delta) + \mathsf{Err}^{\mathsf{corr}}_{\mathsf{SKE}}(\lambda) + \mathsf{Err}^{\mathsf{corr}}_{\mathsf{FHE.Test}}(\lambda).$$

Proof. From correctness of the FHE scheme we have $\mathsf{ct}^{(C)}_i = \mathsf{FHE.Eval}(\mathsf{ct}_i, U_x) \approx \mathsf{FHE.Enc}(\mathsf{sk}_i, C(x))$ and

$$\begin{aligned} \mathsf{ct}^{(\mathsf{Test})}_{i,j} &= \mathsf{FHE.Eval}(\mathsf{ct}^{(C)}_i, \mathsf{SKE.Dec}(., \mathsf{ct}^{(\mathsf{lock})}_{i,j})) \\ &\approx \mathsf{FHE.Enc}(\mathsf{sk}_i, \mathsf{SKE.Dec}(C(x), \overline{\mathsf{ct}}^{(\mathsf{lock})}_{i,j})) \end{aligned}$$

with probability of failure bounded by $\mathsf{Err}^{\mathsf{corr}}_{\mathsf{FHE.Eval}}(\lambda)$ for each $i \in [n]$ and $j \in [m]$.

If $C(x) = \mathsf{lock}$, then we have $\mathsf{ct}^{(\mathsf{Test})}_{i,j} \approx \mathsf{FHE.Enc}(\mathsf{sk}_i, \mathsf{F}_j(\mathsf{sk}_{(i \bmod n)+1}))$ and $\mathtt{Test}([\mathsf{ct}^{(\mathsf{Test})}_{i,j}]^{n,m}_{i=1,j=1}) = 1$ with probability failure bounded by $\mathsf{Err}^{\mathsf{corr}}_{\mathsf{FHE.Test}}(\lambda)$.

If $C(x) \neq \mathsf{lock}$, then we have $\mathsf{ct}_{i,j}^{(\mathsf{Test})} \approx \mathsf{FHE.Enc}(\mathsf{sk}_i, \widetilde{\mathsf{msg}}_{i,j})$, where the plaintext is $\widetilde{\mathsf{msg}}_{i,j} = \mathsf{SKE.Dec}(C(x), \overline{\mathsf{ct}}_{i,j}^{\mathsf{lock}})$. From correctness of the SKE scheme we have that there exists $i \in [n]$ and all $j \in [m]$ such that $\widetilde{\mathsf{msg}}_{i,j} \neq \mathsf{F}_j(\mathsf{sk}_{(i \bmod n)+1})$ with probability at least $1 - \mathsf{Err}_{\mathsf{SKE}}^{\mathsf{corr}}(\lambda)$. Consequently, we have $\mathtt{Test}([\mathsf{ct}_{i,j}^{\mathsf{Test}}]_{i=1,j=1}^{n,m}) = 0$ with probability of failure bounded by $\mathsf{Err}_{\mathsf{FHE.Test}}^{\mathsf{corr}}(\lambda)$.

To summarize we have the probability of failure from the lockable obfuscation $\mathsf{Err}_{\mathsf{LObf}}^{\mathsf{corr}}(\lambda) \leq n \cdot m \cdot \mathsf{Err}_{\mathsf{FHE.Eval}}^{\mathsf{corr}}(\lambda) + \mathsf{Err}_{\mathsf{SKE}}^{\mathsf{corr}}(\lambda) + \mathsf{Err}_{\mathsf{FHE.Test}}^{\mathsf{corr}}(\lambda)$.

Theorem 4 (Security). *Let $\mathcal{D}$ be a class of distribution ensembles $\{D_\lambda\}_{\lambda \subset \mathbb{N}}$ that sample* $(\mathsf{lock}, C) \leftarrow_{\mathsf{D}} \mathsf{D}_\lambda$, *with* $C : \{0,1\}^\kappa \mapsto \{0,1\}^\eta$, $\mathsf{lock} \in \{0,1\}^\eta$ *and* $\kappa, \eta = \mathsf{poly}(\lambda)$. *Let* SKE *be a* $\mathcal{D}$-RandCt *secure symmetric key encryption scheme, and* FHE *be a* IND-CPA *secure fully homomorphic encryption scheme. Then,* LObf *given by Construction 2, is* $\mathcal{D}$-DVBB *secure.*

Proof. To prove security, we define the simulator to compute the FHE ciphertexts as encryptions of 0, and choose the SKE ciphertexts uniformly at random. Note that the simulator requires only the circuit's dimensions and the size of the lock key.

The hybrid argument is the same as in the proof of Theorem 2, except with the following changes. The hybrids $(i-1) \cdot m + j$ for $i \in [n]$ and $j \in [m]$ is as we define below. After hybrid $n \cdot m$ come hybrids $n \cdot m + i$ for $i \in [n]$ that are the same as the hybrids $2 \cdot n \cdot m + i$ in the proof of Theorem 2. Note that the hybrids $n \cdot m + (i-1) \cdot m + j$ from the proof of Theorem 2, are missing as we no longer use those encryptions.

Now the hybrids $(i-1) \cdot m + j$ that we need to redefine are as follows.

Hybrid $(i-1) \cdot m + j$**:** For $i \in [n]$ and $j \in [m]$ we choose the ciphertext $\overline{\mathsf{ct}}_{i,j}^{(\mathsf{lock})} \leftarrow_{\mathsf{R}} \{0,1\}^{\ell_{\mathsf{sk}}}$ from the uniform distribution instead of computing it as $\overline{\mathsf{ct}}_{i,j}^{(\mathsf{lock})} \leftarrow \mathsf{SKE.Enc}(\lambda, \mathsf{lock}, \mathsf{F}_j(\mathsf{sk}_{(i \bmod n)+1}))$.

Claim. If an adversary A distinguishes between Hybrid $(i-1) \cdot m + j$ and Hybrid $(i-1) \cdot m + j - 1$, then there exists a distinguisher D, that uses A to break $\mathcal{D}$-RandCt security of SKE. We have

$$\left| \Pr[\mathcal{H}_{(i-1)\cdot m+j}] - \Pr[\mathcal{H}_{(i-1)\cdot m+j-1}] \right| = \mathsf{Adv}_{\mathsf{D},\mathsf{SKE}}^{\mathcal{D}\text{-}\mathsf{RandCt}}(\lambda).$$

Proof. First, the solver generates all secret keys of the FHE scheme. For $i' \in [n]$ and $j' \in [m]$ such that $(i'-1) \cdot m + j' < (i-1) \cdot m + j$ the solver chooses $\overline{\mathsf{ct}}_{i',j'}^{(\mathsf{lock})} \leftarrow_{\mathsf{R}} \{0,1\}^{\ell_{\mathsf{sk}}}$ uniformly at random. For $(i'-1) \cdot m + j' > (i-1) \cdot m + j$, the solver queries $\overline{\mathsf{ct}}_{i',j'}^{(\mathsf{lock})} \leftarrow \mathcal{O}(\mathsf{lock}, \mathsf{F}_{j'}(\mathsf{sk}_{(i' \bmod n)+1}))$. Finally, the solver submits $\mathsf{msg} = \mathsf{F}_j(\mathsf{sk}_{(i \bmod n)+1})$ as the challenge, and obtains $\overline{\mathsf{ct}}_{i,j}^{(\mathsf{lock})}$. The rest of the obfuscated program is computed as given by the specification. Then if the adversary outputs that it is in Hybrid $(i-1) \cdot m + j - 1$, then the solver answers that the encrypted message is msg. Otherwise, the solver answers that the ciphertext is uniformly random.

In summary we have that the advantage to distinguish between Hybrid 0 and Hybrid $n \cdot m + n$ is $\mathsf{Adv}^{\mathsf{DVBB}}_{\mathsf{A,LObf}} \leq n \cdot m \cdot \mathsf{Adv}^{\mathcal{D}\text{-}\mathsf{RandCt}}_{\mathsf{D,SKE}}(\lambda) + n \cdot \mathsf{Adv}^{\mathsf{IND\text{-}CPA}}_{\mathsf{D,FHE}}(\lambda)$.

Remark 1 (Relaxing the Security Requirement on the SKE *Scheme).* From the proof of Hybrids $[1, n \cdot m]$ in the proofs of Theorem 2 and Theorem 4, we observe that we need $\mathcal{D}$-IND-CPA (resp. $\mathcal{D}$-RandCt) because we need to encrypt multiple FHE secret keys using the same lock key. Note that in the special case of key dependent message insecure fully homomorphic encryption where $n = 1$ and $m = 1$, we can relax the requirement on SKE to $\mathcal{D}$-semantic security (resp. weak $\mathcal{D}$-pseudorandom ciphertext). Furthermore, for $\mathcal{D}$ being the class of uniform distributions, we can efficiently implement SKE as a one-time pad.

4.2 Extending to Multi-bit Messages

In this section, we show variants of our lockable obfuscation scheme capable of returning larger messages instead of only a single bit. We show that it is enough to publish encryptions of the bits of the message, and then use the multiplicative homomorphism and the cycle tester to test which bit is encrypted. We extend the idea and show that circular insecure, fully homomorphic encryption schemes are naturally susceptible to key recovery attacks. Finally, we note that we can exploit a full key recovery attack to reduce further the number of ciphertexts that constitute the obfuscated program.

Construction 3 (Multibit Lockable Obfuscation). *Let* $\mathsf{LObf} = (\mathtt{Obf}, \mathtt{Eval})$ *be the lockable obfuscation as given by Construction 1 or Construction 2. Let* $C : \{0,1\}^\kappa \mapsto \{0,1\}^\eta$ *be a circuit and let* $\widehat{C} \leftarrow \mathsf{LObf}.\mathtt{Setup}(\lambda, C, \mathsf{lock})$ *for* $\mathsf{lock} \in \{0,1\}^\eta$. *Denote as* $\mathsf{msg}[l] \in \{0,1\}$ *for* $l \in [\ell_{\mathsf{msg}}]$ *the lth bit of a message* msg. *For the message* $\mathsf{msg} \in \{0,1\}^{\ell_{\mathsf{msg}}}$ *where* $\ell_{\mathsf{msg}} = \mathsf{poly}(\lambda)$, *we extend the obfuscated circuit as follows.*

- *The* Obf *algorithm additionally computes* $\mathsf{ct}^{(\mathsf{msg})}_{i,l} \leftarrow \mathsf{FHE.Enc}(\mathsf{sk}_i, \mathsf{msg}[l])$ *for all* $i \in [n]$ *and* $l \in [\ell_{\mathsf{msg}}]$. *The extended program is*
  - $\widehat{C} = \left([\mathsf{ct}_i]_{i=1}^n, [\mathsf{ct}^{(\mathsf{msg})}_{i,l}]_{i=1,l=1}^{n,\ell_{\mathsf{msg}}}, [\mathsf{ct}^{(\mathsf{lock})}_{i,j}]_{i=1,j=1}^{n,m}\right)$ *for base Construction 1, and*
  - $\widehat{C} = \left([\mathsf{ct}_i]_{i=1}^n, [\mathsf{ct}^{(\mathsf{msg})}_{i,l}]_{i=1,l=1}^{n,\ell_{\mathsf{msg}}}, [\overline{\mathsf{ct}}^{(\mathsf{lock})}_{i,j}]_{i=1,j=1}^{n,m}\right)$ *for base Construction 2.*
- *The* Eval *algorithm upon computing* $\mathsf{ct}^{(\mathsf{Test})}_{i,j}$ *as in Construction 1 or Construction 2, restores the message* msg *as follows.*
  1. *If* $\mathsf{FHE.Test}([\mathsf{ct}^{(\mathsf{Test})}_{i,j}]_{i=1,j=1}^{n,m}) = 0$, *then return* $\perp$.
  2. *For all* $l \in [\ell_{\mathsf{msg}}]$ *do*
     - *For* $i \in [n]$ *and* $j \in [m]$ *compute*
$$\mathsf{ct}^{(\mathsf{Test,msg})}_{i,j,l} \leftarrow \mathsf{FHE.Eval}\left([\mathsf{ct}^{(\mathsf{Test})}_{i,j}, \mathsf{ct}^{(\mathsf{msg})}_{i,l}], \mathtt{Mul}(.,.)\right).$$
     - *Set* $\mathsf{msg}[l] = \mathsf{FHE.Test}\left([\mathsf{ct}^{(\mathsf{Test,msg})}_{i,j,l}]_{i=1,j=1}^{n,m}\right)$.

Theorem 5 (Correctness). *For all* $\lambda \in \mathbb{N}$, *all* $C : \{0,1\}^\kappa \mapsto \{0,1\}^\eta$, *all* $\mathsf{lock} \in \{0,1\}^\eta$ *and* $\mathsf{msg} \in \{0,1\}^{\ell_{\mathsf{msg}}}$, LObf *given by Construction 3 is a polynomially efficient and correct lockable obfuscation with correctness error*

$$\mathsf{Err}^{\mathsf{corr}}_{\mathsf{LObf}}(\lambda) \leq n \cdot m \cdot \ell_{\mathsf{msg}} \cdot \mathsf{Err}^{\mathsf{corr}}_{\mathsf{FHE.Eval}}(\lambda, \delta) + \ell_{\mathsf{msg}} \cdot \mathsf{Err}^{\mathsf{corr}}_{\mathsf{FHE.Test}}(\lambda) + \mathsf{Err}^{\mathsf{corr}}_{\mathsf{SKE}}(\lambda).$$

Proof. Again, polynomial efficiency follows from polynomial efficiency of the underlying primitives. The proofs of correctness for both versions that are based on Construction 1 and Construction 2, follow the proofs of Theorem 2 and Theorem 4, respectively, until the ciphertexts $\mathsf{ct}^{(\mathsf{Test})}_{i,j}$ are computed. Remind that for $C(x) = \mathsf{lock}$ we have $\mathsf{ct}^{(\mathsf{Test})}_{i,j} \approx \mathsf{FHE.Enc}(\mathsf{sk}_i, \mathsf{F}_j(\mathsf{sk}_{(i \bmod n)+1}))$. Then from Construction 3 we have

$$\begin{aligned}\mathsf{ct}^{(\mathsf{Test},\mathsf{msg})}_{i,j,l} &= \mathsf{FHE.Eval}([\mathsf{ct}^{(\mathsf{Test})}_{i,j}, \mathsf{ct}^{(\mathsf{msg})}_{i,l}], \mathtt{Mul}(.,.)) \\ &\approx \mathsf{FHE.Enc}(\mathsf{sk}_i, \mathsf{F}_j(\mathsf{sk}_{(i \bmod n)+1}) \cdot \mathsf{msg}[l])\end{aligned}$$

with probability failure $\mathsf{Err}^{\mathsf{corr}}_{\mathsf{FHE.Eval}}(\lambda, \delta)$ for all $i \in [n]$, $j \in [m]$ and $l \in [\ell_{\mathsf{msg}}]$. Therefore, if $\mathsf{msg}[l] = 0$, then $\mathtt{Test}([\mathsf{ct}^{(\mathsf{Test},\mathsf{msg})}_{i,j,l}]^{n,m}_{i=1,j=1}) = 0$, and if $\mathsf{msg}[j] = 1$, then $\mathsf{FHE.Test}([\mathsf{ct}^{(\mathsf{Test},\mathsf{msg})}_{i,j,l}]^{n,m}_{i=1,j=1}) = 1$, with probability of failure $\mathsf{Err}^{\mathsf{corr}}_{\mathsf{FHE.Test}}(\lambda)$.

If $C(x) \neq \mathsf{lock}$, then we have $\mathsf{ct}^{(\mathsf{Test},\mathsf{msg})}_{i,j,l} \approx \mathsf{FHE.Enc}(\mathsf{sk}_i, \widetilde{\mathsf{msg}}_{i,j})$, where the plaintext is $\widetilde{\mathsf{msg}}_{i,j} = \mathsf{SKE.Dec}(C(x), \overline{\mathsf{ct}}^{\mathsf{lock}}_{i,j})$. From correctness of the SKE scheme we have that there exists $i \in [n]$ and all $j \in [m]$ such that $\widetilde{\mathsf{msg}}_{i,j} \neq \mathsf{F}_j(\mathsf{sk}_{(i \bmod n)+1})$ with probability at least $1 - \mathsf{Err}^{\mathsf{corr}}_{\mathsf{SKE}}(\lambda)$. Consequently, we have that, even if $\mathsf{msg}[l]= 1$, the vector $[\mathsf{ct}^{(\mathsf{Test},\mathsf{msg})}_{i,j,l}]^{n,m}_{i=1,j=1}$ does not encode a cycle, and the tester returns 0 with probability failure bounded by $\mathsf{Err}^{\mathsf{corr}}_{\mathsf{FHE.Test}}(\lambda)$ and the $\mathsf{LObf.Eval}$ algorithm outputs $\perp$.

Note that in the case $C(x) \neq \mathsf{lock}$, the circuit evaluated by the FHE is smaller, however we upperbound the error with $\mathsf{Err}^{\mathsf{corr}}_{\mathsf{FHE.Eval}}(\lambda, \delta)$. Furthermore, in the case $C(x) = \mathsf{lock}$, SKE always returns the correct message, but we upperbound the probability of failure with $\mathsf{Err}^{\mathsf{corr}}_{\mathsf{SKE}}(\lambda)$.

To summarize, we have that the message extraction may fail with probability at least $n \cdot m \cdot \ell_{\mathsf{msg}} \cdot \mathsf{Err}^{\mathsf{corr}}_{\mathsf{FHE.Eval}}(\lambda) + \ell_{\mathsf{msg}} \cdot \mathsf{Err}^{\mathsf{corr}}_{\mathsf{FHE.Test}}(\lambda) + \mathsf{Err}^{\mathsf{corr}}_{\mathsf{SKE}}(\lambda)$.

Theorem 6 (Security). *Let* SKE *be a* $\mathcal{D}$-IND-CPA *secure symmetric key encryption scheme when using Construction 1 as base, or* $\mathcal{D}$-RandCt *secure when using Construction 2 as base. Let* FHE *be a* IND-CPA *secure fully homomorphic encryption scheme. Then,* LObf *given by Construction 1, is* $\mathcal{D}$-DVBB *secure.*

Proof. The proof of Theorem 6 follows the proofs of Theorem 2 and Theorem 4 depending which base construction is used, except with the following changes.

The simulator works as in Theorem 6 or Theorem 4 but it additionally computes $\mathsf{ct}^{(\mathsf{msg})}_{i,l}$ as encryptions of zero. Let L be the number of the last hybrid in the proof of Theorem 2 or Theorem Theorem 4. We additionally define the following sequence of hybrids.

Hybrid $L + n \cdot (i-1) + l$: For $i \in [n]$ and $l \in [\ell_{\mathsf{msg}}]$, instead of computing $\mathsf{ct}_{i,l}^{(\mathsf{msg})} \leftarrow \mathsf{FHE.Enc}(\mathsf{sk}_i, \mathsf{msg}[l])$, we compute $\mathsf{ct}_{i,l}^{(\mathsf{msg})} \leftarrow \mathsf{FHE.Enc}(\mathsf{sk}_i, 0)$.

Claim. If an adversary A distinguishes between Hybrid $L + n \cdot (i-1) + l$ and Hybrid $L + n \cdot (i-1) + l - 1$, then there exists a distinguisher D, that uses A to break IND-CPA security of FHE. We have

$$\left| \Pr[\mathcal{H}_{L+n\cdot(i-1)+l}] - \Pr[\mathcal{H}_{L+n\cdot(i-1)+l-1}] \right| = \mathsf{Adv}_{\mathsf{D},\mathsf{FHE}}^{\mathsf{IND\text{-}CPA}}(\lambda).$$

Proof. First, the solver generates all secret keys of the FHE scheme except sk_i. The solver generates all ciphertexts as in Hybrid $L + n \cdot (i-1) + l - 1$, except for the ciphertext $\mathsf{ct}_{i,l}^{(\mathsf{msg})}$. To obtain $\mathsf{ct}_{i,l}^{(\mathsf{msg})}$ the solver sets the challenge query as $\mathsf{msg}_0 = \mathsf{msg}[l]$ and $\mathsf{msg}_1 = 0$. All other ciphertexts for the secret key are obtained by querying $\mathcal{O}$ on messages as in Hybrid $L + n \cdot (i-1) + l - 1$.

If the adversary outputs that it is Hybrid $L+n\cdot(i-1)+l-1$, then the solver answers that the encrypted message is msg_0. Otherwise, the solver answers that the message is msg_1.

Finally, we have that for

- the base Construction 1, the adversary's advantage of distinguish between hybrid 0 and hybrid $L + n \cdot \ell_{\mathsf{msg}}$ is

$$\mathsf{Adv}_{\mathsf{A},\mathsf{LObf}}^{\mathsf{DVBB}} \leq n \cdot m \cdot \mathsf{Adv}_{\mathsf{D},\mathsf{SKE}}^{\mathcal{D}\text{-}\mathsf{IND\text{-}CPA}}(\lambda) + n \cdot (m + \ell_{\mathsf{msg}}) \cdot \mathsf{Adv}_{\mathsf{D},\mathsf{FHE}}^{\mathsf{IND\text{-}CPA}}(\lambda)$$

and for

- the base Construction 2, the adversary's advantage of distinguish between hybrid 0 and hybrid $L + n \cdot \ell_{\mathsf{msg}}$ is

$$\mathsf{Adv}_{\mathsf{A},\mathsf{LObf}}^{\mathsf{DVBB}} \leq n \cdot m \cdot \mathsf{Adv}_{\mathsf{D},\mathsf{SKE}}^{\mathcal{D}\text{-}\mathsf{RandCt}}(\lambda) + n \cdot (1 + \ell_{\mathsf{msg}}) \cdot \mathsf{Adv}_{\mathsf{D},\mathsf{FHE}}^{\mathsf{IND\text{-}CPA}}(\lambda)$$

Key Recovery Attack. We show that given a key cycle for any circular insecure fully homomorphic encryption, it is possible to decode the key material. The idea follows from Construction 3.

Construction 4 (The Key Recovery Attack). *Let* FHE = (`Setup`, `Enc`, `Dec`, `Eval`, `Test`) *be a fully homomorphic encryption scheme with a cycle tester. We build the algorithm* `KeyRecovery` *as follows:*

`KeyRecovery`($[\mathsf{ct}_i]_{i=1,j=1}^{n,m}$): *Takes as input a vector of ciphertexts* $[\mathsf{ct}_{i,j}]_{i=1,j=1}^{n,m}$ *and returns a vector* $[\widetilde{\mathsf{sk}}_{i,j}]_{i=1,j=1}^{n,m}$.

1. *Let* $\ell \geq \lceil \log_2 \mathsf{F}_j(.) \rceil$ *for all* $j \in [m]$.
2. *For* $i \in [n]$, $j \in [m]$ *and* $l \in \ell$
   - *Compute* $\mathsf{ct}_l^{(\mathsf{Bit},i,j)} \leftarrow \mathsf{FHE.Eval}(\mathsf{ct}_{i,j}, \mathtt{GetBit}(.,l))$, *where* $\mathtt{GetBit}(x,l)$ *is a circuit that returns the* l*th bit of* x.
   - *For* $i' \in [n]$ *and* $j' \in [m]$

- *If $i' = i$, then set*

$$\mathsf{ct}_{i',j'}^{(\mathsf{Test},i,j)} \leftarrow \mathsf{FHE.Eval}\big([\mathsf{ct}_{l,i'}^{(\mathsf{Bit},i,j)}, \mathsf{ct}_{i',j'}], \mathtt{Mul}(.,.)\big).$$

- *Otherwise set* $\mathsf{ct}_{i',j'}^{(\mathsf{Test},i,j)} \leftarrow \mathsf{ct}_{i',j'}$.

  – *Set* $\widetilde{b}_{i,j,l} \leftarrow \mathtt{Test}\big([\mathsf{ct}_{i',j'}^{(\mathsf{Test},i,j)}]_{i'=1,j'=1}^{n,m}\big)$.

3. *For $i \in [n]$ and $j \in [m]$ compute* $\widetilde{\mathsf{sk}}_{i,j} \leftarrow \sum_{l=1}^{\ell} \widetilde{b}_{i,j,l} \cdot 2^{l-1}$.
4. *Return* $[\widetilde{\mathsf{sk}}_{i,j}]_{i=1,j=1}^{n,m}$.

Theorem 7 (Correctness). *For $i \in [n]$ and $j \in [m]$ let $\mathsf{ct}_{i,j} \approx \mathsf{FHE.Enc}(\mathsf{sk}_i, \mathsf{F}_j(\mathsf{sk}_{(i \bmod n)+1}))$. Let C_{KR} be the circuit that* `KeyRecovery` *homomorphically computes on each ciphertext $\mathsf{ct}_{i,j}$ until it obtains $\mathsf{ct}_{i',j'}^{(\mathsf{Test},i,j)}$. Denote as δ the depth of C_{KR}. Let $[\widetilde{\mathsf{sk}}_{i,j}]_{i=1,j=1}^{n,m} \leftarrow \mathtt{KeyRecovery}([\mathsf{ct}_{i,j}]_{i=1,j=1}^{n,m})$. Then the equation $\widetilde{\mathsf{sk}}_{i,j} = \mathsf{F}_j(\mathsf{sk}_{(i \bmod n)+1})$ holds for all $i \in [n]$ and all $j \in [m]$ with probability $1 - \big(\mathsf{Err}_{\mathsf{FHE.Eval}}^{\mathsf{corr}}(\lambda, \delta) + \mathsf{Err}_{\mathsf{FHE.Test}}^{\mathsf{corr}}(\lambda)\big)$.*

Proof. Let us denote as $b_{i,j,l} \in \{0,1\}$ the bits which satisfy $\mathsf{F}_j(\mathsf{sk}_{(i \bmod n)+1}) = \sum_{l=1}^{\ell} b_{(i \bmod n)+1,j,l} \cdot 2^{l-1}$. From correctness of the FHE we have that $\mathsf{ct}_l^{(\mathsf{Bit},i,j)} = \mathsf{FHE.Eval}(\mathsf{ct}_{i,j}, \mathtt{GetBit}(.,l)) \approx \mathsf{FHE.Enc}(\mathsf{sk}_i, b_{i,j,l})$.

Again from correctness of the FHE we have

$$\begin{aligned}\mathsf{ct}_{i',j'}^{(\mathsf{Test},i,j)} &= \mathsf{FHE.Eval}\big([\mathsf{ct}_{l,i'}^{(\mathsf{Bit},i,j)}, \mathsf{ct}_{i',j'}], \mathtt{Mul}(.,.)\big)\\ &\approx \mathsf{FHE.Enc}\big(\mathsf{sk}_{i'}, b_{i,j,l} \cdot \mathsf{F}_{j'}(\mathsf{sk}_{(i' \bmod n)+1})\big),\end{aligned}$$

for $i' = i$. For $i' \neq i$, we set $\mathsf{ct}_{i',j'}^{(\mathsf{Test},i,j)} = \mathsf{ct}_{i,j}$. Now observe that the vector $[\mathsf{ct}_{i',j'}^{(\mathsf{Test},i,j)}]_{i'=1,j'=1}^{n,m}$ decrypts to the same messages as the vector $[\mathsf{ct}_{i,j}]_{i=1,j=1}^{n,m}$ if $b_{i,j,l} = 1$. If $b_{i,j,l} = 0$, then the ciphertexts $\mathsf{ct}_{i,j'}^{(\mathsf{Test},i,j)}$ are ciphertexts of 0, and the cycle is broken. Hence from correctness of the cycle tester we have $\widetilde{b}_{i,j,l} = 0$ if $b_{i,j,l} = 0$, since $\mathsf{ct}_{i',j'}^{(\mathsf{Test},i,j)} \approx \mathsf{FHE.Enc}(\mathsf{sk}_{i'}, 0)$, and $\widetilde{b}_{i,j,l} = 1$ if $b_{i,j,l} = 1$, since $\mathsf{ct}_{i',j'}^{(\mathsf{Test},i,j)} \approx \mathsf{FHE.Enc}(\mathsf{sk}_{i'}, \mathsf{F}_{j'}(\mathsf{sk}_{(i' \bmod n)+1}))$. Finally, from the definition we have that $\widetilde{\mathsf{sk}}_{i,j} = \sum_{l=1}^{\ell} \widetilde{b}_{i,j,l} \cdot 2^{l-1} = \mathsf{F}_j(\mathsf{sk}_{(i \bmod n)+1})$.

Remark 2 (Further simplification of Multibit Lockable Obfuscation). At this point we believe it is easy to see, that we can reduce the size of the obfuscated program given by Construction 3, by publishing $\mathsf{ct}_{\mathsf{msg}} \leftarrow \mathsf{FHE.Enc}(\mathsf{sk}_1, \mathsf{msg})$ instead of $[\mathsf{ct}_{\mathsf{msg}_i,j}]_{j=1}^{\ell_{\mathsf{msg}}})]_{i=1}^{n}$. The idea to decrypt the message from $\mathsf{ct}_{\mathsf{msg}}$, is to run the attack given by Construction 3, i.e., recover all secret keys for the FHE scheme, including sk_1. Note that we assume that it is feasible to recover the secret keys given $[\mathsf{F}_j(\mathsf{sk}_{(i \bmod n)+1})]_{i=1,j=1}^{n,m}$. Finally, we compute $\mathsf{msg} \leftarrow \mathsf{FHE.Dec}(\mathsf{sk}_1, \mathsf{ct}_{\mathsf{msg}})$.

5 Conclusions

We believe that our lockable obfuscators are intuitive and easy to understand. Our algorithms exemplify, alongside the work from Kluczniak [Klu20], that circular insecure encryption is a useful building block for advanced cryptographic primitives. It is worth noting that circular insecure encryption was previously constructed solely out of theoretical curiosity.

As mentioned in the introduction, the main aim of this paper is to introduce and analyze a general methodology of building lockable obfuscators. In particular, we leave concrete instantiations of our methods to future work. An exciting direction would be whether, for instance, we can use existing fully homomorphic encryption schemes together with the cycle testers in [BHW15,KW16,AP16] to build more efficient lockable obfuscation without the need to obfuscate branching programs.

Funding. This work has been partially funded/supported by the German Ministry for Education and Research through funding for the project CISPA-Stanford Center for Cybersecurity (Funding number 16KIS0927).

References

[ABBC10] Acar, T., Belenkiy, M., Bellare, M., Cash, D.: Cryptographic agility and its relation to circular encryption. In: Gilbert, H. (ed.) EUROCRYPT 2010. LNCS, vol. 6110, pp. 403–422. Springer, Heidelberg (2010). https://doi.org/10.1007/978-3-642-13190-5_21

[ADN+10] Alwen, J., Dodis, Y., Naor, M., Segev, G., Walfish, S., Wichs, D.: Public-key encryption in the bounded-retrieval model. In: Gilbert, H. (ed.) EUROCRYPT 2010. LNCS, vol. 6110, pp. 113–134. Springer, Heidelberg (2010). https://doi.org/10.1007/978-3-642-13190-5_6

[Agr19] Agrawal, S.: Indistinguishability obfuscation without multilinear maps: new methods for bootstrapping and instantiation. In: Ishai, Y., Rijmen, V. (eds.) EUROCRYPT 2019. LNCS, vol. 11476, pp. 191–225. Springer, Cham (2019). https://doi.org/10.1007/978-3-030-17653-2_7

[AGV09] Akavia, A., Goldwasser, S., Vaikuntanathan, V.: Simultaneous hardcore bits and cryptography against memory attacks. In: Reingold, O. (ed.) TCC 2009. LNCS, vol. 5444, pp. 474–495. Springer, Heidelberg (2009). https://doi.org/10.1007/978-3-642-00457-5_28

[AJL+19] Ananth, P., Jain, A., Lin, H., Matt, C., Sahai, A.: Indistinguishability obfuscation without multilinear maps: new paradigms via low degree weak pseudorandomness and security amplification. In: Boldyreva, A., Micciancio, D. (eds.) CRYPTO 2019. LNCS, vol. 11694, pp. 284–332. Springer, Cham (2019). https://doi.org/10.1007/978-3-030-26954-8_10

[AKPW13] Alwen, J., Krenn, S., Pietrzak, K., Wichs, D.: Learning with rounding, revisited. In: Canetti, R., Garay, J.A. (eds.) CRYPTO 2013. LNCS, vol. 8042, pp. 57–74. Springer, Heidelberg (2013). https://doi.org/10.1007/978-3-642-40041-4_4

[AL20] Ananth, P., La Placa, R.L.: Secure quantum extraction protocols. In: Pass, R., Pietrzak, K. (eds.) TCC 2020. LNCS, vol. 12552, pp. 123–152. Springer, Cham (2020). https://doi.org/10.1007/978-3-030-64381-2_5

[AP16] Alamati, N., Peikert, C.: Three's compromised too: circular insecurity for any cycle length from (ring-)LWE. In: Robshaw, M., Katz, J. (eds.) CRYPTO 2016. LNCS, vol. 9815, pp. 659–680. Springer, Heidelberg (2016). https://doi.org/10.1007/978-3-662-53008-5_23

[BDGM20a] Brakerski, Z., Döttling, N., Garg, S., Malavolta, G.: Candidate iO from homomorphic encryption schemes. In: Canteaut, A., Ishai, Y. (eds.) EUROCRYPT 2020. LNCS, vol. 12105, pp. 79–109. Springer, Cham (2020). https://doi.org/10.1007/978-3-030-45721-1_4

[BDGM20b] Brakerski, Z., Döttling, N., Garg, S., Malavolta, G.: Factoring and pairings are not necessary for iO: circular-secure LWE suffices. Cryptology ePrint Archive, Report 2020/1024 (2020). https://eprint.iacr.org/2020/1024

[BG10] Brakerski, Z., Goldwasser, S.: Circular and leakage resilient public-key encryption under subgroup indistinguishability. In: Rabin, T. (ed.) CRYPTO 2010. LNCS, vol. 6223, pp. 1–20. Springer, Heidelberg (2010). https://doi.org/10.1007/978-3-642-14623-7_1

[BGI+01] Barak, B., et al.: On the (Im)possibility of obfuscating programs. In: Kilian, J. (ed.) CRYPTO 2001. LNCS, vol. 2139, pp. 1–18. Springer, Heidelberg (2001). https://doi.org/10.1007/3-540-44647-8_1

[BGI+12] Barak, B., et al.: On the (im)possibility of obfuscating programs. J. ACM **59**(2), 1–48 (2012)

[BHJ+19] Barak, B., Hopkins, S.B., Jain, A., Kothari, P., Sahai, A.: Sum-of-squares meets program obfuscation, revisited. In: Ishai, Y., Rijmen, V. (eds.) EUROCRYPT 2019. LNCS, vol. 11476, pp. 226–250. Springer, Cham (2019). https://doi.org/10.1007/978-3-030-17653-2_8

[BHW15] Bishop, A., Hohenberger, S., Waters, B.: New circular security counterexamples from decision linear and learning with errors. In: Iwata, T., Cheon, J.H. (eds.) ASIACRYPT 2015. LNCS, vol. 9453, pp. 776–800. Springer, Heidelberg (2015). https://doi.org/10.1007/978-3-662-48800-3_32

[BKM+18] Bishop, A., Kowalczyk, L., Malkin, T., Pastro, V., Raykova, M., Shi, K.: A simple obfuscation scheme for pattern-matching with wildcards. In: Shacham, H., Boldyreva, A. (eds.) Advances in Cryptology - CRYPTO 2018. Part III, volume 10993 of Lecture Notes in Computer Science, pp. 731–752. Springer, Heidelberg (2018)

[BKP19] Bitansky, N., Khurana, D., Paneth, O.: Weak zero-knowledge beyond the black-box barrier. In: Charikar, M., Cohen, E. (eds.) 51st Annual ACM Symposium on Theory of Computing, pp. 1091–1102. ACM Press, June 2019

[BKSW18] Badrinarayanan, S., Khurana, D., Sahai, A., Waters, B.: Upgrading to functional encryption. In: Beimel, A., Dziembowski, S. (eds.) TCC 2018. LNCS, vol. 11239, pp. 629–658. Springer, Cham (2018). https://doi.org/10.1007/978-3-030-03807-6_23

[BLMZ19] Bartusek, J., Lepoint, T., Ma, F., Zhandry, M.: New techniques for obfuscating conjunctions. In: Ishai, Y., Rijmen, V. (eds.) EUROCRYPT 2019. LNCS, vol. 11478, pp. 636–666. Springer, Cham (2019). https://doi.org/10.1007/978-3-030-17659-4_22

[BLSV18] Brakerski, Z., Lombardi, A., Segev, G., Vaikuntanathan, V.: Anonymous IBE, leakage resilience and circular security from new assumptions. In: Nielsen, J.B., Rijmen, V. (eds.) EUROCRYPT 2018. LNCS, vol. 10820, pp. 535–564. Springer, Cham (2018). https://doi.org/10.1007/978-3-319-78381-9_20

[BR13] Brakerski, Z., Rothblum, G.N.: Obfuscating conjunctions. In: Canetti, R., Garay, J.A. (eds.) CRYPTO 2013. LNCS, vol. 8043, pp. 416–434. Springer, Heidelberg (2013). https://doi.org/10.1007/978-3-642-40084-1_24

[BS16] Bellare, M., Stepanovs, I.: Point-function obfuscation: a framework and generic constructions. In: Kushilevitz, E., Malkin, T. (eds.) TCC 2016. LNCS, vol. 9563, pp. 565–594. Springer, Heidelberg (2016). https://doi.org/10.1007/978-3-662-49099-0_21

[BS20] Bitansky, N., Shmueli, O.: Post-quantum zero knowledge in constant rounds. In: Makarychev, K., Makarychev, Y., Tulsiani, M., Kamath, G., Chuzhoy, J. (eds.) 52nd Annual ACM Symposium on Theory of Computing, pp. 269–279. ACM Press, June 2020

[BVWW16] Brakerski, Z., Vaikuntanathan, V., Wee, H., Wichs, D.: Obfuscating conjunctions under entropic ring LWE. In: Sudan, M. (ed.) ITCS 2016: 7th Conference on Innovations in Theoretical Computer Science, pp. 147–156. Association for Computing Machinery, January 2016

[BW19] Beullens, W., Wee, H.: Obfuscating simple functionalities from knowledge assumptions. In: Lin, D., Sako, K. (eds.) PKC 2019. LNCS, vol. 11443, pp. 254–283. Springer, Cham (2019). https://doi.org/10.1007/978-3-030-17259-6_9

[Can97] Canetti, R.: Towards realizing random oracles: hash functions that hide all partial information. In: Kaliski, B.S. (ed.) CRYPTO 1997. LNCS, vol. 1294, pp. 455–469. Springer, Heidelberg (1997). https://doi.org/10.1007/BFb0052255

[CD08] Canetti, R., Dakdouk, R.R.: Obfuscating point functions with multibit output. In: Smart, N. (ed.) EUROCRYPT 2008. LNCS, vol. 4965, pp. 489–508. Springer, Heidelberg (2008). https://doi.org/10.1007/978-3-540-78967-3_28

[CGH12] Cash, D., Green, M., Hohenberger, S.: New definitions and separations for circular security. In: Fischlin, M., Buchmann, J., Manulis, M. (eds.) PKC 2012. LNCS, vol. 7293, pp. 540–557. Springer, Heidelberg (2012). https://doi.org/10.1007/978-3-642-30057-8_32

[CKVW10] Canetti, R., Tauman Kalai, Y., Varia, M., Wichs, D.: On symmetric encryption and point obfuscation. In: Micciancio, D. (ed.) TCC 2010. LNCS, vol. 5978, pp. 52–71. Springer, Heidelberg (2010). https://doi.org/10.1007/978-3-642-11799-2_4

[CRV10] Canetti, R., Rothblum, G.N., Varia, M.: Obfuscation of hyperplane membership. In: Micciancio, D. (ed.) TCC 2010. LNCS, vol. 5978, pp. 72–89. Springer, Heidelberg (2010). https://doi.org/10.1007/978-3-642-11799-2_5

[CVW+18a] Chen, Y., Vaikuntanathan, V., Waters, B., Wee, H., Wichs, D.: Traitor-tracing from LWE made simple and attribute-based. In: Beimel, A., Dziembowski, S. (eds.) TCC 2018. LNCS, vol. 11240, pp. 341–369. Springer, Cham (2018). https://doi.org/10.1007/978-3-030-03810-6_13

[CVW18b] Chen, Y., Vaikuntanathan, V., Wee, H.: GGH15 beyond permutation branching programs: proofs, attacks, and candidates. In: Shacham, H., Boldyreva, A. (eds.) CRYPTO 2018. LNCS, vol. 10992, pp. 577–607. Springer, Cham (2018). https://doi.org/10.1007/978-3-319-96881-0_20

[DGK+10] Dodis, Y., Goldwasser, S., Tauman Kalai, Y., Peikert, C., Vaikuntanathan, V.: Public-key encryption schemes with auxiliary inputs. In: Micciancio, D. (ed.) TCC 2010. LNCS, vol. 5978, pp. 361–381. Springer, Heidelberg (2010). https://doi.org/10.1007/978-3-642-11799-2_22

[DHLW10] Dodis, Y., Haralambiev, K., López-Alt, A., Wichs, D.: Efficient public-key cryptography in the presence of key leakage. In: Abe, M. (ed.) ASIACRYPT 2010. LNCS, vol. 6477, pp. 613–631. Springer, Heidelberg (2010). https://doi.org/10.1007/978-3-642-17373-8_35

[DKL09] Dodis, Y., Kalai, Y.T., Lovett, S.: On cryptography with auxiliary input. In: Mitzenmacher, M. (ed.) 41st Annual ACM Symposium on Theory of Computing, pp. 621–630. ACM Press, May/June 2009

[DORS08] Dodis, Y., Ostrovsky, R., Reyzin, L., Smith, A.: Fuzzy extractors: how to generate strong keys from biometrics and other noisy data. SIAM J. Comput. **38**(1), 97–139 (2008)

[DP08] Dziembowski, S., Pietrzak, K.: Leakage-resilient cryptography. In: 49th Annual Symposium on Foundations of Computer Science, pp. 293–302. IEEE Computer Society Press, October 2008

[DRS04] Dodis, Y., Reyzin, L., Smith, A.: Fuzzy extractors: how to generate strong keys from biometrics and other noisy data. In: Cachin, C., Camenisch, J.L. (eds.) EUROCRYPT 2004. LNCS, vol. 3027, pp. 523–540. Springer, Heidelberg (2004). https://doi.org/10.1007/978-3-540-24676-3_31

[DS05] Dodis, Y., Smith, A.: Correcting errors without leaking partial information. In: Gabow, H.N., Fagin, R. (eds.) 37th Annual ACM Symposium on Theory of Computing, pp. 654–663. ACM Press, May 2005

[Gen09] Gentry, C.: Fully homomorphic encryption using ideal lattices. In: Mitzenmacher, M. (ed.) 41st Annual ACM Symposium on Theory of Computing, pp. 169–178. ACM Press, May/June 2009

[GGH15] Gentry, C., Gorbunov, S., Halevi, S.: Graph-induced multilinear maps from lattices. In: Dodis, Y., Nielsen, J.B. (eds.) TCC 2015. LNCS, vol. 9015, pp. 498–527. Springer, Heidelberg (2015). https://doi.org/10.1007/978-3-662-46497-7_20

[GJLS20] Gay, R., Jain, A., Lin, H., Sahai, A.: Indistinguishability obfuscation from simple-to-state hard problems: new assumptions, new techniques, and simplification. Cryptology ePrint Archive, Report 2020/764 (2020). https://eprint.iacr.org/2020/764

[GKPV10] Goldwasser, S., Kalai, Y.T., Peikert, C., Vaikuntanathan, V.: Robustness of the learning with errors assumption. In: Yao, A.C.-C. (ed.) Innovations in Computer Science - ICS 2010, Tsinghua University, Beijing, China, 5–7 January 2010. Proceedings, pp. 230–240. Tsinghua University Press (2010)

[GKVW20] Goyal, R., Koppula, V., Vusirikala, S., Waters, B.: On perfect correctness in (lockable) obfuscation. In: Pass, R., Pietrzak, K. (eds.) TCC 2020. LNCS, vol. 12550, pp. 229–259. Springer, Cham (2020). https://doi.org/10.1007/978-3-030-64375-1_9

[GKW17a] Goyal, R., Koppula, V., Waters, B.: Lockable obfuscation. In: Umans, C. (ed.) 58th Annual Symposium on Foundations of Computer Science, pp. 612–621. IEEE Computer Society Press, October 2017

[GKW17b] Goyal, R., Koppula, V., Waters, B.: Separating IND-CPA and circular security for unbounded length key cycles. In: Fehr, S. (ed.) PKC 2017. LNCS, vol. 10174, pp. 232–246. Springer, Heidelberg (2017). https://doi.org/10.1007/978-3-662-54365-8_10

[GKW17c] Goyal, R., Koppula, V., Waters, B.: Separating semantic and circular security for symmetric-key bit encryption from the learning with errors assumption. In: Coron, J.-S., Nielsen, J.B. (eds.) EUROCRYPT 2017. LNCS, vol. 10211, pp. 528–557. Springer, Cham (2017). https://doi.org/10.1007/978-3-319-56614-6_18

[GKW18] Goyal, R., Koppula, V., Waters, B.: Collusion resistant traitor tracing from learning with errors. In: Diakonikolas, I., Kempe, D., Henzinger, M. (eds.) 50th Annual ACM Symposium on Theory of Computing, pp. 660–670. ACM Press, June 2018

[GP20] Gay, R., Pass, R.: Indistinguishability obfuscation from circular security. Cryptology ePrint Archive, Report 2020/1010 (2020). https://eprint.iacr.org/2020/1010

[HG01] Howgrave-Graham, N.: Approximate integer common divisors. In: Silverman, J.H. (ed.) CaLC 2001. LNCS, vol. 2146, pp. 51–66. Springer, Heidelberg (2001). https://doi.org/10.1007/3-540-44670-2_6

[HH09] Haitner, I., Holenstein, T.: On the (Im)possibility of key dependent encryption. In: Reingold, O. (ed.) TCC 2009. LNCS, vol. 5444, pp. 202–219. Springer, Heidelberg (2009). https://doi.org/10.1007/978-3-642-00457-5_13

[HILL99] HÅstad, J., Impagliazzo, R., Levin, L.A., Luby, M.: A pseudorandom generator from any one-way function. SIAM J. Comput. **28**(4), 1364–1396 (1999)

[HLR07] Hsiao, C.-Y., Lu, C.-J., Reyzin, L.: Conditional computational entropy, or toward separating pseudoentropy from compressibility. In: Naor, M. (ed.) EUROCRYPT 2007. LNCS, vol. 4515, pp. 169–186. Springer, Heidelberg (2007). https://doi.org/10.1007/978-3-540-72540-4_10

[HPS98] Hoffstein, J., Pipher, J., Silverman, J.H.: NTRU: a ring-based public key cryptosystem. In: Buhler, J.P. (ed.) ANTS 1998. LNCS, vol. 1423, pp. 267–288. Springer, Heidelberg (1998). https://doi.org/10.1007/BFb0054868

[JLMS19] Jain, A., Lin, H., Matt, C., Sahai, A.: How to leverage hardness of constant-degree expanding polynomials over $\mathbb{R}$ to build $i\mathcal{O}$. In: Ishai, Y., Rijmen, V. (eds.) EUROCRYPT 2019. LNCS, vol. 11476, pp. 251–281. Springer, Cham (2019). https://doi.org/10.1007/978-3-030-17653-2_9

[JLS20] Jain, A., Lin, H., Sahai, A.: Indistinguishability obfuscation from well-founded assumptions. Cryptology ePrint Archive, Report 2020/1003 (2020). https://eprint.iacr.org/2020/1003

[Klu20] Kluczniak, K.: Witness encryption from garbled circuit and multi-key fully homomorphic encryption techniques. Cryptology ePrint Archive, Report 2020/1502 (2020). https://eprint.iacr.org/2020/1502

[Klu21] Kluczniak, K.: Lockable obfuscation from circularly insecure fully homomorphic encryption. Cryptology ePrint Archive, Report 2021/1324 (2021). https://ia.cr/2021/1324

[KRW15] Koppula, V., Ramchen, K., Waters, B.: Separations in circular security for arbitrary length key cycles. In: Dodis, Y., Nielsen, J.B. (eds.) TCC 2015. LNCS, vol. 9015, pp. 378–400. Springer, Heidelberg (2015). https://doi.org/10.1007/978-3-662-46497-7_15

[KW16] Koppula, V., Waters, B.: Circular security separations for arbitrary length cycles from LWE. In: Robshaw, M., Katz, J. (eds.) CRYPTO 2016. LNCS, vol. 9815, pp. 681–700. Springer, Heidelberg (2016). https://doi.org/10.1007/978-3-662-53008-5_24

[KY18] Komargodski, I., Yogev, E.: Another step towards realizing random oracles: non-malleable point obfuscation. In: Nielsen, J.B., Rijmen, V. (eds.) EUROCRYPT 2018. LNCS, vol. 10820, pp. 259–279. Springer, Cham (2018). https://doi.org/10.1007/978-3-319-78381-9_10

[LPR10] Lyubashevsky, V., Peikert, C., Regev, O.: On ideal lattices and learning with errors over rings. In: Gilbert, H. (ed.) EUROCRYPT 2010. LNCS, vol. 6110, pp. 1–23. Springer, Heidelberg (2010). https://doi.org/10.1007/978-3-642-13190-5_1

[LPS04] Lynn, B., Prabhakaran, M., Sahai, A.: Positive results and techniques for obfuscation. In: Cachin, C., Camenisch, J.L. (eds.) EUROCRYPT 2004. LNCS, vol. 3027, pp. 20–39. Springer, Heidelberg (2004). https://doi.org/10.1007/978-3-540-24676-3_2

[LPST16] Lin, H., Pass, R., Seth, K., Telang, S.: Indistinguishability obfuscation with non-trivial efficiency. In: Cheng, C.-M., Chung, K.-M., Persiano, G., Yang, B.-Y. (eds.) PKC 2016. LNCS, vol. 9615, pp. 447–462. Springer, Heidelberg (2016). https://doi.org/10.1007/978-3-662-49387-8_17

[LT17] Lin, H., Tessaro, S.: Indistinguishability obfuscation from trilinear maps and block-wise local PRGs. In: Katz, J., Shacham, H. (eds.) CRYPTO 2017. LNCS, vol. 10401, pp. 630–660. Springer, Cham (2017). https://doi.org/10.1007/978-3-319-63688-7_21

[NS09] Naor, M., Segev, G.: Public-key cryptosystems resilient to key leakage. In: Halevi, S. (ed.) CRYPTO 2009. LNCS, vol. 5677, pp. 18–35. Springer, Heidelberg (2009). https://doi.org/10.1007/978-3-642-03356-8_2

[Pie09] Pietrzak, K.: A leakage-resilient mode of operation. In: Joux, A. (ed.) EUROCRYPT 2009. LNCS, vol. 5479, pp. 462–482. Springer, Heidelberg (2009). https://doi.org/10.1007/978-3-642-01001-9_27

[RAD+78] Rivest, R.L., Adleman, L., Dertouzos, M.L., et al.: On data banks and privacy homomorphisms. Found. Secure Comput. **4**(11), 169–180 (1978)

[Reg05] Regev, O.: On lattices, learning with errors, random linear codes, and cryptography. In: Gabow, H.N., Fagin, R. (eds.) 37th Annual ACM Symposium on Theory of Computing, pp. 84–93. ACM Press, May 2005

[Rot13] Rothblum, R.D.: On the circular security of bit-encryption. In: Sahai, A. (ed.) TCC 2013. LNCS, vol. 7785, pp. 579–598. Springer, Heidelberg (2013). https://doi.org/10.1007/978-3-642-36594-2_32

[Wee05] Wee, H.: On obfuscating point functions. In: Gabow, H.N., Fagin, R. (eds.) 37th Annual ACM Symposium on Theory of Computing, pp. 523–532. ACM Press, May 2005

[WW20] Wee, H., Wichs, D.: Candidate obfuscation via oblivious LWE sampling. Cryptology ePrint Archive, Report 2020/1042 (2020). https://eprint.iacr.org/2020/1042

[WZ17] Wichs, D., Zirdelis, G.: Obfuscating compute-and-compare programs under LWE. In: Umans, C. (ed.) 58th Annual Symposium on Foundations of Computer Science, pp. 600–611. IEEE Computer Society Press, October 2017

[YZ16] Yu, Yu., Zhang, J.: Cryptography with auxiliary input and trapdoor from constant-noise LPN. In: Robshaw, M., Katz, J. (eds.) CRYPTO 2016. LNCS, vol. 9814, pp. 214–243. Springer, Heidelberg (2016). https://doi.org/10.1007/978-3-662-53018-4_9

[Zha16] Zhandry, M.: The magic of ELFs. In: Robshaw, M., Katz, J. (eds.) CRYPTO 2016. LNCS, vol. 9814, pp. 479–508. Springer, Heidelberg (2016). https://doi.org/10.1007/978-3-662-53018-4_18

Financially Backed Covert Security

Sebastian Faust[1], Carmit Hazay[2], David Kretzler[1], and Benjamin Schlosser[1](✉)

[1] Technical University of Darmstadt, Darmstadt, Germany
{sebastian.faust,david.kretzler,benjamin.schlosser}@tu-darmstadt.de
[2] Bar-Ilan University, Ramat Gan, Israel
carmit.hazay@biu.ac.il

Abstract. The security notion of *covert security* introduced by Aumann and Lindell (TCC'07) allows the adversary to successfully cheat and break security with a fixed probability $1-\epsilon$, while with probability ϵ, honest parties detect the cheating attempt. Asharov and Orlandi (ASIACRYPT'12) extend covert security to enable parties to create publicly verifiable evidence about misbehavior that can be transferred to any third party. This notion is called *publicly verifiable covert security* (PVC) and has been investigated by multiple works. While these two notions work well in settings with known identities in which parties care about their reputation, they fall short in Internet-like settings where there are only digital identities that can provide some form of anonymity.

In this work, we propose the notion of *financially backed covert security* (FBC), which ensures that the adversary is financially punished if cheating is detected. Next, we present three transformations that turn PVC protocols into FBC protocols. Our protocols provide highly efficient judging, thereby enabling practical judge implementations via smart contracts deployed on a blockchain. In particular, the judge only needs to non-interactively validate a single protocol message while previous PVC protocols required the judge to emulate the whole protocol. Furthermore, by allowing an interactive punishment procedure, we can reduce the amount of validation to a single program instruction, e.g., a gate in a circuit. An interactive punishment, additionally, enables us to create financially backed covert secure protocols without any form of common public transcript, a property that has not been achieved by prior PVC protocols.

Keywords: Covert Security · Multi-Party Computation (MPC) · Public Verifiability · Financial Punishment

1 Introduction

Secure multi-party computation (MPC) protocols allow a set of parties to jointly compute an arbitrary function f on private inputs. These protocols guarantee privacy of inputs and correctness of outputs even if some of the parties are corrupted by an adversary. The two standard adversarial models of MPC are

G. Hanaoka et al. (Eds.): PKC 2022, LNCS 13178, pp. 99–129, 2022.
https://doi.org/10.1007/978-3-030-97131-1_4

semi-honest and *malicious* security. While semi-honest adversaries follow the protocol description but try to derive information beyond the output from the interaction, malicious adversaries can behave in an arbitrary way. MPC protocols in the malicious adversary model provide stronger security guarantees at the cost of significantly less efficiency. As a middle ground between good efficiency and high security Aumann and Lindell introduced the notion of *security against covert adversaries* [AL07]. As in the malicious adversary model, corrupted parties may deviate arbitrarily from the protocol specification but the protocol ensures that cheating is detected with a fixed probability, called *deterrence factor* ϵ. The idea of covert security is that adversaries fear to be detected, e.g., due to reputation issues, and thus refrain from cheating.

Although cheating can be detected in covert security, a party of the protocol cannot transfer the knowledge about malicious behavior to other (external) parties. This shortcoming was addressed by Asharov and Orlandi [AO12] with the notion of *covert security with public verifiability* (PVC). Informally, PVC enables honest parties to create a publicly verifiable certificate about the detected malicious behavior. This certificate can subsequently be checked by any other party (often called *judge*), even if this party did not contribute to the protocol execution. The idea behind this notion is to increase the deterrent effect by damaging the reputation of corrupted parties publicly. PVC secure protocols for the two-party case were presented by [AO12, KM15, ZDH19, HKK+19]. Recently, Damgård et al. [DOS20] showed a generic compiler from semi-honest to publicly verifiable covert security for the two-party setting and gave an intuition on how to extend their compiler to the multi-party case. Full specifications of generic compilers from semi-honest to publicly verifiable covert security for multi-party protocols were presented by Faust et al. [FHKS21] and Scholl et al. [SSS21].

Although PVC seems to solve the shortcoming of covert security at first glance, in many settings PVC is not sufficient; especially, if only a digital identity of the parties is known, e.g., in the Internet. In such a setting, a real party can create a new identity without suffering from a damaged reputation in the sequel. Hence, malicious behavior needs to be punished in a different way. A promising approach is to use existing cryptocurrencies to directly link cheating detection to financial punishment without involving trusted third parties; in particular, cryptocurrencies that support so-called *smart contracts*, i.e., programs that enable the transfer of assets based on predefined rules. Similar to PVC, where an external judge verifies cheating by checking a certificate of misbehavior, we envision a smart contract that decides whether a party behaved maliciously or not. In this setting, the task of judging is executed over a distributed blockchain network keeping it incorruptible and verifiable at the same time. Since every instruction executed by a smart contract costs fees, it is highly important to keep the amount of computation performed by a contract small. This aspect is not solely important for execution of smart contracts but in all settings where an external judge charges by the size of the task it gets. Due to this constraint, we cannot straightforward adapt PVC protocols to work in this setting, since detection of malicious behavior in existing PVC protocols is performed in a naive way that requires the judge to recompute a whole protocol execution.

Related Work. While combining MPC with blockchain technologies is an active research area (e.g., [KB14, BK14, ADMM14]) none of these works deal with realizing the judging process of PVC protocols over a blockchain. The only work connecting covert security with financial punishment thus far is by Zhu et al. [ZDH19], which we describe in a bit more detail below. They combine a two-party garbling protocol with an efficient judge that can be realized via a smart contract. Their construction leverages strong security primitives, like a malicious secure oblivious transfer for the transmission of input wires, to ensure that cheating can only occur during the transmission of the garbled circuit and not in any other part of the two-party protocol. By using a binary search over the transmitted circuit, the parties narrow down the computation step under dispute to a single circuit gate. This process requires $O(\log(|C|))$ interactions, where $|C|$ denotes the circuit size, and enables the judge to resolve the dispute by recomputing only a single circuit gate.

While the approach of Zhu et al. [ZDH19] provides an elegant way to reduce the computational complexity of the judge in case cheating is restricted to a single message, it falls short if multiple messages or even a whole protocol execution is under dispute. As a consequence, their construction is limited in scalability and generality, since it is only applicable to two-party garbling protocols, i.e., neither other semi-honest two-party protocols nor more parties are supported.

Generalizing the ideas of [ZDH19] to work for other protocol types and the multi-party case requires us to address several challenges. First, in [ZDH19] the transmitted garbled circuit under dispute is the result of the completely non-interactive garbling process. In contrast, many semi-honest MPC protocols (e.g., [GMW87, BMR90]) consist of several rounds of interactions that need to be all considered during the verification. Interactivity poses the challenge that multiple messages may be under dispute and the computation of messages performed by parties may depend on data received in previous rounds. Hence, verifications of messages need to consider local computations and internal states of the parties that depend on all previous communication rounds. This task is far more complex than verifying a single public message. Second, supporting more than two parties poses the challenge of resolving a dispute about a protocol execution during which parties might not know the messages sent between a subset of other parties. Third, the transmitted garbled circuit in [ZDH19] is independent of the parties private inputs. Considering protocols where parties provide secret inputs or messages that depend on these inputs, requires a privacy-preserving verification mechanism to protect parties' sensitive data.

1.1 Contribution

Our first contribution is to introduce a new security notion called *financially backed covert security* (FBC). This notion combines a covertly secure protocol with a mechanism to financially punish a corrupted party if cheating was detected. We formalize financial security by adding two properties to covert security, i.e., *financial accountability* and *financial defamation freeness*. Our notion is similar to the one of PVC; in fact, PVC adds reputational punishment to covert security via *accountability* and *defamation freeness*. In order to lift these properties to the financial context, FBC requires deposits from all parties and allows for an interactive judge. We present two security games to formalize our introduced properties. While the properties are close to accountability and defamation freeness of PVC, our work for the first time explicitly presents formal security games for these security properties, thereby enabling us to rigorously reason about financial properties in PVC protocols. We briefly compare our new notion to the security definition of Zhu et al. [ZDH19], which is called *financially secure computation*. Zhu et al. follow the approach of simulation-based security by presenting an ideal functionality for two parties that extends the ideal functionality of covert security. In contrast, we present a game-based security definition that is not restricted to the two-party case. While simulation-based definitions have the advantage of providing security under composition, proving a protocol secure under their notion requires to create a full simulation proof which is an expensive task. Instead, our game-based notion allows to re-use simulation proofs of all existing covert and PVC protocols, including future constructions, and to focus on proving financial accountability and financial defamation freeness in a standalone way.

We present transformations from different classes of PVC protocols to FBC protocols. While we could base our transformations on covert protocols, FBC protocols require a property called *prevention of detection dependent abort*, which is not always guaranteed by a covert protocol. The property ensures that a corrupted party cannot abort after learning that her cheating will be detected without leaving publicly verifiable evidence. PVC protocols always satisfy prevention of detection dependent abort. So, by basing our transformation on PVC protocols, we inherit this property.

While the mechanism utilized by [ZDH19] to validate misbehavior is highly efficient, it has only been used for non-interactive algorithms so far, i.e., to validate correctness of the garbling process. We face the challenge of extending this mechanism over an interactive protocol execution while still allowing for efficient dispute resolution such that the judge can be realized via a smart contract. In order to tackle these challenges, we present a novel technique that enables efficient validation of arbitrary complex and interactive protocols given the randomness and inputs of all parties. What's more, we can allow for private inputs if a public transcript of all protocol messages is available. We utilize only standard cryptographic primitives, in particular, commitments and signatures.

We differentiate existing PVC protocols according to whether the parties provide private inputs or not. The former protocols are called *input-dependent* and the latter ones *input-independent*. Input-independent protocols are typically used to generate correlated randomness. Further, all existing PVC protocols incorporate some form of common public transcript. Input-dependent protocols require a common public transcript of messages. In contrast, for input-independent protocols, it is enough to agree on the hashes of all sent messages. While it is not clear, if it is possible to construct PVC protocols without any form of public transcript, we construct FBC protocols providing this property. We achieve this by exploiting the interactivity of the judge, which is non-interactive in PVC. Based on the above observations, we define the following three classes of FBC protocols, for which we present transformations from PVC protocols.

Class 1: The first class contains *input-independent* protocols during which parties learn hashes of all protocol messages such that they agree on a common *transcript of message hashes.*

Class 2: The second class contains *input-dependent* protocols with a public *transcript of messages.* In contrast to class 1, parties may provide secret inputs and share a common view on all messages instead of a common view on hashes only.

Class 3: The third class contains input-independent protocols where parties do not learn any information about messages exchanged between a subset of other parties (cf. class 1). As there are no PVC protocol fitting into this class, we first convert PVC protocols matching the requirements of class 1 into protocols without public transcripts and second leverage an interactive punishment procedure to transform the resulting protocols into FBC protocols without public transcripts. Our FBC protocols benefit from this property since parties have to send all messages only to the receiver and not to all other parties. This effectively reduces the concrete communication complexity by a factor depending on the number of parties. In the optimistic case, if there is no cheating, we get this benefit without any overhead in the round complexity.

For each of our constructions, we provide a formal specification and a rigorous security analysis; the ones of the second class can be found in the full version of this paper. This is in contrast to the work of [ZDH19] which lacks a formal security analysis for financially secure computation. We stress that all existing PVC multi-party protocols can be categorized into class 1 and 2. Additionally, by combining any of the transformations from [DOS20, FHKS21, SSS21], which compile semi-honest protocols into PVC protocols, our constructions can be used to transform these protocol into FBC protocols.

The resulting FBC protocols for class 1 and 2 allow parties to non-interactively send evidence about malicious behavior to the judge. As the judge entity in these two classes is non-interactive, techniques from our transformations are of independent interest to make PVC protocols more efficient. Since, in contrast to class 1 and 2, there is no public transcript present in protocols of class 3, we design an interactive process involving the judge entity to generate evidence about malicious behavior. For all protocols, once the evidence is interactively or non-interactively created, the judge can efficiently resolve the dispute by recomputing only a single protocol message regardless of the overall computation size. We can further reduce the amount of validation to a single program instruction, e.g., a gate in a circuit, by prepending an interactive search procedure. This extension is presented in the full version of this paper.

Finally, we provide a smart contract implementation of the judging party in Ethereum and evaluate its gas costs (cf. Sect. 8). The evaluation shows the practicability, e.g., in the three party setting, with optimistic execution costs of 533 k gas. Moreover, we show that the dispute resolution of our solution is highly scalable in regard to the number of parties, the number of protocol rounds and the protocol complexity.

1.2 Technical Overview

In this section, we outline the main techniques used in our work and present the high-level ideas incorporated into our constructions. We start with on overview of the new notion of *financially backed covert security*. Then, we present a first attempt of a construction over a blockchain and outline the major challenges. Next, we describe the main techniques used in our constructions for PVC protocols of classes 1 and 2 and finally elaborate on the bisection procedure required for the more challenging class 3.

Financially Backed Covert Security. We recall that, a publicly verifiable covertly secure (PVC) protocol $(\pi_{\mathsf{cov}}, \mathsf{Blame}, \mathsf{Judge})$ consists of a covertly secure protocol π_{cov}, a blaming algorithm Blame and a judging algorithm Judge. The blaming algorithm produces a certificate cert in case cheating was detected and the judging algorithm, upon receiving a valid certificate, outputs the identity of the corrupted party. The algorithm Judge of a PVC protocol is explicitly defined as non-interactive. Therefore, cert can be transferred at any point in time to any third party that executes Judge and can be convinced about malicious behavior if the algorithm outputs the identity of a corrupted party.

In contrast to PVC, *financially backed covert security* (FBC) works in a model where parties own assets which can be transferred to other parties. This is modelled via a ledger entity $\mathcal{L}$. Moreover, the model contains a trusted judging party $\mathcal{J}$ which receives deposits before the start of the protocol and adjudicates in case of detected cheating. We emphasize that the entity $\mathcal{J}$, which is a single trusted entity interacting with all parties, is not the same as the algorithm Judge of a PVC protocol, which can be executed non-interactively by any party. An FBC protocol $(\pi'_{\mathsf{cov}}, \mathsf{Blame}', \mathsf{Punish})$ consists of a covertly secure protocol π'_{cov}, a blaming algorithm Blame' and an interactive punishment protocol Punish. Similar to PVC, the blaming algorithm Blame' produces a certificate cert' that is used as an input to the interactive punishment protocol. Punish is executed between the parties and the judge $\mathcal{J}$. If all parties behave honestly during the execution of π'_{cov}, $\mathcal{J}$ sends the deposited coins back to all parties after the execution of Punish. In case cheating is detected during π'_{cov}, the judge $\mathcal{J}$ burns the coins of the cheating party.

First Attempt of an Instantiation Over a Blockchain. Blockchain technologies provide a convenient way of handling monetary assets. In particular, in combination with the execution of smart contracts, e.g., offered by Ethereum [W+14], we envision to realize the judging party $\mathcal{J}$ as a smart contract. A first attempt of designing the punishment protocol is to implement $\mathcal{J}$ in a way, that the judge just gets the certificate generated by the PVC protocol's blame algorithm and executes the PVC protocol's Judge-algorithm. However, the Judge-algorithm of all existing PVC protocols recomputes a whole protocol instance and compares the output with a common transcript on which all parties agree beforehand. As computation of a smart contract costs money in form of transaction fees, recomputing a whole protocol is prohibitively expensive. Therefore, instead of recomputing the whole protocol, we aim for a punishment protocol that facilitates a judging party $\mathcal{J}$ which needs to recompute just a single protocol step or even a single program instruction, e.g., a gate in a circuit. The resulting judge becomes efficient in a way that it can be practically realized via a smart contract.

FBC Protocols with Efficient Judging from PVC Protocols. In this work, we present three transformations from PVC protocols to FBC protocols. Our transformations start with PVC protocols providing different properties which we use to categorize these protocols into three classes. We model the protocol execution in a way such that every party's behavior is deterministically defined by her input, her randomness and incoming messages. More precisely, we define the initial state of a party as her input and some randomness and compute the next state according to the state of the previous round and the incoming messages of the current round. Our first two transformations build on PVC protocols where the parties share a public transcript of the exchanged messages resp. message hashes. Additionally, parties send signed commitments on their intermediate states to all parties. The opening procedure ensures that correctly created commitments can be opened – falsely created commitments open to an invalid state that is interpreted as an invalid message. By sending the internal state of some party P_m for a single round together with the messages received by P_m in the same round to the judging party, the latter can efficiently verify malicious behavior by recomputing just a single protocol step. The resulting punishment protocol is efficient and can be executed without contribution of the cheating party.

Interactive Punishment Protocol to Support Private Transcripts. Our third transformation compiles input-independent PVC protocols with a public transcript into protocols where no public transcript is known to the parties. The lack of a public transcript makes the punishment protocol more complicated. Intuitively, since an honest party has no signed information about the message transcript, she cannot provide verifiable data about the incoming message used to calculate a protocol step. Therefore, we use the technique of an interactive bisection protocol which was first used in the context of verifiable computing by Canetti et al. [CRR11] and subsequently by many further constructions [KGC+18, TR19, ZDH19, EFS20]. While the bisection technique is very efficient to narrow down disagreement, it was only used for non-interactive algorithms so far. Hence, we extend this technique to support also interactive protocols. In particular, in our work, we use a bisection protocol to allow two parties to efficiently agree on a common message history. To this end, both parties, the accusing and the accused one, create a Merkle tree of their emulated message history up to the disputed message and submit the corresponding root. If they agree on the message history, the accusation can be validated by reference to this history. If they disagree, they perform a bisection search over the proposed history that determines the first message in the message history, they disagree on, while automatically ensuring that they agree on all previous messages. Hence, the judge can verify the message that the parties disagree on based on the previous messages they agree on. At the end of both interactions, the judge can efficiently resolve the dispute by recomputing just a single step.

2 Preliminaries

We start by introducing notation and cryptographic primitives used in our construction. Moreover, we provide the definition of covert security and publicly verifiable covert security in the full version of this paper.

We denote the computational security parameter by κ. Let n be some integer, then $[n] = \{1, \ldots, n\}$. Let $i \in [n]$, then we use the notation $j \neq i$ for $j \in [n] \setminus \{i\}$. A function $\mathsf{negl}(n) : \mathbb{N} \to \mathbb{R}$ is *negligible* in n if for every positive integer c there exists an integer n_0 such that $\forall n > n_0$ it hols that $\mathsf{negl}(n) < \frac{1}{n^c}$. We use the notation $\mathsf{negl}(n)$ to denote a negligible function.

We define $\mathsf{REAL}_{\pi,\mathcal{A}(z),\mathcal{I}}(\bar{x}, 1^\kappa)$ to be the output of the execution of an n-party protocol π executed between parties $\{P_i\}_{i\in[n]}$ on input $\bar{x} = \{x_i\}_{i\in[n]}$ and security parameter κ, where $\mathcal{A}$ on auxiliary input z corrupts parties $\mathcal{I} \subset \{P_i\}_{i\in[n]}$. We further specify $\mathsf{OUTPUT}_j(\mathsf{REAL}_{\pi,\mathcal{A}(z),\mathcal{I}}(\bar{x}, 1^\kappa))$ to be the output of party P_j for $j \in [n]$.

Our protocol utilizes a signature scheme $(\mathsf{Generate}, \mathsf{Sign}, \mathsf{Verify})$ that is *existentially unforgeable under chosen-message attacks.* We assume that each party executes the $\mathsf{Generate}$-algorithm to obtain a key pair $(\mathsf{pk}, \mathsf{sk})$ before the protocol execution. Further, we assume that all public keys are published and known to all parties while the secret keys are kept private. To simplify the protocol description we denote signed messages with $\langle x \rangle_i$ instead of $(x, \sigma := \mathsf{Sign}_{\mathsf{sk}_i}(x))$. The verification is therefore written as $\mathsf{Verify}(\langle x \rangle_i)$ instead of $\mathsf{Verify}_{\mathsf{pk}_i}(x, \sigma)$. Further, we make use of a hash function $H(\cdot) : \{0,1\}^* \to \{0,1\}^\kappa$ that is collision resistant.

We assume a synchronous communication model, where communication happens in rounds and all parties are aware of the current round. Messages that are sent in some round k arrive at the receiver in round $k+1$. Since we consider a rushing adversary, the adversary learns the messages sent by honest parties in round k in the same round and hence can adapt her own messages accordingly. We denote a message sent from party P_i to party P_j in round k of some protocol instance denoted with ℓ as $\mathsf{msg}_{(\ell,k)}^{(i,j)}$. The hash of this message is denoted with $\mathsf{hash}_{(\ell,k)}^{(i,j)} := H(\mathsf{msg}_{(\ell,k)}^{(i,j)})$.

A *Merkle tree* over an ordered set of elements $\{x_i\}_{i\in[N]}$ is a labeled binary hash tree, where the i-th leaf is labeled by x_i. We assume N to be an integer power of two. In case the number of elements is not a power of two, the set can be padded until N is a power of two. For construction of Merkle trees, we make use of the collision-resistant hash function $H(\cdot) : \{0,1\}^* \rightarrow \{0,1\}^\kappa$.

Formally, we define a Merkle tree as a tuple of algorithms ($\mathsf{MTree}, \mathsf{MRoot}, \mathsf{MProof}, \mathsf{MVerify}$). Algorithm MTree takes as input a computational security parameter κ as well as a set of elements $\{x_i\}_{i\in[N]}$ and creates a Merkle tree mTree. To ease the notation, we will omit the security parameter and implicitly assume it to be provided. Algorithm MRoot takes as input a Merkle tree mTree and returns the root element root of tree mTree. Algorithm MProof takes as input a leaf x_j and Merkle tree mTree and creates a Merkle proof σ showing that x_j is the j-th leaf in mTree. Algorithm $\mathsf{MVerify}$ takes as input a proof σ, an index i, a root root and a leaf x^* and returns true iff x^* is the i-the leaf of a Merkle tree with root root.

A Merkle Tree satisfies the following two requirements. First, for each Merkle tree mTree created over an arbitrary set of elements $\{x_i\}_{i\in[N]}$, it holds that for each $j \in [N]$ $\mathsf{MVerify}(\mathsf{MProof}(x_j, \mathsf{mTree}), j, \mathsf{MRoot}(\mathsf{mTree}), x_j) = \mathsf{true}$. We call this property *correctness*. Second, for each Merkle tree mTree with root $\mathsf{root} := \mathsf{MRoot}(\mathsf{mTree})$ created over an arbitrary set of elements $\{x_i\}_{i\in[N]}$ with security parameter κ it holds that for each polynomial time algorithm adversary $\mathcal{A}$ outputting an index j^*, leaf $x^* \neq x_{j^*}$ and proof σ^* the probability that $\mathsf{MVerify}(\sigma^*, j^*, \mathsf{MRoot}(\mathsf{mTree}), x^*) = \mathsf{true}$ is $\mathsf{negl}(\kappa)$. We call this property *binding*.

3 Financially Backed Covert Security

In the following, we specify the new notion of *financially backed covert security*. This notion extends covert security by a mechanism of financial punishment. More precisely, once an honest party detects cheating of the adversary during the execution of the covertly secure protocol, there is some corrupted party that is financial punished afterwards. The financial punishment is realized by an interactive protocol Punish that is executed directly after the covertly secure protocol. In order to deal with monetary assets, financially backed covertly secure protocols depend on a public ledger $\mathcal{L}$ and a trusted judge $\mathcal{J}$. The former can be realized by distributed ledger technologies, such as blockchains, and the latter by a smart contract executed on the said ledger. In the following, we describe the role of the ledger and the judging party, formally define financially backed covert security and outline techniques to prove financially backed covert security.

3.1 The Ledger and Judge

An inherent property of our model is the handling of assets and asset transfers based on predefined conditions. Nowadays, distributed ledger technologies like blockchains provide convenient means to realize this functionality. We model the handling of assets resp. coins via a ledger entity denoted by $\mathcal{L}$. The entity stores a balance of coins for each party and transfers coins between parties upon request. More precisely, $\mathcal{L}$ stores a balance $b_i^{(t)}$ for each party P_i at time t. For the security definition presented in Sect. 3.2, we are in particular interested in the balances before the execution of the protocol π, i.e., $b_i^{(\mathsf{pre})}$, and after the execution of the protocol Punish, i.e., $b_i^{(\mathsf{post})}$. The balances are public such that every party can query the amount of coins for any party at the current time. In order to send coins to another party, a party interacts with $\mathcal{L}$ to trigger the transfer.

While we consider the ledger as a pure storage of balances, we realize the conditional transfer of coins based on some predefined rules specified by the protocol Punish via a judge $\mathcal{J}$. In particular, $\mathcal{J}$ constitutes a trusted third party that interacts with the parties of the covertly secure protocol. More precisely, we require that each party sends some fixed amount of coins as deposit to $\mathcal{J}$ before the covertly secure protocol starts. During the covertly secure protocol execution, the judge keeps the deposited coins but does not need to be part of any interaction. After the execution of the covertly secure protocol, the judge plays an important role in the punishment protocol Punish. In case any party detects cheating during the execution of the covertly secure protocol, $\mathcal{J}$ acts as an adjudicator. If there is verifiable evidence about malicious behavior of some party, the judge financially punishes the corrupted party by withholding her deposit. Eventually, $\mathcal{J}$ will reimburse all parties with their deposits except those parties that have been proven to be malicious. The rules according to which parties are considered malicious and hence according to which the coins are reimbursed or withhold need to be specified by the protocol Punish.

Finally, we emphasize that both entities the ledger $\mathcal{L}$ and the judge $\mathcal{J}$ are considered trusted. This means, the correct functionality of these entities cannot be distorted by the adversary.

3.2 Formal Definition

We work in a model in which a ledger $\mathcal{L}$ and a judge $\mathcal{J}$ as explained above exist. Let π' be an n-party protocol that is covertly secure with deterrence factor ϵ. Let the number of corrupted parties that is tolerated by π' be $m < n$ and the set of corrupted parties be denoted by $\mathcal{I}$. We define π as an extension of π', in which all involved parties transfer a fixed amount of coins, d, to $\mathcal{J}$ before executing π'. Additionally, after the execution of π', all parties execute algorithm Blame which on input the view of the honest party outputs a certificate and broadcasts the generated certificate – still as part of π. The certificate is used for both proving malicious behavior, if detected, and defending against being accused for malicious behavior.

After the execution of π, all parties participate in the protocol Punish. In case honest parties detected misbehavior, they prove said misbehavior to $\mathcal{J}$ such that $\mathcal{J}$ can punish the malicious party. In case a malicious party blames an honest one, the honest parties participate to prove their correct behavior. Either way, even if there is no blame at all, all honest parties wait to receive their deposits back, which are reimbursed by $\mathcal{J}$ at the end of the punishment protocol Punish.

Definition 1 (Financially backed covert security). *We call a triple* $(\pi, \mathsf{Blame}, \mathsf{Punish})$ *an n-party* financially backed covertly secure protocol with deterrence factor ϵ *computing some function* f *in the* $\mathcal{L}$ *and* $\mathcal{J}$ *model, if the following security properties are satisfied:*

1. ***Simulatability with*** ϵ***-deterrent:*** *The protocol* π *(as described above) is secure against a covert adversary according to the strong explicit cheat formulation with* ϵ*-deterrent and non-halting detection accurate.*
2. ***Financial Accountability:*** *For every PPT adversary* $\mathcal{A}$ *corrupting parties* P_i *for* $i \in \mathcal{I} \subset [n]$, *there exists a negligible function* $\mu(\cdot)$ *such that for all* $(\bar{x}, z) \in (\{0,1\})^{n+1}$ *the following holds:*
If for any honest party $P_h \in [n] \backslash \mathcal{I}$ *it holds that* $\mathsf{OUTPUT}_h(\mathsf{REAL}_{\pi,\mathcal{A}(z),\mathcal{I}}(\bar{x}, 1^{\kappa})) = \mathsf{corrupted}_*$ [1], *then* $\exists\, m \in \mathcal{I}$ *such that:*
$$\Pr[b_m^{(\mathsf{post})} = b_m^{(\mathsf{pre})} - d] > 1 - \mu(\kappa),$$
where d *denotes the amount of deposited coins per party.*
3. ***Financial Defamation Freeness:*** *For every PPT adversary* $\mathcal{A}$ *corrupting parties* P_i *for* $i \in \mathcal{I} \subset [n]$, *there exists a negligible function* $\mu(\cdot)$ *such that for all* $(\bar{x}, z) \in (\{0,1\})^{n+1}$ *and all* $j \in [n] \setminus \mathcal{I}$ *the following holds:*
$$\Pr[b_j^{(\mathsf{post})} < b_j^{(\mathsf{pre})}] < \mu(\kappa).$$

Remark 1. For simplicity, we assume that the adversary does not transfer coins after sending the deposit to $\mathcal{J}$. This assumption can be circumvented by restating financial accountability such that the sum of the balances of all corrupted parties (not just the ones involved in the protocol) is reduced by d.

3.3 Proving Security of Financially Backed Covert Security

Our notion of financially backed covert security (FBC) consists of three properties. The simulatability property requires the protocol π, which augments the covertly secure protocol π', to be covertly secure as well. This does not automatically follows from the security of π', in particular since π includes the broadcast of certificates in case of detected cheating. Showing simulatability of π guarantees that the adversary does not learn sensitive information from the certificates. Showing that a protocol π satisfies the simulatability property is proven via a simulation proof. In contrast, we follow a game-based approach to formally prove financial accountability and financial defamation freeness. To this end, we introduce two novel security games, $\mathsf{Exp}^{\mathsf{FA}}$ and $\mathsf{Exp}^{\mathsf{FDF}}$, in the following. Although these two properties are similar to the accountability and defamation freeness properties of PVC, we are the first to introduce formal security games for any of these properties. While we focus on financial accountability and financial

[1] We use the notation $\mathsf{corrupted}_*$ to denote that the output of P_h is $\mathsf{corrupted}_i$ for some $i \in \mathcal{I}$. We stress that i does not need to be equal to m of the financial accountability property.

defamation freeness, we note that our approach and our security games can be adapted to suit for the security properties of PVC as well.

Both security games are played between a challenger $\mathcal{C}$ and an adversary $\mathcal{A}$. We define the games in a way that allows us to abstract away most of the details of π. In particular, we parameterize the games by two inputs, one for the challenger and one for the adversary. The challenger's input contains the certificates $\{\mathsf{cert}_i\}_{i\in[n]\setminus\mathcal{I}}$ of all honest parties generated by the Blame-algorithm after the execution of π while the adversary's input consists of all malicious parties' views $\{\mathsf{view}_i\}_{i\in\mathcal{I}}$. By introducing the certificates as inputs to the game, we can prove financial accountability and financial defamation freeness independent from proving simulatability of protocol π.

Throughout the execution of the security games, the adversary executes one instance of the punishment protocol Punish with the challenger that takes over the roles of all honest and trusted parties, i.e., the honest protocol parties P_h for $h \notin \mathcal{I}$, the judge $\mathcal{J}$, and the ledger $\mathcal{L}$. To avoid an overly complex challenger description, we define those parties as separated entities that can be addressed by the adversary separately and are all executed by the challenger: $\{\mathtt{P_h}\}_{\mathtt{h}\in[n]\setminus\mathcal{I}}$, J, and L. In case any entity is supposed to act pro-actively and does not only wait to react to malicious behavior, the entity is invoked by the challenger. Communication between said entities is simulated by the challenger. The adversary acts on behalf of the corrupted parties.

Financial Accountability Game. Intuitively, financial accountability states that whenever any honest party detects cheating, there is some corrupted party that loses her deposit. Therefore, we require that the output of all honest parties was $\mathsf{corrupted}_m$ for $m \in \mathcal{I}$ in the execution of π. If this holds, the security game executes Punish as specified by the FBC protocol. Before the execution of Punish, the challenger asks the ledger for the balances of all parties and stores them as $\{b_i^{(\mathsf{prePunish})}\}_{i\in[n]}$. Note that prePunish denotes the time before Punish but after the whole protocol already started. This means, relating to Definition 1, the security deposits are already transferred to $\mathcal{J}$, i.e., $b_i^{\mathsf{prePunish}} = b_i^{\mathsf{pre}} - d$. After the execution, the challenger $\mathcal{C}$ again reads the balances of all parties storing them as $\{b_i^{(\mathsf{post})}\}_{i\in[n]}$. If $b_m^{(\mathsf{post})} = b_m^{(\mathsf{prePunish})} + d$ for all $m \in \mathcal{I}$, i.e., all corrupted parties get their deposits back, the adversary wins and $\mathcal{C}$ outputs 1, otherwise $\mathcal{C}$ outputs 0. A protocol satisfies the financial accountability property as stated in Definition 1 if for each adversary $\mathcal{A}$ running in time polynomial in κ the probability that $\mathcal{A}$ wins game $\mathsf{Exp}^{\mathsf{FA}}$ is at most negligible, i.e., if $\Pr[\mathsf{Exp}^{\mathsf{FA}}(\mathcal{A},\kappa) = 1] \leq \mathsf{negl}(\kappa)$.

Financial Defamation Freeness Game. Intuitively, financial defamation freeness states that an honest party can never lose her deposit as a result of executing the Punish protocol. The security game is executed in the same way as the financial accountability game. It only differs in the winning conditions for the adversary. After the execution $\mathcal{C}$ checks the balances of the honest parties. If $b_h^{(\mathsf{post})} < b_h^{(\mathsf{prePunish})} + d$ for at least one $h \in [n] \setminus \mathcal{I}$, the adversary wins and the challenger outputs 1, otherwise $\mathcal{C}$ outputs 0. A protocol satisfies the financial defamation freeness property as stated in Definition 1 if for each adversary $\mathcal{A}$ running in time polynomial in κ the probability that $\mathcal{A}$ wins game $\mathsf{Exp}^{\mathsf{FDF}}$ is at most negligible, i.e. if $\Pr[\mathsf{Exp}^{\mathsf{FDF}}(\mathcal{A}, \kappa) = 1] \leq \mathsf{negl}(\kappa)$.

4 Features of PVC Protocols

We present transformations from different classes of *publicly verifiable covertly secure* multi-party protocols (PVC) to *financially backed covertly secure* protocols (FBC). As our transformations make use of concrete features of the PVC protocol (e.g., the exchanged messages), we cannot use the PVC protocol in a block-box way. Instead, we model the PVC protocol in an abstract way, stating features that are required by our constructions. In the remainder of this section, we present these features in detail and describe how we model them. We note that all existing PVC multi-party protocols [DOS20, FHKS21, SSS21] provide the features specified in this section.

4.1 Cut-and-Choose

Although not required per definition of PVC, a fundamental technique used by all existing PVC protocols is the *cut-and-choose* approach that leverages a semi-honest protocol by executing t instances of the semi-honest protocol in parallel. Afterwards, the views (i.e., input and randomness) of the parties is revealed in s instances. This enables parties to detect misbehavior with probability $\epsilon = \frac{s}{t}$. PVC protocols can be split into protocols where parties provide private inputs and those where parties do not have secret data. While cut-and-choose for input-independent protocols, i.e., those where parties do not have private inputs, work as explained on a high level before, the approach must be utilized in such a way that input privacy is guaranteed for input-dependent protocols. However, for both classes of protocols, a cheat detection probability of $\epsilon = \frac{s}{t}$ can be achieved. We elaborate more on the two variants and provide details about them in the full version of this paper.

4.2 Verification of Protocol Executions

An important feature of PVC protocols based on cut-and-choose is to enable parties to verify the execution of the opened protocol instances. This requires parties to emulate the protocol messages and compare them with the messages exchanged during the real execution. In order to emulate honest behavior, we need the protocol to be derandomized.

Derandomization of the Protocol Execution. In general, the behavior of each party during some protocol execution depends on the party's private input, its random tape and all incoming messages. In order to enable parties to check the behavior of other parties in retrospect, the actions of all parties need to be made deterministic. To this end, we require the feature of a PVC protocol that all random choices of a party P_i in a protocol instance are derived from some random seed seed_i using a pseudorandom generator (PRG). The seed seed_i is fixed before the beginning of the execution. It follows that the generated outgoing messages are computed deterministically given the seed seed_i, the secret input and all incoming messages.

State Evolution. Corresponding to our communication model (cf. Sect. 2), the internal states of the parties in a semi-honest protocol instance evolve in rounds. For each party P_i, for $i \in [n]$, and each round $k > 0$ the protocol defines a state transition $\mathsf{computeRound}_k^i$ that on input the previous internal state $\mathsf{state}_{(k-1)}^{(i)}$ and the set of incoming messages $\{\mathsf{msg}_{(k-1)}^{(j,i)}\}_{j \neq i}$ computes the new internal state $\mathsf{state}_{(k)}^{(i)}$ and the set of outgoing messages $\{\mathsf{msg}_{(k)}^{(i,j)}\}_{j \neq i}$. Based on the derandomization feature, the state transition is deterministic, i.e., all random choices are derived from a random seed included in the internal state of a party. Each party starts with an initial internal state that equals its random seed seed_i and its secret input x_i. In case no secret input is present (i.e., in the input-independent setting) or no message is sent, the value is considered to be a dummy symbol ($\bot$). We denote the set of all messages sent during a protocol instance by *protocol transcript*. Summarizing, we formally define

$$\mathsf{state}_{(0)}^{(i)} \leftarrow (\mathsf{seed}_i, x_i)$$

$$\{\mathsf{msg}_{(0)}^{(j,i)}\}_{j \in [n] \setminus \{i\}} \leftarrow \{\bot\}_{j \in [n] \setminus \{i\}}$$

$$(\mathsf{state}_{(k)}^{(i)}, \{\mathsf{msg}_{(k)}^{(i,j)}\}_{j \in [n] \setminus \{i\}}) \leftarrow \mathsf{computeRound}_k^i(\mathsf{state}_{(k-1)}^{(i)}, \{\mathsf{msg}_{(k-1)}^{(j,i)}\}_{j \in [n] \setminus \{i\}}).$$

Protocol Emulation. In order to check for malicious behavior, parties locally emulate the protocol execution of the opened instances and compare the set of computed messages with the received ones. In case some involved parties are not checked (e.g., in the input-dependent setting), the emulation gets their messages as input and assumes them to be correct. In this case, in order to ensure that each party can run the emulation, it is necessary that each party has access to all messages sent in the opened instance (cf. Sect. 4.4).

To formalize the protocol emulation, we define for each n-party protocol π with R rounds two emulation algorithms. The first algorithm $\mathsf{emulate}_\pi^{\mathsf{full}}$ emulates all parties while the second algorithm $\mathsf{emulate}_\pi^{\mathsf{part}}$ emulates only a partial subset of the parties and considers the messages of all other parties as correct. We formally define them as

$$(\{\mathsf{msg}_{(k)}^{(i,j)}\}_{k,i,j \neq i}, \{\mathsf{state}_{(k)}^{(i)}\}_{k,i}) \leftarrow \mathsf{emulate}_\pi^{\mathsf{full}}(\{\mathsf{state}_{(0)}^{(i)}\}_i) \quad \text{and}$$

$$(\{\mathsf{msg}_{(k)}^{(i,j)}\}_{k,i,j \neq i}, \{\mathsf{state}_{(k)}^{(\hat{i})}\}_{k,\hat{i}}) \leftarrow \mathsf{emulate}_\pi^{\mathsf{part}}(O, \{\mathsf{state}_{(0)}^{(\hat{i})}\}_{\hat{i}}, \{\mathsf{msg}_{(k)}^{(i^*,j)}\}_{k,i^*,j \neq i^*})$$

where $k \in [R]$, $i, j \in [n]$, $\hat{i} \in O$ and $i^* \in [n] \setminus O$. O denotes the set of opened parties.

4.3 Deriving the Initial States

As a third feature, we require a mechanism for the parties of a PVC protocol to learn the initial states of all opened parties in order to perform the protocol emulation (cf. Sect. 4.2). Since PVC prevents detection dependent abort, parties learn the initial state even if the adversary aborts after having learned the cut-and-choose selection. Existing multi-party PVC protocols provide this feature by either making use of oblivious transfer or time-lock puzzles as in [DOS20] resp. [FHKS21,SSS21]. We elaborate on these protocols in the full version of this paper.

To model this behavior formally, we define the abstract tuples $\mathsf{initData}^{\mathsf{core}}$ and $\mathsf{initData}^{\mathsf{aux}}$ as well as the algorithm $\mathsf{deriveInit}$. $\mathsf{initData}^{\mathsf{core}}_{(i)}$ represents data each party holds that should be signed by P_i and can be used to derive the initial state of party P_i in a single protocol instance (e.g., a signed time-lock puzzle). $\mathsf{initData}^{\mathsf{aux}}_{(i)}$ represents the additional data all parties receive during the PVC protocol that can be used to interpret $\mathsf{initData}^{\mathsf{core}}_{(i)}$ (e.g., the verifiable solution of the time-lock puzzle). Finally, $\mathsf{deriveInit}$ is an algorithm that on input $\mathsf{initData}^{\mathsf{core}}_{(i)}$ and $\mathsf{initData}^{\mathsf{aux}}_{(i)}$ derives the initial state of party P_i (e.g., verifying the solution of the puzzle). Instead of outputting an initial state, the algorithm $\mathsf{deriveInit}$ can also output bad or $\bot$. The former states that party P_i misbehaved during the PVC protocol by providing inconsistent data. The symbol $\bot$ states that the input to $\mathsf{deriveInit}$ has been invalid which can only occur if $\mathsf{initData}^{\mathsf{core}}_{(i)}$ or $\mathsf{initData}^{\mathsf{aux}}_{(i)}$ have been manipulated.

Similar to commitment schemes, our abstraction satisfies a *binding* and *hiding* requirement, i.e., it is computationally *binding* and computationally *hiding*. The binding property requires that the probability of any polynomial time adversary finding a tuple (x, y_1, y_2) such that $\mathsf{deriveInit}(x, y_1) \neq \bot$, $\mathsf{deriveInit}(x, y_2) \neq \bot$, and $\mathsf{deriveInit}(x, y_1) \neq \mathsf{deriveInit}(x, y_2)$ is negligible. The hiding property requires that the probability of a polynomial time adversary finding for a given $\mathsf{initData}^{\mathsf{core}}$ a $\mathsf{initData}^{\mathsf{aux}}$ such that $\mathsf{deriveInit}(\mathsf{initData}^{\mathsf{core}}, \mathsf{initData}^{\mathsf{aux}}) \neq \bot$ is negligible.

4.4 Public Transcript

A final feature required by PVC protocols of class 1 and 2 is the availability of a common public transcript. We define three levels of transcript availability. First, a *common public transcript of messages* ensures that all parties hold a common transcript containing all messages that have been sent during the execution of a protocol instance. Every protocol can be transformed to provide this feature by requiring all parties to send all messages to all other parties and defining a fixed ordering on the sent messages – we consider an ordering of messages by the round they are sent, the index of the sender, and the receiver's index in this sequence. If messages should be secret, each pair of parties executes a secure key exchange as part of the protocol instance and then encrypts messages with the established keys. Agreement is achieved by broadcasting signatures on the transcript, e.g., via signing the root of a Merkle tree over all message hashes as discussed in [FHKS21] and required in our transformations. Second, a *common public transcript of hashes* ensures that all parties hold a common transcript containing the hashes of all messages sent during the execution of a protocol instance. This feature is achieved similar to the transcript of messages but parties only send message hashes to all parties that are not the intended receiver. Finally, the *private transcript* does not require any agreement on the transcript of a protocol instance.

Currently, all existing multi-party PVC protocols either provide a common public transcript of messages [DOS20, FHKS21] or a common public transcript of hashes [SSS21]. However, [DOS20] and [FHKS21] can be trivially adapted to provide just a common public transcript of hashes.

5 Building Blocks

In this section, we describe the building blocks for our financially backed covertly secure protocols. In the full version of this paper, we show security of the building blocks and that incorporating the building blocks into the PVC protocol does not affect the protocol's security.

5.1 Internal State Commitments

To realize the judge in an efficient way, we want it to validate just a single protocol step instead of validating a whole instance. Existing PVC protocols prove misbehavior in a naive way by allowing parties to show that some other party P_j had an initial state $\mathsf{state}^{(j)}_{(0)}$. Based on the initial state, the judge recomputes the whole protocol instance. In contrast to this, we incorporate a mechanism that allows parties to prove that P_j has been in state $\mathsf{state}^{(j)}_{(k)}$ in a specific round k where misbehavior was detected. Then, the judge just needs to recompute a single step. To this end, we require that parties commit to each intermediate internal state during the execution of each semi-honest instance in a publicly verifiable way. In particular, in each round k of each semi-honest instance ℓ, each party P_i sends a hash of its internal state to all other parties using a collision-resistant hash function $H(\cdot)$, i.e., $H(\mathsf{state}^{(i)}_{(\ell,k)})$. At the end of a protocol instance each party P_h creates a Merkle tree over all state hashes, i.e., $\mathsf{sTree}_\ell := \mathsf{MTree}(\{\mathsf{hash}^{(i)}_{(\ell,k)}\}_{k\in[R],i\in[n]})$, and broadcasts a signature on the root of this tree, i.e., $\left\langle \mathsf{MRoot}(\mathsf{sTree}_\ell)\right\rangle_h$.

5.2 Signature Encoding

Our protocol incorporates signatures in order to provide evidence to the judge $\mathcal{J}$ about the behavior of the parties. Without further countermeasures, an adversary can make use of signed data across multiple instances or rounds, e.g., she could claim that some message msg sent in round k has been sent in round k' using the signature received in round k. To prevent such an attack, we encode signed data by prefixing it with the corresponding indices before being signed. Merkle tree roots are prefixed with the instance index ℓ. Message hashes are prefixed with ℓ, the round index k, the sender index i and the receiver index j. Initial state commitments ($\mathsf{initData}^{\mathsf{core}}_{(\ell,i)}$) are prefixed with ℓ and the index i of the party who's initial state the commitment refers to. The signature verification algorithm automatically checks for correct prefixing. The indices are derived from the super- and subscripts. If one index is not explicitly provided, e.g., in case only one instance is executed, the index is assumed to be 1.

5.3 Bisection of Trees

Our constructions make heavily use of Merkle trees to represent sets of data. This enables parties to efficiently prove that chunk of data is part of a set by providing a Merkle proof showing that the chunk is a leaf of the corresponding Merkle tree. In case two parties disagree about the data of a Merkle tree which should be identical, we use a bisection protocol Π_{BS} to narrow down the dispute to the first leaf of the tree on which they disagree. This helps a judging party to determine the lying party by just verifying a single data chunk in contrast to checking the whole data. The technique of bisecting was first used by Canetti et al. [CRR11] in the context of verifiable computing. Later, the technique was used in [KGC+18,TR19,EFS20].

The protocol is executed between a party P_b with input a tree mTree_b, a party P_m with input a tree mTree_m and a trusted judge $\mathcal{J}$ announcing three public inputs: root^j, the root of mTree_j as claimed by P_j for $j \in \{b, m\}$, and width, the width of the trees, i.e., the number of leaves. The protocol returns the index z of the first leaf at which mTree_b and mTree_m differentiate, the leaf hash^m_z at position z of mTree_m, and the common leaf $\mathsf{hash}_{(z-1)}$ at position $z-1$. The latter is $\perp$ if $z = 1$. Let $\mathsf{node}(\mathsf{mTree}, x, y)$ be the node of a tree mTree at position x of layer y – positions start with 1. The protocol is executed as follows:

Protocol Bisection Π_{BS}

1. $\mathcal{J}$ initializes layer variable $y := 1$, position variable $x := 1$, last agreed hash $\mathsf{hash}^a := \perp$, and $\mathsf{depth} := \lceil \log_2(\mathsf{width}) \rceil + 1$
2. All parties repeat this step while $y \le \mathsf{depth}$:
   (a) Both P_j (for $j \in \{b, m\}$) send $\mathsf{hash}^j := \mathsf{node}(\mathsf{mTree}_j, x, y)$ and $\sigma^j := \mathsf{MProof}(\mathsf{hash}^j, \mathsf{mTree}_j)$ to $\mathcal{J}$.
   (b) If $\mathsf{MVerify}(\mathsf{hash}^j, x, \mathsf{root}^j, \sigma^j) = \mathsf{false}$ (for $j \in \{b, m\}$), $\mathcal{J}$ discards the message from P_j.
   (c) If $y = \mathsf{depth}$, $\mathcal{J}$ keeps hash^b and hash^m and sets $y = y + 1$.
   (d) If $y < \mathsf{depth}$ and $\mathsf{hash}^b = \mathsf{hash}^m$, $\mathcal{J}$ sets $x = (2 \cdot x) + 1$ and $y = y + 1$.
   (e) If $y < \mathsf{depth}$ and $\mathsf{hash}^b \neq \mathsf{hash}^m$, $\mathcal{J}$ sets $x = (2 \cdot x) - 1$ and $y = y + 1$.
3. If $\mathsf{hash}^b = \mathsf{hash}^m$
   - $\mathcal{J}$ sets $z := x + 1$ and $\mathsf{hash}_{(z-1)} := \mathsf{hash}_b$.
   - P_m sends $\mathsf{hash}^m_z := \mathsf{node}(\mathsf{mTree}_m, z, \mathsf{depth})$ and $\sigma := \mathsf{MProof}(\mathsf{hash}^m_z, \mathsf{mTree}_m)$ to $\mathcal{J}$.
   - If $\mathsf{MVerify}(\mathsf{hash}^m_z, z, \mathsf{root}, \sigma) = \mathsf{false}$, $\mathcal{J}$ discards. Otherwise $\mathcal{J}$ stores hash^m_z.
4. If $\mathsf{hash}^b \neq \mathsf{hash}^m$
   - $\mathcal{J}$ sets $z := x$ and $\mathsf{hash}^m_z := \mathsf{hash}^m$. If $z = 1$, $\mathcal{J}$ sets $\mathsf{hash}_{(z-1)} := \perp$, and the protocol jumps to step 5.

– P_m sends $\mathsf{hash}_{(z-1)} := \mathsf{node}(\mathsf{mTree}_m, z-1, \mathsf{depth})$ and $\sigma := \mathsf{MProof}(\mathsf{hash}_{(z-1)}, \mathsf{mTree}_m)$ to $\mathcal{J}$.
– If $\mathsf{MVerify}(\mathsf{hash}_{(z-1)}, z-1, \mathsf{mTree}_m, \sigma) = \mathsf{false}$, $\mathcal{J}$ discards. Otherwise, $\mathcal{J}$ keeps $\mathsf{hash}_{(z-1)}$.

5. $\mathcal{J}$ announces public outputs z, hash^m_z and $\mathsf{hash}_{(z-1)}$.

6 Class 1: Input-Independent with Public Transcript

Our first transformation builds on input-independent PVC protocols where all parties possess a common public transcript of hashes (cf. Sect. 4.4) for each checked instance. Since the parties provide no input in these protocols, all parties can be opened. The set of input-independent protocols includes the important class of preprocessing protocols. In order to speed up MPC protocols, a common approach is to split the computation in an *offline* and an *online* phase. During the offline phase, precomputations are carried out to set up some correlated randomness. This phase does not require the actual inputs and can be executed continuously. In contrast, the online phase requires the private inputs of the parties and consumes the correlated randomness generated during the offline phase to speed up the execution. As the online performance is more time critical, the goal is to put as much work as possible into the offline phase. Prominent examples following this approach are the protocols of Damgård et al. [DPSZ12, DKL+13] and Wang et al. [WRK17a, WRK17b, YWZ20]. Input-independent PVC protocols with a public transcript can be obtained from semi-honest protocols using the input-independent compilers of Damgård et al. [DOS20] and Faust et al. [FHKS21].

In order to apply our construction to an input-independent PVC protocol, π^{pp}, we require π^{pp} to provide some features presented in Sect. 4 and to have incorporated some of the building blocks described in Sect. 5. First, we require the PVC protocol to be based on the cut-and-choose approach (cf. Sect. 4.1). Second, we require the actions of each party P_i in a protocol execution to be deterministically determined by a random seed (cf. Sect. 4.2). Third, we require that all parties learn the initial states of all other parties in the opened protocol instances (cf. Sect. 4.3). To this end, the parties receive signed data (e.g., a commitment and decommitment value) to derive the initial states of the other parties. Fourth, parties need to commit to their intermediate internal states during the protocol executions in a publicly verifiable way (cf. Sect. 5.1). Finally, all signed data match the encoded form specified in Sect. 5.2.

In order to achieve the public transcript of hashes and the commitments to the intermediate internal states, parties exchange additional data in each round. Formally, whenever some party P_h in round k of protocol instance ℓ transitions to a state $\mathsf{state}^{(h)}_{(\ell,k)}$ with the outgoing messages $\{\mathsf{msg}^{(h,i)}_{(\ell,k)}\}_{i \in [n] \setminus \{h\}}$, then it actually sends the following to P_i:

$$(\mathsf{msg}^{(h,i)}_{(\ell,k)}, \{\mathsf{hash}^{(h,j)}_{(\ell,k)} := H(\mathsf{msg}^{(h,j)}_{(\ell,k)})\}_{j \in [n] \setminus \{h,i\}}, \mathsf{hash}^{(h)}_{(\ell,k)} := H(\mathsf{state}^{(h)}_{(\ell,k)}))$$

Let O denote the set of opened instances. We summarize the aforementioned requirements by specifying the data that the view of any honest party P_h includes. It contains signed data to derive the initial state of all parties for the opened instances (1a), a Merkle tree over the hashes of all messages exchanged within a single instance for all instances (1b), a Merkle tree over the hashes of all intermediate internal states of a single instance for all instances (1c), and signatures from each party over the roots of the message and state trees (1d):

$$\{(\langle \mathsf{initData}^{\mathsf{core}}_{(i,\ell)} \rangle_i, \mathsf{initData}^{\mathsf{aux}}_{(i,\ell)})\}_{\ell \in O, i \in [n]}, \tag{1a}$$

$$\{\mathsf{mTree}_\ell\}_{\ell \in [t]} := \{\mathsf{MTree}(\{\mathsf{hash}^{(i,j)}_{(\ell,k)}\}_{k \in [R], i \in [n], j \neq i})\}_{\ell \in [t]}, \tag{1b}$$

$$\{\mathsf{sTree}_\ell\}_{\ell \in [t]} := \{\mathsf{MTree}(\{\mathsf{hash}^{(i)}_{(\ell,k)}\}_{k \in [R], i \in [n]})\}_{\ell \in [t]} \tag{1c}$$

$$\{\langle \mathsf{MRoot}(\mathsf{mTree}_\ell) \rangle_i\}_{i \in [n], \ell \in [t]} \text{ and } \{\langle \mathsf{MRoot}(\mathsf{sTree}_\ell) \rangle_i\}_{i \in [n], \ell \in [t]}. \tag{1d}$$

We next define the blame algorithm that takes the specified view as input and continue with the description of the punishment protocol afterwards.

The Blame Algorithm. At the end of protocol π^{PP}, all parties execute the blame algorithm $\mathsf{Blame}^{\mathsf{PP}}$ to generate a certificate cert. The resulting certificate is broadcasted and the honest party finishes the execution of π^{PP} by outputting cert. The certificate is generated as follows:

Algorithm $\mathsf{Blame}^{\mathsf{PP}}$

1. P_h runs $\mathsf{state}^{(i)}_{(\ell,0)} = \mathsf{deriveInit}(\mathsf{initData}^{\mathsf{core}}_{(i,\ell)}, \mathsf{initData}^{\mathsf{aux}}_{(i,\ell)})$ for each $i \in [n], \ell \in O$. Let $\mathcal{B}$ be the set of all tuples $(\ell, 0, m, 0)$ such that $\mathsf{state}^{(m)}_{(\ell,0)} = \mathsf{bad}$. If $\mathcal{B} \neq \emptyset$, goto step 4.
2. P_h emulates for each $\ell \in O$ the protocol executions on input the initial states from all parties to obtain the expected messages and the expected intermediate states of all parties, i.e., $(\{\mathsf{msg}^{(i,j)}_{(\ell,k)}\}_{k \in [R], i \in [n], j \neq i}, \{\mathsf{state}^{(i)}_{(\ell,k)}\}_{k,i,j}) := \mathsf{emulate}^{\mathsf{full}}(\{\mathsf{state}^{(i)}_{(\ell,0)}\}_{i \in [n]})$.
3. Let $\mathcal{B}$ be the set of all tuples (ℓ, k, m, i) such that $H(\mathsf{msg}^{(m,i)}_{(\ell,k)}) \neq \mathsf{hash}^{(m,i)}_{(\ell,k)}$ or $H(\mathsf{state}^{(m)}_{(\ell,k)}) \neq \mathsf{hash}^{(m)}_{(\ell,k)}$ – where $\mathsf{hash}^{(m,i)}_{(\ell,k)}$ and $\mathsf{hash}^{(m)}_{(\ell,k)}$ are extracted from mTree_ℓ or sTree_ℓ respectively. In case of an incorrect state hash, set $i = 0$.
4. If $\mathcal{B} = \emptyset$ P_h outputs cert $:= \bot$. Otherwise, P_h picks the tuple (ℓ, k, m, i) from $\mathcal{B}$ with the smallest ℓ, k, m, i in this sequence, sets $k' := k - 1$ and defines variables as follows – variables that are not explicitly defined are set to $\bot$.

(Always): $ids := (\ell, k, m, i)$

$$\mathsf{initData} := (\langle \mathsf{initData}^{\mathsf{core}}_{(\ell,m)} \rangle_m, \mathsf{initData}^{\mathsf{aux}}_{(\ell,m)})$$

$$\mathsf{root}^{\mathsf{state}} := \langle \mathsf{MRoot}(\mathsf{sTree}_\ell) \rangle_m$$

$$\mathsf{root}^{\mathsf{msg}} := \langle \mathsf{MRoot}(\mathsf{mTree}_\ell) \rangle_m$$

(If $k > 0$): $\mathsf{state}_{out} := (\mathsf{hash}^{(m)}_{(\ell,k)}, \mathsf{MProof}(\mathsf{hash}^{(m)}_{(\ell,k)}, \mathsf{sTree}_\ell))$

$$\mathsf{msg}_{out} := (\mathsf{hash}^{(m,i)}_{(\ell,k)}, \mathsf{MProof}(\mathsf{hash}^{(m,i)}_{(\ell,k)}, \mathsf{mTree}_\ell))$$

(If $k > 1$): $\mathsf{state}_{in} := (\mathsf{state}^{(m)}_{(\ell,k')}, \mathsf{MProof}(H(\mathsf{state}^{(m)}_{(\ell,k')}), \mathsf{sTree}_\ell))$

$$\mathcal{M}_{in} := \{(\mathsf{msg}^{(j,m)}_{(\ell,k')}, \mathsf{MProof}(H(\mathsf{msg}^{(j,m)}_{(\ell,k')}), \mathsf{mTree}_\ell))\}_{j\in[n]}$$

5. Output $\mathsf{cert} := (ids, \mathsf{initData}, \mathsf{root}^{\mathsf{state}}, \mathsf{root}^{\mathsf{msg}}, \mathsf{state}_{in}, \mathcal{M}_{in}, \mathsf{state}_{out}, \mathsf{msg}_{out})$.

The Punishment Protocol. Each party P_i (for $i \in [n]$) checks if $\mathsf{cert} \neq \bot$. If this is the case, P_i sends cert to $\mathcal{J}^{\mathsf{pp}}$. Otherwise, P_i waits till time T to receive her deposit back. Timeout T is set such that the parties have sufficient time to submit a certificate after the execution of π^{pp} and $\mathsf{Blame}^{\mathsf{pp}}$. The judge $\mathcal{J}^{\mathsf{pp}}$ is described in the following. The validation algorithms wrongMsg and wrongState and the algorithm getIndex can be found in the full version of this paper. We stress that the validation algorithms wrongMsg and wrongState don't need to recompute a whole protocol execution but only a single step. Therefore, $\mathcal{J}^{\mathsf{pp}}$ is very efficient and can, for instance, be realized via a smart contract. To be more precise, the judge is execution without any interaction and runs in computation complexity linear in the protocol complexity. By allowing logarithmic interactions between the judge and the parties, we can further reduce the computation complexity to logarithmic in the protocol complexity. This can be achieved by applying the efficiency improvement described in the full version of this paper.

Judge $\mathcal{J}^{\mathsf{pp}}$

Initialization: The judge has access to public variables n, t, T and the set of parties $\{P_i\}_{i\in[n]}$. Further, it maintains a set cheaters initially set to $\emptyset$. Prior to the execution of π^{pp}, $\mathcal{J}^{\mathsf{pp}}$ has received d coins from each party P_i.

Proof verification: Wait until time T_1 to receive $((\ell, k, m, i), \mathsf{initData}, \langle \mathsf{root}^{\mathsf{state}}_{(\ell)} \rangle_m, \langle \mathsf{root}^{\mathsf{msg}}_{(\ell)} \rangle_m, \mathsf{state}_{in}, \mathcal{M}_{in}, \mathsf{state}_{out}, (\mathsf{hash}, \sigma))$ and do:

1. If $P_m \in$ cheaters, abort.
2. Parse initData to $(\langle \mathsf{initData}^{\mathsf{core}}_{(\ell,m)} \rangle_m, \mathsf{initData}^{\mathsf{aux}}_{(\ell,m)})$ and set $\mathsf{state}_0 = \mathsf{deriveInit}(\mathsf{initData}^{\mathsf{core}}_{(\ell,m)}, \mathsf{initData}^{\mathsf{aux}}_{(\ell,m)})$. If $\mathsf{Verify}(\langle \mathsf{initData}^{\mathsf{core}}_{(\ell,m)} \rangle_m) = \mathsf{false}$ or $\mathsf{state}_0 = \bot$, abort. If $\mathsf{state}_0 = \mathsf{bad}$, add P_m to cheaters and stop.
3. If $\mathsf{Verify}(\langle \mathsf{root}^{\mathsf{state}}_{(\ell)} \rangle_m) = \mathsf{false}$ or $\mathsf{Verify}(\langle \mathsf{root}^{\mathsf{msg}}_{(\ell)} \rangle_m) = \mathsf{false}$, abort.
4. If $i = 0$ and $\mathsf{wrongState}(\mathsf{state}_0, \mathsf{state}_{in}, \mathsf{state}_{out}, \mathcal{M}_{in}, \mathsf{root}^{\mathsf{state}}_{(\ell)}, \mathsf{root}^{\mathsf{msg}}_{(\ell)}, \ell, k, m) = \mathsf{true}$, add P_m to cheaters.

5. If $i > 0$, $\mathsf{MVerify}(\mathsf{hash}, \mathsf{getIndex}(k, m, i), \mathsf{root}^{\mathsf{msg}}_{(\ell)}, \sigma) = \mathsf{true}$ and $\mathsf{wrongMsg}(\mathsf{state}_0, \mathsf{state}_{in}, \mathsf{hash}, \mathcal{M}_{in},, \mathsf{root}^{\mathsf{state}}_{(\ell)}, \mathsf{root}^{\mathsf{msg}}_{(\ell)}, \ell, m, k, i) = \mathsf{true}$, add P_m to cheaters.

Timeout: At time T_1, send d coins to each party $P_i \notin$ cheaters.

6.1 Security

Theorem 1. *Let* $(\pi^{\mathsf{pp}}, \cdot, \cdot)$ *be an n-party publicly verifiable covert protocol computing function f with deterrence factor* ϵ *satisfying the view requirements stated in Eq.* (1a)–(1d). *Further, let the signature scheme* (Generate, Sign, Verify) *be existentially unforgeable under chosen-message attacks, the Merkle tree satisfies the binding property and the hash function H be collision resistant. Then the protocol* π^{pp} *together with algorithm* $\mathsf{Blame}^{\mathsf{pp}}$, *protocol* $\mathsf{Punish}^{\mathsf{pp}}$ *and judge* $\mathcal{J}^{\mathsf{pp}}$ *satisfies financially backed covert security with deterrence factor* ϵ *according to Definition 1.*

We formally prove Theorem 1 in the full version of this paper.

7 Class 3: Input-Independent with Private Transcript

At the time of writing, there exists no PVC protocol without public transcript that could be directly transformed into an FBC protocol. Moreover, it is not clear, if it is possible to construct a PVC protocol without a public transcript. Instead, we present a transformation from an input-independent PVC protocol with public transcript into an FBC protocol without any form of common public transcript. As in our first transformation, we start with an input-independent PVC protocol π_3^{pvc} that is based on cut-and-choose where parties share a common public transcript. Due to the input-independence, all parties of the checked instances can be opened. However, unlike our first transformation, which utilizes the public transcript, we remove this feature from the PVC protocol as part of the transformation. We denote the protocol that results by removing the public transcript feature from π_3^{pvc} by π_3. Without having a public transcript, the punishment protocol becomes interactive and more complicated. Intuitively, without a public transcript it is impossible to immediately decide if a message that deviates from the emulation is maliciously generated or is invalid because of a received invalid messages. Note that we still have a common public tree of internal state hashes in our exposition. However, the necessity of this tree can also be removed by applying the techniques presented here that allow us to remove the common transcript.

In order to apply our construction to a protocol π_3, we require almost the same features of π_3 as demanded in our first transformation (cf. Sect. 6). For the sake of exposition, we outline the required features here again and point out the differences. First, we require π_3 to be based on the cut-and-choose approach (cf. Sect. 4.1). Second, we require the actions of each party P_i in a semi-honest instance execution to be deterministically determined by a random seed (cf. Sect. 4.2). Third, we require that all parties learn the initial states of all other parties in the opened protocol instances (cf. Sect. 4.3). To this end, the parties receive signed data (e.g., a commitment and decommitment value) to derive the initial states of the other parties. Fourth, parties need to commit to their intermediate internal states during the protocol executions in a publicly verifiable way (cf. Sect. 5.1). Finally, all signed data match the encoded form specified in Sect. 5.2.

In contrast to the transformation in Sect. 6 we no longer require from protocol π_3 that the parties send all messages or message hashes to all other parties. Formally, whenever some party P_h in round k of protocol instance ℓ transitions to a state $\mathsf{state}_{(\ell,k)}^{(h)}$ with the outgoing messages $\{\mathsf{msg}_{(\ell,k)}^{(h,i)}\}_{i\in[n]\setminus\{h\}}$, then it actually sends the following to P_i:

$$(\langle \mathsf{msg}_{(\ell,k)}^{(h,i)} \rangle_h, \mathsf{hash}_{(\ell,k)}^{(h)} := H(\mathsf{state}_{(\ell,k)}^{(h)}))$$

Let O be the set of opened instances. We summarize the aforementioned requirements by specifying the data that the view of any honest party P_h after the execution of π_3 includes. The view contains data to derive the initial state of all parties which is signed by each party for each party and every opened instance, i.e.,

$$\{(\langle \mathsf{initData}_{(i,\ell)}^{\mathsf{core}} \rangle_j, \mathsf{initData}_{(i,\ell)}^{\mathsf{aux}})\}_{\ell\in O, i\in[n], j\in[n]}, \tag{2a}$$

a Merkle tree over the hashes of all intermediate internal states of a single instance for all instances, i.e.,

$$\{\mathsf{sTree}_\ell\}_{\ell\in[t]} := \{\mathsf{MTree}(\{\mathsf{hash}_{(\ell,k)}^{(i)}\}_{k\in[R], i\in[n]})\}_{\ell\in[t]}, \tag{2b}$$

signatures from each party over the roots of the state trees, i.e.,

$$\{\langle \mathsf{MRoot}(\mathsf{sTree}_\ell) \rangle_i\}_{i\in[n], \ell\in[t]} \tag{2c}$$

and the signed incoming message, i.e.,

$$\mathcal{M} := \{\langle \mathsf{msg}_{(\ell,k)}^{(i,h)} \rangle_i\}_{\ell\in[t], k\in[R], i\in[n]\setminus\{h\}}. \tag{2d}$$

The Blame Algorithm. At the end of protocol π_3, all parties first execute an evidence algorithm Evidence to generate partial certificates cert′. The partial certificate is a candidate to be used for the punishment protocol and is broadcasted to all other parties as part of π_3. In case the honest party detects cheating in several occurrences, the party picks the occurrence with the smallest indices (ℓ, k, m, i) (in this sequence). The algorithm to generate partial certificates Evidence is formally described as follows:

Algorithm Evidence

1. P_h runs $\mathsf{state}^{(i)}_{(\ell,0)} = \mathsf{deriveInit}(\mathsf{initData}^{\mathsf{core}}_{(i,\ell)}, \mathsf{initData}^{\mathsf{aux}}_{(i,\ell)})$ for each $i \in [n], \ell \in O$. Let $\mathcal{B}$ be the set of all tuples $(\ell, 0, m, 0)$ such that $\mathsf{state}^{(m)}_{(\ell,0)} = \mathsf{bad}$. If $\mathcal{B} \neq \emptyset$, goto step 4.
2. P_h emulates for each $\ell \in O$ the protocol executions on input the initial states from all parties to obtain the expected messages and the expected intermediate states of all parties, i.e., $(\{\widetilde{\mathsf{msg}}^{(i,j)}_{(\ell,k)}\}_{k\in[R],i\in[n],j\neq i}, \{\mathsf{state}^{(i)}_{(\ell,k)}\}_{k,i,j}) := \mathsf{emulate}^{\mathsf{full}}(\{\mathsf{state}^{(i)}_{(\ell,0)}\}_{i\in[n]})$.
3. Let $\mathcal{B}$ be the set of all tuples (ℓ, k, m, h) such that $\mathsf{msg}^{(m,h)}_{(\ell,k)} \neq \widetilde{\mathsf{msg}}^{(m,h)}_{(\ell,k)}$ or $H(\mathsf{state}^{(m)}_{(\ell,k)}) \neq \mathsf{hash}^{(m)}_{(\ell,k)}$ – where $\mathsf{msg}^{(m,h)}_{(\ell,k)}$ and $\mathsf{hash}^{(m)}_{(\ell,k)}$ are taken from $\mathcal{M}$ or sTree_ℓ respectively. In case of an invalid state, set $h = 0$.
4. Pick the tuple (ℓ, k, m, i) from $\mathcal{B}$ with the smallest ℓ, k, m, i in this sequence. If $k > 0$ set $\mathsf{msg}_{out} := \langle \mathsf{msg}^{(m,i)}_{(\ell,k)} \rangle_m$. Otherwise, set $\mathsf{msg}_{out} := \perp$.
5. Output partial certificate $(ids, \mathsf{msg}_{out})$.

Since π_3 does not contain a public transcript of messages, parties can only validate their own incoming message instead of all messages as done in previous approaches. Hence, it can happen that different honest parties generate and broadcast different partial certificates. Therefore, all parties validate the incoming certificates, discard invalid ones and pick the partial certificate cert' with the smallest indices (ℓ, k, m, i) (in this sequence) as their own. If no partial certificate has been received or created, parties set $\mathsf{cert}' := \perp$.

Finally, each honest party executes the blame algorithm $\mathsf{Blame}^{\mathsf{sp}}$ to create the full certificate that is used for both, blaming a malicious party and defending against incorrect accusations. As in this scenario the punishment protocol requires input of accused honest parties, the blame algorithm returns a certificate even if no malicious behavior has been detected, i.e., if $\mathsf{cert}' = \perp$. The final certificate is generated by appending following data from the view to the certificate: $\{(\langle \mathsf{initData}^{\mathsf{core}}_{(i,\ell)} \rangle_j, \mathsf{initData}^{\mathsf{aux}}_{(i,\ell)})\}_{\ell\in O,i\in[n],j\in[n]}$ (cf. Eq. 2a), $\{\mathsf{sTree}_\ell\}_{\ell\in[t]}$ (cf. Eq. 2b), and $\{\langle \mathsf{MRoot}(\mathsf{sTree}_\ell) \rangle_i\}_{i\in[n],\ell\in[t]}$ (cf. Eq. 2c). All the appended data is public and does not really need to be broadcasted. However, in order to match the formal specification, all parties broadcast their whole certificate. If $\mathsf{cert}' \neq \perp$, the honest party outputs in addition to the certificate $\mathsf{corrupted}_m$.

To ease the specification of the punishment protocol in which parties derive further data from the certificates, we define an additional algorithm $\mathsf{mesHistory}$ that uses the messages obtained during the emulation $(\widetilde{\mathsf{msg}})^2$ to compute the message history up to a specific round k' (inclusively) of instance ℓ. We structure the message history in two layers. For each round $k^* < k'$, parties create a Merkle tree of all messages emulated in this round. These trees constitute the bottom layer. On the top layer, parties create a Merkle tree over the roots of the bottom layer trees. This enables parties to agree on all messages of one round making

[2] Formally, parties need to re-execute the emulation, as we do not allow them to use any data not included in the certificate.

it easier to submit Merkle proofs for messages sent in this round. The message history is composed of the following variables:

$$\begin{aligned}\{\mathsf{mTree}^{\mathsf{round}}_{k^*}\}_{k^*\in[k']} &:= \{\mathsf{MTree}(\{H(\widetilde{\mathsf{msg}}^{(i,j)}_{(\ell,k^*)})\}_{i\in[n],j\neq i})\}_{k^*\in[k']}\\ \mathsf{mTree}_{k'} &:= \mathsf{MTree}(\{\mathsf{MRoot}(\mathsf{mTree}^{\mathsf{round}}_{k^*}\}_{k^*\in[k']})\\ \mathsf{root}^{\mathsf{msg}}_{k'} &:= \mathsf{MRoot}(\mathsf{mTree})\end{aligned}$$

Additionally, if $\mathsf{cert}' \neq \perp$, parties compute the following:

$$\begin{aligned}&\text{(Always):} && \mathsf{initData} := (\langle \mathsf{initData}^{\mathsf{core}}_{(\ell,m)}\rangle_m, \mathsf{initData}^{\mathsf{aux}}_{(\ell,m)})\\ &&& \mathsf{root}^{\mathsf{state}} := \langle \mathsf{MRoot}(\mathsf{sTree}_\ell)\rangle_m\\ &\text{(If } k>0\text{):} && \mathsf{state}_{out} := (\mathsf{hash}^{(m)}_{(\ell,k)}, \mathsf{MProof}(\mathsf{hash}^{(m)}_{(\ell,k)}, \mathsf{sTree}_\ell))\\ &\text{(If } k>1\text{):} && \mathsf{state}_{in} := (\mathsf{state}^{(m)}_{(\ell,k')}, \mathsf{MProof}(H(\mathsf{state}^{(m)}_{(\ell,k')}), \mathsf{sTree}_\ell))\\ &&& (\{\mathsf{mTree}^{\mathsf{round}}_{k^*}\}_{k^*\in[k']}, \mathsf{mTree}_{k'}, \mathsf{root}^{\mathsf{msg}}_{k'}) := \mathsf{mesHistory}(k',\ell)\\ &&& \sigma_{k'} := \mathsf{MProof}(\mathsf{MRoot}(\mathsf{mTree}^{\mathsf{round}}_{k'}), \mathsf{mTree}_{k'}))\\ &&& \mathcal{M}_{in} := \{(\widetilde{\mathsf{msg}}^{(j,m)}_{(\ell,k')}, \mathsf{MProof}(H(\widetilde{\mathsf{msg}}^{(j,m)}_{(\ell,k')}), \mathsf{mTree}^{\mathsf{round}}_{k'}))\}_{j\in[n]}\end{aligned}$$

The Punishment Protocol. The main difficulty of constructing a punishment protocol $\mathsf{Punish}^{\mathsf{sp}}$ for this scenario is that there is no publicly verifiable evidence about messages like a common transcript used in the previous transformations. Hence, incoming messages required for the computation of a particular protocol step cannot be validated directly. Instead, the actions of all parties need to be validated against the emulated actions based on the initial states. This leads to the problem that deviations from the protocol can cause later messages of other honest parties to deviate from the emulated ones as well. Therefore, it is important that the judge disputes the earliest occurrence of misbehavior.

We divide the punishment protocol $\mathsf{Punish}^{\mathsf{sp}}$ into three phases. First, the judge determines the earliest accusation of misbehavior. To this end, if $\mathsf{cert} \neq \perp$ all parties start by sending tuple *ids* from cert to $\mathcal{J}^{\mathsf{sp}}$ and the judge selects the tuple with the smallest indices (ℓ, k, m, i). This mechanism ensures that either the first malicious message or malicious state hash received by an honest party is disputed or the adversary blames some party at an earlier point. To look ahead, if the adversary blames an honest party at an earlier point, the punishment will not be successful and the malicious blamer will be punished for submitting an invalid accusation. If the adversary blames another malicious party, either one of them will be punished. This mechanism ensures that if an honest party submits an accusation, a malicious party will be punished, even if it is not the honest party's accusation that is disputed.

If there has not been any accusation submitted in the first phase, $\mathcal{J}^{\mathsf{sp}}$ reimburses all parties. Otherwise, $\mathcal{J}^{\mathsf{sp}}$ defines a blamer P_b, the party that has submitted the earliest accusation, and an accused party P_m. P_b either accuses misbehavior in the initial state, the first round, or in some later round. For the former two, misbehavior can be proven in a straightforward way, similar to our first construction. For the latter, P_b is supposed to submit a proof containing the hash of a tree of the message history up to the disputed round k. P_m can accept or decline the message history depending on whether the tree corresponds to the one emulated by P_m or not. If the tree is accepted, the certificate can be validated as in previous scenarios, with the only difference that incoming messages are validated with respect to the submitted message history tree instead of the common public transcript. In case any party does not respond in time, this party is considered maliciously and is financially punished.

If the message history is declined, the protocol transitions to the third phase. Parties P_b and P_m together with $\mathcal{J}^{\mathsf{sp}}$ execute a bisection search in the message history tree to find the first message they disagree on (cf. Sect. 5.3). By definition they agree on all messages before the disputed one – we call these messages the *agreed sub-tree*. At this step, $\mathcal{J}^{\mathsf{sp}}$ can validate the disputed message of the history tree (not the one disputed in the beginning) the same way as done in previous constructions with the only difference that incoming messages are validated with respect to the agreed sub-tree.

The number of interactions is logarithmic while the computation complexity of the judge is linear in the protocol complexity. We can further reduce the computation complexity to be logarithmic in the protocol complexity while still having logarithmic interactions using the efficiency improvements described in the full version of this paper. The judge is defined as follows:

Protocol $\mathsf{Punish}^{\mathsf{sp}}$

Phase 1: Determine earliest accusation

1. If $\mathsf{cert} \neq \bot$, P_h sends $ids := (\ell, k, m, i)$ taken from cert to $\mathcal{J}^{\mathsf{sp}}$ which stores (ℓ, k, m, i, h).
2. $\mathcal{J}^{\mathsf{sp}}$ waits till time T to receive message (ℓ, k, m, i) from parties P_b for $b \in [n]$. If no accusations have been received, $\mathcal{J}^{\mathsf{sp}}$ sends d coins to each party at time T. Otherwise, $\mathcal{J}^{\mathsf{sp}}$ picks the *smallest* tuple (ℓ, k, m, i, b) (ordered in this sequence), sets $k' := k - 1$ and continues with Phase 2.

Timeout: If its P_j's turn for $j \in \{b, m\}$ and P_j does not respond with a valid message, i.e., one that is not discarded, in time, P_j is considered malicious and $\mathcal{J}^{\mathsf{sp}}$ terminates by sending d coins to all parties but P_j.

Phase 2: First evidence

3. If $k < 2$, P_b sends $(\mathsf{initData}, \mathsf{root}^{\mathsf{state}}, \mathsf{state}_{out}, \langle \mathsf{msg}_{(\ell,k)}^{(m,i)} \rangle_m)$ taken from cert to $\mathcal{J}^{\mathsf{sp}}$
   (a) $\mathcal{J}^{\mathsf{sp}}$ parses $\mathsf{initData}$ to $(\langle \mathsf{initData}_{(\ell,m)}^{\mathsf{core}} \rangle_m, \mathsf{initData}_{(\ell,m)}^{\mathsf{aux}})$ and sets $\mathsf{state}_0 = \mathsf{deriveInit}(\mathsf{initData}_{(\ell,m)}^{\mathsf{core}}, \mathsf{initData}_{(\ell,m)}^{\mathsf{aux}})$. If $\mathsf{Verify}(\langle \mathsf{initData}_{(\ell,m)}^{\mathsf{core}} \rangle_m) = \mathsf{false}$ or $\mathsf{state}_0 = \bot$, $\mathcal{J}^{\mathsf{sp}}$ discards. If $\mathsf{state}_0 = \mathsf{bad}$, $\mathcal{J}^{\mathsf{sp}}$ terminates by sending d coins to all parties but P_m.
   (b) If $\mathsf{Verify}(\langle \mathsf{root}_{(\ell)}^{\mathsf{state}} \rangle_m) = \mathsf{false}$, $\mathcal{J}^{\mathsf{sp}}$ discards.
   (c) If $i = 0$ and $\mathsf{wrongState}(\mathsf{state}_0, \bot, \mathsf{state}_{out}, \emptyset, \mathsf{root}_{(\ell)}^{\mathsf{state}}, \bot, \ell, k, m) = \mathsf{false}$, $\mathcal{J}^{\mathsf{sp}}$ discards.
   (d) If $i > 0$, $\mathsf{Verify}(\langle \mathsf{msg}_{(\ell,k)}^{(m,i)} \rangle_m) = \mathsf{false}$ or $\mathsf{wrongMsg}(\mathsf{state}_0, \bot, H(\mathsf{msg}_{(\ell,k)}^{(m,i)}), \emptyset, \mathsf{root}_{(\ell)}^{\mathsf{state}}, \bot, \ell, m, k, i) = \mathsf{false}$, $\mathcal{J}^{\mathsf{sp}}$ discards.

(e) $\mathcal{J}^{\mathsf{sp}}$ terminates by sending d coins to all parties but P_m.

4. Otherwise, P_b sends $(\mathsf{root}^{\mathsf{state}}, \mathsf{state}_{in}, \mathsf{state}_{out}, \langle \mathsf{root}_{(\ell)}^{\mathsf{state}} \rangle_m, \mathsf{root}^{\mathsf{msg}}, \mathsf{root}_{k'}^{\mathsf{round}}, \sigma_{k'}, \mathcal{M}_{in}, \mathsf{msg}_{out})$ taken from cert to $\mathcal{J}^{\mathsf{sp}}$.
   (a) P_m executes $\mathsf{mesHistory}(k-1, \ell)$. Let $\widetilde{\mathsf{root}}^{\mathsf{msg}}$ be the root of the emulated message history tree. If $\mathsf{root}^{\mathsf{msg}} \neq \widetilde{\mathsf{root}}^{\mathsf{msg}}$ P_m sends $\widetilde{\mathsf{root}}^{\mathsf{msg}}$ to $\mathcal{J}^{\mathsf{sp}}$. Otherwise, P_m sends $(\bot)$.
   (b) If $\widetilde{\mathsf{root}}^{\mathsf{msg}}$ received by P_m does not equal $\bot$, $\mathcal{J}^{\mathsf{sp}}$ jumps to phase 3.
   (c) $\mathcal{J}^{\mathsf{sp}}$ checks that $\mathsf{Verify}(\langle \mathsf{root}_{(\ell)}^{\mathsf{state}} \rangle_m) = \mathsf{true}$ and $\mathsf{MVerify}(\mathsf{root}_{k'}^{\mathsf{round}}, k', \mathsf{root}^{\mathsf{msg}}, \sigma_{k'}) = \mathsf{true}$ and discards otherwise.
   (d) If $i = 0$ and $\mathsf{wrongState}(\bot, \mathsf{state}_{in}, \mathsf{state}_{out}, \mathcal{M}_{in}, \mathsf{root}_{(\ell)}^{\mathsf{state}}, \mathsf{root}_{k'}^{\mathsf{round}}, \ell, k, m) = \mathsf{false}$, $\mathcal{J}^{\mathsf{sp}}$ discards.
   (e) If $i > 0$, $\mathsf{Verify}(\langle \mathsf{msg}_{(\ell,k)}^{(m,i)} \rangle_m) = \mathsf{false}$ or $\mathsf{wrongMsg}(\mathsf{state}_0, \mathsf{state}_{in}, H(\mathsf{msg}_{(\ell,k)}^{(m,i)}), \mathcal{M}_{in},, \mathsf{root}_{(\ell)}^{\mathsf{state}}, \mathsf{root}_{k'}^{\mathsf{round}}, \ell, m, k, i) = \mathsf{false}$, $\mathcal{J}^{\mathsf{sp}}$ discards.
   (f) $\mathcal{J}^{\mathsf{sp}}$ terminates by sending d coins to all parties but P_m.

Phase 3: Dispute the message tree

5. Parties P_b, P_m and $\mathcal{J}^{\mathsf{sp}}$ run bisection sub-protocol Π_{BS} on the top-level tree. P_b's input is the tree with root $\mathsf{root}^{\mathsf{msg}}$; P_m's the one with root $\widetilde{\mathsf{root}}^{\mathsf{msg}}$. $\mathcal{J}^{\mathsf{sp}}$ announces public inputs $\mathsf{root}^{\mathsf{msg}}$ and width of $\mathsf{root}^{\mathsf{msg}}$, $width := k'$. The output is the first round they disagree on k_2, the agreed hash $\mathsf{root}_{k_2'}^{\mathsf{round}}$ of leaf with index $k_2' := k_2 - 1$ and the hash $\mathsf{root}_{(b,k_2)}^{\mathsf{round}}$ of leaf with index k_2 as claimed by P_m.
6. Parties P_m, P_b and $\mathcal{J}^{\mathsf{sp}}$ run bisection sub-protocol Π_{BS} on the low-level tree. Both, P_m and P_b take as input $\mathsf{mTree}_{k_2}^{\mathsf{round}}$ from their certificate. $\mathcal{J}^{\mathsf{sp}}$ announces public inputs $\mathsf{root}_{(b,k_2)}^{\mathsf{round}}$ and the width of the low level tree $width'n \times (n-1)$. The output is the index x of the first message they disagree on and the hash of this message hash_x as claimed by P_m. The index of the sender of the disputed message is $m_2 := \lceil \frac{x}{n-1} \rceil$ and the index of the receiver $i_2 = x \mod (n-1)$ if $m_2 > (x \mod (n-1))$ and $i_2 := (x \mod (n-1)) + 1$ otherwise.
7. Party P_b define variables as follows – variables that are not explicitly defined are set to $\bot$.

$$\text{(Always):}\quad \mathsf{initData}^2 := (\langle \mathsf{initData}_{(\ell,m_2)}^{\mathsf{core}} \rangle_m, \mathsf{initData}_{(\ell,m_2)}^{\mathsf{aux}})$$
$$\mathsf{root}^{\mathsf{state}} := \langle \mathsf{MRoot}(\mathsf{sTree}_\ell) \rangle_m$$
$$\text{(If } k_2 > 1\text{):}\quad \mathsf{state}_{in}^2 := (\mathsf{state}_{(\ell,k_2')}^{(m_2)}, \mathsf{MProof}(H(\mathsf{state}_{(\ell,k_2')}^{(m_2)}), \mathsf{sTree}_\ell))$$
$$\mathcal{M}_{in}^2 := \{(\mathsf{msg}_{(\ell,k_2')}^{(j,m_2)}, \mathsf{MProof}(H(\mathsf{msg}_{(\ell,k_2')}^{(j,m_2)}), \mathsf{mTree}_{k_2'}^{\mathsf{round}}))\}_{j\in[n]}$$

   and sends $(\mathsf{initData}^2, \langle \mathsf{MRoot}(\mathsf{sTree}_\ell) \rangle_m, \mathsf{state}_{in}^2, \mathcal{M}_{in}^2)$ to $\mathcal{J}^{\mathsf{sp}}$.
8. $\mathcal{J}^{\mathsf{sp}}$ parses $\mathsf{initData}^2$ to $(\langle \mathsf{initData}_{(\ell,m_2)}^{\mathsf{core}} \rangle_m, \mathsf{initData}_{(\ell,m_2)}^{\mathsf{aux}})$ and sets $\mathsf{state}_{(0)}^{(m_2)} := \mathsf{deriveInit}(\mathsf{initData}_{(\ell,m_2)}^{\mathsf{core}}, \mathsf{initData}_{(\ell,m_2)}^{\mathsf{aux}})$. If $\mathsf{Verify}(\langle \mathsf{root}_{(\ell)}^{\mathsf{state}} \rangle_m) = \mathsf{false}$, $\mathsf{Verify}(\langle \mathsf{initData}_{(\ell,m_2)}^{\mathsf{core}} \rangle_m) = \mathsf{false}$ or $\mathsf{state}_{(0)}^{(m_2)} \in \{\bot, \mathsf{bad}\}$, $\mathcal{J}^{\mathsf{sp}}$ discards.
9. If $\mathsf{wrongMsg}(\mathsf{state}_{(0)}^{(m_2)}, \mathsf{state}_{in}^2, \mathsf{hash}_x, \mathcal{M}_{in}^2, \mathsf{root}_{(\ell)}^{\mathsf{state}}, \mathsf{root}_{k_2'}^{\mathsf{round}}, \ell, m_2, k_2, i_2) = \mathsf{false}$, $\mathcal{J}^{\mathsf{sp}}$ discards.
10. $\mathcal{J}^{\mathsf{sp}}$ terminates by sending d coins to all parties but P_m.

7.1 Security

Theorem 2. *Let* $(\pi_3^{\mathsf{pvc}}, \mathsf{Blame}^{\mathsf{pvc}}, \mathsf{Judge}^{\mathsf{pvc}})$ *be an* n*-party publicly verifiable covert protocol computing function* f *with deterrence factor* ϵ *satisfying the view requirements stated in Eq.* (2)*. Further,* π_3^{pvc} *generates a common public transcript of hashes that is only used for* $\mathsf{Blame}^{\mathsf{pvc}}$ *and* $\mathsf{Judge}^{\mathsf{pvc}}$*. Let* π_3 *be a protocol that is equal to* π_3^{pvc} *but does not generate a common transcript and instead of calling* $\mathsf{Blame}^{\mathsf{pvc}}$ *executes the blame procedure explained above (including execution of* Evidence *and* $\mathsf{Punish}^{\mathsf{sp}}$*). Further, let the signature scheme* (Generate, Sign, Verify) *be existentially unforgeable under chosen-message attacks, the Merkle tree satisfies the binding property, the hash function* H *be collision resistant and the bisection protocol* Π_{BS} *be correct. Then, the protocol* π_3*, together with algorithm* $\mathsf{Blame}^{\mathsf{sp}}$*, protocol* $\mathsf{Punish}^{\mathsf{sp}}$ *and judge* $\mathcal{J}^{\mathsf{sp}}$ *satisfies financially backed covert security with deterrence factor* ϵ *according to Definition 1.*

We formally prove Theorem 2 in the full version of this paper.

8 Evaluation

In order to evaluate the practicability of our protocols, i.e., to show that the judging party can be realized efficiently via a smart contract, we implemented the judge of our third transformation (cf. Sect. 7) for the Ethereum blockchain and measured the associated execution costs. We focus on the third setting, the verification of protocols with a private transcript, since we expect this scenario to be the most expensive one due to the interactive punishment procedure. Further, we have extended the transformation such that the protocol does not require a public transcript of state hashes.

Our implementation includes the efficiency features described in the full version of this paper. In particular, we model the calculation of each round's and party's computeRound function as an arithmetic circuit and compress disputed calculations and messages using Merkle trees. The latter are divided into 32-byte chunks which constitute the leave of the Merkle tree. The judge only needs to validate either the computation of a single arithmetic gate or the correctness of a single message chunk of a sent or received message together with the corresponding Merkle tree proofs. The proofs are logarithmic in the size of the computation resp. the size of a message. Messages are validated by defining a mapping from each chunk to a gate in the corresponding computeRound function.

In order to avoid redundant deployment costs, we apply a pattern that allows us to deploy the contract code just once and for all and create new independent instances of our FBC protocol without deploying further code. When starting a new protocol instance, parties register the instance at the existing contract which occupies the storage for the variables required by the new instance, e.g., the set of involved parties. Further, we implement the judge to be agnostic to the particular semi-honest protocol executed by the parties – recall that our FBC protocol wraps around a semi-honest protocol that is subject to the cut-and-choose technique. Every instance registered at the judge can involve a different

Table 1. Costs for deployment, instance registration and optimistic execution.

Protocol steps	n	Cost	
		Gas	USD
`Deployment`		4 775 k	639.91
`New instance`	2	287 k	38.41
`New instance`	3	308 k	41.30
`New instance`	5	351 k	47.05
`New instance`	10	458 k	61.43
`Honest execution`	2	178 k	23.92
`Honest execution`	3	224 k	30.07
`Honest execution`	5	316 k	42.38
`Honest execution`	10	546 k	73.14

Table 2. Worst-case execution costs.

Gates	Chunks	R	n	Cost	
				Gas	USD
10	10	10	3	1 780 k	238.58
1 000	10	10	3	2 412 k	323.25
1 M	10	10	3	3 512 k	470.55
1 B	10	10	3	4 782 k	640.75
1 T	10	10	3	6 182 k	828.35
10	10	10	3	1 785 k	239.14
100	100	10	3	2 086 k	279.61
1 000	1 000	10	3	2 422 k	324.55
100	10	10	3	2 081 k	278.91
100	10	10	4	2 223 k	297.86
100	10	10	7	2 442 k	327.29
100	10	10	10	2 659 k	356.34
100	10	10	50	4 764 k	638.35
100	10	3	3	1 878 k	251.65
100	10	10	3	2 074 k	277.88
100	10	100	3	2 403 k	322.04
100	10	1 000	3	2 834 k	379.79

Gates: Number of gates in the circuit of each computeRound function.
Chunks: Number of chunks in each message.
R: Number of communication rounds.
n: Number of parties.

number of parties and define its own semi-honest protocol. This means that the same judge contract can be used for whatever semi-honest protocol our FBC protocol instance is based on, e.g., for both the generation of Beaver triples and garbled circuits. Parties simply define for each involved party and each round the computeRound function as a set of gates, aggregate all gates into a Merkle tree and submit the tree's root upon instance registration.

We perform all measurements on a local test environment. We setup the local Ethereum blockchain with *Ganache* (core version 2.13.2) on the latest supported hard fork, Muir Glacier. The contract is compiled to EVM byte code with *solc* (version 0.8.1, optimized on 20 runs). As common, we measure the efficiency of the smart contracts via its gas consumption – this metric directly translates to execution costs. Further, we estimate USD costs based on the prices (gas to ETH and ETH to USD) on Aug. 20, 2021 [Eth21, Coi21]. For comparison, a simple Ether transfer costs 21,000 gas resp. 2,81 USD.

In Table 1, we display the costs of the deployment, the registration of a new instance and the optimistic execution without any disputes. The costs of these steps only depend on the number of parties. In Table 2, we display the worst-case costs of a protocol execution for different protocol parameters, i.e., complexity of the computeRound functions, message size, communication rounds and number of parties. In order to determine the worst-case costs, we measured different dispute patterns, e.g., disputing sent messages or disputing gates of the computeRound functions, and picked the pattern with the highest costs. The execution costs, both optimistic and worst case, incorporate all protocol steps, incl. the secure funding of the instance. We exclude the derivation of the initial seeds as this step strongly depends on the underlying PVC protocol.

In the optimistic case, the costs of executing our protocol are similar to the ones of [ZDH19]. The authors report a gas consumption of 482 k gas while our protocol consumes between 465 k and 1 M gas, depending on the number of parties – recall that the protocol of [ZDH19] is restricted to the two-party setting. This overhead in our protocol when considering more than two parties is mainly introduced by the fact that [ZDH19] does assume a single deposit while our implementation requires each party to perform a deposit.

Unfortunately, we cannot compare worst-case costs directly, as the protocol of [ZDH19] validates the consistency of a fixed data structure, i.e., a garbled circuit, while our implementation validates the correctness of the whole protocol execution. In particular, [ZDH19] performs a bisection over the garbled circuit while we perform two bisections, first over the message history and then over the computation generating the outgoing messages; such a message might for example be a garbled circuit. Further, [ZDH19] focuses on a boolean circuit, while we model the computeRound function as an arithmetic circuit – as the EVM always stores data in 32-byte words, it does not make sense to model the function as a boolean circuit. Although not directly comparable, we believe the protocol of [ZDH19] to be more efficient for the special case of a two-party garbling protocol, as the protocol can exploit the fact that a dispute is restricted to a single message, i.e., the garbled circuit, and the data structure of this message is fixed such that the dispute resolution can be optimized to said data structure.

Our measurements indicate that the worst-case costs of each scenario are always defined by a dispute pattern that does not dispute a message chunk but a gate of the computeRound functions. This is why the message chunks have no influence on the worst-case execution costs. Of course, this observation might be violated if we set the number of chunks much higher than the number of gates. However, it does not make sense to have more message chunks than gates because each message chunk needs to be mapped to a gate of the computeRound function defining the value of said chunk.

Both, the number of rounds and the number of parties increase the maximal size of the disputed message history and, hence, the depth of the bisected history tree. As the depth of the bisected tree grows logarithmic in the tree size, our protocol is highly scalable in the number of parties and rounds.

Finally, we note that we understand our implementation as a research prototype showing the practicability of our protocol. We are confident that additional engineering effort can further reduce the gas consumption of our contract.

Acknowledgments. The first, third, and fourth authors were supported by the German Federal Ministry of Education and Research (BMBF) *iBlockchain project* (grant nr. 16KIS0902), by the Deutsche Forschungsgemeinschaft (DFG, German Research Foundation) *SFB 1119 - 236615297 (CROSSING Project S7)*, by the BMBF and the Hessian Ministry of Higher Education, Research, Science and the Arts within their joint support of the *National Research Center for Applied Cybersecurity ATHENE*, and by Robert Bosch GmbH, by the Economy of Things Project. The second author was supported by the BIU Center for Research in Applied Cryptography and Cyber

Security in conjunction with the Israel National Cyber Bureau in the Prime Minister's Office, and by ISF grant No. 1316/18.

References

[ADMM14] Andrychowicz, M., Dziembowski, S., Malinowski, D., Mazurek, L.: Secure multiparty computations on bitcoin. In: IEEE SP (2014)

[AL07] Aumann, Y., Lindell, Y.: Security against covert adversaries: efficient protocols for realistic adversaries. In: TCC (2007)

[AO12] Asharov, G., Orlandi, C.: Calling out cheaters: covert security with public verifiability. In: Wang, X., Sako, K. (eds.) ASIACRYPT 2012. LNCS, vol. 7658, pp. 681–698. Springer, Heidelberg (2012). https://doi.org/10.1007/978-3-642-34961-4_41

[BK14] Bentov, I., Kumaresan, R.: How to use bitcoin to design fair protocols. In: Garay, J.A., Gennaro, R. (eds.) CRYPTO 2014. LNCS, vol. 8617, pp. 421–439. Springer, Heidelberg (2014). https://doi.org/10.1007/978-3-662-44381-1_24

[BMR90] Beaver, D., Micali, S., Rogaway, P.: The round complexity of secure protocols (extended abstract). In: STOC (1990)

[Coi21] CoinMarketCap. Ethereum (ETH) price (2021). https://coinmarketcap.com/currencies/ethereum/

[CRR11] Canetti, R., Riva, B., Rothblum, G.N.: Practical delegation of computation using multiple servers. In: CCS (2011)

[DKL+13] Damgård, I., Keller, M., Larraia, E., Pastro, V., Scholl, P., Smart, N.P.: Practical covertly secure MPC for dishonest majority – or: breaking the SPDZ limits. In: Crampton, J., Jajodia, S., Mayes, K. (eds.) ESORICS 2013. LNCS, vol. 8134, pp. 1–18. Springer, Heidelberg (2013). https://doi.org/10.1007/978-3-642-40203-6_1

[DOS20] Damgård, I., Orlandi, C., Simkin, M.: Black-box transformations from passive to covert security with public verifiability. In: Micciancio, D., Ristenpart, T. (eds.) CRYPTO 2020. LNCS, vol. 12171, pp. 647–676. Springer, Cham (2020). https://doi.org/10.1007/978-3-030-56880-1_23

[DPSZ12] Damgård, I., Pastro, V., Smart, N., Zakarias, S.: Multiparty computation from somewhat homomorphic encryption. In: Safavi-Naini, R., Canetti, R. (eds.) CRYPTO 2012. LNCS, vol. 7417, pp. 643–662. Springer, Heidelberg (2012). https://doi.org/10.1007/978-3-642-32009-5_38

[EFS20] Eckey, L., Faust, S., Schlosser, B.: OptiSwap: fast optimistic fair exchange. In: ASIA CCS (2020)

[Eth21] Etherscan. Ethereum Average Gas Price Chart (2021). https://etherscan.io/chart/gasprice

[FHKS21] Faust, S., Hazay, C., Kretzler, D., Schlosser, B.: Generic compiler for publicly verifiable covert multi-party computation. In: Canteaut, A., Standaert, F.-X. (eds.) EUROCRYPT 2021. LNCS, vol. 12697, pp. 782–811. Springer, Cham (2021). https://doi.org/10.1007/978-3-030-77886-6_27

[GMW87] Goldreich, O., Micali, S., Wigderson, A.: How to play ANY mental game or a completeness theorem for protocols with honest majority. In: STOC (1987)

[HKK+19] Hong, C., Katz, J., Kolesnikov, V., Lu, W., Wang, X.: Covert security with public verifiability: faster, leaner, and simpler. In: Ishai, Y., Rijmen, V. (eds.) EUROCRYPT 2019. LNCS, vol. 11478, pp. 97–121. Springer, Cham (2019). https://doi.org/10.1007/978-3-030-17659-4_4

[KB14] Kumaresan, R., Bentov, I.: How to use bitcoin to incentivize correct computations. In: CCS (2014)

[KGC+18] Kalodner, H.A., Goldfeder, S., Chen, X., Matthew Weinberg, S., Felten, E.W.: Arbitrum: scalable, private smart contracts. In: USENIX Security (2018)

[KM15] Kolesnikov, V., Malozemoff, A.J.: Public verifiability in the covert model (almost) for free. In: Iwata, T., Cheon, J.H. (eds.) ASIACRYPT 2015. LNCS, vol. 9453, pp. 210–235. Springer, Heidelberg (2015). https://doi.org/10.1007/978-3-662-48800-3_9

[SSS21] Scholl, P., Simkin, M., Siniscalchi, L.: Multiparty computation with covert security and public verifiability. IACR Cryptology ePrint Archive (2021)

[TR19] Teutsch, J., Reitwießner, C.: A scalable verification solution for blockchains. CoRR, abs/1908.04756 (2019)

[W+14] Wood, G., et al.: Ethereum: A secure decentralised generalised transaction ledger. Ethereum project yellow paper (2014)

[WRK17a] Wang, X., Ranellucci, S., Katz, J.: Authenticated garbling and efficient maliciously secure two-party computation. In: CCS (2017)

[WRK17b] Wang, X., Ranellucci, S., Katz, J.: Global-scale secure multiparty computation. In: CCS (2017)

[YWZ20] Yang, K., Wang, X., Zhang, J.: More efficient MPC from improved triple generation and authenticated garbling. In: CCS (2020)

[ZDH19] Zhu, R., Ding, C., Huang, Y.: Efficient publicly verifiable 2pc over a blockchain with applications to financially-secure computations. In: CCS (2019)

Lifting Standard Model Reductions to Common Setup Assumptions

Ngoc Khanh Nguyen[1(✉)], Eftychios Theodorakis[2,3(✉)], and Bogdan Warinschi[2,4]

[1] IBM Research Europe – Zurich and ETH Zurich, Zurich, Switzerland
nkn@zurich.ibm.com
[2] DFINITY, Zurich, Switzerland
crypto@eftychis.org
[3] Dicrypt, San Francisco, USA
[4] University of Bristol, Bristol, UK
csxbw@bristol.ac.uk

Abstract. In this paper we show that standard model black-box reductions naturally lift to various setup assumptions, such as the random oracle (ROM) or ideal cipher model. Concretely, we prove that a black-box reduction from a security notion P to security notion Q in the standard model can be turned into a non-programmable black-box reduction from $P_{\mathcal{O}}$ to $Q_{\mathcal{O}}$ in a model with a setup assumption $\mathcal{O}$, where $P_{\mathcal{O}}$ and $Q_{\mathcal{O}}$ are the natural extensions of P and Q to a model with a setup assumption $\mathcal{O}$.

Our results rely on a generalization of the recent framework by Hofheinz and Nguyen (PKC 2019) to support primitives which make use of a trusted setup. Our framework encompasses standard idealized settings like the random oracle and the ideal cipher model. At the core of our main result lie novel properties of negligible functions that can be of independent interest.

1 Introduction

Security reductions. In this paper we investigate the interplay between security reductions and setup assumptions. *Security reductions* [15] are perhaps the single most powerful idea that underlies modern cryptography. Roughly speaking, a security reduction is an algorithm which turns an adversary that breaks some protocol Q into one which breaks some underlying primitive P^1. If such a reduction exists, it follows that if P is secure, then so is Q, so the security of a complex system is reduced to that of its underlying components. Here, and throughout the paper, P and Q are understood as *security notions*; that is classes of instantiations together with an experiment which defines their security. Furthermore, reductions correspond to specific constructions which turn an instance of P into an instance of Q.

[1] We do not attempt to make a sharp distinction between primitives and protocols. We use the terms primitive and protocol loosely and only to emphasize that one employs the other in its design. P may also stand for cryptographic assumption, e.g. factorization is hard, just as Q may stand for a more involved primitive, e.g. authenticated encryption.

G. Hanaoka et al. (Eds.): PKC 2022, LNCS 13178, pp. 130–160, 2022.
https://doi.org/10.1007/978-3-030-97131-1_5

The landscape of reductions has been carefully mapped via a taxonomy introduced by Reingold, Trevisan and Vadhan (RTV) [22] and later refined by Baecher, Brzuska, and Fischlin [1]. In its latest incarnation, the taxonomy identifies three components relevant to reductions, namely, the construction, the adversary and the instance used in the construction, and classifies reductions depending on how they access these components. Of central interest in this taxonomy are the so-called "black-box" reductions where the reduction only gets oracle access (i.e. only input/output) to the adversary; further variants distinguish between how the reduction accesses the construction and the instance of the primitive used in the construction. Indeed, with only very few exceptions, the cryptographic practice employs black-box reductions. Not only are these reductions simpler to design but black-box access to the adversary and the instance enables a hierarchical modular design, thereby helping tame the inherent complexity of cryptographic designs.

Setup assumptions. For efficiency reasons, or to circumvent impossibility results, concrete instantiations of cryptographic constructs often rely on setup assumptions. That is, constructions make use of already set-up trusted components. Well-known examples of such assumptions include the random beacon model [21], the random oracle [3], the ideal cipher model [23], the common random string model [4], and its common reference string variant. Other examples include the quantum random oracle [5] or access to specific hardware [9,14,20].

Reductions may use setup assumptions in fundamental ways. They may track the adversary's queries towards the random oracle and program the output of random oracles at dynamically identified inputs. They can access a trapdoor associated to a common random string which allows them to decrypt adversarial ciphertexts or equivocate commitments.

In this paper we are interested in the interplay between reductions and security assumptions. Most of the previous work on classifying reductions does not explicitly surface the use of setup assumptions and, a priori, are set in the standard (vanilla) model. A notable exception is the work of Fischlin et al. [13] who extends the black-box separation techniques to get impossibility results for various constructions even in settings with a (or with variants of the) random oracle model.

The problem. In this paper we investigate the interaction between reductions and setup assumptions from a different perspective which we detail below. For concreteness, in our motivating discussion we use the random oracle as an example setup assumption under consideration. Nonetheless, our work treats generically other settings as well.

Assume that we have already designed a black-box reduction from some protocol Q to a primitive P. The reduction is in the standard model. Then consider protocol $Q_{\mathcal{O}}$ which uses in its construction instantiations of the primitive $P_{\mathcal{O}}$ which potentially rely on the random oracle $\mathcal{O}$. Can we conclude something about the security of $Q_{\mathcal{O}}$? Put differently, does a black-box reduction from Q to

P in the standard model *lift* to a reduction from $Q_{\mathcal{O}}$ to $P_{\mathcal{O}}$? And what, and how does one define the extension of $P_{\mathcal{O}}$ to the random oracle, in the first place?

We contend that the answer is far from obvious. The first obstacle is a syntactic one. Observe that an adversary against $Q_{\mathcal{O}}$ makes queries that exercise the functionality of the protocol yet also queries the random oracle. The reduction from Q to P "knows" how to deal with the former type of queries but makes no provisions for the latter type. We consider the natural extension of the standard model reduction to a non-programming random oracle reduction, where the reduction simply forwards the queries and answers between the adversary and the random oracle.

The second obstacle is more substantial. How would one argue that the random oracle reduction works? Since the existence of the standard model reduction is the only available handle one would need to relate the event that a random oracle adversary wins to the event that a standard adversary wins. However, there is a fundamental difference between the standard model setting and the random oracle one.

In the standard model the only information available to the adversary about the internal state of the protocol is whatever can be inferred from their communication mediated by the security game. In the random oracle model, however, the adversary and the protocol indirectly share state through their joint access to the random oracle. With this in mind, it is unclear how to map events from the joint-state setting to the standard model or, indeed, whether this is even possible. It is conceivable that the adversary manages to break the protocol *because* of the shared state and this is something which the standard model reduction may not even account for. Looking ahead, we show how to bypass these obstacles and provide a positive answer to the question we posed above. We detail our results next.

2 Our contributions

FORMAL FOUNDATIONS. Our first contribution is a framework which allows to talk about "lifting" notions and reductions between notions from the standard model to a model with setup assumptions. Our starting point is the recent framework of Hofheinz and Nguyen [16], who in turn build on the work of Reingold, Trevisan, and Vadhan [22]. In their framework, the notion of a primitive has two key ingredients: i) a set theoretic notion of an *instance* (essentially the set of all instantiations for the primitive), and ii) an explicit notion of a *security* game – defined as an interactive (oracle) Turing machine (and an associated advantage function). We extend this framework in two ways. First, we formalize *setup assumptions* as a mathematical object, essentially as family of distributions over sets of functions. Later in the section, we outline a number of technical challenges we need to overcome to make this approach rigorous, and make our definitions precise and general. One can then extend arbitrary security games to include setup assumptions by providing to the adversary (and the primitive) black-box access to a function; which is sampled in an eager manner (from a computational perspective) according to the distribution(s) before the execution begins. Our abstract approach subsumes many of the widely used setup assumptions including the random oracle model, the CRS model, and the ideal cipher model.

Second, we provide a careful treatment of the notion of primitive instances. Both [22] and [16] define instances of a primitive as arbitrary sets of Turing machines. This approach is too abstract for our purposes since it does not give rise to a meaningful way of lifting the notion of an instantiation from the standard model to the random oracle model. A more concrete definition is necessary that allows one to explicitly define correctness and security membership sets for the primitives. We opt for identifying primitive instances by considering an explicit *correctness* game associated to the primitive.

With these extensions in place, we can then rigorously define the extension of a particular cryptographic notion to a specific setup assumption and the lifting of a reduction from the standard model to a model with a setup assumption.

MAIN RESULT. Our main result establishes that fully black-box reductions in the standard model indeed *do* lift to setup assumptions. That is, if a standard model reduction from some protocol Q to some primitive P exists, then the reduction (or rather its canonical extension) also "works" in the setup assumption. The proof of this result is along the following lines. Once an individual instance of the setup assumption is fixed, then the adversary can be viewed as an adversary in the standard model with the instance of the setup hardwired in its code; the same observation holds for the primitive. One can therefore establish a relation between the success of the reduction and the success of the adversary, for each individual instance of the setup assumption. The crux of the proof is to show how to "aggregate" the distinct individual bounds on advantage functions to get a bound on the adversary's advantage when the setup is sampled according to its defining distribution.

A related and somewhat simpler case of this problem is to show that instantiating a protocol with a *correct* instance of the primitive with a setup assumption yields a *correct* instance of the protocol (with a setup assumption). We cast both of these problems as a generic property of (countable) sets of certain type of families of negligible functions.

TECHNICAL CHALLENGES. As it soon becomes clear in the paper, we require a lot of mathematical machinery, and it is instructive to understand the source of some of the complications we deal with. In particular, there are two related challenges rooted in an interesting interplay between fully black-box reductions and random oracles: (i) how to define a generic notion of a setup assumption and (ii) how to define the adversary's advantage. Recall that a fully black-box reduction "works" even if the adversary against the protocol is unbounded. In particular, the reduction needs to work even for an adversary that with some small probability does not stop and instead keeps on querying the random oracle on increasingly larger inputs. How should one then define the advantage of the adversary? The difficulty here is identifying the underlying sample space of the experiment since an unbounded adversary will essentially require an unbounded random tape.

This discussion also sheds some light on our modeling of a setup assumption. Intuitively, we would like to define a setup assumption simply as a function from some domain X to some co-domain Y to which the different parties involved in the execution get access. The function would need to be sampled, eagerly, at the beginning of the execution. This intuitively appealing approach does not work for the type of infinite execution in the above discussion. For the random oracle model we would have $X = Y = \{0,1\}^*$ and it's not clear how to sample from this space "uniformly at random" as one would expect.

Our solution is to view the setup as a family of sampling algorithms indexed by a natural number ℓ. For each ℓ the setup is sampled from finite sets of functions with (now bounded) domain X_ℓ and range Y. Our formalization enforces that $X_\ell \subseteq X_{\ell+1}$ and that sampling is "consistent" across the parameters, that is the distribution on $Y^{X_{\ell+1}}$ extends naturally the distribution on Y^{X_ℓ}. For each parameter ℓ we define a corresponding execution model where the execution of the game aborts if either the adversary or the construction queries the setup on a point outside X_ℓ. With these bounds in place, we can rigorously show the sample space, required by the setup assumption, is well-defined, and the advantage of the adversary for each individual parameter is well defined and converges. That is the corresponding sums parameterized over ℓ converge and thus it makes sense to define the notions of adversarial advantage and correctness.

APPLICATIONS. In order to illustrate the practicality of our main result, we present the following simple example. Consider the Lamport construction of a one-time (OT) signature scheme out of a one-way function (OWF). Let us call the generic construction $\mathsf{Lamp}[\cdot]$. The traditional reduction shows that $\mathsf{Lamp}[f]$ is a secure OT signature scheme if f is a OWF: for any OWF instance f, an adversary against $\mathsf{Lamp}[f]$ can be used in a black-box way to break f. Note that the reduction allows to establish the security of OT signature instances of the form $\mathsf{Lamp}[f]$ *only for instantiations* of f in the standard model.

Consider now an OWF instance which uses a random oracle (RO), e.g. consider the construction $g^{\mathcal{O}}$, where g simply forwards its inputs to the random oracle $\mathcal{O}$ and returns the result. We claim that, given the state of the art, it is not possible to immediately conclude $\mathsf{Lamp}[g^{\mathcal{O}}]$ is a secure OT signature. Indeed, one cannot draw any rigorous conclusions from existing results: even brushing under the carpet that $g^{\mathcal{O}}$ is "obviously" a OWF, the key observation is that the scheme $\mathsf{Lamp}[g^{\mathcal{O}}]$ is a scheme in the RO model. So, the existing reduction does not apply. It is here where our main result is useful: it lifts the reduction from the standard model to the random oracle model and allows us to conclude that the security of $\mathsf{Lamp}[f]$ reduces to that of f, even if f is a construction in the RO.

Obviously, one can re-establish the security of $\mathsf{Lamp}[g^{\mathcal{O}}]$ directly, in the random oracle, but that would require a new proof where one would have to redo the interesting part of the reduction.

To give another example, consider the black-box construction of a NM-CPA scheme out of a semantically secure scheme by Choi, Soled, Malkin, and Wee

[10]. For brevity we shall call the construction CSMW. Their result shows that CSMW[Enc] is an NM-CPA scheme for any semantically secure scheme in the standard model.

Consider now the instantiation of CSMW[BR] where BR is the concrete semantically secure scheme from the original RO paper by Bellare and Rogaway [2], i.e. for a trapdoor permutation f then $\mathrm{Enc}(m) = f(r)||H(r) \oplus m$. Our results allow one to conclude that CSMW[BR] is an NM-CPA scheme in the RO model. Without this contribution, one would have to the best of our knowledge provide a direct reduction to the security of f[2]. Generally, our results expose the concrete security gap, yet the theorems allow for abstract, and relatively simple, proofs as shown in Sect. 5.5.

Discussion. Our main result shows how to lift fully black-box reductions set in the standard model to a model with a setup. In particular, we rely in a reasonably strong way on the fact that such reductions can deal with unbounded adversaries – at some point we need to hardwire a potentially large table (representing the setup) into adversaries and implementations. Consequently, the resulting constructions may not be efficient anymore. In turn this implies that our result does not immediately extend to a reduction which is only guaranteed to work for efficient adversaries e.g. [1, Section 2.6]. That would be extending our result to BBBa reductions using the terminology of [1]. Restricting our results to such a setting would, however, allow us to avoid many complications that the unbounded nature of the random oracle causes, as outlined above.

An intriguing question is whether our results extend to the case where starting reduction/construction is already in a model with already an idealized setup (as opposed to the standard model). In particular, answering this question raises the question of how idealized models interact/compose. We leave both of these questions to further work.

Related work. The closest work to ours is the work of Hofheinz and Nguyen [16]. They introduce a generic framework for abstractly specifying games (and security reductions) and use it to study the relation between single instance and multi-instance security of primitives. Our work extends their framework with setup assumptions and explicit correctness games, and we study a different extension of the reduction. A somewhat related line of work studies "relativizing" reductions [1,18,22]. This concept borrowed from complexity theory is about establishing relations of the type: if primitive P can be instantiated (securely) then primitive Q can also be instantiated (securely). Such a relation "relativizes" if the statement holds even if the adversaries against P and Q have access to an arbitrary oracle Π. Although apparently related, the focus and results of that line of work are quite different.

RTV [22] assumed probabilistic polynomial time oracle machines when introducing relativizing reductions. In particular, they asserted that for a primitive

[2] Note that this would incorporate the reduction in CSMW as well as some specific, potentially smarter way, of answering RO queries of the adversary against CSMW[BR].

with oracle access to exist there must be a PPTOM machine that can compute it and that no PPTOM machine breaks it (see Definition 2 in the full version of [22] or definition 5 of [1]). Lifting does not have that restriction, and is as such a more general and flexible notion. A lifted reduction holds even if the adversary performs a countable number of queries from an infinite query space. Furthermore, we do not require an efficient implementation in the idealized model (see Definition 5). The same holds for the security definition – even though as is standard we define here security via a PPT game – one may transfer our result to non-polynomial time security settings. As such our tooling and approach can accommodate oracle querying with non-trivial, non-finite, underlying probability distributions.

Note also the difference is one of intent. In relativizing reductions, the security of the primitive under question is not impacted by the choice of oracle the adversary has access to. The reduction must hold *for any* oracle. This of course can rule out such reductions due to oracle separation results. In our work we focus on a particular idealized model and inquire if we can "lift" the security to this idealized model.

A rich line of research, also originating in the seminal work of Rudich and Impagliazzo [18] and continuing with the works of Boneh and Venkatesan [6], Simon [24] and Hsiao and Reyzin [17] has developed a number of black-box separation techniques. These can be used to show negative results of the type: no black-box construction of protocol Q out of primitive P exists, or conversely that no black-box reduction from Q to P exists. Such results are important to rule out minimal assumption for the existence of Q, or identify the need for non-black box constructions but do not serve as support for drawing positive results.

3 Preliminaries

3.1 Notation

For two arbitrary sets X and Y we write Y^X for the set of all functions from X to Y. Let $\mathbb{N} = \{0, 1, 2, 3, \dots, \}$ be the set of natural numbers. We use $\lambda \in \mathbb{N}$ to denote the security parameter, which is a natural number; we assume that it is implicitly provided to all algorithms in the unary representation 1^λ, unless stated otherwise.

We use the shorthand PPT for the Probabilistic Polynomial Time algorithms – in the (unary) security parameter λ. We describe $(y_1, \dots) \leftarrow_\$ \mathcal{A}(1^\lambda, x_1, \dots; r)$ as an event when $\mathcal{A}$ gets $(1^\lambda, x_1, \dots)$ as input, uses fresh random coins r and outputs $(y_1, \dots)$. If $\mathcal{A}$ is deterministic then we simply write $(y_1, \dots) \leftarrow \mathcal{A}(1^\lambda, x_1, \dots)$. Let us write $\mathcal{A}^B$ to denote that $\mathcal{A}$ has black-box access to algorithm B, meaning it sees only its input-output behaviour. The notation $\mathcal{A}^{(\cdot)}$ means that $\mathcal{A}$ expects a black-box access to some other algorithm. Similarly as in [13], we highlight that when an algorithm $\mathcal{B}$ is given oracle access to $\mathcal{A}^{\mathcal{O}}$ for a particular oracle $\mathcal{O}$ then $\mathcal{B}$ does not get to answer $\mathcal{A}$'s queries to $\mathcal{O}$. Throughout the paper, $\perp$ denotes an error symbol.

For a finite set S, we denote its cardinality by $|S|$ and write $s \leftarrow_{\$} S$ meaning that we choose an element s from S uniformly at random. For readability, we define $[k] = \{1, \dots, k\}$ for $k \in \mathbb{N}$ and $[a, b] = \{x \in \mathbb{R} : a \leq x \leq b\}$. Set S is countable if there exists an injective map $\phi : S \to \mathbb{N}$.

A function $\epsilon : \mathbb{N} \to \mathbb{R}$ is negligible if for any $c \in \mathbb{N}$, there exists $N \in \mathbb{N}$ such that for all $\lambda \geq N$: $|\epsilon(\lambda)| < 1/\lambda^c$. We write $\mathsf{negl}(\lambda)$ for an unspecified negligible function in λ. In general, we denote with negl to be a set of all negligible functions. Similarly, we define UBnegl to be the set of functions $f : \mathbb{N} \to \mathbb{R}$ which are upper-bounded by a negligible function. Concretely, $f \in \mathsf{UBnegl}$ if and only if there exists $\epsilon(\cdot) \in \mathsf{negl}$ such that $f(\lambda) \leq \epsilon(\lambda)$ for all $\lambda \in \mathbb{N}$. We highlight that functions in UBnegl are not necessarily negligible, e.g. the constant function $f(\lambda) = -1$. By definition of a negligible function we obtain the following lemma.

Lemma 1. *Let $f : \mathbb{N} \to \mathbb{R}$ be a function. Then, the following conditions are equivalent.*

1. $f \in \mathsf{UBnegl}$,
2. *function* $g(\lambda) := \max\{f(\lambda), 0\}$ *is negligible,*
3. *for all* $c \in \mathbb{N}$, *there exists* $N \in \mathbb{N}$ *such that for all* $\lambda \geq N$: $f(\lambda) < 1/\lambda^c$.

3.2 Limits and Suprema

Let A be a (possibly uncountable) set. Then, for a function $f : A \to \mathbb{R}$ we define the supremum $\sup_{a \in A} f(a)$ to be the smallest real number t (if exists) such that $f(a) \leq t$ for all $a \in A$. In this paper, will use the following simple lemmas. For completeness, we provide the proofs in Appendix A.

Lemma 2. *Let A, S be non-empty sets, where S is either finite or countable, and $(f_s)_{s \in S}$ be a sequence of functions $f_s : A \to \mathbb{R}$. If for all $s \in S$, $\sup_{a \in A} f_s(a)$ exists and if $\sup_{(a_s \in A)_{s \in S}} \sum_{s \in S} f_s(a_s)$ exists then*

$$\sum_{s \in S} \sup_{a \in A} f_s(a) = \sup_{(a_s \in A)_{s \in S}} \sum_{s \in S} f_s(a_s).$$

Lemma 3. *Let A be a non-empty set and $(f_a)_{a \in A}$ be a family of non-decreasing functions $f_a : \mathbb{N} \to \mathbb{R}$. Then:*

$$\lim_{k \to +\infty} \sup_{a \in A} f_a(k) = \sup_{a \in A} \lim_{k \to +\infty} f_a(k)$$

assuming $\sup_{a \in A} \lim_{k \to +\infty} f_a(k)$ and $\lim_{k \to +\infty} f_a(k)$ exist for all $a \in A$.

Lemma 4. *Let $f : \mathbb{N} \times \mathbb{N} \to [0, 1]$ be function such that for all $k, \ell \in \mathbb{N}$: $f(k, \ell) \leq f(k+1, \ell)$ and $f(k, \ell) \leq f(k, \ell+1)$. Then, $\lim_{k \to +\infty} \lim_{\ell \to +\infty} f(k, \ell)$ exists and*

$$\lim_{k \to +\infty} \lim_{\ell \to +\infty} f(k, \ell) = \lim_{\ell \to +\infty} \lim_{k \to +\infty} f(k, \ell) = \lim_{k \to +\infty} f(k, k).$$

Lemma 5. *Let S be a non-empty, either finite or countable set and $f : \mathbb{N} \times S \rightarrow [0,1]$ be a function which satisfies $f(k,s) \leq f(k+1,s)$ and*

$$\sum_{s \in S} f(k,s) \in [0,1]$$

for all $k \in \mathbb{N}, s \in S$. Then

$$\sum_{s \in S} \lim_{k \rightarrow +\infty} f(k,s) = \lim_{k \rightarrow +\infty} \sum_{s \in S} f(k,s).$$

3.3 Fully Black-Box Reductions in the Standard Model

We briefly recall the framework on primitives and black-box reductions by Reingold, Trevisan, and Vadhan [22] (RTV). Using their notation, primitive P is a pair $\langle F_P, R_P \rangle$ where F_P is a set of functions $f : \{0,1\}^* \rightarrow \{0,1\}^*$ and R_P is a relation over pairs (f, M) for $f \in F_P$ and machine M. One can think of F_P as implementations of a primitive P and R_P as security conditions on F_P.

Then, there is a *fully black-box* reduction from a primitive $P = \langle F_P, R_P \rangle$ to $Q = \langle F_Q, R_Q \rangle$ if there exist PPT machines G, S such that:

- for every function $f \in F_Q$, $G^f \in F_P$,
- for every function $f \in F_Q$ and every adversary $\mathcal{A}$, $(G^f, \mathcal{A}) \in R_P \implies (f, S^{\mathcal{A}}) \in R_Q$.

Informally, G and S are called the *generic construction* and the *reduction* respectively. As mentioned in [22], this definition of reduction does not apply to non-uniform or information-theoretic notions of security. They also define different types of reductions such as semi-black-box or relativizing reductions.

There is a long line of research on formalising (black-box) reductions [1, 13,16,19]. In this paper we adapt the recently defined notion of fully black-box reductions by Hofheinz and Nguyen [16]. The main difference to the RTV framework is that the security conditions are represented as a security game instead of a set of relations. Thus, Hofheinz and Nguyen could formally define what is meant by "breaking one primitive with about the same success as the other primitive" in terms of probabilities.

Definition 1 ([16]). *A primitive P is a tuple $\langle \mathbb{P}, F_P, R_P, \sigma \rangle$ where:*

- *$\mathbb{P}$ is a pair of sets (A, B)*
- *F_P is a subset of $\{f : A \rightarrow B\}$,*
- *$R_P^{(\cdot,\cdot)}$ is a PPT security algorithm,*
- *$\sigma : \mathbb{N} \rightarrow [0,1]$ is a security threshold.*

We say that f is an implementation of P if $f \in F_P$.

Note that usually we define F_P via the use of correctness games.

Since we do not consider primitives in the multi-instance setting as in [16], we already include the setup S_P in the security algorithm R_P. For readability, in this paper we also do not restrict the input space for R_P to call f, i.e. $C = A$ in [16, Definition 4].

There are two main differences between this definition and the one proposed by RTV. Firstly, $\mathbb{P} = (A, B)$ is a pair of sets which describe the domain and the co-domain. This modification enables to characterize implementations which are defined on more abstract mathematical models (e.g. groups, rings) rather than on $\{0,1\}^*$. Secondly, R_P is now an efficient algorithm which expects black-box access to both an implementation f and an adversary $\mathcal{A}$. One can think of R_P as a security game, e.g. one-wayness or IND-CPA game. Here, we want to associate for each pair $(f, \mathcal{A})$ a value in $[0,1]$ which corresponds to the probability of $\mathcal{A}$ winning the R_P game against f. We recall the definition of an advantage from [16].

Definition 2 ([16]). *Let $P = \langle \mathbb{P}, F_P, R_P, \sigma \rangle$ be a primitive. Take $f \in F_P$ and any algorithm $\mathcal{A}$. We define the advantage of $\mathcal{A}$ in breaking f as*

$$\mathsf{Adv}^P_{f,\mathcal{A}}[(\lambda)] := \Pr\left[1 \leftarrow_\$ R_P^{f,\mathcal{A}}\right] - \sigma(\lambda)$$

where the probability is defined over random coins in the system [3].

We say that $\mathcal{A}$ $P-$breaks f if $\mathsf{Adv}^P_{f,\mathcal{A}}[(\lambda)] \notin \mathsf{UBnegl}$, i.e. there is no negligible function $\epsilon : \mathbb{N} \to \mathbb{R}$ such that $\mathsf{Adv}^P_{f,\mathcal{A}}[(\lambda)] \leq \epsilon(\lambda)$ for all $\lambda \in \mathbb{N}$. Primitive P is called secure if there exists an implementation f of P such that there are no PPT algorithms $\mathcal{A}$ that $P-$break f.

Example 1. We define a primitive corresponding to an IND-CPA secure public-key encryption scheme as $\mathsf{PKE} = \langle \mathbb{P}_{\mathsf{PKE}}, F_{\mathsf{PKE}}, R_{\mathsf{PKE}}, \frac{1}{2} \rangle$ where $\mathbb{P}_{\mathsf{PKE}}$ defines the domain and range for the encryption schemes, R_{PKE} is the IND-CPA game and F_{PKE} the set that contains encryption schemes, which we could define via a "encryption scheme correctness" game.

We briefly explain why we want the advantage to be in UBnegl rather than negl. Note that there are certain types of adversaries, for which their advantage is not negligible, and yet they do not win the security game in the usual sense. For instance, consider a decisional game, e.g. the IND-CPA game, where the adversary has to guess the bit, and set the security threshold $\sigma(\lambda) = \frac{1}{2}$. Then, an adversary $\mathcal{A}$, which simply aborts/loops, certainly will not win the IND-CPA game (the security game cannot detect $\mathcal{A}$ looping since it is only given black-box access). However, its advantage, as defined in Definition 2, will be $0 - \frac{1}{2} = -\frac{1}{2}$, which is not negligible (but still upper-bounded by a negligible function).

Using the definitions above, Hofheinz and Nguyen formalise fully-black box reductions as follows.

[3] Usually, the security threshold function σ is a constant – either 0 or $\frac{1}{2}$.

Definition 3 (Fully Black-Box Reductions). *Let $P = \langle \mathbb{P}_1, F_P, R_P, \sigma \rangle$ and $Q = \langle \mathbb{P}_2, F_Q, R_Q, \tau \rangle$ be primitives. Then, there is a fully black-box reduction from P to Q if there exist PPT algorithms $G^{(\cdot)}, S^{(\cdot)}$ such that:*

- *for every implementation f of Q, G^f is an implementation of P,*
- *for every implementation f of Q and every (unbounded) algorithm $\mathcal{A}$, if $\mathcal{A}$ P-breaks G^f then $S^{\mathcal{A}}$ Q-breaks f.*

4 Average of Negligible Functions

In this section we establish several technical properties of negligible functions which will be crucial when proving our main reduction correspondence result. It is a well known that given a finite set of negligible functions $P = \{f_1, f_2, \ldots, f_n\}$, the average $\frac{1}{n}\sum_{i=1}^{n} f_i$ of these functions is also negligible. We provide a similar result in the setting when the set P is countable.

Informally, suppose we have a function $P : \mathbb{N} \times \mathbb{N} \rightarrow [-1, 1]$ such that for any $f : \mathbb{N} \rightarrow \mathbb{N}$, function $P_f(\lambda) := P(\lambda, f(\lambda))$ is negligible in λ. Then, for any discrete distribution $\mathcal{D}$ on $\mathbb{N}$ and an infinite sequence of independent random variables $X_1, X_2, \ldots \leftarrow_{\$} \mathcal{D}$, the function $\mathbb{E}(P) : \mathbb{N} \rightarrow [-1, 1]$ defined as

$$\mathbb{E}(P)(\lambda) := \mathbb{E}\left(P(\lambda, X_\lambda)\right)$$

is also negligible. Intuitively, this result says that if a set P[4] consists of only negligible functions then the "expectation of all functions", defined as $\mathbb{E}(P)$ and also called informally as the average of P, is also negligible.

Below we state a generalisation of this result. Roughly speaking and using the language from the previous paragraph, it says the following. Assume there exists a correspondence between negligible functions from set Q to set P. If the expectation of Q is negligible then so is the expectation of P. Clearly, by setting the set Q to only contain the zero functions yields the result described above.

To apply these observations in the context of fully black-box reductions, we work with functions in UBnegl (see Sect. 3.1) rather than with negligible functions.

Theorem 1. *Let $k \in \mathbb{N}$, S be a (possibly uncountable) set and $(\mathcal{D}_\lambda)_{\lambda \in \mathbb{N}}$ be a sequence of discrete probability distributions $\mathcal{D}_\lambda : S_\lambda \rightarrow [0, 1]$ over countable sets $S_\lambda \subseteq S$. Take arbitrary functions $P, Q_1, \ldots, Q_k : \mathbb{N} \times S \rightarrow [-1, 1]$. Suppose that for every function $f : \mathbb{N} \rightarrow S$, the following holds:*

$$\forall i \in [k], Q_i(\lambda, f(\lambda)) \in \mathsf{UBnegl} \implies P(\lambda, f(\lambda)) \in \mathsf{UBnegl}.$$

Then, for $X_\lambda \leftarrow_{\$} D_\lambda$ we have

$$\forall i \in [k], \mathbb{E}\left(Q_i(\lambda, X_\lambda)\right) \in \mathsf{UBnegl} \implies \mathbb{E}\left(P(\lambda, X_\lambda)\right) \in \mathsf{UBnegl}.$$

[4] Formally, we mean the set of functions $\{P(\lambda, f(\lambda)) : f \in \{g : \mathbb{N} \rightarrow \mathbb{N}\}\}$.

Proof. Suppose that each $\mathbb{E}(Q_i(\lambda, X_\lambda))$ is upper-bounded by a negligible function. Then, for each $i \in [k]$, we can find an infinite sequence of positive integers $J(i,1) < J(i,2) < \ldots$ such that for every $d \in \mathbb{N}$ and any $\lambda \geq J(i,d)$, $\mathbb{E}(Q_i(\lambda, X_\lambda)) < 1/\lambda^d$. Fix $d \in \mathbb{N}$ and define

$$j_d = \max\{2k+1, \max_{i \in [k]} J(i, d+1)\}.$$

We claim that for every $\lambda \geq j_d$, there exists $a \in S_\lambda$ which satisfies:

$$\forall i \in [k], Q_i(\lambda, a) < 1/\lambda^d.$$

First, we fix arbitrary $i \in [k]$ and $\lambda \geq j_d$. Let

$$M_i = \{a : a \in S_\lambda \wedge Q_i(\lambda, a) < 1/\lambda^d\}.$$

We know that $\mathbb{E}(Q_i(\lambda, X_\lambda)) < 1/\lambda^{d+1}$. Therefore,

$$\frac{\Pr[X_\lambda \in S_\lambda \backslash M_i]}{\lambda^d} \leq \frac{\sum_{a \in S_\lambda \backslash M_i} \Pr[X_\lambda = a]}{\lambda^d} \leq \sum_{a \in S_\lambda} \Pr[X_\lambda = a] \cdot Q_i(\lambda, a) < \frac{1}{\lambda^{d+1}}.$$

In particular, $\Pr[X_\lambda \in S_\lambda \backslash M_i] \leq 1/\lambda$. Then, by the union bound we have:

$$\Pr[\exists i, X_\lambda \in S_\lambda \backslash M_i] \leq k/\lambda \leq 2k/j_d < 1.$$

Hence, $\Pr[\forall i, X_\lambda \in M_i] > 0$ so there exists $a \in S_\lambda$ such that for every $i \in [k], Q_i(\lambda, a) < 1/\lambda^d$. For $\lambda \geq j_d$, let $a(\lambda)$ be the smallest such value.

Next, we prove the following lemma.

Lemma 6. *Let $c \in \mathbb{N}$. Then, there exists a positive integer $d \geq c$, such that there are only finitely many pairs (λ, a) which satisfy the following conditions:*

$$a \in S_\lambda \wedge \forall i, Q_i(\lambda, a) < 1/\lambda^d \wedge P(\lambda, a) \geq 1/\lambda^c. \quad (1)$$

Proof. We prove it by contradiction. Suppose there exists a positive integer c, such that for every $d \geq c$, there are infinitely many pairs (λ, a) which satisfy (1). We construct a function $f : \mathbb{N} \to S$ such that for $i \in [k]$, $Q_i(\lambda, f(\lambda)) \in \mathsf{UBnegl}$ but $P(\lambda, f(\lambda)) \notin \mathsf{UBnegl}$. Then, we get a contradiction.

Fix $d \geq c$. Let us introduce the following notation. First, $L(\ell, d)$ is the smallest $\lambda \geq \ell$ such that there exists an integer a so that (λ, a) satisfies (1). Additionally, denote $R(\ell, d)$ to be the smallest a such that $(L(\ell, d), a)$ satisfies (1). Then, by definition $(L(\ell, d), R(\ell, d))$ satisfy (1). Finally, set $I(c) = j_c$ and $I(d+1) = \max\{j_{d+1}, L(I(d), d) + 1\}$.

We define the function f as follows. For $\lambda < I(c)$, set $f(\lambda) = x$ where x is an arbitrary fixed element in S_λ. Then, for $I(d) \leq \lambda < I(d+1)$, where $d \geq c$, define:

$$f(\lambda) = \begin{cases} R(I(d), d) \text{ if } \lambda = L(I(d), d) \\ a(\lambda) \text{ otherwise.} \end{cases}$$

Recall that $a(\lambda)$ is the smallest value a such that $i \in [k], Q_i(\lambda, a) < 1/\lambda^d$.

We now prove that for each i, $Q_i(\lambda, f(\lambda))$ is upper-bounded by a negligible function. Let $i \in [k]$. By construction, for any $d \in \mathbb{N}$ and $I(d) \leq \lambda < I(d+1)$, we have $Q_i(\lambda, f(\lambda)) < 1/\lambda^d$. Indeed, if $\lambda = L(I(d), d)$ then $(\lambda, f(\lambda))$ satisfies (1). On the other hand, if $\lambda \neq L(I(d), d)$ then since $\lambda \geq I(d) \geq j_d$ we have $Q_i(\lambda, f(\lambda)) = Q_i(\lambda, a(\lambda)) < 1/\lambda^d$.

As a result, for all $\lambda \geq I(d)$ we have $Q_i(\lambda, f(\lambda)) < 1/\lambda^d$. The reason is that for $\lambda \geq I(d)$ there is some $\alpha \geq d$ so that $I(\alpha) \leq \lambda < I(\alpha+1)$. By the observation above, we have $Q_i(\lambda, f(\lambda)) < 1/\lambda^\alpha \leq 1/\lambda^d$. Consequently, $Q_i(\lambda, f(\lambda))$ is upper-bounded by a negligible function.

On the other hand, for all $d \in \mathbb{N}$, we have $P(\lambda, f(\lambda)) \geq 1/\lambda^c$ where $\lambda = L(I(d), d)$. This means that there are infinitely many positive integers λ such that $P(\lambda, f(\lambda)) \geq 1/\lambda^c$. Hence, $P(\lambda, f(\lambda)) \notin \mathsf{UBnegl}$ by Lemma 1. □

Finally, we prove that $\mathbb{E}(P(\lambda, X_\lambda))$ is upper-bounded by a negligible function. Let $c \in \mathbb{N}$ and $c' = c + k + 1$. From Lemma 6 we know that there exists $d \geq c'$ such that there are finitely many pairs (λ, a) satisfying (1). Therefore, there is an integer N, such that for all pairs (λ, a), where $\lambda \geq N$, one of the conditions in (1) does not hold. Now, let $m = \max\{2, j_{2d-1}, N\}$. We claim that for all $\lambda \geq m$, $\mathbb{E}(P(\lambda, X_\lambda)) < 1/\lambda^c$. This would imply that $\mathbb{E}(P(\lambda, X_\lambda)) \in \mathsf{UBnegl}$.

Take any $\lambda \geq m$. Let us compute a lower-bound on $\Pr[X_\lambda \in H : X_\lambda \leftarrow_{\$} D_\lambda]$ where

$$H = \{a \in S_\lambda : \forall i \in [k], Q_i(\lambda, a) < 1/\lambda^d\}.$$

We proceed similarly as before. Let $i \in [k]$. Then, we have $\mathbb{E}(Q_i(\lambda, X_\lambda)) < 1/\lambda^{2d}$ since $m \geq j_{2d-1}$. Denote $H_i = \{a \in S_\lambda : Q_i(\lambda, a) < 1/\lambda^d\}$. Thus,

$$\frac{\Pr[X_\lambda \in S_\lambda \backslash H_i]}{\lambda^d} \leq \frac{\sum_{a \in S_\lambda \backslash H_i} \Pr[X_\lambda = a]}{\lambda^d} \leq \sum_{a \in S_\lambda} \Pr[X_\lambda = a] \cdot Q_i(\lambda, a) < \frac{1}{\lambda^{2d}}.$$

Therefore, $\Pr[X_\lambda \in S_\lambda \backslash H_i] < 1/\lambda^d$. Hence, by the union bound we get:

$$\Pr[\exists i \in [k], X_\lambda \in S_\lambda \backslash H_i] \leq k/\lambda^d$$

and thus $\Pr[X_\lambda \in H] \geq 1 - k/\lambda^d$.

Note that each pair (λ, a), where $a \in H$, satisfies the first two conditions in (1). Since $\lambda \geq m \geq N$, we get that $P(\lambda, a) < 1/\lambda^{c'}$. Therefore, we can upper-bound $\mathbb{E}(P(\lambda, X_\lambda))$ as follows:

$$\begin{aligned}
\mathbb{E}(P(\lambda, X_\lambda)) &\leq \sum_{a \in S_\lambda} \Pr[X_\lambda = a] \cdot P(\lambda, a) \\
&\leq \sum_{a \in H} \Pr[X_\lambda = a] \cdot P(\lambda, a) + \sum_{a \notin H} \Pr[X_\lambda = a] \cdot P(\lambda, a) \\
&< \sum_{a \in H} \Pr[X_\lambda = a] \cdot \frac{1}{\lambda^{c'}} + \sum_{a \notin H} \Pr[X_\lambda = a] \qquad (2) \\
&< \frac{\Pr[X_\lambda \in H]}{\lambda^{c'}} + \Pr[X_\lambda \in S \backslash H] \\
&< 1/\lambda^{c'} + k/\lambda^d \\
&< (k+1)/\lambda^{c+k+1} < 1/\lambda^c.
\end{aligned}$$

Thus, $\mathbb{E}(P(\lambda, X_\lambda)) \in \mathsf{UBnegl}$. □

5 Setup Assumptions

In this section we formalize, generically, the notion of a setup assumption.

Such assumptions are ubiquitous in modern cryptography and include, for instance, popular settings such as the Ideal Cipher model [23], the Common Random String (CRS) [4], the Random Oracle model (ROM) [3]. They allow one to bypass impossibility results or simply yield more efficient schemes.

Before we present our definition, we motivate some of the choices we make. Naively, we could simply attempt to construct a Turing machine that samples a function $X \to Y$ according to some arbitrary distribution, which would encode the expected behaviour of the oracle. The astute reader is soon to notice that several questions arise. How do we pick the domain of the oracle? For example, in the random oracle model the query domain is $\{0,1\}^*$ which is infinite. What is then our sample space?

We cannot sample eagerly such a function. While one implementation might simply query a small number of polynomial length values in the security parameter λ, we must recall that reductions should also work for unbounded adversaries. Indeed, an unbounded adversary might query the oracle infinitely many times, which raises a conundrum.

5.1 Formal Model for Setup Assumptions

Our formalization is heavily influenced by having to solve the Random Oracle case outlined above. We proceed as follows. We model the use of a random oracle (viewed as an infinite random tape) via a sequence of *finite* setups. Each setup being parameterized by some parameter $\ell \in \mathbb{N}$ – think about this parameter as a restriction on the size of the valid inputs to the random oracle. As ℓ tends to infinity, the setup becomes a better approximation of a random oracle.

For this approach to be meaningful we require a few additional ingredients. We define X_ℓ to be the first ℓ elements of X. Clearly $X_\ell \subseteq X_{\ell+1}$ and X_ℓ is an increasingly better approximation of X, as ℓ grows. Thus, we seek that when ℓ goes to infinity, X_ℓ comes close to X. Here we enforce a total order on X. Since we only consider countable sets X, we model this total order by fixing an arbitrary injection ϕ between X and $\mathbb{N}$; the total order on X is then induced by transporting on X the total order on $\mathbb{N}$.

We may now define a setup assumption as a tuple $(X, Y, \phi, \mathcal{M})$ where X and Y are the domain and range for all possible setup instances. The setup generator $\mathcal{M}$ takes as input the usual security parameter λ and a parameter ℓ as above. For each λ and ℓ, the setup generator defines some distribution on the set of functions with domain X_ℓ and range Y.

More importantly, we demand that the distributions defined by $\mathcal{M}$ are *consistent* across the choices of ℓ. That is, a function sampled from $Y^{X_{\ell+1}}$ according to $\mathcal{M}_{\ell+1,\lambda}$, when restricted to X_ℓ has the same distribution as a function sampled from $\mathcal{M}_{\ell,\lambda}$. The intuition behind this restriction is that the functions output by the setup should "behave" the same on all entries on which they are defined, independent of the size of the domain specified by ℓ.

This requirement is important since, for instance, we do not wish that altering the size of the query space to $X_{\ell+1}$ affects the behavior of participants that only queries the setup with entries from X_ℓ. As it will become clear a bit later in the paper (Definition 5), this property is necessary to meaningfully define the adversary advantage when ℓ goes to infinity.

The following definition formalizes the discussion above.

Definition 4 (Setup Assumptions). *Define setup assumption as a tuple $M = (X, Y, \phi, \mathcal{M})$ where X, Y are non-empty countable sets, ϕ is an injective map from X to $\mathbb{N}$ and $\mathcal{M}_{(\cdot,\cdot)}$ is a probabilistic algorithm with the following properties. Namely, given a "length" parameter $\ell \in \mathbb{N}$ and a security parameter $\lambda \in \mathbb{N}$, it outputs a function $\mathcal{O} : X_\ell \to Y$ according to some distribution over Y^{X_ℓ}, where*

$$X_\ell := \{x \in X : \phi(x) < \ell\}.$$

Note that this distribution is still discrete. We further call the setup assumption consistent, if for all $\ell \in \mathbb{N}$ and $a_1, \ldots, a_{|X_\ell|} \in Y$ we have:

$$\Pr\left[\bigwedge_{i=1}^{|X_\ell|} f(x_{\ell,i}) = a_i : f \leftarrow_\$ \mathcal{M}_{\ell,\lambda}\right] = \Pr\left[\bigwedge_{i=1}^{|X_\ell|} g(x_{\ell,i}) = a_i : g \leftarrow_\$ \mathcal{M}_{\ell+1,\lambda}\right]$$

where $X_\ell = \{x_{\ell,1}, \ldots, x_{\ell,|X_\ell|}\}$.

Henceforth, we shall simply refer to consistent sampling setup assumptions simply as setup assumption. When working with primitives in the standard model, we will abuse the notation and write $M = \varnothing$.

5.2 Defining Primitives with Setup Assumptions

We build on our notion of a setup assumption defined in the previous section to formalize models for primitives with setup assumptions.

Before we proceed, we introduce the following notation. Suppose the sampler $\mathcal{M}_{(\cdot,\cdot)}$ of M samples a function $\mathcal{O} : X \to Y$ where X and Y are countable and let $\phi : X \to \mathbb{N}$ be a fixed injective map. Then, for an algorithm $\mathcal{A}^{(\cdot)}$ and function $t : \mathbb{N} \to \mathbb{N}$, we denote $\mathcal{A}_t^{(\cdot)}$ to be the algorithm which behaves identically as $\mathcal{A}^{(\cdot)}$ but if a query $x \in X$ is made to the setup assumption, where $\phi(x) > t(\lambda)$, then it automatically aborts. Recall ϕ is our total ordering function. We call t the threshold function. When t is constant, i.e. $t(\lambda) = \ell$ for all λ, then we slightly abuse notation and simply write $\mathcal{A}_\ell^{(\cdot)}$.

We now present the notion of a primitive equipped with a setup assumption. The definition below, refines Definition 1 in two different ways. It introduces as part of the execution model the setup generator and it introduces an explicit correctness notion for the primitive as an additional separate algorithm.

Definition 5. *Primitive P with a setup assumption M is a tuple $\langle \mathbb{P}, M, C_P, R_P, \sigma \rangle$ where:*

- $\mathbb{P}$ *is a pair of sets* (A, B),
- $M = (X, Y, \phi, \mathcal{M})$ *is the setup assumption defining the oracle* $\mathcal{O}$,
- $C_P^{(\cdot,\cdot)}$ *is a correctness algorithm,*
- $R_P^{(\cdot,\cdot)}$ *is a PPT security algorithm (related to* λ*),*
- $\sigma : \mathbb{N} \to [0, 1]$ *is a security threshold.*

We say that $f^{(\cdot)} : A \to B$ *is an implementation of* P *if for all (unbounded) adversaries* $\mathcal{A}^{(\cdot)}$*:*

$$\lim_{k\to+\infty} \lim_{\ell\to+\infty} \Pr\left[1 \leftarrow C_P^{f_k{}^{\mathcal{O}}, \mathcal{A}_\ell^{\mathcal{O}}}\right]$$

is negligible, where probability is over random coins in the environment and especially $\mathcal{O} \leftarrow_{\$} \mathcal{M}_{\max\{k,\ell\},\lambda}$.

For an implementation $f^{(\cdot)}$ *and any algorithm* $\mathcal{A}^{(\cdot)}$*, we define the advantage of* $\mathcal{A}^{(\cdot)}$ *in breaking* $f^{(\cdot)}$ *as*

$$\mathsf{Adv}_{f,\mathcal{A}}^{P}[(\lambda)] := \lim_{k\to+\infty} \lim_{\ell\to+\infty} \Pr\left[1 \leftarrow_{\$} R_P^{f_k^{\mathcal{O}}, \mathcal{A}_\ell^{\mathcal{O}}}\right] - \sigma(\lambda)$$

where the probability is defined over $\mathcal{O} \leftarrow_{\$} M(\max\{k, \ell\}, \lambda)$ *and the random coins in the system.*

We say that $\mathcal{A}$ P*–breaks* $f^{(\cdot)}$ *if* $\mathsf{Adv}_{\mathcal{O}\leftarrow M,f,\mathcal{A}}^{P}[(\lambda)] \notin \mathsf{UBnegl}$. *Furthermore,* $f^{(\cdot)}$ *is called a secure implementation of* P *if there are no PPT algorithms* $\mathcal{A}^{(\cdot)}$ *that* P*–break* $f^{(\cdot)}$.

A few remarks are in order. First, we argue that the notion of correctness and the adversary advantage are well-defined, in that the limits are guaranteed to exist. This property is established by the following lemma. Its proof (in Appendix A) crucially relies on the consistency property of the setup assumption. Broadly speaking, the property guarantees that the behavior of an adversary (in terms of winning the security game) is monotonic with respect to ℓ. That is, if an adversary wins the game when its query space is X_ℓ (with some probability), then the adversary will win (with at least the same probability) the instance of the game where the query space is $X_{\ell+1}$. This property then gives rise to a monotonically non-decreasing sequence upper-bounded by 1, which implies that the desired limit exists.

Lemma 7. *Let* $f^{(\cdot)}$, $\mathcal{A}^{(\cdot)}$ *and* $\mathcal{R}^{(\cdot,\cdot)}$ *be any function, unbounded adversary and PPT machine respectively. Then, for* $M = (X, Y, \phi, \mathcal{M})$*, the following limit exists:*

$$\lim_{k\to+\infty} \lim_{\ell\to+\infty} F(k, \ell),$$

where

$$F(k, \ell) := \Pr\left[1 \leftarrow_{\$} \mathcal{R}^{f_k{}^{\mathcal{O}}, \mathcal{A}_\ell^{\mathcal{O}}}\right]$$

and the probability is over $\mathcal{O} \leftarrow_{\$} \mathcal{M}_{\max\{k,\ell\},\lambda}$ *and the random coins in the environment.*

The proof of the lemma is presented in Appendix A.5.

Second, the limits in the definition of a correct implementation can be swapped or merged into a single parameter, as hinted at in the introduction, by Lemma 4. Nonetheless, we prefer to keep the present formulation since it is particularly helpful for proving our main theorem (Theorem 3).

Finally, our definition no longer describes implementations of a primitive as functions from some abstract implementation set. Instead, we identify correct implementations as those for which no efficient adversary can win a correctness game C_P[5]. The reason for this departure is that we need to formalize what is the extension of a notion P to a setup assumption. Indeed, above we have essentially shown how to define a game with an abstract setup assumption. Lifting a notion from the standard model to some particular setup comes down to simply replacing the setup assumption M (which is $\varnothing$ for the standard model), appropriately.

5.3 Fully Black-Box Non-programmable Reductions

We now introduce a notion of a fully black-box non-programmable reduction between primitives with setup assumptions.

Definition 6. *Let P and Q be primitives with the setup assumption M. We say that there is a fully black-box non-programmable reduction from P to Q in M (written as $P \overset{M}{\hookrightarrow} Q$) if there exist PPT algorithms $G^{(\cdot)}, S^{(\cdot)}$ such that:*

- *for every implementation $f^{(\cdot)}$ of Q, $G^{f^{(\cdot)}}$ is an implementation of P,*
- *for every implementation $f^{(\cdot)}$ of Q and every (unbounded) algorithm $\mathcal{A}^{(\cdot)}$, if $\mathcal{A}^{(\cdot)}$ P-breaks $G^{f^{(\cdot)}}$ then $S^{\mathcal{A}^{(\cdot)}}$ Q-breaks $f^{(\cdot)}$.*

In the literature, S has access to an external oracle $\mathcal{O}$ instead of $\mathcal{A}$. We call this reduction *non-programmable* since we let $\mathcal{A}$ have access to $\mathcal{O}$ via S, meaning that if the adversary wants to query $\mathcal{O}$, it sends the value to S, S passes it to $\mathcal{O}$ and returns to $\mathcal{A}$ what it got from $\mathcal{O}$. Apart from that, S does not query $\mathcal{O}$ at all. From the perspective of $\mathcal{A}$, this is clearly equivalent to $\mathcal{A}$ having access to $\mathcal{O}$, as illustrated in the definition above. There is another type of reduction called *programmable* [13], where S can simulate an oracle on its own. However, we omit the details in this paper.

5.4 Setup Assumption Extensions

In order to describe our main result, we need to define what it means to "naturally extend "the primitive to a setup assumption M. Hence, we define a notion of a $M-$extension of a primitive.

[5] One side effect of this change is that Definition 5 does not cover a number of potential oddities which can be represented using previous frameworks [16,22], e.g. a primitive where the set of valid instances is defined as some undecidable set of Turing machines. However, these cases are irrelevant for our purpose.

Definition 7. *Let $P = \langle \mathbb{P}_1, \varnothing, C_P, R_P, \sigma \rangle$ be a primitive in the standard model and M be a setup assumption. Then, a $M-$extension $P(M)$ of P is the tuple $P(M) = \langle \mathbb{P}_1, M, C_P, R_P, \sigma \rangle$.*

We can now formalize our main result. Namely, if there exists a fully black-box reduction from P to Q in the standard model, then there also exists a fully black-box reduction from $P(M)$ to $Q(M)$, where M is any setup assumption.

Theorem 2 (Ideal Model Correspondence). *Let P and Q be primitives in the standard model and M be any ideal model. Then, assuming a fully black-box reduction in the standard model implies a fully black-box reduction in the ideal model.*

$$P \hookrightarrow Q \implies P(M) \xrightarrow{M} Q(M).$$

We provide the proof in Sect. 6.

Remark. Let (G, S) be a reduction from P to Q. Intuitively, (G, S) should also be a correct reduction from $P(M)$ to $Q(M)$. However, in the M model, the adversary as well as the implementation have access to some "shared state" which is the external oracle. This, however, is not the case in the standard model. Indeed, this additional advice might help an adversary break $P(M)$ but not $Q(M)$. In Theorem 2 we show that if (G, S) is a *fully black-box* reduction, then it can be extended to a setup assumption representing some ideal model. However, the open question remains whether the same property holds when (G, S) is not fully black-box anymore.

$$\mathcal{A} \; P - \text{breaks} \; G^f \overset{R}{\longleftarrow\!\!\!-\!\!\!\longrightarrow} S^{f,\mathcal{A}} \; Q - \text{breaks} \; f$$
$$\downarrow \qquad\qquad\qquad\qquad\qquad\qquad\qquad \downarrow$$
$$\mathcal{B}^{\mathcal{O}} \; P - \text{breaks} \; G^{f^{\mathcal{O}}} \overset{R}{\hookleftarrow\!\!\!-\!\!\!\rightarrow} S^{f^{\mathcal{O}},\mathcal{B}^{\mathcal{O}}} \; Q - \text{breaks} \; f^{\mathcal{O}}$$

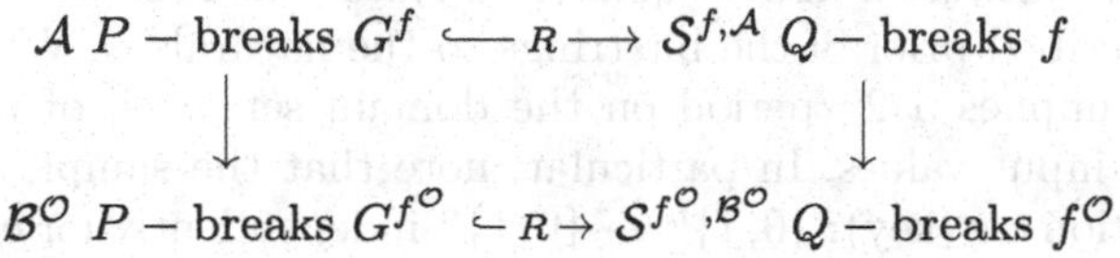

Fig. 1. We prove a correspondence for fully black-box reductions in the standard model to ideal models.

5.5 Common Instantiations of Setup Assumptions

In this section we present common ideal models in the framework we introduced. We also prove they satisfy the consistent sampling property.

THE RANDOM ORACLE MODEL. This model [3] is one of the cornerstones of modern cryptography. A random oracle represents ideal hash functions. When a party queries with a bitstring $\{0,1\}^*$, the random oracle, given a security parameter λ, samples an element from $\{0,1\}^\lambda$ uniformly at random.

Formally, we define a random oracle setup assumption M_{ROM} as the tuple

$$M_{\text{ROM}} = (\{0,1\}^*, \{0,1\}^*, \phi, \mathcal{M}_{\ell,\lambda}^{\text{ROM}})$$

Note we can well-order all bit-strings, for instance as follows: $0, 1, 00, 01, \cdot$. Here, ϕ simply outputs the index of the ordering above. Now define Y to be a set of arbitrary bit-strings with cardinality equal to some polynomial of λ. That is $Y_\lambda = \{0,1\}^{\ell_{\text{out}}(\lambda)}$, for some length function ℓ_{out} – see [8]. Then $\mathcal{M}^{\text{ROM}}_{\ell,\lambda}$ samples from $Y_\lambda^{X_\ell}$ which has cardinality $2^{\ell_{\text{out}}(\lambda)\ell}$. Thus the sampler $\mathcal{M}^{\text{ROM}}_{\ell,\lambda}$ iterates over all ℓ inputs at setup, and for each one picks independently uniformly at random with probability $\frac{1}{2^{\ell_{\text{out}}(\lambda)}}$ an element from Y.

Proposition 1. *The above construction M_{ROM} is a consistent setup assumption.*

Proof. We can easily see that on each instantiation of the setup the sampler picks each element independently at random. Thus, the sampler does not depend on elements ordered after i to pick the value of i. □

THE IDEAL CIPHER MODEL. In the Ideal Cipher Model [23] the participants may access an ideal cipher $\mathsf{enc} : \{0,1\}^k \times \{0,1\}^n \rightarrow \{0,1\}^n$, s.t. enc are random permutations $\{0,1\}^n \rightarrow \{0,1\}^n$ that have been independently and uniformly drawn (with replacement for each key). Recall that the Ideal Cipher model is equivalent to the Random Oracle model [11] (original [12]).

We can define the setup assumption for an (k, n)-ideal cipher similarly to ROM above.

$$M_{IC} = \left(\{0,1\}^* \times \{0,1\}^*, \{0,1\}^*, \phi : \{0,1\}^* \times \{0,1\}^* \rightarrow \mathbb{N}, \mathcal{M}^{\text{IC}}_{\ell,\lambda}\right).$$

For simplicity we just set k above equal to λ. Note that here we use the normal ordering as described prior of the bitstrings to the naturals ϕ. We order strings similarly. This implies a 2^n period on the domain set: each of the 2^λ keys is paired with 2^n input values. In particular, note that the sampler $\mathcal{M}^{\text{IC}}_{\ell,\lambda}$ has to pick a permutation $\mathsf{enc}(\text{key}) : \{0,1\}^n \rightarrow \{0,1\}^n$ independently for each key. Note that n might depend on the security parameter λ.

Proposition 2. *The above setup assumption M_{IC} satisfies the consistent sampling property.*

Proof. Assume the normal ordering as discussed above. First for each new key (of the 2^k) we sample a new random permutation. Thus, we need only to show that while sampling a permutation for $0 \leq \ell < 2^n$ the consistent sampling property holds. We can generalize for each of the keyed permutations. Without loss of generality, if $\ell < 2^n - 1$, observe that the sampling process of the ℓ'th query element of $X_{\ell+1}$ does not depend on the $\ell + 1$ value (it depends only on some of the elements of $X_{\ell-1}$ (if $\ell > 0$) – as we sample without replacement. □

THE COMMON REFERENCE STRING MODEL (CRS) In the Common Reference String model, a generalization of the Common Random String [4] the oracle provides access to a common value that is sampled from some arbitrary desired distribution specific to the protocol. Namely, following the definition of [7] on setup the oracle samples $d \leftarrow_{\$} \mathcal{D}_\lambda$ and sends it to the querying party. For each subsequent query the oracle responds with d.

Formally, for a CRS model with distribution $\mathcal{D}_\lambda$ over a countable set D, we define the following setup assumption M_{CRS}

$$M_{\text{CRS}} = (\{0\}, D, \phi : \{0\} \to \mathbb{N}, \mathcal{M}^{\text{CRS}}_{\ell,\lambda})$$

We simply define $\phi(0) = 0$ and define the sampler $\mathcal{M}^{\text{CRS}}_{\ell,\lambda}$ to sample d from $\mathcal{D}_\lambda$ and return $\mathcal{O} : 0 \mapsto d$.

Proposition 3. *The above setup assumption M_{CRS} satisfies the consistent sampling property.*

Proof. It follows immediately from the observation that the sampling process is independent of the parameter ℓ. □

6 Proof of Theorem 2

We prove our main claim via Theorems 3 and 4. Namely, we show that if (G, S) is a fully black-box reduction from primitives P to Q in the standard model then (i) G is a generic construction in the setup assumption M and (ii) for every implementation $f^{(\cdot)}$ of $Q(M)$ and every (unbounded) algorithm $\mathcal{A}^{(\cdot)}$, if $\mathcal{A}^{(\cdot)}$ $P(M)$-breaks $G^{f^{(\cdot)}}$ then $S^{\mathcal{A}^{(\cdot)}}$ $Q(M)$-breaks $f^{(\cdot)}$.

6.1 Generic Construction Theorem

We first prove a vital lemma about satisfying correctness with functions with access to a bounded oracle random tape.

Lemma 8. *Let P be a primitive in the setup assumption $M = (X, Y, \phi, \mathcal{M})$, $f^{(\cdot)}$ be a function and* OA *be the set of all unbounded adversaries with oracle access. Then, $f^{(\cdot)}$ is an implementation of P if and only if* $\mathsf{Corr}_P(f)$ *is negligible, where:*

$$\mathsf{Corr}_P(f)(\lambda) = \sup_{\mathcal{A} \in \mathsf{OA}} \lim_{k \to +\infty} \lim_{\ell \to +\infty} \Pr\left[1 \leftarrow_{\$} C_P^{f_k^{\mathcal{O}}(\lambda), \mathcal{A}_\ell^{\mathcal{O}}(\lambda)}\right]$$

and $\mathcal{O} \leftarrow_{\$} \mathcal{M}_{\max\{k,\ell\},\lambda}$.

Proof. Clearly, if $\mathsf{Corr}_P(f)(\lambda)$ is negligible then for any adversary $\mathcal{A}$ we have

$$\lim_{k \to +\infty} \lim_{\ell \to +\infty} \Pr\left[1 \leftarrow_{\$} C_P^{f_k^{\mathcal{O}}(\lambda), \mathcal{A}_\ell^{\mathcal{O}}(\lambda)}\right] \le \mathsf{Corr}_P(f)(\lambda).$$

Thus, $f^{(\cdot)}$ is an implementation of P.

Now, suppose that $f^{(\cdot)}$ is an implementation of P. Note that by definition of supremum, we can find a sequence of adversaries $\mathcal{A}_1, \mathcal{A}_2, \ldots$ indexed by λ such that for all λ:

$$\mathsf{Corr}_P(f)(\lambda) \le \lim_{k \to +\infty} \lim_{\ell \to +\infty} \Pr\left[1 \leftarrow_{\$} C_P^{f_k^{\mathcal{O}}(\lambda), \mathcal{A}_{\lambda,\ell}^{\mathcal{O}}(\lambda)}\right] + \frac{1}{2^\lambda}.$$

Hence, let us pick an adversary $\mathcal{A}$ which given λ runs $\mathcal{A}_\lambda$. Since $f^{(\cdot)}$ is an implementation of P, we know that $\lim_{k\to+\infty}\lim_{\ell\to+\infty}\Pr\left[1 \leftarrow_{\$} C_P^{f_k^{\mathcal{O}}(\lambda),\mathcal{A}_\ell^{\mathcal{O}}(\lambda)}\right]$ is negligible and therefore so is $\mathsf{Corr}_P(f)(\lambda)$. □

For convenience, we continue using OA to denote the set of all unbounded adversaries with oracle access henceforth.

Theorem 3. *Let (G, S) be a fully black-box reduction from P to Q in the standard model and $M = (X, Y, \phi, \mathcal{M})$ be a setup assumption. Then, for every implementation $f^{(\cdot)}$ of $Q(M)$, $G^{f^{(\cdot)}}$ is an implementation of $P(M)$.*

Proof. Let us first fix $\lambda \in \mathbb{N}$ and $f^{(\cdot)}$ be an implementation of $Q(M)$. We first prove that there exists a function $t : \mathbb{N} \to \mathbb{N}$ such that f_t is also an implementation of $Q(M)$ and if $G^{f_t^{(\cdot)}}$ is an implementation of $P(M)$ then so is $G^{f^{(\cdot)}}$.

Lemma 9. *For any function $f^{(\cdot)}$, there exists $t : \mathbb{N} \to \mathbb{N}$ which satisfies the following properties:*

- *$f^{(\cdot)}$ is an implementation of $Q(M)$ if and only if $f_t^{(\cdot)}$ is an implementation of $Q(M)$.*
- *$G^{f^{(\cdot)}}$ is an implementation of $P(M)$ if and only if $G^{f_t^{(\cdot)}}$ is an implementation of $P(M)$.*

Proof. We prove the statement by construction. Let $f^{(\cdot)}$ be any function and $\lambda \in \mathbb{N}$. Then, by Lemma 3 we have

$$\begin{aligned}\mathsf{Corr}_{Q(M)}(f)(\lambda) &= \sup_{\mathcal{A}\in\mathsf{OA}}\lim_{k\to+\infty}\lim_{\ell\to+\infty}\Pr\left[1 \leftarrow_{\$} C_P^{f_k^{\mathcal{O}}(\lambda),\mathcal{A}_\ell^{\mathcal{O}}(\lambda)}\right]\\ &= \lim_{k\to+\infty}\sup_{\mathcal{A}\in\mathsf{OA}}\lim_{\ell\to+\infty}\Pr\left[1 \leftarrow_{\$} C_P^{f_k^{\mathcal{O}}(\lambda),\mathcal{A}_\ell^{\mathcal{O}}(\lambda)}\right]\\ &= \lim_{k\to+\infty} c_k\end{aligned} \tag{3}$$

where

$$c_k = \sup_{\mathcal{A}\in\mathsf{OA}}\lim_{\ell\to+\infty}\Pr\left[1 \leftarrow_{\$} C_P^{f_k^{\mathcal{O}}(\lambda),\mathcal{A}_\ell^{\mathcal{O}}(\lambda)}\right].$$

Therefore, there exists an integer N_1 such that for all $n \geq N_1$

$$|c_n - \mathsf{Corr}_{Q(M)}(f)(\lambda)| < \frac{1}{2^\lambda}.$$

Note that

$$\begin{aligned}c_n &= \sup_{\mathcal{A}\in\mathsf{OA}}\lim_{\ell\to+\infty}\Pr\left[1 \leftarrow_{\$} C_P^{f_n^{\mathcal{O}}(\lambda),\mathcal{A}_\ell^{\mathcal{O}}(\lambda)}\right]\\ &= \lim_{k\to+\infty}\sup_{\mathcal{A}\in\mathsf{OA}}\lim_{\ell\to+\infty}\Pr\left[1 \leftarrow_{\$} C_P^{f_{\min\{n,k\}}^{\mathcal{O}}(\lambda),\mathcal{A}_\ell^{\mathcal{O}}(\lambda)}\right]\\ &= \sup_{\mathcal{A}\in\mathsf{OA}}\lim_{k\to+\infty}\lim_{\ell\to+\infty}\Pr\left[1 \leftarrow_{\$} C_P^{f_{\min\{n,k\}}^{\mathcal{O}}(\lambda),\mathcal{A}_\ell^{\mathcal{O}}(\lambda)}\right] = \mathsf{Corr}_{Q(M)}(f_n)(\lambda).\end{aligned} \tag{4}$$

Similarly, one can find $N_2 \in \mathbb{N}$ such that for all $n \geq N_2$:

$$|\mathsf{Corr}_{P(M)}\left(G^{f_n}\right)(\lambda) - \mathsf{Corr}_{P(M)}\left(G^{f}\right)(\lambda)| < \frac{1}{2^\lambda}.$$

Let us set $t(\lambda) := \max\{N_1, N_2\}$. Then, the statement holds by construction and Lemma 8. □

Next, we select t as in the lemma above and define the "relevant tape" as a sequence of sets $T_1, T_2, \ldots$ defined as:

$$T_\lambda = X_{t(\lambda)} = \{x \in X : \phi_\lambda(x) < t(\lambda)\}.$$

For simplicity, we index T_λ as follows $T_\lambda = \{x_{\lambda,1}, \ldots, x_{\lambda,|T_\lambda|}\}$. Define:

$$S_\lambda = Y^{|T_\lambda|} \text{ and } S = \bigcup_{\lambda \in \mathbb{N}} S_\lambda.$$

Then, we set the distribution $D_\lambda : S_\lambda \to [0,1]$ as

$$D_\lambda(y_1, \ldots, y_{|T_\lambda|}) := \Pr\left[\forall i \in [|T_\lambda|], \mathcal{O}(x_{\lambda,i}) = y_i : \mathcal{O} \leftarrow_\$ \mathcal{M}\left(t(\lambda), \lambda\right)\right].$$

Since T_λ is finite, the distribution is discrete. Moreover, by consistency of setup assumptions we get that for all $\ell \geq t(\lambda)$:

$$D_\lambda(y_1, \ldots, y_{|T_\lambda|}) = \Pr\left[\forall i \in [|T_\lambda|], \mathcal{O}(x_{\lambda,i}) = y_i : \mathcal{O} \leftarrow_\$ \mathcal{M}\left(\ell, \lambda\right)\right].$$

Now, we define

$$Q(\lambda, \boldsymbol{y}) = \begin{cases} \sup_{\mathcal{A} \in \mathsf{OA}} \lim_{\ell \to +\infty} \Pr\left[1 \leftarrow_\$ C_Q^{f_t^{\mathcal{O}}(\lambda), \mathcal{A}_\ell^{\mathcal{O}}(\lambda)} \middle| \forall i, \mathcal{O}(x_{\lambda,i}) = y_i\right] & \text{if } \boldsymbol{y} \in S_\lambda \\ 0 \text{ otherwise} \end{cases}$$

and similarly

$$P(\lambda, \boldsymbol{y}) = \begin{cases} \sup_{\mathcal{A} \in \mathsf{OA}} \lim_{\ell \to +\infty} \Pr\left[1 \leftarrow_\$ C_P^{G^{f_t^{\mathcal{O}}}(\lambda), \mathcal{A}_\ell^{\mathcal{O}}(\lambda)} \middle| \forall i, \mathcal{O}(x_{\lambda,i}) = y_i\right] & \text{if } \boldsymbol{y} \in S_\lambda \\ 0 \text{ otherwise.} \end{cases}$$

Here, the probabilities are defined over $\mathcal{O} \leftarrow_\$ \mathcal{M}_{\max\{\ell, t(\lambda)\}, \lambda}$ and the random coins in the system. One argues similarly as in Lemma 7 that functions P and Q are well-defined.

We claim that for any $g : \mathbb{N} \to S$, we have

$$Q(\lambda, g(\lambda)) \in \mathsf{UBnegl} \implies P(\lambda, g(\lambda)) \in \mathsf{UBnegl}.$$

Indeed, suppose that $Q(\lambda, g(\lambda)) \in \mathsf{UBnegl}$. By construction, we have $0 \leq Q(\lambda, g(\lambda)) \leq 1$ for all $\lambda \in \mathbb{N}$ and thus this function is negligible.

We define the function f_t^g with hardwired oracle queries g as follows. Given a security parameter λ, it behaves identically as in $f_t^{(\cdot)}$ but when f "queries an oracle" on input $x_{\lambda,i} \in T_\lambda$, it gets y_i where $g(\lambda) = (y_1, \dots, y_{|T_\lambda|}) \in S_\lambda$. On the other hand, for λ so that $g(\lambda) \notin S_\lambda$, we set f_t^g to simply abort.

By construction, $\mathsf{Corr}_Q(f_t^g) = Q(\lambda, g(\lambda))$ is negligible and therefore, f_t^g is an implementation of Q. Since G is a generic construction in the standard model, we have that $G^{f_t^g}$ is an implementation of P, i.e. $\mathsf{Corr}_Q(G^{f_t^g})$ is negligible. As a consequence, $P(\lambda, g(\lambda))$ is negligible and in particular $P(\lambda, g(\lambda)) \in \mathsf{UBnegl}$.

We are now ready to apply Theorem 1 for $k = 1$. Note that for $Z_\lambda \leftarrow_\$ D_\lambda$ we have

$$\begin{aligned}
&\mathbb{E}(Q(\lambda, Z_\lambda)) \\
&\quad = \sum_{\boldsymbol{y} \in S_\lambda} Q(\lambda, \boldsymbol{y}) \cdot \Pr[Z_\lambda = \boldsymbol{y}] \\
&\quad = \sum_{\boldsymbol{y} \in S_\lambda} \sup_{\mathcal{A} \in \mathsf{OA}} \lim_{\ell \to +\infty} \Pr\left[1 \leftarrow_\$ C_Q^{f_t^{\mathcal{O}}(\lambda), \mathcal{A}_\ell^{\mathcal{O}}(\lambda)} \middle| \forall i, \mathcal{O}(x_{\lambda,i}) = y_i\right] \cdot \Pr[Z_\lambda = \boldsymbol{y}]
\end{aligned} \tag{5}$$

which, by Lemma 2, is equal to

$$\sup_{(\mathcal{A}_y) \in \mathsf{OA}^{|S_\lambda|}} \sum_{\boldsymbol{y} \in S_\lambda} \lim_{\ell \to +\infty} \Pr\left[1 \leftarrow_\$ C_Q^{f_t^{\mathcal{O}}(\lambda), \mathcal{A}_{y,\ell}^{\mathcal{O}}(\lambda)} \middle| \forall i, \mathcal{O}(x_{\lambda,i}) = y_i\right] \cdot \Pr[Z_\lambda = \boldsymbol{y}].$$

We claim that

$$\mathbb{E}(Q(\lambda, Z_\lambda)) = \sup_{\mathcal{A} \in \mathsf{OA}} \lim_{\ell \to +\infty} \Pr\left[1 \leftarrow_\$ C_Q^{f_t^{\mathcal{O}}(\lambda), \mathcal{A}_\ell^{\mathcal{O}}(\lambda)}\right].$$

First, take any unbounded adversary $\mathcal{A} \in \mathsf{OA}$. Then, by Lemma 5:

$$\lim_{\ell \to +\infty} \Pr\left[1 \leftarrow_\$ C_Q^{f_t^{\mathcal{O}}(\lambda), \mathcal{A}_\ell^{\mathcal{O}}(\lambda)}\right] \tag{6}$$

$$= \lim_{\ell \to +\infty} \sum_{\boldsymbol{y} \in S_\lambda} \Pr\left[1 \leftarrow_\$ C_Q^{f_t^{\mathcal{O}}(\lambda), \mathcal{A}_\ell^{\mathcal{O}}(\lambda)} \middle| \forall i, \mathcal{O}(x_{\lambda,i}) = y_i\right] \cdot \Pr[Z_\lambda = \boldsymbol{y}] \tag{7}$$

$$= \sum_{\boldsymbol{y} \in S_\lambda} \lim_{\ell \to +\infty} \Pr\left[1 \leftarrow_\$ C_Q^{f_t^{\mathcal{O}}(\lambda), \mathcal{A}_\ell^{\mathcal{O}}(\lambda)} \middle| \forall i, \mathcal{O}(x_{\lambda,i}) = y_i\right] \cdot \Pr[Z_\lambda = \boldsymbol{y}] \tag{8}$$

$$\leq \sum_{\boldsymbol{y} \in S_\lambda} \sup_{\mathcal{A} \in \mathsf{OA}} \lim_{\ell \to +\infty} \Pr\left[1 \leftarrow_\$ C_Q^{f_t^{\mathcal{O}}(\lambda), \mathcal{A}_\ell^{\mathcal{O}}(\lambda)} \middle| \forall i, \mathcal{O}(x_{\lambda,i}) = y_i\right] \cdot \Pr[Z_\lambda = \boldsymbol{y}] \tag{9}$$

$$\leq \mathbb{E}(Q(\lambda, Z_\lambda)). \tag{10}$$

Then, by definition of supremum we have

$$\mathbb{E}(Q(\lambda, Z_\lambda)) \geq \sup_{\mathcal{A} \in \mathsf{OA}} \lim_{\ell \to +\infty} \Pr\left[1 \leftarrow_\$ C_Q^{f_t^{\mathcal{O}}(\lambda), \mathcal{A}_\ell^{\mathcal{O}}(\lambda)}\right].$$

On the other hand, let us select any sequence of adversaries $(\mathcal{A}_{\boldsymbol{y}})_{\boldsymbol{y}\in S_\lambda}$. We construct an adversary $\mathcal{A}$ which first calls the external oracle $\mathcal{O}$ on all inputs in T_λ and given $\boldsymbol{y} = (y_1, \ldots, y_{|T_\lambda|})$, where $\mathcal{O}(x_{\lambda,i}) = y_i$, it runs $\mathcal{A}_{\boldsymbol{y}}$. Then, we have

$$\sum_{\boldsymbol{y}\in S_\lambda} \lim_{\ell\to+\infty} \Pr\left[1 \leftarrow_\$ C_Q^{f_t^{\mathcal{O}}(\lambda),\mathcal{A}_{\boldsymbol{y},\ell}^{\mathcal{O}}(\lambda)} \middle| \forall i, \mathcal{O}(x_{\lambda,i}) = y_i\right] \cdot \Pr[Z_\lambda = \boldsymbol{y}] \tag{11}$$

$$= \lim_{\ell\to+\infty} \sum_{\boldsymbol{y}\in S_\lambda} \Pr\left[1 \leftarrow_\$ C_Q^{f_t^{\mathcal{O}}(\lambda),\mathcal{A}_{\boldsymbol{y},\ell}^{\mathcal{O}}(\lambda)} \middle| \forall i, \mathcal{O}(x_{\lambda,i}) = y_i\right] \cdot \Pr[Z_\lambda = \boldsymbol{y}] \tag{12}$$

$$= \lim_{\ell\to+\infty} \Pr\left[1 \leftarrow_\$ C_Q^{f_t^{\mathcal{O}}(\lambda),\mathcal{A}_\ell^{\mathcal{O}}(\lambda)}\right]. \tag{13}$$

Consequently, $\mathbb{E}(Q(\lambda, Z_\lambda)) \leq \sup_{\mathcal{A}\in\mathsf{OA}} \lim_{\ell\to+\infty} \Pr\left[1 \leftarrow_\$ C_Q^{f_t^{\mathcal{O}}(\lambda),\mathcal{A}^{\mathcal{O}}(\lambda)}\right]$ and the claim holds. In particular,

$$\mathbb{E}(Q(\lambda, Z_\lambda)) = \mathsf{Corr}_{Q(M)}(f_t)(\lambda) \in \mathsf{UBnegl}.$$

Thus, by Theorem 1, $\mathbb{E}(P(\lambda, Z_\lambda)) \in \mathsf{UBnegl}$. Note that $\mathbb{E}(P(\lambda, Z_\lambda)) \in [0,1]$ for all λ, and consequently this function is also negligible. By arguing similarly as before, we get that $\mathbb{E}(P(\lambda, Z_\lambda)) = \mathsf{Corr}_{Q(M)}(G^{f_t})(\lambda)$ and thus, G^f is an implementation of $P(M)$ by Lemmas 8 and 9. □

6.2 Reduction Theorem

Theorem 4. *Let (G, S) be a fully black-box reduction from P to Q in the standard model and M be an external oracle. Then, for every implementation $f^{(\cdot)}$ of $Q(M)$ and every adversary $\mathcal{A}^{(\cdot)}$, if $\mathcal{A}^{(\cdot)}$ $P(M)$-breaks $G^{f^{(\cdot)}}$ then $S^{\mathcal{A}^{(\cdot)}}$ $Q(M)$-breaks $f^{(\cdot)}$.*

Proof. We prove the statement by contrapositive. First, we will need an extension of Lemma 9.

Lemma 10. *For any implementation $f^{(\cdot)}$ of $Q(M)$ and adversary $\mathcal{A}^{(\cdot)}$, there exists $t : \mathbb{N} \to \mathbb{N}$ such that for all $\lambda \in \mathbb{N}$:*

- *$f_t^{(\cdot)}$ is an implementation of $Q(M)$.*
- $|\mathsf{Adv}_{G^f,\mathcal{A}}^{P(M)}[(\lambda)] - \mathsf{Adv}_{G^{f_t},\mathcal{A}_t}^{P(M)}[(\lambda)]| < \frac{1}{2^\lambda}$.
- $|\mathsf{Adv}_{f,S^{\mathcal{A}}}^{Q(M)}[(\lambda)] - \mathsf{Adv}_{f_t,S^{\mathcal{A}_t}}^{Q(M)}[(\lambda)]| < \frac{1}{2^\lambda}$.

Proof. We prove the statement by construction. Let $f^{(\cdot)}$ and $\mathcal{A}^{(\cdot)}$ be any implementation of $Q(M)$ and adversary respectively, and $\lambda \in \mathbb{N}$. First, the proof of Lemma 9 says that there exists $N_0 \in \mathbb{N}$ such that for all $n \geq N_0$:

$$|\mathsf{Corr}_{Q(M)}(f_n)(\lambda) - \mathsf{Corr}_{Q(M)}(f)(\lambda)| < \frac{1}{2^\lambda}.$$

On the other hand, by definition of the advantage and Lemma 4

$$\begin{aligned}\mathsf{Adv}^{Q(M)}_{f,S^{\mathcal{A}}}[(\lambda)] &= \lim_{k\to+\infty} \Pr\left[1 \leftarrow_{\$} R_Q^{f_k^{\mathcal{O}},S^{\mathcal{A}_k^{\mathcal{O}}}}\right] - \sigma_Q(\lambda) \\ &= \lim_{k\to+\infty} c_k \end{aligned} \tag{14}$$

where $\sigma_Q(\lambda)$ is the security threshold for Q and

$$c_k = \Pr\left[1 \leftarrow_{\$} R_Q^{f_k^{\mathcal{O}},S^{\mathcal{A}_k^{\mathcal{O}}}}\right] - \sigma_Q(\lambda) = \mathsf{Adv}^{Q(M)}_{f_k,S^{\mathcal{A}_k}}[(\lambda)]$$

for $k \in \mathbb{N}$. This means there exists $N_1 \in \mathbb{N}$ such that for all $n \geq N_1$:

$$|c_n - \mathsf{Adv}^{Q(M)}_{f,S^{\mathcal{A}}}[(\lambda)]| < 1/2^\lambda.$$

One can similarly compute such N_2 for G^f. Let us set $t(\lambda) = \max\{N_0, N_1, N_2\}$. Then, the statement holds by construction. □

Fix an implementation $f^{(\cdot)}$ of $Q(M)$ and adversary $\mathcal{A}^{(\cdot)}$ such that $\mathsf{Adv}^{Q(M)}_{f,S^{\mathcal{A}}}[(\lambda)] \in \mathsf{UBnegl}$ is bounded by a negligible function. Let us select t as in the lemma above. Then, $f_t^{(\cdot)}$ is an implementation of $Q(M)$ and $\mathsf{Adv}^{Q(M)}_{f_t,S^{\mathcal{A}_t}}[(\lambda)] \in \mathsf{UBnegl}$ as well.

Define the "relevant tape" as a sequence of sets $T_1, T_2, \ldots$ as:

$$T_\lambda = X_{t(\lambda)} = \{x \in \mathcal{X}_\lambda : \phi_\lambda(x) \leq t(\lambda)\}.$$

For simplicity, we write $T_\lambda = \{x_{\lambda,1}, \ldots, x_{\lambda,|T_\lambda|}\}$. Denote

$$S_\lambda = \mathcal{Y}_\lambda^{|T_\lambda|} \text{ and } S = \bigcup_{\lambda\in\mathbb{N}} S_\lambda.$$

Then, we define the distribution $D_\lambda : S_\lambda \to [0,1]$ as

$$D_\lambda(y_1, \ldots, y_{|T_\lambda|}) := \Pr[\forall i \in [|T_\lambda|], \mathcal{O}(x_{\lambda,i}) = y_i : \mathcal{O} \leftarrow_{\$} \mathcal{M}_{t(\lambda),\lambda}].$$

Since $|T_\lambda|$ is finite, the distribution is discrete. As before, consistency of a setup assumption implies that for all $\ell \geq t(\lambda)$:

$$D_\lambda(y_1, \ldots, y_{|T_\lambda|}) = \Pr[\forall i \in [|T_\lambda|], \mathcal{O}(x_{\lambda,i}) = y_i : \mathcal{O} \leftarrow_{\$} \mathcal{M}_{\ell,\lambda}].$$

Next, we introduce the following functions:

$$Q_1(\lambda, \boldsymbol{y}) = \begin{cases} \Pr\left[1 \leftarrow_{\$} R_Q^{f_t^{\mathcal{O}},S^{\mathcal{A}_t^{\mathcal{O}}}} \middle| \forall i \in [|T_\lambda|], \mathcal{O}(x_{\lambda,i}) = y_i\right] - \sigma_Q(\lambda) \text{ if } \boldsymbol{y} \in S_\lambda \\ 0 \text{ otherwise} \end{cases},$$

$$Q_2(\lambda, \boldsymbol{y}) = \begin{cases} \sup_{\mathcal{B} \in \mathsf{OA}} \lim_{\ell \to +\infty} \Pr\left[1 \leftarrow_{\$} C_Q^{f_t^{\mathcal{O}}(\lambda), \mathcal{B}_\ell^{\mathcal{O}}(\lambda)} \middle| \forall i, \mathcal{O}(x_{\lambda,i}) = y_i \right] & \text{if } \boldsymbol{y} \in S_\lambda \\ 0 \text{ otherwise} \end{cases}$$

and similarly

$$P(\lambda, \boldsymbol{y}) = \begin{cases} \Pr\left[1 \leftarrow_{\$} R_P^{G^{f_t^{\mathcal{O}}}, \mathcal{A}_t^{\mathcal{O}}} \middle| \forall i \in [|T_\lambda|], \mathcal{O}(x_{\lambda,i}) = y_i \right] - \sigma_P(\lambda) \text{ if } \boldsymbol{y} \in S_\lambda \\ 0 \text{ otherwise} \end{cases}.$$

Clearly, for any $\lambda \in \mathbb{N}$ and $\boldsymbol{y} \in S$ we have

$$-1 \leq Q_1(\lambda, \boldsymbol{y}), Q_2(\lambda, \boldsymbol{y}), P(\lambda, \boldsymbol{y}) \leq 1.$$

Let $g : \mathbb{N} \to S$. In order to apply Theorem 1 we need to prove that

$$Q_i(\lambda, g(\lambda)) \in \mathsf{UBnegl} \text{ for } i = 1, 2 \implies P(\lambda, g(\lambda)) \in \mathsf{UBnegl}.$$

Similarly as before, we define the function f_t^g with hardwired oracle queries g in the following way. Given a security parameter λ, it behaves identically as in $f_t^{(\cdot)}$ but when f "queries an oracle" on input $x_{\lambda,i} \in T_\lambda$, it gets y_i where $g(\lambda) = (y_1, \ldots, y_{|T_\lambda|}) \in S_\lambda$. However, for λ so that $g(\lambda) \notin S_\lambda$, we set f_t^g to simply abort. Similarly, we define $\mathcal{A}_t^g$. It is easy to see that

$$Q_1(\lambda, g(\lambda)) = \mathsf{Adv}_{f_t^g, S^{\mathcal{A}_t^g}}^{Q(M)}[(\lambda)].$$

Suppose $Q_i(\lambda, g(\lambda)) \in \mathsf{UBnegl}$ for $i = 1, 2$. This implies that (i) $\mathsf{Adv}_{f_t^g, S^{\mathcal{A}_t^g}}^{Q(M)}[(\lambda)]$ is upper-bounded by a negligible function and (ii) f_t^g is an implementation of Q in the standard model because

$$Q_2(\lambda, g(\lambda)) = \mathsf{Corr}_{Q(M)}(f_t^g)(\lambda) \in \mathsf{UBnegl}$$

and $\mathsf{Corr}_{Q(M)}(f_t^g)(\lambda) \in [0, 1]$ for all λ. Since (G, S) is a fully black-box reduction from P to Q in the standard model, we have that $\mathsf{Adv}_{G^{f_t^g}, \mathcal{A}_t^g}^{Q(M)}[(\lambda)]$ is upper-bounded by a negligible function as well – this is indeed equal to $P(\lambda, g(\lambda))$.

We can now apply Theorem 1 for $k = 2$ with functions defined above. We observe that by the Law of Total Probability, $\mathbb{E}(Q_1(\lambda, Z_\lambda))$ is equal to

$$\sum_{\boldsymbol{y} \in S_\lambda} \left(\Pr\left[1 \leftarrow_{\$} R_Q^{f_t^{\mathcal{O}}, S^{\mathcal{A}_t^{\mathcal{O}}}} \middle| \forall i \in [|T_\lambda|], \mathcal{O}(x_{\lambda,i}) = y_i \right] - \sigma_Q(\lambda) \right) \cdot \Pr[Z_\lambda = \boldsymbol{y}].$$

Hence, we get

$$\mathbb{E}(Q_1(\lambda, Z_\lambda)) = \Pr\left[1 \leftarrow_{\$} R_Q^{f_t^{\mathcal{O}}, S^{\mathcal{A}_t^{\mathcal{O}}}}\right] - \sigma_Q(\lambda) = \mathsf{Adv}_{f_t, S^{\mathcal{A}_t}}^{Q(M)}[(\lambda)].$$

Since $\mathsf{Adv}^{Q(M)}_{f_t,S^{\mathcal{A}_t}}[(\lambda)]$ is upper-bounded by a negligible function, then so is $\mathbb{E}(Q_1(\lambda, Z_\lambda))$. Similarly as in the proof of Theorem 3, one argues that

$$\mathbb{E}(Q_2(\lambda, Z_\lambda)) = \mathsf{Corr}_{Q(M)}(f_t)(\lambda).$$

Since $f_t^{(\cdot)}$ is an implementation of $Q(M)$, this function is negligible. Hence, by Theorem 1, we have $\mathbb{E}(P(\lambda, Z_\lambda)) \in \mathsf{UBnegl}$ which directly implies that $\mathsf{Adv}^{P(M)}_{G^{f_t},\mathcal{A}_t}[(\lambda)]$ is upper-bounded by a negligible function. Finally, $\mathsf{Adv}^{P(M)}_{G^f,\mathcal{A}}[(\lambda)] \in \mathsf{UBnegl}$ by Lemma 10 and thus the statement holds.

Acknowledgments:. We would like to thank all the anonymous reviewers for their helpful suggestions which may also guide future work. Work was conducted while Eftychios Theodorakis was at DFINITY U.S. Research. Ngoc Khanh Nguyen was supported by the EU H2020 ERC Project 101002845 PLAZA.

A Supporting Proofs

A.1 Proof of Lemma 2

Firstly, we observe that for all $(a_s)_{s\in S} \in A^{|S|}$ we have:

$$\sum_{s\in S} f_s(a_s) \leq \sum_{s\in S} \sup_{a\in A} f_s(a)$$

and by definition of supremum we have

$$\sup_{(a_s)_{s\in S}\in A^{|S|}} \sum_{s\in S} f_s(a_s) \leq \sum_{s\in S} \sup_{a\in A} f_s(a).$$

Now, suppose there exists $\varepsilon > 0$ such that

$$\sum_{s\in S} \sup_{a\in A} f_s(a) = \sup_{(a_s)_{s\in S}\in A^{|S|}} \sum_{s\in S} f_s(a_s) + \varepsilon.$$

Let $\phi : S \to \mathbb{N}$ be an injective map. Then, by definition of supremum, for each $s \in S$ we can find an element $a_s \in A$ such that:

$$\sup_{a\in A} f_s(a) < f_s(a_s) + \varepsilon_{\phi(s)}$$

where ε_i is defined as $\varepsilon_i = (\varepsilon/2) \cdot (1/2)^i$ for $i \in \mathbb{N}$. Hence, we get:

$$\begin{aligned}\sum_{s\in S} \sup_{a\in A} f_s(a) &< \sum_{s\in S} f_s(a_s) + \sum_{s\in S} \varepsilon_{\phi(s)} \\ &< \sup_{(a_s)_{s\in S}\in A^{|S|}} \sum_{s\in S} f_s(a_s) + \sum_{i\in\mathbb{N}} \varepsilon_i \\ &< \sup_{(a_s)_{s\in S}\in A^{|S|}} \sum_{s\in S} f_s(a_s) + \varepsilon\end{aligned} \tag{15}$$

which leads to a contradiction.

A.2 Proof of Lemma 3

Let $\varepsilon > 0$. Then, there exists $\alpha \in A$ such that

$$\sup_{a\in A} \lim_{k\to+\infty} f_a(k) \leq \lim_{k\to+\infty} f_\alpha(k) + \varepsilon/2.$$

Next, there exists $N \in \mathbb{N}$ so that for all $n \geq N$:

$$|\lim_{k\to+\infty} f_\alpha(k) - f_\alpha(n)| < \varepsilon/2.$$

Since f_α is non-decreasing, we get

$$0 \leq \lim_{k\to+\infty} f_\alpha(k) - f_\alpha(n) < \varepsilon/2.$$

Therefore:

$$\sup_{a\in A} \lim_{k\to+\infty} f_a(k) - \varepsilon/2 \leq \lim_{k\to+\infty} f_\alpha(k) < f_\alpha(n) + \varepsilon/2 \leq \sup_{a\in A} f_a(n) + \varepsilon/2.$$

On the other hand, for any n, $\sup_{a\in A} \lim_{k\to+\infty} f_a(k) \geq \sup_{a\in A} f_a(n)$ since f_a is non-decreasing for all $a \in A$. Hence, for $n \geq N$ we have:

$$0 \leq \sup_{a\in A} \lim_{k\to+\infty} f_a(k) - \sup_{a\in A} f_a(n) < \varepsilon/2 + \varepsilon/2 = \varepsilon$$

and consequently, $\lim_{k\to+\infty} \sup_{a\in A} f_a(k) = \sup_{a\in A} \lim_{k\to+\infty} f_a(k)$.

A.3 Proof of Lemma 4

Denote $a_k = \lim_{\ell\to+\infty} f(k,\ell)$ and $b_\ell = \lim_{k\to+\infty} f(k,\ell)$. The monotonocity property and the fact that $f(k,\ell) \leq 1$ for all $k,\ell \in \mathbb{N}$ implies that sequences $(a_k),(b_\ell)$ are well-defined and they are non-decreasing. Moreover, $a_k, b_\ell \leq 1$ for all k,ℓ. Thus, $a = \lim_{k\to+\infty} a_k$ and $b = \lim_{\ell\to+\infty} b_\ell$ do exist. Then, for all $k,\ell \in \mathbb{N}$ we have $f(k,\ell) \leq a_k \leq a$ and hence

$$b_\ell = \lim_{k\to+\infty} f(k,\ell) \leq a$$

for all ℓ. In particular, $b = \lim_{\ell\to+\infty} b_\ell \leq a$. One similarly proves that $a \leq b$.

Lastly, we need to show that $c = a$ where $c := \lim_{k\to+\infty} f(k,k)$. It is easy to see that for $k \in \mathbb{N}$ we have $f(k,k) \leq a_k$ and thus $c = \lim_{k\to+\infty} f(k,k) \leq \lim_{k\to+\infty} a_k = a$. On the other hand, for every k and ℓ we have $f(k,\ell) \leq c$. Thus, $a_k = \lim_{\ell\to+\infty} f(k,\ell) \leq c$ for all k and consequently, $a \leq c$. Hence, $a = b = c$.

A.4 Proof of Lemma 5

The statement is easy to prove when S is finite. Hence, suppose there is a bijective map $\phi : \mathbb{N} \to S$ and define a function $g : \mathbb{N} \times \mathbb{N} \to [0,1]$ as $g(k,\ell) = \sum_{i=0}^{\ell} f(k,\phi(i))$. Note that for all k,ℓ we have $g(k,\ell) \leq g(k+1,\ell)$

and $g(k,\ell) \leq g(k,\ell+1)$. Then, by Lemma 4 and the fact that the limit of a finite sum is a sum of limits, we have:

$$\begin{aligned}
\lim_{k\to+\infty} \sum_{s\in S} f(k,s) &= \lim_{k\to+\infty} \lim_{\ell\to+\infty} g(k,\ell) \\
&= \lim_{\ell\to+\infty} \lim_{k\to+\infty} g(k,\ell) \\
&= \lim_{\ell\to+\infty} \lim_{k\to+\infty} \sum_{i=0}^{\ell} f(k,\phi(i)) \qquad (16)\\
&= \lim_{\ell\to+\infty} \sum_{i=0}^{\ell} \lim_{k\to+\infty} f(k,\phi(i)) \\
&= \sum_{s\in S} \lim_{k\to+\infty} f(k,s).
\end{aligned}$$

A.5 Proof of Lemma 7

Clearly, $F(k,\ell) \in [0,1]$. We just need to show that for all $k,\ell \in \mathbb{N}$ we have $F(k,\ell) \leq F(k,\ell+1)$ and $F(k,\ell) \leq F(k+1,\ell)$. Then, the statement follows directly from Lemma 4.

Let us fix $k,\ell \in \mathbb{N}$. Let us define $\mathcal{B}_{\ell+1}$ which behaves exactly as $\mathcal{A}_{\ell+1}$ but when it queries $x \in S$ such that $\phi(x) = \ell+1$, it also aborts. Hence, we have

$$\Pr\left[1 \leftarrow_\$ \mathcal{R}^{f_k{}^{\mathcal{O}},\mathcal{B}_{\ell+1}^{\mathcal{O}}}\right] \leq \Pr\left[1 \leftarrow_\$ \mathcal{R}^{f_k{}^{\mathcal{O}},\mathcal{A}_{\ell+1}^{\mathcal{O}}}\right] = F(k,\ell+1).$$

Now, by the consistency property of the setup assumption, the view of $\mathcal{B}_{\ell+1}$ given an oracle $\mathcal{O} \leftarrow_\$ \mathcal{M}_{\max\{k,\ell+1\},\lambda}$ is exactly the same as $\mathcal{A}_\ell$ given $\mathcal{O} \leftarrow_\$ \mathcal{M}_{\max\{k,\ell\},\lambda}$. Therefore

$$F(k,\ell) = \Pr\left[1 \leftarrow_\$ \mathcal{R}^{f_k{}^{\mathcal{O}},\mathcal{A}_\ell^{\mathcal{O}}}\right] = \Pr\left[1 \leftarrow_\$ \mathcal{R}^{f_k{}^{\mathcal{O}},\mathcal{B}_{\ell+1}^{\mathcal{O}}}\right].$$

Similarly, one proves $F(k,\ell) \leq F(k+1,\ell)$.

References

1. Baecher, P., Brzuska, C., Fischlin, M.: Notions of black-box reductions, revisited. In: Sako, K., Sarkar, P. (eds.) ASIACRYPT 2013. LNCS, vol. 8269, pp. 296–315. Springer, Heidelberg (2013). https://doi.org/10.1007/978-3-642-42033-7_16
2. Bellare, M., Rogaway, P.: Random oracles are practical: a paradigm for designing efficient protocols. In: Ashby, V., (ed.), ACM CCS 93, pp. 62–73. ACM Press, November 1993
3. Bellare, M., Rogaway, P.: Entity authentication and key distribution. In: Stinson, D.R. (ed.) CRYPTO 1993. LNCS, vol. 773, pp. 232–249. Springer, Heidelberg (1994). https://doi.org/10.1007/3-540-48329-2_21

4. Blum, M., Feldman, P., Micali, S.: Proving security against chosen ciphertext attacks. In: Goldwasser, S. (ed.) CRYPTO 1988. LNCS, vol. 403, pp. 256–268. Springer, New York (1990). https://doi.org/10.1007/0-387-34799-2_20
5. Boneh, D., Dagdelen, Ö., Fischlin, M., Lehmann, A., Schaffner, C., Zhandry, M.: Random oracles in a quantum world. In: Lee, D.H., Wang, X. (eds.) ASIACRYPT 2011. LNCS, vol. 7073, pp. 41–69. Springer, Heidelberg (2011). https://doi.org/10.1007/978-3-642-25385-0_3
6. Boneh, D., Venkatesan, R.: Breaking RSA may not be equivalent to factoring. In: Nyberg, K. (ed.) EUROCRYPT 1998. LNCS, vol. 1403, pp. 59–71. Springer, Heidelberg (1998). https://doi.org/10.1007/BFb0054117
7. Canetti, R., Fischlin, M.: Universally composable commitments. In: Kilian, J. (ed.) CRYPTO 2001. LNCS, vol. 2139, pp. 19–40. Springer, Heidelberg (2001). https://doi.org/10.1007/3-540-44647-8_2
8. Canetti, R., Goldreich, O., Halevi, S.: The random oracle methodology, revisited. Cryptology ePrint Archive, Report 1998/011 (1998). http://eprint.iacr.org/1998/011
9. Chaum, D., Pedersen, T.P.: Wallet databases with observers. In: Brickell, E.F. (ed.) CRYPTO 1992. LNCS, vol. 740, pp. 89–105. Springer, Heidelberg (1993). https://doi.org/10.1007/3-540-48071-4_7
10. Choi, S.G., Dachman-Soled, D., Malkin, T., Wee, H.: Black-box construction of a non-malleable encryption scheme from any semantically secure one. In: Canetti, R. (ed.) TCC 2008. LNCS, vol. 4948, pp. 427–444. Springer, Heidelberg (2008). https://doi.org/10.1007/978-3-540-78524-8_24
11. Coron, J.-S., Holenstein, T., Künzler, R., Patarin, J., Seurin, Y., Tessaro, S.: How to build an ideal cipher: the indifferentiability of the Feistel construction. J. Cryptol. **29**(1), 61–114 (2016)
12. Coron, J.-S., Patarin, J., Seurin, Y.: The random oracle model and the ideal cipher model are equivalent. In: Wagner, D. (ed.) CRYPTO 2008. LNCS, vol. 5157, pp. 1–20. Springer, Heidelberg (2008)
13. Fischlin, M., Lehmann, A., Ristenpart, T., Shrimpton, T., Stam, M., Tessaro, S.: Random oracles with(out) programmability. In: Abe, M. (ed.) ASIACRYPT 2010. LNCS, vol. 6477, pp. 303–320. Springer, Heidelberg (2010). https://doi.org/10.1007/978-3-642-17373-8_18
14. Goldwasser, S., Kalai, Y.T., Rothblum, G.N.: One-time programs. In: Wagner, D. (ed.) CRYPTO 2008. LNCS, vol. 5157, pp. 39–56. Springer, Heidelberg (2008). https://doi.org/10.1007/978-3-540-85174-5_3
15. Goldwasser, S., Micali, S.: Probabilistic encryption. J. Comput. Syst. Sci. **28**(2), 270–299 (1984)
16. Hofheinz, D., Nguyen, N.K.: On tightly secure primitives in the multi-instance setting. In: Lin, D., Sako, K. (eds.) PKC 2019. LNCS, vol. 11442, pp. 581–611. Springer, Cham (2019). https://doi.org/10.1007/978-3-030-17253-4_20
17. Hsiao, C.-Y., Reyzin, L.: Finding collisions on a public road, or do secure hash functions need secret coins? In: Franklin, M. (ed.) CRYPTO 2004. LNCS, vol. 3152, pp. 92–105. Springer, Heidelberg (2004). https://doi.org/10.1007/978-3-540-28628-8_6
18. Impagliazzo, R., Rudich, S.: Limits on the provable consequences of one-way permutations. In: Proceedings of the Twenty-First Annual ACM Symposium on Theory of Computing, pp. 44–61 (1989)
19. Impagliazzo, R., Rudich, S.: Limits on the provable consequences of one-way permutations. In: 21st ACM STOC, pp. 44–61. ACM Press, May 1989

20. Katz, J.: Universally composable multi-party computation using tamper-proof hardware. In: Naor, M. (ed.) EUROCRYPT 2007. LNCS, vol. 4515, pp. 115–128. Springer, Heidelberg (2007). https://doi.org/10.1007/978-3-540-72540-4_7
21. Rabin, M.O.: Transaction protection by beacons. J. Comput. Syst. Sci. **27**(2), 256–267 (1983)
22. Reingold, O., Trevisan, L., Vadhan, S.: Notions of reducibility between cryptographic primitives. In: Naor, M. (ed.) TCC 2004. LNCS, vol. 2951, pp. 1–20. Springer, Heidelberg (2004). https://doi.org/10.1007/978-3-540-24638-1_1
23. Shannon, C.E.: Communication theory of secrecy systems. Bell Syst. Tech. J. **28**(4), 656–715 (1949)
24. Simon, D.R.: Finding collisions on a one-way street: can secure hash functions be based on general assumptions? In: Nyberg, K. (ed.) EUROCRYPT 1998. LNCS, vol. 1403, pp. 334–345. Springer, Heidelberg (1998). https://doi.org/10.1007/BFb0054137

Encryption

Efficient Lattice-Based Inner-Product Functional Encryption

Jose Maria Bermudo Mera[1], Angshuman Karmakar[1], Tilen Marc[2,3](✉), and Azam Soleimanian[4,5]

[1] imec -COSIC, KU Leuven, Leuven, Belgium
{Jose.Bermudo,Angshuman.Karmakar}@esat.kuleuven.be
[2] Faculty of Mathematics and Physics, University of Ljubljana, Ljubljana, Slovenia
tilen.marc@xlab.si
[3] XLAB d.o.o, Ljubljana, Slovenia
[4] Equipe Grace, LIX, École Polytechnique, Palaiseau, France
soleimanian@lix.polytechnique.fr
[5] INRIA, Saclay, Palaiseau, France

Abstract. In the recent years, many research lines on Functional Encryption (FE) have been suggested and studied regarding the functionality, security, or efficiency. Nevertheless, an open problem on a basic functionality, the single-input inner-product (IPFE), remains: can IPFE be instantiated based on the Ring Learning With Errors (RLWE) assumption?

The RLWE assumption provides quantum-resistance security while in comparison with LWE assumption gives significant performance and compactness gains. In this paper we present the first RLWE-based IPFE scheme. We carefully choose strategies in the security proofs to optimize the size of parameters. More precisely, we develop two new results on ideal lattices. The first result is a variant of Ring-LWE, that we call multi-hint extended Ring-LWE, where some hints on the secret and the noise are given. We present a reduction from RLWE problem to this variant. The second tool is a special form of Leftover Hash Lemma (LHL) over rings, known as Ring-LHL.

To demonstrate the efficiency of our scheme we provide an optimized implementation of RLWE-based IPFE scheme and show its performance on a practical use case.

We further present new compilers that, combined with some existing ones, can transfer a single-input FE to its (identity-based, decentralized) multi-client variant with linear size of the ciphertext (w.r.t the number of clients).

Keywords: Functional Encryption · Inner-Product · Lattice-Based Cryptography · Learning with Errors over Ring · Multi-Client Functional Enryption

G. Hanaoka et al. (Eds.): PKC 2022, LNCS 13178, pp. 163–193, 2022.
https://doi.org/10.1007/978-3-030-97131-1_6

1 Introduction

Functional Encryption (FE) [11,29] is an extended form of traditional public-key encryption, which can overcome the all-or-nothing access, inherent to the public-key encryption. It allows an authorized user holding a functional-key sk_f to get a function of the message as $f(m)$, by applying sk_f to the encryption of the message m. The functionality provided by this primitive can be useful in practical scenarios such as cloud computing and computation over encrypted data without interactions. The FE schemes supporting general computation circuits either are secure only against a bounded numbers of collusions [19,20], or rely on strong primitives [16]. More importantly, they all suffer from severe inefficiency.

For these reasons a research area emerged with the goal of designing FE with limited but still wide classes of functionalities that are efficient enough to be implemented and used in practice. Particularly, FE for Inner-Product (IP) functionality [4,7], is one of the most popular special cases of FE.

Inner-Product FE (IPFE) [4,7] is a special case of FE supporting the inner-product functionality. In an IPFE scheme the message is a vector $\mathbf{x} \in \mathcal{M}^n$ encrypted as ct_x and the decryption-key sk_y is associated with a n-dimensional vector $\mathbf{y}$. The decryption (of ct_x using sk_y) gets $\langle \mathbf{x}, \mathbf{y} \rangle$, i.e. the inner-product.

IPFE is a well studied problem which is already instantiated based on different assumptions such as the *Decisional Diffie-Helman* (DDH), *Decisional Composite Reminder* (DCR), and *Learning With Errors* (LWE) [4,7] assumption. Despite of all the progress in this field, it has still remained an open problem to present an efficient IPFE based on quantum-secure assumptions. The only quantum-secure assumption that an IPFE has been realized on, is LWE assumption [4,7] with the resulting public key IPFE construction being computationally demanding.

Security of FE. Indistinguishability (IND) [11] is the standard security notion for FE. Informally, it says that an adversary given a ciphertext ct_{m^b}, for $b \xleftarrow{R} \{0,1\}$, cannot distinguish between challenges m^0 and m^1, even if it has access to decryption-keys $\mathsf{sk}_{f_1}, \ldots, \mathsf{sk}_{f_k}$, for $k = \text{poly}(\kappa)$, conditioned on $f_i(m^0) = f_i(m^1)$.

One can further consider two kinds of IND-security: selective and adaptive. In selective-IND (sel-IND), the adversary is restricted to submit its challenges m^0 and m^1 at the very beginning of the game and before seeing the public-key, while in adaptive-IND there is no such restriction.

Multi-Client FE (MCFE) is a stronger form of FE where the data comes from different sources and therefore each client should be able to encrypt its data individually and without thrusting other clients [14]. This means that the security definition of multi-client FE considers corruptions of users as well. Multi-client is usually defined w.r.t to a label set, which brings more flexibility, in the sense that ciphertexts can be combined if and only if they are encrypted under the same label. This is necessary for many applications since otherwise an adversary could mix ciphertexts that were not intended so. In fact, in many applications data may have already been defined w.r.t a label, such as a time-stamp (e.g. monthly data) or others.

Decentralized MCFE (DMCFE) avoids the need for a trusted authority who has access to all the secret keys in the system in order to generate the functional keys [3,14]. Particularly, in DMCFE, the clients take the role of authority together, without trusting each other.

Lattice-Based IPFE. Informally, a lattice $\mathcal{L}$ is a discrete subset of $\mathbb{R}^n$ which can be generated by (integer) linear combinations of several vectors, known as the basis. In this setting, the nice variety of computationally-hard problems against quantum adversaries make it interesting for the cryptography purpose [8].

The problem of Learning With Errors (LWE) [32] discusses solving a system of noisy equations and is known to be as hard as standard hard lattice-problems in the worst case. This problem is usually used as a bridge between cryptosystems and standard hard lattice-problems. Agrawal et al. [7] proposed an IPFE relying on hardness of LWE problem. Unfortunately, due to the large-dimension matrices in the LWE problem (leading to the large keys and slow operations), the resulting construction is not truly practical. The scheme of [4] suffers from similar issues while it is only selectively-secure. In [35], authors tried to improve the standard deviation of error term (by using re-randomization technique of [22] instead of using multi-hint extended LWE assumption), but the size of the public key still grows quadratically w.r.t the length of the message and the LWE-parameter n.

RLWE. The Ring-LWE (RLWE) problem, introduced by Lyubashevsky et al. [26], is the problem of distinguishing between two distributions in a special ring of polynomials R_q:

$$(a, as + e) \quad \text{and} \quad (a, u)$$

with $a, u \xleftarrow{R} \mathsf{R}_q$, the secret $s \leftarrow \chi$, and noise $e \leftarrow \chi$, where χ is a special distribution over the ring, and all the samples share the same secret s. It was introduced as a more efficient and compact version of LWE problem, which can be defined in a similar way, but simply over $\mathbb{Z}_q$ (i.e., $a, s \in \mathbb{Z}_q^n, e, u \in \mathbb{Z}_q$) rather than R_q.

Note that the hardness of RLWE depends on the choice of ring R_q and distribution χ. In [26] it was shown that RLWE, with properly chosen parameters, is as hard as standard hard lattice problems.

Due to its compact form, relying on RLWE usually leads to practical encryption systems with smaller keys. Thanks to the Fast Fourier Transform, multiplication in rings can be further accelerated. Moreover, the ring structure allows to encrypt multiple messages in parallel allowing SIMD type of calculations on encrypted data. These properties make RLWE one of the most interesting and competitive assumptions to develop a post-quantum cryptosystem based on [13,34].

Challenges and Contributions

Although RLWE can provide significant efficiency gains, reducing the security of an encryption systems to RLWE assumption is usually more complicated and tricky, compared with the ones based on LWE. The main obstacles here are: either the lack of common cryptographic-tools compatible with the ring structure, or the lack of variants of RLWE (which are as hard as RLWE) compatible with certain encryption systems. In comparison, LWE is a better understood problem with several variants, and thanks to its matrix-based structure in $\mathbb{Z}_q$, it can be more easily combined with other tools and assumptions during security proofs.

Primary Task: In this work, we study the IPFE cryptosystem and the required tools for the security reduction from IPFE to RLWE.

Secondary Task: We optimize, implement and further extend the scheme to make it applicable to real-world use cases. This includes extending the IPFE scheme to its MCFE and DMCFE versions through new general compilers, implementing it in a highly optimized way, and demonstrating its benefits (including SIMD processing) on a machine learning task.

The first IPFE scheme based on quantum-secure assumption was developed in [4]. This scheme is based on the LWE assumption and proved to be selectively secure. In [7], authors presented an adaptively secure IPFE scheme relying on the same assumption. To extend the security to the adaptive case, they used a variant of LWE assumption, named multi-hint extended-LWE (mhe-LWE) in which some hints on the noise terms are considered. The mhe-LWE says that samples are still indistinguishable from uniform, even given these hints. They proved a reduction from mhe-LWE to LWE problem, for a proper choice of parameters. This variant of LWE is then used directly in the security proof of their IPFE scheme, where hints help to simulate the queries. In the first step, by mhe-LWE, they manage to insert a uniformly random vector in the ciphertext. But as this randomness is multiplied by another vector, in the second step, they still need to apply the Leftover Hash Lemma (LHL) to get a uniform term in the ciphertext.

In this work we follow a somewhat similar approach, while due to the algebraic structure of RLWE and the mentioned obstacles, the details need to be crafted carefully. We build our required tools step by step, namely we extend the similar variants of mhe-LWE and LHL over rings (called mhe-RLWE and Ring-LHL respectively). Our mhe-RLWE assumption not only supports the hints over the error but also over the secret. This property gives special flexibility in the security proof to still improve the size of the parameters. We then construct two IPFE schemes based on RLWE assumption: an adaptively secure whose security proof employs mhe-RLWE and Ring-LHL, and a more efficient but just selectively secure scheme relying only on mhe-RLWE. Thanks to the extra property of our mhe-RLWE, we can remove the need for the Ring-LHL in the security proof of our selective IPFE. Our security proof for the adaptive IPFE avoids the complex entropy discussion appeared in the previous works [4,7,35] and consequently improves the size of the public key.

Contribution 1. We present a ring version of mhe-LWE that we call mhe-RLWE. The mhe-RLWE problem is to distinguish two RLWE samples, given additional information on the secret and noise term through some hints of a special form. More precisely:

- The task of mhe-RLWE is to distinguish between the distributions

  $$(a, ar+f, (e_i, s_i, e_i r + g_i, s_i f + h_i)_{i\in[\ell]}) \text{ and } (a, u, (e_i, s_i, e_i r + g_i, s_i f + h_i)_{i\in[\ell]}).$$

  where a, u are uniformly sampled from R_q, polynomials r, f, g_i, h_i are sampled from Gaussian distributions, and s_i, e_i with $\|s_i\|_\infty, \|e_i\|_\infty \leq C$ are arbitrary polynomials with bounded coefficients.

In comparison with mhe-LWE, where hints are scalar products $\langle s_i, f\rangle$ with (high dimensional) vectors s_i sampled from a specific distribution τ, in mhe-RLWE hints are ring products of the form $s_i f + h_i$ with s_i arbitrary bounded elements of R_q and additional noise h_i is introduced. An important observation is that our mhe-RLWE not only includes hints over the noise but also over the secret, which makes it of independent interest and flexible to be used in more complex cryptosystems. Moreover, the reduction from mhe-LWE to LWE requires $m = \Omega(n \log n)$ samples, which directly affects the performance and the size of the keys in IPFE scheme, while no such requirement is needed in mhe-RLWE.

Intuitively, to prove the reduction from mhe-RLWE to RLWE, the main idea is that for a given RLWE sample $(a, b = ar + f)$ one can sample additional randomnesses r', f', g'_i, h'_i from specific distributions, so that $(a, b' = b + ar' + f', (e_i, s_i, e_i r' + g'_i, s_i f' + h'_i))$ has the right distribution to be submitted to the mhe-RLWE solver.

To show that the distribution obtained in this way is statistically close to the the one in the real game, we generalize a lemma expressing that the sum of two particular discrete Gaussian distributions (one on $\mathbb{Z}^n$ and the other one on a sub-lattice) is (close to) Gaussian. Intuitively, we define these distributions based on values e_i, jointly sample polynomials r', g'_i and use the mentioned lemma to show that hints $e_i r' + g'_i$ and simulated secret $r + r'$ have the right distribution (similarly for the hints over the error). The reduction is not trivial by itself as one needs to build the correct lattice allowing to apply the mentioned lemma.

The second required tool (to develop our RLWE-based IPFE scheme) is a ring version of LHL (Ring-LHL). Informally, in Ring-LHL the main goal is to show that the distribution $\sum_{i=1}^k a_i t_i \in \mathsf{R}_q$ is close to uniform when $\boldsymbol{a} = (a_1, \ldots, a_k)$ is fixed with a_i uniformly sampled from the ring and $\boldsymbol{t} = (t_1, \ldots, t_k)$ is sampled from a distribution with high min-entropy over the ring. In [34], authors presented a special case of Ring-LHL where $\boldsymbol{t}$ is sampled from a Gaussian distribution and no extra information is available.

For our RLWE-based IPFE, Ring-LHL is needed to show that $\sum_{i=1}^k a_i t_i$ is close to uniform even in the presence of additional information leaking on $\boldsymbol{t}$ through the public-key. While the result from [34] enjoys small entropy demands on values t_i and small value k, it can not handle the information leakage. On the other hand, the result from [23] is theoretically sufficient and can handle the leakage, however, it suffers from large parameters, specially the size of k (length of vector $\boldsymbol{a}$) is of order of the security parameter. There are still similar versions of Ring-LHL (such as [27]) but due to the need for clear and efficient choice of parameters, we propose a special version of Ring-LHL which manages to handle the information leaking from the public-key and still enjoys small parameters. In fact, we generalize the Ring-LHL version of [34] from $(\boldsymbol{a}, \langle \boldsymbol{a}, \boldsymbol{t} \rangle)$ to the matrix-coefficient $(\boldsymbol{A}, \boldsymbol{At})$, which is enough for our aim in the security proof of IPFE.

Contribution 2. Apart from relying on LWE, both schemes [4] and [7] require LHL to insert a uniform term in the ciphertext. We present two IPFE constructions based on RLWE, our first IPFE scheme is selectively-secure with smaller parameters, while our second scheme is adaptively-secure. The compactness of RLWE brings two benefits to our schemes: it not only improves the efficiency of encryption in general, but also allows for parallel encryptions while the computational-complexity does not grow by the number of encryptions. Technically, this means a single decryption returns a matrix-multiplication, rather than an inner-product value.

For each of our schemes we follow a somehow different proof technique. Particularly, in our first construction, for the sake of a higher efficiency, we avoid the use of Ring-LHL in the security proof. More precisely, in our selectively-secure IPFE (sel-IPFE) scheme, at the first step, we use mhe-RLWE which leads to the appearance of a term $u \cdot s_i$ in the ciphertext associated with the i-th slot, where $u \in \mathsf{R}_q$ is uniform and $s_i \in \mathsf{R}$ is the secret-key sampled from Gaussian distribution. Then in the second step, we change the structure of the secret-key in an indistinguishable way, which is only possible in the selective setting. This new structure allows us to remove the secret s_i from the functional-key, while it is still present in the public-key $\mathsf{pk}_i = as_i + e_i$. Having the noise term in the public-key and an extra noise in the ciphertext allow us to see s_i as the secret for two samples of RLWE in the public-key and in the ciphertext . Thus we rely on two samples of RLWE rather than relying on Ring-LHL.

For our adaptively secure IPFE, the first step is similar to the one in sel-IPFE while here $\boldsymbol{u}$ and $\boldsymbol{s}_i$ belong to R_q^m (vector-of-polynomials). Then we step back to the selective-game and change the structure of $\boldsymbol{s}_i$ to get rid of it in the functional-key. Interestingly, we have the freedom to come back to the adaptive-game via a mechanism similar to the Complexity Leveraging (CL) and without losing any factor of the security. The prominent observation here is that after stepping back to the selective-security, all of our upcoming games (in the sequence of the games) are statistically-indistinguishable, thanks to the use of Ring-LHL rather than RLWE assumption (unlike how we proceeded in our sel-IPFE). This means all these games can be upgraded to their adaptive versions by the correct setting of the parameters in the statistical arguments. The approach is similar to the one in [35] based on LWE assumption. But we manage to avoid a rather complicated entropy discussion, needed for their version of leftover hash lemma, since it results in a big parameter m reflected in the size of the public key. Instead, we indistinguishably change the generation of the secret key and remove it from the functional key.

This simplifies the proof, since we can use our simple extension of Ring-LHL for $\boldsymbol{A} = (\begin{bmatrix} \boldsymbol{a} \\ \boldsymbol{u} \end{bmatrix})$ to replace $\boldsymbol{as}_i$ and $\boldsymbol{us}_i$ with uniform values, respectively, in the public-key and in the ciphertext. In Ring-LHL with $\boldsymbol{A} \in \mathsf{R}_q^{k \times m}$, the only condition on m is that $m \geq k+1$, where in our case $k = 2$. Thus, we can consider $m = 3$, which means that in comparison with our sel-IPFE the size of the key increases only by a constant size. The use of Ring-LHL demands the variance of secrets to be greater than the one in the selective case, but still giving a reasonable efficiency.

In Fig. 1 we present a general comparison of our scheme with related works.

Contribution 3. We provide an efficient implementation to substantiate our claims of efficiency. Our scheme needs large polynomials where each coefficient can span multiple machine words. Further, the number of polynomial multiplications required in our inner-product functional scheme increases linearly with the length of the vectors. To overcome this, we provide a residue number system based implementation using Chinese remainder theorem and number theoretic transform based multiplication. We further show how the construction of the functional encryption scheme can be exploited to speed-up the multiplication. To reduce the risk of side-channel attacks we avoid all secret dependent branching and use a state-of-the-art constant-time discrete Gaussian sampler to generate error and secret polynomials. Finally, we show using a real-world use case that our work can be helpful for providing practical solutions for privacy-preserving machine learning applications.

	$\vert\mathsf{mpk}\vert$	$\vert\mathsf{msk}\vert$	$\vert\mathsf{ct}\vert$	$\vert\mathsf{sk}_f\vert$
ALS16 [7]	$O(n^2 \log^2 q + \ell n \log q)$	$O(\ell n \log^2 q)$	$O(n \log q^2 + \ell \log q)$	$O(n \log^2 q)$
ABDP15 [4]	$O((n+\ell)n \log^2 q)$	$O(\ell n \log q)$	$O((n+\ell) \log q)$	$O(n \log q)$
RLWE-FE	$O(\ell n \log q)$	$O(\ell n \log q)$	$O(\ell n \log q)$	$O(n \log q)$

	Setup	Encryption	KeyGen	Decryption
ALS16 [7]	$O(\ell n^2 \log q)$	$O(n^2 \log q + \ell n)$	$O(\ell n \log q)$	$O(n \log q + \ell)$
ABDP15 [4]	$O(\ell n^2 \log q)$	$O((\ell+n)n \log q)$	$O(\ell n)$	$O(\ell + n)$
RLWE-FE	$O(\ell n \log n)$	$O(\ell n \log n)$	$O(\ell n)$	$O(\ell n + n \log n)$

Fig. 1. Complexity comparison with related works. Upper and bottom part of the table respectively present the space and time complexity where the operations are in $\mathbb{Z}_q$. Value ℓ is the length of the message-vector, n and q are LWE or RLWE parameters. Since in our adaptively-secure FE scheme $m = 3$, all the above complexity arguments are the same for both of our schemes. However, other parameters, such as the choice of standard deviations, are different.

Contribution 4. In order to bring our IPFE scheme closer to the practical use, we extend our scheme to a (D)MCFE scheme without significantly increasing its complexity. In [6], the authors presented a general compiler to transfer a single-input IPFE to a multi-input IPFE[1]. Later in [3] it was argued that the resulting scheme is also secure against corruptions (removing the trust among the users), while still it does not support labels. In practice labels are needed to prevent undesired mixing of ciphertexts. Hence in this paper, we additionally develop a compiler which can transfer a multi-input FE supporting corruptions (but not labels) to a multi-client scheme (supporting labels). Similar outcome can be achieved with a compiler from [2], but with the ciphertext-size growing quadratically w.r.t the number of clients. On the other hand, one can built a MCFE based on RLWE in a non black-box way, similar to the MCFE scheme in [5] which is based on LWE problem. More precisely, the construction is based on LWE with rounding, which, intuitively, needs a bigger modulus q. Our compiler would not change the size of the modulus or the ciphertext.

The main idea of the construction in [6] is that, to encrypt a message $\mathbf{x}_i$ one indeed encrypts the message $\mathbf{x}_i + \boldsymbol{u}_i$ by the single-input IPFE scheme, where $\boldsymbol{u}_i$ is the secret key of user i. The functional key sk_f has two main parts one to apply the decryption of IPFE and the other one to remove terms involved with $\boldsymbol{u}_i$. Our compiler extends this idea to the labeled multi-client setting (in RO model) by adding another secret key $H(\boldsymbol{u}'_i, \gamma)$ such that the client i now encrypts $\mathbf{x}_i + \boldsymbol{u}_i + H(\boldsymbol{u}'_i, \gamma)$. This leads to what is known as identity-based MCFE where each functional key is associated with a label (or identity) γ as $\mathsf{sk}_{f,\gamma}$. Let ℓ be the number of clients, L be the number of issued labels and m be the number of different vectors $\mathbf{y}$ for which the functional key is issued. Then our scheme results in a joint ciphertext of size ℓL and a functional key of size mL, while the general compiler of [2] generates ciphertexts of size $\ell^2 L$ and functional key of size m. This means for the applications which ℓ is big, our scheme obtains a much better efficiency. This can include the applications such as aggregation and analyse of data from thousands of clients (health centers, data servers, etc.) during one year such that the data is processed daily (i.e., $n = 10000$ and $L = 365$)). Moreover, the fact that the functional key depends on γ can be seen as a kind of fine-grained access control, that can be use even data encrypted in parallel in one ciphertext.

In [3], authors present a general compiler to transfer a MCFE to a decentralized MCFE scheme, when the underlying scheme satisfies a special form of the functional key. More in details, at the setup phase the vector $\mathbf{0}$ is shared among the clients such that $\boldsymbol{v}_i$ is the secret key of the client i and $\sum \boldsymbol{v}_i = \mathbf{0}$. Then the functional key sk_f, which has a inner-product form $\mathsf{sk}_f = \sum_i \langle \boldsymbol{u}_i, \mathbf{y}_i \rangle$, is decentralized via generating $\langle \boldsymbol{u}_i, \mathbf{y}_i \rangle + \langle \boldsymbol{v}_i, \mathbf{y} \rangle$ by the i-th client. For our MCFE scheme, since the secret key $H(\boldsymbol{u}'_i, \gamma)$ depends on γ we can not directly apply their compiler over our scheme. To go around this problem we present a generalized distributed sum (GDSum) protocol which allows us to generate functions $H_i(\gamma)$ (depending on a label γ) such that $\sum H_i(\gamma) = 0$. We use GDSum as a building block to extend the compiler of [3] to an identity-based DMCFE. Finally, we show that our RLWE-based IPFE scheme has all the required

[1] Multi-input FE can be seen as a weaker version of MCFE where it may not support labels or corruptions.

properties to be used in our compilers, and so be extended to a identity-based MCFE or DMCFE scheme based on RLWE assumption.

2 Preliminaries

2.1 Notations

In this paper we shall denote with R a polynomial ring $\mathsf{R} = \mathbb{Z}[x]/\Phi$ where Φ is an irreducible polynomial. For the sake of simplicity (and implementation) Φ will be equal to $x^n + 1$, where n is a power of 2. We shall use a standard notation R_q to denote $\mathsf{R}/q\mathsf{R} = \mathbb{Z}_q[x]/\Phi$. The modulus q is chosen such that polynomial Φ of degree n factors into n distinct linear polynomials over $\mathbb{Z}_q$, i.e. $\Phi = \prod_i \phi_i$, where each ϕ_i is linear. Therefore, by Chinese Remainder Theorem (CRT), the ring R_q factors into n ideals and can be written as $\mathsf{R}_q \cong \prod_i \mathsf{R}_q/\phi_i$. Since each R_q/ϕ_i is isomorphic to $\mathbb{Z}_q$, this gives an isomorphism between R_q and $\mathbb{Z}_q^n$. The latter is specifically useful in the Ring-LHL argument, and consequently for our adaptively secure IPFE scheme. Moreover, if Φ factors as explained, then the multiplication of elements in R_q can be implemented particularly eficient in time $O(n \log n)$ using so called Fast Fourier Transform, which is important for a practical performance.

For $a \in \mathsf{R}$ (or $a \in \mathsf{R}_q$) a polynomial of degree less than n, we shall denote $\boldsymbol{a} \in \mathbb{Z}^n$ (or $\boldsymbol{a} \in \mathbb{Z}_q^n$) the vector of the coefficients of a, and vice versa. When the coefficients of a are sampled from some distribution χ we write $a \leftarrow \chi$. In this paper, $[\ell]$ stands for the set $\{1, \dots, \ell\}$ and $\|\boldsymbol{v}\|_\infty$ and $\|\boldsymbol{v}\|$ stand for the infinity and Euclidean norm, respectively. We write $x \xleftarrow{R} X$ to show that the element x is sampled uniformly at random from the set X. The security parameter is denoted by κ (which is independent from parameters for RLWE problem).

2.2 Discrete Gaussian Distribution

In this section we give a definition of the discrete Gaussian distribution and present some results regarding it that will be used latter in the paper.

Definition 1. *A discrete Gaussian distribution $D_{\Lambda,\sqrt{\Sigma},\boldsymbol{c}}$, for $\boldsymbol{c} \in \mathbb{R}^n$, Σ a positive semi-definite matrix in $\mathbb{R}^{n\times n}$, and $\Lambda \subset \mathbb{Z}^n$ a lattice, is a distribution with values in Λ and probabilities*

$$\Pr(X = \boldsymbol{x}) \propto \exp(-\frac{1}{2}(\boldsymbol{x} - \boldsymbol{e})^T \Sigma^+ (\boldsymbol{x} - \boldsymbol{e})).$$

Note that Σ^+ denotes the pseudoinverse of a matrix. If $\Lambda = \mathbb{Z}^n$ we shall write just $D_{\sqrt{\Sigma},\boldsymbol{c}}$. Furthermore, if $\boldsymbol{c} = 0$, then we shall write just $D_{\sqrt{\Sigma}}$, and if $\sqrt{\Sigma} = \sigma I_n$ for $\sigma \in \mathbb{R}^+$ and I_n an identity matrix, we write D_σ.

We define $\rho_B(\boldsymbol{x}) = \exp(-\boldsymbol{x}^T (BB^T)^{-1}\boldsymbol{x})$. It follows directly from the definition that for any invertible matrix β it holds $\rho_{\sqrt{\Sigma}}(\beta^{-1}\boldsymbol{x}) = \rho_{\beta\sqrt{\Sigma}}(\boldsymbol{x})$. For a lattice Λ we shall write $\rho_B(\Lambda) = \sum_{\boldsymbol{x}\in\Lambda} \rho_B(\boldsymbol{x})$.

We have the following useful fact showing that values from a discrete Gaussian distribution can be bounded.

Lemma 1 ([24]). *For any $k > 0$, $\Pr_{x \leftarrow D_\sigma}[|x| > \sqrt{k}\sigma] \leq 2e^{-k/2}$. (one dimension Gaussian)*

For any lattice $\mathcal{L}$ and positive real $\epsilon > 0$, the *smoothing parameter* $\eta_\epsilon(\mathcal{L})$ is the smallest real $s > 0$ such that $\rho_{s^{-1}I}(\widehat{\mathcal{L}} \setminus \{0\}) \leq \epsilon$ where $\widehat{\mathcal{L}} := \{\boldsymbol{w} : \langle \boldsymbol{w}, \mathcal{L} \rangle \subset \mathbb{Z}\}$ is the dual of $\mathcal{L}$.

Lemma 2 ([4,18]). *Let Σ be a positive semi-definite matrix. For every $\mathbf{c} \in \mathbb{R}^n$ in the span of Σ it holds $\rho_{\sqrt{\Sigma}}(\mathbf{c} + \mathbb{Z}^n) = \rho_{\sqrt{\Sigma}}(\mathbb{Z}^n)\mu_{\mathbf{c}}$, for some $\mu_{\mathbf{c}} \in [\frac{1-\epsilon}{1+\epsilon}, 1]$, as long as $\sqrt{\Sigma} \geq \eta_\epsilon(\mathbb{Z}^n)$.*

Discrete Gaussian distribution has many nice properties, for example: its samples can be easily bounded, and sampling from it is computationally feasible. It is well known that the sum of continuous independent Gaussian distributions is also Gaussian. The following lemma discusses that the sum of *discrete* Gaussian variables is (close to) Gaussian under certain conditions over Gaussian parameters. A special case of this lemma was proved and used in [4].

Lemma 3. *Let $L(B) \subseteq \mathbb{Z}^n$ be a sub-lattice with dimension k whose basis is given by the columns of $(n \times k)$-matrix B. Let $\Sigma \in \mathbb{R}^{n \times n}$ be a positive definite matrix and define $\Sigma' = \sigma'^2 BB^T$. Then sampling $\mathbf{e}$ from a discrete Gaussian distribution $D_{\sqrt{(\Sigma+\Sigma')}}$ is indistinguishable from sampling $\mathbf{e} = \mathbf{e_1} + \mathbf{e_2}$, where $\mathbf{e_1}$ is sampled from $D_{\sqrt{\Sigma}}$ and $\mathbf{e_2} \in L(B)$ is independently sampled from $D_{\sqrt{\Sigma'}}$, as long as the eigenvalues of $\Gamma_{\Sigma,\Sigma'} := \sqrt{\sigma'^2 I_k - \sigma'^4 B^T(\Sigma + \Sigma')^{-1}B}$ are greater than the smoothing parameter $\eta_\epsilon(\mathbb{Z}^k)$.*

Proof. Define

$$\Sigma'' = \begin{bmatrix} \Sigma & 0 \\ 0 & \sigma'^2 I_k \end{bmatrix}, \beta = [I_n \; B], \beta' = \begin{bmatrix} I_n & B \\ X^T & I_k + X^T B \end{bmatrix}, X = -\sigma'^2(\Sigma + \Sigma')^{-1}B$$

Defining $\Sigma''' = (\beta'\sqrt{\Sigma''})(\beta'\sqrt{\Sigma''})^T$ we have by a simple calculation

$$\Sigma''' = \begin{bmatrix} \Sigma + \Sigma' & 0 \\ 0 & \sigma'^2 I_k - \sigma'^4 B^T(\Sigma + \Sigma')^{-1}B \end{bmatrix}.$$

Let $\boldsymbol{e_1}$ be sampled from $D_{\sqrt{\Sigma}}$ and $\boldsymbol{e_2}$ be sampled from $D_{\sigma' I_k}$. Let $\boldsymbol{e} = \boldsymbol{e_1} + B\boldsymbol{e_2}$. Notice that sampling $\boldsymbol{e}_3 \in L(B)$ from $D_{\sqrt{\Sigma'}}$ is by definition equivalent to sampling $B\boldsymbol{e_2}$ where $\boldsymbol{e_2}$ is sampled from $D_{\sigma' I_k}$. Let $\boldsymbol{e'} = \begin{bmatrix} \boldsymbol{e_1} \\ \boldsymbol{e_2} \end{bmatrix}$, and notice that $\boldsymbol{e'}$ is sampled from $D_{\sqrt{\Sigma''}}$. Now

$$\begin{aligned}
\Pr(e = z) &= \Pr(\beta e' = z) \\
&= \sum_{s\in\mathbb{Z}^k} \Pr(\beta' e' = \begin{bmatrix} z \\ X^T z + s \end{bmatrix}) = \sum_{s\in\mathbb{Z}^k} \Pr(e' = \beta'^{-1} \begin{bmatrix} z \\ X^T z + s \end{bmatrix}) \\
&\propto \sum_{s\in\mathbb{Z}^k} \rho_{\sqrt{\Sigma''}}(\beta'^{-1} \begin{bmatrix} z \\ X^T z + s \end{bmatrix}) \propto \sum_{s\in\mathbb{Z}^k} \rho_{\beta'\sqrt{\Sigma''}}(\begin{bmatrix} z \\ X^T z + s \end{bmatrix}) \\
&\propto \sum_{s\in\mathbb{Z}^k} \rho_{\sqrt{\Sigma+\Sigma'}}(z)\rho_{\sqrt{\sigma'^2 I_k - \sigma'^4 B^T(\Sigma+\Sigma')^{-1}B}}(X^T z + s) \\
&\propto \rho_{\sqrt{\Sigma+\Sigma'}}(z)\rho_{\sqrt{\sigma'^2 I_k - \sigma'^4 B^T(\Sigma+\Sigma')^{-1}B}}(X^T z + \mathbb{Z}^k) \\
&\propto \rho_{\sqrt{\Sigma+\Sigma'}}(z)\rho_{\sqrt{\sigma'^2 I_k - \sigma'^4 B^T(\Sigma+\Sigma')^{-1}B}}(\mathbb{Z}^k)\mu_z \quad \text{by Lemma 2} \\
&\propto \rho_{\sqrt{\Sigma+\Sigma'}}(z)\mu_z, \ \text{for } \mu_z \in [\frac{1-\epsilon}{1+\epsilon}, 1]
\end{aligned}$$

where Lemma 2 can be applied as long as the eigenvalues of matrix $\Gamma_{\Sigma,\Sigma'} > \eta_\epsilon(\mathbb{Z}^k)$, where $\Gamma_{\Sigma,\Sigma'} := \sqrt{\sigma'^2 I_k - \sigma'^4 B^T(\Sigma+\Sigma')^{-1}B}$. □

We shall be using Lemma 3 in the following cases. We will have $\Sigma = \sigma^2 I_n - \sigma'^2 BB^T, \Sigma' = \sigma'^2 BB^T$ so that $\Sigma + \Sigma' = \sigma^2 I_n$. Then

$$\sqrt{\sigma'^2 I_k - \sigma'^4 B^T(\Sigma+\Sigma')^{-1}B} = \sigma' \sqrt{I_k - \frac{\sigma'^2}{\sigma^2} BB^T}$$

which is $> \eta_\epsilon(\mathbb{Z}^k)$ for example if $\sigma^2 = 2||\sigma'^2 BB^T||$ and $\sigma' > 2\eta_\epsilon(\mathbb{Z}^k)$, but more specific bounds can be derived as well.

2.3 RLWE Problem

In the seminal work [26], the authors introduced RLWE problem and study its hardness. In the following we define RLWE problem, while one can consult [26] for the choice of the parameters in the reduction from SIVP, a standard hard lattice-problem, to RLWE.

Definition 2 ((Decisional) RLWE[2]). *The Ring Learning With Errors problem, w.r.t the ring R_q and the distribution D_σ, is to distinguish between two following distributions with the secret $s \leftarrow D_\sigma$ fixed for all the samples,*

$$D = \{(a, as+e) \ : \ a \xleftarrow{R} \mathsf{R}_q, \ e \leftarrow D_\sigma\}, \qquad D' = \{(a, u) \ : \ a, u \xleftarrow{R} \mathsf{R}_q\}$$

2.4 Functional Encryption

This section discusses the syntax of a FE scheme and its security notion.

Definition 3 (Functional Encryption scheme). *A FE scheme parameterized by $\rho = (X, Y, Z, f)$ for functionality $f : X \times Y \to Z$, is defined by four following algorithms.*

[2] Here we have considered a special form of RLWE which would be used in this paper.

- $(\mathsf{mpk}, \mathsf{msk}) \leftarrow \mathsf{Setup}(1^\kappa)$: *where* Setup *receives security parameter* κ, *and returns a pair of master public and secret key. The public-key implicitly defines the functionality-parameter* ρ.
- $\mathsf{ct} \leftarrow \mathsf{Enc}(\mathsf{mpk}, \mathbf{x})$: *where* Enc *receives the master public-key* mpk *and a message* $\mathbf{x} \in X$, *and it returns a ciphertext* ct.
- $\mathsf{sk}_y \leftarrow \mathsf{KeyGen}(\mathsf{msk}, \mathbf{y})$: *where* KeyGen *receives the master secret-key* msk *and function* $\mathbf{y} \in Y$, *then it returns a functional-key* sk_y.
- $Y := \mathsf{Dec}(\mathsf{ct}, \mathsf{sk})$: *it receives a ciphertext* ct *and a functional-key* sk, *and returns* $\perp$ *or a value in the range of* f.

Correctness. For a correct execution of the above encryption system, $\mathsf{Dec}(\mathsf{ct}, \mathsf{sk}_F)$ would return $f_{\mathbf{y}}(\mathbf{x})$ with overwhelming probability, where $\mathsf{ct} \leftarrow \mathsf{Enc}(\mathsf{mpk}, \mathbf{x})$ and $\mathsf{sk}_y \leftarrow \mathsf{KeyGen}(\mathsf{msk}, \mathbf{y})$. For the inner-product functionality we have $f_{\mathbf{y}}(\mathbf{x}) = \langle \mathbf{x}, \mathbf{y} \rangle = \sum_{i \in [\ell]} x_i y_i$, where $\mathbf{x} \in \mathcal{M}_1^\ell, \mathbf{y} \in \mathcal{M}_2^\ell$ for some $\mathcal{M}_1^\ell, \mathcal{M}_2^\ell$ message and function space.

Security Notion. Following the standard security notion for FE [4,11], the game $\mathsf{IND}^b_{\mathcal{A}}(1^\kappa)$ between the adversary $\mathcal{A}$ and challenger is defined as follows, where $b \xleftarrow{R} \{0,1\}$.

- *Initialize:* The challenger runs $(\mathsf{msk}, \mathsf{mpk}) \leftarrow \mathsf{Setup}(1^\kappa)$ and send mpk to $\mathcal{A}$.
- *Query*: The adversary adaptively submits queries $\mathbf{y}$ and receives the response $\mathsf{sk}_y = \mathsf{KeyGen}(\mathsf{msk}, \mathbf{y})$ from the challenger.
- *Challenge*: The adversary submits messages $\mathbf{x}^0, \mathbf{x}^1$, the challenger runs $\mathsf{ct} \leftarrow \mathsf{Enc}(\mathsf{mpk}, \mathbf{x}^b)$ and returns it to $\mathcal{A}$. The challenge should satisfy the constraint $f_{\mathbf{y}}(\mathbf{x}^0) = f_{\mathbf{y}}(\mathbf{x}^1)$ for all the previously issed queries $\mathbf{y}$.
- *Query*: The adversary adaptively submits queries $\mathbf{y}$ and receives the response $\mathsf{sk}_y = \mathsf{KeyGen}(\mathsf{msk}, \mathbf{y})$, where the queries $\mathbf{y}$ should satisfy the constraint $f_{\mathbf{y}}(\mathbf{x}^0) = f_{\mathbf{y}}(\mathbf{x}^1)$.
- *Finalize*: The adversary outputs a bit b' as its guess for the bit b.

We say a FE scheme is (adaptively) indistinguishable-secure (IND-secure), if for any PPT adversary $\mathcal{A}$ there is a negligible function negl such that,

$$\mathsf{Adv}^{\mathsf{FE}}_{\mathcal{A}}(\mathsf{IND}^b_{\mathcal{A}}) = |\Pr[\mathsf{IND}^1_{\mathcal{A}}(1^\kappa) = 1] - \Pr[\mathsf{IND}^0_{\mathcal{A}}(1^\kappa) = 1]| \leq \mathrm{negl}(\kappa)$$

Moreover, we say that a FE scheme is selectively secure, if the adversary submits its challenges $(\mathbf{x}^0, \mathbf{x}^1)$ at the very beginning of the game before seeing the public-key.

2.5 Multi-Client FE

In a MCFE scheme data comes from different clients and each client encrypts its data individually. Here we present the standard syntax of MCFE scheme and then clarify its identity-based version.

Definition 4 (Multi-Client Functional Encryption). *Let* f *be a functionality (indexed by* ρ*), and* $\mathsf{Labels} = \{0,1\}^*$ *or* $\{\perp\}$ *be a set of labels. A multi-client functional encryption scheme (MCFE) for the functionality* f *and the label set* Labels *is a tuple of four algorithms* $\mathsf{MCFE} = (\mathsf{Setup}, \mathsf{KeyGen}, \mathsf{Enc}, \mathsf{Dec})$:

$\mathsf{Setup}(1^\kappa, 1^\ell, 1^k)$: *Takes as input a security parameter* κ*, the number of clients* ℓ*, vectors dimension* k *and generates public parameters* pp*. The public parameters implicitly define the functionality-index* ρ*. It outputs* ℓ *secret-keys* $\{\mathsf{ek}_i\}_{i\in[\ell]}$*, the master secret-key* $\mathsf{msk} = \{\mathsf{ek}_i\}_{i\in[\ell]}$ *and* pp *(all other algorithms take public parameters* pp*).*

$\mathsf{KeyGen}(\mathsf{msk}, \mathbf{y})$: *Takes the master secret-key* msk *and a function* $\mathbf{y}$*, and outputs a functional-key* sk_y*.*

$\mathsf{Enc}(\mathsf{ek}_i, \mathbf{x}_i, \gamma)$: *it receives the secret key* ek_i *and a label* $\gamma \in \mathsf{Labels}$ *and the message* $\mathbf{x}_i \in \mathcal{M}^k$ *to encrypt, it outputs the ciphertext* $\mathsf{ct}_{i,\gamma}$*.*

$\mathsf{Dec}(\mathsf{sk}_y, \mathsf{ct}_{1,\gamma}, \ldots, \mathsf{ct}_{\ell,\gamma})$: *Takes as input a functional-key* sk_y *and* ℓ *ciphertexts* $\mathsf{ct}_{i,\gamma}$ *under the same label* γ *and outputs* $\perp$ *or a value in range* f*.*

A MCFE *scheme is correct, if for all* $\kappa, \ell, k \in \mathbb{N}$*, functionality* f*,* $\gamma \in \mathsf{Labels}$*, messages* $\mathbf{x}_i$*, when* $(\mathsf{pp}, \{\mathsf{ek}_i\}_{i\in\ell}, \mathsf{msk}) \leftarrow \mathsf{Setup}(1^\kappa, 1^\ell, 1^k)$*,* $\mathsf{sk}_y \leftarrow \mathsf{KeyGen}(\mathsf{msk}, \mathbf{y})$*, and* $\mathsf{ct}_{i,\gamma} \leftarrow \mathsf{Enc}(\mathsf{ek}_i, \mathbf{x}_i, \gamma)$ *we have*

$$\Pr[\mathsf{Dec}(\mathsf{sk}_y, \{\mathsf{ct}_{i,\gamma}\}_{i\in[\ell]}) = f_y(\mathbf{x}_1, \ldots, \mathbf{x}_\ell)] = 1.$$

If the algorithm KeyGen receives the label γ as input, we call the scheme an *identity-based MCFE scheme*, where the functional key can be applied only over the ciphertexts which share the same identity used in the functional key. Indeed, here the identity is the label.[3]

The security notion allows encryption queries on each individual slot i and the adversary can corrupt chosen clients, while the privacy of uncorrupted clients is still preserved.

3 New Results on Ideal Lattices

In this section we present our new results on lattices which are used in the security proof of our IPFE constructions and might be of independent interest.

3.1 Multi-hint Extended RLWE Problem

We define a variant of the RLWE problem where additional information about the secrets and the noise is given through some hints. These hints are of the form $e_i r + g_i$ and $s_i f + h_i$, where $e_i, s_i \in \mathsf{R}$ are arbitrary, but with bounded norm $||s_i||_\infty, ||e_i||_\infty \leq C$ for some $C > 0$, and g_i, h_i are sampled from the same distribution as r and f. We give a formal definition below.

Definition 5 (multi-hint extended RLWE (mhe-RLWE)). *Let* $s_i, e_i \in \mathsf{R}$ *be arbitrary such that* $||s_i||_\infty, ||e_i||_\infty \leq C$ *for some* $C > 0$*, and fixed by the adversary in advance. Assume that* $a, u \in \mathsf{R}_q$ *are uniformly sampled, and* $r, f, g_i, h_i \in \mathsf{R}_q$ *sampled from* $D_{\delta I_n}$ *for* $i \in [l]$*, all by the challenger. The multi hint extended RLWE problem is to distinguish the tuples*

$$(a, ar + f, (e_i, s_i, e_i r + g_i, s_i f + h_i)_{i\in[l]}) \text{ and } (a, u, (e_i, s_i, e_i r + g_i, s_i f + h_i)_{i\in[l]}).$$

[3] The syntax of MIFE without label is defined similarly removing the labels from the syntax of MCFE.

We prove that, for properly chosen parameters, mhe-RLWE problem is at least as hard as the standard RLWE problem. Note that its hardness depends on the choice of R_q (implicitly on n and q), bound C and Gaussian parameter δ. Values s_i, e_i can be chosen arbitrary and if $s_i = e_i = 0$ for all $i \in [l]$, then the problem corresponds to the standard RLWE problem.

Theorem 1. *Let R_q, σ be such that the RLWE problem in R_q is hard, assuming the secret and errors are sampled from $D_{\sigma I_n}$. Then mhe-RLWE problem with bound C and Gaussian parameter δ is hard, when $\sigma\sqrt{1-\frac{1}{\delta^2}(\sigma n C\sqrt{l+2})^2} > \eta_\epsilon(\mathbb{Z}^{n+nl})$.*

Proof. We start by analyzing the distributions of the variables in the definition. Let Δ be a $(n+nl)\times(n+nl)$ diagonal matrix with values δ^2 on the diagonal, i.e. $\Delta = \delta^2 I_{n+ln}$. Sampling r, g_i from $D_{\delta I_n}$ is by definition indistinguishable from sampling a vector $(\boldsymbol{r}, \boldsymbol{g_1}, \ldots, \boldsymbol{g_l})$ from $D_{\sqrt{\Delta}}$.

Each multiplication $T_{e_i}(x) = e_i x \in \mathsf{R}$ for $e_i, x \in \mathsf{R}$ (as a linear function from R to R) can be represented as a matrix multiplication $E_i\boldsymbol{x}$ (and thus a liner function from $\mathbb{Z}^n$ to $\mathbb{Z}^n$) for some matrix E_i of dimension $n \times n$, independent of x. Let $\bar{\Lambda}$ be a subspace of $\mathbb{R}^{n+nl}$ defined on all the vectors $\boldsymbol{v} = (\boldsymbol{r}, -E_1\boldsymbol{r}, \ldots, -E_l\boldsymbol{r})$ for arbitrary $\boldsymbol{r} \in \mathsf{R}$. Then $\Lambda = \mathbb{Z}^{n+nl} \cap \bar{\Lambda}$ is precisely the sub-lattice of all vectors $(\boldsymbol{r}, \boldsymbol{g_1}, \ldots, \boldsymbol{g_l})$ for which the hints $e_i r + g_i = 0$.

Then elements of Λ can be written as $L\boldsymbol{r}$ for $r \in \mathsf{R}$, where L is a matrix of dimension $(n+nl)\times n$ as follows:

$$L = \begin{bmatrix} I \\ -E_1 \\ -E_2 \\ \vdots \\ -E_l \end{bmatrix}$$

When r is sampled from a Gaussian distribution $D_{\sigma I_n}$, the distribution of vector $L\boldsymbol{r}$ is $D_{\Lambda,\sqrt{B}}$, where the positive semi-definite matrix associated with Λ is defined as $B = \sigma^2 LL^T$.

Now we define matrix $A = \Delta - B$, that will be later used as a Gaussian parameter. We claim that matrix A is positive semi-definite, assuming the bounds from the theorem hold.

We use the following result to prove A is positive semi-definite for a proper choice of parameters. Recall that a matrix is $X = [x_{ij}]$ is diagonally dominated if $|x_{ii}| \geq \sum_{j\neq i}|x_{ij}|$ for any i. By a classical result from linear algebra, if a symmetric matrix X with real components is diagonally dominated, then A is positive semi-definite. Since A is symmetric with real components, it is enough to prove that A is diagonally dominated and the claim follows. Note that by the condition $\|e_i\|_\infty \leq C$ we have $\|E_iE_j\|_\infty \leq nC^2$, meaning that each component of E_iE_j is bounded by nC^2. By the definition of $A = \Delta - B$, we have $|A_{ii}| \geq \delta^2 - \sigma^2 nC^2$ and $\sum_{j\neq i}|A_{ij}| \leq \sigma^2(l-1)n^2C^2 + \sigma^2(n-1)nC^2 + \sigma^2 nC \leq \sigma^2 n^2 C^2(l+1)$. Thus if $\delta \geq \sigma n C\sqrt{l+2}$ the matrix A is a diagonally dominated matrix. The assumption $\sigma\sqrt{1-\frac{1}{\delta^2}(\sigma n C\sqrt{l+2})^2} > \eta_\epsilon(\mathbb{Z}^{n+nl})$ implies the latter.

A similar analysis can be made for vectors $(\boldsymbol{f}, \boldsymbol{h}_1, \ldots, \boldsymbol{h}_l)$ that are also chosen from a Gaussian distribution with matrix parameter Δ. We would get positive semi-definite matrices A' and B' such that $A' = \Delta - B'$ and elements sampled from B' are in the sub-lattice of vectors of the form $(\boldsymbol{f}, -S_1\boldsymbol{f}, \ldots, -S_l\boldsymbol{f})$ with probability as if $\boldsymbol{f}$ was sampled from $D_{\sigma I_n}$, where S_i is a matrix representation of s_i.

Now, we are ready to reduce the security of mhe-RLWE to the security of the RLWE problem. Let $\mathcal{A}$ and $\mathcal{B}$ be the adversary respectively to the problem mhe-RLWE and RLWE. Assume the adversary $\mathcal{B}$ is given a RLWE sample (a, b), where b is either uniformly sampled or calculated as $b = ar + f$, where r, f are sampled from $D_{\sigma I_n}$. We show how the adversary $\mathcal{B}$ uses the adversary $\mathcal{A}$ to win its game.

The adversary $\mathcal{A}$ chooses arbitrary e_i, s_i such that $\|e_i\|_\infty, \|s_i\|_\infty \leq C, i \in [l]$ and gives them to $\mathcal{B}$. Based on e_i, s_i, the adversary $\mathcal{B}$ samples $(\boldsymbol{r}', \boldsymbol{g}_1', \ldots, \boldsymbol{g}_l')$ from $D_{\sqrt{A}}$ and $(\boldsymbol{f}', \boldsymbol{h}_1', \ldots, \boldsymbol{h}_l')$ from $D_{\sqrt{A'}}$ (as described above). Then it calculates $b' = b + ar' + f'$ as the sample and $e_i r' + g_i'$, and $s_i f' + h_i'$ as hints, for $i \in [l]$ and sends them to $\mathcal{A}$. When $\mathcal{A}$ outputs a bit β as its guess, $\mathcal{B}$ outputs the same bit β.

If b was chosen uniformly at random, the distribution of b' is uniformly random. In the other case, $b' = a(r + r') + (f + f')$. To finish the proof we need to confirm that the distributions of b' and the hints are indistinguishable from the ones defined for mhe-RLWE.

Define $r^* = r + r'$, $f^* = f + f'$, $g_i = -e_i r + g_i'$, and $h_i = -s_i f + h_i'$. Note that this values are needed only to argue about the distributions of secrets and hints and are not known to $\mathcal{B}$, since r and f were chosen by the RLWE challenger. More precisely, if b in RLWE challenge was chosen uniformly at random, one can think of r and f as arbitrary sampled from $D_{\delta I_n}$. Since r is sampled from $D_{\sigma I_n}$, the distribution of vector $(\boldsymbol{r}, -\boldsymbol{e_1 r}, \ldots, -\boldsymbol{e_l r})$ is as if it was sampled from $D_{\sqrt{B}}$. On the other hand, the vector $(\boldsymbol{r}', \boldsymbol{g}_1', \ldots, \boldsymbol{g}_l')$ is sampled from $D_{\sqrt{A}}$. Since A and B are positive semi-definite and $A + B = \Delta$, Lemma 3 implies that the distribution of $(r + r', g_1, \ldots, g_l)$ is indistinguishable from being sampled from D_Δ, which is the same as the distribution we have in the assumption. In fact, Lemma 3 can be applied since $\Gamma_{A,B} = \sigma\sqrt{I_{n+nl} - \frac{\sigma^2}{\delta^2}LL^T} \geq \sigma\sqrt{1 - \frac{1}{\delta^2}(\sigma n C\sqrt{l+2})^2} > \eta_\epsilon(\mathbb{Z}^{n+nl})$, by assumption.

A similar arguments show that $(f + f', h_1, \ldots, h_l)$ are also indistinguishable from being sampled from D_Δ.

Since $b' = a(r + r') + (f + f') = ar^* + f^*$ this shows that b' has the right distribution. On the other hand,

$$e_i r^* + g_i = e_i(r + r') - e_i r + g_i' = e_i r' + g_i'$$
$$s_i f^* + h_i = s_i(f + f') - s_i f + h_i' = s_i f' + h_i'.$$

Thus also the hints have the right distribution, and even though g_i and h_i are defined w.r.t. r and f, the hints are independent of r and f. This finishes the proof. □

3.2 Leftover Hash Lemma in Rings

Let $\boldsymbol{A} \in \mathsf{R}_q^{k \times m}$ be a $k \times m$ matrix with elements from R_q. The goal of this section is to show that, with properly chosen parameters, the distribution of values $\boldsymbol{At} \in \mathsf{R}_q^k$, where $\boldsymbol{t} \in \mathsf{R}_q^m$ comes from a discrete Gaussian distribution, is close to uniform. This will be an important building block in designing an adaptively secure IPFE scheme in Sect. 5, but might as well be of an independent interest. Our result generalizes the result in [34], from $k = 1$ to an arbitrary k. We follow closely the ideas as well as notation used in [34].

Theorem 2. *Let n be a power of 2 such that $\Phi = x^n + 1$ splits into n linear factors modulo a prime q. Let $k \geq 1, m \geq 1 + k, \epsilon > 0, \delta \in (0, 1/2)$ and $\boldsymbol{t} \in \mathsf{R}_q^m$ sampled from $D_{\mathbb{Z}^{mn},\sigma}$ with $\sigma \geq \sqrt{n \ln(2mn(1 + 1/\delta))/\pi} q^{\frac{k}{m} + \frac{\epsilon}{k}}$. Then except for at most a fraction of $2^n q^{-\epsilon n} (\frac{q^{mk}}{(q^m-1)(q^m-q)\cdots(q^m-q^{k-1})})^n$ of all $\boldsymbol{A} \in (\mathsf{R}_q^{k \times m})^*$ the distance to the uniformity of $\boldsymbol{At} = (\sum_{i=1}^m a_{1,i} t_i, \ldots, \sum_{i=1}^m a_{k,i} t_i)$ is $\leq 2\delta$. This implies,*

$$\Delta[\boldsymbol{A}, \boldsymbol{At}; U((\mathsf{R}_q^{k \times m})^*, \mathsf{R}_q^k)] \leq 2\delta + 2^n q^{-\epsilon n} (\frac{q^{mk}}{(q^m - 1)(q^m - q) \cdots (q^m - q^{k-1})})^n$$

4 Selectively-Secure IPFE Based on RLWE

Our IPFE construction is inspired by the LWE-based IPFE schemes from [4,7], but here we rely on the RLWE assumption to improve the efficiency. Our construction allows to encrypt ℓ-dimensional non-negative vectors, where infinity norms of the message $\mathbf{x}$ and the function $\mathbf{y}$ are bounded by B_x and B_y, respectively. We let K be greater than the maximal value of the resulting inner product i.e., $K > \ell B_x B_y$. We first describe the construction and postpone the parameters-setting, required for the correctness and the security, to Sect. 4.2.

Construction:

- **Setup:** We sample uniformly at random $a \in \mathsf{R}_q$ and elements $\{s_i \in \mathsf{R} \mid i \in [\ell]\}, \{e_i \in \mathsf{R} \mid i \in [\ell]\}$ from D_{σ_1}. Then $\mathsf{msk} = \{s_i \mid i \in [\ell]\}$ is the master secret-keys and the public-key is $\mathsf{mpk} = (a, \{\mathsf{pk}_i \mid i \in [\ell]\})$, where $\mathsf{pk}_i = as_i + e_i \in \mathsf{R}_q$.
- **Encryption:** To encrypt a vector $\mathbf{x} = (x_1, \ldots, x_\ell) \in \mathbb{Z}^\ell$ with $\|\mathbf{x}\|_\infty \leq B_x$ we sample polynomials r and $f_0 \in \mathsf{R}_q$ from D_{σ_2}, and polynomials $\{f_i \in \mathsf{R}_q \mid i \in [\ell]\}$ independently from D_{σ_3}. We fix 1_R to be the identity element of R_q (or it can be a polynomial of degree $n - 1$ with all coefficients equal $1 \in \mathbb{Z}_q$) and calculate: $\mathsf{ct}_0 = ar + f_0 \in \mathsf{R}_q$, $\mathsf{ct}_i = \mathsf{pk}_i r + f_i + \lfloor q/K \rfloor x_i 1_\mathsf{R} \in \mathsf{R}_q$. Then $(\mathsf{ct}_0, \{\mathsf{ct}_i\}_{i \in [\ell]})$ is the encryption of $\mathbf{x}$.
- **KeyGen:** To generate a decryption key associated with $\mathbf{y} = (y_1, \ldots, y_\ell) \in \mathbb{Z}^\ell$ such that $\|y\|_\infty < B_y$, we calculate $\mathsf{sk}_y = \sum_{i=1}^\ell y_i s_i \in \mathsf{R}$.
- **Decryption:** To decrypt $(\mathsf{ct}_0, \{\mathsf{ct}_i\}_{i \in [\ell]})$ using sk_y and $\mathbf{y}$ we calculate $d = (\sum_{i=1}^\ell y_i \mathsf{ct}_i) - \mathsf{ct}_0 \mathsf{sk}_y \mod \mathsf{R}_q$. Then d should be close to $\lfloor q/K \rfloor \langle \mathbf{x}, \mathbf{y} \rangle 1_\mathsf{R}$ (a bit perturbed coefficients) and we can extract $\langle \mathbf{x}, \mathbf{y} \rangle$.

Correctness. We can write d as follows, by replacing ciphertexts and the functional key.

$$d = \sum_i (y_i e_i r + y_i f_i + f_0 y_i s_i) + \lfloor q/K \rfloor x_i y_i 1_{\mathsf{R}} = \mathsf{noise} + \lfloor q/K \rfloor \langle x, y \rangle 1_{\mathsf{R}}$$

For the correctness we need $\|\mathsf{noise}\|_\infty < \lfloor q/2K \rfloor$. By Lemma 1, for the security parameter κ, with overwhelming probability we have, $\|e_i\|_\infty, \|s_i\|_\infty \leq \sqrt{\kappa}\sigma_1$, also $\|r\|_\infty, \|f_0\|_\infty \leq \sqrt{\kappa}\sigma_2$ and $\|f_i\|_\infty \leq \sqrt{\kappa}\sigma_3$. Thus,

$$\left\| \sum_i y_i(e_i r + f_i + f_0 s_i) \right\|_\infty < \ell(2n\kappa\sigma_1\sigma_2 + \sqrt{\kappa}\sigma_3)B_y$$

Meaning that for the correctness we need $\ell(2n\kappa\sigma_1\sigma_2 + \sqrt{\kappa}\sigma_3)B_y < \lfloor q/2K \rfloor$.

Game	Description	justification
$\mathbf{G}_0$	$s_i \xleftarrow{R} D_{\sigma_1} \quad e_i \xleftarrow{R} D_{\sigma_1}$ $\mathsf{pk}_i = as_i + e_i \quad \mathsf{ct}_0 = ar + f_0$ $\mathsf{sk} = \sum_i y_i s_i \quad \mathsf{ct}_i = \mathsf{pk}_i r + f_i + \lfloor q/K \rfloor x_i^b 1_{\mathsf{R}}$	Real Game
$\mathbf{G}_1$	$s_i \xleftarrow{R} D_{\sigma_1} \quad e_i \xleftarrow{R} D_{\sigma_1}$ $\mathsf{pk}_i = as_i + e_i \quad \mathsf{ct}_0 = ar + f_0$ $\mathsf{sk} = \sum_i y_i s_i \quad \mathsf{ct}_i = \mathsf{ct}_0 s_i - f_0 s_i + e_i r + f_i + \lfloor q/K \rfloor x_i^b 1_{\mathsf{R}}$	Identical
$\mathbf{G}_2$	$\mathsf{pk}_i = as_i + e_i \quad \boxed{\mathsf{ct}_0 = u + ar + f_0}$ $\mathsf{sk} = \sum y_i s_i \quad \mathsf{ct}_i = \mathsf{ct}_0 s_i - f_0 s_i + e_i r + f_i + \lfloor q/K \rfloor x_i^b 1_{\mathsf{R}}$	mhe-RLWE
$\mathbf{G}_3$	$\mathsf{pk}_i = as_i + e_i \quad \mathsf{ct}_0 = u + ar + f_0$ $\mathsf{sk} = \sum y_i s_i \quad \mathsf{ct}_i = \mathsf{pk}_i r + us_i + f_i + \lfloor q/K \rfloor x_i^b 1_{\mathsf{R}}$	Identical
$\mathbf{G}_4$	$\boxed{s_i = s^* \alpha_i + s'_i} \quad \boxed{f_i = f^* \alpha_i + f'_i} \quad \boxed{e_i = e^* \alpha_i + e'_i}, \quad \alpha_i = (x_i^1 - x_i^0)$ $\mathsf{pk}_i = \mathsf{pk}_i = as_i + e_i \quad \mathsf{ct}_0 = u + ar + f_0$ $\mathsf{sk} = \sum_i y_i s_i \quad \mathsf{ct}_i = \mathsf{pk}_i r + us_i + f_i + \lfloor q/K \rfloor x_i^b 1_{\mathsf{R}}$	Stati. argu.
$\mathbf{G}_5$	$\mathsf{ct}_0 = u + ar + f_0$ $\mathsf{pk}_i = (as^* + e^*)\alpha_i + as'_i + e'_i \quad \mathsf{ct}_i = (as^* + e^*)r + (us^* + f^*)\alpha_i +$ $\mathsf{sk} = \sum_i y_i s'_i \quad (as'_i + e'_i)r + us'_i + f'_i + \lfloor q/K \rfloor x_i^b 1_{\mathsf{R}}$	Identical.
$\mathbf{G}_6$	$\mathsf{ct}_0 = u + ar + f_0$ $\mathsf{pk}_i = \boxed{u'}\alpha_i + as'_i + e'_i \quad \mathsf{ct}_i = \boxed{u'}r + \boxed{u''}\alpha_i +$ $\mathsf{sk} = \sum_i y_i s'_i \quad (as'_i + e'_i)r + us'_i + f'_i + \lfloor q/K \rfloor x_i^b 1_{\mathsf{R}}$	RLWE independent of b

Fig. 2. Overview of games for selectively-secure IPFE.

4.1 Security Proof

The following theorem proves the selective security of our construction. For the proof, we first rewrite ct_i based on ct_0 simply by replacing pk_i with its value $as_i + e_i$. This leads to the appearance of the term $\mathsf{ct}_0 s_i$ in the ciphertext, alongside some leakages on r and f_0. We try to formulate these leakages as the hints in the mhe-RLWE assumption, which from there by applying mhe-RLWE, we manage to replace $\mathsf{ct}_0 s_i$ with us_i for a uniform polynomial u. Note that s_i is appearing in the public-key, ciphertext and also the functional-key. To remove this term in the public-key and the ciphertext, one can see s_i as the secret for RLWE samples (with a, u as the coefficients) together with the noise terms present in the public-key and the ciphertext. Thus intuitively, all we need is to remove s_i from the functional-key (mainly because there is no error term in the functional-key, we cannot see s_i as the secret for RLWE samples here). For this, we (indistinguishably) change the structure of s_i to $s^*(x_i^1 - x_i^0) + s_i'$ allowing to remove s^* from the functional-key (thanks to the constraint $\langle \mathbf{y}, \mathbf{x}^1 - \mathbf{x}^0 \rangle = 0$) and looking at s^* as the secret for two samples of RLWE appearing in the ciphertext and in the public-key. This means a uniform term appears in the ciphertext which hides the bit b.

Theorem 3. *The IPFE scheme from Sect. 4 is sel-IND secure, for a proper choice of parameters (see Sect. 4.2). More precisely,*

$$\mathsf{Adv}_{\mathcal{A}}^{\mathsf{FE}}(\text{sel-}IND_{\mathcal{A}}^{b}) \leq \mathsf{Adv}_{\mathcal{B}}^{\mathsf{mheRLWE}}(\kappa) + \mathsf{Adv}_{\mathcal{B}'}^{\mathsf{RLWE}} + negl(\kappa).$$

where negl comes from a statistical arguments.

Proof. We define the following sequence of the games which are also summarized in Fig. 2. The first game is the real game associated with bit b, while the last game is independent of bit b. We will show that each two adjacent games are indistinguishable. Then since the last game is independent of b, the advantage of the adversary in the real game is negligible. The formal descriptions of games is given as follows.

$\boxed{\mathbf{G}_0}$: is the real game associated with the bit $b \xleftarrow{R} \{0,1\}$.

$\boxed{\mathbf{G}_1}$: is the same as game $\mathbf{G}_0$ when ct_i is computed using ct_0 (by replacing pk_i with $as_i + e_i$). Namely, $\mathsf{ct}_i = \mathsf{ct}_0 s_i - f_0 s_i + e_i r + f_i + \lfloor q/K \rfloor x_i^b 1_{\mathsf{R}}$.
Clearly, $\mathsf{Adv}_{\mathcal{A},\mathbf{G}_0}^{\mathsf{FE}}(\kappa) = \mathsf{Adv}_{\mathcal{A},\mathbf{G}_1}^{\mathsf{FE}}(\kappa)$

$\boxed{\mathbf{G}_2}$: is similar to the game $\mathbf{G}_1$ except that $\mathsf{ct}_0 = ar + f_0$ is replaced with $\mathsf{ct}_0 = u + ar + f_0$ for a uniformly sampled $u \in R_q$.
Here we rely on the mhe-RLWE assumption. The hints of the mhe-RLWE problem are leaked through values ct_i where we replace f_i with $g_i - h_i$ where h_i and g_i are sampled from the same distribution $D_{\delta I_n}$. This is possible if in Lemma 3 the positive definite matrices $\Sigma = \Sigma' = \delta I_n$ satisfy the condition $\Gamma_{\Sigma,\Sigma'} \geq \eta_\epsilon(\mathbb{Z}^n)$ for $\epsilon = 2^{-k}$. Meaning that we should set $\sigma_3 = \sqrt{2}\delta$ where δ is such that the mhe-RLWE assumption holds and also satisfies $\Gamma_{\delta I_n, \delta I_n} \geq \eta_\epsilon(\mathbb{Z}^n)$. So, by these conditions,

$$|\mathsf{Adv}_{\mathcal{A},\mathbf{G}_2}^{\mathsf{FE}}(\kappa) - \mathsf{Adv}_{\mathcal{A},\mathbf{G}_1}^{\mathsf{FE}}(\kappa)| \leq \mathsf{Adv}_{\mathcal{B}}^{\mathsf{mheRLWE}}(\kappa) + 2\epsilon.$$

$\boxed{\mathbf{G}_3}$: is the same as game $\mathbf{G}_2$ when ct_i is computed using pk_i (instead of ct_0). Namely, $\mathsf{ct}_i = \mathsf{pk}_i r + us_i + f_i + \lfloor q/K \rfloor x_i^b 1_{\mathsf{R}}, \quad \mathsf{ct}_0 = u + ar + f_0$.
Obviously, $\mathsf{Adv}_{\mathcal{A},\mathbf{G}_3}^{\mathsf{FE}}(\kappa) = \mathsf{Adv}_{\mathcal{A},\mathbf{G}_2}^{\mathsf{FE}}(\kappa)$

To proceed to the next game, we first define the matrices $\boldsymbol{S}$, $\boldsymbol{E}$ and $\boldsymbol{F}$. Recall that the master secret-key is a vector of polynomials $(s_1, \ldots, s_\ell)$ where each polynomial is in R_q. This means one call represent the master secret-key via a matrix $\boldsymbol{S}$ of dimension $\ell \times n$, where the i-th row is the vector-representation of polynomial s_i i.e., $\boldsymbol{S} = \left(\begin{bmatrix} \boldsymbol{s}_1 \\ \vdots \\ \boldsymbol{s}_\ell \end{bmatrix}\right)$. We shall call $\bar{\mathbf{s}}_j$ the j-th column of matrix $\boldsymbol{S}$. Similarly matrices $\boldsymbol{E}$ and $\boldsymbol{F}$ are defined corresponding to the noise vectors $(e_1, \ldots, e_\ell)$ and $(f_1, \ldots, f_\ell)$. Consequently, $\bar{\boldsymbol{e}}_j$ and $\bar{\boldsymbol{f}}_j$ can be defined as the j-th columns of $\boldsymbol{E}$ and $\boldsymbol{F}$ (res.). Now we define the next game as follows.

$\boxed{\mathbf{G}_4}$: is similar to the game $\mathbf{G}_3$, except that, $\bar{\mathbf{s}}_j = (s_{1j}, \ldots, s_{lj})$, $\bar{\boldsymbol{e}}_j = (e_{1j}, \ldots, e_{lj})$ (note that s_{ij} is the j-th coordinate of polynomial s_i when s_i is seen as a vector) and $\bar{\boldsymbol{f}}_j = (f_{1j}, \ldots, f_{lj})$ for $s_{ij}, e_{ij} \leftarrow D_{\sigma_1}$ and $f_{ij} \leftarrow D_{\sigma_3}$, are respectively replaced with $s_j^*\boldsymbol{\alpha} + \bar{\mathbf{s}}'_j$, $e_j^*\boldsymbol{\alpha} + \bar{\boldsymbol{e}}'_j$ and $f_j^*\boldsymbol{\alpha} + \bar{\boldsymbol{f}}'_j$ where $\boldsymbol{\alpha} = \mathbf{x}^1 - \mathbf{x}^0$, such that scalars s_j^*, e_j^*, f_j^* are sampled as $s_j^*, e_j^* \leftarrow D_{\sigma'}$, $f_j^* \leftarrow D_{\sigma''}$ and vectors $\bar{\mathbf{s}}'_j, \bar{\boldsymbol{e}}'_j, \bar{\boldsymbol{f}}'_j$ are sampled as $\bar{\mathbf{s}}'_j, \bar{\boldsymbol{e}}'_j \leftarrow D_\Sigma$, and $\bar{\boldsymbol{f}}'_j \leftarrow D_{\Sigma'}$ where $\Sigma = \sigma_1^2 I_\ell - \sigma'^2\boldsymbol{\alpha}^T\boldsymbol{\alpha}$, $\Sigma' = \sigma_3^2 I_\ell - \sigma''^2\boldsymbol{\alpha}^T\boldsymbol{\alpha}$ and σ', σ'' are positive values.

To show that this game is indistinguishable from its previous game, we apply Lemma 3. Note that since $\|\boldsymbol{\alpha}\|_\infty \leq 2B_x$, if $\sigma_1 > \sqrt{\ell}2B_x\sigma'$ and $\sigma_3 > \sqrt{\ell}2B_x\sigma''$, then matrices Σ and Σ' are positive definite which is the only requirement in Lemma 3. Thus we have,

$$|\mathsf{Adv}^{\mathsf{FE}}_{\mathcal{A},\mathbf{G}_4}(\kappa) - \mathsf{Adv}^{\mathsf{FE}}_{\mathcal{A},\mathbf{G}_3}(\kappa)| \leq 2n(2\epsilon + \epsilon')$$

where $\epsilon, \epsilon' = 2^{-\kappa}/n$ come from applying Lemma 3 respectively for $\bar{\mathbf{s}}_j, \bar{\boldsymbol{e}}_j$ and $\bar{\boldsymbol{f}}_j$ with parameters $\sigma_1, \sigma_3, \sigma', \sigma''$ satisfying $\Gamma_{\Sigma,\sigma'^2\boldsymbol{\alpha}^T\boldsymbol{\alpha}} \geq \eta_\epsilon(\mathbb{Z}^n)$ and $\Gamma_{\Sigma',\sigma''^2\boldsymbol{\alpha}^T\boldsymbol{\alpha}} \geq \eta_\epsilon(\mathbb{Z}^n)$ for $j = 1, \ldots, n$.

Now note that with the mentioned changes in the game $\mathbf{G}_4$, one can rewrite $\boldsymbol{s}_i$ (i.e., i-th row of $\boldsymbol{S}$) as $\boldsymbol{s}_i = \boldsymbol{s}^*\alpha_i + \boldsymbol{s}'_i$ where $\boldsymbol{s}^* = (s_1^*, \ldots, s_n^*)$, $\boldsymbol{s}'_i = (s'_{i1}, \ldots, s'_{in})$ and s'_{ij} is the i-th component of vector $\bar{s}'_j$. Similarly we have, $\boldsymbol{e}_i = \boldsymbol{e}^*\alpha_i + \boldsymbol{e}'_i$ and $\boldsymbol{f}_i = \boldsymbol{f}^*\alpha_i + \boldsymbol{f}'_i$. In the next game, we will use the polynomial representation of the above vectors.

$\boxed{\mathbf{G}_5}$: is the same as game $\mathbf{G}_4$ where in pk_i, ct_i and sk_y, we have replaced s_i, e_i and f_i with their new values from game $\mathbf{G}_4$. Thus,

$$\mathsf{pk}_i = (as^* + e^*)\alpha_i + as'_i + e'_i, \quad \mathsf{sk}_y = \sum_i y_i s'_i$$

$$\mathsf{ct}_i = (as^* + e^*)r + (us^* + f^*)\alpha_i + (as'_i + e'_i)r + us'_i + f'_i + \lfloor q/K \rfloor x_i^b 1_{\mathsf{R}}.$$

Since the adversary can query only for $\mathbf{y}$, with $\langle \mathbf{y}, \boldsymbol{\alpha} \rangle = 0$, the key sk_y can be rewritten without the term $\boldsymbol{s}^*$. We have, $\mathsf{Adv}^{\mathsf{FE}}_{\mathcal{A},\mathbf{G}_5}(\kappa) = \mathsf{Adv}^{\mathsf{FE}}_{\mathcal{A},\mathbf{G}_4}(\kappa)$

$\boxed{\mathbf{G}_6}$: is similar to the game $\mathbf{G}_5$ except that, in pk_i and ct_i values $as^* + e^*$ and $us^* + f^*$ are respectively replaced with uniform polynomials u' and u''. Thus,

$$\mathsf{pk}_i = u'\alpha_i + as'_i + e'_i, \quad \mathsf{sk}_y = \sum_i y_i s'_i$$

$$\mathsf{ct}_i = u'r + u''\alpha_i + (as'_i + e'_i)r + us'_i + f'_i + \lfloor q/K \rfloor x_i^b 1_{\mathsf{R}}$$

We claim that relying on RLWE assumption $\mathbf{G}_6$ is indistinguishable from $\mathbf{G}_5$. Let $\mathcal{B}$ be the attacker to the RLWE problem with two samples (a, b) and (u, b'), it can simply simulate game $\mathbf{G}_6$ when it has received uniform samples $b = u'$ and $b' = u''$, and it simulates game $\mathbf{G}_5$ when it has received samples with RLWE structures $b = as^* + e^*$ and $b = us^* + f^*$. This is due to the fact that s^*, e^* and f^* have not appeared anywhere else (individually) and the adversary $\mathcal{B}$ can simulate all other required variables by herself simply by sampling from proper distributions. Therefore,

$$|\mathsf{Adv}^{\mathsf{FE}}_{\mathcal{A},\mathbf{G}_6}(\kappa) - \mathsf{Adv}^{\mathsf{FE}}_{\mathcal{A},\mathbf{G}_5}(\kappa)| \leq \mathsf{Adv}^{\mathsf{RLWE}}_{\mathcal{B}}(\kappa)$$

Note that here f^* and e^* need to be from the same distribution i.e., $\sigma'' = \sigma'$.

Adversary-advantage in Game $\mathbf{G}_6$. Now we show that in game $\mathbf{G}_6$ the advantage of the adversary is zero. This complete the proof. Note that,

$$\begin{aligned} u''\alpha_i + \lfloor q/K \rfloor x_i^b 1_{\mathsf{R}} &= u''(x_i^1 - x_i^0) + \lfloor q/K \rfloor x_i^b 1_{\mathsf{R}} \\ &= \lfloor q/K \rfloor (\lfloor q/K \rfloor^{-1} u''(x_i^1 - x_i^0) + x_i^0 1_{\mathsf{R}} + b(x_i^1 - x_i^0) 1_{\mathsf{R}}) \\ &= \lfloor q/K \rfloor ((\lfloor q/K \rfloor^{-1} u'' + b 1_{\mathsf{R}})(x_i^1 - x_i^0) + x_i^0 1_{\mathsf{R}}) \\ &= \lfloor q/K \rfloor (\hat{u}(x_i^1 - x_i^0) + x_i^0 1_{\mathsf{R}}), \end{aligned}$$

where $\lfloor q/K \rfloor^{-1}$ is the inverse of $\lfloor q/K \rfloor$ in $\mathbb{Z}_q$ and $\hat{u}$ is uniformly sampled from R_q. The last equality (which is due to the uniformity of u'') shows that in the game $\mathbf{G}_6$, the values $\mathsf{ct} = (\mathsf{ct}_0, \mathsf{ct}_i)_i$ do not depend on the bit b and consequently the advantage of the adversary in this game is 0.

Remark 1. Note that if one wants to encrypt a matrix $\boldsymbol{X}$ rather than a vector $\mathbf{x}$, a trivial solution is to run the encryption separately for each row of the matrix. This means that the encryption of a matrix with m rows needs $O(mT)$-computations, where $O(T)$ is the computational-complexity of one encryption-run. An interesting property of our scheme is that one can use the provided compactness in the encryption to encrypt a matrix $\boldsymbol{X}$ only by $O(T)$ computational-complexity. For this we just need to define vector 1^k_{R} for $k \in [n]$ as the polynomial of degree $k-1$ in R_q with all the coefficients zero except $(k-1)$th coefficient equals 1. Then ct_i would be as $\mathsf{ct}_i = \mathsf{pk}_i r + f_i + \lfloor q/K \rfloor \sum_{k \in [n]} x_i^k 1^k_{\mathsf{R}}$, where $\mathbf{x}^k = (x_i^k)_i$ is the kth row of $\boldsymbol{X}$ and $\boldsymbol{X}$ has ℓ columns and maximum n rows. The security proof is still working with some small editions: we define $\boldsymbol{\alpha}^k = \mathbf{x}^1_k - \mathbf{x}^0_k$ associated with kth row of $\boldsymbol{X}$. Then in $\mathbf{G}_4$, we define the new structure of matrices $\boldsymbol{S}, \boldsymbol{E}, \boldsymbol{F}$ w.r.t all the vectors $\boldsymbol{\alpha}^k$. More precisely, jth column of $\boldsymbol{S}$ would be replaced with $\sum_{k \in [n]} s^*_{j,k} \boldsymbol{\alpha}^k + \bar{\mathbf{s}}'_{j,k}$ where $s^*_{j,k}, \bar{\mathbf{s}}'_{j,k}$ are sampled independently for each index k.

4.2 Parameters Setting for Selectively-Secure IPFE

Here we overview the requirement for the parameters for our selectively-secure IPFE scheme, where κ and n are two separate security parameters (theoretically, one can consider them equal, but we aimed for the efficient implementation).

Correctness. Needs $\ell(2n\kappa\sigma_1\sigma_2 + \sqrt{\kappa}\sigma_3)B_y < \lfloor q/2K \rfloor$ and $q > K > lB_xB_y$.
Transition from $\mathbf{G}_1$ to $\mathbf{G}_2$. Needs $\sigma_3 = \sqrt{2}\sigma_2$, $\Gamma_{\sigma_2 I_n, \sigma_2 I_n} \geq \eta_\epsilon(\mathbb{Z}^n)$ with $\epsilon = 2^{-\kappa}$ (where matrix Γ is defined in Lemma 3) and also all the parameter setting from mhe-RLWE assumption i.e., $\sigma\sqrt{1 - \frac{1}{\sigma_2^2}(\sigma n C\sqrt{\ell+2})^2} > \eta_\epsilon(\mathbb{Z}^{n+n\ell})$ where $\|s_i\|_\infty, \|e_i\|_\infty \leq C$ and σ is the parameter for the hardness of RLWE. By Lemma 1, one can set $C = \sqrt{\kappa}\sigma_1$.
Transition from $\mathbf{G}_3$ to $\mathbf{G}_4$. Needs $\sigma_1 > \sqrt{\ell}2B_x\sigma'$ and $\sigma_3 \geq \sqrt{\ell}2B_x\sigma''$ for non-negatives σ' and σ'' where $\sigma_1, \sigma_3, \sigma', \sigma''$ satisfy $\Gamma_{\Sigma_j, \sigma'^2\alpha^T\alpha} \geq \eta_\epsilon(\mathbb{Z}^n)$ and $\Gamma_{\Sigma'_j, \sigma''^2\alpha^T\alpha} \geq \eta_{\epsilon}(\mathbb{Z}^n)$ with $\epsilon, \epsilon' = 2^{-\kappa}/n$.
Transition from $\mathbf{G}_5$ to $\mathbf{G}_6$. Needs the parameter for the hardness of RLWE where the secret and error are from the distribution $D_{\sigma' I_n}$ and $\sigma' = \sigma''$.
Hardness of RLWE. As we saw we need the parameters q, R, σ and σ' to satisfy the conditions for the hardness of RLWE. We use the bounds from [26] (Theorem 3.6 of [26]), thus set $\mathsf{R} = \mathbb{Z}[x]/(x^n+1)$, n is a power of 2, $q = 1 \mod 2n$ and $\sigma = \alpha q(n/\log n)^{1/4}$ and $\sigma' = \alpha' q(2n/\log(2n))^{1/4}$ where $\alpha \leq \sqrt{\log n/n}$, $\alpha' \leq \sqrt{\log n/n}$ and $\sqrt{\alpha q} \geq \omega(\log n)$, $\sqrt{\alpha' q} \geq \omega(\log n)$.

5 Adaptively Secure IPFE Based on RLWE

Here we modify the construction to lift the security to the adaptive case. The main difference from our selectively-secure construction is that here each secret key s_i and the public parameter a are vectors-of-polynomials rather than two single polynomials. Again the non-negative messages $\mathbf{x}$ and functions $\mathbf{y}$ are bounded by B_x and B_y, respectively, and let K be greater than the maximum value of the inner-product i.e., $K > \ell B_x B_y$.

Construction:

- **Setup:** Let R, R_q be as before. For each $i \in [\ell]$ sample $\boldsymbol{s}_i = (s_{i1}, \ldots, s_{im}) \in \mathsf{R}^m$ where each $s_{ij} \in \mathsf{R}$ is sampled from $D_{\sigma_1 I_n}$. Sample $\boldsymbol{a} = (a_1, \ldots, a_m) \in \mathsf{R}_q^m$ uniformly at random. Check if at least one a_i is invertible in R_q; if not, refuse $\boldsymbol{a}$ and sample it again[4]. Finally, $\mathsf{msk} = \{\boldsymbol{s}_i \mid i \in [\ell]\}$ is the secret-key and the public-key is $\mathsf{mpk} = (\boldsymbol{a}, \{pk_i \mid i \in [\ell]\})$, where $\mathsf{pk}_i = \langle \boldsymbol{a}, \boldsymbol{s}_i \rangle = \sum_j a_j s_{ij}$.
- **Encrypt:** To encrypt a vector $\mathbf{x} = (x_1, \ldots, x_\ell) \in \mathbb{Z}^\ell$ with $\|\mathbf{x}\|_\infty \leq B_x$ sample $r \in R_q$ from $D_{\sigma_2 I_n}$ and $\boldsymbol{f}_0 = (f_{01}, \cdots, f_{0m}) \in R_q^m$ from $D_{\sigma_2 I_{nm}}$, and $\{f_i \in \mathsf{R}_q \mid i \in [\ell]\}$ each from $D_{\sigma_3 I_n}$. Then

$$\mathbf{ct}_0 = \boldsymbol{a}r + \boldsymbol{f}_0 = (a_1 r + f_{01}, \ldots, a_m r + f_{0m}), \quad \mathsf{ct}_i = \mathsf{pk}_i r + f_i + \lfloor q/K \rfloor x_i 1_{\mathsf{R}}.$$

  Check if at least one element of $\mathbf{ct}_0$ is invertible in R_q and that $\mathbf{ct}_0$ is not a multiple of $\boldsymbol{a}$ (over R_q); if this is not the case, resample r, $\boldsymbol{f}_0$ and recompute $\mathbf{ct}_0, \mathsf{ct}_i$ until the latter holds. The ciphertext is $(\mathbf{ct}_0, \{\mathsf{ct}_i\}_{i \in [\ell]})$.

[4] This step would be done efficiently, since the probability that a_i is invertible, is non-negligible.

- **KeyGen:** To generate the decryption key associated with $\mathbf{y} = (y_1, \ldots, y_\ell) \in \mathbb{Z}^\ell$ where $\|\mathbf{y}\|_\infty < B_y$, we calculate

$$\mathsf{sk}_y = \sum_{i=1}^{\ell} y_i s_i = (\sum_{i=1}^{\ell} y_i s_{i1}, \ldots, \sum_{i=1}^{\ell} y_i s_{im}) \in \mathsf{R}^m$$

- **Decryption:** To decrypt the ciphertext $(\mathbf{ct}_0, \{\mathsf{ct}_i\}_{i\in[\ell]})$ by the decryption key sk_y, compute: $d = (\sum_{i=1}^{\ell} y_i \mathsf{ct}_i) - \langle \mathbf{ct}_0, \mathsf{sk}_y \rangle$. Then d should be close to $\lfloor q/K \rfloor \langle \mathbf{x}, \mathbf{y} \rangle 1_R$ (a bit perturbed coefficients) and we can extract $\langle \mathbf{x}, \mathbf{y} \rangle$.

Correctness. Similar to the correctness proof in our sel-IPFE, one can verify that we need $\left\|\sum_i (y_i f_i - y_i \langle \boldsymbol{f}_0, \boldsymbol{s}_i \rangle)\right\|_\infty < \lfloor q/2K \rfloor$ or equivalently, $\ell B_y(\sqrt{\kappa}\sigma_3 + mn\kappa\sigma_1\sigma_2) < \lfloor q/2K \rfloor$.

We claim that this modified version of our IPFE scheme is adaptively-secure. For the proof we use an extended version of mhe-RLWE assumption associated with polynomially-many samples (rather-than a single sample). We also use Theorem 2 which provides us with the required variant of Ring-LHL.

The first steps of the proof are similar to the security proof of our sel-IPFE, namely, we follow a similar sequence of the games from $\mathbf{G}_0$ to $\mathbf{G}_4$. But in the next games instead of using two samples of RLWE, we use Ring-LHL. The reason for this is that the indistiguishability of proceeding games relies only on statistical arguments and so one can upgrade the security to the adaptive version by a technique similar to the complexity leveraging (CL) even for a large value $(B_x)^\ell$ (while applying CL on the computational arguments needs polynomial-size $(B_x)^\ell$).

Theorem 4. *Our modified IPFE scheme is adaptively-secure, for proper choice of parameters.*

Similarly as in the selective case, also the adaptively secure scheme can simply be extended to allow encrypting vectors in parallel.

6 Multi-client IPFE

In this section we present all the needed results to lift our scheme to a multi-client setting. In particular, we present a compiler built upon the compiler of multi-input IPFE (MIFE) scheme of [6], supporting corruptions [3], to transfer a IPFE to its identity-based MCFE version. First, we recall the compiler of [6]. here FE is a single-input IPFE scheme.

Compiler of [6] (MIFE-Compiler): From Single-Input to Multi-Input IPFE.

- $\mathsf{Setup}(1^\kappa, 1^\ell, 1^k)$: it chooses $\boldsymbol{u}_i \xleftarrow{R} \mathbb{Z}_q^k$ and runs $(\mathsf{mpk}'_i, \mathsf{msk}'_i) \leftarrow \mathsf{FE.Setup}(1^\kappa, 1^k)$ for each $i \in [\ell]$. It outputs $\mathsf{msk}_i = (\mathsf{msk}'_i, \boldsymbol{u}_i)$ as the secret key of user i, $\mathsf{msk} = (\mathsf{msk}_i)_i$ as the master key and $\mathsf{pp} = (\mathsf{mpk}'_i)_i$.

- $\mathsf{KeyGen}(\mathsf{msk}, \mathbf{y})$: for $\mathbf{y} = (\mathbf{y}_1, \ldots, \mathbf{y}_\ell)$ where $\mathbf{y}_i \in \mathbb{Z}_q^k$, it runs $\mathsf{sk}_{i,y} \leftarrow \mathsf{FE.KeyGen}(\mathsf{msk}'_i, \mathbf{y}_i)$ for $i \in [\ell]$ and sets $\mathsf{sk}'_y = \sum_i \boldsymbol{u}_i \mathbf{y}_i$. Then it outputs $\mathsf{sk}_y = ((\mathsf{sk}_{i,y})_i, \mathsf{sk}'_y)$.
- $\mathsf{Enc}(\mathsf{msk}_i, \mathbf{x}_i)$: for $\mathbf{x}_i \in \mathbb{Z}_q^k$, it runs $\mathsf{ct}_i \leftarrow \mathsf{FE.Enc}(\mathsf{msk}'_i, \mathbf{x}_i + \boldsymbol{u}_i)$ and outputs ct_i.
- $\mathsf{Dec}((\mathsf{ct}_i)_i, \mathsf{sk}_y)$: it runs $D_i \leftarrow \mathsf{FE.Dec}_1(\mathsf{ct}_i, \mathsf{sk}_{i,y})$ for $i \in [\ell]$. Then it outputs $\mathsf{FE.Dec}_2(\sum_i D_i + \mathcal{E}(-\mathsf{sk}'_y, 0))$.

The compiler can be used on any IPFE scheme with the following properties:

Property 1 (2-step decryption with a linear encoding). The decryption algorithm of IPFE is a 2-step decryption (i.e., $\mathsf{Dec}(\mathsf{ct}, \mathsf{sk}) = \mathsf{Dec}_2(\mathsf{Dec}_1(\mathsf{ct}, \mathsf{sk}))$, where $\mathsf{Dec}_1(\mathsf{ct}, \mathsf{sk}) = \mathcal{E}(\langle x, y\rangle, \text{noise}))$. That is, the first step outputs an encoding of inner-product and in the second step it extracts the inner-product from the mentioned encoding. Additionally, the encoding also has a linear property.[5]

Property 2 (linear encryption). Let Enc be the encryption algorithm of IPFE scheme. Then there exists a deterministic algorithm Add, such that the two following distributions of $\mathsf{Enc}(\mathsf{msk}, \mathbf{x}_1 + \mathbf{x}_2)$ and $\mathsf{Add}(\mathsf{Enc}(\mathsf{msk}, \mathbf{x}_1), \mathbf{x}_2)$ are identical. Informally, given the message $\mathbf{x}_2$ and the encryption of $\mathbf{x}_1$, one can compute the encryption of $\mathbf{x}_1 + \mathbf{x}_2$:

In our RLWE-based IPFE scheme, Dec_1 outputs the inner-product added by a noise term, then Dec_2 removes the noise. Encoding is defined as adding the noise which is linear. It is easy to see that the encryption is linear.

We now present our compiler to build an identity-based MCFE (from MIFE allowing corruptions). In the following construction $H : (U, \mathsf{Labels}) \rightarrow \mathbb{Z}_q^k$ is a hash function (later modeled as a random oracle).

Our Compiler (MCFE-Compiler): From Multi-Input to identity-based Multi-Client IPFE.

- $\mathsf{Setup}(1^\kappa, 1^\ell, 1^k)$: it chooses $\boldsymbol{u}'_i \stackrel{R}{\leftarrow} U$ and runs $(\mathsf{mpk}'_i, \mathsf{msk}'_i)_{i\in[\ell]} \leftarrow \mathsf{MIFE.Setup}(1^\kappa, 1^\ell, 1^k)$. It outputs $\mathsf{msk}_i = (\mathsf{msk}'_i, \boldsymbol{u}'_i)$ as the secret key of user i, $\mathsf{msk} = (\mathsf{msk}_i)_i$ as the master key and $\mathsf{pp} = (\mathsf{mpk}'_i)_i$.
- $\mathsf{KeyGen}(\mathsf{msk}, \mathbf{y}, \gamma)$: it runs $\mathsf{sk}_y = ((\mathsf{sk}_{i,y})_i, \mathsf{sk}'_y) \leftarrow \mathsf{MIFE.KeyGen}(\mathsf{msk}, \mathbf{y})$ and sets $\mathsf{sk}''_{y,\gamma} = \mathsf{sk}'_y + \sum_i H(\boldsymbol{u}'_i, \gamma)\mathbf{y}_i$. Then it outputs $\mathsf{sk}_{y,\gamma} = ((\mathsf{sk}_{i,y})_i, \mathsf{sk}''_{y,\gamma})$.
- $\mathsf{Enc}(\mathsf{msk}_i, \mathbf{x}_i, \gamma)$: it runs $\mathsf{ct}_{i,\gamma} \leftarrow \mathsf{MIFE.Enc}(\mathsf{msk}_i, \mathbf{x}_i + H(\boldsymbol{u}'_i, \gamma))$ and outputs $\mathsf{ct}_{i,\gamma}$.
- $\mathsf{Dec}((\mathsf{ct}_{i,\gamma})_i, \mathsf{sk}_{y,\gamma})$: it runs $D_\gamma \leftarrow \mathsf{MIFE.Dec}((\mathsf{ct}_{i,\gamma})_i, (\{\mathsf{sk}_{i,y}\}_i, \mathsf{sk}''_{y,\gamma}))$ and outputs D_γ

In the security proof of the above compiler, we use Property 2, used also for the compiler of [6].

[5] For the sake of simplicity, here we gave an informal description of this property. An interested reader can see [6] for the formal one. The formal description guarantees the correctness of the MIFE scheme w.r.t the general IPFE, and is not used in the proof of security.

Theorem 5. *In the above compiler (from MIFE with corruptions to identity-based MCFE), if MIFE is secure, then our construction is a secure MCFE against static corruptions.*[6]

The proof proceeds through a sequence of games defined w.r.t to the labels issued by the adversary. For a fixed label γ we change the messages $\mathbf{x}_{i,\gamma}^0$ encrypted under the label γ to $\mathbf{x}_{i,\gamma}^1$ for all i. To ensure that such changes are indistinguishable, we rely on the security of MIFE. For encryption queries w.r.t γ the simulator answers by relaying them to the MIFE-challenger, and it programs the random oracle queries as $H(\boldsymbol{u}_i', \gamma') = \boldsymbol{r}_{i,\gamma'} - \boldsymbol{u}_i$, for $\gamma' \neq \gamma$, while $\boldsymbol{r}_{i,\gamma'}$ is randomly chosen. This allows to remove the term $\boldsymbol{u}_i$ from the encryption, which is the only unknown part to the simulator, and simulate the queries correctly.

Finally, we argue that our RLWE based scheme can be used in the above compilers.

Proposition 1. *The MIFE-compiler and the MCFE-compiler applied on our IPFE schemes in Sect. 4 or Sect. 5 result in a secure and correct MCFE scheme.*

We further can extend our identity-based MCFE scheme to its decentralized version, where we use the compiler of [3], but we modify the compiler and the security proof for the case that the secret key is involved with the label as well (which is the case in our scheme). One can see that our IPFE scheme has the required properties to be used in this compiler as well.

Batching in (D)MCFE: As stated in Remark 1, our RLWE scheme supports encrypting multiple messages in parallel. This property is preserved with (D)MCFE compilers described in this section. To be precise, each encrypted row needs to be masked (as described above) separately. Furthermore, identity-based (D)MCFE allows us to derive functional keys depending on a chosen label. If one encrypts multiple rows in parallel with different labels, a functional key will decrypt only the ones with the matching label. This allows fine-grained control on a batch of messages.

7 Practical Instantiation

In this section, we demonstrate the efficiency and practicality of our scheme with concrete instantiations. We provide different parameter sets with different levels of security and strategies for a very efficient implementation. Finally, we apply our scheme for a privacy preserving machine learning application of identifying digits from encrypted images. The implementation is publicly available at https://github.com/fentec-project/IPFE-RLWE.

[6] Note that we are specifically using MIFE scheme of [6] and it is not any possible MIFE scheme in RO model.

7.1 Implementation

Similar to other RLWE based schemes, the two major components of our scheme are polynomial multiplication and noise sampling. However, from the computational point of view the most challenging task here is to efficiently implement multiple polynomial multiplications and multiple sampling of secret and error polynomials which grow linearly with ℓ. Here, we describe our approach for efficient implementation of these components, all running in constant-time.

Discrete Gaussian Sampling: Our scheme uses discrete Gaussian distribution to sample error and secret vectors. A non-constant-time sampler leaks sensitive information about these secret vectors that can break the cryptosystem. There are three choices for constant time sampling i) linear-searching of CDT (Cumulative Distribution Table) table [12], ii) bit-sliced sampler [21], and iii) constant-time binary sampling [37]. The first two methods are very efficient for smaller (< 10) standard deviations but do not scale very well for larger standard deviations. Moreover, they need different tables or minimized Boolean expressions for different samplers. One can use convolutions to first sample from smaller distributions and then combine them to generate a sample from a distribution with larger standard deviation [30]. However, this method is less efficient compared to the constant-time binary sampling described by Zhao et al. [37]. In this method, to generate a sample from D_σ, first a sample from a base distribution $x \xleftarrow{R} D^+_{\sigma_0}$ is generated. Next, an integer k is fixed such that $\sigma = k\sigma_0$ and a integer y is sampled uniformly from $[0, \cdots, k-1]$. Finally, a rejection sampling on $z = kx + y$ with the acceptance probability $p = \exp(\frac{-y(y+2kx)}{2\sigma^2})$ is performed. It can be easily shown that the samples generated in this way are *statistically close* to discrete Gaussian distribution with Gaussian parameter σ. To generate a sample from D_σ a randomly generated sign bit is applied on z. The rejection sampling is performed using a Bernoulli sampler. If the base sampling algorithm $D^+_{\sigma_0}$ and the Bernoulli sampler are constant-time this method runs in constant-time. In our implementation to generate samples from $\sigma_1 = k_1\sigma_0$, $\sigma_2 = k_2\sigma_0$, and $\sigma_3 = k_3\sigma_0$, we use the constant-time Bernoulli sampler proposed by Zhao et al. [37] for different values of k and σ. The uniform sampler has also been updated for different values of k. Finally, a linear-search based CDT sampling algorithm has been used for the constant-time base sampler. Using the bit-sliced algorithm to instantiate the base sampler might improve the efficiency to some extent but we leave this as future work.

CRT Representation: Due to the correctness and security constraints of our scheme, the modulus q required in all variants of our scheme is quite large (≥ 64 bits). Similar to homomorphic encryption implementations [33] we adapted the residual number system based polynomial arithmetic using Chinese remainder theorem to avoid the naive and relatively slow multi-precision arithmetic. We choose a chain of moduli $q_0, q_1, \ldots, q_{n_p-1}$ such that $q = q_0 \cdot q_1 \cdots q_{n_p-1}$. All the inputs, outputs, and intermediate values are stored as elements in rings R_{q_i} instead of R_q. As all the q_i are less than 32 bits long this replaces the expensive multi-precision polynomial arithmetic with simple and efficient single-precision arithmetic. We only need to revert to R_q while extracting the value d at the end of decryption operation. We use Garner's algorithm and GNU multi-precision library to accomplish this.

Polynomial Arithmetic: We use Number theoretic transform (NTT) based polynomial multiplication in our scheme since it is an in-place algorithm and runs in $O(n \log n)$ time complexity where n is the length of the polynomial. Specifically, we used the NTT with *negative wrapped convolution* [25] which produces the result of the multiplication reduced by $1 + x^n$ without any extra memory.

For a power-of-two n and prime modulus q_i, such that $q_i \equiv 1 \mod 2n$, the multiplication of two polynomials $a, b \in \mathsf{R}_{q_i}$ can be calculated as $NTT^{-1}(NTT(a) \circ NTT(b))$ where NTT and NTT^{-1} are forward and inverse NTT transformations respectively and $\circ$ denotes the component-wise multiplication of two vectors. Computationally, the forward and the inverse NTT transformation are the prevalent components of the whole $O(n \log n)$ time multiplication. We observe that one of the multiplicands, i.e. a in **Setup** and r in **Encrypt** stays same for all the $\ell + 1$ multiplications, Hence we precompute and store NTT(a) and NTT(r). This saves ℓ NTT transformations in each case. Also, the public polynomial a is random in R_{q_i}. As NTT transformation of a random vector is also random, we can assume the a is already in the NTT domain.

NTT or NTT^{-1} transformation algorithms require applying bit-reversal permutations before or after each transformation. As our polynomials are quite large and the number of multiplications is linear in ℓ, this requirement induces a significant overhead. To overcome this problem we followed the same strategy as Pöppelman et al. [31]. We used the *decimation-in-time* NTT based on Cooley-Tukey [15] butterfly which requires input in normal ordering but produces output in bit-reversed ordering. For the inverse transformation we switch to *decimation-in-frequency* NTT based on Gentleman-Sande [17] butterfly, which accepts the input in bit-reversed ordering and produces the output in normal ordering. Hence, applying these transformations in conjunction eliminates the need for bit-reversal step.

Other: There are two common strategies to generate pseudo-random numbers in cryptographic implementations: using extended output function like Keccak [10] or using block ciphers in counter mode. Since our target platform is equipped with AES-NI (Advanced Encryption Standard New Instructions), we decided to use AES in CTR mode for fast generation of cryptographically secure pseudo-random numbers. Further, we have chosen our NTT friendly primes $q_i, i \in [0, n_p - 1]$ of the form $2^i - 2^j + 1$. Due to their special structure it is possible to perform fast modular reduction similar to Mersenne primes with these primes.

7.2 Parameters and Performance

We propose three sets of parameters in Table. 1 depending with different values of ℓ, B_x, and B_y. Here we have considered the selectively secure scheme described in Sect. 4.2. We calculate the concrete security of our scheme based on the underlying hardness of a RLWE instance. That is, we deduce our functional encryption with parameters $(n, q, \sigma_1, \sigma_2, \sigma_3, \ell, B_x, B_y)$ scheme offers $\mathcal{S}$ bits of security if the the underlying RLWE instance with (n, q, σ) offers $\mathcal{S}$ bits of security. Here, the parameters $(n, q, \sigma_1, \sigma_2, \sigma_3, \ell, B_x, B_y)$ and (n, q, σ) are related to satisfy the security constraints delineated in Sect. 4.2.

Performance: Table. 1 also lists the performance of different operations of our scheme. We benchmarked on a single core of an Intel i9-9880H processor running at maximum 4.8GHz frequency. The code has been compiled using GCC-9.3 with optimization flags `-O3 -fomit-frame-pointer -march=native` on Ubuntu 18.04.

7.3 Machine Learning on Encrypted Data and Other Use Cases

To demonstrate the efficiency of our scheme, we use it in a real world application of FE. We perform a task of classification with a simple machine learning model, but on encrypted data using our IPFE. In particular, we evaluate logistic regression on MNIST dataset, recognizing handwritten digits in images. This task involves computing 10 linear functions on a 785-dimensional vectors, where the complexity of computation is bounded with $B_x = 4$ and $B_y = 16$.

Table 1. Parameters and performance of the RLWE based FE scheme. The security has been calculated using the LWE estimator tool [9].

Security level	PQ Security	FE Bounds	Gaussian Parameters	Ring Parameters	CRT moduli	Time (ms)
Low	76.3	$B_x : 2$ $B_y : 2$ $\ell : 64$	$\sigma_1 : 33$ $\sigma_2 : 59473921$ $\sigma_3 : 118947840$	$n : 2048$ $\lceil \log q \rceil : 66$	$q_1 : 2^{14} - 2^{12} + 1$ $q_2 : 2^{23} - 2^{17} + 1$ $q_3 : 2^{29} - 2^{18} + 1$	Setup:26 Enc:16 KG:0.27 Dec:1
Medium	119.2	$B_x : 4$ $B_y : 16$ $\ell : 785$	$\sigma_1 : 225.14$ $\sigma_2 : 258376412.19$ $\sigma_3 : 516752822.39$	$n : 4096$ $\lceil \log q \rceil : 86$	$q_1 : 2^{24} - 2^{14} + 1$ $q_2 : 2^{31} - 2^{17} + 1$ $q_3 : 2^{31} - 2^{24} + 1$	Setup:589 Enc:381 KG:22 Dec:17
High	246.2	$B_x : 32$ $B_y : 32$ $\ell : 1024$	$\sigma_1 : 2049$ $\sigma_2 : 5371330561$ $\sigma_3 : 10742661120$	$n : 8192$ $\lceil \log q \rceil : 101$	$q_1 : 2^{17} - 2^{14} + 1$ $q_2 : 2^{20} - 2^{14} + 1$ $q_3 : 2^{32} - 2^{20} + 1$ $q_4 : 2^{32} - 2^{30} + 1$	Setup:1743 Enc:1388 KG:70 Dec:45

Parameters in Table. 1 for medium level of security (129 bit of PQ Security) were chosen to fit this use-case. Hence it takes approx. 381 ms to encrypt an image (vector representation) of this size and only 170 ms to evaluate the model, i.e. we need to perform 10 decryptions to properly classify an image. In fact, as explained in Remark 1, one can encrypt with one encryption-run multiple images simultaneously, in our case up to 4096 images. Evaluating the model would classify all the images at once, without a major change in the complexity.

Other: We would like to additionally highlight possible practical scenarios where our scheme excels over other known schemes. On one hand, single-input public key RLWE based IPFE is particularly useful when multiple data from the same source is processed with FE, due to its batching property. This could be, for example, streams of data (e.g. a video, see [1] where a single-input public key scheme was used) processed in some fixed intervals, or learning a ML model [36] where IPFE can be used on an encrypted dataset, usually evaluating the same function on batches. On the other hand, the data itself might be structured as a matrix. In [28], a DMCFE scheme was proposed for a privacy preserving location tracking. Users in a decentralized way, for each possible location, encrypt 0 or 1 indicating their presence. Using IPFE, averages (heatmaps) can be computed, where RLWE batching can be used to cover, say, 4096 locations with one ciphertext, outperforming known FE schemes.

Acknowledgements. The authors were supported by EU's Horizon 2020 FENTEC project. Angshuman Karmakar is funded by FWO (Research Foundation - Flanders) as junior post-doctoral fellow (contract number 203056 / 1241722N LV). Tilen Marc is supported by ARRS projects P1-0297, N1-0095, J1-1693, N1-0218 and Horizon 2020 KRAKEN project. Azam Soleimanian benefited from the support of the Chair ≪Blockchain & B2B Platforms≫, led by l'X - Ecole polytechnique and the Fondation de l'Ecole polytechnique, sponsored by Capgemini, Nomadics Lab and Caisse des dépôts.

References

1. https://fentec.eu/content/motion-detection-and-local-decision-making
2. Abdalla, M., Benhamouda, F., Gay, R.: From single-input to multi-client inner-product functional encryption. In: Galbraith, S.D., Moriai, S. (eds.) ASIACRYPT 2019. LNCS, vol. 11923, pp. 552–582. Springer, Cham (2019). https://doi.org/10.1007/978-3-030-34618-8_19
3. Abdalla, M., Benhamouda, F., Kohlweiss, M., Waldner, H.: Decentralizing inner-product functional encryption. In: Lin, D., Sako, K. (eds.) PKC 2019. LNCS, vol. 11443, pp. 128–157. Springer, Cham (2019). https://doi.org/10.1007/978-3-030-17259-6_5
4. Abdalla, M., Bourse, F., De Caro, A., Pointcheval, D.: Simple functional encryption schemes for inner products. In: Katz, J. (ed.) PKC 2015. LNCS, vol. 9020, pp. 733–751. Springer, Heidelberg (2015). https://doi.org/10.1007/978-3-662-46447-2_33

5. Abdalla, M., Bourse, F., Marival, H., Pointcheval, D., Soleimanian, A., Waldner, H.: Multi-client inner-product functional encryption in the random-oracle model. Cryptology ePrint Archive, Report 2020/788 (2020). https://eprint.iacr.org/2020/788
6. Abdalla, M., Catalano, D., Fiore, D., Gay, R., Ursu, B.: Multi-input functional encryption for inner products: function-hiding realizations and constructions without pairings. In: Shacham, H., Boldyreva, A. (eds.) CRYPTO 2018. LNCS, vol. 10991, pp. 597–627. Springer, Cham (2018). https://doi.org/10.1007/978-3-319-96884-1_20
7. Agrawal, S., Libert, B., Stehlé, D.: Fully secure functional encryption for inner products, from standard assumptions. In: Robshaw, M., Katz, J. (eds.) CRYPTO 2016. LNCS, vol. 9816, pp. 333–362. Springer, Heidelberg (2016). https://doi.org/10.1007/978-3-662-53015-3_12
8. Ajtai, M.: Generating hard instances of lattice problems (extended abstract). In: 28th ACM STOC, pp. 99–108. ACM Press, May 1996. https://doi.org/10.1145/237814.237838
9. Albrecht, M.R., et al.: Estimate all the LWE, NTRU schemes! In: Catalano, D., De Prisco, R. (eds.) SCN 2018. LNCS, vol. 11035, pp. 351–367. Springer, Cham (2018). https://doi.org/10.1007/978-3-319-98113-0_19
10. Bertoni, G., Daemen, J., Peeters, M., Van Assche, G.: Keccak. In: Johansson, T., Nguyen, P.Q. (eds.) EUROCRYPT 2013. LNCS, vol. 7881, pp. 313–314. Springer, Heidelberg (2013). https://doi.org/10.1007/978-3-642-38348-9_19
11. Boneh, D., Sahai, A., Waters, B.: Functional encryption: definitions and challenges. In: Ishai, Y. (ed.) TCC 2011. LNCS, vol. 6597, pp. 253–273. Springer, Heidelberg (2011). https://doi.org/10.1007/978-3-642-19571-6_16
12. Bos, J.W., Costello, C., Naehrig, M., Stebila, D.: Post-quantum key exchange for the TLS protocol from the ring learning with errors problem. In: 2015 IEEE Symposium on Security and Privacy, pp. 553–570. IEEE Computer Society Press, May 2015. https://doi.org/10.1109/SP.2015.40
13. Brakerski, Z., Vaikuntanathan, V.: Fully homomorphic encryption from ring-LWE and security for key dependent messages. In: Rogaway, P. (ed.) CRYPTO 2011. LNCS, vol. 6841, pp. 505–524. Springer, Heidelberg (2011). https://doi.org/10.1007/978-3-642-22792-9_29
14. Chotard, J., Dufour Sans, E., Gay, R., Phan, D.H., Pointcheval, D.: Decentralized multi-client functional encryption for inner product. In: Peyrin, T., Galbraith, S. (eds.) ASIACRYPT 2018. LNCS, vol. 11273, pp. 703–732. Springer, Cham (2018). https://doi.org/10.1007/978-3-030-03329-3_24
15. Cooley, J.W., Tukey, J.W.: An algorithm for the machine calculation of complex fourier series. Math. Comput. **19**(90), 297–301 (1965). http://www.jstor.org/stable/2003354
16. Garg, S., Gentry, C., Halevi, S., Raykova, M., Sahai, A., Waters, B.: Candidate indistinguishability obfuscation and functional encryption for all circuits. In: 54th FOCS, pp. 40–49. IEEE Computer Society Press, October 2013. https://doi.org/10.1109/FOCS.2013.13
17. Gentleman, W.M., Sande, G.: Fast fourier transforms: for fun and profit. AFIPS Conference Proceedings, vol. 29, pp. 563–578. AFIPS / ACM / Spartan Books, Washington D.C. (1966). https://doi.org/10.1145/1464291.1464352
18. Gentry, C., Peikert, C., Vaikuntanathan, V.: Trapdoors for hard lattices and new cryptographic constructions. In: Ladner, R.E., Dwork, C. (eds.) 40th ACM STOC, pp. 197–206. ACM Press, May 2008. https://doi.org/10.1145/1374376.1374407

19. Goldwasser, S., Kalai, Y.T., Popa, R.A., Vaikuntanathan, V., Zeldovich, N.: Reusable garbled circuits and succinct functional encryption. In: Boneh, D., Roughgarden, T., Feigenbaum, J. (eds.) 45th ACM STOC, pp. 555–564. ACM Press, June 2013. https://doi.org/10.1145/2488608.2488678
20. Gorbunov, S., Vaikuntanathan, V., Wee, H.: Functional encryption with bounded collusions via multi-party computation. In: Safavi-Naini, R., Canetti, R. (eds.) CRYPTO 2012. LNCS, vol. 7417, pp. 162–179. Springer, Heidelberg (2012). https://doi.org/10.1007/978-3-642-32009-5_11
21. Karmakar, A., Roy, S.S., Reparaz, O., Vercauteren, F., Verbauwhede, I.: Constant-time discrete gaussian sampling. IEEE Trans. Comput. **67**(11), 1561–1571 (2018). https://doi.org/10.1109/TC.2018.2814587
22. Katsumata, S., Yamada, S.: Partitioning via non-linear polynomial functions: more compact IBEs from ideal lattices and bilinear maps. In: Cheon, J.H., Takagi, T. (eds.) ASIACRYPT 2016. LNCS, vol. 10032, pp. 682–712. Springer, Heidelberg (2016). https://doi.org/10.1007/978-3-662-53890-6_23
23. Liu, F.-H., Wang, Z.: Rounding in the rings. In: Micciancio, D., Ristenpart, T. (eds.) CRYPTO 2020. LNCS, vol. 12171, pp. 296–326. Springer, Cham (2020). https://doi.org/10.1007/978-3-030-56880-1_11
24. Lyubashevsky, V.: Lattice signatures without trapdoors. In: Pointcheval, D., Johansson, T. (eds.) EUROCRYPT 2012. LNCS, vol. 7237, pp. 738–755. Springer, Heidelberg (2012). https://doi.org/10.1007/978-3-642-29011-4_43
25. Lyubashevsky, V., Micciancio, D., Peikert, C., Rosen, A.: SWIFFT: a modest proposal for FFT hashing. In: Nyberg, K. (ed.) FSE 2008. LNCS, vol. 5086, pp. 54–72. Springer, Heidelberg (2008). https://doi.org/10.1007/978-3-540-71039-4_4
26. Lyubashevsky, V., Peikert, C., Regev, O.: On ideal lattices and learning with errors over rings. In: Gilbert, H. (ed.) EUROCRYPT 2010. LNCS, vol. 6110, pp. 1–23. Springer, Heidelberg (2010). https://doi.org/10.1007/978-3-642-13190-5_1
27. Lyubashevsky, V., Peikert, C., Regev, O.: A toolkit for ring-LWE cryptography. In: Johansson, T., Nguyen, P.Q. (eds.) EUROCRYPT 2013. LNCS, vol. 7881, pp. 35–54. Springer, Heidelberg (2013). https://doi.org/10.1007/978-3-642-38348-9_3
28. Marc, T., Stopar, M., Hartman, J., Bizjak, M., Modic, J.: Privacy-enhanced machine learning with functional encryption. In: Sako, K., Schneider, S., Ryan, P.Y.A. (eds.) ESORICS 2019. LNCS, vol. 11735, pp. 3–21. Springer, Cham (2019). https://doi.org/10.1007/978-3-030-29959-0_1
29. O'Neill, A.: Definitional issues in functional encryption. Cryptology ePrint Archive, Report 2010/556 (2010). https://eprint.iacr.org/2010/556
30. Pöppelmann, T., Ducas, L., Güneysu, T.: Enhanced lattice-based signatures on reconfigurable hardware. In: Batina, L., Robshaw, M. (eds.) CHES 2014. LNCS, vol. 8731, pp. 353–370. Springer, Heidelberg (2014). https://doi.org/10.1007/978-3-662-44709-3_20
31. Pöppelmann, T., Oder, T., Güneysu, T.: High-performance ideal lattice-based cryptography on 8-Bit ATxmega microcontrollers. In: Lauter, K., Rodríguez-Henríquez, F. (eds.) LATINCRYPT 2015. LNCS, vol. 9230, pp. 346–365. Springer, Cham (2015). https://doi.org/10.1007/978-3-319-22174-8_19
32. Regev, O.: On lattices, learning with errors, random linear codes, and cryptography. In: Gabow, H.N., Fagin, R. (eds.) 37th ACM STOC, pp. 84–93. ACM Press, May 2005. https://doi.org/10.1145/1060590.1060603
33. Microsoft SEAL (release 3.4). https://github.com/Microsoft/SEAL, microsoft Research, Redmond, WA, October 2019

34. Stehlé, D., Steinfeld, R.: Making NTRU as secure as worst-case problems over ideal lattices. In: Paterson, K.G. (ed.) EUROCRYPT 2011. LNCS, vol. 6632, pp. 27–47. Springer, Heidelberg (2011). https://doi.org/10.1007/978-3-642-20465-4_4
35. Wang, Z., Fan, X., Liu, F.-H.: FE for inner products and its application to decentralized ABE. In: Lin, D., Sako, K. (eds.) PKC 2019. LNCS, vol. 11443, pp. 97–127. Springer, Cham (2019). https://doi.org/10.1007/978-3-030-17259-6_4
36. Xu, R., Joshi, J.B., Li, C.: Cryptonn: Training neural networks over encrypted data. In: 2019 IEEE 39th International Conference on Distributed Computing Systems (ICDCS), pp. 1199–1209 (2019). https://doi.org/10.1109/ICDCS.2019.00121
37. Zhao, R.K., Steinfeld, R., Sakzad, A.: FACCT: fast, compact, and constant-time discrete gaussian sampler over integers. IEEE Trans. Comput. **69**(1), 126–137 (2020). https://doi.org/10.1109/TC.2019.2940949

The Direction of Updatable Encryption Does Matter

Ryo Nishimaki(✉)

NTT Corporation, Tokyo, Japan
ryo.nishimaki.zk@hco.ntt.co.jp

Abstract. We introduce a new definition for key updates, called backward-leak uni-directional key updates, in updatable encryption (UE). This notion is a variant of uni-directional key updates for UE. We show that existing secure UE schemes in the bi-directional key updates setting are not secure in the backward-leak uni-directional key updates setting. Thus, security in the backward-leak uni-directional key updates setting is *strictly* stronger than security in the bi-directional key updates setting. This result is in sharp contrast to the equivalence theorem by Jiang (Asiacrypt 2020), which says security in the bi-directional key updates setting is equivalent to security in the existing uni-directional key updates setting. We call the existing uni-directional key updates "forward-leak uni-directional" key updates to distinguish two types of uni-directional key updates in this paper.

We also present two UE schemes with the following features.

- The first scheme is post-quantum secure in the backward-leak uni-directional key updates setting under the learning with errors assumption.
- The second scheme is secure in the no-directional key updates setting and based on indistinguishability obfuscation and one-way functions. This result solves the open problem left by Jiang (Asiacrypt 2020).

Keywords: updatable encryption · key update · lattice

1 Introduction

1.1 Background

Updatable Encryption. Updatable encryption (UE) is a variant of secret key encryption (SKE) where we can periodically update a secret key and a ciphertext. More specifically, a secret key k_e is generated at each period, called epoch. Here, e denotes an index of an epoch. We can generate a conversion key $\Delta_{\mathsf{e}+1}$ that converts a ciphertext under k_e (key at epoch e) to one under $\mathsf{k}_{\mathsf{e}+1}$ (key at epoch $\mathsf{e}+1$). Such a conversion key is called update token and generated from two successive secret keys $\mathsf{k}_\mathsf{e}, \mathsf{k}_{\mathsf{e}+1}$. Roughly speaking, UE security guarantees that confidentiality holds even after some old (and even new) keys and tokens are corrupted as long as trivial winning conditions are not triggered. Adversaries

G. Hanaoka et al. (Eds.): PKC 2022, LNCS 13178, pp. 194–224, 2022.
https://doi.org/10.1007/978-3-030-97131-1_7

trivially win if a target secret key is corrupted or a target ciphertext can be converted into a ciphertext under a corrupted secret key. In this study, we focus on ciphertext-independent updates UE, where we can generate an update token only from two secret keys [LT18, KLR19, BDGJ20, Jia20].[1]

A serious threat to encryption is key leakage. In that case, no security is guaranteed by standard encryption. Key updating is a standard solution to guarantee security even after key leakage. However, the issue is how to update a ciphertext generated by an old key. A naive solution is decrypting all ciphertexts by the old key and re-encrypt them by a new key. However, it incurs significant efficiency loss. Moreover, if we save encrypted data in outsourced storage such as cloud servers, we need to download all ciphertexts from the server, decrypt and re-encrypt them, and upload them again to keep the new key secret. Update tokens of UE solve this problem since if we provide the server with an update token, it can directly convert old ciphertexts into new ones without the new key.

Confidentiality is the primary concern in UE. Confidentiality of UE has been improved to capture realistic attack models [EPRS17, LT18, KLR19, BDGJ20, CLT20] since after UE was introduced [BLMR13]. In particular, Lehman and Tackmann formalized trivially leaked information from corrupted keys and tokens as *the direction of key updates* [LT18]. Although previous works proposed UE schemes with improved confidentiality, most do not focus on preventing information leakage from corrupted keys and tokens. We will explain the detail of the information leakage below. In this work, we focus on the direction of key updates and try to minimize leaked information from update tokens to improve UE confidentiality.

Direction of Key and Ciphertext Updates. Directions of key updates describe information leakage that UE schemes cannot avoid. If an adversary has Δ_{e+1} and k_e, it might be able to obtain k_{e+1}. Most existing UE schemes cannot prevent this attack. In particular, in all existing (ciphertext-independent) UE schemes, we cannot avoid leaking a secret key from both directions [LT18, KLR19, BDGJ20, Jia20]. That is, we can extract k_{e+1} (resp. k_e) from Δ_{e+1} and k_e (resp. k_{e+1}). This setting is defined as *bi-directional* key updates [EPRS17, LT18]. Lehman and Tackmann also defined *uni-directional* key updates, where we can extract k_{e+1} from k_e and Δ_{e+1} (forward direction inference). In other words, this setting means adversaries might not be able to infer k_e from k_{e+1} and Δ_{e+1}. Uni-directional key updates are more preferable than bi-directional ones since a token leaks less information. More information leakage triggers more trivial winning conditions in confidentiality games for UE.

At first glance, secure UE with uni-directional key updates is stronger than one with bi-directional key updates. However, Jiang proved that secure UE with bi-directional key updates *is equivalent to* one with uni-directional key updates [Jia20] (we call Jiang's equivalence theorem in this paper). Jiang also presented the first post-quantum UE scheme with bi-directional key updates [Jia20].

---

[1] The other variant is ciphertext-dependent updates UE, where we need not only two secret keys but also a part of ciphertext (called header) to generate a token [BLMR13, EPRS17, BEKS20]. Ciphertext-independent updates UE is more efficient.

A natural question is: Why do we consider only one-way uni-directional key updates? That is, we can consider a variant of uni-directional key updates where we can extract $\mathsf{k_e}$ from $\mathsf{k_{e+1}}$ and $\Delta_{\mathsf{e+1}}$ (backward direction inference). To distinguish two versions of uni-directional key updates, we call the existing definition *forward-leak uni-directional* key updates and our new one *backward-leak uni-directional* key updates. The backward-leak uni-directional key updates setting has never been studied in the UE literature, but it seems to be a valid setting. It is natural to think the latest key is the most important since the reason why we update keys is that the current and older keys might be leaked. In the forward-leak setting, we must protect older keys to protect newer keys *even if older ciphertexts are deleted.* This is undesirable. However, in the backward-leak setting, we need to protect only the latest key if older ciphertexts are properly deleted. Therefore, the backward-leak key updates are more suitable for UE than the forward-leak key updates.

A related issue is the direction of ciphertext updates. It describes whether we can convert ciphertext into one in an older epoch (downgrading ciphertext) by using an update token or not. If we can both update and downgrade ciphertexts by using a token, we say a UE scheme provides bi-directional ciphertext updates. If we can update but cannot downgrade ciphertexts by using a token, we say a UE scheme provides uni-directional ciphertext updates. UE with uni-directional ciphertext updates is more desirable since older epoch keys might be leaked, and downgrading ciphertexts leaks more information. However, all existing (ciphertext-independent) UE schemes provide bi-directional ciphertext updates.

Thus, the first main question of this study is as follows.

Q1. *Is UE with backward-leak uni-directional key updates strictly stronger than UE with bi-directional key updates?*

We affirmatively answer the first question in this work. Then, the next natural question is as follows.

Q2. *Can we achieve a (post-quantum) UE scheme with backward-leak uni-directional key updates and uni-directional ciphertext updates?*

We also affirmatively answer the second question.

Another natural question is whether we can prevent adversaries from inferring secret keys from both directions or not. That is, even if adversaries have $\mathsf{k_{e+1}}$ (resp. $\mathsf{k_e}$) and $\Delta_{\mathsf{e+1}}$, they cannot infer $\mathsf{k_e}$ (resp. $\mathsf{k_{e+1}}$). Such key updates are called *no-directional* key updates [Jia20]. Jiang left this question as an open problem. Thus, the last question in this work is as follows.

Q3. *Can we achieve a UE scheme with no-directional key updates (and uni-directional ciphertext updates)?*

We solve this open question in this work.

1.2 Our Contribution

The first contribution of our work is a definitional work. We define a new definition of key updates, which we call backward-leak uni-directional key updates. In addition, we prove that UE with backward-leak uni-directional key updates is *strictly stronger* than bi-directional key updates (and forward-leak uni-directional key updates). More specifically, we show that there are UE schemes with bi-directional key updates that are not secure in the *backward-leak* uni-directional key updates setting. This is in sharp contrast to Jiang's equivalence theorem [Jia20] explained above.

The second contribution is that we present two new constructions of UE. The features of our UE schemes are as follows.

- The first scheme is a UE scheme with backward-leak uni-directional key updates and secure under the learning with errors (LWE) assumption, which is known as a post-quantum assumption. This scheme satisfies confidentiality against CPA and ciphertext updates are randomized.
- The second scheme is a UE scheme with no-directional key updates and based on one-way functions (OWFs) and indistinguishability obfuscation (IO). This scheme satisfies confidentiality against CPA and ciphertext updates are randomized.

These are the first UE schemes with stronger key updates. Note that all our schemes provide uni-directional ciphertext updates (i.e., cannot downgrade ciphertext into older epoch ones). The first scheme is implementable since it is directly constructed from lattices. Although the second scheme is a theoretical construction,[2] it solves the open question left by Jiang [Jia20].

Both schemes satisfy r-IND-UE-CPA security, which was defined by Boyd, Davies, Gjøsteen, and Jiang [BDGJ20]. However, we consider the backward-leak uni-directional or no-directional settings. See Sect. 2 for the definitions.

1.3 Related Work

We often use "forward-leak uni-/backward-leak uni-/bi-/no-directional UE" to refer to UE with forward-leak uni-/backward-leak uni-/bi-/no-directional key updates in this paper.

Ciphertext-independent Updates UE. Lehman and Tackmann introduce post-compromise security for UE and refine previous security notions. Those are close to the definitions in this paper. They also present an efficient *bi-directional* UE scheme based on the DDH assumption [LT18]. Klooß, Lehmann, and Rupp present a CCA-secure *bi-directional* UE scheme based on the DDH assumption in the ROM and RCCA-secure *bidirectional* UE schemes based on the SXDH

[2] Note that Jain, Lin,and Sahai achieve IO from well-founded assumptions, the SXDH, LWE, a variant of LPN, and PRG in NC^0 [JLS21]. See their paper for the detail of the assumptions.

assumption [KLR19]. Boyd et al. integrate and refine previous security notions and present CCA-secure *bi-directional* UE schemes with deterministic ciphertext updates based on the DDH assumption in the ideal cipher model [BDGJ20]. Jiang studies relationships among various models for UE and presents a *bi-directional* UE scheme based on the LWE assumption [Jia20]. All these schemes provide bi-directional ciphertext updates (a token enables us to update and downgrade a ciphertext).

Ciphertext-dependent Updates UE. Boneh, Lewi, Montgomery, and Raghunathan introduce the notion of UE in the ciphertext-dependent updates setting and present a *bi-directional* UE scheme based on key homomorphic PRFs [BLMR13]. Everspaugh, Paterson, Ristenpart, and Scott define stronger security notions for UE and present *bi-directional* UE schemes that satisfy those notions [EPRS17]. Chen, Li, and Tang introduce a stronger CCA security notion by considering malicious re-encryption attacks and present *bi-directional* UE schemes that satisfy the stronger CCA security [CLT20]. Boneh, Eskandarian, Kim, and Shih improve security notions by Everspaugh et al. [EPRS17] and present efficient *bi-directional* UE schemes [BEKS20].

UE in Constructive Cryptography. Levy-dit-Vehel and Roméas study security notions for UE in the constructive cryptography framework and explore the right security notion for UE [LR21]. Fabrega, Maurer, and Mularczyk also study security notions for UE in the constructive cryptography framework, generalize previous definitions, and discover new security-efficiency trade-offs. [FMM21].

Concurrent and Independent Work. Slamanig and Striecks [SS21] concurrently and independently proposed a UE scheme.[3] Their scheme is a pairing-based no-directional scheme. They define a stronger model for UE, where we can set an expiry epoch $\mathsf{e}_\perp$ to a ciphertext. If we update a ciphertext with expiry epoch $\mathsf{e}_\perp$ by using a token $\Delta_{\mathsf{e}+1}$ such that $\mathsf{e}+1 > \mathsf{e}_\perp$, the updated ciphertext can no longer be decrypted. Due to this stronger model, Jiang's equivalence theorem [Jia20] does not necessarily hold. The scheme provides uni-directional ciphertext updates. The sharp differences between their work and ours are as follows. Let T be the maximum number of epochs.

- Their no-directional scheme is secure *in the expiry model under the SXDH assumption*, and the ciphertext and key size are $O(\log^2 T)$ and $O(\log^2 T)$, respectively. Our no-directional scheme is secure if IO exists, but the ciphertext and key size do *not depend on* T. Our no-directional scheme is not practical since it relies on IO. Our uni-directional scheme is *post-quantum secure with backward-leak* key updates, and the ciphertext and key size do *not depend on* T.

[3] Their paper [SS21] appeared on Cryptology ePrint archive right after the initial version of this paper (https://eprint.iacr.org/2021/221/20210311:210911) appeared on Cryptology ePrint archive. The comparison here is based on the latest versions of their and our papers.

1.4 Technical Overview

In this section, we present a high-level overview of our technique.

Direction of Key Updates. As we introduce in Sect. 1.1, we can consider two types of uni-directional tokens, forward-leak and backward-leak uni-directional tokens. If we can infer in both directions, we call bi-directional token. In the definitions of confidentiality for UE, trivial winning conditions of adversaries depend on those token variations.

We show the following adversary against existing bi-directional UE schemes: (1) s/he triggers the trivial winning condition of the forward-leak uni-directional key updates setting. (2) s/he does not trigger the trivial winning condition of the backward-leak uni-directional key updates. (3) s/he trivially breaks confidentiality of the schemes in the backward-leak uni-directional key updates. Therefore, existing bi-directional UE schemes are not secure in the backward-leak uni-directional key updates setting. The best way to understand the separation result is looking at an example described in Sect. 3.3.

In this section, we explain the source of the difference between the two settings. First, we recall that UE needs the power of public key encryption (PKE) such as the DDH assumption. We can find this fact in all existing ciphertext-independent UE schemes [LT18, KLR19, BDGJ20, Jia20]. Alamati, Montgomery, and Patranabis [AMP19] prove that ciphertext-independent UE implies PKE. By this fact, we can assume that an epoch key $\mathsf{k_e}$ consists of a secret part $\mathsf{sk_e}$ and a public key part $\mathsf{pk_e}$. As an example, in RISE scheme [LT18], $\mathsf{sk_e} = x_\mathsf{e} \in \mathbb{Z}_p$, $\mathsf{pk_e} = g^{x_\mathsf{e}} \in \mathbb{G}$, and $\Delta_{\mathsf{e}+1} = x_{\mathsf{e}+1}/x_\mathsf{e}$ where g is a generator of a prime-order group $\mathbb{G}$. It is easy to see the token is a bi-directional token.

The direction of key updates depends on how to generate a token. A simple but crucial observation is that we must use $\mathsf{sk_e}$ to generate $\Delta_{\mathsf{e}+1}$. Otherwise, $\Delta_{\mathsf{e}+1}$ does not have the power of decrypting and converting a ciphertext at epoch e. On the other hand, we do not necessarily need $\mathsf{sk_{e+1}}$ to generate $\Delta_{\mathsf{e}+1}$ since we can generate a ciphertext at epoch $\mathsf{e}+1$ by using $\mathsf{pk_{e+1}}$.

The relation between the direction types and how to generate a token is as follows. A forward-leak uni-directional token means $\Delta_{\mathsf{e}+1}$ explicitly contains information about $\mathsf{sk_{e+1}}$. By combining the observation above, $\Delta_{\mathsf{e}+1}$ should contain information about $\mathsf{sk_e}$ and $\mathsf{sk_{e+1}}$ in the forward-leak uni-directional key updates setting. In addition, we can update an older epoch ciphertext into a newer epoch ciphertext and attack the new one if the newer epoch key is revealed. In other words, we can attack older epoch ciphertext even if older epoch keys are not revealed (backward-leak inference is not possible in this setting). The key inference direction could be the same as the ciphertext update direction. By this observation, it is natural that Jiang's equivalence theorem holds.

On the other hand, a backward-leak uni-directional token means $\Delta_{\mathsf{e}+1}$ explicitly contains information about $\mathsf{sk_e}$. It is possible to generate $\Delta_{\mathsf{e}+1}$ from $\mathsf{sk_e}$ and $\mathsf{pk_{e+1}}$ based on the observations so far. Thus, a backward-leak uni-directional token could hide information about $\mathsf{sk_{e+1}}$ and prevent the forward inference. In addition, this property prevents downgrading a ciphertext into an older epoch ciphertext. Thus, even if an older epoch key is revealed, we cannot necessarily attack the newer epoch ciphertexts since downgrading ciphertext and forward-leak inference are impossible. The key inference direction is opposite to the ciphertext update direction. This property is in sharp contrast to the forward-leak setting. Therefore, triggers of trivial winning conditions are different in these two settings. An intuition behind our separation result is based on those observations. See Sect. 3.3 for the detail. Those observations are the starting points of our UE scheme in the backward-leak uni-directional key updates setting. See the next paragraph for an overview.

Our Backward-Leak Uni-Directional Key Updates Scheme. Roughly speaking, a token $\Delta_{\mathsf{e}+1}$ is a homomorphic encryption of sk_{e} under a public key $\mathsf{pk}_{\mathsf{e}+1}$ in our backward-leak uni-directional UE scheme. To update a ciphertext $\mathsf{ct}_{\mathsf{e}} \leftarrow \mathsf{Enc}(\mathsf{pk}_{\mathsf{e}}, \mu)$ at epoch e, we homomorphically decrypt ct_{e} by using $\Delta_{\mathsf{e}+1} = \mathsf{Enc}(\mathsf{pk}_{\mathsf{e}+1}, \mathsf{sk}_{\mathsf{e}})$ and obtain $\mathsf{Enc}(\mathsf{pk}_{\mathsf{e}+1}, \mu)$. It is easy to see that if we have $\Delta_{\mathsf{e}+1}$ and $\mathsf{sk}_{\mathsf{e}+1}$, we can obtain sk_{e} by decryption. However, it is difficult to infer $\mathsf{sk}_{\mathsf{e}+1}$ from $\Delta_{\mathsf{e}+1}$ and sk_{e} since $\mathsf{sk}_{\mathsf{e}+1}$ is not used to generate $\Delta_{\mathsf{e}+1}$. By the security of PKE, it is difficult to obtain $\mathsf{sk}_{\mathsf{e}+1}$ from $\mathsf{pk}_{\mathsf{e}+1}$. To achieve confidentiality for UE, we need to re-randomize tokens and updated ciphertext. This is also possible by using the homomorphic property. Although we use the homomorphic property of lattice-based encryption in our construction, we do not need fully homomorphic encryption (FHE). We use the key-switching technique [BV14, BV11] and the noise smudging technique [AJL+12] to directly achieve secure UE from the LWE assumption. This idea is inspired by uni-directional proxy re-encryption schemes based on lattices [Gen09, ABPW13, CCL+14, NX15].

To prove confidentiality, we need to erase information about $\mathsf{sk}_{\mathsf{e}^*}$ where e^* is the target epoch (otherwise, we cannot use confidentiality under $\mathsf{pk}_{\mathsf{e}^*}$). However, secret keys are linked to update tokens. Thus, we need to gradually erase secret keys in update tokens from new ones to old ones. That is, we change $\mathsf{Enc}(\mathsf{pk}_{\mathsf{e}+1}, \mathsf{sk}_{\mathsf{e}})$ into $\mathsf{Enc}(\mathsf{pk}_{\mathsf{e}+1}, 0^{|\mathsf{sk}_{\mathsf{e}}|})$. Once this change is done, we can change $\mathsf{Enc}(\mathsf{pk}_{\mathsf{e}}, \mathsf{sk}_{\mathsf{e}-1})$ into $\mathsf{Enc}(\mathsf{pk}_{\mathsf{e}}, 0^{|\mathsf{sk}_{\mathsf{e}-1}|})$, and so forth. Note that there exists an epoch e_{r} where $\Delta_{\mathsf{e}_{\mathsf{r}}+1}$ is not corrupted such that $\mathsf{e}^* \leq \mathsf{e}_{\mathsf{r}}$ as long as adversaries do not trigger the trivial winning conditions. We can start the erasing process from e_{r} since $\mathsf{sk}_{\mathsf{e}_{\mathsf{r}}}$ is not used anywhere. This proof outline is reminiscent of the proof technique for multi-hop universal proxy re-encryption [DN21].

Our No-Directional Key Updates Scheme. A no-directional token leaks information about neither k_{e} nor $\mathsf{k}_{\mathsf{e}+1}$. To protect k_{e} and $\mathsf{k}_{\mathsf{e}+1}$, we obfuscate an update circuit. We consider a secret key encryption (SKE) scheme $\mathsf{SKE}.(\mathsf{Gen}, \mathsf{Enc}, \mathsf{Dec})$ and the following circuit R. Two different secret keys $\mathsf{sk}_{\mathsf{e}}, \mathsf{sk}_{\mathsf{e}+1} \leftarrow \mathsf{SKE}.\mathsf{Gen}(1^{\lambda})$ are hard-coded in R. R takes a ciphertext $\mathsf{ct}_{\mathsf{e}} \leftarrow \mathsf{SKE}.\mathsf{Enc}(\mathsf{sk}_{\mathsf{e}}, \mu)$ as an input, computes $\mu = \mathsf{SKE}.\mathsf{Dec}(\mathsf{sk}_{\mathsf{e}}, \mathsf{ct}_{\mathsf{e}})$, and outputs $\mathsf{ct}_{\mathsf{e}+1} \leftarrow \mathsf{SKE}.\mathsf{Enc}(\mathsf{sk}_{\mathsf{e}+1}, \mu)$. A token is an obfuscated circuit of $\mathsf{R}[\mathsf{sk}_{\mathsf{e}}, \mathsf{sk}_{\mathsf{e}+1}]$ (notation $[\mathsf{sk}_{\mathsf{e}}, \mathsf{sk}_{\mathsf{e}+1}]$ denotes that $(\mathsf{sk}_{\mathsf{e}}, \mathsf{sk}_{\mathsf{e}+1})$ are hard-coded). This scheme works as a UE scheme. Intuitively, a token does not leak information about hard-coded secret keys due to obfuscation security. However, we do not know how to prove confidentiality of the scheme above.

To prove security, we instantiate the SKE scheme and obfuscation above with puncturable pseudorandom functions (PRFs) and IO [SW21], respectively. That is, a secret key is a PRF key K, and a ciphertext is $(t, y \oplus \mu) := (\mathsf{PRG}(r), \mathsf{PRF}(\mathsf{K}, \mathsf{PRG}(r)) \oplus \mu)$ where PRG is a pseudorandom generator (PRG) and $r \leftarrow \{0,1\}^{\tau}$. We slightly modified the update circuit above so that it takes not only a ciphertext at epoch e but also randomness $r_{\mathsf{e}+1}$ for a ciphertext at the next epoch. That is, we use a circuit $\mathsf{C}_{\mathsf{re}}[\mathsf{K}_{\mathsf{e}}, \mathsf{K}_{\mathsf{e}+1}]((t,c), r_{\mathsf{e}+1})$ that decrypts (t,c) by K_{e} and encrypts the result by $\mathsf{K}_{\mathsf{e}+1}$ and $r_{\mathsf{e}+1}$. By using this particular scheme and the punctured programming technique with IO security [SW21], we can prove confidentiality of our no-directional UE scheme.

The issue is how to simulate update tokens in security proofs. Note that a UE secret key at epoch e is linked only to UE tokens Δ_{e} and $\Delta_{\mathsf{e}+1}$ in the construction above. In our no-directional scheme, to change target ciphertexts into random ones, we use pseudorandomness of a PRF key $\mathsf{K}_{\mathsf{e}^*}$, which is a UE key $\mathsf{k}_{\mathsf{e}^*}$ at epoch e^*. In the security game of pseudorandomness at punctured points, the adversary is given y^* and a punctured key $\mathsf{K}_{\mathsf{e}^*}\{t^*\}$ where t^* is chosen by the adversary and tries to distinguish y^* is $\mathsf{PRF}(\mathsf{K}_{\mathsf{e}^*}, t^*)$ or random. The punctured key enables us to evaluate the PRF at all inputs except the punctured point t^*. By using $\mathsf{K}_{\mathsf{e}^*}\{t^*\}$, we can simulate tokens Δ_{e} and $\Delta_{\mathsf{e}+1}$ for all inputs except (r, y) such that $t^* = \mathsf{PRG}(r)$. The issue is that we cannot evaluate the PRF at t^*. However, we can overcome this issue by the standard exception handling technique since t^* can be randomly chosen by the reduction due to PRG security and $y^* = \mathsf{PRF}(\mathsf{K}_{\mathsf{e}^*}, t^*)$ is given as a target in the pseudorandomness game. We can construct functionally equivalent circuits by using $\mathsf{K}_{\mathsf{e}^*}\{t^*\}$, t^*, y^*, and exceptional handling. The exceptional handling cannot be detected by IO security. Thus, we can simulate update tokens and use pseudorandomness to prove confidentiality.

Organization. In Sect. 2, we review the syntax and security definitions of UE. Sect. 3 defines a new definition of uni-directional key updates (backward-leak uni-directional key updates) and shows that it is strictly stronger than those of bi-directional and forward-leak uni-directional key updates. In Sect. 4, we present our UE scheme with backward-leak uni-directional key updates based on the LWE problem and prove its security. In Sect. 5, we present our UE scheme with no-directional key updates. Due to space limitations, we omit many details in this version. Please see the full version [Nis21] for them.

2 Updatable Encryption

In this section, we briefly review the syntax and definitions of UE.

Syntax

Definition 2.1. *An updatable encryption scheme* UE *for message space* $\mathcal{M}$ *consists of a tuple of PPT algorithms* ($\mathsf{UE.Setup}$, $\mathsf{UE.KeyGen}$, $\mathsf{UE.Enc}$, $\mathsf{UE.Dec}$, $\mathsf{UE.TokGen}$, $\mathsf{UE.Upd}$).

$\mathsf{UE.Setup}(1^\lambda) \rightarrow \mathsf{pp}$: *The setup algorithm takes as input the security parameter and outputs a public parameter* pp. *(This algorithm is an option for UE.)*

$\mathsf{UE.KeyGen}(\mathsf{pp}) \rightarrow \mathsf{k_e}$: *The key generation algorithm takes as input the public parameter and outputs an epoch key* $\mathsf{k_e}$.

$\mathsf{UE.Enc}(\mathsf{k}, \mu) \rightarrow \mathsf{ct}$: *The encryption algorithm takes as input an epoch key and a plaintext* μ *and outputs a ciphertext* ct.

$\mathsf{UE.Dec}(\mathsf{k}, \mathsf{ct}) \rightarrow \mu'$: *The decryption algorithm takes as input an epoch key and a ciphertext and outputs a plaintext* μ' *or* $\perp$.

$\mathsf{UE.TokGen}(\mathsf{k_e}, \mathsf{k_{e+1}}) \rightarrow \Delta_{\mathsf{e}+1}$: *The token generation algorithm takes as input two keys of successive epochs* e *and* $\mathsf{e}+1$ *and outputs a token* $\Delta_{\mathsf{e}+1}$.

$\mathsf{UE.Upd}(\Delta_{\mathsf{e}+1}, \mathsf{ct_e}) \rightarrow \mathsf{ct_{e+1}}$: *The update algorithm takes as input a token* $\Delta_{\mathsf{e}+1}$ *and a ciphertext* $\mathsf{ct_e}$ *and outputs a ciphertext* $\mathsf{ct_{e+1}}$.

Let T *be the maximum number of the epoch.*

Security Experiments. We review security definitions for UE in this section.

Definition 2.2 (Correctness). *For any* $\mu \in \mathcal{M}$, *for* $0 \leq \mathsf{e}_1 \leq \mathsf{e}_2 \leq T$, *it holds that*

$$\Pr[\mathsf{UE.Dec}(\mathsf{k}_{\mathsf{e}_2}, \mathsf{ct}_{\mathsf{e}_2}) \neq \mu] \leq \mathsf{negl}(\lambda),$$

where $\mathsf{pp} \leftarrow \mathsf{UE.Setup}(1^\lambda)$, $\mathsf{k}_{\mathsf{e}_1}, \ldots, \mathsf{k}_{\mathsf{e}_2} \leftarrow \mathsf{UE.KeyGen}(\mathsf{pp})$, $\mathsf{ct}_{\mathsf{e}_1} \leftarrow \mathsf{UE.Enc}(\mathsf{k}_{\mathsf{e}_1}, \mu)$, *and* $\Delta_{i+1} \leftarrow \mathsf{UE.TokGen}(\mathsf{k}_i, \mathsf{k}_{i+1})$, $\mathsf{ct}_{i+1} \leftarrow \mathsf{UE.Upd}(\Delta_{i+1}, \mathsf{ct}_i)$ *for* $i \in [\mathsf{e}_1, \mathsf{e}_2 - 1]$.

Definition 2.3 (Confidentiality for Updatable Encryption [BDGJ20, Jia20]**).** *For* $\mathsf{x} \in \{\mathsf{d}, \mathsf{r}\}$, $\mathsf{atk} \in \{\mathsf{cpa}, \mathsf{cca}\}$, *the game* $\mathsf{Exp}^{\mathsf{x\text{-}ind\text{-}ue\text{-}atk}}_{\Sigma,\mathcal{A}}(\lambda, b)$ *is formalized as follows.*

- *Invoke* Setup *and set* $\mathsf{phase} := 0$.
- *Let* $\mathcal{O} := \mathcal{O}.\{\mathsf{Enc}, \mathsf{Next}, \mathsf{Upd}, \mathsf{Corr}, \mathsf{Chall}, \mathsf{Upd}\widetilde{\mathsf{C}}\}$ *if* $\mathsf{atk} = \mathsf{cpa}$. *If* $\mathsf{atk} = \mathsf{cca}$, $\mathcal{O}.\mathsf{Dec}$ *is also added in* $\mathcal{O}$.
- *Run* $\mathsf{coin}' \leftarrow \mathcal{A}^{\mathcal{O}}(1^\lambda)$.
- *If* $((\mathcal{K}^* \cap \mathcal{C}^* \neq \emptyset) \vee (\mathsf{x} = \mathsf{d} \wedge (\mathsf{e}^* \in \mathcal{T}^* \vee \mathcal{O}.\mathsf{Upd}(\overline{\mathsf{ct}})$ *is invoked*))) *then* $\mathsf{twf} := 1$
- *If* $\mathsf{twf} = 1$ *then* $\mathsf{coin}' \leftarrow \{0, 1\}$
- *return* coin'

We say a UE scheme is x*-IND-UE-*atk *secure if it holds*

$$\mathsf{Adv}^{\mathsf{x\text{-}ind\text{-}ue\text{-}atk}}_{\Sigma,\mathcal{A}}(\lambda) := |\Pr[\mathsf{Exp}^{\mathsf{x\text{-}ind\text{-}ue\text{-}atk}}_{\Sigma,\mathcal{A}}(\lambda, 0) = 1] - \Pr[\mathsf{Exp}^{\mathsf{x\text{-}ind\text{-}ue\text{-}atk}}_{\Sigma,\mathcal{A}}(\lambda, 1) = 1]| \leq \mathsf{negl}(\lambda).$$

The definitions of oracles are described in Fig. 1.

The prefix d and r in the definition above indicate that we consider UE schemes with *deterministic* and *randomized* update algorithms, respectively.

Leakage Sets. We introduce leakage sets. Adversaries can obtain secret keys, update tokens, challenge-equal ciphertexts from oracles. We record epochs in the following sets to maintain which epoch key/token/challenge-equal-ciphertext was given to adversaries.

- $\mathcal{K}$: Set of epochs where $\mathcal{A}$ corrupted the epoch key via $\mathcal{O}.\mathsf{Corr}$.
- $\mathcal{T}$: Set of epochs where $\mathcal{A}$ corrupted the update token via $\mathcal{O}.\mathsf{Corr}$.
- $\mathcal{C}$: Set of epochs where $\mathcal{A}$ obtained a challenge-equal ciphertext via $\mathcal{O}.\mathsf{Chall}$ or $\mathcal{O}.\mathsf{Upd}\widetilde{\mathsf{C}}$.

$\underline{\mathsf{Setup}(1^\lambda)}$:

- $\mathsf{k}_0 \leftarrow \mathsf{UE.KeyGen}(1^\lambda)$
- $\Delta_0 := \perp; \mathsf{e}, \mathsf{cnt}, \mathsf{twf} := 0$
- $\mathcal{L}, \widetilde{\mathcal{L}}, \mathcal{C}, \mathcal{K}, \mathcal{T} := \emptyset$

$\underline{\mathcal{O}.\mathsf{Enc}(\mu)}$:

- $\mathsf{cnt} := \mathsf{cnt} + 1$
- $\mathsf{ct} \leftarrow \mathsf{UE.Enc}(\mathsf{k_e}, \mu)$
- $\mathcal{L} := \mathcal{L} \cup \{(\mathsf{cnt}, \mathsf{ct}, \mathsf{e}; \mu)\}$
- **return** ct

$\underline{\mathcal{O}.\mathsf{Dec}(\mathsf{ct})}$:

- $\mu'/\perp \leftarrow \mathsf{UE.Dec}(\mathsf{k_e}, \mathsf{ct})$
- **if** $\Big((\mathsf{x} = \mathsf{d} \wedge (\mathsf{ct}, \mathsf{e}) \in \widetilde{\mathcal{L}}^*)$
  $\vee (\mathsf{x} = \mathsf{r} \wedge (\mu', \mathsf{e}) \in \widetilde{\mathcal{Q}}^*)\Big)$
  then $\mathsf{twf} := 1$
- **return** μ' **or** $\perp$

$\underline{\mathcal{O}.\mathsf{Next}()}$:

- $\mathsf{e} := \mathsf{e} + 1$
- $\mathsf{k_e} \leftarrow \mathsf{UE.KeyGen}(1^\lambda)$
- $\Delta_\mathsf{e} \leftarrow \mathsf{UE.TokGen}(\mathsf{k_{e-1}}, \mathsf{k_e})$
- **if** $\mathsf{phase} = 1$
  then $\mathsf{ct}^*_\mathsf{e} \leftarrow \mathsf{UE.Upd}(\Delta_\mathsf{e}, \mathsf{ct}^*_{\mathsf{e}-1})$

$\underline{\mathcal{O}.\mathsf{Upd}(\mathsf{ct}_{\mathsf{e}-1})}$:

- **if** $(j, \mathsf{ct}_{\mathsf{e}-1}, \mathsf{e}-1; \mu) \notin \mathcal{L}$
  then return $\perp$
- $\mathsf{ct_e} \leftarrow \mathsf{UE.Upd}(\Delta_\mathsf{e}, \mathsf{ct}_{\mathsf{e}-1})$
- $\mathcal{L} := \mathcal{L} \cup \{(\mathsf{cnt}, \mathsf{ct_e}, \mathsf{e}; \mu)\}$
- **return** $\mathsf{ct_e}$

$\underline{\mathcal{O}.\mathsf{Corr}(\mathsf{mode}, \widehat{\mathsf{e}})}$:

- **if** $\widehat{\mathsf{e}} > \mathsf{e}$ **then return** $\perp$
- **if** $\mathsf{mode} = \mathsf{key}$
  then $\mathcal{K} := \mathcal{K} \cup \{\widehat{\mathsf{e}}\}$
  return $\mathsf{k}_{\widehat{\mathsf{e}}}$
- **if** $\mathsf{mode} = \mathsf{token}$
  then $\mathcal{T} := \mathcal{T} \cup \{\widehat{\mathsf{e}}\}$
  return $\Delta_{\widehat{\mathsf{e}}}$

$\underline{\mathcal{O}.\mathsf{Chall}(\overline{\mu}, \overline{\mathsf{ct}})}$:

- **if** $\mathsf{phase} = 1$ **then return** $\perp$
- $\mathsf{phase} := 1; \mathsf{e}^* := \mathsf{e}$
- **if** $(\cdot, \overline{\mathsf{ct}}, \mathsf{e}^* - 1; \overline{\mu}_1) \notin \mathcal{L}$
  then return $\perp$
- **if** $b = 0$
  then $\mathsf{ct}^*_{\mathsf{e}^*} \leftarrow \mathsf{UE.Enc}(\mathsf{k}_{\mathsf{e}^*}, \overline{\mu})$
  else $\mathsf{ct}^*_{\mathsf{e}^*} \leftarrow \mathsf{UE.Upd}(\Delta_{\mathsf{e}^*}, \overline{\mathsf{ct}})$
- $\mathcal{C} := \mathcal{C} \cup \{\mathsf{e}^*\}$
- $\widetilde{\mathcal{L}} := \widetilde{\mathcal{L}} \cup \{(\mathsf{ct}^*_{\mathsf{e}^*}, \mathsf{e}^*)\}$
- **return** $\mathsf{ct}^*_{\mathsf{e}^*}$

$\underline{\mathcal{O}.\mathsf{Upd}\widetilde{\mathsf{C}}()}$:

- **if** $\mathsf{phase} \neq 1$ **then return** $\perp$
- $\mathcal{C} := \mathcal{C} \cup \{\mathsf{e}\}$
- $\widetilde{\mathcal{L}} := \widetilde{\mathcal{L}} \cup \{(\mathsf{ct}^*_\mathsf{e}, \mathsf{e})\}$
- **return** ct^*_e

$\underline{\mathcal{O}.\mathsf{Try}(\mathsf{ct}^*)}$:

- $\mu'/\perp \leftarrow \mathsf{UE.Dec}(\mathsf{k_e}, \mathsf{ct}^*)$
- **if** $(\mathsf{e} \in \mathcal{K}^* \vee (\mathsf{atk} = \mathsf{ctxt} \wedge (\mathsf{ct}^*, \mathsf{e}) \in \mathcal{L}^*)$
  $\vee (\mathsf{atk} = \mathsf{ptxt} \wedge (\mu', \mathsf{e}) \in \mathcal{Q}^*))$
  then $\mathsf{twf} := 1$
- **if** $\mu' \neq \perp$ **then** $\mathsf{win} := 1$

Fig. 1. The behavior of oracles in security experiments for updatable encryption. Leakages sets $\mathcal{L}, \widetilde{\mathcal{L}}, \mathcal{L}^*, \widetilde{\mathcal{L}}^*, \mathcal{C}, \mathcal{K}, \mathcal{K}^*, \mathcal{T}, \mathcal{T}^*, \mathcal{Q}, \mathcal{Q}^*, \widetilde{\mathcal{Q}}^*$ are defined in Sect. 2.

We also record ciphertexts given via oracles to maintain which (updated) ciphertexts adversaries obtained.

- $\mathcal{L}$: Set of non-challenge ciphertexts $(\mathsf{cnt}, \mathsf{ct}, \mathsf{e}; \mu)$ returned via $\mathcal{O}.\mathsf{Enc}$ or $\mathcal{O}.\mathsf{Upd}$, where cnt is a query index incremented by each invocation of $\mathcal{O}.\mathsf{Enc}$, ct is the given ciphertext, e is the epoch where the query happens, and μ is the queried plaintext or the plaintext in the queried ciphertext.
- $\widetilde{\mathcal{L}}$: Set of challenge-equal ciphertexts $(\mathsf{ct}^*_{\mathsf{e}}, \mathsf{e})$ returned via $\mathcal{O}.\mathsf{Chall}$ or $\mathcal{O}.\mathsf{Upd}\widetilde{\mathsf{C}}$, where $\mathsf{ct}^*_{\mathsf{e}}$ is the given challenge-equal ciphertext and e is the epoch where the query happens.

In the deterministic update setting, where algorithm Upd is deterministic, an updated ciphertext is uniquely determined by a token and a ciphertext. Thus, we consider extended ciphertext sets $\mathcal{L}^*$ and $\widetilde{\mathcal{L}}^*$ inferred from $\mathcal{L}$ and $\widetilde{\mathcal{L}}$, respectively, by using $\mathcal{T}$. Regarding $\mathcal{L}^*$, we only need information about the ciphertext and epoch. That is, $\mathcal{L}^*$ consists of sets of a ciphertext and an epoch index.

In the randomized update setting, where algorithm Upd is probabilistic, an update ciphertext is not uniquely determined. Thus, we consider sets of plaintexts of which adversaries have ciphertexts.

- $\mathcal{Q}^*$: Set of plaintexts (μ, e) such that the adversary obtained or could generate a ciphertext of μ at epoch e.
- $\widetilde{\mathcal{Q}}^*$: Set of challenge plaintexts $\{(\overline{\mu}, \mathsf{e}), (\overline{\mu}_1, \mathsf{e})\}$, where $(\overline{\mu}, \overline{\mathsf{ct}})$ is the query to $\mathcal{O}.\mathsf{Chall}$ and $\overline{\mu}_1$ is the plaintext in $\overline{\mathsf{ct}}$. The adversary obtained or could generate a challenge-equal ciphertext of $\overline{\mu}$ or $\overline{\mu}_1$ at epoch e.

Inferred Leakage Sets. Lehman and Tackmann [LT18] presented the bookkeeping technique to analyze the epoch leakage sets. We maintain leaked information by the technique in security games.

Key Leakage. Adversaries can infer some information from leakage sets $\mathcal{K}$ and $\mathcal{T}$. Here, "infer" means that adversaries can trivially extract some secret information from given keys and tokens. For example, in the ElGamal-based UE scheme by Lehman and Tackmann (called RISE) [LT18], a secret key at epoch e is $k_{\mathsf{e}} \in \mathbb{Z}_p$ where p is a prime and a token is $\Delta_{\mathsf{e}+1} = k_{\mathsf{e}+1}/k_{\mathsf{e}} \in \mathbb{Z}_p$. Thus, we can easily extract k_{e} from $\Delta_{\mathsf{e}+1}$ and $k_{\mathsf{e}+1}$ (and vice versa).

Inferred information depends on the direction of key updates. In previous works on UE, there are three types of directions of key updates, called bi/uni/no-directional key updates. Formally, for $\mathsf{kk} \in \{\mathsf{no}, \mathsf{uni}, \mathsf{bi}\}$, we consider the following kk-directional key update setting.

Definition 2.4 (Direction of Key Update). *We define inferred leakage key sets. The sets depend on the setting of key updates.*

- *No-directional key updates:* $\mathcal{K}^*_{\mathsf{no}} := \mathcal{K}$.
- *Uni-directional key updates:*

$$\mathcal{K}^*_{\mathsf{uni}} := \{\mathsf{e} \in [0, \ell] \mid \mathsf{CorrK}(\mathsf{e}) = \mathsf{true}\}$$

where $\mathsf{CorrK}(\mathsf{e}) = \mathsf{true} \Leftrightarrow (\mathsf{e} \in \mathcal{K}) \vee (\mathsf{CorrK}(\mathsf{e}-1) \wedge \mathsf{e} \in \mathcal{T})$

- *Bi-directional key updates:*

$$\mathcal{K}^*_{\mathsf{bi}} := \{\mathsf{e} \in [0, \ell] \mid \mathsf{CorrK}(\mathsf{e}) = \mathsf{true}\}$$

where $\mathsf{CorrK}(\mathsf{e}) = \mathsf{true} \Leftrightarrow (\mathsf{e} \in \mathcal{K}) \vee (\mathsf{CorrK}(\mathsf{e}-1) \wedge \mathsf{e} \in \mathcal{T}) \vee (\mathsf{CorrK}(\mathsf{e}+1) \wedge \mathsf{e}+1 \in \mathcal{T})$

Token Leakage. If two successive keys are leaked, a token generated from those keys is also inferred.

Definition 2.5 (Inferred Token Sets). *For* $\mathsf{kk} \in \{\mathsf{no}, \mathsf{uni}, \mathsf{bi}\}$,

$$\mathcal{T}^*_{\mathsf{kk}} := \{\mathsf{e} \in [0, \ell] \mid (\mathsf{e} \in \mathcal{T}) \vee (\mathsf{e} \in \mathcal{K}^*_{\mathsf{kk}} \wedge \mathsf{e} - 1 \in \mathcal{K}^*_{\mathsf{kk}})\}$$

Challenge-Equal Ciphertext Leakage. We can update ciphertexts by using tokens. That is, we can obtain updated ciphertexts generated from a challenge ciphertext via leaked tokens. To check whether a challenge ciphertext can be converted into a ciphertext under a corrupted key, we maintain challenge-equal ciphertext epochs defined below.

Definition 2.6 (Direction of Ciphertext Update). *We define two types of challenge-equal ciphertext epoch sets. For* $\mathsf{kk} \in \{\mathsf{no}, \mathsf{uni}, \mathsf{bi}\}$,

- *Uni-directional ciphertext updates:*

$$\mathcal{C}^*_{\mathsf{kk},\mathsf{uni}} := \{\mathsf{e} \in [0, \ell] \mid \mathsf{ChallEq}(\mathsf{e}) = \mathsf{true}\}$$

where $\mathsf{ChallEq}(\mathsf{e}) = \mathsf{true} \Leftrightarrow (\mathsf{e} \in \mathcal{C}) \vee (\mathsf{ChallEq}(\mathsf{e} - 1) \wedge \mathsf{e} \in \mathcal{T}^*_{\mathsf{kk}})$
- *Bi-directional ciphertext updates:*

$$\mathcal{C}^*_{\mathsf{kk},\mathsf{bi}} := \{\mathsf{e} \in [0, \ell] \mid \mathsf{ChallEq}(\mathsf{e}) = \mathsf{true}\}$$

where $\mathsf{ChallEq}(\mathsf{e}) = \mathsf{true} \Leftrightarrow (\mathsf{e} \in \mathcal{C}) \vee (\mathsf{ChallEq}(\mathsf{e} - 1) \wedge \mathsf{e} \in \mathcal{T}^*_{\mathsf{kk}}) \vee (\mathsf{ChallEq}(\mathsf{e} + 1) \wedge \mathsf{e} + 1 \in \mathcal{T}^*_{\mathsf{kk}})$

By considering directions of key/ciphertext updates, we can consider variants of security notions for UE [Jia20].

Definition 2.7 **((kk, cc)-variant of confidentiality** [Jia20]**).** *Let* UE *be a UE scheme. Then the* (kk, cc)-notion *advantage, for* $\mathsf{kk} \in \{\mathsf{no}, \mathsf{uni}, \mathsf{bi}\}$, $\mathsf{cc} \in \{\mathsf{uni}, \mathsf{bi}\}$ *and* notion $\in$ {r-ind-ue-cpa, d-ind-ue-cpa, r-ind-ue-cca, d-ind-ue-cca}, *of an adversary* $\mathcal{A}$ *against* UE *is defined as*

$$\mathsf{Adv}^{(\mathsf{kk},\mathsf{cc})\text{-}\mathsf{notion}}_{\mathsf{UE},\mathcal{A}}(1^\lambda) := |\Pr[\mathsf{Exp}^{(\mathsf{kk},\mathsf{cc})\text{-}\mathsf{notion}}_{\mathsf{UE},\mathcal{A}}(\lambda, 0) = 1] - \Pr[\mathsf{Exp}^{(\mathsf{kk},\mathsf{cc})\text{-}\mathsf{notion}}_{\mathsf{UE},\mathcal{A}}(\lambda, 1) = 1]|,$$

where $\mathsf{Exp}^{(\mathsf{kk},\mathsf{cc})\text{-}\mathsf{notion}}_{\mathsf{UE},\mathcal{A}}(\lambda, b)$ *is the same as the experiment* $\mathsf{Expt}^{\mathsf{notion}}_{\mathsf{UE},\mathcal{A}}(\lambda, b)$ *in Definition 2.3 except for all leakage sets are both in the* kk*-directional key updates and* cc*-directional ciphertext updates.*

Trivial Winning Condition. Adversaries trivially win the security game if we can convert a challenge ciphertext into a ciphertext under a corrupted key. Thus, we need to define trivial winning conditions.

For all confidentiality games in Definition 2.3, the trivial winning condition $\mathcal{K}^* \cap \mathcal{C}^* \neq \emptyset$ is checked since if the condition holds, adversaries can win the game by decrypting a challenge-equal ciphertext by using a corrupted key.

For all confidentiality games for deterministic update UE, the trivial winning condition $\widetilde{\mathsf{e}} \in \mathcal{T}^* \vee$ "$\mathcal{O}.\mathsf{Upd}(\overline{\mathsf{ct}})$ is queried" is checked since if the condition holds, adversaries can win the game by checking the challenge ciphertext is equal to an updated ciphertext generated from the token and a queried ciphertext to $\mathcal{O}.\mathsf{Chall}$.

We need to consider other trivial winning conditions in the CCA setting (both for randomized and deterministic updates) and integrity setting. However, we do not consider these settings in this work. We do not explain those conditions. See the paper by Jiang [Jia20] for the detail.

Firewall and Insulated Region

Definition 2.8 (Firewall [LT18, KLR19, BDGJ20, Jia20]**).** *An insulated region with firewalls* fwl *and* fwr *is a consecutive sequence of epochs* $[\mathsf{fwl}, \mathsf{fwr}]$ *for which:*

- *No key in the sequence of epochs* $[\mathsf{fwl}, \mathsf{fwr}]$ *is corrupted. That is, it holds* $[\mathsf{fwl}, \mathsf{fwr}] \cap \mathcal{K} = \emptyset$.
- *The tokens* Δ_{fwl} *and* $\Delta_{\mathsf{fwr}+1}$ *are not corrupted if they exist. That is, it holds* $\mathsf{fwl}, \mathsf{fwr}+1 \notin \mathcal{T}$.
- *All tokens* $(\Delta_{\mathsf{fwl}+1}, \ldots, \Delta_{\mathsf{fwr}})$ *are corrupted. That is,* $[\mathsf{fwl}+1, \mathsf{fwr}] \subseteq \mathcal{T}$.

Definition 2.9 (Insulated Region [LT18, KLR19, BDGJ20, Jia20]**).** *The union of all insulated regions is defined as* $\mathcal{IR} := \bigcup_{[\mathsf{fwl},\mathsf{fwr}] \in \mathcal{FW}} [\mathsf{fwl}, \mathsf{fwr}]$, *where* $\mathcal{FW}$ *is the set of insulated region with firewalls.*

On Security Definitions. Boyd et al. prove that r-IND-UE-CPA implies both the standard CPA security for UE and unlinkability of updated ciphertext. See their paper [BDGJ20] for the detail.

3 Backward-Leak Uni-Directional Key Update and Relations

3.1 Definition

We introduce a new notion for the direction of key updates in this section. The notion is categorized in uni-directional key updates, but the direction is the opposite of the uni-directional key updates in Definition 2.4.

Definition 3.1 (Uni-Directional Key Update (revisited)). *We define two types of uni-directional key updates. One is the same as that in Definition 2.4. To distinguish two types of uni-directional key updates, we rename the original one in Definition 2.4 to* forward-leak uni-directional *key updates. The definitions of two notions are as follows.*

- *forward-leak uni-directional key updates:* $\mathcal{K}^*_{\mathsf{f\text{-}uni}} := \mathcal{K}^*_{\mathsf{uni}}$.
- *backward-leak uni-directional key updates:*

$$\mathcal{K}^*_{\mathsf{b\text{-}uni}} := \{\mathsf{e} \in [0, \ell] \mid \mathsf{CorrK(e)} = \mathsf{true}\}$$

where $\mathsf{CorrK(e)} = \mathsf{true} \Leftrightarrow (\mathsf{e} \in \mathcal{K}) \vee (\mathsf{CorrK(e+1)} \wedge \mathsf{e}+1 \in \mathcal{T})$

By using the definition above, we can consider Definition 2.5 and 2.6 for $\mathsf{kk} \in \{\mathsf{no}, \mathsf{f\text{-}uni}, \mathsf{b\text{-}uni}, \mathsf{bi}\}$. We illustrate leaked information in the setting of forward/backward-leak uni-directional key updates settings in Fig. 2.

set	e − 1	e	e + 1
$\mathcal{K}^*_{\mathsf{f\text{-}uni}}$	×	✓	inferred
$\mathcal{T}^*_{\mathsf{f\text{-}uni}}$		✓	✓

set	e − 1	e	e + 1
$\mathcal{K}^*_{\mathsf{b\text{-}uni}}$	inferred	✓	×
$\mathcal{T}^*_{\mathsf{b\text{-}uni}}$		✓	✓

Fig. 2. Inferred keys in the forward-leak/backward-leak uni-directional key updates settings. Symbol ✓ means the key/token was given via $\mathcal{O}.\mathsf{Corr}$. Symbol × means we cannot trivially obtain the information. The text "inferred" means we can trivially extract the information from given values.

3.2 Observations on Definitions

On the Meaningfulness of Backward-Leak Uni-Directional Key Updates. First of all, all ciphertext-independent UE schemes rely on public key encryption power in some sense [LT18,BDGJ20,Jia20].[4] This fact is endorsed by the result by Alamati, Montgomery, and Patranabis [AMP19], which shows any ciphertext-independent UE scheme that is forward and post-compromise secure implies PKE. Thus, we can assume that an epoch key consists of a secret key part $\mathsf{sk_e}$ and a public key part $\mathsf{pk_e}$.

To achieve the ciphertext update mechanism of UE, a token $\Delta_{\mathsf{e}+1}$ must include information about $\mathsf{sk_e}$ since an update algorithm essentially decrypts a ciphertext at epoch e and generates a ciphertext for epoch $\mathsf{e}+1$. The question is: "Do we really need $\mathsf{sk_{e+1}}$ for updating a ciphertext from e to $\mathsf{e}+1$?". The answer is no. The point is that we need only the public key part of an epoch key to generate a ciphertext in most existing ciphertext-independent UE schemes. Thus, we might be able to construct an update token by using only $\mathsf{sk_e}$ and $\mathsf{pk_{e+1}}$. More specifically, we might be able to transform a ciphertext for epoch e by using encryption of $\mathsf{sk_e}$ under $\mathsf{pk_{e+1}}$ and homomorphic properties.

[4] Everspaugh et al. [EPRS17] presented a ciphertext-independent UE scheme from authenticated encryption (AE). However, they assume an AE scheme is secure against related key attacks. So far, it seems that we need the power of public key encryption (such as DDH) to achieve related key secure AE [HLL16]. In addition, Everspaugh et al. retracted the ciphertext-independent construction in their full version paper (https://eprint.iacr.org/2017/527/20180903:192110).

This is what we do in Sect. 4. This insight comes from a few constructions of uni-directional proxy re-encryption [Gen09, ABPW13, CCL+14, NX15].

Based on the observations above, we can say the backward-leak uni-directional key updates setting is natural. If a token Δ_{e+1} is generated by using $(\mathsf{sk}_e, \mathsf{pk}_{e+1})$, it is likely we can infer sk_e from Δ_{e+1} and sk_{e+1} (our backward-leak uni-directional scheme is an example). However, it might be difficult to extract information about sk_{e+1} from sk_e and Δ_{e+1} since only pk_{e+1} is embedded in Δ_{e+1}. In fact, it is difficult in our backward-leak uni-directional scheme.

In the forward-leak uni-directional key updates setting, we assume that it is easy to infer sk_{e+1} from Δ_{e+1} and sk_e. In some sense, this says sk_{e+1} is directly embedded in Δ_{e+1}. We might be able to execute bi-directional key/ciphertext updates if a token enables us to update a ciphertext (in the forward direction). Here, "directly embedded" means that a secret key is not encrypted. In fact, in all existing UE schemes bi-directional (and forward-leak uni-directional) key updates, sk_{e+1} is directly embedded in Δ_{e+1} [LT18, KLR19, BDGJ20, Jia20]. In addition, generating a token Δ_{e+1} from sk_{e+1} and pk_e is unnatural since it is unlikely such Δ_{e+1} can update a ciphertext under pk_e.

Note that the argument above does not consider obfuscation [BGI+12]. If we can somehow obfuscate secret keys in a token, it could be difficult to infer secret keys in the token even if we use those secret keys to generate the token. This is what we do in Sect. 5 to achieve a no-directional key updates scheme.

As we argue in Sect. 1.1, backward-leak uni-directional key updates are more suitable than forward-leak ones in practice. In fact, we prove that confidentiality in the backward-leak uni-directional key updates setting is *strictly* stronger than that in the forward-leak uni-directional key updates setting.

On Meaningful Combination with Bi/Uni-Directional Ciphertext Updates. For ciphertext updates, it is natural to consider only the uni-directional ciphertext updates in Definition 2.6 since updating ciphertext should go forward direction due to the nature of UE. Of course, we can define another uni-directional ciphertext updates (called "backward uni-directional" or "downgrade-only" ciphertext updates), but it is not meaningful.

Jiang considered a setting where key updates are uni-directional (this is forward-leak uni-directional by our definition) and ciphertext updates are bi-directional. This is meaningful only in the forward-leak uni-directional key updates since forward-leak uni-directional and bi-directional key updates are equivalent by Jiang's result. However, it is unnatural to consider bi-directional ciphertext updates with *backward-leak* uni-directional key updates. This is because we show that backward-leak uni-directional key updates are strictly stronger than bi-directional key updates. In addition, it is difficult to use Δ_{e+1} to convert a ciphertext under k_{e+1} into one under k_e in the backward-leak uni-directional key updates setting. This observation affects a theorem proved by Jiang [Jia20, Theorem 3.2 in the ePrint ver.] (Theorem 3.5 in this paper), which we explain later.

Relaxed Firewall. As we observed above, it is natural to consider uni-directional ciphertext updates in the backward uni-directional key updates setting. In this setting, adversaries cannot convert a ciphertext at the challenge epoch into a ciphertext at an older epoch by using tokens. Thus, even if a token Δ_{fwl} at a left firewall fwl is given to adversaries when a challenge epoch is in between fwl and fwr, adversaries cannot obtain a challenge-equal ciphertext at an epoch whose secret key is corrupted. We define this modified firewall notion as relaxed firewall below.

Definition 3.2 (Relaxed Firewall). *A relaxed insulated region with relaxed firewalls* fwl *and* fwr *is a consecutive sequence of epochs* $[\mathsf{fwl}, \mathsf{fwr}]$ *for which:*

- *No key in the sequence of epochs* $[\mathsf{fwl}, \mathsf{fwr}]$ *is corrupted. That is, it holds* $[\mathsf{fwl}, \mathsf{fwr}] \cap \mathcal{K} = \emptyset$.
- *The token* $\Delta_{\mathsf{fwr}+1}$ *is not corrupted if they exist. That is, it holds* $\mathsf{fwr} + 1 \notin \mathcal{T}$.
- *All tokens* $(\Delta_{\mathsf{fwl}}, \dots, \Delta_{\mathsf{fwr}})$ *can be corrupted. That is,* $[\mathsf{fwl}, \mathsf{fwr}] \subseteq \mathcal{T}$.

The difference from Definition 2.8 is that Δ_{fwl} can be corrupted.

Definition 3.3 (Relaxed Insulated Region). *The union of all relaxed insulated regions is defined as* $\mathsf{r}\mathcal{IR} := \bigcup_{[\mathsf{fwl},\mathsf{fwr}] \in \mathsf{r}\mathcal{FW}} [\mathsf{fwl}, \mathsf{fwr}]$, *where* $\mathsf{r}\mathcal{FW}$ *is the set of relaxed insulated region with relaxed firewalls.*

As we will see in the proof of Theorem 3.4, there exists an epoch such that it is set as the challenge ciphertext epoch (does not trigger the trivial winning condition), but not in a firewall area under Definition 2.8 (the original definition of firewall). In the example in Fig. 3, which will appear later, epoch $\{5\}$ is such an area. Therefore, we introduce the modified notion.

Summary of Observations. We summarize possible combinations for token generation and directions of key and ciphertext updates in Table 1. Note that we do not consider using obfuscation in this table. In each field, possible types are written. In the key update column, "forward-leak? or bi?" means that it can be forward-leak, but in this case, it might not be able to update a ciphertext in the forward direction. If it can update, it essentially includes $\mathsf{sk_e}$ and should be bi-directional. In the ciphertext update column, "backward-leak? or bi?" means that it can be backward, but it does not fit the nature of UE, and if it can be forward, it essentially has the power of bi-directional updates. That is, the second-row case could collapse to the first-row case in Table 1 if the second case works as UE (ciphertext updates are in the forward direction). Lastly, "?" means that we do not know whether this type can update a ciphertext or not (or it is unlikely that the type can update a ciphertext).

All previous ciphertext-independent updates UE schemes fall into the first row category. Our scheme in Sect. 4 falls into the third row category. There might be a hope that we can achieve a no-directional UE scheme by using obfuscation-like techniques (but without obfuscation) in the third row case. It is an interesting open question.

Table 1. Possible combinations for token generation from pk or sk and its relationship to possible directions of key updates and ciphertext updates.

use pk or sk	key update type	ct update type
$\mathsf{TokGen}(\mathsf{sk_e}, \mathsf{sk_{e+1}})$	bi	bi
$\mathsf{TokGen}(\mathsf{pk_e}, \mathsf{sk_{e+1}})$	forward-leak? or bi?	backward? or bi?
$\mathsf{TokGen}(\mathsf{sk_e}, \mathsf{pk_{e+1}})$	backward-leak	forward
$\mathsf{TokGen}(\mathsf{pk_e}, \mathsf{pk_{e+1}})$	no	?

3.3 Relationships

We show that bi-directional key updates does not imply backward-leak uni-directional key updates in this section. More precisely, we prove the following

Theorem 3.1. *There exist secure r-IND-UE-CPA UE schemes in the bi-directional key updates setting that are not r-IND-UE-CPA in the backward-leak uni-directional key updates setting.*

On the Equivalence Between Bi-Directional and Uni-Directional Key Updates. First, we review a simple fact. It is easy to see that the following theorem holds by the definition of confidentiality (Definition 2.3).

Theorem 3.2. *If a UE scheme is r-IND-UE-CPA in the backward-leak uni-directional, forward-leak uni-directional, or no-directional key updates setting, it is also r-IND-UE-CPA secure in the bi-directional key updates setting.*

Next, we review Jiang's equivalence theorem.

Theorem 3.3 ([Jia20, **Theorem 2**]). *Let* UE *be an UE scheme and* $\mathsf{notion} \in \{\mathsf{d\text{-}ind\text{-}ue\text{-}cpa}, \mathsf{r\text{-}ind\text{-}ue\text{-}cpa}, \mathsf{d\text{-}ind\text{-}ue\text{-}cca}, \mathsf{r\text{-}ind\text{-}ue\text{-}cca}, \mathsf{int\text{-}ctxt}, \mathsf{int\text{-}ptxt}\}$*. For any* $\mathsf{kk}, \mathsf{kk}' \in \{\mathsf{f\text{-}uni}, \mathsf{bi}\}$, $\mathsf{cc}, \mathsf{cc}' \in \{\mathsf{uni}, \mathsf{bi}\}$, *and any* $(\mathsf{kk}, \mathsf{cc})$-$\mathsf{notion}$ *adversary* $\mathcal{A}$ *against* UE, *there exists a* $(\mathsf{kk}', \mathsf{cc}')$-$\mathsf{notions}$ *adversary* $\mathcal{B}$ *against* UE *such that*

$$\mathsf{Adv}_{\mathsf{UE},\mathcal{A}}^{(\mathsf{kk},\mathsf{cc})\text{-}\mathsf{notion}}(1^\lambda) = \mathsf{Adv}_{\mathsf{UE},\mathcal{B}}^{(\mathsf{kk}',\mathsf{cc}')\text{-}\mathsf{notion}}(1^\lambda).$$

The key lemma for proving Jiang's theorem (Theorem 3.3) for the confidentiality case is the following.

Lemma 3.1 ([Jia20, **Lemma 6**]). *For any* $\mathcal{K}, \mathcal{T}, \mathcal{C}$, *we have* $\mathcal{K}^*_{\mathsf{f\text{-}uni}} \cap \mathcal{C}^*_{\mathsf{f\text{-}uni},\mathsf{uni}} \neq \emptyset \Leftrightarrow \mathcal{K}^*_{\mathsf{bi}} \cap \mathcal{C}^*_{\mathsf{bi},\mathsf{bi}} \neq \emptyset$.

See Definition 2.6 and 3.1 for the sets in the lemma. Note that this lemma holds for *forward-leak* uni-directional key updates. We show a counterexample to this lemma (for confidentiality) in the case of the *backward-leak* uni-directional key updates setting.

		0		{1}		2		3		4		5		{6		7}		8
$\mathcal{K}$		✓		×		×		×		✓		×		×		×		✓
$\mathcal{T}$	×		×		×		✓		✓		✓		×		✓		×	
$\mathcal{K}^*_{\mathsf{bi}}$		✓		×		**✓**		**✓**		✓		**✓**		×		×		✓
$\mathcal{T}^*_{\mathsf{bi}}$	×		×		×		✓		✓		✓		×		✓		×	
$\mathcal{K}^*_{\mathsf{f\text{-}uni}}$		✓		×		$\underline{\times}$		$\underline{\times}$		✓		**✓**		×		×		✓
$\mathcal{T}^*_{\mathsf{f\text{-}uni}}$	×		×		×		✓		✓		✓		×		✓		×	
$\mathcal{K}^*_{\mathsf{b\text{-}uni}}$		✓		×		**✓**		**✓**		✓		$\underline{\times}$		×		×		✓
$\mathcal{T}^*_{\mathsf{b\text{-}uni}}$	×		×		×		✓		✓		✓		×		✓		×	

Fig. 3. Example of leakage sets in the setting of bi/forward/backward-leak uni-directional key updates where $\mathcal{K} := \{0, 4, 8\}$, $\mathcal{T} := \{3, 4, 5, 7\}$, $\mathcal{IR} = \{1, 6, 7\}$. Here, × and ✓ indicates an epoch key or token is not corrupted and corrupted, respectively. The boldface check mark **✓** indicates an epoch key or token is inferred from other corrupted keys/tokens.

Counterexample in Backward-Leak Uni-Directional Key Updates Setting. Looking at an example is the best thing to understand relationships. We consider an example of epoch key leakage sets in Fig. 3.

In the example in Fig. 3, the firewall area is $\mathcal{IR} = \{1, 6, 7\}$. The difference between the bi-directional setting and forward-leak uni-directional setting is the epochs 2 and 3. The difference between the bi-directional setting and backward-leak uni-directional setting is the epoch 5. (Both differences are underlined in Fig. 3.) We investigate each difference in the forward/backward-leak uni-directional settings.

The case of bi/forward-leak uni-directional key updates: First, we consider the bi/forward-leak uni-directional key updates settings. If we set $\mathcal{C} = \{3\}$, it holds $\mathcal{C}^*_{\mathsf{bi},\mathsf{bi}} = \{2, 3, 4, 5\}$ and $\mathcal{C}^*_{\mathsf{f\text{-}uni},\mathsf{uni}} = \{3, 4, 5\}$. Thus, $\mathcal{K}^*_{\mathsf{bi}} \cap \mathcal{C}^*_{\mathsf{bi},\mathsf{bi}} = \{2, 3, 4, 5\} \neq \emptyset$ and $\mathcal{K}^*_{\mathsf{f\text{-}uni}} \cap \mathcal{C}^*_{\mathsf{f\text{-}uni},\mathsf{uni}} = \{4, 5\} \neq \emptyset$. If we set $\mathcal{C} = \{5\}$, it holds that $\mathcal{K}^*_{\mathsf{bi}} \cap \mathcal{C}^*_{\mathsf{bi},\mathsf{bi}} = \{2, 3, 4, 5\} \neq \emptyset$ and $\mathcal{K}^*_{\mathsf{f\text{-}uni}} \cap \mathcal{C}^*_{\mathsf{f\text{-}uni},\mathsf{uni}} = \{5\} \neq \emptyset$. This is consistent with Lemma 3.1 (Jiang's Lemma 6 [Jia20]). Note that if we set $\mathcal{C} = \{2\}$, we obtain a similar result to $\mathcal{C} = \{3\}$.

The case of bi/backward-leak uni-directional key updates: Next, we consider the bi/backward-leak uni-directional key updates settings. If we set $\mathcal{C} = \{3\}$, it holds $\mathcal{C}^*_{\mathsf{bi},\mathsf{bi}} = \{2, 3, 4, 5\}$ and $\mathcal{C}^*_{\mathsf{b\text{-}uni},\mathsf{uni}} = \{3, 4, 5\}$ since Δ_5 is given even though k_5 is not given in the backward-leak uni-directional setting. Thus, it holds $\mathcal{K}^*_{\mathsf{bi}} \cap \mathcal{C}^*_{\mathsf{bi},\mathsf{bi}} = \{2, 3, 4, 5\} \neq \emptyset$ and $\mathcal{K}^*_{\mathsf{b\text{-}uni}} \cap \mathcal{C}^*_{\mathsf{b\text{-}uni},\mathsf{uni}} = \{3, 4\} \neq \emptyset$. However, if we set $\mathcal{C} = \{5\}$, the difference between forward/backward directional key updates is clear. Now, $\mathcal{K}^*_{\mathsf{bi}} \cap \mathcal{C}^*_{\mathsf{bi},\mathsf{bi}} = \{2, 3, 4, 5\} \neq \emptyset$, but $\mathcal{K}^*_{\mathsf{b\text{-}uni}} \cap \mathcal{C}^*_{\mathsf{b\text{-}uni},\mathsf{uni}} = \emptyset$ since we cannot infer k_5 (the key at epoch 5) due to the definition of backward-leak uni-directional key updates (we cannot go to forward direction even if we are given k_4 and Δ_5.). This means that even if we set $\mathcal{C} = \{5\}$, the trivial winning condition is not triggered in the backward-leak uni-directional setting. However, the trivial winning condition in the bi-directional setting is triggered. Therefore, this is a counterexample to Lemma 3.1 (Jiang's Lemma 6 [Jia20]) when we use the definition of *backward-leak* uni-directional key updates.

By using the example above, we immediately obtain the following theorem.

Theorem 3.4. *The ciphertext-independent UE schemes Lehman and Tackmann [LT18], Boyd et al. [BDGJ20], and Jiang [Jia20] do not satisfy confidentiality in the* backward-leak *uni-directional setting.*

Proof. We use the leakage sets example $\mathcal{K}$ and $\mathcal{T}$ in Fig. 3 and set $\mathcal{C} = \{5\}$. This does not trigger the trivial winning condition in the backward-leak uni-directional setting. However, an adversary can infer k_5 by using k_4 and Δ_5 in the *bi-directional key updates* schemes described in the theorem statement. Thus, the adversary trivially wins the confidentiality game in the backward-leak uni-directional setting since a challenge ciphertext is encrypted under k_5. ■

By Theorem 3.4 and the results by Lehman and Tackmann [LT18], Boyd et al. [BDGJ20], and Jiang [Jia20], we immediately obtain Theorem 3.1 since they show that their schemes satisfy confidentiality in the bi-directional key updates setting. Therefore, surprisingly (or unsurprisingly), UE with backward-leak uni-directional (and no-directional) key updates is *strictly stronger* than UE with bi-directional key updates by Theorems 3.1 and 3.2.

On Equivalence Between No/Uni/Bi-Directional Key Updates in Bi-Directional Ciphertext Update Setting. We give an observation on the equivalence theorem about no-directional key updates. Jiang also proves the following theorem.

Theorem 3.5 ([Jia20, **Theorem 3.2 in the ePrint ver.**]). *Let* UE *be an UE scheme and* $\mathsf{notion} \in \{\mathsf{d\text{-}ind\text{-}ue\text{-}cpa}, \mathsf{r\text{-}ind\text{-}ue\text{-}cpa}, \mathsf{d\text{-}ind\text{-}ue\text{-}cca}, \mathsf{r\text{-}ind\text{-}ue\text{-}cca}\}$. *For any* $(\mathsf{no}, \mathsf{bi})\text{-}\mathsf{notion}$ *adversary* $\mathcal{A}$ *against* UE, *there exists a* $(\mathsf{f\text{-}uni}, \mathsf{bi})\text{-}\mathsf{notions}$ *adversary* $\mathcal{B}$ *against* UE *such that*

$$\mathsf{Adv}_{\mathsf{UE},\mathcal{A}}^{(\mathsf{no},\mathsf{bi})\text{-}\mathsf{notion}}(1^\lambda) = \mathsf{Adv}_{\mathsf{UE},\mathcal{B}}^{(\mathsf{f\text{-}uni},\mathsf{bi})\text{-}\mathsf{notion}}(1^\lambda).$$

This theorem seems to contradict our conclusion above, which says UE with no-directional key updates is strictly stronger than UE with forward-leak uni-directional key updates. Recall that no-directional key updates is stronger than backward-leak uni-directional key updates. We also note that bi-directional key updates and forward-leak uni-directional key updates are equivalent.

The source of the puzzle above comes from the fact that the theorem holds for *bi-directional ciphertext* updates. The key lemma for proving Jiang's theorem above (Theorem 3.5) is the following.

Lemma 3.2 ([Jia20, **Lemma 3.15 in the ePrint ver.**]). *For any* $\mathcal{K}, \mathcal{T}, \mathcal{C}$, *we have* $\mathcal{K}^*_{\mathsf{f\text{-}uni}} \cap \mathcal{C}^*_{\mathsf{f\text{-}uni},\mathsf{bi}} \neq \emptyset \Rightarrow \mathcal{K}^*_{\mathsf{no}} \cap \mathcal{C}^*_{\mathsf{no},\mathsf{bi}} \neq \emptyset$.

The proof of the lemma above heavily relies on the bi-directional ciphertext update setting. As we argued in Sect. 3.2, it is unnatural to consider bi-directional ciphertext updates with backward-leak uni-directional (and no-directional) key updates. Thus, if we exclude such an unnatural or artificial setting, the equivalence theorem above (Theorem 3.5), which is counterintuitive, does not hold in the case of the backward-leak uni-directional key updates setting.

4 Construction with Backward-Leak Uni-Directional Key Update

In this section, we present a backward-leak uni-directional key update scheme from the LWE assumption.

4.1 Scheme Description and Design Idea

We present a UE scheme with backward-leak uni-directional key updates based on the Regev PKE scheme [Reg09], and denoted by RtR. A proxy re-encryption scheme by Nishimaki and Xagawa [NX15] inspired this construction idea.

The ciphertext update technique is based on the key-switching technique [BV14,BV11,BGV14]. In particular, we use that for multi-bit plaintexts [BGH13]. In the following, we denote a plaintext by $\boldsymbol{\mu} \in \{0,1\}^{\ell}$ and error distributions by χ and χ_{ns}.

A Variant of Regev PKE Scheme. We review a variant of Regev PKE scheme [Reg09] in the multi-user settings.

- $\mathsf{Setup}(1^{\lambda})$: Choose $\boldsymbol{A} \leftarrow \mathbb{Z}_q^{m \times n}$ and output $\mathsf{pp} := (\boldsymbol{A}, 1^{\lambda}, 1^n, 1^m, 1^{\ell}, q, \chi, \chi_{\mathsf{ns}})$.
- $\mathsf{Reg.Gen}(\mathsf{pp})$: Choose $\boldsymbol{S} \leftarrow \mathbb{Z}_q^{n \times \ell}$ and $\boldsymbol{X} \leftarrow \chi^{m \times \ell}$, compute $\boldsymbol{B} := \boldsymbol{AS} + \boldsymbol{X} \in \mathbb{Z}_q^{m \times \ell}$, and outputs $\mathsf{pk} = \boldsymbol{B}$ and $\mathsf{sk} = \boldsymbol{S}$.
- $\mathsf{Reg.Enc}(\mathsf{pk}, \boldsymbol{\mu})$: Choose $\boldsymbol{r} \leftarrow \{-1,+1\}^m$ and $\boldsymbol{e}' \leftarrow \chi_{\mathsf{ns}}^{\ell}$ and output $(\boldsymbol{u}, \boldsymbol{c}) := (\boldsymbol{rA}, \boldsymbol{rB} + \boldsymbol{e}' + \lfloor q/2 \rfloor \boldsymbol{\mu})$.
- $\mathsf{Reg.Dec}(\mathsf{sk}, (\boldsymbol{u}, \boldsymbol{c}))$ Compute $\boldsymbol{d} := \boldsymbol{c} - \boldsymbol{uS}$ and output $\boldsymbol{\mu} := \lfloor (2/q)\boldsymbol{d} \rceil \bmod 2$.

Key-switching Technique. We review the key-switching technique in the multi-bit version for our update algorithm. Let $\eta := \lceil \lg q \rceil$. We give the definitions of the binary-decomposition algorithm $\mathsf{BD}(\cdot)$ and the powers-of-2 algorithm $\mathsf{P2}(\cdot)$.

- $\mathsf{BD}(\boldsymbol{x} \in \mathbb{Z}_q^n)$: It decomposes $\boldsymbol{x} = \sum_{k=1}^{\eta} 2^{k-1}\boldsymbol{u}_k$, where $\boldsymbol{u}_k \in \{0,1\}^n$, and outputs $(\boldsymbol{u}_1, \boldsymbol{u}_2, \ldots, \boldsymbol{u}_{\eta}) \in \{0,1\}^{n\eta}$.
- $\mathsf{P2}(\boldsymbol{s} \in \mathbb{Z}_q^{n \times 1})$: It outputs $[1, 2, \ldots, 2^{\eta-1}]^{\top} \otimes \boldsymbol{s} = [\boldsymbol{s}; 2\boldsymbol{s}; \ldots; 2^{\eta-1}\boldsymbol{s}] \in \mathbb{Z}_q^{n\eta \times 1}$, where $\otimes$ denotes the standard tensor product. We extend the domain of $\mathsf{P2}$ by setting $\mathsf{P2}([\boldsymbol{s}_1 \ldots \boldsymbol{s}_{\ell}] \in \mathbb{Z}_q^{n \times \ell}) = [\mathsf{P2}(\boldsymbol{s}_1) \ldots \mathsf{P2}(\boldsymbol{s}_{\ell})] \in \mathbb{Z}_q^{n\eta \times \ell}$.

By the definition, it holds that $\mathsf{BD}(\boldsymbol{x}) \cdot \mathsf{P2}(\boldsymbol{S}) = \boldsymbol{x} \cdot \boldsymbol{S} \in \mathbb{Z}_q^{\ell}$ for any $\boldsymbol{x} \in \mathbb{Z}_q^n$ and $\boldsymbol{S} \in \mathbb{Z}_q^{n \times \ell}$.

Let $\boldsymbol{S}_{\mathsf{e}}, \boldsymbol{S}_{\mathsf{e}+1} \in \mathbb{Z}_q^{n \times \ell}$ be two secret keys at epoch $\mathsf{e}, \mathsf{e}+1$, respectively. The key-switching technique enables us to homomorphically decrypt a ciphertext at epoch e and obtain a ciphertext at epoch $\mathsf{e}+1$ by using encryption of $\boldsymbol{S}_{\mathsf{e}}$ under the key at epoch $\mathsf{e}+1$. More formally, the key-switching matrix $\boldsymbol{M}_{\mathsf{e}+1}$ is $[\boldsymbol{A}' \mid \boldsymbol{A}'\boldsymbol{S}_{\mathsf{e}+1} + \boldsymbol{Y}] + [\boldsymbol{O} \mid -\mathsf{P2}(\boldsymbol{S}_{\mathsf{e}})]$, where $\boldsymbol{A}' \leftarrow \mathbb{Z}_q^{n\eta \times n}$, $\boldsymbol{Y} \leftarrow \chi^{n\eta \times \ell}$. To update a ciphertext $(\boldsymbol{u}, \boldsymbol{c})$ under $\boldsymbol{S}_{\mathsf{e}}$ to one under $\boldsymbol{S}_{\mathsf{e}+1}$, we compute $(\boldsymbol{u}', \boldsymbol{c}') = (\boldsymbol{0}, \boldsymbol{c}) + \mathsf{BD}(\boldsymbol{u})\boldsymbol{M}_{\mathsf{e}+1}$. By simple calculation, we have that

$$\begin{aligned}(\boldsymbol{u}', \boldsymbol{c}') &= (\boldsymbol{0}, \boldsymbol{c}) + \mathsf{BD}(\boldsymbol{u})\left([\boldsymbol{A}' \mid \boldsymbol{A}'\boldsymbol{S}_{\mathsf{e}+1} + \boldsymbol{Y}] + [\boldsymbol{O} \mid -\mathsf{P2}(\boldsymbol{S}_{\mathsf{e}})]\right) \\ &= (\mathsf{BD}(\boldsymbol{u})\boldsymbol{A}', \boldsymbol{c} - \boldsymbol{u}\boldsymbol{S}_{\mathsf{e}} + \mathsf{BD}(\boldsymbol{u})\boldsymbol{A}'\boldsymbol{S}_{\mathsf{e}+1} + \mathsf{BD}(\boldsymbol{u}) \cdot \boldsymbol{Y}).\end{aligned}$$

To decrypt ciphertext by secret key $\boldsymbol{S}_{\mathsf{e}+1}$, we compute

$$\begin{aligned}\boldsymbol{c}' - \boldsymbol{u}'\boldsymbol{S}_{\mathsf{e}+1} &= \boldsymbol{c} - \boldsymbol{u}\boldsymbol{S}_{\mathsf{e}} + \mathsf{BD}(\boldsymbol{u})\boldsymbol{A}'\boldsymbol{S}_{\mathsf{e}+1} + \mathsf{BD}(\boldsymbol{u}) \cdot \boldsymbol{Y} - \mathsf{BD}(\boldsymbol{u})\boldsymbol{A}'\boldsymbol{S}_{\mathsf{e}+1} \\ &= \boldsymbol{c} - \boldsymbol{u}\boldsymbol{S}_{\mathsf{e}} + \mathsf{BD}(\boldsymbol{u}) \cdot \boldsymbol{Y}.\end{aligned}$$

Thus, the decryption is correct if the magnitude of additional noises $\mathsf{BD}(\boldsymbol{u}) \cdot \boldsymbol{Y}$ is small.

Backward-Leak Uni-Directional Update. In fact, we do not need the secret key $\boldsymbol{S}_{\mathsf{e}+1}$ at epoch $\mathsf{e}+1$ for update. We set $\boldsymbol{B}_{\mathsf{e}+1} = \boldsymbol{A}\boldsymbol{S}_{\mathsf{e}+1} + \boldsymbol{Y}_{\mathsf{e}+1}$, which we call the public key part of the key at epoch $\mathsf{e}+1$. We choose $\boldsymbol{R}_{\mathsf{e}+1} \leftarrow \{-1, +1\}^{n\eta \times m}$ and compute an update token

$$\begin{aligned}\boldsymbol{M}_{\mathsf{e}+1} &= \boldsymbol{R}_{\mathsf{e}+1}[\boldsymbol{A} \mid \boldsymbol{B}_{\mathsf{e}+1}] + [\boldsymbol{O} \mid -\mathsf{P2}(\boldsymbol{S}_{\mathsf{e}})] \\ &= [\boldsymbol{A}' \mid \boldsymbol{A}'\boldsymbol{S}_{\mathsf{e}+1} + \boldsymbol{Y}'] + [\boldsymbol{O} \mid -\mathsf{P2}(\boldsymbol{S}_{\mathsf{e}})],\end{aligned}$$

where $\boldsymbol{A}' = \boldsymbol{R}_{\mathsf{e}+1}\boldsymbol{A}$ and $\boldsymbol{Y}' = \boldsymbol{R}_{\mathsf{e}+1}\boldsymbol{Y}_j$. By using $\boldsymbol{M}_{\mathsf{e}+1}$, we can update ciphertext $(\boldsymbol{u}, \boldsymbol{c})$ at epoch e. Thus, even if given the key $\boldsymbol{S}_{\mathsf{e}}$ at epoch e and the token $\boldsymbol{M}_{\mathsf{e}+1}$, we cannot infer $\boldsymbol{S}_{\mathsf{e}+1}$ since only the public key part $\boldsymbol{B}_{\mathsf{e}+1}$ (this is pseudorandom by the LWE assumption) of the key at epoch $\mathsf{e}+1$ is embedded in $\boldsymbol{M}_{\mathsf{e}+1}$. Note that $\boldsymbol{S}_{\mathsf{e}}$ and $\boldsymbol{S}_{\mathsf{e}+1}$ are independently chosen. However, if given the key $\boldsymbol{S}_{\mathsf{e}+1}$ at epoch $\mathsf{e}+1$ and the token $\boldsymbol{M}_{\mathsf{e}+1}$, we can easily infer $\boldsymbol{S}_{\mathsf{e}}$ since $\boldsymbol{S}_{\mathsf{e}}$ is encrypted under $\boldsymbol{S}_{\mathsf{e}+1}$. Thus, this update mechanism is a backward-leak uni-directional key update and uni-directional ciphertext update.

How to Achieve Randomized Update. The update algorithm above is deterministic. To re-randomize an updated ciphertext, we set the update token as $\boldsymbol{M}_{\mathsf{e}+1}$ and $\boldsymbol{B}_{\mathsf{e}+1}$, which is the public key part at epoch $\mathsf{e}+1$. First, we convert ciphertext $(\boldsymbol{u}, \boldsymbol{c})$ at epoch e into $(\boldsymbol{u}', \boldsymbol{c}')$ using $\boldsymbol{M}_{\mathsf{e}+1}$ as above and masking $(\boldsymbol{u}', \boldsymbol{c}')$ with a new ciphertext $(\tilde{\boldsymbol{u}}, \tilde{\boldsymbol{v}}) := \tilde{\boldsymbol{r}}[\boldsymbol{A} \mid \boldsymbol{B}_{\mathsf{e}+1}]$ of the plaintext $\boldsymbol{0}$. This is not enough for confidentiality since it includes information about $\boldsymbol{B}_{\mathsf{e}+1}$ and is not random. To overcome this issue, we randomize $[\boldsymbol{A} \mid \boldsymbol{B}_{\mathsf{e}+1}]$ into $\boldsymbol{N}_{\mathsf{e}+1} = \boldsymbol{R}'_{\mathsf{e}+1} \cdot [\boldsymbol{A} \mid \boldsymbol{B}_{\mathsf{e}+1}]$, where $\boldsymbol{R}'_{\mathsf{e}+1} \leftarrow \{-1, +1\}^{m \times m}$ and add it to $\Delta_{\mathsf{e}+1}$. Since the matrix $\boldsymbol{N}_{\mathsf{e}+1}$ consists of m ciphertexts of the message $\boldsymbol{0}$, this is pseudorandom. The update token consists of key-switching matrix $\boldsymbol{M}_{\mathsf{e}+1}$ and randomized matrix $\boldsymbol{N}_{\mathsf{e}+1}$.

Backward-Leak Uni-Directional Key Update Scheme. A UE scheme, RtR, is defined as follows:

$\mathsf{Setup}(1^\lambda)$:
1. Choose $\boldsymbol{A} \leftarrow \mathbb{Z}_q^{m\times n}$.
2. Output $\mathsf{pp} := (\boldsymbol{A}, 1^\lambda, 1^n, 1^m, 1^\ell, q, \chi, \chi_{\mathsf{ns}})$.

$\mathsf{Gen}(\mathsf{pp})$:
1. Generate $(\boldsymbol{B}_{\mathsf{e}}, \boldsymbol{S}_{\mathsf{e}}) \leftarrow \mathsf{Reg.Gen}(1^\lambda)$.
2. Output $\mathsf{k_e} := (\mathsf{sk_e}, \mathsf{pk_e}) := (\boldsymbol{S}_{\mathsf{e}}, \boldsymbol{B}_{\mathsf{e}})$.

$\mathsf{Enc}(\mathsf{k_e}, \boldsymbol{\mu} \in \{0,1\}^\ell)$:
1. Parse $\mathsf{k_e} = (\boldsymbol{S}_{\mathsf{e}}, \boldsymbol{B}_{\mathsf{e}})$.
2. Generate $(\boldsymbol{u}, \boldsymbol{c}) \leftarrow \mathsf{Reg.Enc}(\boldsymbol{B}_{\mathsf{e}}, \boldsymbol{\mu})$.
3. Output $\mathsf{ct} := (\boldsymbol{u}, \boldsymbol{c}) \in \mathbb{Z}_q^n \times \mathbb{Z}_q^\ell$.

$\mathsf{Dec}(\mathsf{k_e}, \mathsf{ct})$:
1. Parse $\mathsf{k_e} = (\boldsymbol{S}_{\mathsf{e}}, \boldsymbol{B}_{\mathsf{e}})$ $\mathsf{ct} = (\boldsymbol{u}, \boldsymbol{c})$.
2. Compute and output $\boldsymbol{\mu} \leftarrow \mathsf{Reg.Dec}(\boldsymbol{S}_{\mathsf{e}}, \mathsf{ct})$.

$\mathsf{TokGen}(\mathsf{k_e}, \mathsf{k_{e+1}})$:
1. Parse $\mathsf{k_e} = (\boldsymbol{S}_{\mathsf{e}}, \boldsymbol{B}_{\mathsf{e}})$ and $\mathsf{k_{e+1}} = (\boldsymbol{S}_{\mathsf{e+1}}, \boldsymbol{B}_{\mathsf{e+1}})$.
2. Compute $\boldsymbol{M}_{\mathsf{e+1}} := \boldsymbol{R}_{\mathsf{e+1}} \cdot [\boldsymbol{A} \mid \boldsymbol{B}_{\mathsf{e+1}}] + [\boldsymbol{O} \mid -\mathsf{P2}(\boldsymbol{S}_{\mathsf{e}})]$, where $\boldsymbol{R}_{\mathsf{e+1}} \leftarrow \{-1,+1\}^{n\eta\times m}$.
3. Compute $\boldsymbol{N}_{\mathsf{e+1}} := \boldsymbol{R}'_{\mathsf{e+1}} \cdot [\boldsymbol{A} \mid \boldsymbol{B}_{\mathsf{e+1}}]$, where $\boldsymbol{R}'_{\mathsf{e+1}} \leftarrow \{-1,+1\}^{m\times m}$.
4. Output $\Delta_{\mathsf{e+1}} := (\boldsymbol{M}_{\mathsf{e+1}}, \boldsymbol{N}_{\mathsf{e+1}})$.

$\mathsf{Upd}(\Delta_{\mathsf{e+1}}, \mathsf{ct_e})$:
1. Parse $\Delta_{\mathsf{e+1}} = (\boldsymbol{M}_{\mathsf{e+1}}, \boldsymbol{N}_{\mathsf{e+1}})$ and $\mathsf{ct_e} = (\boldsymbol{u}_{\mathsf{e}}, \boldsymbol{c}_{\mathsf{e}})$.
2. Compute $(\boldsymbol{u}', \boldsymbol{c}') := \mathsf{BD}(\boldsymbol{u}_{\mathsf{e}})\boldsymbol{M}_{\mathsf{e+1}}$;
3. Compute $(\tilde{\boldsymbol{u}}, \tilde{\boldsymbol{v}}) := \tilde{\boldsymbol{r}} \cdot \boldsymbol{N}_{\mathsf{e+1}}$, where $\tilde{\boldsymbol{r}} \leftarrow \{-1,+1\}^m$;
4. Output $\mathsf{ct_{e+1}} := (\bar{\boldsymbol{u}}, \bar{\boldsymbol{c}}) := (\boldsymbol{u}' + \tilde{\boldsymbol{u}}, \boldsymbol{c}_{\mathsf{e}} + \boldsymbol{c}' + \tilde{\boldsymbol{v}})$.

For notational convenience, we call $\mathsf{pk_e} = \boldsymbol{B}_{\mathsf{e}}$ and $\mathsf{sk_e} = \boldsymbol{S}_{\mathsf{e}}$ public key and secret key of epoch e, respectively. Note that we can run Enc without $\mathsf{sk_e} = \boldsymbol{S}_{\mathsf{e}}$ (we need only $\mathsf{pk_e} = \boldsymbol{B}_{\mathsf{e}}$). We also note that we can run $\mathsf{TokGen}(\mathsf{k_e}, \mathsf{k_{e+1}})$ without $\mathsf{sk_{e+1}}$ (we need only $\mathsf{pk_{e+1}}$ and $\mathsf{sk_e}$).

The scheme is correct and r-IND-UE-CPA secure. We prove the following theorems in Sects. 4.2 and 4.3. Let T be the maximum number of the epoch.

Theorem 4.1. *Let χ and χ_{ns} be B-bounded and B'-bounded distributions, respectively, such that $B/B' = \mathsf{negl}(\lambda)$ and $m = 2n\lg q + \omega(\sqrt{\lg\lambda})$. Suppose that $(1 + n\eta + m)mB + B' \leq q/4T$. Then* RtR *is correct.*

Theorem 4.2. *Suppose that $m \geq (n+\ell)\lg q + \omega(\lg\lambda)$. Under the* LWE$(n, q, \chi)$ *assumption,* RtR *is r-IND-UE-CPA secure in the backward-leak uni-directional setting. That is, $\mathsf{Adv}^{\mathsf{(b\text{-}uni,uni)\text{-}r\text{-}ind\text{-}ue\text{-}cpa}}_{\mathsf{RtR},\mathcal{A}}(1^\lambda) \leq \mathsf{negl}(\lambda)$.*

4.2 Correctness

We give rough estimations on B-bounded and B'-bounded distributions χ and χ_{ns}, respectively, for simplicity. However, if we set $\chi = \bar{\Psi}_\alpha$ or $D_{\mathbb{Z},s}$, we can obtain tighter bounds.

Proof of Theorem. 4.1. The theorem follows from Prop. 4.1 and 4.2 below. ∎

Proposition 4.1. *The scheme is correct for the encryption algorithm if* $mB + B' < q/4$.

Proposition 4.2. *The scheme is correct for the update algorithm if* $(1 + n\eta + m)mB + B' < q/4T$.

Those correctness easily follows from the proof by Regev [Reg09]. We omit them due to space limitations. See the full version for the proofs.

4.3 Confidentiality

We show RtR is r-IND-UE-CPA in the backward-leak uni-directional setting. Although it is trivial that RtR satisfies uni-directional ciphertext updates from its security, we confirm it below.

Lemma 4.1. *If* (Setup, Reg.Gen, Reg.Enc, Reg.Dec) *is IND-CPA secure PKE, adversaries cannot convert a ciphertext under a public key* $\mathsf{pk}_{\mathsf{e}+1}$ *into one under a public key* pk_{e} *even if they are given* $\Delta_{\mathsf{e}+1}$.

Proof. We construct an algorithm $\mathcal{B}$ that breaks IND-CPA security under $\mathsf{pk}_{\mathsf{e}+1}$ by using an adversary $\mathcal{D}$ that converts a ciphertext under $\mathsf{pk}_{\mathsf{e}+1}$ into one under pk_{e} by using $(\mathsf{pk}_{\mathsf{e}}, \mathsf{sk}_{\mathsf{e}})$, $\mathsf{pk}_{\mathsf{e}+1}$, and $\Delta_{\mathsf{e}+1}$.

First, $\mathcal{B}$ is given $\mathsf{pk}_{\mathsf{e}+1}$. $\mathcal{B}$ generates $(\mathsf{pk}_{\mathsf{e}}, \mathsf{sk}_{\mathsf{e}})$ and $\Delta_{\mathsf{e}+1} \leftarrow \mathsf{TokGen}(\mathsf{sk}_{\mathsf{e}}, \mathsf{pk}_{\mathsf{e}+1})$, selects any (m_0, m_1), sends (m_0, m_1) to its challenger, and receives a target ciphertext $\mathsf{ct}^* \leftarrow \mathsf{Reg.Enc}(\mathsf{pk}_{\mathsf{e}+1}, m_b)$ where $b \leftarrow \{0,1\}$. Next, $\mathcal{B}$ sends $((\mathsf{pk}_{\mathsf{e}}, \mathsf{sk}_{\mathsf{e}}), \Delta_{\mathsf{e}+1}, \mathsf{ct}^*)$ to $\mathcal{D}$. $\mathcal{D}$ outputs a ciphertext ct' under pk_{e}. Then, $\mathcal{B}$ computes $m' \leftarrow \mathsf{Reg.Dec}(\mathsf{sk}_{\mathsf{e}}, \mathsf{ct}')$ by using sk_{e} and if $m' = m_{b'}$, it outputs b'.

It is easy to see that if $\mathcal{D}$ can convert ct^* into a ciphertext under pk_{e}, $\mathcal{B}$ outputs $b' = b$. This completes the proof. ∎

Second, we look at the detail of the update procedure again. By simple calculation, we obtain

$$\begin{aligned}
(\bar{\boldsymbol{u}}, \bar{c}) &= (\boldsymbol{0}, \boldsymbol{c}_{\mathsf{e}}) + \mathsf{BD}(\boldsymbol{u}_{\mathsf{e}}) \cdot \boldsymbol{M}_{\mathsf{e}+1} + \tilde{\boldsymbol{r}} \cdot \boldsymbol{N}_{\mathsf{e}+1} \\
&= (\boldsymbol{r}^{\dagger}\boldsymbol{A}, \boldsymbol{r}^{\dagger}\boldsymbol{B}_{\mathsf{e}+1} + \boldsymbol{e}'_{\mathsf{e}} + \boldsymbol{r}\boldsymbol{X}_{\mathsf{e}} + \lfloor q/2 \rfloor \boldsymbol{\mu}) \text{ where } \boldsymbol{r}^{\dagger} := \mathsf{BD}(\boldsymbol{u}_{\mathsf{e}})\boldsymbol{R}_{\mathsf{e}+1} + \tilde{\boldsymbol{r}}\boldsymbol{R}'_{\mathsf{e}+1} \\
&\overset{\mathsf{s}}{\approx} (\boldsymbol{r}^{\dagger}\boldsymbol{A}, \boldsymbol{r}^{\dagger}\boldsymbol{B}_{\mathsf{e}+1} + \boldsymbol{e}'_{\mathsf{e}} + \lfloor q/2 \rfloor \boldsymbol{\mu}).
\end{aligned} \tag{1}$$

The last equation (statistical indistinguishability) holds by the noise smuding lemma [AJL+12]. This equation shows that we can simulate an update ciphertext by using the original ciphertext, its plaintext and randomness, the new epoch public key, and *randomness* for generating the token $\Delta_{\mathsf{e}+1}$ (not the token itself).

To show the security, we define auxiliary algorithms for simulation.

$\mathsf{Hyb.Upd}(\mathsf{ct_e}, \boldsymbol{B}_{\mathsf{e}+1}, \boldsymbol{\mu}; \boldsymbol{e}'_{\mathsf{e}}, (\boldsymbol{R}_{\mathsf{e}+1}, \boldsymbol{R}'_{\mathsf{e}+1}))$:
- Parse $\mathsf{ct_e} = (\boldsymbol{u}_{\mathsf{e}}, \boldsymbol{c}_{\mathsf{e}})$.
- Choose $\tilde{\boldsymbol{r}} \leftarrow \{-1, +1\}^m$ and set $\boldsymbol{r}^{\dagger} := \mathsf{BD}(\boldsymbol{u}_{\mathsf{e}})\boldsymbol{R}_{\mathsf{e}+1} + \tilde{\boldsymbol{r}}\boldsymbol{R}'_{\mathsf{e}+1}$.
- Set $\mathsf{ct}_{\mathsf{e}+1} := (\bar{\boldsymbol{u}}, \bar{\boldsymbol{c}}) := (\boldsymbol{r}^{\dagger}\boldsymbol{A}, \boldsymbol{r}^{\dagger}\boldsymbol{B}_{\mathsf{e}+1} + \boldsymbol{e}'_{\mathsf{e}} + \lfloor q/2 \rfloor \boldsymbol{\mu})$.
- Output $(\mathsf{ct}_{\mathsf{e}+1}; \boldsymbol{e}'_{\mathsf{e}})$.

$\mathsf{Sim.Gen}(\mathsf{pp})$:
- Choose and output $\mathsf{pk_e} := \boldsymbol{B}^{+}_{\mathsf{e}} \leftarrow \mathbb{Z}_q^{m \times \ell}$.

$\mathsf{Sim.TokGen}(\mathsf{pp})$:
- Choose and output $\Delta^{+}_{\mathsf{e}+1} := (\boldsymbol{M}^{+}_{\mathsf{e}+1}, \boldsymbol{N}^{+}_{\mathsf{e}+1}) \leftarrow \mathbb{Z}_q^{n\eta \times (n+\ell)} \times \mathbb{Z}_q^{m \times (n+\ell)}$.

$\mathsf{Sim.Upd}(\mathsf{pp})$:
- Choose and output $\mathsf{ct}_{\mathsf{e}+1} := (\bar{\boldsymbol{u}}, \bar{\boldsymbol{c}}) \leftarrow \mathbb{Z}_q^n \times \mathbb{Z}_q^{\ell}$.

$\mathsf{Sim.Enc}(\mathsf{pp})$:
- Choose and output $\mathsf{ct_e} := (\bar{\boldsymbol{u}}, \bar{\boldsymbol{c}}) \leftarrow \mathbb{Z}_q^n \times \mathbb{Z}_q^{\ell}$.

Lemma 4.2. $\mathsf{Upd}(\Delta_{\mathsf{e}+1}, \mathsf{ct_e}) \overset{\mathsf{s}}{\approx} \mathsf{Hyb.Upd}(\mathsf{ct_e}, \boldsymbol{B}_{\mathsf{e}+1}, \boldsymbol{\mu}; \boldsymbol{e}'_{\mathsf{e}}, (\boldsymbol{R}_{\mathsf{e}+1}, \boldsymbol{R}'_{\mathsf{e}+1}))$

By Eq. (1), Lemma 4.2 immediately holds. That is, we can simulate $\mathcal{O}.\mathsf{Upd}(\mathsf{ct_e})$ by using $\mathsf{Hyb.Upd}(\mathsf{ct_e}, \boldsymbol{B}_{\mathsf{e}+1}, \boldsymbol{\mu}; \boldsymbol{e}'_{\mathsf{e}}, (\boldsymbol{R}_{\mathsf{e}+1}, \boldsymbol{R}'_{\mathsf{e}+1}))$.

We follow the firewall technique [LT18, KLR19, BDGJ20, Jia20] to prove security, but we use the relaxed firewall notion in Definition 3.2.

Proof of Theorem 4.2. Let T be the upper bound of the number of epoch. We consider a sequence of hybrid games. First, we define the following hybrid game:

$\mathsf{Hyb}_i(b)$: This is the same as $\mathsf{Exp}^{\mathsf{(b\text{-}uni,uni)\text{-}r\text{-}ind\text{-}ue\text{-}cpa}}_{\mathsf{RtR},\mathcal{A}}(\lambda, b)$ except the following difference: When the adversary sends a query $(\overline{\mu}, \overline{\mathsf{ct}})$ to $\mathcal{O}.\mathsf{Chall}$ or an empty query to $\mathcal{O}.\mathsf{Upd}\widetilde{\mathsf{C}}$ at epoch j,
- for $j < i$, return an honestly generated challenge-equal ciphertext. That is, if $b = 0$, $\mathsf{UE.Enc}(\mathsf{k}_{\tilde{\mathsf{e}}}, \overline{\mu})$ else $\mathsf{UE.Upd}(\Delta_{\tilde{\mathsf{e}}}, \overline{\mathsf{ct}})$.
- for $j \geq i$, return a random ciphertext.

It is easy to see that $\mathsf{Hyb}_{T+1}(b)$ is the same as the original r-INE-UE-CPA game in the backward-leak uni-directional setting $\mathsf{Exp}^{\mathsf{(b\text{-}uni,uni)\text{-}r\text{-}ind\text{-}ue\text{-}cpa}}_{\mathsf{RtR},\mathcal{A}}(\lambda, b)$. Let $U(\lambda)$ be a random variable distributed uniformly in $[0, T]$, by the standard hybrid argument, we have

$$\begin{aligned}\mathsf{Adv}^{\mathsf{(b\text{-}uni,uni)\text{-}r\text{-}ind\text{-}ue\text{-}cpa}}_{\mathsf{RtR},\mathcal{A}}(\lambda) \leq\ & (T+1)|\Pr[\mathsf{Hyb}_{U(\lambda)+1}(1) = 1] - \Pr[\mathsf{Hyb}_{U(\lambda)}(1) = 1]| \\ & + (T+1)|\Pr[\mathsf{Hyb}_{U(\lambda)+1}(0) = 1] - \Pr[\mathsf{Hyb}_{U(\lambda)}(0) = 1]|,\end{aligned}$$

where we use $\Pr[U(\lambda) = i] = 1/(T+1)$. Note that $\mathsf{Hyb}_0(0) = \mathsf{Hyb}_0(1)$ trivially holds since all challenge-equal ciphertexts are random ciphertexts. Thus, our goal is to prove $|\Pr[\mathsf{Hyb}_{U(\lambda)+1}(b) = 1] - \Pr[\mathsf{Hyb}_{U(\lambda)}(b) = 1]| \leq \mathsf{negl}(\lambda)$ for $b \in \{0, 1\}$.

Hereafter, we write $\mathsf{Hyb}_i(b)$ instead of $\mathsf{Hyb}_{U(\lambda)}(b)$ for simplicity. Next, we define the following hybrid game:

$\mathsf{Hyb}'_i(b)$: This is the same as $\mathsf{Hyb}_i(b)$ except that the game chooses $\mathsf{fwl}, \mathsf{fwr} \leftarrow [0, T]$. If the adversary corrupts k_j such that $j \in [\mathsf{fwl}, \mathsf{fwr}]$ or $\Delta_{\mathsf{fwr}+1}$, the game aborts.

The guess is correct with probability $1/(T+1)^2$. We have

$$|\Pr[\mathsf{Hyb}_i(b) = 1] - \Pr[\mathsf{Hyb}_{i-1}(b)]| \leq (T+1)^2 |\Pr[\mathsf{Hyb}'_i(b) = 1] - \Pr[\mathsf{Hyb}'_{i-1}(b) = 1]|.$$

If $|\Pr[\mathsf{Hyb}'_{U(\lambda)+1}(b) = 1] - \Pr[\mathsf{Hyb}'_{U(\lambda)}(b) = 1]| \leq \mathsf{negl}(\lambda)$, we complete the proof of Theorem 4.2. ■

Lemma 4.3. *If the LWE assumption holds, it holds that* $|\Pr[\mathsf{Hyb}'_{i+1}(b) = 1] - \Pr[\mathsf{Hyb}'_i(b) = 1]| \leq \mathsf{negl}(\lambda)$.

Proof. Note that the difference between these two games appears when the challenge query is sent at epoch i, so we can assume $\widetilde{\mathsf{e}} = i$. We start from $\mathsf{Hyb}'_{i+1}(b)$ and gradually change it to $\mathsf{Hyb}'_i(b)$. We define another sequence of games.

$\mathsf{Hyb}^{\mathsf{r}}_i(b)$: This is the same as $\mathsf{Hyb}'_i(b)$ except that we use the hybrid update algorithm $\mathsf{Hyb.Upd}$ to simulate $\mathcal{O}.\mathsf{Upd}$. More precisely, $\mathcal{O}.\mathsf{Upd}(\mathsf{ct}_{\mathsf{e}-1})$ act as follows:
- If $(\cdot, \mathsf{ct}_{\mathsf{e}-1}, \mathsf{e}-1; \boldsymbol{e}'_{\mathsf{e}-1}; \boldsymbol{\mu}) \notin \mathcal{L}$, then return $\bot$
- Otherwise, $(\mathsf{ct}_{\mathsf{e}}, \boldsymbol{e}'_{\mathsf{e}}) \leftarrow \mathsf{Hyb.Upd}(\mathsf{ct}_{\mathsf{e}-1}, \boldsymbol{B}_{\mathsf{e}}, \boldsymbol{\mu}; \boldsymbol{e}'_{\mathsf{e}-1}, (\boldsymbol{R}_{\mathsf{e}}, \boldsymbol{R}'_{\mathsf{e}}))$.
- $\mathcal{L} := \mathcal{L} \cup \{(\cdot, \mathsf{ct}_{\mathsf{e}}, \mathsf{e}; \boldsymbol{e}'_{\mathsf{e}}, \boldsymbol{\mu})\}$.

Note that $\boldsymbol{R}_{\mathsf{e}}$ and $\boldsymbol{R}'_{\mathsf{e}}$ are randomness used in TokGen, so anyone can choose them. Simulators internally choose and record them.

Proposition 4.3. $|\Pr[\mathsf{Hyb}'_i(b) = 1] - \Pr[\mathsf{Hyb}^{\mathsf{r}}_i(b) = 1]| \leq \mathsf{negl}(\lambda)$.

It is easy to see Prop. 4.3 holds by Lemma 4.2. The next goal is proving $|\Pr[\mathsf{Hyb}^{\mathsf{r}}_{i+1}(b) = 1] - \Pr[\mathsf{Hyb}^{\mathsf{r}}_i(b) = 1]| \leq \mathsf{negl}(\lambda)$. We define the following games.

$\mathsf{G}_j(i, b)$: This is the same as $\mathsf{Hyb}^{\mathsf{r}}_i(b)$ except the following difference.
- For $i \leq k < j$, pk_k and Δ_k are honestly generated as in the real.
- For $\mathsf{fwr} \geq k \geq j$, pk_k and Δ_k are uniformly random.

That is, we gradually erase information about UE secret keys from newer epochs to older epochs. We note that $j \in [i, \mathsf{fwr}+1]$ and i is fixed. By the definition, we have

$$\mathsf{G}_{\mathsf{fwr}+1}(i+1, b) = \mathsf{Hyb}^{\mathsf{r}}_{i+1}(b) \text{ and } \mathsf{G}_{\mathsf{fwr}+1}(i, b) = \mathsf{Hyb}^{\mathsf{r}}_i(b). \tag{2}$$

We prove that

$$|\Pr[\mathsf{G}_{j+1}(i+1, b) = 1] - \Pr[\mathsf{G}_j(i+1, b) = 1]| \leq \mathsf{negl}(\lambda) \text{ for } j \in [i, \mathsf{fwr}] \tag{3}$$

$$|\Pr[\mathsf{G}_i(i+1, b) = 1] - \Pr[\mathsf{G}_i(i, b) = 1]| \leq \mathsf{negl}(\lambda) \tag{4}$$

$$|\Pr[\mathsf{G}_{j+1}(i, b) = 1] - \Pr[\mathsf{G}_j(i, b) = 1]| \leq \mathsf{negl}(\lambda) \text{ for } j \in [i, \mathsf{fwr}]. \tag{5}$$

From these equations, we immediately obtain

$$|\Pr[\mathsf{G}_{\mathsf{fwr}+1}(i+1,b)=1]-\Pr[\mathsf{G}_{\mathsf{fwr}+1}(i,b)]|\leq \mathsf{negl}(\lambda).$$

By combining this with Prop. 4.3 and Eq. (2), we obtain what we want to prove (Lemma 4.3). Thus, all we must do is proving Eqs. (3) to (5).

First, we prove Eq. (3). We define a few hybrid games as follows.

- $\mathsf{Game}\text{-}0(b)$: This is the same as $\mathsf{G}_{j+1}(i+1,b)$. At this point, public keys and tokens of epochs in $[i,j]$ are real values while those at epochs in $[j+1,\mathsf{fwr}]$ are already random values.
- $\mathsf{Game}\text{-}1(b)$: This is the same as $\mathsf{Game}\text{-}0(b)$ except that we modify the public key part of epoch j. We use $\boldsymbol{B}_j^+ \leftarrow \mathbb{Z}_q^{m\times\ell}$ instead of $\boldsymbol{B}_j$ such that $(\boldsymbol{S}_j,\boldsymbol{B}_j)\leftarrow \mathsf{Reg.Gen}(1^\lambda)$. Note that we do not use the secret key $\boldsymbol{S}_j$ of epoch j anywhere in this game since Δ_{j+1} is already a random value.
- $\mathsf{Game}\text{-}2(b)$: This is the same as $\mathsf{Game}\text{-}1(b)$ except that we modify the token generation algorithm for token Δ_j. We use $\Delta_j := (\boldsymbol{M}_j^+,\boldsymbol{N}_j^+)\leftarrow \mathbb{Z}_q^{n\eta\times(n+\ell)}\times \mathbb{Z}_q^{m\times(n+\ell)}$ instead of $(\boldsymbol{M}_j,\boldsymbol{N}_j)\leftarrow \mathsf{TokGen}(\mathsf{k}_{j-1},\mathsf{k}_j)$.

Obviously, $\mathsf{Game}\text{-}2(b)$ is the same as $\mathsf{G}_j(i+1,b)$. It is easy to see if we prove the following, we complete the proof of Eq. (3).

Proposition 4.4. *If the LWE assumption holds, it holds that* $|\Pr[\mathsf{Game}\text{-}1(b)=1]-\Pr[\mathsf{G}_{j+1}(i+1,b)=1]|\leq \mathsf{negl}(\lambda)$.

Proposition 4.5. *It holds that* $|\Pr[\mathsf{Game}\text{-}2(b)=1]-\Pr[\mathsf{Game}\text{-}1(b)=1]|\leq \mathsf{negl}(\lambda)$.

We will prove these propositions above later.

Next, we prove Eq. (4). The only difference between $\mathsf{G}_i(i+1,b)$ and $\mathsf{G}_i(i,b)$ is the challenge-equal ciphertext at epoch i. That is, $\mathsf{G}_i(i,b)$ is the same as $\mathsf{G}_i(i+1,b)$ except that we modify the challenge-equal ciphertext for b at epoch i. We use $(\bar{\boldsymbol{u}},\bar{\boldsymbol{c}})\leftarrow \mathbb{Z}_q^n\times\mathbb{Z}_q^\ell$ instead of $(\bar{\boldsymbol{u}},\bar{\boldsymbol{c}})\leftarrow \mathsf{Upd}(\Delta_i^+,\overline{\mathsf{ct}})$ (the case $b=1$) or $(\bar{\boldsymbol{u}},\bar{\boldsymbol{c}})\leftarrow \mathsf{Enc}(\mathsf{k}_i,\overline{\mu}_0)$ (the case $b=0$). We prove the following proposition later.

Proposition 4.6. *It holds that* $|\Pr[\mathsf{G}_i(i+1,b)=1]-\Pr[\mathsf{G}_i(i,b)=1]|\leq \mathsf{negl}(\lambda)$.

Lastly, we prove Eq. (5). Once the challenge-equal ciphertext at epoch i becomes random, we need to go back to games where public keys and tokens are real. In $\mathsf{G}_j(i,b)$ for $j\in[i,\mathsf{fwr}]$, publics keys and tokens (from epochs j to fwr) are also random. We need to change them from random to real since we need to arrive at Hyb_i^r, where public keys and tokens are real (but ciphertext at epoch i is random). Thus, we need to prove Eq. (5). These backward transitions are possible by using the proof of Eq. (3) in a reverse manner. We summarize how public keys, update tokens, and challenge-equal ciphertexts at epoch i are generated in Fig. 4.

Thus, we complete the proof of Lemma 4.3 if we prove Prop. 4.4 to 4.6. We write those proofs below. ■

Value	$\mathsf{G}_{i+1}(i+1,b)$	Game-1	Game-2 = $\mathsf{G}_i(i+1,b)$	$\mathsf{G}_i(i,b)$
pk_i	$\mathsf{Reg.Gen}(1^\lambda)$	$\underline{\mathsf{Sim.Gen(pp)}}$	$\mathsf{Sim.Gen(pp)}$	$\mathsf{Sim.Gen(pp)}$
Δ_i	$\mathsf{TokGen}(\mathsf{sk}_{i-1},\mathsf{pk}_i)$	$\mathsf{TokGen}(\mathsf{sk}_{i-1},\mathsf{pk}_i)$	$\underline{\mathsf{Sim.TokGen(pp)}}$	$\mathsf{Sim.TokGen(pp)}$
$\mathsf{ct}^*_{i,1}$	$\mathsf{Upd}(\Delta_i,\mathsf{ct}_{i-1})$	$\mathsf{Upd}(\Delta_i,\mathsf{ct}_{i-1})$	$\underline{\mathsf{Upd}(\Delta_i^+,\mathsf{ct}_{i-1})}$	$\underline{\mathsf{Sim.Upd(pp)}}$
$\mathsf{ct}^*_{i,0}$	$\mathsf{Enc}(\mathsf{pk}_i,\overline{\mu}_0)$	$\mathsf{Enc}(\mathsf{pk}_i,\overline{\mu}_0)$	$\mathsf{Enc}(\mathsf{pk}_i,\overline{\mu}_0)$	$\underline{\mathsf{Sim.Enc(pp)}}$

Fig. 4. The differences of public keys, update tokens, challenge-equal ciphertexts at epoch i in hybrid games. We focus the case where $i = \widetilde{\mathsf{e}}$.

Proofs of Core Propositions. We give the proofs of Prop. 4.4 to 4.6.

Proof of Prop. 4.4. We construct a reduction $\mathcal{B}$ that solves the LWE problem by using the distinguisher $\mathcal{A}$ for the two games.

Recall that the key k_j of epoch j consists of $(\mathsf{sk}_j, \mathsf{pk}_j)$. $\mathcal{B}$ is given an LWE instance $(\boldsymbol{A}, \boldsymbol{B})$ and set $\boldsymbol{B}_j := \boldsymbol{B}$. That is, $\boldsymbol{B}$ is used as the public key pk_j of epoch j. Note that $\mathcal{B}$ can simulate all values in epoch $k \in [0,T] \setminus [\mathsf{fwl}, \mathsf{fwr}]$ since all values in epoch k (outside the firewall) are independent of the secret key of epoch j. (Note that such values may be related to the public key of epoch j via tokens.) That is, $\mathcal{B}$ can choose the secret key $\boldsymbol{S}_k$. We also note that $\mathcal{B}$ can simulate $\mathcal{O}.\mathsf{Upd}$ by using $\mathsf{Hyb.Upd}$. In $[\mathsf{fwl}, \mathsf{fwr}]$, values are related to the secret key $\boldsymbol{S}$ behind $\boldsymbol{B}$. However, in $\mathsf{G}_{j+1}(i+1,b)$ (and $\mathsf{Game}\text{-}1(b)$), all values in $[j+1, \mathsf{fwr}]$ are uniformly random values. Note that the original update token Δ_{j+1} needs sk_j and pk_{j+1}. However, Δ_{j+1} was already changed to Δ^+_{j+1}, which is uniformly random value, and we do not need sk_j.

Thus, the issue is how to simulate values in epoch j' such that $j' \in [\mathsf{fwl}, j]$ (including the case where $\mathsf{fwl} = j$). As we see in the definition of TokGen, we do not need sk_j to generate Δ_j and $\mathcal{B}$ can simulate Δ_j. Therefore, $\mathcal{B}$ can also simulate $\mathsf{ct}^*_{j,b}$ for both $b = 0, 1$. For $j'' \in [\mathsf{fwl}, j-1]$, public keys and tokens are not related to sk_j. Thus, $\mathcal{B}$ chooses $\boldsymbol{S}_{j''}$ and can simulate all values $(\mathsf{pk}_{j''}, \Delta_{j''}, \mathsf{ct}^*_{j'',b})$ by using the normal algorithms.

If $\boldsymbol{B} = \boldsymbol{AS} + \boldsymbol{X}$ where $\boldsymbol{S} \leftarrow \mathbb{Z}_q^{n\times\ell}$ and $\boldsymbol{X} \leftarrow \chi^{m\times\ell}$, the distribution is the same as $\mathsf{G}_{i+1}(i+1,b)$. If $\boldsymbol{B}$ is uniformly random, the distribution is the same as $\mathsf{Game}\text{-}1(b)$. Therefore, $\mathcal{B}$ distinguish the instance if $\mathcal{A}$ distinguishes the two games. This completes the proof. ∎

Proof of Prop. 4.5. The difference between these two games is as follows:
$\mathsf{Game}\text{-}1(b)$: $\Delta_j = (\boldsymbol{M}_j, \boldsymbol{N}_j)$:

$$\boldsymbol{M}_j := \boldsymbol{R}_j \cdot [\boldsymbol{A} \mid \boldsymbol{B}_j] + [\boldsymbol{O} \mid -\mathsf{P2}(\boldsymbol{S}_{j-1})], \boldsymbol{N}_j := \boldsymbol{R}'_j \cdot [\boldsymbol{A} \mid \boldsymbol{B}_j],$$

where $\boldsymbol{R}_j \leftarrow \{-1,+1\}^{n\eta\times m}, \boldsymbol{R}'_j \leftarrow \{-1,+1\}^{m\times m}$.
$\mathsf{Game}\text{-}2(b)$: $\Delta^+_j = (\boldsymbol{M}^+_j, \boldsymbol{N}^+_j)$: $(\boldsymbol{M}^+_j, \boldsymbol{N}^+_j) \leftarrow \mathbb{Z}_q^{n\eta\times(n+\ell)} \times \mathbb{Z}_q^{m\times(n+\ell)}$.

In $\mathsf{Game}\text{-}1(b)$ and $\mathsf{Game}\text{-}2(b)$, the public key $\boldsymbol{B}_j \leftarrow \mathbb{Z}_q^{m\times\ell}$ is uniformly random. Thus, we can apply the leftover hash lemma and these differences are statistically indistinguishable. This completes the proof. ∎

Proof of Prop. 4.6. The difference between these two games is as follows: For $b = 1$,

$\mathsf{G}_i(i+1,1)$: $\mathsf{ct}^*_{i,1} = (\bar{\boldsymbol{u}}, \bar{\boldsymbol{c}})$: $(\boldsymbol{u}' + \tilde{\boldsymbol{u}}, \boldsymbol{c}_{i-1} + \boldsymbol{c}' + \tilde{\boldsymbol{v}}) = (\boldsymbol{0}, \boldsymbol{c}_{i-1}) + \mathsf{BD}(\boldsymbol{u}_i)\boldsymbol{M}_i^+ + \tilde{\boldsymbol{r}}\boldsymbol{N}_i^+$, where $\tilde{\boldsymbol{r}} \leftarrow \{-1,+1\}^m$. where $\tilde{\boldsymbol{r}} \leftarrow \{-1,+1\}^m$.

$\mathsf{G}_i(i,1)$: $\mathsf{ct}^*_{i,1} = (\bar{\boldsymbol{u}}, \bar{\boldsymbol{c}})$: $(\bar{\boldsymbol{u}}, \bar{\boldsymbol{c}}) \leftarrow \mathbb{Z}_q^n \times \mathbb{Z}_q^\ell$.

In $\mathsf{G}_i(i+1,b)$ and $\mathsf{G}_i(i,b)$, $\boldsymbol{N}_i^+$ is uniformly random. Thus, we can apply the leftover hash lemma and these differences are statistically indistinguishable. For $b = 0$,

$\mathsf{G}_i(i+1,0)$: $\mathsf{ct}^*_{i,0} = (\boldsymbol{u}, \boldsymbol{c})$: $(\boldsymbol{r}\boldsymbol{A}_i, \boldsymbol{r}\boldsymbol{B}_i^+ + \boldsymbol{e}' + \lfloor q/2 \rfloor \boldsymbol{\mu}_0)$, where $\boldsymbol{A} \leftarrow \mathbb{Z}_q^{m\times}$, $\boldsymbol{r} \leftarrow \{-1,+1\}^m$, $\boldsymbol{e}' \leftarrow \chi_{\mathsf{ns}}^\ell$, and $\boldsymbol{B}_i^+ \leftarrow \mathbb{Z}_q^{m\times\ell}$. where $\boldsymbol{A} \leftarrow \mathbb{Z}_q^{m\times}$, $\boldsymbol{r} \leftarrow \{-1,+1\}^m$, $\boldsymbol{e}' \leftarrow \chi_{\mathsf{ns}}^\ell$, and $\boldsymbol{B}_i^+ \leftarrow \mathbb{Z}_q^{m\times\ell}$.

$\mathsf{G}_i(i,0)$: $\mathsf{ct}^*_{i,0} = (\boldsymbol{u}, \boldsymbol{c})$: $(\boldsymbol{u}, \boldsymbol{c}) \leftarrow \mathbb{Z}_q^n \times \mathbb{Z}_q^\ell$.

In $\mathsf{G}_i(i+1,b)$ and $\mathsf{G}_i(i,b)$, the public key $\boldsymbol{B}_i^+ \leftarrow \mathbb{Z}_q^{m\times\ell}$ is uniformly random. Thus, we can apply the leftover hash lemma and these differences are statistically indistinguishable. This completes the proof. ■

5 Construction with No-Directional Key Update

5.1 Scheme Description

We present a no-directional key update scheme $\mathsf{UE}_{\mathsf{io}}$ from puncturable PRFs and IO. Let $\mathsf{PRF} : \{0,1\}^\lambda \times \{0,1\}^n \to \{0,1\}^\ell$ and $\mathsf{PRG} : \{0,1\}^\tau \to \{0,1\}^n$. We will set $\tau := \lambda$, $n := 2\lambda$.

$\mathsf{Setup}(1^\lambda)$: Does nothing.

$\mathsf{KeyGen}(1^\lambda)$:
- Generate $\mathsf{K} \leftarrow \mathsf{PRF.Gen}(1^\lambda)$ and output $\mathsf{k_e} := \mathsf{K}$.

$\mathsf{TokGen}(\mathsf{k_e}, \mathsf{k_{e+1}})$
- Generate and output $\Delta_{\mathsf{e}+1} \leftarrow i\mathcal{O}(\mathsf{C_{re}}[\mathsf{k_e}, \mathsf{k_{e+1}}])$ where circuit $\mathsf{C_{re}}$ is described in Fig. 5.

$\mathsf{Enc}(\mathsf{k_e}, \mu \in \{0,1\}^\ell)$:
- Choose $r \leftarrow \{0,1\}^\tau$ and compute $t := \mathsf{PRG}(r)$.
- Compute $y := \mathsf{PRF}(\mathsf{K}, t)$ and output $\mathsf{ct} := (t, y \oplus \mu)$.

$\mathsf{Dec}(\mathsf{k_e}, \mathsf{ct})$:
- Parse $\mathsf{k_e} = \mathsf{K}$ $\mathsf{ct} = (t, c)$.
- Compute $\mu' := c \oplus \mathsf{PRF}(\mathsf{K}, t)$ and output μ'.

$\mathsf{Upd}(\Delta_{\mathsf{e}+1}, \mathsf{ct_e})$
- Parse $\Delta_{\mathsf{e}+1} = i\mathcal{O}(\mathsf{C_{re}}[\mathsf{k_e}, \mathsf{k_{e+1}}])$ and choose $r_{\mathsf{e}+1} \leftarrow \{0,1\}^\tau$.
- Compute and output $(t, c) := i\mathcal{O}(\mathsf{C_{re}}[\mathsf{k_e}, \mathsf{k_{e+1}}])(\mathsf{ct_e}, r_{\mathsf{e}+1})$.

Theorem 5.1. $\mathsf{UE}_{\mathsf{io}}$ *is an r-IND-UE-CPA secure UE scheme in the no-directional key updates setting.*

We omit the proof due to space limitations. See the full version.

Update Function $\mathsf{C}_{\mathsf{re}}[\mathsf{k}_{\mathsf{e}}, \mathsf{k}_{\mathsf{e}+1}](\mathsf{ct}_{\mathsf{e}}, r_{\mathsf{e}+1})$

Hardwired: $\mathsf{k}_{\mathsf{e}}, \mathsf{k}_{\mathsf{e}+1}$.
Input: A ciphertext ct_{e} and randomness $r_{\mathsf{e}+1} \in \{0,1\}^{\tau}$.
Padding: This circuit is padded to size $\mathsf{pad}_{\mathsf{T}} := \mathsf{pad}_{\mathsf{T}}(\lambda)$, which is determined in analysis.

1. Parse $\mathsf{ct}_{\mathsf{e}} = (t_{\mathsf{e}}, c_{\mathsf{e}})$
2. Compute $\mu' := c_{\mathsf{e}} \oplus \mathsf{PRF}(\mathsf{k}_{\mathsf{e}}, t_{\mathsf{e}})$.
3. Compute $t' := \mathsf{PRG}(r_{\mathsf{e}+1})$ and $y' := \mathsf{PRF}(\mathsf{k}_{\mathsf{e}+1}, t')$
4. Return $\mathsf{ct}_{\mathsf{e}+1} := (t', y' \oplus \mu')$.

Fig. 5. The description of C_{re}

Acknowledgments. The author would like to thank Fuyuki Kitagawa for giving a pointer to the right reference about an RKA-secure AE scheme. The author also thanks anonymous reviewers of PKC 2022 for useful comments.

References

[ABPW13] Aono, Y., Boyen, X., Phong, L.T., Wang, L.: Key-private proxy re-encryption under LWE. In: Paul, G., Vaudenay, S. (eds.) INDOCRYPT 2013. LNCS, vol. 8250, pp. 1–18. Springer, Cham (2013). https://doi.org/10.1007/978-3-319-03515-4_1

[AJL+12] Asharov, G., Jain, A., López-Alt, A., Tromer, E., Vaikuntanathan, V., Wichs, D.: Multiparty computation with low communication, computation and interaction via threshold FHE. In: Pointcheval, D., Johansson, T. (eds.) EUROCRYPT 2012. LNCS, vol. 7237, pp. 483–501. Springer, Heidelberg (2012). https://doi.org/10.1007/978-3-642-29011-4_29

[AMP19] Alamati, N., Montgomery, H., Patranabis, S.: Symmetric primitives with structured secrets. In: Boldyreva, A., Micciancio, D. (eds.) CRYPTO 2019. LNCS, vol. 11692, pp. 650–679. Springer, Cham (2019). https://doi.org/10.1007/978-3-030-26948-7_23

[BDGJ20] Boyd, C., Davies, G.T., Gjøsteen, K., Jiang, Y.: Fast and secure updatable encryption. In: Micciancio, D., Ristenpart, T. (eds.) CRYPTO 2020. LNCS, vol. 12170, pp. 464–493. Springer, Cham (2020). https://doi.org/10.1007/978-3-030-56784-2_16

[BEKS20] Boneh, D., Eskandarian, S., Kim, S., Shih, M.: Improving speed and security in updatable encryption schemes. In: Moriai, S., Wang, H. (eds.) ASIACRYPT 2020. LNCS, vol. 12493, pp. 559–589. Springer, Cham (2020). https://doi.org/10.1007/978-3-030-64840-4_19

[BGH13] Brakerski, Z., Gentry, C., Halevi, S.: Packed ciphertexts in LWE-based homomorphic encryption. In: Kurosawa, K., Hanaoka, G. (eds.) PKC 2013. LNCS, vol. 7778, pp. 1–13. Springer, Heidelberg (2013). https://doi.org/10.1007/978-3-642-36362-7_1

[BGI+12] Barak, B., et al.: On the (im)possibility of obfuscating programs. J. ACM, **59**(2), 6:1–6:48 (2012)

[BGV14] Brakerski, Z., Vaikuntanathan, C.G.V.: (Leveled) fully homomorphic encryption without bootstrapping. ACM Trans. Comput. Theory **6**(3), 13:1–13:36 (2014)

[BLMR13] Boneh, D., Lewi, K., Montgomery, H., Raghunathan, A.: Key homomorphic PRFs and their applications. In: Canetti, R., Garay, J.A. (eds.) CRYPTO 2013. LNCS, vol. 8042, pp. 410–428. Springer, Heidelberg (2013). https://doi.org/10.1007/978-3-642-40041-4_23

[BV11] Brakerski, Z., Vaikuntanathan, V.: Fully homomorphic encryption from Ring-LWE and security for key dependent messages. In: Rogaway, P. (ed.) CRYPTO 2011. LNCS, vol. 6841, pp. 505–524. Springer, Heidelberg (2011). https://doi.org/10.1007/978-3-642-22792-9_29

[BV14] Brakerski, Z., Vaikuntanathan, V.: Efficient fully homomorphic encryption from (standard) LWE. SIAM J. Comput. **43**(2), 831–871 (2014)

[CCL+14] Chandran, N., Chase, M., Liu, F.-H., Nishimaki, R., Xagawa, K.: Re-encryption, functional re-encryption, and multi-hop re-encryption: a framework for achieving obfuscation-based security and instantiations from lattices. In: Krawczyk, H. (ed.) PKC 2014. LNCS, vol. 8383, pp. 95–112. Springer, Heidelberg (2014). https://doi.org/10.1007/978-3-642-54631-0_6

[CLT20] Chen, L., Li, Y., Tang, Q.: CCA updatable encryption against malicious re-encryption attacks. In: Moriai, S., Wang, H. (eds.) ASIACRYPT 2020. LNCS, vol. 12493, pp. 590–620. Springer, Cham (2020). https://doi.org/10.1007/978-3-030-64840-4_20

[DN21] Döttling, N., Nishimaki, R.: Universal proxy re-encryption. In: Garay, J.A. (ed.) PKC 2021. LNCS, vol. 12710, pp. 512–542. Springer, Cham (2021). https://doi.org/10.1007/978-3-030-75245-3_19

[EPRS17] Everspaugh, A., Paterson, K., Ristenpart, T., Scott, S.: Key rotation for authenticated encryption. In: Katz, J., Shacham, H. (eds.) CRYPTO 2017. LNCS, vol. 10403, pp. 98–129. Springer, Cham (2017). https://doi.org/10.1007/978-3-319-63697-9_4

[FMM21] Fabrega, A., Maurer, U., Mularczyk, M.: A fresh approach to updatable symmetric encryption. IACR Cryptol. ePrint Arch. **2021**, 559 (2021)

[Gen09] Gentry, C.: A fully homomorphic encryption scheme. PhD thesis, Stanford University (2009). crypto.stanford.edu/craig

[HLL16] Han, S., Liu, S., Lyu, L.: Efficient KDM-CCA secure public-key encryption for polynomial functions. In: Cheon, J.H., Takagi, T. (eds.) ASIACRYPT 2016. LNCS, vol. 10032, pp. 307–338. Springer, Heidelberg (2016). https://doi.org/10.1007/978-3-662-53890-6_11

[Jia20] Jiang, Y.: The direction of updatable encryption does not matter much. In: Moriai, S., Wang, H. (eds.) ASIACRYPT 2020. LNCS, vol. 12493, pp. 529–558. Springer, Cham (2020). https://doi.org/10.1007/978-3-030-64840-4_18

[JLS21] Jain, A., Lin, H., Sahai, A.: Indistinguishability obfuscation from well-founded assumptions. In: STOC 2021 (2021)

[KLR19] Klooß, M., Lehmann, A., Rupp, A.: (R)CCA secure updatable encryption with integrity protection. In: Ishai, Y., Rijmen, V. (eds.) EUROCRYPT 2019. LNCS, vol. 11476, pp. 68–99. Springer, Cham (2019). https://doi.org/10.1007/978-3-030-17653-2_3

[LR21] Levy-dit-Vehel, F., Roméas, M.: A composable look at updatable encryption. IACR Cryptol. ePrint Arch. **2021**, 538 (2021)

[LT18] Lehmann, A., Tackmann, B.: Updatable encryption with post-compromise security. In: Nielsen, J.B., Rijmen, V. (eds.) EUROCRYPT 2018. LNCS, vol. 10822, pp. 685–716. Springer, Cham (2018). https://doi.org/10.1007/978-3-319-78372-7_22

[Nis21] Nishimaki, R.: The direction of updatable encryption does matter. IACR Cryptol. ePrint Arch. 221 (2021)

[NX15] Nishimaki, R., Xagawa, K.: Key-private proxy re-encryption from lattices, revisited. IEICE Trans. **98**-A(1), 100–116 (2015)

[Reg09] Egev, O.: On lattices, learning with errors, random linear codes, and cryptography. J. ACM **56**(6), 34:1–34:40 (2009)

[SS21] Slamanig, D., Striecks, C.: Puncture 'Em all: stronger updatable encryption with no-directional key updates. IACR Cryptol. ePrint Arch. **2021**, 268 (2021)

[SW21] Sahai, A., Waters, B.: How to use indistinguishability obfuscation: deniable encryption, and more. SIAM J. Comput. **50**(3), 857–908 (2021)

Leakage-Resilient IBE/ABE with Optimal Leakage Rates from Lattices

Qiqi Lai[1,2], Feng-Hao Liu[3], and Zhedong Wang[4(✉)]

[1] School of Computer Science, Shaanxi Normal University, Xi'an, China
laiqq@snnu.edu.cn

[2] State Key Laboratory of Integrated Service Networks, Xidian University, Xi'an, China

[3] Florida Atlantic University, Boca Raton, FL, USA
fenghao.liu@fau.edu

[4] School of Cyber Science and Engineering, Shanghai Jiao Tong University, Shanghai, China
wzdstill@sjtu.edu.cn

Abstract. We derive the first adaptively secure IBE and ABE for t-CNF, and selectively secure ABE for general circuits from lattices, with $1 - o(1)$ leakage rates, in the both relative leakage model and bounded retrieval model (BRM).

To achieve this, we first identify a new fine-grained security notion for ABE – partially adaptive/selective security, and instantiate this notion from LWE. Then, by using this notion, we design a new key compressing mechanism for identity-based/attributed-based weak hash proof system (IB/AB-wHPS) for various policy classes, achieving (1) succinct secret keys and (2) adaptive/selective security matching the existing non-leakage resilient lattice-based designs. Using the existing connection between weak hash proof system and leakage resilient encryption, the succinct-key IB/AB-wHPS can yield the desired leakage resilient IBE/ABE schemes with the optimal leakage rates in the relative leakage model. Finally, by further improving the prior analysis of the compatible locally computable extractors, we can achieve the optimal leakage rates in the BRM.

1 Introduction

Leakage-resilient cryptography aims to create crypto systems that maintain security even when partial information of the secret key is leaked. This line of studies is motivated by both theoretic curiosities and perhaps more importantly, real-world scenarios, where some secure crypto systems might be completely broken if some partial key leakage is given to the attackers. One famous example is the *side-channel attacks* where the adversary can obtain leakage from measuring some physical behavior of an implementation, e.g., [1,27]. Another source of leakage comes from imperfect erasure where the attacker can obtain partial information before the content is completely erased, e.g., the *cold boot attacks* [23]. On the other hand, leakage resilience can be used to achieve security for other more complicated systems. For example, in the design of non-malleable codes,

G. Hanaoka et al. (Eds.): PKC 2022, LNCS 13178, pp. 225–255, 2022.
https://doi.org/10.1007/978-3-030-97131-1_8

the work [17,26,31] leveraged leakage resilience to prove non-malleability. Therefore, leakage resilience has been an active research subject for the community, e.g., [4–6,8,16,25,33], to name a few.

Main Goal. As motivated above, we aim to determine how to derive encryption schemes with better leakage rates, stronger security, and more expressive access control functionalities. More specifically, our goal is to construct leakage resilient encryption schemes in both the relative leakage model and the bounded retrieval model (BRM) with (1) optimal leakage rates, i.e., $1 - o(1)$, (2) post-quantum security and (3) more fine-grained access control, i.e., IBE and ABE for various classes of policy functions.

The Leakage Models. Various leakage models have been studied in the literature, capturing information leaked to the adversary. This work focuses on a simple yet general model called the *bounded-leakage model* (also known as the *memory leakage model*), allowing the attacker to learn arbitrary information about the secret key sk, as long as the number of leaked bits is bounded by some parameter ℓ. This model has drawn a lot of attentions (e.g., [4,5,25,33]) for its elegance and simplicity, and can be used as a building block towards more sophisticated and realistic models, such as the continual leakage model [9,14] (see [25]). Thus, understanding this model is not only of theoretic interests but also a necessary step towards realizing security for broader physical attacks.

The bounded leakage model would require $\ell < |\mathsf{sk}|$, as otherwise, the attacker can trivially obtain the whole secret key, and thus no meaningful security can be attained. To further characterize this requirement, there are two important models studied in the literature that treat the relation between ℓ and sk in a different way: (1) *relative leakage model*, and (2) *bounded retrieval model* (BRM).

In the former, the secret key and public-key are chosen in the same way as a standard crypto system (not necessary leakage resilient), and then the leakage parameter ℓ would be determined. The latter model generalizes the former by considering ℓ as an independent parameter whose growth (essentially) only goes with $|\mathsf{sk}|$, but would barely affect the other parameters, such as the public-key size, encryption running time, and ciphertext size. Basically, both models can scale up ℓ to allow an arbitrarily long leakage. But their difference is that the former would require to scale up the security parameter and thus all the other parameters, while the latter would only scale up the secret-key size and keep the other parameters essentially the same. Thus, constructions in the BRM is more desirable yet more challenging.

Leakage rate, i.e., the ratio $\ell/|\mathsf{sk}|$, is an important measure of efficiency for crypto systems in these two models. Particularly, rate $1-o(1)$ is the best we can hope for – in order to tolerate ℓ bits of leakage, the system only needs to scale $|\mathsf{sk}|$ slightly larger than ℓ, optimizing the security/efficiency tradeoff.

Current State of the Arts and Challenges. We first notice that for the pre-quantum settings, leakage resilience can be achieved via the beautiful framework – *dual system encryption*, even for IBE/ABE and with optimal leakage rates, e.g., [28]. However, current instantiations of the dual system encryption are all group-based [11,20,28,29,41,42], and thus cannot defend against quantum algorithms. It is an interesting yet extremely challenging open question how to instantiate a dual system from a post-quantum candidate, such as LWE or LPN.

For post-quantum leakage resilient encryption schemes, we notice that there are some limitations of the current techniques in achieving the optimal leakage rate beyond the basic PKE. In prior work, there have been constructed LWE/LPN-based PKE schemes with leakage rates $1-o(1)$, e.g., [10,13], but their ideas do not generalize to more advanced settings, such as IBE and ABE. In a subsequent work, Hazay et al. [25] proposed a unified framework, showing that (1) PKE implies leakage resilient PKE in the relative leakage model, and (2) IBE implies leakage resilient PKE/IBE in the BRM. Moreover, the leakage resilient IBE achieves the same level of adaptive/selective security as that of the underlying IBE. Their idea can be generalized to construct leakage resilient ABE, but this approach inherently yields a very low leakage rate (i.e., $1/O(\lambda)$).

A recent work [35] somewhat mitigated this issue by improving the leakage rates, yet at the cost of weaker security guarantees for the post-quantum instantiations. Particularly, they construct LWE-based leakage resilient IBE schemes in both the relative leakage model and the BRM, achieving $1-o(1)$ leakage rate in the former and $1-O(1)$ (for any arbitrarily small constant) in the latter. Their improvement relies on a novel *key-compression mechanism* that shortens the secret key length required in the framework of Hazay et al. [25]. Due to some technical limitation in the mechanism, their IBE scheme however, can only achieve the selective security. From these works [25,35], we see a tradeoff between security and leakage rate, i.e., either we have an adaptively secure IBE with a low leakage rate, or a selectively secure IBE with a higher leakage rate.

Main Question. In this work, we aim to further determine whether the tradeoff between (selective/adaptive) security and leakage rates as above is inherent. Particularly, we ask the following:

> *Can we achieve the optimal leakage rate* $(1-o(1))$ *for* IBE *(and* ABE *) in both relative and bounded retrieval models with security matching existing non-leakage resilient* IBE *(*ABE *), under* LWE*?*

1.1 Our Contributions

In this work, we give positive answers in many settings of the main question. Our central idea is a refinement of the framework of [25,35] by designing a new key compression mechanism from ABE *with succinct keys.* Below we describe our contributions in more details.

- As a warm-up, we propose a new leakage model for ABE that incorporates parameters ℓ and ω, where ℓ is the number of bits allowed to leak per key and ω is the number of keys the adversary can leak. We note that for PKE and IBE, there is only one possible secret key corresponding to the challenge id.

In this case, it is without loss of generality to just consider $\omega = 1$. However, for the ABE setting, there could be many possible secret keys corresponding to the challenge attribute, so specifying ω is natural and necessary in the leakage model. We call a scheme (ℓ, ω)-leakage resilient if the scheme can tolerate leakage on ω keys, each within ℓ bits.

- Next, we design improved instantiations of attribute-based weak hash proof system (AB-wHPS), which generalizes (identity-based) weak hash proof system [5,25] by associating each ciphertext with an attribute and each secret key with a policy function. Particularly, we construct lattice-based AB-wHPS from ABE for various function classes, achieving two important new features: (1) succinct secret keys, i.e., the secret key length is $|f| + o(|f|)$ where f is the policy function, and (2) security matching currently the best known lattice-based ABE schemes (not necessarily leakage resilient). More specifically, we construct adaptively secure AB-wHPS for the class of comparison functions (which is the IB-wHPS) and the class t-CNF*[1], and selectively secure AB-wHPS for general circuits.
- By using AB-wHPS for class $\mathcal{F}$ with *succinct keys*, we are able to construct $(\ell, 1)$-leakage resilient ABE for $\mathcal{F}$, with leakage rate $\ell/|\mathsf{sk}| = (1 - o(1))$ in the relative leakage model.
  We view AB-wHPS with succinct key as an improved key compression mechanism from prior works [25,35] in the following two aspects: (1) AB-wHPS has better expressibility of policy function (the prior work [35] can only express the comparison function), and (2) we can derive adaptively secure AB-wHPS with succinct keys for classes which we have adaptively secure (non-leakage resilient) ABE. Prior to our work, for lattice-based schemes, we only had either a selectively secure IB-wHPS with succinct secret keys [35] or an adaptively secure IB-wHPS with non-succinct keys [25].
- From our AB-wHPS, we can further derive $(\ell, 1)$-leakage resilient ABE in the BRM, via an amplification and a connection with locally computable extractors as pointed out by [25]. However, prior compatible locally computable extractors [5] can only achieve $1 - O(1)$ leakage rate for an arbitrarily small constant. To achieve $1 - o(1)$ leakage rate, we improve the prior analysis [5] by refining their proof technique via the framework of Vadhan [40].
- Finally, we present a bootstrapping mechanism that generalizes our prior $(\ell, 1)$-leakage resilient ABE schemes to (ℓ, ω)-leakage resilient schemes for any bounded polynomial ω, in both relative leakage model and bounded retrieval model. The resulting leakage rate is still optimal (i.e., $1 - o(1)$) against block leakage functions, a slightly more restricted class.

1.2 Overview of Our Techniques

Our central insight is a new key-compression mechanism for the framework in [25]. To illustrate our new idea, we first briefly review the prior framework [25]

[1] This is the dual class of t-CNF where the function is an assignment x and attribute is a description of t-CNF. We use the dual class as we are working on Key-policy ABE while the prior work [38] worked on Ciphertext-policy ABE.

and point out the barrier of their leakage rates. Then we will describe our new ideas for the improvement.

(Weak) Hash Proof System. A hash proof system can be described as a key encapsulation mechanism that consists of four algorithms $(\mathsf{Setup}, \mathsf{Encap}, \mathsf{Encap}^*, \mathsf{Decap})$: (1) Setup outputs a key pair $(\mathsf{pk}, \mathsf{sk})$, (2) $\mathsf{Encap}(\mathsf{pk})$ outputs a pair (CT, k) where k is a key encapsulated in a "valid" ciphertext CT, (3) $\mathsf{Encap}^*(\mathsf{pk})$ outputs an "invalid" ciphertext CT^*, and (4) $\mathsf{Decap}(\mathsf{sk}, \mathsf{CT})$ outputs a key k'. A (weak) hash proof system requires the following:

- **Correctness.** For a valid ciphertext CT, Decap always outputs the encapsulated key $k' = k$, i.e., $\mathsf{Decap}(\mathsf{sk}, \mathsf{CT}) = k$, where $(\mathsf{CT}, k) \xleftarrow{\$} \mathsf{Encap}(\mathsf{pk})$.
- **Ciphertext Indistinguishability.** Valid ciphertexts and invalid ciphertexts are computationally indistinguishable, *even given the secret key.* This condition is essential for achieving leakage resilience [5,33].
- **Universality.** The decapsulation of an invalid ciphertext has information entropy, even for unbounded adversaries. Here, the randomness of invalid decapsulation comes from randomness in generating secret keys. A weak HPS (wHPS) only requires this property to hold for a random invalid ciphertext, i.e. $\mathsf{CT}^* \xleftarrow{\$} \mathsf{Encap}^*(\mathsf{pk})$, while a full-fledged HPS requires this to hold for any invalid ciphertext.

As noted in prior work [5], a wHPS already suffices to achieve leakage resilience, though it is not sufficient for the CCA2 security, for which the HPS was originally intended to design [12]. Roughly speaking, the leakage resilient scheme derived from wHPS [5,25,33] can tolerate $\ell \approx |k| - \lambda$ bits of leakage, i.e., the length of encapsulated key minus security parameter, and thus the leakage rate of the derived encryption scheme would be $\ell/|\mathsf{wHPS.sk}| \approx \frac{|k|-\lambda}{|\mathsf{wHPS.sk}|}$.

Moreover, the idea can be generalized to IB-wHPS and AB-wHPS where an additional id or attribute $\boldsymbol{x}$ is associated with the ciphertext, and id or a policy function f is associated with the secret key. In the same way [25], IB-wHPS and AB-wHPS suffice to derive leakage resilient IBE and ABE.

wHPS from Any PKE and Generalizations [25]**.** While there were several instantiations of wHPS from specific assumptions [5,33], Hazay et al. [25] showed somewhat surprisingly, any PKE implies wHPS. Their construction [25] can be thought as the following two steps: (1) construct a basic wHPS that only outputs 1 bit (or $\log \lambda$-bits), (2) amplify the output of the wHPS via parallel repetition. As pointed out in the work [25], parallel repetition might not amplify HPS in general, yet it does for wHPS as required in the application of leakage resilience.

The basic wHPS is simple: given any $\mathsf{PKE} = (\mathsf{Enc}, \mathsf{Dec})$, the $\mathsf{wHPS.pk}$ consists of two public keys $\mathsf{pk}_0, \mathsf{pk}_1$ from PKE, and $\mathsf{wHPS.sk}$ is (b, sk_b) for a random bit b where sk_b corresponds to pk_b. The Encap algorithm outputs a valid ciphertext $\mathsf{CT} = (\mathsf{Enc}_{\mathsf{pk}_0}(k), \mathsf{Enc}_{\mathsf{pk}_1}(k))$ to encapsulate a uniformly random key $k \in \{0, 1\}$. The Encap^* algorithm outputs an invalid ciphertext $\mathsf{CT}^* = (\mathsf{Enc}_{\mathsf{pk}_0}(k), \mathsf{Enc}_{\mathsf{pk}_1}(1-k))$ for a uniformly random bit k. With a parallel repetition of n times, i.e.,

$\mathsf{wHPS}_{\|}.\mathsf{pk} := \{\mathsf{pk}_{i,0}, \mathsf{pk}_{i,1}\}_{i\in[n]}$ and $\mathsf{wHPS}_{\|}.\mathsf{sk} := \{(i, b_i), \mathsf{sk}_{i,b_i}\}_{i\in[n]}$, we can get a $\mathsf{wHPS}_{\|}$ with $|k| = n$ for an arbitrarily large $n \gg \lambda$, and thus a leakage resilient encryption that tolerates $\ell = n - \lambda \approx n - o(|\mathsf{wHPS}_{\|}.\mathsf{sk}|)$.

Naturally, this elegant approach can be generalized to construct IB-wHPS and AB-wHPS for class $\mathcal{F}$ from any IBE and ABE for $\mathcal{F}$, and the (adaptive/selective) security of the IB-wHPS and AB-wHPS matches the underlying IBE and ABE. Therefore, this framework provides a powerful way to design leakage resilient IBE and ABE from any IBE and ABE that can tolerate an arbitrarily large leakage ℓ.

Technical Challenges from Prior Work. This technique of [25] achieves almost everything one would desire, except for the leakage rate. The main reason comes from the secret key size of $\mathsf{wHPS}_{\|}$, which is also scaled up by the parallel repetition, resulting in a low leakage rate as $\frac{\ell}{|\mathsf{wHPS}_{\|}.\mathsf{sk}|} = \frac{n-o(|\mathsf{wHPS}_{\|}.\mathsf{sk}|)}{|\mathsf{wHPS}_{\|}.\mathsf{sk}|} \approx \frac{n-o(n|\mathsf{PKE.sk}|)}{n|\mathsf{PKE.sk}|} \approx \frac{1}{|\mathsf{PKE.sk}|}$. To further improve the rate, it suffices to decrease $|\mathsf{wHPS.sk}|$ as observed by [35]. In particular, if we can shrink the secret key size of the wHPS to roughly $|\mathsf{wHPS}_{\|}.\mathsf{sk}| \approx n + |\mathsf{PKE.sk}|$, then the leakage rate would be $\frac{n-o(|\mathsf{wHPS}_{\|}.\mathsf{sk}|)}{|\mathsf{wHPS}_{\|}.\mathsf{sk}|} \approx \frac{n-o(n+|\mathsf{PKE.sk}|)}{n+|\mathsf{PKE.sk}|} \approx 1 - o(1)$, for sufficiently large n. Therefore, now the goal becomes to design a compact form of $\mathsf{wHPS}_{\|}.\mathsf{sk}$ that can encode n possible keys in a succinct way.

The work [35] achieved this goal and the more general IB-wHPS by proposing a novel key compression mechanism from a new primitive called *multi*-IBE. Then they instantiated the required multi-IBE from *inner-product encryption* (IPE) [3, 11, 42] with succinct keys. However, for lattice-based IPE schemes [3], only the selective security can be achieved under currently known techniques. Thus, the work [35] can only derive selectively secure leakage resilient IBE from lattices.

At this point, we summarize two limitations from the prior key compression mechanism [35]: (1) the approach is tied to IBE/IB-HPS, and it is unclear whether we can further generalize the technique for further expressive policies, i.e., ABE; (2) the lattice-based instantiations are only selectively secure under currently known techniques. Below we show our new ideas to break these limitations.

Our New Key Compression Mechanism. We first present a new key compression mechanism that can be generalized to more expressive policy functions, i.e., ABE. To illustrate our core insight, we first describe how to use the technique of key-policy (KP)-ABE to encode $\mathsf{wHPS}_{\|}.\mathsf{sk}$ succinctly. The idea can be naturally generalized to compress IB-wHPS and AB-wHPS. To facilitate further discussions, we first recall the concept of KP-ABE.

In a KP-ABE scheme, a secret key is associated with a policy function $f : \{0,1\}^* \to \{0,1\}$, and a ciphertext is associated with an attribute $\boldsymbol{x}$. The secret key can decrypt and recover the encrypted message if and only if $f(\boldsymbol{x}) = 1$.

Now we explain our key compression mechanism. Let us describe the format of a valid ciphertext of $\mathsf{wHPS}_{\|}$ as $\mathsf{CT} := \left\{\mathsf{Enc}_{\mathsf{pk}_{i,0}}(k_i), \mathsf{Enc}_{\mathsf{pk}_{i,1}}(k_i)\right\}_{i\in[n]}$, and a secret key is of the form $\{(i, b_i), \mathsf{sk}_{i,b_i}\}_{i\in[n]}$. From another angle looking at the ciphertext, we can view the indices (i, b)'s as attributes in an ABE, i.e. $\mathsf{CT} := \{\mathsf{ABE.Enc}(\mathsf{mpk}, (i, 0), k_i), \mathsf{ABE.Enc}(\mathsf{mpk}, (i, 1), k_i)\}_{i \in [n]}$. Then we can use a single ABE secret key to encode the set of keys $\{(i, b_i), \mathsf{sk}_{i,b_i}\}_{i \in [n]}$ as follows. Let $\boldsymbol{b} = (b_1, b_2, \ldots, b_n) \in \{0,1\}^n$ be a binary vector, and define the following policy function $g_{\boldsymbol{b}}(i, z) = 1$ iff $b_i = z$ for each $i \in [n]$. In this way, only this set of attributes $\{(i, b_i)\}_{i \in [n]}$ satisfies the policy function $g_{\boldsymbol{b}}$, so the ABE decryption algorithm with $\mathsf{sk}_{g_{\boldsymbol{b}}}$ can successfully recover the encrypted messages from $\{\mathsf{ABE.Enc}(\mathsf{mpk}, (i, b_i), k_i)\}_{i \in [n]}$. The other part of the ciphertext, i.e., $\{\mathsf{ABE.Enc}(\mathsf{mpk}, (i, 1 - b_i), k_i)\}_{i \in [n]}$ is hidden by the security of the ABE. This approach can be naturally extended to the setting of IB-wHPS and AB-wHPS by adding an additional string $\boldsymbol{x} \in \{0,1\}^*$ (either an ID or general attribute) to the existing attributes as above, resulting in ciphertexts of the form $\mathsf{CT} := \{\mathsf{ABE.Enc}(\mathsf{mpk}, (\boldsymbol{x}, i, 0), k_i), \mathsf{ABE.Enc}(\mathsf{mpk}, (\boldsymbol{x}, i, 1), k_i)\}_{i \in [n]}$. It is not hard to check these designs satisfy the requirements of (IB/AB)-wHPS.

Here we can conclude: (1) $\mathsf{sk}_{g_{\boldsymbol{b}}}$ is functionally equivalent to the set of secret keys $\{(i, b_i), \mathsf{sk}_{i,b_i}\}_{i \in [n]}$, and (2) as long as $\mathsf{sk}_{g_{\boldsymbol{b}}}$ has a succinct representation, i.e., $|\mathsf{sk}_{g_{\boldsymbol{b}}}|$ only depends on the depth but not the size of the function $g_{\boldsymbol{b}}$ when $g_{\boldsymbol{b}}$ is given, we can achieve the optimal leakage rate. We can instantiate the desired ABE by the lattice-based schemes [7,22], and consequently derive a PKE/IBE/ABE with the optimal rate in the relative leakage model.

Adaptive Security for Various Function Classes. A careful reader may already observe that the underlying ABE schemes of [7,22] do not achieve adaptive security, and neither do the IB-wHPS and AB-wHPS as constructed above. Moreover, it seems that lattice-based ABE that supports the computation $g_{\boldsymbol{b}}(\cdot)$ with succinct keys (e.g., general circuits [7,22]) can only achieve selective security. Thus, existing techniques plus the above approach do not suffice for our goal on adaptive security.

To overcome the limitation, we further observe that our constructions of IB-wHPS and AB-wHPS above actually *do not* require the full adaptive security of the whole attribute $(\boldsymbol{x}, (i, b))$ from the underlying ABE. We only need the selective security over the second part (i, b), as this part is generated by the honest key generation algorithm, instead of being challenged by the adversary.

With this insight, we define a more fine-grained security notion that considers partially adaptive/selective security over partitioned attributes $(\boldsymbol{x}, (i, b))$. Intuitively, if the underlying ABE is adaptively (or selectively) secure over $\boldsymbol{x}$ and *selective secure* over (i, b), then we can prove the AB-wHPS is adaptively (resp. selectively) secure. Furthermore we instantiate the required partially adaptive-selective ABE for various function classes. As a result, we obtain an adaptively secure IB-wHPS and AB-wHPS for t-CNF*, and selectively secure AB-wHPS for general circuits. This matches the function classes for which we know how to construct adaptively secure ABE without leakage.

Application. Our AB-wHPS with succinct keys immediately yields a $(\ell, 1)$-leakage resilient ABE with leakage rate $1 - o(1)$ in the relative leakage model, followed from the framework [25]. More specifically, by using our adaptively secure AB-wHPS for the comparison function (i.e., IB-wHPS) and the t-CNF* functions, we get leakage resilient and adaptively secure ABE for these classes with optimal leakage rates. Additionally, we can have selectively secure leakage resilient ABE for general circuits, with leakage rate $1 - o(1)$.

Extension I. As pointed out by [25], we can further derive $(\ell, 1)$-leakage resilient ABE in the BRM from AB-wHPS, via an amplification and a connection with locally computable extractors [40]. However, the analysis from prior compatible locally computable extractors only yields $1 - O(1)$ rate for the leakage resilient encryption scheme. It was left as an interesting open question by [35] how to improve the analysis of the extractor. We solve this open question by improving the analysis of the sampler [5] required by the general construction of Vadhan [40]. With our improved analysis, we are able to achieve $1 - o(1)$ leakage rate in the BRM.

Extension II. Finally, we show how to derive (ℓ, ω)-leakage resilient ABE with the optimal leakage rate in the block leakage setting for both relative model and BRM, for any bounded polynomial ω. Inspired by the work [21], we derive a new bootstrapping mechanism by connecting secret sharing with our AB-wHPS. We leave it as an interesting open question how to achieve leakage resilient ABE even for an unbounded polynomial ω.

1.3 Other Related Work

AB-wHPS has been studied to construct leakage resilient ABE schemes in [43,44]. Particularly, in [43], the authors focus on AB-wHPS supporting linear secret sharing schemes as the policy function class, from the pre-quantum decisional bilinear Diffie-Hellman assumption. The work in [44] constructed an AB-wHPS from a post-quantum, i.e., LWE, assumption. However, the constructions only achieve selective security for linear secret sharing schemes. And both of these related work only consider security in the relative leakage model. Compared with the prior works, our design/analysis approach is more modular, supporting broader function classes and/or stronger (adaptive) security.

2 Preliminaries

We use several standard mathematical notations, whose detailed descriptions are deferred to the full version of this paper, due to space limit.

2.1 Attribute-Based Encryption (ABE)

Definition 2.1 (ABE [37]). *An attribute-based encryption (*ABE*) scheme for a function class $\mathcal{F}_\lambda = \{f : \mathcal{X}_\lambda \to \{0,1\}\}$ consists of four algorithms* $\mathsf{ABE}.\{\mathsf{Setup}, \mathsf{KeyGen}, \mathsf{Enc}, \mathsf{Dec}\}$ *as follows.*

- **Setup.** $\mathsf{ABE.Setup}(1^\lambda)$ *takes a security parameter λ as input, and generates a pair of master public key and master secret key* $(\mathsf{mpk}, \mathsf{msk})$*, where* mpk *contains the attribute space $\mathcal{X}_\lambda$, message space $\mathcal{M}$ and ciphertext space $\mathcal{CT}$.*
- **Key generation.** $\mathsf{ABE.KeyGen}(f, \mathsf{msk})$ *takes as input a function $f \in \mathcal{F}_\lambda$ and the master secret key* msk*, and generates a secret key (f, sk_f). Without loss of generality, we think the secret key contains two parts, the function description f, and an extra sk_f. The secret key is succinct if $|\mathsf{sk}_f| = o(|f|)$. When the context is clear, we often omit the description of f.*
- **Encryption.** $\mathsf{ABE.Enc}(\mathsf{mpk}, \boldsymbol{x}, \mu)$ *takes as input the master public key* mpk*, an attribute $\boldsymbol{x} \in \mathcal{X}_\lambda$ and a message $\mu \in \mathcal{M}$, and outputs a ciphertext $\mathsf{ct} \in \mathcal{CT}$.*
- **Decryption.** $\mathsf{ABE.Dec}(\mathsf{sk}_f, \mathsf{ct})$ *takes as input a secret key sk_f and a ciphertext c, and outputs $\mu \in \mathcal{M}$ if $f(\boldsymbol{x}) = 1$ and $\perp$ if $f(\boldsymbol{x}) = 0$, where $\boldsymbol{x}$ is the corresponding attribute used to generate* ct.

Correctness. We require that for all $f \in \mathcal{F}$, $\boldsymbol{x} \in \mathcal{X}_\lambda$, $\mu \in \mathcal{M}$, for correctly generated $(\mathsf{mpk}, \mathsf{msk}) \stackrel{\$}{\leftarrow} \mathsf{ABE.Setup}(1^\lambda)$, $\mathsf{sk}_f \stackrel{\$}{\leftarrow} \mathsf{ABE.KeyGen}(\mathsf{msk}, f)$ and $\mathsf{ct} \stackrel{\$}{\leftarrow} \mathsf{ABE.Enc}(\mathsf{mpk}, \boldsymbol{x}, \mu)$, it holds that

- if $f(\boldsymbol{x}) = 1$, $\Pr[\mathsf{ABE.Dec}(\mathsf{sk}_f, \mathsf{ct}) = \mu] \geq 1 - \mathsf{negl}(\lambda)$.
- if $f(\boldsymbol{x}) = 0$, $\Pr[\mathsf{ABE.Dec}(\mathsf{sk}_f, \mathsf{ct}) = \perp] \geq 1 - \mathsf{negl}(\lambda)$.

Leakage Resilience in the Relative Leakage Model

Next, we give the formal definition of leakage-resilient key-policy ABE.

Definition 2.2 (Leakage-Resilient ABE). *A leakage-resilient* ABE *with attribute space $\mathcal{X}_\lambda$ for a class of functions $\mathcal{F}_\lambda = \{f : \mathcal{X}_\lambda \to \{0,1\}\}$ in the relative leakage model consists of four algorithms* $\mathsf{ABE}.\{\mathsf{Setup}, \mathsf{KeyGen}, \mathsf{Enc}, \mathsf{Dec}\}$*, which are parameterized by a security parameter λ and leakage parameters ℓ, ω. In particular, (ℓ, ω)-leakage-resilient security can be defined by the following experiment.*

Experiment $\mathbf{Exp}^{\mathsf{LR}}_{\mathsf{ABE},\mathcal{A}}(\lambda, \ell, \omega)$

Attribute Challenge: *In the setting of selective case, $\mathcal{A}$ chooses an challenge attribute $x^* \in \mathcal{X}_\lambda$ before the Setup stage and sends it to $\mathcal{C}$; In the setting of adaptive case, $\mathcal{A}$ chooses an challenge $x^* \in \mathcal{X}_\lambda$ in the challenge stage, and sends it to $\mathcal{C}$.*

Test Stage 1: *$\mathcal{A}$ adaptively queries the challenger $\mathcal{C}$ with function $f \in \mathcal{F}_\lambda$. For each query, $\mathcal{C}$ responds with (f, sk_f) if $f(x^*) \neq 1$ and $\perp$ otherwise.*

ω-Leakage Queries Stage: *$\mathcal{A}$ adaptively queries the challenger $\mathcal{C}$ with q pairs (f_i, h_i) for $i \in [\omega]$, where f_i is a policy function such that $f_i(x^*) = 1$, and $h_i : \{0,1\}^* \to \{0,1\}^\ell$ is a leakage function. The adversary gets $h_i(\mathsf{sk}_{f_i})$ from $\mathcal{C}$.*

Challenge Stage: *$\mathcal{A}$ chooses two messages $\mu_0, \mu_1 \in \mathcal{M}$ and sends them to $\mathcal{C}$. Then $\mathcal{C}$ chooses $b \xleftarrow{\$} \{0,1\}$ and computes $\mathsf{ct}_b \xleftarrow{\$} \mathsf{ABE.Enc}(\mathsf{mpk}, x^*, \mu_b)$. Finally, $\mathcal{C}$ returns ct_b to $\mathcal{A}$.*

Test Stage 2: *$\mathcal{A}$ adaptively queries the challenger $\mathcal{C}$ with function $f \in \mathcal{F}_\lambda$. Then $\mathcal{C}$ responds with $(f, \mathsf{sk}_{\mathsf{id},f})$ if $f(x^*) \neq 1$ and $\perp$ otherwise.*

Output: *The adversary $\mathcal{A}$ outputs a bit $b' \in \{0,1\}$.*

We define the advantage of $\mathcal{A}$ in the above experiment[2] *to be*

$$\mathbf{Adv}^{\mathsf{LR}}_{\mathsf{ABE},\mathcal{A}}(\lambda, \ell, \omega) = |\Pr[b = b'] - 1/2| .$$

The scheme is (ℓ, ω)-leakage resilient if for any PPT *adversary $\mathcal{A}$, we have $\mathbf{Adv}^{\mathsf{LR}}_{\mathsf{ABE},\mathcal{A}}(\lambda, \ell, \omega) \leq \mathsf{negl}(\lambda)$, and the leakage rate of this* ABE *is $\frac{\ell}{|\mathsf{sk}|}$.*

Furthermore, the scheme is abbreviated as ℓ-leakage resilient if $\omega = 1$ in the above experiment.

Remark 2.3. *We use the parameter ω to denote the number of different challenge keys that can be conducted leakage queries. For* PKE *and* IBE*, we have $\omega = 1$ as for these two settings, there is a unique challenge key corresponding to the challenge attribute. For the more general* ABE*, there might be many different "1"-keys corresponding to the challenge attribute. Thus, this parameter ω would be an important specification for the leakage resilient* ABE.

Remark 2.4. *In our security model, the adversary can obtain leakage on ω secret keys adaptively one after another. The secret keys would then form a block-source under the leakage.*[3] *We note that it is possible to generalize the model where the leakage function takes inputs all the ω secret keys. In this work, we focus mainly on the block-source setting, as it already captures many useful scenarios.*

[2] Notice that in the above experiment $\mathbf{Exp}^{\mathsf{LR}}_{\mathsf{ABE},\mathcal{A}}(\lambda, \ell, \omega)$, we allow the adversary to interleave key queries in *Test Stage 1* and leakage queries in *ω-Leakage queries Stage*, in an arbitrary way.

[3] For the case that $\mathsf{sk} := S = (S_1, \ldots, S_m)$ is an $m \times e$ block source as in [39], we define leakage functions $f_i : \{0,1\}^* \to \{0,1\}^\ell$ independently for each block S_i with all $i \in [m]$. We say $(f_1, \ldots, f_m)$ are block leakage functions, if the min-entropy of S_i is still large enough even given leakage $(f_1(S_1), \ldots, f_{i-1}(S_{i-1}))$ for any $i \in [m]$. Clearly, when $m = 1$, this is the trivial case in Definition 2.2. Here, we call $\frac{m\ell}{|\mathsf{sk}|}$ the block leakage rate of the corresponding scheme.

Leakage Resilience in the BRM.
Below, we generalize to the setting of ABE the definition of leakage-resilience in the BRM by Alwen et al. [5].

Definition 2.5. (ABE in the BRM). *An* ABE *for attribute space* $\mathcal{X}_\lambda$ *and policy function class* $\mathcal{F} := \{\mathcal{X}_\lambda \to \{0,1\}\}$ *is* (ℓ, ω)*-leakage resilient in the* BRM *if its master public-key size, ciphertext size, encryption time and decryption time (and the number of secret-key bits used by decryption) are independent of the leakage-bound* ℓ*. Besides, in the leakage resilient experiment, the adversary is allowed to conduct key leakage attacks on* ω *secret keys corresponding to the challenge attribute. More formally, there exist polynomials* mpksize, ctsize, encT, decT*, such that, for any polynomial* ℓ *and any* $(\mathsf{mpk}, \mathsf{msk}) \xleftarrow{\$} \mathsf{ABE.Setup}(1^\lambda, 1^{\ell(\lambda)})$, $\boldsymbol{x} \in \mathcal{X}_\lambda$, $\mu \in \mathcal{M}$, $\mathsf{ct} \xleftarrow{\$} \mathsf{ABE.Enc}(\mathsf{mpk}, \boldsymbol{x}, \mu)$*, the scheme satisfies:*

1. *Master public-key size is* $|\mathsf{mpk}| \leq O(\mathsf{mpksize}(\lambda))$*, ciphertext size is* $|\mathsf{ct}| \leq O(\mathsf{ctsize}(\lambda, |\mu|))$.
2. *Run-time of* $\mathsf{ABE.Enc}(\mu, \mathsf{pk})$ *is bounded by* $O(\mathsf{encT}(\lambda, |\mu|))$.
3. *Run-time of* $\mathsf{ABE.Dec}(\mathsf{ct}, \mathsf{sk}_f)$ *and the number of bits of* sk_f *used in this decryption bounded by* $O(\mathsf{decT}(\lambda, |\mu|))$*, where* $\mathsf{sk}_f \xleftarrow{\$} \mathsf{ABE.KeyGen}(\mathsf{msk}, f)$ *with* $f \in \mathcal{F}$ *such that* $f(\boldsymbol{x}) = 1$*. Here we assume that the secret key* sk_f *is stored in a random access memory (RAM), and the decryption algorithm* $\mathsf{ABE.Dec}(\mathsf{ct}, \cdot)$ *only needs to read partial bits of* sk_f *to decrypt.*

The leakage rate of this scheme is defined as $\frac{\ell}{|\mathsf{sk}_f|}$*. Furthermore, the scheme is abbreviated as* ℓ*-leakage resilient if the parameter* $\omega = 1$ *in the experiment.*

Policy Function Classes. This work considers three function classes: (1) ID comparison functions, (2) t-CNF* formulas, and (3) general circuits. (1) and (3) are clear from the literature. We elaborate on (2). First we present the definition of the function class t-CNF.

Definition 2.6 (t-CNF [38]). *A* t-CNF *policy* $f : \{0,1\}^\ell \to \{0,1\}$ *is a set of classes* $f = \{(T_i, f_i)\}_i$*, where for all* $i, T_i \subseteq [\ell], |T_i| = t$ *and* $f_i : \{0,1\}^t \to \{0,1\}$*. For all* $x \in \{0,1\}^\ell$ *the value of* $f(x)$ *is computed as* $f(x) = \bigwedge_i f_i(x_{T_i})$*, where* x_T *is the length-*t *bit-string consisting of the bits of* x *in the indices* T*. A function class* $\mathcal{F}$ *is* t-CNF *if it consists only of* t-CNF *policies for some fixed* $\ell \in \mathbb{N}$ *and a constant* $t \leq \ell$*. If* $\mathcal{F}$ *is a* t-CNF *class, we say that* t *is the* CNF *locality of* $\mathcal{F}$*.*

In this paper, we use the "dual" form of t-CNF, called t-CNF*. The use of the dual version is because the prior work [38] worked on the ciphertext-policy ABE for t-CNF, and this work presents the result in the key-policy setting.

Definition 2.7 (t-CNF*). *For any* $x \in \{0,1\}^\ell$ *(the domain of* t-CNF*), let* $U_x(\cdot)$ *denote the function for which* x *is hardwired into* $U_x(\cdot)$*, and* $U_x(\cdot)$ *takes* $f \in t$-CNF *as input and outputs* $U_x(f)$ *such that* $U_x(f) = f(x)$*.* $U_x(\cdot)$ *is uniquely determined by* x*. We denote the function class* $\{U_x(\cdot)\}$ *as* t-CNF*.

2.2 Entropy and Extractors

Definition 2.8 (Min-Entropy). *The min-entropy of a random variable* X*, denoted as* $H_\infty(X)$ *is defined as* $H_\infty(x) = -\log\left(\max_{x_0 \in X} \Pr[x = x_0]\right)$.

Definition 2.9 (Average-Conditional Min-Entropy [15]**).** *The average-conditional min-entropy of a random variable* X *conditioned on a correlated variable* Z*, denoted as* $H_\infty(X|Z)$ *is defined as*

$$H_\infty(X|Z) = -\log\left(\mathbb{E}_{z \leftarrow Z}[\max_x \Pr[X = x|Z = z]]\right) = -\log\left(\mathbb{E}_{z \leftarrow Z}[2^{H_\infty[X|Z=z]}]\right).$$

This notion of conditional min-entropy measures the best guess for X by an adversary that may observe an average-case correlated variable Z.

Lemma 2.10 ([15])**.** *Let* X,Y,Z *be arbitrarily correlated random variables where the support of* Y *has at most* 2^ℓ *elements. Then* $H_\infty(X|(Y,Z)) \geq H_\infty(X|Z) - \ell$*. In particular,* $H_\infty(X|Y) \geq H_\infty(X) - \ell$.

We also give the definition of randomness extractors [34], which is somewhat stronger than the average-case strong extractor [15].

Definition 2.11 (Randomness Extractor). *An efficient function* $\mathsf{Ext} : \mathcal{X} \times \mathcal{S} \rightarrow \mathcal{Y}$ *is a* (v, ε)*-extractor if for all (correlated) random variable* X, Z *such that the support of* X *is* $\mathcal{X}$ *and* $H_\infty(X|Z) \geq v$*, we have* $\Delta((Z, S, \mathsf{Ext}(X; S)), (Z, S, Y)) \leq \varepsilon$*, where* S *(also called the seed) and* Y *are distributed uniformly and independently over their domains* $\mathcal{S}, \mathcal{Y}$ *respectively.*

Theorem 2.12 ([15])**.** *Let* $\mathcal{H} = \{h_s : \mathcal{X} \rightarrow \mathcal{Y}\}_{s \in \mathcal{S}}$ *be a universal family of hash functions meaning that for all* $x = x' \in \mathcal{X}$ *we have* $\Pr_{s \leftarrow \mathcal{S}}[h_s(x) = h_s(x')] \leq \frac{1}{|\mathcal{Y}|}$*. Then* $\mathsf{Ext}(x, s) \stackrel{def}{=} h_s(x)$*, is a* (v, ε)*-extractor for any parameter* $v \geq \log|\mathcal{Y}| + 2\log(1/\varepsilon)$.

3 Attribute-Based Weak Hash Proof Systems

In this section, we first present a generalization of the weak hash proof system called *attribute-based* weak hash proof system (AB-wHPS). This notion associates attributes and policy functions to the system following the spirit of attribute-based encryption. Next, we show how to construct AB-wHPS from ABE that achieves the property of *succinct keys*, which is the key to leakage resilience with the optimal rate. With a new fine-grained approach, we are able to achieve AB-wHPS with selective security for general circuits, adaptive security of identity comparison functions (i.e., identity-based wHPS), and adaptive security for t-CNF* functions[4], from lattices. This would imply lattice-based leakage resilient, adaptively secure PKE, IBE, ABE for t-CNF*, and selectively secure ABE for general circuits, all with the optimal rate, matching the best known non-leakage resilient selectively/adaptively secure constructions.

[4] We use a "dual" variant of the CNF functions as we discussed in the introduction. The formal definition is presented in Sect. 2.1.

3.1 Formal Definition of Attribute-Based wHPS

We first present the formal definition of an AB-wHPS.

Definition 3.1 (AB-wHPS). *An attribute-based weak hash proof system (*AB-wHPS*) for an attribute space $\mathcal{X}_\lambda = \{0,1\}^*$ and a class of functions $\mathcal{F}_\lambda = \{f : \mathcal{X}_\lambda \to \{0,1\}\}$ consists of five algorithms* AB-wHPS.{Setup, KeyGen, Encap, Encap*, Decap}*:*

- **Setup.** AB-wHPS.Setup(1^λ) *takes a security parameter λ as input, and generates a pair of master public key and master secret key* (mpk, msk). *The attribute space $\mathcal{X}_\lambda$ and the encapsulated key space $\mathcal{K}$ are determined by* mpk.
- **Key generation.** AB-wHPS.KeyGen (f, msk) *takes as input a function $f \in \mathcal{F}_\lambda$ and the master secret key* msk, *and generates a secret key* (f, sk_f). *Without loss of generality, we think the secret key contains two parts, the function description f, and an extra sk_f. The secret key is succinct if $|\mathsf{sk}_f| = o(|f|)$. When the context is clear, we often omit the description of f.*
- **Valid encapsulation.** AB-wHPS.Encap(mpk, $\boldsymbol{x}$) *takes as input the master public key* mpk *and an attribute $\boldsymbol{x} \in \mathcal{X}_\lambda$, and outputs a valid ciphertext* CT *and its corresponding encapsulated key $k \in \mathcal{K}$.*
- **Invalid encapsulation.** AB-wHPS.Encap*(mpk, $\boldsymbol{x}$) *takes as input the master public key* mpk *and $\boldsymbol{x} \in \mathcal{X}_\lambda$, and outputs an invalid ciphertext* CT*.
- **Decapsulation.** AB-wHPS.Decap(sk_f, CT) *takes as input a secret key sk_f and a ciphertext* CT, *and deterministically outputs $k \in \mathcal{K}$ if $f(\boldsymbol{x}) = 1$ and $\perp$ if $f(\boldsymbol{x}) = 0$, where $\boldsymbol{x}$ is the corresponding attribute used to generate* CT.

Furthermore, an AB-wHPS needs to satisfy three properties: correctness, ciphertext indistinguishability, and universality.

Correctness. For (mpk, msk) $\xleftarrow{\$}$ AB-wHPS.Setup(λ), any $\boldsymbol{x} \in \mathcal{X}_\lambda$ and any $f \in \mathcal{F}_\lambda$ such that $f(\boldsymbol{x}) = 1$, we have

$$\Pr\Big[k = k' \Big| \mathsf{sk}_f \xleftarrow{\$} \text{AB-wHPS.KeyGen}(f, \mathsf{msk}),$$
$$(\mathsf{CT}, k) \xleftarrow{\$} \text{AB-wHPS.Encap}(\mathsf{mpk}, \boldsymbol{x}), k' = \text{AB-wHPS.Decap}(\mathsf{sk}_f, c)\Big] = 1.$$

Ciphertext Indistinguishability. For any challenge attribute $\boldsymbol{x}^*$, valid/in-valid ciphertexts output by AB-wHPS. Encap(mpk, $\boldsymbol{x}^*$) and AB-wHPS.Encap*(mpk, $\boldsymbol{x}^*$) are indistinguishable, even given one secret "1-key" sk_f such that $f(\boldsymbol{x}^*) = 1$ and perhaps many "0-keys" $\mathsf{sk}_{f'}$ such that $f'(\boldsymbol{x}^*) = 0$. More formally, this indistinguishability is always described by the experiment between an adversary $\mathcal{A}$ and a challenger $\mathcal{C}$ in Table 1.

We define the advantage of $\mathcal{A}$ in the above game to be $\mathbf{Adv}^{\text{AB-wHPS}}_{\Pi,\mathcal{A},\mathcal{F}_\lambda}(\lambda) = |\Pr[\mathcal{A}\ wins] - 1/2|$. The indistinguishability means that $\mathbf{Adv}^{\text{AB-wHPS}}_{\Pi,\mathcal{A},\mathcal{F}_\lambda}(\lambda) \leq \mathsf{negl}(\lambda)$.

Remark 3.2 *In this definition, we require ciphertext indistinguishability to hold even given a single* sk_f *such that* $f(\boldsymbol{x}^*) = 1$. *This suffices to achieve leakage resilient* PKE, IBE, *and* $(\ell, 1)$*-leakage resilient* ABE *directly, and* (ℓ, ω)*-leakage resilient* ABE *for any bounded-polynomial* ω *via a bootstrapping procedure (ref. Sect. 6), where* $\ell \approx (1 - o(1))|\mathsf{sk}_f|$.

Universality. We need one additional information theoretic property, requiring that for any adversary with public parameters, the decapsulation of an invalid ciphertext has information entropy. We define this property in as follow.

Definition 3.3. (Universal AB-wHPS). *We say that an* AB-wHPS *is* $(l, \bar{w})$*-universal, if for any attribute* $\boldsymbol{x} \in \mathcal{X}_\lambda$, $(\mathsf{mpk}, \mathsf{msk}) \xleftarrow{\$} \mathsf{AB\text{-}wHPS.Setup}(1^\lambda)$, *and* $\mathsf{CT}^* \xleftarrow{\$} \mathsf{AB\text{-}wHPS.Encap}^*(\mathsf{mpk}, \boldsymbol{x})$, *it holds*

$$H_\infty(\mathsf{AB\text{-}wHPS.Decap}(\mathsf{CT}^*, \mathsf{sk}_f)|\mathsf{mpk}, \mathsf{msk}, \mathsf{CT}^*, \boldsymbol{x}) \geq \bar{w},$$

where $\mathsf{sk}_f = \mathsf{AB\text{-}wHPS.KeyGen}(f, \mathsf{msk})$ *with* $f(\boldsymbol{x}) = 1$, *and* l *is the bit-length of the decapsulated value from* $\mathsf{AB\text{-}wHPS.Decap}(\mathsf{CT}^*, \mathsf{sk})$.

Table 1. X

Valid/Invalid Ciphertext Indistinguishability Experiment
Attribute Challenge: In the setting of selective case, $\mathcal{A}$ chooses an challenge attribute $\boldsymbol{x}^* \in \mathcal{X}_\lambda$ before the Setup stage and sends it to $\mathcal{C}$; In the setting of adaptive case, $\mathcal{A}$ chooses a challenge $\boldsymbol{x}^* \in \mathcal{X}_\lambda$ in any arbitrary stage before the challenge stage, and sends it to $\mathcal{C}$.
Setup: The challenger $\mathcal{C}$ gets a pair of $(\mathsf{mpk}, \mathsf{msk})$ by running $\mathsf{AB\text{-}wHPS.Setup}(1^\lambda)$, and sends mpk to $\mathcal{A}$.
Test Stage 1: $\mathcal{A}$ adaptively queries the challenger $\mathcal{C}$ with $f \in \mathcal{F}_\lambda$, and $\mathcal{C}$ responds with (f, sk_f).
Challenge Stage: $\mathcal{C}$ selects $b \xleftarrow{\$} \{0, 1\}$.
If $b = 0$, $\mathcal{C}$ computes $(\mathsf{CT}, k) \xleftarrow{\$} \mathsf{AB\text{-}wHPS.Encap}(\mathsf{mpk}, \boldsymbol{x}^*)$.
If $b = 1$, $\mathcal{C}$ computes $\mathsf{CT} \xleftarrow{\$} \mathsf{AB\text{-}wHPS.Encap}^*(\mathsf{mpk}, \boldsymbol{x}^*)$.
Then $\mathcal{C}$ returns CT to $\mathcal{A}$.
Test Stage 2: $\mathcal{A}$ adaptively queries the challenger $\mathcal{C}$ with $f \in \mathcal{F}$. Then $\mathcal{C}$ responds with (f, sk_f).
Output: $\mathcal{A}$ outputs a bit $b' \in \{0, 1\}$. $\mathcal{A}$ wins the experiment, if $b = b'$ and at most one of $\mathcal{A}$'s key queries f satisfies $f(\boldsymbol{x}^*) = 1$.

3.2 Fine-Grained Security Notions and General Construction of AB-wHPSfrom ABE

In this section, we present how to construct AB-wHPS from ABE. To achieve adaptive security for several subclasses of policy functions, we present a more fine-grained approach as follows. We first define a notion called partially selective/adaptive security over partitioned attributes. Next we show for a *specific class* $\mathcal{G}$, if an ABE is (X, sel)-secure for class $\mathcal{F} \wedge_{\|} \mathcal{G}$ for X $\in$ {sel, ada}, then we can construct an X-secure AB-wHPS for $\mathcal{F}$. Moreover, suppose the underlying ABE has succinct keys, so does the AB-wHPS. In the next section, we show instantiations of (ada, sel)-secure ABE for various function classes. Below we elaborate on the notations and the new security definition.

Definition 3.4. *Let* $\mathcal{F}_1 = \{f_1 : \mathcal{X}_1 \to \{0,1\}\}$ *and* $\mathcal{F}_2 = \{f_2 : \mathcal{X}_2 \to \{0,1\}\}$ *be two function classes. We define the operator* $\wedge_{\|}$ *over two function classes as follow:* $\mathcal{F} := \mathcal{F}_1 \wedge_{\|} \mathcal{F}_2$ *is a function class that consists of function maps* $\mathcal{X}_1 \times \mathcal{X}_2 \to \{0,1\}$*, where each function* $f_{f_1,f_2} \in \mathcal{F}$ *is indexed by two functions* $f_1 \in \mathcal{F}_1$ *and* $f_2 \in \mathcal{F}_2$ *such that on input* $\boldsymbol{x} = (\boldsymbol{x}_1, \boldsymbol{x}_2) \in \mathcal{X}_1 \times \mathcal{X}_2$*,* $f_{f_1,f_2}(\boldsymbol{x}) = f_1(\boldsymbol{x}_1) \wedge f_2(\boldsymbol{x}_2)$.

Using this composed function class in Definition 3.4, we can naturally consider any combination of selective/adaptive security for ABE as follows.

Definition 3.5. (Partial Selective/Adaptive Security). *For any* ABE *with the attribute space* $\mathcal{X}_1 \times \mathcal{X}_2$ *for the policy function class* $\mathcal{F} := \mathcal{F}_1 \wedge_{\|} \mathcal{F}_2$ *defined as in Definition 3.4, we define partial selective/adaptive security as follows:*

- ada-sel *security: For any challenge attribute* $\boldsymbol{x}^* = (\boldsymbol{x}_1^*, \boldsymbol{x}_2^*) \in \mathcal{X}_1 \times \mathcal{X}_2$*,* $\boldsymbol{x}_1^*$ *is chosen adaptively but* $\boldsymbol{x}_2^*$ *is chosen selectively in the corresponding indistinguishability experiment.*
- sel-ada *security: For any challenge attribute* $\boldsymbol{x}^* = (\boldsymbol{x}_1^*, \boldsymbol{x}_2^*) \in \mathcal{X}_1 \times \mathcal{X}_2$*,* $\boldsymbol{x}_1^*$ *is chosen selectively and* $\boldsymbol{x}_2^*$ *is chosen adaptively in the corresponding indistinguishability experiment.*

This notion also captures the standard selective (or adaptive) security as sel-sel *(or* ada-ada*) security, where both parts of the challenge attribute are chosen selectively (or adaptively).*

Remark 3.6. *In this work, we need a slightly weaker version of the partial selective/adaptive security from* ABE *– the adversary is only allowed to query one key* (f, g) *such that* $f(x_1^*) = 1$ *and* $g(x_2^*) = 0$*. The other keys are of the form* (f', g') *such that* $f'(x_1^*) = 0$*. Therefore, throughout this work we will use this slightly weaker version by default.*

Remark 3.7. *In the same way, we can define the partial selective/adaptive ciphertext indistinguishability for* AB-wHPS.

Remark 3.8. *This definition can be defined recursively. For example, the first part* $\mathcal{F}_1$ *can also consists of two parts, i.e.,* $\mathcal{F}_1 = \mathcal{F}_{1,1} \wedge_{\|} \mathcal{F}_{1,2}$*. In this case, we can consider* (X-Y)-Z *security for any combination of* X, Y, Z $\in$ {sel, ada}.

To construct our desired AB-wHPS for $\mathcal{F}$, we need an ABE for $\mathcal{F} \wedge_{\|} \mathcal{G}$ for this specific $\mathcal{G}$ as we describe below.

Definition 3.9. *Let $m = m(\lambda)$ and $n = n(\lambda)$ be two integer parameters, and we define a function class $\mathcal{G} = \{g : [n] \times [m] \to \{0,1\}\}$ as follows. Each function $g_{\boldsymbol{y}} \in \mathcal{G}$ is indexed by a vector $\boldsymbol{y} = (y_1, \ldots, y_n)^\top \in [m]^n$, and $g_{\boldsymbol{y}}(x_1, x_2) = 1$ if and only if $x_2 = y_{x_1}$.*

Remark 3.10. *The class $\mathcal{G}$ can be captured by boolean circuits with input length $\log n + \log m$, and depth within $O(\log(n+m))$, i.e., $\bigvee_{i\in[n]}(i \stackrel{?}{=} x_1) \wedge (y_i \stackrel{?}{=} x_2)$.*

Given this particular class $\mathcal{G}$ (with parameters m, n) defined in Definition 3.9 and a class $\mathcal{F}$, we show how to use ABE for $\mathcal{F} \wedge_{\|} \mathcal{G}$ to construct AB-wHPS for $\mathcal{F}$. For different classes $\mathcal{F}$'s, the AB-wHPS can be used to further derive leakage resilient PKE, IBE, and ABE.

Construction 3.11 (AB-wHPS from ABE). *Let $\Pi_{\mathsf{ABE}} = \mathsf{ABE}.\{\mathsf{Setup}, \mathsf{KeyGen}, \mathsf{Enc}, \mathsf{Dec}\}$ be an ABE scheme with attribute-space $\tilde{\mathcal{X}}_\lambda = \mathcal{X}_\lambda \times \mathcal{X}'_\lambda = \{0,1\}^* \times \{[n] \times [m]\}$, message-space $\mathcal{M} = \mathbb{Z}_m$ and ciphertext space $\mathcal{CT}$ for the policy-function class $\mathcal{F} \wedge_{\|} \mathcal{G}$ for the class $\mathcal{G}$ as in Definition 3.9 with parameters m, n. Then, an AB-wHPS $\Pi_{\mathsf{AB\text{-}wHPS}}$ with attribute space $\mathcal{X}_\lambda = \{0,1\}^*$ and the encapsulated-key-space $\mathcal{K} = \mathbb{Z}_m^n$ for the policy-function class $\mathcal{F} = \{f : \{0,1\}^* \to \{0,1\}\}$ can be constructed as follows:*

- $\mathsf{AB\text{-}wHPS.Setup}(1^\lambda)$: *Given the security parameter λ as input, the algorithm runs $\mathsf{ABE.Setup}$ to generate $(\mathsf{mpk}^{\mathsf{ABE}}, \mathsf{msk}^{\mathsf{ABE}}) \stackrel{\$}{\leftarrow} \mathsf{ABE.Setup}(1^\lambda)$, and outputs $\mathsf{mpk} := \mathsf{mpk}^{\mathsf{ABE}}$ and $\mathsf{msk} := \mathsf{msk}^{\mathsf{ABE}}$.*
- $\mathsf{AB\text{-}wHPS.KeyGen}(\mathsf{msk}, f)$: *Given a master secret-key $\mathsf{msk} := \mathsf{msk}^{\mathsf{ABE}}$ and a function $f \in \mathcal{F}$ as input, the algorithm first chooses a random vector $\boldsymbol{y} \stackrel{\$}{\leftarrow} [m]^n$, and sets $\hat{f} := \hat{f}_{f, g_{\boldsymbol{y}}} \in \mathcal{F} \wedge_{\|} \mathcal{G}$. Then the algorithm runs $\mathsf{ABE.KeyGen}$ to generate $\mathsf{sk}_{\hat{f}}^{\mathsf{ABE}} \stackrel{\$}{\leftarrow} \mathsf{ABE.KeyGen}(\mathsf{msk}^{\mathsf{ABE}}, \hat{f})$, and outputs $\mathsf{sk}_f := (\hat{f}, \mathsf{sk}_{\hat{f}}^{\mathsf{ABE}})$ as the secret key for f. Note that the description of $\hat{f}$ can be expressed as $(f, \boldsymbol{y})$*
- $\mathsf{AB\text{-}wHPS.Encap}(\mathsf{mpk}, \boldsymbol{x})$: *Given a master public-key mpk and an attribute $\boldsymbol{x} \in \{0,1\}^*$ as input, the algorithm first samples a random vector $\boldsymbol{k} = (k_1, \ldots, k_n)^\top \in \mathbb{Z}_m^n$, and then runs $\mathsf{ABE.Enc}$ mn times with attributes $\boldsymbol{x}_{i,j} = (\boldsymbol{x}, i, j) \in \{0,1\}^* \times [n] \times [m]$ to set*

$$\mathsf{CT} := \{\mathsf{ct}_{i,j} \stackrel{\$}{\leftarrow} \mathsf{ABE.Enc}(\mathsf{mpk}, \boldsymbol{x}_{i,j}, k_i)\}_{(i,j)\in[n]\times[m]} \in \mathcal{CT}^{n\times m}, \text{ i.e.,}$$

$$\mathsf{CT} := \begin{bmatrix} \mathsf{ABE.Enc}(\boldsymbol{x}_{1,1}, k_1) & \ldots & \mathsf{ABE.Enc}(\boldsymbol{x}_{1,j}, k_1) & \ldots & \mathsf{ABE.Enc}(\boldsymbol{x}_{1,m}, k_1) \\ \vdots & \ddots & \vdots & \ddots & \vdots \\ \mathsf{ABE.Enc}(\boldsymbol{x}_{n,1}, k_n) & \ldots & \mathsf{ABE.Enc}(\boldsymbol{x}_{n,j}, k_n) & \ldots & \mathsf{ABE.Enc}(\boldsymbol{x}_{n,m}, k_n) \end{bmatrix}.$$

Finally, the algorithm outputs $(\mathsf{CT}, \boldsymbol{k})$.

- $\mathsf{AB\text{-}wHPS.Encap}^*(\mathsf{mpk}, \boldsymbol{x})$: *Given a master public-key* mpk *and an attribute* $\boldsymbol{x} \in \{0,1\}^*$ *as input, the algorithm first samples a random vector* $\boldsymbol{k} = (k_1, \ldots, k_n)^\top \in \mathbb{Z}_m^n$, *and then runs* ABE.Enc *mn times with attributes* $\boldsymbol{x}_{i,j} = (\boldsymbol{x}, i, j)$ *to set*

$$\mathsf{CT}^* := \{\mathsf{ct}^*_{i,j} \xleftarrow{\$} \mathsf{ABE.Enc}(\mathsf{mpk}, \boldsymbol{x}_{i,j}, k_i + j)\}_{(i,j)\in[n]\times[m]} \in \mathcal{CT}^{n\times m}, \text{ i.e.,}$$

$$\mathsf{CT}^* \coloneqq \begin{bmatrix} \mathsf{ABE.Enc}(\boldsymbol{x}_{1,1}, k_1{+}1) \ldots \mathsf{ABE.Enc}(\boldsymbol{x}_{1,j}, k_1{+}j) \ldots \mathsf{ABE.Enc}(\boldsymbol{x}_{1,m}, k_1{+}m) \\ \vdots \qquad \ddots \qquad \vdots \qquad \ddots \qquad \vdots \\ \mathsf{ABE.Enc}(\boldsymbol{x}_{n,1}, k_n{+}1) \ldots \mathsf{ABE.Enc}(\boldsymbol{x}_{n,j}, k_n{+}j) \ldots \mathsf{ABE.Enc}(\boldsymbol{x}_{n,m}, k_n{+}m) \end{bmatrix},$$

where the addition $k_i + j$ *is performed over* $\mathbb{Z}_m$. *The algorithm outputs* CT^*.
- $\mathsf{AB\text{-}wHPS.Decap}(\mathsf{sk}_f, \mathsf{CT})$: *Given a secret key* $\mathsf{sk}_f := (\boldsymbol{y}, \mathsf{sk}_{\hat{f}}^{\mathsf{ABE}})$ *and* $\mathsf{CT} := \{\mathsf{ct}_{i,j}\}_{(i,j)\in[n]\times[m]}$ *as input, the algorithm runs* ABE.Dec *to compute* $k_i = \mathsf{ABE.Dec}(\mathsf{sk}_{\hat{f}}^{\mathsf{ABE}}, \mathsf{ct}_{i,y_i})$ *for all* $i \in [n]$, *and then outputs* $\boldsymbol{k} = (k_1, \ldots, k_n)^\top$, *if* $\hat{f}(\boldsymbol{x}, i, y_i) = f(\boldsymbol{x}) \wedge g_{\boldsymbol{y}}(i, y_i) = 1$ *for all* $i \in [n]$, *and* $\perp$ *otherwise.*

Intuitively, our attribute design (the class $\mathcal{G}$) allows the secret key to open one ciphertext per row while keeps the others secret. For the valid encapsulation, all ciphertexts in a row encrypts the same element, while for the invalid encapsulation, they encrypt different elements. As the secret key can only open one per row, an adversary cannot distinguish a valid from an invalid encapsulation, even given the secret key.

Our AB-wHPS secret key would be of length $|\hat{f}_{f,g_{\boldsymbol{y}}}| + s(\hat{f}_{f,g_{\boldsymbol{y}}}) = |\boldsymbol{y}| + |f| + s(\hat{f}_{f,g_{\boldsymbol{y}}}) = n \log m + |f| + s(\hat{f}_{f,g_{\boldsymbol{y}}})$, where $s(\cdot)$ is the key-size function (of the extra part, excluding the function description) of the underlying ABE. If the underlying ABE has succinct keys, i.e., $s(f) = o(|f|)$, then our AB-wHPS secret would have size $n \log m + |f| + s(\hat{f}_{f,g_{\boldsymbol{y}}}) = n \log m + |f| + o(n \log m + |f|)$. By setting sufficiently large n, m, we can achieve ABE with the optimal leakage rate, ref. Sect. 4.

Next we present the following theorem. Due to space limit, we defer the full proof to the full version, due to space limit.

Theorem 3.12. (AB-wHPS from ABE). *Suppose* Π_{ABE} *is a secure* ABE *scheme with attribute space* $\bar{\mathcal{X}}_\lambda = \mathcal{X}_\lambda \times \mathcal{X}'_\lambda = \{0,1\}^* \times \{[n] \times [m]\}$ *for the function class* $\mathcal{F} \wedge_{\|} \mathcal{G}$, *where* $\mathcal{G}$ *is the class as in Definition 3.9 with parameters* m, n, *then the construction* $\Pi_{\mathsf{AB\text{-}wHPS}}$ *described above is an* $(n \log m, n \log m)$*-universal* AB-wHPS *with the attribute space* $\mathcal{X}_\lambda$ *and the encapsulated-key-space* $\mathcal{K} = \mathbb{Z}_m^n$, *for the function class* $\mathcal{F}$. *Furthermore,*

- *if the* ABE *is* X*-sel secure for* X $\subset$ {sel, ada}, *then the* AB-wHPS *is* X *secure;*
- *if the key-size (of the extra part, excluding the function description) of the* ABE *scheme for policy function* f *is* $s(f)$, *then the key size of the* AB-wHPS *for* f *is* $n \log m + |f| + s(\hat{f}_{f,g_{\boldsymbol{y}}})$, *where* $s(\cdot)$ *is the key-size function (of the extra part, excluding the function description) of the underlying* ABE.

3.3 Instantiations of AB-wHPSfrom Lattices

Now we show how to instantiate the required underlying ABE. By combining the work [7] with [2] or [38], we get ABE for the following three classes.

Theorem 3.13. *Assuming* LWE, *then there exist:*

1. ada-sel-*secure* ABE *for* $\mathcal{I} \wedge_{||} \mathcal{G}$, *where* $\mathcal{I}$ *is the comparison function (*IBE*).*
2. ada-sel-*secure* ABE *for* t-CNF* $\wedge_{||} \mathcal{G}$, *where* t-CNF* *is the dual of the* t *conjunctive normal form formula. (Ref. Sect. 2.1.)*
3. sel-sel *secure* ABE *for* $\mathcal{F} \wedge_{||} \mathcal{G}$, *where* $\mathcal{F}$ *is the general boolean circuits.*

In all three cases, the size of the secret keys (excluding the function description) depends only on the depth of the circuit but not the size.

We present the constructions in full version for completeness. As a direct corollary of this theorem, we obtain the following AB-wHPS from lattices.

Corollary 3.14. *Assuming* LWE, *there exists* AB-wHPS *that is*

1. *adaptively secure for the comparison functions;*
2. *adaptively secure for* t-CNF* *functions.*
3. *selectively secure for general circuits.*

Moreover, the secret key size (excluding the function description) of the AB-wHPS *only depends on the depth of the function, but not the size.*

4 Optimal-Rate Leakage-Resilient Encryption Schemes in the Relative Leakage Model

Prior work (e.g., Naor and Segev [33], Alwen et al. [5], and Hazay et al. [25]) showed how to construct leakage resilient PKE/IBE from wHPS/IB-wHPS in the relative model. The construction can be generalized to construct leakage resilient ABE from AB-wHPS in the same spirit. To further achieve the optimal leakage rate, we observe that all we need is an AB-wHPS with succinct keys (which do not depend on the function size). This is what we construct in Sect. 3.2, i.e., Construction 3.11, Theorem 3.12, AB-wHPS and the underlying ABE instantiations in Corollary 3.14.

Construction 4.1. *Let* Π =AB-wHPS.{Setup, KeyGen, Encap, Encap*, Decap} *be a* $(\log|\mathcal{K}|, \log|\mathcal{K}|)$*-universal* AB-wHPS *with the encapsulated-key-space* $\mathcal{K}$ *and attribute space* $\mathcal{X} = \{0,1\}^*$ *for a class of policy functions* $\mathcal{F} = \{f : \{0,1\}^* \to \{0,1\}\}$. *Let* $\mathsf{Ext} : \mathcal{K} \times \mathcal{S} \to \mathcal{M}$ *be a* $(\log|\mathcal{K}| - \ell, \varepsilon)$*-extractor, where three sets* $\mathcal{K}, \mathcal{S}, \mathcal{M}$ *are efficient ensembles,* $\ell = \ell(\lambda)$ *is some parameter and* $\varepsilon = \varepsilon(\lambda) = \mathsf{negl}(\lambda)$ *is negligible. Furthermore, assume that* $\mathcal{M}$ *is an additive group. Then, a leakage-resilient* ABE *scheme* $\Pi_{\mathcal{F}} = \Pi_{\mathcal{F}}$.{Setup, KeyGen, Enc, Dec} *with message space* $\mathcal{M}$ *and policy function class* $\mathcal{F}$ *can be constructed as follows:*

- $\Pi_{\mathcal{F}}.\mathsf{Setup}(1^\lambda)$: *The algorithm runs* $(\mathsf{mpk}^\Pi, \mathsf{msk}^\Pi) \xleftarrow{\$} \Pi.\mathsf{Setup}(1^\lambda)$, *and outputs* $\mathsf{mpk} := \mathsf{mpk}^\Pi$, *and* $\mathsf{msk} := \mathsf{msk}^\Pi$.
- $\Pi_{\mathcal{F}}.\mathsf{KeyGen}(\mathsf{msk}, f)$: *Given a master secret-key* msk *and a function* $f \in \mathcal{F}$ *as input, the algorithm runs* AB-wHPS.KeyGen *to generate and output* (f, sk_f^Π), *where* $\mathsf{sk}_f := \mathsf{sk}_f^\Pi \xleftarrow{\$} \text{AB-wHPS.KeyGen}(\mathsf{msk}, f)$.
- $\Pi_{\mathcal{F}}.\mathsf{Enc}(\mathsf{mpk}, \boldsymbol{x}, \mu)$: *Given a master public-key* mpk, *an attribute* $\boldsymbol{x} \in \mathcal{X} = \{0,1\}^*$, *and a message* $\mu \in \mathcal{M}$ *as input, the algorithm runs* AB-wHPS.Encap *to generate* $(\mathsf{CT}', k) \leftarrow \text{AB-wHPS.Encap}(\mathsf{mpk}, \boldsymbol{x})$, *and then samples* $s \xleftarrow{\$} \mathcal{S}$. *Furthermore, the algorithm computes and outputs*

$$\mathsf{ct} = (s, \mathsf{ct}_0, \mathsf{ct}_1) = (s, \mathsf{CT}', \mu + \mathsf{Ext}(k, s)).$$

- $\Pi_{\mathcal{F}}.\mathsf{Dec}(\mathsf{sk}_f, \mathsf{ct})$: *Given a ciphertext* $\mathsf{ct} = (s, \mathsf{ct}_0, \mathsf{ct}_1)$ *and a secret key* sk_f *as input, the algorithm runs* AB-wHPS.Decap *to generate* $k = \text{AB-wHPS.Decap}(\mathsf{sk}_f, \mathsf{ct}_0)$, *and then output* $\mu = \mathsf{ct}_1 - \mathsf{Ext}(k, s)$.

Our construction achieves a leakage resilient ABE, and can be re-calibrated into a leakage resilient PKE/IBE. We summarize the results in the following theorem, and defer the full proof to the full version, due to space limit.

Theorem 4.2. *Assume* Π *is a selectively (or adaptively, resp.) secure* $(\log|\mathcal{K}|, \log|\mathcal{K}|)$*-universal* AB-wHPS *for the policy function class* $\mathcal{F}$, *and* $\mathsf{Ext} : \mathcal{K} \times \mathcal{S} \to \mathcal{M}$ *be a* $(\log|\mathcal{K}| - \ell, \mathsf{negl}(\lambda))$*-extractor. Then the above* ABE *scheme* $\Pi_{\mathcal{F}} = \Pi_{\mathcal{F}}.\{\mathsf{Setup}, \mathsf{KeyGen}, \mathsf{Enc}, \mathsf{Dec}\}$ *for* $\mathcal{F}$ *is a selectively (or adaptively, resp.)* $\ell(\lambda)$*-leakage resilient attribute-based encryption scheme for the policy function class* $\mathcal{F}$ *in the relative-leakage model. Particularly,* $\Pi_{\mathcal{F}}$ *is aslo*

- *an* $\ell(\lambda)$*-leakage-resilient* PKE *in the relative-leakage model, if* $\mathcal{F}$ *contains only a single function that always outputs* 1.
- *an* $\ell(\lambda)$*-leakage-resilient* IBE *in the relative-leakage model, if* $\mathcal{F}$ *contains the following comparison functions, i.e., each function* $f_{\boldsymbol{y}} \in \mathcal{F}$ *is indexed by a vector* $\boldsymbol{y}$, *and* $f_{\boldsymbol{y}}(\boldsymbol{x}) = 1$ *if and only if* $\boldsymbol{y} = \boldsymbol{x}$.

Combining Theorem 3.12 and Theorem 4.2, we obtain the following results. Assume there exists a sel-sel (or ada-sel) secure ABE scheme with the message space $\mathbb{Z}_m$ for the function class $\mathcal{F} \wedge_{\|} \mathcal{G}$, where $\mathcal{G}$ is the class as in Definition 3.9 with parameters m, n, and the key-length (of the extra part, excluding the function description of f) of this underlying ABE scheme for policy function f is $s(f)$. Then the allowed leakage length of the above leakage resilient ABE (or IBE or PKE) scheme $\Pi_{\mathcal{F}}$ for the function class $\mathcal{F}$ is $\ell = (n \log m - 2\lambda)$ and the key-length of $\Pi_{\mathcal{F}}$ for f is $|\mathsf{sk}_f| = n \log m + |f| + s(\hat{f}_{f,g_y})$.

Furthermore, if the secret key size $s(\hat{f}_{f,g_y})$ is succinct, i.e., $s(\hat{f}_{f,g_y}) = o(|f_{f,g_y}|) = o(n \log m + |f|)$, then we can set sufficiently large n, m such that $n \log m = \omega(|f|)$. Consequently, the leakage rate of this scheme $\Pi_{\mathcal{F}}$ is $\frac{n \log m - 2\lambda}{n \log m + |f| + s(\hat{f}_{f,g_y})} = \frac{1 - \frac{2\lambda}{n \log m}}{1 + \frac{s(\hat{f}_{f,g_y}) + |f|}{n \log m}} \approx 1 - o(1)$, achieving the desired optimal leakage rate.

Finally, by combining Corollary 3.14 and Theorem 4.2, we obtain the following Corollary.

Corollary 4.3. *Assuming* LWE, *for all polynomial* $S = \mathsf{poly}(\lambda)$, *there exist* $1 - o(1)$ *leakage resilient* ABE *schemes in the relative leakage model, which are*

1. *adaptively secure for the comparison functions;*
2. *adaptively secure for* t-CNF* *functions of size up to* S;
3. *selectively secure for general circuits of size up to* S.

Remark 4.4. *We note that our ABE schemes are leakage resilient even if the policy function goes beyond the size bound* S. *The leakage rate would still be* $1 - o(1)$ *for a slightly restricted class that leaks* $n \log m - 2\lambda$ *on the part* $\boldsymbol{y}$, *the whole description of* f, *and the extra part of* sk_f^{Π} *(excluding the function description) of the underlying* AB-wHPS. *This is more restrictive than functions that leak* $n \log m - 2\lambda + |f|$ *from the whole secret key.*

5 Extension I: Optimal-Rate Leakage-Resilient Encryption Schemes in the BRM

In this section, we present how to use AB-wHPS to construct optimal-rate leakage resilient ABE in the BRM. We follow the structure of [5,25] by first amplifying the hash proof system and then combining it with a locally computable extractor [40]. In particular, we first amplify AB-wHPS through parallel repetition and random sampling in Sect. 5.1. Then, in Sect. 5.2, we generalize the notion of locally computable extractor by Vadhan [40] into one with larger alphabets, and show that a refined analysis of this tool can be used to derive $1 - o(1)$ leakage rate in the BRM, improving the prior analysis [5,35] that can only achieve a constant leakage rate. Finally in Sect. 5.3, we present the overall construction of our leakage resilient ABE in the BRM with the optimal leakage rate.

5.1 Amplification of AB-wHPS

Definition 5.1. *Let* n' *be a positive integer, and* $\mathcal{H} = \{h : [n'] \to \{0,1\}\}$ *be a function class where each function* $h_y \in \mathcal{H}$ *is indexed by a value* $y \in [n']$, *and* $h_y(x) = 1$ *if and only if* $x = y$.

Construction 52. (Construction of Amplified AB-wHPS.). *Let* $\Pi =$ AB-wHPS.{Setup, KeyGen, Encap, Encap*, Decap} *be an* AB-wHPS *with the encapsulated-key-space* $\mathcal{K}$ *and attribute space* $\mathcal{X} = \{0,1\}^* \times [n']$ *for a class of functions* $\mathcal{F} \wedge_{\|} \mathcal{H}$, *and let* $t \leq n'$ *be a positive integer. Then a new* AB-wHPS $\Pi_{\|}^{n',t}$ *with attribute space* $\{0,1\}^*$ *and the encapsulated-key-space* $\mathcal{K}^t$ *for the function class* $\mathcal{F}$ *can be constructed.*

- $\Pi_{\|}^{n',t}.\mathsf{Setup}(1^\lambda)$: *The algorithm runs* $(\mathsf{mpk}^{\Pi}, \mathsf{msk}^{\Pi}) \xleftarrow{\$} \Pi.\mathsf{Setup}(1^\lambda)$, *and outputs* $\mathsf{mpk} := \mathsf{mpk}^{\Pi}$, *and* $\mathsf{msk} := \mathsf{msk}^{\Pi}$.

- $\Pi_{\|}^{n',t}$.KeyGen(msk, f): *Given a function* $f \in \mathcal{F}$, *the algorithm first sets* $\hat{f}^i = \hat{f}^i_{f,h_i} \in \mathcal{F} \wedge_{\|} \mathcal{H}$ *for every* $i \in [n']$, *and runs* AB-wHPS.KeyGen n' *times to generate* $\mathsf{sk}_{\hat{f}^i} \xleftarrow{\$} \Pi.\mathsf{KeyGen}(\mathsf{msk}^{\Pi}, \hat{f}^i)$ *for* $i \in [n']$. *The algorithm outputs*

$$\mathsf{sk}_f := \left(\mathsf{sk}_{\hat{f}^1}, \mathsf{sk}_{\hat{f}^2}, \ldots, \mathsf{sk}_{\hat{f}^{n'}}\right).$$

- $\Pi_{\|}^{n',t}$.Encap(mpk, $\boldsymbol{x}$): *Given* mpk *and an attribute* $\boldsymbol{x} \in \{0,1\}^*$ *as input, the algorithm chooses a random subset* $\boldsymbol{r} := \{r_1, \ldots, r_t\} \subseteq [n']$ *and computes*

$$(\mathsf{CT}_i, k_i) \xleftarrow{\$} \Pi.\mathsf{Encap}(\mathsf{mpk}, (\boldsymbol{x}, r_i)) \text{ for all } i \in [t].$$

The algorithm finally outputs $\mathsf{CT} := (\boldsymbol{r}, \mathsf{CT}_1, \ldots, \mathsf{CT}_t)$ *and* $\boldsymbol{k} = (k_1, \ldots, k_t)^\top$.
- $\Pi_{\|}^{n',t}$.Encap*(mpk, $\boldsymbol{x}$): *Given* mpk *and an attribute* $\boldsymbol{x} \in \{0,1\}^*$ *as input, the algorithm chooses a random subset* $\boldsymbol{r} := \{r_1, \ldots, r_t\} \subseteq [n']$ *and computes*

$$\mathsf{CT}_i \xleftarrow{\$} \Pi.\mathsf{Encap}^*(\mathsf{mpk}, (\boldsymbol{x}, r_i)) \text{ for all } i \in [t].$$

Finally, the algorithm outputs $\mathsf{CT} := (\boldsymbol{r}, \mathsf{CT}_1, \ldots, \mathsf{CT}_t)$.
- $\Pi_{\|}^{n',t}$.Decap(sk_f, CT): *Given a ciphertext* $\mathsf{CT} := (\boldsymbol{r}, \mathsf{CT}_1, \ldots, \mathsf{CT}_t)$ *and a secret key* $\mathsf{sk}_f := \left(\mathsf{sk}_{\hat{f}^1}, \mathsf{sk}_{\hat{f}^2}, \ldots, \mathsf{sk}_{\hat{f}^{n'}}\right)$, *the algorithm runs* Π.Decap *to generate* $k_i = \Pi.\mathsf{Decap}(\mathsf{sk}_{\hat{f}^{r_i}}, \mathsf{CT}_i)$ *for* $i \in [t]$, *and outputs* $\boldsymbol{k} = (k_1, \ldots, k_t)^\top$ *if* $\hat{f}^{r_i}(\boldsymbol{x}, r_i) = 1$ *for all* $i \in [t]$. *Otherwise, the algorithm outputs* $\perp$.

Next, we present the following amplification theorem, which is essential an extension of the work [5]. Due to space limit, we defer the full proof to the full version of this paper.

Theorem 5.3. *Assume* Π *is an* (l, w)*-universal* AB-wHPS *with the encapsulated-key-space* $\mathcal{K}$ *for* $\mathcal{F} \wedge_{\|} \mathcal{H}$. *Then the above amplified construction of* $\Pi_{\|}^{n',t}$ *is an* $(t \cdot l, t \cdot w)$*-universal* AB-wHPS *with the encapsulated-key-set* $\mathcal{K}^t$ *for* $\mathcal{F}$. *Furthermore,*

- *if the underlying* Π *is selectively (or adaptively) secure, then the* $\Pi_{\|}^{n',t}$ *is also selectively (or adaptively) secure;*
- *if the secret-key-size of* Π *scheme for the policy function* f *is* $(|f| + s(f))$,[5] *then the secret-key size of the* $\Pi_{\|}^{n',t}$ *for* f *is* $n' \times (|f| + \log n' + s(\hat{f}_{f,h}))$.

Combining Theorem 3.12 and Theorem 5.3, we obtain the following corollary.

Corollary 5.4. *Assume there exists an* ABE *scheme with the message space* $\mathbb{Z}_m$ *for the function class* $\mathcal{F} \wedge_{\|} \mathcal{H} \wedge_{\|} \mathcal{G}$, *where* $\mathcal{G}$ *with parameters* m, n *and* $\mathcal{H}$ *with parameter* n' *are as Definitions 3.9 and 5.1, then there exists an amplified* AB-wHPS *with the encapsulated-key-space* $\mathbb{Z}_m^t$ *for the function class* $\mathcal{F}$.

[5] Recall that the function $s(f)$ denotes the size of the extra part of the secret key, excluding the description of the function.

5.2 Locally Computable Extractor

Definition 5.5 (Locally Computable Extractor, Definition 6 in [40]). *An extractor* $\mathsf{Ext} : \{0,1\}^n \times \{0,1\}^d \to \{0,1\}^v$ *is said to be* t*-locally computable if for every* $r \in \{0,1\}^d$, $\mathsf{Ext}(\boldsymbol{x}, r)$ *depends only on* t*-bits of* $\boldsymbol{x} \in \{0,1\}^n$.

For our application (constructing leakage-resilient encryption in the BRM), we need a generalized variant of the above notion. Let $\boldsymbol{x} \in \{0,1\}^{nk}$ be a vector. We can view it as a concatenation of n vectors $\boldsymbol{x}_i \in \{0,1\}^k$ for $i \in [n]$, i.e., $\boldsymbol{x} = (\boldsymbol{x}_1^\top, \ldots, \boldsymbol{x}_n^\top)^\top$. In this case, each $\boldsymbol{x}_i \in \{0,1\}^k$ can be viewed as a symbol of some larger alphabet, i.e., $\Gamma = \{0,1\}^k$, and we will need a locally computable extractor for Γ as follow.

Definition 5.6 (Locally Computable Extractor for Larger Alphabets). *Let* $\Gamma = \{0,1\}^k$ *be some alphabet. An extractor* $\mathsf{Ext} : \Gamma^n \times \{0,1\}^d \to \{0,1\}^v$ *is* t*-locally computable with respect to* Γ *if for every* $\boldsymbol{r} \in \{0,1\}^d$, $\mathsf{Ext}(\boldsymbol{x}, \boldsymbol{r})$ *depends only on* t *symbols of* $\boldsymbol{x} = (\boldsymbol{x}_1^\top, \ldots, \boldsymbol{x}_n^\top)^\top \in \Gamma^n$.

Generally, a locally computable extractor can be obtained in two steps [40]: (1) the extractor uses part of the seed to select t bits (or symbols) of $\boldsymbol{x}$, and (2) the remaining seed is used to apply a standard extractor on the selected bits/symbols in the previous step. Vadhan [40] showed that as long as the selection in step (1) achieves an average sampler, then the combined steps would achieve a locally computable extractor. We summarize the result of Vadhan [40] below. We first recall the notion of an average sampler.

Definition 5.7 (Average Sampler, Definition 8 in [40]). *A function* $\mathrm{Samp} : \{0,1\}^r \to [n]^t$ *is a* (μ, θ, γ) *average sampler if for every function* $f : [n] \to [0,1]$ *with average value* $\frac{1}{n}\sum_i f(i) \geq \mu$,

$$\Pr_{(i_1,\ldots,i_t) \xleftarrow{\$} \mathrm{Samp}(U_r)} \left[\frac{1}{t} \sum_{j=1}^{t} f(i_j) < \mu - \theta \right] \leq \gamma.$$

Next, we present a theorem by Vadhan in [40] that describes detailed requirements for a locally computable extractor.

Theorem 5.8 (Theorem 10 in [40]). *Suppose that* $\mathrm{Samp} : \{0,1\}^r \to [n]^t$ *is a* (μ, θ, γ) *average sampler with distinct samples for* $\mu = (\delta - 2\tau)/\log(1/\tau)$ *and* $\theta = \tau/\log(1/\tau)$, *and* $\mathsf{Ext} : \{0,1\}^t \times \{0,1\}^d \to \{0,1\}^v$ *is a strong* $((\delta - 3\tau)t, \varepsilon)$ *extractor. Define* $\mathsf{Ext}' : \{0,1\}^n \times \{0,1\}^{r+d} \to \{0,1\}^v$ *by*

$$\mathsf{Ext}'(\boldsymbol{x}, (\boldsymbol{y}_1, \boldsymbol{y}_2)) = \mathsf{Ext}(\boldsymbol{x}_{\mathrm{Samp}(\boldsymbol{y}_1)}, \boldsymbol{y}_2).$$

Then Ext' *is a* t*-local strong* $(\delta n, \varepsilon + \gamma + 2^{-\Omega(\tau n)})$ *extractor.*

As we mentioned above, our application needs a locally computable extractor for larger alphabets, which may not be implied directly from Theorem 5.8. To tackle this issue, we define the following sampling procedure **Sampler 1** that outputs t distinct symbols of samples, and then prove that **Sampler 1** is in fact a good average sampler as needed in Theorem 5.8. This would imply a locally computable extractor for larger alphabets as required in our application.

Notations for the Sampling. Before describing the algorithm, we set up some notations as follows. Let $\Gamma = \{0,1\}^k$ and $\boldsymbol{x} = (\boldsymbol{x}_1^\top, \ldots, \boldsymbol{x}_n^\top)^\top \in \Gamma^n$ be a vector of n symbols, where $\boldsymbol{x}_i = (x_{i1}, x_{i2}, \ldots, x_{ik})^\top \in \Gamma = \{0,1\}^k$ for $i \in [n]$. Let S denote a subset of $[n] \times [k]$, i.e. S contains tuples $(i,j) \in [n] \times [k]$ as its elements. In this case, we define $\boldsymbol{x}_S = \{x_{ij}\}_{(i,j)\in S}$. Then, we define **Sampler 1** as below.

Sampler 1: Sample a random subset R of $[n]$ that contains t *distinct* elements, i.e., $R = \{r_1, \ldots, r_t\}$, and output $S := \{(r_i, j)\}_{i\in[t], j\in[k]}$. Then we derive the following lemma.

Lemma 5.9. *For any* $\lambda \in \mathbb{Z}$, $\mu, \theta \in (0,1]$ *and* $\gamma = 2\lambda \exp(-t\theta^2/4) + \left(\frac{t(t-1)}{2n}\right)^\lambda$, ***Sampler 1*** *is a* (μ, θ, γ) *averaging sampler.*

Proof. According to the natural bijection between $[nk]$ and $[n]\times[k]$, to prove that **Sampler 1** is a good average sampler as Definition 5.7, it suffices to show that for any $f : [n] \times [k] \to [0,1]$ such that $\frac{1}{nk}\sum_{i\in[n], j\in[k]} f(i,j) \geq \mu$, the following inequality holds:

$$\Pr_{S \xleftarrow{\$} \textbf{Sampler 1}}\left[\frac{1}{|S|}\sum_{(i,j)\in S} f(i,j) < \mu - \theta\right] \leq \gamma. \tag{1}$$

It might be hard to prove inequality (1) directly, since all blocks output by **Sampler 1** are distinct. To handle this issue, we then define the following **Sampler 2** through using "sample with replacement" and rejection sampling. It is not hard to show that these two procedures are statistically close. Furthermore, by using use a Chernoff bound argument, we show that **Sampler 2** is a good average sampler as required in Theorem 5.8. Thus, we conclude that **Sampler 1** with any strong extractor yields a locally computable extractor for larger alphabets.

Sampler 2:

1. Sample $R = \{r_1, \ldots, r_t\}$ from $[n]^t$ uniformly at random.
   - If all elements are distinct, then output $S := \{(r_i, j)\}_{i\in[t], j\in[k]}$ and terminate.
2. Otherwise, i.e., there is a repeated element, discard the whole sample and redo Step 1.
   Note. the algorithm will only redo Step 1 up to λ times. If the algorithm does not produce an output by then, then output $\perp$.

Next we analyze **Sampler 1** and **Sampler 2** by the following two claims. Due to space limit, we defer the full proof to the full version of this paper.

Claim 5.10. *For a set X consisting of $n = n(\lambda)$ different blocks and the parameters $t = t(\lambda)$ such that $t(t-1) < n$, the output distributions of Sample 1 and Sample 2 are statistically close.*

Claim 5.11. *For any μ, t, θ, n, Sampler 2 is a (μ, θ, γ) average sampler conditioned on non-$\perp$ output, where $\gamma = 2\lambda \exp(-t\theta^2/4)$.*

The proof of the lemma follows by the above Claims 5.10 and 5.11. □

Furthermore, by applying the **Sample 1** to Theorem 5.8 with the following parameters setting, we derive the following theorem.

Parameter Setting. Taking λ as the security parameter, we set all the parameters in the following way: $k = \mathsf{poly}(\lambda), n = \mathsf{poly}(\lambda), t = \lambda \log^3(nk), \delta = \frac{1}{\log(nk)}, \tau = \frac{1}{6\log(nk)}, \mu = \frac{2}{3\log(nk)\log(6\log(nk))}, \theta = \frac{1}{6\log(nk)\log(6\log(nk))}, \gamma = 2\lambda\exp(-t\theta^2/4) + \left(\frac{t(t-1)}{2n}\right)^{\lambda}, \varepsilon = \mathsf{negl}(\lambda)$.

Theorem 5.12. *Let $\Gamma = \{0,1\}^k$, $\mathrm{Samp} : \{0,1\}^r \to [n]^t$ be the* ***Sampler 1*** *(as a (μ, θ, γ) average sampler), and let $\mathsf{Ext} : \Gamma^t \times \{0,1\}^d \to \{0,1\}^v$ be a strong $((\delta - 3\tau)tk, \varepsilon)$ extractor. Define $\mathsf{Ext}' : \Gamma^n \times \{0,1\}^{r+d} \to \{0,1\}^v$ as*

$$\mathsf{Ext}'(\boldsymbol{x}, (\boldsymbol{y}_1, \boldsymbol{y}_2)) = \mathsf{Ext}(\boldsymbol{x}_{\mathrm{Samp}(\boldsymbol{y}_1)}, \boldsymbol{y}_2).$$

Then Ext' is a t-block-local strong $(\delta nk, \varepsilon + \gamma + 2^{-\Omega(\tau n)})$ extractor, where $\varepsilon + \gamma + 2^{-\Omega(\tau n)} = \mathsf{negl}(\lambda)$ according to the setting of parameters.

5.3 Leakage-Resilient Encryption in the Bounded-Retrieval Model

In this section, we construct leakage-resilient encryption schemes in the BRM, through combining an random extractor with an amplified AB-wHPS presented in Sect. 5.1. Below, we give the specific construction of leakage resilient ABE scheme in the BRM from an amplified AB-wHPS.

Construction 513. (Construction in the) BRM). *Let $\Pi = \mathsf{AB\text{-}wHPS}.\{\mathsf{Setup}, \mathsf{KeyGen}, \mathsf{Encap}, \mathsf{Encap}^*, \mathsf{Decap}\}$ be an amplified AB-wHPS with integer parameters n', t, the encapsulated-key-space $\mathcal{K}^t$ and attribute space $\mathcal{X} = \{0,1\}^*$ for a class of policy functions $\mathcal{F} = \{f : \{0,1\}^* \to \{0,1\}\}$. Let $\mathsf{Ext} : \mathcal{K}^t \times \mathcal{S} \to \mathcal{M}$ be a strong extractor, where three sets $\mathcal{K}, \mathcal{S}, \mathcal{M}$ are efficient ensembles, k denotes the size of $\mathcal{K}$. Furthermore, assume that $\mathcal{M}$ is an additive group. Then, an ABE scheme $\Pi_{\mathcal{F}} = \Pi_{\mathcal{F}}.\{\mathsf{Setup}, \mathsf{KeyGen}, \mathsf{Enc}, \mathsf{Dec}\}$ with message space $\mathcal{M}$ and policy function class $\mathcal{F}$ can be constructed as follows:*

- *$\Pi_{\mathcal{F}}.\mathsf{Setup}(1^\lambda)$: The algorithm runs $(\mathsf{mpk}^{\Pi}, \mathsf{msk}^{\Pi}) \xleftarrow{\$} \Pi.\mathsf{Setup}(1^\lambda)$, and outputs $\mathsf{mpk} := \mathsf{mpk}^{\Pi}$, and $\mathsf{msk} := \mathsf{msk}^{\Pi}$.*
- *$\Pi_{\mathcal{F}}.\mathsf{KeyGen}(\mathsf{msk}, f)$: $\Pi_{\mathcal{F}}.\mathsf{KeyGen}(\mathsf{msk}, f)$: Given a master secret-key msk and a function $f \in \mathcal{F}$ as input, the algorithm runs $\mathsf{sk}_f^{\Pi} \xleftarrow{\$} \mathsf{AB\text{-}wHPS.KeyGen}(\mathsf{msk}, f)$ and output $\mathsf{sk}_f := \mathsf{sk}_f^{\Pi}$.*

- $\Pi_{\mathcal{F}}.\mathsf{Enc}(\mathsf{mpk}, \boldsymbol{x}, \mu)$: *Given a master public-key* mpk, *an attribute* $\boldsymbol{x} \in \{0,1\}^*$ *and a message* $\mu \in \mathcal{M}$ *as input, the algorithm runs* AB-wHPS.Encap *to generate* $(\mathsf{CT}', \boldsymbol{k}) \leftarrow$AB-wHPS.Encap$(\mathsf{mpk}, \boldsymbol{x})$ *with* $\boldsymbol{k} \in \mathcal{K}^t$, *and then samples* $s \xleftarrow{\$} \mathcal{S}$. *Furthermore, the algorithm computes and outputs*

$$\mathsf{ct} = (s, \mathsf{ct}_0, \mathsf{ct}_1) = (s, \mathsf{CT}', \mu + \mathsf{Ext}(\boldsymbol{k}, s)).$$

- $\Pi_{\mathcal{F}}.\mathsf{Dec}(\mathsf{sk}_f, \mathsf{ct})$: *Given a ciphertext* $\mathsf{ct} = (s, \mathsf{ct}_0, \mathsf{ct}_1)$ *and a secret key* sk_f *as input, the algorithm runs* AB-wHPS.Decap *to generate* $\boldsymbol{k} =$ AB-wHPS. Decap$(\mathsf{sk}_f, \mathsf{ct}_0)$ *with* $\boldsymbol{k} \in \mathcal{K}^t$, *and then output* $\mu = \mathsf{ct}_1 - \mathsf{Ext}(\boldsymbol{k}, s)$.

Parameter Setting. For security parameter λ, we set the system parameters as follows: $k = \mathsf{poly}(\lambda), n' = \mathsf{poly}(\lambda), t = \lambda \log^3(n'k)$, $\delta = \frac{1}{\log(n'k)}, \tau = \frac{1}{6\log(n'k)}, \varepsilon = \mathsf{negl}(\lambda)$. Moreover, for the proof of leakage-resilience in the BRM, we let $\mathsf{Ext} : \mathcal{K}^t \times \mathcal{S} \to \mathcal{M}$ be a $((\delta - 3\tau)tk, \varepsilon)$-extractor.

Next, we prove that the construction is a leakage resilient ABE in the BRM. Our proof uses a technique of locally computable extractors [40], i.e., Theorem 5.12, in a black-box way. Due to the space limit, we defer the detailed proof to the full version of this paper.

Theorem 5.14. *Assume* Π *is a selectively (or adaptively, resp.) secure amplified* AB-wHPS *with integer parameters* $n', t = \lambda \log^3(n'k)$ *for the policy function class* $\mathcal{F}$, *and* $\mathsf{Ext} : \mathcal{K}^t \times \mathcal{S} \to \mathcal{M}$ *be a strong extractor. Then the above* ABE *scheme* $\Pi_{\mathcal{F}} = \Pi_{\mathcal{F}}.\{\mathsf{Setup}, \mathsf{KeyGen}, \mathsf{Enc}, \mathsf{Dec}\}$ *for* $\mathcal{F}$ *is a selectively (or adaptively, resp.)* ℓ*-leakage-resilient attribute-based encryption scheme with message space* $\mathcal{M}$ *in the* BRM *where* $\ell = kn' - \frac{kn'}{\log(kn')}$.

Particularly, $\Pi_{\mathcal{F}}$ *is also*

- *an* ℓ*-leakage-resilient public-key encryption scheme in the* BRM *with* $\ell = kn' - \frac{kn'}{\log(kn')}$, *if* $\mathcal{F}$ *contains only a single function that always outputs* 1.
- *a selectively (or adaptively, resp.)* ℓ*-leakage-resilient identity-based encryption scheme in the* BRM *with* $\ell = kn' - \frac{kn'}{\log(kn')}$, *if* $\mathcal{F}$ *contains the following comparison functions, i.e., each function* $f_{\boldsymbol{y}} \in \mathcal{F}$ *is indexed by a vector* $\boldsymbol{y}$, *and* $f_{\boldsymbol{y}}(\boldsymbol{x}) = 1$ *if and only if* $\boldsymbol{y} = \boldsymbol{x}$.

Moreover,

1. *Public-key (resp. master public-key) size of* $\Pi_{\mathcal{F}}$ *is the same as that of* Π, *which is not dependent on leakage parameter* ℓ.
2. *The locality-parameter is* $t = \lambda \log^3(n'k)$. *Thus, the size of secret-key accessed during decryption depends on* t, *but not* ℓ.
3. *The ciphertext-size/encryption-time/decryption-time of* $\Pi_{\mathcal{F}}$ *depends on* t, *but not* ℓ.

Combining Corollary 5.4 and Theorem 5.14, we obtain the following results. Assume there exists an ABE scheme with the message space $\mathbb{Z}_m$ for the function class $\mathcal{F} \wedge_{||} \mathcal{H} \wedge_{||} \mathcal{G}$, where $\mathcal{G}$ with parameters m, n and $\mathcal{H}$ with parameter n' are as defined in Definitions 3.9 and 5.1, and the key-length (of the extra part, excluding the function description of f) of this underlying ABE scheme for policy function f is $s(f)$. Then the largest allowed leakage length of the above ABE (or IBE or PKE) scheme $\Pi_{\mathcal{F}}$ for the function class $\mathcal{F}$ is $\ell = (kn' - \frac{kn'}{\log(kn')})$ with $k = n \log m$ and the key-length of $\Pi_{\mathcal{F}}$ for f is $|\mathsf{sk}_f| = n'(n \log m + \log n' + |f| + s(\hat{f}_{f,h,g_y}))$.

Furthermore, if the secret key size $s(\hat{f}_{f,h,g_y})$)is succinct, i.e., $s(\hat{f}_{f,h,g_y}) = o(|\hat{f}_{f,h,g_y}|) = o(n \log m + \log n' + |f|)$, then we can set sufficiently large n, m, n' such that $(\log n' + |f|) = o(n \log m)$. Consequently, the leakage rate of this scheme $\Pi_{\mathcal{F}}$ is $\frac{kn' - \frac{kn'}{\log(kn')}}{n'(n \log m + \log n' + |f| + s(\hat{f}_{f,h,g_y}))} = \frac{1 - \frac{1}{\log(nn' \log m)}}{1 + \frac{\log n' + |f| + s(\hat{f}_{f,h,g_y})}{n \log m}} \approx 1 - o(1)$, achieving the desired optimal leakage rate.

Finally, by combining Corollary 3.14 and Theorem 5.14, we obtain the following Corollary.

Corollary 5.15. *Assuming* LWE, *for all polynomial* $S = \mathsf{poly}(\lambda)$, *there exist* $1 - o(1)$ *leakage resilient* ABE *schemes in the* BRM, *which are*

1. *adaptively secure for the comparison functions;*
2. *adaptively secure for* t-CNF* *functions of size up to* S;
3. *selectively secure for general circuits of size up to* S.

For unbounded polynomial S, our schemes are still leakage resilient with the optimal rate for a smaller function class. See Remark 4.4 for the discussion.

6 Extension II: Leakage on Multiple Keys

Our prior ABE constructions from AB-wHPS only achieve leakage resilience in the one-key setting where the adversary can only leak on one of the all possible decrypting keys with respect to the challenge attribute. In this section, we show how to achieve leakage resilience in the *multiple-key* setting where the attacker can obtain leakage on ω possible decrypting keys for any bounded polynomial ω. Our construction leverages the normal AB-wHPS (where the ciphertext indistinguishability holds when the adversary gets one decrypting key) and a threshold secret sharing scheme, following the bootstrapping idea of the work [21].

Construction 61. (Extended Leakage Resilient ABE). *Let* $\Pi = \Pi.\{\mathsf{Setup}, \mathsf{KeyGen}, \mathsf{Encap}, \mathsf{Encap}^*, \mathsf{Decap}\}$ *be a* $(\log |\mathcal{K}|, \log |\mathcal{K}|)$*-universal* AB-wHPS *with the encapsulated-key-space* $\mathcal{K}$ *and attribute space* $\mathcal{X} = \{0,1\}^*$ *for a class of policy functions* $\mathcal{F} = \{f : \{0,1\}^* \to \{0,1\}\}$. *Let* $\mathsf{Ext} : \mathcal{K} \times \mathcal{S} \to \mathcal{M}$ *be a* $(\log |\mathcal{K}| - \ell, \varepsilon)$*-extractor, where* $\mathcal{K}, \mathcal{S}, \mathcal{M}$ *are efficient ensembles,* $\ell = \ell(\lambda)$ *is some parameter and* $\varepsilon = \varepsilon(\lambda) = \mathsf{negl}(\lambda)$ *is negligible. In addition, let* $(\mathsf{Share}, \mathsf{Rec})$ *be a* $(\hat{t}+1)$*-out-of-n threshold secret sharing scheme with respect to secret domain* $\mathcal{M}$, *an additive group.*

Then, a leakage-resilient ABE *scheme* $\Pi_{\mathcal{F}} = \Pi_{\mathcal{F}}.\{\mathsf{Setup}, \mathsf{KeyGen}, \mathsf{Enc}, \mathsf{Dec}\}$ *with message space* $\mathcal{M}$ *for policy function class* $\mathcal{F}$ *can be constructed as follows:*

- $\Pi_{\mathcal{F}}.\mathsf{Setup}(1^\lambda, n)$: *The algorithm runs* $(\mathsf{mpk}_i^{\Pi}, \mathsf{msk}_i^{\Pi}) \xleftarrow{\$} \Pi.\mathsf{Setup}(1^\lambda)$ *for every* $i \in [n]$, *and outputs* $\mathsf{mpk} := \{\mathsf{mpk}_i^{\Pi}\}_{i\in[n]}$ *and* $\mathsf{msk} := \{\mathsf{msk}_i^{\Pi}\}_{i\in[n]}$.
- $\Pi_{\mathcal{F}}.\mathsf{KeyGen}(\mathsf{msk}, f)$: *Given a master secret-key* $\mathsf{msk} := \{\mathsf{msk}_i^{\Pi}\}_{i\in[n]}$ *and a function* $f \in \mathcal{F}$ *as input, the algorithm first chooses a random subset of cardinality* $\hat{t}+1$, *i.e.,* $\Gamma = \{r_1, \ldots, r_{\hat{t}+1}\} \subseteq [n]$, *and then runs* $\mathsf{sk}_f^{(r_i)} \xleftarrow{\$} \Pi.\mathsf{KeyGen}(\mathsf{msk}_{r_i}^{\Pi}, f)$ *for* $i \in [\hat{t}+1]$. *Finally, the algorithm outputs*

$$\mathsf{sk}_f := (\Gamma, \mathsf{sk}_f^{(r_1)}, \ldots, \mathsf{sk}_f^{(r_{\hat{t}+1})}).$$

- $\Pi_{\mathcal{F}}.\mathsf{Enc}(\mathsf{mpk}, \boldsymbol{x}, \mu)$: *Given a master public-key* $\mathsf{mpk} := \{\mathsf{mpk}_i^{\Pi}\}_{i\in[n]}$, *an attribute* $\boldsymbol{x} \in \mathcal{X} = \{0,1\}^*$ *and a message* $\mu \in \mathcal{M}$ *as input, the algorithm first runs* $(\mu_1, \ldots, \mu_n) \xleftarrow{\$} \mathsf{Share}(\mu)$. *Furthermore, the algorithm runs* $\Pi.\mathsf{Encap}$ *to generate* $(\mathsf{CT}_i, k_i) \xleftarrow{\$} \Pi.\mathsf{Encap}(\mathsf{mpkmpk}_i, \boldsymbol{x})$ *for every* $i \in [n]$. *Next, the algorithm samples* $s_1, \ldots, s_n \xleftarrow{\$} \mathcal{S}$, *and outputs*

$$\begin{aligned}\mathsf{ct} &= (s_1, \ldots, s_n, \mathsf{ct}_1, \ldots, \mathsf{ct}_n, \mathsf{ct}_{n+1}, \ldots, \mathsf{ct}_{2n})\\ &= (s_1, \ldots, s_n, \mathsf{CT}_1, \ldots, \mathsf{CT}_n, \mu_1 + \mathsf{Ext}(k_1, s_1), \ldots, \mu_n + \mathsf{Ext}(k_n, s_n)).\end{aligned}$$

- $\Pi_{\mathcal{F}}.\mathsf{Dec}(\mathsf{sk}_f, \mathsf{ct})$: *Given a ciphertext* $\mathsf{ct} = (\{s_i\}_{i\in[n]}, \{\mathsf{ct}_i\}_{i\in[2n]})$ *and a secret key* $\mathsf{sk}_f = (\Gamma, \{\mathsf{sk}_f^{(r_i)}\}_{i\in[\hat{t}+1]})$ *as input, the algorithm first runs* $\Pi.\mathsf{Decap}$ *to generate* $k_{r_i} = \Pi.\mathsf{Decap}(\mathsf{sk}_f^{(r_i)}, \mathsf{ct}_{r_i})$ *and* $\mu_{r_i} = \mathsf{ct}_{n+r_i} - \mathsf{Ext}(k_{r_i}, s_{r_i})$ *for every* $i \in [\hat{t}+1]$. *Then, the algorithm outputs* $\mu = \mathsf{Rec}(\mu_{r_1}, \ldots, \mu_{r_{\hat{t}+1}})$.

Parameter Setting. For security parameter λ, given any $\omega = \mathsf{poly}(\lambda)$, we set $\hat{t} = \Theta(\omega^2\lambda)$ and $n = \Theta(\omega^2\hat{t})$. For details, we refer readers to the full version of this paper.

Our construction achieves a leakage resilient ABE in the multiple key setting. We summarize the results in the following theorem, and defer the full proof to the full version, duc to space limit.

Theorem 6.2. *Assume* Π *is a selectively (or adaptively, resp.) secure* $(\log|\mathcal{K}|, \log|\mathcal{K}|)$*-universal* AB-wHPS *for the policy function class* $\mathcal{F}$, *and* $\mathsf{Ext} : \mathcal{K} \times \mathcal{S} \to \mathcal{M}$ *be a* $(\log|\mathcal{K}| - \ell, \mathsf{negl}(\lambda))$*-extractor. Then the above* ABE *scheme* $\Pi_{\mathcal{F}} = \Pi_{\mathcal{F}}.\{\mathsf{Setup}, \mathsf{KeyGen}, \mathsf{Enc}, \mathsf{Dec}\}$ *for* $\mathcal{F}$ *is a selectively (or adaptively, resp.)* $(\ell(\lambda), \omega(\lambda))$*-leakage resilient attribute-based encryption scheme for* $\mathcal{F}$ *in the relative-leakage model, for any fixed bounded polynomial* $\omega(\lambda) = \mathsf{poly}(\lambda)$.

The corresponding leakage rate is $\frac{\ell(\lambda)}{(\hat{t}+1)(|\mathsf{sk}_f|+\log n)}$. *Furthermore, when the underlying secret keys* $(\mathsf{sk}_f^{(r_1)}, \ldots, \mathsf{sk}_f^{(r_{\hat{t}+1})})$ *form a block source under each leakage function, the corresponding leakage rate is* $\frac{\ell(\lambda)}{(|\mathsf{sk}_f|+\log n)}$.

Combining Theorem 3.12 and Theorem 6.2, we obtain the following results. Assume there exists an sel-ada/sel-sel (or ada-ada/ada-sel) secure ABE scheme with the message space $\mathbb{Z}_{\bar{m}}$ for the function class $\mathcal{F} \wedge_{\parallel} \mathcal{G}$, where $\mathcal{G}$ is the class as in Definition 3.9 with parameters $\bar{m}, \bar{n}$, and the key-length (of the extra part, excluding the function description of f) of this underlying ABE scheme for policy function f is $s(f)$. Then the allowed leakage length of the above leakage resilient ABE scheme $\Pi_{\mathcal{F}}$ with parameters $n, \hat{t}, \omega$ as in the above paragraph setting for the function class $\mathcal{F}$ is $\ell = (\bar{n}\log\bar{m} - 2\lambda)$ and the key-length of $\Pi_{\mathcal{F}}$ for f is $|\mathsf{sk}_f| = (\hat{t}+1)(\log n + \bar{n}\log\bar{m} + |f| + s(\hat{f}_{f,g_y}))$.

Furthermore, if the secret key size $s(\hat{f}_{f,g_y})$ is succinct, i.e., $s(\hat{f}_{f,g_y}) = o(\bar{n}\log\bar{m} + |f|)$, then we can set sufficiently large $n, \bar{m}, \bar{n}$ such that $(\log n + |f|) = o(\bar{n}\log\bar{m})$. Consequently, when the underlying secret keys form a block source under each leakage function, the corresponding leakage rate of this scheme $\Pi_{\mathcal{F}}$ is $\frac{\bar{n}\log\bar{m} - 2\lambda}{\log n + \bar{n}\log\bar{m} + |f| + s(\hat{f}_{f,g_y})} = \frac{1 - \frac{2\lambda}{\bar{n}\log\bar{m}}}{1 + \frac{\log n + |f| + s(\hat{f}_{f,g_y})}{\bar{n}\log\bar{m}}} \approx 1 - o(1)$, achieving the desired optimal leakage rate.

Finally, by combining Corollary 3.14 and Theorem 6.2, we obtain the following Corollary.

Corollary 6.3. *Assuming* LWE, *for any* $S = \mathsf{poly}(\lambda)$ *and* $\omega = \mathsf{poly}(\lambda)$, *there exist* (ℓ, ω)*-leakage resilient* ABE*'s in the relative leakage model, which are*

1. *adaptively secure for* t-CNF^* *functions of size up to* S*;*
2. *selectively secure for general circuits of size up to* S*.*

Moreover, when the underlying secret keys form a block source under the each leakage function, the corresponding leakage rate is $1 - o(1)$.

Furthermore, we can also achieve similar results in the BRM. By combining Corollary 3.14, Theorem 5.3 and Theorem 6.2, we obtain the following corollary.

Corollary 6.4. *Assuming* LWE, *for any polynomial* $S = \mathsf{poly}(\lambda)$ *and* $\omega = \mathsf{poly}(\lambda)$, *there exist* (ℓ, ω)*-leakage resilient* ABE *schemes in the* BRM, *which are*

1. *adaptively secure for* t-CNF^* *functions of size up to* S*;*
2. *selectively secure for general circuits of size up to* S*.*

Moreover, when the underlying secret keys form a block source under the each leakage function, the corresponding leakage rate is $1 - o(1)$.

Acknowledgements. We would like to thank the reviewers of PKC 2022 for their insightful advices. Qiqi Lai is supported by the National Natural Science Foundation of China (62172266, 61802241, U2001205), the National Cryptography Development Foundation during the 13th Five-year Plan Period (MMJJ20180217), and the Fundamental Research Funds for the Central Universities (GK202103093).

Feng-Hao Liu and Zhedong Wang are supported by the NSF Career Award CNS-1942400.

References

1. Agrawal, D., Archambeault, B., Rao, J.R., Rohatgi, P.: The EM side—channel(s). In: Kaliski, B.S., Koç, K., Paar, C. (eds.) CHES 2002. LNCS, vol. 2523, pp. 29–45. Springer, Heidelberg (2003). https://doi.org/10.1007/3-540-36400-5_4
2. Agrawal, S., Boneh, D., Boyen, X.: Efficient lattice (H)IBE in the standard model. In: Gilbert [19], pp. 553–572
3. Agrawal, S., Freeman, D.M., Vaikuntanathan, V.: Functional encryption for inner product predicates from learning with errors. In: Lee, D.H., Wang, X. (eds.) ASIACRYPT 2011. LNCS, vol. 7073, pp. 21–40. Springer, Heidelberg (2011). https://doi.org/10.1007/978-3-642-25385-0_2
4. Akavia, A., Goldwasser, S., Vaikuntanathan, V.: Simultaneous hardcore bits and cryptography against memory attacks. In: Reingold, O. (ed.) TCC 2009. LNCS, vol. 5444, pp. 474–495. Springer, Heidelberg (2009). https://doi.org/10.1007/978-3-642-00457-5_28
5. Alwen, J., Dodis, Y., Naor, M., Segev, G., Walfish, S., Wichs, D.: Public-key encryption in the bounded-retrieval model. In: Gilbert [19], pp. 113–134
6. Alwen, J., Dodis, Y., Wichs, D.: Leakage-resilient public-key cryptography in the bounded-retrieval model. In: Halevi [24], pp. 36–54
7. Boneh, D., et al.: Fully key-homomorphic encryption, arithmetic circuit ABE and compact garbled circuits. In: Nguyen, P.Q., Oswald, E. (eds.) EUROCRYPT 2014. LNCS, vol. 8441, pp. 533–556. Springer, Heidelberg (2014). https://doi.org/10.1007/978-3-642-55220-5_30
8. Brakerski, Z., Goldwasser, S.: Circular and leakage resilient public-key encryption under subgroup indistinguishability. In: Rabin, T. (ed.) CRYPTO 2010. LNCS, vol. 6223, pp. 1–20. Springer, Heidelberg (2010). https://doi.org/10.1007/978-3-642-14623-7_1
9. Brakerski, Z., Kalai, Y.T., Katz, J., Vaikuntanathan, V.: Overcoming the hole in the bucket: Public-key cryptography resilient to continual memory leakage. In: FOCS 2010 [18], pp. 501–510
10. Brakerski, Z., Lombardi, A., Segev, G., Vaikuntanathan, V.: Anonymous IBE, leakage resilience and circular security from new assumptions. In: Nielsen, J.B., Rijmen, V. (eds.) EUROCRYPT 2018. LNCS, vol. 10820, pp. 535–564. Springer, Cham (2018). https://doi.org/10.1007/978-3-319-78381-9_20
11. Chen, J., Gay, R., Wee, H.: Improved dual system ABE in prime-order groups via predicate encodings. In: Oswald, E., Fischlin, M. (eds.) EUROCRYPT 2015. LNCS, vol. 9057, pp. 595–624. Springer, Heidelberg (2015). https://doi.org/10.1007/978-3-662-46803-6_20
12. Cramer, R., Shoup, V.: Universal hash proofs and a paradigm for adaptive chosen ciphertext secure public-key encryption. In: Knudsen, L.R. (ed.) EUROCRYPT 2002. LNCS, vol. 2332, pp. 45–64. Springer, Heidelberg (2002). https://doi.org/10.1007/3-540-46035-7_4
13. Dodis, Y., Goldwasser, S., Kalai, Y.T., Peikert, C., Vaikuntanathan, V.: Public-key encryption schemes with auxiliary inputs. In: Micciancio [32], pp. 361–381
14. Dodis, Y., Haralambiev, K., Lopez-Alt, A., Wichs, D.: Cryptography against continuous memory attacks. In: FOCS 2010 [18], pp. 511–520
15. Dodis, Y., Ostrovsky, R., Reyzin, L., Smith, A.D.: Fuzzy extractors: How to generate strong keys from biometrics and other noisy data. SIAM J. Comput. **38**(1), 97–139 (2008)

16. Dziembowski, S.: On forward-secure storage. In: Dwork, C. (ed.) CRYPTO 2006. LNCS, vol. 4117, pp. 251–270. Springer, Heidelberg (2006). https://doi.org/10.1007/11818175_15
17. Faust, S., Mukherjee, P., Nielsen, J.B., Venturi, D.: Continuous non-malleable codes. In: Lindell [30], pp. 465–488
18. 51st FOCS. IEEE Computer Society Press, October 2010
19. Gilbert, H. (ed.): EUROCRYPT 2010. LNCS, vol. 6110. Springer, Heidelberg (2010). https://doi.org/10.1007/978-3-642-13190-5
20. Gong, J., Chen, J., Dong, X., Cao, Z., Tang, S.: Extended nested dual system groups, revisited. In: Cheng, C.-M., Chung, K.-M., Persiano, G., Yang, B.-Y. (eds.) PKC 2016. LNCS, vol. 9614, pp. 133–163. Springer, Heidelberg (2016). https://doi.org/10.1007/978-3-662-49384-7_6
21. Gorbunov, S., Vaikuntanathan, V., Wee, H.: Functional encryption with bounded collusions via multi-party computation. In: Safavi-Naini and Canetti [36], pp. 162–179
22. Gorbunov, S., Vinayagamurthy, D.: Riding on asymmetry: efficient ABE for branching programs. In: Iwata, T., Cheon, J.H. (eds.) ASIACRYPT 2015. LNCS, vol. 9452, pp. 550–574. Springer, Heidelberg (2015). https://doi.org/10.1007/978-3-662-48797-6_23
23. Haldermany, J.A.: Lest we remember: cold boot attacks on encryption keys. Commun. ACM **52**(5), 91–98 (2008)
24. Halevi, S. (ed.): CRYPTO 2009. LNCS, vol. 5677. Springer, Heidelberg (2009)
25. Hazay, C., López-Alt, A., Wee, H., Wichs, D.: Leakage-resilient cryptography from minimal assumptions. In: Johansson, T., Nguyen, P.Q. (eds.) EUROCRYPT 2013. LNCS, vol. 7881, pp. 160–176. Springer, Heidelberg (2013). https://doi.org/10.1007/978-3-642-38348-9_10
26. Kiayias, A., Liu, F.-H., Tselekounis, Y.: Practical non-malleable codes from l-more extractable hash functions. In: Weippl, E.R., Katzenbeisser, S., Kruegel, C., Myers, A.C., Halevi, S. (eds.) ACM CCS 16, pp. 1317–1328. ACM Press, Oct. (2016)
27. Kocher, P.C.: Timing attacks on implementations of Diffie-Hellman, RSA, DSS, and other systems. In: Koblitz, N. (ed.) CRYPTO 1996. LNCS, vol. 1109, pp. 104–113. Springer, Heidelberg (1996). https://doi.org/10.1007/3-540-68697-5_9
28. Lewko, A., Rouselakis, Y., Waters, B.: Achieving leakage resilience through dual system encryption. In: Ishai, Y. (ed.) TCC 2011. LNCS, vol. 6597, pp. 70–88. Springer, Heidelberg (2011). https://doi.org/10.1007/978-3-642-19571-6_6
29. Lewko, A.B., Waters, B.: New techniques for dual system encryption and fully secure HIBE with short ciphertexts. In: Micciancio [32], pp. 455–479
30. Lindell, Y. (ed.): TCC 2014. LNCS, vol. 8349. Springer, Heidelberg (2014)
31. Liu, F.-H., Lysyanskaya, A.: Tamper and leakage resilience in the split-state model. In: Safavi-Naini and Canetti [36], pp. 517–532
32. Micciancio, D. (ed.): TCC 2010. LNCS, vol. 5978. Springer, Heidelberg (2010)
33. Naor, M., Segev, G.: Public-key cryptosystems resilient to key leakage. In: Halevi [24], pp. 18–35
34. Nisan, N., Zuckerman, D.: Randomness is Linear in Space. Academic Press Inc. (1996)
35. Nishimaki, R., Yamakawa, T.: Leakage-resilient identity-based encryption in bounded retrieval model with nearly optimal leakage-ratio. In: Lin, D., Sako, K. (eds.) PKC 2019. LNCS, vol. 11442, pp. 466–495. Springer, Cham (2019). https://doi.org/10.1007/978-3-030-17253-4_16
36. Safavi-Naini, R., Canetti, R. (eds.): CRYPTO 2012. LNCS, vol. 7417. Springer, Heidelberg (2012)

37. Sahai, A., Waters, B.: Fuzzy identity-based encryption. In: Cramer, R. (ed.) EUROCRYPT 2005. LNCS, vol. 3494, pp. 457–473. Springer, Heidelberg (2005). https://doi.org/10.1007/11426639_27
38. Tsabary, R.: Fully secure attribute-based encryption for t-CNF from LWE, pp. 62–85
39. Vadhan, S.P.: Pseudorandomness. Found. Trends Theor. Comput. Sci. **7**(1–3), 1–336 (2012)
40. Vadhan, S.P.: On constructing locally computable extractors and cryptosystems in the bounded storage model. In: Boneh, D. (ed.) CRYPTO 2003. LNCS, vol. 2729, pp. 61–77. Springer, Heidelberg (2003). https://doi.org/10.1007/978-3-540-45146-4_4
41. Waters, B.: Dual system encryption: realizing fully secure IBE and HIBE under simple assumptions. In: Halevi [24], pp. 619–636
42. Wee, H.: Dual system encryption via predicate encodings. In: Lindell [30], pp. 616–637
43. Zhang, L., Zhang, J., Mu, Y.: Novel leakage-resilient attribute-based encryption from hash proof system. Comput. J. **60**(4), 541–554 (2016)
44. Zhang, M., Zhang, Y., Su, Y., Huang, Q., Mu, Y.: Attribute-based hash proof system under learning-with-errors assumption in obfuscator-free and leakage-resilient environments. IEEE Syst. J. **11**(2), 1018–1026 (2017)

Encapsulated Search Index: Public-Key, Sub-linear, Distributed, and Delegatable

Erik Aronesty[1], David Cash[2], Yevgeniy Dodis[3], Daniel H. Gallancy[1], Christopher Higley[1], Harish Karthikeyan[3(✉)], and Oren Tysor[1]

[1] Atakama, Atakama, Chile
[2] University of Chicago, Chicago, USA
[3] New York University, New York City, USA
harish@nyu.edu

Abstract. We build the first *sub-linear* (in fact, potentially constant-time) *public-key* searchable encryption system:

- server can publish a public key PK.
- anybody can build an encrypted index for document D under PK.
- client holding the index can obtain a token z_w from the server to check if a keyword w belongs to D.
- search using z_w is almost as fast (e.g., sub-linear) as the non-private search.
- server granting the token does not learn anything about the document D, beyond the keyword w.
- yet, the token z_w is specific to the pair (D, w): the client does not learn if other keywords $w' \neq w$ belong to D, or if w belongs to other, freshly indexed documents D'.
- server cannot fool the client by giving a wrong token z_w.

We call such a primitive *Encapsulated Search Index* (ESI). Our ESI scheme can be made (t, n)-distributed among n servers in the best possible way: *non-interactive*, verifiable, and resilient to any coalition of up to $(t-1)$ malicious servers. We also introduce the notion of *delegatable* ESI and show how to extend our construction to this setting.

Our solution — including public indexing, sub-linear search, delegation, and distributed token generation — is deployed as a commercial application by a real-world company.

1 Introduction

Imagine the user Alice has a powerful but potentially insecure device, which we call *Desktop*. Since the Desktop is insecure (at least when not used by Alice), Alice cannot permanently store any secret keys on the Desktop. Instead, all the secret keys she will need for her work should be stored on a more secure, but weaker device, which we call *Phone*.

Y. Dodis–Partially supported by gifts from VMware Labs and Google, and NSF grants 1619158, 1319051, 1314568.

G. Hanaoka et al. (Eds.): PKC 2022, LNCS 13178, pp. 256–285, 2022.
https://doi.org/10.1007/978-3-030-97131-1_9

Alice works on the Desktop and periodically generates large documents D_1, $D_2 \ldots$, that she might want to index separately.[1] Since the documents are sensitive, Alice will always keep the indices encrypted, with the secret key stored on the Phone (and capable of supporting multiple documents $D_1, D_2, \ldots$ with the same key). Moreover, when the Phone approves her search request for keyword w inside the document D, the token z_w should only tell if $w \in D$, but will not reveal anything else: either about different keywords w' in D, or the same keyword w for another document D' (that Alice indexed separately).

ENCAPSULATED SEARCH INDEX. In order to solve the above motivating application, we will introduce a new primitive, which we term *Encapsulated Search Index* (ESI). As we will illustrate in Sect. 1.3, ESI is different than previously studied primitives in the area of searchable encryption. But for now, we informally summarize the main functionality and security properties of ESI (see also Definition 1):

- Phone can generate secret key SK, and send public key PK to the Desktop.
- Given PK and document D, Desktop can build an encrypted index E for D, and a "compact" handle c.
- D is then encrypted and erased (together with any local randomness created during the process), and Desktop only remembers E, c and PK.
- Desktop can ask the Phone's permission to search for keyword w in D, by sending it w and the compact handle c.
- If approved, the Phone will use the secret key SK to grant token $z = z(w, c, SK)$ to the Desktop.
- The Phone does not learn anything beyond w from the handle c. This should hold *information-theoretically*.
- The Desktop can verify that the token z indeed corresponds to w, and, if so, use E, c, z and PK to correctly learn if $w \in D$. In particular, the Phone cannot cause the Desktop to output a wrong answer (beyond denial of service).
- The token z is specific to the pair (D, w): the Desktop does not learn if other keywords $w' \neq w$ belong to D, or if w belongs to other, freshly indexed documents D'.
- While each tuple (E, c) is specific to the document D, the same (PK, SK) pair should work for future documents D', without compromising security.

Remark 1. For simplicity, we had the Desktop serve the role of both index creator and the storage location with the Phone serving the role of the search approver. However, the same could be generalized to the setting where the storage location is a company server, a trusted Desktop is the index creator, and the Phone is the search approver — all three being different parties.

Additionally, in a good ESI, the overall search by the Desktop is much faster than the number of keywords in D. In fact, ideally, the bulk of the search should

[1] In fact, our solution will allow for generating secure indices even outside the Desktop, possibly by different parties. But for simplicity, we discuss the already interesting setting where Alice herself generates indices on the Desktop.

be done by the Desktop using any *non-private* dictionary structure, while the interaction between the Phone and the Desktop should have constant size/complexity, independent of $|D|$. Our main construction will have this property.

EXTENSIONS OF ESI. For applications, we would also like to consider various extensions of ESI.

First, to mitigate Alice's worry that her Phone might be compromised, she might want to use a secure indexing scheme that is "friendly" to distributed implementation. For example, she might wish to secretly share her master key between her Phone, Laptop, and iPad (which we call *mobile devices* to differentiate them from the Desktop) in a way that she gets the token whenever two of them approve her search request. Moreover, this process should be *non-interactive*. The Desktop will send a request "Do you authorize to search document D for keyword w?" to each of the n mobile devices, and gets the token z_w the moment $t \leq n$ of them respond affirmatively. Moreover, the Desktop can separately verify the authenticity of each of the shares from the mobile devices (which is why it does not need to wait for all n to respond). The resulting notion of *threshold ESI* is formalized and can be found in the full version of the paper [3]. This would correspond to the setting of multiple devices serving the role of the search approver.

Second, Alice might wish to delegate her searching ability to another user Bob, without the need to re-index the document. (A special case of this scenario is Bob being "Alice with a new Phone".) In this case, Alice does not want to freshly re-index the document, meaning that the encrypted index E should not change. Instead, she only wants to convert the compact "handle" c corresponding to her PK to a new compact handle c' corresponding to Bob's public key PK'. Once this conversion is done, Bob can use the pair (E, c') with his Phone to search for keywords in the same document D. We formalize several flavors of such *delegatable ESI* in the full version of the paper [3].

Finally, we might want to have the ability to update the index E by adding and deleting the keyword. In an *updatable ESI*, formalized in the full version of the paper [3], the token z_w sent by Phone is also sufficient for the Desktop to update E to E' accordingly: remove, w if w was in D, or add it if it was not. This does not affect the handle c.

1.1 Our Main Tool: Encapsulated Verifiable Random Function

NAIVE SOLUTION. Before introducing our solution approach, it is helpful to start with the naive solution which almost works. The Phone can generate a (PK, SK) pair for a chosen-ciphertext-attack (CCA) secure encryption scheme. To index a document D, the Desktop can choose a seed k for a pseudorandom function (PRF) F_k, and generate a standard (non-private) index E by replacing each keyword $w \in D$ with the PRF value $y = F_k(w)$. These values are pseudorandom (hence, also distinct w.h.p.); thus, index E will not reveal any information about D except the number of keywords N.

The Desktop will finally generate a ciphertext c encrypting k under PK, and then erase the PRF key k. To get token for keyword w, the Desktop will send the tuple (c, w) to the Phone, which will decrypt c to get k, and return $y = F_k(w)$.

This naive solution satisfies our efficiency property and almost all the security properties. For example, the value c is independent of the document D, so the Phone does not learn anything about the document (including search results). Similarly, the Desktop cannot use the token y to learn about other keyword w', as $y' = F_k(w')$ is pseudorandom given $y = F_k(w)$. The only basic property missing is verifiability: the Desktop cannot tell if the value y indeed corresponds to w. This can be fixed by replacing PRF F_K with a *verifiable random function* (VRF) [35]. A VRF has its own public-secret key pair (pk, sk). For each input w, the owner of sk can produce not only the function value $y = F_{sk}(w)$, but also a "proof" $z = z(sk, w)$. This proof can convince the verifier (who only knows pk) that the value y is correct, while still leaving other yet "unproven" output $y' = F_{sk}(w')$ pseudorandom. While initial treatment of VRF focused on the "standard model" constructions [23,24,34,35], VRFs are quite efficient in the random oracle model. In particular, several such efficient constructions are given the CFRG VRF standard [29,30].

Deficiencies of the Naive Solution. While the composition of VRF and CCA encryption indeed works for the most basic ESI notion — and shows that *sublinear search can be meaningfully combined with public indexing*[2] — it seems too inflexible for our two main extensions: threshold ESI and delegatable ESI.

For threshold ESI, achieving "decrypt-then-evaluate-VRF" functionality *non-interactively* appears quite challenging with the current state-of-the-art. In particular, a natural way to accomplish this task would be to combine some non-interactive threshold CCA-decryption with a non-interactive threshold VRF implementation. Each of these advanced primitives is highly non-trivial but exists in isolation. For example, the works of [7,12] show how to achieve non-interactive CCA-secure decryption in bilinear map groups. Unfortunately (for our purposes), both of these constructions encrypt elements of the "target bilinear group" $\mathbb{G}_1$ (see the full version [3].). Thus, to get a non-interactive threshold ESI scheme we will need to build a non-interactive threshold VRF in which the secret key resides in the bilinear target group $\mathbb{G}_1$. No such construction is known, however. In fact, we are aware of only two recent non-interactive threshold VRF schemes, both proposed by [26].[3] Unfortunately, both of these constructions have the secret key over the standard group $\mathbb{Z}_p$, and cannot be composed with the schemes of [7,12]. Hence, we either need to build a new (threshold) VRF with secret keys residing in $\mathbb{G}_1$, or build a new, *non-interactive*[4] threshold CCA decryption with keys residing in $\mathbb{Z}_p$. Both options seem challenging.

For delegatable ESI, our definitions (and the overall application) require an efficient procedure S-Check(PK_1, c_1, PK_2, c_2) to check that the new handle c_2

[2] ESI is the first searchable encryption primitive to do so; see Sect. 1.3.

[3] As other prior distributed VRFs were either interactive [23,33], or had no verifiability [2,36] or offered no formal model/analysis [16,17,21,32,41].

[4] E.g., we cannot use the interactive threshold Cramer-Shoup [19] construction of [13].

was indeed delegated from c_1. The naive delegation scheme of decrypting c_1 to get VRF key sk, and then re-encrypting sk with PK_2 does not have such efficient verifiability. We could try to attach a non-interactive zero-knowledge (NIZK) proof for this purpose, but such proof might be quite inefficient, especially with chosen *ciphertext* secure encryptions c_1 and c_2.

OUR NEW TOOL: ENCAPSULATED VRF. Instead of tying our hands with the very specific and inflexible "CCA-encrypt-VRF-key" solution, we introduce a general primitive we call *encapsulated VRF* (EVRF). This primitive abstracts the core of the naive solution, but without insisting on a particular implementation. Intuitively, an EVRF allows the Phone to publish a public key PK, keep secret key SK private so that the Desktop can use PK to produce a ciphertext C and trapdoor key T in a way that for any input w, the correct VRF value y on w can be efficiently evaluated in two different ways:

(a) Phone: using secret key SK and ciphertext C.
(b) Desktop: using trapdoor T.

In addition, if the Desktop erased T and only remembers C, PK, and w:

(c) Phone can produce a proof z convincing Desktop that the value y is correct.
(d) Without such proof, the value y will look pseudorandom to the Desktop.

These properties are formalized in Definition 2. It is then easy to see that we can combine any EVRF with a non-private dictionary data structure, by simply replacing each keyword w with EVRF output y, just as in the naive solution. See Construction 2. Moreover, this construction is very friendly to all our extensions. If the EVRF is a threshold (resp. delegatable) — see Definitions 3, 4, — then we get threshold (resp. delegatable) ESI. Similarly, if the non-private data structure allows updates, our ESI construction is updatable.

To summarize, to efficiently solve all the variants of our Encapsulated Search Index scenario, we just need to build a *custom* EVRF which overcomes the difficulties we faced with the naive composition of VRF and CCA encryption.

1.2 Our EVRF Constructions

This is precisely what we accomplish: we build a simple and efficient EVRF under the Bilinear Decisional Diffie-Hellman (BDDH) assumption [9], in the random oracle model. Our basic EVRF is given in Construction 1. It draws a lot of inspiration and resemblance to the original Boneh-Franklin IBE (BF-IBE) [9], but with a couple of important tweaks. In essence, we observe that BF-IBE key encapsulation produces the ciphertext $R = g^r$ which is independent of the "target identity". Hence, we can use this value R as "part of identity" $\mathsf{ID} = (R, w)$, where w is our input/keyword, and still have a meaningful "ID-based secret key" z_w corresponding to this identity. On the usability level, this trick allows the index generator to produce the value $R = g^r$ before any of subsequent EVRF inputs (keywords in our application) w will be known. On a technical level, it allows us to "upgrade" BF-IBE from a chosen-plaintext attack (CPA) to CCA security for free.

Additionally, in Sect. 6.2 we show that our VRF construction easily lends itself to very simple, non-interactive threshold EVRF (which gives threshold ESI), by using Shamir's Secret Sharing [42], Feldman VSS [25], and the fact that the correctness of all computations is easily verified using the pairing. The resulting (t, n)-threshold implementation, given in Construction 3, is the best possible: it is non-interactive and every share is individually verifiable, which allows computing the output the moment t correct shares are obtained.

Finally, Sects. 7.2, 7.3, 7.4 extend our basic EVRF to various levels of delegatable EVRFs (which yield corresponding delegatable ESIs). All our constructions have a very simple delegation procedure, including a simple "equivalence" check to test if two handles correspond to the same EVRF under two different keys (which was challenging in the naive construction). The most basic delegatable EVRF in Sects. 7.2 (Construction 4) is shown secure under the same BDDH assumption as the underlying EVRF. It assumes that all delegations are performed by non-compromised devices.

To handle delegation to/from an untrusted device, we modify our underlying EVRF construction to also include "BLS Signature" [11], to ensure that the sender "knew" the value r used to generate the original handle $R = g^r$. See Sect. 7.3 and Construction 5. This new construction is shown to have "unidirectional" delegation security under the same BDDH assumption. Finally, we show that the same construction can be shown to satisfy even stronger levels of "bidirectional" delegation security, albeit under slightly stronger variants of BDDH we justify in the generic group model (see Sects. 7.3, 7.4).

1.3 ESI vs Other Searchable Encryption Primitives

The notion of ESI is closely related to other searchable encryption primitives: most notably, *Searchable Symmetric Encryption* (SSE) [5,15,20,22,22,28] and *Public-Key Encrypted Keyword Search* (PEKS) [1,4,8,10,40,44]. Just like ESI, SSE and PEKS achieve the most basic property of any searchable encryption scheme, which we call *index privacy*: knowledge of encrypted index E and several tokens z_w does not reveal information about keywords w' for which no tokens were yet given. I.e., the keywords in the index that have not been searched so far continue to remain private. Otherwise, the SSE/PEKS primitives have some notable differences from ESI. We discuss them below, simultaneously arguing why SSE/PEKS does not suffice for our application.

Setting of SSE. As suggested by its name, in this setting the index creator is the same party as the search approver, meaning that both parties must know the secret key SK which is hidden from the Desktop storing the index. On the positive, this restriction allows for some additional properties which are hard or even impossible in the public-indexing setting of the ESI (and PEKS; see below). First, they allow for "universal searching", where the search approver can produce the token z_w without getting the document-specific handle c: such token allows to simultaneously search different indices $E_1, E_2, \ldots$ corresponding to different documents $D_1, D_2, \ldots$.[5]

Second, one can talk about so-called "hidden queries" [22] which essentially captures the idea of "keyword-privacy". Specifically, the adversary who knows the index E and keyword token z should not learn if z corresponds to keywords w_0 or keyword w_1.[6] With public-key indexing, such a strong semantic-security guarantee is impossible, at least when combined with universal searching: the adversary can always generate the index for some document D_0 containing w_0 and not w_1 and then test if z works on this index.

We notice that "keyword privacy" and universal searching are not important for our motivating application. In fact, w is generated by Alice when using the Desktop (and will be erased when no longer relevant). Moreover, our verifiability property of the ESI explicitly requires that the Desktop can check that the token z_w is correct, explicitly at odds with keyword privacy. Additionally, when Alice sees the prompt on her phone asking if it is OK to search for the keyword w, she generally wants to know in what context (i.e., to what document D) this search would apply; and will not want a compromised token z_w to search a more sensitive document D'. Thus, we do not insist on universal searching either in the ESI setting.

On the other hand, the biggest limitation of SSE — the inability to perform public-key indexing, — makes it inapplicable to our motivating application. First, at the time of index creation, Alice already has the entire document D she wants to index on the Desktop, and she does not want to transmit this gigantic document to the Phone, have the Phone spend hours indexing it (or possibly run out of memory doing so), and then send the (also gigantic) index back to the Desktop. Second, even if efficiency was not an issue, Alice is not willing to fully trust her Phone either. For example, while Alice hopes that the Phone is more secure than the Desktop, it might be possible that the Phone is compromised as well. In this case, Alice wants the (compromised) Phone to only learn which keywords w she is searching for, but not to learn anything else about the document D (including if her searches were successful!). Moreover, even if Alice had a secure channel between the Desktop and the Phone, she does not want to use SSE and send-then-erase the corresponding secret key. Indeed, this method requires the phone to store a separate secret key for each document and also does not allow other parties to generate encrypted indexes for different files — a convenient feature Alice might find handy in the future.

To sum up, Alice wants to generate the entire encrypted index E on her Desktop (and then erase/encrypt the document D), without talking to the Phone,

---

[5] From an application perspective, universal and document-specific setting are incomparable, as some application might want to restrict which keywords are allowed for different databases. On a technical level, however, a universal scheme can always be converted to a document-specific one, by prefixing the keyword with the name of the document D. Thus, universal searching is more powerful.

[6] Unfortunately, as surveyed by Cash *et al.* [14] and further studied by [20,31] (and others), *all* SSE schemes in the literature do not achieve the strongest possible keyword privacy and suffer from various forms of information leakage.

and only contact the Phone to help authorize subsequent keyword searches. This means that SSE is inapplicable, and we must use public-key cryptography.

SETTING OF PEKS. In a different vein, PEKS allows Alice to publish a public-key PK allowing anybody to create her encrypted index. Akin to SSE, PEKS also demand universal searching, meaning that the token z_w can be produced independently of the (handle c for the) document D. This means that strong keyword privacy is impossible (and, thus, not required) in PEKS.

More significantly for our purposes, this feature makes searching *inherently slow*: not as an artifact of the existing PEKS scheme, but as already mandated even by the *syntax* of PEKS. Specifically, to achieve universality, the index is created by indexing each keyword $w' \in D$ one-by-one (using PK), and then the token z_w can only be used to test each such "ciphertext" e separately, to see whether or not it corresponds to $w' = w$. Thus, inherently slow searching makes PEKS inapplicable as well for our motivating application. In contrast, the searching in the ESI is (required to be!) document-specific. As a result, we will be able to achieve the sublinear searching we desire.

SUMMARY COMPARISON. Summarizing the above discussion (see Table 1), we can highlight five key properties of a given searchable encryption scheme: public-key indexing, sublinear search, universal search, keyword privacy, and index privacy. All of ESI/SSE/PEKS satisfy (appropriate form) of index privacy, and differ — sometimes by choice (ESI) or necessity (PEKS) — in terms of keyword privacy. So the most interesting three dimensions separating them are public-key indexing, sublinear search, and universal search, where (roughly) each primitive achieves two out of three. For our purposes, however, *ESI is the first primitive which combines public-key indexing and sublinear search*, which is precisely the setting of our motivating example.

Table 1. A comparison of SSE, PEKS, and ESI.

	SSE	PEKS	ESI
Public-Key Indexing	✗	✓	✓
Sublinear Search	✓	✗	✓
Universal Index	✓	✓	✗
Index Privacy	✓	✓	✓
Keyword Privacy	✓(partial)	✗(impossible)	✗(by choice!)

2 Preliminaries

NOTATION. In this paper, we let k be a security parameter. We employ the standard cryptographic model in which protocol participants are modeled by probabilistic polynomial (in k) time Turing machines (PPTs). We use poly(k) to denote a polynomial function, and negl(k) to refer to a negligible function in the security parameter k. For a distribution X, we use $x \leftarrow X$ to denote that

x is a random sample drawn from distribution X. For a set S we use $x \leftarrow S$ to denote that x is chosen uniformly at random from the set S. Additionally, we use the equality operator to denote a deterministic algorithm, and the $\rightarrow, \leftarrow$ operation to indicate a randomized algorithm.

Further, our EVRF constructions will use some "cryptographic hash function(s)" $H, H' : \{0,1\}^* \rightarrow \mathbb{G}$ mapping arbitrary-length strings (denoted $\{0,1\}^*$) to elements of the bilinear group $\mathbb{G}$. We produce a formal discussion about bilinear groups in the full version of our paper [3]. The key property of these groups are that: for all $u, v \in \mathbb{G}$ and $x, y \in \mathbb{Z}$, we have $e(u^x, v^y) = e(u, v)^{xy}$. In our security proofs, where we reduce EVRF security to an appropriate assumption, we model the cryptographic hash functions as random oracles.

3 Encapsulated Search Index

We begin by formally introducing the new primitive of *standard* Encapsulated Search Index in Sect. 3.1, defining its syntax and security. We also consider extensions to this primitive, adding features such as distribution, delegation, and update. Due to space constraints, we defer the discussions to the full version of the paper [3].

3.1 Standard Encapsulated Search Index

We discussed, at length, the motivating application or setting for the primitive we call as Encapsulated Search Index in Sect. 1.
For visual simplicity, for the remainder of this section we will use upper-case letters (D, E, Y, etc.) to denote objects whose size can depend on the size of document D (with the exception of various keys SK, PK, etc.), and by lower-case letters (c, s, r, z, w, etc.) objects whose size is constant.

In the definition below, we let k be a security parameter, PPT stand for probabilistic polynomial-time Turing machines, poly(k) to denote a polynomial function, and negl(k) to refer to a negligible function in the security parameter k.

Definition 1. *An Encapsulated Search Index (ESI) is a tuple of PPT algorithms* ESI = (KGen, Prep, Index, S-Split, S-Core, Finalize) *such that:*

- KGen$(1^k) \rightarrow (PK, SK)$*: outputs the public/secret key pair.*
- Prep$(PK) \rightarrow (s, c)$*: outputs compact representation c, and trapdoor s.*
- Index$(s, D) = E$*: outputs the encrypted index E for a document D using the trapdoor s.*
- S-Split$(PK, c') = r'$*: outputs a handle r' from the representation c'.*
- S-Core$(SK, r', w) = z'$*: outputs a partial result z' from the handle r'.*
- Finalize$(PK, E', c', z', w) = \beta \in \{0, 1, \perp\}$*: outputs* 1 *if the word w is present in the original document D,* 0 *if not present, and $\perp$ if the partial output z' is inconsistent.*

Before we define the security properties, it is useful to define the following short-hand functions:

- $\textsc{BldIdx}(PK, D) = (\textsc{Index}(s, D), c)$, *where* $(s, c) \leftarrow \textsc{Prep}(PK)$.
- $\textsc{S-Prove}(PK, SK, c, w) = \textsc{S-Core}(SK, \textsc{S-Split}(PK, c), w)$.
- $\textsc{Search}(PK, SK, (E, c), w) = \textsc{Finalize}(PK, E, c, \textsc{S-Prove}(SK, c, w), w)$.

We require the following security properties from this primitive:

1. ***Correctness:*** *with prob.* 1 *(resp.* $(1 - negl(k))$*) over randomness of* KGen *and* Prep*, for all documents* D *and keywords* $w \in D$ *(resp.* $w \notin D$*):*
$$\textsc{Search}(PK, SK, \textsc{BldIdx}(PK, D), w) = \begin{cases} 1 & \text{if } w \in D \\ 0 & \text{if } w \notin D \end{cases}$$
2. ***Uniqueness:*** *there exist no values* (PK, E, c, z_1, z_2, w) *such that* $b_1 \neq \bot$, $b_2 \neq \bot$ *and* $b_1 \neq b_2$*, where:*
$$b_1 = \textsc{Finalize}(PK, E, c, z_1, w); \quad b_2 = \textsc{Finalize}(PK, E, c, z_2, w)$$
3. ***CCA Security:*** *We require that for any PPT algorithm* $\mathcal{A} = (\mathcal{A}_1, \mathcal{A}_2)$ *the following holds, where* $\mathcal{A}$ *does not make the query* $\textsc{S-Prove}(PK, SK, c^*, w)$ *with* $w \in (D_1 \backslash D_2) \cup (D_2 \backslash D_1)$ *and* $|D_1| = |D_2|$*, for variables* SK, c^*, D_1, D_2, w *defined below:*
$$\Pr\left[b = b' \left| \begin{array}{c} (PK, SK) \leftarrow \textsc{KGen}(1^k); \\ (D_1, D_2, st) \leftarrow \mathcal{A}_1^{\textsc{S-Prove}(PK, SK, \cdot, \cdot)}(PK); \\ b \leftarrow \{0, 1\}; \\ (E^*, c^*) \leftarrow \textsc{BldIdx}(PK, D_b); \\ b' \leftarrow \mathcal{A}_2^{\textsc{S-Prove}(PK, SK, \cdot, \cdot)}(E^*, c^*, st) \end{array} \right. \right] \leq \frac{1}{2} + negl(k)$$
4. ***Privacy-Preserving***[7]*: We require that for any PPT Algorithm* $\mathcal{A} = (\mathcal{A}_1, \mathcal{A}_2)$ *which outputs documents* D_1, D_2 *such that* $|D_1| = |D_2|$ *for variables* D_1, D_2 *defined below, the following holds:*
$$\Pr\left[b = b' \left| \begin{array}{c} (PK, SK) \leftarrow \textsc{KGen}(1^k); \\ (D_1, D_2, st) \leftarrow \mathcal{A}_1(PK, SK); \\ b \leftarrow \{0, 1\}; \\ (E^*, c^*) \leftarrow \textsc{BldIdx}(PK, D_b); \\ b' \leftarrow \mathcal{A}_2(c^*, st) \end{array} \right. \right] \leq \frac{1}{2} + negl(k)$$

Remark 2. We want to ensure that an honest representation c_1 will not collide with another honest representation c_2. With this, we can ensure that honestly generated documents do not conflict. If there is a non-trivial chance of such a collision, then one can simply generate c_2 until collision with the challenge c_1. With this collision, and with knowledge of trapdoor T_2, one can trivially break security.

[7] It is easy to see that our syntax guarantees that any ESI construction is *unconditionally* **Privacy-Preserving** (even with knowledge of SK), for the simple reason that Prep that produces c does not depend on the input document D. Thus, we will never explicitly address this property, but list it for completeness, as it is important for our motivating application.

Remark 3. For efficiency, we will want SEARCH to run in time $O(\log N)$ or less, where N is the size of the document D. In fact, our main construction will have S-PROVE run in time $O(1)$, independent of the size of the document, and FINALIZE would run in time at most $O(\log N)$, depending on the non-cryptographic data structure we use.

3.2 Extensions to ESI

THRESHOLD ESI. We extend the definition of the standard Encapsulated Search Index to achieve support for distributed token generation. To do this, we introduce a new algorithm called KG-VERIFY that aims to verify if the output of the KGEN algorithm is correct, and replace FINALIZE with two more fined-grained procedures S-VERIFY and S-COMBINE. The formal discussion about the syntax and security of this primitive can be found in the full version of the paper [3].

DELEGATABLE ESI. We can also extend the definition of the standard Encapsulated Search Index to achieve support for delegation. Informally, Encapsulated Search Index is delegatable if there are two polynomial-time procedures S-DEL, S-CHECK that work as follows: S-DEL that achieves the delegation wherein it takes as input a representation c corresponding to one key pair and produces a representation c' corresponding to another key pair; S-CHECK helps verify if a delegation was performed correctly. The formal discussion about the syntax and security of this primitive, including several definitional subtleties, can be found in the full version of the paper [3].

UPDATABLE ESI. We can further extend the definition of the standard Encapsulated Search Index to support a use-case where one might want to remove a word, or add a word to the document D, without having to necessarily recompute the entire index. To achieve this, we need an additional algorithm called UPDATE that can produce a new index E' after performing an `action` relating to word w in original index E, using the same token z_w used for searching. The formal discussion about the syntax and security of this primitive can be found in the full version of the paper [3].

4 Encapsulated Verifiable Random Functions (EVRFs)

As mentioned earlier, we use a new primitive called Encapsulated Verifiable Random Function to build the encapsulated search index. In this section, we begin by introducing this primitive in Sect. 4.1. In Sect. 4.2, we present an overview of extensions to this primitive. Later sections in paper contained detailed expositions on the extensions.

4.1 Standard EVRFs

Intuitively, an EVRF allows the receiver Alice to publish a public key PK and keep secret key SK private so that any sender Bob can use PK to produce a ciphertext C and trapdoor key T in a way such that for any input x, the correct VRF value y on x can be efficiently evaluated in two different ways:

(a) Alice can evaluate y using secret key SK and ciphertext C.
(b) Bob can evaluate y using trapdoor T.

In addition, for any third party Charlie who knows C, PK and x:

(c) Alice can produce a proof z convincing Charlie that the value y is correct.
(d) Without such proof, the value y will look pseudorandom to Charlie.

Definition 2. *An* Encapsulated Verifiable Random Function *(EVRF) is a tuple of PPT algorithms* EVRF $=$ (Gen, Encap, Comp, Split, Core, Post) *such that:*

- $\textsc{Gen}(1^k) \to (PK, SK)$*: outputs the public/secret key pair.*
- $\textsc{Encap}(PK) \to (C, T)$*: outputs ciphertext C and trapdoor T.*
- $\textsc{Comp}(T, x) = y$*: evaluates EVRF on input x, using trapdoor T.*
- $\textsc{Split}(PK, C') = R'$*: outputs a handle from full ciphertext C'.*
  Note, this preprocessing is independent of the input x, can depend on the public key PK, but not *on the secret key SK.*[8]
- $\textsc{Core}(SK, R', x) = z'$*: evaluates partial EVRF output on input x, using the secret key SK and handle R'.*
- $\textsc{Post}(PK, z', C', x) = y' \cup \perp$*: outputs either the EVRF output from the partial output z', or $\perp$.*

Before we define the security properties, it is useful to define the following shorthand functions:

- $\textsc{Prove}(PK, SK, C, x) = \textsc{Core}(SK, \textsc{Split}(PK, C), x)$
- $\textsc{Eval}(PK, SK, C, x) = \textsc{Post}(PK, \textsc{Prove}(SK, C, x), C, x)$

We require the following security properties:

1. ***Evaluation-Correctness****: with prob.* 1 *over randomness of* Gen *and* Encap*, for honestly generated ciphertext C and for all inputs x,*

$$\textsc{Comp}(T, x) = \textsc{Eval}(PK, SK, C, x)$$

2. ***Uniqueness****: there exist no values (PK, C, x, z_1, z_2) s.t. $y_1 \neq \perp, y_2 \neq \perp$, and $y_1 \neq y_2$ where*

$$y_1 = \textsc{Post}(PK, z_1, C, x), \quad y_2 = \textsc{Post}(PK, z_2, C, x)$$

[8] The algorithm Split is not technically needed, as one can always set $R = C$. In fact, this will be the case for our EVRF in Sect. 5.1. However, one could envision EVRF constructions where the Split procedure can do a non-trivial (input-independent) part of the overall Prove $=$ Core(Split) procedure, and without the need to know the secret key SK. This will be the case for some of the delegatable EVRFs we consider in Sect. 7.1.

3. ***Pseudorandomness under*** Core ***(\$-Core)****: for any PPT algorithm $\mathcal{A} = (\mathcal{A}_1, \mathcal{A}_2)$, where $\mathcal{A}$ does not make query (C, x) to* Prove$(PK, SK, \cdot, \cdot)$*, for variables SK, C, x defined below, the following holds:*

$$\Pr\left[b = b' \;\middle|\; \begin{array}{c} (PK, SK) \leftarrow \textsc{Gen}(1^k); \\ (C, T) \leftarrow \textsc{Encap}(PK); \\ (x, st) \leftarrow \mathcal{A}_1^{\textsc{Prove}(PK,SK,\cdot,\cdot)}(PK, C); \\ y_0 = \textsc{Comp}(T, x);\;\; y_1 \leftarrow \{0,1\}^{|y_0|}; \\ b \leftarrow \{0,1\};\;\; b' \leftarrow \mathcal{A}_2^{\textsc{Prove}(PK,SK,\cdot,\cdot)}(y_b, st) \end{array} \right] \leq \frac{1}{2} + \mathit{negl}(k)$$

We present a construction of our EVRF in Sect. 5.1.

Remark 4. We note that any valid ciphertext C implicitly defines a standard verifiable random function (VRF). In particular, the value $z = \textsc{Prove}(SK, C, x)$ could be viewed as the VRF proof, which is accepted iff $\textsc{Post}(PK, z, C, x) \neq \perp$.

Remark 5. We reiterate that our pseudorandomness definition does not give the attacker "unguarded" access to the Core procedure, but only "Split-guarded" access to Prove = Core(Split). This difference does not matter when the Split procedure just sets $R = C$. However, when Split is non-trivial, the owner of SK (Alice) can only outsource it to some outside server (Charlie) if it trusts Charlie and the authenticity (but not privacy) of the channel between Alice and Charlie.

4.2 Extensions to EVRFs

Threshold EVRF. In the earlier definition, we had a single secret key SK. With possession of this secret key, one can evaluate the EVRF on any input x. Therefore, it becomes imperative to protect the key from leakage. Indeed, it is natural to extend our early definition to cater to the setting of a distributed evaluation of the EVRF. The key difference in the definition of threshold EVRF from the earlier definition is that the Post algorithm is now formally split into the share verification algorithm Shr-Vfy and the final evaluation algorithm Combine. The formal discussion about the syntax and security of this primitive can be found in Sect. 6.1.

Delegatable EVRF. Next, we extend the definition of *standard* EVRFs to the setting where the EVRF owner could delegate its evaluation power to another key. Recall that a standard EVRF has the following algorithms: Gen, Encap, Comp, Split, Core, Post. Delegation, therefore, implies that one can convert a ciphertext C_1 for key pair (PK_1, SK_1) to ciphertext C_2 for a different key pair (PK_2, SK_2) which encapsulates the same VRF, i.e.,

$$\forall x, \textsc{Eval}(PK_1, SK_1, C_1, x) = \textsc{Eval}(PK_2, SK_2, C_2, x) \tag{1}$$

where $\textsc{Eval}(PK, SK, C, x) = \textsc{Post}(PK, \textsc{Prove}(SK, c, x), C, x)$. The formal discussion about the syntax and security of this primitive can be found in Sect. 7.1.

Protocol Standard EVRF

$\text{Gen}(1^k)$
- Sample $a \in_r \mathbb{Z}_p^*$
- Compute $A = g^a \in \mathbb{G}$.
- **return** $SK = a$ and $PK = (g, A)$.

$\text{Encap}(PK)$
- Parse $PK = (g, A)$.
- Sample $r \in_r \mathbb{Z}_p^*$.
- Compute $R = g^r, S = A^r$.
- **return** $C = R$, $T = (R, S)$.

$\text{Comp}(T, x)$
- Parse $T = (R, S)$.
- Compute $y = e(H(R, x), S)$.
- **return** y.

$\text{Split}(PK, C')$
- Parse $PK = (g, A)$, $C' = R'$.
- **return** R'.

$\text{Core}(SK, C', x)$
- Parse $SK = a, C' = R'$.
- Compute $z = H(R', x)^a$.
- **return** z.

$\text{Post}(PK, z, C', x)$
- Parse $PK = (g, A)$, $C' = R'$
- **if** $e(z, g) \neq e(H(R', x), A)$ **then**
  - **return** $\perp$.
- **else**
  - Compute $y' = e(z, R')$.
  - **return** y'.

Construction 1. Standard EVRF = (Gen, Encap, Comp, Split, Core, Post).

5 Our Constructions

We begin by presenting the standard EVRF construction in Sect. 5.1. We then present a generic construction of our ESI in Sect. 5.2.

5.1 Standard EVRF

We now present the standard EVRF construction, presented in Construction 1.

Security Analysis. To check **Evaluation-Correctness**, we observe that $A^r = g^{ar} = R^a$, and by the bilinearity we have:

$$\text{Comp}(T = (R, S), x) = e(H(R, x), S) = e(H(R, x), A^r)$$

From our earlier observation, we get that:

$$e(H(R, x), A^r) = e(H(R, x), R^a) = e(H(R, x)^a, R) = e(z, R)$$

This is the same as $\text{Post}(A, \text{Core}(a, \text{Split}(A, R), x), R, x)$ which concludes the proof.

To prove **Uniqueness**, consider any tuple $(PK = A, C = R, x, z_1, z_2)$. Further, let $y_1 = \text{Post}(A, z_1, R, x)$ and $y_2 = \text{Post}(A, z_2, R, x)$. If $y_1 \neq \perp$ and $y_2 \neq \perp$, then we have that $e(z_1, g) = e(H(R, x), A) = e(z_2, g)$. From definition of bilinear groups, we get that $z_1 = z_2$. Consequently, $y_1 = e(z_1, R) = e(z_2, R) = y_2$.

Finally, we can prove the following result in the full version of the paper [3].

Theorem 1. *The standard* EVRF *given in Construction 1 satisfies the **\$-Core** property under the* BDDH *assumption in the random oracle model.*

5.2 Generic Construction of Encapsulated Search Index

Non-private Dictionary Data Structure. Our generic construction will use the simplest kind of non-cryptographic dictionary which allows one to preprocess some set D into some data structure E so that membership queries

Protocol Generic ESI Construction

KGEN(1^k)

Run EVRF.GEN(1^k) $\rightarrow (PK, SK)$.
return PK, SK.

PREP(PK)

Run EVRF.ENCAP(PK) $\rightarrow (C, T)$.
return $c = C$ and $s = T$.

INDEX(s, D)

for $w \in D$ **do**
Compute y_w= EVRF.COMP(s, w).
Compute $Y = \{y_w | w \in D\}$.
Run DS.CONSTRUCT(Y) $\rightarrow E$.
return E.

S-SPLIT(PK, c')

Run EVRF.SPLIT(PK, c') $= r'$.
return r'.

S-CORE(SK, r', w)

Run EVRF.CORE(SK, r', w) $= z'$.
return z'.

FINALIZE(PK, E', c', z', w)

Run EVRF.POST(PK, z', c', w) $= y'$.
if $y' = \perp$ **then**
return $\perp$.
else
return DS.FIND(E', y').

Construction 2. Generic ESI = (KGEN, PREP, INDEX, S-SPLIT, S-CORE, FINALIZE).

$w \in D$ can be answered in sub-linear time in $N = |D|$. In particular, a classic instantiation of such a dictionary could be any balanced search trees with search time $O(\log N)$. If a small probability of error is allowed, we could also use faster data structures, such as hash tables [18], Bloom filters [6,37,38] or cuckoo hash [39], whose search takes expected time $O(1)$. The particular choice of the non-cryptographic dictionary will depend on the application, which is a nice luxury allowed by our generic composition.

Formally, a non-private dictionary DS = (CONSTRUCT, FIND) is any data structure supporting the following two operations:

- CONSTRUCT(D) $\rightarrow E$: outputs the index E on an input document D.
- FIND(E, w) $\rightarrow \{0, 1\}$: outputs 1 if w is present in D, and 0 otherwise. We assume perfect correctness for $w \in D$, and allow negligible error probability for $w \notin D$.

OUR COMPOSITION. We show that Encapsulated Search Index can be easily built from any such non-cryptographic dictionary DS = (CONSTRUCT, FIND) and and EVRF = (GEN, ENCAP, COMP, SPLIT, CORE, POST). This composition is given below in Construction 2.

EFFICIENCY. By design, the SEARCH operation of our composition inherits the efficiency of the non-cryptographic dictionary DS. In particular, it is $O(\log |D|)$ with standard balanced search trees and could become potentially $O(1)$ with probabilistic dictionaries, such as hash tables or Bloom filters.

SECURITY ANALYSIS. The **Correctness** and **Uniqueness** properties of the above construction trivially follows from the respective properties of the underlying EVRF and DS. In particular, we get negligible error probability for $w \notin D$ either due to unlikely EVRF collision between y_w and $y_{w'}$ for some $w' \in D$, or a false positive of the DS. In the full version of the paper [3] we prove the following theorem:

Theorem 2. *If* EVRF *satisfies the* ***\$-Core*** *property, then Encapsulated Search Index is* ***CCA*** *secure. Further, if the* EVRF *(resp.* DS *) is threshold and/or delegatable, the resulting ESI inherits the same.*

6 Threshold Encapsulated Verifiable Random Functions

In this section, we formally introduce the primitive known as a Threshold EVRF in Sect. 6.1. We then present a construction of Threshold EVRF in Sect. 6.2 but defer the security proof due to space constraints. The proof can be found in the full version of the paper [3].

6.1 Definition of Threshold (or Distributed) EVRFs

Definition 3. *A* (t, n)-Threshold EVRF *is a tuple of PPT algorithms* TEVRF = (Gen, Gen-Vfy, Encap, Comp, Split, D-Core, Shr-Vfy, Combine) *such that:*

- Gen$(1^k, t, n) \rightarrow (PK, \boldsymbol{SK} = (sk_1, \ldots, sk_n), \boldsymbol{VK} = (vk_1, \ldots, vk_n))$*: outputs the public key* PK*, a vector of secret shares* $\boldsymbol{SK}$*, and public shares* $\boldsymbol{VK}$*.*
- Gen-Vfy$(PK, \mathbf{VK}) = \beta \in \{0, 1\}$*: verifies that the output of* Gen *is indeed valid.*
- Encap$(PK) \rightarrow (C, T)$*: outputs ciphertext* C *and trapdoor* T*.*
- Comp$(T, x) = y$*: evaluates EVRF on input* x*, using trapdoor* T*.*
- Split$(PK, n, C') = (R'_1, \ldots R'_n)$*: outputs* n *handles* $R'_1, \ldots, R'_n$ *from full ciphertext* C'*.*
- D-Core$(sk_i, R'_i, x) = z'_i$*: evaluates EVRF share on input* x*, using handle* R'_i *and secret key share* sk_i*.*
- Shr-Vfy$(PK, vk_i, z'_i, x) = \beta \in \{0, 1\}$*: verifies that the share produced by the party* i *is valid.*
- Combine$(PK, C', z'_{i_1}, \ldots, z'_{i_t}, x) = y'$*: uses the partial evaluations* $z'_{i_1}, \ldots, z'_{i_t}$ *to compute the final value of EVRF on input* x*.*[9]

Before we define the security properties, it is useful to define the following short-hand functions:

- Prove$(\mathbf{SK}, i, C, x) =$ D-Core(sk_i, R_i, x)*, where* $(R_1, \ldots, R_n) =$ Split(PK, n, C)*.*
- Eval$(\mathbf{SK}, i_1, \ldots, i_t, C, x)$*: For* $j = 1 \ldots t$*, compute* $z_{i_j} =$ Prove$(\mathbf{SK}, i_j, C, x)$*. Output* $\perp$ *if, for some* $1 \leq j \leq t$*,* Shr-Vfy$(PK, vk_{i_j}, z_{i_j}, x) = 0$*. Otherwise, output* Combine$(PK, C, z_{i_1}, \ldots, z_{i_t}, x)$*.*

We require the following security properties:

1. ***Distribution-Correctness:***
   (a) with prob. 1 over randomness of Gen$(1^k, t, n) \rightarrow (PK, \mathbf{SK}, \mathbf{VK})$*,* Gen-Vfy$(PK, \mathbf{VK}) = 1$
   (b) with prob. 1 over randomness of Gen *and* Encap*, for honestly generated ciphertext* C*:* Eval$(\mathbf{SK}, i_1, \ldots, i_t, C, x) =$ Comp(T, x)

[9] Without loss of generality, we will always assume that all the t partial evaluations z'_i satisfy Shr-Vfy$(PK, vk_i, z'_i) = 1$ (else, we output $\perp$ before calling Combine). See also the definition of Eval below to explicitly model this assumption.

2. ***Uniqueness:*** *there exists no values* $(PK, \mathbf{VK}, C, x, Z_1, Z_2)$ *where* $Z_1 = ((i_1, z_{i_1}), \ldots, (i_t, z_{i_t}))$ *and* $Z_2 = ((j_1, z_{j_1}), \ldots, (j_t, z_{j_t}))$. *s.t.*
   (a) $\textsc{Gen-Vfy}(PK, \mathbf{VK}) = 1$
   (b) *for* $k = 1, \ldots, t$*:*
   - $\textsc{Shr-Vfy}(PK, vk_{i_k}, z_{i_k}, x) = 1$.
   - $\textsc{Shr-Vfy}(PK, vk_{j_k}, z_{j_k}, x) = 1$.

   (c) *Let* $\mathbf{Z}_i = (z_{i_1}, \ldots, z_{i_t})$ *and* $\mathbf{Z}_j = (z_{j_1}, \ldots, z_{j_t})$. *Then,*

$$\textsc{Combine}(PK, C, \mathbf{Z}_i, x) \neq \textsc{Combine}(PK, C, \mathbf{Z}_j, x)$$

3. ***Pseudorandomness under D-Core ($-DCore):*** *for any PPT algorithm* $\mathcal{A} = (\mathcal{A}_0, \mathcal{A}_1, \mathcal{A}_2)$, *where* $\mathcal{A}$ *does not make query* (j, C, x) *to* $\textsc{Prove}(\mathbf{SK}, \cdot, \cdot, \cdot)$, *for* $j \notin \{i_1, \ldots, i_{t-1}\}$ *for variables* $i_1, \ldots, i_{t-1}, \mathbf{SK}, C, x$ *defined below,*

$$\Pr\left[b = b' \;\middle|\; \begin{array}{c} \{i_1, \ldots, i_{t-1}, st\} \leftarrow \mathcal{A}_0(1^k, t, n); \\ (PK, \mathbf{SK}, \mathbf{VK}) \leftarrow \textsc{Gen}(1^k, t, n); \\ (C, T) \leftarrow \textsc{Encap}(PK); \\ (R_1, \ldots, R_n) = \textsc{Split}(PK, n, C); \\ (x, st) \leftarrow \mathcal{A}_1^{\textsc{Prove}(\mathbf{SK}, \cdot, \cdot, \cdot)}(PK, C, \mathbf{VK}, \mathbf{SK}', st) \\ y_0 = \textsc{Comp}(T, x); \;\; y_1 \leftarrow \{0,1\}^{|y_0|}; \\ b \leftarrow \{0,1\}; \;\; b' \leftarrow \mathcal{A}_2^{\textsc{Prove}(SK, \cdot, \cdot)}(y_b, st) \end{array} \right] \leq \frac{1}{2} + negl(k)$$

   where $\mathbf{SK}' = (sk_{i_1}, \ldots, sk_{i_{t-1}})$.

We present a construction of our threshold EVRF in Sect. 6.2.

Remark 6. For simplicity, in the above definition, we assume honest key generation and do not explicitly address distributed key generation. Even with this simplification, the existence of the Gen-Vfy algorithm ensures the users of the system that the public key $(PK, \mathbf{VK})$ is "consistent"and was generated properly. Moreover, our construction, given in Sect. 6.2, can easily achieve efficient distributed key generation using techniques of Gennaro *et al.* [27].

Remark 7. Note that when $t = n = 1$, our threshold EVRF implies the the standard EVRF definition (Definition 2), where Post algorithm first runs Shr-Vfy on the single share z and then, if successful, runs Combine to produce the final output y. For $n > 1$, however, we find it extremely convenient that we can separately check the validity of each share, and be guaranteed to compute the correct output the moment t servers return consistent (i.e., Shr-Vfy'ed) shares z_i.

6.2 Construction of Threshold (or Distributed) EVRFs

Our non-interactive threshold EVRF is given in Construction 3. It combines elements of our standard EVRF from Construction 1 with the ideas of Shamir's Secret Sharing [42], Feldman VSS [25], and the fact that the correctness of all computations is easily verified using the pairing.

Protocol Non-Interactive Threshold EVRF

GEN(1^k)

Sample a random $(t - 1)$ degree polynomial $f \in \mathbb{Z}_p^*[X]$.
Compute $a = f(0)$, $A_0 = g^a$.
for $i = 1, \ldots, n$ **do**
  Compute $a_i = f(i), A_i = g^{a_i}$.
return $PK = (g, A_0)$, $\mathbf{SK} = (a_1, \ldots, a_n)$, $\mathbf{VK} = (A_1, \ldots, A_n)$,
with server i getting secret key $sk_i = a_i$ and verification key $vk_i = A_i$.

GEN-VFY($PK, \mathbf{VK}$)

Parse $PK = (g, A_0), \mathbf{VK} =, (A_1, \ldots, A_n))$.
for $i = t, \ldots, n$ **do**
  Compute Lagrange coefficients $\lambda_{i,0} \ldots, \lambda_{i,t-1}$ s.t. $f(i) = \sum_{j=0}^{t-1} \lambda_{i,j} \cdot f(j)$.
  Each $\lambda_{i,j}$ is a fixed constant.
  if $A_i \neq \prod_{j=0}^{t-1} A_j^{\lambda_{i,j}}$ **then**
    return 0
return 1

ENCAP(PK)

Parse $PK = (g, A_0)$.
Sample $r \in_r \mathbb{Z}_p^*$.
Compute $R = g^r, S = A_0^r$.
return ciphertext $C = R$ and trapdoor $T = (R, S)$.

COMP(T, x)

Parse $T = (R, S)$.
Compute $y = e(H(R, x), S)$.
return y.

SPLIT(PK, C')

Parse $PK = (g, A_0)$, $C' = R'$.
return $R'_1 = R', \ldots, R'_n = R'$.

D-CORE(SK_i, R'_i, x)

Parse $SK_i = a_i, R'_i = R'$.
Compute partial output $z_i = H(R'_i, x)^{a_i}$.
return z_i.

SHR-VFY(PK, VK_i, z'_i, x)

Parse $PK = (g, A_0), VK_i = A_i$.
if $e(z'_i, g) \neq e(H(R'_i, x), A_i)$ **then**
  return $\perp$.

COMBINE($PK, C', z'_{i_1}, \ldots, z'_{i_t}, x$)

Parse $PK = (g, A_0)$, $C' = R'$.
Compute Lagrange coefficients $\lambda_1 \ldots, \lambda_t$ s.t. $f(0) = \sum_{j=1}^{t} \lambda_j \cdot f(i_j)$.
Note that these λ_j's only depend on indices $i_1, \ldots, i_t$.
Compute $z' = \prod_{j=1}^{t} (z'_{i_j})^{\lambda_j}$.
return $y = e(z', R')$.

Construction 3. TEVRF = (GEN, GEN-VFY, ENCAP, COMP, SPLIT, D-CORE, SHR-VFY, COMBINE).

Security Analysis. To check **Distribution-Correctness**, we observe that $A = g^a$, $S = g^{ar}$, and $R = g^r$. Therefore, COMP$(T = (R, S), x) = e(H(R, x), S) = e(H(R, x), g)^{ar}$. By definition, we have that:

$$\text{EVAL}(PK, \mathbf{SK}, i_1, \ldots, i_t, R, x) = e(\prod_{j=1}^{t} z_{i_j}^{\lambda_j}, R)$$

$$e(\prod_{j=1}^{t} z_{i_j}^{\lambda_j}, R) = e(\prod_{j=1}^{t} H(R, x)^{a_{i_j} \cdot \lambda_j}, R) = e(H(R, x)^{\sum_{j=1}^{t} a_{i_j} \cdot \lambda_j}, R)$$

However, we know that $a = \sum_{j=1}^{t} a_{i_j} \cdot \lambda_j$. Therefore,

$$e(H(R, x)^{\sum_{j=1}^{t} a_{i_j} \cdot \lambda_j}, R) = e(H(R, x)^a, g^r) = e(H(R, x), g)^{ar}$$

To check **Uniqueness**, we are given: $(PK, \mathbf{VK} = (vk_1, \ldots, vk_n), R, x, Z_1, Z_2)$ where $Z_1 = ((i_1, z_{i_1}), \ldots, (i_t, z_{i_t}))$ and $Z_2 = ((j_1, z_{j_1}), \ldots, (j_t, z_{j_t}))$.

- GEN-VFY$(PK, \mathbf{VK}) = 1$ implies that $a_0, a_1, \ldots, a_n$ where $g^{a_0} = PK$ and $g^{a_i} = vk_i$ all lie on a consistent polynomial f of degree $t - 1$. Thus, there exist $\lambda_1, \ldots, \lambda_t \in \mathbb{Z}_p$ such that $f(0) = \sum_{\ell=1}^{t} \lambda_\ell \cdot f(i_\ell)$ and $\lambda'_1, \ldots, \lambda'_t \in \mathbb{Z}_p$ such that $f(0) = \sum_{\ell=1}^{t} \lambda_\ell \cdot f(j_\ell)$. Therefore, we have that:

$$A = \prod_{\ell=1}^{t} vk_{i_\ell}{}^{\lambda_\ell} = \prod_{\ell=1}^{t} vk_{j_\ell}{}^{\lambda'_\ell} \tag{2}$$

- We also know that for $\ell = 1, \ldots, t$, $\textsc{Shr-Vfy}(PK, vk_{i_\ell}, z_{i_\ell}, x) = 1$ and $\textsc{Shr-Vfy}(PK, vk_{j_\ell}, z_{j_\ell}, x) = 1$. Therefore, we have that for $\ell = 1, \ldots, t$:

$$e(z_{i_\ell}, g) = e(H(R,x), vk_{i_\ell});\ e(z_{j_\ell}, g) = e(H(R,x), vk_{j_\ell}) \tag{3}$$

- We will now show that the 2 outputs of COMBINE must be equal. Here we we will write $R = g^r$ for some r,

$$\textsc{Combine}(PK, R, z_{i_1}, \ldots, z_{i_t}, x) = e(\prod_{\ell=1}^{t} z_{i_\ell}^{\lambda_\ell}, R) = \prod_{\ell=1}^{t} e(z_{i_\ell}, g)^{r \cdot \lambda_\ell}$$

From Eq. (3):

$$\prod_{\ell=1}^{t} e(z_{i_\ell}, g)^{r \cdot \lambda_\ell} = \prod_{\ell=1}^{t} e(H(R,x), vk_{i_\ell})^{r \cdot \lambda_\ell} = e\left(H(R,x), \prod_{\ell=1}^{t} vk_{i_\ell}^{\lambda_\ell}\right)^r$$

From Eq. (2), we have that:

$$e(H(R,x), \prod_{\ell=1}^{t} vk_{i_\ell}^{\lambda_\ell})^r = e(H(R,x), \prod_{\ell=1}^{t} vk_{j_\ell}^{\lambda'_\ell})^r = \prod_{\ell=1}^{t} e(H(R,x), vk_{j_\ell})^{r \cdot \lambda'_\ell}$$

We again use Eq. (3) to conclude the proof. Finally, we prove the following result in the full version of the paper [3].

Theorem 3. *If Construction 1 satisfies the **\$-Core** property of standard* EVRF*, then Construction 3 satisfies the **\$-DCore** property of threshold* EVRF*. By Theorem 1, it follows that Construction 3 satisfies the **\$-DCore** property under the* BDDH *assumption in the random oracle model.*

7 Delegatable Encapsulated Verifiable Random Functions

In this section, we formally introduce the primitive known as a Delegatable EVRF in Sect. 7.1. This definition captures different levels of delegatability and we present constructions that satisfy these levels in Sects. 7.2, 7.3, and 7.4. The security proofs are deferred to the appendix.

7.1 Definition of Delegatable EVRFs

In this work, we will be interested in a stronger type of delegatable EVRFs where anybody can check if two ciphertexts C_1 and C_2 "came from the same place". This is governed by the "comparison" procedure $\textsc{Same}(PK_1, C_1, PK_2, C_2)$ which outputs 1 only if Eq. (1) holds. This procedure will have several uses. First, it allows the owner of SK_2 to be sure that the resulting ciphertext C_2 indeed encapsulates the same VRF under PK_2 as C_1 does under PK_1. Second, it will allow us to cleanly define a "trivial" attack on the pseudorandomness of delegatable EVRFs. See also Remark 9.

We define three levels of pseudorandomness security for delegatable EVRFs.

Definition 4. *An* $EVRF = (\text{Gen}, \text{Encap}, \text{Comp}, \text{Split}, \text{Core}, \text{Post})$ *is* delegatable *if there exists polynomial-time procedures* Del *and* Same, *such that:*

- $\text{Del}(SK_1, C_1, SK_2) = C_2$ *for the (default)* secretly-delegatable *variant;*
- $\text{Del}(SK_1, C_1, PK_2) = C_2$ *for the* publicly-delegatable *variant.*
- $\text{Same}(PK_1, C_1, PK_2, C_2) = \beta \in \{0, 1\}$.

Before we define the security properties, it is useful to define the following shorthand functions:

- $\text{Prove}(SK_i, C, x) = \text{Core}(SK_i, \text{Split}(PK_i, C), x)$
- $\text{Eval}(SK, C, x) = \text{Post}(PK, \text{Prove}(SK, C, x), C, x)$

In addition to the standard EVRF *properties of **Evaluation-Correctness** and **Uniqueness** , we require the following security properties from a delegatable* EVRF*:*

1. ***Delegation-Completeness:*** *for any valid* (PK_1, SK_1), (PK_2, SK_2), *and ciphertext* C_1,
$$\text{Del}(SK_1, C_1, SK_2/PK_2) = C_2 \implies \text{Same}(PK_1, C_1, PK_2, C_2) = 1$$
2. ***Delegation-Soundness:*** *for any valid* $(PK_1, SK_1), (PK_2, SK_2)$, *and ciphertexts* C_1, C_2
$$\text{Same}(PK_1, C_1, PK_2, C_2) = 1 \implies \forall x\ \text{Eval}(SK_1, C_1, x) = \text{Eval}(SK_2, C_2, x)$$
Moreover, if we have $PK_1 = PK_2$, *then* $C_1 = C_2$.
3. ***Pseudorandomness under Core (\$-Core):*** *for any legal PPT attacker* $\mathcal{A} = (\mathcal{A}_1, \mathcal{A}_2)$, *where legality of* $\mathcal{A}$ *and appropriate delegation oracle(s)* $\mathcal{O}$ *are defined separately for each notion:*
$$\Pr\left[b = b' \;\middle|\; \begin{array}{c} (1, PK_1) \leftarrow \text{Reg}(1^k); \\ (C_1, T_1) \leftarrow \text{Encap}(PK_1); \\ (x, st) \leftarrow \mathcal{A}_1^{\text{Reg},\text{HProve},\mathcal{O}}(PK_1, C_1); \\ y_0 = Comp(T_1, x); \;\; y_1 \leftarrow \{0,1\}^{|y_0|}; \\ b \leftarrow [0,1]; \;\; b' \leftarrow \mathcal{A}_2^{\text{Reg},\text{HProve},\mathcal{O}}(y_b, st) \end{array} \right] \le \frac{1}{2} + negl(k)$$

(a) ***Basic-\$-Core:*** $\mathcal{A}$ *has 1 delegation oracle* $\mathcal{O} = \text{HDel}$.
Legality of $\mathcal{A}$*: no call to* $\text{HProve}(i, C', x)$ *s.t.*
$\text{Same}(PK_1, C_1, PK_i, C') = 1$.

(b) ***Uni-\$-Core**: $\mathcal{A}$ has 2 delegation oracles* $\mathcal{O} = (\text{HDEL}, \text{OUTDEL})$.
Legality of $\mathcal{A}$*: no call to* $\text{HPROVE}(i, C', x)$ *or*
$\text{OUTDEL}(i, C', *)$ *s.t.* $\text{SAME}(PK_1, C_1, PK_i, C') = 1$.
(c) ***Bi–\$-Core**: $\mathcal{A}$ has 3 delegation oracles*
$\mathcal{O} = (\text{HDEL}, \text{OUTDEL}, \text{INDEL})$.
Legality of $\mathcal{A}$*: same as that of **Uni-\$-Core**.*

Now, we can define the oracles. As alluded to earlier, there are significant subtleties in both the syntax and security of such a primitive. We defer this exposition to the appendix for want of space. This discussion can be found in the full version of the paper [3].

To adequately capture these nuances, we define the following oracles to the attacker:

1. $\text{REG}(1^k)$: registration oracle. It maintains a global variable q, initially 0, counting the number of non-compromised users. A call to REG: (a) increments q; (b) calls $(PK_q, SK_q) \leftarrow \text{GEN}(1^k)$, (c) records this tuple (q, PK_q, SK_q) in a global table not accessible to the attacker; (d) returns (q, PK_q) to the attacker.
2. $\text{HPROVE}(i, C, x)$: honest evaluation oracle. Here $1 \leq i \leq q$ is an index, C is a ciphertext, and x in an input. The oracle returns $\text{PROVE}(SK_i, C, x) = \text{CORE}(SK_i, \text{SPLIT}(PK_i, C), x)$.
3. $\text{HDEL}(i, C, j)$: honest delegation oracle. Here $1 \leq i, j \leq q$ are two indices, and C is a ciphertext. The oracle returns $C' = \text{DEL}(SK_i, C, SK_j)$ (or $\text{DEL}(SK_i, C, PK_j)$ in the publicly-delegatable case).
4. $\text{OUTDEL}(i, C, SK/PK)$: "Out" delegation oracle. Here $1 \leq i \leq q$ is an index, C is a ciphertext, and PK or SK (depending on whether scheme is publicly-delegatable or not) is any public/secret key chosen by the attacker. The oracle returns $C' = \text{DEL}(SK_i, C, SK/PK)$.
5. $\text{INDEL}(SK, C, i)$: "In" delegation oracle. Here $1 \leq i \leq q$ is an index, and C is a ciphertext, and SK is any secret key chosen by the attacker. The oracle returns $C' = \text{DEL}(SK, C, SK_i)$. Notice, this oracle is interesting only in the secretly-delegatable case.

Remark 8. **Delegation-Completeness** and **Delegation-Soundness** easily imply **Delegation-Correctness** which was advocated in Eq. (1):

$$\text{DEL}(SK_1, C_1, SK_2/PK_2) = C_2 \implies \forall x\ \text{EVAL}(SK_1, C_1, x) = \text{EVAL}(SK_2, C_2, x)$$

Remark 9. The legality condition on the attacker is necessary, as evaluating EVRF on the "same" ciphertext C' as the challenge ciphertext C_1 breaks pseudorandomness (by delegation-soundness). However, it leaves open the possibility for the attacker to find such equivalent ciphertext C' *without building some explicit "delegation path"* from the challenge ciphertext C_1. Indeed, in the full version of the paper [3], we will give an even stronger legality condition on $\mathcal{A}$, and some (but not all) of our schemes will meet it. For applications, however, we do not envision this slight definitional gap to make any difference. Namely, the higher-level application will anyway need some mechanism to disallow any "trivial" attacks. We expect this mechanism will explicitly use our SAME procedure, rather than keep track of the tree of "delegation paths" originating from C_1, which could quickly become unmanageable.

Remark 10. It is easy to observe the following implications:

$$\textbf{Bi–\$-Core} \implies \textbf{Uni-\$-Core} \implies \textbf{Basic-\$-Core} \implies \textbf{\$-Core}$$

Here, the last implication uses the fact that C_1 is the only ciphertext equivalent to C_1 under PK_1. Thus, bidirectional delegation security is the strongest of all the notions.

Remark 11. One could also consider EVRFs which are simultaneously threshold and delegatable. In this case, n_1 servers for the sender's EVRFs will communicate with n_2 servers for the receiver's EVRF to help convert a ciphertext C_1 for the sender EVRF into a corresponding ciphertext C_2 for the receiver EVRF. We leave this extension to future work.

7.2 Construction of Basic Delegatable EVRF

We now show that our original EVRF Construction 1 can be extended to make it basic-delegatable. The idea is to separate the role of the "handle" R hashed under H inside the CORE procedure from the one used in the preprocessing. For technical reasons explained below, we will also hash the public key A when evaluating the EVRF. The construction is presented as Construction 4.

OBSERVATIONS. We notice that, since $R = D$ initially, the resulting EVRF before the delegation is the same as the one we defined in Sect. 5.1, except (a) we also include the public key A under the hash H during both ENCAP and CORE; and (b) we perform the delegation check $e(A', R') \stackrel{?}{=} e(A, D')$ in the split procedure SPLIT, which is trivially true initially, as $A' = A$ and $R' = D' = R$. Thus, **Evaluation-Correctness** trivially holds, as before. For the same reason, **Uniqueness** trivially holds as well.

The importance of change (a) comes from the fact that challenge ciphertext $C = (A, R, D)$ no longer includes only the value R, even though the value R would be all that is needed to actually evaluate our EVRF, had we not included A under the hash H. In particular, the attacker $\mathcal{A}$ given challenge $C = (A, R, R)$, can easily produce $C' \neq C$ by setting $C' = (A^2, R, R^2)$. C' passes the delegation check $e(A^2, R) = e(A, R^2)$, but clearly produces the same partial output $z = H(R, x)^a$ as the challenge ciphertext, trivially breaking the **\$-Core** property. Instead, by also hashing the public key, the oracle call PROVE(C', x) would return $z' = H(A^2, R, x)^a$, which is now unrelated to $z = H(A, R, x)^a$, foiling the trivial attack.

The importance of change (b) comes from ensuring that a valid ciphertext (A', R', D') determines the value D' *information-theoretically* from the values (A', R') (and the public key A), because the condition $e(A', R') = e(A, D')$

Protocol Basic Delegatable EVRF

GEN(1^k)

Sample $a \in_r \mathbb{Z}_p^*$
Compute $A = g^a \in \mathbb{G}$.
return $SK = a$ and $PK = (g, A)$.

ENCAP(PK)

Parse $PK = (g, A)$.
Sample $r \in_r \mathbb{Z}_p^*$.
Compute $R = D = g^r, S = A^r$.
return ciphertext $C = (A, R, D)$ and trapdoor $T = (A, R, S)$.

COMP(T, x)

Parse $T = (A, R, S)$.
Compute $y = e(H(A, R, x), S)$.
return y.

DEL(SK_1, C_1, SK_2)

Parse $SK_1 = a_1, SK_2 = a_2, C_1 = (A, R, D_1)$.
if $e(A, R) \neq e(g^{a_1}, D_1)$ **then**
  return $\perp$.
else
  Compute $D_2 = D_1^{a_1/a_2}$ where $a_1/a_2 = a_1 \cdot (a_2)^{-1} \mod p$.
  return $C_2 = (A, R, D_2)$.

SPLIT(PK, C')

Parse $PK = (g, A)$, $C' = (A, R', D')$.
if $e(A', R') \neq e(A, D')$ **then**
  return $\perp$.
else
  return (A', R').

CORE(SK, C', x)

Parse $SK = a, C' = (A', R', D')$.
Compute partial output $z = H(A', R', x)^a$.
return z.

POST(PK, z', C', x)

Parse $PK = (g, A)$, $C' = (A', R', D')$
if $e(z', g) \neq e(H(A', R', x), A)$ **then**
  return $\perp$.
else
  Compute full output $y' = e(z', D')$.
  return y'.

SAME(PK_1, C_1, PK_2, C_2)

Parse $PK_1 = (g, A_1), PK_2 = (g, A_2), C_1 = (A, R, D_1), C_2 = (A', R', D_2)$.
if $(A, R) \neq (A', R')$ or $e(A_1, D_1) \neq e(A_2, D_2)$ **then**
  return $\perp$.

Construction 4. Basic Delegatable DEVRF$_1$ = (GEN, ENCAP, COMP, SPLIT, CORE, POST, DEL, SAME).

uniquely determines D'. Thus, it is OK that the CORE procedure only passes the values (A', R') under the random oracle H.

DELEGATION. To check **Delegation-Completeness**, notice that valid delegation of (A, R, D_1) outputs (A', R', D_2), where $(A', R') = (A, R)$ and $D_2 = D_1^{a_1/a_2}$, which implies that

$$e(A_2, D_2) = e(g^{a_2}, D_1^{a_1/a_2}) = e(g^{a_1}, D_1) = e(A_1, D_1)$$

which means SAME$(A_1, (A, R, D_1), A_2, (A', R', D_2)) = 1$ indeed.

For **Delegation-Soundness**, given $C_1 = (A, R, D_1)$ and $C_2 = (A', R', D_2)$ satisfying $(A', R') = (A, R)$ and $e(A_1, D_1) = e(A_2, D_2)$, we can see that the delegation checks $e(A, R) \stackrel{?}{=} e(A_1, D_1)$ and $e(A', R') \stackrel{?}{=} e(A_2, D_2)$ are either both false or true simultaneously. Moreover, by writing $A_1 = A_2^{a_1/a_2}$, the second equation implies that $D_2 = D_1^{a_1/a_2}$. In particular, if $A_1 = A_2$, we have $C_1 = C_2$; and, in general, when $(A', R') = (A, R)$ and $D_2 = D_1^{a_1/a_2}$, for any x, we know: EVAL$(a_2, (A, R, D_2), x) = e(H(A, R, x)^{a_2}, D_2)$.

However, that can be rewritten as

$$e(H(A, R, x)^{a_2}, D_1^{a_1/a_2}) = e(H(A, R, x)^{a_2}, D_1^{a_1/a_2}) = e(H(A, R, x)^{a_1}, D_1)$$

which concludes the proof.

We reiterate that though our delegation is secretly-delegatable, as D_2 depends on a_2, in practice the owner Alice of a_1 will simply send the trapdoor value $T_1 = D_1^{a_1}$ to the owner Bob of a_2 over secure channel (say, encrypted under a separate public key), and Bob can then compute $D_2 = T_1^{1/a_2}$. In particular, this does not leak any extra information beyond (D_2, a_2) to Bob, as $T_1 = D_2^{a_2}$ is efficiently computable from D_2 and a_2. Also, the delegation check does not require any of the secret keys. Despite that, it ensures that only properly delegated ciphertexts can be securely re-delegated again. We will critically use to prove the following:

Theorem 4. *The basic delegatable EVRF, given in Construction 4, satisfies the **Basic-\$-Core** property under the* BDDH *assumption in the random oracle model.*

The proof of the above theorem is deferred to full version of paper [3].

DELEGATION ATTACK ON STRONGER LEGALITY. We briefly mentioned in Sect. 7.1 that one could require a stronger legality condition to say that the only way to distinguish the evaluation of C on x from random is to honestly delegate C to some honest user (possibly iteratively), getting ciphertext C', and then ask this user to evaluate EVRF on x.

Here we show that our construction does not satisfy this notion. Consider challenge ciphertext $C_1 = (A_1, R_1, R_1)$ under public key A_1. Construct $C_1' = (A_1, R_1^2, R_1^2)$. C_1' will satisfy the delegation check, so we could ask to delegate C' to public key A_2. We get $C_2' = (A_1, R_1^2, (R_1^2)^{a_1/a_2}) = (A_1, R_1^2, (R_1^{a_1/a_2})^2)$. By taking square roots from the last two components, we get $C_2 = (A_1, R_1, R_1^{a_1/a_2})$. Notice, $\text{SAME}(A_1, C_1, A_2, C_2) = 1$ is true, so our original definition does *not* permit the attacker to evaluate $\text{HPROVE}(2, C_2, x)$ (which clearly breaks the scheme). However, since we obtained C_2 *without* asking the delegate C_1 itself (instead, we asked a different ciphertext C_1'), the stronger notion would have allowed the attacker to call $\text{HPROVE}(2, C_2, x)$ and break the scheme.

7.3 Construction of Uni- And Bidirectional Delegatable EVRF

Next, we extend the construction from the previous EVRF construction to also handle delegation *to* (and, under a stronger assumption, *from*) potentially untrusted parties. The idea is to add a "BLS signature" [11] σ in the ENCAP procedure which will prove that the initial ciphertext was "well-formed". This makes it hard for the attacker to maul a valid initial ciphertext C into a related ciphertext C', whose delegation might compromise the security of C. The public verifiability of the signature σ will also make it easy to add a "signature check" to the "delegation check" we already used in our scheme, to ensure that the appropriate pseudorandomness property is not compromised. This is presented as Construction 5.

Protocol Delegatable EVRF

<u>$\text{Gen}(1^k)$</u>

Sample $a \in_r \mathbb{Z}_p^*$
Compute $A = g^a \in \mathbb{G}$.
return $SK = a$ and $PK = (g, A)$.

<u>$\text{Encap}(PK)$</u>

Parse $PK = (g, A)$.
Sample $r \in_r \mathbb{Z}_p^*$.
Compute $R = D = g^r, S = A^r, \sigma = H'(A, R)^r$.
return ciphertext $C = (A, R, D, \sigma)$ and trapdoor $T = (A, R, S)$.

<u>$\text{Comp}(T, x)$</u>

Parse $T = (A, R, S)$.
Compute $y = e(H(A, R, x), S)$.
return y.

<u>$\text{Del}(SK_1, C_1, SK_2)$</u>

Parse $SK_1 = a_1, SK_2 = a_2, C_1 = (A, R, D_1, \sigma)$.
if $e(A, R) \neq e(g^{a_1}, D_1)$ or $e(H'(A, R), R) \neq e(\sigma, g)$ **then**
  return $\perp$.
else
  Compute $D_2 = D_1^{a_1/a_2}$ where $a_1/a_2 = a_1 \cdot (a_2)^{-1}$ mod p.
  return $C_2 = (A, R, D_2)$.

<u>$\text{Split}(PK, C')$</u>

Parse $PK = (g, A)$, $C' = (A', R', D', \sigma')$.
if $e(A', R') \neq e(A, D')$ or $e(H'(A', R'), R') \neq e(\sigma', g)$ **then**
  return $\perp$.
else
  return (A', R').

<u>$\text{Core}(SK, C', x)$</u>

Parse $SK = a, C' = (A', R', D', \sigma')$.
Compute partial output $z = H(A', R', x)^a$.
return z.

<u>$\text{Post}(PK, z', C', x)$</u>

Parse $PK = (g, A)$, $C' = (A', R', D', \sigma')$
if $e(z', g) \neq e(H(A', R', x), A)$ **then**
  return $\perp$.
else
  Compute full output $y' = e(z', D')$.
  return y'.

<u>$\text{Same}(PK_1, C_1, PK_2, C_2)$</u>

Parse $PK_1 = (g, A_1), PK_2 = (g, A_2), C_1 = (A, R, D_1, \sigma), C_2 = (A', R', D_2, \sigma')$.
if $(A, R, \sigma) \neq (A', R', \sigma')$ or $e(A_1, D_1) \neq e(A_2, D_2)$ **then**
  return $\perp$.

Construction 5. $\text{DEVRF}_2 = (\text{Gen}, \text{Encap}, \text{Comp}, \text{Split}, \text{Core}, \text{Post}, \text{Del}, \text{Same})$.

Security Analysis. Since DEVRF_2 is essentially the same as DEVRF_1, its correctness follows the same argument. In particular, we notice that the original signature σ indeed satisfies our signature check:

$$e(H'(A, R), R) = e(H'(A, R), g^r) = e(H'(A, R)^r, g) = e(\sigma, g)$$

Similar to the delegation check, the signature check, $e(H'(A', R'), R') \stackrel{?}{=} e(\sigma', g)$, is important to ensure that the value σ' is information-theoretically determined from the value (A', R'), so it is fine to not include σ under H.

Also, since the delegation procedure Del simply copies the values A, R and σ, and only modifies the value D_1, the **Delegation-Completeness** and **Delegation-Soundness** of DEVRF_2 holds as it did for DEVRF_1, since the signature check is not affected by changing D_1 to $D_2 = D_1^{a_1/a_2}$. In particular, similar to the delegation checks, both signature checks are either simultaneously true or false.

More importantly, in the full version of the paper [3], we also show how the addition of the "BLS signature" σ and the new signature check allow us to prove the following theorem:

Theorem 5. *The delegatable EVRF given in Construction 5 satisfies the* ***Uni-\$-Core*** *property under the* BDDH *assumption in the random oracle model.*

Finally, we also show that the same construction also satisfies the strongest *bidirectional-delegation* security, but now under a much stronger iBDDH assumption. In fact, for this result, we will even show a *stronger legality* condition mentioned earlier: the only way to break DEVRF_2 is to trivially delegate it "out" to the attacker, or delegate it to the honest user, and then ask the user to evaluate on challenge x. We define this formally in the full version of the paper [3], where we also show the following result:

Theorem 6. *The delegatable EVRF given in Construction 5 satisfies the **Bi–$-Core** property under the interactive* iBDDH *assumption in the random oracle model. It satisfies the strongest possible legality condition for the attacker (see [3]).*

7.4 Construction of One-time Delegatable EVRF

Note that the bidirectional-delegation security of Construction 5 relied on a very strong inversion-oracle BDDH (iBDDH) assumption, which is interactive and not well studied. For applications where we only guarantee security after a single delegation, we could prove bidirectional-delegation under a much reasonable extended BDDH (eBDDH) assumption. More precisely, any party P is "safe" to do any number of "out-delegations" to other, potentially untrusted parties P', but should only accept "in-delegation" from such an untrusted P' only if the delegated ciphertext C' was created directly for P' (and not delegated to P' from somewhere else).

More formally, the one-time delegation scheme we present here is identical to the unidirectional-delegation scheme from the previous section, except we replace the "delegation check" ($e(A, R) \stackrel{?}{=} e(A_1, D_1)$) by a stricter "equality check"($(A, R) \stackrel{?}{=} (A_1, D_1)$) which means that the ciphertext C_1 was directly created for public key $A_1 = A$. We call the resulting 1-time-delegatable construction DEVRF_3. In the full version of the paper [3] we show that DEVRF_3 satisfies bidirectional-delegation security, but now under a much weaker (non-interactive) eBDDH assumption:

Theorem 7. *The* one-time *delegatable* DEVRF_3 *above satisfies the **Bi–$-Core** property under the* eBDDH *assumption in the random oracle model. It satisfies the strongest possible legality condition for the attacker (see [3]).*

We stress that our 1-time delegatable scheme could in principle be delegated further, if the stricter delegation check $(A, R) \stackrel{?}{=} (A_1, D_1)$ is replaced by the original check $e(A, R) \stackrel{?}{=} e(A_1, D_1)$. However, by doing so the party receiving the EVRF from some untrusted source must rely on the stronger iBDDH complexity assumption.

8 Conclusion and Final Thoughts

In this work we introduce the idea of an encapsulated search index (ESI) that offers support for public-indexing and where the search takes sub-linear time. We also presented a generic construction of ESI from another primitive known as encapsulated verifiable random functions (EVRF). We further detailed meaningful extensions to both ESI and EVRF with support for delegation and distribution. We presented constructions of a standard EVRF and its various extensions. Indeed, obtain the following Theorem as a corollary of Theorem 2, and by using any updatable sub-linear DS with an appropriate (delegatable and/or threshold) EVRF from the earlier sections, we get:

Theorem 8. *We have an updatable* ESI *(see [3]) which*

(a) maintains the efficiency of the non-cryptographic DS*;*
(b) has non-interactive (t, n) *threshold implementation for token generation (by using* TEVRF*); and*
(c) achieves either of the following delegation security levels in the random oracle model:
  - ***Basic CCA secure*** *under* BDDH *assumption (by using* DEVRF_1*)*
  - ***Uni CCA secure*** *under* BDDH *assumption (by using* DEVRF_2*)*
  - ***Bi CCA secure*** *under* iBDDH *assumption (by using* DEVRF_2*)*
  - ***One Time CCA secure*** *under* eBDDH *assumption (by using* DEVRF_3*)*

COMMERCIAL PRODUCT. This theorem forms the backbone of a commercially available product that has been in the market since 2020. It serves over two-dozen enterprise customers, with the largest having over 100 users. At a high level, the commercial application is essentially the motivating application described in the Introduction, but with a few pragmatic extensions.

The code is production quality and has been deployed without any noticeable performance degradation, even for large files. Note that a typical mobile device has the capability to compute 10,000 elliptic curve multiplications (which is needed in our partial decryption step) per second, with the help of multiple cores. This number is only expected to go up with further technological advancements such as the growth of mobile GPUs. In the search functionality, a user can enter one or several keywords. The system then sequentially searches each file using the ESI that has been built leading to a total complexity proportional to the product of the number of keywords, the number of files, and the ESI search time. By using a blinded bloom filter as the data structure, the application achieves a constant time search dictionary.[10] Currently, searching 1000 files with up to 4 keywords (or 2000 files with a maximum of 2 keywords) can be accomplished in about 2 s on a standard mobile phone. The application already uses the distributed token generation and the search delegation capabilities of our underlying ESI. We present additional details in the full version of the paper [3].

References

1. Abdalla, M., et al.: Searchable encryption revisited: consistency properties, relation to anonymous IBE, and extensions. In: Shoup, V. (ed.) CRYPTO 2005. LNCS, vol. 3621, pp. 205–222. Springer, Heidelberg (2005). https://doi.org/10.1007/11535218_13

[10] Of course, the indexing step is proportional to the size of the file.

2. Agrawal, S., Mohassel, P., Mukherjee, P., Rindal, P.: DiSE: distributed symmetric-key encryption. In: Lie, D., Mannan, M., Backes, M., Wang, X.F. (eds.), ACM CCS 2018, pp. 1993–2010. ACM Press, October 2018
3. Aronesty, E., et al.: Encapsulated search index: Public-key, sub-linear, distributed, and delegatable. https://cs.nyu.edu/~dodis/ps/esi.pdf (2021)
4. Baek, J., Safavi-Naini, R., Susilo, W.: Public key encryption with keyword search revisited. In: Gervasi, O., Murgante, B., Laganà, A., Taniar, D., Mun, Y., Gavrilova, M.L. (eds.) ICCSA 2008. LNCS, vol. 5072, pp. 1249–1259. Springer, Heidelberg (2008). https://doi.org/10.1007/978-3-540-69839-5_96
5. Bellovin, S.M., Cheswick, W.R.: Privacy-enhanced searches using encrypted bloom filters. Cryptology ePrint Archive, Report 2004/022 (2004). http://eprint.iacr.org/2004/022
6. Bloom, B.H.: Space/time trade-offs in hash coding with allowable errors. Commun. ACM **13**(7), 422–426 (1970)
7. Boneh, D., Boyen, X., Halevi, S.: Chosen ciphertext secure public key threshold encryption without random oracles. In: Pointcheval, D. (ed.) CT-RSA 2006. LNCS, vol. 3860, pp. 226–243. Springer, Heidelberg (2006). https://doi.org/10.1007/11605805_15
8. Boneh, D., Di Crescenzo, G., Ostrovsky, R., Persiano, G.: Public key encryption with keyword search. In: Cachin, C., Camenisch, J.L. (eds.) EUROCRYPT 2004. LNCS, vol. 3027, pp. 506–522. Springer, Heidelberg (2004). https://doi.org/10.1007/978-3-540-24676-3_30
9. Boneh, D., Franklin, M.: Identity-based encryption from the Weil pairing. SIAM J. Comput. **32**(3), 586–615 (2003)
10. Boneh, D., Kushilevitz, E., Ostrovsky, R., Skeith, W.E.: Public key encryption that allows PIR queries. In: Menezes, A. (ed.) CRYPTO 2007. LNCS, vol. 4622, pp. 50–67. Springer, Heidelberg (2007). https://doi.org/10.1007/978-3-540-74143-5_4
11. Boneh, D., Lynn, B., Shacham, H.: Short signatures from the Weil pairing. In: Boyd, C. (ed.) ASIACRYPT 2001. LNCS, vol. 2248, pp. 514–532. Springer, Heidelberg (2001). https://doi.org/10.1007/3-540-45682-1_30
12. Boyen, X., Mei, Q., Waters, B.: Direct chosen ciphertext security from identity-based techniques. In: Atluri, V., Meadows, C., Juels, A. (eds.), ACM CCS 2005, pp. 320–329. ACM Press, November 2005
13. Canetti, R., Goldwasser, S.: An efficient *threshold* public key cryptosystem secure against adaptive chosen ciphertext attack (Extended abstract). In: Stern, J. (ed.) EUROCRYPT 1999. LNCS, vol. 1592, pp. 90–106. Springer, Heidelberg (1999). https://doi.org/10.1007/3-540-48910-X_7
14. Cash, D., Grubbs, P., Perry, J., Ristenpart, T.: Leakage-abuse attacks against searchable encryption. In: Ray, I., Li, N., Kruegel, C. (eds.), ACM CCS 2015, pp. 668–679. ACM Press, October 2015
15. Chang, Y.-C., Mitzenmacher, M.: Privacy preserving keyword searches on remote encrypted data. In: Ioannidis, J., Keromytis, A., Yung, M. (eds.) ACNS 2005. LNCS, vol. 3531, pp. 442–455. Springer, Heidelberg (2005). https://doi.org/10.1007/11496137_30
16. Cloudflare. Cloudflare Randomness Beacon docs. https://developers.cloudflare.com/randomness-beacon/
17. Corestar. corestario/tendermint, October 2020. original-date: 2018-12-19T13:33:15Z
18. Cormen, T.H., Leiserson, C.E., Rivest, R.L., Stein, C.: Introduction to Algorithms, 3rd edition. The MIT Press, Cambridge (2009)

19. Cramer, R., Shoup, V.: A practical public key cryptosystem provably secure against adaptive chosen ciphertext attack. In: Krawczyk, H. (ed.) CRYPTO 1998. LNCS, vol. 1462, pp. 13–25. Springer, Heidelberg (1998). https://doi.org/10.1007/BFb0055717
20. Curtmola, R., Garay, J., Kamara, S., Ostrovsky, R.: Searchable symmetric encryption: improved definitions and efficient constructions. In: Juels, A., Wright, R.N., De Capitani di Vimercati, S. (eds.), ACM CCS 2006, pp. 79–88. ACM Press, October/November 2006
21. DAOBet. DAOBet (ex - DAO.Casino) to Deliver On-Chain Random Beacon Based on BLS Cryptography, May 2019. https://daobet.org/blog/on-chain-random-generator/
22. Song, D.X., Wagner, D., Perrig, A.: Practical techniques for searches on encrypted data. In: Proceeding 2000 IEEE Symposium on Security and Privacy. S P 2000, pp. 44–55 (2000)
23. Dodis, Y.: Efficient construction of (Distributed) verifiable random functions. In: Desmedt, Y.G. (ed.) PKC 2003. LNCS, vol. 2567, pp. 1–17. Springer, Heidelberg (2003). https://doi.org/10.1007/3-540-36288-6_1
24. Dodis, Y., Yampolskiy, A.: A verifiable random function with short proofs and keys. In: Vaudenay, S. (ed.) PKC 2005. LNCS, vol. 3386, pp. 416–431. Springer, Heidelberg (2005). https://doi.org/10.1007/978-3-540-30580-4_28
25. Feldman, F.A.: Fast spectral tests for measuring nonrandomness and the DES. In: Pomerance, C. (ed.) CRYPTO 1987. LNCS, vol. 293, pp. 243–254. Springer, Heidelberg (1988). https://doi.org/10.1007/3-540-48184-2_22
26. Galindo, D., Liu, J., Ordean, M., Wong, J.M.: Fully distributed verifiable random functions and their application to decentralised random beacons. Cryptology ePrint Archive, Report 2020/096 (2020). https://eprint.iacr.org/2020/096
27. Gennaro, R., Jarecki, S., Krawczyk, H., Rabin, T.: Secure distributed key generation for discrete-log based cryptosystems. J. Cryptology **20**(1), 51–83 (2007)
28. Goh, E.J.: Secure indexes. Cryptology ePrint Archive, Report 2003/216 (2003). http://eprint.iacr.org/2003/216
29. Goldberg, S., Naor, M., Papadopoulos, D., Reyzin, L., Vasant, S., Ziv, A.: NSEC5: Provably preventing DNSSEC zone enumeration. In: NDSS 2015. The Internet Society, February 2015
30. Goldberg, S., Reyzin, L., Papadopoulos, D., Včelák, J.: Verifiable Random Functions (VRFs). Internet-Draft draft-irtf-cfrg-vrf-07, Internet Engineering Task Force, June 2020. Work in Progress
31. Kamara, S., Papamanthou, C., Roeder, T.: Dynamic searchable symmetric encryption. In: Yu, T., Danezis, G., Gligor, V.D. (eds.), ACM CCS 2012, pp. 965–976. ACM Press, October 2012
32. Keep. The Keep Random Beacon: An Implementation of a Threshold Relay, 2020. https://docs.keep.network/random-beacon/
33. Kuchta, V., Manulis, M.: Unique aggregate signatures with applications to distributed verifiable random functions. In: Abdalla, M., Nita-Rotaru, C., Dahab, R. (eds.) CANS 2013. LNCS, vol. 8257, pp. 251–270. Springer, Cham (2013). https://doi.org/10.1007/978-3-319-02937-5_14
34. Lysyanskaya, A.: Unique signatures and verifiable random functions from the DH-DDH separation. In: Yung, M. (ed.) CRYPTO 2002. LNCS, vol. 2442, pp. 597–612. Springer, Heidelberg (2002). https://doi.org/10.1007/3-540-45708-9_38
35. Micali, S., Rabin, M.O., Vadhan, S.P.: Verifiable random functions. In: 40th FOCS, pp. 120–130. IEEE Computer Society Press, October 1999

36. Naor, M., Pinkas, B., Reingold, O.: Distributed pseudo-random functions and KDCs. In: Stern, J. (ed.) EUROCRYPT 1999. LNCS, vol. 1592, pp. 327–346. Springer, Heidelberg (1999). https://doi.org/10.1007/3-540-48910-X_23
37. Naor, M., Yogev, E.: Tight bounds for sliding bloom filters. Algorithmica **73**(4), 652–672 (2015)
38. Pagh, A., Pagh, R., Rao, S.S.: An optimal bloom filter replacement. In: Proceedings of the Sixteenth Annual ACM-SIAM Symposium on Discrete Algorithms, SODA 2005, pp. 823–829, USA, Society for Industrial and Applied Mathematics (2005)
39. Pagh, R., Rodler, F.F.: Cuckoo hashing. J. Algorithms **51**(2), 122–144 (2004)
40. Rhee, H.S., Park, J.H., Susilo, W., Lee, D.H.: Improved searchable public key encryption with designated tester. In: Li, W., Susilo, W., Tupakula, U.K., Safavi-Naini, R., Varadharajan, V. (eds.), ASIACCS 09, pp. 376–379. ACM Press, March 2009
41. Schindler, P., Judmayer, A., Stifter, N., Weippl, E.: ETHDKG: distributed key generation with ethereum smart contracts. Cryptology ePrint Archive, Report 2019/985 (2019). https://eprint.iacr.org/2019/985
42. Shamir, A.: How to share a secret. Commun. ACM **22**(11), 612–613 (1979)
43. Stern, J. (ed.): EUROCRYPT 1999. LNCS, vol. 1592. Springer, Heidelberg (1999). https://doi.org/10.1007/3-540-48910-X
44. Zhou, Y., Li, N., Tian, Y., An, D., Wang, L.: Public key encryption with keyword search in cloud: a survey. Entropy **22**(4), 421 (2020)

KDM Security for the Fujisaki-Okamoto Transformations in the QROM

Fuyuki Kitagawa(✉) and Ryo Nishimaki

NTT Corporation, Tokyo, Japan
{fuyuki.kitagawa.yh,ryo.nishimaki.zk}@hco.ntt.co.jp

Abstract. Key dependent message (KDM) security is a security notion that guarantees confidentiality of communication even if secret keys are encrypted. KDM security has found a number of applications in practical situations such as hard-disk encryption systems, anonymous credentials, and bootstrapping of fully homomorphic encryption. Recently, it also found an application in quantum delegation protocols as shown by Zhang (TCC 2019).

In this work, we investigate the KDM security of existing practical public-key encryption (PKE) schemes proposed in the quantum random oracle model (QROM). Concretely, we study a PKE scheme whose KEM is constructed by using Fujisaki-Okamoto (FO) transformations in the QROM. FO transformations are applied to IND-CPA secure PKE schemes and yield IND-CCA secure key encapsulation mechanisms (KEM). Then, we show the following results.

- We can reduce the KDM-CPA security in the QROM of a PKE scheme whose KEM is derived from any of the FO transformations proposed by Hofheinz et al. (TCC 2017) to the IND-CPA security of the underlying PKE scheme, without square root security loss. For this result, we use one-time-pad (OTP) as DEM to convert KEM into PKE.
- We can reduce the KDM-CCA security in the QROM of a PKE scheme whose KEM is derived from a single variant of the FO transformation proposed by Hofheinz et al. (TCC 2017) to the IND-CPA security of the underlying PKE scheme, without square root security loss. For this result, we use OTP-then-MAC construction as DEM to convert KEM into PKE. Also, we require a mild injectivity assumption for the underlying IND-CPA secure PKE scheme.

In order to avoid square root security loss, we use a double-sided one-way to hiding (O2H) lemma proposed by Kuchta et al. (EUROCRYPT 2020). In the context of KDM security, there is a technical hurdle for using double-sided O2H lemma due to the circularity issue. Our main technical contribution is to overcome the hurdle.

1 Introduction

1.1 Background

Post-quantum security is emerging as a de facto standard since quantum technology has been making rapid progress. In particular, since the NIST post-quantum

G. Hanaoka et al. (Eds.): PKC 2022, LNCS 13178, pp. 286–315, 2022.
https://doi.org/10.1007/978-3-030-97131-1_10

cryptography standardization project started, IND-CCA security in the quantum random oracle model (QROM) have been extensively studied to design practical and post-quantum secure public-key encryption (PKE) [BHH+19, AHU19, HKSU20, JZM19a, HHK17, JZC+18, SXY18, TU16, KSS+20]. IND-CCA [RS92, DDN00] is the gold standard security notion for PKE since chosen-ciphertext attacks are realistic in many practical applications [Ble98]. The random oracle model (ROM) [BR93] is an idealized model where hash functions are modeled as ideal random functions in security proofs. This idealized model helps us to design extremely efficient cryptographic primitives. In the QROM [BDF+11], a random oracle query is a superposition query since adversaries are modeled as quantum polynomial-time algorithms and hash functions are locally computable.

Although IND-CCA is suitable for many practical applications, a stronger security goal than standard confidentiality is required in some settings. Key-dependent message (KDM) security [BRS03] is such an example. KDM security guarantees that adversaries cannot distinguish encryption of $f_0(\mathsf{sk})$ from encryption of $f_1(\mathsf{sk})$ where sk is a secret key and f_0, f_1 are arbitrary functions. The KDM situation is realistic in hard disk encryption systems like BitLocker [BHHO08] and bootstrapping fully homomorphic encryption [Gen09]. We also use KDM secure encryption as a building block of cryptographic primitives and protocols such as anonymous credentials [CL01]. In particular, (non-adaptive) KDM secure secret-key encryption (SKE) against quantum adversaries is used to achieve delegation of quantum computation [Zha19]. The KDM situation also naturally arises in formal verification of cryptographic protocols [AR02].

Thus, a natural question is:

Can we achieve practical KDM-CPA/CCA secure PKE in the QROM?

or

Do existing practical IND-CPA/CCA secure PKE satisfy KDM security in the QROM?

The difficulty of this question depends on what level of security and efficiency we achieve.

Security analysis in the QROM usually deviates from one in the classical ROM. One significant issue is that, in the QROM, we cannot directly use the observability of the classical ROM, which says reduction algorithms can observe input points where adversaries make random oracle queries. In the QROM, reduction algorithms need to measure superposition queries to observe random oracle queries, but this prevents reduction since adversaries can detect measurement. Superposition queries also prevent us from straightforwardly applying the adaptive programming technique. These problems make it more challenging to achieve CCA and KDM security in the QROM since each property is one of the crucial properties in the proofs for CCA and KDM [FO13, KMHT16]. New techniques have been proposed to solve the security-proof problems in the QROM. The one-way to hiding (O2H) lemma [Unr15] and its variants [AHU19, BHH+19, KSS+20] are the most well-known useful tools to solve the problem above and achieve secure encryption in the QROM.

Roughly speaking, the (original) O2H lemma is as follows. A quantum distinguisher $\mathcal{A}$ is given oracle access to an oracle $\mathcal{O}$, which is either a random function $H : X \rightarrow Y$ or $G : X \rightarrow Y$ such that $\forall x \notin S$, $H(x) = G(x)$. Let z be a random classical string or quantum state ((G, H, S, z) may have an arbitrary distribution). Let $\mathcal{D}$ be a quantum algorithm that is given input z and oracle access to H, measures $\mathcal{A}$'s query, and outputs the result. The distinguishing advantage of $\mathcal{A}$, $\epsilon_{\mathcal{A}}$, is bounded by the *square root* of the search advantage of $\mathcal{D}$, $\epsilon_{\mathcal{D}}$, that finds an element in S.[1] All O2H lemmas except the variant by Kuchta, Sakzad, Stehlé, Steinfeld, and Sun [KSS+20] incur a square root security loss. A square root security loss significantly degrades the performance of cryptographic primitives since we need to use much longer security parameters for building blocks to guarantee a reasonable security level, say, 128-bit security.[2] Thus, to achieve practical KDM secure PKE schemes, we should avoid a square root loss. When we focus on tight security, both security advantages and the running time of reductions are crucial factors. However, in most PKE schemes (and all our schemes), the overhead of running time of reductions is only additive and is not a dominant factor. Thus, we focus on security loss.

At first glance, the O2H lemma by Kuchta et al. [KSS+20] (denoted by O2H with MRM) seems to immediately answer our question since it does not incur a square root security loss. However, this is not the case. O2H with MRM is a variation of the *double-sided* O2H lemma by Bindel, Hamburg, Hövelmanns, Hülsing, and Persichetti [BHH+19], where $\mathcal{D}$ is given oracle access to *both H and G*. Thus, in O2H with MRM, $\mathcal{D}$ is given oracle access to a random oracle H and *a modified random oracle G*. This is not an issue for proving IND-CPA/CCA security. However, it is a serious issue for proving KDM security because correlated information about secret keys could remain in the modified random oracle G in known proofs for KDM in the classical ROM. See Sect. 1.4 for the detail. Kuchta et al. [KSS+20] left relaxing their double-sided O2H with MRM to a single-sided variant as an open question. However, that question remains elusive. In the KDM setting, we cannot directly apply a double-sided type O2H lemma. Achieving KDM security with a double-sided O2H lemma is of independent interest. Thus, our question is more precisely described as follows.

Can we achieve practical KDM-CPA/CCA secure PKE without a square root security loss in the QROM?

or

Do existing practical IND-CPA/CCA secure PKE satisfy KDM security without a square root security loss in the QROM?

1.2 Our Result

In this work, we affirmatively answer the question above. We prove the following.

[1] Here, we ignore security loss by the number of queries and constants for simplicity.

[2] Saito, Xagawa, and Yamakawa [SXY18] estimate that we need 376-bit security of underlying trapdoor functions for 128-bit security of the IND-CCA KEM scheme by Boneh et al. [BDF+11] if the number of queries is 2^{60} due to a square root security loss.

- We can obtain KDM-CPA secure PKE without a square root security loss by applying a Fujisaki-Okamoto transformation (denoted by FO) [FO13, HHK17] to IND-CPA secure PKE and combining one-time pad (OTP) as DEM.
- We can obtain KDM-CCA secure PKE without a square root security loss by applying an FO [FO13, BHH+19] to IND-CPA secure PKE and combining OTP and strong one-time MAC[3] (that is, OTP-then-MAC) as DEM.

Note that our goal is PKE (not KEM) since we can consider the KDM setting only in PKE. We need OTP to achieve PKE since FO yields KEM [FO13, HHK17]. Our results are extremely versatile since we can convert IND-CPA secure PKE to KDM-CPA/CCA secure PKE by the well-known general transformations. FO yields practical KEM/PKE schemes and is employed in many candidates of the NIST PQC standardization to achieve CCA security. Note that we do not need the perfect correctness of the building block PKE. However, for the result on KDM-CCA secure PKE, we require that a derandomized version of the building block PKE is injective as in the CCA schemes in some previous works [BHH+19, KSS+20]. Bindel et al. argue that injectivity is commonly satisfied by many practical IND-CPA secure lattice based schemes [BHH+19]. We also note that we use PKE in the multi-user setting [BBM00] as the building block PKE in the transformation since the KDM setting is the multi-user setting by default.[4]

To explain our result more precisely, we recall that an FO can be decomposed into two transformations T and U. This was first observed by Hofheinz, Hövelmanns, and Kiltz [HHK17]. In this work, we adopt variants of T and U defined by Bindel et al. [BHH+19]. The only difference between the transformations by Hofheinz et al. and those by Bindel et al. is that the validity check by encryption in the decryption algorithm is performed as a part of T in the former while it is performed as a part of U in the latter. Thus, the resulting FO is the same regardless of which definitions of T and U we use.

T transformation transforms an IND-CPA secure PKE scheme into an OW-CPA secure deterministic PKE scheme. U transformation transforms an OW-CPA secure deterministic PKE scheme into an IND-CCA secure KEM. Regarding U, there are six variants, $\mathsf{U}^{\perp}$, $\mathsf{U}^{\not\perp}$, $\mathsf{U}^{\perp,\mathtt{keyconf}}$, $\mathsf{U}^{\perp}_{m}$, $\mathsf{U}^{\not\perp}_{m}$, and $\mathsf{U}_m^{\perp,\mathtt{keyconf}}$. Here, $\perp$ and $\not\perp$ mean explicit and implicit rejection in decryption, respectively, and no subscript and subscript m mean a hash function takes a ciphertext as a part of the input or not. Superscript `keyconf` (key confirmation) means that we add a hash value of a plaintext to a ciphertext and check the hash value in decryption. Bindel et al. [BHH+19] prove that $\mathsf{U}^{\perp}$, $\mathsf{U}^{\not\perp}$, and $\mathsf{U}^{\perp,\mathtt{keyconf}}$ yield IND-CCA KEM if and only if $\mathsf{U}^{\perp}_{m}$, $\mathsf{U}^{\not\perp}_{m}$, and $\mathsf{U}_m^{\perp,\mathtt{keyconf}}$ yield IND-CCA KEM, respectively. It does not matter whether a hash function takes a ciphertext as the input or not. This is also the case in the context of KDM security since the prove can be done via simple mappings between random functions. Thus, in this work, we focus on $\mathsf{U}^{\perp}_{m}$, $\mathsf{U}^{\not\perp}_{m}$, and $\mathsf{U}_m^{\perp,\mathtt{keyconf}}$.

[3] Strong one-time MAC unconditionally exists.

[4] We can achieve PKE in the ℓ-user setting with advantage ϵ' from standard PKE with advantage ϵ such that $\epsilon' \approx \ell \cdot \epsilon$.

Table 1. Summary of our results. Here, $\mathsf{U}^{\perp}_{m,\mathtt{OTP}}$ and $\mathsf{U}^{\perp,\mathtt{keyconf}}_{m,\mathtt{OTP+MAC}}$ denote $\mathsf{U}^{\perp}_{m}$ with OTP and $\mathsf{U}^{\perp,\mathtt{keyconf}}_{m}$ with OTP-then-MAC, respectively. Let ϵ_{Σ} and d_F be the attacker advantage in scheme Σ and the query depth of queries to random oracle F, respectively. Note that $d_F \leq q_F$ where q_F is the number of random oracle queries. We use PKE in the multi-user setting for the building block PKE (denoted by PKE). Open Q. means that it is an open question whether we can achieve KDM-CCA security by using $\mathsf{U}^{\not\perp}_{m,\mathtt{OTP}}[\mathsf{PKE}_1, H]$ transformation.

Transformation	Security implication	Security bound	Condition
$\mathsf{PKE}_1 := \mathsf{T}_{\mathsf{HKG}}[\mathsf{PKE}, G]$ (Sect. 5)	IND-CPA ⇒ SDM-OW-RSA	$O(d_G \cdot \epsilon_{\mathsf{PKE}})$	none
$\mathsf{U}^{\perp}_{m,\mathtt{OTP}}[\mathsf{PKE}_1, H]$ (Sect. 4)	SDM-OW-RSA ⇒ KDM-CPA	$O(d_H \cdot \epsilon_{\mathsf{PKE}_1})$	none
$\mathsf{U}^{\perp}_{m,\mathtt{OTP}}[T[\mathsf{PKE}, G], H]$ (Sect. 6)	IND-CPA ⇒ KDM-CPA	$O(d_H \cdot d_G \cdot \epsilon_{\mathsf{PKE}})^{\mathrm{a}}$	none
$\mathsf{U}^{\not\perp}_{m,\mathtt{OTP}}[T[\mathsf{PKE}, G], H]$	IND-CPA ⇒ KDM-CPA	$O(d_H \cdot d_G \cdot \epsilon_{\mathsf{PKE}})^{\mathrm{a}}$	none
$\mathsf{U}^{\perp,\mathtt{keyconf}}_{m,\mathtt{OTP+MAC}}[\mathsf{PKE}_1, H]$ ([KN21])	SDM-OW-RSA ⇒ KDM-CCA	$O(d_H \cdot \epsilon_{\mathsf{PKE}_1})$	injectivity
$\mathsf{U}^{\perp,\mathtt{keyconf}}_{m,\mathtt{OTP+MAC}}[T[\mathsf{PKE}, G], H]$ ([KN21])	IND-CPA ⇒ KDM-CCA	$O(d_H \cdot d_G \cdot \epsilon_{\mathsf{PKE}})^{\mathrm{a}}$	injectivity
$\mathsf{U}^{\not\perp}_{m,\mathtt{OTP}}[\mathsf{PKE}_1, H]$	open Q. ⇒ KDM-CCA	open Q	open Q

[a] This is a simplified bound. See Sect. 6 for the detail.

To solve the correlated information problem above, we introduce a new security notion called *seed-dependent message one-wayness against related seed attacks (SDM-OW-RSA)*. This notion is a technical contribution and plays a crucial role in this work (defined in Sect. 2.3). Then, we show that if we apply the $\mathsf{U}^{\perp}_{m}$ transformation to SDM-OW-RSA deterministic PKE, the resulting scheme is KDM-CPA secure by combining OTP as DEM. We also show that if we apply $\mathsf{U}^{\perp,\mathtt{keyconf}}_{m}$ to SDM-OW-RSA secure deterministic PKE with injectivity, the resulting scheme is KDM-CCA secure by combining OTP-then-MAC as DEM. Although we need O2H with MRM in this part to avoid a square root security loss, we can overcome the double-sided oracle issue due to SDM-OW-RSA security.

In order to complete the proof for the KDM security of FO transformations, we go to the following path. We first introduce a variant of T that we call T transformation with hash key generation $\mathsf{T}_{\mathsf{HKG}}$, and show that if we apply $\mathsf{T}_{\mathsf{HKG}}$ to IND-CPA PKE, the resulting deterministic PKE scheme satisfies SDM-OW-RSA without square root security loss. Combined with the above, we see that $\mathsf{U}^{\perp}_{m}$ (resp. $\mathsf{U}^{\perp,\mathtt{keyconf}}_{m}$) together with $\mathsf{T}_{\mathsf{HKG}}$ can be used to obtain a KDM-CPA (resp. KDM-CCA) secure PKE scheme from an IND-CPA secure PKE scheme without square root loss. Finally, we show that $\mathsf{T}_{\mathsf{HKG}}$ in those constructions can be replaced with T, thus prove the KDM security of FO transformations.

Although we omit in this paper, we can see that we can prove the KDM-CPA security without a square root security loss even if we use $\mathsf{U}^{\not\perp}_{m}$ instead of $\mathsf{U}^{\perp}_{m}$. Interestingly, if we use $\mathsf{U}^{\not\perp}_{m}$ instead of $\mathsf{U}^{\perp,\mathtt{keyconf}}_{m}$, it is not clear whether we can prove the KDM-CCA security without a square root loss. In the IND-CCA case, $\mathsf{U}^{\not\perp}_{m}$ provides us with IND-CCA security without a square root security loss [KSS+20, BHH+19]. See Sect. 1.4 for the detail. We summarize these results in Table 1.

1.3 Related Work

Our work is the first study on KDM secure *PKE in the QROM*. Our work also focuses on *tighter reductions*. Zhang constructs a non-adaptive KDM-CPA *SKE* scheme in the QROM to achieve delegation of quantum computation [Zha19].

Backes, Dürmuth, and Unruh [BDU08] study the KDM security of the OAEP transformation [BR95] in the classical ROM. They prove that OAEP is KDM-secure in the classical ROM if the underlying trapdoor permutation is partial-domain one-way. Note that there is no post-quantum secure trapdoor permutation so far. Davies and Stam [DS14] study the KDM security in the KEM/DEM framework. They prove that if a key derivation function (KDF) is used in between the KEM and DEM part and the KDF function is modelled as a classical random oracle, the resulting PKE scheme is KDM-secure. See the reference for security requirements. Kitagawa, Matsuda, Hanaoka, and Tanaka [KMHT16] prove that the FO transformation [FO13] satisfies KDM-CCA security in the classical ROM.[5] These works studied KDM security in the classical ROM basically prove KDM security by eliminating key dependency of plaintexts by random oracle programming.

We also briefly introduce previous works on IND-CCA secure PKE/KEM in the QROM. Let ϵ and ϵ_{bb} be the advantages of IND-CCA PKE/KEM and the building block, respectively. Let q_H be the number of random oracle queries (and we set $d_H := q_H$ for simplicity). Below, we omit "IND-CCA" and "in the QROM" since all results are about them. We also ignore the differences between FO and FO variants.

Boneh et al. [BDF+11] use a KEM variant of Bellare-Rogaway transformation [BR93] to obtain their KEM from trapdoor functions and $\epsilon \approx q_H\sqrt{\epsilon_{\mathsf{bb}}}$. Targhi and Unruh [TU16] use FO to obtain their PKE from OW-CPA PKE and $\epsilon \approx q_H^{1.5}\sqrt[4]{\epsilon_{\mathsf{bb}}}$. They also use an OAEP variant to obtain their PKE from partial domain trapdoor injective OWFs and $\epsilon \approx \mathrm{poly}(q_H)\sqrt[8]{\epsilon_{\mathsf{bb}}}$. Hofheinz et al. [HHK17] present modular analysis for FO, but their KEM does not improve the construction by Targhi and Unruh. Saito et al. [SXY18] use FO to obtain their KEM from disjoint simulatable deterministic PKE and $\epsilon \approx \epsilon_{\mathsf{bb}}$. They also obtain their KEM from IND-CPA PKE with perfect correctness and $\epsilon \approx q_H\sqrt{\epsilon_{\mathsf{bb}}}$. Jiang, Zhang, Chen, Wang, and Ma [JZC+18] use FO and obtain their KEM from OW-CPA PKE and $\epsilon \approx q_H\sqrt{\epsilon_{\mathsf{bb}}}$. Jiang, Zhang, and Ma [JZM19a] achieve the same bound as those by Jiang et al. [JZC+18] and Saito et al. [SXY18] by using the same assumptions and FO with explicit rejection. Ambainis, Hamburg, and Unruh [AHU19] prove an improved variant of the original O2H lemma (semi-classical O2H lemma) and its bound is $\epsilon_{\mathcal{A}} \approx \sqrt{q_H}\sqrt{\epsilon_{\mathcal{D}}}$ (the query loss is improved). The semi-classical O2H lemma leads to KEM with improved bounds in the query part [AHU19,HKSU20,JZM19b]. Bindel et al. [BHH+19] prove the double-sided O2H lemma whose bound is $\epsilon_{\mathcal{A}} \approx \sqrt{\epsilon_{\mathcal{D}}}$. They use FO to obtain their KEM from IND-CPA PKE with injectivity, but its bound is essentially the same as that of schemes using the semi-classical O2H lemma. Kuchta et al. [KSS+20]

[5] Precisely speaking, the FO transformations studied in the context of QROM are somewhat different from the original FO transformation [FO13].

prove O2H with MRM and obtain their KEM from IND-CPA PKE with injectivity via FO, and $\epsilon \approx q_H^2 \epsilon_{\mathsf{bb}}$.

1.4 Technical Overview

We provide the technical overview of this work. Our goal here is to show that the KDM security in the QROM of the PKE scheme $\mathsf{U}^{\perp}_{m,\mathtt{OTP}}(\mathsf{T}(\mathsf{PKE}, G_{\mathsf{enc}}), H)$[6] can be reduced to the IND-CPA security of the underlying PKE without square root security loss. Roughly speaking, the difficulty is that in the setting of KDM security, double-sided O2H lemmas [BHH+19,KSS+20] cannot be applied straightforwardly, which is currently the only tool that enables us to circumvent square root security loss in the QROM.

We first explain how we circumvent square root security loss and prove the KDM security in the QROM of the PKE scheme $\mathsf{U}^{\perp}_{m,\mathtt{OTP}} = \mathsf{U}^{\perp}_{m,\mathtt{OTP}}(\mathsf{dPKE}, H)$ whose ciphertext is described as

$$(\mathsf{dEnc}(\mathsf{pk}, s), H(s) \oplus m),$$

where dEnc is the encryption algorithm of a deterministic PKE scheme dPKE with the message space $\mathcal{M}$, $s \leftarrow \mathcal{M}$, and H is a random oracle. We identify that the KDM security in the QROM of $\mathsf{U}^{\perp}_{m,\mathtt{OTP}}$ can be reduced without square root loss to the security notion of dPKE that we call seed-dependent message one-wayness (SDM-OW security). Then, we explain that the SDM-OW security in the QROM of a tweaked version of $\mathsf{T} = \mathsf{T}(\mathsf{PKE}, G_{\mathsf{enc}})$ can be reduced to the IND-CPA security of the underlying PKE scheme PKE without square root security loss. We call the tweaked version T transformation with hash key generation $\mathsf{T}_{\mathtt{HKG}} = \mathsf{T}_{\mathtt{HKG}}(\mathsf{PKE}, (G_{\mathsf{kg}}, G_{\mathsf{enc}}))$ where G_{kg} and G_{enc} are random oracles. From these facts, we see that the KDM security in the QROM of $\mathsf{U}^{\perp}_{m,\mathtt{OTP}}(\mathsf{T}_{\mathtt{HKG}}(\mathsf{PKE}, (G_{\mathsf{enc}}, G_{\mathsf{kg}})), H)$ can be reduced to the IND-CPA security of PKE without square root security loss. Finally, we state that the KDM security of $\mathsf{U}^{\perp}_{m,\mathtt{OTP}}(\mathsf{T}(\mathsf{PKE}, G_{\mathsf{enc}}), H)$ immediately follows from the KDM security of $\mathsf{U}^{\perp}_{m,\mathtt{OTP}}(\mathsf{T}_{\mathtt{HKG}}(\mathsf{PKE}, (G_{\mathsf{enc}}, G_{\mathsf{kg}})), H)$.

Below, we start with how to prove the KDM security of $\mathsf{U}^{\perp}_{m,\mathtt{OTP}}$ in the classical ROM. For simplicity, in this overview, we consider the following simplified KDM security. Given a ciphertext of $f_b(\mathsf{sk})$, any adversary cannot predict b correctly better than random guessing, where $b \leftarrow \{0,1\}$ is the challenge bit and f_0 and f_1 are any a-priori fixed two functions. The actual KDM security requires indistinguishability holds for multiple pairs of functions adaptively chosen by an adversary under multiple public and secret key pairs.

KDM Security of $\mathsf{U}^{\perp}_{m,\mathtt{OTP}}$ *in the Classical ROM.* Let $\mathcal{A}$ be an adversary. $\mathcal{A}$ is given the challenge ciphertext and the random oracle access, which are described as

$$CT : (\mathsf{dEnc}(\mathsf{pk}, s), H(s) \oplus f_b(\mathsf{sk})) \quad \text{and} \quad RO : H(x).$$

---

6 We again note that we use variants of T and U transformations defined by [BHH+19] in this work.

We first make a conceptual change to the security game so that the challenge ciphertext and the random oracle are described as

$$CT : (\mathsf{dEnc}(\mathsf{pk}, s), u) \quad \text{and} \quad RO : V(x) = \begin{cases} u \oplus f_b(\mathsf{sk}) & (\text{if } x = s) \\ H(x) & (\text{otherwise}), \end{cases}$$

where u is a uniformly chosen value independent of H and $f_b(\mathsf{sk})$. We can confirm that this is a purely conceptual change since V behaves as a random function and the challenge ciphertext is computed as $(\mathsf{dEnc}(\mathsf{pk}, s), V(s) \oplus f_b(\mathsf{sk})) = (\mathsf{dEnc}(\mathsf{pk}, s), u)$. Therefore, it does not change $\mathcal{A}$'s advantage. Then, we further change the security game so that $\mathcal{A}$ gets access to H instead of V, but the challenge ciphertext is still generated using V. Thus, the challenge ciphertext is not changed from $(\mathsf{dEnc}(\mathsf{pk}, s), u)$. In other words, except for the generation of the challenge ciphertext, we program the output value of the random oracle at point s from $V(s) = u \oplus f_b(\mathsf{sk})$ into $H(s)$. The view of $\mathcal{A}$ is now

$$CT = (\mathsf{dEnc}(\mathsf{pk}, s), u) \quad \text{and} \quad RO : H(x).$$

We see that in the final game, the challenge bit b is completely hidden from the view of $\mathcal{A}$, and thus $\mathcal{A}$'s advantage is 0. Therefore, we must estimate how much the advantage of $\mathcal{A}$ is changed by the above programming of the random oracle. From the difference lemma[7], this can be bounded by the probability that $\mathcal{A}$ queries s to H in the final security game. In the final game, information of $f_b(\mathsf{sk})$ is completely eliminated from the view of $\mathcal{A}$. Thus, we can use the security of dPKE in order to estimate the probability. Concretely, the probability is estimated by using the OW-CPA security of dPKE. This completes the proof. Of course, square root security loss does not occur in this proof.

KDM Security of $\mathsf{U}^{\perp}_{m,\mathtt{OTP}}$ *in the QROM?* When we try to prove KDM security of $\mathsf{U}^{\perp}_{m,\mathtt{OTP}}$ in the QROM, we need a different tool from the difference lemma. This is because "the probability that $\mathcal{A}$ queries s to H" is not well-defined in this case since $\mathcal{A}$ can make a query to the random oracle in super-position. In the QROM, in many cases, we can use one-way to hiding (O2H) lemma [Unr15] and its variants [AHU19, BHH+19, KSS+20] as drop-in replacements of the difference lemma in the security proof done in the classical ROM. Roughly speaking, the O2H lemma guarantees that there exists an extractor $\mathcal{D}$ such that the distinguishing gap caused by a programming of a quantumly-accessible random oracle can be bounded by the probability that $\mathcal{D}$ extracts the programmed point. O2H lemma is classified into two categories. The first one is a single-sided O2H lemma where $\mathcal{D}$ gets access to either pre-programmed or post-programmed random oracles. The other one is a double-sided O2H lemma where $\mathcal{D}$ gets access to both of them. In order to circumvent the square root security loss, we currently need to use double-sided O2H lemma proposed in [KSS+20] called O2H with measure-rewind-measure (MRM) lemma.

[7] The lemma states that if $\Pr[A \wedge \neg C] = \Pr[B \wedge \neg C]$, $|\Pr[A] - \Pr[B]| \le \Pr[C]$ holds for any events A,B, and C.

Suppose to prove KDM security of $\mathsf{U}^{\perp}_{m,\mathtt{OTP}}$ in the QROM, we follow the same strategy as the case of the classical ROM (i.e., make a conceptual change and program V into H) and use O2H lemma instead of the difference lemma. Since our goal here is to prove the KDM security of $\mathsf{U}^{\perp}_{m,\mathtt{OTP}}$ in the QROM without square root security loss, we use O2H lemma with MRM. By doing so, we can say that there exists a QPT extractor $\mathcal{D}$ such that

$$\left|\Pr\left[1 \leftarrow \mathcal{A}^{|V\rangle}(z)\right] - \Pr\left[1 \leftarrow \mathcal{A}^{|H\rangle}(z)\right]\right| \leq 4d \cdot \Pr\left[s \leftarrow \mathcal{D}^{|V,H\rangle}(z)\right],$$

where $z = (\mathsf{dEnc}(\mathsf{pk}, s), u)$ and d is the query depth of $\mathcal{A}$ to the random oracle.[8] Thus, if we can in turn bound the probability $\Pr[s \leftarrow \mathcal{D}^{|V,H\rangle}(z)]$ by using the security of the underlying dPKE, we can complete the entire security proof. However, it turns out that it cannot be done straightforwardly using the OW-CPA security of dPKE as before. The reason is that since $\mathcal{D}$ has access to not only H but also V that has information of $f_b(\mathsf{sk})$, it is not clear whether we can use the OW-CPA security of dPKE. Recall that in the proof in the classical ROM case, when estimating "the probability that $\mathcal{A}$ queries s to H" using the OW-CPA security of dPKE, information of $f_b(\mathsf{sk})$ is eliminated from the view of $\mathcal{A}$ since $\mathcal{A}$ does not have access to V.

In summary, in the proof in the classical ROM, we can successfully reduce the KDM security of $\mathsf{U}^{\perp}_{m,\mathtt{OTP}}$ to the OW-CPA security of dPKE by eliminating information of $f_b(\mathsf{sk})$ using programming of the random oracle. However, in the case of the QROM, if we use O2H with MRM lemma, it seems difficult to eliminate the information of $f_b(\mathsf{sk})$ by programming the random oracle. This is because we finally need to handle the extractor $\mathcal{D}$ who gets access to both pre-programmed and post-programmed random oracles.

Note that even if V does not have information of $f_b(\mathsf{sk})$, it might not be clear whether an OW-CPA adversary can simulate two random oracles V and H at the same time for $\mathcal{D}$. The reason is that the differing point s of the two random oracles is the solution of the OW-CPA game itself. This problem can be handled by using the correctness of dPKE. As shown by [LW21], the correctness of dPKE implies that under a randomly generated key $(\mathsf{pk}, \mathsf{sk})$, a randomly generated message m does not have a collision, that is another message m' such that $\mathsf{dEnc}(\mathsf{pk}, m) = \mathsf{dEnc}(\mathsf{pk}, m')$, with overwhelming probability. If $\mathsf{ct} = \mathsf{dEnc}(\mathsf{pk}, s)$ has unique pre-image s, the OW-CPA adversary can check the condition "if $x = s$" by checking "if $\mathsf{dEnc}(\mathsf{pk}, x) = \mathsf{ct}$" (in super-position), thus can simulate V and H at the same time if V does not have information of $f_b(\mathsf{sk})$.

Reduction to SDM-OW Security. Although it seems difficult to bound the probability $\Pr[s \leftarrow \mathcal{D}^{|V,H\rangle}(z)]$ using the OW-CPA security of dPKE, we show that it can be bounded if dPKE satisfies *SDM-OW security* introduced in this work. Hereafter, we assume that the message space $\mathcal{M}$ of dPKE is an abelian group with the operation "+" and the random coin space of the key generation algorithm dKG of dPKE is contained in $\mathcal{M}$. Then, SDM-OW security is a security

[8] The notation $\mathcal{A}^{|O\rangle}$ indicates that $\mathcal{A}$ is allowed to make a query to O in super-position. Also, for the definition of query depth, see Sect. 3.

notion that guarantees that given $(s, \mathsf{dEnc}(\mathsf{pk}, r + s))$, an adversary cannot compute $r + s$, where $s \leftarrow \mathcal{M}$, and $r \in \mathcal{M}$ is the random coin used to generate $(\mathsf{pk}, \mathsf{sk})$ (i.e., $(\mathsf{pk}, \mathsf{sk}) \leftarrow \mathsf{dKG}(1^\lambda; r)$).

The estimation is done after adding the following changes to z and V that do not affect the view of $\mathcal{D}$. First, we replace s in z and V with $r + s$, where $r \in \mathcal{M}$ is the random coin used to generate $(\mathsf{pk}, \mathsf{sk})$. Namely, we change z and V as

$$z = (\mathsf{dEnc}(\mathsf{pk}, r + s), u) \quad \text{and} \quad V(x) = \begin{cases} u \oplus f_b(\mathsf{sk}) & (\text{if } x = r + s) \\ H(x) & (\text{otherwise}). \end{cases} \tag{1}$$

This change does not affect the view of $\mathcal{D}$ since s is chosen uniformly at random and independently of r. Then, we further replace V with the following

$$V(x) = \begin{cases} u \oplus \widehat{f_b}(x) & (\text{if } x = r + s) \\ H(x) & (\text{otherwise}), \end{cases} \tag{2}$$

where $\widehat{f_b}$ is a function that is given x as an input, computes $(\mathsf{pk}, \mathsf{sk}) \leftarrow \mathsf{KG}(1^\lambda; x - s)$, and outputs $f_b(\mathsf{sk})$. We can check that V in Eq. (1) and V in Eq. (2) are functionally equivalent. Thus, this change also does not affect the view of $\mathcal{D}$. Moreover, we finally replace the condition "if $x = s + r$" in V with "if $\mathsf{dEnc}(\mathsf{pk}, x) = \mathsf{dEnc}(\mathsf{pk}, r + s)$". As noted before, this can be justified from the correctness of dPKE.

We see that by the above changes, z and V (i.e., the entire view of $\mathcal{D}$) can now be simulated by an SDM-OW adversary $\mathcal{B}$ who is given $(s, \mathsf{dEnc}(\mathsf{pk}, r+s))$. Moreover, $\mathcal{B}$ can break the SDM-OW security if the simulated $\mathcal{D}$ successfully extracts the differing point of V and H, that is, $r+s$. This means that $\Pr\left[s \leftarrow \mathcal{D}^{|V,H\rangle}(z)\right]$ can be bounded by using the SDM-OW security of dPKE.

From the above arguments, we see that the KDM security of $\mathsf{U}^{\perp}_{m,\mathtt{OTP}}$ in the QROM can be reduced to the SDM-OW security of dPKE without square root security loss.

SDM-OW Security of a Variant of T. We next explain the SDM-OW security of $\mathsf{T}_{\mathtt{HKG}} = \mathsf{T}_{\mathtt{HKG}}(\mathsf{PKE}, (G_{\mathtt{kg}}, G_{\mathtt{enc}}))$ can be reduced to the IND-CPA security of the underlying PKE scheme PKE without square roof security loss, where $G_{\mathtt{kg}}$ and $G_{\mathtt{enc}}$ are random oracles. $\mathsf{T}_{\mathtt{HKG}}$ is a tweaked version of $T = T(\mathsf{PKE}, G_{\mathtt{enc}})$ transformation. T transformation converts a (randomized) IND-CPA secure PKE scheme into an OW-CPA secure deterministic PKE scheme. The encryption algorithm of T is described as $\mathsf{Enc}(\mathsf{pk}, m; G_{\mathtt{enc}}(m))$, where Enc is the encryption algorithm of the underlying PKE. The key generation and decryption algorithms of T are those of PKE themselves. In $\mathsf{T}_{\mathtt{HKG}}$, we also generate a key pair $(\mathsf{pk}, \mathsf{sk})$ by using a random coin generated by the random oracle $G_{\mathtt{kg}}$, that is, $(\mathsf{pk}, \mathsf{sk}) \leftarrow \mathsf{KG}(1^\lambda; G_{\mathtt{kg}}(r))$, where $r \leftarrow \mathcal{M}$.

Bindel et al. [BHH+19] showed that the OW-CPA security of T can be reduced to the IND-CPA security of PKE without square root security loss. The important thing is that the target security notion is one-wayness (not indistinguishability) here. Essentially, Bindel et al. avoided the square root security loss

by relying on the fact that if the target security notion is one-wayness and the starting security notion is indistinguishability, we can avoid square root security loss by using *single-sided* O2H lemma called semi-classical O2H lemma [AHU19]. In this work, we show that such a reduction to IND-CPA security without square root loss is possible even when we prove $\mathsf{T}_{\mathtt{HKG}}$'s SDM-OW security, which can be seen as one-wayness for a kind of key dependent messages. In fact, there is no difficulty based on the circularity issue as before since we use single-sided O2H lemma in this step, *not double-sided* one. Roughly speaking, when we use single-sided O2H lemma, we can eliminate correlations between keys, encryption random coins, and plaintexts by random oracle programming in the security proof even in the context of QROM. We give the overview of this proof in Sect. 5.2. More specifically, we provide a high-level idea of how to solve the correlations after we describe a few hybrid games for the proof, and complete the proof.
The KDM Security of $\mathsf{U}^{\perp}_{m,\mathtt{OTP}}(\mathsf{T}(\mathsf{PKE}, G_{\mathtt{enc}}), H)$. From the discussions so far, we see that the KDM security of $\mathsf{U}^{\perp}_{m,\mathtt{OTP}}(\mathsf{T}_{\mathtt{HKG}}(\mathsf{PKE}, (G_{\mathtt{kg}}, G_{\mathtt{enc}})), H)$ can be reduced to the IND-CPA security of PKE without square root security loss. This immediately implies the same holds for $\mathsf{U}^{\perp}_{m,\mathtt{OTP}}(\mathsf{T}(\mathsf{PKE}, G_{\mathtt{enc}}), H)$. This is because adversaries cannot detect whether the public and secret key pair is generated using a random oracle or not. The KDM security of $\mathsf{U}^{\perp}_{m,\mathtt{OTP}}(\mathsf{T}(\mathsf{PKE}, G_{\mathtt{enc}}), H)$ can be reduced to that of $\mathsf{U}^{\perp}_{m,\mathtt{OTP}}(\mathsf{T}_{\mathtt{HKG}}(\mathsf{PKE}, (G_{\mathtt{kg}}, G_{\mathtt{enc}})), H)$.

Remarks.

- In the actual security game of KDM security, an adversary can choose a pair of functions (f_0, f_1) adaptively and obtain a ciphertext of $f_b(\mathsf{sk})$ multiple times under the existence of multiple key pairs. Also, to capture a wide range of usage scenarios, we allow those functions to get access to random oracles. We handle these issues by using the adaptive reprogramming technique for QROM [Unr14] and introducing a security notion we call SDM-OW-RSA security which is an extension of SDM-OW security.
- Our proof technique is also compatible with KDM-CCA security. Concretely, we can prove the KDM-CCA security of a PKE scheme constructed by using $\mathsf{U}^{\perp,\mathtt{keyconf}}_{m} = \mathsf{U}^{\perp,\mathtt{keyconf}}_{m}(\mathsf{dPKE}, H)$ [BHH+19] as KEM and OTP-then-MAC as DEM without square root security loss. We assume the underlying dPKE is SDM-OW-RSA secure and additionally satisfies injectivity. The security proof is a combination of our proof for the KDM security of $\mathsf{U}^{\perp}_{m,\mathtt{OTP}}$ and the proof for the IND-CCA security of $\mathsf{U}^{\perp,\mathtt{keyconf}}_{m}$ by [BHH+19, KSS+20]. Thus, we mainly focus on KDM-CPA security in this version, and we provide the results on KDM-CCA security in [KN21].

  As shown by [BHH+19], $\mathsf{U}^{\perp,\mathtt{keyconf}}_{m}$ and $\mathsf{U}^{\not\perp}_{m}$ are IND-CCA secure KEMs that are compatible with double-sided O2H lemma such as O2H lemma with MRM. To use $\mathsf{U}^{\perp,\mathtt{keyconf}}_{m}$ as the KEM part in the above construction is essential. If we use $\mathsf{U}^{\not\perp}_{m}$ as the KEM part, it seems difficult to prove the KDM-CCA security of the construction. $\mathsf{U}^{\not\perp}_{m}$ returns a random value generated by using pseudo-random functions (PRF) if the decryption algorithm detects a given ciphertext is not valid to make it possible to simulate the decryption oracle without using secret keys. In the KDM-CCA security game of a PKE scheme whose KEM part is $\mathsf{U}_m^{\not\perp}$, the keys of PRF are also encrypted. In that case, we cannot use the security of PRF and cannot simulate the decryption oracle. It is an interesting open problem to prove KDM-CCA security of a PKE scheme whose KEM part is $\mathsf{U}_m^{\not\perp}$ without square root security loss.

- Our proof strategy explained so far can be realized more easily for SKE where the secret key is used for encryption. A ciphertext of a simple SKE scheme is $(s, H(\mathsf{sk}\|s) \oplus m)$, where H is a random oracle. The simple scheme has a good structure to apply our proof strategy because the secret key sk can be recovered from the differing point $\mathsf{sk}\|s$ when programming the random oracle in the security proof. Zhang [Zha19] showed the non-adaptive KDM security of the SKE scheme with security bound $\sqrt{\frac{\mathrm{poly}(q, q_{\mathsf{kdm}}, q_f, \ell)}{2^\lambda}}$, where q is the number of random oracle queries, q_{kdm} is the number of KDM queries, q_f is the number of random oracle queries by KDM functions, ℓ is the number of secret keys, and λ is the length of sk. Using our proof strategy, we can prove the non-adaptive KDM security of the SKE scheme with security bound roughly $\frac{\mathrm{poly}(q, q_{\mathsf{kdm}}, q_f, \ell)}{2^\lambda}$. We formally prove it in [KN21]. The proof of this is much easier than the proof of our main construction $\mathsf{U}_{m,\mathsf{OTP}}^{\perp}$. The former can be a warming-up for the latter.
- We do not directly prove the KDM security of $\mathsf{U}_{m,\mathsf{OTP}}^{\perp}(\mathsf{T}(\mathsf{PKE}, G_{\mathsf{enc}}), H)$, and first prove that of $\mathsf{U}_{m,\mathsf{OTP}}^{\perp}(\mathsf{T}_{\mathsf{HKG}}(\mathsf{PKE}, (G_{\mathsf{kg}}, G_{\mathsf{enc}})), H)$. If we directly prove the former in a modular way, we think we would need to introduce a more complicated security notion for deterministic PKE schemes. We believe that the introduction of $\mathsf{T}_{\mathsf{HKG}}$ makes our presentation simpler and more modular.
- In this work, we focus on PKE schemes whose DEM is OTP for a technical reason. As we saw above, for our strategy, it is important that DEM has a non-committing property in the sense that we can move an encrypted plaintext from the ciphertext to the key. Although our technique can be used to not only OTP but also any DEM with non-committing property, it is an interesting open question to prove KDM security of FO transformation with any DEM without square root security loss.

2 Preliminaries

2.1 Notations

In this paper, for a finite set X and a distribution D, $x \leftarrow X$ denotes selecting an element from X uniformly at random, $x \leftarrow D$ denotes sampling an element x according to D. Let $y \leftarrow \mathsf{A}(x)$ denotes assigning to y the output of a probabilistic or deterministic algorithm A on an input x. When we explicitly show that A uses randomness r, we write $y \leftarrow \mathsf{A}(x; r)$. When A is allowed to get access to an oracle O, we write $y \leftarrow \mathsf{A}^O(x)$. Let $[a]$ and $[a, b]$ denote the sets of integers $\{1, \cdots, a\}$ and $\{a, \cdots, b\}$, respectively. λ denote a security parameter. PPT and QPT algorithms stand for probabilistic polynomial-time algorithms and polynomial-time quantum algorithms, respectively. Let negl denote a negligible function.

2.2 Public-Key Encryption

A public-key encryption (PKE) scheme PKE is a three tuple (KG, Enc, Dec) of PPT algorithms. Let $\mathcal{M}$ be the message space of PKE. The key generation algorithm KG, given a security parameter 1^λ, outputs a public key pk and a secret key sk. The encryption algorithm Enc, given a public key pk and message $m \in \mathcal{M}$, outputs a ciphertext CT. The decryption algorithm Dec, given a secret key sk and ciphertext CT, outputs a message $\tilde{m} \in \{\bot\} \cup \mathcal{M}$.

Definition 2.1 (Correctness of PKE). *We say that* PKE *is δ-correct if*

$$\mathbb{E}\left[\max_{m\in\mathcal{M}} \Pr[\mathsf{Dec}(\mathsf{sk}, \mathsf{Enc}(\mathsf{pk}, m; r)) \neq m] \middle| (\mathsf{pk}, \mathsf{sk}) \leftarrow \mathsf{KG}(1^\lambda), r \leftarrow \mathcal{R}\right] \leq \delta \ ,$$

where $\mathcal{R}$ is the random coin space of Enc. *If* PKE *is constructed in the random oracle model, the expectation is taken over the choice of* $(\mathsf{pk}, \mathsf{sk}) \leftarrow \mathsf{KG}(1^\lambda)$ *and the random oracle.*

We say that PKE is deterministic PKE if $\mathsf{Enc}(\mathsf{pk}, \cdot)$ is a deterministic function. We introduce the correctness notion that is specific to deterministic PKE. In addition to the ordinary correctness above, it requires that under a randomly generated key (pk, sk), a randomly generated message m does not have a collision, that is another message m' such that $\mathsf{dEnc}(\mathsf{pk}, m) = \mathsf{dEnc}(\mathsf{pk}, m')$. This correctness notion is useful when we use double-sided O2H lemmas [BHH+19, KSS+20].

Definition 2.2 (Correctness of deterministic PKE). *We say that a deterministic PKE scheme* $\mathsf{dPKE} = (\mathsf{dKG}, \mathsf{dEnc}, \mathsf{dDec})$ *with the message space $\mathcal{M}$ is (δ_1, δ_2)-correct if it is δ_1-correct and it holds that*

$$\Pr\left[\exists m' \in \mathcal{M} \ : \ \mathsf{dEnc}(\mathsf{pk}, m') = \mathsf{dEnc}(\mathsf{pk}, m) | (\mathsf{pk}, \mathsf{sk}) \leftarrow \mathsf{dKG}(1^\lambda), m \leftarrow \mathcal{M}\right] \leq \delta_2 \ .$$

If dPKE *is constructed in the random oracle model, the probability is taken over the choice of* $(\mathsf{pk}, \mathsf{sk}) \leftarrow \mathsf{dKG}(1^\lambda)$, $m \leftarrow \mathcal{M}$, *and the random oracle.*

We introduce a multi-instance and multi-challenge version of IND-CPA security for PKE that we denote as IND-m-CPA security.

Definition 2.3 (IND-m-CPA security for PKE). *Let* PKE = (KG, Enc, Dec) *be a PKE scheme. We define* $\mathsf{Exp}^{\mathsf{ind\text{-}m\text{-}cpa}}_{\mathsf{PKE},\ell,\mathcal{A}}(1^\lambda)$ *for an adversary $\mathcal{A}$ as follows.*

Initialize: *First, the challenger chooses a challenge bit $b \leftarrow \{0,1\}$. Next, the challenger generates $(\mathsf{pk}^k, \mathsf{sk}^k) \leftarrow \mathsf{KG}(1^\lambda)$ for every $k \in [\ell]$. The challenger executes $b' \leftarrow \mathcal{A}^{O_{\mathrm{IND}}}((\mathsf{pk}^k)_{k\in[\ell]})$.*

$O_{\mathbf{IND}}$: *On the i-th call with input $(k_i, \mathsf{m}_{i,0}, \mathsf{m}_{i,1})$, where $k_i \in [\ell]$ and $|\mathsf{m}_{i,0}| = |\mathsf{m}_{i,1}|$, it returns $\mathsf{ct}_i \leftarrow \mathsf{Enc}(\mathsf{pk}^{k_i}, \mathsf{m}_{i,b})$.*

Finalize: *The challenger outputs 1 if $b = b'$ and 0 otherwise.*

We say that PKE *is IND-m-CPA secure if for any polynomial $\ell = \ell(\lambda)$ and QPT adversary $\mathcal{A}$, we have* $\mathsf{Adv}^{\mathsf{ind\text{-}m\text{-}cpa}}_{\mathsf{PKE},\ell,\mathcal{A}}(\lambda) = \left|\Pr\left[1 \leftarrow \mathsf{Exp}^{\mathsf{ind\text{-}m\text{-}cpa}}_{\mathsf{PKE},\ell,\mathcal{A}}(1^\lambda)\right] - \frac{1}{2}\right| = \mathsf{negl}(\lambda)$.

We introduce the definition of KDM-CPA security for PKE.

Definition 2.4 (KDM-CPA security for PKE). *Let* $\mathsf{PKE} = (\mathsf{KG}, \mathsf{Enc}, \mathsf{Dec})$ *be a PKE scheme. We define* $\mathsf{Exp}^{\mathsf{kdm\text{-}cpa}}_{\mathsf{PKE},\ell,\mathcal{A}}(1^\lambda)$ *for an adversary* $\mathcal{A}$ *as follows.*

Initialize: *First, the challenger chooses a challenge bit* $b \xleftarrow{r} \{0,1\}$*. Next, the challenger generates* $(\mathsf{pk}^k, \mathsf{sk}^k) \leftarrow \mathsf{KG}(1^\lambda)$ *for every* $k \in [\ell]$*. The challenger sets* $\mathbf{sk} := (\mathsf{sk}^1, \ldots, \mathsf{sk}^\ell)$*, and executes* $b' \leftarrow \mathcal{A}^{O_{\mathsf{KDM}}}((\mathsf{pk}^k)_{k\in[\ell]})$*.*

O_{KDM}**:** *On the i-th call with input* $(k_i, f_{i,0}, f_{i,1})$*, where* $k_i \in [\ell]$ *and* $f_{i,0}$ *and* $f_{i,1}$ *are efficiently computable functions with the same output length, it returns* $\mathsf{ct}_i \leftarrow \mathsf{Enc}(\mathsf{pk}^{k_i}, f_{i,b}(\mathbf{sk}))$*.*

Finalize: *The challenger outputs* 1 *if* $b = b'$ *and* 0 *otherwise.*

We say that PKE *is KDM-CPA secure if for any polynomial* $\ell = \ell(\lambda)$ *and QPT adversary* $\mathcal{A}$*, we have*

$$\mathsf{Adv}^{\mathsf{kdm\text{-}cpa}}_{\mathsf{PKE},\ell,\mathcal{A}}(\lambda) = \left|\Pr\left[1 \leftarrow \mathsf{Exp}^{\mathsf{kdm\text{-}cpa}}_{\mathsf{PKE},\ell,\mathcal{A}}(1^\lambda)\right] - \frac{1}{2}\right| = \mathsf{negl}(\lambda).$$

Remark 2.1 (KDM security in QROM). In order to capture a wide variety of situations, we allow KDM functions to get access to random oracles if the scheme is constructed in the (quantum) random oracle model. We allow only classical access random oracles for KDM functions, while adversaries get access to random oracles in super-position. This setting is sufficient when honest entities are classical.

2.3 SDM-OW-RSA Security

We introduce a new security notion *seed-dependent message one-wayness against related seed attacks (SDM-OW-RSA security).* This notion plays a crucial role in achieving KDM security from IND-m-CPA security in the QROM without square roof security loss.

Definition 2.5 (SDM-OW-RSA security for PKE). *Let* $\mathsf{PKE} = (\mathsf{KG}, \mathsf{Enc}, \mathsf{Dec})$ *be a PKE scheme such that the message space* $\mathcal{M}$ *is an abelian group with the operation* $+$*, and the random coin space of* KG *is* $\mathcal{M}$*. We define* $\mathsf{Exp}^{\mathsf{sdm\text{-}ow\text{-}rsa}}_{\mathsf{PKE},\ell,q_{\mathsf{sdm}},\mathcal{A}}(1^\lambda)$ *for an adversary* $\mathcal{A}$ *as follows.*

Initialize: *The challenger first generates* $r \leftarrow \mathcal{M}$*. The challenger then generates* $\Delta^k \leftarrow \mathcal{M}$ *and* $(\mathsf{pk}^k, \mathsf{sk}^k) \leftarrow \mathsf{KG}(1^\lambda; r + \Delta^k)$ *for every* $k \in [\ell]$*. Next, for every* $k \in [\ell]$ *and* $i \in [q_{\mathsf{sdm}}]$*, the challenger generates* $s_{i,k} \leftarrow \mathcal{M}$ *and computes* $\mathsf{ct}_{i,k} \leftarrow \mathsf{Enc}\left(\mathsf{pk}^k, r + s_{i,k}\right)$*. Finally, the challenger executes* $T \leftarrow \mathcal{A}((\mathsf{pk}^k, \Delta^k)_{k\in[\ell]}, (s_{i,k}, \mathsf{ct}_{i,k})_{i\in[q_{\mathsf{sdm}}],k\in[\ell]})$*.*

Finalize: *The challenger outputs* 1 *if and only if* T *contains* r' *such that* $r' = r + s_{i,k}$ *holds for some* $i \in [q_{\mathsf{sdm}}]$ *and* $k \in [\ell]$*.*

We say that PKE *is SDM-OW-RSA secure if for any polynomial* $\ell = \ell(\lambda)$ *and* $q_{\mathsf{sdm}} = q_{\mathsf{sdm}}(\lambda)$ *and QPT adversary* $\mathcal{A}$*, we have*

$$\mathsf{Adv}^{\mathsf{sdm\text{-}ow\text{-}rsa}}_{\mathsf{PKE},\ell,\mathcal{A}}(\lambda) = \Pr\left[1 \leftarrow \mathsf{Exp}^{\mathsf{sdm\text{-}ow\text{-}rsa}}_{\mathsf{PKE},\ell,\mathcal{A}}(1^\lambda)\right] = \mathsf{negl}(\lambda).$$

3 Quantum Random Oracle and Useful Lemmas

Given a function $H : X \to Y$, a quantum-accessible oracle O of H is modeled by a unitary transformation U_H operating on two registers *in* and *out*, in which $|x\rangle |y\rangle$ is mapped to $|x\rangle |y \oplus H(x)\rangle$, where $\oplus$ denotes XOR group operation on Y. Following [AHU19, BHH+19, KSS+20], we model a quantum algorithm $\mathcal{A}$ making parallel queries to a quantum oracle O as a quantum algorithm making $d \le q$ queries to an oracle $O^{\otimes n}$ consisting of $n = q/d$ parallel copies of oracle O. Given an input state of n pairs of *in*/*out* registers $|x_1\rangle |y_1\rangle \cdots |x_n\rangle |y_n\rangle$, the oracle $O^{\otimes n}$ maps it to the state $|x_1\rangle |y_1 \oplus H(x_1)\rangle \cdots |x_n\rangle |y_n \oplus H(x_n)\rangle$. We call d the algorithm's query depth, n the parallelization factor, and $q = n \cdot d$ the total number of oracle queries. We write $\mathcal{A}^{|O\rangle}$ to denote that the algorithm $\mathcal{A}$'s oracle O is a quantum-accessible oracle.

Simulation of Quantum Random Oracles. In this paper, following many previous works in the QROM, we give quantum-accessible random oracles to reduction algorithms if needed. This is just a convention. We can efficiently simulate quantum-accessible random oracles perfectly by using $2q$-wise independent hash function [Zha12], where q is the number of queries to the quantum-accessible random oracles by an adversary.

3.1 One-Way to Hiding (O2H) Lemma

Definition 3.1 (Punctured oracle). *Let $F : X \to Y$ be any function, and $S \subset X$ be a set. The oracle $F \setminus S$("F punctured by S") takes as input a value $x \in X$. It first computes whether $x \in S$ into an auxiliary register and measures it. Then it computes $F(x)$ and returns the result. Let* $\mathtt{Find}$ *be the event that any of the measurements returns* 1.

Lemma 3.1 (Semi-classical O2H [AHU19, Theorem 1]**).** *Let $G, H : X \to Y$ be random functions, z be a random value, and $S \subseteq X$ be a random set such that $G(x) = H(x)$ for every $x \notin S$. The tuple (G, H, S, z) may have arbitrary joint distribution. Furthermore, let $\mathcal{A}$ be a quantum oracle algorithm. Let* $\mathtt{Ev}$ *be any classical event. Then we have*

$$\left|\sqrt{\Pr\left[\mathtt{Ev} : \mathcal{A}^{|G\rangle}(z)\right]} - \sqrt{\Pr\left[\mathtt{Ev} \wedge \neg\mathtt{Find} : \mathcal{A}^{|H\setminus S\rangle}(z)\right]}\right| \le \sqrt{(d+1) \cdot \Pr\left[\mathtt{Find} : \mathcal{A}^{|H\setminus S\rangle}(z)\right]} \ ,$$

where d is the query depth of $\mathcal{A}$ for G and $H \setminus S$.

Lemma 3.2 (Search in semi-classical oracle [AHU19, Theorem 2]**).** *Let $H : X \to Y$ be a random function, let z be a random value, and let $S \subset X$ be a random set. (H, S, z) may have arbitrary joint distribution. Let $\mathcal{A}$ be a quantum oracle algorithm. If for each $x \in X$, $\Pr[x \in S] \le \epsilon$ (conditioned on H and z), then we have*

$$\Pr\left[\mathtt{Find} : \mathcal{A}^{|H\setminus S\rangle}(z)\right] \le 4q\epsilon \ ,$$

where q is the number of queries to $H \setminus S$ by $\mathcal{A}$.

Note that the above lemma is originally introduced in [AHU19], but we use a variant that is closer to Lemma 4 in [BHH+19].

Lemma 3.3 (Adapted version of O2H with MRM [KSS+20, Lemma 3.3]**).** *Let $G, H : X \to Y$ be functions, and $S \subseteq X$ be a set such that $G(x) = H(x)$ for every $x \notin S$. Also, let z be a value and O_{aux} be a function. The tuple $(G, H, S, z, O_{\mathsf{aux}})$ may have arbitrary joint distribution. Furthermore, let $\mathcal{A}$ be a quantum oracle algorithm. Then we can construct an algorithm $\mathcal{D}$ such that*

- *The running time of $\mathcal{D}$ is roughly three times longer than that of $\mathcal{A}$. Moreover, if $\mathcal{A}$ makes at most q queries to G and H with query depth d, $\mathcal{D}$ makes at most $O(q)$ queries to each of those oracles with query depth $O(d)$, and outputs a list $T \subseteq X$ of size at most $O(q)$.*
- *It holds that*

$$\left|\Pr\left[1 \leftarrow \mathcal{A}^{|G,O_{\mathsf{aux}}\rangle}(z)\right] - \Pr\left[1 \leftarrow \mathcal{A}^{|H,O_{\mathsf{aux}}\rangle}(z)\right]\right|$$
$$\leq 4d \cdot \Pr\left[T \cap S \neq \emptyset : T \leftarrow \mathcal{D}^{|G,H,O_{\mathsf{aux}}\rangle}(z)\right],$$

where d is the query depth of $\mathcal{A}$ for the first oracle.

Remark 3.1 (On the difference from the original version). There are some differences between Lemma 3.3 and the original O2H lemma with MRM [KSS+20, Lemma 3.3]. First, in Lemma 3.3, we allow the algorithm $\mathcal{A}$ to get access to an additional oracle O_{aux}, which is not explicitly appeared in the original version. Second, in Lemma 3.3, we explicitly state the size of $\mathcal{D}$'s output T is at most $O(q)$ while the original lemma does not refer to the size of T. For the first one, it is easy to see that even if we introduce such an additional oracle, the lemma still holds. (This extension is used in also [LW21].) For the second, the concrete extractor $\mathcal{D}$ constructed in [KSS+20] satisfies this condition. Since we need the upper bound on the size of T in order to estimate the security bound in our proof, we place the requirement.

3.2 Additional Lemma

The following lemma is a multi-point version of adaptive reprogramming of QRO used in the proof of adaptive O2H lemma [Unr14, Lemma 14 in the eprint version]. We need it to handle KDM queries that are adaptively made. We provide the proof of it in [KN21].

Lemma 3.4 (Adaptive reprogramming of QRO). *We consider the following $\mathsf{Exp}^{\mathsf{adp\text{-}prog}}_{\mathcal{Y}_{\mathsf{prog}},\mathcal{A}}(1^\lambda)$*

Initialization: *The challenger first generates the challenge bit $b \leftarrow \{0,1\}$ and a fresh random oracle $V_0 : X \to Y$. Then, the challenger executes $b' \leftarrow \mathcal{A}^{|V_0\rangle, O_{\mathsf{prog}}}(1^\lambda)$, where O_{prog} is defined as follows.*

O_{prog}: *On the i-th call, it first generates* $s_i \leftarrow X$. *If* $b = 0$, *it just returns* $(s_i, V_0(s_i))$. *Otherwise, it generates* $u_i \leftarrow Y$, *updates the random oracle* $\mathcal{A}$ *gets access into* V_i *defined as*

$$V_i(x) = \begin{cases} u_j & (\textit{if } x = s_j \textit{ holds for some } j \le i) \\ H(x) & (\textit{otherwise}), \end{cases}$$

and returns $(s_i, V_i(s_i)) = (s_i, u_i)$.

Finalization: *The challenger outputs* 1 *if* $b = b'$ *and* 0 *otherwise.*

Then, for any integer q_{prog} *and an oracle algorithm* $\mathcal{A}$ *that makes at most* q *queries to* O_{b}, *we have* $\left|\Pr\left[1 \leftarrow \mathsf{Exp}^{\mathsf{adp\text{-}prog}}_{q_{\mathsf{prog}},\mathcal{A}}(1^\lambda)\right] - \frac{1}{2}\right| \le \frac{2q \cdot q_{\mathsf{prog}}}{\sqrt{|X|}}$.

4 KDM-CPA Security of $\mathsf{U}^{\not\perp}_m$ with OTP as DEM

In this section, we show that the KDM-CPA security in the QROM of a PKE scheme $\mathsf{U}^{\not\perp}_{m,\mathsf{OTP}} = \mathsf{U}^{\not\perp}_{m,\mathsf{OTP}}(\mathsf{dPKE}, H)$ can be reduced to the SDM-OW-RSA security of the underlying dPKE without square root security loss. $\mathsf{U}^{\not\perp}_{m,\mathsf{OTP}}$ is constructed by using $\mathsf{U}^{\not\perp}_m(\mathsf{dPKE}, H)$ [BHH+19] as KEM and OTP as DEM. Since we focus on KDM-*CPA* security here, $\mathsf{U}^{\not\perp}_{m,\mathsf{OTP}}$ omits the ciphertext validity check by re-encryption in the decryption algorithm, which is performed in $\mathsf{U}^{\not\perp}_m$.

4.1 Construction

Construction 4.1. Let $\mathsf{dPKE} = (\mathsf{dKG}, \mathsf{dEnc}, \mathsf{dDec})$ be a deterministic PKE scheme whose message space is $\mathcal{M}$. We assume that $\mathcal{M}$ is an abelian group and denote the operation in $\mathcal{M}$ as $+$. Let $H : \mathcal{M} \rightarrow \{0,1\}^*$ be a hash function. We construct $\mathsf{U}^{\not\perp}_{m,\mathsf{OTP}} = (\mathsf{KG}, \mathsf{Enc}, \mathsf{Dec})$ as follows.

$\mathsf{KG}(1^\lambda)$: Return $(\mathsf{pk}, \mathsf{sk}) \leftarrow \mathsf{dKG}(1^\lambda)$.

$\mathsf{Enc}(\mathsf{pk}, \mathsf{m})$: Generate $s \leftarrow \mathcal{M}$ and compute $\mathsf{ct} \leftarrow \mathsf{dEnc}(\mathsf{pk}, s)$ and $t = H(s) \oplus \mathsf{m}$. Return $\mathsf{CT} = (\mathsf{ct}, t)$.

$\mathsf{Dec}(\mathsf{sk}, \mathsf{CT}')$: Parse $\mathsf{CT}' = (\mathsf{ct}', t')$, compute $s' \leftarrow \mathsf{dDec}(\mathsf{sk}, \mathsf{ct}')$, and return $\perp$ if $s' = \perp$. Otherwise, return $t' \oplus H(s')$.

We see that if dPKE is (δ_1, δ_2)-correct, then $\mathsf{U}^{\not\perp}_{m,\mathsf{OTP}}$ is δ_1-correct for any δ_1.

4.2 Security Proof

We prove the following theorem.

Theorem 4.2. *Let* $\ell = \ell(\lambda)$ *be a polynomial and* dPKE *be a* (δ_1, δ_2)*-correct deterministic PKE. Let* $\mathcal{A}$ *be a QPT adversary against the KDM-CPA security of* $\mathsf{U}^{\not\perp}_{m,\mathsf{OTP}} = \mathsf{U}^{\not\perp}_{m,\mathsf{OTP}}(\mathsf{dPKE}, H)$ *making* q *(superposition) random oracle queries to* H *with query depth* d *and* q_{kdm} *(classical) queries to* O_{KDM}. *Also, let* q_f *be the* *upper bound of the total number of (classical) random oracle queries made by KDM functions. Then, there exists a QPT adversary $\mathcal{B}$ such that*

$$\mathsf{Adv}^{\mathsf{kdm\text{-}cpa}}_{\mathsf{U}^{\perp}_{m,\mathsf{OTP}},\ell,\mathcal{A}}(1^\lambda) \leq 4d \cdot \mathsf{Adv}^{\mathsf{sdm\text{-}ow\text{-}rsa}}_{\mathsf{dPKE},\ell,q_{\mathsf{kdm}},\mathcal{B}}(1^\lambda) + \frac{4(q+q_f)q_{\mathsf{kdm}}}{\sqrt{|\mathcal{M}|}} + (4d+1) \cdot q_{\mathsf{kdm}} \cdot \delta_2 \ . \tag{3}$$

Proof. We complete the proof using hybrid games. Let $\mathtt{SUC}_X$ be the event that the final output is 1 in Game X. We assume that $\mathcal{A}$ makes at least one KDM query before the first set of random oracle queries and between d^*-th set of random oracle queries and (d^*+1)-th set of random oracle queries for every $d^* \in [d-1]$. This assumption is without loss of generality in the sense that any adversary can be transformed into one satisfying this condition without changing the number and depth of random oracle queries.

Game 1: This is $\mathsf{Exp}^{\mathsf{kdm\text{-}cpa}}_{\mathsf{U}^{\perp}_{m,\mathsf{OTP}},\ell,\mathcal{A}}(1^\lambda)$.

Initialize: First, the challenger chooses a challenge bit $b \leftarrow \{0,1\}$. The challenger also generates a fresh random oracle H. Next, the challenger generates $(\mathsf{pk}^k, \mathsf{sk}^k) \leftarrow \mathsf{dKG}(1^\lambda)$ for every $k \in [\ell]$. The challenger sets $\mathbf{sk} := (\mathsf{sk}^1, \ldots, \mathsf{sk}^\ell)$ and $\mathbf{pk} := (\mathsf{pk}^1, \ldots, \mathsf{pk}^\ell)$, and executes $b' \leftarrow \mathcal{A}^{|H\rangle, O_{\mathtt{KDM}}}(\mathbf{pk})$. $O_{\mathtt{KDM}}$ behaves as follows.

$O_{\mathtt{KDM}}$: On the i-th call with input $(k_i, f_{i,0}, f_{i,1})$, it returns CT_i generated as follows.

1. Generate $s_i \leftarrow \mathcal{M}$ and compute $\mathsf{ct}_i \leftarrow \mathsf{dEnc}(\mathsf{pk}^{k_i}, s_i)$.
2. Compute $t_i = H(s_i) \oplus f^H_{i,b}(\mathbf{sk})$.
3. Set $\mathsf{CT}_i \leftarrow (\mathsf{ct}_i, t_i)$.

Finalize: The challenger outputs 1 if $b = b'$ and 0 otherwise.

Game 2: This is the same as Game 1 except the behavior of $O_{\mathtt{KDM}}$. In this game, $O_{\mathtt{KDM}}$ adaptively reprograms the random oracle that $\mathcal{A}$ (and functions queried by $\mathcal{A}$) gets access every time it is invoked. The detailed description is as follows.

$O_{\mathtt{KDM}}$: On input $(k_i, f_{i,0}, f_{i,1})$, it returns CT_i generated as follows.

1. Generate $s_i \leftarrow \mathcal{M}$ and compute $\mathsf{ct}_i \leftarrow \mathsf{dEnc}(\mathsf{pk}^{k_i}, s_i)$.
2. Generate $u_i \leftarrow \{0,1\}^*$ and compute $t_i = u_i \oplus f^{V_{i-1}}_{i,b}(\mathbf{sk})$.
3. Set $\mathsf{CT}_i \leftarrow (\mathsf{ct}_i, t_i)$.

Also, it updates the random oracle into

$$V_i(x) = \begin{cases} u_j & (\text{if } \exists j \leq i \ : \ x = s_j) \\ H(x) & (\text{otherwise}), \end{cases}$$

From Lemma 3.4, we have $|\Pr[\mathtt{SUC}_1] - \Pr[\mathtt{SUC}_2]| = \frac{4(q+q_f)q_{\mathsf{kdm}}}{\sqrt{\mathcal{M}}}$.

Game 3: This game is the same as Game 2 except that u_i is replaced with $u_i \oplus f^{V_{i-1}}_{i,b}(\mathbf{sk})$ for every $i \in [q_{\mathsf{kdm}}]$. More concretely, the behavior of $O_{\mathtt{KDM}}$ is changed as follows.

$O_{\mathtt{KDM}}$: On input $(k_i, f_{i,0}, f_{i,1})$, it returns CT_i generated as follows.
1. Generate $s_i \leftarrow \mathcal{M}$ and compute $\mathsf{ct}_i \leftarrow \mathsf{dEnc}(\mathsf{pk}^{k_i}, s_i)$.
2. Generate $u_i \leftarrow \{0,1\}^*$ and $\underline{\text{set } t_i \leftarrow u_i}$.
3. Set $\mathsf{CT}_i \leftarrow (\mathsf{ct}_i, t_i)$.

Also, it updates the random oracle into

$$V_i(x) = \begin{cases} \underline{u_j \oplus f_{j,b}^{V_{j-1}}(\mathbf{sk})} & (\text{if } \exists j \le i \ : \ x = s_j) \\ H(x) & (\text{otherwise}), \end{cases}$$

This change does not affect the view of $\mathcal{A}$ since u_i is chosen uniformly at random and independently of $f_{i,b}^{V_{i-1}}(\mathbf{sk})$ for every $i \in [q_{\mathtt{kdm}}]$. Thus, we have $|\Pr[\mathtt{SUC}_2] - \Pr[\mathtt{SUC}_3]| = 0$.

Game 4: This game is the same as Game 3 except for the following. The challenger first generates $r \leftarrow \mathcal{M}$. The challenger then generates $\Delta^1, \ldots, \Delta^\ell \leftarrow \mathcal{M}$ and generates $(\mathsf{pk}^k, \mathsf{sk}^k) \leftarrow \mathsf{dKG}(1^\lambda; r + \Delta^k)$ for every $k \in [\ell]$.

The above change does not affect the view of $\mathcal{A}$ since the distribution of $(\mathsf{pk}^k, \mathsf{sk}^k)_{k\in[\ell]}$ does not change. Thus, we have $|\Pr[\mathtt{SUC}_3] - \Pr[\mathtt{SUC}_4]| = 0$.

Game 5: This game is the same as Game 4 except that s_i is replaced with $r + s_i$. More concretely, the challenger generates ct_i as $\mathsf{ct}_i \leftarrow \mathsf{dEnc}(\mathsf{pk}^{k_i}, \underline{r + s_i})$ for every $i \in [q_{\mathtt{kdm}}]$. Also, the challenger sets V_i as

$$V_i(x) = \begin{cases} u_j \oplus f_{j,b}^{V_{j-1}}(\mathbf{sk}) & (\text{if } \exists j \le i \ : \ \underline{x = r + s_j}) \\ H(x) & (\text{otherwise}) \end{cases}$$

for every $i \in [q_{\mathtt{kdm}}]$.

We have $|\Pr[\mathtt{SUC}_4] - \Pr[\mathtt{SUC}_5]| = 0$ since this change also does not affect the view of $\mathcal{A}$.

From the next game, we use the function $\widehat{f}_{i,b}$ described in Fig. 1. $\widehat{f}_{i,b}$ is designed so that it computes $f_{i,b}^{V_{i-1}}(\mathbf{sk})$ if it has oracle access to H and is given $r + s_i$ as an input. For this aim, $\widehat{f}_{i,b}^H$ sequentially computes V_j from $V_1, V_2, ..., V_{i-1}$ using H. They are denoted as $\widehat{V}_j$ in the description of $\widehat{f}_{i,b}^H$. Here, the computation of $\widehat{V}_j$ by $\widehat{f}_{j,b}^H$ is local, and thus $\widehat{f}_{j,b}^H$ does not perform the updates of the random oracle that $\mathcal{A}$ gets access.

Game 6: For every $i \in [q_{\mathtt{kdm}}]$, we define a function . Then, Game 6 is the same as Game 5 except that the challenger sets V_i as

$$V_i(x) = \begin{cases} \underline{u_j \oplus \widehat{f}_{j,b}^H(x)} & (\text{if } \exists j \le i \ : \ x = r + s_j) \\ H(x) & (\text{otherwise}) \end{cases}$$

for every $i \in [q_{\mathtt{kdm}}]$.

$$\widehat{f}_{i,b}^{H}\left[(s_j, u_j, f_{j,b})_{j\in[i]}, (\Delta^k)_{k\in[\ell]}\right](x):$$

Hardwired: $(s_j, u_j, f_{j,b})_{j\in[i]}, (\Delta^k)_{k\in[\ell]}$.
Oracle H.
Input: $x \in \mathcal{M}$.

1. Compute $w = x - s_i$ and $(\mathsf{pk}^k, \mathsf{sk}^k) \leftarrow \mathsf{dKG}(1^\lambda; w + \Delta^k)$ for every $k \in [\ell]$, and set $\mathbf{sk} = (\mathsf{sk}^1, \ldots, \mathsf{sk}^\ell)$.
2. Repeat the following from $j = 1$ to $i - 1$, where $\widehat{V}_0 = H$.
   (a) Compute $v_j = u_j \oplus f_{j,b}^{\widehat{V}_{j-1}}(\mathbf{sk})$.
   (b) Set $\widehat{V}_j$ as
$$\widehat{V}_j(x') = \begin{cases} v_{j'} & (\text{if } \exists j' \in [q_{\mathsf{kdm}}] : j' \leq j \text{ and } x' = w + s_{j'}) \\ H(x') & (\text{otherwise}). \end{cases}$$
3. Return $f_{i,b}^{\widehat{V}_{i-1}}(\mathbf{sk})$.

Fig. 1. The description of $\widehat{f}_{i,b}^{H}$.

Since $\widehat{f}_{i,b}$ correctly computes $f_{i,b}^{V_{i-1}}(\mathbf{sk})$ if it has oracle access to H and is given $r + s_i$ as an input for every $i \in [q_{\mathsf{kdm}}]$, the functionality of V_i does not change between Game 5 and 6 for every $i \in [q_{\mathsf{kdm}}]$. Therefore, we have $|\Pr[\mathsf{SUC}_5] - \Pr[\mathsf{SUC}_6]| = 0$.

Game 7: This game is the same as Game 6 except that for every $i \in [q_{\mathsf{kdm}}]$, V_i is defined as

$$V_i(x) = \begin{cases} u_j \oplus \widehat{f}_{j,b}^{H}(x) & (\text{if } \exists j \leq i : \underline{\mathsf{dEnc}(\mathsf{pk}^{k_j}, x) = \mathsf{ct}_j}) \\ H(x) & (\text{otherwise}). \end{cases}$$

If ct_i has a unique pre-image $r + s_i$ under pk^{k_i} for every $i \in [q_{\mathsf{kdm}}]$, the functionality of V_i does not change for every $i \in [q_{\mathsf{kdm}}]$ between Game 6 and 7. Thus, from the correctness of dPKE, we have $|\Pr[\mathsf{SUC}_6] - \Pr[\mathsf{SUC}_7]| \leq q_{\mathsf{kdm}} \cdot \delta_2$.

At Game 7, $\mathcal{A}$ can obtain information of the challenge bit b only through d sets of random oracle queries. Below, we use d more hybrid games and remove information of b from those d sets of random oracle queries one by one.

Game 7+d^* ($d^* = 1, \ldots, d$): This is the same game as Game 7 except $O_{\mathtt{KDM}}$ defers updating the random oracle. Concretely, $O_{\mathtt{KDM}}$ does not update the random oracle until $\mathcal{A}$ makes the d^*-th set of random oracle queries. The detailed description of $O_{\mathtt{KDM}}$ is as follows.

$O_{\mathtt{KDM}}$: On input $(k_i, f_{i,0}, f_{i,1})$, it returns CT_i generated as follows.
1. Generate $s_i \leftarrow \mathcal{M}$ and compute $\mathsf{ct}_i \leftarrow \mathsf{dEnc}(\mathsf{pk}^{k_i}, r + s_i)$.
2. Generate $u_i \leftarrow \{0,1\}^*$ and set $t_i \leftarrow u_i$.

3. Set $\mathsf{CT}_i \leftarrow (\mathsf{ct}_i, t_i)$.

Also, if $\mathcal{A}$ already makes d^*-th set of queries to the random oracle, it updates the random oracle into

$$V_i(x) = \begin{cases} u_j \oplus \widehat{f}^H_{j,b}(x) & (\text{if } \exists j \leq i \ : \ \mathsf{dEnc}(\mathsf{pk}^{k_j}, x) = \mathsf{ct}_j) \\ H(x) & (\text{otherwise}). \end{cases}$$

We have $\left|\Pr[\mathtt{SUC}_{7+d}] - \frac{1}{2}\right| = 0$ since in Game 7+d, the view of $\mathcal{A}$ is completely independent of b. In order to estimate $|\Pr[\mathtt{SUC}_{7+d^*-1}] - \Pr[\mathtt{SUC}_{7+d^*}]|$ for every $d^* \in [d]$, we consider the following procedure Setup_{d^*}.

Setup_{d^*}: First, the challenger chooses a challenge bit $b \leftarrow \{0,1\}$. The challenger also generates a fresh random oracle H. Next, the challenger generates $(\mathsf{pk}^k, \mathsf{sk}^k) \leftarrow \mathsf{dKG}(1^\lambda; r + \Delta^k)$, where $r \leftarrow \mathcal{M}$ and $\Delta^k \leftarrow \mathcal{M}$ for every $k \in [\ell]$. The challenger sets $\mathbf{pk} := (\mathsf{pk}^1, \ldots, \mathsf{pk}^\ell)$, and executes $\mathcal{A}^{|H\rangle, O_{\mathtt{KDM}}}(\mathbf{pk})$ just before $\mathcal{A}$ makes the d^*-th set of random oracle queries. $O_{\mathtt{KDM}}$ behaves as follows.

$O_{\mathtt{KDM}}$: On input $(k_i, f_{i,0}, f_{i,1})$, it returns CT_i generated as follows.
1. Generate $s_i \leftarrow \mathcal{M}$ and compute $\mathsf{ct}_i \leftarrow \mathsf{dEnc}(\mathsf{pk}^{k_i}, r + s_i)$.
2. Generate $u_i \leftarrow \{0,1\}^*$ and set $t_i \leftarrow u_i$.
3. Set $\mathsf{CT}_i \leftarrow (\mathsf{ct}_i, t_i)$.

Let $\mathcal{A}$ makes i^* KDM queries before d^*-th set of random oracle queries. Then, the challenger sets V_{i^*} as

$$V_{i^*}(x) = \begin{cases} u_j \oplus \widehat{f}^H_{j,b}(x) & (\text{if } \exists j \leq i^* \ : \ \mathsf{dEnc}(\mathsf{pk}^{k_j}, x) = \mathsf{ct}_j) \\ H(x) & (\text{otherwise}) \end{cases}$$

and $S_{i^*} = \{x | \exists j \in [i^*] \ : \ \mathsf{dEnc}(\mathsf{pk}^{k_j}, x) = \mathsf{ct}_j\}$. The challenger also generates $s_{i,k} \leftarrow \mathcal{M}$ and generates $\mathsf{ct}_{i,k} \leftarrow \mathsf{dEnc}(\mathsf{pk}^k, r + s_{i,k})$ for every $i \in [i^* + 1, q_{\mathtt{kdm}}]$ and $k \in [\ell]$. The challenger then sets

$$z = (|st\rangle, b, \mathbf{pk}, (\Delta^k)_{k\in[\ell]}, (k_i, f_{i,b}, s_i, \mathsf{ct}_i, u_i)_{i\in[i^*]}, (s_{i,k}, \mathsf{ct}_{i,k})_{i\in[i^*+1, q_{\mathtt{kdm}}], k\in[\ell]}), \quad (4)$$

where $|st\rangle$ is the internal state of $\mathcal{A}$ at this point. The challenger outputs $(V_{i^*}, H, S_{i^*}, z, O_{\mathsf{aux}} = H)$.

Also, we consider the following QPT algorithm $\mathcal{A}_{d^*}$ that has oracle access to $O \in \{V_{i^*}, H\}$ and $O_{\mathsf{aux}} = H$.

$\mathcal{A}_{d^*}$: Given an input z, $\mathcal{A}_{d^*}$ parse it as Eq. (4) and executes $\mathcal{A}^{|O\rangle, O_{\mathtt{KDM}}}$ from $\mathcal{A}$'s d^*-th set of random oracle queries using $|st\rangle$ as the internal state of $\mathcal{A}$ at that point. $\mathcal{A}_{d^*}$ simulates $O_{\mathtt{KDM}}$ as follows.

$O_{\mathtt{KDM}}$: On input $(k_i, f_{i,0}, f_{i,1})$, it returns CT_i generated as follows.
1. Set $\mathsf{ct}_i \leftarrow \mathsf{ct}_{i,k_i}$ (and set $s_i \leftarrow s_{i,k_i}$).
2. Generate $u_i \leftarrow \{0,1\}^*$ and set $t_i \leftarrow u_i$.

3. Set $\mathsf{CT}_i \leftarrow (\mathsf{ct}_i, t_i)$.

Also, it updates the random oracle that $\mathcal{A}$ gets access into

$$V_i(x) = \begin{cases} u_j \oplus \widehat{f}^H_{j,b}(x) & (\text{if } \exists j \leq i \ : \ \mathsf{dEnc}(\mathsf{pk}^{k_j}, x) = \mathsf{ct}_j) \\ H(x) & (\text{otherwise}). \end{cases}$$

When $\mathcal{A}$ terminates with output b', $\mathcal{A}_{d^*}$ outputs 1 if $b = b'$ and 0 otherwise.

Suppose we execute Setup_{d^*} and $\mathcal{A}_{d^*}$ successively. They simulate the view of $\mathcal{A}$ in Game $7 + d^* - 1$ (resp. Game $7 + d^*$) if $O = V_{i^*}$ (resp. $O = H$). Also, $\mathcal{A}_{d^*}$ outputs 1 if and only if the output of the simulated games is 1. Thus, we have $\Pr[\mathtt{SUC}_{7+d^*-1}] = \Pr\left[1 \leftarrow \mathcal{A}_{d^*}^{|O=V_{i^*}, O_{\mathrm{aux}}=H\rangle}(z) : \mathsf{Setup}_{d^*}\right]$ and $\Pr[\mathtt{SUC}_{7+d^*}] = \Pr\left[1 \leftarrow \mathcal{A}_{d^*}^{|O=H, O_{\mathrm{aux}}=H\rangle}(z) : \mathsf{Setup}_{d^*}\right]$. From Lemma 3.3, there exists a QPT algorithm $\mathcal{D}_{d^*}$ such that

$$|\Pr[\mathtt{SUC}_{7+d^*-1}] - \Pr[\mathtt{SUC}_{7+d^*}]| \leq 4 \cdot \Pr\left[T \cap S_{i^*} \neq \emptyset \;\middle|\; T \leftarrow \mathcal{D}_{d^*}^{|V_{i^*}, H, O_{\mathrm{aux}}=H\rangle}(z), \mathsf{Setup}_{d^*}\right].$$

Note that $\mathcal{A}_{d^*}$ makes queries to $O \in \{V_{i^*}, H\}$ with depth 1 by the following reason. $\mathcal{A}_{d^*}$ is supposed to simulate Game $7 + d^* - 1$ (resp. Game $7 + d^*$) for $\mathcal{A}$ from the point that $\mathcal{A}$ makes d^*-th set of random oracle queries when $\mathcal{A}_{d^*}$ gets access to $O = V_{i^*}$ (resp. $O = H$). The answers to $\mathcal{A}$'s $(d^* + 1)$ to d-th set of random oracle queries are identical between Game $7+d^*-1$ and $7+d^*$. (Here, $\mathcal{A}$ makes at least one KDM query between the d^*-th and $(d^* + 1)$-th set of random oracle queries due to the assumption. Thus, they are answered using an updated random oracle.) $\mathcal{A}_{d^*}$ can simulate them by using $O_{\mathrm{aux}} = H$ and information included in z. Therefore, $\mathcal{A}_{d^*}$ uses its oracle O only for answering to $\mathcal{A}$'s d^*-th set of random oracle queries, and thus $\mathcal{A}_{d^*}$'s query depth to O is 1.

We bound the right-hand side probability. Using $\mathcal{D}_{d^*}$, we construct the following adversary $\mathcal{B}_{d^*}$ against the SDM-OW-RSA security of dPKE.

$\mathcal{B}_{d^*}$: Given $\mathbf{pk} = (\mathsf{pk}^1, \ldots, \mathsf{pk}^\ell)$, $(\Delta^k)_k$, and $(s_{i,k}, \mathsf{ct}_{i,k})_{i \in [q_{\mathrm{kdm}}], k \in [\ell]}$, $\mathcal{B}_{d^*}$ first simulates Setup_{d^*}. $\mathcal{B}_{d^*}$ chooses a challenge bit $b \leftarrow \{0,1\}$ and prepares a fresh random oracle H. $\mathcal{B}_{d^*}$ then executes $\mathcal{A}^{|H\rangle, O_{\mathrm{KDM}}}(\mathbf{pk})$ just before $\mathcal{A}$ makes the d^*-th set of random oracle queries, where O_{KDM} is simulated as follows.

O_{KDM}: On input $(k_i, f_{i,0}, f_{i,1})$, it returns CT_i generated as follows.

1. Set $\mathsf{ct}_i \leftarrow \mathsf{ct}_{i,k_i}$ (and set $s_i \leftarrow s_{i,k_i}$).
2. Generate $u_i \leftarrow \{0,1\}^*$ and set $t_i \leftarrow u_i$.
3. Set $\mathsf{CT}_i \leftarrow (\mathsf{ct}_i, t_i)$.

Let $\mathcal{A}$ makes i^* KDM queries before d^*-th set of random oracle queries. Then, $\mathcal{B}_{d^*}$ sets V_{i^*} as

$$V_{i^*}(x) = \begin{cases} u_j \oplus \widehat{f}^H_{j,b}(x) & (\text{if } \exists j \leq i^* \ : \ \mathsf{dEnc}(\mathsf{pk}^{k_j}, x) = \mathsf{ct}_j) \\ H(x) & (\text{otherwise}). \end{cases}$$

$\mathcal{B}_{d^*}$ also sets

$$z = (|st\rangle, b, \mathbf{pk}, (\Delta^k)_{k \in [\ell]}, (k_i, f_{i,b}, s_i, \mathsf{ct}_i, u_i)_{i \in [i^*]}, (s_{i,k}, \mathsf{ct}_{i,k})_{i \in [i^*+1, q_{\mathrm{kdm}}], k \in [\ell]}),$$

where $|st\rangle$ is the internal state of $\mathcal{A}$ at this point. Finally, $\mathcal{B}_{d^*}$ outputs $T \leftarrow \mathcal{D}_{d^*}^{|V_{i^*}, H, O_{\mathrm{aux}}=H\rangle}(z)$.

$\mathcal{B}_{d^*}$ perfectly simulates a successive execution of Setup_{d^*} and $\mathcal{D}_{d^*}$. Also, in the simulated execution, if $T \cap S_{i^*} \neq \emptyset$ occurs and ct_i has a unique pre-image $r + s_i$ under pk^{k_i} for every $i \in [q_{\mathsf{kdm}}]$, $\mathcal{B}_{d^*}$ wins. Thus, we have

$$Pr[T \cap S_{i^*} \neq \emptyset : T \leftarrow \mathcal{D}_{d^*}^{|V_{i^*}, H, O_{\mathsf{aux}}=H\rangle}(z), \mathsf{Setup}_{d^*}] \leq \mathsf{Adv}^{\mathsf{sdm\text{-}ow\text{-}rsa}}_{\mathsf{dPKE},\ell,q_{\mathsf{kdm}},\mathcal{B}_{d^*}}(1^\lambda) + q_{\mathsf{kdm}} \cdot \delta_2.$$

By setting $\mathcal{B}$ as $\mathcal{B}_{d^*}$ such that $\mathsf{Adv}^{\mathsf{sdm\text{-}ow\text{-}rsa}}_{\mathsf{dPKE},\ell,q_{\mathsf{kdm}},\mathcal{B}_{d^*}}(1^\lambda) \leq \mathsf{Adv}^{\mathsf{sdm\text{-}ow\text{-}rsa}}_{\mathsf{dPKE},\ell,q_{\mathsf{kdm}},\mathcal{B}}(1^\lambda)$ for every $d^* \in [d]$, we see that there exists a QPT $\mathcal{B}$ that satisfies Eq. (3). □ (Theorem 4.2)

5 SDM-OW-RSA Secure Deterministic PKE

In this section, we show that the SDM-OW-RSA security in the QROM of a tweaked version of T transformation [BHH+19] can be reduced to the IND-CPA security of the underlying PKE scheme.

5.1 Construction

Construction 5.1. Let $\mathsf{PKE} = (\mathsf{KG}, \mathsf{Enc}, \mathsf{Dec})$ be a PKE scheme whose message space is an abelian group $\mathcal{M}$ with the operation $+$. We also let the random coin space of KG and Enc be $\mathcal{R}_{\mathsf{kg}}$ and $\mathcal{R}_{\mathsf{enc}}$, respectively. Let $G = (G_{\mathsf{kg}}, G_{\mathsf{enc}})$ be a pair of hash functions, where $G_{\mathsf{kg}} : \mathcal{M} \to \mathcal{R}_{\mathsf{kg}}$ and $G_{\mathsf{enc}} : \mathcal{M} \to \mathcal{R}_{\mathsf{enc}}$. We construct T transformation with hash key generation $\mathsf{T}_{\mathsf{HKG}} = \mathsf{T}_{\mathsf{HKG}}(\mathsf{PKE}, G) = (\mathsf{dKG}, \mathsf{dEnc}, \mathsf{dDec})$ as follows.

$\mathsf{dKG}(1^\lambda; r)$: Return $(\mathsf{pk}, \mathsf{sk}) \leftarrow \mathsf{KG}(1^\lambda; G_{\mathsf{kg}}(r))$.
$\mathsf{dEnc}(\mathsf{pk}, \mathsf{m})$: Return $\mathsf{ct} \leftarrow \mathsf{Enc}(\mathsf{pk}, \mathsf{m}; G_{\mathsf{enc}}(\mathsf{m}))$.
$\mathsf{dDec}(\mathsf{sk}, \mathsf{CT})$: Return $\mathsf{m} \leftarrow \mathsf{Dec}(\mathsf{sk}, \mathsf{ct})$.

Recall that we define a deterministic PKE scheme is (δ_1, δ_2)-correct if it is δ_1-correct, and under a randomly generated key $(\mathsf{pk}, \mathsf{sk})$, the probability that a randomly generated message m has a collision, that is, another message m' such that $\mathsf{dEnc}(\mathsf{pk}, m) = \mathsf{dEnc}(\mathsf{pk}, m')$ is bounded by δ_2. Under this definition, as shown by [LW21, Lemma 4], $T(\mathsf{PKE}, G_{\mathsf{enc}})$ is $(\delta, 2\delta)$-correct if PKE is δ-correct for any δ. We can easily see that the correctness of $\mathsf{T}_{\mathsf{HKG}}(\mathsf{PKE}, G)$ can be reduced to that of $\mathsf{T}(\mathsf{PKE}, G_{\mathsf{enc}})$, and thus $\mathsf{T}_{\mathsf{HKG}}(\mathsf{PKE}, G)$ is $(\delta, 2\delta)$-correct if PKE is δ-correct for any δ.

5.2 Security Proof

We prove the following theorem.

Theorem 5.2. *Let $\ell = \ell(\lambda)$ and $q_{\mathsf{sdm}} = q_{\mathsf{sdm}}(\lambda)$ be polynomials and* PKE *be a PKE scheme. Let $\mathcal{A}$ be a QPT adversary against SDM-OW-RSA security of $\mathsf{T}_{\mathsf{HKG}} = \mathsf{T}_{\mathsf{HKG}}(\mathsf{PKE}, G)$ making total q (superposition) random oracle queries to G_{kg} and G_{enc} with query depth d, and outputs a list of size at most t as the final output. Then, there exists a QPT adversary $\mathcal{B}$ such that*

$$\mathsf{Adv}^{\mathsf{sdm\text{-}ow\text{-}rsa}}_{\mathsf{T}_{\mathsf{HKG}},\ell,q_{\mathsf{sdm}},\mathcal{A}}(\lambda) \leq (d+2) \cdot \left(2 \cdot \mathsf{Adv}^{\mathsf{ind\text{-}m\text{-}cpa}}_{\mathsf{PKE},\ell,\mathcal{B}}(1^\lambda) + \frac{4(q+t)\ell(q_{\mathsf{sdm}}+1)}{|\mathcal{M}|}\right) + \frac{\ell q_{\mathsf{sdm}}(\ell q_{\mathsf{sdm}} - 1)}{2|\mathcal{M}|}. \quad (5)$$

Proof. Without loss of generality, we assume that $\mathcal{A}$ makes random oracle queries to a single random oracle $G = G_{\mathsf{kg}} \times G_{\mathsf{enc}}$ instead of separate two random oracles G_{kg} and G_{enc} in the security games. Let $\widehat{\mathcal{A}}$ be a QPT adversary that runs in the same way as $\mathcal{A}$ except that before it terminates, $\widehat{\mathcal{A}}$ computes and discards $G(r')$ for all r' contained in $\mathcal{A}$'s final output T. Then, $\widehat{\mathcal{A}}$ makes at most $q + t$ queries to G with query depth $d + 1$, and we have $\mathsf{Adv}^{\mathsf{sdm\text{-}ow\text{-}rsa}}_{\mathsf{T}_{\mathsf{HKG}},\ell,q_{\mathsf{sdm}},\mathcal{A}}(\lambda) = \mathsf{Adv}^{\mathsf{sdm\text{-}ow\text{-}rsa}}_{\mathsf{T}_{\mathsf{HKG}},\ell,q_{\mathsf{sdm}}\widehat{\mathcal{A}}}(\lambda)$. We estimate the latter using hybrid games. Let $\mathtt{SUC}_X$ be the event that the final output is 1 in Game X.

Game 1: This is $\mathsf{Exp}^{\mathsf{sdm\text{-}ow\text{-}rsa}}_{\mathsf{T}_{\mathsf{HKG}},\ell,q_{\mathsf{sdm}},\widehat{\mathcal{A}}}(1^\lambda)$.

Initialize: The challenger generates $r \leftarrow \mathcal{M}$ and generates $(\mathsf{pk}^k, \mathsf{sk}^k) \leftarrow \mathsf{KG}(1^\lambda; G_{\mathsf{kg}}(r + \Delta^k))$, where $\Delta^k \leftarrow \mathcal{M}$ for every $k \in [\ell]$. Then, for every $k \in [\ell]$ and $i \in [q_{\mathsf{sdm}}]$, the challenger generates $s_{i,k} \leftarrow \mathcal{M}$ and computes $\mathsf{ct}_{i,k} \leftarrow \mathsf{Enc}(\mathsf{pk}^k, r + s_{i,k}; G_{\mathsf{enc}}(r + s_{i,k}))$. The challenger executes $T \leftarrow \widehat{\mathcal{A}}^{|G\rangle}((\mathsf{pk}^k, \Delta^k)_{k\in[\ell]}, (s_{i,k}, \mathsf{ct}_{i,k})_{i\in[q_{\mathsf{sdm}}],k\in[\ell]})$.

Finalize: The challenger outputs 1 if and only if T contains r' such that $r' = r + s_{i,k}$ holds for some $i \in [q_{\mathsf{sdm}}]$ and $k \in [\ell]$.

Game 2: This game is the same as Game 1 except the followings. First, if there exists a pair $(s_{i,k}, s_{i',k'})$ such that $s_{i,k} = s_{i',k'}$, the challenger immediately outputs 0 as the final output of the game. Also, $G = G_{\mathsf{kg}} \times G_{\mathsf{enc}}$ is replaced with

$$V(x) = \begin{cases} \underline{u^k} & \underline{(\text{if } \exists k \in [\ell] \ :\ x = r + \Delta^k)} \\ \underline{v_{i,k}} & \underline{(\text{if } \exists i \in [q_{\mathsf{kdm}}] \text{ and } k \in [\ell] \ :\ x = r + s_{i,k})} \\ G(x) & (\text{otherwise}), \end{cases}$$

where $u^k, v_{i,k} \leftarrow \mathcal{R}_{\mathsf{kg}} \times \mathcal{R}_{\mathsf{enc}}$ for every $k \in [\ell]$ and $i \in [q_{\mathsf{kdm}}]$.

We have $|\Pr[\mathtt{SUC}_1] - \Pr[\mathtt{SUC}_2]| = \frac{\ell q_{\mathsf{sdm}}(\ell q_{\mathsf{sdm}}-1)}{2|\mathcal{M}|}$ since Game 1 and 2 are identical unless there exists a pair $(s_{i,k}, s_{i',k'})$ such that $s_{i,k} = s_{i',k'}$. Below, we let $S = \{r + \Delta^k\}_{k\in[\ell]} \cup \{r + s_{i,k}\}_{i\in[q_{\mathsf{sdm}}],k\in[\ell]}$.

Before proceeding the hybrid games, We provide the high level overview of the rest of games. In Game 2, the key generation randomness $G_{\mathsf{kg}}(r + \Delta^k)$ and encryption randomness $G_{\mathsf{enc}}(r + s_{i,k})$ correlate with the encrypted plaintexts $r + s_{i,k}$. Thus, next, at transition from Game 2 to 3, we eliminate the correlation by programming the random oracle. Concretely, in Game 3, the above randomnesses are generated by using V, but $\widehat{\mathcal{A}}$ gets access to only the punctured oracle $G \setminus S$, not V. In order to justify the programming, we use semi-classical O2H lemma (Lemma 3.1). By doing so, we can justify the programming without square root security loss, and obtain $\Pr[\mathtt{SUC}_2] \leq (d+2)\Pr[\mathtt{Find}_3]$, where $\mathtt{Find}_X$ be the event that the punctured oracle $G \setminus S$ returns 1 in Game X. Thus, all we have to do is to bound $\Pr[\mathtt{Find}_3]$. At Game 3, from the view of $\mathcal{A}$, the key generation randomness and encryption randomness are uniformly random strings that are independent of r, that is, u^k and $v_{i,k}$. Namely, the correlation issue above are solved. Thus, at transition from Game 3 to 4, we use the IND-m-CPA security of PKE, and eliminate information of r from $\mathsf{ct}_{i,k}$. In Game 4, except the punctured oracle $G \setminus S$, r is completely hidden from the view of $\widehat{\mathcal{A}}$. Therefore, by using Lemma 3.2, we can bound $\Pr[\mathtt{Find}_4]$ and complete the proof.

Game 3: This game is the same as Game 2 except that $\widehat{\mathcal{A}}$ gets access to the punctured oracle $G \setminus S$. $(\mathsf{pk}^k, \mathsf{sk}^k)$ and $\mathsf{ct}_{i,k}$ are still generated using V for every $k \in [\ell]$ and $i \in [q_{\mathtt{sdm}}]$.

Let $\mathtt{Find}_X$ be the event that the punctured oracle $G \setminus S$ returns 1 in Game X. From the definition of $\widehat{\mathcal{A}}$, we have $\Pr[\mathtt{SUC}_3 \wedge \neg\mathtt{Find}_3] = 0$. Thus, we have

$$\sqrt{\Pr[\mathtt{SUC}_2]} = \left| \sqrt{\Pr[\mathtt{SUC}_2]} - \sqrt{\Pr[\mathtt{SUC}_3 \wedge \neg\mathtt{Find}_3]} \right| .$$

By applying Lemma 3.1, we obtain

$$\left| \sqrt{\Pr[\mathtt{SUC}_2]} - \sqrt{\Pr[\mathtt{SUC}_3 \wedge \neg\mathtt{Find}_3]} \right| \leq \sqrt{(d+2) \cdot \Pr[\mathtt{Find}_3]} .$$

Therefore, we also obtain $\Pr[\mathtt{SUC}_2] \leq (d+2)\Pr[\mathtt{Find}_3]$.

Game 4: This game is the same as Game 3 except that $\mathsf{ct}_{i,k}$ is generated as $\mathsf{ct}_{i,k} \leftarrow \mathsf{Enc}(\mathsf{pk}^k, 0)$ for every $k \in [\ell]$ and $i \in [q_{\mathtt{sdm}}]$.

In order to estimate $|\Pr[\mathtt{Find}_3] - \Pr[\mathtt{Find}_4]|$, using $\widehat{\mathcal{A}}$, we construct the following QPT adversary $\mathcal{B}$ against the IND-m-CPA security of PKE. In the description, a function Test takes a value x and a set X as inputs and outputs 1 if $x \in X$ and 0 otherwise.

Initialize: Given $(\mathsf{pk}^k)_k$, $\mathcal{B}$ first generates $r \leftarrow \mathcal{M}$. $\mathcal{B}$ then generates $\Delta^k \leftarrow \mathcal{M}$ for every $k \in [\ell]$, $s_{i,k} \leftarrow \mathcal{M}$ for every $i \in [q_{\mathtt{sdm}}]$ and $k \in [\ell]$, and a fresh random oracle G. If there exists a pair $(s_{i,k}, s_{i',k'})$ such that $s_{i,k} = s_{i',k'}$, $\mathcal{B}$ outputs 0 and terminates. Next, for every $i \in [q_{\mathtt{sdm}}]$ and $k \in [\ell]$, $\mathcal{B}$ queries $(k, r + s_{i,k}, 0)$ to its oracle $O_{\mathtt{IND}}$ and obtains $\mathsf{ct}_{i,k}$. Finally, $\mathcal{B}$ sets $b' = 0$ and executes $T \leftarrow \widehat{\mathcal{A}}^{|G\setminus S\rangle}((\mathsf{pk}^k, \Delta^k)_{k\in[\ell]}, (s_{i,k}, \mathsf{ct}_{i,k})_{i\in[q_{\mathtt{sdm}}],k\in[\ell]})$, where $G \setminus S$ is simulated as follows.

$G \setminus S$: When $\widehat{\mathcal{A}}$ makes a (superposition) query $|x\rangle |y\rangle$ to $G \setminus S$, $\mathcal{B}$ first computes $|x\rangle |y\rangle |\mathsf{Test}(x, S)\rangle$ and measures $|\mathsf{Test}(x, S)\rangle$. If the result is 0, $\mathcal{B}$ just returns $|x\rangle |y \oplus G(x)\rangle$ to $\widehat{\mathcal{A}}$. Otherwise, $\mathcal{B}$ set the value of b' to 1, and returns $|x\rangle |y \oplus G(x)\rangle$ to $\widehat{\mathcal{A}}$.

Finalize: If $\widehat{\mathcal{A}}$ terminates, $\mathcal{B}$ terminates with output b'.

Let the challenge bit in $\mathsf{Exp}^{\mathsf{ind\text{-}m\text{-}cpa}}_{\mathsf{PKE},\ell,\mathcal{B}}$ be b. $\mathcal{B}$ perfectly simulates Game 3 and 4 for $\mathcal{A}$ when $b = 0$ and $b = 1$, respectively. Also, $\mathcal{B}$ outputs $b' = 1$ if and only if $\mathtt{Find}_3$ and $\mathtt{Find}_4$ occur in the simulated Games. Thus, we have

$$\begin{aligned}\mathsf{Adv}^{\mathsf{ind\text{-}m\text{-}cpa}}_{\mathsf{PKE},\ell,\mathcal{B}}(1^\lambda) &= \frac{1}{2}|\Pr[b'=1|b=0]-\Pr[b'=1|b=1]| \\ &= \frac{1}{2}|\Pr[\mathtt{Find}_3]-\Pr[\mathtt{Find}_4]| \ .\end{aligned}$$

Finally, we bound $\Pr[\mathtt{Find}_4]$. In Game 4, conditioned on $(\mathsf{pk}^k, \Delta^k)_{k\in[\ell]}$ and $(s_{i,k}, \mathsf{ct}_{i,k})_{i\in[q_{\mathsf{sdm}}],k\in[\ell]}$, we have $\Pr_{r\leftarrow\mathcal{M}}[m \in S] \le \frac{\ell(q_{\mathsf{sdm}}+1)}{|\mathcal{M}|}$ for any $m \in \mathcal{M}$. Thus, from Lemma 3.2, we obtain $\Pr[\mathtt{Find}_4] \le \frac{4(q+t)\ell(q_{\mathsf{sdm}}+1)}{|\mathcal{M}|}$.

Overall, we see that there exists a QPT $\mathcal{B}$ that satisfies Eq. (5). □
(Theorem 5.2)

6 Conclusion: KDM Security of FO Transformations

In the conclusion, we show that the KDM security in the QROM of FO transformations can be reduced to the IND-CPA security of the underlying PKE scheme without square root security loss.

We first provide the security bound for the KDM-CPA security of the PKE scheme $\mathsf{U}^{\perp}_{m,\mathtt{OTP}}(\mathsf{T}_{\mathtt{HKG}}(\mathsf{PKE}, G), H)$ in terms of the IND-m-CPA security of the underlying PKE. In order to capture the most general setting, we allow adversaries for the KDM-CPA security of $\mathsf{U}^{\perp}_{m,\mathtt{OTP}}(\mathsf{T}_{\mathtt{HKG}}(\mathsf{PKE}, G), H)$ and KDM functions queried by them to get access to not only H but also G. The access to G by an adversary does not affect the security proof provided in Sect. 4.2 since H and G are independent random oracles. Then, the following theorem holds.

Theorem 6.1. *Let $\ell = \ell(\lambda)$ be a polynomial and PKE be a δ-correct PKE scheme. Let $\mathcal{A}_{\mathsf{kdm}}$ be an adversary for the KDM-CPA security of $\mathsf{U}^{\perp}_{m,\mathtt{OTP}}(\mathsf{T}_{\mathtt{HKG}}(\mathsf{PKE}, G), H)$ making q_{kdm} KDM queries. Suppose $\mathcal{A}_{\mathsf{kdm}}$ makes at most q^G (resp. q^H) super-position random oracle queries to G (resp. H) with query depth d^G (resp. d^H). Also, suppose KDM functions queried by $\mathcal{A}_{\mathsf{kdm}}$ makes at most q_f^G (resp. q_f^H) classical random oracle queries to G (resp. H). Then, there exists a QPT adversary $\mathcal{A}_{\mathsf{ind}}$ such that*

$$\begin{aligned}&\mathsf{Adv}^{\mathsf{kdm\text{-}cpa}}_{\mathsf{U}^{\perp}_{m,\mathtt{OTP}}(\mathsf{T}_{\mathtt{HKG}}(\mathsf{PKE},G),H),\ell,\mathcal{A}_{\mathsf{kdm}}}(1^\lambda)\\ &\le 4d^H \cdot O(d^G + d^H \cdot q_f^G)\left(2\cdot \mathsf{Adv}^{\mathsf{ind\text{-}m\text{-}cpa}}_{\mathsf{PKE},\ell,\mathcal{A}_{\mathsf{ind}}}(1^\lambda) + \frac{O(q^G + q^H\cdot(\ell+q_f^G))\cdot\ell\cdot(q_{\mathsf{kdm}}+1)}{|\mathcal{M}|}\right)\\ &\quad + \frac{2d^H\ell q_{\mathsf{kdm}}(\ell q_{\mathsf{kdm}}-1)}{|\mathcal{M}|} + \frac{4(q^H+q_f^H)q_{\mathsf{kdm}}}{\sqrt{|\mathcal{M}|}} + 2(4d^H+1)\cdot q_{\mathsf{kdm}}\cdot\delta \ . \qquad (6)\end{aligned}$$

Proof. We estimate the number of queries to G made by $\mathcal{B}_{d^*}$ appeared in the proof of Theorem 4.2 when $\mathcal{A}_{\mathsf{kdm}}$ is used inside of it. First, $\mathcal{B}_{d^*}$ make $O(q^G)$ queries with depth $O(d^G)$ in order to simulate queries to G made by $\mathcal{D}_{d^*}$. Also, every time $\mathcal{D}_{d^*}$ makes a query to V_{i^*}, $\mathcal{B}_{d^*}$ needs to make at most $O(\ell + q_f^G)$ queries to G with depth $O(q_f^G)$ in order for the computation of $\widehat{f}_{i,b}$. Since $\mathcal{D}_{d^*}$ makes at most $O(q^H)$ queries to V_{i^*} with depth $O(d^H)$, to simulate $\mathcal{D}_{d^*}$'s queries to V_{i^*}, $\mathcal{B}_{d^*}$ needs to make at most $O(q^H \cdot (\ell + q_f^G))$ queries to G with query depth $O(d^H \cdot q_f^G)$. Therefore, $\mathcal{B}_{d^*}$ makes at most $O(q^G + q^H \cdot (\ell + q_f^G))$ queries to G with query depth $O(d^G + d^H \cdot q_f^G)$. This holds for every $d^* \in [d]$. Also, Since $\mathcal{D}_{d^*}$ outputs a list of size $O(q^H)$, so does $\mathcal{B}_{d^*}$ for every $d^* \in [d]$. From this fact and Theorem 4.2 and 5.2, we see that there exists a QPT $\mathcal{A}_{\mathsf{ind}}$ that satisfies Eq. (6). □ (Theorem 6.1)

Remark 6.1 (On the value of q_f^G and q_f^H.). Note that the values of q_f^G and q_f^H are determined depending on usage scenarios and independent of the adversary's behavior. For example, in the usage scenario where we need only circular security such as anonymous credential [CL01], we can set $q_f^G = q_f^H = 0$. In that case, the multiplicative term of $\mathsf{Adv}^{\mathsf{ind\text{-}m\text{-}cpa}}_{\mathsf{PKE},\ell,\mathcal{A}_{\mathsf{ind}}}(1^\lambda)$ in Eq. (6) is roughly the square of the query depth of $\mathcal{A}_{\mathsf{kdm}}$ to the random oracles. It is asymptotically the same as the multiplicative term appeared in the proof of IND-CCA secure KEM using O2H lemma with MRM [KSS+20]. In order to capture a wide range of applications, we allow KDM functions to get access to the random oracles in this work, but we think q_f^G and q_f^H are not large in many applications.

Let $\mathsf{FO}^{\perp}_{m,\mathsf{OTP}}(\mathsf{PKE}, G_{\mathsf{enc}}, H)$ be a PKE scheme constructed by combining the KEM $\mathsf{U}^{\perp}_{m}(\mathsf{T}(\mathsf{PKE}, G_{\mathsf{enc}}), H)$ with OTP as DEM. From Theorem 6.1, we can show that $\mathsf{FO}^{\perp}_{m}(\mathsf{PKE}, G_{\mathsf{enc}}, H)$ satisfies KDM-CPA security with asymptotically the same security loss with respect to the underlying IND-m-CPA secure PKE as Eq. (6). Concretely, we have the following theorem.

Theorem 6.2. *Let $\ell = \ell(\lambda)$ be a polynomial and* PKE *be a PKE scheme. Let $\mathcal{A}_{\mathsf{kdm}}$ be an adversary for the KDM-ATK security of $\mathsf{FO}^{\perp}_{m,\mathsf{OTP}}(\mathsf{PKE}, G_{\mathsf{enc}}, H)$ where ATK $\in$ {CPA, CCA}. Then, for* $\mathsf{atk} \in \{\mathsf{cpa}, \mathsf{cca}\}$, *there exists an adversary $\mathcal{A}'_{\mathsf{kdm}}$ such that*

$$\mathsf{Adv}^{\mathsf{kdm\text{-}atk}}_{\mathsf{FO}^{\perp}_{m,\mathsf{OTP}}(\mathsf{PKE},G_{\mathsf{enc}},H),\ell,\mathcal{A}_{\mathsf{kdm}}}(1^\lambda) \le \mathsf{Adv}^{\mathsf{kdm\text{-}atk}}_{\mathsf{U}^{\perp}_{m,\mathsf{OTP}}(\mathsf{T}_{\mathsf{HKG}}(\mathsf{PKE},G),H),\ell,\mathcal{A}'_{\mathsf{kdm}}}(1^\lambda) + \frac{\ell(\ell-1)}{2|\mathcal{M}|} .$$

Proof. Suppose we modify the security game $\mathsf{Exp}^{\mathsf{kdm\text{-}atk}}_{\mathsf{FO}^{\perp}_{m,\mathsf{OTP}},\ell,\mathcal{A}_{\mathsf{kdm}}}(1^\lambda)$ so that the k-th key pair $(\mathsf{pk}^k, \mathsf{sk}^k)$ is generated by using $G_{\mathsf{kg}}(r^k)$ as the random coin for KG for every $k \in [\ell]$, where $G_{\mathsf{kg}} : \mathcal{M} \to \mathcal{R}_{\mathsf{kg}}$ is a random oracle and $r^k \leftarrow \mathcal{M}$ for every $k \in [\ell]$. If $r^1, \ldots, r^\ell$ are mutually different, then the distribution of ℓ key pairs does not change from the view of $\mathcal{A}_{\mathsf{kdm}}$ by this modification. We emphasize that $\mathcal{A}_{\mathsf{kdm}}$ does not have access to G_{kg}. By the modification, $\mathcal{A}_{\mathsf{kdm}}$'s advantage is changed at most $\frac{\ell(\ell-1)}{2|\mathcal{M}|}$. We can see that we can easily construct an adversary $\mathcal{A}'_{\mathsf{kdm}}$ such that $\mathsf{Adv}^{\mathsf{kdm\text{-}atk}}_{\mathsf{U}^{\perp}_{m,\mathsf{OTP}}(\mathsf{T}_{\mathsf{HKG}}(\mathsf{PKE},G),H),\ell,\mathcal{A}'_{\mathsf{kdm}}}(1^\lambda)$ is exactly the same as $\mathcal{A}_{\mathsf{kdm}}$' advantage in the modified game. Therefore, we obtain the theorem. □ (Theorem 6.2)

Thus, we see that the KDM-CPA security of $\mathsf{FO}^{\perp}_{m,\mathsf{OTP}}(\mathsf{PKE}, G_{\mathsf{enc}}, H)$ is reduced to that of $\mathsf{U}^{\perp}_{m,\mathsf{OTP}}(\mathsf{T}_{\mathsf{HKG}}(\mathsf{PKE}, G), H)$ with additional security loss $\frac{\ell(\ell-1)}{2|\mathcal{M}|}$ which is absorbed by the additive term of Eq. (6).

Extension to KDM-CCA Security. In the main body of this paper, we focused on KDM-CPA security. Our proof technique is also compatible with KDM-CCA security. Concretely, we can prove the KDM-CCA security of a PKE scheme constructed by using a variant of $\mathsf{U}_m^{\perp}$ called $\mathsf{U}_m^{\perp,\mathtt{keyconf}} = \mathsf{U}_m^{\perp,\mathtt{keyconf}}(\mathsf{dPKE}, H)$ as KEM and OTP-then-MAC as DEM without square root security loss if the underlying dPKE is SDM-OW-RSA secure and additionally satisfies injectiveness. The security proof is a combination of our proof for the KDM-CPA security of $\mathsf{U}_{m,\mathtt{OTP}}^{\perp}$ and the proof for the IND-CCA security of $\mathsf{U}_m^{\perp,\mathtt{keyconf}}$ by [BHH+19,KSS+20]. We provide the formal description of this construction and security proof for the KDM-CCA security of it in [KN21].

By following a similar argument as the case of KDM-CPA security, we can show that the KDM-CCA security of the KEM $\mathsf{FO}_m^{\perp,\mathtt{keyconf}}(\mathsf{PKE}, G_{\mathtt{enc}}, H) = \mathsf{U}_m^{\perp,\mathtt{keyconf}}(T(\mathsf{PKE}, G_{\mathtt{enc}}), H)$ combined with OTP-then-MAC as DEM, can be reduced to the IND-CPA security of PKE. The multiplicative term in the security bound with respect to the underlying PKE is roughly the same as Eq. (6) though some additive terms are added to the security bound.

Acknowledgments. The authors thank Takashi Yamakawa for helpful comments.

References

[AHU19] Ambainis, A., Hamburg, M., Unruh, D.: Quantum security proofs using semi-classical Oracles. In: Boldyreva, A., Micciancio, D. (eds.) CRYPTO 2019. LNCS, vol. 11693, pp. 269–295. Springer, Cham (2019). https://doi.org/10.1007/978-3-030-26951-7_10

[AR02] Abadi, M., Rogaway, P.: Reconciling Two Views of Cryptography (The Computational Soundness of Formal Encryption). J. Cryptol. **15**(2), 103–127 (2002)

[BBM00] Bellare, M., Boldyreva, A., Micali, S.: Public-Key Encryption in a Multi-user Setting: Security Proofs and Improvements. In: Preneel, B. (ed.) EUROCRYPT 2000. LNCS, vol. 1807, pp. 259–274. Springer, Heidelberg (2000). https://doi.org/10.1007/3-540-45539-6_18

[BDF+11] Boneh, D., Dagdelen, Ö., Fischlin, M., Lehmann, A., Schaffner, C., Zhandry, M.: Random Oracles in a Quantum World. In: Lee, D.H., Wang, X. (eds.) ASIACRYPT 2011. LNCS, vol. 7073, pp. 41–69. Springer, Heidelberg (2011). https://doi.org/10.1007/978-3-642-25385-0_3

[BDU08] Backes, M., Dürmuth, M., Unruh, D.: OAEP Is Secure under Key-Dependent Messages. In: Pieprzyk, J. (ed.) ASIACRYPT 2008. LNCS, vol. 5350, pp. 506–523. Springer, Heidelberg (2008). https://doi.org/10.1007/978-3-540-89255-7_31

[BHH+19] N. Bindel, M. Hamburg, K. Hövelmanns, A. Hülsing, E. Persichetti. Tighter Proofs of CCA Security in the Quantum Random Oracle Model. In: TCC 2019, Part II, volume 11892 of LNCS, pages 61–90. 2019

[BHHO08] Boneh, D., Halevi, S., Hamburg, M., Ostrovsky, R.: Circular-Secure Encryption from Decision Diffie-Hellman. In: Wagner, D. (ed.) CRYPTO 2008. LNCS, vol. 5157, pp. 108–125. Springer, Heidelberg (2008). https://doi.org/10.1007/978-3-540-85174-5_7

[Ble98] D. Bleichenbacher. Chosen Ciphertext Attacks Against Protocols Based on the RSA Encryption Standard PKCS #1. In CRYPTO'98, volume 1462 of LNCS, pages 1–12. 1998.

[BR93] Bellare, M., Rogaway, P.: Random Oracles are Practical: A Paradigm for Designing Efficient Protocols. In ACM CCS **93**, 62–73 (1993)

[BR95] M. Bellare and P. Rogaway. Optimal Asymmetric Encryption. In EUROCRYPT'94, volume 950 of LNCS, pages 92–111. 1995.

[BRS03] Black, J., Rogaway, P., Shrimpton, T.: Encryption-scheme security in the presence of key-dependent messages. In: Nyberg, K., Heys, H. (eds.) SAC 2002. LNCS, vol. 2595, pp. 62–75. Springer, Heidelberg (2003). https://doi.org/10.1007/3-540-36492-7_6

[CL01] Camenisch, J., Lysyanskaya, A.: An Efficient System for Non-transferable Anonymous Credentials with Optional Anonymity Revocation. In: Pfitzmann, B. (ed.) EUROCRYPT 2001. LNCS, vol. 2045, pp. 93–118. Springer, Heidelberg (2001). https://doi.org/10.1007/3-540-44987-6_7

[DDN00] Dolev, D., Dwork, C., Naor, M.: Nonmalleable Cryptography. SIAM J. Comput. **30**(2), 391–437 (2000)

[DS14] Davies, G.T., Stam, M.: KDM Security in the Hybrid Framework. In: Benaloh, J. (ed.) CT-RSA 2014. LNCS, vol. 8366, pp. 461–480. Springer, Cham (2014). https://doi.org/10.1007/978-3-319-04852-9_24

[FO13] Fujisaki, E., Okamoto, T.: Secure Integration of Asymmetric and Symmetric Encryption Schemes. J. Cryptol. **26**(1), 80–101 (2011). https://doi.org/10.1007/s00145-011-9114-1

[Gen09] Gentry, C.: A fully homomorphic encryption scheme. Ph.D. thesis, Stanford University (2009). crypto.stanford.edu/craig

[HHK17] Hofheinz, D., Hövelmanns, K., Kiltz, E.: A modular analysis of the Fujisaki-Okamoto transformation. In: Kalai, Y., Reyzin, L. (eds.) TCC 2017. LNCS, vol. 10677, pp. 341–371. Springer, Cham (2017). https://doi.org/10.1007/978-3-319-70500-2_12

[HKSU20] Hövelmanns, Kathrin, Kiltz, Eike, Schäge, Sven, Unruh, Dominique: Generic authenticated key exchange in the quantum random Oracle model. In: Kiayias, Aggelos, Kohlweiss, Markulf, Wallden, Petros, Zikas, Vassilis (eds.) PKC 2020. LNCS, vol. 12111, pp. 389–422. Springer, Cham (2020). https://doi.org/10.1007/978-3-030-45388-6_14

[JZC+18] H. Jiang, Z. Zhang, L. Chen, H. Wang, and Z. Ma. IND-CCA-Secure Key Encapsulation Mechanism in the Quantum Random Oracle Model, Revisited. In CRYPTO 2018, Part III, volume 10993 of LNCS, pages 96–125. 2018

[JZM19a] Jiang, H., Zhang, Z., Ma, Z.: Key encapsulation mechanism with explicit rejection in the quantum random Oracle model. In: Lin, D., Sako, K. (eds.) PKC 2019. LNCS, vol. 11443, pp. 618–645. Springer, Cham (2019). https://doi.org/10.1007/978-3-030-17259-6_21

[JZM19b] Jiang, H., Zhang, Z., Ma, Z.: Tighter security proofs for generic key encapsulation mechanism in the quantum random Oracle model. In: Ding, J., Steinwandt, R. (eds.) PQCrypto 2019. LNCS, vol. 11505, pp. 227–248. Springer, Cham (2019). https://doi.org/10.1007/978-3-030-25510-7_13

[KMHT16] F. Kitagawa, T. Matsuda, G. Hanaoka, and K. Tanaka. On the Key Dependent Message Security of the Fujisaki-Okamoto Constructions. In *PKC 2016, Part I*, volume 9614 of *LNCS*, pages 99–129. 2016

[KN21] Kitagawa, F., Nishimaki, R.: KDM Security for the Fujisaki-Okamoto Transformations in the QROM. IACR Cryptol. ePrint Arch., p. 1200 (2021)

[KSS+20] V. Kuchta, A. Sakzad, D. Stehlé, R. Steinfeld, and S. Sun. Measure-Rewind-Measure: Tighter Quantum Random Oracle Model Proofs for One-Way to Hiding and CCA Security. In EUROCRYPT 2020, Part III, volume 12107 of LNCS, pages 703–728. 2020

[LW21] Liu, X., Wang, M.: QCCA-Secure Generic Key Encapsulation Mechanism with Tighter Security in the Quantum Random Oracle Model. In: Garay, J.A. (ed.) PKC 2021. LNCS, vol. 12710, pp. 3–26. Springer, Cham (2021). https://doi.org/10.1007/978-3-030-75245-3_1

[RS92] Rackoff, C., Simon, D.R.: Non-Interactive Zero-Knowledge Proof of Knowledge and Chosen Ciphertext Attack. In: Feigenbaum, J. (ed.) CRYPTO 1991. LNCS, vol. 576, pp. 433–444. Springer, Heidelberg (1992). https://doi.org/10.1007/3-540-46766-1_35

[SXY18] Saito, T., Xagawa, K., Yamakawa, T.: Tightly-secure key-encapsulation mechanism in the quantum random Oracle model. In: Nielsen, J.B., Rijmen, V. (eds.) EUROCRYPT 2018. LNCS, vol. 10822, pp. 520–551. Springer, Cham (2018). https://doi.org/10.1007/978-3-319-78372-7_17

[TU16] Targhi, E.E., Unruh, D.: Post-quantum security of the Fujisaki-Okamoto and OAEP transforms. In: Hirt, M., Smith, A. (eds.) TCC 2016. LNCS, vol. 9986, pp. 192–216. Springer, Heidelberg (2016). https://doi.org/10.1007/978-3-662-53644-5_8

[Unr14] Unruh, D.: Quantum Position Verification in the Random Oracle Model. In: Garay, J.A., Gennaro, R. (eds.) CRYPTO 2014. LNCS, vol. 8617, pp. 1–18. Springer, Heidelberg (2014). https://doi.org/10.1007/978-3-662-44381-1_1

[Unr15] Unruh, D.: Revocable quantum timed-release encryption. J. ACM **62**(6), 49:1–49:76 (2015)

[Zha12] Zhandry, M.: Secure Identity-Based Encryption in the Quantum Random Oracle Model. In: Safavi-Naini, R., Canetti, R. (eds.) CRYPTO 2012. LNCS, vol. 7417, pp. 758–775. Springer, Heidelberg (2012). https://doi.org/10.1007/978-3-642-32009-5_44

[Zha19] Zhang, J.: Delegating quantum computation in the quantum random Oracle model. In: Hofheinz, D., Rosen, A. (eds.) TCC 2019. LNCS, vol. 11892, pp. 30–60. Springer, Cham (2019). https://doi.org/10.1007/978-3-030-36033-7_2

A New Security Notion for PKC in the Standard Model: Weaker, Simpler, and Still Realizing Secure Channels

Wasilij Beskorovajnov[1], Roland Gröll[1], Jörn Müller-Quade[1,2,3], Astrid Ottenhues[2,3], and Rebecca Schwerdt[2,3](✉)

[1] FZI Research Center for Information Technology, Karlsruhe, Germany
{beskorovajnov,groell}@fzi.de

[2] Karlsruhe Institute of Technology (KIT), Karlsruhe, Germany

[3] KASTEL Security Research Labs, Karlsruhe, Germany
{mueller-quade,ottenhues,schwerdt}@kit.edu

Abstract. Encryption satisfying CCA2 security is commonly known to be unnecessarily strong for realizing secure channels. Moreover, CCA2 constructions in the standard model are far from being competitive practical alternatives to constructions via random oracle. A promising research area to alleviate this problem are weaker security notions—like IND-RCCA secure encryption or IND-atag-wCCA secure tag-based encryption—which are still able to facilitate secure message transfer (SMT) via authenticated channels.

In this paper we introduce the concept of sender-binding encryption (SBE), unifying prior approaches of SMT construction in the universal composability (UC) model. We furthermore develop the corresponding non-trivial security notion of IND-SB-CPA and formally prove that it suffices for realizing SMT in conjunction with authenticated channels. Our notion is the weakest so far in the sense that it generically implies the weakest prior notions—RCCA and atag-wCCA—without additional assumptions, while the reverse is not true. A direct consequence is that IND-stag-wCCA, which is strictly weaker than IND-atag-wCCA but stronger than our IND-SB-CPA, can be used to construct a secure channel.

Finally, we give an efficient IND-SB-CPA secure construction in the standard model from IND-CPA secure double receiver encryption (DRE) based on McEliece. This shows that IND-SB-CPA security yields simpler and more efficient constructions in the standard model than the weakest prior notions, i.e., IND-atag-wCCA and IND-stag-wCCA.

Keywords: Secure message transfer · Authenticated channel · Tag-based encryption · IND-CPA · IND-CCA2 · CCA2 Relaxations · Universal composability · McEliece

G. Hanaoka et al. (Eds.): PKC 2022, LNCS 13178, pp. 316–344, 2022.
https://doi.org/10.1007/978-3-030-97131-1_11

1 Introduction

The construction of secure channels is one of the main goals of cryptography. Among the milestones that have been reached to this end are public-key cryptosystems by Diffie and Hellman [18], semantic security by Goldwasser and Micali [22] (today referred to as chosen plaintext attack (CPA)), and the stronger adaptive chosen ciphertext attack (CCA2) by Rackoff and Simon [29].

Nowadays, CCA2 secure public key encryption (PKE) is a cornerstone of many protocols realizing secure channels for our daily life applications. One of the most typical applications is the encryption of e-mails. This is usually realized by implementations of either the S/MIME [32] or OpenPGP [7] standard. Both standards utilize a public key infrastructure (PKI) and digital signatures to realize authenticated channels. Hence we see that widespread applications of secure message transfer (SMT) integrally use authenticated channels and a PKI in addition to encryption. secure message transfer (SMT) is an abstraction of authenticated and encrypted communication in the universal composability (UC) model. How secure message transfer (SMT) can be utilized in practical real world scenarios can be seen for example in [30].

It is widely known that CCA2 is unnecessarily strong to construct SMT when authenticated channels are already present [11]. In addition many concrete CCA2 constructions either lack efficiency to be considered practical constructions or were only proven secure within the random oracle model (ROM), which has inherent problems, e.g., that some constructions which can be proven secure in the ROM are insecure with any implementation of the random oracle [10]. We would like to point out that we do not question the usefulness of the ROM despite its shortcomings. However, we consider the exploration of alternatives just as important and therefore focus on constructions proven secure in the standard model in this work. Hence the following question arises:

What is the weakest security definition in order to establish a secure channel in the standard model if we assume existing authenticated channels?

In an attempt to answer this question we find a non-trivial relaxation of the weakest prior notions of replayable chosen ciphertext attack (RCCA) from [11] and adaptive-tag weakly chosen ciphertext attack (atag-wCCA) from [26], which were both shown to be weaker than CCA2 and used to construct secure channels. While this work does not provide an ultimate answer to this question—i.e., we do not prove that our definition, labeled indistinguishability under senderbinding chosen plaintext attack (IND-SB-CPA), is the weakest possible and hence necessary—we show IND-SB-CPA to be sufficient in the sense that any encryption protocol satisfying this security can be used directly to UC-realize SMT using authenticated channels.

Although this is an interesting theoretic result, we argue that for more relevancy the previous question needs to be accompanied by the following:

Can weaker security notions lead to simpler and more efficient constructions of a secure channel in the standard model?

In the current state of affairs, tag-based encryption (TBE) is an attractive choice for constructing efficient CCA2 secure PKE in the standard model as already the weakest established TBE security notion, indistinguishability under selective-tag weakly chosen ciphertext attack (IND-stag-wCCA), was shown by Kiltz [23] to yield a transformation to CCA2 secure PKE by adding one-time signatures for example. We show that IND-stag-wCCA secure TBE does not actually require prior transformation to CCA2 secure PKE in order to construct secure channels: By deriving the new concept of sender-binding encryption (SBE) from TBE we are able to construct secure channels directly from IND-stag-wCCA secure encryption. The intuition behind SBE is to tie ciphertexts not only to the receiver as with classic PKE notions, but to the sending/encrypting party as well.

Somewhat surprisingly, via IND-SB-CPA secure SBE we are also able to construct secure channels from double receiver encryption (DRE) which only satisfies CPA security and soundness. CPA secure DRE was initially introduced by Diament et al. [17] to facilitate message transmission from one sender to two different receivers and allows for interesting applications such as security puzzles for denial of service countermeasures. Subsequently, Chow et al. [14] introduced the property of soundness for DRE, and proved it to be crucial for some applications such as plaintext awareness (PA). Our DRE-based protocol allows for a much simpler and more efficient encryption than IND-stag-wCCA secure TBE for constructing secure channels and hence allows us to answer the second question in the positive.

One caveat of the construction via DRE is that we require an extended PKI that realizes the *key registration with knowledge (KRK)* functionality. This guarantees that users of the PKI have knowledge of their private keys. While this is not a common functionality of PKIs in use today, there are first protocol drafts like OTRv4[1] which utilize deniable authenticated key exchange protocols that rely on the KRK functionality. In this case those are DAKEZ and XZDH due to Unger and Goldberg [33].

As discussed in the next section the two questions we raise have partially been considered in prior works. In this paper we make considerable headway towards answering both of them.

1.1 Related Work

In this section we firstly analyze the current scientific landscape of security notions for SMT construction with authenticated channels. We then discuss the most promising prior constructions to efficiently achieve these security notions.

A PKE satisfying CCA2 security was already shown by Canetti in [9] to realize SMT in the UC framework by communicating confidentially over authenticated channels. On the other hand CCA2 was also shown by Canetti et al. [11] to be unnecessarily strong for this purpose. Hence relaxations of CCA2 came into focus. Among these relaxations is indistinguishability under replayable

[1] https://github.com/otrv4/otrv4/blob/master/otrv4.md.

chosen ciphertext attack (IND-RCCA), introduced by Canetti, Krawczyk and Nielsen in [11] where they show that IND-RCCA suffices to UC-realize SMT using authenticated channels. IND-RCCA differs from CCA2 in the characteristic that the ability to generate ciphertexts, which decrypt to the same plaintext as the test ciphertext, does not help the adversary to win the game. We provide the formal notions of IND-RCCA in Appendix B.1 of the full version of this paper [3]. Recently, Badertscher et al. [1] examined IND-RCCA and variations of it using the constructive cryptography framework to construct a confidential channel—a strictly weaker notion than SMT. They concluded that IND-RCCA is not sufficient to realize confidential channels when using the authenticated channel for public key transfer only. They introduce a stronger security definition to solve this problem whereas we, like the original IND-RCCA paper, assume authentication for every message transfer.

Another direction to achieve weaker security definitions is that of TBE which was introduced by MacKenzie, Reiter and Yang [26]. They introduced the notion of tag-based non-malleability, which is nowadays known as indistinguishability under adaptive-tag weakly chosen ciphertext attack (IND-atag-wCCA) security for TBE. The authors show that an IND-atag-wCCA secure TBE scheme is also sufficient to realize SMT when provided with authenticated channels. A relaxation, IND-stag-wCCA, has been shown to facilitate CCA2 constructions with the additional usage of a one-time signature scheme [5] or a message authentication code combined with a commitment scheme [6]. Both constructions are originally meant for identity based encryption (IBE), but Kiltz showed in [23] how to adapt these for the TBE setting. So far IND-stag-wCCA secure TBE has not been shown, however, to directly facilitate SMT.

Let us now look at how efficiently these security notions can be achieved without employing the ROM. The most efficient general construction paradigms nowadays are the lossy trapdoor functions by Peikert and Waters [28], the correlated products by Rosen and Segev [31] and the very similar k-repetition by Döttling et al. [19][2], the Cramer-Shoup-like constructions [15] and the adaptive trapdoor functions [25]. More efficient constructions of SMT can be built upon TBE. The—to the best of our knowledge—most efficient code-based TBE schemes nowadays are due to Kiltz [23], Kiltz, Masny and Pietrzak [24], Cheng et al. [13] and Yu et al. [34]. In their schemes, the notion of IND-stag-wCCA security for TBE is required, which can be used to construct CCA2 schemes by adding one-time signatures or message authentication codes and commitments as mentioned above.

Regarding both of our research questions we see that although some progress was made in previous works there is still a lot of room for improvement. In the following section we highlight this paper's contribution towards closing this gap.

[2] In spite of being a generic paradigm this work was applied only to McEliece so far.

1.2 Our Contribution

In this paper we develop the new security notion of IND-SB-CPA, which is the weakest so far to UC-realize SMT in conjunction with authenticated channels. We also give a concrete efficient construction of an IND-SB-CPA secure SBE scheme in the standard model. An overview of this five-part contribution is illustrated in Fig. 1. The five contribution parts correspond to the Sects. 2 to 6:

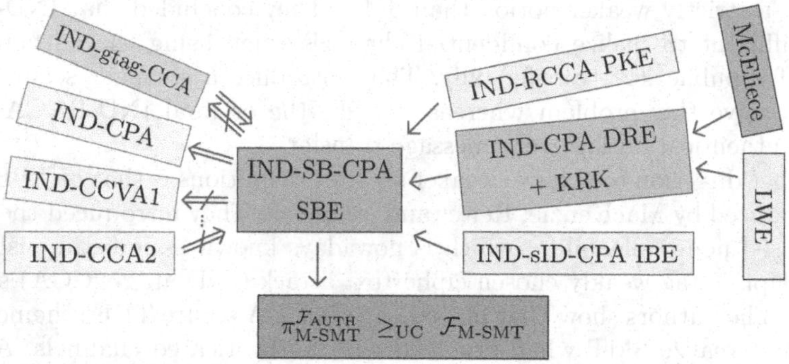

Fig. 1. Overview of our contribution

- In Sect. 2 we firstly provide the unifying definition of SBE, capturing all prior ways to construct SMT from authenticated channels and some form of encryption. A direct consequence is that all of the TBE notions, reformulated as SBE, directly construct SMT from authenticated channels. We then go on to develop the new game-based security notion of IND-SB-CPA. This is explicitly tailored to be as weak as possible while still only requiring authenticated channels to facilitate SMT. We achieve this by binding ciphertexts to sending parties.
- Section 3 presents a generic transformation from an indistinguishability under chosen plaintext attack (IND-CPA) secure DRE scheme with key registration to an IND-SB-CPA secure SBE scheme. To the extent of our knowledge it was not previously known how CPA secure DRE could be used to realize SMT. Appendix E of the full version of this paper [3] presents further generic transformations based on IND-RCCA secure PKE and indistinguishability under selective identity chosen plaintext attack (IND-sID-CPA) secure IBE.
- In Sect. 4 we construct an IND-CPA secure and sound DRE scheme from a McEliece variant. In conjunction with Sect. 3 this can be used to implement SMT in a more efficient and simpler way than known so far. To the extent of our knowledge we are the first to construct a McEliece-based DRE with soundness. Moreover, we show an improvement of a factor 5 regarding the size of the public key, which is mostly due to the avoidance of relying solely

on the (low-noise) learning parity with noise (LPN) assumption. Additionally, we provide another (2-repetition) McEliece construction and one from LWE-based binding encryption in Appendix F of the full version of this paper [3]. All our constructions are proven secure in the standard model.

- In Sect. 5 we finally construct a protocol which combines IND-SB-CPA security with authenticated channels. This protocol is subsequently proven to UC-realize SMT under static corruption by a malicious adversary.
- Section 6 highlights the theoretical relation between IND-SB-CPA and TBE security notions—in particular that the new notion of IND-SB-CPA is implied by the weakest known TBE security. Appendix G.2 of the full version of this paper [3] expands on this theoretic classification by comparing IND-SB-CPA to classic PKE indistinguishability notions from CPA to CCA2.

1.3 Preliminaries

Firstly, let us note that all notations and abbreviations we use can be looked up in Appendix A. We talk about different *game-based security notions* for various types of encryption schemes throughout this paper. While we would expect the reader to be familiar with the standard definitions of IND-CPA/-CCA2 etc., we provide formal definitions of all notions for your convenience in Appendix B of the full version of this paper [3]—in particular the more involved ones pertaining, e.g., to DRE, TBE and IBE schemes including security, correctness and soundness definitions.

In this work we use DRE as a building block for our construction. DRE encrypts a plaintext to two ciphertexts using two different public keys with the guarantee, that these ciphertexts decrypt to the same plaintext. Formally a DRE scheme consists of three probabilistic polynomial time (PPT) algorithms $(\mathtt{gen}, \mathtt{enc}, \mathtt{dec})$ and the function $\mathtt{f}_{\text{Key}}$, which checks if the key pair (sk, pk) is well-formed.

$$\begin{aligned}
\mathtt{gen}: &\quad 1^\lambda \mapsto (sk, pk)\\
\mathtt{enc}: &\quad (pk_1, pk_2, m) \mapsto c\\
\mathtt{dec}: &\quad (sk_i, pk_1, pk_2, c) \mapsto m \text{ where } i \in \{1, 2\}\\
\mathtt{f}_{\text{Key}}: &\quad (sk, pk) \mapsto \begin{cases}\mathsf{true}\\ \mathsf{false}.\end{cases}
\end{aligned}$$

TBE extends public key encryption by adding a tag to the encryption and decryption algorithms. This tag contains additional information and is a simple string. Formally a TBE scheme with message space $\mathbf{M}$ and tag space $\mathbf{T}$ consists of three PPT algorithms $(\mathtt{gen}, \mathtt{enc}, \mathtt{dec})$.

$$\begin{aligned}
\mathtt{gen}: &\quad (1^\lambda) \mapsto (sk, pk)\\
\mathtt{enc}: &\quad (pk, t, m) \mapsto c\\
\mathtt{dec}: &\quad (sk, t, c) \mapsto m \in \mathbf{M} \cup \{\bot\}
\end{aligned}$$

The weakest security notion of TBE so far is IND-stag-wCCA introduced by Kiltz [23]. This and further definitions of TBE security can be found in the full version of this paper [3]. The TBE notion IND-gtag-wCCA—which we start from to develop our notion of IND-SB-CPA security—is explicitly given in Sect. 2.

For readers who are not intimately familiar with the concept of *simulation-based security* or *universal composability* we also briefly recap the ideal/real-paradigm as well as UC in Appendix C of the full version of this paper [3]. More detailed explanations can be found, for instance, in [8,9]. As there have been conflicting definitions, we explicitly state formal definitions for the *ideal functionalities* of $\mathcal{F}_{\text{AUTH}}$, $\mathcal{F}_{\text{M-SMT}}$ and $\mathcal{F}_{\text{KRK}}$. For $\mathcal{F}_{\text{AUTH}}$ and $\mathcal{F}_{\text{M-SMT}}$ these can be found in Sect. 5 and additionally with further discussion in Appendix D of the full version of this paper [3]. The definition for $\mathcal{F}_{\text{KRK}}$ can be found in Appendix D of the full version as well.

2 IND-SB-CPA Security

SMT is commonly realized by combining an IND-CCA2 secure PKE or an IND-atag-wCCA secure TBE scheme with authenticated channels. As highlighted in Sect. 1, however, both of those security notions seem to be unnecessarily strong and restrictive for this application. In this observation we are hardly the first (cp. Sect. 1.1) as there are previous efforts to relax security notions with the aim to facilitate SMT—like the RCCA relaxation of CCA2 and efforts to use IND-stag-wCCA secure TBE.

In this section we introduce the concept of SBE and our new security notion of IND-SB-CPA. It is even weaker than the IND-atag-wCCA relaxation IND-stag-wCCA but still captures the security needed for secure message transfer via authenticated channels. Although the term SBE has not previously been defined, all prior realizations of SMT via authenticated channels (based on CCA2, RCCA, atag-wCCA or selective-tag weakly chosen ciphertext attack (stag-wCCA)) work by constructing an SBE scheme from the underlying encryption scheme. We therefore regard this as a long overdue unifying definition which is central for the topic of SMT construction.

Definition 1 (Sender-binding encryption (SBE)). *The interface of an SBE scheme is given by a set of three PPT algorithms* $(\texttt{gen}, \texttt{enc}, \texttt{dec})$*:*

$$\begin{aligned} \texttt{gen}: &\quad 1^\lambda \mapsto (sk, pk) \\ \texttt{enc}: &\quad (pk, S, m) \mapsto c \\ \texttt{dec}: &\quad (sk, S, c) \mapsto m. \end{aligned}$$

We expect an SBE scheme to fulfill the notion of correctness, i.e. that whenever $(sk, pk) \leftarrow \texttt{gen}(1^\lambda)$*, then*

$$m = \texttt{dec}(sk, S, \texttt{enc}(pk, S, m)).$$

Some remarks are in order about this use case definition of SBE.

In addition to the inputs present in any common PKE scheme, encryption and decryption algorithms use the encrypting party's ID S[3] as well. The ID of a party represents the identification information used within the system. This might be the public key itself, the party's actual name, their e-mail address etc. This does not only bind a ciphertext to the receiving party who holds the secret key and is able to decrypt the ciphertext—as any PKE scheme does—but also to the party who created the encryption.

However, binding a ciphertext to the ID of a sending/encrypting party alone does not yet yield obvious benefits. Even if a specific party ID is specified by the protocol, party IDs are public knowledge and malicious parties can insert any ID they want. SBE starts to unfold its benefit when used in conjunction with IDs that are associated with authenticated channels. This channel reliably indicates the true sender S of a message. Checking this against the sender ID bound to the received ciphertext prevents (honest sender) replay attacks, i.e., that this message was just copied from another (unwitting) sender. The terminology "sender-binding" stems from the example application of SMT via authenticated channels where this is taken to be the encrypting/sending party. Of course there might be other use cases for SBE where the encrypting party does not constitute a "sender". But throughout this paper (whenever we talk about SBE) we use R and "receiver" to denote the party owning the keys $(sk_R, pk_R) := (sk, pk)$, and S and the term "sender" for the party whose ID is input on encryption and decryption.

Given the definition of an SBE scheme we still need to arrive at a meaningful corresponding security notion. The intuitive way to construct an SBE scheme is to use a TBE scheme where the tag space $\mathbf{T}$ is chosen to be the set of party IDs $\mathbf{P}$. Even a TBE scheme with arbitrary tag space $\mathbf{T}$ can easily be used for

$\mathsf{Exp}^{\mathbf{IND\text{-}gtag\text{-}wCCA}}_{\mathbf{TBE},\mathcal{A}}$

(1) $t^* \xleftarrow{R} \mathbf{T}$
$(sk, pk) \leftarrow \mathbf{gen}(1^\lambda)$

(2) $(st, m_0, m_1) \leftarrow \mathcal{A}^{\mathsf{dec}(sk,\cdot,\cdot)^a}(t^*, pk)$

(3) $b \xleftarrow{R} \{0,1\}$
$c^* \leftarrow \mathbf{enc}(pk, t^*, m_b)$

(4) $b^* \leftarrow \mathcal{A}^{\mathsf{dec}(sk,\cdot,\cdot)^a}(st, c^*)$

(5) Return 1 if $b = b^*$, else return 0

[a] Decryption outputs $\perp$ for tags $t^* \in \{S, R\}$.

Fig. 2. The IND-gtag-wCCA TBE game.

[3] For the encryption mechanism we will sometimes omit the explicit input of the ID S if it is clear from the context which party S is conducting the encryption.

SBE as long as the tag space is as least as large as the set $\mathbf{P}$ of participating parties. To do so a public and injective function $\mathbf{P} \hookrightarrow \mathbf{T}$ is chosen to translate party IDs into tags. Hence to develop a security notion for SBE we start from the TBE notion indistinguishability under given-tag weakly chosen ciphertext attack (IND-gtag-wCCA). This is an intuitive weakening of the previously considered IND-stag-wCCA, with the only difference being that the adversary is not allowed to choose the challenge tag but is instead given a random tag by the challenger:

Definition 2 (IND-gtag-wCCA). *A TBE scheme* (gen, enc, dec) *satisfies IND-gtag-wCCA security, if and only if for any PPT adversary $\mathcal{A}_{gtag\text{-}CCA}$ the advantage to win the IND-gtag-wCCA game shown in Fig. 2 is negligible in λ.*

Using party IDs as tags in TBE provides a special meaning to these tags. It is this additional meaning which induces the changes we make to IND-gtag-wCCA to arrive at our new notion of IND-SB-CPA for SBE: We now additionally have a connection between tags and key pairs, as any party ID (tag) is associated to the key pair of this party. Hence there is another ID/tag R corresponding to the key pair $(sk_R, pk_R) = (sk, pk)$ and another key pair (sk_S, pk_S) corresponding to the party $S = t^*$. As we are aiming towards the weakest possible notion from which to construct SMT we let both of those be chosen by the challenger instead of giving the adversary any more power. Depending on the underlying encryption scheme it is possible that keys may not be generated independently of the ID (think, e.g., of IBE schemes) or that public keys are used as IDs themselves. Hence we assume the challenger to randomly generate/draw keys and IDs in

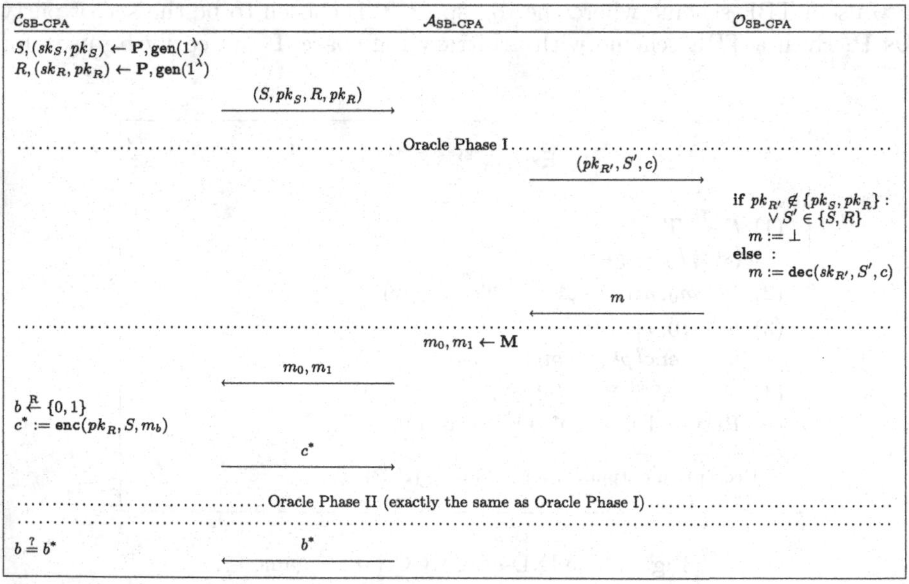

Fig. 3. The IND-SB-CPA game for SBE

a consistent fashion. With the additional key pair (sk_S, pk_S) we also need to define how much decryption power the adversary gets for these keys in the two oracle phases. We choose this intuitively to be symmetric with the challenge keys (sk_R, pk_R). Because this gives a weaker notion and is still enough for SMT we restrict decryption not only for the challenge tag S but for R as well. All in all this adjustment of IND-gtag-wCCA to SBE yields the following definition:

Definition 3 (IND-SB-CPA). *An SBE scheme* $(\mathtt{gen}, \mathtt{enc}, \mathtt{dec})$ *satisfies IND-SB-CPA security, if and only if for any PPT adversary* $\mathcal{A}_{\text{SB-CPA}}$ *the advantage to win the IND-SB-CPA game shown in Fig. 3 is negligible in* λ.

Within this context of SBE, the new security notion of IND-SB-CPA has a very straight forward intuition: If it was possible to alter a ciphertext $c \leftarrow \mathtt{enc}(pk, S, m)$ to some c' which successfully decrypted under another sender ID S' (i.e. $\mathtt{dec}(sk_R, S', c') \neq \bot$), replay attacks would be possible. Let us look at this in a bit more detail. From Fig. 3 we see that the adversary is provided with perfect knowledge (via oracle or its own power) about any ciphertext which involves any other party than just S and R. About communication between S and R, on the other hand, the adversary learns nothing—with the natural exception that encryption only requires public knowledge and can therefore be conducted by the adversary as well. A directed version—where the adversary can additionally decrypt messages from R to S (but not from S to R)—would also naturally suggest itself. But as mentioned before our choice of a symmetric version is strictly weaker as well as sufficient for SMT construction. Having no decryption possibilities for the channel (S to R) along which the challenge ciphertext is sent justifies classifying IND-SB-CPA as some form of CPA security. For more thoughts on these classifications see Appendix G.3 of the full version of this paper [3].

We thoroughly investigate the relationships between IND-SB-CPA and other game-based notions in Sect. 6 and Appendix G.2 of the full version of this paper [3]. In the next section we show that IND-SB-CPA is not merely of academic interest by giving a generic example construction for IND-SB-CPA secure SBE via DRE.

3 Transformation from DRE to SBE

In this section we generically construct an IND-SB-CPA secure SBE scheme from DRE. Further generic constructions as well as more involved discussions of this DRE construction—particular about the use of KRK—can be found in the full version of this paper [3].

Originally meant to encrypt a message to two receivers, we use DRE in such a way, that one of those ciphertexts is encrypted using the public key of the sender. This, together with the usage of PKIs using KRK results in an encryption where the sender is aware of the plaintext. Without KRK there is no guarantee that the sender has knowledge of the private key corresponding to his public key, so this awareness could not be guaranteed. A possible realization of the KRK functionality is that the PKI demands a zero-knowledge proof of knowledge about the secret key when registering the public key. While this is a possibly expensive operation it only needs to be done once while registering.

We require the underlying DRE scheme to be sound, IND-CPA secure and compatible with the key registration functionality $\mathcal{F}_{\text{KRK}}$. For the definition of DRE, its soundness, and the definition of $\mathcal{F}_{\text{KRK}}$ we refer the reader to Appendices B.4 and D of the full version of this paper [3] respectively. This transformation will broaden our intuitive understanding of the new notion as well as provide a background for the concrete DRE construction we discuss in Sect. 4. We furthermore use the transformation in Sect. 6 to show that IND-SB-CPA does not in fact imply IND-gtag-wCCA but is a strictly weaker security notion.

Although DRE was initially devised to facilitate message transmission from one sender to two different receivers, choosing one of the receivers to be the sender itself provides a way to bind the ciphertext to the sender and to achieve an IND-SB-CPA secure SBE scheme.

One small caveat of using DRE is the need for key registration with knowledge: If we can not make sure the sender knows a key pair, ciphertexts encrypted under this key will not establish a reliable connection between ciphertext and sender. Hence we employ the ideal functionality $\mathcal{F}_{\text{KRK}}$. To do so, however, we need to make sure the underlying DRE scheme is compatible:

Remark 1. Throughout this section we will assume DRE schemes to permit efficiently computable boolean functions $\texttt{f}_{\text{Key}}$. On input of a (possible) key pair (sk, pk) this function decides whether the keys "belong together", i.e., whether they could have been output by the encryption scheme's key generation algorithm or might just be an unrelated pair of values:

$$\texttt{f}_{\text{Key}} : (sk, pk) \mapsto \begin{cases} \mathsf{true}, & (sk, pk) \leftarrow \texttt{gen}(1^\lambda) \\ \mathsf{false}, & \text{else.} \end{cases}$$

This is necessary for the scheme to be used in conjunction with the registration functionality $\mathcal{F}_{\text{KRK}}$. In Appendix D of the full version of this paper [3] we discuss $\mathcal{F}_{\text{KRK}}$ a bit more and also see that we can easily dispose of the need for a function $\texttt{f}_{\text{Key}}$ if we are happy for the registration functionality to (partially) generate the keys for the registering parties.

Let $(\texttt{gen}, \texttt{enc}, \texttt{dec})$ be an IND-CPA secure DRE scheme which admits a function $\texttt{f}_{\text{Key}}$. We define a new encryption scheme $(\texttt{Gen}, \texttt{Enc}, \texttt{Dec})$:

$\texttt{Gen}(1^\lambda)$ executed by party P:
- $(sk, pk) \leftarrow \texttt{gen}(1^\lambda)$.
- Register (sk, pk) with $\mathcal{F}_{\text{KRK}}^{\texttt{f}_{\text{Key}}}$.

$\hookrightarrow$ Return $(SK, PK) := ((sk, pk), P)$.

$\texttt{Enc}(PK_R, S, m) = \texttt{Enc}(R, S, m)$ executed by party S:
- Retrieve pk_R and pk_S from $\mathcal{F}_{\text{KRK}}^{\texttt{f}_{\text{Key}}}$.

$\hookrightarrow$ Return $c \leftarrow \texttt{enc}(pk_R, pk_S, m)$.

$\texttt{Dec}(SK_R, S, c) = \texttt{Dec}((sk_R, pk_R), S, c)$ executed by party R:
- Retrieve pk_S from $\mathcal{F}_{\text{KRK}}^{\texttt{f}_{\text{Key}}}$.

$\hookrightarrow$ Return $m := \texttt{dec}(sk_R, pk_R, pk_S, c)$.

Let us give some intuition about the construction before we move on to formalities. Choosing one of the receivers for DRE to be the sender itself and having them encrypt a message under its own key might seem counterintuitive at first, but has one crucial benefit: It guarantees to the other (actual) receiver that even if the sender might not have constructed the ciphertext themselves but rather copied it from somewhere else, they have knowledge about the plaintext since they are able to decrypt as well. This is guaranteed by the registration with $\mathcal{F}_{\text{KRK}}^{\texttt{f}_{\text{Key}}}$ in conjunction with the soundness property of the underlying DRE scheme. In addition to showing that this construction does in fact satisfy IND-SB-CPA security, we provide a discussion in Appendix E of the full version of this paper [3] on what properties exactly we need from DRE and how this is related to registration-based plaintext awareness (RPA).

Lemma 1. *In the* $\mathcal{F}_{KRK}^{\texttt{f}_{Key}}$ *hybrid model* $(\texttt{Gen}, \texttt{Enc}, \texttt{Dec})$ *is an IND-SB-CPA secure SBE scheme.*

Proof. Assuming that $(\texttt{gen}, \texttt{enc}, \texttt{dec})$ is a sound DRE scheme with key function $\texttt{f}_{\text{Key}}$ and assuming we have an adversary $\mathcal{A}_{\text{SB-CPA}}$ who has non-negligible success probability in winning the IND-SB-CPA game with respect to $(\texttt{Gen}, \texttt{Enc}, \texttt{Dec})$, we construct an adversary $\mathcal{A}_{\text{DRE-CPA}}$ with non-negligible success probability in winning the DRE IND-CPA game with respect to $(\texttt{gen}, \texttt{enc}, \texttt{dec})$. Note that in this case, $\mathcal{A}_{\text{DRE-CPA}}$ not only fields $\mathcal{A}_{\text{SB-CPA}}$'s queries to $\mathcal{O}_{\text{SB-CPA}}$ but also plays the role of $\mathcal{F}_{\text{KRK}}^{\texttt{f}_{\text{Key}}}$ and has therefore access to registered keys. In the reduction shown in Fig. 4 we do not explicitly state this, but all interactions with $\mathcal{F}_{\text{KRK}}^{\texttt{f}_{\text{Key}}}$ are handled exactly as the functionality itself would. The only exceptions are that an instantaneous $\texttt{ok}$ is assumed whenever the functionality would ask the adversary for some permission and that in the first phase the adversary $\mathcal{A}_{\text{DRE-CPA}}$ itself "registers" the keys pk_S and pk_R for S and R respectively without providing corresponding secret keys.

Since $\mathcal{A}_{\text{DRE-CPA}}$ has access to the internal state of $\mathcal{F}_{\text{KRK}}^{\texttt{f}_{\text{Key}}}$, they can look up the keys $(sk_{S'}, pk_{S'})$ for any oracle query (R', S', c). If no such keys have been registered, decryption of the ciphertext would result in $\perp$. If keys have been registered, they can be used to correctly decrypt the ciphertext as the soundness

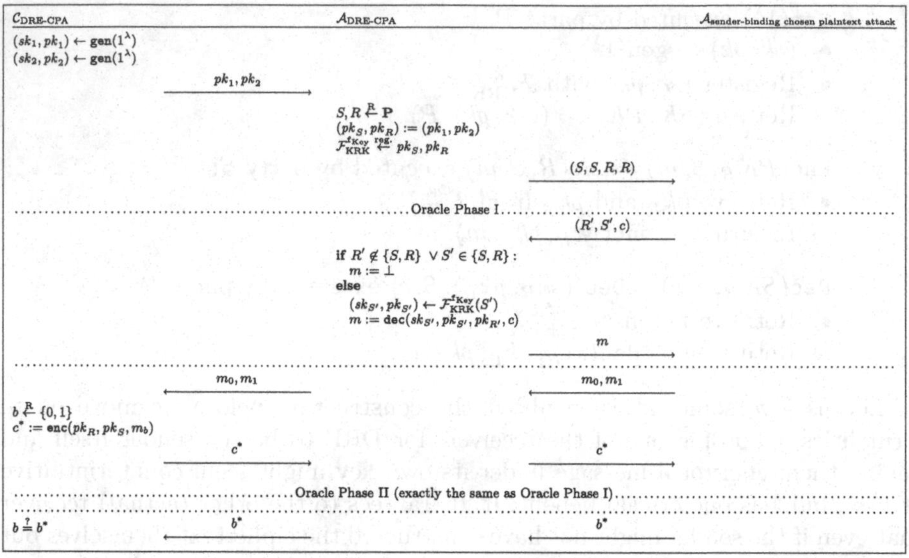

Fig. 4. Reduction for DRE construction

of DRE (see Appendix B.4 of the full version of this paper [3] for definition) guarantees

$$\mathsf{dec}(sk_{S'}, pk_{S'}, pk_{R'}, c) = \mathsf{dec}(sk_{R'}, pk_{R'}, pk_{S'}, c).$$

Hence it is no problem for $\mathcal{A}_{\text{DRE-CPA}}$ to respond with correct decryptions exactly as $\mathcal{O}_{\text{SB-CPA}}$ would. This gives $\mathcal{A}_{\text{DRE-CPA}}$ the same non-negligible success probability as $\mathcal{A}_{\text{SB-CPA}}$. □

This newfound utility for IND-CPA secure DRE schemes provides the motivational background for the next section, which in turn shows the relevance of our theoretical construction for the efficient construction of SMT in the standard model.

4 Efficient DRE Construction from McEliece and LPN

In this section we present an efficient way to construct an IND-CPA secure and sound DRE scheme from the McEliece and LPN assumptions and discuss how our construction improves the state of the art of SMT realizations in the standard model based on the McEliece and LPN assumptions. Moreover, to the extent of our knowledge we are the first to construct a DRE based on these assumptions. More details on our construction as well as further constructions via 2-repetition McEliece and learning with errors (LWE)-based binding encryption can be found in Appendix F of the full version of this paper [3].

Construction. Our DRE scheme can be seen as an augmentation of a construction from Kiltz et al. [24]. In this the authors propose a creative construction of a low-noise LPN-based TBE scheme, which they show to be IND-stag-wCCA secure. In the appendix of [24] the authors introduce a simplified variant of their IND-stag-wCCA secure construction, which is only IND-CPA secure. We use this simplified variant as a basis for our own construction. In order to establish the soundness property we add a second encryption of the randomness and exploit the randomness recovery to perform the consistency check. Moreover, we change the trapdoor mechanism to the one from the McEliece cryptosystem over Goppa codes. Hence we define our DRE scheme $(\mathtt{gen}, \mathtt{enc}, \mathtt{dec})$ as follows:

- `gen` Generate the McEliece secret key $sk := (S, G', P)$ and corresponding public key $pk := (G, C)$ where $G := SG'P$ and C is a random binary matrix.
- `enc` Sample a fresh random vector s, fresh error vectors e, e_R, e_S and encrypt s for both sender S and receiver R, i.e., $c_S := s \cdot G_S \oplus e_S$ and $c_R := s \cdot G_R \oplus e_R$. Mask the encoded message m with the noisy product $s \cdot C_S \oplus e$, i.e. $c' = s \cdot C_S \oplus e \oplus Encode(m)$ and output $c := (c_R, c_S, c')$ as the ciphertext.
- `dec` The receiver recovers the randomness s from c_R with textbook McEliece decryption, verifies the hamming weight $wgt(s \cdot G_S \oplus c_S) < t$ and unmasks $Encode(m) \oplus e = c' \oplus s \cdot C_S$. Finally, the receiver decodes and outputs the message m.

For the encoding and decoding we propose to use a suitable Goppa code, which is fixed for all parties. More details can be found in Appendix F of the full version of this paper [3].

Theorem 1. *The DRE scheme* $(\mathtt{gen}, \mathtt{enc}, \mathtt{dec})$ *is IND-CPA secure, given that both the McEliece indistinguishability assumption and the learning parity with noise decisional problem (LPNDP) hold. In particular, let $\mathcal{A}$ be an IND-CPA adversary against the cryptosystem. Then there is a distinguisher $\mathcal{B}$ for Goppa codes and a distinguisher $\mathcal{D}$ for the LPNDP, such that for all $\lambda \in \mathbb{N}$*

$$\mathsf{Adv}_{\mathcal{A}}^{CPA}(\lambda) \leq \mathsf{Adv}_{\mathcal{D}}^{LPNDP_\theta(3n,l)}(\lambda) + 2 \times \mathsf{Adv}_{\mathcal{B}_R,G_R}^{IND}(\lambda).$$

Theorem 2. *The DRE scheme* $(\mathtt{gen}, \mathtt{enc}, \mathtt{dec})$ *satisfies DRE soundness.*

The proofs and formal definitions of assumptions and experiments can be found in Appendix F of the full version of this paper [3] as well. Note also, that this DRE scheme admits an efficiently computable function $\mathtt{f}_{\mathrm{Key}}$ as required for the use with $\mathcal{F}_{\mathrm{KRK}}$ (cp. Sect. 3):

$$\mathtt{f}_{\mathrm{Key}} : ((S, P, G'), (G, C)) \mapsto \begin{cases} \mathsf{true}, & G = SG'P \\ \mathsf{false}, & \text{else.} \end{cases}$$

In conjunction with Theorems 1 and 2 our DRE scheme satisfies all requirements for the generic transformation to IND-SB-CPA given in Sect. 3. Hence we can use it to efficiently achieve SMT if combined with authenticated channels.

Discussion. Considering that one of the third round finalists of the post-quantum cryptography (PQC) standardization by the NIST[4] is a McEliece variant based on Goppa codes we expect this mechanism to have significantly better parameters than cryptosystems that are based solely on the (low noise) LPN assumption. We argue, however, that our construction may as well be realized with the sole (low noise) LPN assumption or the Niederreiter cryptosystem [27]. Also, a similar augmentation of the randomness recovering variant of the dual Regev [21] cryptosystem may yield a very similar construction of DRE based on LWE. Currently, the Niederreiter cryptosystem seems the most promising as it was already shown in [20] that the trapdoor function is one-way under k-correlated input. The tightness loss is expected to be a factor of 3 regarding the number of LPNDP samples and a factor of 2 regarding the indistinguishability assumption. Therefore, we expect our construction of DRE to have roughly the same parameters as their single receiver IND-CPA counterparts without the soundness. An algebraic comparison of the public keys and the ciphertext from our work and the current state of the art in [24] and [34] can be found in Table 1.

Table 1. Comparison of public keys and ciphertext between [24,34] and this work.

Construction	Public Key	Ciphertext
Kiltz et al. [24]	$(A, B_0, B_1, C) \in (\mathbb{Z}_2^{m \times n'})^3 \times \mathbb{Z}_2^{l' \times n'}$	$(c, c_0, c_1, c_2) \in (\mathbb{Z}_2^m)^3 \times \mathbb{Z}_2^{l'}$
Yu et al. [34]	$(A, B_0, B_1, C) \in \mathbb{Z}_2^{\overline{n} \times \overline{n}} \times (\mathbb{Z}_2^{q \times \overline{n}})^2 \times \mathbb{Z}_2^{\overline{l} \times \overline{n}}$	$(c, c_0, c_1, c_2) \in (\mathbb{Z}_2^{\overline{n}}) \times (\mathbb{Z}_2^q)^2 \times \mathbb{Z}_2^{\overline{l}}$
This Work	$(G, C) \in \mathbb{Z}_2^{l \times n} \times \mathbb{Z}_2^{l \times n}$	$(c_R, c_S, c') \in (\mathbb{Z}_2^n)^3$

At this point some remarks are necessary to understand the comparisons more thoroughly. For the sake of simplicity we will give rough estimations of the respective public key sizes. Kiltz et al. [24] require for their dimensions that $m \geq 2n'$ and $l' \geq m$, where n' is the dimension of the low-noise LPN secret. Current estimations suggest that cryptosystems based on low-noise LPN to have rather large dimensions, e.g., [16] suggest for 80 bits of security $n' = 9000$ when the noise is $\mu = 0.0044$. Therefore, setting $n' = 9000$ leads to the smallest possible $m = 18000$ and $l' = 18000$ and results in a public key size of roughly 77 megabyte.

Yu et al. [34] improved the construction of [24] in such a way that it may be based on constant noise LPN assuming sub-exponential hardness. Current estimations of concrete constant noise LPN hardness suggest much smaller dimensions than in the low-noise variant, e.g., [4] suggest for 80 bits of security $\overline{n} = 1280$ and noise level of $\mu = 0.05$, which meets the restriction from [34] that $\mu \leq 0.1$. The crucial parameter is, however, the choice of an $\alpha > 0$ as this parameter controls the dimension $q = O(\overline{n}^{6 \cdot \alpha + 1})$, which means that minimizing α will minimize the size of the public key. In order to estimate α as small as possible we take the formula $\beta = \frac{1}{2} - \frac{1}{\overline{n}^{3 \cdot \alpha}}$, which controls the number $\beta \cdot q$ of bit flipping errors that a suitable error correcting code will correct. For the

[4] National Institute of Standards and Technology.

sake of simplicity we set $\alpha = 0.04$, which is almost the minimal possible α for an $\overline{n} = 1280$, and get approximately $q = 7127$. Finally, fixing the remaining dimension $\overline{l} = \overline{n}$ we get a public key size of roughly 2.5 megabyte, which is a substantial improvement compared to [24].

For classic McEliece constructions Bernstein et al. [2] suggests for 80 bits of security to utilize [1632, 1269] Goppa codes. Setting $n = 1632$ and $l = 1269$ in this work leads to a public key size of roughly 505 kilobyte, which is roughly factor 5 smaller than previous works.

We would like to point out that constructions from [24] and [34] are not directly comparable to our construction because we rely on the additional indistinguishability assumption of Goppa codes from random linear codes. However, all three constructions are code-based and implement a secure channel such that (rough) estimations of concrete sizes regarding the same security level may help to understand the improvement.

5 Realizing $\mathcal{F}_{\text{M-SMT}}$ from IND-SB-CPA and $\mathcal{F}_{\text{AUTH}}$

In this section we show that IND-SB-CPA secure SBE suffices in conjunction with authenticated channels to realize SMT. We prove this in the universal composability (UC) model of Canetti [9] (which is explained in more detail in Appendix C of the full version of this paper [3]) using *static corruptions* only. This means that the adversary chooses which parties to corrupt at the start of the protocol execution and not adaptively as the computation proceeds. We provide the formal definitions of the UC functionalities $\mathcal{F}_{\text{AUTH}}$ for authenticated channels and $\mathcal{F}_{\text{M-SMT}}$ for SMT to clarify which exact definitions we use. The latter deals with multiple receivers, multiple senders *and* multiple messages rather than working with a multi-session extension (cp. [12]) of a functionality $\mathcal{F}_{\text{SMT}}$ which only transmits a single message. Note that this is just a technical difference but essentially equivalent to the base of many arisen different definitions for SMT over the past. For more detailed discussions on these ideal functionalities see Appendix D of the full version of this paper [3].

$\mathcal{F}_{\text{AUTH}}$

Provides:
Single-receiver single-message single-sender authenticated message transfer with constant message size.

Behaviour:

- Upon invocation with input $(\texttt{send}, sid, R, m)$ from some party S, send backdoor message $(\texttt{send}, sid, S, R, m)$ to the adversary $\mathcal{A}$.
- Upon receiving $(\texttt{send ok}, sid)$ from adversary $\mathcal{A}$: If not yet generated output, then output $(\texttt{sent}, sid, S, R, m)$ to R.
- Ignore all further inputs.

$\mathcal{F}_{\text{M-SMT}}$

Provides:
Multi-receiver multi-message multi-sender secure message transfer with constant message size.
State:
Function $p_{\text{Msg}} : \mathbf{SID} \times \mathbf{MID} \to \mathbf{M} \times \mathbf{P}^2$ of pending messages.
Behaviour:

- Upon receiving $(\texttt{send}, sid, R, m)$ from some party S, draw fresh mid, send $(\texttt{send}, sid, mid, S, R)$ to the adversary $\mathcal{A}$ and append $(sid, mid) \mapsto (m, S, R)$ to p_{Msg}.
- Upon receiving $(\texttt{send ok}, sid, mid)$ from the adversary, look up $(m, S, R) := p_{\text{Msg}}(sid, mid)$. If it exists, output $(\texttt{sent}, sid, S, m)$ to R.

We will proceed towards the goal of realizing SMT in three stages: Firstly, we define a candidate protocol $\pi^{\mathcal{F}_{\text{AUTH}}}_{\text{M-SMT}}$ in the $\mathcal{F}_{\text{AUTH}}$-hybrid model which utilizes an IND-SB-CPA secure SBE scheme. Secondly, we construct a simulator $\mathcal{S}_{\text{M-SMT}}$ aiming to provide indistinguishability between the candidate protocol and the SMT functionality $\mathcal{F}_{\text{M-SMT}}$. The last step is formally proving that in the $\mathcal{F}_{\text{AUTH}}$-hybrid model indistinguishability from $\mathcal{F}_{\text{M-SMT}}$ is actually achieved by $\pi^{\mathcal{F}_{\text{AUTH}}}_{\text{M-SMT}}$ in conjunction with $\mathcal{S}_{\text{M-SMT}}$.

Protocol $\pi^{\mathcal{F}_{\text{AUTH}}}_{\text{M-SMT}}$ Let $(\texttt{gen}, \texttt{enc}, \texttt{dec})$ be an IND-SB-CPA secure SBE scheme. From this we define a secure message transfer protocol $\pi^{\mathcal{F}_{\text{AUTH}}}_{\text{M-SMT}}$ as follows: Whenever a party S wants to securely transmit a message m to some party R, they essentially send the encryption $c \leftarrow \texttt{enc}(pk_R, S, m)$ over an authenticated channel to R. When a party R receives a ciphertext c over an authenticated channel from some party S, they decrypt it via $m := \texttt{dec}(sk_R, S, c)$. Although this general principle is very simple, many details—e.g. regarding key generation—need to be taken into account. The formal definition looks as follows:

$\pi^{\mathcal{F}_{\text{AUTH}}}_{\text{M-SMT}}$

Realizes:
Multi-receiver multi-message multi-sender secure message transfer with constant message size.

Parameters:

- IND-SB-CPA secure SBE scheme $(\texttt{gen}, \texttt{enc}, \texttt{dec})$ with message size l and ciphertext length l'.
- Functionality $\mathcal{F}_{\text{AUTH}}$.

State of Party P:

- Function $p_{\mathsf{Cred}} : \mathbf{SID} \to \mathbf{SK} \times \mathbf{PK}$ of own credentials.
- Function $p_{\mathsf{Pk}} : \mathbf{SID} \times \mathbf{P} \to \mathbf{PK}$ of known public keys.
- Function $p_{\mathsf{Send}} : \mathbf{SID} \times \mathbf{P} \to \mathbf{M}^*$ of pending messages.

Behaviour of Party P:

\\ Being asked to initialize

- Upon receiving output $(\mathtt{sent}, sid_{\mathrm{AUTH}}, S, P, (\mathtt{init}, sid))$ from $\mathcal{F}_{\mathrm{AUTH}}$, if there is no entry $p_{\mathsf{Cred}}(sid)$ yet:
  (1) $(sk, pk) \leftarrow \mathtt{gen}(1^\lambda)$.
  (2) Append $sid \mapsto (sk, pk)$ to p_{Cred}.
  (3) For each party $P' \neq P$: Draw fresh sid'_{AUTH} and call $\mathcal{F}_{\mathrm{AUTH}}$ with input $(\mathtt{send}, sid'_{\mathrm{AUTH}}, P', (\mathtt{inited}, sid, pk))$.

\\ Receiving keys and sending stored messages

- Upon receiving output $(\mathtt{sent}, sid_{\mathrm{AUTH}}, P', P, (\mathtt{inited}, sid, pk_{P'}))$ from $\mathcal{F}_{\mathrm{AUTH}}$, if there is no entry $p_{\mathsf{Pk}}(sid, P')$ yet:
  (1) Append $(sid, P') \mapsto pk_{P'}$ to p_{Pk}.
  (2) For any $m \in p_{\mathsf{Send}}(sid, P')$:
    (1) Remove m from $p_{\mathsf{Send}}(sid, P')$.
    (2) $c \leftarrow \mathtt{enc}(pk_{P'}, P, m)$.
    (3) Draw fresh sid_{AUTH}.
    (4) Call $\mathcal{F}_{\mathrm{AUTH}}$ with input $(\mathtt{send}, sid_{\mathrm{AUTH}}, P', (sid, c))$.

\\ Sending messages

- Upon receiving input $(\mathtt{send}, sid, R, m)$ with $m \in \{0,1\}^l$ from environment $\mathcal{Z}$:
  - If $R = P$ report output $(\mathtt{sent}, sid, P, m)$ to the environment.
  - Else if no entry $p_{\mathsf{Pk}}(sid, R)$ exists yet:
    (1) Append m to $p_{\mathsf{Send}}(sid, R)$.
    (2) Draw fresh sid_{AUTH}.
    (3) Call $\mathcal{F}_{\mathrm{AUTH}}$ with input $(\mathtt{send}, sid_{\mathrm{AUTH}}, R, (\mathtt{init}, sid))$.
  - Else:
    (1) $pk_R := p_{\mathsf{Pk}}(sid, R)$.
    (2) $c \leftarrow \mathtt{enc}(pk_R, P, m)$.
    (3) Draw fresh sid_{AUTH}.
    (4) Call $\mathcal{F}_{\mathrm{AUTH}}$ with input $(\mathtt{send}, sid_{\mathrm{AUTH}}, R, (sid, c))$.

\\ Receiving messages

- Upon receiving output $(\mathtt{sent}, sid_{\mathrm{AUTH}}, S, R, (sid, c))$ from $\mathcal{F}_{\mathrm{AUTH}}$:
  (1) Look up $pk_S := p_{\mathsf{Pk}}(sid, S)$. If this does not exist, abort.
  (2) $m \leftarrow \mathtt{dec}(sk, S, c)$.
  (3) Report output $(\mathtt{sent}, sid, S, m)$ to the environment $\mathcal{Z}$.

Simulator $\mathcal{S}_{\text{M-SMT}}$. According to the real/ideal paradigm explained in Appendix C of the full version of this paper [3], our protocol $\pi_{\text{M-SMT}}^{\mathcal{F}_{\mathrm{AUTH}}}$ realizes secure message transfer if and only if for any (dummy) adversary $\mathcal{A}$ interacting with the real protocol, there exists a simulator $\mathcal{S}$ interacting with the ideal functionality $\mathcal{F}_{\text{M-SMT}}$ such that no environment $\mathcal{Z}$ can distinguish between executions in the real and ideal world. We now construct such a simulator $\mathcal{S}_{\text{M-SMT}}$ which we will later show to achieve indistinguishability for $\pi_{\text{M-SMT}}^{\mathcal{F}_{\text{AUTH}}}$ and $\mathcal{F}_{\text{M-SMT}}$.

The main idea of the simulator $\mathcal{S}_{\text{M-SMT}}$ is that it simulates the protocol behaviour of all parties and the hybrid functionality $\mathcal{F}_{\text{AUTH}}$ in its head. It takes inputs to and reports messages and outputs from these in-the-head parties to $\mathcal{Z}$ on the one hand and uses them on the other hand to interface with the ideal functionality $\mathcal{F}_{\text{M-SMT}}$. The only case in which the simulator does not have sufficient knowledge to perfectly simulate the protocol in their head is when an honest party S sends a message m to another honest party R: The simulator has no way of knowing the actual message m. In this case $\mathcal{S}_{\text{M-SMT}}$ reports an encryption $c \leftarrow \texttt{enc}(pk_R, S, 0)$ of zero to have been send instead.

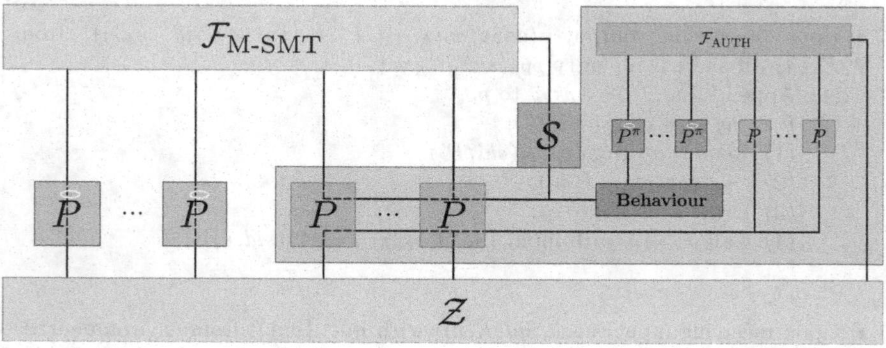

Fig. 5. Overview of Simulator $\mathcal{S}$

The overall construction of $\mathcal{S}_{\text{M-SMT}}$ is shown in Fig. 5. Again there are some more details to keep track of (especially regarding the box labeled "Behaviour" in Fig. 5) so we provide a more formal definition as well:

$\mathcal{S}_{\text{M-SMT}}$

Realizes:
Multi-receiver multi-message multi-sender secure message transfer with constant message size.

Parameters:

- Security parameter λ.
- IND-SB-CPA secure SBE scheme $(\texttt{gen}, \texttt{enc}, \texttt{dec})$.

In-the-head Parties:

- Functionality $\mathcal{F}_{\text{AUTH}}$. This functionality communicates in-the-head with all honest in-the-head parties as well as with the environment $\mathcal{Z}$ as adversary.
- Copies of honest parties running the protocol $\pi_{\text{M-SMT}}^{\mathcal{F}_{\text{AUTH}}}$, which we will denote as P^{π}. These parties communicate in-the-head with the in-the-head functionality $\mathcal{F}_{\text{AUTH}}$. Their interface to the environment is played by the simulator (defined in "Behaviour" below).
- Dummy corrupted parties. Whenever the simulator is asked by the environment to call the functionality $\mathcal{F}_{\text{AUTH}}$ in the name of a corrupted party, this in-the-head dummy calls the in-the-head functionality correspondingly and reports all outputs back to the environment $\mathcal{Z}$.

State:

- Everything the in-the-head parties store in their states.

Behaviour:

\\ Self-communication

- Upon receiving ($\texttt{send}$, sid, mid, P, P) from $\mathcal{F}_{\text{M-SMT}}$ to $\mathcal{A}$ for honest party P, call $\mathcal{F}_{\text{M-SMT}}$ with input ($\texttt{send ok}$, sid, mid).

\\ Message from honest to honest party

- Upon receiving ($\texttt{send}$, sid, mid, S, R) from $\mathcal{F}_{\text{M-SMT}}$ to $\mathcal{A}$ for honest parties $S \neq R$:
  - Start in-the-head party S^{π} with input ($\texttt{send}$, $sid, R, 0$) from the environment $\mathcal{Z}$.
  - If in-the-head party R^{π} at some point reports output ($\texttt{sent}$, $sid, S, 0$), call $\mathcal{F}_{\text{M-SMT}}$ with input ($\texttt{send ok}$, sid, mid).[5]

\\ Message from honest to corrupted party

- Upon receiving ($\texttt{send}$, sid, mid, S, R) from $\mathcal{F}_{\text{M-SMT}}$ to $\mathcal{A}$ for honest party S and corrupted party R:
  1. Call $\mathcal{F}_{\text{M-SMT}}$ with input ($\texttt{send ok}$, sid, mid).
  2. Receive output ($\texttt{sent}$, sid, S, m) from $\mathcal{F}_{\text{M-SMT}}$ to R.
  3. Start in-the-head party S^{π} with input ($\texttt{send}$, sid, R, m) from the environment $\mathcal{Z}$.

\\ Message from corrupted to honest party

- Upon in-the-head honest party R^{π} reporting output ($\texttt{sent}$, sid, S, m) for corrupted party S:
  1. Call $\mathcal{F}_{\text{M-SMT}}$ with input ($\texttt{send}$, sid, R, m) in the name of S.
  2. Receive output ($\texttt{send}$, sid, mid, S, R) from $\mathcal{F}_{\text{M-SMT}}$ to $\mathcal{A}$.
  3. Call $\mathcal{F}_{\text{M-SMT}}$ with input ($\texttt{send ok}$, sid, mid).

---

[5] At this point we assume the simulator to track the protocol executions in their head so they know which *mid* to use. For readability purposes we refrained from introducing notation to explicitly store this.

Security Theorem and Proof. The last thing left to do is to prove that under static corruption the simulator $\mathcal{S}_{\text{M-SMT}}$ does in fact achieve indistinguishability between $\pi_{\text{M-SMT}}^{\mathcal{F}_{\text{AUTH}}}$ and $\mathcal{F}_{\text{M-SMT}}$ in the $\mathcal{F}_{\text{AUTH}}$-hybrid model. To do so we will reduce this indistinguishability to the IND-SB-CPA security of the underlying SBE scheme. I.e. assuming there is an environment $\mathcal{Z}$ which can efficiently distinguish a real execution of $\pi_{\text{M-SMT}}^{\mathcal{F}_{\text{AUTH}}}$ from an ideal experiment with $\mathcal{F}_{\text{M-SMT}}$ and $\mathcal{S}_{\text{M-SMT}}$ (with non-negligible probability) we construct an adversary $\mathcal{A}_{\text{SB-CPA}}$ who can win the IND-SB-CPA game with non-negligible probability.

To achieve this let us first take a closer look at what a successfully distinguishing environment needs to do:

Remark 2. From the definition of the simulator $\mathcal{S}_{\text{M-SMT}}$ we immediately see that if an environment $\mathcal{Z}$ is able to distinguish executions of $\mathcal{F}_{\text{M-SMT}}$ and $\pi_{\text{M-SMT}}^{\mathcal{F}_{\text{AUTH}}}$, it can only do so by messages between honest parties $S \neq R$. In this case the simulator prompts its in-the-head sender S^{π} to send a message 0 to R instead of the actual message m (which the simulator does not know). The environment will therefore receive from $\mathcal{F}_{\text{AUTH}}$ (played by $\mathcal{S}_{\text{M-SMT}}$) a message

$$\Big(\textsf{send}, sid_{\text{AUTH}}, S, R, \big(sid, \textsf{enc}(pk_R, S, 0)\big)\Big)$$

in the ideal execution, while it receives in the protocol execution the message

$$\Big(\textsf{send}, sid_{\text{AUTH}}, S, R, \big(sid, \textsf{enc}(pk_R, S, m)\big)\Big).$$

In all other cases the simulator can perfectly mimic the protocol execution by playing the relevant parties and functionalities in its head.[6]

Let us restrict the distinguishing possibilities even more by introducing a sequence of hybrid games and showing that we only need to consider distinguishability of two consecutive hybrids:

Definition 4 (Hybrids H_k). *Let $k \in \mathbb{N}_0$ be a natural number. The hybrid H_k represents the execution set-up where almost all interactions are handled as in the real world execution of $\pi_{\text{M-SMT}}^{\mathcal{F}_{AUTH}}$. Note that Remark 2 guarantees that these are the same as in the ideal world, apart from encryptions of messages between honest parties. Now the only difference between an execution of $\pi_{\text{M-SMT}}^{\mathcal{F}_{AUTH}}$ and H_k is the following: For the first k messages m_i $(i \leq k)$ between two honest parties $R_i \neq S_i$, the output from $\mathcal{F}_{AUTH}$ to the environment $\mathcal{Z}$*

$$\Big(\textsf{send}, sid_{AUTH}, S_i, R_i, \big(sid, \textsf{enc}(pk_{R_i}, S_i, 0)\big)\Big)$$

contains an encryption of zeros—as it would in the ideal execution with simulator $\mathcal{S}_{\text{M-SMT}}$—instead of an encryption of the real message m_i.
Note that H_0 is equal to the real world execution of $\pi_{\text{M-SMT}}^{\mathcal{F}_{AUTH}}$ and H_∞ (where encryptions of zeros are used for all messages m_i, $i \in \mathbb{N}$) is equal to the ideal world execution of $\mathcal{F}_{\text{M-SMT}}$ with $\mathcal{S}_{\text{M-SMT}}$.

[6] Please convince yourself from the definition of the simulator $\mathcal{S}_{\text{M-SMT}}$ that it has all the knowledge required for simulation and that activations/outputs of $\mathcal{F}_{\text{M-SMT}}$ will actually occur at the right times.

Lemma 2. *Let there be an environment $\mathcal{Z}$ which distinguishes real and ideal world. Then there is a $\kappa \in \mathbb{N}$ and an environment $\mathcal{Z}_\kappa$ which distinguishes hybrids $H_{\kappa-1}$ and H_κ.*

Proof. By definition $\mathcal{Z}$ distinguishes executions in hybrids H_0 and H_∞. Since $\mathcal{Z}$ is PPT, there is a polynomial $p_\mathcal{Z}$ which bounds its runtime, i.e. $\mathcal{Z}$ takes at most $p_\mathcal{Z}(\lambda)$ steps. In particular $\mathcal{Z}$ can request no more than $p_\mathcal{Z}(\lambda)$ messages to be sent between honest parties, and hence executions of $\mathcal{Z}$ in H_∞ and H_k are the same for all $k > p_\mathcal{Z}(\lambda)$. Hence by transitivity of indistinguishability (here we require the chain from H_0 to H_∞ to actually be finite by the argument before), there is an $\kappa \in \mathbb{N}$ such that H_κ and $H_{\kappa-1}$ are not indistinguishable. □

With this preparatory work, we are finally ready to prove that our protocol $\pi^{\mathcal{F}_{\text{AUTH}}}_{\text{M-SMT}}$ does in fact realize secure message transfer:

Theorem 3. *Under static corruption, $\pi^{\mathcal{F}_{AUTH}}_{M\text{-}SMT}$ is a UC-realization of $\mathcal{F}_{M\text{-}SMT}$ in the $\mathcal{F}_{AUTH}$-hybrid model, if the underlying SBE scheme satisfies IND-SB-CPA security. I.e.*

$$\pi^{\mathcal{F}_{AUTH}}_{M\text{-}SMT} \geq_{UC} \mathcal{F}_{M\text{-}SMT}.$$

Proof. Assume there is an environment $\mathcal{Z}$ which distinguishes between executions of $\pi^{\mathcal{F}_{\text{AUTH}}}_{\text{M-SMT}}$ and $\mathcal{F}_{\text{M-SMT}}$. By Lemma 2 there is a $\kappa \in \mathbb{N}$ such that $\mathcal{Z}$ distinguishes hybrids $H_{\kappa-1}$ and H_κ with non-negligible probability. We now construct and adversary $\mathcal{A}_{\text{SB-CPA}}$ from $\mathcal{Z}$ which has non-negligible probability to win the IND-SB-CPA game. First $\mathcal{A}_{\text{SB-CPA}}$ receives (S, pk_S, R, pk_R) from $\mathcal{C}_{\text{SB-CPA}}$. Then it starts $\mathcal{Z}$ in it's head, playing all other parties. Again by Remark 2, $\mathcal{Z}$ needs to register at least two honest parties (and send a message between them) to distinguish. For the two honest parties R and S (randomly chosen by the challenger), $\mathcal{A}_{\text{SB-CPA}}$ does not generate fresh credentials as the honest parties would do, but rather uses pk_S and pk_R from $\mathcal{C}_{\text{SB-CPA}}$.

It is no problem that $\mathcal{A}_{\text{SB-CPA}}$ does not know sk_R, sk_S. The only case they are used is when a corrupted party sends a message to R or S, i.e. when one of them receives output $(\texttt{sent}, sid_{\text{AUTH}}, P, R/S, (sid, c))$ for some corrupted party P from the functionality $\mathcal{F}_{\text{AUTH}}$. In this case $\mathcal{A}_{\text{SB-CPA}}$ promts the oracle $\mathcal{O}_{\text{SB-CPA}}$ with input (pk_S, P, c). Note that it is $P \notin \{S, R\}$. Hence $\mathcal{O}_{\text{SB-CPA}}$ by definition responds with the decryption $m := \texttt{dec}(sk_{S/R}, P, c)$ and $\mathcal{A}_{\text{SB-CPA}}$ can let the simulator call $\mathcal{F}_{\text{M-SMT}}$ with input $(\texttt{send}, sid, S/R, m)$ in the name of P as usual.

For the first $\kappa - 1$ messages which are sent between two honest parties, we report encryptions of 0 instead, when $\mathcal{Z}$ asks the adversary to see the content of the communication channel. When $\mathcal{Z}$ asks for the κ-th message m_κ to be sent, $\mathcal{A}_{\text{SB-CPA}}$ does the following:

- If m_κ is not a message from S to R, give up.
- If m_κ is to be sent from S to R, hand messages 0 and m_κ to $\mathcal{C}_{\text{SB-CPA}}$ and receive challenge c^*. Report c^* as communication channel content to $\mathcal{Z}$.

From now on, when a message m is sent between two honest parties, always report an encryption of m as channel content instead of 0 as before. When $\mathcal{Z}$

stops and reports it has run in the hybrid H_κ, report bit $b = 0$ to $\mathcal{C}_{\text{SB-CPA}}$, if $\mathcal{Z}$ decides on $H_{\kappa-1}$, report $b = 1$. □

6 Relation Between IND-SB-CPA and TBE Notions

We have presented the new notion of IND-SB-CPA for SBE in Sect. 2, given some intuition on what this notion implies and broadened the intuitive understanding by a generic example construction in Sect. 3. What is still missing from the picture is a formal classification of how this notion directly relates to other security notions. To fill this gap we firstly examine the connection between IND-SB-CPA and TBE security notions in this section.

In Appendix G.2 of the full version of this paper [3] we also look at the implications between IND-SB-CPA and classical PKE IND notions ranging from CPA to CCA2.

First note that although the notion of IND-gtag-wCCA has not been defined prior to this work it is an obvious relaxation of IND-stag-wCCA security—which was the weakest TBE notion considered so far. The proofs for the (non-)implications between IND-gtag-wCCA and IND-stag-wCCA can be found in Appendix G.1 of the full version of this paper [3].

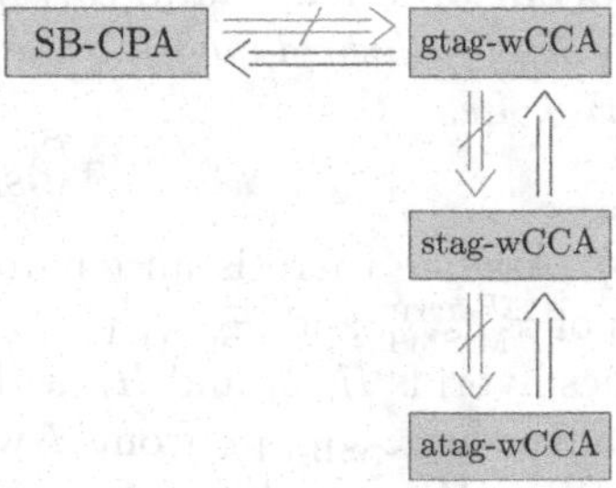

Fig. 6. Relationship to TBE notions

In this section we concentrate on the relationship between IND-SB-CPA and IND-gtag-wCCA. To compare the two notions we assume the tag space $\mathbf{T}$ considered for IND-gtag-wCCA to be equal to a set $\mathbf{P}$ of party IDs. Of course a bijection between the two is sufficient as well, but we compare the notions for tag and ID spaces of the same size. An overview is shown in Fig. 6.

Lemma 3. *IND-SB-CPA* $\Leftarrow$ *IND-gtag-wCCA.*

Proof. Let $(\texttt{gen}, \texttt{enc}, \texttt{dec})$ be a TBE scheme. Under assumption of an efficient adversary $\mathcal{A}_{\text{SB-CPA}}$ with non-negligible probability to win the IND-SB-CPA security game, we will construct an efficient adversary $\mathcal{A}_{\text{gtag-wCCA}}$ who has the same success probability in the IND-gtag-wCCA game. An overview of the construction can be found in Fig. 7.

After being handed an ID S as the challenge tag and a public key pk, the adversary $\mathcal{A}_{\text{gtag-wCCA}}$ determines an ID R matching the public key $pk = pk_R$ and generates a key pair (sk_S, pk_S) matching the ID S. Depending on the specific scheme, these might, e.g., involve some key registration or be completely independent of one another. The IDs and public keys (S, pk_S, R, pk_R) are handed on to $\mathcal{A}_{\text{SB-CPA}}$. Any valid oracle queries $(pk_{R'}, S', c)$ from $\mathcal{A}_{\text{SB-CPA}}$ (i.e., those with $S' \notin \{S, R\}$ and $pk_{R'} \in \{pk_S, pk_R\}$) are answered in one of two ways: If pk'_R is equal to the challenge key pk_R, the query (S', c) is forwarded to $\mathcal{A}_{\text{gtag-wCCA}}$'s

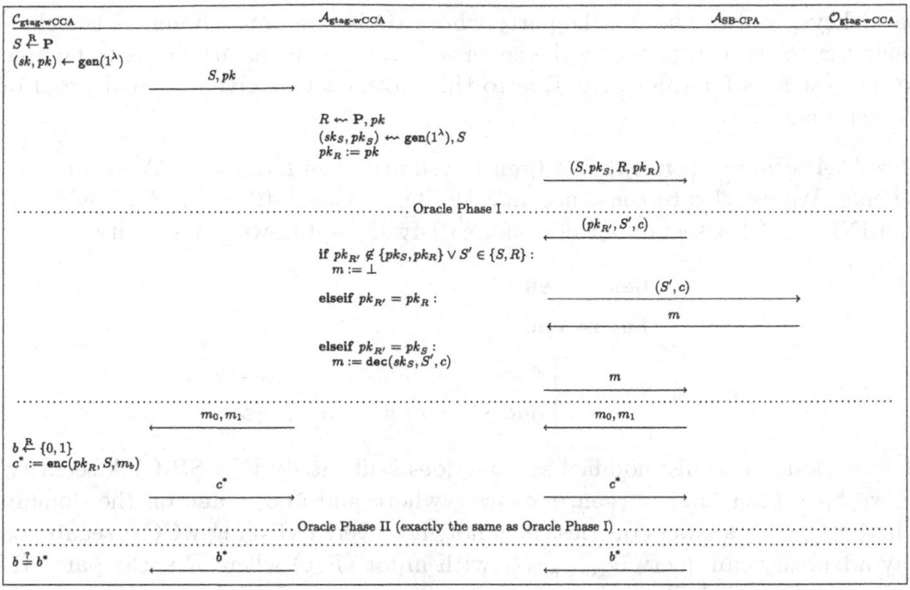

$\mathcal{C}_{\text{gtag-wCCA}}$
$\mathcal{A}_{\text{gtag-wCCA}}$
$\mathcal{A}_{\text{SB-CPA}}$
$\mathcal{O}_{\text{gtag-wCCA}}$
$S \xleftarrow{R} \mathbf{P}$
$(sk, pk) \leftarrow \text{gen}(1^\lambda)$
S, pk
$R \leftarrow \mathbf{P}, pk$
$(sk_S, pk_S) \leftarrow \text{gen}(1^\lambda), S$
$pk_R := pk$
(S, pk_S, R, pk_R)
Oracle Phase I
$(pk_{R'}, S', c)$
if $pk_{R'} \notin \{pk_S, pk_R\} \vee S' \in \{S, R\}$:
$m := \bot$
elseif $pk_{R'} = pk_R$:
(S', c)
m
elseif $pk_{R'} = pk_S$:
$m := \text{dec}(sk_S, S', c)$
m
m_0, m_1
m_0, m_1
$b \xleftarrow{R} \{0, 1\}$
$c^* := \text{enc}(pk_R, S, m_b)$
c^*
c^*
Oracle Phase II (exactly the same as Oracle Phase I)
$b \stackrel{?}{=} b^*$
b^*
b^*

Fig. 7. Reduction for IND-SB-CPA $\Leftarrow$ IND-gtag-wCCA

own oracle $\mathcal{O}_{\text{gtag-wCCA}}$. Otherwise, $\mathcal{A}_{\text{gtag-wCCA}}$ uses it's secret key sk_S to perform the decryption itself. In both cases the challenge is answered exactly like an oracle $\mathcal{O}_{\text{SB-CPA}}$ would. After forwarding the messages m_0, m_1 and the challenge ciphertext c^* between $\mathcal{A}_{\text{SB-CPA}}$ and $\mathcal{C}_{\text{gtag-wCCA}}$, the oracle phase is repeated exactly as before. Finally, the bit b^* which $\mathcal{A}_{\text{SB-CPA}}$ outputs is forwarded as well. If the adversary $\mathcal{A}_{\text{SB-CPA}}$ wins, so will $\mathcal{A}_{\text{gtag-wCCA}}$. □

Lemma 4. *IND-SB-CPA $\not\Rightarrow$ IND-gtag-wCCA.*

Proof. Let us consider the DRE-based example $(\texttt{Gen}, \texttt{Enc}, \texttt{Dec})$ from Sect. 3 again. In Lemma 1 we have already shown that this scheme is IND-SB-CPA secure. To prove our current claim it remains to be shown that $(\texttt{Gen}, \texttt{Enc}, \texttt{Dec})$ does not satisfy IND-gtag-wCCA security. We do so by constructing an efficient adversary $\mathcal{A}_{\text{gtag-wCCA}}$ which has non-negligible probability of winning the IND-gtag-wCCA security game. Firstly the challenger $\mathcal{C}_{\text{gtag-wCCA}}$ chooses a random party ID $S \in \mathbf{P}$, generates the challenge key pair (SK_R, PK_R) and registers it for some party R. On input of S, PK_R, the adversary $\mathcal{A}_{\text{gtag-wCCA}}$ generates a fresh key pair (SK_S, PK_S), and register this key pair with $\mathcal{F}_{\text{KRK}}$ in the name of S. Now the adversary chooses random messages $m_0 \neq m_1$ for the challenge and receives $c^* = \texttt{Enc}(PK_R, S, m_b)$. Due to DRE soundness the adversary can now decrypt the challenge as $m_b = \texttt{Dec}(SK_S, R, c^*)$ and win the IND-gtag-wCCA game with probability one. □

Although this proof is instructing for the intuitive understanding of SBE schemes since it relies on the fact that there is a connection between tags and party keys, it also relies on the party whose ID is randomly chosen as the challenge tag to be corruptible by the adversary. I.e. the adversary needs to be able to register keys for this party. Due to this caveat let us give a second proof of the lemma:

Proof (Alternative version). Let $(\texttt{gen}, \texttt{enc}, \texttt{dec})$ be an IND-SB-CPA secure SBE scheme. We use this to construct an SBE/TBE scheme $(\texttt{Gen}, \texttt{Enc}, \texttt{Dec})$ which is still IND-SB-CPA secure but does not satisfy IND-gtag-wCCA security:

$$\texttt{Gen} := \texttt{gen}$$

$$\texttt{Enc} := \texttt{enc}$$

$$\texttt{Dec}(sk, S, c) := \begin{cases} \texttt{dec}(sk, S, c) || sk & , sk = sk_S \\ \texttt{dec}(sk, S, c) || 0 \cdots 0 & , \text{else.} \end{cases}$$

It is obvious that this modified scheme does still satisfy IND-SB-CPA security, as we have $(\texttt{Gen}, \texttt{Enc}) = (\texttt{gen}, \texttt{enc})$ everywhere and $\texttt{Dec} = \texttt{dec}$ on the domain where $\mathcal{O}_{\text{SB-CPA}}$ answers queries. It is not, however, IND-gtag-wCCA secure, as any adversary can query $\mathcal{O}_{\text{gtag-wCCA}}$ with input (R, c) where R is the party ID corresponding to challenge key pk_R and c is an arbitrary ciphertext. The oracle will hand back sk_R which can be used to decrypt the challenge ciphertext c^* and win the security game every time. □

7 Conclusion

In this work we have introduced the concept of sender-binding encryption and developed the corresponding new security notion of IND-SB-CPA. We showed IND-SB-CPA security to be sufficient for UC-realizing secure message transfer (SMT) when combined with authenticated channels. Furthermore the direct implication from Sect. 6 and generic transformations from Appendix E of the full version of this paper [3] show that it is currently the weakest known notion with this property. Additionally we provided a generic transformation for IND-SB-CPA via IND-CPA secure double receiver encryption (DRE) in conjunction with key registration with knowledge. In particular this construction from DRE yields an efficient practical instantiation based on McEliece in the standard model.

For future work we see several directions to further this line of research. Although we know IND-SB-CPA to be weaker than prior notions which realize SMT via authenticated channels, it remains to be shown whether it constitutes the weakest possible notion to do so. It is also far from obvious that our current practical constructions are the most efficient to satisfy IND-SB-CPA security. More effort in this direction might prove fruitful as well.

Acknowledgments. We thank Björn Kaidel for fruitful initial discussions. We thank the PKC 2022 anonymous reviewers for their valuable feedback. The work presented in this paper has been funded by the German Federal Ministry of Education and Research (BMBF) under the project "PQC4MED" (ID 16KIS1044) and by KASTEL Security Research Labs.

A Notations and Abbreviations

This section can be used to look up all notations and abbreviations employed throughout this paper.

A.1 Notations

$\xleftarrow{R}$	Uniformly randomly drawn from
$\hookrightarrow$	Output
$\geq_{UC}$	Securely UC-realizes
$\bot$	Invalid/failed
$\mathcal{A}$	Adversary
Adv	Advantage
aux	Auxiliary input/output
b	Bit from $\{0,1\}$
$\mathcal{C}$	Challenger
c	Ciphertext
c^*	Challenge ciphertext
$\mathbf{c}$	Vectors
$\mathtt{dec}/\mathtt{Dec}$	Decryption algorithm
$\mathcal{E}$	Encryption scheme
$\mathtt{enc}/\mathtt{Enc}$	Encryption algorithm
Exp	Experiment
$\mathtt{ext}$	Key extraction algorithm
$\mathcal{F}$	Ideal functionality
$\mathtt{f}_{\mathrm{ID}}/\mathtt{F}_{\mathrm{ID}}$	ID function
$\mathtt{f}_{\mathrm{Key}}/\mathtt{F}_{\mathrm{Key}}$	Boolean key function
$\mathtt{f}_{\mathbf{PK}}$	Key function $sk \mapsto pk$
G	Matrices
$\mathtt{gen}/\mathtt{Gen}$	Key generation algorithm
goal	Goal of the adversary
id/ID	Protocol party ID
$\mathbf{ID}$	Set of all IDs
$\mathtt{init}$	Asking to initialize
$\mathtt{inited}$	Initialization done
k	Binary key length
λ	Security parameter
l	Message length
l'	Ciphertext length
m	Message
M	Message space
$\mathtt{message}$	$\mathcal{F}$ message variable
mid	Message ID
$\mathbf{MID}$	Set of all message IDs
mpk	IBE master public key
msk	IBE master secret key
n	Security parameter for McEliece
$\mathcal{O}$	Oracle
π	Protocol
$\pi^{\mathcal{F}_{\mathrm{AUTH}}}_{\text{M-SMT}}$	M-SMT protocol
P	Party
$\mathbf{P}$	Set of all parties
$\mathbb{P}$	Probability
pk/PK	Public key
$\mathbf{PK}$	Set of all public keys
pow	Power of the adversary
pr	Boolean prefix function
R	Receiver
$\mathbf{R}$	Set of all registered parties
$\mathtt{receiver}$	Message *receiver*
$\mathtt{register}$	Asking to be registered
$\mathtt{register\ ok}$	Registration allowed
$\mathtt{registered}$	Registration done
$\mathtt{retrieve}$	Asking to retrieve credentials
$\mathtt{retrieve\ ok}$	Retrieval allowed
$\mathtt{retrieved}$	Retrieval done
$resp$	Oracle response
S	Sender
$\mathcal{S}$	Simulator
$\mathcal{S}_{\text{M-SMT}}$	Simulator for $\pi^{\mathcal{F}_{\mathrm{AUTH}}}_{\text{M-SMT}}$
scp	Scope of adversary's power
$\mathtt{send}$	Asking to send message
$\mathtt{send\ ok}$	Transmission allowed
$\mathtt{sent}$	Message sent
set	Setting of security game
sid	Session ID
$\mathbf{SID}$	Set of all session IDs
sk/SK	Secret key
$\mathbf{SK}$	Set of all secret keys
$\mathtt{stray}$	Message *stray*
$test$	Special response of $\mathcal{O}_{\mathrm{RCCA}}$
usk	User secret key
$\mathcal{Z}$	Environment

A.2 Abbreviations

CCA2 adaptive chosen ciphertext attack
CPA chosen plaintext attack
DAKEZ Deniable authenticated key exchange with zero-knowledge
DRE double receiver encryption
IBE identity based encryption
IF ideal functionality
IND indistinguishability
IND-CCA2 indistinguishability under adaptive chosen ciphertext attack
IND-CPA indistinguishability under chosen plaintext attack
IND-gtag-wCCA indistinguishability under given-tag weakly chosen ciphertext attack
gtag-wCCA given-tag weakly chosen ciphertext attack
IND-stag-wCCA indistinguishability under selective-tag weakly chosen ciphertext attack
stag-wCCA selective-tag weakly chosen ciphertext attack
IND-RCCA indistinguishability under replayable chosen ciphertext attack
IND-sID-CPA indistinguishability under selective identity chosen plaintext attack
IND-SB-CPA indistinguishability under sender-binding chosen plaintext attack
IND-atag-wCCA indistinguishability under adaptive-tag weakly chosen ciphertext attack
atag-wCCA adaptive-tag weakly chosen ciphertext attack
KRK key registration with knowledge
LPN learning parity with noise
LPNDP learning parity with noise decisional problem
LWE learning with errors
M-SMT multiple secure message transfer
OTR Off-the-Record
PA plaintext awareness
PKE public key encryption
PKI public key infrastructure
PPT probabilistic polynomial time
PQC post-quantum cryptography
RCCA replayable chosen ciphertext attack
ROM random oracle model
RPA registration-based plaintext awareness
SBE sender-binding encryption
SMT secure message transfer
TBE tag-based encryption
UC universal composability
XZDH Extended Zero-knowledge Diffie-Hellman

References

1. Badertscher, C., Maurer, U., Portmann, C., Rito, G.: Revisiting (R)CCA security and replay protection. IACR Cryptol, pp. 177 (2020). ePrint Arch. 2020. https://eprint.iacr.org/2020/177
2. Bernstein, D.J., Lange, T., Peters, C.: Attacking and defending the McEliece cryptosystem. In: Buchmann, J., Ding, J. (eds.) PQCrypto 2008. LNCS, vol. 5299, pp. 31–46. Springer, Heidelberg (2008). https://doi.org/10.1007/978-3-540-88403-3_3
3. Beskorovajnov, W., Groll, R., Muller-Quade, J., Ottenhues, A., Schwerdt, R.: A new security notion for PKC in the standard model: weaker, simpler, and still realizing secure channels, cryptology. ePrint Archive, Report 2021/1649 (2021). https://ia.cr/2021/1649

4. Bogos, S., Tramer, F., Vaudenay, S.: On solving LPN using BKW and variants. IACR Cryptol. ePrint Arch. (2015). http://eprint.iacr.org/2015/049
5. Boneh, D., Canetti, R., Halevi, S., Katz, J.: Chosen-ciphertext security from identity-based encryption. SIAM J. Comput. **36**(5), 1301–1328 (2007)
6. Boneh, D., Katz, J.: Improved efficiency for CCA-secure cryptosystems built using identity-based encryption. In: Menezes, A. (ed.) CT-RSA 2005. LNCS, vol. 3376, pp. 87–103. Springer, Heidelberg (2005). https://doi.org/10.1007/978-3-540-30574-3_8
7. Callas, J., Donnerhacke, L., Finney, H., Shaw, D., Thayer, R.: OpenPGP Message Format. RFC 4880, pp. 1–90 (2007). https://doi.org/10.17487/RFC4880
8. Canetti, R.: Security and Composition of Multi-party Cryptographic Protocols, Cryptology ePrint Archive, Report 1998/018 (1998). https://eprint.iacr.org/1998/018
9. Canetti, R.: Universally composable security: a new paradigm for cryptographic protocols. In: 42nd FOCS, pp. 136–145. IEEE Computer Society Press (2001). https://doi.org/10.1109/SFCS.2001.959888
10. Canetti, R., Goldreich, O., Halevi, S.: The Random Oracle Methodology, Revisited, Cryptology ePrint Archive, Report 1998/011 (1998). https://eprint.iacr.org/1998/011
11. Canetti, R., Krawczyk, H., Nielsen, J.B.: Relaxing chosen-ciphertext security. In: Boneh, D. (ed.) CRYPTO 2003. LNCS, vol. 2729, pp. 565–582. Springer, Heidelberg (2003). https://doi.org/10.1007/978-3-540-45146-4_33
12. Canetti, R., Rabin, T.: Universal composition with joint state. In: Boneh, D. (ed.) CRYPTO 2003. LNCS, vol. 2729, pp. 265–281. Springer, Heidelberg (2003). https://doi.org/10.1007/978-3-540-45146-4_16
13. Cheng, H., Li, X., Qian, H., Yan, D.: Simpler CCA secure PKE from LPN problem without double-trapdoor. In: Naccache, D., Xu, S., Qing, S., Samarati, P., Blanc, G., Lu, R., Zhang, Z., Meddahi, A. (eds.) ICICS 2018. LNCS, vol. 11149, pp. 756–766. Springer, Cham (2018). https://doi.org/10.1007/978-3-030-01950-1_46
14. Chow, S.S.M., Franklin, M.K., Zhang, H.: Practical dual-receiver encryption - soundness, complete non-malleability, and applications. In: Benaloh, J. (ed.) CT-RSA 2014. LNCS, pp. 85–105. Springer, Heidelberg (2014). https://doi.org/10.1007/978-3319-04852-9
15. Cramer, R., Shoup, V.: Design and analysis of practical public-key encryption schemes secure against adaptive chosen ciphertext attack. SIAM J. Comput. **33**(1), 167–226 (2003)
16. Damgard, I., Park, S.: Is Public-Key Encryption Based on LPN Practical? IACR Cryptol. ePrint Arch. (2012). http://eprint.iacr.org/2012/699
17. Diament, T., Lee, H.K., Keromytis, A.D., Yung, M.: The dual receiver cryptosystem and its applications. In: Atluri, V., Pfitzmann, B., McDaniel, P. (eds.) ACM CCS 2004, pp. 330–343. ACM Press (2004). https://doi.org/10.1145/1030083
18. Diffie, W., Hellman, M.E.: New directions in cryptography. IEEE Trans. Inf. Theory **22**(6), 644–654 (1976)
19. Dottling, N., Dowsley, R., Mxiller-Quade, J., Nascimento, A.C.A.: A CCA2 Secure Variant of the McEliece Cryptosystem, Cryptology ePrint Archive, Report 2008/468 (2008). https://eprint.iacr.org/2008/468
20. Freeman, D.M., Goldreich, O., Kiltz, E., Rosen, A., Segev, G.: More constructions of lossy and correlation-secure trapdoor functions. In: Nguyen, P.Q., Pointcheval, D. (eds.) PKC 2010. LNCS, vol. 6056, pp. 279–295. Springer, Heidelberg (2010). https://doi.org/10.1007/978-3-642-13013-7_17

21. Gentry, C., Peikert, C., Vaikuntanathan, V.: Trapdoors for hard lattices and new cryptographic constructions. In: Ladner, R.E., Dwork, C. (eds.) 40th ACM STOC, pp. 197–206. ACM Press (2008). https://doi.org/10.1145/1374376.1374407
22. Goldwasser, S., Micali, S.: Probabilistic encryption. J. Comput. Syst. Sci. **28**(2), 270–299 (1984)
23. Kiltz, E.: Chosen-ciphertext security from tag-based encryption. In: Halevi, S., Rabin, T. (eds.) TCC 2006. LNCS, vol. 3876, pp. 581–600. Springer, Heidelberg (2006). https://doi.org/10.1007/11681878_30
24. Kiltz, E., Masny, D., Pietrzak, K.: Simple chosen-ciphertext security from low-noise LPN. In: Krawczyk, H. (ed.) PKC 2014. LNCS, vol. 8383, pp. 1–18. Springer, Heidelberg (2014). https://doi.org/10.1007/978-3-642-54631-0_1
25. Kiltz, E., Mohassel, P., O'Neill, A.: Adaptive trapdoor functions and chosen-ciphertext security. In: Gilbert, H. (ed.) EUROCRYPT 2010. LNCS, vol. 6110, pp. 673–692. Springer, Heidelberg (2010). https://doi.org/10.1007/978-3-642-13190-5_34
26. MacKenzie, P.D., Reiter, M.K., Yang, K.: Alternatives to non-malleability: definitions, constructions, and applications (extended ebstract). In: Naor, M. (ed.) TCC 2004. LNCS, pp. 171–190. Springer, Heidelberg (2004). https://doi.org/10.1007/9783-540-24638-1
27. Nojima, R., Imai, H., Kobara, K., Morozov, K.: Semantic security for the McEliece cryptosystem without random oracles. Des. Codes Cryptogr. **49**(1–3), 289–305 (2008). https://doi.org/10.1007/sl0623-008-9175-9
28. Peikert, C, Waters, B.: Lossy trapdoor functions and their applications. In: Ladner, R.E., Dwork, C. (eds.) 40th ACM STOC, pp. 187–196. ACM Press (2008). https://doi.org/10.1145/1374376.1374406
29. Rackoff, O., Simon, D.R.: Non-interactive zero-knowledge proof of knowledge and chosen ciphertext attack. In: Feigenbaum, J. (ed.) CRYPTO'91. LNCS, pp. 433–444. Springer, Heidelberg (1992). https://doi.org/10.1007/3-540-46766-1_35
30. Rill, J.: Towards Applying Cryptographic Security Models to Real-World Systems. Karlsruhe Institute of Technology, Germany (2020)
31. Rosen, A., Segev, G.: Chosen-ciphertext security via correlated products. In: Reingold, O. (ed.) TCC 2009. LNCS, vol. 5444, pp. 419–436. Springer, Heidelberg (2009). https://doi.org/10.1007/978-3-642-00457-5_25
32. Schaad, J., Ramsdell, B., Turner, S.: Secure/multipurpose internet mail extensions (S/MIME) version 4.0 message specification. RFC 8551, pp. 1–63 (2019). https://doi.org/10.17487/RFC8551
33. Unger, N., Goldberg, I.: Improved strongly deniable authenticated key exchanges for secure messaging. PoPETs **2018**(1), 21–66 (2018)
34. YU, Y., Zhang, J.: Cryptography with auxiliary input and trapdoor from constant-noise LPN. In: Robshaw, M., Katz, J. (eds.) CRYPTO 2016. LNCS, vol. 9814, pp. 214–243. Springer, Heidelberg (2016). https://doi.org/10.1007/978-3-662-53018-4_9

Signatures

Lattice-Based Signatures with Tight Adaptive Corruptions and More

Jiaxin Pan[1(✉)] and Benedikt Wagner[2]

[1] Department of Mathematical Sciences, NTNU - Norwegian University of Science and Technology, Trondheim, Norway
jiaxin.pan@ntnu.no

[2] CISPA Helmholtz Center for Information Security, Saarbrücken, Germany
benedikt.wagner@cispa.de

Abstract. We construct the *first* tightly secure signature schemes in the multi-user setting with adaptive corruptions from lattices. In stark contrast to the previous tight constructions whose security is solely based on number-theoretic assumptions, our schemes are based on the Learning with Errors (LWE) assumption which is supposed to be post-quantum secure. The security of our scheme is independent of the numbers of users and signing queries, and it is in the non-programmable random oracle model. Our LWE-based scheme is *compact*, namely, its signatures contain only a constant number of lattice vectors.

At the core of our construction are a new abstraction of the existing lossy identification (ID) schemes using dual-mode commitment schemes and a refinement of the framework by Diemert et al. (PKC 2021) which transforms a lossy ID scheme to a signature using sequential OR proofs. In combination, we obtain a tight generic construction of signatures from dual-mode commitments in the multi-user setting. Improving the work of Diemert et al., our new approach can be instantiated using not only the LWE assumption, but also an isogeny-based assumption. We stress that our LWE-based lossy ID scheme in the intermediate step uses a conceptually different idea than the previous lattice-based ones.

Of independent interest, we formally rule out the possibility that the aforementioned "ID-to-Signature" methodology can work tightly using parallel OR proofs. In addition to the results of Fischlin et al. (EUROCRYPT 2020), our impossibility result shows a qualitative difference between both forms of OR proofs in terms of tightness.

Keywords: Digital signatures · identification schemes · multi-user security · tightness · OR proofs · commitments · lattice · isogeny · impossibility result

---

J. Pan—Supported by the Research Council of Norway under Project No. 324235.
B. Wagner—This work was done while the second author was a student at Karlsruhe Institute of Technology (Germany) and was doing an internship with the first author at NTNU (Norway).

G. Hanaoka et al. (Eds.): PKC 2022, LNCS 13178, pp. 347–378, 2022.
https://doi.org/10.1007/978-3-030-97131-1_12

1 Introduction

TIGHT SECURITY. Security of modern cryptographic constructions is established by security reductions. A reduction is an efficient algorithm $\mathcal{R}$ that uses an efficient algorithm $\mathcal{A}$ against the security of scheme X as a subroutine, and if $\mathcal{A}$ can break the security of X, then $\mathcal{R}$ can solve the computational problem Y. Thus, the hardness of Y implies the security of X. More precisely, we obtain $\epsilon_{\mathcal{A}}/t_{\mathcal{A}} \leq L \cdot \epsilon_{\mathcal{R}}/t_{\mathcal{R}}$, where $\mathcal{A}$ runs in time $t_{\mathcal{A}}$ and has success probability $\epsilon_{\mathcal{A}}$, and $\mathcal{R}$ runs in time $t_{\mathcal{R}}$ and has success probability $\epsilon_{\mathcal{R}}$. Here L is a polynomial in the security parameter λ, which we call the security loss. Asymptotically, any polynomial L is sufficient to show security. However, when we instantiate the scheme in a theoretically sound manner, the concrete L has impact on the setup of the system parameters. In particular, the smaller L is, the shorter the parameters will be. If L is a small constant, we call the reduction *tight* (e.g. [8,9]). Many works (e.g. [12,16,26]) also consider a relaxed tightness notion, called "*almost tight*", where L depends at most linearly on the security parameter λ. We do not distinguish these two notions, but are precise about the security loss of our scheme in our security theorem and when we compare it with the related work.

SIGNATURES IN MULTI-USER SETTING. Digital Signatures play a central role in modern public-key cryptography. The standard security notion is unforgeability against chosen-message attacks [32] (denoted by CMA security) which states that no efficient adversary can forge a signature on a new message after adaptively asking signatures for arbitrary messages. This is defined in a single-user setting where only one public key is involved. A seemingly more realistic notion is CMA security in the multi-user setting with adaptive corruptions (denoted by $\mathsf{MU\text{-}CMA\text{-}Corr}$ security). Here, adversary $\mathcal{A}$ receives N public keys, can adaptively ask for signatures and additionally can corrupt some of the corresponding secret keys, and in the end it outputs a forgery for an uncorrupted user. This is also named $\mathsf{MU\text{-}EUF\text{-}CMA}^{\mathsf{corr}}$ security in [6,31]. We note that there is a weaker notion of multi-user security considered in [41,49] ($\mathsf{MU\text{-}CMA}$ security) where secret key corruptions are not allowed.

$\mathsf{MU\text{-}CMA\text{-}Corr}$ security is an interesting notion to consider. The most important reason is that $\mathsf{MU\text{-}CMA\text{-}Corr}$ security captures the actual security requirements of many applications that use digital signatures as a building block. A well-known example is authenticated key exchange (AKE) protocols which use signatures to authenticate protocol transcripts. Standard AKE security models (such as the Bellare-Rogaway [10] and Canetti-Krawczyk [14] models) are in multi-user settings and allow adversaries to corrupt signing keys of some honest users. In particular, the work of Bader et al. [6] proposed the first tightly $\mathsf{MU\text{-}CMA\text{-}Corr}$ secure signature schemes and used it to construct the first tightly secure AKE protocol. The notion of $\mathsf{MU\text{-}CMA\text{-}Corr}$ has been used in many of its subsequent works [31,38,43] for constructing more efficient AKE protocols, and the notion is also used to prove the tight security of real-world protocols [20,22]. Tight security is of particular interest for these protocols, since they often have massive amount of users involved. Nevertheless, understanding and constructing efficient tightly MU-CMA-Corr secure signature schemes are fundamental research questions.

ON ACHIEVING TIGHT MU-CMA-Corr SECURITY. In general, CMA security can only *non-tightly* imply MU-CMA-Corr security by a guessing argument. The resulting reduction will lose a factor linear in the number of users, N. This is similar for the implication from MU-CMA to MU-CMA-Corr.

Many of the tightly secure signature schemes in the literature established their tightness in the weaker sense, namely, either tight CMA security (for instance, [11,26]) or tight MU-CMA security (for instance, [41,49]). None of them will lead to a tightly MU-CMA-Corr secure scheme. Furthermore, Bader et al. [7] even proved that tight MU-CMA-Corr is impossible to achieve if the signature satisfies certain properties. These properties are satisfied by most signature schemes, and thus constructing tightly MU-CMA-Corr secure signature schemes is very challenging.

To the best of our knowledge, signature schemes in [1,5,6,21,31,35] are the only exceptions with tight MU-CMA-Corr security. They all base their security on number-theoretic assumptions (such as the Diffie-Hellman assumption in pairing groups and φ-Hiding assumption), which leads to insecurity in the presence of a powerful quantum adversary. It is also worth mentioning that very recently Han et al. [35] identified a gap in the security proof of the compact and tightly MU-CMA-Corr-secure scheme in [6] and closed this gap by following the blueprint of the pairing-based HIBE scheme in [42].

We highlight that the tight lattice-based signature schemes in [2,11,12] and isogeny-based scheme in [24] are only in the single-user setting. It is not clear how to translate them tightly to the multi-user setting with adaptive corruptions. Hence, currently, there is no tightly MU-CMA-Corr secure signature scheme from post-quantum assumptions.

OUR GOAL AND ITS DIFFICULTIES. We aim at constructing *compact* lattice-based signature schemes with tight MU-CMA-Corr security. In this paper, *"compact"* means that the signature contains only a small constant number of lattice vectors and has size independent of the message length, which is in contrast to less efficient tree-based constructions.

As remarked above, there exist tight constructions of MU-CMA-Corr secure signature schemes. However, we argue why it is inherently difficult to extend them in realizing our goal:

- First, generic constructions in [5,6] and [1, Section 9.2] require some extractability of the underlying proof system. Such a proof system is hard to construct in a compact and tightly secure manner using lattices. For instance, one can use the Unruh proof system [55] that is tightly secure and extractable, but its proof size is at least linear in the security parameter. This can only give us a scheme with linear-size signatures.
- Second, the tree-based construction from one-time signatures in [1, Section 9.3] can give us a tight lattice-based construction, but it is not compact and has signature size linear in the message length.

- Third, in [21] a generic construction was proposed by transforming a lossy identification (ID) scheme [2] to a tightly MU-CMA-Corr secure signature scheme using the sequential OR proof technique [4,25]. As pointed out by the authors, this transformation requires additional properties of the lossy ID scheme which are not obvious how to achieve using lattices.
- Last, the specific schemes in [31,35] crucially rely on number-theoretic assumptions and the underlying algebraic structure. More precisely, [31] requires the Decisional Diffie-Hellman (DDH) assumption and a proof system for the equality of discrete logarithms, and the compact scheme in [35] requires an algebraic MAC with affine structures.

1.1 Our Contributions

We construct the *first* compact lattice-based signature schemes with tight MU-CMA-Corr security in the random oracle model. Their security is based on the Learning with Errors (LWE) assumption, and their security loss is independent of the number of users and signing queries. Furthermore, our security proofs do not program a random oracle. We also give an instantiation of our approach in the isogeny setting to show its flexibility. Unfortunately, the resulting signature scheme in the isogeny setting is not compact.

We have three tight lattice-based schemes, and they are all constructed from our generic approach. One of them is almost tight, and the other two are fully tight. All three schemes have public key size and signature size independent of the message length. We note that our fully tight schemes (see our full version) contain linearly (in λ) many lattice vectors in signatures, but independent of the message length. In Table 1 we compare the efficiency and concrete security of our schemes with some well-known efficient signature schemes in the random oracle model. Asymptotically, the signature size of our almost tight scheme is comparable to non-tight constructions, such as Lyubashevsky [44] and Ducas et al. [23], which require the rewinding technique. Due to the tightness of our scheme, it may have shorter signatures than these schemes. We stress that the main purpose of this work is taking the first theoretical step to study whether and how a tightly MU-CMA-Corr secure compact signature scheme from lattices is possible. We are optimistic that the efficiency of our schemes can be further improved.

Our schemes are constructed by a generic transformation that tightly turns a dual-mode commitment scheme into a MU-CMA-Corr secure signature. Our transformation contains two technical contributions, an abstraction of the existing lossy ID schemes and a refinement of the framework of Diemert et al. [21] which used the *sequential* OR proofs of Abe et al. [4] and Fischlin et al. [25]. The abstraction is a generic transformation from dual-mode commitment to lossy ID, and the existing lossy ID schemes [1,2,15,34] are concrete instantiations of our transformation. More importantly, this yield a new construction based on the LWE assumption using a conceptually new approach. Together with our refinement of the Diemert et al. framework, our tight lattice-based signature schemes are obtained.

Table 1. Overview of lattice-based signature schemes in the random oracle model. Here, Q denotes an upper bound on the number of signature and random oracle queries and λ is the security parameter. The security loss is up to constants and with respect to N-MU-CMA-Corr security. The modulus is denoted by $q = \mathsf{poly}(n)$ and $M = n{\cdot}m{\cdot}\lceil \log q \rceil$ denotes the size of an $n \times m$ matrix, $m = \Theta(n \log q)$, T denotes the size of a trapdoor for such a matrix and z the size of an element in $\mathbb{Z}_q$.

Scheme	Assumption	Loss	$\lvert\mathsf{sk}\rvert$	$\lvert\mathsf{pk}\rvert$	$\lvert\sigma\rvert$
GPV [29]	SIS	N	T	M	mz
Lyu [44]	SIS	$QN/\mathsf{Adv}_{\mathcal{A}}$	mn	$n^2z + M$	$\omega(\log \lambda) + mz$
DDLL [23]	SIS	$QN/\mathsf{Adv}_{\mathcal{A}}$	M	$mn + M$	$m + n + mz$
AFLT [2]	RLWE	N	$2nz$	nz	$3nz$
KLS [40]	MLWE	N	$2knz$	k^2nz	$3knz$
Ours (Fig. 6)	LWE	λ	$1 + T$	$4M$	$(4n + 2m)z$
Ours (full version)	LWE	1	$1 + T$	$2M$	$(2n^2 + 2nm)z$
Ours (full version)	LWE	1	$1 + T$	$2M$	$2n(M + T)$

We stress that our approach is more general than Diemert et al.. To show this, we implement our approach with isogenies. For readability, we present our scheme using the (general) Group Action Diffie-Hellman assumption, which captures the post-quantum secure isogeny-based assumption used in [24,54], Decisional CSIDH. We detail our technical approach and show how it improves the existing literature in Sect. 1.2. We will mostly focus on the lattice-based construction for simplicity.

LIMITATION OF PARALLEL OR PROOFS. Complementing these positive results, we show the advantage of sequential OR proofs by formally proving the limitation of its natural counterpart, parallel OR proofs of Cramer et al. [18], in constructing tightly secure signatures. More precisely, we prove that it is impossible to tightly turn an ID scheme into a MU-CMA-Corr secure signature using parallel OR proofs Cramer et al., if the underlying ID scheme satisfies some mild properties. We note that these properties are satisfied by many ID schemes, including the DDH-based lossy ID scheme [15]. We establish this impossibility result using meta-reduction techniques [1,7,17]. We note that our impossibility result does not apply to more generic but less efficient OR-proof-based tight construction in [6], since they use the OR-proof ideas in a different manner.

Our result is very different to the previous impossibility results [7,17,37,39] about tight signatures, and it enriches our understanding on constructing tight signature schemes. More precisely, Bader et al. [7] show that, if a signature scheme has signatures that are either unique or rerandomizable over the whole signature space, it will not have a tight reduction. Here we note that the work of Bader et al. [7] summarized results [17,37,39]. Clearly, signature schemes from parallel OR proofs are neither unique nor rerandomizable. Thus, their approach cannot be directly applied here, while our work is the *first* tightness impossibility result applicable to non-unique and non-rerandomizable signatures.

1.2 Technical Details

We provide more details about our generic construction of tightly MU-CMA-Corr secure signatures. Our generic construction has two steps: It first transforms a dual-mode commitment scheme to a lossy ID scheme, and then from a lossy ID scheme to a MU-CMA-Corr secure signature scheme via sequential OR proofs. Both steps are tight. Figure 1 gives an figurative overview of this framework.

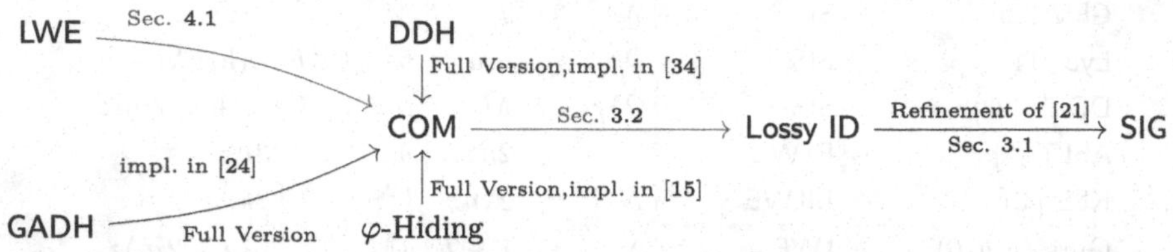

Fig. 1. Overview of our construction. All implications are tight. New implications are marked with red, and new implications that implicitly exist in previous work are marked with blue. The assumption GADH is a generic assumption about group actions, capturing isogeny-based assumptions. (Color figure online)

<u>Our Starting Point: The Diemert et al. (DGJL) Approach [21].</u> The DGJL approach transforms a lossy ID scheme into a tightly MU-CMA-Corr secure signature scheme using sequential OR proofs. A lossy ID scheme is a canonical three-move ID scheme (or, equivalently, a Σ protocol [19]). Additionally, a lossy ID scheme has two sets of public keys, lossy keys and normal ones. It requires that under a lossy public key even an unbounded adversary cannot impersonate an honest user. For tight MU-CMA-Corr security, the DGJL approach required that, given multiple keys of a lossy ID scheme, it is hard to tell whether they all are lossy or normal. This is a property can be tightly satisfied by the random self-reducibility of DDH- and φ-Hiding-based schemes in [15,34], but not the lattice-based ones. It is the main reason why their approach cannot be implemented from lattices. We call this property multi-key lossiness. Our main technical goal is to find a lattice-based lossy ID scheme with tight multi-key lossiness.

<u>From Dual-Mode Commitment to Lossy ID.</u> We take a closer look at the existing lattice-based lossy ID schemes, and they are based on the Ring-LWE [2] and Module-LWE [40] assumptions. To tightly achieve multi-key lossiness, we need the random self-reducibility (RSR) of these structured LWE assumptions. Unfortunately, it is not known how to rerandomize these structured LWE instances. We suppose this is inherent, since if the RSR was possible then the hardness of Ring-LWE would not depend on the number of samples in the current worst-case to average-case reduction [46]. However, for plain LWE assumption the number of samples does not influence security [13,27,50,52], i.e. we have RSR. Hence, we want to construct a lossy ID scheme based on the (plain) LWE

assumption. A natural direction is to take the idea of these Ring-LWE and Module-LWE schemes and implement them directly using the plain LWE assumption. We suppose this cannot work, since in these schemes the ring structure is crucial for proving lossiness[1].

Instead, our approach uses a dual-mode commitment scheme which can be constructed from the plain LWE assumption. Roughly speaking, a dual-mode commitment scheme has two indistinguishable modes, hiding and binding. In the hiding mode, there exists a (private) trapdoor that can open a commitment to any message. In the binding mode, a commitment can be opened to only one message, which is a statistical property and similar to public-key encryption.

Our high-level idea can be described in a simple manner: The commitment key is the public key of the lossy ID scheme. The hiding commitment key is the normal public key of our lossy ID scheme, and the binding commitment key is the lossy key. In the protocol, a prover P holds the commitment trapdoor and its first move to the verifier V is a random commitment. After that, V returns a random message and asks P to open the previous commitment to the given message. If P sends back a valid opening for that in the third move, V will accept.

The correctness is implied by the hiding mode of the commitment scheme. In the binding mode (which is the lossy mode of the ID scheme), a commitment can only be opened to only one message, and thus even an unbounded adversary cannot successfully complete the interaction, since our message space is exponentially large.

We modify the Regev encryption scheme [52] to construct this dual-mode commitment scheme. In particular, we are able to show that multiple hiding commitment keys are tightly indistinguishable from the binding ones, which implies tight multi-key lossiness of the resulting ID scheme. Interestingly, the resulting lossy ID scheme is the first lattice-based lossy ID scheme without using the rejection sampling technique [44].

Moreover, we show that many well-known lossy ID schemes [1,2,15,24,34] are obtained from dual-mode commitment schemes. In particular, we give a new analysis of the isogeny-based scheme in [24] to show that it is tightly multi-key lossy. It will give us the first tightly MU-CMA-Corr secure signature scheme from isogenies. We remark that this scheme is non-compact, since it requires parallel repetitions for soundness of the underlying ID scheme.

<u>FROM LOSSY ID TO SIGNATURES.</u> Equipped with our lattice-based lossy ID scheme, we can transform it to a tightly MU-CMA-Corr secure signature scheme using sequential OR proofs. We note that this cannot be done using parallel OR proofs by our impossibility result.

Our transformation follows the blueprint of the DGJL framework, but we adapt it to be suitable for our ID schemes. An important modification is our

[1] A trivial solution to argue lossiness with plain LWE is to have an ID scheme with single bit challenges, but that will result in a non-compact scheme with linear-size signatures, since for such an ID scheme we need to repeat $O(\lambda)$ times to get soundness (where λ is the security parameter).

transformation requires universal honest-verifier zero-knowledge (uHVZK) property of the underlying lossy ID, instead of injective simulators as in [21]. This is more natural, as lossy ID schemes from dual-mode commitments do not necessarily have an injective simulator, but uHVZK. Our work shows that injective simulator is not necessary for tight MU-CMA-Corr security, but uHVZK is enough. Further, in contrast to [21], we allow the lossy keys to be correlated, which is necessary for the analysis of the isogney-based scheme. Another (minor) adaptation is to tolerate correctness errors. This is a property which lattice-based constructions always have. Thus, our refinements make it possible to instantiate the DGJL framework based on a wider class of assumptions.

Similar to the DGJL framework, our security proof does not program the random oracle. Different to them, our resulting signature scheme does not have strong MU-CMA-Corr security, but it can be tightly turned into a strongly secure scheme using one-time signatures [45] and the known transformation [53].

OPEN PROBLEMS. We leave further improving the efficiency of our schemes as an open problem. Random oracles used in our proofs are classical, and it is an interesting direction to extend our approach in the quantum random oracle model, or even without random oracles. We also leave constructing tight and compact signatures from isogenies as an open problem.

2 Preliminaries

We denote the security parameter by $\lambda \in \mathbb{N}$. All algorithms will get 1^λ implicitly as input. A probabilistic algorithm $\mathcal{A}$ is said to be PPT (probabilistic polynomial time) if its running time $\mathbf{T}(\mathsf{A})$ can be bounded by a polynomial in its input size. We make use of standard asymptotic notation for positive functions such as ω and O. A function $\nu : \mathbb{N} \to \mathbb{R}$ is negligible in its input λ if $\nu \in \lambda^{-\omega(1)}$. The term $\mathsf{negl}(\lambda)$ always denotes a negligible function. If a function ν is at least $1 - \mathsf{negl}(\lambda)$, we say that it is overwhelming. If $\mathcal{D}$ is a distribution, we write $x \leftarrow \mathcal{D}$ to state that x is sampled from $\mathcal{D}$. If S is a finite set, the notation $x \stackrel{\$}{\leftarrow} S$ states that x is sampled uniformly random from S. The statistical distance of distributions $\mathcal{D}_1, \mathcal{D}_2$ on support $\mathcal{X}$ is defined as $\frac{1}{2}\sum_{x\in\mathcal{X}} |\Pr[\mathcal{D}_1 = x] - \Pr[\mathcal{D}_2 = x]|$. If it is negligible in λ, we say the distributions are statistically close. The notation $y \leftarrow \mathsf{A}(x)$ means that the variable y is assigned to the output of algorithm A on input x. Sometimes we make the randomness used by an algorithm explicit by writing $y = \mathsf{A}(x; r)$ if $r \in \{0,1\}^*$ is $\mathsf{A}'s$ randomness. If we want to state that y is a possible output of A on input x, we write $y \in \mathsf{A}(x)$. In all code-based security games, numerical values are assumed to be implicitly initialized as 0, sets and lists as $\emptyset$. If $\mathbf{G}$ is a game, we write $\mathbf{G}_\Pi^{\mathcal{A}}(1^\lambda) \Rightarrow b$ to state that the game $\mathbf{G}$ outputs $b \in \{0,1\}$ considering the adversary $\mathcal{A}$ and the scheme Π. Whenever we deal with statistically negligible terms, we denote them by Greek letters, e.g. $\varepsilon_{\mathcal{A}}$. For computationally negligible terms we use notation like $\mathsf{Adv}^{\mathsf{G}}_{\mathcal{A},\Pi}(\lambda)$. Throughout the paper, we always denote the number of users or keys in a scheme by N. We implicitly assume that it is bounded by a polynomial in the security parameter.

Matrices and (column) vectors are written in bold letters. The Euclidean norm of a vector $\mathbf{v}$ is denoted by $\|\mathbf{v}\|$, and the spectral norm of a matrix $\mathbf{A}$ is denoted by $s_1(\mathbf{A})$. By $[n] := \{1, \ldots, n\}$ we denote the set of the first n natural numbers.

We present the standard background on lattices in the full version.

COMMITMENT SCHEMES. A dual-mode commitment scheme is a commitment scheme with two indistinguishable key generation modes, inducing statistically binding and hiding commitments, respectively. Additionally, the latter mode outputs a trapdoor that allows to open commitments to arbitrary messages.

Definition 1 (Dual-Mode Commitment Scheme). *A dual-mode $(\varepsilon_\mathsf{b}, \varepsilon_\mathsf{t}, N)$-commitment scheme is a tuple of PPT algorithms* $\mathsf{CMT} = (\mathsf{Setup}, \mathsf{TSetup}, \mathsf{Gen}, \mathsf{TGen}, \mathsf{Com}, \mathsf{TCom}, \mathsf{Open}, \mathsf{TCol})$ *with the following syntax:*

- $\mathsf{Setup}(1^\lambda)$ *outputs global system parameters* par. *We assume that* par *implicitly defines sets* $\mathcal{K}, \mathcal{M}, \mathcal{C}, \mathcal{D}$ *of keys, messages, commitments and decommitments, respectively. All algorithms related to* CMT *take at least implicitly* par *as input.*
- $\mathsf{Gen}(\mathsf{par}, 1^N)$ *outputs* N *commitment keys* $\mathsf{ck}_1, \ldots, \mathsf{ck}_N \in \mathcal{K}$.
- $\mathsf{Com}(\mathsf{ck}, \mathsf{m})$ *outputs a commitment* $\mathsf{c} \in \mathcal{C}$ *and a decommitment* $\mathsf{dc} \in \mathcal{D}$.
- $\mathsf{Open}(\mathsf{ck}, \mathsf{m}, \mathsf{dc}, \mathsf{c})$ *is deterministic and outputs* $b \in \{0, 1\}$.
- TSetup *has the same output types as* Setup *and additionally implicitly defines a set* $\mathcal{T}$ *of trapdoors.*
- $\mathsf{TGen}(\mathsf{par})$ *outputs a commitment key* $\mathsf{ck} \in \mathcal{K}$ *and a trapdoor* $\mathsf{td} \in \mathcal{T}$.
- $\mathsf{TCom}(\mathsf{ck}, \mathsf{td})$ *outputs a commitment* $\mathsf{c} \in \mathcal{C}$ *and a state* St.
- $\mathsf{TCol}(\mathsf{ck}, \mathsf{td}, St, \mathsf{m})$ *outputs* $\mathsf{dc}' \in \mathcal{D}$.

We say that CMT *is* ρ*-complete if for all* $\mathsf{par} \in \mathsf{TSetup}(1^\lambda), (\mathsf{ck}, \mathsf{td}) \in \mathsf{TGen}(\mathsf{par}), \mathsf{m} \in \mathcal{M}$ *we have that* $\Pr\left[\mathsf{Open}(\mathsf{ck}, \mathsf{m}, \mathsf{dc}, \mathsf{c}) = 1 \mid (\mathsf{c}, \mathsf{dc}) \leftarrow \mathsf{Com}(\mathsf{ck}, \mathsf{m})\right] \geq \rho$.
Finally, the following security properties should hold:

- ***Key Indistinguishability:*** *The following advantage is negligible for all PPT algorithms* $\mathcal{A}$*:*

$$\mathsf{Adv}^{N\text{-keydist}}_{\mathcal{A},\mathsf{CMT}}(\lambda) :=$$
$$\left|\Pr\left[\mathcal{A}(\mathsf{par}, \mathsf{ck}_1, \ldots, \mathsf{ck}_N) = 1 \;\middle|\; \begin{array}{r}\mathsf{par} \leftarrow \mathsf{Setup}(1^\lambda),\\ (\mathsf{ck}_1, \ldots, \mathsf{ck}_N) \leftarrow \mathsf{Gen}(\mathsf{par}, 1^N)\end{array}\right]\right.$$
$$\left.-\Pr\left[\mathcal{A}(\mathsf{par}, \mathsf{ck}_1, \ldots, \mathsf{ck}_N) = 1 \;\middle|\; \begin{array}{r}\mathsf{par} \leftarrow \mathsf{TSetup}(1^\lambda),\\ (\mathsf{ck}_i, \mathsf{td}_i) \leftarrow \mathsf{TGen}(\mathsf{par}), i \in [N]\end{array}\right]\right|.$$

- ε_t*-**Trapdoor Property:*** *For all* $\mathsf{par} \in \mathsf{TSetup}(1^\lambda), (\mathsf{ck}, \mathsf{td}) \in \mathsf{TGen}(\mathsf{par}), \mathsf{m} \in \mathcal{M}$ *the following distributions have statistical distance at most* ε_t*:*

$$\{(\mathsf{c}, \mathsf{m}, \mathsf{dc}) \mid (\mathsf{c}, \mathsf{dc}) \leftarrow \mathsf{Com}(\mathsf{ck}, \mathsf{m})\}$$

and

$$\{(\mathsf{c}, \mathsf{m}, \mathsf{dc}) \mid (\mathsf{c}, St) \leftarrow \mathsf{TCom}(\mathsf{ck}, \mathsf{td}), \mathsf{dc} \leftarrow \mathsf{TCol}(\mathsf{ck}, \mathsf{td}, St, \mathsf{m})\}.$$

– (ε_b, N)-**Statistically Binding:** *The following probability is at most* ε_b:

$$\Pr\left[\exists i \in [N], c \in \mathcal{C}, m \neq m' \in \mathcal{M} : \begin{array}{l} \exists dc \in \mathcal{D} : \mathsf{Open}(\mathsf{ck}_i, m, dc, c) = 1 \\ \wedge \ \exists dc' \in \mathcal{D} : \mathsf{Open}(\mathsf{ck}_i, m', dc', c) = 1 \end{array}\right],$$

where the probability is taken over

$$\mathsf{par} \leftarrow \mathsf{Setup}(1^\lambda), (\mathsf{ck}_1, \ldots, \mathsf{ck}_N) \leftarrow \mathsf{Gen}(\mathsf{par}, 1^N).$$

SIGNATURE SCHEMES. We define the standard notion of signature schemes and their security.

Definition 2 (Digital Signature Scheme). *A signature scheme is a tuple of PPT algorithms* $\mathsf{SIG} = (\mathsf{Setup}, \mathsf{Gen}, \mathsf{Sig}, \mathsf{Ver})$, *where*

– $\mathsf{Setup}(1^\lambda)$ *outputs global system parameters* par. *We assume that* par *implicitly defines sets* $\mathcal{K}_p, \mathcal{K}_s, \mathcal{M}, \mathcal{S}$ *of public keys, secret keys, messages and signatures, respectively. All algorithms related to* SIG *take at least implicitly* par *as input.*
– $\mathsf{Gen}(\mathsf{par})$ *outputs public and secret key* $(\mathsf{pk}, \mathsf{sk}) \in \mathcal{K}_p \times \mathcal{K}_s$.
– $\mathsf{Sig}(\mathsf{sk}, m)$ *returns a signature* $\sigma \in \mathcal{S}$.
– $\mathsf{Ver}(\mathsf{pk}, m, \sigma)$ *is deterministic and returns* $b \in \{0, 1\}$.

We say that SIG *is* ρ-*complete, if for all* $\mathsf{par} \in \mathsf{Setup}(1^\lambda)$, *all* $(\mathsf{pk}, \mathsf{sk}) \in \mathsf{Gen}(\mathsf{par})$, *all* $m \in \mathcal{M}$ *we have* $\Pr[\mathsf{Ver}(\mathsf{pk}, m, \sigma) = 1 \mid \sigma \leftarrow \mathsf{Sig}(\mathsf{sk}, m)] \geq \rho$.

Definition 3 (Multi-user Security). *Consider a signature scheme* $\mathsf{SIG} = (\mathsf{Setup}, \mathsf{Gen}, \mathsf{Sig}, \mathsf{Ver})$, *let* $N \in \mathbb{N}$ *be a natural number and consider the game* N-**MU-CMA-Corr** *given in Fig. 2. We say that* SIG *is* N-**MU-CMA-Corr** *secure, if for every PPT adversary* $\mathcal{A}$ *the following advantage is negligible in* λ:

$$\mathsf{Adv}_{\mathcal{A},\mathsf{SIG}}^{N\text{-MU-CMA-Corr}}(\lambda) := \Pr\left[N\text{-}\mathbf{MU}\text{-}\mathbf{CMA}\text{-}\mathbf{Corr}_{\mathsf{SIG}}^{\mathcal{A}}(\lambda) \Rightarrow 1\right].$$

In addition, the notion N-**MU-CMA** *is defined similarly, but* $\mathcal{A}$ *does not get access to the oracle* KEY.

Game N-**MU-CMA-Corr**$_{\mathsf{SIG}}^{\mathcal{A}}(\lambda)$	**Oracle** KEY(i)
01 $\mathsf{par} \leftarrow \mathsf{Setup}(1^\lambda)$	08 $\mathcal{L}_{id} := \mathcal{L}_{id} \cup \{i\}$
02 **for** $i \in [N] : (\mathsf{pk}_i, \mathsf{sk}_i) \leftarrow \mathsf{Gen}(\mathsf{par})$	09 **return** sk_i
03 $O := (\mathsf{SIG}, \mathsf{KEY})$	
04 $(i^*, m^*, \sigma^*) \leftarrow \mathcal{A}^O(\mathsf{par}, (\mathsf{pk}_i)_{i=1}^N)$	**Oracle** SIG(i, m)
05 **if** $i^* \in \mathcal{L}_{id}$: **return** 0	10 $\sigma \leftarrow \mathsf{Sig}(\mathsf{sk}_i, m)$
06 **if** $\exists \sigma : (i^*, m^*, \sigma) \in \mathcal{L}_m$: **return** 0	11 $\mathcal{L}_m := \mathcal{L}_m \cup \{(i, m, \sigma)\}$
07 **return** $\mathsf{Ver}(\mathsf{pk}_{i^*}, m^*, \sigma^*)$	12 **return** σ

Fig. 2. The games **MU-CMA, MU-CMA-Corr** for a signature scheme SIG and an adversary $\mathcal{A}$. The shaded statement is only executed in game **MU-CMA-Corr**.

IDENTIFICATION SCHEMES. Here, we introduce identification schemes and their properties, where we extend the notions of [2, 40] to the multi-user setting.

Definition 4 (Canonical Identification Scheme). *A canonical identification scheme* ID *is defined as a tuple of PPT algorithms* $\mathsf{ID} := (\mathsf{ISetup}, \mathsf{IGen}, \mathsf{P} := (\mathsf{P}_1, \mathsf{P}_2), \mathsf{V})$, *with the following properties:*

- $\mathsf{ISetup}(1^\lambda)$ *outputs global system parameters* par. *We assume that* par *implicitly defines a set* ChSet, *the set of challenges and sets* $\mathsf{CmtSet}, \mathsf{RspSet}$. *All algorithms related to* ID *take at least implicitly* par *as input.*
- $\mathsf{IGen}(\mathsf{par})$ *returns public and secret key* $(\mathsf{pk}, \mathsf{sk})$.
- $\mathsf{P} := (\mathsf{P}_1, \mathsf{P}_2)$ *is split into two algorithms.* $\mathsf{P}_1(\mathsf{sk})$ *returns a commitment* $\mathsf{cmt} \in \mathsf{CmtSet}$ *and a state* St; $\mathsf{P}_2(\mathsf{sk}, \mathsf{ch}, St)$ *returns a response* $\mathsf{rs} \in \mathsf{RspSet}$.
- $\mathsf{V}(\mathsf{pk}, \mathsf{cmt}, \mathsf{ch}, \mathsf{rs})$ *is deterministic and outputs* $b \in \{0, 1\}$.

Given ID *as above, we define transcript generation as follows:*

Alg $\mathsf{Tran}(\mathsf{pk}, \mathsf{sk}, \mathsf{ch})$

$(\mathsf{cmt}, St) \leftarrow \mathsf{P}_1(\mathsf{sk}), \mathsf{rs} \leftarrow \mathsf{P}_2(\mathsf{sk}, \mathsf{ch}, St)$

if $\mathsf{rs} = \perp$: $(\mathsf{cmt}, \mathsf{ch}) = (\perp, \perp)$

return $(\mathsf{cmt}, \mathsf{ch}, \mathsf{rs})$

We say that ID *is* ρ*-complete, if for all* $\mathsf{par} \in \mathsf{ISetup}(1^\lambda)$, *all* $(\mathsf{pk}, \mathsf{sk}) \in \mathsf{IGen}(\mathsf{par})$ *we have*

$$\Pr\left[\mathsf{V}(\mathsf{pk}, \mathsf{cmt}, \mathsf{ch}, \mathsf{rs}) = 1 \;\middle|\; \begin{array}{c} \mathsf{ch} \xleftarrow{\$} \mathsf{ChSet} \\ (\mathsf{cmt}, \mathsf{ch}, \mathsf{rs}) \leftarrow \mathsf{Tran}(\mathsf{par}, \mathsf{pk}, \mathsf{sk}, \mathsf{ch}) \end{array}\right] \geq \rho.$$

From now on, without loss of generality, we assume that V *accepts an honestly generated transcript if and only if* $\mathsf{P}_2(\mathsf{sk}, \mathsf{ch}, St) \neq \perp$. *This can be assumed as the algorithm* P_2 *can call* V *to check the transcript itself before returning* rs.

For the following definitions, we let $\mathsf{ID} = (\mathsf{ISetup}, \mathsf{IGen}, \mathsf{P} = (\mathsf{P}_1, \mathsf{P}_2), \mathsf{V})$ be a canonical identification scheme.

Definition 5 (Special Honest Verifier Zero-Knowledge). *We say that* ID *is* $\varepsilon_{\mathsf{zk}}$*-special honest verifier zero-knowledge (HVZK) if there is a PPT algorithm* Sim *such that for all* $\mathsf{par} \in \mathsf{ISetup}(1^\lambda)$, *all* $(\mathsf{pk}, \mathsf{sk}) \in \mathsf{IGen}(\mathsf{par})$ *the following distributions have statistical distance at most* $\varepsilon_{\mathsf{zk}}$:

$$\{(\mathsf{cmt}, \mathsf{ch}, \mathsf{rs}) \leftarrow \mathsf{Tran}(\mathsf{pk}, \mathsf{sk}, \mathsf{ch}) \mid \mathsf{ch} \xleftarrow{\$} \mathsf{ChSet}\}$$

and

$$\{(\mathsf{cmt}, \mathsf{ch}, \mathsf{rs}) \mid \mathsf{ch} \xleftarrow{\$} \mathsf{ChSet}, (\mathsf{cmt}, \mathsf{rs}) \leftarrow \mathsf{Sim}(\mathsf{pk}, \mathsf{ch})\}.$$

We also introduce a slightly stronger version of HVZK, called universal special honest verifier zero-knowledge (uHVZK), where the distributions should be the same for every challenge. Clearly, uHVZK implies HVZK.

Definition 6 (Universal Special Honest Verifier Zero-Knowledge). *We say that* ID *is* $\varepsilon_{\mathsf{zk}}$*-universal special honest verifier zero-knowledge (uHVZK) if there is a PPT algorithm* Sim *such that for all* $\mathsf{par} \in \mathsf{ISetup}(1^\lambda)$, *all* $(\mathsf{pk}, \mathsf{sk}) \in \mathsf{IGen}(\mathsf{par})$ *and all* $\mathsf{ch} \in \mathsf{ChSet}$ *the following distributions have statistical distance at most* $\varepsilon_{\mathsf{zk}}$:

$$\{(\mathsf{cmt}, \mathsf{ch}, \mathsf{rs}) \leftarrow \mathsf{Tran}(\mathsf{pk}, \mathsf{sk}, \mathsf{ch})\} \text{ and } \{(\mathsf{cmt}, \mathsf{ch}, \mathsf{rs}) \mid (\mathsf{cmt}, \mathsf{rs}) \leftarrow \mathsf{Sim}(\mathsf{pk}, \mathsf{ch})\}.$$

Definition 7 (Multi-Key Lossiness). *Let N be a natural number. We say that* ID *is* $(\varepsilon_{\mathsf{mkl}}, N)$*-multi-key lossy, if there exists a PPT algorithm* LIGen *which takes the number of users* 1^N *as input and returns system parameters* par *and public keys* $\mathsf{pk}_1, \ldots, \mathsf{pk}_N$ *such that the following holds:*

- *For every PPT algorithm* $\mathcal{D}$*, the following advantage is negligible in* λ*:*

$$\mathsf{Adv}_{\mathcal{D},\mathsf{ID}}^{N\text{-keydist}}(\lambda) :=$$
$$\left| \Pr\left[\mathcal{D}(\mathsf{par}, \mathsf{pk}_1, \ldots, \mathsf{pk}_N) = 1 \,\middle|\, \begin{array}{c} \mathsf{par} \leftarrow \mathsf{ISetup}(1^\lambda) \\ (\mathsf{pk}_i, \mathsf{sk}_i) \leftarrow \mathsf{IGen}(\mathsf{par}), i \in [N] \end{array}\right]\right.$$
$$\left. - \Pr\left[\mathcal{D}(\mathsf{par}, \mathsf{pk}_1, \ldots, \mathsf{pk}_N) = 1 \,\middle|\, (\mathsf{par}, \mathsf{pk}_1, \ldots, \mathsf{pk}_N) \leftarrow \mathsf{LIGen}(1^N)\right] \right|.$$

- *The following inequality holds:*

$$\mathbb{E}\left[\max_{i \in [N]} \max_{\mathsf{cmt}} \Pr_{\mathsf{ch}}\left[\exists \mathsf{rs} \in \mathsf{RspSet} : \mathsf{V}(\mathsf{pk}_i, \mathsf{cmt}, \mathsf{ch}, \mathsf{rs}) = 1\right]\right] \le \varepsilon_{\mathsf{mkl}},$$

where we take the expectation, maximum and probability over

$$(\mathsf{par}, \mathsf{pk}_1, \ldots, \mathsf{pk}_N) \leftarrow \mathsf{LIGen}(1^N), \mathsf{cmt} \in \mathsf{CmtSet}, \mathsf{ch} \xleftarrow{\$} \mathsf{ChSet},$$

respectively. That is, if the keys are generated in this lossy way, for every unbounded adversary the advantage of successfully completing the protocol with respect to any user is bounded by $\varepsilon_{\mathsf{mkl}}$*.*

Note that N-multi-key lossiness for $N = 1$ is just lossiness as defined in [2].

Remark 1 (Correlation of Lossy Keys). Note that in our definition of multi-key lossiness, we define one algorithm that outputs N lossy keys, whereas the definition in [21] is with regards to N keys that are generated via N independent invocations of the lossy key generator. We claim that our definition is more general, as it also captures the possibility that the N lossy keys are somehow correlated. As long as the expectation in our definition is bounded, this correlation is not a problem. In fact, in some cases it is only possible to tightly achieve key indistinguishability if the lossy keys are correlated, see our instantiation from group actions in the full version.

3 Tight Signatures from Sequential or Proofs, Revisited

In this section we will generically construct a signature scheme with tight security in presence of adaptive corruptions. First, we show that sequential OR proofs can be used to construct signatures with this strong form of security from lossy identification schemes. Then, we introduce a new generic construction of lossy identification schemes from dual-mode commitments.

3.1 Generic Construction of Signatures in the Multi-user Setting

Let $\mathsf{ID} := (\mathsf{ISetup}, \mathsf{IGen}, \mathsf{P} := (\mathsf{P}_1, \mathsf{P}_2), \mathsf{V})$ be a canonical identification scheme with challenge set ChSet. We use $\ell \in \mathbb{N}$ to model multiple attempts to compute a signature for schemes with non-perfect completeness. Assuming that ID is uHVZK, we construct a signature scheme $\mathsf{SIG}_s[\mathsf{ID}, \mathsf{H}, \ell]$ with random oracle $\mathsf{H} : \{0,1\}^* \to \mathsf{ChSet}$ and message space $\{0,1\}^*$ using the sequential OR proof technique as defined in Fig. 3.

Intuitively, in the sequential OR proof signature, the challenge of one instance is computed as the hash of the commitment of the other instance. To break the circularity, the HVZK simulator is used on the instance for which the signer does not know a secret key. Note that the construction is a combination of the constructions in [2,25], in a sense that we combine the sequential OR proof from [25] with the lossy identification framework and the repetition as in [2]. Completeness is straight-forward.

Alg $\mathsf{Gen}(\mathsf{par})$	**Alg** $\mathsf{Sig}(\mathsf{sk}, m)$
01 $(\mathsf{pk}_0, \mathsf{sk}_0) \leftarrow \mathsf{IGen}(\mathsf{par})$	11 $ctr := 0$
02 $(\mathsf{pk}_1, \mathsf{sk}_1) \leftarrow \mathsf{IGen}(\mathsf{par})$	12 **while** $ctr \leq \ell \wedge (\mathsf{rs}_0 = \perp \vee \mathsf{rs}_1 = \perp)$:
03 $b \xleftarrow{\$} \{0,1\}, \mathsf{sk} := (b, \mathsf{sk}_b)$	13 $\quad ctr := ctr + 1$
04 $\mathsf{pk} := (\mathsf{pk}_0, \mathsf{pk}_1)$	14 $\quad (\mathsf{cmt}_b, St_b) \leftarrow \mathsf{P}_1(\mathsf{sk}_b)$
05 **return** $(\mathsf{pk}, \mathsf{sk})$	15 $\quad \mathsf{ch}_{1-b} \leftarrow \mathsf{H}(b, \mathsf{pk}, \mathsf{cmt}_b, m)$
	16 $\quad (\mathsf{cmt}_{1-b}, \mathsf{rs}_{1-b}) \leftarrow \mathsf{Sim}(\mathsf{pk}_{1-b}, \mathsf{ch}_{1-b})$
Alg $\mathsf{Ver}(\mathsf{pk}, m, \sigma)$	17 $\quad \mathsf{ch}_b \leftarrow \mathsf{H}(1 - b, \mathsf{pk}, \mathsf{cmt}_{1-b}, m)$
06 $\mathsf{ch}_1 \leftarrow \mathsf{H}(0, \mathsf{pk}, \mathsf{cmt}_0, m)$	18 $\quad \mathsf{rs}_b \leftarrow \mathsf{P}_2(\mathsf{sk}_b, \mathsf{ch}_b, St_b)$
07 $\mathsf{ch}_0 \leftarrow \mathsf{H}(1, \mathsf{pk}, \mathsf{cmt}_1, m)$	19 **if** $\mathsf{rs}_0 = \perp \vee \mathsf{rs}_1 = \perp$: **return** $\perp$
08 $v_0 \leftarrow \mathsf{V}(\mathsf{pk}_0, \mathsf{cmt}_0, \mathsf{ch}_0, \mathsf{rs}_0)$	20 **return** $\sigma := (\mathsf{cmt}_0, \mathsf{cmt}_1, \mathsf{rs}_0, \mathsf{rs}_1)$
09 $v_1 \leftarrow \mathsf{V}(\mathsf{pk}_1, \mathsf{cmt}_1, \mathsf{ch}_1, \mathsf{rs}_1)$	
10 **return** $(v_0 \wedge v_1)$	

Fig. 3. The signature scheme $\mathsf{SIG}_s[\mathsf{ID}, \mathsf{H}, \ell] = (\mathsf{Setup}, \mathsf{Gen}, \mathsf{Sig}, \mathsf{Ver})$ for a canonical identification scheme $\mathsf{ID} := (\mathsf{ISetup}, \mathsf{IGen}, \mathsf{P} := (\mathsf{P}_1, \mathsf{P}_2), \mathsf{V})$ with HVZK simulator Sim, where $\mathsf{Setup} := \mathsf{ISetup}$.

Theorem 1. *Let* ID *be a canonical identification scheme. If* ID *is* $\varepsilon_{\mathsf{zk}}$-*uHVZK and* $(\varepsilon_{\mathsf{mkl}}, N)$-*multi-key lossy for negligible* $\varepsilon_{\mathsf{zk}}, \varepsilon_{\mathsf{mkl}}$, *then* $\mathsf{SIG}_s[\mathsf{ID}, \mathsf{H}, \ell]$ *is* N-MU-CMA-$Corr$ *secure, with a tight reduction. More precisely, for any adversary* $\mathcal{A}$ *making at most* Q_S *signing queries,* Q_C *secret key queries and* Q_H *hash queries (including the indirect ones induced by signing queries), there exists an adversary* $\mathcal{D}$ *such that* $\mathbf{T}(\mathcal{D}) \approx \mathbf{T}(\mathcal{A})$ *and*

$$\mathsf{Adv}_{\mathcal{A}, \mathsf{SIG}_s[\mathsf{ID}, \mathsf{H}, \ell]}^{N\text{-}MU\text{-}CMA\text{-}Corr}(\lambda) \leq 2 \cdot \mathsf{Adv}_{\mathcal{D}, \mathsf{ID}}^{N\text{-}keydist}(\lambda) + 2 \cdot (Q_H + 2)^2 \cdot \varepsilon_{\mathsf{mkl}} + 3 \cdot \ell \cdot Q_S \cdot \varepsilon_{\mathsf{zk}}.$$

Due to space limitation and its similarities with [21] we postpone the proof to the full version.

Similar to the above result, we can show that the Fiat-Shamir transformation applied to a multi-key lossy identification scheme leads to a tightly secure signature scheme in the multi-user setting without corruptions. We postpone this result to the full version.

3.2 Generic Construction of Lossy Identification Schemes

In this section we show a relation between (multi-key) lossy identification schemes and dual-mode commitments. Note that it is well-known how to use canonical identification schemes to build standard commitment schemes [36]. This section shows that this can be used to understand lossy identification in a novel way. In combination with the result from the previous section, we obtain an N-MU-CMA-Corr secure signature scheme from a dual-mode commitment in a tight way. Let $\mathsf{CMT} = (\mathsf{Setup}, \mathsf{TSetup}, \mathsf{Gen}, \mathsf{TGen}, \mathsf{Com}, \mathsf{TCom}, \mathsf{Open}, \mathsf{TCol})$ be a dual-mode commitment with message space $\mathcal{M}$. We construct a canonical identification scheme $\mathsf{ID}[\mathsf{CMT}]$ in Fig. 4.

The intuition is that the prover sends a random commitment and is challenged with a random element from the message space. Then the prover needs to open the commitment for the challenge message. If the prover knows the trapdoor of the dual-mode commitment, this is no problem. On the other hand, if the commitment key is in binding mode, opening the commitment for the challenge message is infeasible.

Alg $\mathsf{LIGen}(1^N)$
- $\mathsf{par} \leftarrow \mathsf{Setup}(1^\lambda)$
- $(\mathsf{ck}_1, \ldots, \mathsf{ck}_N) \leftarrow \mathsf{Gen}(\mathsf{par}, 1^N)$
- **for** $i \in [N] : \mathsf{pk}_i := \mathsf{ck}_i$
- **return** $(\mathsf{par}, \mathsf{pk}_1, \ldots, \mathsf{pk}_N)$

Alg $\mathsf{P}_1(\mathsf{sk} = \mathsf{td})$
- $(\mathsf{c}, St) \leftarrow \mathsf{TCom}(\mathsf{pk}, \mathsf{sk})$
- **return** $(\mathsf{cmt} := \mathsf{c}, St)$

Alg $\mathsf{P}_2(\mathsf{sk}, \mathsf{ch}, St)$
- $\mathsf{dc} \leftarrow \mathsf{TCol}(\mathsf{pk}, \mathsf{sk}, St, \mathsf{ch})$
- **return** dc

Alg $\mathsf{V}(\mathsf{pk}, \mathsf{cmt}, \mathsf{ch}, \mathsf{rs})$
- $\mathsf{c} := \mathsf{cmt}, \mathsf{m} := \mathsf{ch}, \mathsf{dc} := \mathsf{rs}$
- **return** $\mathsf{Open}(\mathsf{pk}, \mathsf{m}, \mathsf{dc}, \mathsf{c})$

Alg $\mathsf{Sim}(\mathsf{pk}, \mathsf{ch})$
- $(\mathsf{c}, \mathsf{dc}) \leftarrow \mathsf{Com}(\mathsf{pk}, \mathsf{ch})$
- **return** $(\mathsf{cmt} := \mathsf{c}, \mathsf{rs} := \mathsf{dc})$

Fig. 4. The identification scheme $\mathsf{ID}[\mathsf{CMT}] = (\mathsf{ISetup} := \mathsf{TSetup}, \mathsf{IGen} := \mathsf{TGen}, \mathsf{P}, \mathsf{V})$ with challenge set $\mathsf{ChSet} := \mathcal{M}$ and related algorithms Sim, LIGen for a given dual-mode commitment $\mathsf{CMT} = (\mathsf{Setup}, \mathsf{TSetup}, \mathsf{Gen}, \mathsf{TGen}, \mathsf{Com}, \mathsf{TCom}, \mathsf{Open}, \mathsf{TCol})$ with message space $\mathcal{M}$.

Lemma 1 (uHVZK and Completeness). *If* CMT *is a* ρ*-complete dual-mode* $(\varepsilon_{\mathsf{bind}}, \varepsilon_{\mathsf{trap}}, N)$*-commitment scheme, then* $\mathsf{ID}[\mathsf{CMT}]$ *is* $\varepsilon_{\mathsf{zk}}$*-uHVZK and* ρ'*-complete, where* $\varepsilon_{\mathsf{zk}} \leq \varepsilon_{\mathsf{trap}}$ *and* $\rho' \geq \rho - \varepsilon_{\mathsf{trap}}$.

Proof. By definition of a dual-mode commitment scheme, the following distributions have statistical distance at most $\varepsilon_{\mathsf{trap}}$ for any $\mathsf{m} \in \mathcal{M}$:

$$\{(\mathsf{c}, \mathsf{m}, \mathsf{dc}) \mid (\mathsf{c}, \mathsf{dc}) \leftarrow \mathsf{Com}(\mathsf{ck}, \mathsf{m})\}$$

and

$$\{(\mathsf{c}, \mathsf{m}, \mathsf{dc}) \mid (\mathsf{c}, St) \leftarrow \mathsf{TCom}(\mathsf{ck}, \mathsf{td}), \mathsf{dc} \leftarrow \mathsf{TCol}(\mathsf{ck}, \mathsf{td}, St, \mathsf{m})\},$$

and the former is exactly the distribution output by Sim on input $\mathsf{ch} = \mathsf{m}$, and the latter is exactly the distribution of a real transcript using m as the challenge. The completeness of CMT now implies that V accepts a simulated transcript output by Sim with probability at least ρ. Thus, a real transcript will be accepted with probability at least $\rho - \varepsilon_{\mathsf{trap}}$, which finishes the proof. □

Lemma 2 (Multi-Key Lossiness). *If* CMT *is a dual-mode* $(\varepsilon_{\mathsf{bind}}, \varepsilon_{\mathsf{trap}}, N)$*-commitment scheme, then* $\mathsf{ID}[\mathsf{CMT}]$ *is* $(\varepsilon_{\mathsf{mkl}}, N)$*-multi-key lossy, where*

$$\varepsilon_{\mathsf{mkl}} \le \varepsilon_{\mathsf{bind}} + 1/|\mathcal{M}|.$$

In particular, for every PPT algorithm $\mathcal{A}$ *there exists a PPT algorithm* $\mathcal{B}$*, such that* $\mathbf{T}(\mathcal{B}) \approx \mathbf{T}(\mathcal{A})$ *and*

$$\mathsf{Adv}^{N\text{-keydist}}_{\mathcal{A},\mathsf{ID}[\mathsf{CMT}]}(\lambda) \le \mathsf{Adv}^{N\text{-keydist}}_{\mathcal{B},\mathsf{CMT}}(\lambda).$$

Proof. As $(\mathsf{ISetup}, \mathsf{IGen}) = (\mathsf{TSetup}, \mathsf{TGen})$ and LIGen combines the outputs of Setup and Gen, distinguishing lossy and honest keys of $\mathsf{ID}[\mathsf{CMT}]$ is exactly equivalent to distinguishing commitment keys generated via $\mathsf{Setup}, \mathsf{Gen}$ and $\mathsf{TSetup}, \mathsf{TGen}$. Thus, the reduction $\mathcal{B}$ is trivial. It remains to show the statement about $\varepsilon_{\mathsf{mkl}}$. To this end, let $(\mathsf{par}, \mathsf{pk}_1, \ldots, \mathsf{pk}_N) \leftarrow \mathsf{LIGen}(1^N)$, which is the same as writing

$$\mathsf{par} \leftarrow \mathsf{Setup}(1^\lambda), (\mathsf{ck}_1, \ldots, \mathsf{ck}_N) \leftarrow \mathsf{Gen}(\mathsf{par}, 1^N).$$

Define the event E of finding a collision for some $i \in [N]$ as

$$\begin{aligned}\mathsf{E} := (\exists i \in [N], \mathsf{c} \in \mathcal{C}, \mathsf{m}, \mathsf{m}' \in \mathcal{M}, \mathsf{dc}, \mathsf{dc}' \in \mathcal{D} :\\ \mathsf{m} \ne \mathsf{m}' \wedge \mathsf{Open}(\mathsf{ck}_i, \mathsf{m}, \mathsf{dc}, \mathsf{c}) = 1 \wedge \mathsf{Open}(\mathsf{ck}_i, \mathsf{m}', \mathsf{dc}', \mathsf{c}) = 1).\end{aligned}$$

By definition of the (multi-key) binding property, we know that $\Pr[\mathsf{E}] \le \varepsilon_{\mathsf{bind}}$. We can rewrite this event E in terms of $\mathsf{ID}[\mathsf{CMT}]$:

$$\begin{aligned}\exists i \in [N], \mathsf{cmt} \in \mathsf{CmtSet}, \mathsf{ch}, \mathsf{ch}' \in \mathsf{ChSet}, \mathsf{rs}, \mathsf{rs}' \in \mathsf{RspSet} :\\ \mathsf{ch} \ne \mathsf{ch}' \wedge \mathsf{V}(\mathsf{pk}_i, \mathsf{cmt}, \mathsf{ch}, \mathsf{rs}) = \mathsf{V}(\mathsf{pk}_i, \mathsf{cmt}, \mathsf{ch}', \mathsf{rs}') = 1.\end{aligned}$$

Define the random variable W as

$$\mathsf{W} := \max_{i \in [N]} \max_{\mathsf{cmt} \in \mathsf{CmtSet}} \Pr_{\mathsf{ch} \xleftarrow{\$} \mathsf{ChSet}} [\exists \mathsf{rs} \in \mathsf{RspSet} : \mathsf{V}(\mathsf{pk}_i, \mathsf{cmt}, \mathsf{ch}, \mathsf{rs}) = 1].$$

Then, note that $\neg\mathsf{E}$ implies that for any $i \in [N]$ and $\mathsf{cmt} \in \mathsf{CmtSet}$ there is at most one challenge such that there is a valid response for it (with respect to pk_i). Hence

$$\mathbb{E}[\mathsf{W} \mid \neg\mathsf{E}] \leq 1/|\mathcal{M}|.$$

To finish our proof, we need to bound the expectation of W:

$$\begin{aligned}\mathbb{E}[\mathsf{W}] = \mathbb{E}[\mathsf{W} \mid \mathsf{E}]\Pr[\mathsf{E}] + \mathbb{E}[\mathsf{W} \mid \neg\mathsf{E}]\Pr[\neg\mathsf{E}] &\leq 1 \cdot \varepsilon_{\mathsf{bind}} + \mathbb{E}[\mathsf{W} \mid \neg\mathsf{E}] \cdot 1\\ &\leq \varepsilon_{\mathsf{bind}} + 1/|\mathcal{M}|.\end{aligned}$$

□

4 Instantiations

In the previous sections we showed how to tightly transform any (multi-key) dual-mode commitment scheme into a signature scheme with security in presence of corruptions. We will now construct such dual-mode commitment schemes based on a variety of assumptions, including LWE and isogenies.

4.1 Instantiation Based on LWE

Our scheme $\mathsf{CMT}_{\mathsf{LWE}}$ based on the LWE assumption is presented in Fig. 5. It is inspired by the classical lattice cryptosystem by Regev [52] and its extension to multiple bits from [51]. It makes use of parameters $n, m \in \mathbb{N}$ and $q \in \mathbb{P}$ and a parameter $k \in \mathbb{N}, k \in \Theta(\lambda)$, as well as Gaussian widths $s_0, s > 0$. For the trapdoor algorithms (see [47][2]) to work, we need to ensure that

$$\begin{aligned}&m \geq 3(n+k)\lceil \log q \rceil\\ &s \geq C_1 \cdot \sqrt{s_0^2 C_0^2(\sqrt{m-w}+\sqrt{w})^2+1} \cdot \omega(\sqrt{\log(n+k)}),\end{aligned}$$

where $w = (n+k)\lceil \log q \rceil$. Additionally, we need a parameter $0 < \alpha < 1$ with $\alpha < 1/(4sm)$ and $\alpha q \geq 2\sqrt{n}$, which is used for setting up statistically binding keys.

Lemma 3 (Completeness, Trapdoor Property). *The scheme* $\mathsf{CMT}_{\mathsf{LWE}}$ *is* ρ*-complete and satisfies the* ε_{t}*-trapdoor property with* $\rho \geq 1 - \mathsf{negl}(\lambda)$ *and* $\varepsilon_{\mathsf{t}} \leq \mathsf{negl}(\lambda)$.

Proof. Let $(\mathsf{ck} = \mathbf{A}, \mathsf{td} = \mathbf{T_A}) \leftarrow \mathsf{TGen}(\mathsf{par})$. First, we show that commitments and decommitments generated using the trapdoor are accepted with overwhelming probability, then we show the trapdoor property. In combination, this also implies completeness.

First, let $(\mathbf{u}, St) \leftarrow \mathsf{TCom}(\mathsf{ck}, \mathsf{td}), \mathbf{m} \in \{0,1\}^k, \mathsf{TCol}(\mathsf{ck}, \mathsf{td}, St, \mathbf{m})$. The properties of $\mathsf{GenTrap}$ ensure that $\mathbf{A}$ is statistically close to uniform. By the definition

[2] For the exact statements we use, we refer to the full version of our paper.

Alg $\mathsf{TGen}(\mathsf{par})$

$(\mathbf{A}, \mathbf{T_A}) \leftarrow \mathsf{GenTrap}(1^{n+k}, 1^m, s_0, q)$

$\mathsf{ck} := \mathbf{A} \in \mathbb{Z}_q^{(n+k)\times m}, \mathsf{td} := \mathbf{T_A}$

return $(\mathsf{ck}, \mathsf{td})$

Alg $\mathsf{Gen}(\mathsf{par}, 1^N)$

$\bar{\mathbf{S}} \xleftarrow{\$} \mathbb{Z}_q^{n\times k}$

for $i \in [N]$:

$\quad \bar{\mathbf{A}}_i \xleftarrow{\$} \mathbb{Z}_q^{n\times m}, \bar{\mathbf{E}}_i \leftarrow D_{\mathbb{Z},\alpha q}^{m\times k}$

$\quad \mathsf{ck}_i := \mathbf{A}_i := \begin{bmatrix} \bar{\mathbf{A}}_i \\ \bar{\mathbf{S}}^t \bar{\mathbf{A}}_i + \bar{\mathbf{E}}_i^t \end{bmatrix}$

return $(\mathsf{ck}_1, \ldots, \mathsf{ck}_N)$

Alg $\mathsf{Com}(\mathsf{ck}, \mathbf{m})$

$\mathbf{z} \leftarrow D_{\mathbb{Z}^m,s}, \mathbf{u} := \mathbf{Az} + \begin{bmatrix} \mathbf{0} \\ \lfloor q/2 \rceil \cdot \mathbf{m} \end{bmatrix}$

if $\|\mathbf{z}\| > s \cdot \sqrt{m}$: **return** $\perp$

return $(\mathsf{c} := \mathbf{u}, \mathsf{dc} := \mathbf{z})$

Alg $\mathsf{TCom}(\mathsf{ck}, \mathsf{td})$

$\mathbf{u} \xleftarrow{\$} \mathbb{Z}_q^{n+k}$

return $(\mathbf{u}, St := \mathbf{u})$

Alg $\mathsf{TCol}(\mathsf{ck}, \mathsf{td}, St, \mathbf{m})$

$\mathbf{y} := \mathbf{u} - \begin{bmatrix} \mathbf{0} \\ \lfloor q/2 \rceil \cdot \mathbf{m} \end{bmatrix}$

$\mathbf{z} \leftarrow \mathsf{SampleD}(\mathbf{A}, \mathbf{T_A}, \mathbf{y}, s)$

if $\|\mathbf{z}\| > s \cdot \sqrt{m}$: **return** $\perp$

return $\mathbf{z}$

Alg $\mathsf{Open}(\mathsf{ck}, \mathbf{m}, \mathbf{z}, \mathbf{u})$

if $\|\mathbf{z}\| > s \cdot \sqrt{m}$: **return** 0

if $\mathbf{Az} + \begin{bmatrix} \mathbf{0} \\ \lfloor q/2 \rceil \cdot \mathbf{m} \end{bmatrix} \neq \mathbf{u}$:

$\quad$ **return** 0

return 1

Fig. 5. The dual-mode commitment $\mathsf{CMT_{LWE}} = (\mathsf{Setup}, \mathsf{TSetup}, \mathsf{Gen}, \mathsf{TGen}, \mathsf{Com}, \mathsf{TCom}, \mathsf{Open}, \mathsf{TCol})$ with message space $\mathcal{M} = \{0,1\}^k$, where $\mathsf{Setup} = \mathsf{TSetup}$ sets parameters par as in the text.

of algorithm TCol and algorithm $\mathsf{SampleD}$ we have that $\mathbf{z}$ is distributed statistically close to $D_{\Lambda_{\mathbf{y}}^{\perp}(\mathbf{A}),s}$, where $\mathbf{y} = \mathbf{u} - [\mathbf{0}^t | \lfloor q/2 \rceil \cdot \mathbf{m}^t]^t$. It follows by definition of $\Lambda_{\mathbf{y}}^{\perp}(\mathbf{A})$ that we have

$$\mathbf{Az} = \mathbf{y} = \mathbf{u} - \begin{bmatrix} \mathbf{0} \\ \lfloor q/2 \rceil \cdot \mathbf{m} \end{bmatrix} \Longrightarrow \mathbf{Az} + \begin{bmatrix} \mathbf{0} \\ \lfloor q/2 \rceil \cdot \mathbf{m} \end{bmatrix} = \mathbf{u},$$

and with overwhelming probability (see [28,48]) $\|\mathbf{z}\| \leq s \cdot \sqrt{m}$ (implying that the transcript is not $\perp$), which makes Open accept.

For the second part, note that the aborting condition $\|\mathbf{z}\| > s \cdot \sqrt{m}$ is given in Com and in the execution of $\mathsf{TCom}, \mathsf{TCol}$, hence we only have to show that for every $\mathbf{m}$ the distributions

$$\mathcal{D}_1 := \left\{ (\mathbf{u}, \mathbf{m}, \mathbf{z}) \,\middle|\, \mathbf{u} \xleftarrow{\$} \mathbb{Z}_q^{n+k}, \mathbf{z} \leftarrow \mathsf{SampleD}(\mathbf{A}, \mathbf{T_A}, \mathbf{u} - \begin{bmatrix} \mathbf{0} \\ \lfloor q/2 \rceil \cdot \mathbf{m} \end{bmatrix}, s) \right\}$$

and

$$\mathcal{D}_2 := \left\{ (\mathbf{u}, \mathbf{m}, \mathbf{z}) \,\middle|\, \mathbf{u} := \mathbf{Az} + \begin{bmatrix} \mathbf{0} \\ \lfloor q/2 \rceil \cdot \mathbf{m} \end{bmatrix}, \mathbf{z} \leftarrow D_{\mathbb{Z}^m,s} \right\}$$

are statistically close. Notice that in both distributions, $\mathbf{u}$ is uniquely determined by $\mathbf{m}$ and $\mathbf{y} := \mathbf{u} - [\mathbf{0}^t | \lfloor q/2 \rceil \cdot \mathbf{m}^t]^t$ and $\mathbf{y}$ by $\mathbf{m}$ and $\mathbf{u}$, which means we can instead bound the statistical distance between

$$\mathcal{D}_1' := \{ (\mathbf{y}, \mathbf{z}) \,|\, \mathbf{y} \xleftarrow{\$} \mathbb{Z}_q^{n+k}, \mathbf{z} \leftarrow \mathsf{SampleD}(\mathbf{A}, \mathbf{T_A}, \mathbf{y}, s) \}$$

and

$$\mathcal{D}_2' := \{(\mathbf{y}, \mathbf{z}) \,|\, \mathbf{y} := \mathbf{A}\mathbf{z}, \mathbf{z} \leftarrow D_{\mathbb{Z}^m,s}\}.$$

Standard lattice trapdoor techniques (see [28,48]) imply that these are statistically close, which finishes the proof. □

Lemma 4 (Key Indistinguishability). *Let $N = \mathsf{poly}(\lambda)$ be a natural number. Then $\mathsf{CMT_{LWE}}$ satisfies key indistinguishability, under the $\mathsf{LWE}_{n,q,D_{\mathbb{Z},\alpha q}}$ assumption, where for every PPT algorithm $\mathcal{A}$ there exists a PPT algorithm $\mathcal{B}$, such that $\mathbf{T}(\mathcal{B}) \approx \mathbf{T}(\mathcal{A})$ and*

$$\mathsf{Adv}^{N\text{-keydist}}_{\mathcal{A},\mathsf{CMT_{LWE}}}(\lambda) \leq k \cdot \mathsf{Adv}^{\mathsf{LWE}_{n,q,D_{\mathbb{Z},\alpha q}}}_{\mathcal{B}}(\lambda) + \mathsf{negl}(\lambda).$$

Due to space limitations, we postpone the proof to the full version.

Lemma 5 (Binding Property). *For any $N = \mathsf{poly}(\lambda)$ the scheme $\mathsf{CMT_{LWE}}$ is $(\varepsilon_{\mathsf{b}}, N)$-statistically binding, with $\varepsilon_{\mathsf{b}} \leq \mathsf{negl}(\lambda)$.*

Proof. Consider the random experiment

$$\mathsf{par} \leftarrow \mathsf{Setup}(1^\lambda), (\mathsf{ck}_1, \ldots, \mathsf{ck}_N) \leftarrow \mathsf{Gen}(\mathsf{par}, 1^N).$$

Fix some user $i \in [N]$ and some commitment $\mathbf{u}$. We show that with high probability, there is at most one challenge $\mathbf{m}$ for which there is a decommitment $\mathbf{z}$ that makes Open accept: Consider the matrix $\bar{\mathbf{S}} \in \mathbb{Z}_q^{n\times k}$ used in Gen and set $\mathbf{S} := [-\bar{\mathbf{S}}^t \mid \mathbf{I}_k] \in \mathbb{Z}_q^{k\times(n+k)}$. Then we have $\mathbf{S}\mathbf{A}_i = \bar{\mathbf{E}}_i^t$. Now consider accepting pairs $(\mathbf{u}, \mathbf{m}, \mathbf{z}), (\mathbf{u}, \mathbf{m}', \mathbf{z}')$ of commitment, message and decommitment and denote $\mathbf{A} := \mathbf{A}_i, \mathbf{E} := \bar{\mathbf{E}}_i$ for simplicity. Let $\mathbf{e}_j$ denote the j-th column of $\mathbf{E}$ for $j \in [k]$. By definition of Open, we have $\|\mathbf{z}\|, \|\mathbf{z}'\| \leq s\sqrt{m}$ and

$$\mathbf{A}\mathbf{z} + \begin{bmatrix} \mathbf{0} \\ \lfloor q/2 \rceil \cdot \mathbf{m} \end{bmatrix} = \mathbf{u} = \mathbf{A}\mathbf{z}' + \begin{bmatrix} \mathbf{0} \\ \lfloor q/2 \rceil \cdot \mathbf{m}' \end{bmatrix}.$$

Multiplying with $\mathbf{S}$ from the left this implies

$$\mathbf{E}^t\mathbf{z} + \lfloor q/2 \rceil \cdot \mathbf{m} = \mathbf{E}^t\mathbf{z}' + \lfloor q/2 \rceil \cdot \mathbf{m}' \Longrightarrow \lfloor q/2 \rceil \cdot \mathbf{m} - \lfloor q/2 \rceil \cdot \mathbf{m}' = \mathbf{E}^t(\mathbf{z}' - \mathbf{z}).$$

Looking at the absolute value of each coordinate $j \in [k]$ of this equality individually we see that

$$\{\lfloor q/2 \rceil, 0\} \ni \left|\lfloor q/2 \rceil \cdot m_j - \lfloor q/2 \rceil \cdot m_j'\right| = \left|\mathbf{e}_j^t(\mathbf{z}' - \mathbf{z})\right| \leq 2s\sqrt{m}\|\mathbf{e}_j\| \leq 2s\alpha q m,$$

where the last inequality holds with overwhelming probability, as $\mathbf{e}_j \leftarrow D^m_{\mathbb{Z},\alpha q}$. By our assumption $\alpha < 1/(4sm)$, this term is less than $q/2$, hence it is 0. This means that $m_j = m_j'$. In summary, we have that with overwhelming probability there is only one message $\mathbf{m}$ for which there exists a decommitment $\mathbf{z}$ that makes Open accept. This holds for any i and any $\mathbf{u}$ and the claim follows. □

To satisfy all the requirements of the previous analysis, we can set

$$k := n, \qquad m := 6n\lceil \log q \rceil, \qquad \alpha := \frac{1}{5C^*} m^{-3/2} \cdot \omega(\sqrt{\log n})^{-2},$$
$$4n^3 \leq q \leq n^4, \qquad s_0 = \omega(\sqrt{\log n}), \qquad s := C^* \cdot \sqrt{m} \cdot \omega(\sqrt{\log n})^2,$$

where $C^* := \sqrt{8} \cdot C_0 \cdot C_1$ is chosen such that s satisfies the requirement. Then especially the hardness of LWE is supported by worst-case to average case reductions, i.e. $\alpha q \geq 2\sqrt{n}$. Also, Bertrand's postulate implies that there is such a prime number q between $4n^3$ and $8n^3$, which is upper bounded by n^4 for all reasonable n.

Remark 2 (On Complete Tightness). Let us sketch two variants of turning the above ideas into a completely tight scheme. The first variant is to start with the single bit version of the above scheme, i.e. use $k = 1$. Unfortunately, with such a constant message space, the statement of Lemma 2 becomes useless and lossiness is not guaranteed anymore. The solution is to repeat $\Theta(n)$ many instances with the same key in parallel and to accept only if all of the instances accept. Then uHVZK can be seen for each instance independently and our message space is large enough to apply Lemma 2. The second variant is to use commitments resulting from [30,33] instead of the Regev-based construction we used here. In this variant a commitment for $\mathbf{x} \in \{0,1\}^k$ with decommitment $\mathbf{R}$ is $\mathbf{C} := \mathbf{AR} + \mathbf{x}^t \otimes \mathbf{G}$. It can be proven that this is also a dual-mode commitment scheme, using the same ideas we used here. We postpone a formal description of these variants to the full version.

We will now instantiate our generic construction in Sect. 3 with the dual-mode commitment scheme $\mathsf{CMT}_{\mathsf{LWE}}$. As it has negligible completeness error, $\ell = 1$ repetition of the sequential OR proof is sufficient. The final tightly N-MU-CMA-Corr secure signature scheme is presented in Fig. 6. Note that signatures contain a linear number of elements from $\mathbb{Z}_q$. The signature schemes based on the completely tight dual-mode commitments mentioned above are formally presented in the full version.

4.2 Instantiation Based on Isogenies

We show how to instantiate our approach in the isogeny setting. In [24] a lossy identification scheme is based on an isogeny assumption is presented. Our new analysis shows that this can be obtained from a dual-mode commitment scheme. More importantly, we are able to show tight multi-user security. Here, we use the subtle fact that our definition allows lossy keys to be correlated. Applying our approach leads to the first tightly MU-CMA-Corr secure signature scheme based on isogenies.

We can also show that the previously known lossy ID schemes [2,15,34,41] are concrete instantiations of our transformation in Sect. 3.2. Due to space limitations, we postpone these results to the full version.

Alg $\mathsf{Gen}(\mathsf{par})$

$(\mathbf{A}_0, \mathbf{T}_0) \leftarrow \mathsf{GenTrap}(1^{2n}, 1^m, s_0, q)$
$(\mathbf{A}_1, \mathbf{T}_1) \leftarrow \mathsf{GenTrap}(1^{2n}, 1^m, s_0, q)$
$b \stackrel{\$}{\leftarrow} \{0,1\}, \mathsf{sk} := (b, \mathbf{T}_b)$
$\mathsf{pk} := (\mathbf{A}_0, \mathbf{A}_1)$
return $(\mathsf{pk}, \mathsf{sk})$

Alg $\mathsf{Ver}(\mathsf{pk}, \mathsf{m}, \sigma = (\mathbf{u}_0, \mathbf{u}_1, \mathbf{z}_0, \mathbf{z}_1))$

$\mathbf{m}_1 \leftarrow \mathsf{H}(0, \mathsf{pk}, \mathbf{u}_0, \mathsf{m})$
$\mathbf{m}_0 \leftarrow \mathsf{H}(1, \mathsf{pk}, \mathbf{u}_1, \mathsf{m})$
if $\|\mathbf{z}_0\| > s \cdot \sqrt{m}$: **return** 0
if $\|\mathbf{z}_1\| > s \cdot \sqrt{m}$: **return** 0
if $\mathbf{A}_0\mathbf{z}_0 + \begin{bmatrix} \mathbf{0} \\ \lfloor q/2 \rceil \cdot \mathbf{m}_0 \end{bmatrix} \neq \mathbf{u}_0$:
  return 0
if $\mathbf{A}_1\mathbf{z}_1 + \begin{bmatrix} \mathbf{0} \\ \lfloor q/2 \rceil \cdot \mathbf{m}_1 \end{bmatrix} \neq \mathbf{u}_1$:
  return 0
return 1

Alg $\mathsf{Sig}(\mathsf{sk}, \mathsf{m})$

let $\sigma = (b, \mathbf{T}_b)$
$\mathbf{u}_b \stackrel{\$}{\leftarrow} \mathbb{Z}_q^{2n}$
$\mathbf{m}_{1-b} \leftarrow \mathsf{H}(b, \mathsf{pk}, \mathbf{u}_b, \mathsf{m})$
$\mathbf{z}_{1-b} \leftarrow D_{\mathbb{Z}^m, s}$
$\mathbf{u}_{1-b} := \mathbf{A}_{1-b}\mathbf{z}_{1-b} + \begin{bmatrix} \mathbf{0} \\ \lfloor q/2 \rceil \cdot \mathbf{m}_{1-b} \end{bmatrix}$
$\mathbf{m}_b \leftarrow \mathsf{H}(1-b, \mathsf{pk}, \mathbf{u}_{1-b}, \mathsf{m})$
$\mathbf{y}_b := \mathbf{u}_b - \begin{bmatrix} \mathbf{0} \\ \lfloor q/2 \rceil \cdot \mathbf{m}_b \end{bmatrix}$
$\mathbf{z}_b \leftarrow \mathsf{SampleD}(\mathbf{A}_b, \mathbf{T}_b, \mathbf{y}_b, s)$
if $\|\mathbf{z}_0\| > s \cdot \sqrt{m}$: **return** $\perp$
if $\|\mathbf{z}_1\| > s \cdot \sqrt{m}$: **return** $\perp$
return $\sigma := (\mathbf{u}_0, \mathbf{u}_1, \mathbf{z}_0, \mathbf{z}_1)$

Fig. 6. The signature scheme $\mathsf{SIG}_s[\mathsf{ID}[\mathsf{CMT}_{\mathsf{LWE}}], \mathsf{H}, 1] = (\mathsf{Setup}, \mathsf{Gen}, \mathsf{Sig}, \mathsf{Ver})$, where Setup sets parameters as in Sect. 4.1.

5 Impossibility Result for Parallel or Proofs

In this section, we consider a canonical identification scheme $\mathsf{ID} = (\mathsf{ISetup}, \mathsf{IGen}, \mathsf{P} := (\mathsf{P}_1, \mathsf{P}_2), \mathsf{V})$ with challenge set ChSet and a random oracle $\mathsf{H} : \{0,1\}^* \to \mathsf{ChSet}$. Recall that sequential OR proofs can be used to construct MU-CMA-Corr secure signatures in a tight way (see the previous sections). Here, we show that a similar tight result for parallel OR proofs $\mathsf{SIG}_p[\mathsf{ID}, \mathsf{H}]$ defined in Fig. 7 is unlikely. For simplicity, we assume perfect completeness and hence only $l = 1$ repetition of the signing procedure. We will consider reductions without rewinding that use the adversary as a black box. First, we fix an intermediate security notion and the assumptions about the underlying identification scheme. After that we state and prove our impossibility result.

SECURITY NOTIONS AND ASSUMPTIONS. We will now define a security notion for digital signature scheme, which is weaker than N-MU-CMA-Corr security. Here, the adversary can only corrupt statically and can not ask for signatures. To be more precise, for a given signature scheme, the security game picks N (distinct) public keys pk_i and corresponding secret keys sk_i and sends all public keys to the adversary. Then the adversary can pick an index $j \in [N]$ and gets all sk_i, except sk_j from the game. Finally, the adversary has to return a valid forgery (m^*, σ^*) for pk_j. Note that there is a straightforward tight reduction, showing that if SIG is N-MU-CMA-Corr secure, then it is also N-MU-CMA-S secure. Thus, to prove that there is no tight proof of N-MU-CMA-Corr security of a signature scheme SIG, it is sufficient to show the same for N-MU-CMA-S security.

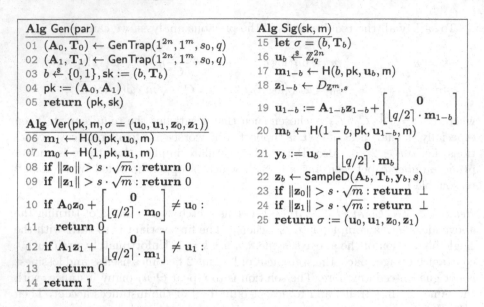

Alg $\mathsf{Gen}(\mathsf{par})$

$(\mathsf{pk}_0, \mathsf{sk}_0) \leftarrow \mathsf{IGen}(\mathsf{par})$
$(\mathsf{pk}_1, \mathsf{sk}_1) \leftarrow \mathsf{IGen}(\mathsf{par})$
$b \xleftarrow{\$} \{0,1\}, \mathsf{sk} := (b, \mathsf{sk}_b)$
return $(\mathsf{pk} := (\mathsf{pk}_0, \mathsf{pk}_1), \mathsf{sk})$

Alg $\mathsf{Ver}(\mathsf{pk}, \mathsf{m}, \sigma)$

$\mathsf{ch} \leftarrow \mathsf{H}(\mathsf{pk}, \mathsf{cmt}_0, \mathsf{cmt}_1, \mathsf{m})$
if $\mathsf{ch}_0 \oplus \mathsf{ch}_1 \neq \mathsf{ch}$: **return** 0
$v_0 \leftarrow \mathsf{V}(\mathsf{pk}_0, \mathsf{cmt}_0, \mathsf{ch}_0, \mathsf{rs}_0)$
$v_1 \leftarrow \mathsf{V}(\mathsf{pk}_1, \mathsf{cmt}_1, \mathsf{ch}_1, \mathsf{rs}_1)$
return $(v_0 \wedge v_1)$

Alg $\mathsf{Sig}(\mathsf{sk}, \mathsf{m})$

$(\mathsf{cmt}_b, St_b) \leftarrow \mathsf{P}_1(\mathsf{par}, \mathsf{sk}_b)$
$\mathsf{ch}_{1-b} \xleftarrow{\$} \mathsf{ChSet}$
$(\mathsf{cmt}_{1-b}, \mathsf{rs}_{1-b}) \leftarrow \mathsf{Sim}(\mathsf{pk}_{1-b}, \mathsf{ch}_{1-b})$
$\mathsf{ch} \leftarrow \mathsf{H}(\mathsf{pk}, \mathsf{cmt}_0, \mathsf{cmt}_1, \mathsf{m})$
$\mathsf{ch}_b := \mathsf{ch} \oplus \mathsf{ch}_{1-b}$
$\mathsf{rs}_b \leftarrow \mathsf{P}_2(\mathsf{sk}_b, \mathsf{ch}_b, St_b)$
if $\mathsf{rs}_0 = \perp \vee \mathsf{rs}_1 = \perp$: **return** $\perp$
$\sigma := (\mathsf{cmt}_0, \mathsf{cmt}_1, \mathsf{ch}_0, \mathsf{ch}_1, \mathsf{rs}_0, \mathsf{rs}_1)$
return σ

Fig. 7. The signature scheme $\mathsf{SIG}_p[\mathsf{ID}, \mathsf{H}] = (\mathsf{Setup}, \mathsf{Gen}, \mathsf{Sig}, \mathsf{Ver})$ for a canonical identification scheme $\mathsf{ID} := (\mathsf{ISetup}, \mathsf{IGen}, \mathsf{P} := (\mathsf{P}_1, \mathsf{P}_2), \mathsf{V})$ with HVZK simulator Sim, where $\mathsf{Setup} := \mathsf{ISetup}$.

Game N-**MU-CMA-S**$^{\mathcal{A}}_{\mathsf{SIG}}(\lambda)$

$\mathsf{par} \leftarrow \mathsf{Setup}(1^\lambda)$
for $i \in [N]$: $(\mathsf{pk}_i, \mathsf{sk}_i) \leftarrow \mathsf{Gen}(\mathsf{par})$ // Assume pk_i's pairwise distinct
$(j, St_{\mathcal{A}}) \leftarrow \mathcal{A}_1(\mathsf{par}, (\mathsf{pk}_i)_{i \in [N]})$
if $j \notin [N]$: **return** 0
$(\mathsf{m}^*, \sigma^*) \leftarrow \mathcal{A}_2(St_{\mathcal{A}}, (\mathsf{sk}_i)_{i \in [N] \setminus \{j\}})$
return $\mathsf{Ver}(\mathsf{pk}_j, \mathsf{m}^*, \sigma^*)$

Fig. 8. Game **MU-CMA-S** for a signature scheme $\mathsf{SIG} = (\mathsf{Setup}, \mathsf{Gen}, \mathsf{Sig}, \mathsf{Ver})$, used in the proof of the impossibility result in Sect. 5. We assume that the keys $\mathsf{pk}_1, \ldots, \mathsf{pk}_N$ are pairwise distinct.

Definition 8 (Static Multi-user Security). *Let* $\mathsf{SIG} = (\mathsf{Setup}, \mathsf{Gen}, \mathsf{Sig}, \mathsf{Ver})$ *be a signature scheme and* $N \in \mathbb{N}$ *be a natural number. Consider the game* **MU-CMA-S** *given in Fig. 8. We say that* SIG *is* N-MU-CMA-S *secure, if for every PPT adversary* $\mathcal{A} = (\mathcal{A}_1, \mathcal{A}_2)$ *the following advantage is negligible in* λ*:*

$$\mathsf{Adv}^{N\text{-}\mathsf{MU}\text{-}\mathsf{CMA}\text{-}\mathsf{S}}_{\mathcal{A},\mathsf{SIG}}(\lambda) := \Pr\left[N\text{-}\mathbf{MU}\text{-}\mathbf{CMA}\text{-}\mathbf{S}^{\mathcal{A}}_{\mathsf{SIG}}(\lambda) \Rightarrow 1\right].$$

Next, we define some properties the underlying identification scheme ID should have, in order to apply our impossibility result. These are similar to the ones defined in [7]. However, in our case they need to hold for the underlying identification scheme and not for the resulting signature scheme as it would be required for applying the result of [7] directly. For the rest of the section, we denote the set of secret keys for a given public key pk with respect to some parameters par, which should be clear from the context, of an identification scheme by $\mathcal{SK}(\mathsf{pk})$. More formally $\mathcal{SK}(\mathsf{pk}) := \{\mathsf{sk} \mid (\mathsf{pk}, \mathsf{sk}) \in \mathsf{IGen}(\mathsf{par})\}$.

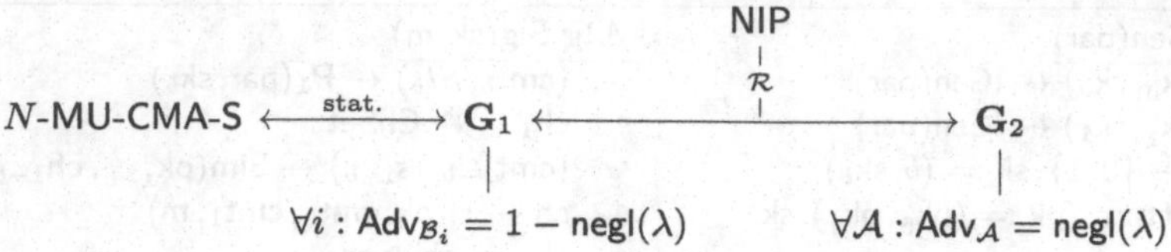

Fig. 9. Overview of a typical cryptographic proof, summarized by two games $\mathbf{G}_1, \mathbf{G}_2$, where $\mathbf{G}_1$ is statistically close to the real game. Here, a reduction $\mathcal{R}$ to the problem NIP is used to interpolate between the games. We will show meta-reductions $\mathcal{B}_i$, that have a high advantage in $\mathbf{G}_1$, whereas every adversary has negligible advantage in $\mathbf{G}_2$.

Definition 9 (Verifiability). *Let* $\mathsf{ID} = (\mathsf{ISetup}, \mathsf{IGen}, \mathsf{P}, \mathsf{V})$ *be a canonical identification scheme. We say that* ID *is parameter-verifiable if there is a deterministic polynomial time algorithm* VerP *such that for all* par*:*

$$\mathsf{VerP}(\mathsf{par}) = 1 \iff \mathsf{par} \in \mathsf{ISetup}(1^\lambda).$$

Further, we say that ID *is key-verifiable if there is a deterministic polynomial time algorithm* VerK *such that for all* $\mathsf{par} \in \mathsf{ISetup}(1^\lambda)$ *and* pk, sk*:*

$$\mathsf{VerK}(\mathsf{par}, \mathsf{pk}, \mathsf{sk}) = 1 \iff (\mathsf{pk}, \mathsf{sk}) \in \mathsf{IGen}(\mathsf{par}).$$

Definition 10 (Key-Rerandomization). *Let* $\mathsf{ID} = (\mathsf{ISetup}, \mathsf{IGen}, \mathsf{P}, \mathsf{V})$ *be a canonical identification scheme. We say that* ID *is key-rerandomizable if there is a PPT algorithm* RerandK *such that for all* $\mathsf{par} \in \mathsf{ISetup}(1^\lambda)$ *and all* $(\mathsf{pk}, \mathsf{sk}) \in \mathsf{IGen}(\mathsf{par})$ *the key* $\mathsf{sk}' \leftarrow \mathsf{RerandK}(\mathsf{par}, \mathsf{pk}, \mathsf{sk})$ *is distributed uniformly over* $\mathcal{SK}(\mathsf{pk})$.

We note that these properties are quite natural and are satisfied for example by the Chaum-Pedersen (CP) lossy identification scheme [15], which is easy to see.

Example 1. The parameters of the CP scheme are the description of a cyclic group $\mathbb{G}$ of prime order p and two generators $g_1, g_2 \in \mathbb{G}$. To check the validity of these parameters, one simply has to check that g_1 and g_2 are not the identity element and that p is prime. Hence, CP is parameter-verifiable. The secret key is a single exponent $x \in \mathbb{Z}_p$, sampled uniformly at random, and the public key is $(X, Y) := (g_1^x, g_2^x)$. Given x, g_1, g_2, X, Y it is trivial to check if this relation is satisfied, showing key-verifiability. Moreover, such an x is unique for given X, Y, g_1, g_2, which implies that CP is also key-rerandomizable.

Reduction Syntax. Before defining reductions, we need to define the undelying problem, where we follow the notation in [3,7].

Definition 11 (Non-Interactive Problem). *A non-interactive computational problem is a triple of algorithms* $\mathsf{NIP} = (\mathsf{T}, \mathsf{V}, \mathsf{U})$, *where*

- $\mathsf{T}(1^\lambda)$ *takes the security parameter as input and outputs an instance* c *and a witness* w.

Alg $\mathcal{R}^{\mathcal{A}}(c)$ // **Simulate MU-CMA-S**
$\rho_{\mathcal{R}} \xleftarrow{\$} \{0,1\}^z$
$(St_{\mathcal{R}}, \mathsf{par}, (\mathsf{pk}_i)_{i\in[N]}) \leftarrow \mathcal{R}_1(c; \rho_{\mathcal{R}})$
$(j, St_{\mathcal{A}}) \leftarrow \mathcal{A}_1^{\mathsf{H}}(\mathsf{par}, (\mathsf{pk}_i)_{i\in[N]})$
$(St_{\mathcal{R}}, (\mathsf{sk}_i)_{i\in[N]\setminus\{j\}}) \leftarrow \mathcal{R}_2(St_{\mathcal{R}}, j)$
$(\mathsf{m}^*, \sigma^*) \leftarrow \mathcal{A}_2^{\mathsf{H}}(St_{\mathcal{A}}, (\mathsf{sk}_i)_{i\in[N]\setminus\{j\}})$
return $\mathcal{R}_3(St_{\mathcal{R}}, j, \mathsf{m}^*, \sigma^*)$

Oracle $\mathsf{H}(\mathsf{query})$
$(St_{\mathcal{R}}, h) \leftarrow \mathcal{R}_{RO}(St_{\mathcal{R}}, \mathsf{query})$
return h

Fig. 10. Syntax of a simple reduction $\mathcal{R} = (\mathcal{R}_1, \mathcal{R}_2, \mathcal{R}_3, \mathcal{R}_{RO})$ in an execution with an adversary $\mathcal{A} = (\mathcal{A}_1, \mathcal{A}_2)$, used in the proof of the impossibility result in Sect. 5. Here, $\mathcal{R}$ simulates the game N-**MU-CMA-S**$_{\mathsf{SIG}}^{\mathcal{A}}$ for $\mathcal{A}$.

- $\mathsf{U}(c)$ *takes an instance* c *as input and outputs a candidate solution* s.
- $\mathsf{V}(c, w, s)$ *takes an instance* c*, a witness* w *and a candidate solution* s *as input and outputs a bit* $b \in \{0,1\}$.

For any algorithm $\mathcal{A}$ *taking* z *bits of randomness, we define the advantage*

$$\begin{aligned}\mathsf{Adv}_{\mathcal{A}}^{\mathsf{NIP}}(\lambda) := |&\Pr\left[\mathsf{V}(c, w, s) = 1 \mid (c, w) \leftarrow \mathsf{T}(1^\lambda), \rho_{\mathcal{A}} \leftarrow \{0,1\}^z, s \leftarrow \mathcal{A}(c; \rho_{\mathcal{A}})\right] \\ &-\Pr\left[\mathsf{V}(c, w, s) = 1 \mid (c, w) \leftarrow \mathsf{T}(1^\lambda), \rho_{\mathsf{U}} \leftarrow \{0,1\}^z, s \leftarrow \mathsf{U}(c; \rho_{\mathsf{U}})\right]|.\end{aligned}$$

Before we formally define simple reductions, we make a convention about cryptographic proofs. A proof can be presented as a sequence of games $\mathbf{G}_i$, where typically $\mathbf{G}_0$ is the original security game and $\mathbf{G}_{i+1}$ results from $\mathbf{G}_i$ by making small changes. In the final game it will be clear that the advantage of an adversary is negligible. If one can show that in every step, changing the game only changes the advantage of the adversary by a negligible amount, the proof is complete. This is shown in one of two ways: Either, one can argue that two subsequent games look statistically close to the adversary, or one uses a reduction that interpolates between the games to show that the advantages are close under some computational assumption. Clearly, we can summarize all the steps into one initial statistical step and one computational step using a reduction $\mathcal{R}$, as it is presented in Fig. 9. Note that this also captures reductions to search problems, as one can always define the final game to reject everything. The reduction solves the computational problem whenever the difference between the advantages in $\mathbf{G}_1$ and $\mathbf{G}_2$ is non-negligible. This means that, when we analyze the advantage of adversaries or meta-reductions, we can focus on $\mathbf{G}_1$, as every (even unbounded) adversary has negligible advantage in $\mathbf{G}_2$. Hence, in our analysis we only have to deal with the case where $\mathcal{R}$'s simulation is statistically close to the real game. With this convention in mind, we can now move towards the definition.

Definition 12 (Simple Reduction). *Let* NIP *be a non-interactive computational problem and* SIG *be a signature scheme. A simple* (NIP, SIG)*-reduction* $\mathcal{R}$ *is an algorithm against* NIP *that has one-time black box-access to an adversary* $\mathcal{A} = (\mathcal{A}_1, \mathcal{A}_2)$ *against the* N-MU-CMA-S *security of* SIG*. In this case,* $\mathcal{R}$ *can be represented by four algorithms* $(\mathcal{R}_1, \mathcal{R}_2, \mathcal{R}_3, \mathcal{R}_{RO})$*, where* $\mathcal{R}_2, \mathcal{R}_3, \mathcal{R}_{RO}$ *are deterministic polynomial time algorithms and* $\mathcal{R}_1$ *is PPT, such that*

- $\mathcal{R}_1(c)$ *takes as input a* NIP *challenge* c *and outputs a state, parameters and public keys* $(St_{\mathcal{R}}, \mathsf{par}, (\mathsf{pk}_i)_{i\in[N]})$.
- $\mathcal{R}_2(St_{\mathcal{R}}, j)$ *takes as input a state* $St_{\mathcal{R}}$ *and an index* $j \in [N]$ *and outputs a new state and secret keys* $(St_{\mathcal{R}}, (\mathsf{sk}_i)_{i\in[N]\setminus\{j\}})$.
- $\mathcal{R}_3(St_{\mathcal{R}}, j, \mathsf{m}^*, \sigma^*)$ *takes as input a state, an index* $j \in [N]$*, a message* m^* *and a signature* σ^* *and outputs a* NIP *solution* s.
- $\mathcal{R}_{RO}(St_{\mathcal{R}}, \mathsf{query})$ *takes as input a state* $St_{\mathcal{R}}$ *and a random oracle query* query *and outputs a new state and a hash value* $(St_{\mathcal{R}}, h)$.

The joint execution of $\mathcal{R}$ *with adversary* $\mathcal{A}$ *is formally given in Fig. 10. We say that* $\mathcal{R}$ *is* $(N, \delta_{\mathcal{R}}, L)$*-simple, if* $\mathcal{R}$*'s simulation has statistical distance at most* $\delta_{\mathcal{R}}$ *from the game* **MU-CMA-S** *and for all* $\mathcal{A}$ *as above, it holds that*

$$\mathsf{Adv}^{\mathsf{NIP}}_{\mathcal{R}^{\mathcal{A}}}(\lambda) \geq L(\lambda, N, \mathsf{Adv}^{N\text{-}\mathsf{MU\text{-}CMA\text{-}S}}_{\mathcal{A},\mathsf{SIG}}(\lambda)).$$

Note that in our definition we can assume that $\mathcal{R}_1$ is the only probabilistic part of the reduction as it can save random coins for $\mathcal{R}_2, \mathcal{R}_3, \mathcal{R}_{RO}$ in the state $St_{\mathcal{R}}$.

<u>Our Impossibility Result.</u> We formalize and prove our impossibility result.

Theorem 2. *Let* ID *be a canonical identification scheme, which is* $\varepsilon_{\mathsf{zk}}$*-HVZK, parameter-verifiable, key-verifiable and key-rerandomizable. Define the signature scheme* $\mathsf{SIG} := \mathsf{SIG}_p[\mathsf{ID}, \mathsf{H}]$*. Then for every* $(N, \delta_{\mathcal{R}}, L)$*-simple* $(\mathsf{NIP}, \mathsf{SIG})$*-reduction* $\mathcal{R} = (\mathcal{R}_1, \mathcal{R}_2, \mathcal{R}_3, \mathcal{R}_{RO})$ *there is an algorithm* $\mathcal{B}$ *such that*

$$\mathsf{Adv}^{\mathsf{NIP}}_{\mathcal{B}}(\lambda) \geq L(\lambda, N, 1) - 2(\delta_{\mathcal{R}} + \varepsilon_{\mathsf{zk}}) - 1/N$$

and $\mathbf{T}(\mathcal{B}) \leq N \cdot \mathbf{T}(\mathcal{R}) + N(N-1)\mathbf{T}(\mathsf{VerK}) + \mathbf{T}(\mathsf{VerP}) + \mathbf{T}(\mathsf{RerandK}) + \mathbf{T}(\mathsf{Sig})$.

Proof. Let $\mathcal{R} = (\mathcal{R}_1, \mathcal{R}_2, \mathcal{R}_3, \mathcal{R}_{RO})$ be a reduction as defined above. To prove our impossibility result, we construct a sequence of adversaries and show that they can win the MU-CMA-S game with high probability. The first few adversaries will be inefficient. However, the final adversary is efficient by rewinding the reduction $\mathcal{R}$. This is a common way to present meta-reductions, although often there is only one inefficient algorithm [7]. Our main task is to show that the success probabilities of the reduction do not change significantly when we move from one adversary to the next. The first adversary $\mathcal{A}^* = (\mathcal{A}^*_1, \mathcal{A}^*_2)$, formally presented in Fig. 11, obtains parameters and keys $\mathsf{par}, (\mathsf{pk}_i)_{i\in[N]}$ from the challenger, samples $j^* \xleftarrow{\$} [N]$ and gives it to the challenger. After obtaining all secret keys except sk_{j^*}, $\mathcal{A}^*$ samples a random secret key with bit 0, i.e. a secret key with respect to $\mathsf{ID}, \mathsf{par}$ and $\mathsf{pk}_{j^*,0}$. Note that this is why $\mathcal{A}^*$ is inefficient. It then signs a random message $\mathsf{m} \xleftarrow{\$} \mathcal{M}$ and returns it. In terms of success probability the following claim is then clear:

Lemma 6. $\mathsf{Adv}^{N\text{-}\mathsf{MU\text{-}CMA\text{-}S}}_{\mathcal{A}^*,\mathsf{SIG}_p[\mathsf{ID},\mathsf{H}]}(\lambda) = 1$.

We will now present and analyze the other adversaries, which are implicitly given as meta-reductions $\mathcal{B}_1, \ldots \mathcal{B}_5$ modeling the adversary and the reduction in their joint execution. That is, they run in the NIP game and use $\mathcal{R}$ as a subroutine. $\mathcal{B}_5$ will be efficient. A formal description can be found in Fig. 13. The changes can be summarized as follows:

- $\mathcal{B}_1$ is as $\mathcal{R}^{\mathcal{A}^*}$ except that $\mathcal{B}_1$ makes the following steps, summarized in the subroutine Rewind in Fig. 12: After obtaining $St_{\mathcal{R},1}$, par and $(\mathsf{pk}_i)_{i\in[N]}$ from $\mathcal{R}_1$ it runs $\mathcal{R}_2$ independently for every $j \in [N]$, stores all secret keys obtained and uses a flag $\mathsf{succ}[j]$ to keep track of those runs in which all secret keys returned by $\mathcal{R}_2$ were valid. Then it samples a random j^* as $\mathcal{A}^*$ does, continues with the j^*-th run as $\mathcal{A}^*$ and returns whatever $\mathcal{R}_3$ returns.
- $\mathcal{B}_2$ additionally checks for an event bad between sampling the index j^* and continuing with the j^*-run. The event occurs if $\mathsf{succ}[j^*] = 1$ and $\mathsf{succ}[j] = 0$ for all other $j \neq j^*$, i.e. $\mathcal{R}$ could only return valid secret keys for one index j^* given to $\mathcal{R}_2$. If the event holds, $\mathcal{B}_2$ aborts.
- $\mathcal{B}_3$ is as $\mathcal{B}_2$ but additionally brute forces a random secret key for $\mathsf{pk}_{j^*,1}$ and then uses both secret keys $\mathsf{sk}_{j^*,0}, \mathsf{sk}_{j^*,1}$ to compute the signature instead of using the algorithm Sim. The computation of the signature with two keys is summarized in Fig. 12.
- $\mathcal{B}_4$ is as $\mathcal{B}_3$, but if bad does not occur, it will have received a valid secret key $(b, \mathsf{sk}_{j^*,b})$ for pk_{j^*} from some execution of $\mathcal{R}_2$ with index $j \neq j^*$. It will use this secret key (rerandomized) to generate the signature instead of a brute forced one. The other key $\mathsf{sk}_{j^*,1-b}$ is still brute forced and Sim is still not used.
- $\mathcal{B}_5$ now uses only the rerandomized $\mathsf{sk}_{j^*,b}$ and the algorithm Sim to generate the signature. Note the $\mathcal{B}_5$ does not brute force any secret key anymore and is efficient. We set $\mathcal{B} := \mathcal{B}_5$.

Alg $\mathcal{A}_1^{*\mathsf{H}}(\mathsf{par}, (\mathsf{pk}_i)_{i\in[N]})$	**Alg** $\mathcal{A}_2^{*\mathsf{H}}(St, (\mathsf{sk}_i = (b_i, \mathsf{sk}_{i,b_i}))_{i\in[N]\setminus\{j^*\}})$
if $\mathsf{VerP}(\mathsf{par}) \neq 1$:	**if** $\exists i \in [N] \setminus \{j^*\} : \mathsf{VerK}(\mathsf{par}, \mathsf{pk}_{i,b_i}, \mathsf{sk}_{i,b_i}) = 0$:
return $\perp$	**return** $\perp$
$j^* \overset{\$}{\leftarrow} [N]$	$\mathsf{sk}_0 \overset{\$}{\leftarrow} \mathcal{SK}(\mathsf{pk}_{j^*,0})$
$St := (\mathsf{par}, (\mathsf{pk}_i)_{i\in[N]}, j^*)$	$\mathsf{m}^* \overset{\$}{\leftarrow} \mathcal{M}, \sigma^* \leftarrow \mathsf{Sig}((0, \mathsf{sk}_0), \mathsf{m}^*)$
return (j^*, St)	**return** (m^*, σ^*)

Fig. 11. The optimal (but inefficient) adversary $\mathcal{A}^* = (\mathcal{A}_1^*, \mathcal{A}_2^*)$, winning the game MU-CMA-S for the signature scheme $\mathsf{SIG}_p[\mathsf{ID}, \mathsf{H}]$.

```
Alg Rewind^R(c)
01 ρ_R ←$ {0,1}^z
02 (St_{R,1}, par, (pk_i)_{i∈[N]}) ← R_1(c; ρ_R)
03 if VerP(par) ≠ 1 : return ⊥
04 succ := [0, . . . , 0]
05 for j ∈ [N]:
06    (St_{R,2,j}, (sk_i)_{i∈[N]\{j}}) ← R_2(St_{R,1}, j)
07    succ[j] := 1
08    for i ∈ [N] \ {j} :
09       let sk_i = (b_i, sk_{i,b_i})
10       if VerK(par, pk_{i,b_i}, sk_{i,b_i}) = 0 :
11          succ[j] := 0
12    if succ[j] = 1 :
13       for i ∈ [N] \ {j} : sk[i] := sk_i
14 return (par, succ[·], sk[·], (St_{R,2,j})_{j∈[N]})
```

```
Alg FakeSign((sk_0, sk_1), m)
15 (cmt_0, St_0) ← P_1(sk_0)
16 (cmt_1, St_1) ← P_1(sk_1)
17 ch_0 ←$ ChSet
18 ch ← H(pk, cmt_0, cmt_1, m)
19 ch_1 := ch_0 ⊕ ch
20 rs_0 ← P_2(sk_0, ch_0, St_0)
21 rs_1 ← P_2(sk_1, ch_1, St_1)
22 if rs_0 =⊥ ∨rs_1 =⊥:
23    return ⊥
24 σ := (cmt_0, cmt_1, ch_0,
         ch_1, rs_0, rs_1)
25 return σ
```

Fig. 12. Subroutines Rewind and FakeSign, used in algorithms $\mathcal{B}_i$ given in Fig. 13.

We will now argue, that the success probability of $\mathcal{R}$ does not significantly change when we change our adversaries.

Lemma 7. $\mathsf{Adv}^{\mathsf{NIP}}_{\mathcal{R}^{\mathcal{A}^*}}(\lambda) = \mathsf{Adv}^{\mathsf{NIP}}_{\mathcal{B}_1}(\lambda)$.

Proof. First, note that the output of $\mathcal{B}_1$ does not depend on the executions of $\mathcal{R}_2(St_{\mathcal{R},1}, j)$ for $j \neq j^*$. That is, only one iteration of the loop in Fig. 12, Line 05 has an influence on the output of $\mathcal{R}_3$ and hence $\mathcal{B}_1$. Considering only this iteration, $\mathcal{R}^{\mathcal{A}^*}$ and $\mathcal{B}_1$ are exactly the same, where it may be worth mentioning that Line 06 in Fig. 13 and Line 06 in Fig. 11 are equivalent conditions. □

Lemma 8. $\left|\mathsf{Adv}^{\mathsf{NIP}}_{\mathcal{B}_1}(\lambda) - \mathsf{Adv}^{\mathsf{NIP}}_{\mathcal{B}_2}(\lambda)\right| \leq 1/N$.

Proof. Note that $\mathcal{B}_1$ and $\mathcal{B}_2$ only differ if the event bad occurs, which implies that $\mathsf{succ}[j^*] = 1$ and $\mathsf{succ}[j] = 0$ for all other $j \neq j^*$. Further, the set of possible j^* satisfying this condition is either empty or has one element. This means that

$$\left|\mathsf{Adv}^{\mathsf{NIP}}_{\mathcal{B}_1}(\lambda) - \mathsf{Adv}^{\mathsf{NIP}}_{\mathcal{B}_2}(\lambda)\right| \leq \Pr[\mathsf{bad}] \leq \frac{1}{N}.$$

□

Lemma 9. $\left|\mathsf{Adv}^{\mathsf{NIP}}_{\mathcal{B}_2}(\lambda) - \mathsf{Adv}^{\mathsf{NIP}}_{\mathcal{B}_3}(\lambda)\right| \leq \delta_{\mathcal{R}} + \varepsilon_{\mathsf{zk}}$.

Proof. Both $\mathcal{B}_2$ and $\mathcal{B}_3$ return $\bot$ if $\mathsf{VerP}(\mathsf{par}) \neq 1$ (see Fig. 12) and also if $\mathsf{bad} = 1$. Therefore we can assume that $\mathsf{par} \in \mathsf{ISetup}(1^\lambda)$. As we assume that the reduction $\mathcal{R}$ simulated a game of statistical distance $\delta_\mathcal{R}$ to the real game, the public key $\mathsf{pk}_{j^*,1}$ is of statistical distance at most $\delta_\mathcal{R}$ to an honest key. Hence with probability at least $1 - \delta_\mathcal{R}$, $\mathcal{B}_3$ will be able to successfully sample a random sk_1 such that $(\mathsf{pk}_{j^*,1}, \mathsf{sk}_1) \in \mathsf{IGen}(\mathsf{par})$. Note that in this case what $\mathcal{R}$ sees is $(\mathsf{m}^*, \sigma^*, \mathsf{query})$ where $\mathsf{m}^* \xleftarrow{\$} \mathcal{M}, \sigma^* \leftarrow \mathsf{FakeSign}((\mathsf{sk}_0, \mathsf{sk}_1), \mathsf{m}^*)$ and $\mathsf{query} = ((\mathsf{pk}_{j^*,0}, \mathsf{pk}_{j^*,1}), \mathsf{cmt}_0, \mathsf{cmt}_1, \mathsf{m}^*)$ is the random oracle query (observable by $\mathcal{R}_{RO}$) that occurs during the run of $\mathsf{FakeSig}$. Similarly, in the execution of $\mathcal{B}_2$ it sees $(\mathsf{m}^*, \sigma^*, \mathsf{query})$ where $\mathsf{m}^* \xleftarrow{\$} \mathcal{M}, \sigma^* \leftarrow \mathsf{Sig}((0, \mathsf{sk}_0), \mathsf{m}^*)$ and $\mathsf{query} = ((\mathsf{pk}_{j^*,0}, \mathsf{pk}_{j^*,1}), \mathsf{cmt}_0, \mathsf{cmt}_1, \mathsf{m}^*)$. Note that the difference is only the way how the transcript $(\mathsf{cmt}_1, \mathsf{ch}_1, \mathsf{rs}_1)$, which is part of σ^*, is generated. Further, query can be efficiently computed without knowing how that transcript was generated. Hence by $\varepsilon_{\mathsf{zk}}$-HVZK, these have statistical distance at most $\varepsilon_{\mathsf{zk}}$, which implies that $\mathcal{R}_3$'s final output in the execution of $\mathcal{B}_3$ is distributed as the same output in $\mathcal{B}_2$, except with probability at most $\varepsilon_{\mathsf{zk}}$. Note that this is the step where the entire argument fails for sequential OR proofs, as the additional value query that $\mathcal{R}$ observes would have an order that allows $\mathcal{R}$ to distinguish (Recall that a sequential OR proof makes two random oracle queries during signing). □

Lemma 10. $\mathsf{Adv}^{\mathsf{NIP}}_{\mathcal{B}_3}(\lambda) = \mathsf{Adv}^{\mathsf{NIP}}_{\mathcal{B}_4}(\lambda)$.

Proof. The only difference between $\mathcal{B}_3$ uses sk_b sampled uniformly random from $\mathcal{SK}(\mathsf{pk}_{j^*,b})$ to generate the signature via $\mathsf{FakeSign}$ and $\mathcal{B}_4$ uses $\mathsf{sk}_b \leftarrow \mathsf{RerandK}(\mathsf{par}, \mathsf{pk}_{j^*,b}, \bar{\mathsf{sk}})$. If bad does not occur, then there will be some $j \neq j^*$, such that $\mathsf{succ}[j] = 1$. Fix the largest such j, then $\mathsf{sk}[j^*] = (b, \bar{\mathsf{sk}})$ is defined and by definition of succ and key-verifiability we have that $(\mathsf{pk}_{j^*,b}, \bar{\mathsf{sk}}) \in \mathsf{IGen}(\mathsf{par})$. By our assumption that ID is key-rerandomizable, we then know that these keys are distributed sk_b as used in $\mathcal{B}_4$ is distributed uniformly over $\mathcal{SK}(\mathsf{pk}_{j^*,b})$, which proves the claim. □

Lemma 11. $\left|\mathsf{Adv}^{\mathsf{NIP}}_{\mathcal{B}_4}(\lambda) - \mathsf{Adv}^{\mathsf{NIP}}_{\mathcal{B}_5}(\lambda)\right| \leq \delta_\mathcal{R} + \varepsilon_{\mathsf{zk}}$.

Proof. The proof is exactly the same as for Lemma 9, applying $\varepsilon_{\mathsf{zk}}$-HVZK to $(\mathsf{pk}_{j^*,1-b}, \mathsf{sk}_{1-b})$. □

In summary, combining all claims we obtain that

$$\mathsf{Adv}^{\mathsf{NIP}}_{\mathcal{B}_5}(\lambda) \geq \mathsf{Adv}^{\mathsf{NIP}}_{\mathcal{R}^{\mathcal{A}^*}}(\lambda) - 2(\delta_\mathcal{R} + \varepsilon_{\mathsf{zk}}) - 1/N,$$

and $\mathcal{B}_5$ is efficient, which proves Theorem 2. □

```
Alg B₁(c), B₂(c)
01 (par, succ[·], sk[·], (St_{R,2,j})_{j∈[N]})
                              ← Rewind^R(c)
02 j* ←$ [N]
03 if succ[j*] ≠ 1 : return 0
04 if ∀j ∈ [N] \ {j*} : succ[j] = 0 :
05     bad := 1, return ⊥
06 sk₀ ←$ SK(pk_{j*,0})
07 m* ←$ M, σ* ← Sig((0, sk₀), m*)
08 return R₃(St_{R,2,j*}, j*, m*, σ*)

Alg B₅(c)
09 (par, succ[·], sk[·], (St_{R,2,j})_{j∈[N]})
                              ← Rewind^R(c)
10 j* ←$ [N]
11 if succ[j*] ≠ 1 : return 0
12 if ∀j ∈ [N] \ {j*} : succ[j] = 0 :
13     bad := 1, return ⊥
14 let sk[j*] = (b, s̄k)
15 sk_b ← RerandK(par, pk_{j*,b}, s̄k)
16 m* ←$ M, σ* ← Sig(sk_b, m*)
17 return R₃(St_{R,2,j*}, j*, m*, σ*)

Alg B₃(c), B₄(c)
18 (par, succ[·], sk[·], (St_{R,2,j})_{j∈[N]})
                              ← Rewind^R(c)
19 j* ←$ [N]
20 if succ[j*] ≠ 1 : return 0
21 if ∀j ∈ [N] \ {j*} : succ[j] = 0 :
22     bad := 1, return ⊥
23 sk₀ ←$ SK(pk_{j*,0})
24 sk₁ ←$ SK(pk_{j*,1})
25 let sk[j*] = (b, s̄k)
26 sk_b ← RerandK(par, pk_{j*,b}, s̄k)
27 m* ←$ M
28 σ* ← FakeSign((sk₀, sk₁), m*)
29 return R₃(St_{R,2,j*}, j*, m*, σ*)
```

Fig. 13. The (inefficient) algorithms $B_1,\ldots,B_4$ and the efficient algorithm B_5 used in the proof of Theorem 2. The subroutines Rewind, FakeSign are given in Fig. 12.

References

1. Abdalla, M., Benhamouda, F., Pointcheval, D.: On the tightness of forward-secure signature reductions. J. Cryptol. **32**(1), 84–150 (2019)
2. Abdalla, M., Fouque, P.-A., Lyubashevsky, V., Tibouchi, M.: Tightly-secure signatures from lossy identification schemes. In: Pointcheval, D., Johansson, T. (eds.) EUROCRYPT 2012. LNCS, vol. 7237, pp. 572–590. Springer, Heidelberg (2012). https://doi.org/10.1007/978-3-642-29011-4_34
3. Abe, M., Groth, J., Ohkubo, M.: Separating short structure-preserving signatures from non-interactive assumptions. In: Lee, D.H., Wang, X. (eds.) ASIACRYPT 2011. LNCS, vol. 7073, pp. 628–646. Springer, Heidelberg (2011). https://doi.org/10.1007/978-3-642-25385-0_34
4. Abe, M., Ohkubo, M., Suzuki, K.: 1-out-of-n signatures from a variety of keys. In: Zheng, Y. (ed.) ASIACRYPT 2002. LNCS, vol. 2501, pp. 415–432. Springer, Heidelberg (2002). https://doi.org/10.1007/3-540-36178-2_26
5. Bader, C.: Efficient signatures with tight real world security in the random-oracle model. In: Gritzalis, D., Kiayias, A., Askoxylakis, I. (eds.) CANS 2014. LNCS, vol. 8813, pp. 370–383. Springer, Cham (2014). https://doi.org/10.1007/978-3-319-12280-9_24
6. Bader, C., Hofheinz, D., Jager, T., Kiltz, E., Li, Y.: Tightly-secure authenticated key exchange. In: Dodis, Y., Nielsen, J.B. (eds.) TCC 2015. LNCS, vol. 9014, pp. 629–658. Springer, Heidelberg (2015). https://doi.org/10.1007/978-3-662-46494-6_26

7. Bader, C., Jager, T., Li, Y., Schäge, S.: On the impossibility of tight cryptographic reductions. In: Fischlin, M., Coron, J.-S. (eds.) EUROCRYPT 2016. LNCS, vol. 9666, pp. 273–304. Springer, Heidelberg (2016). https://doi.org/10.1007/978-3-662-49896-5_10
8. Bellare, M., Boldyreva, A., Micali, S.: Public-key encryption in a multi-user setting: security proofs and improvements. In: Preneel, B. (ed.) EUROCRYPT 2000. LNCS, vol. 1807, pp. 259–274. Springer, Heidelberg (2000). https://doi.org/10.1007/3-540-45539-6_18
9. Bellare, M., Ristenpart, T.: Simulation without the artificial abort: simplified proof and improved concrete security for waters' IBE scheme. In: Joux, A. (ed.) EUROCRYPT 2009. LNCS, vol. 5479, pp. 407–424. Springer, Heidelberg (2009). https://doi.org/10.1007/978-3-642-01001-9_24
10. Bellare, M., Rogaway, P.: Entity authentication and key distribution. In: Stinson, D.R. (ed.) CRYPTO 1993. LNCS, vol. 773, pp. 232–249. Springer, Heidelberg (1994). https://doi.org/10.1007/3-540-48329-2_21
11. Blazy, O., Kakvi, S.A., Kiltz, E., Pan, J.: Tightly-secure signatures from Chameleon Hash functions. In: Katz, J. (ed.) PKC 2015. LNCS, vol. 9020, pp. 256–279. Springer, Heidelberg (2015). https://doi.org/10.1007/978-3-662-46447-2_12
12. Boyen, X., Li, Q.: Towards tightly secure lattice short signature and id-based encryption. In: Cheon, J.H., Takagi, T. (eds.) ASIACRYPT 2016. LNCS, vol. 10032, pp. 404–434. Springer, Heidelberg (2016). https://doi.org/10.1007/978-3-662-53890-6_14
13. Brakerski, Z., Langlois, A., Peikert, C., Regev, O., Stehlé, D.: Classical hardness of learning with errors. In: Boneh, D., Roughgarden, T., Feigenbaum, J. (eds.) 45th ACM STOC, pp. 575–584. ACM Press (June 2013)
14. Canetti, R., Krawczyk, H.: Analysis of key-exchange protocols and their use for building secure channels. In: Pfitzmann, B. (ed.) EUROCRYPT 2001. LNCS, vol. 2045, pp. 453–474. Springer, Heidelberg (2001). https://doi.org/10.1007/3-540-44987-6_28
15. Chaum, D., Pedersen, T.P.: Wallet databases with observers. In: Brickell, E.F. (ed.) CRYPTO 1992. LNCS, vol. 740, pp. 89–105. Springer, Heidelberg (1993). https://doi.org/10.1007/3-540-48071-4_7
16. Chen, J., Wee, H.: Fully, (almost) tightly secure IBE and dual system groups. In: Canetti, R., Garay, J.A. (eds.) CRYPTO 2013. LNCS, vol. 8043, pp. 435–460. Springer, Heidelberg (2013). https://doi.org/10.1007/978-3-642-40084-1_25
17. Coron, J.-S.: Optimal security proofs for PSS and other signature schemes. In: Knudsen, L.R. (ed.) EUROCRYPT 2002. LNCS, vol. 2332, pp. 272–287. Springer, Heidelberg (2002). https://doi.org/10.1007/3-540-46035-7_18
18. Cramer, R., Damgård, I., Schoenmakers, B.: Proofs of partial knowledge and simplified design of witness hiding protocols. In: Desmedt, Y.G. (ed.) CRYPTO 1994. LNCS, vol. 839, pp. 174–187. Springer, Heidelberg (1994). https://doi.org/10.1007/3-540-48658-5_19
19. Damgård, I.: On Σ-protocols (2010). https://cs.au.dk/ivan/Sigma.pdf
20. Davis, H., Günther, F.: Tighter proofs for the SIGMA and TLS 1.3 key exchange protocols. In: ACNS 2021 (2021). https://eprint.iacr.org/2020/1029
21. Diemert, D., Gellert, K., Jager, T., Lyu, L.: More efficient digital signatures with tight multi-user security. In: Garay, J.A. (ed.) PKC 2021. LNCS, vol. 12711, pp. 1–31. Springer, Cham (2021). https://doi.org/10.1007/978-3-030-75248-4_1
22. Diemert, D., Jager, T.: On the tight security of TLS 1.3: theoretically-sound cryptographic parameters for real-world deployments. J. Cryptol. **34**, 1–57 (2020). https://eprint.iacr.org/2020/726

23. Ducas, L., Durmus, A., Lepoint, T., Lyubashevsky, V.: Lattice signatures and bimodal Gaussians. In: Canetti, R., Garay, J.A. (eds.) CRYPTO 2013. LNCS, vol. 8042, pp. 40–56. Springer, Heidelberg (2013). https://doi.org/10.1007/978-3-642-40041-4_3
24. El Kaafarani, A., Katsumata, S., Pintore, F.: Lossy CSI-FiSh: efficient signature scheme with tight reduction to decisional CSIDH-512. In: Kiayias, A., Kohlweiss, M., Wallden, P., Zikas, V. (eds.) PKC 2020, Part II. LNCS, vol. 12111, pp. 157–186. Springer, Heidelberg (May (2020)
25. Fischlin, M., Harasser, P., Janson, C.: Signatures from sequential-OR proofs. In: Canteaut, A., Ishai, Y. (eds.) EUROCRYPT 2020. LNCS, vol. 12107, pp. 212–244. Springer, Cham (2020). https://doi.org/10.1007/978-3-030-45727-3_8
26. Gay, R., Hofheinz, D., Kohl, L., Pan, J.: More efficient (almost) tightly secure structure-preserving signatures. In: Nielsen, J.B., Rijmen, V. (eds.) EUROCRYPT 2018. LNCS, vol. 10821, pp. 230–258. Springer, Cham (2018). https://doi.org/10.1007/978-3-319-78375-8_8
27. Genise, N., Micciancio, D., Peikert, C., Walter, M.: Improved discrete Gaussian and Subgaussian analysis for lattice cryptography. In: Kiayias, A., Kohlweiss, M., Wallden, P., Zikas, V. (eds.) PKC 2020. LNCS, vol. 12110, pp. 623–651. Springer, Cham (2020). https://doi.org/10.1007/978-3-030-45374-9_21
28. Gentry, C., Peikert, C., Vaikuntanathan, V.: Trapdoors for hard lattices and new cryptographic constructions. Cryptology ePrint Archive, Report 2007/432 (2007). https://eprint.iacr.org/2007/432
29. Gentry, C., Peikert, C., Vaikuntanathan, V.: Trapdoors for hard lattices and new cryptographic constructions. In: Ladner, R.E., Dwork, C. (eds.) 40th ACM STOC, pp. 197–206. ACM Press (May 2008)
30. Gentry, C., Sahai, A., Waters, B.: Homomorphic encryption from learning with errors: conceptually-simpler, asymptotically-faster, attribute-based. In: Canetti, R., Garay, J.A. (eds.) CRYPTO 2013. LNCS, vol. 8042, pp. 75–92. Springer, Heidelberg (2013). https://doi.org/10.1007/978-3-642-40041-4_5
31. Gjøsteen, K., Jager, T.: Practical and tightly-secure digital signatures and authenticated key exchange. In: Shacham, H., Boldyreva, A. (eds.) CRYPTO 2018. LNCS, vol. 10992, pp. 95–125. Springer, Cham (2018). https://doi.org/10.1007/978-3-319-96881-0_4
32. Goldwasser, S., Micali, S., Rivest, R.L.: A digital signature scheme secure against adaptive chosen-message attacks. SIAM J. Comput. **17**(2), 281–308 (1988)
33. Gorbunov, S., Vaikuntanathan, V., Wichs, D.: Leveled fully homomorphic signatures from standard lattices. In: Servedio, R.A., Rubinfeld, R. (eds.) 47th ACM STOC, pp. 469–477. ACM Press (June 2015)
34. Guillou, L.C., Quisquater, J.-J.: A "Paradoxical" indentity-based signature scheme resulting from zero-knowledge. In: Goldwasser, S. (ed.) CRYPTO 1988. LNCS, vol. 403, pp. 216–231. Springer, New York (1990). https://doi.org/10.1007/0-387-34799-2_16
35. Han, S., et al.: Authenticated key exchange and signatures with tight security in the standard model. In: Malkin, T., Peikert, C. (eds.) CRYPTO 2021. LNCS, vol. 12828, pp. 670–700. Springer, Cham (2021). https://doi.org/10.1007/978-3-030-84259-8_23
36. Hazay, C., Lindell, Y.: Efficient Secure Two-Party Protocols. ISC. Springer, Heidelberg (2010). https://doi.org/10.1007/978-3-642-14303-8

37. Hofheinz, D., Jager, T., Knapp, E.: Waters signatures with optimal security reduction. In: Fischlin, M., Buchmann, J., Manulis, M. (eds.) PKC 2012. LNCS, vol. 7293, pp. 66–83. Springer, Heidelberg (2012). https://doi.org/10.1007/978-3-642-30057-8_5
38. Jager, T., Kiltz, E., Riepel, D., Schäge, S.: Tightly-secure authenticated key exchange, revisited. In: Canteaut, A., Standaert, F.-X. (eds.) EUROCRYPT 2021. LNCS, vol. 12696, pp. 117–146. Springer, Cham (2021). https://doi.org/10.1007/978-3-030-77870-5_5
39. Kakvi, S.A., Kiltz, E.: Optimal security proofs for full domain hash, revisited. In: Pointcheval, D., Johansson, T. (eds.) EUROCRYPT 2012. LNCS, vol. 7237, pp. 537–553. Springer, Heidelberg (2012). https://doi.org/10.1007/978-3-642-29011-4_32
40. Kiltz, E., Lyubashevsky, V., Schaffner, C.: A concrete treatment of Fiat-Shamir signatures in the quantum random-oracle model. In: Nielsen, J.B., Rijmen, V. (eds.) EUROCRYPT 2018. LNCS, vol. 10822, pp. 552–586. Springer, Cham (2018). https://doi.org/10.1007/978-3-319-78372-7_18
41. Kiltz, E., Masny, D., Pan, J.: Optimal security proofs for signatures from identification schemes. In: Robshaw, M., Katz, J. (eds.) CRYPTO 2016. LNCS, vol. 9815, pp. 33–61. Springer, Heidelberg (2016). https://doi.org/10.1007/978-3-662-53008-5_2
42. Langrehr, R., Pan, J.: Tightly secure hierarchical identity-based encryption. In: Lin, D., Sako, K. (eds.) PKC 2019. LNCS, vol. 11442, pp. 436–465. Springer, Cham (2019). https://doi.org/10.1007/978-3-030-17253-4_15
43. Liu, X., Liu, S., Gu, D., Weng, J.: Two-pass authenticated key exchange with explicit authentication and tight security. In: Moriai, S., Wang, H. (eds.) ASIACRYPT 2020. LNCS, vol. 12492, pp. 785–814. Springer, Cham (2020). https://doi.org/10.1007/978-3-030-64834-3_27
44. Lyubashevsky, V.: Lattice signatures without trapdoors. In: Pointcheval, D., Johansson, T. (eds.) EUROCRYPT 2012. LNCS, vol. 7237, pp. 738–755. Springer, Heidelberg (2012). https://doi.org/10.1007/978-3-642-29011-4_43
45. Lyubashevsky, V., Micciancio, D.: Asymptotically efficient lattice-based digital signatures. J. Cryptol. **31**(3), 774–797 (2018)
46. Lyubashevsky, V., Peikert, C., Regev, O.: On ideal lattices and learning with errors over rings. In: Gilbert, H. (ed.) EUROCRYPT 2010. LNCS, vol. 6110, pp. 1–23. Springer, Heidelberg (2010). https://doi.org/10.1007/978-3-642-13190-5_1
47. Micciancio, D., Peikert, C.: Trapdoors for lattices: simpler, tighter, faster, smaller. In: Pointcheval, D., Johansson, T. (eds.) EUROCRYPT 2012. LNCS, vol. 7237, pp. 700–718. Springer, Heidelberg (2012). https://doi.org/10.1007/978-3-642-29011-4_41
48. Micciancio, D., Regev, O.: Worst-case to average-case reductions based on Gaussian measures. In: 45th FOCS, pp. 372–381. IEEE Computer Society Press (October 2004)
49. Pan, J., Ringerud, M.: Signatures with tight multi-user security from search assumptions. In: Chen, L., Li, N., Liang, K., Schneider, S. (eds.) ESORICS 2020. LNCS, vol. 12309, pp. 485–504. Springer, Cham (2020). https://doi.org/10.1007/978-3-030-59013-0_24
50. Peikert, C.: Public-key cryptosystems from the worst-case shortest vector problem: extended abstract. In: Mitzenmacher, M. (ed.) 41st ACM STOC, pp. 333–342. ACM Press (May/June 2009)

51. Peikert, C., Vaikuntanathan, V., Waters, B.: A framework for efficient and composable oblivious transfer. In: Wagner, D. (ed.) CRYPTO 2008. LNCS, vol. 5157, pp. 554–571. Springer, Heidelberg (2008). https://doi.org/10.1007/978-3-540-85174-5_31
52. Regev, O.: On lattices, learning with errors, random linear codes, and cryptography. In: Gabow, H.N., Fagin, R. (eds.) 37th ACM STOC, pp. 84–93. ACM Press (May 2005)
53. Steinfeld, R., Pieprzyk, J., Wang, H.: How to strengthen any weakly unforgeable signature into a strongly unforgeable signature. In: Abe, M. (ed.) CT-RSA 2007. LNCS, vol. 4377, pp. 357–371. Springer, Heidelberg (2006). https://doi.org/10.1007/11967668_23
54. Stolbunov, A.: Cryptographic schemes based on isogenies. Ph.D. thesis, Norwegian University of Science and Technology (2012)
55. Unruh, D.: Non-interactive zero-knowledge proofs in the quantum random oracle model. In: Oswald, E., Fischlin, M. (eds.) EUROCRYPT 2015. LNCS, vol. 9057, pp. 755–784. Springer, Heidelberg (2015). https://doi.org/10.1007/978-3-662-46803-6_25

Count Me In! Extendability for Threshold Ring Signatures

Diego F. Aranha[1(✉)], Mathias Hall-Andersen[1], Anca Nitulescu[3], Elena Pagnin[2], and Sophia Yakoubov[1]

[1] Aarhus University, Aarhus, Denmark
{dfaranha,ma,sophia.yakoubov}@cs.au.dk
[2] Lund University, Lund, Sweden
elena.pagnin@eit.lth.se
[3] Protocol Labs, Wilmington, USA
anca@protocol.ai

Abstract. Ring signatures enable a signer to sign a message on behalf of a group *anonymously*, without revealing her identity. Similarly, threshold ring signatures allow several signers to sign the same message on behalf of a group; while the combined signature reveals that some threshold t of the group members signed the message, it does not leak anything else about the signers' identities. Anonymity is a central feature in threshold ring signature applications, such as whistleblowing, e-voting and privacy-preserving cryptocurrencies: it is often crucial for signers to remain anonymous even from their fellow signers. When the generation of a signature requires interaction, this is difficult to achieve. There exist threshold ring signatures with non-interactive signing—where signers locally produce *partial* signatures which can then be aggregated—but a limitation of existing threshold ring signature constructions is that all of the signers must agree on the group on whose behalf they are signing, which implicitly assumes some coordination amongst them. The need to agree on a group before generating a signature also prevents others—from outside that group—from endorsing a message by adding their signature to the statement post-factum.

We overcome this limitation by introducing *extendability* for ring signatures, same-message linkable ring signatures, and threshold ring signatures. Extendability allows an untrusted third party to take a signature, and *extend* it by enlarging the anonymity set to a larger set. In the extendable threshold ring signature, two signatures on the same message which have been extended to the same anonymity set can then be combined into one signature with a higher threshold. This enhances signers' anonymity, and enables new signers to anonymously support a statement already made by others.

For each of those primitives, we formalize the syntax and provide a meaningful security model which includes different flavors of anonymous extendability. In addition, we present concrete realizations of each primitive and formally prove their security relying on signatures of knowledge and the hardness of the discrete logarithm problem. We also describe a generic transformation to obtain extendable threshold ring signa-

G. Hanaoka et al. (Eds.): PKC 2022, LNCS 13178, pp. 379–406, 2022.
https://doi.org/10.1007/978-3-030-97131-1_13

tures from same-message-linkable extendable ring signatures. Finally, we implement and benchmark our constructions.

Keywords: Threshold ring signatures · Anonymity · Extendability

1 Introduction

Anonymity has become a requirement in many real-world implementations of cryptographic systems and privacy-enhancing technologies, including electronic voting [24], direct anonymous attestation [9], and private cryptocurrencies [27]. Another compelling scenario is whistleblowing of organizational wrongdoing. In this case, an insider publishes a *secret* in a manner that convinces the public of its authenticity, while having his/her identity protected [25]. In all of these applications, a large *anonymity set*, i.e., set of users who may have performed a certain action, is crucial in order to not reveal who exactly is behind it.

Group signatures enable any member of a given group to sign a message, without revealing which member signed. However, group signatures suffer from the drawback that they require trusted setup for every group. Ring signatures are a manager-free variant of group signatures. They enable individual users to sign messages anonymously on behalf of a dynamically chosen group of users, while hiding the exact identity of the signer(s) [25]. Traditionally, this is enabled by including a "ring" $\mathcal{R}$ of public keys (belonging to all possible signers, including the actual signer) as an input to the signing algorithm; a ring signature does not reveal which of the corresponding secret keys was used to produce it. There are many ways to construct ring signatures using different building blocks: classic RSA [13], bilinear pairings [5,12,30], composite-order groups [7,26], non-interactive zero knowledge [6,20], and, most recently, quantum-safe isogenies and lattices [4,14,18,19].

Threshold ring signatures are a threshold variant of this primitive [8], which allow some t signers to sign a message on behalf of a ring $\mathcal{R}$ of size larger than t. The signature reveals that t members of the ring signed the message, but not the identities of those members. Some threshold ring signature schemes are *flexible* [23], meaning that even after the threshold ring signature has been produced for a given ring $\mathcal{R}$, another signer from that ring can participate, resulting in a threshold ring signature for the same ring $\mathcal{R}$ but with a threshold of $t+1$. However, if a signer from *outside* the ring wants to participate, existing constructions do not support this. All existing constructions of ring and threshold ring signatures have a common limitation: the ring of potential signers is fixed at the time of signature generation. In particular, it is not possible to have the added flexibility of publicly "adjusting" the ring, i.e., to extend the initial ring to a larger one, increasing the anonymity set. Increasing the size of the set of potential signers not only increases the anonymity provided by the signature, but also makes threshold systems easier to realize in practice.

To work in practice, standard threshold ring signatures need all of the signers to independently sign the same message μ with the same ring $\mathcal{R}$, which must include the public keys of all t signers. We are interested in relaxing this implicit synchronization requirement.

1.1 Our Contributions

In this paper, we introduce a new property of (threshold) ring signatures which we call *extendability.* A (threshold) ring signature scheme is *extendable* if it allows anyone to enlarge the set of potential signers of a given signature. Extendable threshold ring signatures are fundamental for whistleblowing, where one party may want to "join the cause" after it becomes public. Extendability, together with flexibility, enables a signer A to join a threshold ring signature which was produced using an anonymity ring $\mathcal{R}$ that does not contain A. This can be done by first extending the existing signature to a new ring $\mathcal{R}' \supseteq \mathcal{R} \cup \{A\}$ which contains both the ring used by previous signers as well as the new signer. Then, thanks to flexibility, the new signer can add their own signature with respect to the new ring $\mathcal{R}'$ (using $\mathbf{sk}_A$). (Of course, an observer who has seen signatures under the old ring $\mathcal{R}$ and under the new ring $\mathcal{R}'$ will be able to determine $\mathcal{R}' \backslash \mathcal{R}$; this is inherent—since an observer can always tell which ring a signature is meant for by attempting verification—and can help that observer narrow down possibilities for the identity of A. However, an observer who has *not* seen a signature under the old ring $\mathcal{R}$ will learn nothing additional about the identity of A.)

In addition to drawing formal models, we give the first constructions of *extendable ring signatures*, *same-message linkable* extendable ring signatures and extendable *threshold* ring signatures. We provide a proof of concept implementation of our construction, benchmark the signing and verification running times as well as the signature size.

Constructions from Signatures of Knowledge and Discrete Log. We build extendable ring signatures and same-message linkable extendable ring signatures using signatures of knowledge. Each signature will include several elements of a group, with the property that all of their discrete logs cannot be known. (This is because the product of the elements gives a discrete log challenge which is part of the public parameters.) A signer signs the message with a *signature of knowledge* that proves that she knows either her own secret key, or the discrete log of one of the elements. The signer uses her secret key for this (and so can use the element for which the discrete log is unknown), but for each of the other signers' public keys in the ring, she includes a signature of knowledge using the discrete log of one of the elements. Because all of the element discrete logs cannot be known, a verifier is convinced that at least one signature of knowledge is produced using a secret key, and that therefore the overall signature was produced by one of the members of the ring.

We build extendable threshold ring signatures similarly, but by choosing the elements in such a way that at least t of their discrete logs cannot be known without revealing the discrete log of a challenge element in the public parameters. We enforce this by placing the elements on a polynomial of appropriate degree.

A Generic Transformation. One might hope to build extendable threshold ring signatures by concatenating t extendable ring signatures; however, we would need to additionally prove to the verifier that the t signatures were produced by t different signers. Building such a proof would require interaction between the signers, and it would be challenging to maintain the proof as the ring is expanded. Instead, we solve this problem using a primitive which we call a *same-message linkable extendable ring signatures*, where, given two signatures on the same message, it is immediately clear whether they were produced by the same signer. Our realizations of this primitive provide linkability without revealing the signer's identity or resorting to additional zero knowledge proofs and can be used to construct extendable threshold ring signatures in a generic way.

Implementation. We provide an implementation that demonstrates the concrete efficiency of our schemes. The benchmarks place our constructions firmly within the realm of practicality: an extendable ring signature for a ring with 2048 members can be created in 0.45 s.

1.2 Related Work

Ring signatures were first introduced by Rivest, Shamir, and Tauman in [25] as a mechanism to leak secrets anonymously. This initial construction was based on trapdoor permutations, but other schemes quickly followed. A threshold version of their scheme was proposed the following year by Bresson *et al.* [8], together with a revised security analysis for the original scheme. By using RSA accumulators and the Fiat-Shamir transform, a ring signature scheme with signature sizes independent of the ring size was later constructed by Dodis *et al.* [13]. (A similar scheme in the threshold setting was described by Munch-Hansen *et al.* [22].) In addition to the hardness of integer factorization, pairing groups were used in early constructions to obtain ring signatures in the conventional [5] and identity-based [30] settings.

The first ring signature constructions were all based on the random oracle model, but alternatives proven secure in the common reference string model were later proposed [12,26], including constructions with sublinear [10] and constant signature size [7]. In the standard model, early constructions were based on 2-round public coin witness-indistinguishable protocols [1], but more recent constructions rely on non-interactive zero-knowledge proofs [6,20].

Threshold ring signature schemes come in many flavors, with many constructions based on RSA and bilinear maps and security based on number-theoretic assumptions [17,28,29]; and post-quantum schemes based both on lattices [3] and coding theory [21]. The post-quantum schemes have traditionally relied on the Fiat-Shamir transform, the quantum security of which is not fully determined. Recent work in threshold ring signatures has provided both improved security definitions [22] and constructions based on the quantum-safe Unruh's transform [15].

2 Background and Preliminaries

Notation. We denote the set of natural numbers by $\mathbb{N}$ and let the computational security parameter of our schemes to be $\lambda \in \mathbb{N}$. We say that a function is *negligible* (in λ), and we denote it by $\mathtt{negl}$, if $\mathtt{negl}(\lambda) = \Omega(\lambda^{-c})$ for any fixed constant $c > 1$. We also say that a probability is *overwhelming* (in λ) if it is greater than or equal to $1 - \mathtt{negl}$. Given two values $a < b$, we denote the list of integer numbers between a and b as $[a, \ldots, b]$. For compactness, when $a = 1$, we simply write $[b]$ for $[1, \ldots, b]$. We denote empty strings as ϵ. Unless otherwise specified, all the algorithms defined throughout this work are assumed to be probabilistic Turing machines that run in polynomial time (abbreviated as PPT). When sampling the value a uniformly at random from a set X, we employ the notation $a \leftarrow_R X$. In our constructions, we denote by $\mathsf{GroupGen}(1^\lambda)$ the algorithm that, given in input the security parameter, outputs the tuple $(p, g, \mathbb{G})$, where p is a 2λ-bit prime; g is a group generator and $\mathbb{G}$ is a description of a group of order p, $\mathbb{G} = \langle g \rangle$. Through out the paper, we assume solving the Discrete Logarithm Problem in $\mathbb{G}$ is computationally hard.

2.1 Main Primitives

Ring Signatures. A ring signature scheme is defined as a tuple of four probabilistic polynomial time algorithms $\mathbf{RS} = (\mathsf{Setup}, \mathsf{KeyGen}, \mathsf{Sign}, \mathsf{Verify})$:

$\mathsf{Setup}(1^\lambda) \rightarrow \mathtt{pp}$: Takes a security parameter λ and outputs a set of public parameters $\mathtt{pp}$. The public parameters are implicitly input to all subsequent algorithms.

$\mathsf{KeyGen}() \rightarrow (\mathtt{pk}, \mathtt{sk})$: Produces a key pair $(\mathtt{pk}, \mathtt{sk})$.

$\mathsf{Sign}(\mu, \{\mathtt{pk}_j\}_{j \in \mathcal{R}}, \mathtt{sk}_i) \rightarrow \sigma$: Takes a message $\mu \in \{0,1\}^*$ to be signed, the set of public keys of the users within the ring of identifiers $\mathcal{R}$, and the secret key $\mathtt{sk}_i$ of the signer $i \in \mathcal{R}$ (i.e., the signer's public key must appear in the set $\{\mathtt{pk}_j\}_{j \in \mathcal{R}}$). Outputs a signature σ.

$\mathsf{Verify}(\mu, \{\mathtt{pk}_i\}_{i \in \mathcal{R}}, \sigma) \rightarrow \mathtt{accept}/\mathtt{reject}$: Takes a message, a set of public keys of the users within a ring, and a signature σ. Outputs $\mathtt{accept}$ or $\mathtt{reject}$, reflecting the validity of the signature σ on the message μ with respect to the ring $\mathcal{R}$.

Naturally, a ring signature scheme should satisfy correctness, meaning that any signature generated by Sign should verify (against the signed message and the original ring). A *secure* ring signature scheme RS must additionally satisfy (a) unforgeability, meaning that no adversary should be able to produce a verifying signature without knowledge of at least one signing key corresponding to a public verification key in the ring, and (b) anonymity, meaning that no adversary should be able to tell from a signature which ring member produced it. We refer to prior work for the formal definitions of a ring signature scheme [8,13,16].

Threshold Ring Signatures. There are many different ways to formalize the threshold ring signature syntax, which force varying degrees of interaction between the t signers. A non-interactive threshold ring signature scheme is defined as a tuple of five probabilistic polynomial time algorithms (Setup, KeyGen, Sign, Combisign, Verify). The algorithms Setup, KeyGen, Sign and Verify are syntactically the same as in a ring signature scheme, with the exceptions that (1) Sign now outputs a *partial* signature σ_i for signer i, and (2) Verify now additionally takes the threshold t as input. The algorithm Combisign, described below, combines t partial signatures into a single threshold signature. It may be run by any third party, as it does not require any signers' secrets.

$\mathsf{Combisign}(\{\sigma_i\}_{i \in \mathcal{S} \subseteq \mathcal{R}}) \to \sigma$: Takes partial signatures $\{\sigma_i\}_{i \in \mathcal{S}}$ from $|\mathcal{S}| = t$ signers, and outputs a combined signature σ.

There are also interactive threshold ring signature schemes. In this case Sign (which in this case also subsumes Combisign) is an interactive protocol run between the signers, which implicitly requires the signers to be aware of one another's identities.

Finally, there is a solution in between, where one signer produces the initial signature, and then the remaining signers pass the signature around, and each "joins" the signature before passing it on. In such a syntax, each signer must only receive (at most) one message from one other signer, and send (at most) one message to one other signer. Instead of Combisign, in such a syntax we have a Join algorithm, described below.

$\mathsf{Join}(\mu, \{\mathtt{pk}_j\}_{j \in \mathcal{R}}, \mathtt{sk}, \sigma) \to \sigma'$: Takes a message μ, a set of public keys $\{\mathtt{pk}_j\}_{j \in \mathcal{R}}$, which includes the public key of the new signer, the new signer's secret key $\mathtt{sk}$, and a signature σ produced by a subset of $\mathcal{R}$ (with threshold level t'). Outputs a modified threshold ring signature σ' with threshold $t' + 1$.

2.2 Main Building Blocks

Signatures of Knowledge. Signatures of Knowledge (SoKs) [11] generalise digital signatures by replacing the public key with an *instance*, or *statement*, in a NP language. A signer can generate a valid signature for a message only if she has a valid witness for the statement.

Syntax. A SoK for an efficiently decidable binary relation $\mathscr{R}$ is defined as a tuple of PPT algorithms $\mathbf{SoK} = (\mathsf{Setup}, \mathsf{Sign}, \mathsf{Verify}, \mathsf{SimSetup}, \mathsf{SimSign})$:

$\mathsf{Setup}(1^\lambda, \mathscr{R}) \to \mathsf{pp}$: Takes a security parameter λ and a binary relation $\mathscr{R}$ and returns public parameters pp. The input pp is implicit to al subsequent algorithms.

$\mathsf{Sign}(\mu, \phi, w) \to \sigma$: Takes as input a message $\mu \in \{0,1\}^*$, a statement ϕ, and a witness w. Outputs a signature σ.

$\mathsf{Verify}(\mu, \phi, \sigma) \to \mathtt{accept}/\mathtt{reject}$: Takes as input a message μ, a statement ϕ, and a signature σ. Outputs `accept` if the the signature is valid, `reject` otherwise.

$\mathsf{SimSetup}(1^\lambda, \mathscr{R}) \rightarrow (\mathtt{pp}, \mathtt{td})$: A simulated setup which takes as input a relation $\mathscr{R}$ and returns public parameters $\mathtt{pp}$ and a trapdoor $\mathtt{td}$.

$\mathsf{SimSign}(\mathtt{td}, \mu, \phi) \rightarrow \sigma'$: A simulated signing algorithm that takes as input a trapdoor $\mathtt{td}$, a message μ and a statement ϕ and returns a simulated signature σ'.

A SoK scheme should satisfy correctness, simulatability and extractability as formally defined in the full version of this paper.

3 Extendable Ring Signatures

Ring signatures enable a signer to generate a signature while hiding her identity within a ring of potential signers. Even though the ring of potential signers $\mathcal{R}$ can be arbitrary[1]—realizing ad-hoc anonymity sets—existing constructions do not let a third party increase the size of $\mathcal{R}$ after the signature is produced. Once a signature is generated, it is not possible to "extend" it to a larger anonymity set; in other words, ring signatures do not allow one to modify a signature and obtain a new signature for the same message but with a wider set of potential signers. Our notion of extendability aims to allow exactly this, while preserving signer anonymity.

3.1 Syntax

An extendable ring signature scheme (ERS) is a ring signature scheme that has an additional algorithm, Extend, that allows any third party to enlarge the ring of potential signers of a given signature:

$\mathsf{Extend}(\mu, \{\mathtt{pk}_i\}_{i\in\mathcal{R}}, \sigma, \{\mathtt{pk}_j\}_{j\in\mathcal{R}'}) \rightarrow \sigma'$: Takes a message, a set of public keys (indexed by the ring $\mathcal{R}$), a signature σ, and a second ring of public keys (indexed by $\mathcal{R}'$). It outputs a modified signature σ' which verifies under $\mathcal{R} \cup \mathcal{R}'$.

Remark 1. Consider an ERS scheme where Extend can be repeatedly applied to extend a signature a polynomial number of times. In this case, we can have a very simple instantiation where Sign always produces a signature for the singleton ring $\{\mathtt{pk}\}$ containing only the signer's public key $\mathtt{pk}$, and Extend is called only on singleton extension rings, i.e., $|\mathcal{R}'| = 1$. A signature for the singleton ring can be extended to any ring by having the signer iteratively apply Extend with a single additional public key.

For the following definitions, we use ladders of rings, i.e., tuples $\mathtt{lad} = (i, \mathcal{R}^{(1)}, \mathcal{R}^{(2)}, \ldots, \mathcal{R}^{(l)})$, where i is a signer identity, and the rings $\mathcal{R}^{(1)}, \mathcal{R}^{(2)}, \ldots, \mathcal{R}^{(l)}$ are all sets of signer identifiers. In addition, we make use of an algorithm $\mathsf{Process}(\mu, \mathsf{L}_{\mathsf{keys}}, \mathtt{lad})$, that we describe in Fig. 1. As the name suggests,

[1] The ring $\mathcal{R}$ should of course contain the signer's identity.

this algorithm processes a ladder $\mathtt{lad}$ on a given message μ using keys from $\mathsf{L}_{\mathsf{keys}}$ (the list of generated keys). Process signs μ using $\mathtt{sk}_i$ under the ring $\mathcal{R}^{(1)}$, and extends the signature to all the subsequent rings (using keys stored in the list $\mathsf{L}_{\mathsf{keys}}$). Process returns an extendable ring signature σ, which is the output of the last operation.

ERS.Process(μ, $\mathsf{L}_{\mathsf{keys}}$, lad)

Parse $\mathtt{lad}$ as $(i, \mathcal{R}^{(1)}, \mathcal{R}^{(2)}, \ldots, \mathcal{R}^{(l)})$

if $i \notin \mathcal{R}^{(1)}$ **return** $\perp$ // make sure all public keys are in $\mathsf{L}_{\mathsf{keys}}$

for $j \in \mathcal{R}^{(1)} \cup \cdots \cup \mathcal{R}^{(l)}$: **if** $(j, \mathtt{pk}_j, \cdot) \notin \mathsf{L}_{\mathsf{keys}}$ **return** $\perp$

// make sure the signer's secret key is available in $\mathsf{L}_{\mathsf{keys}}$

if $\mathtt{sk}_i = \perp$: **return** $\perp$ // make sure $\mathtt{sk}_i$ is not corrupted

// process the instructions in the ladder

$\sigma^{(1)} \leftarrow \mathbf{ERS}.\mathsf{Sign}(\mu, \{\mathtt{pk}_j\}_{j \in \mathcal{R}^{(1)}}, \mathtt{sk}_i)$

for $l' \in [2, \ldots, l]$:

  $\mathcal{R}^{(l')} \leftarrow \mathcal{R}^{(l')} \cup \mathcal{R}^{(l'-1)}$ // enforce rings form an increasing chain

  $\sigma^{(l')} \leftarrow \mathbf{ERS}.\mathsf{Extend}(\mu, \{\mathtt{pk}_j\}_{j \in \mathcal{R}^{(l'-1)}}, \sigma^{(l'-1)}, \{\mathtt{pk}_j\}_{j \in \mathcal{R}^{(l')}})$

$\sigma \leftarrow \sigma^{(l)}$

return σ

Fig. 1. The Process algorithm for extendable ring signatures.

For correctness, we require that any—possibly extended—signature σ output by Process verifies for the given message, under the final ring $\mathcal{R}^{(l)}$.

Definition 1 (Correctness for ERS). *An extendable ring signature scheme ERS is said to be correct if, for all security parameters $\lambda \in \mathbb{N}$, for any message $\mu \in \{0,1\}^*$, for any ladder $\mathtt{lad} = (i, \mathcal{R}^{(1)}, \mathcal{R}^{(2)}, \cdots, \mathcal{R}^{(l)})$ where $i \in \mathcal{R}^{(1)}$ and $l > 0$, it must hold that:*

$$\Pr\left[\begin{array}{r|l} \mathbf{ERS}.\mathsf{Verify}(\mu, \{\mathtt{pk}_j\}_{j\in\mathcal{R}}, \sigma) & \mathcal{R} = \mathcal{R}^{(1)} \cup \cdots \cup \mathcal{R}^{(l)} \\ & \mathsf{pp} \leftarrow \mathbf{ERS}.\mathsf{Setup}(1^\lambda) \\ = \mathsf{accept}\ OR\ \sigma = \perp & \mathsf{L}_{\mathsf{keys}} \leftarrow \{(\mathtt{pk}_j, \mathtt{sk}_j) \leftarrow \mathbf{ERS}.\mathsf{KeyGen}()\}_{j\in\mathcal{R}} \\ & \sigma \leftarrow \mathbf{ERS}.\mathsf{Process}(\mu, \mathsf{L}_{\mathsf{keys}}, \mathtt{lad}) \end{array}\right] = 1$$

3.2 Security Model

Definition 2 (Secure ERS). *An extendable ring signature scheme is secure if it satisfies correctness (Definition 1), unforgeability (Definition 3), anonymity (Definition 4), and some notion of anonymous extendability (described below).*

Unforgeability. Extendable ring signatures inherit their unforgeability requirement from regular ring signatures: no adversary should be able to produce a signature unless they know at least one secret key belonging to a party in the ring. Notably, the unforgeability experiment for ERS (cmEUF, detailed in Figure 2) needs to take into account that the adversary can arbitrarily expand the ring associated to a signature. To rule out trivial attacks derived with this strategy, the adversary does not break unforgeability if the candidate forgery could be generated by extending the outcome of a signing query (line 5 in $\mathsf{Exp}^{\mathrm{cmEUF}}_{\mathcal{A},\mathbf{ERS}}(\lambda)$). Additionally, to account for the key duplication attack (where an adversary registers an existing public key to a new identity), instead of simply checking if the identities in the output ring are among the corrupted ones, the experiment checks if the *public keys* belonging to the parties involved in the adversary's output ring are among the corrupted ones (line 7, Fig. 2).

$\mathsf{Exp}^{\mathrm{cmEUF}}_{\mathcal{A},\mathbf{ERS}}(\lambda)$

```
1 :  L_keys, L_corr, L_sign ← ∅
2 :  pp ← ERS.Setup(1^λ)
3 :  O ← {OSign, OKeyGen, OCorrupt}
4 :  (μ*, R*, σ*) ← A^O(pp)
     // rule out trivial wins due to ring expansion
5 :  if ∃ (μ*, R, ·) ∈ L_sign s.t.
          {pk_j}_{j∈R} ⊆ {pk_j}_{j∈R*}
6 :     return lose
     // rule out trivial wins due to key duplication
7 :  if {pk_j}_{j∈R*} ∩ {pk_j}_{j∈L_corr} ≠ ∅
8 :     return lose
9 :  if Verify(μ*, {pk_j}_{j∈R*}, σ*) = reject
10 :    return lose
11 : return win
```

$\mathcal{O}\mathsf{Corrupt}(i)$

```
1 :  if (i, pk_i, sk_i) ∈ L_keys and sk_i ≠ ⊥
2 :     L_corr ← L_corr ∪ {i}
3 :     return (pk_i, sk_i)
4 :  return ⊥ // if i has not been initialized.
```

$\mathcal{O}\mathsf{KeyGen}(i, \mathsf{pk})$

```
     // standard key generation for a new identifier i
1 :  if pk = ⊥
2 :     (pk_i, sk_i) ← ERS.KeyGen()
3 :     L_keys ← L_keys ∪ {(i, pk_i, sk_i)}
4 :  else
     // A over-writes an identifier with malicious keys
5 :     L_corr ← L_corr ∪ {i}
6 :     pk_i ← pk
7 :     L_keys ← L_keys ∪ {(i, pk_i, ⊥)}
8 :  return pk_i
```

$\mathcal{O}\mathsf{Sign}(\mu, \mathcal{R}, i)$

```
1 :  if (i ∈ L_corr ∨ i ∉ R) :  return ⊥
     // check that all keys in the query are initialized
2 :  for all j ∈ R
3 :     if (j, pk_j, ·) ∉ L_keys
4 :        return ⊥
5 :  σ ← ERS.Sign(μ, {pk_j}_{j∈R}, sk_i)
6 :  L_sign ← L_sign ∪ {(μ, R, i)}
7 :  return σ
```

Fig. 2. Existential unforgeability under chosen message attack for (extendable) ring signatures (security experiment and oracles). Our key generation oracle allows $\mathcal{A}$ to register signers with arbitrary public keys (i.e., it also acts as a registration oracle).

Definition 3 (Unforgeability for ERS). *An extendable ring signature scheme ERS is said to be unforgeable if for all PPT adversaries $\mathcal{A}$ taking part in the unforgeability experiment (*cmEUF *in Fig. 2), the success probability is negligible, i.e.:* $\Pr\left[\mathsf{Exp}^{\mathrm{cmEUF}}_{\mathcal{A},\mathbf{ERS}}(\lambda) = \mathtt{win}\right] \leq \mathbf{negl}$.

Anonymous Extendability. For extendability, we consider security notions related to anonymity (thus the name anonymous extendability). We define an experiment that is general enough to support three different flavors of anonymous extendability: the standard *anonymity* notion, where no extension happens; *weak extendability*, where it is not possible to identify the original subring of an extended signature; and *strong extendability*, where it is not possible to tell what sequence of extensions a signature has undergone.

$\mathsf{Exp}^{\mathrm{ANEXT}}_{\mathcal{A},\mathbf{ERS}}(\lambda)$

1 : $b \leftarrow_R \{0,1\}$
2 : $\mathsf{L_{keys}}, \mathsf{L_{corr}}, \mathsf{L_{sign}} \leftarrow \varnothing$
3 : $\mathsf{pp} \leftarrow \mathbf{ERS}.\mathsf{Setup}(1^\lambda)$
// handle of oracles, for compact notation
4 : $O \leftarrow \{O\mathsf{Sign}, O\mathsf{KeyGen}, O\mathsf{Corrupt}\}$
5 : $(\mu^*, \mathtt{lad}_0^*, \mathtt{lad}_1^*) \leftarrow \mathcal{A}^O(\mathsf{pp})$
6 : $\bar{\sigma} \leftarrow \mathsf{Chal}_b(\mu^*, \mathtt{lad}_0^*, \mathtt{lad}_1^*)$
7 : $b^* \leftarrow \mathcal{A}^O(\bar{\sigma})$
// make sure $\mathcal{A}$ did not corrupt the challenge
// keys during the second query phase
8 : **if** $i_0 \in \mathsf{L_{corr}} \vee i_1 \in \mathsf{L_{corr}}$
9 : **return lose**
10 : **if** $b^* \neq b$
11 : **return lose**
12 : **return win**

$\mathsf{Chal}_b(\mu^*, \mathtt{lad}_0^*, \mathtt{lad}_1^*)$

1 : **parse** $\mathtt{lad}_0^* = (i_0, \mathcal{R}_0^{(1)}, \ldots, \mathcal{R}_0^{(l_0)})$
2 : **parse** $\mathtt{lad}_1^* = (i_1, \mathcal{R}_1^{(1)}, \ldots, \mathcal{R}_1^{(l_1)})$
// challenge signing keys should not be corrupted
3 : **if** $i_0, i_1 \in \mathsf{L_{corr}}$ **return** $\perp$
// sign and extend following the instructions
// in both ladders
4 : $\sigma_0 \leftarrow \mathsf{Process}(\mu, \mathsf{L_{keys}}, \mathtt{lad}_0^*)$
5 : $\sigma_1 \leftarrow \mathsf{Process}(\mu, \mathsf{L_{keys}}, \mathtt{lad}_1^*)$
6 : **if** $\sigma_0 = \perp$ **or** $\sigma_1 = \perp$ **return** $\perp$
// check that ladders end with the same ring
7 : **if** $\mathcal{R}_0^{(1)} \cup \cdots \cup \mathcal{R}_0^{(l_0)} \neq \mathcal{R}_1^{(1)} \cup \cdots \cup \mathcal{R}_1^{(l_1)}$
8 : **return** $\perp$
// set the challenge signature according to b
9 : $\bar{\sigma} \leftarrow \sigma_b$
10 : **return** $\bar{\sigma}$

Fig. 3. Anonymity and anonymous extendability for extendable ring signatures. The oracles OSign, OKeyGen and OCorrupt are defined in Fig. 2.

For standard anonymity we consider adversaries that output ladders ($\mathtt{lad}_0^*, \mathtt{lad}_1^*$ in line 5 of $\mathsf{Exp}^{\mathrm{ANEXT}}_{\mathcal{A},\mathbf{ERS}}$ in Fig. 3) each containing only one ring. To avoid making the game trivial to win, the two rings need to be identical (line 7 of Chal_b). Moreover since the extension algorithm is never called ($l_0 = l_1 = 1$ in this case), it is clear that—with this restriction on the adversary's input to the challenger—our ANEXT experiment is the same as the standard anonymity one.

Definition 4 (Anonymity for ERS). *An extendable ring signature scheme is said to be anonymous if for all PPT adversaries $\mathcal{A}$ taking part in the anonymous extendability experiment (*ANEXT *in Figure 3) and submitting to the challenger ladders of the type* $\mathtt{lad}_0^* = (i_0, \mathcal{R}), \mathtt{lad}_1^* = (i_1, \mathcal{R})$, *it holds that the success probability of $\mathcal{A}$ is negligibly close to random guessing. i.e.,:* $\Pr\left[\mathsf{Exp}_{\mathcal{A},\mathbf{ERS}}^{\mathrm{ANEXT}}(\lambda) = \mathtt{win}\right] \leq \frac{1}{2} + \mathtt{negl}.$

For strong anonymous extendability, we consider adversaries that output any type of ladders that culminate in the same ring. In particular, we could have $l_0 \neq l_1$. Notice that strong anonymous extendability implies both weak anonymous extendability and standard anonymity.

Definition 5 (Strong Anonymous Extendability for ERS). *An extendable ring signature scheme is said to be strongly anonymous extendable if for all PPT adversaries $\mathcal{A}$ taking part in the anonymous extendability experiment (Fig. 3), it holds that:* $\Pr\left[\mathsf{Exp}_{\mathcal{A},\mathbf{ERS}}^{\mathrm{ANEXT}}(\lambda) = \mathtt{win}\right] \leq \frac{1}{2} + \mathtt{negl}.$

We remark that strong extendability implies that the act of extending a ring signature is seamless, i.e., an adversary is not able to distinguish between a fresh ring signature (returned by Sign), and an extension of it (returned by Extend). This is covered in the strong extendability game for $l_0 = 1$ and $l_1 > 1$.

3.3 ERS from Signatures of Knowledge and Discrete Log

In what follows, we exhibit an efficient realization of extendable ring signature scheme from prime order groups and signatures of knowledge.

Our Construction in a Nutshell. The setup generates a prime-order group $\mathbb{G} = \langle g \rangle$, a random group element $H \leftarrow_R \mathbb{G}$ and public parameters for a SoK scheme for the relation

$$\mathscr{R}_{\mathbb{G}}(\phi = (h, \mathtt{pk}), w = x) = \{g^x = h \vee g^x = \mathtt{pk}\}.$$

Intuitively, $\mathscr{R}_{\mathbb{G}}$ requires that the witness be either the discrete log of $\mathtt{pk}$ (which is the corresponding secret key), or the element h. The signing procedure simply samples a random value $\mathtt{td} \leftarrow_R \mathbb{Z}_p$, creates an element $h := H \cdot g^{-\mathtt{td}}$ (which implies that $h \cdot g^{\mathtt{td}} = H$), and computes a signature of knowledge π for $(h, \mathtt{pk})$ using her secret key $\mathtt{sk}$. The signature σ contains $\mathtt{td}$, and a set $P = \{(h, \mathtt{pk}, \pi)\}$. Extending works essentially like signing, except that the extender uses the other kind of witness. Concretely, the extender samples a new $\mathtt{td}'$, computes $h' = g^{\mathtt{td}'}$ and a signature of knowledge π' for the $\mathtt{pk}'$ she wishes to add to the ring, using $\mathtt{td}'$ as the witness. The tuple $(h', \mathtt{pk}', \pi')$ is added to P, and $\mathtt{td}$ is replaced by $\mathtt{td} - \mathtt{td}'$. The verification checks that $H = g^{\mathtt{td}} \cdot \prod h_i$ for all h_i present in P, and that all π_i verify. This ensures that at least one of the π_i was produced using $\mathtt{sk}_i$ as a witness (otherwise we would be able to extract $dlog(H)$). A formal description of this construction is given in Fig. 4.

ERS.Setup(1^λ) $\mapsto$ pp

$(p, g, \mathbb{G}) \leftarrow \mathsf{GroupGen}(1^\lambda)$
SoK.pp $\leftarrow$ **SoK**.Setup($1^\lambda, \mathscr{R}_{\mathbb{G}}$)
$H \leftarrow_R \mathbb{G}$
return pp := (**SoK**.pp, g, H)

ERS.KeyGen() $\mapsto$ (pk, sk)

sk $\leftarrow \mathbb{Z}_p$
pk := g^{sk}
return (sk, pk)

ERS.Sign(μ, sk) $\mapsto \sigma$

td $\leftarrow_R \mathbb{Z}_p$
$h := H \cdot g^{-\mathsf{td}}$
// signer does not know $dlog(h)$
// compute the signature
nonce $\leftarrow_R \{0,1\}^\lambda$
$\phi := (h, \mathsf{pk})$
$w :=$ sk
$\pi \leftarrow$ **SoK**.Sign((nonce, μ), $\mathscr{R}$, ϕ, w)
$P := \{(h, \mathsf{pk}, \pi)\}$
return σ := (nonce, td, P)

ERS.Verify(μ, $\{\mathsf{pk}_j\}_{j \in \mathcal{R}}$, σ) $\mapsto$ **accept/reject**

parse σ = (nonce, td, $P = \{(h_i, \mathsf{pk}_i, \pi_i)\}_{i \in \mathcal{R}'}$)
if $H \neq g^{\mathsf{td}} \cdot \prod_{i \in \mathcal{R}'} h_i$: **return reject**
if $\{\mathsf{pk}_j\}_{j \in \mathcal{R}} \neq \{\mathsf{pk}_i\}_{i \in \mathcal{R}'}$:
  return reject
for $i \in \mathcal{R}'$:
  $\phi_i := (h_i, \mathsf{pk}_i)$
  if SoK.Verify((nonce, μ), $\mathscr{R}$, ϕ_i, π_i) = **reject** :
   return reject
return accept

ERS.Extend(μ, $\{\mathsf{pk}_j\}_{j \in \mathcal{R}}$, σ, pk) $\mapsto \sigma'$

if pk $\in \{\mathsf{pk}_j\}_{j \in \mathcal{R}}$: **return** $\perp$
parse σ = (nonce, td, $P = \{(h_i, \mathsf{pk}_i, \pi_i)\}_{i \in \mathcal{R}'}$)
td$'$ $\leftarrow_R \mathbb{Z}_p$ // pick a trapdoor
td $\leftarrow$ td $-$ td$'$ (mod p)
$h := g^{\mathsf{td}'}$ // to simulate using the trapdoor
$\phi := (h, \mathsf{pk}), w :=$ td$'$
$\pi \leftarrow$ **SoK**.Sign((nonce, μ), $\mathscr{R}$, ϕ, w)
add (h, pk, π) **to** P // update the signature
return σ' := (nonce, td, P)

Fig. 4. Extendable ring signatures from signature of knowledge and discrete log. The relation used by the SoK scheme is $\mathscr{R}_{\mathbb{G}} = \{(\phi, w) = (h, \mathsf{pk}, x) \in \mathbb{G} \times \mathbb{G} \times \mathbb{Z}_p : g^x = h \vee g^x = \mathsf{pk}\}$.

Theorem 1. *Assuming that* **SoK** *is a secure signature of knowledge scheme, and that the discrete log problem is hard in the group* $\mathbb{G}$, *then the scheme* **ERS** = (Setup, KeyGen, Sign, Verify, Extend) *described in Fig. 4 is an extendable ring signature scheme that satisfies* correctness *(Definition 1),* unforgeability *(Definition 3), and* strong anonymous extendability *(Definition 5).*

Proof. The correctness of the construction follows by inspection.

Unforgeability. To prove unforgeability, we present a sequence of hybrid games at the end of which the reduction is able to extract a solution to a discrete logarithm challenge from $\mathcal{A}$'s forgery with high-enough probability. Essentially this involves: embedding a discrete logarithm into H; moving to the simulatable setup for the SoK; replacing all signatures of knowledge with simulated ones; and using the witness extracted from π^* to learn $dlog(H)$. Due to space limitation all details are deferred to the full version of this paper.

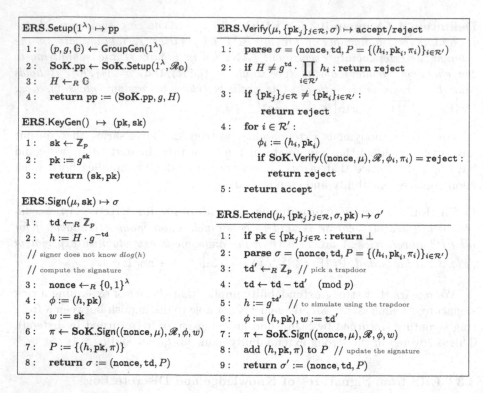

Anonymous Extendability. To prove the strong anonymous extendability of our construction it suffices to show that if an adversary $\mathcal{A}$ can successfully break anonymous extendability, we can build a reduction $\mathcal{B}$ that breaks the security of the signature of knowledge. Imagine that $\mathcal{B}$, playing the role of the challenger, runs the simulated setup for the signature of knowledge, instead of the real setup. This gives $\mathcal{B}$ a trapdoor that allows it to simulate signatures without knowledge of a witness. $\mathcal{B}$ uses this trapdoor to simulate all signatures of knowledge in response to signing queries from $\mathcal{A}$. $\mathcal{B}$ generates the challenge signature with no reference to the ladders. It simply chooses td at random, generates the h_i's as random values such that $g^{\mathtt{td}} \cdot \prod h_i = H$, and uses the trapdoor to simulate all signatures of knowledge. If $\mathcal{A}$ can distinguish $\mathcal{B}$ from an honest challenger, $\mathcal{B}$ can use $\mathcal{A}$ to break the simulatability property of the signature of knowledge. If $\mathcal{A}$ cannot distinguish $\mathcal{B}$ from an honest challenger, since $\mathcal{B}$'s behavior does not depend on choice of b, $\mathcal{A}$ cannot possibly win the anonymous extendability game with probability non-negligibly more than half. □

4 Same-Message Linkable Extendable Ring Signatures

A same-message linkable ring signature scheme (SMLRS) is a ring signature scheme that additionally allows any third party to publicly identify (link) whether two signatures were generated by the same signer for the same message. This means that if the same party signs the same message twice, even for different rings, the two signatures can be linked by any third party.

In what follows, we introduce the notion of *extendable* same-message linkable ring signatures (ESMLRS). We give a security model for this new primitive, and describe an instantiation that builds on our ERS construction from Sect. 3.3.

4.1 Syntax

A same-message linkable extendable ring signature scheme is a tuple of six algorithms **SMLERS** = (Setup, KeyGen, Sign, Verify, Extend, Link). The first five algorithms are inherited from extendable ring signatures. The Link algorithm (described below) allows any verifier to determine whether two signatures on a particular message were produced by the same signer.

$\mathsf{Link}(\mu, (\sigma_0, \{\mathtt{pk}_j\}_{j \in \mathcal{R}_0}), (\sigma_1, \{\mathtt{pk}_j\}_{j \in \mathcal{R}_1})) \rightarrow \{\mathtt{linked}, \mathtt{unlinked}\}$: An algorithm that takes a message μ, two signatures (σ_0, σ_1) and two sets of public keys belonging to members of the rings $\mathcal{R}_0, \mathcal{R}_1$. It outputs linked if σ_0 and σ_1 were produced by the same signer, and unlinked otherwise.

We remark that Link does not necessarily reveal the identity of the common signer if signatures are linked. Next we discuss correctness for extendable same-message linkable ring signature schemes, which encompasses two statements: *extended signatures verify*, which is inherited from correctness for extendable ring signatures (Definition 1); and *extended signatures from different signers are unlinked*, which we formalize in the following definition.

Definition 6 (Cross-Signer Correctness for SMLERS). *For all security parameters $\lambda \in \mathbb{N}$, for any message $\mu \in \{0,1\}^*$, for any two ladders* $\mathtt{lad}_0 = (i_0, \mathcal{R}_0^{(1)}, \ldots, \mathcal{R}_0^{(l_0)})$, $\mathtt{lad}_1 = (i_1, \mathcal{R}_1^{(1)}, \ldots, \mathcal{R}_1^{(l_0)})$ *where* $i_0 \in \mathcal{R}_0^{(1)}$, $i_1 \in \mathcal{R}_1^{(1)}$, $l_0 > 0$, $l_1 > 0$ *and* $i_0 \neq i_1$, *it must hold that:*

$$\Pr\left[\begin{array}{c|l} \mathsf{Link}(\mu, (\sigma_0, \{\mathsf{pk}_j\}_{j \in \mathcal{R}_0}), & \mathcal{R}_0 = \mathcal{R}_0^{(1)} \cup \cdots \cup \mathcal{R}_0^{(l_0)} \\ (\sigma_1, \{\mathsf{pk}_j\}_{j \in \mathcal{R}_1})) \rightarrow \mathtt{unlinked} & \mathcal{R}_1 = \mathcal{R}_0^{(1)} \cup \cdots \cup \mathcal{R}_1^{(l_1)} \\ & \mathsf{pp} \leftarrow \mathsf{Setup}(1^\lambda) \\ & \mathsf{L_{keys}} \leftarrow \{\mathsf{KeyGen}()\}_{j \in \mathcal{R}_0 \cup \mathcal{R}_1} \\ & \sigma_0 \leftarrow \mathsf{Process}(\mu, \mathsf{L_{keys}}, \mathtt{lad}_0) \\ & \sigma_1 \leftarrow \mathsf{Process}(\mu, \mathsf{L_{keys}}, \mathtt{lad}_1) \end{array}\right] = 1 - \mathtt{negl}$$

where Process *is the algorithm described in Fig. 1 except that the ERS algorithms are replaced with the corresponding* **SMLERS** *ones.*

Remark 2. To build some intuition that may come in handy for understanding the security model, the reader might consider the following natural strategy for constructing an extendable same-message linkable ring signature scheme: ensuring that (part of) the signature is unique for every public key and message pair. In other words, the signer's public key and the signed message uniquely determine a part of the ring signature; we will refer to this part as the *linkability tag*. This tag is not modified by ring extensions and can be used to identify if two ring signatures, on the same message, were produced by the same signer simply by checking whether they share the same tag.

4.2 Security Model

A same-message linkable extendable ring signature scheme is an extendable ring signature that additionally satisfies the following properties:

Same-Message One-More Linkability: no set of $(t-1)$ corrupt signers can produce t signatures for the same message which appear pairwise unlinked. (We present this property in Definition 8).

Cross-Message Unlinkability: no adversary can determine whether two signatures for different messages were produced by the same signer. (We present this property in Definition 9).

Definition 7 (Secure SMLERS). *A same-message linkable extendable ring signature scheme (ESMLRS) is* secure *if it satisfies correctness, same-message one-more linkability (Definition 8, which implies unforgeability), and cross-message unlinkability (Definition 9).*

Definition 8 (Same-Message One-more Linkability for SMLERS). *A same-message linkable extendable ring signature scheme ESMLRS is said to be one-more linkable if for all PPT adversaries $\mathcal{A}$ taking part in the same-message one-more linkability experiment* ($\mathsf{Exp}^{\mathrm{omlink}}_{\mathcal{A},\mathbf{SMLERS}}(\lambda)$ *depicted in Fig. 5), it holds that:* $\Pr[\mathsf{Exp}^{\mathrm{omlink}}_{\mathcal{A},\mathbf{SMLERS}}(\lambda) = \mathtt{win}] \leq \mathtt{negl}$.

$\mathsf{Exp}^{\mathrm{omlink}}_{\mathcal{A},\mathbf{SMLERS}}(\lambda)$

$\mathsf{pp} \leftarrow \mathsf{Setup}(1^\lambda)$

$\mathsf{L_{keys}}, \mathsf{L_{corr}}, \mathsf{L_{sign}} \leftarrow \varnothing$

$\mathcal{O} \leftarrow \{\mathcal{O}\mathsf{Sign}, \mathcal{O}\mathsf{KeyGen}, \mathcal{O}\mathsf{Corrupt}\}$

$(\mu^*, \{(\sigma_k^*, \mathcal{R}_k^*)\}_{k\in[1\ldots,t]}) \leftarrow \mathcal{A}^{\mathcal{O}}(\mathsf{pp})$

// $\mathcal{A}$ has never seen a signature for the message and a subring of the forgery rings

if $\exists\ (\mu^*, \mathcal{R}, \cdot) \in \mathsf{L_{sign}}$ *s.t.* $\mathcal{R} \subseteq \mathcal{R}_k^*$ for some $k \in [1, \ldots, t]$ **return lose**

// $\mathcal{A}$ holds at most $t-1$ secret keys, among the keys identified by the forgery rings

if $|(\mathcal{R}_1^* \cup \cdots \cup \mathcal{R}_t^*) \cap \mathsf{L_{corr}}| \geq t$ **return lose**

// all the signatures in the forgery verify (for the same message)

if $\exists\ k \in [1\ldots,t]$ s.t. $\mathsf{Verify}(\mu^*, \{\mathsf{pk}_j\}_{j\in\mathcal{R}_k^*}, \sigma_k^*) = \mathtt{reject}$ **return lose**

// all signatures in the forgery are unlinked (here $k, l \in [1, \ldots, t]$)

if $\exists\ k \neq l$ s.t. $\mathsf{Link}(\mu^*, (\sigma_k^*, \{\mathsf{pk}_j\}_{j\in\mathcal{R}_k^*}), (\sigma_l^*, \{\mathsf{pk}_j\}_{j\in\mathcal{R}_l^*})) = \mathtt{linked}$

return lose

return win

Fig. 5. Security experiment for same-message one-more linkability. The signing, key generation and corruption oracles are as defined in Fig. 2, except that the algorithms for **ERS** are replaced with the corresponding algorithms for **SMLERS**. We recall that the list $\mathsf{L_{sign}}$ of sign-queries contains elements of the form $(\mu, \mathcal{R}, i)$.

Definition 9 (Cross-Message Unlinkability for SMLERS). *A same-message linkable extendable ring signature scheme ESMLRS is said to be cross-message unlinkable if for all PPT adversaries $\mathcal{A}$ taking part in the cross-message unlinkability experiment ($\mathsf{Exp}^{\mathrm{cmunlink}}_{\mathcal{A},\mathbf{SMLERS}}(\lambda)$ depicted in Fig. 6), it holds that the success probability of $\mathcal{A}$ is negligibly close to random guessing, i.e.,:* $\Pr[\mathsf{Exp}^{\mathrm{cmunlink}}_{\mathcal{A},\mathbf{SMLERS}}(\lambda) = \mathtt{win}] \leq \frac{1}{2} + \mathbf{negl}$.

4.3 SMLERS from Signatures of Knowledge and Discrete Log

Our ESMLRS construction builds on the ERS construction in Fig. 4. Since the nuance is limited, we only briefly describe the tweaks needed to transform our ERS into an ESMLRS.

First, we adopt a slightly different relation $\mathscr{R}_{\mathbf{SMLERS}}$:

$$\mathscr{R}_{\mathbf{SMLERS}}\,(\phi = (h, \mathsf{pk}, g', \tau), w = x) = \{g^x = h \vee (g^x = \mathsf{pk} \wedge (g')^x = \tau)\}$$

Notably, the last *AND* not only requires a signer to prove knowledge of the secret key, but it also enforces that the same secret key is used to generate the linkability tag τ. The signatures of knowledge for ESMLRS are with respect to the new relation $\mathscr{R}_{\mathbf{SMLERS}}$.

$\mathsf{Exp}^{\mathrm{cmunlink}}_{\mathcal{A},\mathbf{LRS}}(\lambda)$

$b \leftarrow_R \{0,1\}, \mathsf{L_{keys}}, \mathsf{L_{corr}}, \mathsf{L_{sign}} \leftarrow \emptyset$
$\mathsf{pp} \leftarrow \mathsf{Setup}(1^\lambda)$
$O \leftarrow \{O\mathsf{Sign}, O\mathsf{KeyGen}, O\mathsf{Corrupt}\}$
$(\{\mu_0, \mathcal{R}_0, i_0\}, \{\mu_1, \mathcal{R}_1, i_1\}) \leftarrow \mathcal{A}^O(\mathsf{pp})$
$(\bar{\sigma}_0, \bar{\sigma}_1) \leftarrow \mathsf{Chal}_b(\{\mu_0, \mathcal{R}_0, i_0\}, \{\mu_1, \mathcal{R}_1, i_1\})$
$b^* \leftarrow \mathcal{A}^O(\bar{\sigma}_0, \bar{\sigma}_1)$
// Rule out corruption of challenge identities
if $i_0 \in \mathsf{L_{corr}} \vee i_1 \in \mathsf{L_{corr}}$ **return lose**
// Rule out trivial attacks using Link
if $\mu_0 = \mu_1$ **return lose**
// Rule out trivial attacks using Link
if $(\mu_0, \cdot, i_0) \in \mathsf{L_{sign}} \vee (\mu_0, \cdot, i_1) \in \mathsf{L_{sign}}$
$\vee (\mu_1, \cdot, i_0) \in \mathsf{L_{sign}} \vee (\mu_1, \cdot, i_1) \in \mathsf{L_{sign}}$
  return lose
if $b^* \neq b$ **return lose**
return win

$\mathsf{Chal}_b(\{\mu_0, \mathcal{R}_0, i_0\}, \{\mu_1, \mathcal{R}_1, i_1\})$

// the challenge identities must be uncorrupted
if $i_0 \in \mathsf{L_{corr}} \vee i_1 \in \mathsf{L_{corr}}$
  return $\perp$
// one identity needs to be in both rings
if $i_0 \notin \mathcal{R}_0 \cap \mathcal{R}_1 \vee i_1 \notin \mathcal{R}_1$
  return $\perp$
// signing keys must exist
if $\nexists\, (i_0, \mathbf{pk}_{i_0}, \mathbf{sk}_{i_0}) \in \mathsf{L_{keys}}$ **return** $\perp$
if $\nexists\, (i_1, \mathbf{pk}_{i_1}, \mathbf{sk}_{i_1}) \in \mathsf{L_{keys}}$ **return** $\perp$
// generate a signature
$\bar{\sigma}_0 \leftarrow \mathbf{LRS}.\mathsf{Sign}(\mu_0, \{\mathbf{pk}_i\}_{i \in \mathcal{R}_0}, \mathbf{sk}_{i_0})$
// generate the second signature according to
// the experiment's bit b
$\bar{\sigma}_1 \leftarrow \mathbf{LRS}.\mathsf{Sign}(\mu_1, \{\mathbf{pk}_i\}_{i \in \mathcal{R}_1}, \mathbf{sk}_{i_b})$
return $(\bar{\sigma}_0, \bar{\sigma}_1)$

Fig. 6. Cross-message unlinkability. The signing, key generation and corruption oracles are as defined in Fig. 2, except that the **ERS** algorithms are substituted with the respective **SMLERS** variants.

Second, we modify the Sign algorithm of our ERS in Figure 4 so that it additionally computes $g' := \mathsf{H}(\mu)$ and $\tau := (g')^{\mathbf{sk}}$ for some hash function H, and it includes the linkability tag τ as part of the signature. Finally, the algorithm Link simply compares the linkability tags in the two signatures. It returns `linked` if they are equal, and `unlinked` otherwise.

This scheme can be shown to be same-message one-more linkable (resp. cross-message unlinkable) with only minor modifications to the proof of unforgeability (resp. anonymous extendability) of the extendable ring signature scheme.

5 Extendable Threshold Ring Signatures

Like a traditional threshold ring signature scheme, an *extendable* threshold ring signature scheme enables parties to produce a signature on a message μ for a ring $\mathcal{R}$ showing that at least t of the $|\mathcal{R}|$ potential signers in the ring participated, without revealing which. An extendable threshold ring signature scheme additionally has the following properties:

Flexibility: Given any two threshold signatures σ_0 and σ_1 that verify for the same message μ and for the same ring $\mathcal{R}$, anyone can *non-interactively* combine the signatures to obtain σ. The new signature σ is also a threshold ring signature and its threshold is equal to the total number of unique signers who contributed to at least one of the two signatures. This functionality is provided by the Combine algorithm (below).

Extendability: Given a signature σ on a message μ for the ring $\mathcal{R}$ with threshold t, anyone can *non-interactively* transform σ into a signature σ' on the same message with the same threshold , but for a larger ring $\mathcal{R}' \supseteq \mathcal{R}$. This functionality is provided by Extend (see below).

5.1 Syntax

A non-interactive extendable threshold ring signature scheme (**ETRS**) is defined as a tuple of six PPT algorithms **ETRS** = (Setup, KeyGen, Sign, Verify, Combine, Extend), where the public parameters pp produced by Setup are implicitly available to all other algorithms:

$\mathsf{Setup}(1^\lambda) \to \mathsf{pp}$: Takes a security parameter λ and outputs a set of public parameters pp.

$\mathsf{KeyGen}() \to (\mathsf{pk}, \mathsf{sk})$: Generates a new public and secret key pair.

$\mathsf{Sign}(\mu, \{\mathsf{pk}_i\}_{i \in \mathcal{R}}, \mathsf{sk}) \to \sigma$: Returns a signature with threshold $t = 1$ using the secret key sk corresponding to a public key pk_i with $i \in \mathcal{R}$.

$\mathsf{Verify}(t, \mu, \{\mathsf{pk}_i\}_{i \in \mathcal{R}}, \sigma) \to \mathtt{accept/reject}$: Verifies a signature σ for the message μ against the public keys $\{\mathsf{pk}_i\}_{i \in \mathcal{R}}$ with threshold t.

$\mathsf{Combine}(\mu, \sigma_0, \sigma_1, \{\mathsf{pk}_i\}_{i \in \mathcal{R}}) \mapsto \sigma'$: Combines two signatures σ_0, σ_1 for the same ring $\mathcal{R}$ into a signature σ' with threshold $t = |S_0 \cup S_1|$ where S_0, S_1 is the set of (hidden) signers for σ_0 and σ_1 respectively.

$\mathsf{Extend}(\mu, \sigma, \{\mathsf{pk}_i\}_{i \in \mathcal{R}}, \{\mathsf{pk}_i\}_{i \in \mathcal{R}'}) \mapsto \sigma'$: Extends the signature σ with threshold t for the ring $\mathcal{R}$ into a new signature σ' with threshold t for the larger ring $\mathcal{R} \cup \mathcal{R}'$.

For a somewhat more interactive syntax, we can replace 'Sign&Combine' executions with a Join operation (described in Sect. 2.1). For the sake of formalism, we present our security model only for schemes with Combine and defer the discussion on how to handle Join operations to the Sect. 5.4, where we present a construction that uses the Join operation from signatures of knowledge and the discrete log problem.

For the following definitions, we use ladders lad in a slightly different way than we did in the context of extendable ring signatures (Sect. 3). We generalize lad to support arbitrary sequences of actions that could lead to a valid threshold ring signature (on some fixed message). lad will contain a sequence of tuples of the form (action, input). The first component, action, can take on the values Sign, Combine, or Extend. If action = Sign, we expect input = $(\mathcal{R}, i)$, where $\mathcal{R}$ and i are the ring and signer identity with which the signature should be produced. If action = Combine, we expect input = $(l_1, l_2, \mathcal{R})$, where l_1 and l_2 are indices of two signatures under the same ring $\mathcal{R}$. If action = Extend, we expect input = $(l', \mathcal{R})$, where l' is the index of an existing signature which we will extended to $\mathcal{R}$.

For use in our definitions, we define an algorithm $\mathsf{Process}(\mu, \mathsf{L_{keys}}, \mathtt{lad})$, which processes all of the operations in lad on the message μ (using keys stored in the list $\mathsf{L}_{\mathsf{keys}}$) and returns $(\sigma, t, \mathcal{R})$: the signature returned by the last operation of $\mathtt{lad}$, the corresponding threshold, and the ring that σ verifies under. We define $\mathtt{lad.sr}$ to be the union of all identities and rings in $\mathtt{lad}$. ($\mathtt{sr}$ stands for super-ring.)

We give a formal description of Process in the full version of this paper.

Definition 10 (Correctness for ETRS). *For correctness, we require that for all ladders* $\mathtt{lad}$*, the signature returned by* $\mathsf{Process}(\mathtt{lad})$ *verifies. Formally: for all security parameters* $\lambda \in \mathbb{N}$*, for any message* $\mu \in \{0,1\}^*$*, for any ladder* $\mathtt{lad}$ *of polynomial size identifying a ring* $\mathcal{R} := \mathtt{lad.sr}$ *of public-key identifiers, for any chosen threshold value* $1 \leq t \leq |\mathcal{R}|$*, it holds:*

$$\Pr\left[\begin{array}{c} \mathsf{Verify}(t, \mu, \{\mathsf{pk}_i\}_{i \in \mathcal{R}}, \sigma) \\ = \mathtt{accept}\ \mathit{OR}\ \sigma = \bot \end{array} \middle| \begin{array}{l} \mathsf{pp} \leftarrow \mathsf{Setup}(1^\lambda) \\ \mathsf{L}_{\mathsf{keys}} \leftarrow \{\mathsf{KeyGen}()\}_{j \in \mathtt{lad.sr}} \\ (\sigma, t, \mathcal{R}) \leftarrow \mathsf{Process}(\mu, \mathsf{L}_{\mathsf{keys}}, \mathtt{lad}) \end{array}\right] = 1.$$

5.2 Security Model

Our security definitions are loosely based on the ones given for threshold ring signatures by Munch-Hansen *et al.* [22].

Definition 11 (Secure ETRS). *An extendable threshold ring signature scheme is secure if it satisfies correctness (Definition 10), unforgeability (Definition 12), anonymity (Definition 13), and some notion of anonymous extendability.*

$\mathsf{Exp}^{\mathrm{cmEUF}}_{\mathcal{A},\mathbf{ETRS}}(\lambda)$

$\mathsf{L}_{\mathsf{keys}}, \mathsf{L}_{\mathsf{corr}}, \mathsf{L}_{\mathsf{sign}} \leftarrow \varnothing$

$\mathsf{pp} \leftarrow \mathsf{Setup}(1^\lambda)$

$\mathcal{O} \leftarrow \{\mathcal{O}\mathsf{Sign}, \mathcal{O}\mathsf{KeyGen}, \mathcal{O}\mathsf{Corrupt}\}$

$(t^*, \mu^*, \mathcal{R}^*, \sigma^*) \leftarrow \mathcal{A}^{\mathcal{O}}(\mathsf{pp})$

$q \leftarrow |\{(\mu^*, \mathcal{R}, \cdot) \in \mathsf{L}_{\mathsf{sign}}\ s.t.\ \mathcal{R} \subseteq \mathcal{R}^*)\}|$

// rule out attacks if $\mathcal{A}$ knows too many sk:s or honestly generated signatures for μ^*

if $|\mathcal{R}^* \cap \mathsf{L}_{\mathsf{corr}}| + q \geq t$ **return lose**

// rule out outputs that do not verify

if $\mathsf{Verify}(t, \mu^*, \{\mathsf{pk}_j\}_{j \in \mathcal{R}^*}, \sigma^*) = \mathtt{reject}$ **return lose**

return win

Fig. 7. Existential unforgeability under chosen message attack for (extendable) threshold ring signatures. The key generation, corruption and signing oracles are as in Fig. 2, with the difference that the **ERS** algorithms are substituted with the **ETRS** variants, and the signing oracle now returns partial signatures.

Definition 12 (Unforgeability for ETRS). *An extendable threshold ring signature scheme* **ETRS** *is said to be unforgeable if for all thresholds t, for all PPT adversaries* $\mathcal{A}$ *the success probability in the* cmEUF *experiment in Fig. 7 is* $\Pr\left[\mathsf{Exp}^{\mathrm{cmEUF}}_{\mathcal{A},\mathbf{ETRS}}(\lambda) = \mathtt{win}\right] \leq \mathtt{negl}.$

Just like for extendable ring signatures, the notion of anonymity for extendable threshold ring signatures captures scenarios where the adversary distinguishes fresh (not-extended) signatures, i.e., the challenge will be a threshold ring signature which has not be extended.

$\mathsf{Exp}^{\mathrm{ANEXT}}_{\mathcal{A},\mathbf{ETRS}}(\lambda)$	$\mathsf{Chal}_b(\mu^*, \mathrm{lad}_0^*, \mathrm{lad}_1^*)$
1 : $b \leftarrow_R \{0,1\}$	1 : **if** lad_0^* or lad_1^* is not well-formed
2 : $\mathsf{L}_{\mathsf{keys}}, \mathsf{L}_{\mathsf{corr}}, \mathsf{L}_{\mathsf{sign}} \leftarrow \varnothing$	2 : **return** $\perp$
3 : $\mathsf{pp} \leftarrow \mathbf{ETRS}.\mathsf{Setup}(1^\lambda)$	3 : **if** $\exists i \in \mathrm{lad}_0^*.\mathsf{signers}$ *s.t.* $i \in \mathsf{L}_{\mathsf{corr}}$
4 : $O \leftarrow \{O\mathsf{Sign}, O\mathsf{KeyGen}, O\mathsf{Corrupt}\}$	4 : **return** $\perp$
5 : $(\mu^*, \mathrm{lad}_0^*, \mathrm{lad}_1^*) \leftarrow \mathcal{A}^O(\mathsf{pp})$	5 : **if** $\exists i \in \mathrm{lad}_1^*.\mathsf{signers}$ *s.t.* $i \in \mathsf{L}_{\mathsf{corr}}$
6 : $\bar{\sigma} \leftarrow \mathsf{Chal}_b(\mu^*, \mathrm{lad}_0^*, \mathrm{lad}_1^*)$	6 : **return** $\perp$
7 : $b^* \leftarrow \mathcal{A}^O(\bar{\sigma})$	// make sure the public keys are known / initialized
8 : **if** $\exists i \in \mathrm{lad}_0^*.\mathsf{signers}$ *s.t.* $i \in \mathsf{L}_{\mathsf{corr}}$	7 : **if** $\exists i \in \mathrm{lad}_0^*.\mathsf{sr}$ *s.t.* $(\mathsf{pk}_i, \cdot) \notin \mathsf{L}_{\mathsf{keys}}$
9 : **return lose**	8 : **return** $\perp$
10 : **if** $\exists i \in \mathrm{lad}_1^*.\mathsf{signers}$ *s.t.* $i \in \mathsf{L}_{\mathsf{corr}}$	9 : **if** $\exists i \in \mathrm{lad}_1^*.\mathsf{sr}$ *s.t.* $(\mathsf{pk}_i, \cdot) \notin \mathsf{L}_{\mathsf{keys}}$
11 : **return lose**	10 : **return** $\perp$
12 : **if** $\exists (\mu^*, \cdot, i) \in \mathsf{L}_{\mathsf{sign}}$ for $i \in \mathrm{lad}_0^*.\mathsf{signers}$	11 : $(\sigma_0, t_0, \mathcal{R}_0) \leftarrow \mathsf{Process}(\mu^*, \mathsf{L}_{\mathsf{keys}}, \mathrm{lad}_0)$
13 : **return lose**	12 : $(\sigma_1, t_1, \mathcal{R}_1) \leftarrow \mathsf{Process}(\mu^*, \mathsf{L}_{\mathsf{keys}}, \mathrm{lad}_1)$
14 : **if** $\exists (\mu^*, \cdot, i) \in \mathsf{L}_{\mathsf{sign}}$ for $i \in \mathrm{lad}_1^*.\mathsf{signers}$	// rule out trivial attacks
15 : **return lose**	13 : **if** $\mathcal{R}_0 \neq \mathcal{R}_1$ or $t_0 \neq t_1$
16 : **if** $b^* \neq b$	14 : **return** $\perp$
17 : **return lose**	15 : $\bar{\sigma} \leftarrow \sigma_b$
18 : **return win**	16 : **return** $\bar{\sigma}$

Fig. 8. Anonymity and anonymous extendability for extendable threshold ring signatures. The key generation, corruption and signing oracles are exactly as described in the unforgeability experiment (Fig. 7).

Definition 13 (Anonymity for ETRS). *An extendable threshold ring signature scheme is said to be anonymous if for all PPT adversaries* $\mathcal{A}$ *taking part in the anonymous extendability experiment (ANEXT in Figure 8) and submitting to the challenger two ladders with the structure explained below, it holds that the success probability of* $\mathcal{A}$ *is negligibly close to random guessing, i.e.:*
$$\Pr\left[\mathsf{Exp}^{\mathrm{ANEXT}}_{\mathcal{A},\mathbf{ETRS}}(\lambda) = \mathtt{win}\right] \leq \tfrac{1}{2} + \mathtt{negl}.$$

For anonymity, the ladders submitted by the adversary to the challenger have the following structure (here t denotes the threshold of the scheme): the first t instructions are of the type (Sign, $(\mathcal{R}, i)$)*, where* $\mathcal{R}$ *is the same for all instructions in both ladders, and the signer indexes* i *are all distinct within the same ladder; the last* $(t-1)$ *instructions are of the type* (Combine, $(l_1, l_2, \mathcal{R})$)*, where* $\mathcal{R}$ *is the same for all instructions in both ladders,* $l_1 = 1, 2, \ldots, t-1$*, and* $l_2 = t, t+1, \ldots, 2t-2$.

Our notion of anonymous extendability follows the gist of strong anonymity introduced in Sect. 3.2 for extendable ring signatures, but adapted to the threshold setting.

Definition 14 (Strong Anonymous Extendability for ETRS). *An extendable threshold ring signature scheme ETRS is said to be strongly anonymous extendable if for all PPT adversaries* $\mathcal{A}$ *taking part in the anonymous extendability experiment (*ANEXT *in Fig. 8) and submitting to the challenger ladders with the structure specified below, it holds that the success probability of* $\mathcal{A}$ *is negligibly close to random guessing, i.e.:* $\Pr\left[\mathsf{Exp}^{\mathrm{ANEXT}}_{\mathcal{A}_{\mathrm{sAnon}},\mathbf{ERS}}(\lambda) = \mathtt{win}\right] \leq \frac{1}{2} + \mathtt{negl}$.

For strong anonymous extendability the adversary submits ladders that have the with the following structure: the first t *instructions are of the type* (Sign, $(i, \mathcal{R})$)*, where the signer identities are pairwise distinct within a ladder, and the ring* $\mathcal{R}$ *is the same within the ladder (but possibly different for each ladder); the subsequent* $t-1$ *instructions are of the form* (Combine, $(l_1, l_2, \mathcal{R})$) *or* (Extend, $(l', \mathcal{R}')$)*, where* l_1, l_2 *and* l' *denote indexes.*

Notably, in strong anonymous extendability each ladder may contain an arbitrary (polynomial, and possibly different for each ladder) number of subsequent Extend *instructions, so long the final one of each ladder culminates in the same ring.*

5.3 A Generic Compiler for ETRS from SMLERS

In what follows, we formalize the intuition given in Remark 2 (Section 4.1) on how to generically derive an extendable threshold ring signature scheme from any given same-message linkable extendable ring signature scheme. The compiler is detailed in Fig. 9.

Theorem 2. *Assuming that* **SMLERS** *is a secure same-message linkable extendable ring signature scheme, then the scheme* **ETRS** = (Setup, KeyGen, Sign, Verify, Extend, Combine) *described in Fig. 9 is an extendable threshold ring signature scheme that satisfies* correctness *(Definition 10),* unforgeability *(Definition 12), and* anonymity *(Definition 13).*

We prove Theorem 2 in the full version of this paper.

5.4 ETRS from Signatures of Knowledge and Discrete Log

In what follows we present a somewhat more interactive Extendable Threshold Ring Signature Scheme that supports Join operations and enjoys more compact

$\mathsf{Setup}(1^\lambda) \mapsto \mathsf{pp}$

return **SMLERS**.$\mathsf{Setup}(1^\lambda)$

$\mathsf{KeyGen}() \mapsto (\mathsf{pk}, \mathsf{sk})$

return **SMLERS**.$\mathsf{KeyGen}()$

$\mathsf{Sign}(\mu, \mathsf{sk}, \{\mathsf{pk}_i\}_{i \in \mathcal{R}}) \mapsto \sigma$

return **SMLERS**.$\mathsf{Sign}(\mu, \mathsf{sk}, \{\mathsf{pk}_i\}_{i \in \mathcal{R}})$

$\mathsf{Extend}(\mu, \sigma, \{\mathsf{pk}_i\}_{i \in \mathcal{R}_0}, \{\mathsf{pk}_i\}_{i \in \mathcal{R}_1},) \mapsto \sigma'$

return $\{$**SMLERS**.$\mathsf{Extend}(\{\mathsf{pk}_i\}_{i \in \mathcal{R}_1}, \{\mathsf{pk}_j\}_{j \in \mathcal{R}_2}, \sigma_i)\}_{\sigma_i \in \sigma}$

$\mathsf{Combine}(\mu, \sigma_0, \sigma_1, \{\mathsf{pk}_i\}_{i \in \mathcal{R}}) \mapsto \sigma'$

```
1 : σ'_0 ← {s_0 ∈ σ_0 | ∀s_1 ∈ σ_1 : Link(μ, (s_0, {pk_i}_{i∈R}), (s_1, {pk_i}_{i∈R})) = unlinked}
2 : return σ'_0 ∪ σ_1
```

$\mathsf{Verify}(t, \mu, \{\mathsf{pk}_i\}_{i \in \mathcal{R}}, \sigma) \mapsto \mathtt{accept}/\mathtt{reject}$

```
1 : Parse σ = {s_0, ..., s_ℓ} as a set of signatures // removing duplicates
2 : if |σ| < t return reject
3 : if ∃ s_i ∈ σ : Verify(μ, {pk_i}_{i∈R}, s_i) = reject  return reject
4 : if ∃ (s_i, s_j) ∈ σ × σ : s_i ≠ s_j ∧
        Link(μ, (s_i, {pk_i}_{i∈R}), (s_j, {pk_i}_{i∈R})) = linked  return reject
5 : return accept
```

Fig. 9. Generic compiler for extendable threshold ring signatures from extendable same-message linkable ring signatures.

signatures. Concretely, the size of extended threshold signatures is independent of the threshold t, instead it grows linearly with n' (an upper bound on the ring size). This is an improvement compared to the compiler presented in Fig. 9, which if instantiated using our **SMLERS** from Signatures of Knowledge and Discrete Log of Sect. 4.3, returns signatures of size linear in $t \cdot |\mathcal{R}|$.

Our Construction in a Nutshell. Similarly to the ERS construction of Fig. 4, we work with a prime order group $\mathbb{G}$, with two public elements $g, H \in \mathbb{G}$ and a signature of knowledge for a relation $\mathscr{R}_{\mathbb{G}}$ for knowledge of the discrete logarithm either of a given value h or of a pk.

Let $n' \in \mathbb{N}$ be an upper bound on the ring size. We achieve the threshold functionality by leveraging features of polynomials in a similar way to Shamir secret sharing. Intuitively, the signer samples $n' > 0$ pairs of values $(x_i, \mathtt{td}_i) \in \mathbb{Z}_p \times \mathbb{G}$. These pairs of values define a unique polynomial $f(x)$ of degree n' such that $f(0) = \mathrm{dlog}_g(H)$ and $f(x_i) = \mathtt{td}_i$ for every $i \in [n']$. Of course, since $\mathrm{dlog}_g(H)$ is unknown, our signers don't know the coefficients of this polynomial. However, since polynomial interpolation involves only linear operations (when the

x-coordinates are fixed and known), the signers can interpolate this polynomial *in the exponent* to learn additional points $(\hat{x}, y = g^{f(\hat{x})})$ for any given $\hat{x}$. In order to sign, and later to endorse a statement (Join a signature), the signer is required to produce a signature of knowledge for $\mathscr{R}_{\mathbb{G}}$ for a random point $(\hat{x}, y = g^{f(\hat{x})})$ on the polynomial such that $\hat{x} \notin \{x_i\}_{i\in[n']}$. Crucially, the signer does not know the discrete log of y (i.e., $(\hat{x}, y)$ is not among the 'trapdoored' values $(x_i, g^{\mathtt{td}_i})$), and thus must satisfy the second clause of the relation (proving knowledge of their secret key). On the other hand, to extend a signature, anyone can pick one of the (remaining) 'trapdoored' points $(x_i, \mathtt{td}_i)$, and generate a proof for $\mathscr{R}_{\mathbb{G}}$ by satisfying the first clause (proving knowledge of $\mathtt{td}_i$), to include any $\mathbf{pk}$ in the ring. The pair $(x_i, \mathtt{td}_i)$ is then removed from the list of trapdoors. (In case the owner of $\mathbf{pk}$ later wants to join the signature, the Extend algorithm encrypts $\mathtt{td}_i$ to $\mathbf{pk}$; later, the owner of $\mathbf{pk}$ can recover $\mathtt{td}_i$ and return it to the list of trapdoors before producing a fresh signature of knowledge using her secret key.)

The key idea of our construction is detailed in Fig. 10 (the PolySign subroutine employed in Sign and Join–where this is called using the signer's secret key as w and on a random value $\hat{x}$– and in Extend–where an evaluation point and its corresponding trapdoor are used as $\hat{x}$and w respectively).

For any field $\mathbb{F}$ (often implicit) and $\mathcal{X} \subseteq \mathbb{F}$, $j \in \mathcal{X}$, define the degree $|\mathcal{X}| - 1$ Lagrange polynomial $L_{(\mathcal{X},j)}(X) := \prod_{m\in\mathcal{X}\setminus\{j\}} \frac{X-m}{j-m} \in \mathbb{F}[X]$.

Theorem 3. *Assuming that* **SoK** *is a secure signature of knowledge scheme, and that the discrete log problem is hard in the group* $\mathbb{G}$*, then the scheme*

$\mathsf{PolySign}(P, T, \hat{x}, w, \mathbf{pk}, \mu) \rightarrow (y_{\hat{x}}, \pi)$

// compute values for the Lagrange interpolation

$\mathcal{Z} := \{(0, H)\} \cup \{(x, g^{\mathtt{td}})\}_{(x,\mathtt{td})\in T} \cup \{(x, y)\}_{(x,y,\mathbf{pk},c,\pi)\in P}$

// compute evaluation points for the Lagrange interpolation

$\mathcal{X} := \{x\}_{(x,y)\in\mathcal{Z}}$

// evaluate the polynomial on the input point $\hat{x}$

$y_{\hat{x}} \leftarrow \prod_{(x,y)\in\mathcal{Z}} y^{L_{(\mathcal{X},x)}(\hat{x})}$ // note: $dlog(y_{\hat{x}})$ is unknown because $dlog(H)$ is

$\phi := (\hat{y}, \mathbf{pk}_s)$ // include new poly. value in the statement

// Lagrange interpolation in the exponent over the standard set $\{1,\ldots,n'\}$

for $i \in [n']$: $V_i \leftarrow \prod_{(x,y)\in\mathcal{Z}} y^{L_{(\mathcal{X},x)}(i)}$

$\hat{\mu} := (\mu, \{V_i\}_{i\in[n']})$ // include a 'commitment' to the polynomial in the message

$\pi \leftarrow \mathbf{SoK}.\mathsf{Sign}(\hat{\mu}, \mathscr{R}_{\mathbb{G}}, \phi, w)$

// note: w is given in input to the algorithm, $w = \mathsf{sk}$ for Sign & Join, otherwise $w = \mathsf{td}$

return $(\hat{y}, \pi)$

Fig. 10. Subroutine used in our **ETRS** construction depicted in Fig. 11.

$\mathsf{KeyGen}() \mapsto (\mathsf{pk}, \mathsf{sk})$

$(\mathsf{pk}_s, \mathsf{sk}_s) \leftarrow \mathbf{ERS}.\mathsf{KeyGen}()$
$(\mathsf{pk}_e, \mathsf{sk}_e) \leftarrow \mathbf{PKE}.\mathsf{KeyGen}()$
return $(\mathsf{pk} = (\mathsf{pk}_s, \mathsf{pk}_e), \mathsf{sk} = (\mathsf{sk}_s, \mathsf{sk}_e))$

$\mathsf{Sign}(\mu, \mathsf{sk}) \mapsto \sigma$

$X \leftarrow_R \binom{\mathbb{Z}_p^*}{n'}$ // pick n' distinct evaluation points
$T := \varnothing; \quad P := \varnothing$
for $x \in X$
  $\mathsf{td} \leftarrow_R \mathbb{Z}_p$ // generate trapdoors for poly. values
  $T \leftarrow T \cup \{(x, \mathsf{td})\}$ // populate trapdoor set
$c \leftarrow \mathsf{Enc}(\mathsf{pk}_e, \perp)$ // no info to pass on
$\hat{x} \leftarrow_R \mathbb{Z}_p^* \setminus X$ // pick a new evaluation point
$(y, \pi) \leftarrow \mathsf{PolySign}(P, T, \hat{x}, w := \mathsf{sk}, \mathsf{pk}, \mu)$
$P := \{(\hat{x}, y, \mathsf{pk}_s, \pi, c)\}$
return $\sigma := (T, P)$

$\mathsf{Join}(\mu, \{\mathsf{pk}_j\}_{j \in \mathcal{R}}, \mathsf{sk}, \sigma) \mapsto \sigma'$

// check if current signer's pk_s is in P
if $\exists\ (x, y, \mathsf{pk}, \pi, c) \in P$ *s.t.* $\mathsf{pk} = \mathsf{pk}_s$
// remove simulated proof for the signer who wants to join
  $P \leftarrow P \setminus \{(x, y, \mathsf{pk}_s, \pi, c)\}$
// retrieve trapdoor value
  $\mathsf{td} \leftarrow \mathsf{Dec}(\mathsf{sk}_e, c)$
// add eval. point and td to the set of available trapdoors
  $T \leftarrow T \cup \{(x, \mathsf{td})\}$
$c' \leftarrow \mathsf{Enc}(\mathsf{pk}_e, \perp)$ // no info to pass on
$\hat{x} \leftarrow_R \mathbb{Z}_p^* \setminus X$ // pick a new evaluation point
// interpolate a unique representation of the polynomial
$(y', \pi') \leftarrow \mathsf{PolySign}(P, T, \hat{x}, w := \mathsf{sk}, \mathsf{pk}, \mu)$
$P \leftarrow P \cup \{(\hat{x}, y', \mathsf{pk}_s, \pi', c')\}$
Randomly permute P
return $\sigma := (T, P)$

$\mathsf{Extend}(\mu, \{\mathsf{pk}_j\}_{j \in \mathcal{R}}, \sigma, \mathsf{pk}) \mapsto \sigma'$

if $\mathsf{pk} \in \{\mathsf{pk}_j\}_{j \in \mathcal{R}}$: **return** $\perp$
$(\hat{x}, \hat{\mathsf{td}}) \leftarrow_R T$ // Pick eval-point and trapdoor
$c' \leftarrow \mathsf{Enc}(\mathsf{pk}_e, \hat{\mathsf{td}})$ // enable future endorsing
// interpolate a unique representation of the polynomial
$(y', \pi') \leftarrow \mathsf{PolySign}(P, T, \hat{x}, w := \hat{x}, \mathsf{pk}, \mu)$
$T \leftarrow T \setminus \{(\hat{x}, \hat{\mathsf{td}})\}$ // erase used trapdoor
// Add simulated signature to the set of proofs
$P \leftarrow P \cup \{(\hat{x}, y', \mathsf{pk}_s, \pi', c')\}$
Randomly permute P
return $\sigma' := (T, P)$

$\mathsf{Verify}(t, \mu, \{\mathsf{pk}_j\}_{j \in \mathcal{R}}, \sigma) \mapsto \mathtt{accept/reject}$

if $\{\mathsf{pk}_j\}_{j \in \mathcal{R}} \neq \{\mathsf{pk}_i\}_{(\cdot,\cdot,\mathsf{pk}_i,\cdot,\cdot) \in P}$:
  return reject
// check y's are consistent with a degree n' polynomial
$\mathcal{Z} := \{(0, H)\} \cup \{(x, g^{\mathsf{td}})\}_{(x,\mathsf{td}) \in T}$
$\mathcal{Z} \leftarrow \mathcal{Z} \cup \{(x, y)\}_{(x,y,\mathsf{pk},c,\pi) \in P}$
Pick $\hat{\mathcal{Z}} \subseteq \mathcal{Z}$ *s.t.* $|\hat{\mathcal{Z}}| = n' + 1$
$\mathcal{X} := \{x\}_{(x,y) \in \mathcal{Z}}; \hat{\mathcal{X}} := \{x\}_{(x,y) \in \hat{\mathcal{Z}}}$
for $(x, y) \in \mathcal{Z}$:
  if $y \neq \prod_{(\hat{x},\hat{y}) \in \hat{\mathcal{Z}}} \hat{y}^{L(\hat{\mathcal{X}},\hat{x})(x)}$: **return reject**
// Interpolation over the standard set $\{1,\ldots,n'\}$
for $i \in [n']$: $\quad V_i \leftarrow \prod_{(x,y) \in \mathcal{Z}} y^{L(\mathcal{X},x)(i)}$
$\hat{\mu} := (\mu, \{V_i\}_{i \in [n']})$
for $(x, y, \mathsf{pk}_s, \pi, c) \in P$ // check proofs individually
  $\phi := (y, \mathsf{pk}_s)$
  if $\mathbf{SoK}.\mathsf{Verify}(\hat{\mu}, \mathscr{R}_{\mathbb{G}}, \phi, \pi) = \mathtt{reject}$
    return reject
if $|T| + |P| \geq t + n'$ **return accept**
else return reject

Fig. 11. Extendable threshold ring signatures from signature of knowledge and hardness of discrete log. The **Setup** algorithm is the same as in the **ERS** construction of Fig. 4 (with $\mathscr{R}_{\mathbb{G}} = \{(\phi, w) = (h, \mathsf{pk}, x) \in \mathbb{G} \times \mathbb{G} \times \mathbb{Z}_p : g^x = h \vee g^x = \mathsf{pk}\}$). In the description, $n' > 0$ denotes the maximum amount of times a signature can be extended (it can be set in pp, or chosen upon signing). We always let pk denote the public key corresponding to sk; any algorithm that is given sk as input implicitly has access to pk. The parsing of pk into $(\mathsf{pk}_s, \mathsf{pk}_e)$ (or of pk_i into $(\mathsf{pk}_{s,i}, \mathsf{pk}_{e,i})$), of sk into $(\mathsf{sk}_s, \mathsf{sk}_e)$ and of σ into (T, P) is done implicitly.

ETRS $=$ (Setup, KeyGen, Sign, Verify, Extend, Join) *described in Fig. 11 is an extendable threshold ring signature scheme that satisfies* correctness *(Definition 10),* unforgeability *(Definition 12), and* strong anonymous extendability *(Definition 13).*

We give a proof of Theorem 3 in the full version of this paper. We also describe how we modify the security model to account for the Join there.

Remark 3. Note that a malicious extender can prevent the newly added members of the ring from later joining a signature, simply by not encrypting the correct trapdoor under that new member's public key. This is not captured by our security definitions, but precluding such attacks would be an interesting and valuable extension. We can modify our construction to disallow this by adding a zero knowledge proof that the encrypted value is in fact the discrete log of the h in question.

6 Implementation Results

We have implemented the **ERS**, **SMLERS** and **ETRS** constructions, respectively from Sects. 3, 4.3 and 5, at the 128-bit security level within the RELIC[2] library. The choice of underlying group is the conservative `edwards25519` elliptic curve used in the Ed25519 signature scheme [2]. The benchmarking platform is an Intel Core i7-6700K Skylake @ 4 GHz, with HyperThreading and TurboBoost disabled. Each operation was executed 10^4 times for the smaller rings and 10^2 times for the larger ones. The average times for signature generation and verification, and signature sizes (without point compression) are shown in Figs. 12, 13 and 14, respectively. For ease of exposition, we combined the wall time for the initial signature generation and subsequent joinings or extensions in the plots. A specific binary built by running `make` in `relic/demo/ers-etrs` allows to reproduce our results.

ERS Benchmark. We benchmark our ERS implementation for ring sizes of 1 to 2^{11}. The performance depends on the ring size only, so the number of extensions is always the number of keys. We instantiate the SoK for the relation $\mathscr{R}_{\mathbf{ERS}}$ as a non-interactive Sigma protocol combining an OR-proof with proof of knowledge of the discrete logarithm embedding the message to be signed in the challenge computation.

ETRS Benchmark. We benchmark our ETRS implementation for thresholds of $1, 2, 4, 8$ and ring sizes of 1 to 2^{11}. For the ETRS construction, the quadratic cost of interpolation clearly dominates the signing, joining and verification steps; and explains the additional computational overhead in comparison to the ERS scheme.

ETRS from SMLERS Benchmark. Finally, we include the benchmarks of our generic compiler applied to our SMLERS scheme. We instantiate the SoK for the relation $\mathscr{R}_{\mathbf{SMLERS}}$ as another non-interactive Sigma protocol combining OR-proofs and discrete logarithm proofs by slightly rewriting the statement as $\{(g^x = h \vee g^x = \mathtt{pk}) \wedge (g^x = h \vee (g')^x = \tau)\}$, which allows us to share code with

[2] https://github.com/relic-toolkit/relic

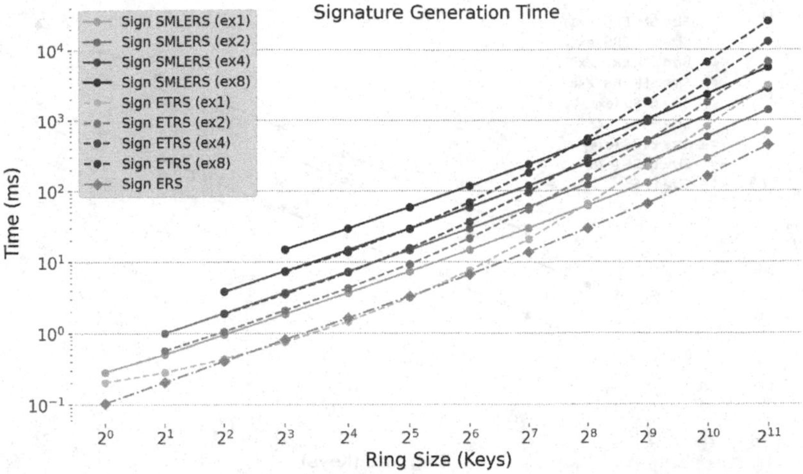

Fig. 12. Clock time for Sign in the three implemented schemes for different thresholds. The signature generation time includes the initial signature generation and subsequent joinings/extensions.

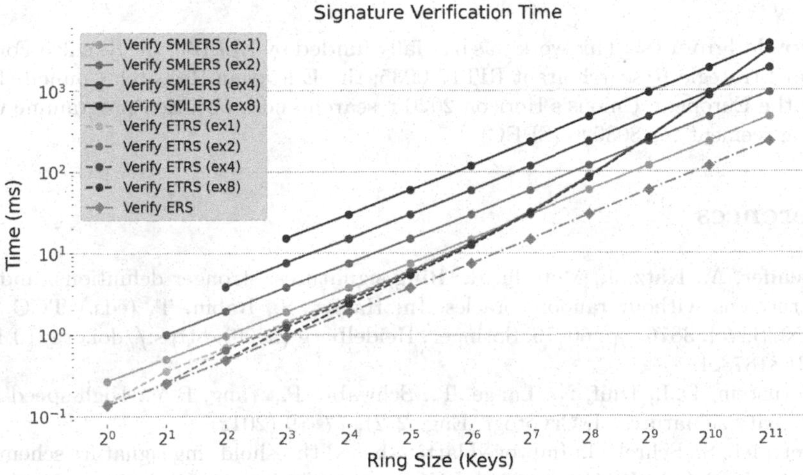

Fig. 13. Clock time for Verify in the three implemented schemes for different thresholds. The verification time is that of verifying the final extended signature.

the ERS implementation. In comparison with the ETRS scheme, the signature sizes are much larger; but the signature and verification times are more efficient for larger rings due to the cost of interpolation in the ETRS scheme.

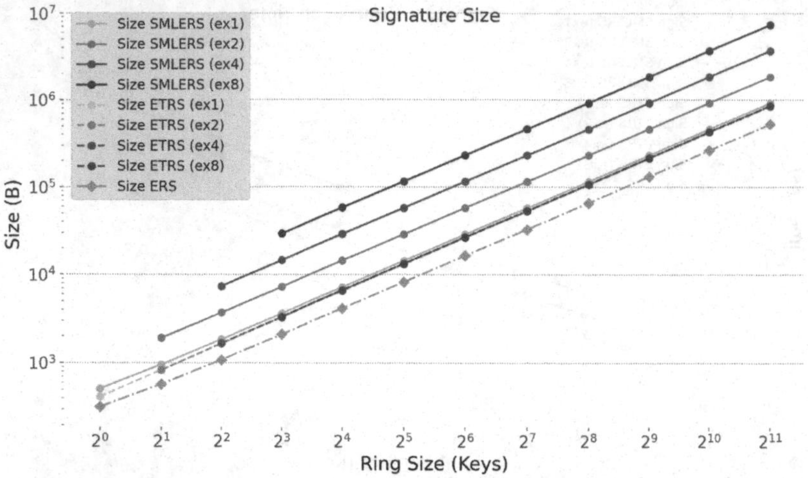

Fig. 14. Signature sizes for all the three implemented schemes, with varying thresholds. In the ETRS scheme, the signature size is independent of the threshold, while in ESMLRS there is a linear dependence.

Acknowledgments. This work was partially funded by ELLIIT; the Swedish Foundation for Strategic Research grant RIT17-0035; the European Research Council (ERC) under the European Unions's Horizon 2020 research and innovation programme under grant agreement No 803096 (SPEC).

References

1. Bender, A., Katz, J., Morselli, R.: Ring signatures: stronger definitions, and constructions without random oracles. In: Halevi, S., Rabin, T. (eds.) TCC 2006. LNCS, vol. 3876, pp. 60–79. Springer, Heidelberg (2006). https://doi.org/10.1007/11681878_4
2. Bernstein, D.J., Duif, N., Lange, T., Schwabe, P., Yang, B.Y.: High-speed high-security signatures. J. Cryptogr. Eng. **2**(2), 77–89 (2012)
3. Bettaieb, S., Schrek, J.: Improved lattice-based threshold ring signature scheme. In: Gaborit, P. (ed.) PQCrypto 2013. LNCS, vol. 7932, pp. 34–51. Springer, Heidelberg (2013). https://doi.org/10.1007/978-3-642-38616-9_3
4. Beullens, W., Katsumata, S., Pintore, F.: Calamari and falafl: logarithmic (linkable) ring signatures from isogenies and lattices. Cryptology ePrint Archive, Report 2020/646 (2020). https://eprint.iacr.org/2020/646
5. Boneh, D., Gentry, C., Lynn, B., Shacham, H.: Aggregate and verifiably encrypted signatures from bilinear maps. In: Biham, E. (ed.) EUROCRYPT 2003. LNCS, vol. 2656, pp. 416–432. Springer, Heidelberg (2003). https://doi.org/10.1007/3-540-39200-9_26
6. Bootle, J., Cerulli, A., Chaidos, P., Ghadafi, E., Groth, J., Petit, C.: Short accountable ring signatures based on DDH. In: Pernul, G., Ryan, P.Y.A., Weippl, E. (eds.) ESORICS 2015. LNCS, vol. 9326, pp. 243–265. Springer, Cham (2015). https://doi.org/10.1007/978-3-319-24174-6_13

7. Bose, P., Das, D., Rangan, C.P.: Constant size ring signature without random oracle. In: Foo, E., Stebila, D. (eds.) ACISP 2015. LNCS, vol. 9144, pp. 230–247. Springer, Cham (2015). https://doi.org/10.1007/978-3-319-19962-7_14
8. Bresson, E., Stern, J., Szydlo, M.: Threshold ring signatures and applications to ad-hoc groups. In: Yung, M. (ed.) CRYPTO 2002. LNCS, vol. 2442, pp. 465–480. Springer, Heidelberg (2002). https://doi.org/10.1007/3-540-45708-9_30
9. Brickell, E.F., Camenisch, J., Chen, L.: Direct anonymous attestation. In: Atluri, V., Pfitzmann, B., McDaniel, P. (eds.) ACM CCS 2004, pp. 132–145. ACM Press (2004)
10. Chandran, N., Groth, J., Sahai, A.: Ring signatures of sub-linear size without random oracles. In: Arge, L., Cachin, C., Jurdziński, T., Tarlecki, A. (eds.) ICALP 2007. LNCS, vol. 4596, pp. 423–434. Springer, Heidelberg (2007). https://doi.org/10.1007/978-3-540-73420-8_38
11. Chase, M., Lysyanskaya, A.: On signatures of knowledge. In: Dwork, C. (ed.) CRYPTO 2006. LNCS, vol. 4117, pp. 78–96. Springer, Heidelberg (2006). https://doi.org/10.1007/11818175_5
12. Chow, S.S.M., Wei, V.K.W., Liu, J.K., Yuen, T.H.: Ring signatures without random oracles. In: Lin, F.C., Lee, D.T., Lin, B.S., Shieh, S., Jajodia, S. (eds.) ASIACCS 2006, pp. 297–302. ACM Press (2006)
13. Dodis, Y., Kiayias, A., Nicolosi, A., Shoup, V.: Anonymous identification in *Ad Hoc* groups. In: Cachin, C., Camenisch, J.L. (eds.) EUROCRYPT 2004. LNCS, vol. 3027, pp. 609–626. Springer, Heidelberg (2004). https://doi.org/10.1007/978-3-540-24676-3_36
14. Esgin, M.F., Steinfeld, R., Sakzad, A., Liu, J.K., Liu, D.: Short lattice-based one-out-of-many proofs and applications to ring signatures. In: Deng, R.H., Gauthier-Umaña, V., Ochoa, M., Yung, M. (eds.) ACNS 2019. LNCS, vol. 11464, pp. 67–88. Springer, Cham (2019). https://doi.org/10.1007/978-3-030-21568-2_4
15. Haque, A., Scafuro, A.: Threshold ring signatures: new definitions and post-quantum security. In: Kiayias, A., Kohlweiss, M., Wallden, P., Zikas, V. (eds.) PKC 2020. LNCS, vol. 12111, pp. 423–452. Springer, Cham (2020). https://doi.org/10.1007/978-3-030-45388-6_15
16. Liu, J.K.: Ring signature. In: Li, K.-C., Chen, X., Susilo, W. (eds.) Advances in Cyber Security: Principles, Techniques, and Applications, pp. 93–114. Springer, Singapore (2019). https://doi.org/10.1007/978-981-13-1483-4_5
17. Liu, J.K., Wong, D.S.: On the security models of (threshold) ring signature schemes. In: Park, C., Chee, S. (eds.) ICISC 2004. LNCS, vol. 3506, pp. 204–217. Springer, Heidelberg (2005). https://doi.org/10.1007/11496618_16
18. Liu, Z., Nguyen, K., Yang, G., Wang, H., Wong, D.S.: A lattice-based linkable ring signature supporting stealth addresses. In: Sako, K., Schneider, S., Ryan, P.Y.A. (eds.) ESORICS 2019. LNCS, vol. 11735, pp. 726–746. Springer, Cham (2019). https://doi.org/10.1007/978-3-030-29959-0_35
19. Lu, X., Au, M.H., Zhang, Z.: Raptor: a practical lattice-based (linkable) ring signature. In: Deng, R.H., Gauthier-Umaña, V., Ochoa, M., Yung, M. (eds.) ACNS 2019. LNCS, vol. 11464, pp. 110–130. Springer, Cham (2019). https://doi.org/10.1007/978-3-030-21568-2_6
20. Malavolta, G., Schröder, D.: Efficient ring signatures in the standard model. In: Takagi, T., Peyrin, T. (eds.) ASIACRYPT 2017. LNCS, vol. 10625, pp. 128–157. Springer, Cham (2017). https://doi.org/10.1007/978-3-319-70697-9_5
21. Melchor, C.A., Cayrel, P.L., Gaborit, P., Laguillaumie, F.: A new efficient threshold ring signature scheme based on coding theory. IEEE Trans. Inf. Theory **57**(7), 4833–4842 (2011)

22. Munch-Hansen, A., Orlandi, C., Yakoubov, S.: Stronger notions and a more efficient construction of threshold ring signatures. Cryptology ePrint Archive, Report 2020/678 (2020). https://eprint.iacr.org/2020/678
23. Okamoto, T., Tso, R., Yamaguchi, M., Okamoto, E.: A k-out-of-n ring signature with flexible participation for signers. Cryptology ePrint Archive, Report 2018/728 (2018). https://eprint.iacr.org/2018/728
24. Patachi, Ş, Schürmann, C.: Eos a universal verifiable and coercion resistant voting protocol. In: Krimmer, R., Volkamer, M., Braun Binder, N., Kersting, N., Pereira, O., Schürmann, C. (eds.) E-Vote-ID 2017. LNCS, vol. 10615, pp. 210–227. Springer, Cham (2017). https://doi.org/10.1007/978-3-319-68687-5_13
25. Rivest, R.L., Shamir, A., Tauman, Y.: How to leak a secret. In: Boyd, C. (ed.) ASIACRYPT 2001. LNCS, vol. 2248, pp. 552–565. Springer, Heidelberg (2001). https://doi.org/10.1007/3-540-45682-1_32
26. Shacham, H., Waters, B.: Efficient ring signatures without random oracles. In: Okamoto, T., Wang, X. (eds.) PKC 2007. LNCS, vol. 4450, pp. 166–180. Springer, Heidelberg (2007). https://doi.org/10.1007/978-3-540-71677-8_12
27. Sun, S.-F., Au, M.H., Liu, J.K., Yuen, T.H.: RingCT 2.0: a compact accumulator-based (linkable ring signature) protocol for blockchain cryptocurrency monero. In: Foley, S.N., Gollmann, D., Snekkenes, E. (eds.) ESORICS 2017. LNCS, vol. 10493, pp. 456–474. Springer, Cham (2017). https://doi.org/10.1007/978-3-319-66399-9_25
28. Tsang, P.P., Wei, V.K., Chan, T.K., Au, M.H., Liu, J.K., Wong, D.S.: Separable linkable threshold ring signatures. In: Canteaut, A., Viswanathan, K. (eds.) INDOCRYPT 2004. LNCS, vol. 3348, pp. 384–398. Springer, Heidelberg (2004). https://doi.org/10.1007/978-3-540-30556-9_30
29. Yuen, T.H., Liu, J.K., Au, M.H., Susilo, W., Zhou, J.: Threshold ring signature without random oracles. In: Cheung, B.S.N., Hui, L.C.K., Sandhu, R.S., Wong, D.S. (eds.) ASIACCS 2011, pp. 261–267. ACM Press (2011)
30. Zhang, F., Kim, K.: ID-based blind signature and ring signature from pairings. In: Zheng, Y. (ed.) ASIACRYPT 2002. LNCS, vol. 2501, pp. 533–547. Springer, Heidelberg (2002). https://doi.org/10.1007/3-540-36178-2_33

A Note on the Post-quantum Security of (Ring) Signatures

Rohit Chatterjee[1(✉)], Kai-Min Chung[2], Xiao Liang[1], and Giulio Malavolta[3]

[1] Stony Brook University, Stony Brook, USA
rochatterjee@cs.stonybrook.edu
[2] Academia Sinica, Taipei, Taiwan
kmchung@iis.sinica.edu.tw
[3] Max Planck Institute for Security and Privacy, Bochum, Germany

Abstract. This work revisits the security of classical signatures and ring signatures in a quantum world. For (ordinary) signatures, we focus on the arguably preferable security notion of *blind-unforgeability* recently proposed by Alagic et al. (Eurocrypt'20). We present two *short* signature schemes achieving this notion: one is in the quantum random oracle model, assuming quantum hardness of SIS; and the other is in the plain model, assuming quantum hardness of LWE with super-polynomial modulus. Prior to this work, the only known blind-unforgeable schemes are Lamport's one-time signature and the Winternitz one-time signature, and both of them are in the quantum random oracle model.

For ring signatures, the recent work by Chatterjee et al. (Crypto'21) proposes a definition trying to capture adversaries with quantum access to the signer. However, it is unclear if their definition, when restricted to the classical world, is as strong as the standard security notion for ring signatures. They also present a construction that only *partially* achieves (even) this seeming weak definition, in the sense that the adversary can only conduct superposition attacks over the messages, but not the rings. We propose a new definition that does not suffer from the above issue. Our definition is an analog to the blind-unforgeability in the ring signature setting. Moreover, assuming the quantum hardness of LWE, we construct a compiler converting any blind-unforgeable (ordinary) signatures to a ring signature satisfying our definition.

Keywords: Blind-Unforgeability · Quantum · Ring Signatures

1 Introduction

Recent advances in quantum computing have uncovered several new threats to the existing body of cryptographic work. As demonstrated several times in the literature (e.g., [1,15,64,65]), building quantum-secure primitives requires

X. Liang—Part of this work was done while visiting Max Planck Institute.

G. Hanaoka et al. (Eds.): PKC 2022, LNCS 13178, pp. 407–436, 2022.
https://doi.org/10.1007/978-3-030-97131-1_14

more than taking existing constructions and replacing the underlying assumptions with post-quantum ones. It usually requires new techniques and analysis. Moreover, for specific primitives, even giving a meaningful security notion against quantum adversaries is a non-trivial task (e.g., [5,17,18,61,67]). This work focuses on *post-quantum security* of digital signature schemes, namely, classical signatures schemes for which we want to protect against quantum adversaries.

Post-quantum Unforgeable Signatures. To build post-quantum secure signature schemes, the first step is to have a notion of unforgeability that protects against adversaries with quantum power. Probably the most natural attempt is to take the standard existential unforgeability (EUF) game, but require unforgeability against all *quantum polynomial-time* (QPT) adversaries (instead of all *probabilistic polynomial-time* (PPT) adversaries). We emphasize that the communication between the EUF challenger and the QPT adversary is still classical. Namely, the adversary is not allowed to query the challenger's circuit in a quantum manner. Herein, we refer to this notion as PQ-EUF. Usually, PQ-EUF can be achieved by existing constructions in the classical setting via replacing the underlying hardness assumptions with quantum-hard ones (e.g., hard problems on lattice or isogeny-based assumptions).

The (Quantum) Random Oracle Model. In the classical setting, the random oracle model (ROM) [11] has been accepted as a useful paradigm to obtain efficient signature schemes. When considering the above PQ-EUF notion in the ROM, two choices arise—one can either allow the adversary *classical* access to the RO (as in the classical setting)[1], or *quantum* access to the RO. The latter was first formalized as the *quantum random oracle model* (QROM) by Boneh et al. [15], who showed that new techniques are necessary to achieve unforgeability against QPT adversaries in this model. Then, a large body of literature has since investigated the PQ-EUF in QROM [6,32,33,42,48,52,62].

One-More Unforgeability vs Bind Unforgeability. Starting from [65], people realize that the definitional approach taken by the above PQ-EUF may not be sufficient to protect against quantum adversaries. The reason is that quantum adversaries may try to attack the concerned protocol/primitive by executing it *quantumly*, even if the protocol/primitive by design is only meant to be executed classically. As argued in existing literature (e.g., [31,36]), such an attack could possibly occur in a situation where the computer executing the classical protocol is a quantum machine, and an adversary somehow manages to observe the communication before measurement. Other examples include adversaries managing to trick a classical device (e.g., a smart card reader) into showing full or partial quantum behavior by, for example, cooling it down and shielding it from any external electromagnetic or thermal interference. Moreover, this concern may also arise in the security reduction (even) w.r.t. classical security games but against QPT adversaries. For example, some constructions may allow the

[1] To avoid confusion, we henceforth denote this model as CROM ("C" for "classical").

adversary to obtain an *indistinguishability obfuscation* of, say, a PRF; the QPT adversary can then implement it as a quantum circuit to conduct superposition attacks. Recently, this issue has received an increasing amount of attention [4,5,9,17,18,23,28,30,36,43–46,59,61,67].

To address the aforementioned security threats to digital signatures, it is reasonable to give the QPT adversary $\mathcal{A}$ *quantum access* to the signing oracle in the EUF game. This raises an immediate question—How should the game decide if $\mathcal{A}$'s final forgery is valid? Recall that in the classical setting (or the PQ-EUF above), the game records all the signing queries made by $\mathcal{A}$; to decide if $\mathcal{A}$ wins, it needs to make sure that $\mathcal{A}$'s final forgery message-signature pair is different from the ones $\mathcal{A}$ learned from the signing oracle. However, this approach does not fit into the quantum setting, since it is unclear how to record $\mathcal{A}$'s *quantum* queries without irreversibly disturbing them.

Boneh and Zhandry [18] proposed the notion of *one-more unforgeability*. This requires that the adversary cannot produce $\mathsf{sq}+1$ valid message-signature pairs with only sq signing queries (an approach previously taken to define blind signatures [57]). When restricted to the classical setting, this definition is equivalent to the standard unforgeability of ordinary signatures, by a simple application of the pigeonhole principle. [18] shows how to convert any PQ-EUF signatures to one-more unforgeable ones using a *chameleon hash function* [49]; it also proves that the PQ-EUF signature scheme by Gentry, Peikert, and Vaikuntanathan [38] (henceforth, GPV) is one-more unforgeable in the QROM, assuming the PRF in that construction is quantum secure (i.e., being a QPRF [65]).

As argued in [5,37], one-more unforgeability does not seem to capture all that we can expect from quantum unforgeability. For example, an adversary may produce a forgery for a message in a subset A of the message space, while making queries to the signing oracle supported on a disjoint subset B. Also, an adversary may make multiple quantum signing queries, but then must consume, say, all of the answers in order to make a single valid forgery. This forgery might be for a message that is different from all the messages in all the superpositions of previous queries. This clearly violates what we intuitively expect for unforgeability, but the one-more unforgeability definition may never rule this out.

To address these problems, Alagic et el. [5] propose *blind-unforgeability* (BU). Roughly, the blind-unforgeability game modifies the (quantum-accessible) signing oracle by asking it to always return "$\perp$" for messages in a "blinded" subset of the message space. The adversary's forgery is considered valid only if it lies in the blinded subset. In this way, the adversary is forced to forge a signature for a message she has not seen a signature before, consistent with our intuition for unforgeability. [5] shows that blind-unforgeability, when restricted to the classical setting, is also equivalent to PQ-EUF; Moreover, it does not suffer from the above problems for one-more unforgeability[2].

In terms of constructions, [5] show that Lamport's one-time signature [50] is BU in the QROM, assuming the OWF is modeled as a (quantum-accessible)

[2] [5] also claimed that blind-unforgeability implies one-more unforgeability. But their proof was flawed [29]. The relation between these two notions is an open problem.

random oracle. Later, [54] show that the Winternitz one-time signature [55] is BU in the QROM, assuming the underlying hash function is modeled as a (quantum-accessible) random oracle. To the best of our knowledge, they are the only schemes known to achieve BU. This gives rise to the following question:

> **Question 1:** *Is it possible to build (multi-time) signature schemes achieving blind-unforgeability, either in the QROM or the plain model?*

Post-quantum Secure Ring Signatures. In a *ring signature* scheme [12,58], a user can sign a message with respect to a *ring* of public keys, with the knowledge of a signing key corresponding to any public key in the ring. It should satisfy two properties: (1) *Anonymity* requires that no user can tell which user in the ring actually produced a given signature; (2) *Unforgeability* requires that no user outside the specified ring can produce valid signatures on behalf of this ring. In contrast to its notional predecessor, *group signatures* [27], no central coordination is required for producing and verfying ring signatures. Due to these features, ring signatures (and their variants) have found natural applications related to whistleblowing, authenticating leaked information, and more recently to cryptocurrencies [56,60], and thus have received extensive attention (see, e.g., [26] and related work therein).

For ring signatures from *latticed-based* assumptions, there exist several constructions in the CROM [3,10,13,34,51,53,60,63], but only two schemes are known in the plain model [21,26]. The authors of [26] also initiate the study of quantum security for ring signatures. They propose a definition where the QPT adversary is allowed quantum access to the signing oracle in both the anonymity and unforgeability game, where the latter is a straightforward adaption of the aforementioned one-more unforgebility for ordinary signatures. As noted in their work, this approach suffers from two disadvantages: (1) Their unforgeability definition seems weak in the sense that, when restricted to the classical setting, it is unclear if their unforgeability is equivalent to the standard one (see Sect. 2.3). This is in contrast to ordinary signatures, for which one-more unforgeability is equivalent to the standard existential unforgeability. (2) Their construction only partially achieves (even) this seemingly weak definition. In more detail, their security proof only allows the adversary to conduct superposition attacks on the messages, but not on the rings. As remarked by the authors, this is not a definitional issue, but rather a limitation of their technique. Indeed, [26] leave it as an open question to have a construction protecting against superposition attacks on both the messages and the rings.

The outlined gap begs the following natural question:

> **Question 2:** *Can we have a proper unforgeability notion for ring signatures that does not suffer from the above disadvantage? If so, can we have a construction achieving such a notion?*

Our Results. In this work, we resolve the aforementioned questions:

1. We show that the GPV signature, which relies on the quantum hardness of SIS (QSIS), can be proven BU-secure in the QROM. Since our adversary has

quantum access to the signing oracle, we also need to replace the PRF in the original GPV scheme with a QPRF, which is also known from QSIS. As will be discussed later in Sect. 2.1, our security proof is almost identical to the proof in [18] for the one-more unforgeability of GPV, except how the desired contradiction is derived in the last hybrid. Interestingly, our proof for BU turns out to be simpler than that in [18] (for one-more unforgeability). We remark that the GPV scheme is *short* (i.e., the signature size only depends on the security parameter, but not the message size).

2. We also construct a BU-secure signature *in the plain model*, assuming quantum hardness of Learning with Errors (QLWE) with super-polynomial modulus. Our construction is inspired by the signature (and adaptive IBE) scheme by Boyen and Li [20]. This signature scheme is also short.
3. We present a new definition of post-quantum security for ring signatures, by extending blind-unforgeability from [5]. We show that this definition, when restricted to the classical setting, is equivalent to the standard security requirements for ring signatures.
4. We build a ring signature satisfying the above definition. Our construction is a compiler that converts any BU (ordinary) signature to a ring signature achieving the definition in Item 3., assuming QLWE.

2 Technical Overview

2.1 BU Signatures in the QROM

We show that the GPV signature scheme from [38] is BU-secure in the QROM. The GPV signature scheme follows the hash-and-sign paradigm and relies crucially on the notion of *preimage sampleable functions* (PSFs). As the name indicates, these functions can be efficiently inverted given a secret inverting key in addition to being efficiently computable. Further, the joint distribution of image-preimage pairs is statistically close, no matter whether the image or the preimage is sampled first. PSFs also provide collision resistance, as well as *preimage min-entropy*: given any image, the set of possible preimages has $\omega(\log \lambda)$ bits of min-entropy, meaning that a specific preimage can only be predicted with negligible chance.

The GPV scheme uses a hash function H modeled as a random oracle. It first hashes the message m using H to obtain a digest h. The signing key includes the PSF secret key, and the signature is a preimage of h (the signing randomness is generated using a quantum secure PRF over the message). To verify a signature, one simply computes its image under the PSF and compares it with the digest.

Notice that in the proof of (post-quantum) blind-unforgeability, the adversary has quantum access to both H and the signing algorithm. To show blind-unforgeability, we will move to a hybrid experiment where the H and the signing algorithm Sign are constructed differently, but their *joint distribution* is statistically close to that in the real execution. To do so, the hybrid will set the signature for a message m to a random preimage from the domain of the PSF (note that this procedure is "de-randomized" using the aforementioned PRF).

To answer an H-oracle query on m, the hybrid will first compute its signature (i.e., the PSF preimage corresponding to m), and then return the PSF evaluation on this signature (aka preimage) as the output of $H(m)$. Observe that, in this hybrid, the (H, Sign) oracles are constructed by first sampling preimages for the PSF, and then evaluating the PSF in the "forward" direction; in contrast, in the real game, the (H, Sign) oracles can be interpreted as sampling a image for PSF first, and then evaluating the PSF in the "reverse" direction using the inverting key. From the property of PSFs given above, these two approaches induce statistically-close joint distributions of (H, Sign) on each (classical) query. A lemma from [18] then shows that these are also indistinguishable to adversaries making polynomially-many *quantum* queries.

So far, our proof is identical to that of [18], where GPV is shown to be one-more unforgeable. This final part is where we differ. In the final hybrid, if the adversary produces a successful forgery for a message in the blind set, only two possibilities arise. Since the image of the signature under the PSF must equal the digest, the signature must either (i) provide a second preimage for h to the one computed by the challenger, creating a collision for the PSF, or (ii) equal the one the challenger itself computes, compromising preimage min-entropy of the PSF. This latter claim requires special attention in [18]. A reduction to the min-entropy condition is not immediate, since it is unclear if the earlier quantum queries of $\mathcal{A}$ already allow $\mathcal{A}$ information about the preimages for the $q + 1$ forgeries it outputs. To handle this, [18] prove a lemma ([18, Lemma 2.6]) showing q quantum queries will not allow $\mathcal{A}$ to predict $q + 1$ preimages, given the min-entropy condition. In contrast, this last argument is superfluous in our case, since the blind unforgeability game *automatically* prevents any information for queries in the blindset from reaching the adversary. We can therefore directly appeal to the min-entropy condition for case (ii) above.

Since our overall construction and proof for the QROM scheme is similar to that in [18], we provide this construction and the corresponding proof in the full version [25] due to space constraints.

2.2 BU Signatures in the Plain Model

We make use of the signature template introduced in [20], which in turn relies on key-homomorphic techniques as used in [22]. We will refer to their homomorphic evaluation procedure as $\mathsf{Eval}_{\mathrm{BV}}$. The scheme uses the 'left-right trapdoor' paradigm. Namely, the verification key contains a matrix $\mathbf{A}$ sampled with a 'trapdoor' basis $\mathbf{T_A}$, and $\mathbf{A}_0, \mathbf{C}_0, \mathbf{A}_1, \mathbf{C}_1$, which can be interpreted as BV encodings of 0 and 1 respectively, as well as similar encodings $\{\mathbf{B}_i\}_{i \in [|k|]}$ of the bits of a key k for a bit-PRF (the use of this PRF is the key innovation in [20]). The corresponding signing key contains $\mathbf{T_A}$. To sign, one computes BV encodings $\mathbf{C}_{M_1}, \ldots, \mathbf{C}_{M_t}$ of a t-bit message M, then computes $\mathbf{A}_{\mathrm{PRF,M}} = \mathsf{Eval}_{\mathrm{BV}}(\{\mathbf{B}_i\}_{i \in [|k|]}, \{\mathbf{C}_j\}_{j \in [t]}, \mathsf{PRF})$. Two signing matrices $\mathbf{F}_{M,b} = [\mathbf{A} \mid \mathbf{A}_b - \mathbf{A}_{\mathrm{PRF,M}}]$ $(\forall b \in \{0, 1\})$ are then generated (crucially, the adversary cannot tell these apart because of the PRF). A signature is a *short non-zero* vector $\sigma \in \mathbb{Z}^{2m}$ satisfying $\mathbf{F}_{M,b} \cdot \sigma = 0$ for any one of the $\mathbf{F}_{M,b}$'s. As pointed out, $\mathbf{T}_\mathbf{A}$ allows the signer to produce a short vector for either $\mathbf{F}_{M,b}$.

To show unforgeability, one constructs a reduction that (i) replaces the left matrix with an SIS challenge (thus losing $\mathbf{T}_\mathbf{A}$), and (ii) replaces the other matrices used to generate the right half with their 'puncturable' versions (e.g., $\mathbf{A}_b$ now becomes $\mathbf{A}\mathbf{R}_b + \mathbf{G}$, where $\mathbf{R}_b$ is an uniform low-norm matrix and $\mathbf{G}$ is the gadget matrix), with the end result being that the matrix $\mathbf{A}_{\mathrm{PRF,M}}$ becomes $\mathbf{A}\mathbf{R}' + \mathbf{G}$ and $\mathbf{F}_{M,b}$ now looks like $[\mathbf{A} \mid \mathbf{A}\mathbf{R} + (b - \mathsf{PRF}_k(M))\mathbf{G}]$ (with $\mathbf{R}, \mathbf{R}'$ being suitable low-norm matrices). The crucial point is this: having sacrificed $\mathbf{T}_\mathbf{A}$, the reduction cannot sign like a normal signer. However it still retains a trapdoor for the gadget matrix $\mathbf{G}$, and for *exactly one* of the $\mathbf{F}_{M,b}$, a term in G survives in the right half. This suffices to obtain a 'right trapdoor', and in turn, valid signatures for any M. On the other hand, a forging adversary lacks the PRF key and so it cannot tell apart $\mathbf{F}_{M,0}$ from $\mathbf{F}_{M,1}$. Thus the forgery must correspond to $\mathbf{F}_{M,\mathsf{PRF}_k(M)}$ with probability around 1/2, and the reduction can use this solution to obtain a short solution for the challenge $\mathbf{A}$.

However, the blind-unforgeability setting differs in several meaningful ways. Here we no longer expect a forgery for any possible message, so the additional machinery to have two signing matrices for every message becomes superfluous. Indeed, for us the challenge is to disallow signing queries in the blindset (even if they are made as part of a query superposition) and to prevent forgeries in the blindset. Accordingly, we interpret the function of the PRF in a different manner. We simply have the bit-PRF act as the characteristic function for the blindset. Then we can extend the approach above to the blind-unforgeability setting very easily: we use a single signing matrix $\mathbf{F}_\mathrm{M} = [\mathbf{A} \mid \mathbf{A}' - \mathbf{A}_{\mathrm{PRF,M}}]$ (where $\mathbf{A}'$ 'encodes 1'). In the reduction, after making changes just as before, we obtain that $\mathbf{F}_\mathrm{M} = \left[\mathbf{A} \mid \mathbf{A}\mathbf{R} - (1 - \mathsf{PRF}_k(M))\mathbf{G}\right]$. For messages where the PRF is not 1, we can answer signing queries using the trapdoor for $\mathbf{G}$; For messages where it is 1, we cannot, and further we can use a forgery for such a message to break the underlying SIS challenge. In effect, the reduction enforces the requisite blindset behavior naturally.

A caveat is that the bit-PRF based approach may not correctly model a blindset, which is a random ε-weight set of messages. Indeed, we require a slight modification of a normal bit-PRF to allow us the necessary latitude in approximating sets of any weight $\varepsilon \in [0, 1]$. Moreover, due to the adversary's quantum access to the signing oracle, this PRF must be quantum-access secure; and to allow the BV homomorphic evaluation, the PRF must have NC^1 implementation. Fortunately, such a *biased* bit-PRF can be built by slightly modifying the PRF from [8], assuming QLWE with super-polynomial modulus.

2.3 Post-quantum Secure Ring Signatures

Defining Post-quantum Security. To reflect the *quantum power* of an QPT adversary $\mathcal{A}$, one needs to give $\mathcal{A}$ quantum access to the signing oracle in the security game. While this is rather straightforward for anonymity, the challenge here is to find a proper notion for unforgeability (thus, here we only focus on the latter). Let us first recall the *classical* unforgeability game for a ring signature. In this game, $\mathcal{A}$ learns a ring $\mathcal{R}$ from the challenger, and then can make two types of queries: (1) by a *corruption query* $(\mathsf{corrupt}, i)$, $\mathcal{A}$ can corrupt a member in $\mathcal{R}$ to learn its secret key; (2) by a *signing query* $(\mathsf{sign}, i, \mathsf{R}^*, m)$, $\mathcal{A}$ can create a ring R^*, specify a member i that is contained in both $\mathcal{R}$ and R^*, and ask the challenger to sign a message m w.r.t. R^* using the signing keys of member i. Notice that R^* may contain (potentially malicious) keys created by $\mathcal{A}$; but as long as the member i is in both R^* and $\mathcal{R}$, the challenger is able to sign m w.r.t. R^*. The challenger also maintains a set $\mathcal{C}$ recording all the members in $\mathcal{R}$ that are corrupted by $\mathcal{A}$. To win the game, $\mathcal{A}$ needs to output a forgery $(\mathsf{R}^*, m^*, \Sigma^*)$ such that $\mathsf{R}^* \subseteq \mathcal{R} \setminus \mathcal{C}$, $\mathsf{RS.Verify}(\mathsf{R}^*, m^*, \Sigma^*) = 1$, and that $\mathcal{A}$ never made a signing query of the form $(\mathsf{sign}, \cdot, \mathcal{R}^*, m^*)$.

To consider quantum attacks, we first require that corruption queries should remain classical. In practice, corruption queries maps to the attack where a ring member is totally taken over by $\mathcal{A}$. Since ring signatures are a de-centralized primitive, corrupting a specific party should not affect other parties in the system. This situation arguably does not change with $\mathcal{A}$'s quantum power. One could of course consider "corrupting a group of users in superposition", but the motivation and practical implications of such corruptions is unclear, and thus we defer it to future research. In this work, we restrict ourselves to classical ring member corruptions.

We will allow $\mathcal{A}$ to conduct superposition attacks over the ring and message. That is, a QPT $\mathcal{A}$ can send singing queries of the form $(\mathsf{sign}, i, \sum \psi_{\mathsf{R},m} |\mathsf{R}, m\rangle)$, where the identity i is classical for the same reason above. Given the argument above, one may wonder why we allow superpositions over R in the signing query. The reason is that unlike for corruption queries, each signing query specifies a specific member i to run the signing algorithm for. No matter what R is, this member will only sign using her own signing key (and this is the only signing key that she knows), and this has nothing to do with other parties in the system[3]. Therefore, superposition attacks over R can be validated just as superposition attacks over m, thus should be allowed.

The next step is to determine the winning condition for QPT adversaries in the above quantum unforgeability game. The approach taken by [26] is to extend the one-more unforgeability from [18] to the ring setting. Concretely, it is required that the adversary cannot produce $(\mathsf{sq} + 1)$ valid signatures by making only sq quantum sign queries. However, there is a caveat. Recall that the R^* in $\mathcal{A}$'s forgery should be a subset of uncorrupted ring members (i.e., $\mathcal{R} \setminus \mathcal{C}$). A natural generalization of the "one-more forgery" approach here is to require that, with sq quantum signing queries, the adversary cannot produce $\mathsf{sq} + 1$ forgery signatures, where *all* the rings contained are subsets of $\mathcal{R} \setminus \mathcal{C}$. This requirement turns out to be so strict that, when restricted to the classical setting, this one-more unforgeability seems to be weaker than the standard unforgeability for ring signatures (more details in Sect. 5.1).

---

[3] Indeed, R may even contain "illegitimate" or "non-existent" members faked by $\mathcal{A}$. Note that we do not require $\mathsf{R} \subseteq \mathcal{R}$.

Our idea is to extend the blind-unforgeability definition to our setting. Specifically, the challenger will create a blind set $B_\varepsilon^{\mathsf{RS}}$ by including in each ring-message pair (R, m) with probability ε. It will then blind the signing algorithm such that it always returns $\perp$ for $(\mathsf{R}, m) \in B_\varepsilon^{\mathsf{RS}}$. In contrast to one-more unforgeability, we will show that this definition, when restricted to the classical setting, is indeed equivalent to the standard unforgeability notion for ring signatures.

Our Construction. Our starting point is the LWE-based construction by Chatterjee et al. [26]. We first recall their construction: the public key consists of a public key for a public-key encryption scheme PKE and a verification key for a standard signature scheme Sig, as well as the first round message of a (bespoke) ZAP argument. To sign a message, one first computes an ordinary signature σ and then encrypts this along with a hash key hk for a specific (SPB) hash. Two such encryptions (c_1, c_2) are produced, along with the second-round message π of the ZAP proving that one of these encryptions is properly computed using a public key that is part of the presented ring. The hash key is extraneous to our concerns here; suffice it to say that it helps encode a 'hash' of the ring into the signature and is a key feature in establishing compactness of their scheme.

To show anonymity, one starts with a signature for i_0, then switches the ciphertexts c_1 and c_2 in turn to be computed using the public key for i_1 while changing the ZAP accordingly. Semantic security ensures that ciphertexts with respect to different public keys are indistinguishable, and WI of the ZAP allows us to switch whichever ciphertext is not being used to prove π, and also to switch a proof for a ciphertext corresponding to i_0 to one corresponding to i_1.

Unforgeability in [26] follows from a reduction to the unforgeability of Sig. Even though their construction uses a custom ZAP that only offers soundness for (effectively) $\mathsf{NP} \cap \mathsf{coNP}$, they develop techniques in this regard to show that even with this ZAP, one can ensure that if an adversary produces a forgery with non-negligible probability, then it also encrypts a valid signature for Sig in one of c_1 or c_2 with non-negligible probability. The reduction can extract this using a corresponding decryption key (which it can obtain during key generation for the experiment) and use this as a forgery for Sig.

The [26] construction can thus in fact be seen as a compiler from ordinary to ring signatures assuming LWE. We use their template as a starting point, but there are significant differences between security notions for standard (classical) ring signatures, and our (quantum) blind-unforgeability setting. We discuss these and how to accomodate them next. The very first change that we require here is to use a blind-unforgeable signature scheme in lieu of Sig, since we reduce unforgeability to that of Sig.

Next, let us discuss post-quantum anonymity. Here, the adversary can make a challenge query that contains a *superposition* over rings and messages. We would like to use the same approach as above, but of course computational indistiguishability is compromised against superposition queries. Two clear strengthenings are needed compared to the classical scheme: first, we need to use pairwise-independent hashing to generate signing randomness (to apply quantum oracle similarity techniques from [18]). Second, we want to ensure statistical similarity of the components c_1, c_2, π (in order to use an aforementioned lemma from [18] which says that pointwise statistically close oracles are indistiguishable even with quantum queries). In particular, PKE needs to be statistically close on different plaintexts, and the WI guarantee for the ZAP needs to be statistical. Fortunately, we can use lossy encryption for the constraint on ciphertexts, and the ZAP from [26] is already statistical WI.

Finally we turn to blind-unforgeability. Here, the things that change are that firstly, we need to switch to injective public keys (instead of lossy ones) to carry over the reduction from the classical case. Further, we forego using SPB hashing, because our techniques require that we sign the message along with the ring, i.e. $\mathsf{Sig.Sign}(sk, \mathsf{R}\|m)$. Thus we end up compromising compactness and using an SPB would serve no purpose. The reason that we need to sign the ring too has to do with how we define the blindset and how the challenger must maintain it in the course of the unforgeability game; this turns out to be more delicate than expected (see related discussion in [25, Section 6.5]). With the modifications above, we can eventually reduce the blind-unforgeability to that of Sig.

3 Preliminaries

Notation. For a set $\mathcal{X}$, let $2^{\mathcal{X}}$ denote the power set of $\mathcal{X}$ (i.e., the set of all subsets of $\mathcal{X}$. Let $\lambda \in \mathbb{N}$ denote the security parameter. A non-uniform QPT adversary is defined by $\{\mathsf{QC}_\lambda, \rho_\lambda\}_{\lambda\in\mathbb{N}}$, where $\{\mathsf{QC}_\lambda\}_\lambda$ is a sequence of polynomial-size non-uniform quantum circuits, and $\{\rho_\lambda\}_\lambda$ is some polynomial-size sequence of mixed quantum states. For any function $F : \{0,1\}^n \to \{0,1\}^m$, "quantum access" will mean that each oracle call to F grants an invocation of the $(n+m)$-qubit unitary gate $|x,t\rangle \mapsto |x, t\oplus F(x)\rangle$; we stipulate that for any $t \in \{0,1\}^*$, we have $t\oplus\perp = \perp$. Symbols $\overset{c}{\approx}$, $\overset{s}{\approx}$ and $\overset{\text{i.d.}}{=\!=}$ are used to denote computational, statistical, and perfect indistinguishability respectively. Computational indistinguishability in this work is by default w.r.t. non-uniform QPT adversaries.

Quantum Oracle Indistinguishability. We will need the following lemmata.

Lemma 1 ([66]). *Let H be an oracle drawn from a $2q$-wise independent distribution. Then, the advantage of any quantum algorithm making at most q queries to H has in distinguishing H from a truly random function is 0.*

Lemma 2 ([18]). *Let $\mathcal{X}$ and $\mathcal{Y}$ be sets, and for each $x \in \mathcal{X}$, let D_x and D'_x be distributions on $\mathcal{Y}$ such that $|D_x - D'_x| \le \varepsilon$ for some value ε that is independent of x. Let $O : \mathcal{X} \to \mathcal{Y}$ be a function where, for each x, $O(x)$ is drawn from D_x, and let $O'(x)$ be a function where, for each x, $O'(x)$ is drawn from $D'(x)$. Then any quantum algorithm making at most q queries to either O or O' cannot distinguish the two, except with probability at most $\sqrt{8C_0 q^3 \varepsilon}$.*

Blind-Unforgeable Signatures. We recall in Definition 1 the definition for blind unforgeable signature schemes in [5]. The authors there provide a formal definition for MACs. We extend it in the natural way to the signature setting.

Definition 1 (Blind-Unforgeable Signatures). *For any security parameter $\lambda \in \mathbb{N}$, let $\mathcal{M}_\lambda$ denote the message space and $\mathcal{T}_\lambda$ denote the signature space. A* blind-unforgeable *signature scheme* Sig *consists of the following PPT algorithms:*

- $\mathsf{Gen}(1^\lambda)$ *outputs a verification and signing key pair (vk, sk).*
- $\mathsf{Sign}(sk, m; r)$ *takes as input a signing key sk, a message $m \in \mathcal{M}_\lambda$, and a randomness r (which we avoid specifying unless pertinent). It outputs a signature $\sigma \in \mathcal{T}_\lambda$.*
- $\mathsf{Verify}(vk, m, \sigma)$ *takes as input a verification key vk, a message $m \in \mathcal{M}_\lambda$ and a signature $\sigma \in \mathcal{T}_\lambda$. It outputs a bit signifying accept (1) or reject (0).*

These algorithms satisfy the following requirements:

1. **Completeness:** *For any $\lambda \in \mathbb{N}$, any (vk, sk) in the range of* $\mathsf{Gen}(1^\lambda)$, *and any $m \in \mathcal{M}_\lambda$, it holds that* $\Pr\left[\mathsf{Verify}(vk, m, \mathsf{Sign}(sk, m)) = 1\right] = 1 - \mathsf{negl}(\lambda)$.
2. **Blind-Unforgeability:** *For any non-uniform QPT adversary $\mathcal{A}$, it holds w.r.t. Experiment 1 that* $\mathsf{PQAdv}^\lambda_{\mathrm{BU}}(\mathcal{A}) := \Pr\left[\mathsf{PQExp}^\lambda_{\mathrm{BU}}(\mathcal{A}) = 1\right] \leq \mathsf{negl}(\lambda)$.

Experiment 1: Blind-Unforgeability Game $\mathsf{PQExp}^\lambda_{\mathrm{BU}}(\mathcal{A})$

1. $\mathcal{A}$ sends a constant $0 \leq \varepsilon \leq 1$ to the challenger;
2. The challenger generates $(vk, sk) \leftarrow \mathsf{Gen}(1^\lambda)$ and provides vk to $\mathcal{A}$.
3. The challenger defines a *blindset* $B^{\mathsf{Sig}}_\varepsilon \subseteq \mathcal{M}_\lambda$ as follows: every $m \in \mathcal{M}_\lambda$ is put in $B^{\mathsf{Sig}}_\varepsilon$ independently with probability ε.
4. $\mathcal{A}$ is allowed to make $\mathsf{poly}(\lambda)$ quantum queries. For each query, the challenger samples a (classical) random string r and performs the following mapping:
$$\sum_{m,t} \psi_{m,t}|m, t\rangle \mapsto \sum_{m,t} \psi_{m,t}|m, t \oplus B^{\mathsf{Sig}}_\varepsilon \mathsf{Sign}(sk, m; r)\rangle,$$
where $B^{\mathsf{Sig}}_\varepsilon\mathsf{Sign}(sk, m; r) = \begin{cases} \bot & \text{if } m \in B^{\mathsf{Sig}}_\varepsilon \\ \mathsf{Sign}(sk, m; r) & \text{otherwise} \end{cases}$.
5. Finally, $\mathcal{A}$ outputs (m^*, σ^*); the challenger checks if: (1) $m^* \in B^{\mathsf{Sig}}_\varepsilon$; (2) $\mathsf{Verify}(vk, m^*, \sigma^*) = 1$. If so, the experiment outputs 1; otherwise, it outputs 0.

3. **Shortness (Optional):** *The signature scheme is short if the signature size is at most a polynomial on the security parameter* and *the logarithm of the message size.*

Remark 1 (One randomness to rule them all). [4]The signing algorithm in our definition samples signing randomness once per every query, as opposed to sampling signing randomness for every classical message in the superposition. This was established as a reasonable definitional choice in [18], where they observed that one could "de-randomize" the signing procedure by simply using a quantum PRF to generate randomness for each possible message in superposition, and use this for signing. We stick with this convention when defining post-quantum security for both ordinary signatures (Definition 1) and ring signatures (Definitions 4 and 5).

[4] Inspired by J. R. R. Tolkien. Indeed, this is a "ring" signature paper.

Remark 2. We let the adversary choose ε. This is equivalent to quantifying over all values of ε as in the definition in [5].

4 Blind-Unforgeable Signatures in the Plain Model

Building Blocks. We assume familiarity with standard lattice-based cryptographic notions and procedures. Here we will recall certain techniques and properties to be directly used in our plain model construction. For standard lattice-related concepts (e.g., parameters, hardness, trapdoors), see the full version [25, Appendix A.1].

We denote the Gram-Schmidt ordered orthogonalization of a matrix $\mathbf{A} \in \mathbb{Z}^{m\times m}$ by $\widetilde{\mathbf{A}}$. For a vector $\mathbf{u}$, we let $||\mathbf{u}||$ denote its ℓ_2 norm. For a matrix $\mathbf{R} \in \mathbb{Z}^{k\times m}$, we define two matrix norms: $||\mathbf{R}||$ denotes the ℓ_2 norm of the largest column of $\mathbf{R}$. Correspondingly, $||\mathbf{R}||_2$ denotes the operator norm of $\mathbf{R}$, defined as $||\mathbf{R}||_2 = \mathsf{sup}_{x\in\mathbb{R}^{m+1}}||\mathbf{Rx}||$. For a prime q, a modular matrix $\mathbf{A} \in \mathbb{Z}_q^{n\times m}$ and vector $\mathbf{u} \in \mathbb{Z}_q^n$, we define the m-dimensional (full rank) lattice $\Lambda_q^{\mathbf{u}}(\mathbf{A}) = \{\mathbf{e} \in \mathbb{Z}^m : \mathbf{Ae} = \mathbf{u} \pmod q\}$. In particular, $\Lambda_q^{\perp}(\mathbf{A})$ denotes the lattice $\Lambda_q^{\mathbf{0}}(\mathbf{A})$.

Lattice Sampling Algorithms. Our construction uses the 'left-right trapdoors' framework introduced in [2,19] which uses two sampling algorithms SampleLeft and SampleRight. The algorithm SampleLeft works as follows:

- *Inputs:* A full-rank matrix $\mathbf{A} \in \mathbb{Z}_q^{n\times m}$ and a short basis $\mathbf{T_A}$ of $\Lambda_q^{\perp}(\mathbf{A})$, along with a matrix $\mathbf{B} \in \mathbb{Z}_q^{n\times m_1}$, a vector $\mathbf{u} \in \mathbb{Z}_q^n$, and a Gaussian parameter s.
- *Output:* Let $\mathbf{F} = [\mathbf{A} \mid \mathbf{B}]$. SampleLeft outputs a vector $\mathbf{d} \in \mathbb{Z}^{m+m_1}$ in $\Lambda_q^{\mathbf{u}}(\mathbf{F})$.

Theorem 1 (SampleLeft **Closeness** [2,24]). *Let $q > 2$, $m > n$ and $s > ||\widetilde{\mathbf{T_A}}|| \cdot \omega(\sqrt{\log(m+m_1)})$. Then* $\mathsf{SampleLeft}(\mathbf{A}, \mathbf{B}, \mathbf{T_A}, \mathbf{u}, s)$ *outputs $\mathbf{d} \in \mathbb{Z}^{m+m_1}$ distributed statistically close to $\mathcal{D}_{\Lambda_q^{\mathbf{u}}(\mathbf{F}),s}$.*

The algorithm SampleRight works as follows:

- *Inputs:* Matrices $\mathbf{A} \in \mathbb{Z}_q^{n\times k}$ and $\mathbf{R} \in \mathbb{Z}_q^{k\times m}$, a full-rank matrix $\mathbf{B} \in \mathbb{Z}_q^{n\times m}$, a short basis $\mathbf{T_B}$ of $\Lambda_q^{\perp}(\mathbf{B})$, a vector $\mathbf{u} \in \mathbb{Z}_q^n$, and a Gaussian parameter s.
- *Output:* Let $\mathbf{F} = [\mathbf{A} \mid \mathbf{AR} + \mathbf{B}]$. It outputs a vector $\mathbf{d} \in \mathbb{Z}^{m+m_1}$ in $\Lambda_q^{\mathbf{u}}(\mathbf{F})$.

Theorem 2 (SampleRight **Closeness** [2]). *Let $q > 2$, $m > n$ and $s > ||\widetilde{\mathbf{T_B}}|| \cdot \omega(\sqrt{\log m})$. Then* $\mathsf{SampleRight}(\mathbf{A}, \mathbf{B}, \mathbf{R}, \mathbf{T_B}, \mathbf{u}, s)$ *outputs $\mathbf{d} \in \mathbb{Z}^{m+k}$ distributed statistically close to $\mathcal{D}_{\Lambda_q^{\mathbf{u}}(\mathbf{F}),s}$.*

Random Sampling Related. The following is a simple corollary of [2, Lemma 4] (see the full version [25, Appendix A.2] for more details).

Corollary 1. *Suppose that $m > (n+1)\log_2 q + \omega(\log n)$ and that $q > 2$ is a prime. Let $\mathbf{R}$ be an $m \times k$ matrix chosen uniformly from $\{-1,1\}^{m\times k} \bmod q$ where $k = k(n)$ is polynomial in n. Let $\mathbf{A}' \in \mathbb{Z}_q^{n\times m}$ be sampled from a distribution statistically close to uniform over $\mathbb{Z}_q^{n\times m}$. Let $\mathbf{R}$ be an $m \times k$ matrix chosen* *uniformly from* $\{-1,1\}^{m \times k} \bmod q$ *where* $k = k(n)$ *is polynomial in* n. *Let* $\mathbf{B}$ *be chosen uniformly in* $\mathbb{Z}_q^{n \times k}$. *Then for all vectors* $\mathbf{w} \in \mathbb{Z}_q^m$, *the distributions* $(\mathbf{A}', \mathbf{A}'\mathbf{R}, \mathbf{R}^\top \mathbf{w})$ *and* $(\mathbf{A}', \mathbf{B}, \mathbf{R}^\top \mathbf{w})$ *are statistically close.*

Key-Homomorphic Evaluation. We briefly recall the matrix key-homomorphic evaluation algorithm, as found in [16,22,39] (see the full version [25, Appendix A.3] for more details). This template evaluates NAND circuits, gate by gate, in a homomorphic manner. For a NAND gate $g(u, v; w)$ with input wires u, v and output wire w, we have (inductively) matrices $\mathbf{A}_u = \mathbf{A}\mathbf{R}_u + x_u\mathbf{G}$, and $\mathbf{A}_v = \mathbf{A}\mathbf{R}_v + x_v\mathbf{G}$ where x_u and x_v are the input bits of u and v, and the evaluation algorithm computes:

$$\mathbf{A}_w = \mathbf{G} - \mathbf{A_u} \cdot \mathbf{G}^{-1}(\mathbf{A}_v) = \mathbf{G} - (\mathbf{A}\mathbf{R}_u + x_u\mathbf{G}) \cdot \mathbf{G}^{-1}(\mathbf{A}\mathbf{R}_v + x_v\mathbf{G}) = \mathbf{A}\mathbf{R}_g + (1 - x_u x_v)\mathbf{G},$$

where $1 - x_u x_v := \mathsf{NAND}(x_u, x_v)$, and $\mathbf{R}_g = -\mathbf{R}_u \cdot \mathbf{G}^{-1}(\mathbf{A}_v) - x_u\mathbf{R}_v$ has low norm if both $\mathbf{R}_u$ and $\mathbf{R}_v$ have low norm.

Biased Bit-QPRF. We need a *quantum-access secure* PRF having a *biased single-bit* output. It should also be implementable by NC^1 circuits. Let us first present the definition.

Definition 2 (Biased Bit-QPRFs). *A biased bit-QPRF on domain* $\{0,1\}^{n(\lambda)}$ *consists of:*

- $\mathsf{Gen}(1^\lambda, \varepsilon)$: *takes as input a constant* $\varepsilon \in [0,1]$, *outputs a key* k_ε;
- $\mathsf{PRF}_{k_\varepsilon}(x)$: *takes as input* $x \in \{0,1\}^{n(\lambda)}$, *outputs a bit* $b \in \{0,1\}$,

such that for any $\varepsilon \in [0,1]$ *and any QPT* $\mathcal{A}$ *having* quantum access *to its oracle,*

$$\left|\Pr\left[k_\varepsilon \leftarrow \mathsf{Gen}(1^\lambda, \varepsilon) : \mathcal{A}^{\mathsf{PRF}_{k_\varepsilon}(\cdot)} = 1\right] - \Pr\left[F \xleftarrow{\$} \mathcal{F}(n(\lambda), \varepsilon) : \mathcal{A}^{F(\cdot)} = 1\right]\right| \le \mathsf{negl}(\lambda),$$

where $\mathcal{F}(n(\lambda), \varepsilon)$ *is the collection of all functions from* $\{0,1\}^{n(\lambda)}$ *to* $\{0,1\}$ *that output* 1 *with probability* ε.

It is known that the NC^1 PRF from [8] is quantum-access secure (i.e., a QPRF) [65]. It can be made biased by standard techniques (e.g., using the standard QPRF to "de-randomize" a ε-biased coin-tossing circuit). Note that the [8] PRF relies on the quantum hardness of LWE with *super-polynomial* modulus.

Our Construction. Our signature scheme uses a biased bit QPRF PRF whose input space $\mathcal{X}$ corresponds to our message space $\mathcal{M}$, and the algorithms SampleLeft, SampleRight given as in Theorem 1 and Theorem 2 respectively, and TrapGen that can sample matrices in $\mathbb{Z}_q^{n \times m}$ statistically close to uniform, along with a corresponding 'short' or 'trapdoor' basis for the associated lattice. The construction is as follows:

Construction 1: Blind-Unforgeable Signatures in the Plain Model
Set message length $t(\lambda)$ and row size $n(\lambda)$ as free parameters (polynomial in λ). PRF key size is set as $k(\lambda)$, and the depth for $\mathsf{C}_{\mathsf{PRF}}$ is given by $d(\lambda)$. We set $m = n^{1+\eta}$ for

proper running of TrapGen, and $\text{sigsize}_\lambda = s\sqrt{2m}$ for the validity of SampleLeft output (to ensure completeness). Set $s = O(4^d m^{3/2})\omega(\sqrt{\log m})$ to ensure statistical closeness of SampleLeft and SampleRight, and correspondingly set $\beta = O(16^d m^{7/2})\omega(\sqrt{\log m})$ and $q = O(16^d m^4)(\omega(\sqrt{\log m}))^2$ to have an overall reduction to an appropriately hard instance of SIS. For further details about these choices, see the full version [25, Section 5.3].

$\text{Gen}(1^\lambda)$:

1. Sample a matrix $\mathbf{A}$ along with a 'trapdoor' basis $\mathbf{T_A}$ for $\Lambda_q^\perp(\mathbf{A})$ using TrapGen.
2. Sample a matrix $\mathbf{A}'$, 'PRF key' matrices $\mathbf{B}_1, \ldots, \mathbf{B}_k$, and 'PRF input' matrices $\mathbf{C}_0, \mathbf{C}_1$ uniformly from $\mathbb{Z}_q^{n \times m}$ (k is the PRF key length).
3. Fix the Gaussian width parameter s as given in parameter selection.
4. Fix a Boolean circuit description $\mathsf{C}_{\mathsf{PRF}}$ of the algorithm $\mathsf{PRF}_{(\cdot)}(\cdot)$.
5. Output $vk = (\mathbf{A}, \mathbf{A}', \{\mathbf{B}_i\}_{i=1}^k, \{\mathbf{C}_0, \mathbf{C}_1\}, \mathsf{PRF}, s, \mathbf{C}_{\mathsf{PRF}})$ and $sk = \mathbf{T_A}$.

$\text{Sign}(sk, vk, M)$: let $(M_1, \ldots, M_t) \in \{0,1\}^t$ be the bit-wise representation of M.

1. Run the [22] evaluation algorithm Eval_{BV} to homomorphically evaluate the circuit $\mathbf{C}_{\mathsf{PRF}}$ using the 'encoded' PRF key bits $\{\mathbf{B}_i\}_{i\in[k]}$ and message bits $\{\mathbf{C}_{M_j}\}_{j\in[t]}$. This yields $\mathbf{A}_{\text{PRF,M}} := \text{Eval}_{\text{BV}}(\mathbf{C}_{\mathsf{PRF}}, \{\mathbf{B}_i\}_{i\in[k]}, \{\mathbf{C}_{M_j}\}_{j\in[t]}) \in \mathbb{Z}_q^{n\times m}$.
2. Set $\mathbf{F}_{\text{M}} := [\mathbf{A} \mid \mathbf{A}' - \mathbf{A}_{\text{PRF,M}}]$; Use SampleLeft to obtain $\mathbf{d}_{\text{M}} \leftarrow \mathcal{D}_{\Lambda_q^\perp(\mathbf{F}_{\text{M}}),s}$.
3. Output $\sigma = \mathbf{d}_{\text{M}} \in \mathbb{Z}_q^{2m}$.

$\text{Verify}(vk, M, \sigma)$:

1. Compute $\mathbf{A}_{\text{PRF,M}}, \mathbf{F}_{\text{M}}$ as before.
2. Check that $\sigma \in \mathbb{Z}_q^{2m}$, $\sigma \neq 0$, and $||\sigma|| \leq \text{sigsize}_\lambda$. If it fails, output 0.
3. If $\mathbf{F}_{\text{M}} \cdot \sigma = 0 \mod q$, output 1, otherwise output 0.

Proof of Security. Completeness follows straightforwardly from the correctness of SampleLeft (Theorem 1) for $\mathcal{D}_{\Lambda_q^\perp(\mathbf{F}),s}$. In the following, we prove BU-security.

Theorem 3. *Let λ denote the security parameter, and* PRF *be a biased bit QPRF as defined in Definition 2 above. If the parameters n, m, q, β, s, d are picked as discussed above, and the $\mathbf{SIS}_{q,\beta,n,m}$ problem is hard for QPT adversaries, then our signature scheme* Sig *constructed as above, with the indicated parameters, satisfies Blind-Unforgeability as in Definition 5.*

Proof. Consider a QPT $\mathcal{A}$ that is able to produce forgeries w.r.t. Sig in the blind-unforgeability challenge. Our proof proceeds using a series of hybrid experiments. In the final hybrid we show a reduction from an adversary producing succesful forgeries to the hardness of $\mathbf{SIS}_{q,\beta,n,m}$. The hybrids are as follows:

Hybrid H_0: This is the blind-unforgeability game (Experiment 1). Namely, for an adversary-specified ε, the challenger manually samples an ε-weight set B_ε over messages, and does not answer queries in B_ε. Signing and verification keys are chosen just as in the ordinary signing procedure.

Hybrid H_1: This hybrid is identical to the previous one, except that we change the ordinary key generation into the following:

1. Sample $\mathbf{A}$ with a 'trapdoor' basis $\mathbf{T_A}$ for $\Lambda_q^{\perp}(\mathbf{A})$ using $\mathsf{TrapGen}$ as before.
2. Sample 'low-norm' matrices: $\mathbf{R}'_{\mathbf{A}}, \{\mathbf{R}_{\mathbf{B}_i}\}_{i=1}^{k}, \mathbf{R}_{\mathbf{C}0}, \mathbf{R}_{\mathbf{C}1} \xleftarrow{\$} \{-1,1\}^{m \times m}$.
3. Let PRF and $\mathsf{C_{PRF}}$ be as before.
4. Sample a PRF key $k_\varepsilon \leftarrow \mathsf{PRF.Gen}(1^\lambda, \varepsilon)$, where $k_\varepsilon = s_1, \ldots, s_k$ (i.e. has length k).
5. Set $\mathbf{A}' = \mathbf{A}\mathbf{R}_{\mathbf{A}'} + \mathbf{G}$, where $\mathbf{G}$ the gadget matrix $\mathbf{G}$, which has a publicly-known trapdoor $\widetilde{\mathbf{T}}_{\mathbf{G}}$.
6. Set $\mathbf{C}_b = \mathbf{A}\mathbf{R}_{\mathbf{C}_b} + b\mathbf{G}$ for $b \in \{0,1\}$, and sample $\mathbf{B}_i \xleftarrow{\$} \mathbb{Z}_q^{n \times m}$ for every $i \in [k]$.
7. Fix the Gaussian width parameter s as before.
8. Output $vk = (\mathbf{A}, \mathbf{A}', \{\mathbf{B}_i\}_{i=1}^{k}, \{\mathbf{C}_0, \mathbf{C}_1\}, s, \mathsf{PRF}, \mathsf{C_{PRF}})$, and $sk = (\mathbf{T_A}, k_\varepsilon)$.

Note that while this hybrid generates a key k_ε, it never uses it.

<u>$H_0 \overset{s}{\approx} H_1$:</u> The only thing that changes (w.r.t. $\mathcal{A}$) is the distribution of the various components $(\mathbf{A}', \mathbf{C}_0, \mathbf{C}_1)$ of the verification key handed out by the challenger. However, by Corollary 1 these distributions are all statistically close to the corresponding distributions in H_0. Note that the verification key is picked at the start of the challenge and provided to $\mathcal{A}$, so there is no scope for $\mathcal{A}$ to have quantum access to these component distributions. Thus the outputs in these hybrids are statistically close.

Hybrid H_2: This hybrid is identical to the previous one, except that we change how the challenger picks the blindset—Instead of manually sampling B_ε as a random ε-weight set, it now sets B_ε to be the set of messages M where $\mathsf{PRF}_{k_\varepsilon}(M)$ is 1 (note that the challenger now possesses k_ε as part of sk, and can compute $\mathsf{PRF}_{k_\varepsilon}(\cdot)$). Observe that the challenger in this hybrid is now efficient.

<u>$H_1 \overset{c}{\approx} H_2$:</u> Note that setup and key generation in H_2 is identical to that in H_1—In particular, the adversary learns *no* information about the key k_ε. The indistinguishability between H_1 and H_2 then follows immediately from the security of the biased bit-QPRF (Definition 2).

Hybrid H_3: This hybrid is identical to the previous one, except that we change how the matrices $\mathbf{B}_i$'s (in Step 6) are generated. Namely, we now set

$$\forall i \in [k], \quad \mathbf{B}_i := \mathbf{A}\mathbf{R}_{\mathbf{B}_i} + s_i \cdot \mathbf{G}.$$

(Recall that s_i is the i-th bit of the k_ε generated in Step 4.)

<u>$H_2 \overset{s}{\approx} H_3$:</u> The only things that change between these hybrids are the matrices $\{\mathbf{B}_i\}_{i \in [k]}$. Again, using Corollary 1 the distributions for $\mathbf{B}_i$ for each $i \in [k]$ are all statistically close to the corresponding distributions in H_2, and just as in the similarity argument between H_2 and H_3, we can conclude that these hybrids too have indistinguishable outputs.

Hybrid H_4: Observe that, starting from H_1, we have:

$$\begin{aligned}\mathbf{F}_{\mathrm{M}} &= [\mathbf{A} \mid \mathbf{A}' - \mathbf{A}_{\mathrm{PRF,M}}] = \left[\mathbf{A} \mid \mathbf{A}' - \mathsf{Eval}_{\mathrm{BV}}(\mathbf{C}_{\mathsf{PRF}}, \{\mathbf{B}_i\}_{i\in[k]}, \{\mathbf{C}_{M_j}\}_{j\in[t]})\right] \\ &= \left[\mathbf{A} \mid \mathbf{A}' - (\mathbf{A}\mathbf{R}_{\mathrm{PRF,M}} + \mathsf{PRF}_{k_\varepsilon}(M)\cdot \mathbf{G})\right] \\ &= \left[\mathbf{A} \mid \mathbf{A}(\mathbf{R}_{\mathbf{A}'} - \mathbf{R}_{\mathrm{PRF,M}}) + (1 - \mathsf{PRF}_{k_\varepsilon}(M))\cdot \mathbf{G}\right].\end{aligned}$$

In this hybrid, we switch to using SampleRight to answer signing queries, instead of using SampleLeft. That is, we run SampleRight using $\mathbf{T}_{\mathbf{G}}$, the publicly available trapdoor for $\mathbf{G}$. Note this means that now the challenger cannot answer queries where the 'right half' of $\mathbf{F}_{\mathrm{M}}$ does not include $\mathbf{G}$, i.e., $\mathsf{PRF}_{k_\varepsilon}(M) = 1$. But due to the way H_2 generate the blindset, such a query is anyway answered with "$\perp$".

<u>$H_3 \overset{c}{\approx} H_4$:</u> We first show that these two hybrids answer signature queries for any *classical* query M in a *statistically* indistinguishable manner. For any query M, there are two cases: (1) if $\mathsf{PRF}_{k_\varepsilon}(M) = 1$, the challengers in both H_3 and H_4 return $\perp$. In this case, these distributions are identical. (2) Else, we have $\mathsf{PRF}_{k_\varepsilon}(M) = 0$. Since $\mathbf{F}_{\mathrm{M}}$ is computed identically in both hybrids, and by Theorem 1 and 2 both SampleLeft and SampleRight sample from distributions statistically close to $\mathcal{D}_{\Lambda_q^\perp(\mathbf{F}_{\mathrm{M}}),s}$, i.e., they are also statistically close to each other. Thus overall the distributions of signatures returned in H_3 and H_4 are statistically close to each other, say with less than distance $\Delta(\lambda)$ (which is negligible in λ). Now since $\mathcal{A}$ is a quantum machine making at most polynomially (say $q(\lambda)$) many quantum queries. Then, we can use Lemma 2 to conclude that $\mathcal{A}$ distinguishes between H_3 and H_4 with probability at most $\sqrt{8C_0q^3\Delta}$, which is negligible.

Hybrid H_5: In this hybrid, the challenger no longer samples $\mathbf{A}$ using TrapGen. Instead, it samples $\mathbf{A}$ uniformly from $\mathbb{Z}_q^{n\times m}$.

<u>$H_4 \overset{s}{\approx} H_5$:</u> This follows immediately from the property of the lattice trapdoor algorithm TrapGen.

Reduction to QSIS. We can now describe our reduction $\mathcal{R}$ in this hybrid:

1. Asks for and recieves a uniform matrix in $\mathbb{Z}_q^{n\times m}$ as the $\mathbf{SIS}_{q,\beta,n,m}$ challenge.
2. Sets $\mathbf{A}$ to be this matrix (instead of sampling $\mathbf{A}$ by itself).
3. When the adversary returns a forgery (M^*, σ^*), $\mathcal{R}$ checks if this is valid, i.e., that (i) $M^* \in B_\varepsilon$, (ii) $\sigma^* \in \mathbb{Z}_q^{2m}$, (iii) $\sigma^* \neq 0$, (iv) $\mathbf{F}_{\mathrm{M}^*} \cdot \sigma^* = 0 \mod q$ and (v) $||\sigma|| \leq \mathsf{sigsize}_\lambda$. If any of these checks fail, it aborts.
4. Represent σ^* as $[\mathbf{d}_1^\top \mid \mathbf{d}_2^\top]^\top$, with $\mathbf{d}_1, \mathbf{d}_2 \in \mathbb{Z}_q^m$. $\mathcal{R}$ computes $\mathbf{e} = \mathbf{d}_1 + \mathbf{R}\mathbf{d}_2$ where $\mathbf{R} = \mathbf{R}_{\mathbf{A}'} - \mathbf{R}_{\mathrm{PRF,M}}$ (we will use this shorthand going forward), and presents $\mathbf{e}$ as its solution to the SIS challenge $\mathbf{A}$.

Now we can prove that $\mathbf{e}$ is indeed an SIS solution with non-negligible probability by an argument very similar as in the final reduction for [20, Theorem 3.1]. Due to space constraints, we present it in the full version [25, Section 5.4]. □

5 Post-quantum Ring Signatures

5.1 Definitions

Classical Ring Signatures. We start by recalling the classical definition of ring signatures [7,12].

Definition 3 (Ring Signature). *A ring signature scheme* RS *is described by a triple of PPT algorithms* $(\mathsf{Gen}, \mathsf{Sign}, \mathsf{Verify})$ *such that:*

- $\mathsf{Gen}(1^\lambda, N)$*: on input a security parameter* 1^λ *and a super-polynomial*[5] N *(e.g.,* $N = 2^{\log^2 \lambda}$*) specifying the maximum number of members in a ring, output a verification and signing key pair* $(\mathsf{VK}, \mathsf{SK})$.
- $\mathsf{Sign}(\mathsf{SK}, \mathsf{R}, m)$*: given a secret key* SK*, a message* $m \in \mathcal{M}_\lambda$*, and a list of verification keys (interpreted as a ring)* $\mathsf{R} = (\mathsf{VK}_1, \cdots, \mathsf{VK}_\ell)$ *as input, and outputs a signature* Σ.
- $\mathsf{Verify}(\mathsf{R}, m, \Sigma)$*: given a ring* $\mathsf{R} = (\mathsf{VK}_1, \ldots, \mathsf{VK}_\ell)$*, message* $m \in \mathcal{M}_\lambda$ *and a signature* Σ *as input, outputs either 0 (rejecting) or 1 (accepting).*

These algorithms satisfy the following requirements:

1. **Completeness:** *for all* $\lambda \in \mathbb{N}$, $\ell \leq N$, $i^* \in [\ell]$*, and* $m \in \mathcal{M}_\lambda$*, it holds that* $\forall i \in [\ell]$ $(\mathsf{VK}_i, \mathsf{SK}_i) \leftarrow \mathsf{Gen}(1^\lambda, N)$ *and* $\Sigma \leftarrow \mathsf{Sign}(\mathsf{SK}_{i^*}, \mathsf{R}, m)$ *where* $\mathsf{R} = (\mathsf{VK}_1, \ldots, \mathsf{VK}_\ell)$*, we have* $\Pr[\mathsf{RS.Verify}(\mathsf{R}, m, \Sigma) = 1] = 1$*, where the probability is taken over the random coins used by* Gen *and* Sign.
2. **Anonymity:** *For any* $Q = \mathsf{poly}(\lambda)$ *and any PPT adversary* $\mathcal{A}$*, it holds w.r.t. Expr. 2 that* $\mathsf{Adv}^{\lambda,Q}_{\mathrm{ANON}}(\mathcal{A}) := \left| \Pr\left[\mathsf{Exp}^{\lambda,Q}_{\mathrm{ANON}}(\mathcal{A}) = 1\right] - 1/2 \right| \leq \mathsf{negl}(\lambda)$.

Experiment 2: Classical Anonymity $\mathsf{Exp}^{\lambda,Q}_{\mathrm{ANON}}(\mathcal{A})$

1. For each $i \in [Q]$, the challenger generates key pairs $(\mathsf{VK}_i, \mathsf{SK}_i) \leftarrow \mathsf{Gen}(1^\lambda, N; r_i)$. It sends $\{(\mathsf{VK}_i, \mathsf{SK}_i, r_i)\}_{i \in [Q]}$ to $\mathcal{A}$;
2. $\mathcal{A}$ sends a challenge to the challenger of the form $(i_0, i_1, \mathsf{R}, m)$.[a] The challenger checks if $\mathsf{VK}_{i_0} \in \mathsf{R}$ and $\mathsf{VK}_{i_1} \in \mathsf{R}$. If so, it samples a uniform bit b, computes $\Sigma \leftarrow \mathsf{Sign}(\mathsf{SK}_{i_b}, \mathsf{R}, m)$, and sends Σ to $\mathcal{A}$.
3. $\mathcal{A}$ outputs a guess b'. If $b' = b$, the experiment outputs 1, otherwise 0.

[a] We stress that R might contain keys that are not generated by the challenger in the previous step. In particular, it might contain maliciously generated keys.

3. **Unforgeability:** *for any* $Q = \mathsf{poly}(\lambda)$ *and any PPT adversary* $\mathcal{A}$*, it holds w.r.t. Experiment 3 that* $\mathsf{Adv}^{\lambda,Q}_{\mathrm{UNF}}(\mathcal{A}) := \Pr\left[\mathsf{Exp}^{\lambda,Q}_{\mathrm{UNF}}(\mathcal{A}) = 1\right] < \mathsf{negl}(\lambda)$.

[5] The N has to be super-polynomial to support rings of *arbitrary* polynomial size.

Experiment 3: Classical Unforgeability $\mathsf{Exp}^{\lambda,Q}_{\mathrm{UNF}}(\mathcal{A})$

1. For each $i \in [Q]$, the challenger generates $(\mathsf{VK}_i, \mathsf{SK}_i) \leftarrow \mathsf{Gen}(1^\lambda, N; r_i)$, and stores these key pairs along with their corresponding randomness. It then sets $\mathcal{VK} = \{\mathsf{VK}_1, \dots, \mathsf{VK}_Q\}$ and initializes a set $\mathcal{C} = \emptyset$.
2. The challenger sends $\mathcal{VK}$ to $\mathcal{A}$.
3. $\mathcal{A}$ can make polynomially-many queries of the following two types:
   - **Corruption query** $(\mathsf{corrupt}, i)$**:** The challenger adds VK_i to the set $\mathcal{C}$ and returns the randomness r_i to $\mathcal{A}$.
   - **Signing query** $(\mathsf{sign}, i, \mathsf{R}, m)$**:** The challenger first checks if $\mathsf{VK}_i \in \mathsf{R}$. If so, it computes $\Sigma \leftarrow \mathsf{Sign}(\mathsf{SK}_i, \mathsf{R}, m)$ and returns Σ to $\mathcal{A}$. It also keeps a list of all such queries made by $\mathcal{A}$.
4. Finally, $\mathcal{A}$ outputs a tuple $(\mathsf{R}^*, m^*, \Sigma^*)$. The challenger checks if: (1) $\mathsf{R}^* \subseteq \mathcal{VK} \setminus \mathcal{C}$; (2) $\mathcal{A}$ never made a signing query of the form $(\mathsf{sign}, \cdot, \mathsf{R}^*, m^*)$; (3) $\mathsf{Verify}(\mathsf{R}^*, m^*, \Sigma^*) = 1$. If so, the experiment outputs 1; otherwise, 0.

We mention that the unforgeability and anonymity properties defined in Definition 3 correspond respectively to the notions of *unforgeability with insider corruption* and *anonymity with respect to full key exposure* presented in [12].

Defining Post-quantum Security. We aim to build a classical ring signature that is secure against adversaries making superposition queries to the signing oracle. Formalizing the security requirements in this scenario is non-trivial. An initial step toward this direction has been taken in [26]. But their definition has certain restrictions (discussed below). In the following, we develop a new definition building on ideas from [26].

Post-quantum Anonymity. Recall that in the classical anonymity game (Experiment 2), the adversary's challenge is a quadruple $(i_0, i_1, \mathsf{R}, m)$. To define post-quantum anonymity, a natural attempt is to allow the adversary to send a superposition over components of quadruple, and to let the challenger respond using the following unitary mapping[6]:

$$\sum_{i_0,i_1,\mathsf{R},m,t} \psi_{i_0,i_1,\mathsf{R},m,t} \left|i_0, i_1, \mathsf{R}, m, t\right\rangle \mapsto \sum_{i_0,i_1,\mathsf{R},m,t} \psi_{i_0,i_1,\mathsf{R},m,t} \left|i_0, i_1, \mathsf{R}, m, t \oplus \mathsf{Sign}(\mathsf{SK}_{i_b}, m, \mathsf{R}; r)\right\rangle.$$

However, as observed in [26], this will lead to an unsatisfiable definition due to an attack from [18]. Roughly speaking, the adversary could use classical values for R, m, and i_1, but she puts a uniform superposition of all valid identities in the register for i_0. After the challenger's signing operation, observe that if $b = 0$, the last register will contain signatures in superposition (as i_0 is in superposition); if $b = 1$, it will contain a classical signature (as i_1 is classical). These two cases can be efficiently distinguished by means of a Fourier transform on the i_0's register followed by a measurement. Therefore, to obtain an achievable notion, we should not allow superpositions over (i_0, i_1).

[6] Of course, the challenger also needs to check if $\mathsf{VK}_{i_0} \in \mathsf{R}$ and $\mathsf{VK}_{i_1} \in \mathsf{R}$. But we can safely ignore this for our current discussion.

Now, $\mathcal{A}$ only has the choice to put superpositions over R and m. The definition in [26] further forbids $\mathcal{A}$ from putting superpositions over R. But this is only because they fail to prove security if superposition attacks on R is allowed. Indeed, they leave open the problem to construct a scheme that protects against superposition attacks on R. In this work, we solve this problem: our definition allows superposition attacks on both R and m.

Definition 4 (Post-quantum Anonymity). *Consider a triple of PPT algorithms* $\mathsf{RS} = (\mathsf{Gen}, \mathsf{Sign}, \mathsf{Verify})$ *that satisfies the same syntax as in Definition 3.* RS *achieves post-quantum anonymity if for any* $Q = \mathsf{poly}(\lambda)$ *and any QPT adversary* $\mathcal{A}$*, it holds w.r.t. Experiment 4 that*

$$\mathsf{PQAdv}^{\lambda,Q}_{\mathrm{ANON}}(\mathcal{A}) := \left|\Pr\left[\mathsf{PQExp}^{\lambda,Q}_{\mathrm{ANON}}(\mathcal{A}) = 1\right] - 1/2\right| \leq \mathsf{negl}(\lambda).$$

Experiment 4: Post-quantum Anonymity $\mathsf{PQExp}^{\lambda,Q}_{\mathrm{ANON}}(\mathcal{A})$

1. For each $i \in [Q]$, the challenger generates key pairs $(\mathsf{VK}_i, \mathsf{SK}_i) \leftarrow \mathsf{RS.Gen}(1^\lambda, N; r_i)$. The challenger sends $\{(\mathsf{VK}_i, \mathsf{SK}_i, r_i)\}_{i\in[Q]}$ to $\mathcal{A}$;
2. $\mathcal{A}$ sends (i_0, i_1) to the challenger, where both i_0 and i_1 are in $[Q]$;
3. $\mathcal{A}$'s challenge query is allowed to be a superposition of rings *and* messages. The challenger picks a random bit b and a random string r. It signs the message using SK_{i_b} and randomness r, while making sure that VK_{i_0} and VK_{i_1} are indeed in the ring specified by $\mathcal{A}$. Formally, the challenger implements the following mapping:
$$\sum_{\mathsf{R},m,t} \psi_{\mathsf{R},m,t} \left|\mathsf{R}, m, t\right\rangle \mapsto \sum_{\mathsf{R},m,t} \psi_{\mathsf{R},m,t} \left|\mathsf{R}, m, t \oplus f(\mathsf{R}, m)\right\rangle,$$
where $f(\mathsf{R}, m) := \begin{cases} \mathsf{RS.Sign}(\mathsf{SK}_{i_b}, R, m; r) & \text{if } \mathsf{VK}_{i_0}, \mathsf{VK}_{i_1} \in R \\ \bot & \text{otherwise} \end{cases}.$
4. $\mathcal{A}$ outputs a guess b'. If $b' = b$, the experiment outputs 1, otherwise 0.

Post-quantum Unforgeability. In the classical unforgeability game (Experiment 3), $\mathcal{A}$ can make both $\mathsf{corrupt}$ and sign queries. As discussed in Sect. 2.3, we do not consider quantum $\mathsf{corrupt}$ queries, or superposition attacks over the identity in $\mathcal{A}$'s sign queries. We also remark that in the unforgeability game, [26] does not allow superpositions over the ring. Instead of a definitional issue, this is again only because they are unable to prove the security of their scheme if superposition attacks on the ring is allowed. In contrast, our construction can be proven secure against such attacks; thus, this restriction is removed from our definition.

To define quantum unforgeability, [26] adapts one-more unforgeability [18] to the ring setting: they require that, with sq quantum signing queries, the adversary cannot produce $\mathsf{sq} + 1$ signatures, where all the rings are subsets of $\mathcal{VK} \setminus \mathcal{C}$. This definition, *when restricted to the classical setting*, seems to be weaker than the standard unforgeability in Definition 3. That is, in the classical setting, any RS satisfying the unforgeability in Definition 3 is also one-more unforgeable; but the reverse direction is unclear (we provide more discussion in

[25, Appendix B]). Instead, our definition extends the blind-unforgeability for ordinary signatures (Definition 1) to the ring setting. We present this version in Definition 5. In contrast to the "one-more" unforgeability, we will show in Lemma 3 that, when restricted to the classical setting, this blind-unforgeability for ring signatures is indeed equivalent to the standard existential unforgeability in Definition 3. Its proof is almost identical to [5, Proposition 2]. Due to space constraints, we put it in [25, Section 6.1.2].

Definition 5 (Post-quantum Blind-Unforgeability). *Consider a triple of PPT algorithms* $\mathsf{RS} = (\mathsf{Gen}, \mathsf{Sign}, \mathsf{Verify})$ *that satisfies the same syntax as in Definition 3. For any security parameter* λ, *let* $\mathcal{R}_\lambda$ *and* $\mathcal{M}_\lambda$ *denote the ring space and message space, respectively.* RS *achieves blind-unforgeability if for any* $Q = \mathsf{poly}(\lambda)$ *and any QPT adversary* $\mathcal{A}$, *it holds w.r.t. Experiment 5 that*

$$\mathsf{PQAdv}^{\lambda,Q}_{\mathrm{BU}}(\mathcal{A}) := \Pr\left[\mathsf{PQExp}^{\lambda,Q}_{\mathrm{BU}}(\mathcal{A}) = 1\right] \leq \mathsf{negl}(\lambda).$$

Experiment 5: Post-quantum Blind-Unforgeability $\mathsf{PQExp}^{\lambda,Q}_{\mathrm{BU}}(\mathcal{A})$

1. $\mathcal{A}$ sends a constant $0 \leq \varepsilon \leq 1$ to the challenger;
2. For each $i \in [Q]$, the challenger generates $(\mathsf{VK}_i, \mathsf{SK}_i) \leftarrow \mathsf{Gen}(1^\lambda, N; r_i)$, and stores these key pairs along with their corresponding randomness. It then sets $\mathcal{VK} = \{\mathsf{VK}_1, \ldots, \mathsf{VK}_Q\}$ and initializes a set $\mathcal{C} = \emptyset$; The challenger sends $\mathcal{VK}$ to $\mathcal{A}$;
3. The challenger defines a *blindset* $B^{\mathsf{RS}}_\varepsilon \subseteq 2^{\mathcal{R}_\lambda} \times \mathcal{M}_\lambda$: every pair $(\mathsf{R}, m) \in 2^{\mathcal{R}_\lambda} \times \mathcal{M}_\lambda$ is put in $B^{\mathsf{RS}}_\varepsilon$ with probability ε;
4. $\mathcal{A}$ can make polynomially-many queries of the following two types:
   - **Classical corruption query** $(\mathsf{corrupt}, i)$**:** The challenger adds VK_i to the set $\mathcal{C}$ and returns the randomness r_i to $\mathcal{A}$.
   - **Quantum Signing query** $(\mathsf{sign}, i, \sum \psi_{\mathsf{R},m,t} |\mathsf{R}, m, t\rangle)$**:** That is, $\mathcal{A}$ is allowed to query the signing oracle on some classical identity i and superpositions over rings and messages. The challenger samples a random string r and performs:
   $$\sum_{\mathsf{R},m,t} \psi_{\mathsf{R},m,t} |\mathsf{R}, m, t\rangle \mapsto \sum_{\mathsf{R},m,t} \psi_{\mathsf{R},m,t} \left|\mathsf{R}, m, t \oplus B^{\mathsf{RS}}_\varepsilon f(\mathsf{R}, m)\right\rangle,$$
   where $B^{\mathsf{RS}}_\varepsilon f(\mathsf{R}, m) := \begin{cases} \bot & \text{if } (\mathsf{R}, m) \in B^{\mathsf{RS}}_\varepsilon \\ f(\mathsf{R}, m) & \text{otherwise} \end{cases}$, and
   $$f(\mathsf{R}, m) := \begin{cases} \mathsf{RS.Sign}(\mathsf{SK}_i, m, \mathsf{R}; r) & \text{if } \mathsf{VK}_i \in \mathsf{R} \\ \bot & \text{otherwise} \end{cases}.$$
5. Finally, $\mathcal{A}$ outputs $(\mathsf{R}^*, m^*, \Sigma^*)$. The challenger checks if: (1) $\mathsf{R}^* \subseteq \mathcal{VK} \setminus \mathcal{C}$; (2) $\mathsf{Verify}(\mathsf{R}^*, m^*, \Sigma^*) = 1$; (3) $(\mathsf{R}^*, m^*) \in B^{\mathsf{RS}}_\varepsilon$. If so, it outputs 1; otherwise, 0.

Lemma 3. *Restricted to (classical) QPT adversaries, a ring signature* RS *scheme is blind-unforgeable (Definition 5) if and only if it satisfies the unforgeability requirement in Definition 3.*

To conclude, we present the complete definition for quantum ring signatures.

Definition 6 (Post-quantum Secure Ring Signatures). *A post-quantum secure ring signature scheme* RS *is described by a triple of PPT algorithms* (Gen, Sign, Verify) *that share the same syntax as in Definition 3. Moreover, they also satisfy the* completeness *requirement in Definition 3, the* post-quantum anonymity *in Definition 4, and the* post-quantum blind-unforgeability *as in Definition 5.*

5.2 Building Blocks

Lossy PKEs with Special Properties. We need the following lossy PKE.

Definition 7 (Special Lossy PKE). *For any security parameter $\lambda \in \mathbb{N}$, let $\mathcal{M}_\lambda$ denote the message space. A special lossy public-key encryption scheme* LE *consists of the following PPT algorithms:*

- $\mathsf{MSKGen}(1^\lambda, Q)$, *on input a number $Q \in \mathbb{N}$, outputs* $(\{\mathsf{pk}_i\}_{i\in[Q]}, \mathsf{msk})$. *We call pk_i's the* injective public keys, *and* msk *the* master secret key.
- $\mathsf{MSKExt}(\mathsf{msk}, \mathsf{pk})$, *on input a master secret key* msk *and an injective public key* pk, *outputs a secret key* sk.
- $\mathsf{KSam}^{\mathsf{ls}}(1^\lambda)$ *outputs key* $\mathsf{pk}_{\mathsf{ls}}$, *which we call* lossy public key.
- $\mathsf{Valid}(\mathsf{pk}, \mathsf{sk})$, *on input a public* pk *and a secret key* sk, *outputs either* 1 *(accepting) or* 0 *(rejecting).*
- $\mathsf{RndExt}(\mathsf{pk})$ *outputs a r which we call* extracted randomness.
- $\mathsf{Enc}(\mathsf{pk}, m)$, *on input a public key* pk, *and a message $m \in \mathcal{M}_\lambda$, outputs* ct.
- $\mathsf{Dec}(\mathsf{sk}, \mathsf{ct})$, *on input a secret key* sk *and a ciphertext ct, outputs m.*

These algorithms satisfy the following properties:

1. **Completeness.** *For any $\lambda \in \mathbb{N}$, any* $(\mathsf{pk}, \mathsf{sk})$ *s.t.* $\mathsf{Valid}(\mathsf{pk}, \mathsf{sk}) = 1$, *and any $m \in \mathcal{M}_\lambda$, it holds that* $\Pr\big[\mathsf{Dec}(\mathsf{sk}, \mathsf{Enc}(\mathsf{pk}, m)) = m\big] = 1$.
2. **Lossiness of lossy keys.** *For any* $\mathsf{pk}_{\mathsf{ls}}$ *in the range of* $\mathsf{KSam}^{\mathsf{ls}}(1^\lambda)$ *and any $m_0, m_1 \in \mathcal{M}_\lambda$, it holds that* $\big\{\mathsf{Enc}(\mathsf{pk}_{\mathsf{ls}}, m_0)\big\}_{\lambda\in\mathbb{N}} \overset{s}{\approx} \big\{\mathsf{Enc}(\mathsf{pk}_{\mathsf{ls}}, m_1)\big\}_{\lambda\in\mathbb{N}}$.
3. **Completeness of Master Secret Keys:** *for any* $Q = \mathsf{poly}(\lambda)$, *it holds that*

$$\Pr\left[(\{\mathsf{pk}_i\}_{i\in[Q]}, \mathsf{msk}) \leftarrow \mathsf{MSKGen}(1^\lambda, Q) : \begin{array}{c}\forall i \in [Q], \mathsf{Valid}(\mathsf{pk}_i, \mathsf{sk}_i) = 1, \\ \textit{where } \mathsf{sk}_i := \mathsf{MSKExt}(\mathsf{msk}, \mathsf{pk}_i)\end{array}\right] \geq 1 - \mathsf{negl}(\lambda).$$

4. **IND of $\mathsf{MSKGen}/\mathsf{KSam}^{\mathsf{ls}}$ mode:** *For any* $Q = \mathsf{poly}(\lambda)$, *the following two distributions are computationally indistinguishable:*
   - $\forall i \in [Q]$, *sample* $\mathsf{pk}_i \leftarrow \mathsf{KSam}^{\mathsf{ls}}(1^\lambda; r_i)$, *then output* $\{\mathsf{pk}_i, r_i\}_{i\in[Q]}$;
   - *Sample* $(\{\mathsf{pk}_i\}_{i\in[Q]}, \mathsf{msk}) \leftarrow \mathsf{MSKGen}(1^\lambda, Q)$ *and output* $\{\mathsf{pk}_i, \mathsf{RndExt}(\mathsf{pk}_i)\}_{i\in[Q]}$.
5. **Almost-Unique Secret Key:** *For any* $Q = \mathsf{poly}(\lambda)$, *it holds that*

$$\Pr\left[(\{\mathsf{pk}_i\}_{i\in[Q]}, \mathsf{msk}) \leftarrow \mathsf{MSKGen}(1^\lambda, Q) : \begin{array}{c}\textit{There exist } i \in [Q] \textit{ and } \mathsf{sk}'_i \textit{ such that} \\ \mathsf{sk}'_i \neq \mathsf{MSKExt}(\mathsf{msk}, \mathsf{pk}_i) \ \wedge \ \mathsf{Valid}(\mathsf{pk}_i, \mathsf{sk}'_i) = 1\end{array}\right] = \mathsf{negl}(\lambda).$$

We propose an instantiation of such a lossy PKE using dual mode LWE commitments [41]. In lossy (statistically hiding) mode, the public key consists of a uniformly sampled matrix $\mathbf{A}$ and a message m is encrypted by computing $\mathbf{AR} + m\mathbf{G}$, where $\mathbf{R}$ is a low-norm matrix and $\mathbf{G}$ is the gadget matrix. Note that the random coins used to sample $\mathbf{A}$ simply consists of the matrix $\mathbf{A}$ itself. Furthermore, we can switch $\mathbf{A}$ to be an LWE-matrix (using some secret vector $\mathbf{s}$) to make the encryption scheme injective. Such a modification is computationally indistinguishable by an invocation of the LWE assumption. Note that this is true also in the presence of the output of $\mathsf{RndExt}(\mathbf{A})$, since the algorithm simply returns $\mathbf{A}$. Furthermore, by setting the dimensions appropriately, the secret $\mathbf{s}$ is uniquely determined by $\mathbf{A}$ with overwhelming probability. Finally, we note that we can define a master secret key for all keys in injective mode using a simple trick: sample a PRF key k and sample the i-th key pair using $\mathsf{PRF}(k, i)$ as the random coins. It is not hard to see that the distribution of public/secret keys is computationally indistinguishable by the pseudorandomness of PRF. Furthermore, given k one can extract the i-th secret key simply by recomputing it.

ZAPs for Super-Complement Languages. As mentioned in Sect. 2.3, [26] uses a ZAP (for $\mathsf{NP} \cap \mathsf{coNP}$) to prove a statement that the (ring) signature contains a ciphertext of a valid signature w.r.t. the building-block signature scheme. Let us denote this language as L. In the security proof, they need to argue that the adversary cannot prove a false statement $x^* \notin L$. However, this L is not necessarily in coNP; thus, there may not exist a non-witness $\widetilde{w}$ for the fact that $x^* \notin L$. Therefore, it is unclear how to use a ZAP for $\mathsf{NP} \cap \mathsf{coNP}$ here. To address this issue, the authors of [26] propose the notion of *super-complement languages.* This notion considers a pair of NP languages $(L, \widetilde{L})$ such that $(x \in \widetilde{L}) \Rightarrow (x \notin L)$. Their ZAP achieves soundness such that the cheating prove cannot prove $x \in L$ (except with negligible probability) once there exists a "non-witness" $\widetilde{w}$ s.t. $(x, \widetilde{w}) \in R_{\widetilde{L}}$. The $\widetilde{L}$ is set to the language the captures some *necessary conditions* for any valid forgery. Thus, a winning adversary will break the soundness of the ZAP, leading to a contradiction.

In the following, we present the original definition of super-complement languages. But we will only need a special case of it (see Remark 3).

Definition 8 (Super-Complement [26]**).** *Let* $(L, \widetilde{L})$ *be two* NP *languages where the elements of* $\widetilde{L}$ *are represented as pairs of bit strings. We say* $\widetilde{L}$ *is a* super-complement *of* L*, if* $\widetilde{L} \subseteq (\{0,1\}^* \setminus L) \times \{0,1\}^*$*. I.e.,* $\widetilde{L}$ *is a super complement of* L *if for any* $x = (x_1, x_2)$*,* $x \in \widetilde{L} \Rightarrow x_1 \notin L$*.*

Notice that, while the complement of L might not be in NP, it must hold that $\widetilde{L} \in \mathsf{NP}$. The language $\widetilde{L}$ is used to define the soundness property. Namely, producing a proof for a statement $x = (x_1, x_2) \in \widetilde{L}$, should be hard. We also use the fact that $\widetilde{L} \in \mathsf{NP}$ to mildly strengthen the soundness property. In more detail, instead of having selective soundness where the statement $x \in \widetilde{L}$ is fixed in advance, we now fix a non-witness $\widetilde{w}$ and let the statement x be adaptively chosen by the malicious prover from all statements which have $\widetilde{w}$ as a witness to their membership in $\widetilde{L}$.

Remark 3. Our application only needs a special case of the general form given in Definition 8—we will only focus on $\widetilde{L}$ where the x_2 part is an empty string. Formally, we consider the special case where $\widetilde{L} \subseteq \{0,1\}^* \backslash L$ (i.e., $x \in \widetilde{L} \Rightarrow x \notin L$).

We now define ZAPs for super-complement languages. We remark that the original definition (and construction) in [26] captures the general $(L, \widetilde{L})$ pairs defined in Definition 8. Since we only need the special case in Remark 3, we will define the ZAP only for this case.

Definition 9 (ZAPs for Special Super-Complement Languages). *Let $L, \widetilde{L} \in \mathsf{NP}$ be the special super-complement language in Remark 3. Let R and $\widetilde{R}$ denote the* NP *relations corresponding to L and $\widetilde{L}$ respectively. Let $\{C_{n,\ell}\}_{n,\ell}$ and $\{\widetilde{C}_{n,\widetilde{\ell}}\}_{n,\widetilde{\ell}}$ be the* NP *verification circuits for L and $\widetilde{L}$ respectively. Let $\widetilde{d} = \widetilde{d}(n, \widetilde{\ell})$ be the depth of $\widetilde{C}_{n,\widetilde{\ell}}$. A* ZAP *for $(L, \widetilde{L})$ is a tuple of PPT algorithms* $(\mathsf{V}, \mathsf{P}, \mathsf{Verify})$ *having the following interfaces (where $1^n, 1^\lambda$ are implicit inputs to* P, Verify*):*

- $\mathsf{V}(1^\lambda, 1^n, 1^{\widetilde{\ell}}, 1^{\widetilde{D}})$*: On input a security parameter λ, statement length n for L, witness length $\widetilde{\ell}$ for $\widetilde{L}$, and* NP *verifier circuit depth upper-bound $\widetilde{D}$ for $\widetilde{L}$, output a first message ρ.*
- $\mathsf{P}(\rho, x, w)$*: On input a string ρ, a statement $x \in \{0,1\}^n$, and a witness w such that $(x, w) \in R$, output a proof π.*
- $\mathsf{Verify}(\rho, x, \pi)$*: On input a string ρ, a statement x, and a proof π, output either 1 (accepting) or 0 (rejecting).*

The following requirements are satisfied:

1. **Completeness:** *For every $x \in L$, every $\widetilde{\ell} \in \mathbb{N}$, every $\widetilde{D} \geq \widetilde{d}(|x|, \widetilde{\ell})$, and every $\lambda \in \mathbb{N}$, it holds that*
$$\Pr\Big[\rho \leftarrow \mathsf{V}(1^\lambda, 1^{|x|}, 1^{\widetilde{\ell}}, 1^{\widetilde{D}}); \pi \leftarrow \mathsf{P}(\rho, x, w) : \mathsf{Verify}(\rho, x, \pi) = 1\Big] = 1.$$
2. **Public coin:** $\mathsf{V}(1^\lambda, 1^n, 1^{\widetilde{\ell}}, 1^{\widetilde{D}})$ *simply outputs a uniformly random string.*
3. **Selective non-witness adaptive-statement soundness:** *For any non-uniform QPT machine P^*_λ, any $n, \widetilde{D} \in \mathbb{N}$, and any non-witness $\widetilde{w} \in \{0,1\}^*$,*
$$\Pr\left[\begin{array}{l}\rho \leftarrow \mathsf{V}(1^\lambda, 1^n, 1^{|\widetilde{w}|}, 1^{\widetilde{D}});\\ (x, \pi^*) \leftarrow P^*_\lambda(\rho)\end{array} : \begin{array}{l}\mathsf{Verify}(\rho, x, \pi^*) = 1 \wedge \\ \widetilde{D} \geq \widetilde{d}(|x|, |\widetilde{w}|) \wedge (x, \widetilde{w}) \in \widetilde{R}\end{array}\right] \leq \mathsf{negl}(\lambda).$$
4. **Statistical witness indistinguishability:** *For every (possibly unbounded) "cheating" verifier $V^* = (V^*_1, V^*_2)$ and every $n, \widetilde{\ell}, \widetilde{D} \in \mathbb{N}$, the probabilities*
$$\Pr[V^*_2(\rho, x, \pi, \zeta) = 1 \ \wedge \ (x, w) \in \mathcal{R} \ \wedge \ (x, w') \in \mathcal{R}]$$
in the following two experiments differ only by $\mathsf{negl}(\lambda)$*:*
   - *in experiment 1, $(\rho, x, w, w', \zeta) \leftarrow V^*_1(1^\lambda, 1^n, 1^{\widetilde{\ell}}, 1^{\widetilde{D}}), \pi \leftarrow \mathsf{P}(\rho, x, w)$;*
   - *in experiment 2, $(\rho, x, w, w', \zeta) \leftarrow V^*_1(1^\lambda, 1^n, 1^{\widetilde{\ell}}, 1^{\widetilde{D}}), \pi \leftarrow \mathsf{P}(\rho, x, w')$.*

Lemma 4. **([26]).** *Assuming QLWE, there exist ZAPs as per Definition 9 for any super-complement language as per Definition 8.*

5.3 Construction

Our construction, shown in Construction 2, relies on the following building blocks: (1) pair-wise independent functions; a Sig satisfying Definition 1; a LE satisfying Definition 7; a ZAP satisfying Definition 9.

We remark that the RS.Sign algorithm runs ZAP on a special super-complement language $(L, \widetilde{L})$, whose definition will appear after the construction in Sect. 5.4. This arrangement is because we find that the language $(L, \widetilde{L})$ becomes easier to understand once the reader has slight familiarity with Construction 2.

Construction 2: Post-quantum Ring Signatures

Let $\widetilde{D} = \widetilde{D}(\lambda, N)$ be the maximum depth of the NP verifier circuit for language $\widetilde{L}$ restricted to statements where the the ring has at most N members, and the security parameter for Sig and LE is λ. Let $n = n(\lambda, \log N)$ denote the maximum size of the statements of language L where the ring has at most N members and the security parameter is λ. Recall that for security parameter λ, secret keys in LE have size $\ell = \ell_{\mathsf{sk}}(\lambda)$. We now describe our ring signature construction:

Key Generation Algorithm $\mathsf{Gen}(1^\lambda, N)$*:*

- sample signing/verification key pair: $(vk, sk) \leftarrow \mathsf{Sig.Gen}(1^\lambda)$;
- sample obliviously an injective public key of LE: $pk \leftarrow \mathsf{LE.KSam}^{\mathsf{ls}}(1^\lambda)$;
- compute the first message $\rho \leftarrow \mathsf{ZAP.V}(1^\lambda, 1^n, 1^{\widetilde{\ell}}, 1^{\widetilde{D}})$ for ZAP;
- output the verification key $\mathsf{VK} := (vk, pk, \rho)$ and signing key $\mathsf{SK} := (sk, vk, pk, \rho)$.

Signing Algorithm $\mathsf{Sign}(\mathsf{SK}, \mathsf{R}, m)$*:*

- parse $\mathsf{R} = (\mathsf{VK}_1, \ldots, \mathsf{VK}_\ell)$; and parse $\mathsf{SK} = (sk, vk, pk, \rho)$;
- compute $\sigma \leftarrow \mathsf{Sig.Sign}(sk, \mathsf{R}\|m)$;
- let $\mathsf{VK} := \mathsf{VK}_i \in R$ be the verification key corresponding to SK;
- sample two pairwise-independent functions PI_1 and PI_2, and compute
$$r_{c_1} = \mathsf{PI}_1(\mathsf{R}\|m), \quad r_{c_2} = \mathsf{PI}_2(\mathsf{R}\|m).$$
- compute $c_1 \leftarrow \mathsf{LE.Enc}(pk, (\sigma, vk); r_{c_1})$ and $c_2 \leftarrow \mathsf{LE.Enc}(pk, 0^{|\sigma|+|vk|}; r_{c_2})$;
- let $\mathsf{VK}_1 = (vk_1, pk_1, \rho_1)$ denote the lexicographically smallest member of R (as a string; note that this is necessarily unique);
- fix statement $x = (\mathsf{R}, m, c_1, c_2)$ and witness $w = (vk, pk, \sigma, r_{c_1})$. We remark that this statement and witness correspond to a super-complement language $(L, \widetilde{L})$ that will be defined in Sect. 5.4. Looking ahead, x with witness w is a statement in the L defined in Eq. (1); x constitutes a statement that is *not* in the $\widetilde{L}$ defined in Eq. 4.
- sample another pairwise-independent function PI_3 and compute $r_\pi = \mathsf{PI}_3(\mathsf{R}\|m)$;
- compute $\pi \leftarrow \mathsf{ZAP.P}(\rho_1, x, w; r_\pi)$;
- output $\Sigma = (c_1, c_2, \pi)$.

Verification Algorithm $\mathsf{Verify}(\mathsf{R}, m, \Sigma)$*:*

- identify the lexicographically smallest verification key VK_1 in R;
- fix $x = (\mathsf{R}, m, c_1, c_2)$; read ρ_1 from VK_1;
- compute and output $\mathsf{ZAP.Verify}(\rho_1, x, \pi)$.

5.4 The Super-Complement Language Proven by the ZAP

We now define the super-complement language $(L, \widetilde{L})$ used in Construction 2. This deviates from the $(L, \widetilde{L})$ defined in [26, Section 5], to accommodate Construction 2.

For a statement of the form $x_1 = (\mathsf{R}, m, c)$ and witness $w = \big(\mathsf{VK} = (vk, pk, \rho), \sigma, r_c\big)$, define relations R_1, R_2, and R_3 as follows:

$$(x_1, w) \in R_1 \Leftrightarrow \mathsf{VK} \in \mathsf{R}, \quad (x_1, w) \in R_2 \Leftrightarrow \mathsf{LE.Enc}(pk, (\sigma, vk); r_c) = c,$$
$$(x_1, w) \in R_3 \Leftrightarrow \mathsf{Sig.Verify}(vk, \mathsf{R} \| m, \sigma) = 1.$$

Next, define the relation R' as $R' := R_1 \cap R_2 \cap R_3$. Let L' be the language corresponding to R'. Define language L as

$$L := \big\{x = (\mathsf{R}, m, c_1, c_2) \;\big|\; (\mathsf{R}, m, c_1) \in L' \vee (\mathsf{R}, m, c_2) \in L'\big\}. \tag{1}$$

Now, we define another language $\widetilde{L}$ and prove that it is a super-complement of L in Claim 1. Let $x_1 = (\mathsf{R}, m, c)$ as above, but let $\widetilde{w} := msk$. Define the following relations:

$$(x_1, \widetilde{w}) \in R_4 \Leftrightarrow \forall j \in [\ell] : \mathsf{LE.Valid}\big(pk_j, \mathsf{LE.MSKExt}(msk, pk_j)\big) = 1 \tag{2}$$

$$(x_1, \widetilde{w}) \in R_5 \Leftrightarrow \begin{cases} \exists \mathsf{VK} \in \mathsf{R} : \mathsf{VK} = (vk, pk, \rho) \text{ such that:} \\ \mathsf{LE.Valid}\big(pk, \mathsf{LE.MSKExt}(msk, pk)\big) = 1 \wedge \\ \mathsf{LE.Dec}\big(\mathsf{LE.MSKExt}(msk, pk), c\big) = (\sigma, vk) \wedge \\ \mathsf{Sig.Verify}(vk, \mathsf{R} \| m, \sigma) = 1 \end{cases} \tag{3}$$

where, for each $j \in [\ell]$, $\mathsf{VK}_j = (vk_j, pk_j, \rho_j)$ is the j-th member in R. Let L_4 and L_5 be the languages corresponding to R_4 and R_5, respectively. Define further the relation $\widehat{R}$ according to $\widehat{R} := R_4 \setminus R_5$, and let $\widehat{L}$ be the corresponding language. Define $\widetilde{L}$ as follows:

$$\widetilde{L} := \{x = (\mathsf{R}, m, c_1, c_2) \mid (\mathsf{R}, m, c_1) \in \widehat{L} \wedge (\mathsf{R}, m, c_2) \in \widehat{L}\}. \tag{4}$$

Following a similar proof as for [26, Lemma 5.1], we can show that $\widetilde{L}$ is indeed a super-complement of L. (The full proof is provided in [25, Section 6.3.1].)

Claim 1. *If* LE *satisfies the completeness defined in Item 1, then* $\widetilde{L}$ *as defined in Eq. (4) is a super-complement of* L *defined in Eq. (1).*

5.5 Proof of Security

The security of Construction 2 can be established following the idea illustrated in Sect. 2.3. Due to space constraints, we refer the reader to [25, Section 6.4] for the formal security proof.

Acknowledgments. We thank the anonymous PKC 2022 reviewers for their valuable comments.

Rohit Chatterjee and Xiao Liang are supported in part by Omkant Pandey's DARPA SIEVE Award HR00112020026 and NSF grants 1907908 and 2028920. Any opinions, findings, and conclusions, or recommendations expressed in this material are those of the author(s) and do not necessarily reflect the views of the United States Government, DARPA, or NSF.

Kai-Min Chung is supported by Ministry of Science and Technology, Taiwan, under Grant No. MOST 109-2223-E-001-001-MY3.

Giulio Malavolta is supported by the German Federal Ministry of Education and Research BMBF (grant 16K15K042, project 6GEM).

References

1. Agarwal, A., Bartusek, J., Goyal, V., Khurana, D., Malavolta, G.: Post-quantum multi-party computation. In: Canteaut, A., Standaert, F.-X. (eds.) EUROCRYPT 2021. LNCS, vol. 12696, pp. 435–464. Springer, Cham (2021). https://doi.org/10.1007/978-3-030-77870-5_16
2. Agrawal, S., Boneh, D., Boyen, X.: Efficient lattice (H)IBE in the standard model. In: Gilbert [40], pp. 553–572. https://doi.org/10.1007/978-3-642-13190-5_28
3. Aguilar Melchor, C., Bettaieb, S., Boyen, X., Fousse, L., Gaborit, P.: Adapting Lyubashevsky's signature schemes to the ring signature setting. In: Youssef, A., Nitaj, A., Hassanien, A.E. (eds.) AFRICACRYPT 2013. LNCS, vol. 7918, pp. 1–25. Springer, Heidelberg (2013). https://doi.org/10.1007/978-3-642-38553-7_1
4. Alagic, G., Brakerski, Z., Dulek, Y., Schaffner, C.: Impossibility of quantum virtual black-box obfuscation of classical circuits. In: Malkin, T., Peikert, C. (eds.) CRYPTO 2021. LNCS, vol. 12825, pp. 497–525. Springer, Cham (2021). https://doi.org/10.1007/978-3-030-84242-0_18
5. Alagic, G., Majenz, C., Russell, A., Song, F.: Quantum-access-secure message authentication via blind-unforgeability. In: Canteaut, A., Ishai, Y. (eds.) EUROCRYPT 2020, Part III. LNCS, vol. 12107, pp. 788–817. Springer, Heidelberg (2020). https://doi.org/10.1007/978-3-030-45727-3_27
6. Ambainis, A., Rosmanis, A., Unruh, D.: Quantum attacks on classical proof systems: the hardness of quantum rewinding. In: 55th FOCS, pp. 474–483. IEEE Computer Society Press (2014). https://doi.org/10.1109/FOCS.2014.57
7. Backes, M., Döttling, N., Hanzlik, L., Kluczniak, K., Schneider, J.: Ring signatures: logarithmic-size, no setup—from standard assumptions. In: Ishai, Y., Rijmen, V. (eds.) EUROCRYPT 2019. LNCS, vol. 11478, pp. 281–311. Springer, Cham (2019). https://doi.org/10.1007/978-3-030-17659-4_10
8. Banerjee, A., Peikert, C., Rosen, A.: Pseudorandom functions and lattices. In: Pointcheval, D., Johansson, T. (eds.) EUROCRYPT 2012. LNCS, vol. 7237, pp. 719–737. Springer, Heidelberg (2012). https://doi.org/10.1007/978-3-642-29011-4_42
9. Bartusek, J., Malavolta, G.: Indistinguishability obfuscation of null quantum circuits and applications. Cryptology ePrint Archive, Report 2021/421 (2021). https://ia.cr/2021/421
10. Baum, C., Lin, H., Oechsner, S.: Towards practical lattice-based one-time linkable ring signatures. In: Naccache, D., et al. (eds.) ICICS 2018. LNCS, vol. 11149, pp. 303–322. Springer, Cham (2018). https://doi.org/10.1007/978-3-030-01950-1_18

11. Bellare, M., Rogaway, P.: Random oracles are practical: a paradigm for designing efficient protocols. In: Denning, D.E., Pyle, R., Ganesan, R., Sandhu, R.S., Ashby, V. (eds.) ACM CCS 1993, pp. 62–73. ACM Press (1993). https://doi.org/10.1145/168588.168596
12. Bender, A., Katz, J., Morselli, R.: Ring signatures: stronger definitions, and constructions without random oracles. In: Halevi, S., Rabin, T. (eds.) TCC 2006. LNCS, vol. 3876, pp. 60–79. Springer, Heidelberg (2006). https://doi.org/10.1007/11681878_4
13. Beullens, W., Katsumata, S., Pintore, F.: Calamari and falafl: logarithmic (linkable) ring signatures from isogenies and lattices. In: Moriai, S., Wang, H. (eds.) ASIACRYPT 2020. LNCS, vol. 12492, pp. 464–492. Springer, Cham (2020). https://doi.org/10.1007/978-3-030-64834-3_16
14. Boldyreva, A., Micciancio, D. (eds.): CRYPTO 2019, Part II, LNCS, vol. 11693. Springer, Heidelberg (2019). https://doi.org/10.1007/978-3-030-26951-7
15. Boneh, D., Dagdelen, Ö., Fischlin, M., Lehmann, A., Schaffner, C., Zhandry, M.: Random oracles in a quantum world. In: Lee, D.H., Wang, X. (eds.) ASIACRYPT 2011. LNCS, vol. 7073, pp. 41–69. Springer, Heidelberg (2011). https://doi.org/10.1007/978-3-642-25385-0_3
16. Boneh, D.: Fully key-homomorphic encryption, arithmetic circuit ABE and compact garbled circuits. In: Nguyen, P.Q., Oswald, E. (eds.) EUROCRYPT 2014. LNCS, vol. 8441, pp. 533–556. Springer, Heidelberg (2014). https://doi.org/10.1007/978-3-642-55220-5_30
17. Boneh, D., Zhandry, M.: Quantum-secure message authentication codes. In: Johansson, T., Nguyen, P.Q. (eds.) EUROCRYPT 2013. LNCS, vol. 7881, pp. 592–608. Springer, Heidelberg (2013). https://doi.org/10.1007/978-3-642-38348-9_35
18. Boneh, D., Zhandry, M.: Secure signatures and chosen ciphertext security in a quantum computing world. In: Canetti, R., Garay, J.A. (eds.) CRYPTO 2013. LNCS, vol. 8043, pp. 361–379. Springer, Heidelberg (2013). https://doi.org/10.1007/978-3-642-40084-1_21
19. Boyen, X.: Lattice mixing and vanishing trapdoors: a framework for fully secure short signatures and more. In: Nguyen, P.Q., Pointcheval, D. (eds.) PKC 2010. LNCS, vol. 6056, pp. 499–517. Springer, Heidelberg (2010). https://doi.org/10.1007/978-3-642-13013-7_29
20. Boyen, X., Li, Q.: Towards tightly secure lattice short signature and id-based encryption. In: Cheon, J.H., Takagi, T. (eds.) ASIACRYPT 2016. LNCS, vol. 10032, pp. 404–434. Springer, Heidelberg (2016). https://doi.org/10.1007/978-3-662-53890-6_14
21. Brakerski, Z., Kalai, Y.T.: A framework for efficient signatures, ring signatures and identity based encryption in the standard model. IACR Cryptol. ePrint Arch, p. 86 (2010). http://eprint.iacr.org/2010/086
22. Brakerski, Z., Vaikuntanathan, V.: Lattice-based FHE as secure as PKE. In: Naor, M. (ed.) ITCS 2014, pp. 1–12. ACM (2014). https://doi.org/10.1145/2554797.2554799
23. Carstens, T.V., Ebrahimi, E., Tabia, G.N., Unruh, D.: On quantum indistinguishability under chosen plaintext attack. IACR Cryptol. ePrint Arch, p. 596 (2020). https://eprint.iacr.org/2020/596
24. Cash, D., Hofheinz, D., Kiltz, E., Peikert, C.: Bonsai trees, or how to delegate a lattice basis. In: Gilbert [40], pp. 523–552. https://doi.org/10.1007/978-3-642-13190-5_27

25. Chatterjee, R., Chung, K.M., Liang, X., Malavolta, G.: A note on the post-quantum security of (ring) signatures. arXiv preprint arXiv:2112.06078 (2021)
26. Chatterjee, R., et al.: Compact ring signatures from learning with errors. In: Malkin, T., Peikert, C. (eds.) CRYPTO 2021. LNCS, vol. 12825, pp. 282–312. Springer, Cham (2021). https://doi.org/10.1007/978-3-030-84242-0_11
27. Chaum, D., van Heyst, E.: Group signatures. In: Davies, D.W. (ed.) EUROCRYPT 1991. LNCS, vol. 547, pp. 257–265. Springer, Heidelberg (1991). https://doi.org/10.1007/3-540-46416-6_22
28. Chevalier, C., Ebrahimi, E., Vu, Q.H.: On the security notions for encryption in a quantum world. IACR Cryptol. ePrint Arch, p. 237 (2020). https://eprint.iacr.org/2020/237
29. Communication, P.: Personal communication with the authors of [amrs20] (2021)
30. Czajkowski, J., Hülsing, A., Schaffner, C.: Quantum indistinguishability of random sponges. In: Boldyreva and Micciancio [14], pp. 296–325. https://doi.org/10.1007/978-3-030-26951-7_11
31. Damgård, I., Funder, J., Nielsen, J.B., Salvail, L.: Superposition attacks on cryptographic protocols. In: Padró, C. (ed.) ICITS 2013. LNCS, vol. 8317, pp. 142–161. Springer, Cham (2014). https://doi.org/10.1007/978-3-319-04268-8_9
32. Don, J., Fehr, S., Majenz, C.: The measure-and-reprogram technique 2.0: multi-round fiat-shamir and more. In: Micciancio, D., Ristenpart, T. (eds.) CRYPTO 2020. LNCS, vol. 12172, pp. 602–631. Springer, Cham (2020). https://doi.org/10.1007/978-3-030-56877-1_21
33. Don, J., Fehr, S., Majenz, C., Schaffner, C.: Security of the Fiat-Shamir transformation in the quantum random-oracle model. In: Boldyreva and Micciancio [14], pp. 356–383. https://doi.org/10.1007/978-3-030-26951-7_13
34. Esgin, M.F., Zhao, R.K., Steinfeld, R., Liu, J.K., Liu, D.: MatRiCT: efficient, scalable and post-quantum blockchain confidential transactions protocol. In: Cavallaro, L., Kinder, J., Wang, X., Katz, J. (eds.) ACM CCS 2019, pp. 567–584. ACM Press (2019). https://doi.org/10.1145/3319535.3354200
35. Fischlin, M., Coron, J.S. (eds.): EUROCRYPT 2016, Part II, LNCS, vol. 9666. Springer, Heidelberg (2016). https://doi.org/10.1007/978-3-662-49896-5
36. Gagliardoni, T., Hülsing, A., Schaffner, C.: Semantic security and indistinguishability in the quantum world. In: Robshaw, M., Katz, J. (eds.) CRYPTO 2016. LNCS, vol. 9816, pp. 60–89. Springer, Heidelberg (2016). https://doi.org/10.1007/978-3-662-53015-3_3
37. Garg, S., Yuen, H., Zhandry, M.: New security notions and feasibility results for authentication of quantum data. In: Katz and Shacham [47], pp. 342–371. https://doi.org/10.1007/978-3-319-63715-0_12
38. Gentry, C., Peikert, C., Vaikuntanathan, V.: Trapdoors for hard lattices and new cryptographic constructions. In: Ladner, R.E., Dwork, C. (eds.) 40th ACM STOC, pp. 197–206. ACM Press (2008). https://doi.org/10.1145/1374376.1374407
39. Gentry, C., Sahai, A., Waters, B.: Homomorphic encryption from learning with errors: conceptually-simpler, asymptotically-faster, attribute-based. In: Canetti, R., Garay, J.A. (eds.) CRYPTO 2013. LNCS, vol. 8042, pp. 75–92. Springer, Heidelberg (2013). https://doi.org/10.1007/978-3-642-40041-4_5
40. Gilbert, H. (ed.): EUROCRYPT 2010, LNCS, vol. 6110. Springer, Heidelberg (2010). https://doi.org/10.1007/978-3-642-13190-5
41. Gorbunov, S., Vaikuntanathan, V., Wichs, D.: Leveled fully homomorphic signatures from standard lattices. In: Servedio, R.A., Rubinfeld, R. (eds.) 47th ACM STOC, pp. 469–477. ACM Press (2015). https://doi.org/10.1145/2746539.2746576

42. Grilo, A.B., Hövelmanns, K., Hülsing, A., Majenz, C.: Tight adaptive reprogramming in the QROM. Cryptology ePrint Archive, Report 2020/1361 (2020). https://eprint.iacr.org/2020/1361
43. Hosoyamada, A., Iwata, T.: 4-round luby-rackoff construction is a qPRP. In: Galbraith, S.D., Moriai, S. (eds.) ASIACRYPT 2019. LNCS, vol. 11921, pp. 145–174. Springer, Cham (2019). https://doi.org/10.1007/978-3-030-34578-5_6
44. Hosoyamada, A., Iwata, T.: On tight quantum security of HMAC and NMAC in the quantum random oracle model. In: Malkin, T., Peikert, C. (eds.) CRYPTO 2021. LNCS, vol. 12825, pp. 585–615. Springer, Cham (2021). https://doi.org/10.1007/978-3-030-84242-0_21
45. Hosoyamada, A., Sasaki, Yu.: Quantum collision attacks on reduced SHA-256 and SHA-512. In: Malkin, T., Peikert, C. (eds.) CRYPTO 2021. LNCS, vol. 12825, pp. 616–646. Springer, Cham (2021). https://doi.org/10.1007/978-3-030-84242-0_22
46. Hosoyamada, A., Yasuda, K.: Building quantum-one-way functions from block ciphers: Davies-Meyer and Merkle-Damgård constructions. In: Peyrin, T., Galbraith, S. (eds.) ASIACRYPT 2018. LNCS, vol. 11272, pp. 275–304. Springer, Cham (2018). https://doi.org/10.1007/978-3-030-03326-2_10
47. Katz, J., Shacham, H. (eds.): CRYPTO 2017, Part II, LNCS, vol. 10402. Springer, Heidelberg (Aug (2017). https://doi.org/10.1007/978-3-319-63688-7
48. Kiltz, E., Lyubashevsky, V., Schaffner, C.: A concrete treatment of Fiat-Shamir signatures in the quantum random-oracle model. In: Nielsen, J.B., Rijmen, V. (eds.) EUROCRYPT 2018. LNCS, vol. 10822, pp. 552–586. Springer, Cham (2018). https://doi.org/10.1007/978-3-319-78372-7_18
49. Krawczyk, H., Rabin, T.: Chameleon signatures. In: Proceedings of the Network and Distributed System Security Symposium, NDSS 2000, San Diego, California, USA. The Internet Society (2000). https://www.ndss-symposium.org/ndss2000/chameleon-signatures/
50. Lamport, L.: Constructing digital signatures from a one-way function. Technical report, Citeseer (1979)
51. Libert, B., Ling, S., Nguyen, K., Wang, H.: Zero-knowledge arguments for lattice-based accumulators: Logarithmic-size ring signatures and group signatures without trapdoors. In: Fischlin and Coron [35], pp. 1–31. https://doi.org/10.1007/978-3-662-49896-5_1
52. Liu, Q., Zhandry, M.: Revisiting post-quantum Fiat-Shamir. In: Boldyreva and Micciancio [14], pp. 326–355. https://doi.org/10.1007/978-3-030-26951-7_12
53. Lyubashevsky, V., Nguyen, N.K., Seiler, G.: SMILE: set membership from ideal lattices with applications to ring signatures and confidential transactions. In: Malkin, T., Peikert, C. (eds.) CRYPTO 2021. LNCS, vol. 12826, pp. 611–640. Springer, Cham (2021). https://doi.org/10.1007/978-3-030-84245-1_21
54. Majenz, C., Manfouo, C.M., Ozols, M.: Quantum-access security of the winternitz one-time signature scheme. arXiv preprint arXiv:2103.12448 (2021)
55. Merkle, R.C.: A certified digital signature. In: Brassard, G. (ed.) CRYPTO 1989. LNCS, vol. 435, pp. 218–238. Springer, New York (1990). https://doi.org/10.1007/0-387-34805-0_21
56. Noether, S.: Ring signature confidential transactions for monero. Cryptology ePrint Archive, Report 2015/1098 (2015). https://eprint.iacr.org/2015/1098
57. Pointcheval, D., Stern, J.: Provably secure blind signature schemes. In: Kim, K., Matsumoto, T. (eds.) ASIACRYPT 1996. LNCS, vol. 1163, pp. 252–265. Springer, Heidelberg (1996). https://doi.org/10.1007/BFb0034852

58. Rivest, R.L., Shamir, A., Tauman, Y.: How to leak a secret. In: Boyd, C. (ed.) ASIACRYPT 2001. LNCS, vol. 2248, pp. 552–565. Springer, Heidelberg (2001). https://doi.org/10.1007/3-540-45682-1_32
59. Song, F., Yun, A.: Quantum security of NMAC and related constructions - PRF domain extension against quantum attacks. In: Katz and Shacham [47], pp. 283–309. https://doi.org/10.1007/978-3-319-63715-0_10
60. Alberto Torres, W.A., et al.: Post-quantum one-time linkable ring signature and application to ring confidential transactions in blockchain (Lattice RingCT v1.0). In: Susilo, W., Yang, G. (eds.) ACISP 2018. LNCS, vol. 10946, pp. 558–576. Springer, Cham (2018). https://doi.org/10.1007/978-3-319-93638-3_32
61. Unruh, D.: Computationally binding quantum commitments. In: Fischlin and Coron [35], pp. 497–527. https://doi.org/10.1007/978-3-662-49896-5_18
62. Unruh, D.: Post-quantum security of fiat-shamir. In: Takagi, T., Peyrin, T. (eds.) ASIACRYPT 2017. LNCS, vol. 10624, pp. 65–95. Springer, Cham (2017). https://doi.org/10.1007/978-3-319-70694-8_3
63. Wang, S., Zhao, R., Zhang, Y.: Lattice-based ring signature scheme under the random oracle model. Int. J. High Perform. Comput. Netw. **11**(4), 332–341 (2018). https://doi.org/10.1504/IJHPCN.2018.10014445
64. Watrous, J.: Zero-knowledge against quantum attacks. In: Kleinberg, J.M. (ed.) 38th ACM STOC, pp. 296–305. ACM Press (2006). https://doi.org/10.1145/1132516.1132560
65. Zhandry, M.: How to construct quantum random functions. In: 53rd FOCS, pp. 679–687. IEEE Computer Society Press (2012). https://doi.org/10.1109/FOCS.2012.37
66. Zhandry, M.: Secure identity-based encryption in the quantum random oracle model. In: Safavi-Naini, R., Canetti, R. (eds.) CRYPTO 2012. LNCS, vol. 7417, pp. 758–775. Springer, Heidelberg (2012). https://doi.org/10.1007/978-3-642-32009-5_44
67. Zhandry, M.: A note on the quantum collision and set equality problems. Quantum Inf. Comput. 15(7&8), 557–567 (2015). https://doi.org/10.26421/QIC15.7-8-2

Logarithmic-Size (Linkable) Threshold Ring Signatures in the Plain Model

Abida Haque[1(✉)], Stephan Krenn[2], Daniel Slamanig[2], and Christoph Striecks[2]

[1] North Carolina State University, Raleigh, USA
ahaque3@ncsu.edu

[2] AIT Austrian Institute of Technology, Vienna, Austria
{stephan.krenn,daniel.slamanig,christoph.striecks}@ait.ac.at

Abstract. A 1-out-of-N ring signature scheme, introduced by Rivest, Shamir, and Tauman-Kalai (ASIACRYPT '01), allows a signer to sign a message as part of a set of size N (the so-called "ring") which are anonymous to any verifier, including other members of the ring. Threshold ring (or "thring") signatures generalize ring signatures to t-out-of-N parties, with $t \geq 1$, who anonymously sign messages and show that they are distinct signers (Bresson et al., CRYPTO'02).

Until recently, there was no construction of ring signatures that both (*i*) had logarithmic signature size in N, and (*ii*) was secure in the plain model. The work of Backes et al. (EUROCRYPT'19) resolved both these issues. However, threshold ring signatures have their own particular problem: with a threshold $t \geq 1$, signers must often reveal their identities to the other signers as part of the signing process. This is an issue in situations where a ring member has something controversial to sign; he may feel uncomfortable requesting that other members join the threshold, as this reveals his identity.

Building on the Backes et al. template, in this work we present the first construction of a thring signature that is logarithmic-sized in N, in the plain model, and does not require signers to interact with each other to produce the thring signature.

We also present a linkable counterpart to our construction, which supports a fine-grained control of linkability. Moreover, our thring signatures can easily be adapted to achieve the recent notions of claimability and repudiability (Park and Sealfon, CRYPTO'19).

1 Introduction

Ring signatures, first introduced by Rivest, Shamir, and Tauman-Kalai [30], allow a member of a set (known as the *ring*) to anonymously sign on behalf of the ring. A verifier can check that a signature comes from one of the ring members, but cannot learn who the actual signer is, a property known as *(signer) anonymity*. Bresson, Stern, and Szydlo [6] generalized ring signatures to t-out-of-N ring signatures (aka threshold ring signatures or *thring signatures*), in which $t \geq 1$ distinct members of an ad-hoc set participate to produce a signature.

G. Hanaoka et al. (Eds.): PKC 2022, LNCS 13178, pp. 437–467, 2022.
https://doi.org/10.1007/978-3-030-97131-1_15

In a (th)ring signature, the ring should be set-up free, i.e., members can join at will by publishing a public key. Anyone can then sign with respect to a ring assembled from available public keys. Despite this open setting, many ring signature schemes need a trusted setup and rely on heuristic assumptions (e.g.,. the random oracle). However, the most desirable setting for an ad-hoc primitive like ring signatures is the plain model. In the plain model, security is based on standard and falsifiable hardness assumptions and no trusted setup is allowed. Also, most ring signature schemes are linear in the size of the ring, which is an issue when ring sizes are large. Recently, Backes et al. (BDH^+ for short) [3] presented an elegant construction of the first logarithmic-sized ring signatures in the plain model.

While the issues of model and signature size appear in ring signatures (see the full version for a discussion on related previous work), thring signatures with $t > 1$ have another issue. In a thring signature, t-out-of-N signers compute a signature with the property that any verifier can check that t distinct parties signed the message without revealing exactly which t members signed. While the t signers are anonymous to anyone *outside their set*, these signers may need to interact to create the signature. Thus, signers are not necessarily anonymous *to each other*. Importantly, concatenating t instances of 1-out-of-N ring signatures does not guarantee distinct signers – the same signer may have signed t times in a row.

Two works avoid interaction among the signers but have other drawbacks. First, Okamoto et al. [27] designed a linear-sized scheme in the random oracle model. Here, ring members can create a 1-out-of-N ring signature themselves, while also showing that they are a new signer. Thus, a list of 1-out-of-N ring signatures forms a threshold ring signature. However, their solution requires a fully trusted party who issues short-term keys to all signers. This is a strong assumption for such an ad-hoc distributed primitive. Second, Liu, Wei, and Wong [23] introduced linkable ring signatures, which allow a verifier to publicly check whether two signatures were produced by the same signer. This could be extended to produce threshold ring signatures. With a list of 1-out-of-N *linkable* ring signatures on a message, the signature verification algorithm checks pairwise that no two signatures in the list are linked to the same ring member without learning the identity of the signers. This approach is generic, but only yields a *one-time* thring signature scheme.

1.1 Our Contribution

In this work we construct thring signatures which are: *(i)* logarithmic-sized in the number of ring members; *(ii)* in the plain model from standard assumptions; *(iii)* and non-interactive, where specifically signers need not know each other.

In more detail:

- We present and prove the first construction of thring signatures where the signature size is *logarithmic* in the number of ring members and *in the plain model*. Our construction is instantiable from falsifiable standard assumptions

without the need for the random oracle heuristic or trusted setup assumptions. Our construction is inspired by the recent results by BDH$^+$ [3] but requires novel ideas and techniques.
- We create a thring signature scheme in a setting where there is no interaction among the mutually anonymous signers. Signers need not know the other signers that participate in a threshold signing, meaning our scheme achieves *strong inter-signer anonymity.* Every signer locally computes a signature and the thring signature is just the collection of the individual signatures. Additionally, our thring signature scheme allows each signer to select their own threshold. We will discuss our solution in Sect. 1.2.

We also adapt the current model of *linkability* of ring signatures and make this model more flexible and fine-grained by using the concept of a *scope* to support *scoped linkability.* We describe scoped linkability in more detail in Sect. 5. We discuss a potential post-quantum instantiation and future directions in Sect. 6.

1.2 Overview of Our Techniques

To give context to our approach and techniques, we describe the approach used by BDH$^+$ [3], which is inspired by the construction of linear-size ring signatures in the plain model due to Bender, Katz, and Morselli [5].

Outline of BDH$^+$ Approach. In BDH$^+$, the ring is $P = (VK^1, \ldots, VK^N)$. To join the ring, a user $s \in [N]$ generates key pairs $(vk_\sigma^s, sk_\sigma^s)$ and (pk^s, sk^s) of a signature scheme and a public-key encryption (PKE) scheme, respectively, and sets the verification and signing key to $VK^s := (vk_\sigma^s, pk^s)$ and $SK := (sk_\sigma^s, sk^s)$. To produce a signature for a message m with respect to R, a signer s computes a signature σ on m using sk_σ^s and encrypts σ under pk^s resulting in a ciphertext ct. The signer samples a random ciphertext ct' (representing another user i of the ring) and generates two hashing keys hk and hk' of a somewhere perfectly binding (SPB) hashing scheme [28] that are *perfectly binding* at position s and i respectively. It computes the hash of the ring R under both hk and hk', obtaining hash values h and h'. SPB hashing allows the signer to collapse a ring R of N verification keys into a ring of just two keys and membership witnesses are of size $\mathcal{O}(\log(N))$. Finally, signer s computes a perfectly sound NIWI proof π using an OR-statement which proves that either (hk, h) binds to a key VK^s and that ct encrypts a signature of m for VK^s or (hk', h') binds to a key VK^i and that ct' encrypts a signature of m for VK^i. A signature has the form $\Sigma = (ct, ct', hk, hk', \pi)$ and verification is straightforward.

For a non-interactive threshold variant, one needs to guarantee that a specific signer cannot contribute more than one signature to a thring signature, but at the same time keep other signatures from the same signer unlinkable. As BDH$^+$ encrypt the conventional signatures (which would identify the actual signer) for anonymity, one signer can sign repeatedly on the same message. While BDH$^+$ do have a linkable version, but as soon as a signer issues two signatures, even on different messages, they can be linked together, which contradicts the anonymity of thring signatures.

Outline of Our Approach. To achieve inter-signer anonymous thring signatures, we follow the BDH^+ template, but our approach requires novel ideas. First, instead of using a signature scheme, we use a verifiable random function (VRF) [25], inspired by the recent work by Park and Sealfon [29].[1] A VRF is a function which outputs a pseudorandom value v and a proof p so that given the input m, the values (v, p) and the corresponding verification key vk everyone can check correctness of the evaluation. However, an output v is still pseudorandom if the proof p is not known. Because the VRF yields a deterministic value v, using v in the signature ensures distinctness of the signers. Meanwhile, we encrypt the proof p. Our approach now enables non-interactive thring signatures, where the signatures are a collection of single 1-out-of-N ring signatures. A verifier can inspect the VRF values for inequality to determine if the signers are distinct. We need an assumption called *key collision resistance* on the VRF, which requires that if the VRF is evaluated under different (honestly generated) verification keys and the same message, the evaluations will not collide. This is a reasonable assumption. Indeed, VRF candidates such as the Dodis-Yampolskiy VRF [13] satisfy this assumption (where key-collision can be seen to be unconditional).

Suppose the only change we make to BDH^+ is replacing a ciphertext with a VRF evaluation v and encrypted proof, and the other one with a random value $\tilde{v}$ in the VRF range with an encryption of a random value. Intuitively, anonymity holds as the values v and $\tilde{v}$ are (pseudo)random and do not leak the signer's identity. Meanwhile, unforgeability is based on the unpredictability of the VRF. However, we cannot use the same proof technique as BDH^+. In BDH^+, the proof of anonymity goes by hybrid game and indistinguishably hops between two OR-clauses to switch from an encrypted signature from user s to an encryption signature from user i. If we use this strategy in our hybrids, we end up at a point where the VRF evaluations of users s and i are at the same time present as values v and $\tilde{v}$ in one signature. Unfortunately, this immediately gives a distinguisher as the adversary can query signatures for the same message and ring both s and i and in the real game one "evaluation" in each signature will be a random string, but here it finds a pair that contains two values from queried signatures at the same time. Such an event is negligible in the real game.

Thus, our second change to change the NIWI to include a third OR clause. This third clause allows us in the anonymity proof to simulate the first two clauses of the OR language and switch the witnesses in the hybrids of the anonymity proof.

Being in the plain model precludes us from using a common reference string (CRS), which would allow us to embed a simulation trapdoor for the anonymity proof. To avoid a CRS, we use the following trick. Each signer s adds an extra secret key sk_{F}^s into her overall secret key and encrypts it, i.e., $E \leftarrow \mathsf{Enc}(pk^s, sk_{\mathsf{F}}^s; r)$, and the ciphertext is added to the public key VK^s. Our

[1] We note that in a concurrent and independent work in [21], Lin and Wang propose a modification of BDH^+ that use VRFs instead of signatures to achieve repudiability. We note that their ideas do not extend to thring signatures and thus their approach cannot be directly compared to our work.

third clause in the OR language now proves that for two non-revealed users s and i (i.e., s and i from the first two OR-clauses) in the ring, it holds that $\mathsf{F}(sk_{\mathsf{F}}^{s}) = sk_{\mathsf{F}}^{i}$, where F is a one-way function (OWF)[2] , i.e., the clause shows that one of the two keys is the image of the other key under F. For honestly generated keys this relation will never be satisfied. However, in the simulation we can now set up user-keys in a way that they satisfy this relationship (without requiring a CRS). We can then use the witness for this clause of the OR proof to switch out the VRF witnesses to random.

Our Approach to Linkable Thring Signatures. With scoped linkability, one may control linking in a fine-grained way. An arbitrary string (the scope) used for signing allows one to link multiple signatures issued with respect to the same scope. While using the compiler by Liu et al. [23] on the linkable version of the BDH^{+} scheme yields linkable thring signatures, it is not clear how to extend this to scoped linkability. One would need to fix the scopes beforehand and make the public keys linear in the number of used scopes. Thus, it would not be possible to support a potential unbounded number of scopes. Besides, the "tagging trick" in BDH^{+} makes their linkable version rather involved.[3] Our linkable thring signatures support an unbounded number of scopes and are a simple modular extension of our basic thring signatures.

We get scoped linkability by adding another VRF key pair to the user's keys and use the evaluation of the VRF on the scope for linking purposes (and fixing the scope in the scheme yields the conventional notion of linkability). We extend the language of the NIWI used for the OR proof to account for this additional VRF.

We use a variant of the folklore technique of extending the language of the proof system to obtain simulation-sound NIZKs [19,31], but use VRFs instead of PRFs or signatures. The additional VRF "signs" a verification key of a strongly unforgeable one-time signature scheme and the corresponding one-time signing key signs the respective partial signature. The signature and the verification key are attached to the respective 1-out-of-N ring signature.

Claimability and Repudiability. Recently, Park and Sealfon in [29] introduced the notions of (un-)repudiability and (un-)claimability for ring signatures and are the first to formalize such definitions. Our constructions satisfy both notions of repudiability and claimability. Details are discussed in the full version.

Flexibility. Okamoto et al. [27] introduced the notion of flexibility. Flexibility means ring members can sign a message themselves and add themselves to a previously computed ring signature if they wish to sign on the same message and ring. However, in [27] the new signers must cooperate with a trusted dealer to achieve this. The way we construct our threshold ring signatures also allows

[2] The restriction is that the domain and range of F is the same.

[3] The evaluation of their JointVerify algorithm which they need to prove with their NIWI, when unrolled gives 480 clauses, where each clause is a conjunction of 5 verification statements of a commitment scheme.

us to achieve flexibility in that new signers can add themselves to an already-created threshold ring signature at any time and thus the threshold t can be extended dynamically (see the full version for a discussion).

Applications. We briefly describe some potential applications for non-interactive thring signatures with inter-signer anonymity and scoped linkability. One interesting practical application for thring signatures is to share cryptocurrency wallets that require no setup and that allow users to have a single key (even if they have multiple wallets) as discussed in [26].

Secondly, linkable ring signatures are a solution to e-voting [32]. Our scheme features scoped linkability, so signers can use the same verification key to vote for candidates in different offices. For example, votes cast under the scope 'mayor' are linkable, so that nobody can double vote for mayor. Meanwhile, votes cast for different scopes remain unlinkable, such as between scopes 'governor' and 'mayor'. As a result, thrings with scoped linkability might be a valuable tool for e-voting.

Finally, one can consider an extension of the whistleblower example from Rivest et al. [30] to the "parliament's problem". Suppose that a member of a national parliament (an MP) would like to submit a controversial bill for a law. The bill is controversial enough that the MP could lose his standing among his own party. However, if enough other members agree to the bill, it will be submitted for an official law. The MP cannot use a ring signature because another MP, wishing to attach their name, can neither add themselves nor submit a new ring signature while still showing that they are a distinct member. It would not be easy for this MP to discover other interested parties. Otherwise, a thring signature with interaction would do. The solution, then, is for the first MP to publish their bill using a thring signature with strong inter-signer anonymity. Now, he need not interact with other members, and any other MP can add themselves by contributing to the thring signature.

Due to lack of space, we defer a discussion of related work to the full version.

2 Preliminaries

We denote the main security parameter by λ. We write $[N] = \{1, \ldots, N\}$, and $\boldsymbol{a} = (a_1, \ldots, a_N)$. $\sqcup$ denotes disjoint union and $\triangle$ denotes symmetric difference. We denote algorithms by, e.g., A, and write $out \leftarrow \mathsf{A}(in)$ to denote that out is assigned the output of the probabilistic algorithm A with input in; Sometimes we make the used random coins r explicit and write $out \leftarrow \mathsf{A}(in; r)$. A function $\mathsf{negl} : \mathbb{N} \rightarrow \mathbb{R}$ is negligible if $\forall k \in \mathbb{N}\ \exists n_0 \in \mathbb{N}\ \forall n > n_0\ :\ \mathsf{negl}(n) \leq n^{-k}$.

For the formal definition properties of the primitives discussed below, we refer the reader to the full version.

Non-Interactive Witness-Indistinguishable Proof Systems. Feige and Shamir [15] first introduced witness-indistinguishable proof systems. We recap the basic notions of non-interactive witness-indistinguishable proofs (NIWIs).

Let $\mathcal{R} \subseteq \mathcal{X} \times \mathcal{Y}$ be an *effective* relation, i.e., $\mathcal{X}$, $\mathcal{Y}$, $\mathcal{R}$ are all efficiently computable. For $(x, \mathsf{w}) \in \mathcal{R}$, x is a *statement*, and w is the *witness*. The language

$\mathcal{L}_\mathcal{R}$ is defined as all statements that have a valid witness in $\mathcal{R}$, i.e., $\mathcal{L}_\mathcal{R} := \{x \mid \exists \mathsf{w} : (x, \mathsf{w}) \in \mathcal{R}\}$.

Definition 1 (Non-interactive Proof System). *Let $\mathcal{R}$ be an effective relation and $\mathcal{L}_\mathcal{R}$ be the language accepted by $\mathcal{R}$. A* non-interactive proof system *for $\mathcal{L}_\mathcal{R}$ is a pair of algorithms* (Prove, Vfy) *where:*

- $\pi \leftarrow \mathsf{Prove}(1^\lambda, x, \mathsf{w})$. *On input a statement x and a witness w, outputs a proof π or $\perp$.*
- $b \leftarrow \mathsf{Vfy}(x, \pi)$. *Given a statement x and a proof π, outputs a bit b.*

NIWIs must satisfy the following three properties. First, *perfect completeness* guarantees that correct statements can always be successfully proven. Second, *perfect soundness* ensures that it is impossible to generate valid proofs for false statements. Finally, *witness indistinguishability* says that, given two valid witnesses for a statement, no efficient adversary can decide which witness was used to compute a proof.

Following BDH$^+$ [3], we only consider NIWIs with bounded *proof-size.* That is, if we require that for any valid proof π generated by $\mathsf{Prove}(1^\lambda, x, \mathsf{w})$, it holds that $|\pi| \leq |C_x|\mathsf{poly}(\lambda)$ for a fixed polynomial $\mathsf{poly}(\cdot)$, where C_x is the verification circuit for the statement x, i.e., $(x, \mathsf{w}) \in \mathcal{R}$ iff $C_x(\mathsf{w}) = 1$.

Verifiable Random Functions. A verifiable random function (VRF) is a pseudo-random function that enables the owner of the secret key to compute a non-interactively verifiable proof for the correctness of its output [25].

Definition 2 (Verifiable Random Function (VRF)). *A verifiable random function is 4-tuple* (Gen, Eval, Prove, Vfy) *where:*

- $(vk, sk) \leftarrow \mathsf{Gen}(1^\lambda)$. *On input the security parameter λ in unary, this PPT algorithm outputs a public verification key vk and corresponding secret key sk.*
- $v \leftarrow \mathsf{Eval}(sk, x)$. *On input the secret key sk and an input value $x \in \{0,1\}^{a(\lambda)}$, this deterministic algorithm outputs a value $v \in \{0,1\}^{b(\lambda)}$.*
- $p \leftarrow \mathsf{Prove}(sk, x)$. *On input the secret key sk and an input value x, this PPT algorithm outputs a proof p.*
- $b \leftarrow \mathsf{Vfy}(vk, x, v, p)$. *On input a verification key vk, an input value x, a value v, and a proof p, this deterministic algorithm outputs a single bit b.*

Here, $a(\lambda)$ and $b(\lambda)$ are polynomially bounded and efficiently computable functions in λ.

VRFs must satisfy the following six properties. First, *complete provability* guarantees that, if an output v and a proof p have been honestly computed on consistent inputs, then p will verify for v. Second, *unique provability* ensures that for all inputs x, a valid proof can only be computed for a unique output value v. Third, *residual pseudorandomness* says that no efficient adversary that sees arbitrarily many VRF evaluations can distinguish outputs on fresh inputs from uniform. Fourth, *residual unpredictability* requires that no efficient adversary that sees arbitrarily many VRF evaluations can compute a correct input and output pair; this is implied by residual pseudorandomness. Fifth, *key privacy* requires that no efficient adversary, only having access to an output but not the corresponding proof, can decide for which public key the output was computed. Finally, we introduce the notion of *key collision resistance* which guarantees that Eval, on input the same message but two different secret keys, will never return the same output value. We note that all required properties are for instance satisfied by the Dodis-Yampolskiy VRF [13]. Other instantiations in the standard model have been proposed by Lysyanskaya [24] and Hofheinz and Jager [20].

Somewhere Perfectly Binding Hashing. Somewhere statistically binding hashes were first introduced by Hubáček and Wichs [28]. Intuitively, such schemes allow one to efficiently commit to a vector (or database). Furthermore, one can generate short openings for individual positions of the vector.

Originally, it was only required that such schemes be *statistically binding* at a single position [28]. BDH$^+$ [3] strengthened this to *perfectly* binding. Furthermore, they introduced private openings to require a secret hashing key to compute a valid opening.

As shown in [3,28] SPB hashes with private local openings in the standard model can be efficiently obtained from any 2-message private information retrieval scheme with fully efficient verifier and perfect correctness. Also, we refer to [3] for DCR and DDH based instantiations of SPB based on [28].

Definition 3 (Somewhere Perfectly Binding (SPB) Hash). *A somewhere perfectly binding hash with private local opening is a tuple of algorithms* (Gen, Hash, Open, Vfy) *where:*

- $(hk, shk) \leftarrow \mathsf{Gen}(1^\lambda, n, \mathsf{i})$. *On input the security parameter* λ *in unary, a maximum database size* n*, and an index* i*, this PPT algorithm outputs public hashing key* hk *and corresponding secret hashing key* shk*.*
- $h \leftarrow \mathsf{Hash}(hk, db)$. *On input a hashing key* hk *and a database* db *of size* n*, this deterministic algorithm outputs a hash value* h*.*
- $\tau \leftarrow \mathsf{Open}(hk, shk, db, j)$. *On input a public and private hashing key* hk *and* shk*, a database* db*, and index* j*, this algorithm outputs witness* τ*.*
- $b \leftarrow \mathsf{Vfy}(hk, h, j, x, \tau)$. *On input a hash key* hk*, a hash value* h*, an index* j*, a value* x *and witness* τ*, this algorithm outputs a single bit* b*.*

SPBs must satisfy the following three properties. First, *correctness* guarantees that for honestly generated keys, hashes, and openings, verification will allows succeed. Second, *somewhere perfectly binding* ensures that if for a specific index i and value x verification succeeds, all valid openings on this position must open to x. Finally, *index hiding* says that no efficient adversary can infer the index i from the public hashing key.

Definition 4 (Public Key Encryption). *A public key encryption scheme is a triple* (Gen, Enc, Dec) *of algorithms over a message space* $M(\lambda)$*, ciphertext space* $C(\lambda)$*, and randomness space* $Rnd(\lambda)$*:*

- $(pk, sk) \leftarrow \mathsf{Gen}(1^\lambda)$. *On input the security parameter* λ *in unary, this PPT algorithm computes a public key* pk *and a corresponding secret key* sk.
- $ct \leftarrow \mathsf{Enc}(pk, m)$. *On input a public key* pk *and a message* $m \in M(\lambda)$, *this PPT algorithm outputs a ciphertext* ct.
- $m \leftarrow \mathsf{Dec}(sk, ct)$. *On input a secret key* sk *and a ciphertext* ct, *this deterministic algorithm outputs a message* m.

We require PKE schemes to satisfy the following three properties. First, *perfect correctness* guarantees that for honestly generated keys and ciphertexts, decryption will always yield the original plaintext. Second, *IND-CPA security* ensures that knowing only the public key, it is computationally infeasible to decide which message is contained in a ciphertext. Finally, *key privacy* says that no efficient adversary, not knowing the secret keys, can decide for which public key a ciphertext has been computed.

Definition 5 (Strong One-Time Signature Scheme). *A strong one-time signature scheme is a triple* (Gen, Sign, Vfy) *of algorithms over a message space* $M(\lambda)$*:*

- $(vk, sk) \leftarrow \mathsf{Gen}(1^\lambda)$. *On input the security parameter* λ *in unary, this PPT algorithm computes a verification key* vk *and a corresponding signing key* sk.
- $\varsigma \leftarrow \mathsf{Sign}(sk, m)$. *On input a signing key* sk *and a message* $m \in M(\lambda)$, *this PPT algorithm outputs a signature* ς.
- $b \leftarrow \mathsf{Vfy}(vk, m, \varsigma)$. *On input a verification key* vk, *a message* m *and a signature* ς, *this deterministic algorithm outputs a single bit* b.

sOTS schemes must satisfy these two properties: First, *correctness* guarantees that for honestly generated keys and signatures, verification will always succeed. Second, *strong unforgeability* ensures that no efficient adversary that can obtain one signature for a given key can produce another valid signature on any message.

Definition 6 (One-Way Function). *A one-way function* F *is defined such that:*

- $y \leftarrow \mathsf{F}(1^\lambda, x)$. *On input the security parameter* λ *in unary and an input value* $x \in \{0,1\}^\lambda$, *this deterministic algorithm computes an output* $y \in \{0,1\}^\lambda$.

OWFs must satisfy the following two properties. First, it must be *efficiently computable*, meaning that there is a polynomial-time algorithm to evaluate the function. Second, it must be *hard to invert*, so that given only an output value y, it is computationally infeasible to find a preimage x^* mapping to this output. Note that there can be multiple x^* for which $\mathsf{F}(x^*) = y$, but it is hard to find any such x^*. One additional requirement that we put on our OWFs is that the range must be a subset of the domain[4].

We define a concept of a *few fixed points* function. We have not seen this particular property in the literature, however a one-way function F is naturally

[4] A one-way permutation where the domain and range are equal can be used here.

a few fixed points function. If not, given $x \leftarrow \{0,1\}^\lambda$, it would be likely that $\mathsf{F}(x) = x$ and an adversary could find a pre-image. This property helps clarity in the unforgeability proof.

Definition 7 (Few fixed points). *A function F is a few fixed points function if $F : \{0,1\}^* \rightarrow \{0,1\}^*$ if* $\Pr[x \leftarrow \{0,1\}^\lambda, F(x) = x] \leq \mathsf{negl}(\lambda)$.

We also introduce a lemma that helps in the unforgeability proof. We provide a lemma that shows that the probability of finding random values that happen to be pre-images in a polynomially-sized list is negligible.

Lemma 1. *If $\mathsf{F} : \{0,1\}^* \rightarrow \{0,1\}^*$ is a one-way function, then the probability that the process: $s = 1, \dots, N$ $x_s \leftarrow \{0,1\}^\lambda$ generates a pair (x_i, x_j) such that $\mathsf{F}(x_i) = x_j$ is negligible in λ (where N is at most* $\mathsf{poly}(\lambda)$*).*

Proof. Given a list $x_1, \dots, x_N$, where each $x_s \leftarrow \{0,1\}^\lambda$ (with replacement) we want to find the probability that there exists $i, j \in [N]$ such that $F(x_i) = x_j$.

Because F is a function, for each value x_i, there is one image: $F(x_i) = y$. Thus, given two values (x_i, x_j), which are chosen uniformly at random, the probability that $x_j = y$ is $\frac{1}{2^\lambda}$.

There are $N(N-1)$ pairs where $i \neq j$.

$$\Pr[x_i, x_j \leftarrow D, F(x_i) = x_j] \leq \mathsf{negl}'(\lambda).$$

Where if $x_i = x_j$, from the few fixed points property we know it's less than $\mathsf{negl}(\lambda)$ and if $x_i \neq x_j$ it is $\frac{1}{2^\lambda}$, which is still a negligible function in λ.

Then we look at the case where $i = j$. There are N such pairs and by definition of few fixed points:

$$\Pr[x_i \leftarrow \{0,1\}^\lambda, F(x_i) = x_j] \leq \mathsf{negl}(\lambda).$$

Adding together, he overall probability of success is $T(\lambda) = \frac{N}{\mathsf{negl}'(\lambda)} + \frac{N(N-1)}{2^\lambda}$. Because N is polynomial in λ, it is much smaller than 2^λ. So we conclude that $T(\lambda)$ is negligible in λ as well.

3 Framework and Security Definitions

3.1 Syntax

We extend the basic ring signature notation of Bender et al. [5] to a thring signature. The notation is summarized in Table 1. Assuming an ordering of all public keys (e.g., lexicographic), we denote the sequence of all public keys as P as a *ring*. A *subring* is a subsequence $R \subseteq P$. Regardless of which members are part of the subring, we always enumerate the subring as $R = (VK^1, \dots, VK^N)$. A set of signers is $S \subseteq [N]$, where $R[S] = \{VK^s\}_{s \in S}$. In a thring signature scheme, a set of signers $S \subseteq [N]$ signs a message $\mathsf{msg} \in \mathcal{M}$ with respect to a subring R. The secret keys of signers are denoted as T.

Table 1. Notation used in the algorithms.

Symbol	Meaning
t^s	Individual threshold of signer s[§]
$\boldsymbol{t}$	$= (t^{i_1}, \ldots, t^{i_{\lvert S \rvert}})$
t_V	Verification threshold
N	Number of members of the ring. Indexed by s.
P	Ordered list of public keys $P = (VK^1, \ldots, VK^N)$.
R	Subring $R \subseteq P$.
S	Set of signers where $S \subseteq [N]$.
T	Secret keys to signers in S, $T = \{sk^s\}_{s \in S}$.
NS	Non-signers where $NS \subseteq [N]$
$\mathcal{M}$	Message space.
λ	Security parameter.

[§] By convention, indices used to distinguish between signers are written as superscripts

Each signer $s \in S$ chooses the minimum number of total signers t^s they require for a valid signature, and the verifier can choose a threshold as well. The sequence of all individual signer thresholds is denoted as $\boldsymbol{t}$. We denote the verification threshold by t_V, e.g., $t_V \leq \lvert \{s : t^s \leq t_V\} \rvert$ for $t^s \in \boldsymbol{t}$. The different thresholds are there to make the scheme as general as possible. This allows for different levels of signatures in different contexts (e.g., a signer may not want her signature to be used if there's not enough support, a verifier might be a potential signer who wants to see that there's enough support before adding her own signature to the set).

For generality, our syntax also considers system parameters *pp* generated by a Setup algorithm (which in our security definitions is always assumed to be honestly executed) allowing one to also model schemes requiring trusted setup in our framework. However, we stress that our instantiations given in Sect. 4 and Sect. 5 *do not require* such a Setup and are in the plain model.

Definition 8 (Threshold Ring Signature Scheme). *A threshold ring signature (thring) scheme is a 4-tuple of algorithms* (Setup, KGen, Sign, Vfy). *A subset of signers S from ring P signs the message* msg $\in \mathcal{M}$ *with respect to a subring R and thresholds $\boldsymbol{t}$.*

- $pp \leftarrow \mathsf{Setup}(1^\lambda)$. *On input the security parameter λ in unary, this PPT algorithm generates public parameters pp. The public parameters are implicit input to all other algorithms and will be omitted when clear from context.*
- $(VK, SK) \leftarrow \mathsf{KGen}(pp)$. *On input the public parameters pp, this PPT algorithm generates a public verification key VK and a corresponding secret key SK for a signer.*
- $\sigma \leftarrow \mathsf{Sign}(\mathsf{msg}, T, R, \boldsymbol{t})$. *On input a message* msg, *a set of secret keys T, a subring R, and a vector of individual thresholds $\boldsymbol{t}$, this potentially interactive PPT procedure outputs a signature σ on* msg.

- $b \leftarrow \mathsf{Vfy}(\mathsf{msg}, R, \sigma, t)$. *On input a message* msg, *a subring* R, *a signature* σ, *and a verification threshold* t, *this deterministic algorithm outputs a bit* b.

3.2 Security Definitions

In this section, we define the security properties for a thring signature scheme: correctness, unforgeability with respect to insider corruption, and inter-signer anonymity with respect to adversarial keys. Our paper is the first feasibility result for non-interactive thrings entirely in the plain model. Because of these requirements, it does not seem easy to achieve the strongest notions of unforgeability and anonymity (as shown in [5]). Namely, we avoid malicious users to satisfy unforgeability and we have anonymity for honest users only.

We first describe a set of oracles. In our security definitions, the adversary may access these oracles in arbitrary interleaf during the corresponding experiments. All oracles have access to the following initially empty sequences or sets: $P, P_{corr}, \mathcal{L}_{\mathsf{signers}}$, and Q. The first sequence P is the ring, and $P_{corr} \subseteq P$ is the subset of corrupted (or malicious) members in the ring. The sequence $\mathcal{L}_{\mathsf{signers}}$ is the triple of the signer, the public key, and the private key. The set Q is the set of signing queries.

- $\mathsf{OKGen}(s)$. On input a signer s, this oracle first checks whether there exists $(s, \cdot, \cdot) \in \mathcal{L}$ and returns $\perp$ if so. Otherwise, it generates a fresh key pair $(VK^s, SK^s) \leftarrow \mathsf{KGen}(pp)$, adds (s, VK^s, SK^s) to $\mathcal{L}_{\mathsf{signers}}$, VK^s to P, and returns VK^s to the adversary.
- $\mathsf{OSign}(\mathsf{msg}, S, R, \boldsymbol{t})$. On input a message msg, a list of signers S, a subring R, and a vector of individual thresholds $\boldsymbol{t}$, this oracle first checks whether $R \subseteq P$ and returns $\perp$ if this is not the case. The oracle then decomposes S to $S = S_{corr} \sqcup S_{hon}$, where S_{corr} denotes corrupted users (i.e., corrupted or registered by $\mathcal{A}$) and S_{hon} denotes honest users. The oracle then engages in an execution of $\mathsf{Sign}(\mathsf{msg}, T, R, \boldsymbol{t})$. The oracle mimics the behavior of honest parties using the secret keys corresponding to S_{hon}, and the adversary participates using S_{corr}. For all honest signers s, the oracle adds $(\mathsf{msg}, R, s, t^s)$ to Q.
- $\mathsf{OCorr}(s)$. On input a signer s, if there exists $(s, VK^s, sk^s) \in \mathcal{L}_{\mathsf{signers}}$, the oracle returns SK^s to the adversary. The oracle adds VK^s to P_{corr}.
- $\mathsf{OReg}(s, VK^s)$. On input a signer s and a public key VK^s, the oracle checks if there exists $(s, \cdot, \cdot) \in \mathcal{L}_{\mathsf{signers}}$ and returns $\perp$ if so. Otherwise, it adds VK^s to P_{corr} and $(s, VK^s, \cdot)$ to $\mathcal{L}_{\mathsf{signers}}$.

Correctness. Correctness guarantees that a signature generated by sufficiently many honest users will always pass the verification algorithm. In our definition, the verification algorithm will check whether the individual thresholds are less than or equal to the verification threshold. This supports the concept of flexibility (see the full version).

Definition 9 (Correctness). *A thring signature scheme is* correct *if there exists a negligible function* $\mathsf{negl}(\lambda)$ *such that for every* $\mathsf{msg} \in \mathcal{M}$, *any subring*

Experiment $\mathsf{SigForge}^{\mathcal{A}}(\lambda)$
$pp \leftarrow \mathsf{Setup}(1^\lambda)$
$(\mathsf{msg}^*, \sigma^*, R^*, t^*) \leftarrow \mathcal{A}^{\mathsf{OKGen},\mathsf{OCorr},\mathsf{OSign}}(pp)$
return 1 if:
$\mathsf{Vfy}(\mathsf{msg}^*, \sigma^*, R^*, t^*) = 1$ and
$R^* \subseteq P$ and
$|U \cup (R^* \cap P_{corr})| < t^*$
where $U = \{VK^s | \exists (\mathsf{msg}^*, R^*, s, t^s) \in Q : t^s \leq t^*\}$
return 0

Fig. 1. Unforgeability

Experiment $\mathsf{Anonymity}^{\mathcal{A}}(\lambda)$
$pp \leftarrow \mathsf{Setup}(1^\lambda)$
$(\mathsf{st}, \mathsf{msg}^*, R^*, S_0^*, S_1^*, \vec{t}) \leftarrow \mathcal{A}^{\mathsf{OKGen},\mathsf{OCorr},\mathsf{OSign},\mathsf{OReg}}(pp)$
$b \leftarrow \{0,1\}$
$T^* = \{SK^s\}$ for $s \in S_b^*$
If any $s \in P_{corr}$ $\mathcal{A}$ will cooperate to create σ_b:
$\sigma_b \leftarrow \mathsf{OSign}(\mathsf{msg}^*, T^*, R^*, \vec{t})$
$b' \leftarrow \mathcal{A}^{\mathsf{OKGen},\mathsf{OCorr},\mathsf{OSign},\mathsf{OReg}}(\mathsf{st}, \sigma_b)$
where OCorr and OSign ignore queries on $S_0^* \triangle S_1^*$ on (msg^*, R^*)
return a random bit if:
$|S_0^*| \neq |S_1^*|$, or
$S_0^* \cup S_1^* \not\subseteq R^*$, or
$(S_0^* \cap P_{corr}) \neq (S_1^* \cap P_{corr})$, or
(msg^*, R^*) has been signed before
return $(b = b')$

Fig. 2. Inter-signer anonymity

and ring such that $R \subseteq P$ (with $|P|$ being polynomially bounded in λ), any set of signers $S \subseteq R$, any vector of individual thresholds $\mathbf{t} = (t^1, \ldots, t^N)$, and any verification threshold t such that $t \leq |\{i : t^i \leq t\}|$, it holds that:

$$\Pr\left[\begin{array}{l} pp \leftarrow \mathsf{Setup}(1^\lambda) \\ \{(VK^s, SK^s) \leftarrow \mathsf{KGen}(pp)\}_{s \in [|P|]} \\ T = \{SK^s\}_{s \in [|P|]} \\ \sigma \leftarrow \mathsf{Sign}(\mathsf{msg}, T, R, \mathbf{t}) \end{array} : \begin{array}{l} R[S] \subseteq P \Longrightarrow \\ \mathsf{Vfy}(\mathsf{msg}, R, \sigma, t) = 0 \end{array}\right] = \mathsf{negl}(\lambda)$$

The scheme is called perfectly correct *iff* $\mathsf{negl}(\lambda) = 0$.

Unforgeability. Intuitively, unforgeability guarantees that an adversary who has corrupted up to $t-1$ signers will not be able to generate a valid signature for threshold t. More precisely, the adversary can adaptively corrupt an arbitrary number of signers and engage in the signing protocol on arbitrary messages with honest users with respect to any thresholds and subrings. The adversary finally outputs a valid message, signature, subring, and threshold msg^*, σ^*, R^*, and t^*. The adversary wins if (1) he did not request OSign for too many honest parties on msg^* and R^* for thresholds less than t^*, and (2) he corrupted fewer than t^* members in R.

Note, we can tolerate corrupted but not *malicious* parties in our scheme. This is since we get inter-signer anonymity by having unique signatures. While this requirement is weaker, it is not unusual among the ring signature definitions (many schemes do not consider malicious parties). The experiment is described in Fig. 1.

Definition 10 (Unforgeability wrt Insider Corruption). *A thring signature scheme satisfies* unforgeability wrt insider corruption *if for all PPT adversaries $\mathcal{A}$ there is a negligible function* $\mathsf{negl}(\lambda)$ *such that* $\Pr[\mathsf{SigForge}^{\mathcal{A}}(\lambda) = 1] \leq \mathsf{negl}(\lambda)$.

Anonymity. Anonymity says that it is infeasible to infer from a valid signature which honest users contributed to the signature generation, or in general to link a signer across different signatures. We protect honest signers' identities even from other signers (*inter-signer anonymity*). We can tolerate malicious keys, even in the challenge sets, so long as both sets have the same malicious parties.

In the anonymity game, the adversary has access to all the oracles. He then requests a signature on the sets S_0^* or S_1^*. He may continue to make OSign and OCorr requests, but the oracle will not respond to queries in the set difference between S_0^* and S_1^*. The experiment is in Fig. 2.

In our scheme, users signing the same message msg with respect to the same subring R but potentially different thresholds are linkable among these signatures. We ensure the threshold by preventing signers from signing the same (msg, R) twice. Thus, in the challenge phase we require new message-ring pairs.

Moreover, a signer who has already signed with respect to a message/ring cannot sign again because the signature needs to be completely *distinct* for new users, which is not possible due to the deterministic part. Thus, if the adversary requests a signature from a specific user in the training phase, he could pinpoint from whom that signature originated. Thus, in the challenge phase we require either that the signature is different from previous signatures or that it verifies for a different message-ring pair.

In some ring signature schemes, an adversary $\mathcal{A}$ cannot identify which user a signature came from *even with knowledge of their secret key*. However, in our scheme, the signature is an output of the VRF, and $\mathcal{A}$ can learn which signer signed a message if he knows all the keys. Thus, we do not achieve this more robust definition.

We also note that the anonymity security definition does not hide the set sizes, but this is usually the case with threshold ring signatures. Unlike in other threshold ring signatures (where after the signature is created, it is not possible to *remove* signers), here the signature can be modified for a lower threshold by removing signatures from the total concatenation.

Due to how we use the VRF in our construction, we cannot achieve the strongest notion of anonymity from Bender et al. [5] (i.e., anonymity against attribution attacks/full key exposure), where the adversary sees all the random coins for generating all the honest keys. However, we do achieve anonymity with respect to adversarially chosen keys [5], which still allows an adversary to join the ring with maliciously generated keys and corrupt users. Although an adversary can de-anonymize corrupt or malicious users, our definition allows us to protect honest users' identities.

Definition 11 (Anonymity wrt adversarial Keys). *A threshold ring signature scheme satisfies* inter-signer anonymity with respect to adversarial keys *if for every PPT adversary $\mathcal{A}$ there exists a negligible function* $\mathsf{negl}(\lambda)$ *such that*

$$\left| \Pr[\mathsf{Anonymity}^{\mathcal{A}}(\lambda) = 1] - \frac{1}{2} \right| \leq \mathsf{negl}(\lambda)\,.$$

4 Our Construction of Threshold Ring Signatures

In this section, we provide an overview of our construction. The formal description of our threshold ring signature scheme TRS is in Fig. 3.

Signing. Suppose that t members of a ring $R = (VK^1, \ldots, VK^N)$ wish to sign a message msg. We identify a signer index $s \in [N]$. Then each signer s locally evaluates the VRF using her private key on the inputs $\mathsf{msg}||R$ and $t^s||\mathsf{msg}||R$. The latter is needed because we allow each signer to choose its own threshold. The signer then encrypts the proofs of these VRF evaluations in ct and ct'. Next, it samples two SPB hashing keys hk^s and hk^i for $i \in [N]$ where $i \neq s$, binding at positions s and i respectively. Next, it calculates $h^i = \mathsf{Hash}_{SPB}(hk^i, R)$ and $h^s = \mathsf{Hash}_{SPB}(hk^s, R)$. Then (hk^s, h^s) and (hk^i, h^i) are commitments to VK^s and VK^i respectively. Finally, the signer computes a NIWI proof (discussed below). Signer s then outputs its signature σ^s as a tuple containing the VRF evaluations, the ciphertexts, hashing keys, the NIWI proof, and its individual threshold. A threshold signature is now a plain concatenation of individual signatures, i.e., $\sigma = (\sigma^1, \ldots, \sigma^t)$.
Verification. To verify a signature for a target threshold t, the verifier on $\sigma = (\sigma^1, \ldots, \sigma^t)$ checks each σ^i for each $1 \leq i \leq t$. It checks to see if the VRF value is different than all previously verified signatures. Then the verifier will check if the NIWI verifies and whether the threshold is less than or equal to his threshold t. The verifier will keep track of how many valid signatures it sees in a list $\mathcal{L}_V$. At the end, if $\mathcal{L}_V$ contains at least t signatures, the verifier will accept.

NIWI. The signer needs to show that one of the following claims is true:

(i) The computations are correct for signer s, i.e., hk^s is binding at position s and commits to R, VK^s and the corresponding secret key was used to evaluate the VRF on $\mathsf{msg}||R$ and $t^s||\mathsf{msg}||R$ resulting in v and v', and the corresponding proofs have been encrypted as ct and ct' under $pk^s_\dagger$. This is the branch for which an honest signer has all necessary keys; OR
(ii) the same computations have been performed correctly for signer i; OR
(iii) the secret keys sk_F of signer s and i satisfy $\mathsf{F}(sk^s_\mathsf{F}) = sk^i_\mathsf{F}$, that hk^s and hk^i have been computed for positions s and i, and that the sk_F are those corresponding to the public keys of s and i. As discussed in Sect. 1.2 this is needed in the anonymity proof (as publishing the VRF evaluations in the plain does no longer work with the technique of [3]) but will never be satisfied for honest keys.

More formally, we denote this language as: $\mathcal{L}' := \mathcal{L}_{\mathcal{R}|_{VK}} \vee \mathcal{L}_{\mathcal{R}|_{VK'}} \vee \mathcal{L}_F$, where $\mathcal{R}|_{VK}$ indicates the following relation $\mathcal{R}$ for a specific key $VK^s = (vk^s, pk^s_\dagger, pk^s_\ddagger, E_s)$. Statements and witnesses have the form:

$$\begin{aligned}
\mathcal{R}|_{VK} : x &= (\mathsf{msg}, R, t^s, v, v', ct, ct', hk^s, h^s)\\
\mathsf{w} &= (VK^s, s, p, p', r_{ct}, r_{ct'}, \tau)\\
\mathcal{R}_F : x &= (R, h^s, h^i, hk^s, hk^i)\\
\mathsf{w} &= (s, i, VK^s, VK^i, \tau^s, \tau^i, sk^s_\mathsf{F}, sk^i_\mathsf{F}, r_{E_s}, r_{E_i})
\end{aligned}$$

The relations are then defined as follows:

$(x, \mathsf{w}) \in \mathcal{R}|_{VK}$ if and only if:

$$\begin{aligned}&\mathsf{Vfy}_{SPB}(hk^s, h^s, s, VK^s, \tau) = 1 \wedge \\ &\mathsf{Enc}_{PKE}(pk_{\dagger}^s, p; r_{ct}) = ct \wedge \\ &\mathsf{Enc}_{PKE}(pk_{\dagger}^s, p'; r_{ct'}) = ct' \wedge \\ &\mathsf{Vfy}_{VRF}(vk^s, \mathsf{msg}||R, v, p) = 1 \wedge \\ &\mathsf{Vfy}_{VRF}(vk^s, t^s||\mathsf{msg}||R, v', p') = 1\end{aligned}$$

$(x, \mathsf{w}) \in \mathcal{R}_F$ if and only if:

$$\begin{aligned}&\mathsf{F}(sk_{\mathsf{F}}^s) = sk_{\mathsf{F}}^i \wedge \\ &\mathsf{Enc}_{PKE}(pk_{\ddagger}^s, sk_{\mathsf{F}}^s; r_{E_s}) = E_s \wedge \\ &\mathsf{Enc}_{PKE}(pk_{\ddagger}^i, sk_{\mathsf{F}}^i; r_{E_i}) = E_i \wedge \\ &\mathsf{Vfy}_{SPB}(hk^s, h^s, s, VK^s, \tau^s) = 1 \wedge \\ &\mathsf{Vfy}_{SPB}(hk^i, h^i, i, VK^i, \tau^i) = 1\end{aligned}$$

Note that an honest signer does not use $(pk_{\ddagger}, sk_{\ddagger})$ for the NIWI proof. As mentioned above, our final language $\mathcal{L}'$ is the OR of two $\mathcal{L}_{\mathcal{R}|_{VK}}$ and $\mathcal{L}_F$. Statements and witnesses for $\mathcal{L}'$ are of the form:

$$x = \begin{pmatrix} \mathsf{msg} & R & v & v' & ct & ct' \\ t & h^s & h^i & hk^s & hk^i & \end{pmatrix} \qquad \mathsf{w} = \begin{pmatrix} VK^s & VK^i & s & i & \tau^s & \tau^i \\ p & p' & sk_{\mathsf{F}}^s & sk_{\mathsf{F}}^i & & \\ r_{ct} & r_{ct'} & r_{E_s} & r_{E_i} & & \end{pmatrix}$$

As our instantiation does not rely on any trusted setup, there is no need for Setup to generate joint parameters. The verifier must know a description of the ring to check the signature. The input of the VRF includes the description of the ring. Thus, it seems that the ring signature must always be linear in the size of the ring. However, if the verifier knows the ring beforehand, the signature need not include the ring description. Alternatively, we can change the domain of the VRF to compute on the hash of the ring instead (this was also noted by Park and Sealfon [29]). For simplicity, we include the ring as input everywhere in our scheme.

4.1 Security of Our Construction

In this section, we provide the formal proofs of each property correctness, unforgeability, and anonymity for the construction TRS.

Theorem 1 (Correctness). *If the underlying NIWI, VRF, PKE, and SPB schemes are correct, and the VRF is key collision free,* TRS *is correct.*

Proof. By construction, all individual signatures are valid. Also, we require that $\sigma^i.v \neq \sigma^j.v$ for all $i \neq j$, which follows directly as otherwise we would have that $\mathsf{Eval}_{VRF}(sk^i, \mathsf{msg}||R) = \mathsf{Eval}_{VRF}(sk^j, \mathsf{msg}||R)$ contradicting to the assumed key collision freeness. □

Theorem 2 (Unforgeability). *If* F *is a one-way function,* VRF *has residual unpredictability and unique provability,* NIWI *has perfect soundness, SPB is somewhere perfectly binding and PKE is perfectly correct, then* TRS *is unforgeable.*

To prove unforgeability, we need to show that a forger $\mathcal{F}$ who knows up to $t-1$ secret keys cannot forge a signature that verifies for t signers. At a high level, because $\mathcal{F}$ needs to provide a valid NIWI proof in the signature, and the NIWI is perfectly sound, the claimed statement must indeed be true. We do not give $\mathcal{F}$ access to the OReg oracle so it is not possible for it to produce keys

Key Generation $\mathsf{Gen}(1^\lambda)$:

$(vk, sk) \leftarrow \mathsf{Gen}_{VRF}(1^\lambda)$;
$(pk_\dagger, sk_\dagger) \leftarrow \mathsf{Gen}_{PKE}(1^\lambda)$;
$(pk_\ddagger, sk_\ddagger) \leftarrow \mathsf{Gen}_{PKE}(1^\lambda)$;
$sk_\mathsf{F} \leftarrow \{0,1\}^\lambda$;
$r_E \leftarrow Rnd_{PKE}$;
$E \leftarrow \mathsf{Enc}_{PKE}(pk_\ddagger, sk_\mathsf{F}; r_E)$;
$VK := (vk, pk_\dagger, pk_\ddagger, E)$;
$SK := (sk, sk_\dagger, sk_\ddagger, r_E, VK)$;
return (VK, SK).

Verification $\mathsf{Vfy}(\mathsf{msg}, R, \sigma, t_V)$:

// Parse each signature in the list;
$\sigma = ((v, v', ct, ct', hk^s, hk^i, \pi, t^i))_{i=1}^{t}$;
Sort list by t^i;
for $i \in [t]$
  $h' := \mathsf{Hash}_{SPB}(hk^s, R)$;
  $h'' := \mathsf{Hash}_{SPB}(hk^i, R)$;
  $x := (\mathsf{msg}, R, v, v', ct, ct', h', h'', hk^s, hk^i)$;
  $b' \leftarrow \mathsf{Vfy}_{NIWI}(x, \pi)$;
  if $b' = 1 \wedge \sigma^i.v \neq \sigma^k.v \ \forall k \in [i-1]$
    $\mathcal{L}_V.\mathsf{append}(t^i)$;
endfor
if $\exists i \geq t_V : \mathcal{L}_V[i] \leq i$ **return** 1;
return 0.

Threshold Signing $\mathsf{Sign}(\mathsf{msg}, T, R, \vec{t})$:

// Note $T = \{SK^s\}$
// Every signer s signs by themselves
// Look at algorithm per each signer s.
$v \leftarrow \mathsf{Eval}_{VRF}(sk^s, \mathsf{msg}||R)$;
$p \leftarrow \mathsf{Prove}_{VRF}(sk^s, \mathsf{msg}||R)$;
$v' \leftarrow \mathsf{Eval}_{VRF}(sk^s, t^s||\mathsf{msg}||R)$;
$p' \leftarrow \mathsf{Prove}_{VRF}(sk^s, t^s||\mathsf{msg}||R)$;
$r_{ct}, r_{ct'} \leftarrow Rnd_{PKE}$;
$ct \leftarrow \mathsf{Enc}_{PKE}(pk^s_\dagger, p; r_{ct})$;
$ct' \leftarrow \mathsf{Enc}_{PKE}(pk^s_\dagger, p'; r_{ct'})$;
$(hk^s, shk^s) \leftarrow \mathsf{Gen}_{SPB}(1^\lambda, N, s)$;
$h^s \leftarrow \mathsf{Hash}_{SPB}(hk^s, R)$;
$\tau^s \leftarrow \mathsf{Open}_{SPB}(hk^s, shk^s, R, s)$;
// Pick other ring member $i \neq s$
$i \in [N] \setminus s$;
$r_{E_s}, r_{E_i} \leftarrow Rnd_{PKE}$;
$(hk^i, shk^i) \leftarrow \mathsf{Gen}_{SPB}(1^\lambda, N, i)$;
$h^i := \mathsf{Hash}_{SPB}(hk^i, R)$;
$\tau^i \leftarrow \mathsf{Open}_{SPB}(hk^i, shk^i, R, i)$;
// Call on the NIWI for language $\mathcal{L}'$
$\pi \leftarrow \mathsf{Prove}_{NIWI}(x, \mathsf{w})$
$\sigma^s := (v, v', ct, ct', hk^s, hk^i, \pi, t^s)$;
// Every signer s broadcasts the signature
broadcast σ^s;
// Final threshold ring signature under set T
return $\sigma = \{\sigma^j\}_{j=1}^{t}$.

Fig. 3. Our threshold ring signature scheme. For notation refer to Table 1.

which satisfy $\mathcal{R}_\mathsf{F}$. $\mathcal{F}$ can, however, corrupt honest users. One possible winning strategy is for $\mathcal{F}$ to find a pair $sk_\mathsf{F}^i, sk_\mathsf{F}^j$ such that $\mathsf{F}(sk_\mathsf{F}^i) = sk_\mathsf{F}^j$. Because F is one-way, such a pair will exist with only negligible probability in the set of users (by Lemma 1).

Then for the other strategy, as $\mathcal{F}$ needs to hold a witness to either $\mathcal{R}|_{VK}$ (or $\mathcal{R}|_{VK'}$) due to the somewhere perfect binding property of the SPB, the forgery must have used the identity of a signer who is a member of the ring. Due to the perfect correctness of the PKE scheme, ct (or ct') contains a valid proof for the respective VRF. Due to the unique provability of the VRF we know that an uncorrupted signer must have generated such a value. Finally, we can reduce unforgeability to the residual unpredictability of the VRF.

Proof. We prove unforgeability via hybrid arguments and a reduction to residual unforgeability.

$\mathcal{H}_0$ to $\mathcal{H}_1$: $\mathcal{H}_0$ is the unforgeability experiment SigForge from Fig. 1. In $\mathcal{H}_1$, the challenger will pick one index i^* ahead of time. We abort on an OCorr request of i^*. When the adversary provides a forgery, he must have used honest keys (created via OKGen queries) in his chosen ring. Since i^* was picked at random, i^* is in the forgery's ring with probability at least $\frac{1}{q_{KG}}$ with q_{KG} the number of users generated by OKGen. Suppose there is an adversary $\mathcal{F}$ who forges in $\mathcal{H}_0$ with some probability. Then $\mathcal{F}$ can forge in $\mathcal{H}_1$ with the same probability (except with a loss of $\frac{1}{q_{KG}}$).

$\mathcal{H}_1$ to $\mathcal{H}_2$: All keys sk_{F} generated via OKGen are chosen in a way that for none of the pairs $(sk^j_{\mathsf{F}}, sk^k_{\mathsf{F}})$ it holds that either $sk^j_{\mathsf{F}} = \mathsf{F}(sk^k_{\mathsf{F}})$ or $sk^k_{\mathsf{F}} = \mathsf{F}(sk^j_{\mathsf{F}})$.

Such a pair existed in $\mathcal{H}_1$ with only negligible probability (Lemma 1), thus the probability of distinguishing between $\mathcal{H}_1$ and $\mathcal{H}_2$ is negligible as well. As the sk^i_{F} are chosen uniformly at random in the original game, here OKGen need only re-sample at random if a collision is found.

Now $\mathcal{R}_{\mathsf{F}}$ can never be satisfied among all the honest keys. In $\mathcal{H}_2$, the forgery $\sigma^* = \{(v, v', ct, ct', hk^s, hk^i, \pi, t^i)\}_{i=1}^t$ needs to use a witness for $\mathcal{R}|_{VK}$ or $\mathcal{R}|_{VK'}$. Due to symmetry of these both cases let us w.l.o.g. assume that $\mathcal{F}$ uses a witness for $\mathcal{R}|_{VK}$. Now by the perfect soundness of the NIWI we know that

$$(\mathsf{msg}, R, t, v, v', ct, ct', hk^{i_0}, h^{i_0}) \in \mathcal{L}|_{VK}.$$

As the SPB is somewhere perfectly binding, we have that $h^{i_0} = \mathsf{Hash}(hk^{i_0}, R)$ and $\mathsf{Vfy}_{SPB}(hk^{i_0}, h^{i_0}, i_0, VK^{s_0}, \tau^{i_0}) = 1$ implies that $R[i_0] = VK^{i_0}$. If we have $i_0 = i^*$, due to the perfect correctness of PKE we have that $(pk^{i^*}_{\dagger}, sk^{i*}_{\dagger})$ are correct for all messages. Then for $p := \mathsf{Dec}(sk^{i*}_{\dagger}, ct)$ and $p' := \mathsf{Dec}(sk^{i*}_{\dagger}, ct')$ the VRF verifications $\mathsf{Vfy}_{VRF}(vk^{i^*}, \mathsf{msg}^*||R^*, v, p) = 1$ and $\mathsf{Vfy}_{VRF}(vk^{i^*}, t^*||\mathsf{msg}^*||R^*, v', p') = 1$. Finally, due to the unique provability of the VRF we know that the values (v, p) and (v', p') are the unique pairs under vk^{i^*} corresponding to inputs $\mathsf{msg}^*||R^*$ and $t^*||\mathsf{msg}^*||R^*$.

Reduction to Residual Unpredictability.

We present a reduction $\mathcal{A}$ to the residual unpredictability of the VRF, which uses $\mathcal{F}$ (as in $\mathcal{H}_2$) as a subroutine.

- $\mathcal{A}$ from challenger $\mathcal{C}_{VRF}$ receives vk which we embed into VK^{i^*}.
- On each request from $\mathcal{F}$: OKGen, OCorr, OSign are as in $\mathcal{H}_2$. But for each VRF evaluation at i^* $\mathcal{A}$ queries $\mathcal{C}_{VRF}^{\mathsf{OEval}(sk,\cdot)}$. Remember that if $\mathcal{F}$ requests OCorr on either i^* then ABORT.
- From a valid forgery σ^* of $\mathcal{F}$, we obtain p and p' for inputs $\mathsf{msg}^*||R^*$ and $t^*||\mathsf{msg}^*||R^*$.
- Output one of $(\mathsf{msg}^*||R^*, v)$ and $(t^*||\mathsf{msg}^*||R^*, v')$ as forgery to $\mathcal{C}_{VRF}$.

If $\mathcal{F}$ made a valid forgery, then with probability $\frac{1}{q_{KG}}$ he picked the index i^*. Because the relationship for F does not hold, the NIWI has perfect soudness, the SPB is somewhere perfectly binding, and the PKE is perfectly correct, $\mathcal{F}$ can make a valid forgery by violating the residual unpredictability of the VRF. Consequently, we can just forward all VRF evaluations for this key in calls to the OSign oracle to the challenger of the VRF and given that the winning condition for the forgery output by the thrings forger are valid, we need to have a fresh evaluation of the VRF, which allows $\mathcal{A}$ to break residual unpredictability.

As $\mathcal{A}$ can break residual unpredictability with at most negligible probability, we see that $\mathcal{F}$ can win in $\mathcal{H}_2$ with at most negligible probability as well. By hybrid argument, we see that $\mathcal{F}$ cannot win in $\mathcal{H}_0$ either except with negligible probability.

□

Theorem 3 (Anonymity). *If SPB is index hiding, PKE has key-privacy and CPA-security,* NIWI *is computationally witness-indistinguishable, and* VRF *has residual pseudorandomness and key-privacy then* TRS *is anonymous.*

Recall the anonymity experiment in Fig. 2. In the training phase, the adversary $\mathcal{A}_{anon}$ queries on OKGen, OSign, OCorr, and OReg. Then in the challenge phase, $\mathcal{A}_{anon}$ submits a message msg, a subring R, and two signing sets $S_0, S_1 \subset R$. The challenger picks one of the signing sets S_b and computes a signature σ. On σ, $\mathcal{A}_{anon}$ guesses which of S_0, S_1 signed the message.

For us, a t-out-of-N thring signature is a collection of t ring signatures, and signatures are independent of each other. Thus, it suffices to show anonymity for a single signer and one can use a hybrid argument to show anonymity for larger thresholds. The probability of distinguishing between two sets of signatures is negligible if distinguishing between two signatures is negligible. Then for the challenge phase, $\mathcal{A}_{anon}$ will produce two indices s_0, s_1, message msg, and ring R.

Over a sequence of hybrids, we transform the signature element by element from one under s_0 to a signature under s_1. By showing that each hybrid is computationally indistinguishable from its predecessor, we see that signatures under s_0 and s_1 are indistinguishable to $\mathcal{A}_{anon}$.

We make changes over the hybrids and justify them in the proofs by using the following properties: *(i)* Changes to hk: the SPB is index-hiding. *(ii)* Changes to ct: the PKE has key-privacy and CPA-security. *(iii)* Changes to the witness used for π: the NIWI is computationally witness-indistinguishable. *(iv)* Changes to the value v: the VRF has residual pseudorandomness.

Proof. Consider the following hybrids:

$\mathcal{H}_0$ to $\mathcal{H}_1$: $\mathcal{H}_0$ is the anonymity experiment in Fig. 2 with challenge bit $b = 0$. The challenger knows ahead of time q_{KG}, the number of queries $\mathcal{A}_{anon}$ will make to OKGen and picks two indices $\mathsf{i}_0, \mathsf{i}_1 \leftarrow [q_{KG}]$ $(\mathsf{i}_0 \neq \mathsf{i}_1)$. If on either $\mathsf{i}_0, \mathsf{i}_1$, $\mathcal{A}_{anon}$ requests OCorr (or chooses these for OReg) then ABORT. Finally, we require that $\mathcal{A}_{anon}$ picks indices $\mathsf{i}_0, \mathsf{i}_1$ equal to the two indices the challenger picked ahead of time. Because $\mathsf{i}_0, \mathsf{i}_1$ were picked randomly, with $\frac{1}{q_{KG}}$ probability these will be the right two indices. An adversary playing in $\mathcal{H}_1$ wins with the same probability as in $\mathcal{H}_0$, except for a multiplicative loss of $\frac{1}{(q_{KG})^2}$.

$\mathcal{H}_1$ to $\mathcal{H}_2$: In this step, the challenger always chooses i_1 as the 'other index' when computing the final challenge signature. As i_1 was uniformly random, this is indistinguishable.

$\mathcal{H}_2$ to $\mathcal{H}_3$: In this step, for OKGen on $\mathsf{i}_0, \mathsf{i}_1$ make sure the secret keys $sk_{\mathsf{F}}^{\mathsf{i}_0}$ and $sk_{\mathsf{F}}^{\mathsf{i}_1}$ are such that $\mathsf{F}(sk_{\mathsf{F}}^{\mathsf{i}_0}) = sk_{\mathsf{F}}^{\mathsf{i}_1}$ holds. This change affects only $sk_{\mathsf{F}}^{\mathsf{i}_0}$ and $sk_{\mathsf{F}}^{\mathsf{i}_1}$, which are hidden in E_{i_0} and E_{i_1} and are never revealed.

$\mathcal{H}_3$ to $\mathcal{H}_4$: Calculate $(v^1, p^1) \leftarrow (\mathsf{Eval}_{VRF}(sk^{\mathsf{i}_1}, \mathsf{msg}||R), \mathsf{Prove}_{VRF}(sk^{\mathsf{i}_1}, \mathsf{msg}||R))$ and $(v'^1, p'^1) \leftarrow (\mathsf{Eval}_{VRF}(sk^{\mathsf{i}_1}, t||\mathsf{msg}||R), \mathsf{Prove}_{VRF}(sk^{\mathsf{i}_1}, t||\mathsf{msg}||R))$, and $\tau^{\mathsf{i}_1} = \mathsf{Open}_{SPB}(hk^{\mathsf{i}_1}, shk^{\mathsf{i}_1}, R, \mathsf{i}_1)$. Then change the witness w:

$$\mathcal{H}_3 \quad \mathsf{w}^0 = (VK^{\mathsf{i}_0}, VK^{\mathsf{i}_1}, \mathsf{i}_0, \mathsf{i}_1, \tau^{\mathsf{i}_0}, \boxed{\tau'}, \boxed{p}, \boxed{p'}, sk_{\mathsf{F}}^{\mathsf{i}_0}, \boxed{sk'_{\mathsf{F}}}, r_{ct}, r_{ct'}, r_{E_0}, r_{E_1})$$

$$\mathcal{H}_4 \quad \widehat{\mathsf{w}}^0 = (VK^{\mathsf{i}_0}, VK^{\mathsf{i}_1}, \mathsf{i}_0, \mathsf{i}_1, \tau^{\mathsf{i}_0}, \boxed{\tau^{\mathsf{i}_1}}, \boxed{p^1}, \boxed{p'^1}, sk_{\mathsf{F}}^{\mathsf{i}_0}, \boxed{sk_{\mathsf{F}}^{\mathsf{i}_1}}, r_{ct}, r_{ct'}, r_{E_0}, r_{E_1})$$

Note that this only makes changes in the *witness* of the NIWI. The values in the signature are only changed in subsequent games. Since the NIWI is witness indistinguishable, these changes are indistinguishable to any adversary. We construct $\mathcal{A}_{WI}$ which uses $\mathcal{A}_{anon}$.

1. $\mathcal{A}_{WI}$ activates $\mathcal{A}_{anon}$. He chooses $\mathsf{i}_0, \mathsf{i}_1$.
2. For each query, he answers as the challenger would.
3. On a challenge $(s_0, s_1, \mathsf{msg}, R)$, if $s_0 = \mathsf{i}_0$ and $s_1 = \mathsf{i}_1$, he calculates $\mathsf{w}^0, \mathsf{w}^0$ as above and sends to the challenger. He gets back π^*.
4. $\mathcal{A}_{WI}$ forwards π^* as part of the signature to $\mathcal{A}_{anon}$.
5. $\mathcal{A}_{WI}$ outputs the same as $\mathcal{A}_{anon}$.

In $\mathcal{H}_3$, the witness is w_0, and in $\mathcal{H}_4$, it is $\widehat{\mathsf{w}}^0$. Then if $\mathcal{A}_{anon}$ wins $\mathcal{H}_3$ and $\mathcal{H}_4$ with different probabilities, then $\mathcal{A}_{WI}$ can win the witness-indistinguishability game with the same probability. Thus, $\mathcal{H}_3$ and $\mathcal{H}_4$ are indistinguishable.

$\mathcal{H}_4$ to $\mathcal{H}_5$: $ct := \mathsf{Enc}_{PKE}(\boxed{pk_{\dagger}^{\mathsf{i}_0}}, p; r_{ct}) \rightarrow ct^1 := \mathsf{Enc}_{PKE}(\boxed{pk_{\dagger}^{\mathsf{i}_1}}, p; r_{ct})$

To show that this change is indistinguishable, we construct an adversary to PKE key privacy $\mathcal{A}_{KP}^{PKE}$.

1. $\mathcal{A}_{KP}^{PKE}$ receives two public keys pk^0, pk^1 from his challenger.
2. $\mathcal{A}_{KP}^{PKE}$ activates $\mathcal{A}_{anon}$. He picks $\mathsf{i}_0, \mathsf{i}_1$. $\mathcal{A}_{KP}^{PKE}$ answers every query as the challenger would have done, except for KGen at i_0 and i_1, where he gives $pk^{\mathsf{i}_0} = pk^0$ and $pk^{\mathsf{i}_1} = pk^1$.
3. Finally, $\mathcal{A}_{anon}$ will request a signature on msg, R.
4. $\mathcal{A}_{KP}^{PKE}$ computes using sk^{i_0}, $p \leftarrow \mathsf{Prove}_{NIWI}(sk^{\mathsf{i}_0}, \mathsf{msg}||R)$. He sends p to his challenger.
5. The challenger will pick $b \leftarrow \{0,1\}$. If $b = 0$, returns $ct^* = ct$ and if $b = 1$, returns $ct^* = ct^1$.
6. $\mathcal{A}_{KP}^{PKE}$ uses ct^* for the signature he gives $\mathcal{A}_{anon}$.
7. Output the same as $\mathcal{A}_{anon}$.

If the challenger picks pk^0, this is the anonymity game as in $\mathcal{H}_4$, but if he picks pk^1 then this is the game as in $\mathcal{H}_5$. Thus, if $\mathcal{A}_{anon}$ wins $\mathcal{H}_4$ and $\mathcal{H}_5$ with different probabilities, then this is the advantage of $\mathcal{A}_{KP}^{PKE}$ winning the PKE key privacy experiment.

$\mathcal{H}_5$ to $\mathcal{H}_6$: $ct' := \mathsf{Enc}_{PKE}(\boxed{pk_{\dagger}^{\mathsf{i}_0}}, p'; r_{ct'}) \rightarrow ct'^1 := \mathsf{Enc}_{PKE}(\boxed{pk_{\dagger}^{\mathsf{i}_1}}, p'; r_{ct'})$

The argument is identical to the transition from $\mathcal{H}_4$ to $\mathcal{H}_5$ with a reduction to PKE key privacy. The only difference is that $p' \leftarrow \mathsf{Prove}_{VRF}(sk^{\mathsf{i}_0}, t||\mathsf{msg}||R)$ and thus we omit details.

$\mathcal{H}_6$ **to** $\mathcal{H}_7$: $ct^1 := \mathsf{Enc}_{PKE}(pk_\dagger^{i_1}, \boxed{p}; r_{ct}) \rightarrow \widehat{ct}^1 := \mathsf{Enc}_{PKE}(pk_\dagger^{i_1}, \boxed{p^1}; r_{ct})$, where $p^1 \leftarrow \mathsf{Prove}_{VRF}(sk^{i_1}, \mathsf{msg}||R)$.

We construct $\mathcal{A}_{CPA}$ which uses $\mathcal{A}_{anon}$ as a subroutine to break CPA security.

1. $\mathcal{A}_{CPA}$ receives pk. $\mathcal{A}_{CPA}$ picks i_0, i_1, activates $\mathcal{A}_{anon}$.
2. For each query by $\mathcal{A}_{anon}$, $\mathcal{A}_{CPA}$ answers as a challenger would, except for OKGen at i_0, where he gives $pk_\dagger^{i_0} = pk$.
3. When $\mathcal{A}_{anon}$ queries on $(s_0, s_1, \mathsf{msg}, R)$ then $\mathcal{A}_{CPA}$ calculates both $p \leftarrow \mathsf{Eval}_{VRF}(sk^{i_0}, \mathsf{msg}||R)$ and $p^1 \leftarrow \mathsf{Eval}_{VRF}(sk^{i_1}, \mathsf{msg}||R)$. He gives p, p^1 to his challenger.
4. Challenger flips $b \leftarrow \{0,1\}$. If $b = 0$ he encrypts p, if $b = 1$ he encrypts p^1. He returns ct^* to $\mathcal{A}_{CPA}$.
5. $\mathcal{A}_{CPA}$ uses ct^* for the signature he gives to $\mathcal{A}_{anon}$.
6. $\mathcal{A}_{CPA}$ outputs the same as $\mathcal{A}_{anon}$.

If the challenger picks p, we are in $\mathcal{H}_6$, if p^1 then $\mathcal{H}_7$. Thus, $\mathcal{A}_{CPA}$ wins the CPA-security experiment with the same advantage as the difference of $\mathcal{A}_{anon}$ winning in $\mathcal{H}_6$ versus winning in $\mathcal{H}_7$.

$\mathcal{H}_7$ **to** $\mathcal{H}_8$: $ct'^1 := \mathsf{Enc}_{PKE}(pk_\dagger^{i_1}, \boxed{p'}; r_{ct}) \rightarrow \widehat{ct}'^1 := \mathsf{Enc}_{PKE}(pk_\dagger^{i_1}, \boxed{p'^1}; r_{ct})$, where $p'^1 \leftarrow \mathsf{Prove}_{VRF}(sk^{i_1}, t||\mathsf{msg}||R)$. The argument is identical to the transition from $\mathcal{H}_6$ to $\mathcal{H}_7$ and thus we omit details.

$$\mathcal{H}_8 \textbf{ to } \mathcal{H}_9\text{: } \sigma = (\boxed{v}, v', \widehat{ct}^1, \widehat{ct}'^1, hk^{i_0}, hk^{i_1}, \pi, t) \rightarrow$$
$$\sigma = (\boxed{v^1}, v', \widehat{ct}^1, \widehat{ct}'^1, hk^{i_0}, hk^{i_1}, \pi, t)$$

where $v^1 \leftarrow \mathsf{Eval}_{VRF}(sk^{i_1}, \mathsf{msg}||P)$.

We show that the change between $\mathcal{H}_8$ and $\mathcal{H}_9$ is indistinguishable using the following reduction to the VRF key privacy.

1. $\mathcal{A}_{KP}^{VRF}$ gets a vk^0, vk^1 from his challenger.
2. $\mathcal{A}_{KP}^{VRF}$ picks i_0, i_1 and activates $\mathcal{A}_{anon}$.
3. $\mathcal{A}_{KP}^{VRF}$ answers every query from $\mathcal{A}_{anon}$. At index i_0 he sets the VRF $vk^{i_0} = vk^0$ and at i_1 he sets $vk^{i_1} = vk^1$.
4. On an OSign query for msg_i, R_i, at i_0: $\mathcal{A}_{KP}^{VRF}$ asks the challenger to return $v \leftarrow \mathsf{Eval}_{VRF}(sk^b, \mathsf{msg}_i||R_i)$
5. When $\mathcal{A}_{anon}$ makes his challenge, $(s_0, s_1, \mathsf{msg}, R)$, then $\mathcal{A}_{KP}^{VRF}$ submits $\mathsf{msg}||R$ to the challenger as his challenge and gets back v^*. He uses this in the signature $\sigma = (v^*, ct, hk, h, \pi)$.

If $b = 0$, then the $\mathcal{A}_{KP}^{VRF}$ uses vk^{i_0} to answer queries. If $b = 1$, then $\mathcal{A}_{KP}^{VRF}$ uses vk^{i_1}. By the VRF's key privacy property, $\mathcal{A}_{KP}^{VRF}$ cannot distinguish between a v from vk^{i_0} and vk^{i_1}. Thus, $\mathcal{H}_8$ and $\mathcal{H}_9$ are indistinguishable.

$\mathcal{H}_9$ **to** $\mathcal{H}_{10}$: $\sigma = (v^1, \boxed{v'}, \widehat{ct}^1, \widehat{ct}'^1, hk^{i_0}, hk^{i_1}, \pi, t) \rightarrow (v^1, \boxed{v'^1}, \widehat{ct}^1, \widehat{ct}'^1, hk^{i_0}, hk^{i_1}, \pi, t)$. The challenger replaces v^1 by $v'^1 \leftarrow \mathsf{Eval}_{PRF}(sk^{i_1}, t||\mathsf{msg}||P)$. The argument is as in $\mathcal{H}_8$ to $\mathcal{H}_9$.

$\mathcal{H}_{10}$ **to** $\mathcal{H}_{11}$: $(hk, shk) \leftarrow \mathsf{Gen}_{SPB}(1^\lambda, N, \boxed{i_0}) \rightarrow hk^1, shk^1 \leftarrow \mathsf{Gen}_{SPB}(1^\lambda, N, \boxed{i_1})$.

Because of the SPB's index-hiding property we can next change the index for which hk is generated from i_0 to i_1. We construct $\mathcal{A}_{IH}$ as an adversary against SPB index hiding which uses $\mathcal{A}_{anon}$ as a subroutine.

1. $\mathcal{A}_{IH}$ picks $(N, \mathsf{i}_0, \mathsf{i}_1, \emptyset)$ (where N is the maximum ring size).
2. $\mathcal{A}_{IH}$ activates $\mathcal{A}_{anon}$ as a subroutine. On each query $\mathcal{A}_{IH}$ answers as the challenger would.
3. Eventually, $\mathcal{A}_{anon}$ requests a signature on i_0, i_1.
4. $\mathcal{A}_{IH}$ produces the signature as described in $\mathcal{H}_{10}$, except for he gives $(N, \mathsf{i}_0, \mathsf{i}_1)$ to the challenger. He uses (hk, shk) from the challenger to create the signature for $\mathcal{A}_{anon}$.
5. $\mathcal{A}_{IH}$ outputs same as $\mathcal{A}_{anon}$.

If $\mathcal{A}_{anon}$ wins with non-negligibly different probabilities in $\mathcal{H}_{10}$ and $\mathcal{H}_{11}$, then $\mathcal{A}_{IH}$ could win the index hiding experiment. We see then that $\mathcal{H}_{10}$ and $\mathcal{H}_{11}$ must be indistinguishable.

$\mathcal{H}_{11}$ to $\mathcal{H}_{12}$: Using $\tau^1 \leftarrow \mathsf{Open}_{SPB}(hk^1, shk^1, R, \mathsf{i}_1)$, select $sk_{\mathsf{F}}^{\mathsf{i}_0}, sk_{\mathsf{F}}^{\mathsf{i}_1}$ randomly when requested for OKGen and change the witness:

$$\mathcal{H}_{11}\ \widehat{\mathsf{w}}^0 = (\ VK^{\mathsf{i}_0}, VK^{\mathsf{i}_1}, \mathsf{i}_0, \mathsf{i}_1\ ,\ \tau^{\mathsf{i}_0}\ ,\ \tau^{\mathsf{i}_1}\ , p^1, p'^1,\ sk_{\mathsf{F}}^{\mathsf{i}_0}\ ,\ sk_{\mathsf{F}}^{\mathsf{i}_1}\ , r_{ct_1}, r_{ct'_1},, r_{E_0}, r_{E_1})$$

$$\mathcal{H}_{12}\ \mathsf{w}^1 = (\ VK^{\mathsf{i}_1}, VK^{\mathsf{i}_0}, \mathsf{i}_1, \mathsf{i}_0\ ,\ \tau^{\mathsf{i}_1}\ ,\ \tau^{\mathsf{i}_0}\ , p^1, p'^1,\ sk_{\mathsf{F}}^{\mathsf{i}_1}\ ,\ sk_{\mathsf{F}}^{\mathsf{i}_0}\ , r_{ct_1}, r_{ct'_1}, r_{E_0}, r_{E_1})$$

and use to compute $\pi^1 \leftarrow \mathsf{Prove}_{NIWI}(x, \mathsf{w}^1)$. This change is indistinguishable because NIWI has witness indistinguishability.

In $\mathcal{H}_{12}$, the challenger is returning a signature for i_1. Because each hybrid is computationally indistinguishable from its predecessor, we see that signatures under s_0 and s_1 are indistinguishable to $\mathcal{A}_{anon}$. □

5 (Scoped) Linkable Thring Signatures

We extend the techniques in TRS to create a *linkable* threshold ring signature scheme LTRS. Linkability [23] means that given two thring signatures for any two messages, one can verify whether (at least one of) the same signers contributed to both signatures. The verification is done via a Link algorithm that takes as input two thring signatures and outputs a bit indicating whether the two signatures are linked.

The security framework and construction presented in the following support *scoped* linkability, where two signatures link if they have been produced by related sets of signers for the same scope (e.g., context information)[5]. Scoped linkability is more fine-grained than linkability: two signatures are linkable if they have been produced w.r.t the same scope, but across different scopes signatures cannot be linked. Scope can be an arbitrary string. Using a scope string fixed in

[5] We note that this concept is not new and has previously been used within anonymous credential systems (cf. [9]), direct anonymous attestation [7] and also in context of traceable ring signatures [16].

the scheme yields the conventional notion of linking. Like BDH$^+$ [3] recently did for ring signatures, we present the first construction of a *linkable* thring signature scheme in the plain model by building upon our thring signature scheme.

The standard security requirements for (scope-)linkable threshold ring signatures are correctness, unforgeability, *scoped linkability*, *linkable anonymity*, and *non-frameability*. Scoped linkability requires that even maliciously generated signatures need to link. With linkable anonymity, while it is possible to see that two signatures come from the same signer, it is not possible to determine which signer it is. Finally, non-frameability requires that an adversary, even after seeing many messages and signatures, cannot generate fresh signatures which will link to signatures that have been generated by honest parties.

Syntax. A linkable threshold ring signature scheme is a 5-tuple of algorithms (Setup, KGen, Sign, Vfy, Link) and an extension of threshold ring signatures, where Sign and Vfy take an extra input sc (the scope). Thus, we do not detail the first four interfaces here. Finally, Link is defined as follows:

- $b \leftarrow \mathsf{Link}(\sigma_1, \sigma_2)$. On input two valid threshold ring signatures for the same scope, this deterministic algorithm outputs a single bit b.

5.1 Properties and Definitions

We now formally define the above mentioned properties.

Scoped Linkability. Intuitively, scoped linkability guarantees that signatures from non-disjoint sets of signers for the same scope will link. This is captured by giving the adversary access to honestly generated keys for a ring of size q (for any q) and have the adversary output $q+1$ valid signatures for the same scope. The adversary wins if none of them link to each other. The definition of linkability is reminiscent of unforgeability (Def. 10): the adversary with only knowledge of q keys cannot create $q+1$ signatures. We have a similar limitation with linkability as we had with unforgeability: our construction has us exclude malicious keys due to our use of $\mathcal{R}_{\mathcal{F}}$. Thus, we miss the situation where the adversary forges signatures using malicious keys, which could be trivially made to link. As before, this is inherent in our scheme due to the use of the VRF and the OWF which allows us to be in the plain model. The formal experiment is provided in Fig. 4.

We note that the proposed signatures will be linkable for different scopes if the same message/ring is signed.

Definition 12 (Scoped Linkability). *A linkable threshold ring signature scheme satisfies* scoped linkability *if for every PPT adversary $\mathcal{A}$ and every q polynomially bounded in λ, there exists a negligible function* $\mathsf{negl}(\lambda)$ *such that*

$$\Pr[\mathsf{ScopedLinkability}^{\mathcal{A}}(\lambda, q) = 1] \leq \mathsf{negl}(\lambda)\,.$$

Non-Frameability. Non-frameability guarantees that no adversary can generate fresh signatures which will link to signatures that have been generated by honest parties. The adversary has access to OCorr and OSign and can receive arbitrarily

Experiment $\mathsf{ScopedLinkability}^{\mathcal{A}}(\lambda, q)$
$pp \leftarrow \mathsf{Setup}(1^\lambda)$
$(vk^s, sk^s) \leftarrow \mathsf{KGen}(pp)$ for $s \in [q]$
$(\{(\mathsf{msg}_i, R_i, \sigma_i, t_i)\}_{i \in [q+1]}, \mathsf{sc}) \leftarrow \mathcal{A}(\{(vk^s, sk^s)\}_{s \in [q]})$
return 1 if:
$\mathsf{Vfy}(\mathsf{msg}_i, R_i, \sigma_i, t_i, \mathsf{sc}) = 1$ for $i \in [q+1]$
$R_i \subseteq \{vk^1, \ldots, vk^s\}$ for $i \in [q+1]$
$\forall i \neq j \in [q+1] \ : \ \mathsf{Link}(\sigma^i, \sigma^j) = 0$
return 0

Fig. 4. Scoped linkability

Experiment $\mathsf{Frameability}^{\mathcal{A}}(\lambda, q)$
$pp \leftarrow \mathsf{Setup}(1^\lambda)$
$(vk^s, sk^s) \leftarrow \mathsf{KGen}(pp)$ for $s \in [q]$
$(\mathsf{st}, \mathsf{msg}^*, R^*, \sigma^*, t^*, \mathsf{sc}) \leftarrow \mathcal{A}^{\mathsf{OCorr}, \mathsf{OSign}}(\{vk^s\}_{s \in [q]})$
where $\sigma^* = (\sigma_1^*, \ldots, \sigma_{n^*}^*)$
$(\mathsf{msg}^\dagger, R^\dagger, \sigma^\dagger, t^\dagger) \leftarrow \mathcal{A}(\mathsf{st}, \{sk^s\}_{s \in [q]})$
where $\sigma^\dagger = (\sigma_1^\dagger, \ldots, \sigma_{n^\dagger}^\dagger)$
return 1 if:
$\mathsf{Vfy}(\mathsf{msg}^*, R^*, \sigma^*, t^*, \mathsf{sc}) = 1$
$\mathsf{Vfy}(\mathsf{msg}^\dagger, R^\dagger, \sigma^\dagger, t^\dagger, \mathsf{sc}) = 1$
$R^* \cup R^\dagger \subseteq P$
$|R^* \cap P_{corr}| < t^*$
$\exists i$ such that σ_i^* was not obtained for (msg^*, R^*) from OSign
$R^* \cap R^\dagger \cap P_{corr} = \emptyset$
$\mathsf{Link}(\sigma^*, \sigma^\dagger) = 1$
return 0

Fig. 5. Non-frameability

many signatures, and finally outputs a strong forgery, i.e., a fresh signature to a new message and subring. The adversary then learns all secret keys and wins if it can generate another signature which links to the former one, if no corrupted user was in the subring for both signatures (as this would allow for trivial attacks).

Definition 13 (Non-Frameability). *A linkable threshold ring signature scheme satisfies* non-frameability *if for every PPT adversary $\mathcal{A}$ and every q polynomially bounded in λ, there exists a negligible function* $\mathsf{negl}(\lambda)$ *such that*

$$\Pr[\mathsf{Frameability}^{\mathcal{A}}(\lambda, q) = 1] \leq \mathsf{negl}(\lambda).$$

In our definition (see Fig. 5 for the formal experiment), we only consider signature schemes where the threshold signature consists of a list of individual signatures (as is also the case in the construction). This is because the same message can be signed for the same subring and scope, but by two disjoint sets of signers. Because of non-interactivity and inter-signer anonymity, the individual contributions of the signature cannot depend on the set of signers, and thus an adversary could create a fresh overall signature by combining parts from both signatures. The adversary could then to trivially win the frameability experiment, if the winning condition only excluded that the overall challenge signature σ^* has not been generated by OSign, while not having a real-world impact. To overcome this problem, we either must drop inter-signer anonymity or require an interactive process.

Linkable Anonymity. For linkable anonymity, it is not possible to decide from which signer in the ring the signatures came from, only what signatures are linked together. We capture this concept formally in the experiment in Fig. 6.

The adversary picks two signing sets S_0, S_1 such that $|S_0| = |S_1$. We can assume that $S_0 \cap S_1 = \emptyset$ without loss of generality. By ordering members of each set, we have a correspondence from user i_k and j_k in S_0, S_1 respectively. We say a key $VK_0^s \in S_0$ is matched with a key $VK_1^s \in S_1$.

Then in one case, all signature queries with signer i_k are signed with i_k. Otherwise, all signature queries of i_k are signed with j_k (and vice versa). Then $\mathcal{A}$ can use Link for any signature gotten from the challenger. If $\mathcal{A}$ requested two signatures for i_k then these two signatures will always link.

Depending on the bit b the challenger generates, the requested signatures on the sets S_0, S_1 have this form: If $b = 0$ then the signers are the ones $\mathcal{A}$ asks for. If $b = 1$ then each signature on $i_k \in S_0$ is replaced with $j_k \in S_1$ (and vice versa). In the end, $\mathcal{A}$ must decide whether the signatures were signed according to what he requested, or whether they were all flipped.

We note a weakness in our scheme: neither S_0 nor S_1 can have a corrupted member in the set. That is, if user i_k is corrupted, then it will be easy for $\mathcal{A}$ to learn whether i_k's key was used to create a signature. Therefore, we have OCorr ignores any calls to users in $S_0 \cup S_1$. This is a rather weak definition in the context of ring signatures, but seems unavoidable when using a deterministic function such as VRFs.

Experiment $\mathsf{LinkableAnonymity}^{\mathcal{A}}(\lambda, q)$
  $pp \leftarrow \mathsf{Setup}(1^\lambda)$
  $(vk^s, sk^s) \leftarrow \mathsf{KGen}(pp)$ for $s \in [q]$
  $b \leftarrow \{0,1\}$
  $(S_0, S_1, \mathsf{st}) \leftarrow \mathcal{A}(\{vk^s\}_{s\in[q]})$
    let $S_0 = \{vk^{i_1}, \ldots, vk^{i_m}\}$ and $S_1 = \{vk^{j_1}, \ldots, vk^{j_m}\}$
  $(S_0^*, S_1^*, \mathsf{msg}^*, R^*, \vec{t}^*, \mathsf{sc}^*, \mathsf{st}) \leftarrow \mathcal{A}^{\mathsf{OSign}, \mathsf{OSign}', \mathsf{OCorr}}(\mathsf{st})$
    where OCorr ignores any calls to users in $S_0 \cup S_1$
    where OSign′ engages in a signing protocol with $\mathcal{A}$ on the given inputs
      mimicking all uncorrupted users
    where OSign ignores calls where $\exists m$ with $vk^{i_m} \in S$ or $vk^{j_m} \in S$ but $\{vk^{i_m}, vk^{j_m}\} \not\subseteq S$, and
      otherwise computes S' by replacing all signers from S_0 with S_1 and vice versa, i.e.,
      with $S' = S \setminus (\{vk^{i_m}\}_{i_m \in S} \cup \{vk^{j_m}\}_{j_m \in S}) \cup (\{vk^{j_m}\}_{i_m \in S} \cup \{vk^{i_m}\}_{j_m \in S})$
      and then engages in signing protocols with $\mathcal{A}$ for sets S and S' ($b = 0$) or S' and S ($b = 1$).
  $\sigma^* \leftarrow \mathsf{Sign}(\mathsf{msg}^*, T_b^*, R^*, \vec{t}^*, \mathsf{sc}^*)$
      where $T_b^* = \{SK^s\}$ for $s \in S$ if $b = 0$ and $s \in S'$ if $b = 1$.
  $b' \leftarrow \mathcal{A}(\mathsf{st}, \sigma^*)$
  return a random bit if:
    (msg^*, R^*) was queried before, or
    (sc^*, S_j') has been queried before for some $j \in \{0,1\}$, or
    $S_0 \cap S_1 \neq \emptyset$
  return $b = b'$

Fig. 6. Linkable anonymity.

Definition 14 (Linkable Anonymity). *A linkable threshold ring signature scheme satisfies* scope-exclusive linkable anonymity *if for every PPT adversary $\mathcal{A}$ and every q polynomially bounded in λ, there exists a negligible function* $\mathsf{negl}(\lambda)$ *such that*

$$\left|\Pr[\mathsf{LinkableAnonymity}^{\mathcal{A}}(\lambda, q) = 1] - \frac{1}{2}\right| \leq \mathsf{negl}(\lambda)\,.$$

5.2 Our Construction

Our threshold ring signature TRS is modular in the sense that we need only to add a few elements to TRS to turn it into a linkable thring signature scheme including the concept of a scope. The full LTRS construction is presented in Fig. 7.

Key Generation $\mathsf{Gen}(1^\lambda)$:

$(vk, sk) \leftarrow \mathsf{Gen}_{VRF}(1^\lambda)$;
$(vk_L, sk_L) \leftarrow \mathsf{Gen}_{VRF}(1^\lambda)$;
$(vk_{mal}, sk_{mal}) \leftarrow \mathsf{Gen}_{VRF}(1^\lambda)$;
$(pk_\dagger, sk_\dagger) \leftarrow \mathsf{Gen}_{PKE}(1^\lambda)$;
$(pk_\ddagger, sk_\ddagger) \leftarrow \mathsf{Gen}_{PKE}(1^\lambda)$;
$sk_{\mathsf{F}} \leftarrow \{0,1\}^\lambda$;
$r_E \leftarrow Rnd_{PKE}$;
$E \leftarrow \mathsf{Enc}_{PKE}(pk_\ddagger, sk_{\mathsf{F}}; r_E)$;
$VK := (vk, vk_L, vk_{mal}, pk_\dagger, pk_\ddagger, E)$;
$SK := (sk, sk_L, sk_{mal}, sk_\dagger, sk_\ddagger, r_E, VK)$;
return (VK, SK).

Verification $\mathsf{Vfy}(\mathsf{msg}, R, \sigma, t_V, \mathsf{sc})$:

// Parse signature;
$\sigma = (\rho, \varsigma, \mathsf{vk}_{sOTS})_{j=1}^{t}$;
$\rho = (v, v', v_L, v_{mal}, ct, ct', ct_L, ct_{mal}, hk^s, hk^i, \pi, t^j, \mathsf{sc}^j)$;
Sort list by t^i;
for $j \in [t]$
  $h' := \mathsf{Hash}_{SPB}(hk^s, R)$;
  $h'' := \mathsf{Hash}_{SPB}(hk^i, R)$;
  $x := (\mathsf{msg}, R, v, v', ct, ct', ct_L, ct_{mal}, h', h'', hk^s, hk^i, \mathsf{sc})$;
  $b \leftarrow \mathsf{Vfy}_{NIWI}(x, \pi)$;
  $b \leftarrow b \wedge \mathsf{Vfy}_{sOTS}(\mathsf{vk}_{sOTS}, \rho, \varsigma)$;
   if $b = 1 \wedge \sigma^j.v \neq \sigma^k.v\ \forall k \in [j-1]$
    $\mathcal{L}_V.\mathsf{append}(t^j)$;
endfor
if $\exists i \geq t_V : \mathcal{L}_V[i] \leq i$ **return** 1;
return 0

Link $\mathsf{Link}(\sigma_1, \sigma_2)$:

Let $t_i := |\sigma_i|, i \in \{1, 2\}$
for $(j, k) \in [t_1] \times [t_2]$
  if $\sigma_1^j.v_L = \sigma_2^k.v_L$ **return** 1
endfor
return 0

Threshold Signing $\mathsf{Sign}(\mathsf{msg}, T, R, \vec{t}, \mathsf{sc})$:

// Every signer $s \in S$, $|S| \geq t$
$v \leftarrow \mathsf{Eval}_{VRF}(sk^s, \mathsf{msg}||R)$;
$p \leftarrow \mathsf{Prove}_{VRF}(sk^s, \mathsf{msg}||R)$;
$v' \leftarrow \mathsf{Eval}_{VRF}(sk^s, t^s||\mathsf{msg}||R)$;
$p' \leftarrow \mathsf{Prove}_{VRF}(sk^s, t^s||\mathsf{msg}||R)$;
$v_L \leftarrow \mathsf{Eval}_{VRF}(sk_L^s, \mathsf{sc})$;
$p_L \leftarrow \mathsf{Prove}_{VRF}(sk_L^s, \mathsf{sc})$;
$(vk_{sOTS}, sk_{sOTS}) \leftarrow \mathsf{Gen}_{sOTS}(1^\lambda)$;
$v_{mal} \leftarrow \mathsf{Eval}_{VRF}(sk_{mal}^s, vk_{sOTS})$;
$p_{mal} \leftarrow \mathsf{Prove}_{VRF}(sk_{mal}^s, vk_{sOTS})$;
$r_{ct}, r_{ct'}, r_L, r_{mal} \leftarrow Rnd_{PKE}$;
$ct \leftarrow \mathsf{Enc}_{PKE}(pk_\dagger^s, p; r_{ct})$;
$ct' \leftarrow \mathsf{Enc}_{PKE}(pk_\dagger^s, p'; r_{ct'})$;
$ct_L \leftarrow \mathsf{Enc}_{PKE}(pk_\dagger^s, p_L; r_L)$;
$ct_{mal} \leftarrow \mathsf{Enc}_{PKE}(pk_\dagger^s, p_{mal}; r_{mal})$;
$(hk^s, shk^s) \leftarrow \mathsf{Gen}_{SPB}(1^\lambda, N, s)$;
$h^s \leftarrow \mathsf{Hash}_{SPB}(hk^s, R)$;
$\tau^s \leftarrow \mathsf{Open}_{SPB}(hk^s, shk^s, R, s)$;
// Pick other ring member $i \neq s$
$i \leftarrow [N] \setminus s$;
$r_{E_0}, r_{E_1} \leftarrow Rnd_{PKE}$
$(hk^i, shk^{i_1}) \leftarrow \mathsf{Gen}_{SPB}(1^\lambda, N, i)$;
$h^i := \mathsf{Hash}_{SPB}(hk^i, R)$;
$\tau^i \leftarrow \mathsf{Open}_{SPB}(hk^{i_1}, shk^{i_1}, R, i)$;
// Call on the NIWI for language $\mathcal{L}'_L$
$\pi \leftarrow \mathsf{Prove}_{NIWI}(x, \mathsf{w})$
$\rho := (v, v', v_L, v_{mal}, ct, ct', ct_L, ct_{mal}, hk^s, hk^i, \pi, t^s, \mathsf{sc})$;
$\varsigma \leftarrow \mathsf{Sign}_{sOTS}(\mathsf{sk}_{sOTS}, \rho)$;
$\sigma^s := (\rho, \varsigma, \mathsf{vk}_{sOTS})$;
// Every signer s broadcasts the signature
broadcast σ^s;
// Final threshold ring signature
return $\sigma = \{\sigma^i\}_{i=1}^t$.

Fig. 7. Linkable threshold ring signature scheme LTRS (changes to TRS highlighted).

Besides TRS keys, we include two VRF keys (vk_L, sk_L) (for linking) and (vk_{mal}, sk_{mal}) (for achieving non-malleability). For signing, a signer additionally evaluates the first VRF on the scope sc to get (v_L, p_L) and encrypts p_L into ct_L. The evaluation on scope is necessary to allow for scoped linkability. Then, it creates a key-pair (vk_{sOTS}, sk_{sOTS}) for a strong one-time signature (sOTS) scheme. The signer evaluates another VRF using sk_{mal} on vk_{sOTS} (i.e., "signs" the verification key) and encrypts p_{mal} into ct_{mal}. The purpose of the second VRF is for non-malleability, i.e., sk_{sOTS} is used to sign the partial signature and the final signature also includes the sOTS signature. As before, the signer evaluates a NIWI:

NIWI. The NIWI consists of the OR of three different languages:

$$\mathcal{L}'_L := (\mathcal{L}_{\mathcal{R}|_{VK}} \wedge \mathcal{L}_{\mathcal{R}_{Link}}) \vee (\mathcal{L}_{\mathcal{R}|_{VK'}} \wedge \mathcal{L}_{\mathcal{R}_{Link'}}) \vee \mathcal{L}_{\mathcal{R}_F}$$

The relation $\mathcal{R}_F$ is identical to the one in TRS and $\mathcal{R}|_{VK}$ is a straightforward adaption of the one in TRS. We added a new language for the relationship $\mathcal{R}_{Link}$, which allows a signer to maintain anonymity and non-frameability: $\mathcal{R}_{Link}(x, \mathsf{w}) \iff$

$$ct_L = \mathsf{Enc}_{PKE}(pk_\dagger, p_L; r_L) \wedge ct_{mal} = \mathsf{Enc}_{PKE}(pk_\dagger, p_{mal}; r_{mal}) \wedge$$
$$\mathsf{Vfy}_{VRF}(vk_L, \mathsf{sc}, v_L, p_L) = 1 \wedge \mathsf{Vfy}_{VRF}(vk_L, vk_{ots}, v_{mal}, p_{mal}) = 1$$

Statements x and witnesses w for $\mathcal{L}'_L$ are of the form:

$$x = \begin{pmatrix} \mathsf{msg} & R & v & v_{mal} & v_L \\ h^s & h^i & hk^s & hk^i & vk_{ots} \\ ct & ct_{mal} & \mathsf{sc} & ct_L & \varsigma_{ots} \end{pmatrix} \qquad \mathsf{w} = \begin{pmatrix} VK^s & VK^{s_1} & s & s_1 & \tau^s & \tau^i \\ & p & p_{mal} & p_L & sk_{\mathsf{F}}^{i_0} & sk_{\mathsf{F}}^{i_1} \\ & r_{ct} & r_{ct'} & r_{E_0} & r_{E_1} & r_L \; r_{mal} \end{pmatrix}$$

5.3 Security of Our Construction

In the following we state the security claims for our (scope) linkable thring signature scheme LTRS. The proofs are along the same lines as those for TRS and therefore omitted; proof sketches can be found inthe full version.

Theorem 4. *If* F *is a OWF,* VRF *has residual unpredictability and unique provability,* NIWI *has perfect soundness, SPB is somewhere perfectly binding and PKE is perfectly correct, SPB is index hiding then* LTRS *is unforgeable.*

Theorem 5. *If* F *is a one-way function, the NIWI has perfect soundness, PKE is perfectly correct, SPB is somewhere perfectly binding, VRF has residual unpredictability and key collision resistance, and sOTS is strongly unforgeable then* LTRS *is non-frameable.*

Theorem 6. *If the NIWI is computationally witness-indistinguishable, PKE has key-privacy and CPA-security, and VRF has key privacy and residual pseudorandomness, then* LTRS *has linkable anonymity.*

Theorem 7. *If the NIWI has perfect soundness, SPB is somewhere perfectly binding, the VRF has unique provability, and PKE is perfectly correct, then* LTRS *is linkable.*

6 Instantiations and Future Directions

Our construction is generic but we have made some choices for convenience, i.e., the use of PKE instead of commitments as key-privacy is a natural well studied notion for PKEs. Thus, for a concrete instantiation there may be a number of choices and possible optimizations, which are outside the scope of this paper. Also, for asymptotics, the general algebraic circuit for the NIWI will have a polynomial expansion in the size of its input. The input is logarithmic in the number of users of the ring, and therefore the overall size of the proof is *polylogarithmic* in the size of the input. This is a natural limitation when relying on general building blocks, an issue that is also present in BDH^+ [3]. We discuss later how this could be circumvented.

Towards Post-Quantum Instantiations. If the instantiations of underlying primitives are post-quantum secure, then our thring signature scheme is also post-quantum secure. Post-quantum VRFs that rely on LWE [17] exist[6] and so do key-private PKE schemes (e.g., based on LWE [22]). Many PKE schemes have key privacy, as this property immediately holds if the ciphertexts are pseudorandom. SPBs can be constructed from somewhere statistically binding hashing (SSBs). BDH^+ show in Appendix A.2 of [2] how to turn two-to-one SSBs into SPBs. There are SSBs that rely only on the existence of a lossy/injective functions. One natural lossy/injective function is one built from the LWE problem [1]. The other building blocks we require are a post-quantum strong one-time signature scheme and OWFs. One example for the former is the Winternitz scheme [8] and for latter there are multiple candidates (e.g., from assumptions such as LWE or SIS or based on symmetric primitives as in Picnic [10] and related signature schemes).

The last concern is whether one can construct NIWIs that are post-quantum secure. While NIWIs in the post-quantum setting are not known, as discussed in a recent work by Chatterjee et al. [11] and based on an observation in [5], the NIWI in the BDH^+ approach (and also ours) can be replaced with a two-message public coin argument systems (ZAPs [14]). This can be done by extending verification keys with the first message of the ZAP (cf. [11]). While ZAPs are known under the LWE assumption [4,18], one requires to rely on subexponential hardness. To achieve standard polynomial hardness, it though might be possible to adapt the recent approach in [11], which uses the BDH^+ approach along with a novel ZAPs for a limited class of languages to achieve compact ring signatures in the plain model from LWE.

Potential Trade-offs. The most challenging part of our approach is proving that a verification key belongs to the ring of verification keys. Like BDH^+ [3], our thring signature is asymptotically logarithmic but due to the insistence of being in the plain model, there are technical sticking points that guide our choice of building blocks. In particular, when we want to use NIWIs we require perfect

[6] Though key privacy and key collision resistance seem natural in this approach, a formal treatment is missing.

soundness and thus like BDH$^+$ [3] rely on SPBs. Clearly, if we move to knowledge sound NIZKs and thus allow a trusted setup (CRS), then we can move to computationally sound versions and in particular accumulators, e.g., Merkle-tree accumulators with log-sized membership witnesses or even ones with constant size. For the latter ones, the accumulators rely on a trusted setup. Using accumulators was already shown to be useful to get compact ring signatures [12] and in concurrent and independent work also more compact thring signatures [26]. However, the latter requires accepting trusted setup and the random oracle heuristic. We expect that our core idea could also be combined with these primitives when accepting these additional assumptions. Another direction to reduce the signature size would be replace the NIWI with a zk-SNARG or zk-SNARK. However, this would again require a trusted setup or the random oracle heuristic and additionally non-falsifiable assumptions in the latter case.

Acknowledgments. We thank anonymous reviewers for their comments. This work was in part funded by the European Union's Horizon 2020 research and innovation programme under grant agreement No. 830929 (CyberSec4Europe) and by the Austrian Science Fund (FWF) and netidee SCIENCE under grant agreement P31621-N38 (PROFET).

References

1. Alwen, J., Krenn, S., Pietrzak, K., Wichs, D.: Learning with rounding, revisited. In: Canetti, R., Garay, J.A. (eds.) CRYPTO 2013. LNCS, vol. 8042, pp. 57–74. Springer, Heidelberg (2013). https://doi.org/10.1007/978-3-642-40041-4_4
2. Backes, M., Döttling, N., Hanzlik, L., Kluczniak, K., Schneider, J.: Ring signatures: Logarithmic-size, no setup - from standard assumptions. Cryptology ePrint Archive, Report 2019/196 (2019)
3. Backes, M., Döttling, N., Hanzlik, L., Kluczniak, K., Schneider, J.: Ring signatures: logarithmic-size, no setup—from standard assumptions. In: Ishai, Y., Rijmen, V. (eds.) EUROCRYPT 2019. LNCS, vol. 11478, pp. 281–311. Springer, Cham (2019). https://doi.org/10.1007/978-3-030-17659-4_10
4. Badrinarayanan, S., Fernando, R., Jain, A., Khurana, D., Sahai, A.: Statistical ZAP arguments. In: Canteaut, A., Ishai, Y. (eds.) EUROCRYPT 2020. LNCS, vol. 12107, pp. 642–667. Springer, Cham (2020). https://doi.org/10.1007/978-3-030-45727-3_22
5. Bender, A., Katz, J., Morselli, R.: Ring signatures: stronger definitions, and constructions without random oracles. J. Cryptol. **22**(1), 114–138 (2009)
6. Bresson, E., Stern, J., Szydlo, M.: Threshold ring signatures and applications to ad-hoc groups. In: Yung, M. (ed.) CRYPTO 2002. LNCS, vol. 2442, pp. 465–480. Springer, Heidelberg (2002). https://doi.org/10.1007/3-540-45708-9_30
7. Brickell, E.F., Camenisch, J., Chen, L.: Direct anonymous attestation. In: ACM CCS (2004)
8. Buchmann, J., Dahmen, E., Ereth, S., Hülsing, A., Rückert, M.: On the security of the winternitz one-time signature scheme. In: Nitaj, A., Pointcheval, D. (eds.) AFRICACRYPT 2011. LNCS, vol. 6737, pp. 363–378. Springer, Heidelberg (2011). https://doi.org/10.1007/978-3-642-21969-6_23

9. Camenisch, J., Krenn, S., Lehmann, A., Mikkelsen, G.L., Neven, G., Pedersen, M.Ø.: Formal treatment of privacy-enhancing credential systems. In: SAC (2015)
10. Chase, M., et al.: Post-quantum zero-knowledge and signatures from symmetric-key primitives. In: ACM CCS (2017)
11. Chatterjee, R., et al.: Compact ring signatures from learning with errors. In: Malkin, T., Peikert, C. (eds.) CRYPTO 2021. LNCS, vol. 12825, pp. 282–312. Springer, Cham (2021). https://doi.org/10.1007/978-3-030-84242-0_11
12. Dodis, Y., Kiayias, A., Nicolosi, A., Shoup, V.: Anonymous identification in *ad hoc* groups. In: Cachin, C., Camenisch, J.L. (eds.) EUROCRYPT 2004. LNCS, vol. 3027, pp. 609–626. Springer, Heidelberg (2004). https://doi.org/10.1007/978-3-540-24676-3_36
13. Dodis, Yevgeniy, Yampolskiy, Aleksandr: A verifiable random function with short proofs and keys. In: Vaudenay, Serge (ed.) PKC 2005. LNCS, vol. 3386, pp. 416–431. Springer, Heidelberg (2005). https://doi.org/10.1007/978-3-540-30580-4_28
14. Dwork, C., Naor, M.: Zaps and their applications. In: 41st FOCS (2000)
15. Feige, U., Shamir, A.: Witness indistinguishable and witness hiding protocols. In: STOC (1990)
16. Fujisaki, Eiichiro, Suzuki, Koutarou: Traceable ring signature. In: Okamoto, Tatsuaki, Wang, Xiaoyun (eds.) PKC 2007. LNCS, vol. 4450, pp. 181–200. Springer, Heidelberg (2007). https://doi.org/10.1007/978-3-540-71677-8_13
17. Goyal, R., Hohenberger, S., Koppula, V., Waters, B.: A generic approach to constructing and proving verifiable random functions. In: Kalai, Y., Reyzin, L. (eds.) TCC 2017. LNCS, vol. 10678, pp. 537–566. Springer, Cham (2017). https://doi.org/10.1007/978-3-319-70503-3_18
18. Goyal, V., Jain, A., Jin, Z., Malavolta, G.: Statistical zaps and new oblivious transfer protocols. In: Canteaut, A., Ishai, Y. (eds.) EUROCRYPT 2020. LNCS, vol. 12107, pp. 668–699. Springer, Cham (2020). https://doi.org/10.1007/978-3-030-45727-3_23
19. Groth, J.: Simulation-sound NIZK proofs for a practical language and constant size group signatures. In: Lai, X., Chen, K. (eds.) ASIACRYPT 2006. LNCS, vol. 4284, pp. 444–459. Springer, Heidelberg (2006). https://doi.org/10.1007/11935230_29
20. Hofheinz, D., Jager, T.: Verifiable random functions from standard assumptions. In: Kushilevitz, E., Malkin, T. (eds.) TCC 2016. LNCS, vol. 9562, pp. 336–362. Springer, Heidelberg (2016). https://doi.org/10.1007/978-3-662-49096-9_14
21. Lin, H., Wang, M.: Repudiable ring signature: Stronger security and logarithmic-size. Cryptology ePrint Archive, Report 2019/1269 (2019)
22. Lindner, R., Peikert, C.: Better key sizes (and attacks) for LWE-based encryption. In: Kiayias, A. (ed.) CT-RSA 2011. LNCS, vol. 6558, pp. 319–339. Springer, Heidelberg (2011). https://doi.org/10.1007/978-3-642-19074-2_21
23. Liu, J.K., Wei, V.K., Wong, D.S.: Linkable spontaneous anonymous group signature for ad hoc groups. In: Wang, H., Pieprzyk, J., Varadharajan, V. (eds.) ACISP 2004. LNCS, vol. 3108, pp. 325–335. Springer, Heidelberg (2004). https://doi.org/10.1007/978-3-540-27800-9_28
24. Lysyanskaya, A.: Unique signatures and verifiable random functions from the DH-DDH separation. In: Yung, M. (ed.) CRYPTO 2002. LNCS, vol. 2442, pp. 597–612. Springer, Heidelberg (2002). https://doi.org/10.1007/3-540-45708-9_38
25. Micali, S., Rabin, M.O., Vadhan, S.P.: Verifiable random functions. In: 40th FOCS (1999)

26. Munch-Hansen, A., Orlandi, C., Yakoubov, S.: Stronger notions and a more efficient construction of threshold ring signatures. In: Longa, P., Ràfols, C. (eds.) LATINCRYPT 2021. LNCS, vol. 12912, pp. 363–381. Springer, Cham (2021). https://doi.org/10.1007/978-3-030-88238-9_18
27. Okamoto, T., Tso, R., Yamaguchi, M., Okamoto, E.: A k-out-of-n ring signature with flexible participation for signers. Cryptology ePrint Archive, Report 2018/728 (2018)
28. Okamoto, T., Pietrzak, K., Waters, B., Wichs, D.: New realizations of somewhere statistically binding hashing and positional accumulators. In: Iwata, T., Cheon, J.H. (eds.) ASIACRYPT 2015. LNCS, vol. 9452, pp. 121–145. Springer, Heidelberg (2015). https://doi.org/10.1007/978-3-662-48797-6_6
29. Park, S., Sealfon, A.: It wasn't me! - repudiability and claimability of ring signatures. In: Boldyreva, A., Micciancio, D. (eds.) CRYPTO 2019. LNCS, vol. 11694, pp. 159–190. Springer, Cham (2019). https://doi.org/10.1007/978-3-030-26954-8_6
30. Rivest, R.L., Shamir, A., Tauman, Y.: How to leak a secret. In: Boyd, C. (ed.) ASIACRYPT 2001. LNCS, vol. 2248, pp. 552–565. Springer, Heidelberg (2001). https://doi.org/10.1007/3-540-45682-1_32
31. Sahai, A.: Simulation-sound non-interactive zero knowledge. Technical report, IBM RESEARCH REPORT RZ 3076 (2000)
32. Tsang, P.P., Wei, V.K.: Short linkable ring signatures for e-voting, e-cash and attestation. In: Deng, R.H., Bao, F., Pang, H.H., Zhou, J. (eds.) ISPEC 2005. LNCS, vol. 3439, pp. 48–60. Springer, Heidelberg (2005). https://doi.org/10.1007/978-3-540-31979-5_5

On Pairing-Free Blind Signature Schemes in the Algebraic Group Model

Julia Kastner[1](✉), Julian Loss[2], and Jiayu Xu[3]

[1] Department of Computer Science, ETH Zurich, Zurich, Switzerland
julia.kastner@inf.ethz.ch
[2] CISPA Helmholtz Center for Information Security, Saarbrücken, Germany
[3] Algorand, Boston, MA, USA
jiayux@uci.edu

Abstract. Studying the security and efficiency of blind signatures is an important goal for privacy sensitive applications. In particular, for large-scale settings (e.g., cryptocurrency tumblers), it is important for schemes to scale well with the number of users in the system. Unfortunately, all practical schemes either 1) rely on (very strong) number theoretic hardness assumptions and/or computationally expensive pairing operations over bilinear groups, or 2) support only a polylogarithmic number of *concurrent* (i.e., arbitrarily interleaved) signing sessions per public key. In this work, we revisit the security of two *pairing-free* blind signature schemes in the Algebraic Group Model (AGM) + Random Oracle Model (ROM). Concretely,

1. We consider the security of Abe's scheme (EUROCRYPT '01), which is known to have a flawed proof in the plain ROM. We adapt the scheme to allow a partially blind variant and give a proof of the new scheme under the discrete logarithm assumption in the AGM+ROM, even for (polynomially many) *concurrent* signing sessions.
2. We then prove that the popular blind Schnorr scheme is secure under the one-more discrete logarithm assumption if the signatures are issued *sequentially*. While the work of Fuchsbauer et al. (EUROCRYPT '20) proves the security of the blind Schnorr scheme for *concurrent* signing sessions in the AGM+ROM, its underlying assumption, ROS, is proven false by Benhamouda et al. (EUROCRYPT '21) when more than *polylogarithmically many* signatures are issued. Given the recent progress, we present the first security analysis of the blind Schnorr scheme in the slightly weaker sequential setting. We also show that our security proof reduces from the weakest possible assumption, with respect to known reduction techniques.

1 Introduction

Blind signatures, first introduced by Chaum [17], are a fundamental cryptographic building block. They find use in many privacy sensitive applications

J. Kastner—Supported by ERC Project PREP-CRYPTO 724307.
J. Loss—Work done while at University of Maryland.
J. Xu—Work done while at George Mason University.

G. Hanaoka et al. (Eds.): PKC 2022, LNCS 13178, pp. 468–497, 2022.
https://doi.org/10.1007/978-3-030-97131-1_16

such as anonymous credentials, eCash, and eVoting. Informally, a blind signature scheme is a interactive protocol between a *user* and a *signer*. Here, the signer holds a secret key sk and the user holds the corresponding public key pk. The goal of the interaction is for the user to learn a signature σ on a message m of its choice such that σ can efficiently be verified using pk. The protocol should ensure two properties [29]: (1) *One-More-Unforgeability:* if the protocol is run ℓ times, the user should not be able to create $\ell + 1$ or more valid signatures (2) *Blindness:* the signer cannot link the transcripts of protocol runs to the signatures that they created. In particular, it does not learn the messages that it signs. In a practical setting, signer and user might however want a more relaxed property to include some shared information, e.g. a date when the signature was issued or an expiration date. To this end, Abe and Fujisaki [2] introduced *Partial Blindness* which guarantees that signatures with the same shared information, the so-called *tag*, are unlinkable to protocol runs using this tag.

In spite of decades of study, the security guarantees of practical blind and partially blind signature schemes remain unsatisfactory. Practical constructions rely on strong number-theoretic hardness assumptions and/or computationally expensive pairing operations over bilinear groups [9,13,21,24,36]. Other constructions rely on weaker assumptions (and no pairings) but allow only for a very small (polylogarithmic) number of signatures to be issued per public key [3,15,27,28,38,40–42]. The reason for this is that the homomorphic structure of these schemes gives rise to the so-called ROS attack (Random inhomogenities in Overdetermined System of equations) when sufficiently many sessions of the scheme are executed concurrently (i.e., if session can be interleaved arbitrarily). Shortly after its discovery by Schnorr [45], Wagner [47] showed how to carry out the ROS attack in sub-exponential time against the Schnorr and Okamoto-Schnorr [35] blind signature schemes.[1] A recent result of Benhamouda et al. [12] improved the parameters of Wagner's attack, presenting the first polynomial-time attack (assuming that polylogarithmically many signing sessions can be opened concurrently).

1.1 Our Results

In this work, we revisit the security properties of two classic blind signature schemes which do not rely on pairings: Schnorr's blind signature scheme [16,44] and Abe's blind signature scheme [1]. Neither of these schemes have meaningful security guarantees if the number of concurrent signing sessions is beyond polylogarithmic (in fact, Abe's blind signature scheme has no security proof at all in a non-generic model of computation). Given the popularity of these schemes, we believe that a reassessment of their security properties is long overdue. We give a summary of our results below.

[1] Although the attack can be formulated for all the aforementioned blind signature schemes, the algebraic structure in the latter two schemes gives rise to an *efficient* attack.

Abe's Scheme. In the first part of our work, we study the concurrent security properties of Abe's blind signature scheme. This scheme was initially proven secure under the DL assumption in the ROM (with blindness holding computationally under the DDH assumption). However, a later work by Abe and Ohkubo [34] pointed out that the original proof contained a flaw and gave a security proof in the generic group model (GGM)+ROM instead. We generalize Abe's scheme to the partially blind setting and prove security of our new scheme in the more realistic AGM+ROM under the DL assumption. (We note that Abe's scheme can be obtained as a special case of our new scheme and thus our proof of security thus applies also to Abe's original scheme). As the work of Abe and Ohkubo is not publicly available, our proof is inspired by Abe's original proof and does not follow the blue print of a 'GGM-style proof.' Instead, we give a more general (and involved) proof that uses the AGM to avoid the rewinding step that causes the problem in Abe's proof. Apart from generalizing Abe's scheme to the partially blind setting, avoiding rewinding has the benefit that our reduction is tight, allowing for relatively practical parameter sizes. We stress that our reduction allows for the scheme to be proven secure with *concurrent signing sessions* and for *polynomially many signatures per tag.*

Schnorr's Scheme. In the second part of our work, we focus on the security of Schnorr's blind signature scheme. As we have already explained, the security of this scheme is completely broken in the concurrent setting for reasonable parameters. In spite of this, the Schnorr scheme continues to be one of the most popular blind signatures due to its simplicity and its efficiency. Hence, it is an important open question to settle what type of security this scheme actually *does achieve (if any).*

We show that the blind Schnorr signature scheme is secure in the algebraic group model (AGM) [22] + random oracle model (ROM) [10] if *signing sessions are sequential*, i.e., if the i-th session is always completed before the $(i+1)$-st session is opened.

In more detail, under the above model assumptions, the blind Schnorr signature scheme is secure against ℓ-sequential one-more-unforgeability (ℓ-SEQ-OMUF) under the ℓ-one-more discrete logarithm (ℓ-OMDL) assumption. This is true even when polynomially many signatures are issued for the same public key pk. We remark that security under sequential signing sessions is still a very meaningful security guarantee and has been explored in prior works (see below). Namely, sequentiality of sessions is easy to ensure (from the signer's perspective) at the expense of some efficiency.

Our result improves upon that of Fuchsbauer et al. [23], which proves that the scheme is secure under the OMDL+ROS assumption (when run concurrently). While the ROS problem is known to be information theoretically hard as long as the number of concurrent signing sessions is polylogarithmic, the recent work of Benhamouda et al. [12] shows a polynomial-time attack for super-polylogarithmically many concurrent signing sessions. Therefore, the blind Schnorr scheme is concurrently secure (in the AGM+ROM) if and only if the signer issues at most polylogarithmically many signatures.

Negative Result (Schnorr). As OMDL is a relatively strong assumption (in fact, [8] showed it is strictly stronger than q-discrete logarithm for known reduction approaches), a natural question is whether it is *actually necessary* for proving Schnorr's scheme secure. We answer this question by showing that our reduction for blind Schnorr signatures in the AGM+ROM is optimal in the sense that it is not possible to reduce ℓ-SEQ-OMUF from $(\ell-1)$-OMDL (or OMDL with any lower dimension).

We use the meta-reduction technique [18] to rule out reductions in a very strong sense: we show that any algebraic reduction that reduces ℓ-SEQ-OMUF from $(\ell-1)$-OMDL in the AGM+ROM, can be turned into an efficient solver against $(\ell-1)$-OMDL. Our result complements that of Baldimtsi and Lysyanskaya [7], which also rules out a certain class of reductions for the blind Schnorr scheme. Concretely, they show that reductions that program the random oracle in a certain predictable way, can be turned into an efficient solver against the underlying hardness assumption. While their approach restricts the type of random oracle programming that the reduction may do, ours allows for arbitrary programming, but restricts the reduction to be algebraic. On the other hand, our (algebraic) reductions may themselves work in the AGM, which further strengthens our result.

1.2 Related Work and Discussion

We have already mentioned several works that study the security of blind signatures in the concurrent signer model. In the sequential model, the work of Baldimtsi and Lysyanskaya [6] proves that an enhanced version of Abe's scheme is secure under DL. Pointcheval and Katz et al. [31,39] give a transformations that apply (among others) to the blind Schnorr and Okamoto-Schnorr scheme. The resulting schemes remain secure even in the concurrent setting, but require communication that grows linear in the number of signatures that have been issued. In terms of practical parameters, these schemes are also significantly less efficient than the schemes we consider here. Fuchsbauer et al. [23] gave a (concurrently secure) scheme under the OMDL and *modified ROS assumption* in the AGM+ROM. The latter assumption asserts the conjectured hardness of an (apparently harder) version of the ROS problem, even given unbounded computing power. Nicolosi et al. [33] use a similar strategy to ours (i.e., by restricting concurrency) to prove security of a proactive two-party signature scheme. Interestingly, they encounter similar issues as we do in our work, if concurrent session are permitted. Drijvers et al. [19] show how a ROS based attack can be applied in the context of multi-signatures (and how it can be overcome at the cost of some efficiency). Finally, various constructions of blind signatures in the standard model exist (e.g., [20,25]), but are usually not considered practical.

The Algebraic Group Model. [22] introduced the *algebraic group model (AGM)* as a formal model to analyze group based cryptosystems. Previous works had considered algebraic algorithms, for example [14,37]. In the AGM, any adversary must output an explanation of how it computed its output group elements from the group elements in its input. Since its introduction, the AGM has been readily adopted [5,8,23,26,32] and has served as a useful tool to prove the security of schemes that would be too difficult to analyze in the plain model. [43] have furthermore extended the AGM to decisional assumptions.

While the AGM is a weakening of the GGM, proofs in the AGM are inherently different from the GGM in the sense that they are reductions from one problem to another instead of showing information-theoretic hardness. From a qualitative point of view, proofs in the AGM provide a weaker form of security than proofs in the plain model, but a much stronger one than proofs in the GGM. The recent work of Agrikola et al. [4] shows that some results from the AGM can be transferred to the standard model using strong but falsifiable assumptions. This suggests that proofs in the AGM indeed hold some meaning for the plain model.

Another benefit of AGM proofs (over GGM proofs) is that they offer more insight into how secure a scheme actually is when deployed in real-world applications, as we explain in the following. In the GGM, a proof consists of establishing bounds on the runtime/success probabilities of an adversary attacking a particular signature scheme. These bounds often look similar for different schemes from an asymptotic point of view. Because of this, they do not give much insight into what computational assumptions are needed for the scheme to remain secure when run in the real world. By comparison, AGM proofs are by means of reduction from a computational assumption and thus can be used to assess the real-world disparities between two schemes that 'look equally secure' in the GGM. As a concrete example, our work gives a security proof for Abe's scheme under the discrete logarithm assumption. By comparison, we show that proving Schnorr's scheme secure (even under sequential signing sessions) requires the much stronger OMDL assumption. Arguably, this makes Abe's scheme the more attractive choice (along with allowing for concurrent sessions) for real world systems. This insight could not have been gained from proving these schemes secure in the GGM.

Open Questions. Our work leaves open the question of what can be proven about both the Abe and Schnorr blind signature schemes in the random oracle model only. Interestingly, the already mentioned work of Baldimtsi and Lysyanskaya [7] rules out a security proof for the blind Schnorr scheme using standard reduction techniques even in the sequential signing model. Namely, their result excludes such a reduction from a computational hardness assumption even if the signer just issues *a single signature* (which trivially restricts the sessions to being sequential). Another interesting direction for future work could be a more fine-grained security analysis (in the AGM+ROM) of the Schnorr scheme in a less restrictive signing model that allows for a low degree of concurrency. Namely, the ROS attack requires a polylogarithmic number of signing sessions to be open *at the same time*. Thus, it might be possible to prove the security of the scheme if, say, up to a constant number of signing sessions may be interleaved at any given point in time. Regarding Abe's scheme, there might yet be a glimmer of hope that the original proof can be salvaged (i.e., without requiring the AGM).

1.3 Organization

We first recall some preliminaries in Sect. 2. In Sect. 3 we introduce our adaption of Abe's scheme to the partially blind setting. We provide a proof of partial blindness under DDH in Sect. 3.1 as well as a proof of one-more-unforgeability in Sect. 3.2. We then provide the proof of sequential security of blind Schnorr signatures in the AGM in Sect. 4 and show that this result is optimal in the number of OMDL-queries in Sect. 4.1.

2 Preliminaries

2.1 Notation and Security Games

Notation. For positive integer n, we write $[n]$ for $\{1, \ldots, n\}$. We write x_j for the j-th entry of vector $\overrightarrow{x}$ and write $x \xleftarrow{\$} \mathcal{X}$ to denote that x is drawn uniformly at random from set $\mathcal{X}$. We denote the security parameter with λ.

Security Games. We use the standard notion of (prose-based) *security games* [11,46] to present our proofs. We denote the binary output of a game $\mathbf{G}$ with an adversary A as $\mathbf{G}^{\mathsf{A}}$ and say that A *wins* $\mathbf{G}$ if $\mathbf{G}^{\mathsf{A}} = 1$.

2.2 the Algebraic Group Model

In the following, let pp be public parameters that describe a group $\mathbb{G}$ of prime order q with generator $\mathbf{g}$. (We assume for simplicity that pp also includes the security parameter λ.) We denote the neutral element by ϵ and write all other group elements in bold face. We further write $\mathbb{Z}_q$ for $\mathbb{Z}/q\mathbb{Z}$.

Definition 1 (Algebraic Algorithm). *We say that an algorithm* A *is* algebraic *if, for any group element* $\mathbf{y} \in \mathbb{G}$ *that it outputs, it also outputs a list of* algebraic coefficients $\overrightarrow{z} \in \mathbb{Z}_q^t$, *i.e.,*

$$(\mathbf{y}, \overrightarrow{z}) \xleftarrow{\$} \mathsf{A}(\overrightarrow{\mathbf{x}})$$

such that

$$\mathbf{y} = \prod \mathbf{x}_i^{z_i}$$

We denote this representation as $[\mathbf{y}]_{\overrightarrow{\mathbf{x}}}$. *For an adversary* A *that has access to oracles during its runtime, we impose the above restriction to all group elements that it outputs to an oracle. Similarly, all group elements that* A *receives through oracle interactions are treated as inputs to* A*; hence, such group elements become part of* $\overrightarrow{\mathbf{x}}$ *when* A *outputs group elements (and hence algebraic coefficients) at a later point.*

In the algebraic group model (AGM), all algorithms are treated as algebraic algorithms. Moreover, we define the *running time* of an algorithm A in the AGM as the *number of group operations* that A performs.

2.3 Hardness Assumptions

We introduce the two main hardness assumptions that we will use in the subsequent sections. As before, we will tacitly assume that some public parameters pp are known and describe a group $\mathbb{G}$ of prime order q with generator $\mathbf{g}$.

Definition 2 (Discrete Logarithm Problem (DLP)). *For an algorithm* A, *we define the game* **DLP** *as follows:*

Setup. *Sample* $x \xleftarrow{\$} \mathbb{Z}_q$ *and run* A *on input* $\mathbf{g}, \mathbf{U} := \mathbf{g}^x$.

Output Determination. *When* A *outputs* x', *return 1 if* $\mathbf{g}^{x'} = \mathbf{U}$. *Otherwise, return 0.*

We define the advantage of A *in* **DLP** *as*

$$\mathsf{Adv}_{\mathsf{A}}^{\mathbf{DLP}} := \Pr\left[\mathbf{DLP}^{\mathsf{A}} = 1\right].$$

Definition 3 (One-More-Discrete Logarithm Problem (OMDL)). *For a stateful algorithm* A *and a positive integer* ℓ, *we define the game* ℓ-**OMDL** *as follows:*

Setup. *Initialize* $C = \emptyset$. *Run* A *on input* $\mathbf{g}$.

Online Phase. A *is given access to the following oracles:*

Oracle chal *takes no input and samples a group element* $\mathbf{y} \xleftarrow{\$} \mathbb{G}$. *It sets* $C := C \cup \{\mathbf{y}\}$ *and returns* $\mathbf{y}$.

Oracle dlog *takes as input a group element* $\mathbf{y}$. *It returns* $\mathrm{dlog}_{\mathbf{g}}\, \mathbf{y}$. *We assume that* **dlog** *can be queried at most* ℓ *many times.*

Output Determination. *When* A *outputs* $(\mathbf{y}_i, x_i)_{i=1}^{\ell+1}$, *return* 1 *if for all* $i \in [\ell+1]$: $\mathbf{y}_i \in C$, $\mathbf{g}^{x_i} = \mathbf{y}_i$, *and* $y_i \neq y_j$ *for all* $j \neq i$. *Otherwise, return* 0.

We define the advantage of A *in* ℓ-**OMDL** *as*

$$\mathsf{Adv}_{\mathsf{A},\ell}^{\mathbf{OMDL}} := \Pr\left[\ell\text{-}\mathbf{OMDL}^{\mathsf{A}} = 1\right].$$

Definition 4 (Decisional Diffie-Hellman Problem (DDH)). *For an algorithm* A *we define the game* **DDH** *as follows:*

Setup. *Sample* $x, y, z \xleftarrow{\$} \mathbb{Z}_q$ *and* $b \xleftarrow{\$} \{0,1\}$. *Run* A *on input* $(\mathbf{g}, \mathbf{g}^x, \mathbf{g}^y, \mathbf{g}^{xy+bz})$

Output Determination. *When* A *outputs* b', *return* 1 *if* $b = b'$ *and* 0 *otherwise.*

We define the advantage of A *in* **DDH** *as*

$$\mathsf{Adv}_{\mathsf{A}}^{\mathbf{DDH}} := \left|\Pr[\mathbf{DDH}^{\mathsf{A}} = 1] - \frac{1}{2}\right|.$$

2.4 (Partially) Blind Signature Schemes

In this section, we introduce the syntax and security definitions of partially blind (three-move) signature schemes [27]. We note that a fully blind signature scheme is a special case of a partially blind signature scheme where there is only one tag info, the empty string. We will refer to schemes where the tag is always the empty string as *blind signature schemes.*

Definition 5 (Three-Move Partially Blind Signature Scheme). *A three-move partially blind signature scheme is a tuple of algorithms* $\mathsf{BS} = (\mathsf{KeyGen}, \mathsf{Sign} := (\mathsf{Sign}_1, \mathsf{Sign}_2), \mathsf{User} := (\mathsf{User}_1, \mathsf{User}_2), \mathsf{Verify})$ *with the following behaviour.*

- *The randomized* key generation algorithm KeyGen *takes as input parameters* pp, *and outputs a public key* pk *and a secret key* sk. *We assume for convenience that* pk *contains* pp *and* sk *contains* pk.
- *The signing algorithm* $\mathsf{Sign} := (\mathsf{Sign}_1, \mathsf{Sign}_2)$ *is split into two algorithms:*
  - *The randomized algorithm* Sign_1 *takes as input a secret key* sk *and a tag* info *and outputs a commitment* C *as well as a state* st_S.
  - *The deterministic algorithm* Sign_2 *takes as input a secret key* sk, *a state* st_S, *and a challenge* e. *It outputs a response* R.
- *The user algorithm* $\mathsf{User} := (\mathsf{User}_1, \mathsf{User}_2)$ *is split into two algorithms:*
  - *The randomized algorithm* User_1 *takes as input a public key* pk, *a message* m, *a tag* info *and a commitment* C. *It outputs a challenge* e *and a state* st_U.
  - *The deterministic algorithm* User_2 *takes as input a public key* pk, *a state* st_U, *and a response* R. *It outputs a signature* σ *or* $\perp$.
- *The deterministic verifier algorithm* Verify *takes as input a public key* pk, *a signature* σ, *and a message* m *and a tag* info. *It outputs either 1 (accept) or 0 (reject).*

Definition 6 (Correctness). *We say that a partially blind signature scheme* $\mathsf{BS} = (\mathsf{KeyGen}, \mathsf{Sign}, \mathsf{User}, \mathsf{Verify})$ *is correct if for all messages* m, *all tags* info *the following holds:*

$$\Pr\left[\mathsf{Verify}(\mathsf{pk}, \mathsf{sig}, m, \mathsf{info}) = 1 : \begin{array}{r} (\mathsf{pk}, \mathsf{sk}) \xleftarrow{\$} \mathsf{KeyGen}(\mathsf{pp}) \\ (C, \mathsf{st}_S) \xleftarrow{\$} \mathsf{Sign}_1(\mathsf{sk}, \mathsf{info}) \\ (e, \mathsf{st}_U) \xleftarrow{\$} \mathsf{User}_1(\mathsf{pk}, m, \mathsf{info}, C) \\ R \xleftarrow{\$} \mathsf{Sign}_2(\mathsf{sk}, \mathsf{st}_S, e) \\ \sigma \xleftarrow{\$} \mathsf{User}_2(\mathsf{pk}, \mathsf{st}_U, R) \end{array}\right] = 1$$

Definition 7 (Partial blindness under chosen keys). *We define* partial blindness *of a three-move partially blind signature scheme* BS *against an adversary* M *via the following game:*

Setup. *Sample* $b \xleftarrow{\$} \{0, 1\}$ *and run* M *on input* pp.

Online Phase. *When* M *outputs messages* $\tilde{m}_0$ *and* $\tilde{m}_1$, $\widetilde{\mathsf{info}}_0$ *and* $\widetilde{\mathsf{info}}_1$, *and a public key* pk, *check if* pk *is a valid*[2] *public key, and* $\widetilde{\mathsf{info}}_0 = \widetilde{\mathsf{info}}_1$. *If so, assign* $m_0 := \tilde{m}_b$, $\mathsf{info}_0 := \widetilde{\mathsf{info}}_0$, $m_1 := \tilde{m}_{1-b}$, *and* $\mathsf{info}_1 := \widetilde{\mathsf{info}}_1$. *If* pk *is not a valid public key or* $\mathsf{info}_0 \neq \mathsf{info}_1$, *abort and output* 0. M *is given access to oracles* $\mathbf{User}_1, \mathbf{User}_2$, *which behave as follows.*

Oracle $\mathbf{User}_1$**:** *On input a bit* b', *and a commitment* C, *if the session* b' *is not yet open, the game marks session* b' *as open and generates a state and challenge as* $(\mathsf{st}_{b'}, e) \xleftarrow{\$} \mathsf{BS.User}_1(\mathsf{pk}, m_{b'}, C, \mathsf{info}_{b'})$. *It returns* e *to the adversary. Otherwise, it returns* $\perp$.

Oracle $\mathbf{User}_2$**:** *On input a response* R *and a bit* b', *if the session* b' *is open, the game creates the signature* $\mathsf{sig}_{b'}$ *as* $\mathsf{sig}_{b'} := \mathsf{BS.User}_2(\mathsf{pk}, \mathsf{st}_{b'}, R)$ *to obtain a signature* $\mathsf{sig}_{b'}$. *It marks session* b' *as closed and outputs* $\mathsf{sig}_{b'}$. *If both sessions are closed and produced signatures, the oracle outputs the two signatures* $\mathsf{sig}_0, \mathsf{sig}_1$ *to the adversary.*

Output Determination. *If both sessions are closed and produced signatures, return* 1 *if the adversary outputs a bit* b^* *s.t.* $b^* = b$. *Otherwise, return* 0.

We define the advantage of M *in game* $\mathbf{BLIND}_{\mathsf{BS}}$ *as*

$$\mathsf{Adv}_{\mathsf{M}}^{\mathbf{BLIND},\mathsf{BS}} := \left|\Pr\left[\mathbf{BLIND}^{\mathsf{M}} = 1\right] - \frac{1}{2}\right|.$$

Definition 8 (ℓ-(Sequential-)One-More-Unforgeability (ℓ-(SEQ-)OMUF)). *For a stateful algorithm* A, *a three-move partially blind signature scheme* BS, *and a positive integer* ℓ, *we define the game* ℓ-$\mathbf{OMUF}_{\mathsf{BS}}$ *(*ℓ-$\mathbf{SEQ}$-$\mathbf{OMUF}_{\mathsf{BS}}$*) as follows:*

Setup. *Sample* $(\mathsf{pk}, \mathsf{sk}) \xleftarrow{\$} \mathsf{BS.KeyGen}(\mathsf{pp})$ *and run* A *on input* $(\mathsf{pk}, \mathsf{pp})$.

Online Phase. A *is given access to the oracles* $\mathbf{Sign}_1$ *and* $\mathbf{Sign}_2$ *that behave as follows.*

Oracle $\mathbf{Sign}_1$**:** *On input* info, *it samples a fresh session identifier* id *(If sequential, it checks if* $\mathtt{session}_{\mathtt{id}-1} = \mathtt{open}$ *and returns* $\perp$ *if yes). If* info *has not been requested before, it initializes a counter* $\ell_{\mathsf{closed,info}} := 0$. *It sets* $\mathtt{session}_{\mathtt{id}} := \mathtt{open}$ *and generates* $(C_{\mathtt{id}}, \mathsf{st}_{\mathtt{id}}) \xleftarrow{\$} \mathsf{BS.Sign}_1(\mathsf{sk}, \mathsf{info})$. *Then it returns* $C_{\mathtt{id}}$ *and* id.

Oracle $\mathbf{Sign}_2$**:** *If* $\sum_{\mathsf{info}} \ell_{\mathsf{closed,info}} < \ell$, $\mathbf{Sign}_2$ *takes as input a challenge* e *and a session identifier* id. *If* $\mathtt{session}_{\mathtt{id}} \neq \mathtt{open}$, *it returns* $\perp$. *Otherwise, it sets* $\ell_{\mathsf{closed,info}} := \ell_{\mathsf{closed,info}} + 1$ *and* $\mathtt{session}_{\mathtt{id}} := \mathtt{closed}$. *Then it generates the response* R *via* $R \xleftarrow{\$} \mathsf{BS.Sign}_2(\mathsf{sk}, \mathsf{st}_{\mathtt{id}}, e)$ *and returns* R.

Output Determination. *When* A *outputs tuples* $(m_1, \sigma_1, \mathsf{info}_1), \ldots, (m_k, \sigma_k, \mathsf{info}_k)$, *return* 1 *if there exists a tag* $\overline{\mathsf{info}}$ *such that* $\big|\{(m_i, \sigma_i, \mathsf{info}_i) \big| \mathsf{info}_i =$

[2] We include this in case the scheme permits such a check - for example, one can think of schemes where the public key consists of group elements, in which case a user may be able to check that the public key consists of valid encodings of group elements. Another example of such a check is in the original version of Abe's scheme [1] where $\mathbf{z} = H_1(\mathbf{g}, \mathbf{h}, \mathbf{y})$ which a user may check.

$\overline{\mathsf{info}}\}\big| \geq \ell_{\mathsf{closed},\overline{\mathsf{info}}} + 1$ *(where by convention* $\ell_{\mathsf{closed},\mathsf{info}} := 0$ *for any* info *that has not been requested to the signing oracles) and for all* $i \in [k]$: $\mathsf{BS.Verify}(\mathsf{pk}, \sigma_i, m_i, \mathsf{info}_i) = 1$ *and* $(m_i, \sigma_i, \mathsf{info}_i) \neq (m_j, \sigma_j, \mathsf{info}_j)$ *for all* $j \neq i$*. Otherwise, return* 0.

We define the advantage of A *in* $\mathbf{OMUF}_{\mathsf{BS}}$ *as*

$$\mathsf{Adv}^{\mathbf{OMUF}}_{\mathsf{A},\mathsf{BS},\ell} := \Pr\left[\ell\text{-}\mathbf{OMUF}^{\mathsf{A}}_{\mathsf{BS}} = 1\right].$$

And, respectively for $\mathbf{SEQ\text{-}OMUF}_{\mathsf{BS}}$

$$\mathsf{Adv}^{\mathbf{SEQ\text{-}OMUF}}_{\mathsf{A},\mathsf{BS},\ell} := \Pr\left[\ell\text{-}\mathbf{SEQ\text{-}OMUF}^{\mathsf{A}}_{\mathsf{BS}} = 1\right].$$

3 Adaption of Abe's Blind Signature Scheme to Allow Partial Blindness

We begin by describing an adaption of Abe's blind signature scheme BSA [1] to the partially blind setting. A figure depicting an interaction between signer and user can be found in the full version [30]. Let again $\mathbb{G}$ be a group of order q with generator $\mathbf{g}$ described by public parameters pp. Let $H_1\colon \{0,1\}^* \to \mathbb{G} \setminus \{\epsilon\}$, $H_2\colon \{0,1\}^* \to \mathbb{G} \setminus \{\epsilon\}$, $H_3\colon \{0,1\}^* \to \mathbb{Z}_q$ be hash functions.

- KeyGen: On input pp, KeyGen samples $\mathbf{h} \xleftarrow{\$} \mathbb{G}$, $x \xleftarrow{\$} \mathbb{Z}_q$ and sets $\mathbf{y} := \mathbf{g}^x$. It sets $\mathsf{sk} := x$, $\mathsf{pk} := (\mathbf{g}, \mathbf{h}, \mathbf{y})$ and returns (sk, pk).
- Sign_1: On input sk, info, Sign_1 samples $\mathsf{rnd} \xleftarrow{\$} \{0,1\}^\lambda$ and $u, d, s_1, s_2 \xleftarrow{\$} \mathbb{Z}_q$. It computes $\mathbf{z} := H_1(\mathsf{pk}, \mathsf{info})$, $\mathbf{z_1} := H_2(\mathsf{rnd})$, $\mathbf{z_2} := \mathbf{z}/\mathbf{z_1}$, $\mathbf{a} := \mathbf{g}^u$, $\mathbf{b_1} := \mathbf{g}^{s_1} \cdot \mathbf{z}_1^d$, $\mathbf{b_2} := \mathbf{h}^{s_2} \cdot \mathbf{z}_2^d$. It returns a commitment $(\mathsf{rnd}, \mathbf{a}, \mathbf{b_1}, \mathbf{b_2})$ and a state $\mathsf{st}_S = (u, d, s_1, s_2, \mathsf{info})$.
- Sign_2: On input a secret key sk, a challenge e, and state $\mathsf{st}_S = (u, d, s_1, s_2, \mathsf{info})$, Sign_2 computes $c := e - d \mod q, r := u - c \cdot \mathsf{sk} \mod q$ and returns the response (c, d, r, s_1, s_2).
- User_1: On input a public key pk and a commitment $(\mathsf{rnd}, \mathbf{a}, \mathbf{b_1}, \mathbf{b_2})$, a tag info, and message m, User_1 does the following. It samples $\gamma \xleftarrow{\$} \mathbb{Z}_q^*$ and $\tau, t_1, t_2, t_3, t_4, t_5 \xleftarrow{\$} \mathbb{Z}_q$. Then, it computes $\mathbf{z} := H_1(\mathsf{pk}, \mathsf{info})$, $\mathbf{z_1} := H_2(\mathsf{rnd})$, $\alpha := \mathbf{a} \cdot \mathbf{g}^{t_1} \cdot \mathbf{y}^{t_2}$, $\zeta := \mathbf{z}^\gamma$, $\zeta_1 := \mathbf{z}_1^\gamma$, $\zeta_2 := \zeta/\zeta_1$. Next, it sets $\beta_1 := \mathbf{b}_1^\gamma \cdot \mathbf{g}^{t_3} \cdot \zeta_1^{t_4}$, $\beta_2 := \mathbf{b}_2^\gamma \cdot \mathbf{h}^{t_5} \cdot \zeta_2^{t_4}$, $\eta := \mathbf{z}^\tau$, and $\varepsilon := H_3(\zeta, \zeta_1, \alpha, \beta_1, \beta_2, \eta, m, \mathsf{info})$. Finally, it computes a challenge $e := \varepsilon - t_2 - t_4 \mod q$, the state $St_U := (\gamma, \tau, t_1, t_2, t_3, t_4, t_5, m)$ and returns e, St_U.
- User_2: On input a public key pk, a response (c, d, r, s_1, s_2) and a state $(\gamma, \tau, t_1, t_2, t_3, t_4, t_5, m)$, User_2 first computes $\rho := r + t_1$, $\omega := c + t_2$, $\sigma_1 := \gamma \cdot s_1 + t_3$, $\sigma_2 := \gamma \cdot s_2 + t_5$, and $\delta := d + t_4$. Then, it computes $\mu := \tau - \delta \cdot \gamma$ and $\varepsilon := H_3(\zeta, \zeta_1, \mathbf{g}^\rho \mathbf{y}^\omega, \mathbf{g}^{\sigma_1} \zeta_1^\delta, \mathbf{h}^{\sigma_2} \zeta_2^\delta, \mathbf{z}^\mu \zeta^\delta, m)$. It returns the signature $\sigma := (\zeta, \zeta_1, \rho, \omega, \sigma_1, \sigma_2, \delta, \mu)$ if $\delta + \omega = \varepsilon$; otherwise, it returns $\perp$.[3]

---

[3] We note that the check for $\varepsilon = \omega + \delta$ implicitly checks that $c + d = e$ as well as $\mathbf{a} = \mathbf{y}^c \mathbf{g}^r, \mathbf{b}_1 = \mathbf{z}_1^d \mathbf{g}^{s_1}, \mathbf{b}_2 = \mathbf{z}_2^d \mathbf{h}^{s_2}$, i.e. it checks that the output of Sign − 2 was valid.

- Verify: On input a public key pk, a signature $(\zeta, \zeta_1, \rho, \omega, \sigma_1, \sigma_2, \delta, \mu)$ and a message m, Verify computes first $\mathbf{z} := H_1(\mathsf{pk}, \mathsf{info})$ and then $\varepsilon := H_3(\zeta, \zeta_1, \mathbf{g}^\rho \mathbf{y}^\omega, \mathbf{g}^{\sigma_1} \zeta_1^\delta, \mathbf{h}^{\sigma_2} \zeta_2^\delta, \mathbf{z}^\mu \zeta^\delta, m, \mathsf{info})$. It returns 1 if $\delta + \omega = \varepsilon$; otherwise, it returns 0.

We note that the only change we made to Abe's scheme is that in our variant, the $\mathbf{z}$ part of the public key is derived as a hash of pk and a tag info instead of as a hash of the other elements of the public key. It is easy to see that by using an empty info this yields the original scheme and thus our proofs about the adapted scheme also apply to the original.

We note that Abe refers to $\mathbf{z}, \mathbf{z}_1, \zeta, \zeta_1$ as the tags of a signing session or signature. However, as we are considering partial blindness, we will refer to them as the *linking components.* By [1], the original scheme is computationally blind under the Decisional Diffie-Hellman assumption. For completeness, we provide a detailed proof of the partial computational blindness of our variant in Sect. 3.1.

3.1 Partial Blindness of the Adapted Abe Scheme

We provide a formal proof of partial blindness under chosen keys for the Abe blind signature scheme. Abe [1] proved the scheme to be blind for keys selected by the challenger.

Lemma 1. *Under the decisional Diffie-Hellman assumption in $\mathbb{G}$, Abe's blind signature scheme* BSA *is computationally blind in the random oracle model.*

Proof. We use similar techniques as [6].
Game $\mathbf{G_1}$. The first game is identical to the blindness game from Definition 7 for Abe's blind signature scheme.

Setup. $\mathbf{G_1}$ samples $b \xleftarrow{\$} \{0,1\}$.
Simulation of oracle H_1. $\mathbf{G_1}$ simulates H_1 by lazy sampling of group elements.
Online Phase. When M outputs a public key $(\mathbf{g}, \mathbf{y}, \mathbf{h})$ and messages $\tilde{m}_0$ and $\tilde{m}_1$, and tags info_0, info_1, $\mathbf{G_1}$ verifies $\mathsf{info}_0 = \mathsf{info}_1$ assigns $m_0 = \tilde{m}_b$ and $m_1 = \tilde{m}_{b-1}$
 Oracle User$_1$. Works the same as described in Definition 7
 Oracle User$_2$. Works the same as described in Definition 7
 Simulation of H_2. H_2 is simulated through lazy sampling
 Simulation of H_3. H_3 is simulated through lazy sampling
Output Determination. As described in Definition 7

The second game replaces the signature for m_0 by a signature that is independent of the run with the signer.
Game $\mathbf{G_2}$. The second game generates the signature on m_0 independently of the corresponding signing session.

Setup. $\mathbf{G_2}$ samples $b \xleftarrow{\$} \{0,1\}$.
Simulation of oracle H_1. $\mathbf{G_2}$ simulates H_1 by lazy sampling of group elements.

Online Phase. When M outputs a public key $(\mathbf{g}, \mathbf{y}, \mathbf{h})$ and messages $\widetilde{m}_0$ and $\widetilde{m}_1$ and $\widetilde{\mathsf{info}}_0, \widetilde{\mathsf{info}}_1$, $\mathbf{G_2}$ verifies that the key is well-formed and that $\widetilde{\mathsf{info}}_0 = \widetilde{\mathsf{info}}_1$ and aborts with output 0 if this check fails. It further assigns $m_0 = \widetilde{m}_b$ and $m_1 = \widetilde{m}_{b-1}$ as well as $\mathsf{info}_0 = \widetilde{\mathsf{info}}_0$ and $\mathsf{info}_1 = \widetilde{\mathsf{info}}_1$.

Oracle User$_1$. For message m_1, the oracle behaves the same as in $\mathbf{G_1}$. For message m_0, it checks that session 0 is not open yet and opens session 0. Then the game picks $\delta, \omega, \sigma_1, \sigma_2, \rho, \mu$ uniformly at random from $\mathbb{Z}_q$. It further draws two random group elements ζ and ζ_1 and sets $\zeta_2 := \zeta/\zeta_1$. It then sets $H_3(\mathbf{y}^{\omega} \cdot \mathbf{g}^{\rho}, \zeta_1^{\delta} \cdot \mathbf{g}^{\sigma_1}, \zeta_2^{\delta} \cdot \mathbf{h}^{\sigma_2}, \zeta^{\delta} \cdot \mathbf{z}^{\mu}, m_0, \mathsf{info}_0) := \delta + \omega$. It draws $e \xleftarrow{\$} \mathbb{Z}_q$ uniformly at random and returns e as a challenge to the adversary.

Oracle User$_2$. For message m_1, the oracle behaves the same as in $\mathbf{G_1}$. For message m_0, on input c, d, r, s_1, s_2, the game does the following checks[4]: $e = d + c$, $\mathbf{a}_0 = \mathbf{g}^r \cdot \mathbf{y}^c$, $\mathbf{b}_{1,0} = \mathbf{g}^{s_1} \cdot \mathbf{z}_{1,0}^d$, $\mathbf{b}_{2,0} = \mathbf{h}^{s_2} \cdot \mathbf{z}_{2,0}^d$. It considers the produced signature to be the one generated in **User$_1$**.

Simulation of H_2. H_2 is simulated through lazy sampling

Simulation of H_3. For values not programmed in **User$_1$**, $\mathbf{G_2}$ simulates H_3 via lazy sampling

Output Determination. As described in Definition 7

Claim 1. The advantage of an adversary B to tell the difference between $\mathbf{G_1}$ and $\mathbf{G_2}$ is $\mathsf{Adv}_{\mathsf{B}}^{\mathbf{G_1},\mathbf{G_2}} = \left|\Pr\left[\mathbf{G_1}^{\mathsf{B}} = 1\right] - \Pr\left[\mathbf{G_2}^{\mathsf{B}} = 1\right]\right| \leq \mathsf{Adv}_{\mathsf{B}'}^{\mathbf{DDH}}$.

Proof. We provide a reduction B′ that receives a random-generator DDH challenge $(\mathbf{W}, \mathbf{X}, \mathbf{Y}, \mathbf{Z})$ and simulates either $\mathbf{G_1}$ or $\mathbf{G_2}$ to the adversary. During the first phase of the online phase, the reduction programs the random oracle H_1 to return values $\mathbf{W}^{f_i}$ $f_i \in \mathbb{Z}_q$. For simulation of H_2, the reduction chooses exponents $g_i \xleftarrow{\$} \mathbb{Z}_q$ and returns values $\mathbf{X}^{g_i}$, yielding uniformly random values from the group $\mathbb{G}$. In **User$_1$** for m_0, when the adversary sends the commitment which contains a random string rnd to be queried to the oracle H_2, the reduction identifies the $g = g_i$ that was used as the random exponent for $\mathbf{z}_1 = \mathbf{X}^g$. Denote further by f the f_i used for generation of $\mathbf{z} = H_1(\mathsf{pk}, \mathsf{info}_1)$. It sets $\zeta = \mathbf{Y}^f$ and $\zeta_1 = \mathbf{Z}^{f \cdot g}$. The reduction then proceeds to generate a signature by programming the random oracle H_3 as described in $\mathbf{G_2}$. For m_1, the reduction participates honestly in the signing protocol. In **User$_2$**, for m_0, the reduction checks that the adversary produces a valid signing transcript as described in $\mathbf{G_2}$. If both interactions yield valid signatures (i.e. the adversary produced a valid transcript for m_0 and a valid signature for m_1), the reduction outputs both signatures, otherwise $\perp$. If the adversary outputs it was playing game $\mathbf{G_1}$, the reduction outputs 0, otherwise it outputs 1.

We argue that if the challenge is a Diffie-Hellman tuple, the reduction simulates $\mathbf{G_1}$ perfectly. For a tuple $\mathbf{W}, \mathbf{W}^a, \mathbf{W}^b, \mathbf{W}^{ab}$, the tuple $\mathbf{z} = \mathbf{W}^f, \mathbf{z}_1 = \mathbf{W}^{a \cdot f \cdot \frac{g}{f}}, \zeta = \mathbf{W}^{b \cdot f}, \zeta_1 = \mathbf{W}^{a \cdot b \cdot f \cdot g}$ is a valid Diffie-Hellman tuple w.r.t generator

[4] We note that these checks need to be done explicitly here, as they are no longer implicitly performed through checking that $\varepsilon = \omega + \delta$.

$\mathbf{W}^f$. Furthermore, the user tags ζ and ζ_1 can be computed from $\mathbf{z}$ and $\mathbf{z}_1$ using blinding factor $\gamma = b$. Furthermore, for any c, d, r, s_1, s_2 and signature components $\omega, \delta, \rho, \sigma_1, \sigma_2, \mu$ there are unique choices of $t_1 = \rho - r, t_2 = \omega - c, t_3 = \sigma_1 - \gamma \cdot s_1, t_4 = \delta - d, t_5 = \sigma_2 - \gamma \cdot s_2, \tau = \mu + \delta \cdot \gamma$ that explain the signature in combination with the transcript. Thus, the produced combination of signature and transcript is identically distributed as an honestly generated signature.

If the challenge is not a Diffie-Hellman tuple, then the reduction simulates $\mathbf{G_2}$ perfectly as the linking components $\zeta_i, \zeta_{1,i}$ look like random group elements and the reduction computes the same steps as $\mathbf{G_2}$ to generate the signatures and its outputs to the adversary. □

We describe the final game $\mathbf{G_3}$ where both signatures are independent from the runs with the signer.

Game $\mathbf{G_3}$

Setup. $\mathbf{G_3}$ samples $b \xleftarrow{\$} \{0, 1\}$.
Simulation of oracle H_1. $\mathbf{G_3}$ simulates H_1 by lazy sampling of group elements.
Online Phase. When M outputs a public key $(\mathbf{g}, \mathbf{y}, \mathbf{h})$ and messages $\tilde{m}_0$ and $\tilde{m}_1$, $\mathbf{G_3}$ verifies that the key is well-formed and checks that $\mathsf{info}_0 = \mathsf{info}_1$ and aborts with output 0 if this check fails. It further assigns $m_0 = \tilde{m}_b$ and $m_1 = \tilde{m}_{b-1}$

Oracle $\mathbf{User}_1$. For session b', the game checks that session b' is not open yet and opens session b'. It sets $\mathbf{z} := H_1(\mathsf{info})$. Then the game picks $\delta, \omega, \sigma_1, \sigma_2, \rho, \mu$ uniformly at random from $\mathbb{Z}_q$. It further draws two random group elements ζ and ζ_1 and sets $\zeta_2 := \zeta/\zeta_1$. It then sets $H_3(\mathbf{y}^\omega \cdot \mathbf{g}^\rho, \zeta_1^\delta \cdot \mathbf{g}^{\sigma_1}, \zeta_2^\delta \cdot \mathbf{h}^{\sigma_2}, \zeta^\delta \cdot \mathbf{z}^\mu, m_{b'}, \mathsf{info}_{b'}) := \delta + \omega$. It draws $e \xleftarrow{\$} \mathbb{Z}_q$ uniformly at random and returns e as a challenge to the adversary.

Oracle $\mathbf{User}_2$. For both sessions (denoted by $i = 0, 1$), on input $c_i, d_i, r_i, s_{1,i}, s_{2,i}$, the game does the following checks: $e_i = d_i + c_i$, $\mathbf{a}_i = \mathbf{g}^{r_i} \cdot \mathbf{y}^{c_i}$, $\mathbf{b}_{1,i} = \mathbf{g}^{s_{1,i}} \cdot \mathbf{z}_{1,i}^{d_i}$, $\mathbf{b}_{2,i} = \mathbf{h}^{s_{2,i}} \cdot \mathbf{z}_{2,i}^{d_i}$. It considers the output signature to be the one generated for this session in $\mathbf{User}_1$.

Simulation of H_2. H_2 is simulated through lazy sampling

Simulation of H_3. For values not programmed in $\mathbf{User}_1$, $\mathbf{G_2}$ simulates H_3 via lazy sampling

Output Determination. As described in Definition 7

Claim 2. The advantage of an adversary B to tell the difference between $\mathbf{G_1}$ and $\mathbf{G_2}$ is $\mathsf{Adv}_{\mathsf{B}'''}^{\mathbf{G_2},\mathbf{G_3}} = \Pr\left[\mathbf{G_2}^{\mathsf{B}'''} = 1\right] - \Pr\left[\mathbf{G_3}^{\mathsf{B}'''} = 1\right] \leq \mathsf{Adv}_{\mathsf{B}''}^{\mathbf{DDH}}$.

Proof. Follows along the same lines as Claim 1, embedding the **DDH** challenge in the signature for m_1 this time. □

In game $\mathbf{G_3}$, the adversary cannot win, as both signatures are completely independent from the two runs. As game $\mathbf{G_3}$ needs to program the random oracle H_3 twice to generate the signatures (this fails with probability at most $\frac{2q_h}{q^4 \cdot 2^{|m_0|}}$, i.e.

if the adversary has made the exact same requests before), we get the following overall advantage of

$$\mathsf{Adv}_{\mathsf{M}}^{\mathbf{BLIND}_{\mathsf{BSA}}} = \frac{2 \cdot q_h}{q^4 \cdot 2^{|m_0|}} + \mathsf{Adv}_{\mathsf{B}'}^{\mathbf{DDH}} + \mathsf{Adv}_{\mathsf{B}''}^{\mathbf{DDH}}$$

□

3.2 One-More-Unforgeability

In the following, we provide a proof for the one-more-unforgeability. Similar to [1] we do this in two steps. First, we show that it is infeasible for an adversary to generate a signature that does not use a tag that corresponds to a closed signing session. (Note that the scheme is only computationally blind, and an unbounded algorithm can link signatures and sessions since $(\mathbf{z}, \mathbf{z}_1, \zeta, \zeta_1)$ forms a DDH tuple. We call such tuples *linking components*, and refer to $\mathbf{z}, \mathbf{z}_1$ as "signer-side" and ζ, ζ_1 as "user-side".) This corresponds to Abe's restrictive blinding lemma. Then, as the main theorem, we show that it is also infeasible for an adversary to win ℓ-**OMUF** by providing two signatures corresponding to the same closed signing session.

Our Techniques. The main idea for both the lemma and the theorem is to use the algebraic representations of the group elements submitted to the random oracle H_3 in combination with the corresponding signature to compute the discrete logarithm of either $\mathbf{y}$ or $\mathbf{h}$ or in the tags $\mathbf{z}$. This fails either when the adversary has not made a hash query for the signature in question, or when the representation of the hash query does not contain more information than the signature, i.e., the exponents in the representation already match the signature. We show that both of these cases only occur with a negligible probability. We simulate the protocol in two different ways. One way is to use the secret key x like an honest signer and try to extract the discrete logarithm of $\mathbf{h}$ or one of the $\mathbf{z}$. The other way is to program the random oracles H_1 and H_2 so that the reduction can use the discrete logarithms of $\mathbf{z}, \mathbf{z}_1, \mathbf{z}_2$ to simulate the other side of the OR-proof for extraction of the secret key. We also use the programming of the random oracles to efficiently identify which signature is the "forgery". This, in combination with not having to run the protocol twice for forking, renders a tight proof.

Comparison to the Original Standard Model Proof by Abe [1]**.** We briefly recall that similar to our proof, the original proof also shows the restrictive blinding lemma first, which, shows that an adversary that wins the **OMUF** game and at the same time produces a signature where $\mathrm{dlog}_\zeta \zeta_1 \neq \mathrm{dlog}_{\mathbf{z}} \mathbf{z}_{1,i}$ for all sessions i, can be used to solve the discrete logarithm problem. The proof uses the forking technique, i.e. it rewinds the adversary to obtain a second set of signatures with different hash responses to H_3. The original proof of the restrictive blinding lemma also uses two signers, one that embeds in $\mathbf{y}$ and signs using the $\mathbf{z}$-side witness, another that embeds in $\mathbf{h}$ and signs using the secret key x.

These two signers are indistinguishable for a single run, however, two forking runs using the same witness reveal the witness being used internally. In particular, a forking pair of runs using the secret key x to sign, cannot be reproduced by a signer that does not know the x-side witness. Therefore, the distribution of signatures obtained from forking runs, in particular the components δ and ω may depend on which witness was used internally. We note that for example in 'honestly generated' signatures (i.e. when the adversary followed the User_1 and User_2 algorithms to generate signatures), the a pair of signatures at the forking hash query reveals exactly the same witness as the signer used to sign while forking, so it is not clear why a similar thing may not also hold for 'dishonestly generated' signatures.

As our reduction for the restrictive blinding lemma works in the AGM, we can avoid the rewinding step. The adversary submits representations of all the group elements contained in a hash query, which gives the reduction information that would otherwise be obtained from the previous run. As the scheme is perfectly witness indistinguishable, the representations submitted by the adversary are independent of the witness used internally. We show in Claim 5, that even a so-called *reduced representation* that does use factors that are only determined after all signing sessions were closed, is likely to reveal enough information for the reduction to be able to solve the discrete logarithm problem.

The Restrictive Blinding Lemma. We first provide a reduction for the restrictive blinding lemma in the AGM + ROM. We therefore define the game ℓ-**RB-OMUF**$_{\mathsf{BSA}}$ as follows:

Setup: Sample keys via $(\mathsf{sk} = x, \mathsf{pk} = (\mathbf{g}, \mathbf{h}, \mathbf{y})) \xleftarrow{\$} \mathsf{BSA.KeyGen}(\mathsf{pp})$.

Online Phase: M is given access to oracles $\mathbf{Sign}_1, \mathbf{Sign}_2$ that emulate the behavior of the honest signer in BSA. It is allowed to arbitrarily many calls to $\mathbf{Sign}_1$ and allowed to make ℓ queries to $\mathbf{Sign}_2$. In addition, it is given access to random oracles H_1, H_2, H_3. Let ℓ_{info} denote the number of interactions that M completes with oracle $\mathbf{Sign}_2$ in this phase for each tag info.

Output Determination: When M outputs a list L of tuples $(m_1, \mathsf{sig}_1, \mathsf{info}_1)$, $\ldots, (m_k, \mathsf{sig}_k, \mathsf{info}_k)$, proceed as follows:

- If the list contains a tuple $(m, \mathsf{sig}, \mathsf{info})$ s.t. $\mathsf{Verify}(\mathsf{pk}, m, \mathsf{sig}, \mathsf{info}) = 0$, or does not contain $\ell_{\overline{\mathsf{info}}} + 1$ pairwise-distinct tuples for some tag $\overline{\mathsf{info}}$, return 0.
- Let $\mathbf{z}_j, \mathbf{z}_{1,j}$ denote the values of $\mathbf{z}$ and $\mathbf{z}_1$ used in the j-th invocation of $\mathbf{Sign}_1$. If there exists $(m, \mathsf{sig}, \overline{\mathsf{info}}) \in L$ with signature components $\zeta \neq \zeta_1$ (equivalently, $\zeta_2 \neq \epsilon$), s.t. for all j with $H_1(\mathsf{pk}, \overline{\mathsf{info}}) = \mathbf{z}_j$ whose sessions were closed with an invocation of $\mathbf{Sign}_2$, $\zeta^{\mathrm{dlog}_{\mathbf{z}_j} \mathbf{z}_{1,j}} \neq \zeta_1$, then return 1. Otherwise, return 0. We call the first signature in L with these mismatched linking components the *special signature*.

Define $\mathsf{Adv}^{\mathbf{RB\text{-}OMUF}}_{\mathsf{M},\ell,\mathsf{BSA}} := \Pr[\ell\text{-}\mathbf{RB\text{-}OMUF}^{\mathsf{M}}_{\mathsf{BSA}} = 1]$. We show that an algebraic forger M that wins ℓ-**RB-OMUF**$_{\mathsf{BSA}}$ can be used to solve the discrete logarithm problem. This reduction is tight and does not require rewinding of the adversary.

Lemma 2 (Restrictive Blinding, see Lemma 3 in [1]). *Let* M *be an algebraic algorithm that runs in time* t_{M}*, makes at most* ℓ *queries to oracle* Sign_2 *in* $\mathbf{RB\text{-}OMUF}_{\mathsf{BSA}}$ *and at most (total)* q_h *queries to* H_1, H_2, H_3*. Then, in the random oracle model, there exists an algorithm* B *s.t.*

$$\begin{aligned}\mathsf{Adv}_{\mathsf{B}}^{\mathbf{DLP}} \geq & \frac{1}{2}\mathsf{Adv}_{\mathsf{M},\ell,\mathsf{BSA}}^{\mathbf{RB\text{-}OMUF}} - \frac{\ell+1}{2q} \\ & - (\frac{3q_h}{q} + \mathsf{Adv}_{\mathsf{R}_1}^{\mathrm{dlog}} + \mathsf{Adv}_{\mathsf{R}_2}^{\mathrm{dlog}} + \mathsf{Adv}_{\mathsf{R}_3}^{\mathrm{dlog}} + \mathsf{Adv}_{\mathsf{R}_4}^{\mathrm{dlog}})\end{aligned}$$

Proof. Let M be as in the lemma statement. As before, we assume w.l.o.g. that M makes exactly ℓ queries to Sign_2 and outputs a list of $\ell+1$ tuples. The proof goes by a series of games, which we describe below.

Game $\mathbf{G_0}$. This is ℓ-$\mathbf{RB\text{-}OMUF}_{\mathsf{BSA}}$.

Game $\mathbf{G_1}$. To define $\mathbf{G_1}$, we first define the following event E_1. E_1 happens if M returns a list L of $\ell+1$ valid signatures on distinct messages $m_1, ..., m_\ell$ and there exists $(m, \mathsf{sig}, \mathsf{info}) = (m, (\zeta, \zeta_1, \rho, \omega, \sigma_1, \sigma_2, \delta, \mu), \mathsf{info}) \in L$ s.t. for all j whose sessions were closed with an invocation of $\mathbf{Sign}_2$, $\zeta^{\mathrm{dlog}_{\mathbf{z}_j} \mathbf{z}_{1,j}} \neq \zeta_1 \wedge \zeta_2 \neq \epsilon$ and M did not make a query of the form $H_3(\zeta, \zeta_1, \mathbf{g}^\rho \mathbf{y}^\omega, \mathbf{g}^{\sigma_1}\zeta_1^\delta, \mathbf{h}^{\sigma_2}\zeta_2^\delta, \mathbf{z}^\mu \zeta^\delta, m, \mathsf{info})$. In the following, we refer to the first tuple $(m, \mathsf{sig}, \mathsf{info}) \in L$ as *the special tuple* for convenience. $\mathbf{G_1}$ is identical to game $\mathbf{G_0}$, except that it aborts when E_1 happens.

Claim 3. $\Pr[E_1] = \frac{\ell+1}{q}$

Proof. The only way for an adversary to succeed without querying H_3 for the signature is by guessing the hash value $\varepsilon = \omega + \delta$. Since there are $\ell+1$ valid signatures in L, the probability of guessing ε correctly for one of them is $\frac{\ell+1}{q}$. □

By the claim, we have that $\mathsf{Adv}_{\mathsf{M}}^{\mathbf{G_1}} \geq \mathsf{Adv}_{\mathsf{M}}^{\mathbf{G_0}} - \frac{\ell+1}{q}$.

Game $\mathbf{G_2}$. Game $\mathbf{G_2}$ is identical to $\mathbf{G_1}$, except that it keeps track of the algebraic representations of group elements submitted to H_3 by M and aborts if a certain event E_2 happens. In the following, we define the event E_2 which depends on these representations.

Simplifying Notations. For each query to H_3, the adversary M submits a set of group elements $\zeta, \zeta_1, \alpha, \beta_1, \beta_2, \eta$ along with a message m and info.

As M is algebraic, it also provides a representation of these group elements to the basis of elements $\mathbf{g}, \mathbf{h}, \mathbf{y}, \vec{\mathbf{z}}, \vec{\mathbf{a}}, \vec{\mathbf{b_1}}, \vec{\mathbf{b_2}}, \vec{\mathbf{z_1}}$ that it has previously obtained via calls to $H_1, H_2, \mathbf{Sign}_1$, or $\mathbf{Sign}_2$. We note that by programming the oracles H_1 and H_2 the reduction knows a representation of its responses $\mathbf{z}_i$ and $\mathbf{z}_{1,i}$. Any element $\mathbf{a}, \mathbf{b}_1, \mathbf{b}_2$ that was returned as reply to a query to $\mathbf{Sign}_1$ can be represented as $\mathbf{a} = \mathbf{y}^c \cdot \mathbf{g}^r, \mathbf{b}_1 = \mathbf{z}_1^d \cdot \mathbf{g}^{s_1}, \mathbf{b}_2 = \mathbf{z}_2^d \cdot \mathbf{h}^{s_2}$. Here, $\mathbf{z}_1, \mathbf{z}_2 = \mathbf{z}/\mathbf{z}_1$ correspond to the call $H_2(\mathrm{rnd})$ made as part of answering this query to $\mathbf{Sign}_1$. This allows us to convert any representation provided by M into a *reduced representation* in the (simpler) basis $\mathbf{g}, \mathbf{h}, \mathbf{y}$. For a group element $\mathbf{o}$, we denote this reduced representation by $[\mathbf{o}]_{\overrightarrow{I}}$ and its components as $g_{[\mathbf{o}]_{\overrightarrow{I}}}, h_{[\mathbf{o}]_{\overrightarrow{I}}}, y_{[\mathbf{o}]_{\overrightarrow{I}}}$, respectively, where

$\vec{I} := (\mathbf{g}, \mathbf{h}, \mathbf{y})$. If M wins, we denote the special message/signature pair in its winning output as $(m, \mathsf{info}, (\zeta, \zeta_1, \rho, \omega, \sigma_1, \sigma_2, \delta, \mu))$. The algebraic coefficients of this tuple define the following integers which we call "preliminary values":

$$\omega' := y_{[\alpha]_{\vec{I}}}$$

$$\delta' := \frac{g_{[\beta_2]_{\vec{I}}} + x \cdot y_{[\beta_2]_{\vec{I}}}}{x \cdot y_{[\zeta_2]_{\vec{I}}} + g_{[\zeta_2]_{\vec{I}}}}$$

$$\delta'' := \frac{h_{[\beta_1]_{\vec{I}}}}{h_{[\zeta_1]_{\vec{I}}}}, \delta''' := \frac{h_{[\eta]_{\vec{I}}}}{h_{[\zeta]_{\vec{I}}}}.$$

We further define the following non-exclusive boolean variables that describe when which of the above values is actually well-defined:

$$C_0 := (\omega' \neq \omega) \qquad C_1 := (\omega' = \omega) \wedge (x \cdot y_{[\zeta_2]_{\vec{I}}} + g_{[\zeta_2]_{\vec{I}}} \neq 0)$$

$$C_2 := (\omega' = \omega) \wedge (h_{[\zeta_1]_{\vec{I}}} \neq 0) \quad C_3 := (\omega' = \omega) \wedge (h_{[\zeta]_{\vec{I}}} \neq 0)$$

Claim 4. $\bigvee_i C_i = 1$.

Proof. Since $\mathbf{G_2^{\mathsf{M}}} = 1 \Rightarrow \zeta_2 \neq \epsilon$, it follows that $x \cdot y_{[\zeta_2]_{\vec{I}}} + g_{[\zeta_2]_{\vec{I}}}$ and $h_{[\zeta_2]_{\vec{I}}}$ cannot both be 0 when $\mathbf{G_2^{\mathsf{M}}} = 1$. Therefore, either $x \cdot y_{[\zeta_2]_{\vec{I}}} + g_{[\zeta_2]_{\vec{I}}} \neq 0$ or $h_{[\zeta_2]_{\vec{I}}} \neq 0$. Moreover, since $[\zeta_2]_{\vec{I}} = [\zeta]_{\vec{I}} - [\zeta_1]_{\vec{I}}$, either $h_{[\zeta_1]_{\vec{I}}} \neq 0$ or $h_{[\zeta]_{\vec{I}}} \neq 0$, whenever $h_{[\zeta_2]_{\vec{I}}} \neq 0$. Therefore, $(h_{[\zeta_1]_{\vec{I}}} \neq 0 \vee h_{[\zeta]_{\vec{I}}} \neq 0 \vee x \cdot y_{[\zeta_2]_{\vec{I}}} + g_{[\zeta_2]_{\vec{I}}} \neq 0) = 1$ and thus $C_1 \vee C_2 \vee C_3 = (\omega' = \omega)$. The lemma follows immediately. □

We now define E_2 as the following event: $\omega' = \omega$, and for any of $\delta', \delta'', \delta'''$, as long as its denominator is not 0 (i.e., it is well-defined), then it is equal to δ. That is,

$$E_2 := (C_0 = 0) \wedge (C_1 = 0 \vee (C_1 = 1 \wedge (\delta' = \delta)))$$
$$\wedge (C_2 = 0 \vee (C_2 = 1 \wedge (\delta'' = \delta))) \wedge (C_3 = 0 \vee (C_3 = 1 \wedge (\delta''' = \delta))).$$

Claim 5. $\Pr[E_2] \leq \frac{3q_h}{q} + \mathsf{Adv}^{\mathrm{dlog}}_{\mathsf{R}_1} + \mathsf{Adv}^{\mathrm{dlog}}_{\mathsf{R}_2} + \mathsf{Adv}^{\mathrm{dlog}}_{\mathsf{R}_3} + \mathsf{Adv}^{\mathrm{dlog}}_{\mathsf{R}_4}$

The proof for this claim can be found in the full version [30].

By the claim, $\mathsf{Adv}^{\mathbf{G_2}}_{\mathsf{M}} \geq \mathsf{Adv}^{\mathbf{G_1}}_{\mathsf{M}} - \frac{3q_h}{q}$.

In the following, we explain how the reduction can simulate game $\mathbf{G_2}$ to the adversary M and win the discrete logarithm game.

Simulation of H_1, H_2, H_3. We begin by describing how S_0, S_1 simulate the random oracles H_1, H_2, H_3. These simulations are common to both S_ι and are performed in the straightforward way using lazy sampling. We assume that the oracles keep respective lists L_i for bookkeeping, where L_i stores input/output pairs. More specifically.

- H_1 and H_2: on each fresh input ξ, H_i samples $v \xleftarrow{\$} \mathbb{Z}_q$ and returns $\mathbf{g}^v$. It stores $(\xi, \mathbf{g}^v, v)$ in L_i.

- H_3 : on each fresh input $(\xi, \cdot)$, H_3 samples $\varepsilon \xleftarrow{\$} \mathbb{Z}_q$ and returns ε. It stores $(\xi, \overrightarrow{\mathrm{rep}}, \varepsilon)$ in L_i.
- On repeated inputs H_i returns whatever it returned the first time that ξ was queried.

Scheduling of Signing Sessions. We assume that each S_i internally schedules sessions with the oracles $\mathbf{Sign}_1$ and $\mathbf{Sign}_2$ as required by $\mathbf{G_2}$. This can be easily implemented by using a fresh session identifier for each new session.

Extracting Equations from Forgery. Suppose that M wins game $\mathbf{G_2}$, i.e., $\mathbf{G_2^M} = 1$. Recall that in this case, M produces a one-more forgery of at least $\ell+1$ valid signatures, after having completed at most ℓ sessions with oracle $\mathbf{Sign}_2$. In addition, we have required that one of the returned tuples $(m, \mathsf{info}, \mathsf{sig})$ be special, i.e., that $\zeta^{\mathrm{dlog}_{\mathbf{z}_j} \mathbf{z}_{1,j}} \neq \zeta_1$ for all $\mathbf{z}_j$ and $\mathbf{z}_{1,j}$ (where again $\mathbf{z}_j$ and $\mathbf{z}_{1,j}$ corresponds to the value of $\mathbf{z}$ and $\mathbf{z}_1$, respectively, derived during the j-th interaction with oracle $\mathbf{Sign}_1$).

From the verification equation of the special signature $(m, \mathsf{info}, \mathsf{sig})$, one obtains the equations $\alpha = \mathbf{g}^{\rho} \cdot \mathbf{y}^{\omega}$, $\beta_1 = \zeta_1^{\delta} \cdot \mathbf{g}^{\sigma_1}$, $\beta_2 = \zeta_2^{\delta} \cdot \mathbf{h}^{\sigma_2}$, $\eta = \mathbf{z}_j^{\mu} \cdot \zeta^{\delta}$. Denoting $w_{0,j} := \mathrm{dlog}\, \mathbf{z}_j$, $w := \mathrm{dlog}\, \mathbf{h}$, we obtain the reduced equations

$$g_{[\alpha]_{\vec{I}}} + x \cdot y_{[\alpha]_{\vec{I}}} + w \cdot h_{[\alpha]_{\vec{I}}} = \rho + x \cdot \omega \tag{1}$$

$$g_{[\beta_1]_{\vec{I}}} + x \cdot y_{[\beta_1]_{\vec{I}}} + w \cdot h_{[\beta_1]_{\vec{I}}} = (g_{[\zeta_1]_{\vec{I}}} + w \cdot h_{[\zeta_1]_{\vec{I}}} + x \cdot y_{[\zeta_1]_{\vec{I}}}) \cdot \delta + \sigma_1 \tag{2}$$

$$g_{[\beta_2]_{\vec{I}}} + x \cdot y_{[\beta_2]_{\vec{I}}} + w \cdot h_{[\beta_2]_{\vec{I}}} = (g_{[\zeta_2]_{\vec{I}}} + w \cdot h_{[\zeta_2]_{\vec{I}}} + x \cdot y_{[\zeta_2]_{\vec{I}}}) \cdot \delta + \sigma_2 \cdot w \tag{3}$$

$$g_{[\eta]_{\vec{I}}} + w \cdot h_{[\eta]_{\vec{I}}} + x \cdot y_{[\eta]_{\vec{I}}} = w_{0,j} \cdot \mu + (g_{[\zeta]_{\vec{I}}} + w \cdot h_{[\zeta]_{\vec{I}}} + x \cdot y_{[\zeta]_{\vec{I}}}) \cdot \delta. \tag{4}$$

We continue by describing simulators S_0 which covers case C_0, and S_1 which covers C_1, C_2, C_3. As we will see, the values c, r, d, s_1, s_2 inside a signature issued as part of a signing query are all known to S_i. Together with the above observations, it is easy for each simulator to convert a query to H_3 into reduced representation. Moreover, the winning tuple in M's output can be identified through knowledge of the logarithms of all $\mathbf{z}_i$ and all $\mathbf{z}_{1,i}$ efficiently.

Case $C_0 = 1$. We describe simulator S_0, which simulates $\mathbf{G_2}$ using w. On input a discrete logarithm instance $\mathbf{U} := \mathbf{g}^x$, it behaves as follows:

Setup: S_0 samples $w \xleftarrow{\$} \mathbb{Z}_q$ and computes the public key pk as $\mathsf{pk} := (\mathbf{g}, \mathbf{h} := \mathbf{g}^w, \mathbf{y} := \mathbf{U})$, which implicitly sets $\mathsf{sk} := x$.

Online Phase. S_0 runs M on input pp, pk and simulates the oracles $\mathbf{Sign}_1$, $\mathbf{Sign}_2$ as described below. In addition, it simulates the oracles H_1, H_2, H_3 as outlined above.

Queries to $\mathbf{Sign}_1$. When M queries $\mathbf{Sign}_1(\mathsf{info})$ to open session sid, S_0 checks in L_1 if $\mathsf{pk}, \mathsf{info}$ has been previously requested from H_1 and if yes sets $w_{0,\mathrm{sid}}$ accordingly, otherwise samples $w_{0,\mathrm{sid}}$ and programs $H_1(\mathsf{pk}, \mathsf{info}) := \mathbf{g}^{w_{0,j}}$. It samples $\mathrm{rnd}_{\mathrm{sid}} \xleftarrow{\$} \{0,1\}^{\lambda}$ and sets $\mathbf{z}_{1,\mathrm{sid}} := \mathbf{g}^{w_{1,\mathrm{sid}}} = H_2(\mathrm{rnd}_{\mathrm{sid}})$, which places the tuple $(\mathrm{rnd}_{\mathrm{sid}}, \mathbf{z}_{1,\mathrm{sid}}, w_{1,\mathrm{sid}})$ into L_2. It then sets $\mathbf{z}_{2,\mathrm{sid}} := \mathbf{z}_{\mathrm{sid}}/\mathbf{z}_{1,\mathrm{sid}}$, $w_{2,\mathrm{sid}} := \frac{w_{0,\mathrm{sid}} - w_{1,\mathrm{sid}}}{w}$, $c_{\mathrm{sid}}, r_{\mathrm{sid}}, u_{1,\mathrm{sid}}, u_{2,\mathrm{sid}} \xleftarrow{\$} \mathbb{Z}_q$, $\mathbf{a}_{\mathrm{sid}} := \mathbf{y}^{c_{\mathrm{sid}}} \cdot \mathbf{g}^{r_{\mathrm{sid}}}$, $\mathbf{b}_{1,\mathrm{sid}} := \mathbf{g}^{u_{1,\mathrm{sid}}}$, $\mathbf{b}_{2,\mathrm{sid}} := \mathbf{h}^{u_{2,\mathrm{sid}}}$ and returns $\mathbf{a}_{\mathrm{sid}}, \mathbf{b}_{1,\mathrm{sid}}, \mathbf{b}_{2,\mathrm{sid}}$.

Queries to Sign$_2$. When M queries **Sign**$_2(\mathrm{sid}, e_{\mathrm{sid}})$, S_0 sets $d_{\mathrm{sid}} := e_{\mathrm{sid}} - c_{\mathrm{sid}}$, $s_{1,\mathrm{sid}} := u_{1,\mathrm{sid}} - d_{\mathrm{sid}} \cdot w_{1,\mathrm{sid}}$, $s_{2,\mathrm{sid}} := u_{2,\mathrm{sid}} - d_{\mathrm{sid}} \cdot w_{2,\mathrm{sid}}$ and returns $c_{\mathrm{sid}}, d_{\mathrm{sid}}, r_{\mathrm{sid}}, s_{1,\mathrm{sid}}, s_{2,\mathrm{sid}}$.

It is straightforward to verify that the above simulation of $\mathbf{G_2}$ is perfect.

Solving the DLP Instance. When M returns $\ell+1$ message signature pairs, S_0 identifies the special signature using the exponents stored in L_2. It retrieves the corresponding hash query to H_3 from L_3 together with representations of $\alpha, \beta_1, \beta_2, \eta$. S_0 uses Eq. (1) and the fact that $C_0 = 1 \Leftrightarrow \omega \neq y_{[\alpha]_{\mathcal{T}}}$, to (efficiently) compute and output the value x as $x = (\rho - g_{[\alpha]_{\mathcal{T}}} - w \cdot h_{[\alpha]_{\mathcal{T}}})/(y_{[\alpha]_{\mathcal{T}}} - \omega)$. (In case $C_0 = 0$, or there is no hash query corresponding to the special signature, it aborts.)

If $C_0 = 1$, then S_0's simulation of $\mathbf{G_2}$ is perfect.

Case $C_0 = 0$. We describe simulator S_1, which simulates $\mathbf{G_2}$ using x. On input a discrete logarithm instance $\mathbf{U} := \mathbf{g}^w$, it behaves as follows.

Setup. S_1 samples $x \xleftarrow{\$} \mathbb{Z}_q$. It sets $\mathsf{pk} := (\mathbf{g}, \mathbf{h} := \mathbf{U}, \mathbf{y} := \mathbf{g}^x)$, $\mathsf{sk} := x$.

Online Phase. S_1 runs M on input pp, pk and simulates the oracles **Sign**$_1$, **Sign**$_2$ as described below. In addition, it simulates the oracles H_1, H_2, H_3 as outlined above.

Queries to Sign$_1$. When M queries **Sign**$_1(\mathsf{info})$ to open session sid, S_1 checks if info was requested to H_1 already and if so sets $w_{0,j}$ accordingly, otherwise it samples $w_{0,j} \xleftarrow{\$} \mathbb{Z}_q$ and sets $H_1(\mathsf{pk}, \mathsf{info}) := w_{0,j}$. It then samples $\mathrm{rnd}_{\mathrm{sid}} \xleftarrow{\$} \{0,1\}^\lambda$ and sets $\mathbf{z}_{1,\mathrm{sid}} := \mathbf{g}^{w_{1,\mathrm{sid}}} = H_2(\mathrm{rnd}_{\mathrm{sid}})$ (hence $w_{1,\mathrm{sid}}$ is known to S_1 from programming H_2). It then samples $u_{\mathrm{sid}}, d_{\mathrm{sid}}, s_{1,\mathrm{sid}}, s_{2,\mathrm{sid}} \xleftarrow{\$} \mathbb{Z}_q$ and sets $\mathbf{a}_{\mathrm{sid}} := \mathbf{g}^{u_{\mathrm{sid}}}$, $\mathbf{b}_{1,\mathrm{sid}} := \mathbf{g}^{s_{1,\mathrm{sid}}} \cdot \mathbf{z}_{1,\mathrm{sid}}^{d_{\mathrm{sid}}}$, $\mathbf{b}_{2,\mathrm{sid}} := \mathbf{h}^{s_{2,\mathrm{sid}}} \cdot \mathbf{z}_{2,\mathrm{sid}}^{d_{\mathrm{sid}}}$ and returns $\mathbf{a}_{\mathrm{sid}}, \mathbf{b}_{1,\mathrm{sid}}, \mathbf{b}_{2,\mathrm{sid}}$.

Queries to Sign$_2$. When M queries **Sign**$_2$ on input $(\mathrm{sid}, e_{\mathrm{sid}})$, S_1 sets $c_{\mathrm{sid}} := e_{\mathrm{sid}} - d_{\mathrm{sid}}$, $r_{\mathrm{sid}} := u_{\mathrm{sid}} - c_{\mathrm{sid}} \cdot x$ and returns $c_{\mathrm{sid}}, d_{\mathrm{sid}}, r_{\mathrm{sid}}, s_{1,\mathrm{sid}}, s_{2,\mathrm{sid}}$

Solving the DLP Instance. When M returns $\ell+1$ message signature pairs, S_1 identifies the special signature using the exponents stored in L_2. It retrieves the corresponding hash query to H_3 from L_3 together with representations of $\alpha, \beta_1, \beta_2, \eta$. If there is no hash query to H_3 corresponding to the special signature, it aborts. Since $C_0 = 0$ it holds that $C_1 = 1 \vee C_2 = 1 \vee C_3 = 1$. S_1 uses one of the following extraction strategies.

If $C_1 = 1$: S_1 uses Eq. (3) and the fact that $C_1 = 1 \Rightarrow (x \cdot y_{[\zeta_2]_{\mathcal{T}}} + g_{[\zeta_2]_{\mathcal{T}}} \neq 0)$, to (efficiently) compute and output the value w as follows. S_1 first computes δ' as $\delta' := (g_{[\beta_2]_{\mathcal{T}}} + x \cdot y_{[\beta_2]_{\mathcal{T}}})/(x \cdot y_{[\zeta_2]_{\mathcal{T}}} + g_{[\zeta_2]_{\mathcal{T}}})$, which gives the equality

$$\delta' \cdot (g_{[\zeta_2]_{\mathcal{T}}} + x \cdot y_{[\zeta_2]_{\mathcal{T}}}) + w \cdot h_{[\beta_2]_{\mathcal{T}}} = g_{[\beta_2]_{\mathcal{T}}} + x \cdot y_{[\beta_2]_{\mathcal{T}}} + w \cdot h_{[\beta_2]_{\mathcal{T}}}. \quad (5)$$

Equations (5) and (3) yield

$$\begin{aligned} \delta' \cdot (g_{[\zeta_2]_{\mathcal{T}}} + x \cdot y_{[\zeta_2]_{\mathcal{T}}}) + w \cdot h_{[\beta_2]_{\mathcal{T}}} &= g_{[\beta_2]_{\mathcal{T}}} + x \cdot y_{[\beta_2]_{\mathcal{T}}} + w \cdot h_{[\beta_2]_{\mathcal{T}}} \\ &= \delta \cdot (g_{[\zeta_2]_{\mathcal{T}}} + x \cdot y_{[\zeta_2]_{\mathcal{T}}} + w \cdot h_{[\zeta_2]_{\mathcal{T}}}) + \sigma_2 \cdot w. \end{aligned}$$

If $h_{[\beta_2]_{\mathcal{T}}} - \delta \cdot h_{[\zeta_2]_{\mathcal{T}}} - \sigma_2 \neq 0$, S_1 outputs $w = ((\delta - \delta') \cdot (g_{[\zeta_2]_{\mathcal{T}}} + x \cdot h_{[\zeta_2]_{\mathcal{T}}}))/(h_{[\beta_2]_{\mathcal{T}}} - \delta \cdot h_{[\zeta_2]_{\mathcal{T}}} - \sigma_2)$. We prove the following claim.

Claim 6. $h_{[\beta_2]_{\mathcal{T}}} - \delta \cdot h_{[\zeta_2]_{\mathcal{T}}} - \sigma_2 \neq 0$.

Proof. Since $C_1 = 1$ and event E_2 does not happen (since otherwise $\mathbf{G}_2^{\mathsf{M}} = 0$), we know that $\delta \neq \delta'$. Hence, it suffices to show that if $\delta \neq \delta'$, then $h_{[\beta_2]_{\mathcal{T}}} - \delta \cdot h_{[\zeta_2]_{\mathcal{T}}} - \sigma_2 \neq 0$. Due to Eq. (3) we get

$$\begin{aligned}\delta' \cdot (g_{[\zeta_2]_{\mathcal{T}}} + x \cdot y_{[\zeta_2]_{\mathcal{T}}}) + w \cdot h_{[\beta_2]_{\mathcal{T}}} &= \delta \cdot (g_{[\zeta_2]_{\mathcal{T}}} + x \cdot y_{[\zeta_2]_{\mathcal{T}}} + w \cdot h_{[\zeta_2]_{\mathcal{T}}}) + \sigma_2 \cdot w \\ &= \delta \cdot (g_{[\zeta_2]_{\mathcal{T}}} + x \cdot y_{[\zeta_2]_{\mathcal{T}}}) + w \cdot h_{[\beta_2]_{\mathcal{T}}},\end{aligned}$$

which yields $(\delta' - \delta) \cdot (g_{[\zeta_2]_{\mathcal{T}}} + x \cdot y_{[\zeta_2]_{\mathcal{T}}}) = 0$. Since $C_1 = 1$, we have $g_{[\zeta_2]_{\mathcal{T}}} + x \cdot y_{[\zeta_2]_{\mathcal{T}}} \neq 0$, which contradicts the assumption that $\delta' \neq \delta$. □

It is easily verified that whenever $C_1 = 1$, S_1's simulation of $\mathbf{G_2}$ is perfect.

If $C_1 = 0$ and $C_2 = 1$: S_1 uses Eq. (2) and the fact that $C_2 = 1 \Leftrightarrow (\omega = y_{[\alpha]_{\mathcal{T}}}) \wedge (h_{[\zeta_1]_{\mathcal{T}}} \neq 0)$, to compute and output the discrete logarithm w of the instance $\mathbf{U}$ as follows. S_1 first computes $\delta'' := \frac{h_{[\beta_1]_{\mathcal{T}}}}{h_{[\zeta_1]_{\mathcal{T}}}}$ which leads to the equality

$$\delta'' \cdot w \cdot h_{[\zeta_1]_{\mathcal{T}}} + g_{[\beta_1]_{\mathcal{T}}} + x \cdot y_{[\beta_1]_{\mathcal{T}}} = g_{[\beta_1]_{\mathcal{T}}} + x \cdot y_{[\beta_1]_{\mathcal{T}}} + w \cdot h_{[\beta_1]_{\mathcal{T}}}. \tag{6}$$

Equations (6) and (2) yield

$$\begin{aligned}&\delta'' \cdot w \cdot h_{[\zeta_1]_{\mathcal{T}}} + g_{[\beta_1]_{\mathcal{T}}} + x \cdot y_{[\beta_1]_{\mathcal{T}}} = g_{[\beta_1]_{\mathcal{T}}} + x \cdot y_{[\beta_1]_{\mathcal{T}}} + w \cdot h_{[\beta_1]_{\mathcal{T}}} \\ &= (g_{[\zeta_1]_{\mathcal{T}}} + w \cdot h_{[\zeta_1]_{\mathcal{T}}} + x \cdot y_{[\zeta_1]_{\mathcal{T}}}) \cdot \delta + \sigma_1.\end{aligned}$$

By the same argument as in the previous case, $\delta \neq \delta''$, and S_1 can compute and output w as $w = (\delta \cdot (g_{[\zeta_1]_{\mathcal{T}}} + x \cdot y_{[\zeta_1]_{\mathcal{T}}}) + \sigma_1 - g_{[\beta_1]_{\mathcal{T}}} + x \cdot y_{[\beta_1]_{\mathcal{T}}})/((\delta - \delta'') \cdot h_{[\zeta_1]_{\mathcal{T}}})$, as $C_2 = 1$ implies that $h_{[\zeta_1]_{\mathcal{T}}} \neq 0$. Moreover, S_1's simulation of $\mathbf{G_2}$ is perfect if $C_2 = 1$ holds.

If $C_1 = C_2 = 0$ and $C_3 = 1$: In this case, S_1 uses Eq. (4) and the fact that $C_3 = 1 \Leftrightarrow (\omega = y_{[\alpha]_{\mathcal{T}}}) \wedge (h_{[\zeta]_{\mathcal{T}}} \neq 0)$, to compute and output the discrete logarithm w of the instance $\mathbf{U}$ as we described below. S_1 computes $\delta''' := h_{[\eta]_{\mathcal{T}}}/h_{[\zeta]_{\mathcal{T}}}$, leading to

$$\delta''' \cdot w \cdot h_{[\zeta]_{\mathcal{T}}} + g_{[\eta]_{\mathcal{T}}} + x \cdot y_{[\eta]_{\mathcal{T}}} = g_{[\eta]_{\mathcal{T}}} + x \cdot y_{[\eta]_{\mathcal{T}}} + w \cdot h_{[\eta]_{\mathcal{T}}}. \tag{7}$$

Equations (4) and (7) imply that

$$\begin{aligned}&\delta''' \cdot w \cdot h_{[\zeta]_{\mathcal{T}}} + g_{[\eta]_{\mathcal{T}}} + x \cdot y_{[\eta]_{\mathcal{T}}} = g_{[\eta]_{\mathcal{T}}} + x \cdot y_{[\eta]_{\mathcal{T}}} + w \cdot h_{[\eta]_{\mathcal{T}}} \\ &= w_0 \cdot \mu + (g_{[\zeta]_{\mathcal{T}}} + w \cdot h_{[\zeta]_{\mathcal{T}}} + x \cdot y_{[\zeta]_{\mathcal{T}}}) \cdot \delta.\end{aligned}$$

As in the previous cases, $\delta \neq \delta'''$, so S_1 can output w by computing $w = (\delta \cdot (g_{[\zeta]_{\mathcal{T}}} + x \cdot y_{[\zeta]_{\mathcal{T}}}) + \mu \cdot w_0 - (g_{[\eta]_{\mathcal{T}}} + x \cdot y_{[\eta]_{\mathcal{T}}}))/((\delta''' - \delta) \cdot h_{[\zeta]_{\mathcal{T}}})$, since $h_{[\zeta]_{\mathcal{T}}} \neq 0$

due to $C_3 = 1$. Moreover, S_1's simulation of $\mathbf{G_2}$ is perfect if $C_3 = 1$ holds. Since both simulators provide a perfect simulation (in their respective cases) and cover all cases that can happen whenever $\mathbf{G_2^M} = 1$, B can run the correct simulator to extract the discrete logarithm with advantage $\mathsf{Adv}_{\mathsf{B}}^{\mathbf{DLP}} \geq \mathsf{Adv}_{\mathsf{M}}^{\mathbf{G_2}}/2$. Moreover, we have $\mathsf{Adv}_{\mathsf{M}}^{\mathbf{G_2}} \geq \mathsf{Adv}_{\mathsf{M}}^{\mathbf{G_1}} - (\frac{3q_h}{q} + \mathsf{Adv}_{\mathsf{R_1}}^{\mathrm{dlog}} + \mathsf{Adv}_{\mathsf{R_2}}^{\mathrm{dlog}} + \mathsf{Adv}_{\mathsf{R_3}}^{\mathrm{dlog}} + \mathsf{Adv}_{\mathsf{R_4}}^{\mathrm{dlog}}) \geq \mathsf{Adv}_{\mathsf{M}}^{\mathbf{G_0}} - (\frac{3q_h}{q} + \mathsf{Adv}_{\mathsf{R_1}}^{\mathrm{dlog}} + \mathsf{Adv}_{\mathsf{R_2}}^{\mathrm{dlog}} + \mathsf{Adv}_{\mathsf{R_3}}^{\mathrm{dlog}} + \mathsf{Adv}_{\mathsf{R_4}}^{\mathrm{dlog}}) - \frac{\ell+1}{q}$. Hence, $t_{\mathsf{B}} \approx t_{\mathsf{M}}$ and

$$\begin{aligned}\mathsf{Adv}_{\mathsf{B}}^{\mathbf{DLP}} \geq & \frac{1}{2}\mathsf{Adv}_{\mathsf{M},\ell,\mathsf{BSA}}^{\mathbf{RB\text{-}OMUF}} - \frac{\ell+1}{2q} \\ & - (\frac{3q_h}{q} + \mathsf{Adv}_{\mathsf{R_1}}^{\mathrm{dlog}} + \mathsf{Adv}_{\mathsf{R_2}}^{\mathrm{dlog}} + \mathsf{Adv}_{\mathsf{R_3}}^{\mathrm{dlog}} + \mathsf{Adv}_{\mathsf{R_4}}^{\mathrm{dlog}})\end{aligned}$$

□

The Main Theorem. In the following, we show that Abe's blind signature scheme has full one-more-unforgeability. We make use of the restrictive blinding lemma to identify the forged signature.

Theorem 1. *Let* M *be an algebraic algorithm that runs in time* t_{M}*, makes at most* ℓ *queries to oracle* $\mathbf{Sign}_2$ *in* ℓ-$\mathbf{OMUF}_{\mathsf{BSA}}$ *and at most (total)* q_h *queries to* H_1, H_2, H_3*. Then, in the random oracle model, there exists an algorithm* B *such that*

$$\begin{aligned}\mathsf{Adv}_{\mathsf{B}}^{\mathbf{DLP}} \geq & \frac{1}{4}\mathsf{Adv}_{\mathsf{M},\ell,\mathsf{BSA}}^{\mathbf{OMUF}} - \frac{3q_h}{q} - \mathsf{Adv}_{\mathsf{R_1}}^{\mathbf{DLP}} - \mathsf{Adv}_{\mathsf{R_2}}^{\mathbf{DLP}} - \mathsf{Adv}_{\mathsf{R_3}}^{\mathbf{DLP}} \\ & - (\mathsf{Adv}_{\mathsf{R'_1}}^{\mathbf{DLP}} + \mathsf{Adv}_{\mathsf{R'_2}}^{\mathbf{DLP}} + \mathsf{Adv}_{\mathsf{R'_3}}^{\mathbf{DLP}} + \mathsf{Adv}_{\mathsf{R'_4}}^{\mathbf{DLP}})\end{aligned}$$

Proof. The proof is similar to the proof of Lemma 2. We give a brief overview, the full proof can be found in the full version [30].

The reduction embeds the discrete logarithm challenge in either $\mathbf{y}$ or all the $\mathbf{z}_j$ and $\mathbf{z}_{1,j}$ by programming the random oracle H_1 and H_2. I.e. on input of a discrete logarithm challenge $\mathbf{U}$, the reduction sets either $\mathbf{y} = \mathbf{U}$ and generates $\mathbf{z}_j, \mathbf{z}_{1,j}, \mathbf{h}$ with known discrete logarithms to base $\mathbf{g}^{v_i}$ for randomly chosen $v_i \xleftarrow{\$} \mathbb{Z}_q$, or the reduction sets $\mathbf{y} = \mathbf{g}^x$ for known $x \xleftarrow{\$} \mathbb{Z}_q$, $\mathbf{h} := \mathbf{g}^v$ for a known $v \in \mathbb{Z}_q$, and generates all $\mathbf{z}_j, \mathbf{z}_{1,j}$ as $\mathbf{U}^{v_i}$ for $v_i \xleftarrow{\$} \mathbb{Z}_q$. This allows the reduction to either generate signatures using its knowledge of the discrete logarithms of $\mathbf{z}_j, \mathbf{z}_{1,j}$, and $\mathbf{h}$, or its knowledge of the secret key x. Due to Lemma 2 we can assume that there is one session that produces two signatures. As the responses for H_2 have been programmed, this session can be identified and a representation of all group elements to $\mathbf{g}, \mathbf{y}, \mathbf{z}_j, \mathbf{z}_{1,j}$ is known to the reduction. Similar to the proof of Lemma 2 the algebraic representations of the group elements submitted in hash queries to H_3 can be used to compute preliminary ω' and $\delta', \delta'', \delta'''$ for both of the special signatures belonging to the same session. As at least one of the signatures was not created through a run of the honest signing protocol, using similar arguments as for the special signature in Lemma 2, thus the witness can be computed by the reduction which yields the statement. □

4 Sequential Unforgeability of Schnorr's Blind Signature Scheme

In this section we show that Schnorr's blind signature scheme satisfies sequential one-more unforgeability under the one-more DL assumption in the AGM. We first recall Schnorr's blind signature scheme BSS below. A figure depicting an interaction can be found in the full version [30].[5] Let $H\colon \{0,1\}^* \to \mathbb{Z}_q$ be a hash function.

- KeyGen: On input pp, KeyGen samples $x \xleftarrow{\$} \mathbb{Z}_q$ and sets $\mathbf{x} := \mathbf{g}^x$. It sets $\mathsf{sk} := x, \mathsf{pk} := \mathbf{x}$ and returns (sk, pk).
- Sign_1: On input sk, Sign_1 samples $r \xleftarrow{\$} \mathbb{Z}_q$ and returns the commitment $\mathbf{r} := \mathbf{g}^r$ and the state $St_S := r$.
- Sign_2: On input a secret key sk, a state $St_S = r$ and a challenge c, Sign_2 computes $s := c \cdot \mathsf{sk} + r \mod q$ and returns the response s.
- User_1: On input a public key pk, a commitment $\mathbf{r}$, and a message m, User_1 does the following. It samples first samples $\alpha, \beta \xleftarrow{\$} \mathbb{Z}_q$. Then, it computes $\mathbf{r}' := \mathbf{r} \cdot \mathbf{g}^\alpha \cdot \mathsf{pk}^\beta$ and $c' := H(\mathbf{r}', m), c := c' + \beta \mod q$. It returns the challenge c and the state $St_U := (\mathbf{r}, c, \alpha, \beta, m)$.
- User_2: On input a public key pk, a state $St_U = (\mathbf{r}, c, \alpha, \beta, m)$, and a response s, User_2 first checks if $\mathbf{g}^s = \mathbf{r} \cdot \mathbf{x}^c$ and returns $\perp$ if not. Otherwise, it computes $\mathbf{r}' := \mathbf{r} \cdot \mathbf{g}^\alpha \cdot \mathsf{pk}^\beta$ and $s' := s + \alpha$ and returns the signature $\sigma := (\mathbf{r}', s')$.
- Verify: On input a public key pk, a signature $\sigma = (\mathbf{r}', s')$ and a message m, Verify computes $c' := H(\mathbf{r}', m)$ and checks whether $g^{s'} = \mathbf{r}' \cdot \mathsf{pk}^{c'}$. If so, it returns 1; otherwise, it returns 0.

Theorem 2. *Let* M *be an algebraic adversary that runs in time* t_M*, makes at most* ℓ *queries to* $\mathbf{Sign}_2$ *in* ℓ-**SEQ-OMUF**$_\mathsf{BSS}$*, and at most* q_h *random oracle queries to* H*. Then there exists an adversary* B *such that*

$$\mathsf{Adv}^{\mathbf{OMDL}}_{\mathsf{B},\ell} \geq \mathsf{Adv}^{\mathbf{SEQ\text{-}OMUF}}_{\mathsf{M},\ell,\mathsf{BSS}} - \frac{q_h^2 + q_h + 2}{2q},$$

and B *runs in time* $t_\mathsf{B} = t_\mathsf{M} + O(\ell + q_h)$.

Proof. Let M be as in the theorem statement. Without loss of generality, we assume that M makes exactly $\ell + 1$ many $\mathbf{Sign}_1()$ and exactly ℓ many $\mathbf{Sign}_2$ queries, and returns exactly $\ell + 1$ valid signatures $(\mathbf{r}_1^*, s_1^*), \ldots, (\mathbf{r}_{\ell+1}^*, s_{\ell+1}^*)$ of messages $m_1^*, \ldots, m_{\ell+1}^*$.[6] We further assume that pairs $(m_1^*, \mathbf{r}_1^*), \ldots, (m_{\ell+1}^*, \mathbf{r}_{\ell+1}^*)$

[5] We use different letters to denote the variables in the scheme than what we used in the previous section Our choices are in line with the standard notation for this scheme.

[6] Since the security game is *sequential* OMUF, and M can make at most ℓ many $\mathbf{Sign}_2$ queries, this implies that M can make at most $\ell + 1$ many $\mathbf{Sign}_1$ queries. Obviously, any adversary who makes less than $\ell + 1$ many $\mathbf{Sign}_1$ queries, or less than ℓ many $\mathbf{Sign}_2$ queries, or returns more than $\ell + 1$ valid signatures, can be turned into an adversary who makes exactly $\ell + 1$ many $\mathbf{Sign}_1$ and exactly ℓ many $\mathbf{Sign}_2$ queries, and returns exactly $\ell + 1$ valid signatures, with the same advantage and roughly the same running time.

are all distinct; otherwise M could not win ℓ-**SEQ-OMUF**$_{\mathsf{BSS}}$ as we prove in the following simple claim.

Claim 7. The pairs $(m_i^*, \mathbf{r}_i^*), \ldots, (m_j^*, \mathbf{r}_j^*)$ are pairwise distinct for all $i, j \in [\ell+1]$.

Proof. Suppose $(m_i^*, \mathbf{r}_i^*) = (m_j^*, \mathbf{r}_j^*)$ for $i \neq j \in [\ell+1]$. If $s_i^* = s_j^*$ then M outputs two identical message/signature pairs, violating the winning condition. Otherwise it cannot be the case that both $(\mathbf{r}_i^*, s_i^*)$ and $(\mathbf{r}_i^*, s_j^*)$ are both valid signatures of m_i^*, since given m_i^* and $\mathbf{r}_i^*$, s_i^* as in the valid signature is uniquely defined. □

Let $\mathbf{x}$ be the public key, $\mathbf{r}_1, \ldots, \mathbf{r}_{\ell+1}$ be the group elements returned by $\mathbf{Sign}_1$, and M's $\mathbf{Sign}_2$ queries be $\mathbf{Sign}_2(c_1), \ldots, \mathbf{Sign}_2(c_\ell)$. The proof goes by a sequence of games, which we describe below. For convenience, we set $\mathsf{Adv}_{\mathsf{M}}^{\mathbf{G_i}} := \Pr[\mathbf{G_i^{\mathsf{M}}} = 1]$.

Game $\mathbf{G_0}$. This is the ℓ-SEQ-OMUF game. We have that

$$\mathsf{Adv}_{\mathsf{M}}^{\mathbf{G_0}} = \mathsf{Adv}_{\mathsf{M},\ell,\mathsf{BSS}}^{\mathbf{SEQ\text{-}OMUF}}.$$

Game $\mathbf{G_1}$. In $\mathbf{G_1}$ we make the following change. When M returns its final outputs $(m_1^*, (\mathbf{r}_1^*, s_1^*)), \ldots, (m_{\ell+1}^*, (\mathbf{r}_{\ell+1}^*, s_{\ell+1}^*))$, together with $\mathbf{r}_i^*$'s algebraic representation $(\gamma_i^*, \xi_i^*, \rho_{i,1}^*, \ldots, \rho_{i,\ell+1}^*)$ based on $\mathbf{g}, \mathbf{x}, \mathbf{r}_1, \ldots, \mathbf{r}_{\ell+1}$, for each $i \in [\ell+1]$ for which $H(\mathbf{r}_i^*, m_i^*)$ is undefined, we emulate a query $c_i^* := H(\mathbf{r}_i^*, m_i^*)$ via lazy sampling. (If M has not seen a certain $\mathbf{r}_j$ when outputting $\mathbf{r}_i^*$, then the game naturally sets $\rho_{i,j}^* = 0$, as M is not allowed to use $\mathbf{r}_j$ as a base.) After that, we define $\chi_i := c_i^* + \xi_i^* - \sum_{j=1}^{\ell} \rho_{i,j}^* c_j$, and abort if $\chi_i = 0$ for all i. (Note that $\rho_{i,\ell+1}^*$ does not appear in the definition of χ_i.)

$\mathbf{G_1}$ and $\mathbf{G_0}$ are identical unless $\chi_i = 0$ for all $i \in [\ell+1]$. Call this event E.

Claim 8. $\Pr[E] \leq \frac{q_h^2 + q_h + 2}{2q}$

Proof. If M does not query $H(\mathbf{r}_i^*, m_i^*)$ for some i, then c_i^* is a uniformly random element of $\mathbb{Z}_q$ in M's view, so $\Pr[\chi_i = 0] = 1/q$.

Next we assume that M queries $H(\mathbf{r}_i^*, m_i^*)$ for all i; call such query the *i-th special query*. Since $(m_i^*, \mathbf{r}_i^*)$ pairs are all distinct, $c_i^* = H(\mathbf{r}_i^*, m_i^*)$ is a uniformly random element in $\mathbb{Z}_q$ (independent of everything else) when M makes the i-th special query. Also, $\mathbf{r}_i^*$'s algebraic representation $(\gamma_i^*, \xi_i^*, \rho_{i,1}^*, \ldots, \rho_{i,\ell+1}^*)$ is already determined when M makes its i-th special query. Any special query is made either during a session which is eventually closed (i.e., between M's j-th $\mathbf{Sign}_1$ query and j-th $\mathbf{Sign}_2$ query for some $j \in [\ell]$), or between two sessions (including before the first session), or during the last session which is never closed (i.e., after M's $(\ell+1)$-th $\mathbf{Sign}_1$ query). We consider these cases separately:

Case C_1. Suppose that there is *any* special query (say the i-th) made (a) between two sessions (including before the first session); say the i-th special query is made after the j_0-th $\mathbf{Sign}_2$ query and before the (j_0+1)-th $\mathbf{Sign}_1$ query, or (b) after the $(\ell+1)$-th $\mathbf{Sign}_1$ query. Consider the time when M makes its i-th special query $H(\mathbf{r}_i^*, m_i^*)$. In case (a), at this point all group elements M has seen are $\mathbf{g}, \mathbf{x}, \mathbf{r}_1, \ldots, \mathbf{r}_{j_0}$, so $\rho_{i,j_0+1}^* = \ldots = \rho_{i,\ell}^* = 0$; furthermore, the algebraic coefficients (for $\mathbf{r}_i^*$) $\xi_i^*, \rho_{i,1}^*, \ldots, \rho_{i,j_0}^*$ are all fixed. Finally, c_j (where $j \in [j_0]$) is fixed when M makes its j-th $\mathbf{Sign}_2$ query, which happens *before* M's i-th special query. Similarly, in case (b), at this point the algebraic coefficients (for $\mathbf{r}_i^*$) $\xi_i^*, \rho_{i,1}^*, \ldots, \rho_{i,\ell+1}^*$ are all fixed, and $c_1, \ldots, c_\ell$ are fixed when M makes its ℓ-th $\mathbf{Sign}_2$ query, which happens *before* M's i-th special query. This means that in both cases (a) and (b), all coefficients in χ_i's expression, except c_i^*, are fixed when M makes its i-th special query. On the other hand, c_i^* is a uniformly random element in $\mathbb{Z}_q$. Therefore, $\Pr[\chi_i = c_i^* + \xi_i^* - \sum_{j=1}^{j_0} \rho_{i,j}^* c_j = 0] = \frac{1}{q}$, for a single $H(\mathbf{r}_i^*, m_i^*)$ query. Since M makes q_h random oracle queries in total, we have that $\Pr[\chi_i = 0 \wedge C_1] \leq \frac{q_h}{q}$, and hence $\Pr[E \wedge C_1] \leq \frac{q_h}{q}$.

Case C_2. Suppose that *all* special queries are made during some session which is eventually closed. Since there are ℓ such sessions and $\ell + 1$ special queries, there is at least one session with at least two special queries during it; say the i-th and $(i+1)$-th special queries are made during the j_0-th session. Consider the time when M makes its $(i+1)$-st special query. At this point all group elements M has seen are $\mathbf{g}, \mathbf{x}, \mathbf{r}_1, \ldots, \mathbf{r}_{j_0}$, so $\rho_{i,j_0+1}^* = \ldots = \rho_{i,\ell}^* = 0$; furthermore, the algebraic coefficients (for $\mathbf{r}_i^*$ and $\mathbf{r}_{i+1}^*$) $\xi_i^*, \rho_{i,1}^*, \ldots, \rho_{i,j_0}^*, \xi_{i+1}^*, \rho_{i+1,1}^*, \ldots, \rho_{i+1,j_0}^*$ are all fixed. The output of M's i-th special query c_i^* is also fixed right after M makes its i-th special query, which happens *before* M's $(i+1)$-th special query. Finally, c_j (where $j \in [j_0 - 1]$) is fixed when M makes its j-th $\mathbf{Sign}_2$ query, which again happens *before* M's $(i+1)$-th special query. (This is because M's $(i+1)$-th special query is made during the j_0-th session, which is started after the j-th session is closed.) This means that all coefficients in χ_i and χ_{i+1}'s expressions, except c_{j_0} and c_{i+1}^*, are fixed when M makes its $(i+1)$-th special query.

Next consider the time when M makes its j_0-th $\mathbf{Sign}_2$ query (i.e., when the j_0-th session is closed). At this point c_{i+1}^* is also fixed, so the only coefficient in χ_i and χ_{i+1}'s expressions which is not fixed is c_{j_0} (to be chosen by M). In sum, the last coefficient fixed is c_{j_0} (chosen by M), and the second last coefficient fixed is c_{i+1}^* (uniformly random in $\mathbb{Z}_q$).

Consider the linear system with unknown c_{j_0}

$$\begin{cases} \chi_i = c_i^* + \xi_i^* - \sum_{j=1}^{j_0} \rho_{i,j}^* c_j = 0, \\ \chi_{i+1} = c_{i+1}^* + \xi_{i+1}^* - \sum_{j=1}^{j_0} \rho_{i+1,j}^* c_j = 0. \end{cases} \tag{8}$$

Denote $A := \begin{pmatrix} \rho_{i,j_0}^* & c_i^* + \xi_i^* - \sum_{j=1}^{j_0-1} \rho_{i,j}^* c_j \\ \rho_{i+1,j_0}^* & c_{i+1}^* + \xi_{i+1}^* - \sum_{j=1}^{j_0-1} \rho_{i+1,j}^* c_j \end{pmatrix}$ and $B := \begin{pmatrix} \rho_{i,j_0}^* \\ \rho_{i+1,j_0}^* \end{pmatrix}$ the augmented matrix and coefficient matrix, respectively, of (8). We first note that if $\rho_{i,j_0}^* = \rho_{i+1,j_0}^* = 0$ all factors in Eq. (8) are fixed when M makes his query. Thus, the probability that $\chi_i = \chi_{i+1} = 0$ is at most $\frac{1}{q}$ over the choice of c_i^* and c_{i+1}^*. In the following we assume that $\rho_{i,j_0}^* \neq 0$ or $\rho_{i+1,j_0}^* \neq 0$. Then

$$\Pr[\chi_i = \chi_{i+1} = 0] = \Pr[c_{j_0} \text{ is the solution of (8)}] \le \Pr[\text{(8) has a solution}]$$
$$= \Pr[\operatorname{rank}(A) = \operatorname{rank}(B)] \le \Pr[\operatorname{rank}(A) \le 1] = \Pr[\det(A) = 0]$$
$$= \Pr\left[\begin{matrix}\rho^*_{i,j_0} c^*_{i+1} + \rho^*_{i,j_0}(\xi^*_{i+1} - \sum_{j=1}^{j_0-1} \rho^*_{i+1,j} c_j) \\ -\rho^*_{i+1,j_0}(c^*_i + \xi^*_i - \sum_{j=1}^{j_0-1} \rho^*_{i,j} c_j) = 0\end{matrix}\right] = \frac{1}{q},$$

for a single pair of $H(\mathbf{r}^*_i, m^*_i)$ and $H(\mathbf{r}^*_{i+1}, m^*_{i+1})$ queries. (The last equation is true because when M makes its $(i+1)$-th special query, c^*_{i+1} is a uniformly random element of $\mathbb{Z}_q$, and all other coefficients are fixed.) Since M makes q_h random oracle queries in total, we have that $\Pr[\chi_i = \chi_{i+1} = 0 \wedge C_2] \le \frac{\binom{q_h}{2}}{q}$, and hence $\Pr[E \wedge C_2] \le \frac{\binom{q_h}{2}}{q}$.

In sum, we have that (let case C_0 be "M does not make the i-th special query for some $i \in [\ell+1]$")

$$\Pr[E] = \Pr[E \wedge C_0] + \Pr[E \wedge C_1] + \Pr[E \wedge C_2]$$
$$\le \frac{1}{q} + \frac{q_h}{q} + \frac{\binom{q_h}{2}}{q} = \frac{q_h^2 + q_h + 2}{2q}.$$

□

By the claim, $\mathsf{Adv}^{\mathbf{G_1}}_{\mathsf{M}} \le \mathsf{Adv}^{\mathbf{G_0}}_{\mathsf{M}} - \frac{q_h^2+q_h+2}{2q}$.

Reduction to ℓ-OMDL. We now upper bound $\mathsf{Adv}^{\mathbf{G_1}}_{\mathsf{M}}$ via a reduction B from **ℓ-OMDL**. B runs on input $(\mathbb{G}, \mathbf{g}, q)$, and is given oracle access to **chal** and **dlog**. B first queries $\mathbf{x} := \mathbf{chal}()$ and runs $\mathsf{M}(\mathbb{G}, \mathbf{g}, q, \mathbf{x})$. B runs the code of $\mathbf{G_1}$ except that (1) on M's j-th $\mathbf{Sign}_1$ query ($j \in [\ell]$), B returns $\mathbf{r}_j := \mathbf{chal}()$; (2) on M's j-th $\mathbf{Sign}_2$ query, B returns $s_j := \mathbf{dlog}(\mathbf{g}, \mathbf{r}_j \cdot \mathbf{x}^{c_j})$. (B answers M's $(\ell+1)$-th $\mathbf{Sign}_1$ query just as in $\mathbf{G_1}$, i.e., by sampling $r_{\ell+1} \xleftarrow{\$} \mathbb{Z}_q$ and returning $\mathbf{r}_{\ell+1} := \mathbf{g}^{r_{\ell+1}}$.) Finally, when M returns its final outputs, if there exists an $i \in [\ell+1]$ s.t. $\chi_i \neq 0$, B computes

$$x := \frac{s^*_i - \gamma^*_i - \sum_{j=1}^{\ell} \rho^*_{i,j} s_j - \rho^*_{i,\ell+1} r_{\ell+1}}{\chi_i}$$

and

$$r_j := s_j - c_j x,$$

and outputs $(x, r_1, \ldots, r_\ell)$. (If $\chi_i = 0$ for all i, B aborts.)

Clearly, B runs in time $t_{\mathsf{M}} + O(\ell + q_h)$. We claim that B wins **ℓ-OMDL** if M wins $\mathbf{G_1}$. Since M is algebraic, we have that

$$\mathbf{r}^*_i = \mathbf{g}^{\gamma^*_i} \cdot \mathbf{x}^{\xi^*_i} \cdot \prod_{j=1}^{\ell} \mathbf{r}_j^{\rho^*_{i,j}} \cdot \mathbf{r}_{\ell+1}^{\rho^*_{i,\ell+1}} = \mathbf{g}^{\gamma^*_i + \rho^*_{i,\ell+1} r_{\ell+1}} \cdot \mathbf{x}^{\xi^*_i} \cdot \prod_{j=1}^{\ell} \mathbf{r}_j^{\rho^*_{i,j}}.$$

On the other hand, since M wins $\mathbf{G_1}$, i.e., $(\mathbf{r}^*_i, s^*_i)$ is a valid forgery on message m^*_i, we have that

$$\mathbf{g}^{s^*_i} = \mathbf{r}^*_i \cdot \mathbf{x}^{c^*_i}.$$

The two equations above combined yield

$$\mathbf{x}^{c_i^*+\xi_i^*} \cdot \prod_{j=1}^{\ell} \mathbf{r}_j^{\rho_{i,j}^*} = \mathbf{g}^{s_i^*-\gamma_i^*-\rho_{i,\ell+1}^* r_{\ell+1}}. \tag{9}$$

By definition of s_j, we have that

$$\mathbf{r}_j = \frac{\mathbf{g}^{s_j}}{\mathbf{x}^{c_j}}, \tag{10}$$

substituting (10) into (9), we get

$$\mathbf{x}^{\chi_i} = \mathbf{x}^{c_i^*+\xi_i^*-\sum_{j=1}^{\ell}\rho_{i,j}^* c_j} = \mathbf{g}^{s_i^*-\gamma_i^*-\sum_{j=1}^{\ell}\rho_{i,j}^* s_j-\rho_{i,\ell+1}^* r_{\ell+1}},$$

so $x = \mathrm{dlog}\,\mathbf{x}$. By (10) again, $r_j = \mathrm{dlog}\,\mathbf{r}_j$. This means that B wins ℓ-**OMDL**. We have that

$$\mathsf{Adv}_{\mathsf{B},\ell}^{\mathbf{OMDL}} = \mathsf{Adv}_{\mathsf{M}}^{\mathbf{G_1}}.$$

We conclude that

$$\mathsf{Adv}_{\mathsf{B},\ell}^{\mathbf{OMDL}} \geq \mathsf{Adv}_{\mathsf{M},\ell,\mathsf{BSS}}^{\mathbf{SEQ\text{-}OMUF}} - \frac{q_h^2+q_h+2}{2q},$$

completing the proof. □

4.1 Optimality of Our Reduction

In this section, we show an impossibility result which states (roughly) that reducing ℓ-sequential one-more unforgeability of Schnorr's blind signature scheme from ℓ-**OMDL** (as shown in Sect. 4) is the best one can hope for. Concretely, we show that any algebraic reduction B that solves $(\ell-1)$-**OMDL** when provided with black-box access to a successful algebraic forger A in ℓ-**SEQ-OMUF**$_{\mathsf{BSS}}$, can be turned into an efficient adversary M against $(\ell-1)$-**OMDL**.

Algebraic Black Boxes. We consider a type of algebraic adversary that, apart from providing algebraic representations for each of its output group elements to the reduction, does not provide any further access (beyond black-box access). In particular, the reduction does not get access to the code of the adversary. This notion was previously put forth and used by Bauer et al. [8].

Theorem 3. [7] *Let* B *be an algebraic reduction that satisfies the following: if algorithm* A *is an algebraic black-box algorithm that runs in time* t_{A} *then*

$$\mathsf{Adv}_{\mathsf{B},\ell-1}^{\mathbf{OMDL}} = \epsilon_{\mathsf{B}}\left(\mathsf{Adv}_{\mathsf{A},\ell,\mathsf{BSS}}^{\mathbf{SEQ\text{-}OMUF}}\right)$$

[7] This theorem even holds for a weaker version of ℓ-**SEQ-OMUF**$_{\mathsf{BSS}}$ where the adversary A is required to output signatures for $\ell+1$ *distinct* messages.

and B *runs in time* $t_B(t_A)$. *(Here,* ϵ_B *and* t_B *are functions in the success probability and running time of* A*). Then there exists an algorithm* M *(the meta-reduction) such that*

$$\mathsf{Adv}^{\mathbf{OMDL}}_{\mathsf{M},\ell-1} \geq \epsilon_\mathsf{B}\left(\left(1-\frac{1}{q}\right)^\ell\right)$$

and M *runs in time* $t_M = t_B(O(\ell^3))$.

Proof Idea. We give a brief overview of the proof here, the detailed proof can be found in the full version [30]. We employ the meta-reduction technique [18]. Our meta-reduction provides the reduction with interfaces from the one-more discrete logarithm game as well as an algebraic black box forger for blind Schnorr signatures. It plays the OMDL game itself and forwards all oracle queries and responses, thereby providing the reduction with the interfaces of an OMDL challenger. The meta-reduction (in the role of the forger) first opens and closes all signing sessions before it makes its first hash query. We note that up to this point the only outputs made by the meta-reduction in the role of the forger have been uniformly random queries to the $\mathbf{Sign}_2$ oracle provided by the reduction, and thus independent of the algebraic representations output by the meta-reduction during the process. It then uses the algebraic representations output by the reduction as well as the responses from $\mathbf{Sign}_2$ to compute the secret key through means of linear algebra. The meta-reduction then starts making queries to the random oracle provided by the reduction and generating signatures, providing the discrete logarithm of its random commitments as a representation. Thus, all representations as well as all queries made by the reduction are independent from the algebraic representations that the reduction provides to the meta-reduction but not a to a real adversary. When the meta-reduction has output its signatures to the reduction, the reduction solves the OMDL challenge. The meta-reduction at this point only forwards the solution to its own OMDL challenger and wins whenever the reduction wins.

Doesn't this also Contradict Sect. 3*?* One may ask if it is possible to apply a similar meta-reduction technique to Abe's blind signature scheme or our partially blind variant, which would contradict our result from Sect. 3. However, this is not possible as the algebraic representations output by the reduction break the witness-indistinguishability of the scheme. The meta-reduction would only be able to compute the witness used by the reduction. Thus, the combination of representations provided by the adversary and signatures provided by the adversary would be dependent on the algebraic representations provided by the reduction.

Acknowledgements. We would like to thank Chenzhi Zhu and Stefano Tessaro for pointing out a flaw in a previous version of Claim 5. We would further like to thank the anonymous reviewers for their helpful feedback.

References

1. Abe, M.: A secure three-move blind signature scheme for polynomially many signatures. In: Pfitzmann, B. (ed.) EUROCRYPT 2001. LNCS, vol. 2045, pp. 136–151. Springer, Heidelberg (2001). https://doi.org/10.1007/3-540-44987-6_9
2. Abe, M., Fujisaki, E.: How to date blind signatures. In: Kim, K., Matsumoto, T. (eds.) ASIACRYPT 1996. LNCS, vol. 1163, pp. 244–251. Springer, Heidelberg (1996). https://doi.org/10.1007/BFb0034851
3. Abe, M., Okamoto, T.: Provably secure partially blind signatures. In: Bellare, M. (ed.) CRYPTO 2000. LNCS, vol. 1880, pp. 271–286. Springer, Heidelberg (2000). https://doi.org/10.1007/3-540-44598-6_17
4. Agrikola, T., Hofheinz, D., Kastner, J.: On instantiating the algebraic group model from falsifiable assumptions. In: Canteaut, A., Ishai, Y. (eds.) EUROCRYPT 2020. LNCS, vol. 12106, pp. 96–126. Springer, Cham (2020). https://doi.org/10.1007/978-3-030-45724-2_4
5. Kılınç Alper, H., Burdges, J.: Two-round trip Schnorr multi-signatures via delinearized witnesses. In: Malkin, T., Peikert, C. (eds.) CRYPTO 2021. LNCS, vol. 12825, pp. 157–188. Springer, Cham (2021). https://doi.org/10.1007/978-3-030-84242-0_7
6. Baldimtsi, F., Lysyanskaya, A.: Anonymous credentials light. In: Sadeghi, A.R., Gligor, V.D., Yung, M. (eds.) ACM CCS 2013, pp. 1087–1098. ACM Press (November 2013)
7. Baldimtsi, F., Lysyanskaya, A.: On the security of one-witness blind signature schemes. In: Sako, K., Sarkar, P. (eds.) ASIACRYPT 2013. LNCS, vol. 8270, pp. 82–99. Springer, Heidelberg (2013). https://doi.org/10.1007/978-3-642-42045-0_5
8. Bauer, B., Fuchsbauer, G., Loss, J.: A classification of computational assumptions in the algebraic group model. In: Micciancio, D., Ristenpart, T. (eds.) CRYPTO 2020. LNCS, vol. 12171, pp. 121–151. Springer, Cham (2020). https://doi.org/10.1007/978-3-030-56880-1_5
9. Bellare, M., Namprempre, C., Pointcheval, D., Semanko, M.: The one-more-RSA-inversion problems and the security of Chaum's blind signature scheme. J. Cryptol. **16**(3), 185–215 (2003)
10. Bellare, M., Rogaway, P.: Random oracles are practical: a paradigm for designing efficient protocols. In: Denning, D.E., Pyle, R., Ganesan, R., Sandhu, R.S., Ashby, V. (eds.) ACM CCS 93, pp. 62–73. ACM Press (November 1993)
11. Bellare, M., Rogaway, P.: Code-based game-playing proofs and the security of triple encryption. Cryptology ePrint Archive, Report 2004/331 (2004). https://eprint.iacr.org/2004/331
12. Benhamouda, F., Lepoint, T., Loss, J., Orrù, M., Raykova, M.: On the (in)security of ROS. In: Canteaut, A., Standaert, F.-X. (eds.) EUROCRYPT 2021. LNCS, vol. 12696, pp. 33–53. Springer, Cham (2021). https://doi.org/10.1007/978-3-030-77870-5_2
13. Boldyreva, A.: Threshold signatures, multisignatures and blind signatures based on the Gap-Diffie-Hellman-Group signature scheme. In: Desmedt, Y.G. (ed.) PKC 2003. LNCS, vol. 2567, pp. 31–46. Springer, Heidelberg (2003). https://doi.org/10.1007/3-540-36288-6_3
14. Boneh, D., Venkatesan, R.: Breaking RSA may not be equivalent to factoring. In: Nyberg, K. (ed.) EUROCRYPT 1998. LNCS, vol. 1403, pp. 59–71. Springer, Heidelberg (1998). https://doi.org/10.1007/BFb0054117

15. Bouaziz-Ermann, S., Canard, S., Eberhart, G., Kaim, G., Roux-Langlois, A., Traoré, J.: Lattice-based (partially) blind signature without restart. Cryptology ePrint Archive, Report 2020/260 (2020). https://eprint.iacr.org/2020/260
16. Brands, S.: Untraceable off-line cash in wallet with observers. In: Stinson, D.R. (ed.) CRYPTO 1993. LNCS, vol. 773, pp. 302–318. Springer, Heidelberg (1994). https://doi.org/10.1007/3-540-48329-2_26
17. Chaum, D.: Blind signatures for untraceable payments. In: Chaum, D., Rivest, R.L., Sherman, A.T. (eds.) Advances in Cryptology, pp. 199–203. Springer, Boston, MA (1983). https://doi.org/10.1007/978-1-4757-0602-4_18
18. Coron, J.-S.: Optimal security proofs for PSS and other signature schemes. In: Knudsen, L.R. (ed.) EUROCRYPT 2002. LNCS, vol. 2332, pp. 272–287. Springer, Heidelberg (2002). https://doi.org/10.1007/3-540-46035-7_18
19. Drijvers, M., et al.: On the security of two-round multi-signatures. In: 2019 IEEE Symposium on Security and Privacy, pp. 1084–1101. IEEE Computer Society Press (May 2019)
20. Fischlin, M.: Round-optimal composable blind signatures in the common reference string model. In: Dwork, C. (ed.) CRYPTO 2006. LNCS, vol. 4117, pp. 60–77. Springer, Heidelberg (2006). https://doi.org/10.1007/11818175_4
21. Fuchsbauer, G., Hanser, C., Slamanig, D.: Practical round-optimal blind signatures in the standard model. In: Gennaro, R., Robshaw, M. (eds.) CRYPTO 2015. LNCS, vol. 9216, pp. 233–253. Springer, Heidelberg (2015). https://doi.org/10.1007/978-3-662-48000-7_12
22. Fuchsbauer, G., Kiltz, E., Loss, J.: The algebraic group model and its applications. In: Shacham, H., Boldyreva, A. (eds.) CRYPTO 2018. LNCS, vol. 10992, pp. 33–62. Springer, Cham (2018). https://doi.org/10.1007/978-3-319-96881-0_2
23. Fuchsbauer, G., Plouviez, A., Seurin, Y.: Blind Schnorr signatures and signed ElGamal encryption in the algebraic group model. In: Canteaut, A., Ishai, Y. (eds.) EUROCRYPT 2020. LNCS, vol. 12106, pp. 63–95. Springer, Cham (2020). https://doi.org/10.1007/978-3-030-45724-2_3
24. Garg, S., Gupta, D.: Efficient round optimal blind signatures. In: Nguyen, P.Q., Oswald, E. (eds.) EUROCRYPT 2014. LNCS, vol. 8441, pp. 477–495. Springer, Heidelberg (2014). https://doi.org/10.1007/978-3-642-55220-5_27
25. Garg, S., Rao, V., Sahai, A., Schröder, D., Unruh, D.: Round optimal blind signatures. In: Rogaway, P. (ed.) CRYPTO 2011. LNCS, vol. 6841, pp. 630–648. Springer, Heidelberg (2011). https://doi.org/10.1007/978-3-642-22792-9_36
26. Ghoshal, A., Tessaro, S.: Tight state-restoration soundness in the algebraic group model. In: Malkin, T., Peikert, C. (eds.) CRYPTO 2021. LNCS, vol. 12827, pp. 64–93. Springer, Cham (2021). https://doi.org/10.1007/978-3-030-84252-9_3
27. Hauck, E., Kiltz, E., Loss, J.: A modular treatment of blind signatures from identification schemes. In: Ishai, Y., Rijmen, V. (eds.) EUROCRYPT 2019. LNCS, vol. 11478, pp. 345–375. Springer, Cham (2019). https://doi.org/10.1007/978-3-030-17659-4_12
28. Hauck, E., Kiltz, E., Loss, J., Nguyen, N.K.: Lattice-based blind signatures, revisited. In: Micciancio, D., Ristenpart, T. (eds.) CRYPTO 2020. LNCS, vol. 12171, pp. 500–529. Springer, Cham (2020). https://doi.org/10.1007/978-3-030-56880-1_18
29. Juels, A., Luby, M., Ostrovsky, R.: Security of blind digital signatures. In: Kaliski, B.S. (ed.) CRYPTO 1997. LNCS, vol. 1294, pp. 150–164. Springer, Heidelberg (1997). https://doi.org/10.1007/BFb0052233
30. Kastner, J., Loss, J., Xu, J.: On pairing-free blind signature schemes in the algebraic group model. Cryptology ePrint Archive, Report 2020/1071 (2020). https://eprint.iacr.org/2020/1071

31. Katz, J., Loss, J., Rosenberg, M.: Boosting the security of blind signature schemes. In: Tibouchi, M., Wang, H. (eds.) Advances in Cryptology, ASIACRYPT 2021. LNCS, vol. 13093. Springer, Cham (2021). https://doi.org/10.1007/978-3-030-92068-5_16
32. Nick, J., Ruffing, T., Seurin, Y.: MuSig2: simple two-round Schnorr multi-signatures. In: Malkin, T., Peikert, C. (eds.) CRYPTO 2021. LNCS, vol. 12825, pp. 189–221. Springer, Cham (2021). https://doi.org/10.1007/978-3-030-84242-0_8
33. Nicolosi, A., Krohn, M.N., Dodis, Y., Mazières, D.: Proactive two-party signatures for user authentication. In: NDSS 2003. The Internet Society (February 2003)
34. Ohkubo, M., Abe, M.: Security of some three-move blind signature schemes reconsidered. In: The 2003 Symposium on Cryptography and Information Security (2003)
35. Okamoto, T.: Provably secure and practical identification schemes and corresponding signature schemes. In: Brickell, E.F. (ed.) CRYPTO 1992. LNCS, vol. 740, pp. 31–53. Springer, Heidelberg (1993). https://doi.org/10.1007/3-540-48071-4_3
36. Okamoto, T.: Efficient blind and partially blind signatures without random oracles. In: Halevi, S., Rabin, T. (eds.) TCC 2006. LNCS, vol. 3876, pp. 80–99. Springer, Heidelberg (2006). https://doi.org/10.1007/11681878_5
37. Paillier, P., Vergnaud, D.: Discrete-log-based signatures may not be equivalent to discrete log. In: Roy, B. (ed.) ASIACRYPT 2005. LNCS, vol. 3788, pp. 1–20. Springer, Heidelberg (2005). https://doi.org/10.1007/11593447_1
38. Papachristoudis, D., Hristu-Varsakelis, D., Baldimtsi, F., Stephanides, G.: Leakage-resilient lattice-based partially blind signatures. IET Inf. Secur. **13**(6), 670–684 (2019)
39. Pointcheval, D.: Strengthened security for blind signatures. In: Nyberg, K. (ed.) EUROCRYPT 1998. LNCS, vol. 1403, pp. 391–405. Springer, Heidelberg (1998). https://doi.org/10.1007/BFb0054141
40. Pointcheval, D., Stern, J.: Provably secure blind signature schemes. In: Kim, K., Matsumoto, T. (eds.) ASIACRYPT 1996. LNCS, vol. 1163, pp. 252–265. Springer, Heidelberg (1996). https://doi.org/10.1007/BFb0034852
41. Pointcheval, D., Stern, J.: New blind signatures equivalent to factorization (extended abstract). In: Graveman, R., Janson, P.A., Neuman, C., Gong, L. (eds.) ACM CCS 1997, pp. 92–99. ACM Press (April 1997)
42. Pointcheval, D., Stern, J.: Security arguments for digital signatures and blind signatures. J. Cryptol. **13**(3), 361–396 (2000)
43. Rotem, L., Segev, G.: Algebraic distinguishers: from discrete logarithms to decisional Uber assumptions. In: Pass, R., Pietrzak, K. (eds.) TCC 2020. LNCS, vol. 12552, pp. 366–389. Springer, Cham (2020). https://doi.org/10.1007/978-3-030-64381-2_13
44. Schnorr, C.P.: Efficient identification and signatures for smart cards. In: Brassard, G. (ed.) CRYPTO 1989. LNCS, vol. 435, pp. 239–252. Springer, New York (1990). https://doi.org/10.1007/0-387-34805-0_22
45. Schnorr, C.P.: Security of blind discrete log signatures against interactive attacks. In: Qing, S., Okamoto, T., Zhou, J. (eds.) ICICS 2001. LNCS, vol. 2229, pp. 1–12. Springer, Heidelberg (2001). https://doi.org/10.1007/3-540-45600-7_1
46. Shoup, V.: Sequences of games: a tool for taming complexity in security proofs. Cryptology ePrint Archive, Report 2004/332 (2004). https://eprint.iacr.org/2004/332
47. Wagner, D.: A generalized birthday problem. In: Yung, M. (ed.) CRYPTO 2002. LNCS, vol. 2442, pp. 288–304. Springer, Heidelberg (2002). https://doi.org/10.1007/3-540-45708-9_19

Efficient Lattice-Based Blind Signatures via Gaussian One-Time Signatures

Vadim Lyubashevsky[1(✉)], Ngoc Khanh Nguyen[1,2], and Maxime Plancon[1,2]

[1] IBM Research, Zurich, Switzerland
[2] ETH Zurich, Zurich, Switzerland

Abstract. Lattice-based blind signature schemes have been receiving some recent attention lately. Earlier efficient 3-round schemes (Asiacrypt 2010, Financial Cryptography 2020) were recently shown to have mistakes in their proofs, and fixing them turned out to be extremely inefficient and limited the number of signatures that a signer could send to less than a dozen (Crypto 2020). In this work we propose a round-optimal, 2-round lattice-based blind signature scheme which produces signatures of length 150 KB. The running time of the signing protocol is linear in the maximum number signatures that can be given out, and this limits the number of signatures that can be signed per public key. Nevertheless, the scheme is still quite efficient when the number of signatures is limited to a few dozen thousand, and appears to currently be the most efficient lattice-based candidate.

Keywords: Lattice cryptography · Blind signatures

1 Introduction

Recent years have seen an influx of efficient lattice-based constructions of various cryptographic primitives. From zero-knowledge proofs [BLS19, YAZ+19, ESLL19, LNS20], to group signatures [dPLS18], and even Monero-like private payment systems [EZS+19, LNS21b], it now appears that a lot of fairly advanced privacy-enhancing constructions can be instantiated based on the potential quantum-safety of lattice problems. Somewhat surprisingly, though, there aren't any practical proposals of blind signatures.

Blind signatures, originally proposed by Chaum [Cha82] consist of an interactive procedure between a user and a signer in which the user would like to obtain the signature of a message μ under the public key of the signer, but not reveal the μ to the signer. Furthermore, after producing some certificate that he indeed has a signature of μ, the signer should not be able to figure out during which interaction this certificate was obtained. And of course, it is also required that the user cannot produce signatures by himself – that is, after interacting k times with the signer, the user should not be able to produce $k+1$ signatures.

A candidate for a 3-round lattice-based blind signature has been proposed by Ruckert [Rüc10], and then improved upon in [ABB20]. The proofs of these

G. Hanaoka et al. (Eds.): PKC 2022, LNCS 13178, pp. 498–527, 2022.
https://doi.org/10.1007/978-3-030-97131-1_17

schemes have, however, recently been shown to be incorrect [HKLN20]. At a high level, the difficulty that was incorrectly overcome was what prevented Pointcheval and Stern [PS00] from giving stronger proofs for Schnorr's blind signature. It recently turned out that the obstacle blocking the proof was real, and the full Schnorr blind signature has been completely broken [BLL+21]. It is thus quite possible that the errors in [Rüc10, ABB20] are not just mistakes in the proof.

There have since been other constructions of blind signatures, such as [HKLN20], which result in signatures being several (dozen) megabytes long and, more importantly, only allow one to securely sign less than a dozen messages per public key. Another recent proposal [ASY21] produces signatures that are almost as short as in regular lattice-based signatures (i.e. a few kilobytes); but the scheme has a few major downsides. The idea behind the scheme is for the user to encrypt his message μ, and then for the signer to run a (modified version of) the Dilithium lattice-based signature scheme [DKL+18] *homomorphically* by employing a fully-homomorphic encryption scheme. The user would then decrypt and reveal the signature. This approach entails evaluating cryptographic hash functions homomorphically. Furthermore, as it is, the scheme is only blind with respect to an honest signer. To protect against a malicious signer, the signer would be required to give a zero-knowledge proof that the homomorphic evaluation of the signing procedure was done correctly. The extremely heavy tools required for communication between the user and signer almost certainly put this scheme into the theoretical category.

1.1 Our Results

We propose a practical two-round lattice-based blind signature scheme with two restrictions. The first is that the signer is required to keep a counter as a state. Secondly, the running time of signature generation and verification is linear in the total number of signatures allowed by the scheme, and so it seems reasonable to put a limit of the total number of signatures to somewhere under 2^{20}.[1]

The signature size is around 150 KB, and the interaction between the user and the signer is approximately 16 MB. The size of the public key is a little over a megabyte. The 150 KB signatures are about 50X longer than the signature size of regular lattice signatures (e.g. [DKL+18, PFH+17], but as far as we're aware these are the shortest (instantiable and having a security proof) blind signatures which are potentially quantum-safe. Even though the communication between the user and the signer is large, all operations are efficient operations on polynomials which have been extensively optimized in recent works on lattice cryptography, and so time-wise, it should be rather efficient. We should mention that the running time of the interaction between the user and the signer is

[1] If one is content with a relaxed definition of blindness where a signature is hidden among T user-signer interactions, then the running time of the scheme can be kept to $O(T)$. This is not a standard definition of a blind signature, but we just mention this possibility in case it's good enough for an application.

independent of the total number of signatures, and it's only the user's offline time after interacting with the signer that is linear in the total number of signatures.

A part of our construction requires the use of lattice-based one-time signatures, and we employ ideas from the scheme in [LM18]. In the current paper, we need to use Gaussian-generated secret keys (because in the scheme, they will be sampled using a trapdoor, and the most efficient such algorithm produces Gaussians) unlike the uniform ones used in that paper, and so we develop a different, and arguably easier, security proof for the one-time signature scheme. The developed techniques for analyzing the security of the one-time signature are then extended to prove security of our blind signature and we believe that they can sometimes be used in lieu of analysis that employs Renyi techniques. We believe that this contribution could be potentially of interest in other works.

1.2 Scheme Overview

Let N be the maximum number of messages that can be signed. For each N, we will create a public key and secret key pair for a one-time signature scheme. The N public key pairs are polynomial vectors $(\mathbf{v}_i, \mathbf{w}_i)$, and the corresponding secret keys are polynomial vectors $(\mathbf{s}_i, \mathbf{y}_i)$ with small coefficients satisfying $\mathbf{A}\mathbf{s}_i = \mathbf{v}_i$ and $\mathbf{A}\mathbf{y}_i = \mathbf{w}_i$. All the polynomials are in the polynomial ring $\mathbb{Z}_q[X]/(X^d + 1)$. The matrix $\mathbf{A}$, which is also part of the public key, is generated by the signer together with a trapdoor which allows him to produce the aforementioned short polynomial vectors $\mathbf{s}_i$ and $\mathbf{y}_i$. The public keys $(\mathbf{v}_i, \mathbf{w}_i)$ are uniformly-random and therefore do not need to be stored, as they can simply be defined as $\mathcal{H}(i) = (\mathbf{v}_i, \mathbf{w}_i)$, where $\mathcal{H}$ is some cryptographic hash function such as SHAKE. Thus the public key size is dominated by $\mathbf{A}$ and is not dependent on N.

The message μ is a polynomial with very small, i.e. $-1/0/1$ coefficients, and the signing process begins by the user sending an encryption $\mathbf{c} = \mathsf{enc}(\mu)$. The signer's goal is to apply a function f to $\mathbf{c}$ such that $\mathsf{dec}(f(\mathbf{c})) = \mathbf{s}_i\mu + \mathbf{y}_i$. The signer thus sends $f(\mathbf{c})$ to the user, and the latter obtains $\mathbf{z} = \mathbf{s}_i\mu + \mathbf{y}_i$ by applying dec. The vector $\mathbf{z}$ has small coefficients and satisfies the relation

$$\mathbf{A}\mathbf{z} = \mathbf{v}_i\mu + \mathbf{w}_i. \tag{1}$$

The vector $\mathbf{z}$ is a signature of μ, but the user cannot reveal it in the clear because that would allow the signer to link the message to the instance during which it was signed. Instead, the user outputs a zero-knowledge proof of knowledge of a $\mathbf{z}$ with small coefficients satisfying (1) for some $(\mathbf{v}_i, \mathbf{w}_i)$ from a set. Such a compact proof, whose size is logarithmic in N, was given in [LNS21b]. Since this proof does not reveal the $\mathbf{z}$ nor the specific $(\mathbf{v}_i, \mathbf{w}_i)$ from the set of public keys, the blindness property is preserved.

The main technical part of this work is showing that for our specific functions $\mathsf{enc}, \mathsf{dec}$, and f, the message μ is hidden, and that $f(\mathbf{c})$ does not leak enough information about the signer's keys $\mathbf{s}_i, \mathbf{y}_i$. In particular, the user who obtains $f(\mathbf{c})$ should not be able to produce two different $(\mathbf{z}, \mu), (\mathbf{z}', \mu')$ satisfying (1).

An easy solution for hiding the μ and not having $f(\mathbf{c})$ leak anything would be to use a circuit-private homomorphic encryption scheme; but this would be overkill. We instead show a solution, which is similar in intuition to the one-time signature proof idea in [LM18], which does not require the secrets $\mathbf{s}_i$ and $\mathbf{y}_i$ to be completely hidden either by drowning them with noise or applying a Renyi entropy argument. Instead, it's enough to show that $\mathbf{z}$ does not leak the exact $\mathbf{s}_i$ and $\mathbf{y}_i$. And in this case, coming up with another signature is as hard as solving the SIS problem.

We now give some more details. To improve readability, we will drop the subscripts i from the secret and public keys. Because all the keys are independent, we can prove things about individual public/secret key pairs. The $\mathsf{enc}(\mu)$ procedure is essentially an LWE public key encryption scheme in which the user both does the encrypting and decrypting. So the public key consists of a random matrix $\mathbf{B}$ and a polynomial vector $\mathbf{b}^T = \mathbf{x}^T\mathbf{B}$, where $\mathbf{x}$ is a polynomial vector with small coefficients. The $\mathsf{enc}(\mu)$ function samples random small-coefficient polynomial vectors $\mathbf{r}, \mathbf{e}$ and a polynomial e', and outputs the ciphertext $(\mathbf{t}, t') = (\mathbf{Br} + p\mathbf{e}, \mathbf{b}^T\mathbf{r} + pe' + \mu)$, where p is a "large-enough" prime. This ciphertext, along with a zero-knowledge proof that it was properly computed (i.e. that $\mathbf{r}, \mathbf{e}, e', \mu$ have small coefficients) is sent to the signer. The zero-knowledge proof can be created using the fairly-efficient recent techniques from [ALS20, ENS20, LNS21a].

The signer now needs to create an encryption of $\mathbf{z} = \mathbf{s}\mu + \mathbf{y}$. He does this by creating an encryption of each coefficient comprising $\mathbf{z}$ independently. In particular, if $\mathbf{s} = \begin{bmatrix} s_1 \\ \dots \\ s_\alpha \end{bmatrix}$ and $\mathbf{y} = \begin{bmatrix} y_1 \\ \dots \\ y_\alpha \end{bmatrix}$, then for each $1 \leqslant j \leqslant \alpha$, the signer computes

$$s_j\mathbf{t} = \mathbf{Br}s_j + p\mathbf{e}s_j \tag{2}$$

$$y_j + s_jt' = \mathbf{b}^T\mathbf{r}s_j + pe's_j + (\mu s_j + y_j). \tag{3}$$

Because $\mathbf{r}, \mathbf{e}, e'$, and s_j have small coefficients, and assuming that all the coefficients of $(\mu s_j + y_j)$ are less than p, the above is an encryption of $(\mu s_j + y_j)$. That is, one would decrypt in the usual way by computing

$$(y_j + s_jt') - \mathbf{x}^T s_j\mathbf{t} \bmod p = \mu s_j + y_j.$$

It's unclear however, whether sending (2) and (3) is secure on the signer's part. That is, he is possibly leaking too much information about $\mathbf{s}$ and $\mathbf{y}$. Instead of (2) and (3), he therefore sends the "masked" equations

$$s_j\mathbf{t} + \mathbf{By}'_j + p\mathbf{y}''_j = \mathbf{B}(\mathbf{r}s_j + \mathbf{y}'_j) + p(\mathbf{e}s_j + \mathbf{y}''_j) \tag{4}$$

$$y_j + s_jt' + \mathbf{b}^T\mathbf{y}'_j + py''' = \mathbf{b}^T(\mathbf{r}s_j + \mathbf{y}'_j) + p(e's_j + y'''_j) + (\mu s_j + y_j), \tag{5}$$

where $\mathbf{y}'_j, \mathbf{y}''_j$, and y'''_j are (vectors of) polynomials with small coefficients. As long as these coefficients are small enough, one should still be able to decrypt $\mu s_j + y_j$ as before. We will now outline the proof showing that an adversary who is able to produce a signature other than $\mu\mathbf{s} + \mathbf{y}$ for the public key $(\mathbf{v}, \mathbf{w})$ and message μ can solve the SIS problem.

In the real scheme, the public key is set as $(\mathbf{v}, \mathbf{w}) = \mathcal{H}(i)$, and then the $\mathbf{s}, \mathbf{y}$ are sampled using a trapdoor for $\mathbf{A}$. In the security proof, we will instead get a random $\mathbf{A}$ from the challenger, sample the $\mathbf{s}, \mathbf{y}$, and then program the random oracle $\mathcal{H}(i) = (\mathbf{v} = \mathbf{A}\mathbf{s}, \mathbf{w} = \mathbf{A}\mathbf{y})$. Because the trap-doored matrix is indistinguishable from uniform [MP12] and the standard deviation of $\mathbf{s}, \mathbf{y}$ is above the smoothing parameter [MR07], the two distributions are indistinguishable. The reduction's goal is to now solve SIS for the matrix $\mathbf{A}$.

Because the reduction knows the secret keys $\mathbf{s}, \mathbf{y}$, it can produce the responses in (4) and (5). Now, suppose that an adversary who sees (4) and (5) is able to create two valid signatures $\mathbf{z}, \mathbf{z}'$ (with small coefficients) for two messages $\mu \neq \mu'$ satisfying[2]

$$\mathbf{A}\mathbf{z} = \mathbf{v}\mu + \mathbf{w} \tag{6}$$

$$\mathbf{A}\mathbf{z}' = \mathbf{v}\mu' + \mathbf{w}. \tag{7}$$

Plugging in $(\mathbf{v} = \mathbf{A}\mathbf{s}, \mathbf{w} = \mathbf{A}\mathbf{y})$ and subtracting, the reduction obtains

$$\mathbf{A}(\mathbf{z} - \mathbf{z}') = \mathbf{A}((\mathbf{s}(\mu - \mu')). \tag{8}$$

Thus, if

$$\mathbf{z} - \mathbf{z}' \neq \mathbf{s}(\mu - \mu'), \tag{9}$$

the reduction extracted a solution to SIS. The crucial part is now proving that the signatures produced by the forger will indeed satisfy this inequality with some non-negligible probability. Notice that if $\mathbf{z} - \mathbf{z}' = \mathbf{s}(\mu - \mu')$, then one has also has extracted $\mathbf{s}$ (because the coefficients of $\mathbf{s}(\mu - \mu')$ are small-enough that no reduction modulo q takes place and so the ring $\mathbb{Z}[X]/(X^d + 1)$ is an integral domain, and so one can simply divide by $\mu - \mu'$). In other words, the reduction can either extract a solution to SIS from the adversary, or the adversary "knows" the value $\mathbf{s}$ that was used by the reduction. The former is the computational assumption upon which the scheme is based, while the latter, we will show, is information-theoretically impossible except with probability at most $1 - \delta$. It's important to point out that the latter holds *for all* views that contain the public key and equations (4) and (5). Therefore, it is impossible for an adversary to always extract the correct $\mathbf{s}$, and so (9) will be satisfied with probability at least δ. So if an adversary succeeds in a forgery with probability ϵ,the reduction will solve SIS with probability $\epsilon\delta$.

We now need to show that that despite knowing the public keys and having access to (4) and (5), the adversary still cannot *information-theoretically* determine the exact value $\mathbf{s}$. Consider the possibility that instead of the vector $\mathbf{s}$, we sampled the vector $\tilde{\mathbf{s}} = \mathbf{s} + \mathbf{u}$, where $\mathbf{u}$ satisfies $\mathbf{A}\mathbf{u} = \mathbf{0}$. This is a valid pre-image for the public key $\mathbf{v} = \mathbf{A}\mathbf{s} = \mathbf{A}(\mathbf{s} + \mathbf{u})$, and in order to also satisfy (4),(5), we would need to have sampled, instead of $\mathbf{y}, \mathbf{y}', \mathbf{y}''$, and y''',

[2] The first signature $\mathbf{z}$ on a message μ is already given to the adversary in (4) and (5), so he really just has to produce a second one.

$$\tilde{\mathbf{y}} = \mathbf{y} - \mu\mathbf{u} \tag{10}$$

$$\tilde{\mathbf{y}}'_j = \mathbf{y}'_j - u_j\mathbf{r} \tag{11}$$

$$\tilde{\mathbf{y}}''_j = \mathbf{y}''_j - u_j\mathbf{e} \tag{12}$$

$$\tilde{y}'''_j = y'''_j - u_j e'. \tag{13}$$

To complete the proof, we need to show that the event that $\mathbf{s}, \mathbf{y}, \mathbf{y}'_j, \mathbf{y}''_j, y'''_j$ are sampled, conditioned on the view of the adversary, is not overly dominant. For simplicity, let's just look at $\mathbf{s}$ and the alternative $\tilde{\mathbf{s}} = \mathbf{s} + \mathbf{u}$; incorporating the $\tilde{\mathbf{y}}, \tilde{\mathbf{y}}', \tilde{\mathbf{y}}'', \tilde{y}'''$ in the analysis is done in a similar manner.

If $\mathbf{s}$ is sampled from $\mathbb{Z}^m$ according to a Gaussian distribution with standard deviation σ – that is the distribution is proportional to $\left(\frac{1}{\sqrt{2\pi}\sigma}\right)^m \cdot \rho_\sigma(\mathbf{x})$, where $\rho_\sigma(\mathbf{x}) = e^{-\|\mathbf{x}\|^2/2\sigma^2}$, then the conditional probability that $\mathbf{s}$ is some $\mathbf{s}^*$ satisfying $\mathbf{v} = \mathbf{A}\mathbf{s}^*$ is

$$\Pr_{\mathbf{s}^*}[\mathbf{s}* = \mathbf{s}|\mathbf{A}\mathbf{s} = \mathbf{v}] = \frac{\rho_\sigma(\mathbf{s})}{\sum\limits_{\mathbf{u}\in\mathbf{\Lambda}} \rho_\sigma(\mathbf{s}-\mathbf{u})} \leqslant \frac{1}{\sum\limits_{\mathbf{u}\in\mathbf{\Lambda}} \rho_\sigma(\mathbf{u})}, \tag{14}$$

where the last inequality is implicit in the proof of [AR04, Lemma 3.2]. In Theorem 3.3, we then show that when $\sigma \approx q^{n/m}$, the above inequality is less than $\frac{1}{2}$, and so even an all-powerful adversary cannot know the exact $\mathbf{s}^*$.

In Sect. 3, as an interlude, we also use the same techniques to give an instantiation of the one-time signature from [LM18] where the secret keys are Gaussians. In particular, the one-time signatures are just the blind signatures without the blinding part and without the user needing to hide the public key that was used to sign the message. That is, there is no user and no equations (4) and (5). The signer simply sends $\mathbf{z} = \mathbf{s}\mu + \mathbf{y}$ as his signature of μ, and the verifier checks that $\|\mathbf{z}\|$ is small and $\mathbf{A}\mathbf{z} = \mathbf{v}\mu + \mathbf{w}$. This is exactly the template from [LM18], but with a different security proof which crucially uses the fact that the secret keys are Gaussian instead of uniform. It seems that both instantiations are about equally efficient, but we include this instantiation in case a Gaussian-based scheme is useful for some application, similarly to how it was extended in this paper.

As a side note, we would like to draw attention to the advantage of our proof over a more "generic" one that would use Renyi entropy arguments (e.g. [BLL+15]) to show that not enough information about $\mathbf{s}$ is leaked in (4) and (5)). Using such arguments would require to set the standard deviations of $\mathbf{y}, \mathbf{y}'$, etc. to be at least as large as $\|\mathbf{s}\mu\|, \|\mathbf{r}s_j\|$, etc. Our proof technique, on the other hand, only needs the standard deviation to be approximately $q^{n/m}$, which is siginficantly smaller because just $\mathbf{s}$ has standard deviation at least that. In fact, somewhat counter-intuitively, one does not even need the "mask" $\mathbf{y}$ to have larger standard deviation than $\|\mathbf{s}\mu\|$. This is a rather different situation than in signature schemes where the role of $\mathbf{y}$ is to make the distribution of $\mathbf{y} + \mathbf{s}\mu$ independent of $\mathbf{s}$.

We remark, however, that our technique cannot replace the Renyi argument everywhere. For our technique to be applicable, the reduction needs to know the secret values when performing the simulation, because we do not make any claims about what the output distribution looks like. Renyi proofs, on the other hand, argue that the resulting distribution is "close-enough" to some distribution which can be sampled without knowing the secret.

2 Preliminaries

2.1 Notation

Let q be an odd prime and λ be a security parameter. In this paper we aim for 128-bit security. Unless stated otherwise, all algorithms are implicitly given a security parameter in unary. The joint execution of two algorithms $\mathcal{A}$ and $\mathcal{B}$ in an interactive protocol with private inputs x to $\mathcal{A}$ and y to $\mathcal{B}$ is written as $(a, b) \leftarrow \langle \mathcal{A}(x), \mathcal{B}(y) \rangle$ where a and b are the private outputs of $\mathcal{A}$ and $\mathcal{B}$ respectively.

We write $x \leftarrow S$ when $x \in S$ is sampled uniformly at random from the finite set S and similarly $x \leftarrow D$ when x is sampled according to the discrete distribution D. The statistical distance between two probability distributions X and Y over a countable set D is defined as $\Delta(X, Y) = \sum_{d \in D} |X(d) - Y(d)|$. For integer $n \in \mathbb{N}$, we define $[n] := \{1, 2, \ldots, n\}$. Given two functions $f, g : \mathbb{N} \to [0, 1]$, we write $f(\mu) \approx g(\mu)$ if $|f(\mu) - g(\mu)| < \mu^{-\omega(1)}$. A function f is negligible if $f \approx 0$. We write $\mathsf{negl}(n)$ to denote an unspecified negligible function in n.

2.2 Lattices

Let $\mathbf{B} = \{\mathbf{b}_1, \ldots, \mathbf{b}_n\}$ consist of n linearly independent vectors. The n-dimensional lattice generated by B is defined as

$$\mathbf{\Lambda} = \mathcal{L}(\mathbf{B}) = \left\{ \sum_{i=1}^{n} c_i \mathbf{b}_i : c_1, \ldots, c_n \in \mathbb{Z} \right\}.$$

The dual lattice of $\mathbf{\Lambda}$ is defined as $\mathbf{\Lambda}^* = \{\mathbf{x} \in \mathbb{R}^n : \forall \mathbf{v} \in \mathbf{\Lambda}, \langle \mathbf{x}, \mathbf{v} \rangle \in \mathbb{Z}\}$. We denote $\tilde{\mathbf{B}}$ to be the Gram-Schmidt orthogonalization of $\mathbf{B}$.

For a power of two d, denote $\mathcal{R}$ and $\mathcal{R}_q$ respectively to be the rings $\mathbb{Z}[X]/(X^d + 1)$ and $\mathbb{Z}_q[X]/(X^d + 1)$. Unless stated otherwise, lower-case letters denote elements in $\mathcal{R}$ or $\mathcal{R}_q$ and bold lower-case (resp. upper-case) letters represent column vectors (resp. matrices) with coefficients in $\mathcal{R}$ or $\mathcal{R}_q$.

For an element $w \in \mathbb{Z}_q$, we write $\|w\|_\infty$ to mean $|w \bmod^{\pm} q|$. Define the ℓ_∞ and ℓ_p norms for $w = w_0 + w_1 X + \ldots + w_{d-1} X^{d-1} \in \mathcal{R}$ as follows:

$$\|w\|_\infty = \max_j \|w_j\|_\infty, \quad \|w\|_p = \sqrt[p]{\|w_0\|_\infty^p + \ldots + \|w_{d-1}\|_\infty^p}.$$

If $w = (w_1, \ldots, w_m) \in \mathcal{R}^k$, then

$$\|\mathbf{w}\|_\infty = \max_j \|w_j\|_\infty, \quad \|\mathbf{w}\|_p = \sqrt[p]{\|w_1\|^p + \ldots + \|w_k\|^p}.$$

By default, $\|\mathbf{w}\| := \|\mathbf{w}\|_2$. Similarly, we define the norms for vectors over $\mathbb{Z}_q$. Denote $S_\gamma = \{x \in \mathcal{R}_q : \|x\|_\infty \leqslant \gamma\}$.

For a matrix $\mathbf{A} \in \mathbb{Z}_q^{n\times m}$, we define the module q-ary lattice as:

$$\mathbf{\Lambda}_q^\perp(\mathbf{A}) := \{\mathbf{x} \in \mathbb{Z}^m : \mathbf{A}\mathbf{x} = \mathbf{0} \bmod q\}.$$

Similarly, when $\mathbf{A} \in \mathcal{R}_q^{n\times m}$ then:

$$\mathbf{\Lambda}_{\mathcal{R}_q}^\perp(\mathbf{A}) := \{\mathbf{x} \in \mathcal{R}^m : \mathbf{A}\mathbf{x} = \mathbf{0} \text{ over } \mathcal{R}_q\}.$$

For a polynomial $f = f_0 + f_1X + \ldots + f_{d-1}X^{d-1} \in \mathcal{R}$, we define the rotation matrix $\mathsf{Rot}(f) \in \mathbb{Z}^{d\times d}$ as:

$$\mathsf{Rot}(f) = \begin{bmatrix} f_0 & -f_{d-1} & \cdots & -f_1 \\ f_1 & f_0 & \cdots & -f_2 \\ \vdots & \vdots & \ddots & \vdots \\ f_{d-1} & f_{d-2} & \cdots & f_0 \end{bmatrix}.$$

Similarly, for a matrix $\mathbf{F} = (f_{i,j}) \in \mathcal{R}_q^{n\times m}$, we define

$$\mathsf{Rot}(\mathbf{F}) = \begin{bmatrix} \mathsf{Rot}(f_{1,1}) & \mathsf{Rot}(f_{1,2}) & \ldots & \mathsf{Rot}(f_{1,m}) \\ \vdots & \vdots & \vdots & \vdots \\ \mathsf{Rot}(f_{n,1}) & \mathsf{Rot}(f_{n,2}) & \ldots & \mathsf{Rot}(f_{n,m}) \end{bmatrix} \in \mathbb{Z}^{nd\times md}.$$

2.3 Discrete Gaussian Distribution on Lattices

For any $\sigma > 0$, we define the Gaussian function on $\mathbb{R}^n$ centered at $\mathbf{c} \in \mathbb{R}^n$ with parameter σ as:

$$\forall \mathbf{x} \in \mathbb{R}^n, \rho_{\sigma,\mathbf{c}}(\mathbf{x}) := \exp\left(-\|\mathbf{x} - \mathbf{c}\|^2/2\sigma^2\right).$$

More generally, if $\sigma = (\sigma_1, \ldots, \sigma^n) \in \mathbb{R}^n_{>0}$ then we define $\rho_{\sigma,\mathbf{c}}(\mathbf{x}) = \prod_{i=1}^n \rho_{\sigma_i,c_i}(x_i)$[3]. When we omit the subscript $\mathbf{c}$, we set $\mathbf{c} = \mathbf{0}$ by default.

Let $\mathbf{c} \in \mathbb{R}^n, \sigma > 0$ and $\mathbf{\Lambda}$ be a n-dimensional lattice. We now define the discrete Gaussian distribution over a lattice $\mathbf{\Lambda}$ as

$$\forall \mathbf{x} \in \mathbf{\Lambda}, D_{\mathbf{\Lambda},\sigma,\mathbf{c}}(\mathbf{x}) := \frac{\rho_{\sigma,\mathbf{c}}(\mathbf{x})}{\rho_{\sigma,\mathbf{c}}(\mathbf{\Lambda})}.$$

As above, we may omit the subscript $\mathbf{c}$. Also, we drop the subscript $\mathbf{\Lambda}$ when $\mathbf{\Lambda} = \mathbb{Z}^n$ and denote it as $D^n_{\sigma,\mathbf{c}}$.

We recall the definition of a smoothing parameter [MR07].

---

[3] One could define the Gaussian function more generally using a covariance matrix. However, we will not need such a general case and thus we omit it for presentation purposes.

Definition 2.1. *Let $\mathbf{\Lambda}$ be an n-dimensional lattice and $\varepsilon > 0$. Then, the smoothing parameter $\eta_\varepsilon(\mathbf{\Lambda})$ is the smallest real $s > 0$ such that $\rho_{\frac{1}{\sqrt{2\pi}s}}(\mathbf{\Lambda}^* \backslash \{\mathbf{0}\}) \leqslant \varepsilon$.*

We will use the following upper-bound on the smoothing parameter.

Lemma 2.2 ([GPV08]). *For any n-dimensional lattice $\mathbf{\Lambda}$ with basis $\mathbf{B}$ and $\varepsilon > 0$, we have:*

$$\eta_\varepsilon(\mathbf{\Lambda}) \leqslant \|\tilde{\mathbf{B}}\| \cdot \sqrt{\ln(2n/(1+1/\varepsilon))/\pi}.$$

The next fact states that the total Gaussian measure on any translation of the lattice is essentially the same.

Lemma 2.3 ([MR07]). *Let $\mathbf{\Lambda}$ be an n-dimensional lattice. Then, for any $\varepsilon \in (0,1)$, $\sigma \geqslant \eta_\varepsilon(\mathbf{\Lambda})$ and $\mathbf{c} \in \mathbb{R}^n$, we have*

$$\rho_{\sigma,\mathbf{c}}(\mathbf{\Lambda}) \in \left[\frac{1-\varepsilon}{1+\varepsilon}, 1\right] \cdot \rho_\sigma(\mathbf{\Lambda}).$$

In this paper we will apply the following simple corollary and provide the proof in the full version of the paper.

Corollary 2.4. *Let $\mathbf{\Lambda}, \mathbf{\Lambda}'$ be n-dimensional lattices and $\mathbf{\Lambda}' \subseteq \mathbf{\Lambda}$. Then, for any $\varepsilon \in (0, \frac{1}{2}]$, $\sigma \geqslant \eta_\varepsilon(\mathbf{\Lambda}')$, define the following probability distributions D_1, D_2:*

- *D_1: first sample $\mathbf{x} \leftarrow D_{\mathbf{\Lambda},\sigma}$ and output $(\mathbf{x}, \mathbf{t} := \mathbf{x} \bmod \mathbf{\Lambda}')$,*
- *D_2: first generate $\mathbf{t}$ uniformly at random from $\mathbf{\Lambda} \backslash \mathbf{\Lambda}'$ and then sample $\mathbf{x} \leftarrow D_{\mathbf{\Lambda},\sigma}$ conditioned on $\mathbf{t} = \mathbf{x} \bmod \mathbf{\Lambda}'$. Output $(\mathbf{x}, \mathbf{t})$.*

Then, $\Delta(D_1, D_2) \leqslant 4\varepsilon$.

We will use the following tail bound from [Ban93,Lyu12].

Lemma 2.5. *Let $m, k > 1, \mathbf{\Lambda}$ be m-dimensional lattice and $\mathbf{c} \in \mathbb{Z}^m$. Then*

1. $\Pr_{z \leftarrow D_\sigma}[|z| > k\sigma] \leqslant 2e^{\frac{-k^2}{2}}$.
2. $\Pr_{\mathbf{z} \leftarrow D_\sigma^m}[\|\mathbf{z}\|_2 > k\sigma\sqrt{m}] \leqslant k^m e^{\frac{m}{2}(1-k^2)}$.
3. $\Pr_{\mathbf{z} \leftarrow D_{\mathbf{\Lambda},\sigma,\mathbf{c}}^m}[\|\mathbf{z}\|_2 > k\sigma\sqrt{m}] \leqslant 2k^m e^{\frac{m}{2}(1-k^2)}$.

2.4 Module-SIS and Module-LWE Problems

Security of our blind signature scheme relies on the well-known computational lattice problems, namely Module-LWE (MLWE) and Module-SIS (MSIS) [LS15]. Both problems are defined over $\mathcal{R}_q$.

Definition 2.6 ($\mathsf{MSIS}_{n,m,B}$). *Given $\mathbf{A} \leftarrow \mathcal{R}_q^{n\times m}$, the* Module-SIS *problem with parameters $n, m > 0$ and $0 < B < q$ asks to find $\mathbf{z} \in \mathcal{R}_q^m$ such that $\mathbf{A}\mathbf{z} = \mathbf{0}$ over $\mathcal{R}_q$ and $0 < \|\mathbf{z}\| \leqslant B$. An algorithm $\mathcal{A}$ is said to have advantage ϵ in solving* $\mathsf{MSIS}_{n,m,B}$ *if*

$$\Pr\left[0 < \|\mathbf{z}\| \leqslant B \wedge \mathbf{A}\mathbf{z} = \mathbf{0} \,\middle|\, \mathbf{A} \leftarrow \mathcal{R}_q^{n\times m};\ \mathbf{z} \leftarrow \mathcal{A}(\mathbf{A})\right] \geqslant \epsilon.$$

Definition 2.7 ($\mathsf{MLWE}_{n,m,\chi}$). *The* Module-LWE *problem with parameters* $n, m > 0$ *and an error distribution* χ *over* $\mathcal{R}$ *asks the adversary* $\mathcal{A}$ *to distinguish between the following two cases: 1)* $(\mathbf{A}, \mathbf{As} + \mathbf{e})$ *for* $\mathbf{A} \leftarrow \mathcal{R}_q^{n\times m}$*, a secret vector* $\mathbf{s} \leftarrow \chi^m$ *and error vector* $\mathbf{e} \leftarrow \chi^n$*, and 2)* $(\mathbf{A}, \mathbf{b}) \leftarrow \mathcal{R}_q^{n\times m} \times \mathcal{R}_q^m$*. Then,* $\mathcal{A}$ *is said to have advantage* ϵ *in solving* $\mathsf{MLWE}_{n,m,\chi}$ *if*

$$\begin{aligned}\big|\Pr\big[b = 1 \,\big|\, \mathbf{A} \leftarrow \mathcal{R}_q^{n\times m}; \mathbf{s} \leftarrow \chi^m; \mathbf{e} \leftarrow \chi^n; b \leftarrow \mathcal{A}(\mathbf{A}, \mathbf{As} + \mathbf{e})\big] \\ - \Pr\big[b = 1 \,\big|\, \mathbf{A} \leftarrow \mathcal{R}_q^{n\times m}; \mathbf{b} \leftarrow \mathcal{R}_q^n; b \leftarrow \mathcal{A}(\mathbf{A}, \mathbf{b})\big]\big| \geqslant \epsilon.\end{aligned} \tag{15}$$

2.5 Blind Signatures

We present a definition of a blind signature where the signer is stateful and a user is allowed to make at most $k = \mathsf{poly}(\lambda)$ queries.

Definition 2.8. *A* k*-time stateful blind signature scheme* BS *consists of PPT algorithms* $\mathsf{BS.KeyGen}$, $\mathsf{BS.Ver}$ *along with two interactive PPT algorithms* $\mathcal{S}$ *and* $\mathcal{U}$ *such that*

- $\mathsf{BS.KeyGen}(1^\lambda, 1^k)$*: given a security parameter* λ *and maximum number of signing queries* k*, it outputs a private/verification key pair* $(\mathsf{sk}, \mathsf{pk})$*,*
- *For* $i \in [k]$*, the joint execution of* $\mathcal{S}(\mathsf{sk}, i)$ *and* $\mathcal{U}(\mathsf{pk}, m)$*, where* $m \in \{0,1\}^*$*, generates an output* σ_i *for the user* $\mathcal{U}$ *and no output for* $\mathcal{S}$*, i.e.*

$$(\perp, \sigma) \leftarrow \langle \mathcal{S}(\mathsf{sk}, i), \mathcal{U}(\mathsf{pk}, m)\rangle$$

- $\mathsf{BS.Ver}(\mathsf{pk}, m, \sigma)$*: given a verification key* pk*, message* m *and signature* σ*, it outputs a bit* b*.*

The main difference from previous works is the fact that $\mathcal{S}$ has the additional input i which can be seen as a state. Indeed, if the message m and random coins in the system are fixed, then it might still be the case that for $i \neq j$, the interaction between $\mathcal{S}(\mathsf{sk}, i)$ and $\mathcal{U}(\mathsf{pk}, m)$ would be different than the interaction between $\mathcal{S}(\mathsf{sk}, j)$ and $\mathcal{U}(\mathsf{pk}, m)$.

In general, blind signatures must satisfy three properties: (i) correctness, (ii) blindness and (iii) one-more unforgeability. We adapt these standard properties to k-time stateful blind signatures in an intuitive way.

Definition 2.9 (Correctness). *A* k*-time stateful blind signature scheme* BS *is correct if for any* k *messages* $m_1, \ldots, m_k \in \{0,1\}^*$*,* $(\mathsf{sk}, \mathsf{pk}) \leftarrow \mathsf{BS.KeyGen}(1^\lambda)$*, and* σ_i *output by* $\mathcal{U}$ *in the joint execution between* $\mathcal{S}(\mathsf{sk}, i)$ *and* $\mathcal{U}(\mathsf{pk}, m_i)$ *for* $i \in [k]$*, it holds that* $\forall i \in [k], \mathsf{BS.Ver}(\mathsf{pk}, m_i, \sigma_i) = 1$ *with probability* $1 - \mathsf{negl}(\lambda)$*.*

Definition 2.10 (Blindness). *A* k*-time stateful blind signature scheme* BS *is blind every PPT algorithm* $\mathcal{S}^*$ *wins the following blindness game with negligible probability:*

1. $(\mathsf{sk}, \mathsf{pk}) \leftarrow \mathcal{S}^*$.
2. $\mathcal{S}^*$ *provides two distinct messages* m_0, m_1.
3. $b \leftarrow \{0,1\}$.
4. $\mathcal{S}^*$ *interacts concurrently with* $\mathcal{U}_0 = \mathcal{U}(\mathsf{pk}, m_b)$ *and* $\mathcal{U}_1 = \mathcal{U}(\mathsf{pk}, m_{1-b})$.
5. *If either* $\mathcal{U}_0$ *or* $\mathcal{U}_1$ *abort, then* $(\sigma_0, \sigma_1) = (\perp, \perp)$. *Otherwise, denote* σ_b *and* σ_{1-b} *to be the outputs of* $\mathcal{U}_0$ *and* $\mathcal{U}_1$ *respectively. Then,* $\mathcal{S}^*$ *is given* (σ_0, σ_1).
6. $\mathcal{S}^*$ *returns a bit* b'. *It wins the blindness game if* $b = b'$.

In this paper we consider blindness in the malicious signer model i.e. an adversary gets to choose its own keys.

Definition 2.11 (One-More Unforgeability). *A k-time stateful blind signature scheme* BS *is one-more unforgeable if every PPT algorithm* $\mathcal{U}^*$ *wins the following one-more unforgeability game with negligible probability:*

1. $(\mathsf{sk}, \mathsf{pk}) \leftarrow \mathsf{BS.KeyGen}(1^\lambda)$ *and* $\mathcal{U}^*$ *is given* pk.
2. $\mathcal{U}^*$ *interacts with* ℓ *signers* $\mathcal{S}(\mathsf{sk}, 1), \ldots, \mathcal{S}(\mathsf{sk}, \ell)$ *where* $\ell \leqslant k$.
3. $\mathcal{U}^*$ *outputs* $\ell + 1$ *pairs* (m_i, σ_i) *where* $i \in [\ell + 1]$.
4. *Algorithm* $\mathcal{U}^*$ *wins the one-more unforgeability game if* $\forall i \in [\ell + 1]$, *it holds that* $\mathsf{BS.Ver}(\mathsf{pk}, m_i, \sigma_i) = 1$.

2.6 Lattice-Based NIZKs

We will use the LANES framework for efficient (non-interactive) arguments of knowledge for proving linear and multiplicative relations between committed messages developed in [ALS20, ENS20, LNS21a][4]. In this paper we are interested in the following two relations.

Verifiable Encryption. We want to prove that a ciphertext was constructed correctly. More concretely, let μ be a binary polynomial, p be prime, $\mathbf{r} \in S_\gamma^m$ and $\mathbf{e} \in S_\gamma^{n+1}$ be randomness and error vectors respectively. Then, given public keys $\mathbf{B} \in \mathcal{R}_q^{n \times m}, \mathbf{b} \in \mathcal{R}_q^m$ and valid ciphertext $\mathbf{t} \in \mathcal{R}_q^{n+1}$, we want to prove that

(i) μ is a binary polynomial,
(ii) $\mathbf{r}$ and $\mathbf{e}$ have coefficients between $-\gamma$ and γ,
(iii) $\begin{pmatrix} \mathbf{B} \\ \mathbf{b}^T \end{pmatrix} \mathbf{r} + p\mathbf{e} + \begin{pmatrix} \mathbf{0} \\ \mu \end{pmatrix} = \mathbf{t}$.

One observes that (i) and (ii) are multiplicative relations and (iii) is a linear relation. These statements can be efficiently proven using protocols from [ENS20, LNS21a]. We will denote the verifiable encryption proof as $\pi_{\mathsf{enc}}((\mathbf{B}, \mathbf{b}, \mathbf{t}), (\mathbf{r}, \mathbf{e}, \mu))$.

[4] We refer to [ENS20, LNS21a] for more details on the protocol.

One-Out-of-Many Proof. Our blind signature will consist of the one-out-of-many proof [GK15], i.e. a proof that one of the elements of a public set is a commitment to zero. In our setting, we want to prove that, given a matrix $\mathbf{A} \in \mathcal{R}_q^{n\times m}$ and a public finite set U of vectors in $\mathcal{R}_q^n$, we know a vector $\mathbf{s} \in \mathcal{R}_q^m$ which has small coefficients and $\mathbf{As} \in U$. As shown in [GK15], this concept is closely related to ring signatures.

Very recently, Lyubashevsky et al. [LNS21b] proposed an efficient one-out-of-many proof based on the LANES framework where the communication size is logarithmic in the size of U. We will apply the non-interactive protocol from [LNS21b, Section 3.2] and denote this proof as $\pi_{\in}((\mathbf{A}, U), \mathbf{s})$.

3 Lattice Based One-Time Signature Revisited

An important building block of our blind signature is the lattice-based one-time signature construction by Lyubashevsky and Micciancio [LM18] using modules lattices. However, we modify the original scheme so that the secret keys are chosen from a discrete Gaussian distribution rather than picked uniformly at random. The main motivation for such a change is that it mixes well with other building blocks (e.g. trapdoor sampling [MP12]) described in the next section.

The one-time signature is defined by the following algorithms:

- **Key Generation**: sample matrix $\mathbf{A} \leftarrow \mathcal{R}_q^{n\times m}$ uniformly at random and a secret key $\mathbf{y} \leftarrow \mathcal{D}_{\sigma_y}^{md}, \mathbf{s} \leftarrow \mathcal{D}_{\sigma_s}^{md}$. Then, the public key is a pair $\mathsf{pk} = (\mathbf{A}, \mathbf{w} := \mathbf{Ay}, \mathbf{v} := \mathbf{As})$ and its corresponding secret key is $\mathsf{sk} = (\mathbf{y}, \mathbf{s})$.
- **Signing**: given a binary polynomial $\mu \in \{0,1\}^d \subset \mathcal{R}_q$ as a message and a secret key $(\mathbf{y}, \mathbf{s})$, it outputs $\mathbf{z} = \mathbf{y} + \mu\mathbf{s}$.
- **Verification**: given a binary polynomial $\mu \in \mathcal{R}_q$, public key $(\mathbf{A}, \mathbf{w}, \mathbf{v})$ and a signature $\mathbf{z}$, it checks whether $\|\mathbf{z}\| \leqslant (\sigma_y + d\sigma_s)\sqrt{2md}$ and $\mathbf{Az} = \mathbf{w} + \mu\mathbf{v}$.

Correctness and security of the one-time signature can be summarised with the following theorem. We provide the full proof in the full version of the paper.

Theorem 3.1. *Let $m \geqslant 6(\lambda+1)/d$. Then, the one-time signature scheme above is correct. Concretely, the verification algorithm always accepts signatures produced by the legitimate signer with an overwhelming probability.*

For unforgeability, suppose that $\sigma_y \geqslant q^{n/m}\sqrt{2ed} + 2$, $\sigma_s \geqslant q^{n/m}\sqrt{2e} + 2$ and $q > 4d\sigma_s\sqrt{2md}$. If there is an adversary $\mathcal{A}$ which succeeds in breaking the strong unforgeability game of the one-time signature scheme with probability γ, then there exists an algorithm that can solve $\mathsf{MSIS}_{n,m,2(\sigma_y+d\sigma_s)\sqrt{2md}}$ with probability at least $\gamma/3 - \mathsf{negl}(\lambda)$ in essentially the same running time as the forgery attack.

For readability, we first provide a sketch for the unforgeability proof. Namely, assume there is an adversary $\mathcal{A}$ which succeeds in breaking the strong unforgeability game of the one-time signature scheme. We can then construct an algorithm $\mathcal{B}$ for solving MSIS as follows. Given a uniformly random matrix $\mathbf{A}$, the algorithm samples $\mathbf{y} \leftarrow \mathcal{D}_{\sigma_y}^{md}, \mathbf{s} \leftarrow \mathcal{D}_{\sigma_s}^{md}$ and sets $\mathbf{w} = \mathbf{Ay}$ and $\mathbf{v} = \mathbf{As}$. Next,

$\mathcal{B}$ outputs $(\mathbf{A}, \mathbf{w}, \mathbf{v})$. When $\mathcal{A}$ asks a signing query on input μ, $\mathcal{B}$ answers with $\mathbf{z} = \mathbf{y} + \mu\mathbf{s}$. Finally, $\mathcal{A}$ outputs a forgery $(\mu', \mathbf{z}')$. Assuming that it is valid, $\mathcal{B}$ outputs a potential solution $\mathbf{z}' - (\mathbf{y} + \mu'\mathbf{s})$. Now, given $\mathbf{A}, \mathbf{w}, \mathbf{v}, \mu, \mathbf{z}$, the adversary $\mathcal{A}$ does not know which $(\mathbf{y}, \mathbf{s})$ from the following set was used:

$$S = \{(\mathbf{y}', \mathbf{s}') : \mathbf{A}\mathbf{y}' = \mathbf{w}, \mathbf{A}\mathbf{s}' = \mathbf{v}, \mathbf{z} = \mathbf{y}' + \mu\mathbf{s}'\}.$$

To this end, we will prove that the probability of picking $(\mathbf{y}, \mathbf{s})$ when sampling from a discrete Gaussian distribution restricted to S (which is a coset of a lattice as shown below) is sufficiently small, e.g. 1/2 when standard deviations σ_y, σ_s are chosen properly.

Let us fix $\mathbf{A}, \mathbf{y}, \mathbf{s}, \mu$. We provide tools to compute an upper-bound on the following probability:

$$\Pr\left[\mathbf{y}^* = \mathbf{y} \wedge \mathbf{s}^* = \mathbf{s} : (\mathbf{y}^*, \mathbf{s}^*) \leftarrow D_{\Lambda^{\perp}_{\mathcal{R}_q}(\mathbf{X}),\sigma,\mathbf{c}}\right] \tag{16}$$

where $\sigma = (\sigma_y, \ldots, \sigma_y, \sigma_s, \ldots, \sigma_s) \in \mathbb{R}^{2m}_{>0}$,

$$\mathbf{X} = \begin{pmatrix} \mathbf{A} & \mathbf{0} \\ \mathbf{0} & \mathbf{A} \\ 1 \cdot \mathbf{I}_m & \mu \cdot \mathbf{I}_m \end{pmatrix} \in \mathcal{R}_q^{(2n+m)\times 2m} \text{ and } \mathbf{c} = -\begin{pmatrix} \mathbf{y} \\ \mathbf{s} \end{pmatrix} \in \mathcal{R}_q^{2m}.$$

These techniques will be crucial for proving not only unforgeability for the one-time signature but also for one-more unforgeability of the blind signature presented in the next section.

We start with the following technical lemma.

Lemma 3.2. *Let* $\mathbf{M} \in \mathbb{Z}^{m\times n}$ *and* $\mathbf{\Lambda}$ *be an* n*-dimensional lattice. Then, for any* $\sigma \in \mathbb{R}^m_{>0}$, $\mathbf{s} \in \mathbb{R}^m$ *we have:*

$$\frac{\rho_\sigma(\mathbf{s})}{\sum_{\mathbf{z}\in\mathbf{\Lambda}} \rho_\sigma(\mathbf{M}\mathbf{z})} \leqslant \frac{\rho_\sigma(\mathbf{s})}{\sum_{\mathbf{z}\in\mathbf{\Lambda}} \rho_\sigma(\mathbf{s} + \mathbf{M}\mathbf{z})} \leqslant \frac{1}{\sum_{\mathbf{z}\in\mathbf{\Lambda}} \rho_\sigma(\mathbf{M}\mathbf{z})}.$$

Proof. Inequality on the left follows directly from [MR07, Lemma 2.9] and the fact that $\mathbf{M\Lambda}$ is an m-dimensional lattice. The inequality on the right is essentially implicit in the proof of [AR04, Lemma 3.2], but for completeness, we give a proof of a slightly generalized statement needed in this work. Let us partition $\mathbf{\Lambda}\backslash\{\mathbf{0}\}$ into two sets $\mathbf{\Lambda}_1$ and $\mathbf{\Lambda}_2$, such that $\mathbf{x} \in \mathbf{\Lambda}_1$ if and only $-\mathbf{x} \in \mathbf{\Lambda}_2$. Clearly, $|\mathbf{\Lambda}_1| = |\mathbf{\Lambda}_2|$. Then, for $\mathbf{z} \in \mathbf{\Lambda}_1$ we have:

$$\begin{aligned}
\rho_\sigma(\mathbf{s} + \mathbf{M}\mathbf{z}) + \rho_\sigma(\mathbf{s} - \mathbf{M}\mathbf{z}) &= e^{-\sum_{i=1}^m \frac{s_i^2 + \langle \mathbf{m}_i, \mathbf{z}\rangle^2}{2\sigma_i^2}} \cdot \left(e^{\sum_{i=1}^m \frac{2\langle \mathbf{m}_i, \mathbf{z}\rangle}{2\sigma_i^2}} + e^{-\sum_{i=1}^m \frac{2\langle \mathbf{m}_i, \mathbf{z}\rangle}{2\sigma_i^2}}\right) \\
&\geqslant 2e^{-\sum_{i=1}^m \frac{s_i^2 + \langle \mathbf{m}_i, \mathbf{z}\rangle^2}{2\sigma_i^2}} \\
&\geqslant 2\rho_\sigma(\mathbf{s})\rho_\sigma(\mathbf{M}\mathbf{z}) \\
&\geqslant \rho_\sigma(\mathbf{s}) \cdot (\rho_\sigma(\mathbf{M}\mathbf{z}) + \rho_\sigma(-\mathbf{M}\mathbf{z}))
\end{aligned}$$

where for the first inequality we used the fact that $x + x^{-1} \geqslant 2$ for any $x > 0$. Hence,

$$\begin{aligned}\sum_{\mathbf{z}\in\mathbf{\Lambda}} \rho_\sigma(\mathbf{s}+\mathbf{Mz}) &= \rho_\sigma(\mathbf{s}) + \sum_{\mathbf{z}\in\mathbf{\Lambda}_1} (\rho_\sigma(\mathbf{s}+\mathbf{Mz}) + \rho_\sigma(\mathbf{s}-\mathbf{Mz})) \\ &\geqslant \rho_\sigma(\mathbf{s}) + \sum_{\mathbf{z}\in\mathbf{\Lambda}_1} \rho_\sigma(\mathbf{s})\cdot(\rho_\sigma(\mathbf{Mz}) + \rho_\sigma(-\mathbf{Mz})) \\ &\geqslant \rho_\sigma(\mathbf{s})\left(1 + \sum_{\mathbf{z}\in\mathbf{\Lambda}_1} (\rho_\sigma(\mathbf{Mz}) + \rho_\sigma(-\mathbf{Mz}))\right) \\ &\geqslant \rho_\sigma(\mathbf{s}) \sum_{\mathbf{z}\in\mathbf{\Lambda}} \rho_\sigma(\mathbf{Mz}).\end{aligned}$$

Thus, the statement holds. □

We are ready to present a theorem that says for which parameters the probability in (16) is upper-bounded by 1/2.

Theorem 3.3. *Let* $\mathbf{A} \in \mathbb{Z}_q^{n\times m}$ *and* $\mathbf{M} \in \mathbb{Z}^{k\times m}$ *be arbitrary matrices and denote* $\mathbf{m}_i \in \mathbb{Z}^m$ *to be the i-th row of* $\mathbf{M}$. *Furthermore, suppose* $\sigma = (\sigma_1, \ldots, \sigma_k)$ *satisfies* $\sigma_i \geqslant q^{n/m}\sqrt{\frac{ek}{m}}\|\mathbf{m}_i\|_1 + 2$ *for* $i \in [k]$. *Then, for any* $\mathbf{s} \in \mathbb{R}^k$, *we have:*

$$\frac{\rho_\sigma(\mathbf{s})}{\sum_{\mathbf{z}\in\mathbf{\Lambda}_q^\perp(\mathbf{A})} \rho_\sigma(\mathbf{s}+\mathbf{Mz})} \leqslant \frac{1}{2}.$$

Proof. By Lemma 3.2 we only need to show that $\sum_{\mathbf{z}\in\mathbf{\Lambda}_q^\perp(\mathbf{A})} \rho_\sigma(\mathbf{Mz}) \geqslant 2$. Let us set $\gamma = \lceil \frac{1}{2}\sqrt{e}q^{n/m} \rceil$ and define the set U as follows:

$$U = \left\{\mathbf{u} \in \mathbf{\Lambda}_q^\perp(\mathbf{A})\backslash\{\mathbf{0}\} : \|\mathbf{u}\| \leqslant 2\gamma\right\}.$$

First, we lower-bound the cardinality of U. By the pigeonhole principle, there exist at least $\ell + 1 \geqslant (2\gamma)^m/q^n + 1$ vectors $\mathbf{u}_1, \ldots, \mathbf{u}_{\ell+1}$ such that for each $j \in [\ell+1]$, $\|\mathbf{u}_j\|_\infty \leqslant \gamma$ and $\mathbf{Au}_1 = \mathbf{Au}_2 = \ldots = \mathbf{Au}_\ell$. Hence, for all $i \in [\ell]$, we have $\mathbf{u}_i - \mathbf{u}_{l+1} \in U$. Consequently, $|U| \geqslant \ell = (2\gamma)^m/q^n$ and

$$\begin{aligned}\sum_{\mathbf{z}\in\mathbf{\Lambda}_q^\perp(\mathbf{A})} \rho_\sigma(\mathbf{Mz}) &\geqslant 1 + \sum_{\mathbf{z}\in U} \rho_\sigma(\mathbf{Mz}) \\ &\geqslant 1 + \sum_{\mathbf{z}\in U} \exp\left(-\sum_{i=1}^k \frac{\langle \mathbf{m}_i, \mathbf{z}\rangle^2}{2\sigma_i^2}\right) \\ &\geqslant 1 + \sum_{\mathbf{z}\in U} \exp\left(-\sum_{i=1}^k \frac{4\gamma^2\|\mathbf{m}_i\|_1^2}{2\sigma_i^2}\right) \\ &\geqslant 1 + |U|\cdot\exp\left(-\sum_{i=1}^k \frac{2\gamma^2\|\mathbf{m}_i\|_1^2}{\sigma_i^2}\right) \\ &\geqslant 1 + \frac{(2\gamma)^m}{q^n}\exp\left(-\sum_{i=1}^k \frac{2\gamma^2\|\mathbf{m}_i\|_1^2}{\sigma_i^2}\right).\end{aligned}$$

Since, we assumed that $\sigma_i \geqslant 2\gamma\sqrt{k/m}\|\mathbf{m}_i\|_1$ and $\gamma \geqslant \frac{1}{2}\sqrt{e}q^{n/m}$, we obtain:

$$\begin{aligned}\sum_{\mathbf{z}\in\mathbf{\Lambda}_q^\perp(\mathbf{A})} \rho_\sigma(\mathbf{Mz}) &\geqslant 1 + \frac{(2\gamma)^m}{q^n}\exp\left(-\sum_{i=1}^{k}\frac{m}{2k}\right)\\ &\geqslant 1 + \frac{(2\gamma)^m}{q^n}\exp\left(-\frac{m}{2}\right)\\ &\geqslant 1 + \exp\left(\frac{m}{2}\right)\exp\left(-\frac{m}{2}\right)\\ &\geqslant 2\end{aligned}$$

which concludes the proof. □

Finally, to compute the probability in (16), we note that:

$$\Pr[\mathbf{y}^* = \mathbf{y} \wedge \mathbf{s}^* = \mathbf{s}] = D_{\mathbf{\Lambda}_q^\perp(\mathbf{X}),\sigma,\mathbf{c}}(\mathbf{0},\mathbf{0}) = \frac{\rho_\sigma(\mathbf{y},\mathbf{s})}{\rho_\sigma((\mathbf{y},\mathbf{s}) + \mathbf{\Lambda}_q^\perp(\mathbf{X}))}$$

Note for every $\mathbf{u} \in \mathbf{\Lambda}_{\mathcal{R}_q}^\perp(\mathbf{A})$, we have $(\mu\mathbf{u}, -\mathbf{u}) \in \mathbf{\Lambda}_q^\perp(\mathbf{X})$. Therefore,

$$\frac{\rho_\sigma(\mathbf{y},\mathbf{s})}{\rho_\sigma((\mathbf{y},\mathbf{s}) + \mathbf{\Lambda}_q^\perp(\mathbf{X}))} \leqslant \frac{\rho_\sigma(\mathbf{y},\mathbf{s})}{\sum_{\mathbf{u}\in\mathbf{\Lambda}_{\mathcal{R}_q}^\perp(\mathbf{A})}\rho_\sigma\left((\mathbf{y},\mathbf{s}) + \begin{bmatrix}\mu\cdot\mathbf{I}_m\\ -\mathbf{I}_m\end{bmatrix}\mathbf{u}\right)}.$$

Since we set $\sigma_y \geqslant q^{n/m}\sqrt{2ed} + 2$, $\sigma_s \geqslant q^{n/m}\sqrt{2e} + 2$, we can apply Theorem 3.3 for $\sigma = (\sigma_y, \ldots, \sigma_y, \sigma_s, \ldots, \sigma_s) \in \mathbb{R}^{2md}$,

$$\mathbf{A} := \mathsf{Rot}(\mathbf{A}) \in \mathbb{Z}_q^{nd\times md} \text{ and } \mathbf{M} := \mathsf{Rot}\left(\begin{bmatrix}\mu\cdot\mathbf{I}_m\\ -\mathbf{I}_m\end{bmatrix}\right) \in \mathbb{Z}^{2md\times md}.$$

We refer to the full version of the paper for a more rigorous proof of Theorem 3.1.

4 The Blind Signature

In this section, we define our blind signature scheme. A blind signature scheme has two parties interacting: a user and a server (or signer), so the user produces a signature under the public key of the server. The security of a blind signature scheme is captured by two properties properly defined in Definitions 2.10 and 2.11: Blindness and One-More Unforgeability. Blindness informally requires that the server is unable to link a signature to the interaction during which this signature was produced. One-More Unforgeability informally says that after some number ℓ of interactions with the server, the user is not able to produce $\ell + 1$ signatures.

The strategy of our blind signature scheme is as follows: the public key is a collection of N public keys of the one-time signature scheme defined in the previous Sect. 3. To keep the user/server interaction "blind", the user sends an encryption of his message, together with a NIZK proof that the ciphertext is well-formed. This encryption scheme is such that the server can homomorphically compute (somewhat efficiently) an encryption of the one-time signature under the i-th public key. This way, the user receives an encryption of a one-time signature of his message, but the response from the server hides its i-th secret key enough so the user can only produce one signature per interaction. Again, to preserve blindness, instead of giving away directly his one-time signature, he gives a NIZK proof of knowledge of a valid one-time signature to one of the public keys.

4.1 Definition of the Encryption Scheme

In this subsection, we define the first building block of our blind signature scheme: an encryption scheme. This encryption scheme shall be secure against Chosen Plaintext Attacks (we prove in Lemma 4.2 that the distribution of the ciphertext is indistinguishable from uniform) and allow the server to compute a one-time signature of the message while masking his secret key. The proofs of the latter statement is postponed to Sect. 5. We also define a multi-dimensional decryption algorithm Dec for better readability of the blind signature protocol Fig. 2.

Notations. Throughout this subsection, we use n, m for dimensions, prime modulus q' and prime p. Please note that the modulus used in the encryption scheme differs from the one we use in the remaining of the blind signature scheme.

Algorithm 1. $\mathsf{KeyGen}()$:

1: $\mathbf{B} \leftarrow \mathcal{R}_{q'}^{n\times m}$
2: $\mathbf{x} \leftarrow \{-\gamma, \ldots, \gamma\}^n$
3: $\mathbf{b}^T = \mathbf{x}^T\mathbf{B} \mod q'$
4: $\mathsf{pk}_{\mathsf{enc}} = (\mathbf{B}, \mathbf{b})$
5: $\mathsf{sk}_{\mathsf{enc}} = \mathbf{x}$
6: **return** $(\mathsf{pk}_{\mathsf{enc}}, \mathsf{sk}_{\mathsf{enc}})$

Algorithm 2. $\mathsf{enc}(\mathsf{pk}_{\mathsf{enc}}, \mu)$:

1: $(\mathbf{r}, \mathbf{e}, e') \leftarrow \{-\gamma, \ldots, \gamma\}^m \times \{-\gamma, \ldots, \gamma\}^n \times \{-\gamma, \ldots, \gamma\}$
2: $\mathbf{t} = p\mathbf{B}\mathbf{r} + p\mathbf{e} \mod q'$
3: $t' = p\mathbf{b}^T\mathbf{r} + pe' + \mu \mod q'$
4: **return** $(\mathbf{t}, t')$

Algorithm 3. $\mathsf{dec}(\mathsf{sk}_{\mathsf{enc}}, \mathbf{t}, t')$:

1: $z = t' - \mathbf{x}^T\mathbf{t} \mod q'$
2: **return** $z \mod p$

Theorem 4.1. *The encryption scheme defined through Algorithms 1 to 3 is correct. More precisely, if* $\|\mu\|_\infty \leqslant \lfloor p/2 \rfloor$, $(\mathsf{pk}_{\mathsf{enc}}, \mathsf{sk}_{\mathsf{enc}}) = \mathsf{KeyGen}()$ *and*

$$(nd\gamma + 1)\gamma \leqslant \frac{q'}{2p} - 1/2, \tag{17}$$

then $\mathsf{dec}(\mathsf{sk}_{\mathsf{enc}}, \mathbf{t}, t') = \mu$.

Proof. We compute $z = t' - \mathbf{x}^T\mathbf{t}$. We have :

$$z = p\mathbf{b}^T\mathbf{r} + p\mathbf{e}' + \mu - \mathbf{x}^T(p\mathbf{B}\mathbf{r} + p\mathbf{e}) \tag{18}$$

$$= \mu + p(e' - \mathbf{x}^T\mathbf{e}). \tag{19}$$

Since we assumed $(nd\gamma + 1)\gamma \leqslant \frac{q'}{2p} - 1/2$ and $\|\mu\|_\infty \leqslant p/2$, then $\|\mu + p(e' - \mathbf{x}^T\mathbf{e})\|_\infty \leqslant q'/2$, therefore there is no reduction modulo q' in $\mu + p(e' - \mathbf{x}^T\mathbf{e})$ and hence $z = \mu + p(e' - \mathbf{x}^T\mathbf{e}) \mod p = \mu$. □

Algorithm 4. $\mathsf{Dec}(\mathsf{sk}_{\mathsf{enc}}, \mathbf{T}, \mathbf{t}')$:

1: $z^T = \mathbf{t}'^T - \mathbf{x}^T\mathbf{T} \mod q'$
2: **return** $z \mod p$

Lemma 4.2.
Let μ *be some message,* $(\mathsf{pk}, \mathsf{sk}) \leftarrow \mathsf{KeyGen}$*, and* $(\mathbf{t}, t') = \mathsf{enc}(\mathsf{pk}, \mu)$*. Then* $\mathbf{t}, t'$ *is indistinguishable from uniform under* $\mathsf{MLWE}_{m,n-m,S_\gamma}$ *and* $\mathsf{MLWE}_{n+1,m,S_\gamma}$[5].

Proof. We define a sequence of games.

G_0: In this game, the adversary $\mathcal{A}$ wins if he distinguishes honest samples $(\mathsf{pk}, \mathsf{sk}) \leftarrow \mathsf{KeyGen}$, $(\mathbf{t}, t') = \mathsf{enc}(\mathsf{pk}, \mu)$ from $(\mathsf{pk}, \mathsf{sk}) \leftarrow \mathsf{KeyGen}$, $(\mathbf{t}, t') \leftarrow \mathcal{R}_q^n \times \mathcal{R}_q$.

G_1: This game is the same as the previous one, except in the key generation, $\mathbf{b}$ is sampled uniformly random. This game is indistinguishable from the previous one under $\mathsf{MLWE}_{m,n-m,S_\gamma}$.

[5] We remind the reader that the encryption scheme's variables and computations are done over $\mathcal{R}_q$, and therefore the MLWE problem is $\mod q$, and S_γ here is those $r \in \mathcal{R}_q$ such that $|r| \leqslant \gamma$.

G_2: This game is the same as the previous one, except $\mathbf{Br}$ and $\mathbf{b}^T\mathbf{r}$ are sampled uniformly random. This game is indistinguishable from the previous one under $\mathsf{MLWE}_{n+1,m,S_\gamma}$.

G_3: This game is the same as the previous one, except $\mathbf{t}, t'$ are sampled uniformly random. This game is identical to the previous one.

G_4: This game is the same as the previous one, except the public key is honestly sampled from KeyGen. This game is indistinguishable from the previous one under $\mathsf{MLWE}_{m,n,S_\gamma}$.

The result follows from summing up the advantages. □

4.2 Description of the Scheme

We describe in Fig. 1 the setup algorithm for the server, the setup algorithm for the user is simply 1) Run KeyGen to generate a key pair for the encryption scheme 2) Run the setup algorithm for the zero-knowledge proofs $\pi_{\mathsf{enc}}, \pi_\in$ (notice that the public parameters for π_{enc} and $\pi_\in$ must be independent so as to preserve blindness), and finally in Fig. 2 we describe our blind signature scheme. The verification algorithm is the verification algorithm of the NIZK $\pi_\in$. The scheme contains two verification steps: the verification of the well-formedness of the ciphertext π_{enc} by the server and the verification of valid one-time signature $\mathbf{z}$ such that $\mathbf{Az} = \mu\mathbf{v}_j + \mathbf{w}_j$ by the user. A non-succeeding verification implies abortion of the scheme.

Notations. We let q, q' be a prime moduli (q' is the modulus for the encryption, which will be greater than q, the modulus for the blind signature), p be a prime which shall be smaller than q' but greater than the messages to be encrypted, and N a real number corresponding to the number of blind signatures. We introduce a dimension α which is the height of the public matrix $\mathbf{A}$, and $\sigma_\mathbf{s}, \sigma_\mathbf{y}, \sigma'$ which are standard deviations for the Gaussian distributions. One can think of $\sigma_\mathbf{y}$ as d times greater than $\sigma_\mathbf{s}$ so that $\|\mu\mathbf{s}\| \simeq \|\mathbf{y}\|$. For a matrix $\mathbf{A} \in \mathcal{R}_q^{n\times m}$ and a vector $\mathbf{u} \in \mathcal{R}_q^n$, we write $\Lambda_\mathbf{u}^\perp(\mathbf{A})$ the lattice $\{\mathbf{s} \in \mathcal{R}_q^m \mid \mathbf{As} = \mathbf{u}\}$. We omit the subscript $\mathbf{u}$ when $\mathbf{u} = \mathbf{0}$. For the sake of clarity, we write $\sqrt[3]{q} = \lfloor \sqrt[3]{q} \rfloor$. We define a gadget vector $\mathbf{g} = (1\ \sqrt[3]{q}\ \sqrt[3]{q}^2)$, which we use to define the gadget matrix

$$\mathbf{G} = \begin{bmatrix} \mathbf{g}^T & & & \\ & \mathbf{g}^T & & \\ & & \ddots & \\ & & & \mathbf{g}^T \end{bmatrix}.$$

5 Security Proof

In this section, we prove the correctness and security of our blind signature. In Sect. 5.1, we prove the correctness of the homomorphic computation of the server

$$
\begin{aligned}
&\mathbf{R} \leftarrow (S_1^{\alpha\times\alpha})^{2\times 3}\\
&\mathbf{A}' \leftarrow \mathcal{R}_q^{\alpha\times 2\alpha},\ \mathbf{A} = [\mathbf{A}'\,|\mathbf{A}'\mathbf{R} - \mathbf{G}] \in \mathcal{R}_q^{\alpha\times 5\alpha}\\
&\mathsf{seed} \leftarrow \{0,1\}^\lambda,\ (\mathbf{v}_i, \mathbf{w}_i)_{1\leqslant i\leqslant N} = \mathsf{PRNG}(\mathsf{seed}) \qquad (20)\\
&\mathsf{pk}_{\mathsf{Server}} = (\mathbf{A}, \mathsf{seed}),\ \text{seed which expands through PRNG to } (\mathbf{v}_i, \mathbf{w}_i)_{1\leqslant i\leqslant N}\\
&\mathsf{sk}_{\mathsf{Server}} = \mathbf{R}
\end{aligned}
$$

Fig. 1. ServerKeyGen() :

on the user's ciphertext, from which we infer the correctness of the blind signature scheme. In Sect. 5.2, we prove the blindness and one-more unforgeability of our blind signature scheme.

5.1 Blind Computation on the Ciphertext

We first prove in Lemma 5.1 that if both parties follow the protocol honestly, then with overwhelming probability, the user successfully decrypts $\mathbf{z} = \mu\mathbf{s}_i + \mathbf{y}_i$. Next, we prove in Theorem 5.2 that this yields the correctness of the blind signature scheme.

Lemma 5.1. *We use notations from Fig. 2. If the user and the server follow the protocol on Fig. 2 honestly and if*

$$24\sigma' + d\gamma(n+1) \leqslant \frac{q'}{2p} - \frac{1}{2} \text{ and } 12d\sigma_{\mathbf{s}} + 12\sigma_{\mathbf{y}} \leqslant p/2,$$

then with overwhelming probability $\mathsf{Dec}(\mathsf{sk}_{\mathsf{enc}}, \mathbf{F}, \mathbf{f}')^T = \mathbf{y}_i + \mu\mathbf{s}_i$.

Proof. First, we notice that $\begin{cases} \mathbf{F} = p\mathbf{B}(\mathbf{r}\mathbf{s}_i^T + \mathbf{Y}) + p(\mathbf{e}\mathbf{s}_i^T + \mathbf{Y}') \\ \mathbf{f}^T = p\mathbf{b}(\mathbf{r}\mathbf{s}_i^T + \mathbf{Y}) + p(e'\mathbf{s}_i^T + \mathbf{y}''^T) + \mu\mathbf{s}_i^T + \mathbf{y}_i^T \end{cases}$
Let us write $\bar{\mathbf{Y}} = \mathbf{r}\mathbf{s}_i^T + \mathbf{Y}, \bar{\mathbf{Y}}' = \mathbf{e}\mathbf{s}_i^T + \mathbf{Y}', \bar{\mathbf{y}} = e'\mathbf{s}_i^T + \mathbf{y}''^T$ and $\bar{\mu} = \mu\mathbf{s}_i^T + \mathbf{y}_i^T$. Then, the decryption $\mathsf{Dec}(\mathsf{sk}_{\mathsf{enc}}, \mathbf{F}, \mathbf{f})$ is given by

$$
\begin{aligned}
\mathsf{Dec}(\mathsf{sk}_{\mathsf{enc}}, \mathbf{F}, \mathbf{f}) &= p\mathbf{b}^T\bar{\mathbf{Y}} + p\bar{\mathbf{Y}}' + \bar{\mu} - \mathbf{x}^T(p\mathbf{B}\bar{\mathbf{Y}} + p\bar{\mathbf{Y}}') \mod p\\
&= \bar{\mu} + p(\bar{\mathbf{y}} - \mathbf{x}^T\bar{\mathbf{Y}}') \mod p.
\end{aligned}
$$

Since we assumed $12d\sigma_{\mathbf{s}} + 12\sigma_{\mathbf{y}} \leqslant p/2$, then with overwhelming probability we have $\|\bar{\mu}\|_\infty \leqslant p/2$. Moreover, we assumed $24\sigma' + d\gamma(n+1) \leqslant \frac{q'}{2p} - \frac{1}{2}$, hence $\|\bar{\mu} + \bar{\mathbf{y}} - \mathbf{x}^T\bar{\mathbf{Y}}'\|_\infty \leqslant \frac{q'}{2p} - \frac{1}{2}$, and therefore $\mathsf{Dec}(\mathsf{sk}_{\mathsf{enc}}, \mathbf{F}, \mathbf{f}) = \bar{\mu}$. □

Theorem 5.2. *The blind signature scheme defined in Fig. 2 is correct. More precisely, if both parties follow the protocol honestly, then the produced signature passes verification with overwhelming probability.*

Server		User
State i, $\mathsf{sk}_{\mathsf{Server}} = \mathbf{R}$		message μ, $\mathsf{sk}_{\mathsf{enc}}$
		$(\mathbf{t}, t') = \mathsf{enc}(\mathsf{pk}_{\mathsf{enc}}, \mu)$
		$\pi_{\mathsf{enc}} = \pi_{\mathsf{enc}}((\mathbf{B}, \mathbf{b}, (\mathbf{t}, t'), (\mathbf{r}, (\mathbf{e}, e'), \mu))$
	$\xleftarrow{\mathbf{t}, t', \pi_{\mathsf{enc}}, \mathsf{pk}_{\mathsf{enc}}}$	
Verify π_{enc}		
$\Lambda_i = \Lambda^{\perp}_{\mathbf{v}_i}(\mathbf{A}),\ \Lambda'_i = \Lambda^{\perp}_{\mathbf{w}_i}(\mathbf{A})$		
$(\mathbf{s}_i, \mathbf{y}_i) \leftarrow D_{\Lambda_i, \sigma_{\mathbf{s}}} \times D_{\Lambda'_i, \sigma_{\mathbf{y}}}$		
$\mathbf{Y}, \mathbf{Y}', \mathbf{y}'' \leftarrow D_{\sigma'}^{m \times 5\alpha} \times D_{\sigma'}^{n \times 5\alpha} \times D_{\sigma'}^{5\alpha}$ (21)		
$\mathbf{F} = \mathbf{t}\mathbf{s}_i^T + p\mathbf{B}\mathbf{Y} + p\mathbf{Y}'$ (22)		
$\mathbf{f}'^T = \mathbf{y}_i^T + t'\mathbf{s}_i^T + p\mathbf{b}^T\mathbf{Y} + p\mathbf{y}''$ (23)		
Update state $i = i + 1$ (24)		
	$\xrightarrow{\mathbf{F}, \mathbf{f}'}$	
		$\mathbf{z} = \mathsf{Dec}(\mathsf{sk}_{\mathsf{enc}}, \mathbf{F}, \mathbf{f}')$ (25)
		Verify that $\exists j \leqslant N,\ \mathbf{A}\mathbf{z} = \mu\mathbf{v}_j + \mathbf{w}_j$
		$\mathsf{BlindSig}(\mu) = \pi_{\in}(\mathbf{A}, (\mathbf{w}_j + \mu\mathbf{v}_j)_{1 \leqslant j \leqslant N}, \mathbf{z})$

Fig. 2. Blind signature scheme

Proof. We only need to prove that the vector $\mathbf{z}$ recovered by the user verifies $\mathbf{A}\mathbf{z} \in \{\mathbf{w}_i + \mu\mathbf{v}_i,\ 1 \leqslant i \leqslant N\}$, so the non-interactive zero-knowledge proof $\pi_{\in}$ that the user computes as the blind signature passes verification. We chose parameters such that it follows directly from Lemma 5.1 that we have $\mathbf{z} = \mathbf{y}_i + \mu\mathbf{s}_i$, and therefore $\mathbf{A}\mathbf{z} = \mathbf{w}_i + \mu\mathbf{v}_i$ where i is the state of the server when he responded to the user's query. □

5.2 Blindness and One-More Unforgeability of the Blind Signature Scheme

The main Theorem of this subsection is Theorem 5.4. We prove blindness directly from a sequence of games, proving that the blindness game is indistinguishable from a game that is independent of the messages. The proof of one-more unforgeability is broken down in 2 parts: first we reduce the one-more unforgeability game to another game OMUF^*. Next, we prove that with rewindable access to an adversary $\mathcal{A}$ with winning probability ϵ, one has probability $O(\epsilon)$ to solve $\mathsf{MSIS}_{\alpha,5\alpha,B}$ for some short bound B.

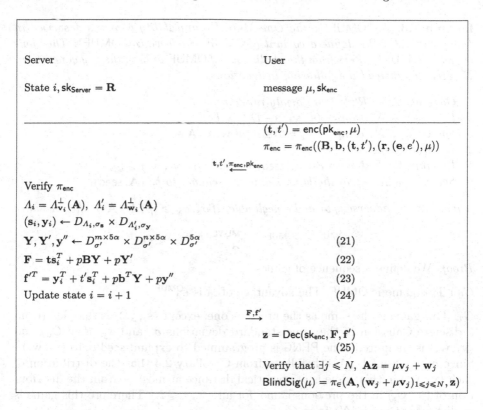

Lemma 5.3. *Let* OMUF *be the One-More Unforgeability game as described in Definition 2.11. We define a variant of* OMUF *which we call* OMUF*. *The challenger of* OMUF* *differs from the challenger of* OMUF *only in the key generation. He executes instead the following instructions:*

1. *Generate* $\mathbf{A} \leftarrow \mathcal{R}_q^{\alpha \times 5\alpha}$ *uniformly random*
2. *For* $1 \leqslant i \leqslant N$, *sample* $(\mathbf{s}_i, \mathbf{y}_i) \leftarrow D_{\sigma_{\mathbf{s}}}^{5\alpha} \times D_{\sigma_{\mathbf{y}}}^{5\alpha}$
3. *For* $1 \leqslant i \leqslant N$, *compute* $\mathbf{v}_i = \mathbf{A}\mathbf{s}_i$ *and* $\mathbf{w}_i = \mathbf{A}\mathbf{w}_i$
4. *Generate a* seed
5. *Program the* PRNG *so* PRNG(seed) *expands to* $(\mathbf{v}_i, \mathbf{w}_i)_{1 \leqslant i \leqslant N}$
6. *Set the public key of the blind signature scheme to be* $(\mathbf{A}, \mathsf{seed})$.

Then, for any adversary $\mathcal{A}$ *and* ϵ *negligible, if* $\sigma_{\mathbf{s}}, \sigma_{\mathbf{y}} \geqslant \eta_\epsilon(\Lambda^\perp(\mathbf{A}))$, *then we have*

$$\epsilon_{\mathcal{A}}^{\mathsf{OMUF}} \leqslant \epsilon_{\mathcal{A}}^{\mathsf{OMUF}^*} + \epsilon_{\mathcal{A}}^{\mathsf{MLWE}_{\alpha,\alpha,S_1}} + 4N\epsilon.$$

Proof. We define a sequence of games:

G_0 : This game is OMUF. The advantage of $\mathcal{A}$ is $\epsilon_{\mathcal{A}}^{\mathsf{OMUF}}$.

G_1: This game is the same as the previous one, except $(\mathbf{s}_i, \mathbf{y}_i)_i$ is sampled (from a discrete Gaussian of the same standard deviations $\sigma_{\mathbf{s}}$ and $\sigma_{\mathbf{y}}$ as in G_0) and $(\mathbf{v}_i, \mathbf{w}_i)$ is computed. The PRNG is programmed to expand seed onto $(\mathbf{v}_i, \mathbf{w}_i)_i$. Since $\sigma_{\mathbf{s}}, \sigma_{\mathbf{y}} \geqslant \eta_\epsilon(\Lambda^\perp(\mathbf{A}))$, it follows from Corollary 2.4 that the distribution of each $(\mathbf{v}_i, \mathbf{w}_i)$ in this game is at statistical distance at most 4ϵ from the distribution of $(\mathbf{v}_i, \mathbf{w}_i)$ in the previous game, for all $1 \leqslant i \leqslant N$. Therefore this game is at distance at most $4N\epsilon$ from G_0.

G_2: This game is the same as the previous one, except the public matrix $\mathbf{A}$ is sampled uniformly random $\mathbf{A} \leftarrow \mathcal{R}_q^{\alpha \times 5\alpha}$. This game is indistinguishable from G_1 under $\mathsf{MLWE}_{\alpha,\alpha,S_1}$.

The last game G_2 is OMUF*, hence the adversary $\mathcal{A}$ has advantage $\epsilon_{\mathcal{A}}^{\mathsf{OMUF}^*}$ against G_2, and the result follows from summing up the advantages. □

The strategy of the one-more unforgeability proof is roughly speaking to rely on the security of our one-time signature from Sect. 3. More precisely, the reduction $\mathcal{B}$ plays the OMUF* with $\mathcal{A}$. Similarly as in the unforgeability reduction of the one-time signature, $\mathcal{B}$ knows one preimage $\mu\mathbf{s} + \mathbf{y}$ of $\mu\mathbf{v} + \mathbf{w}$, and extracts a second one $\mathbf{z}$ from $\mathcal{A}$'s forgery[6]. We cannot argue straight away that $\mathbf{z} - (\mathbf{s}\mu + \mathbf{y})$ is a non-zero solution to MSIS for the public matrix $\mathbf{A}$, since $\mathcal{A}$ may have learnt from the extra information - or hints that $\mathcal{B}$ gave away when sending the ciphertext $(\mathbf{F}, \mathbf{f})$. Indeed, we have

$$\mathbf{F} = \mathbf{t}\mathbf{s}_i^T + p\mathbf{B}\mathbf{Y} + p\mathbf{Y}' = p\mathbf{B}(\mathbf{r}\mathbf{s}_i^T + \mathbf{Y}) + p(\mathbf{e}\mathbf{s}_i^T + \mathbf{Y}')$$
$$\mathbf{f}^T = \mathbf{y}_i + t'\mathbf{s}_i^T + p\mathbf{b}^T\mathbf{Y} + p\mathbf{y}'' = p\mathbf{b}(\mathbf{r}\mathbf{s}_i^T + \mathbf{Y}) + p(e'\mathbf{s}_i^T + \mathbf{y}''^T) + \mathbf{z}.$$

[6] The forgery is one of the unexpected signatures, which exists since the adversary is expected to produce at most ℓ signatures from ℓ interactions.

The masks $\mathbf{Y}, \mathbf{Y}', \mathbf{y}''$ hide the secret values $\mathbf{r}\mathbf{s}_i^T, \mathbf{e}\mathbf{s}_i^T, e'\mathbf{s}_i^T$, but we need to take into account the amount of leakage these hints represent. In other word, what is the winning probability of the adversary to the one-time signature when the signer provides hints? We decided to write Theorem 3.3, which is the foundation of the unforgeability proof of our one-time signature in a general fashion, which encompasses the case with extra hints. The one-more unforgeability proof then boils down to an application of Theorem 3.3.

Theorem 5.4. *The blind signature scheme defined in Fig. 2 verifies blindness and one-more unforgeability.*

For blindness, we have the following:

$$\epsilon_{\mathcal{A}}^{blind} \leqslant \epsilon_{\mathcal{A}}^{ZK(\pi_{\mathsf{enc}})} + \epsilon_{\mathcal{A}}^{ZK(\pi_{\in})} + \epsilon_{\mathcal{A}}^{\mathsf{MLWE}_{m,n,S_\gamma}} + \epsilon_{\mathcal{A}}^{\mathsf{MLWE}_{n+m,m,S_\gamma}}.$$

For One-More Unforgeability, if $\sigma_{\mathbf{s}} \geqslant 2 + q^{1/5}\sqrt{(m+n+3)}$, $\sigma_{\mathbf{y}} \geqslant 2 + q^{1/5}\sqrt{(m+n+3)d}, \sigma' \geqslant 2 + q^{1/5}\sqrt{(m+n+3)\gamma d}$ *and* $\mathcal{A}$ *is an adversary with winning probability* ϵ *against* OMUF*, *then there exists an algorithm* $\mathcal{B}$ *that with rewindable black-box access to* $\mathcal{A}$ *can solve* $\mathsf{MSIS}_{\alpha,5\alpha,B}$ *with winning probability at least* $\frac{\epsilon}{2N}$, *where* $B = 24\kappa_{\in}(d\sigma_{\mathbf{s}} + \sigma_{\mathbf{y}}) + 2B_{\in}$, $B_{\in}$ *is the bound on the norm verification of the membership proof and* $\delta =$. *This statement combined with Lemma 5.3 gives the One-More Unforgeability of the scheme.*

Proof. Blindness.
We define a sequence of games.

G_0: This game is the blindness game Definition 2.10. The adversary sends $\mathsf{pk}_{\mathsf{Server}}$ to the challenger $\mathcal{B}$. The challenger runs UserKeyGen twice. He sends $\mathsf{pk}_0, \mathsf{pk}_1$ to the adversary $\mathcal{A}$. Then, the adversary sends two messages m_0, m_1 of his choice to $\mathcal{B}$, which picks a random bit b. The adversary and the challenger produce $\sigma_0 = \mathsf{BlindSig}(m_0)$ (respectively $\sigma_1 = \mathsf{BlindSig}(m_1)$), and we write $\mathbf{t}_0, t_0', \pi_{\mathsf{enc}}^0, \mathbf{F}_0, \mathbf{f}_0$ (respectively $\mathbf{t}_1, t_1, \pi_{\mathsf{enc}}^1, \mathbf{F}_1, \mathbf{f}_1$) the transcript of their communications. The verification step from the user ensures that the decryption of $\mathbf{F}_0, \mathbf{f}_0$ (respectively $\mathbf{F}_1, \mathbf{f}_1$) is a valid $\mathbf{z}$[7]. The users send (σ_b, σ_{1-b}) to the adversary. The adversary wins if he outputs b.

G_1: This game is the same as the previous one, except the challengers runs the simulator of the zero-knowledge proof π_{enc} to produce $\pi_{\mathsf{enc}}^0, \pi_{\mathsf{enc}}^1$. This game is indistinguishable from G_0 under the zero-knowledge property of π_{enc}.

G_2: This game is the same as the previous one except $\mathbf{t}_0, t_0', \mathbf{t}_1, t_1'$ are replaced with uniformly random samples. This game is indistinguishable from G_1 under $\mathsf{MLWE}_{m,n,S_\gamma}$ and $\mathsf{MLWE}_{n+m,m,S_\gamma}$ by Lemma 4.2.

G_3: This game is the same as the previous one, except $\pi_{\in}^0$ and $\pi_{\in}^1$ are generated using the simulator from the zero-knowledge proof of $\pi_{\in}$. This game is indistinguishable from G_2 under the zero-knowledge property of $\pi_{\in}$. This game is independent of b, and therefore, the advantage of $\mathcal{A}$ against G_4 is 0.

[7] Notice that due to this verification step, our definition of blindness is stronger than honest-signer blindness.

The result follows from summing up the advantages.

One-More Unforgeability.
Let $\mathcal{A}$ be an adversary to the OMUF^* game with winning probability ϵ. We describe an efficient algorithm $\mathcal{B}$ that with rewindable black-box access to $\mathcal{A}$ solves $\mathsf{MSIS}_{\alpha,5\alpha,B}$ with $B = 24\kappa_{\in}(d\sigma_{\mathbf{s}} + \sigma_{\mathbf{y}}) + 2B_{\in}$.

First, $\mathcal{B}$ receives an $\mathsf{MSIS}_{\alpha,5\alpha,B}$ instance $\mathbf{A} \in \mathcal{R}_q^{\alpha\times 5\alpha}$. Then, $\mathcal{B}$ will execute the following instructions:

1. For $1 \leqslant i \leqslant N$, generate $\mathbf{s}_i, \mathbf{y}_i \leftarrow D_{\sigma_{\mathbf{s}}}^{5\alpha} \times D_{\sigma_{\mathbf{y}}}^{5\alpha}$.
2. For $1 \leqslant i \leqslant N$, set $\mathbf{v}_i = \mathbf{A}\mathbf{s}_i$, $\mathbf{w}_i = \mathbf{A}\mathbf{y}_i$ and set $\mathbf{v}_j = \mathbf{v}$.
3. Sample a random seed.
4. Program the PRNG on input seed such that $\mathsf{PRNG}(\mathsf{seed}) = (\mathbf{v}_i, \mathbf{w}_i)_{1\leqslant i\leqslant N}$.
5. Send the public key $(\mathbf{A}, \mathsf{seed})$ to the adversary $\mathcal{A}$.

Notice that since $\mathbf{A}$ is an $\mathsf{MSIS}_{\alpha,5\alpha,B}$ instance, it is uniformly random and the distribution of the public key that the adversary $\mathcal{A}$ receives is identical to OMUF^*. Next, the adversary sends some number ℓ of queries $(\mathbf{t}_i, t'_i, \pi^i_{\mathsf{enc}})$ to $\mathcal{B}$. The algorithm $\mathcal{B}$ computes honest responses $(\mathbf{F}_i, \mathbf{f}_i)$ and sends them to $\mathcal{A}$. The adversary has probability at least ϵ to succeed in producing $\ell + 1$ valid signatures, which he sends to $\mathcal{B}$ if he indeed succeeds.

Next, algorithm $\mathcal{B}$ picks a uniformly random index $1 \leqslant j \leqslant \ell + 1$, and runs the extractor $\mathcal{E}$ from the membership proof upon reception of the j-th signature from $\mathcal{A}$. This way, $\mathcal{B}$ extracts an index i, a message μ, a vector $\mathbf{z}$ and a challenge difference $\bar{c}$ such that $\mathbf{A}\mathbf{z} = \bar{c}(\mu\mathbf{v}_i + \mathbf{w}_i)$. We remind that from key generation, $\mathcal{B}$ also knows $\mathbf{z}' = \bar{c}(\mu\mathbf{s}_i + \mathbf{y}_i)$ which verifies the same equation as the extracted $\mathbf{z}$. Three options are possible:

1. The adversary had an interaction with $\mathcal{B}$ on the public key $\mathbf{v}_i, \mathbf{w}_i$ for the message μ, at the end of which the decryption of $\mathcal{B}$'s response $\mathbf{F}_i, \mathbf{f}_i$ is $\mathbf{z}$.
2. The adversary had an interaction with $\mathcal{B}$ on the public key $\mathbf{v}_i, \mathbf{w}_i$ for any message, at the end of which the decryption of $\mathcal{B}$'s response $\mathbf{F}_i, \mathbf{f}_i$ is not $\mathbf{z}$.
3. The adversary never had an interaction with $\mathcal{B}$ on the public $\mathbf{v}_i, \mathbf{w}_i$.

Since $\mathcal{A}$ had ℓ interactions with $\mathcal{B}$ but managed to produce $\ell + 1$ signatures, at least one of these signatures is in option 2) or 3). With probability at least $1/(\ell + 1) \geqslant 1/N$, option 2) or 3) happened, otherwise $\mathcal{B}$ fails and aborts[8].

[8] It seems that $\mathcal{A}$ could send directly the index of the unexpected signature to $\mathcal{B}$. This would save a factor $1/N$ in the winning probability of $\mathcal{B}$ while seemingly keeping the hardness of the forgery the same.

Option 3) is harder for the adversary than option 2), so we will only deal with the latter. Let us assume that $i, \mu, \mathbf{z}, \bar{c}$ are from option 2). We assume that the adversary $\mathcal{A}$ is able to collect the masks $\mathbf{Y} + \mathbf{r}_i\mathbf{s}_i^T, \mathbf{Y}' + \mathbf{e}\mathbf{s}_i^T, \mathbf{y}'' + e'\mathbf{s}_i^T$. We gather these 3 equations in the form $\boldsymbol{\omega} + \mathbf{P}\mathbf{s}_i = \mathbf{x}$, where $\boldsymbol{\omega}, \mathbf{x} \in \mathcal{R}_q^{5\alpha(m+n+1)}$, and $\mathbf{P}$ is the matrix of the linear function that depends on $\mathbf{r}, \mathbf{e}, e'$ such that $\mathbf{P}\mathbf{s} = (s_1\mathbf{r}\ s_2\mathbf{r}\ \ldots\ s_1\mathbf{e}\ s_2\mathbf{e}\ \ldots\ s_1e'\ s_2e'\ \ldots)$. Both $\mathbf{P}$ and $\mathbf{x}$ are known to the adversary. Since the adversary is able to reconstruct $\mathbf{F}_i, \mathbf{f}_i$ from $\mathbf{X}$, we claim that this assumption is without loss of generality.

The vector $\mathbf{z} - \mathbf{z}'$ (remind that $\mathbf{z}' = \bar{c}(\mu\mathbf{s}_i + \mathbf{y}_i)$ is informally $\mathcal{B}$'s signature of μ times $\bar{c}$) is $\mathcal{B}$'s candidate for $\mathsf{MSIS}_{\alpha,5\alpha,B}$. Indeed,

$$\mathbf{A}(\mathbf{z} - \mathbf{z}') = \bar{c}(\mu\mathbf{v}_i + \mathbf{w}_i) - \bar{c}(\mu\mathbf{A}\mathbf{s}_i + \mathbf{A}\mathbf{y}_i) = 0.$$

Remains to prove i) that the probability that $\mathbf{z} = \mathbf{z}'$ is not negligibly close to 1, and ii) that $\mathbf{z} - \mathbf{z}'$ is shorter than B. First, for i), we introduce the following lattice coset

$$\Lambda = \left\{ (\mathbf{s}, \mathbf{y}, \boldsymbol{\omega}) \in \mathcal{R}_q^{5\alpha} \times \mathcal{R}_q^{5\alpha} \times \mathcal{R}_q^{(n+m+1)5\alpha}, \left\{ \begin{aligned} \mathbf{A}\mathbf{s} &= \mathbf{v}_i \\ \mathbf{A}\mathbf{y} &= \mathbf{w}_i \\ \mu_i\mathbf{s} + \mathbf{y}_i &= \mathbf{z}_i \\ \mathbf{P}\mathbf{s}^T + \boldsymbol{\omega} &= \mathbf{x} \end{aligned} \right\} \right\}.$$

We claim that all of $\mathcal{A}$'s information on $(\mathbf{s}_i, \mathbf{y}_i)$ is contained in the statement that $(\mathbf{s}_i, \mathbf{y}_i, \boldsymbol{\omega})$ are drawn from χ, which is $D_{\sigma_\mathbf{s}}^{5\alpha} \times D_{\sigma_\mathbf{y}}^{5\alpha} \times D_{\sigma'}^{(m+n+1)5\alpha}$ restricted to Λ. Let $(\mathbf{s}'_i, \mathbf{y}'_i, \boldsymbol{\omega}')$ be random variables following χ, and let $\boldsymbol{\zeta}(\mathbf{s}'_i, \mathbf{y}'_i, \boldsymbol{\omega}') = \mu\mathbf{s}'_i + \mathbf{y}'_i$. Notice that for some $\boldsymbol{\zeta}^* \in \mathcal{R}_q^{5\alpha}$, there can be only one tuple $(\mathbf{s}^*, \mathbf{y}^*, \boldsymbol{\omega}^*)$ in the support of χ such that $\boldsymbol{\zeta}^* = \mu\mathbf{s}^* + \mathbf{y}^*$. We have

$$\begin{aligned} \mathbb{P}(\mathbf{z} = \mathbf{z}') &= \mathbb{P}(\mathbf{z} = \boldsymbol{\zeta}(\mathbf{s}_i, \mathbf{y}_i, \boldsymbol{\omega}_i)) \\ &\leqslant \mathbb{P}(\boldsymbol{\zeta}(\mathbf{s}'_i, \mathbf{y}'_i, \boldsymbol{\omega}') = \boldsymbol{\zeta}(\mathbf{s}_i, \mathbf{y}_i, \boldsymbol{\omega}_i)) \\ &\leqslant \mathbb{P}((\mathbf{s}'_i, \mathbf{y}'_i, \boldsymbol{\omega}'_i) = (\mathbf{s}_i, \mathbf{y}_i, \boldsymbol{\omega}_i)) \\ &\leqslant \chi(\mathbf{s}_i, \mathbf{y}_i, \boldsymbol{\omega}_i). \end{aligned}$$

To finish the proof of i), we prove that

$$\max_{(\mathbf{s}'_i, \mathbf{y}'_i, \boldsymbol{\omega}'_i)} \chi(\mathbf{s}'_i, \mathbf{y}'_i, \boldsymbol{\omega}'_i) \leqslant \delta, \tag{26}$$

for some constant δ that is not negligibly close to 1. This fact follows from Theorem 3.3 applied to the rotations of the matrices $\mathbf{A}$, and

$$\mathbf{M} = \begin{bmatrix} \mathbf{I}_{5\alpha} \\ -\mu\mathbf{I}_{5\alpha} \\ -\mathbf{P} \end{bmatrix}.$$

The reason is we have

$$\chi(\mathbf{s}_i^*, \mathbf{y}_i^*, \boldsymbol{\omega}_i^*) = \frac{\rho_{\sigma_{\mathbf{s}}}(\mathbf{s}_i^*)\rho_{\sigma_{\mathbf{y}}}(\mathbf{y}_i^*)\rho_{\sigma'}(\boldsymbol{\omega}_i^*)}{\sum_{\mathbf{z}=(\mathbf{z}_1,\mathbf{z}_2,\mathbf{z}_3)\in\Lambda} \rho_{\sigma_{\mathbf{s}}}(\mathbf{z}_1)\rho_{\sigma_{\mathbf{y}}}(\mathbf{z}_2)\rho_{\sigma'}(\mathbf{z}_3)}.$$

Now, note that for every $\mathbf{u} \in \Lambda^{\perp}(\mathbf{A})$, the vector $\mathbf{Mu}$ is such that $(\mathbf{s}_i^*, \mathbf{y}_i^*, \boldsymbol{\omega}_i^*) + \mathbf{Mu} \in \Lambda$. This means that $\mathsf{rot}(M)$ is a valid matrix for Theorem 3.3. If we take $\sigma_{\mathbf{s}} \geqslant 2 + q^{1/5}\sqrt{(m+n+3)}$, $\sigma_{\mathbf{y}} \geqslant 2 + q^{1/5}\sqrt{(m+n+3)d}$ and $\sigma' \geqslant 2 + q^{1/5}\sqrt{(m+n+3)\gamma d}$, then Theorem 3.3 ensures $\delta \leqslant 1/2$.

We now prove ii): $\mathbf{z}$ has the length of the extracted vector from the set membership proof. With $B_{\in}$ the bound on the norm verification of the membership proof, we have $\|\mathbf{z}\| \leqslant 2B_{\in}$. On the other hand, $\mathcal{B}$'s private signature $\mathbf{z}' = \bar{c}(\mu\mathbf{s}_i + \mathbf{y}_i)$ is such that $\|\mathbf{z}'\| \leqslant 24\kappa_{\in}(d\sigma_{\mathbf{s}} + \sigma_{\mathbf{y}})$, where $\kappa_{\in}$ is a bound on the Hamming weight of the challenge difference $\bar{c}$ of the membership proof. Pluging together the inequalities yields ii), which in turn completes the One-More Unforgeability proof. □

Remark on Standard Deviation Bounds. Theorem 3.3 gives lower bounds on the standard deviation of the secrets such that the maximum probability of the secret distribution (which is a multi-dimensionnal Gaussian) is 1/2. As it turns out in our case, there is another lower bound on the standard deviations $\sigma_{\mathbf{s}}$ and $\sigma_{\mathbf{y}}$ given by the smoothing parameter for trapdoor sampling, which is greater than the one for one-more unforgeability. Therefore, the actual maximum probability is lower than 1/2, which gives us some more room to decrease the standard deviation σ' of the hints. We leave this remark as a possible optimization of the parameters, that would slightly reduce the communication cost of the blind signature.

6 Parameter Selection

In this section we instantiate our blind signature for at most $N = 2^{18}$ signing queries and aim for 128-bit security (see Fig. 3 and 4). To this end, we measure the hardness of MSIS and MLWE with the root Hermite factor δ and aim for $\delta \approx 1.0043$. For computing hardness of the latter problem, we use the LWE Estimator by Albrecht et al. [APS15]. We refer to [LNS21a, Section 3.3] and [LNS21b, Appendix C] for a detailed explanation on the parameter selection for π_{enc} and $\pi_{\in}$ respectively.

Parameter	Definition	Instantiation
N	maximum number of signing queries	2^{18}
d	dimension of the ring $\mathcal{R}$	128
q	modulus for the blind signature	$\approx 2^{64}$
q'	modulus for the encryption	$\approx 2^{128}$
α	height of the matrix $\mathbf{A} = [\mathbf{A}'\vert\mathbf{A}'\mathbf{R} - \mathbf{G}]$	21
σ_y	standard deviation for sampling $\mathbf{y}$	$\approx 2^{30}$
σ_s	standard deviation for sampling $\mathbf{s}$	$\approx 2^{30}$
n	height of the encryption public key matrix $\mathbf{B}$	80
m	width of the encryption public key matrix $\mathbf{B}$	40
γ	maximum coefficient of the $\mathbf{x}, \mathbf{r}$ and errors $\mathbf{e}, e'$	4
p	additional prime number, less than q', used for encryption	$\approx 2^{43}$
σ'	standard deviation used to sample maskings $\mathbf{Y}, \mathbf{Y}'$ and $\mathbf{y}''$	$\approx 2^{26}$

Fig. 3. Definition and concrete numbers for parameters used in the blind signature construction.

Dimensions and Moduli. Firstly, we choose the ring dimension $d = 128$ and moduli $(q, q') = (\approx 2^{64}, \approx 2^{128})$[9]. Next, we want to make sure that $\mathbf{A} = [\mathbf{A}'|\mathbf{A}'\mathbf{R} - \mathbf{G}]$ is indistinguishable from a random matrix over $\mathcal{R}_q$. Hence, we choose $\alpha = 21$ such that $\mathsf{MLWE}_{\alpha,\alpha,S_1}$ is hard. Then, in order to apply Micciancio-Peikert trapdoor sampling [MP12], we need the standard deviations σ_s, σ_y to be at least $2(s_1(\mathbf{R}) + 1)\sqrt{\lceil q^{2/3} \rceil + 1}$ where s_1 is the operator norm. Similarly as in [dPLS18, Section 2.6], we found experimentally that for a structured matrix $\mathbf{R} \in S_1^{2\alpha \times 3\alpha}$, $s_1(\mathbf{R}) \leqslant 6\sqrt{\alpha d}$ with a high probability. Note that the other lower bound for σ_y, σ_s in Theorem 5.4 is smaller than the one necessary for trapdoor sampling. Hence, in this scenario we will set $\sigma := \sigma_s = \sigma_y = 13\sqrt{\alpha d\left(\lceil q^{2/3} \rceil + 1\right)}$.

Encryption Scheme. We now focus on parameters for the encryption scheme. In order to ensure the property that both the public key and the ciphertext are indistinguishable from random, we need $\mathsf{MLWE}_{m,n-m,S_\gamma}$ and $\mathsf{MLWE}_{n+1,m,S_\gamma}$ to be hard. We set $n = 2m$ and thus these two problems are almost equally hard. Since $q' \approx 2^{128}$, we pick $(n, m) = (80, 40)$ and $\gamma = 4$. Then we set $p = 12d\sigma_s + 12\sigma_y$ and $\sigma' = 2 + q^{1/5}\sqrt{(m + n + 3)}\gamma d$. For such a large $q' \approx 2^{128}$, correctness conditions from Lemma 5.1 follow easily.

Verifiable Encryption. We turn to computing the proof sizes for π_{enc} and $\pi_{\in}$. Let us focus on the former one first. Let $\tilde{n} := m + (n + 1) + 1$ be the

[9] More specifically, we choose $q \approx 2^{64}$ for which $X^d + 1$ splits into quadratic terms modulo q. This makes sure the one-out-of-many proof $\pi_{\in}$ from [LNS21b] does not need any repetitions.

number polynomials in the vector $(\mathbf{r}, \mathbf{e}, e', \mu)$ and $\tilde{\alpha} = 2\gamma + 1$[10]. Then, in order to prove π_{enc} (see Sect. 2.6), we apply the framework from [LNS21a]. As discussed in [LNS21a, Section 3.3], the proof with soundness error $1/q' \approx 2^{-128}$, i.e. no repetitions, has size upper-bounded by:

$$(\tilde{n} + \tilde{\kappa} + \tilde{\alpha} + 1)d \log q' + (\tilde{\lambda} + \tilde{n} + \tilde{\kappa} + \tilde{\alpha})d \log(12\mathfrak{s}) \text{ bits}$$

The standard deviation[11]. $\mathfrak{s}$ is set as $\mathfrak{s} = d\sqrt{(\tilde{\lambda} + \tilde{n} + \tilde{\kappa} + \tilde{\alpha})d}$. Then, $\tilde{\kappa}$ and $\tilde{\lambda}$ are chosen such that $\mathsf{MSIS}_{\tilde{\kappa}, \tilde{\lambda}+\tilde{n}+\tilde{\kappa}+\tilde{\alpha}, 8d\beta}$ and $\mathsf{MLWE}_{\tilde{n}+\tilde{\kappa}+\tilde{\alpha}, \tilde{\lambda}, \chi^d}$ are hard[12], where $\beta = \mathfrak{s}\sqrt{2(\tilde{\lambda} + \tilde{n} + \tilde{\kappa} + \tilde{\alpha})d}$ and χ is the distribution on $\{-1, 0, 1\}$ where ± 1 both have probability 5/16 and 0 has probability 6/16. To further reduce the proof size, we apply the Dilithium compression described in [LNS21a, Appendix B].

Communication Complexity. In order to compute total communication size, we calculate the total size of public key and ciphertexts sent by both the user $\mathcal{U}$ and the signer $\mathcal{S}$. Note that $\mathcal{U}$ sends $m + n + 1$ elements in $\mathcal{R}_q$. On the other hand, $\mathcal{S}$ outputs back $5\alpha(n + 1)$ polynomials. Hence, the total communication size, excluding π_{enc}, is

$$(m + (5\alpha + 1)(n + 1)) \log q' \text{ bits.}$$

Signature Size. Finally, to estimate the signature size, we need to look at the one-out-of-many proof $\pi_{\in}$. Let us set $m' = 2$, i.e. $(\log q)^{m'+1} = 2^{18} = N$. As described in [LNS21b, Appendix C], the proof size of $\pi_{\in}$ can be bounded by:

$$(\kappa' + \alpha + 2m' + 2)d \log q + 5\alpha d \log(12\mathfrak{s}') + (\kappa' + \lambda' + \alpha + 2m' + 2)d \log(12\mathfrak{s}'')$$

bits. We set $\mathfrak{s}' = d(d+1)\sigma\sqrt{10\alpha d}$ and $\mathfrak{s}'' = d\sqrt{(\kappa' + \lambda' + \alpha + 2m' + 2)d}$. Then, κ' and λ' are chosen such that $\mathsf{MSIS}_{\kappa', \kappa'+\lambda'+\alpha+2m'+2, 8d\beta''}$ and $\mathsf{MLWE}_{\kappa'+\alpha+2m'+2, \lambda', \chi^d}$ are hard where $\beta'' = \mathfrak{s}''\sqrt{2(\kappa' + \lambda' + \alpha + 2m' + 2)d}$. Eventually, in order to ensure one-more-unforgeability, we check that $\mathsf{MSIS}_{\alpha, 5\alpha, 2\mathfrak{s}'\sqrt{2(\kappa'+\lambda'+\alpha+2m'+2)d}}$ is a hard problem. As before, we apply the Dilithium compression technique when computing the signature/proof size.

Reducing the Public Key Size. We observe that the public key contains the matrix $\mathbf{A}'\mathbf{R}$ which cannot be generated from the seed. It consists of $3\alpha^2$

[10] Intuitively, $\tilde{\alpha}$ represents how many garbage polynomials we need to prove that coefficients a polynomial are exactly between $-\gamma$ and γ. For example, if one wants to prove ternary coefficients, we need three garbage polynomials.

[11] For simplicity, we neglect the size of a challenge polynomial since it has a negligible impact on the total proof size.

[12] Actually, the zero-knowledge property of the protocol in [LNS21a] reduces to the so-called Extended-MLWE problem. However, as argued in [LNS21a], this problem should still be almost as hard as the plain MLWE.

Public key	Secret key	Signature	Communication
1.3MB	75KB	150KB	16MB

Fig. 4. Public key, user secret key, signature sizes and communication complexity of our blind signature scheme.

polynomials in $\mathcal{R}_q$ and for parameters selected above, the total public key size is above 1 MB as presented in Fig. 4. In order to reduce the public key size, we apply the technique by Lyubashevsky et al. [LNPS21] where one can decrease the value of α at the cost of increasing the ring dimension d[13]. Then, one observes that the equations over $\mathcal{R}_q$ which we are interested in, can be equivalently written over the ring $\mathbb{Z}_q[X]/(X^{128}+1)$ and then proven using e.g. [ALS20, LNS21a]. However, as a drawback of having a large ring dimension, we would obtain slightly larger signatures and communication complexity.

Acknowledgement. We would like to thank anonymous reviewers for the useful feedback. This work was supported by the EU H2020 ERC Project 101002845 PLAZA.

References

[ABB20] Alkeilani Alkadri, N., El Bansarkhani, R., Buchmann, J.: BLAZE: practical lattice-based blind signatures for privacy-preserving applications. In: Bonneau, J., Heninger, N. (eds.) FC 2020. LNCS, vol. 12059, pp. 484–502. Springer, Cham (2020). https://doi.org/10.1007/978-3-030-51280-4_26

[ALS20] Attema, T., Lyubashevsky, V., Seiler, G.: Practical product proofs for lattice commitments. In: Micciancio, D., Ristenpart, T. (eds.) CRYPTO 2020. LNCS, vol. 12171, pp. 470–499. Springer, Cham (2020). https://doi.org/10.1007/978-3-030-56880-1_17

[APS15] Albrecht, M.R., Player, R., Scott, S.: On the concrete hardness of learning with errors. Cryptology ePrint Archive, Report 2015/046 (2015). https://eprint.iacr.org/2015/046

[AR04] Aharonov, D., Regev, O.: Lattice problems in NP cap coNP. In: FOCS, pp. 362–371. IEEE Computer Society (2004)

[ASY21] Agrawal, S., Stehlé, D., Yadav, A.: Towards practical and round-optimal lattice-based threshold and blind signatures. IACR Cryptology ePrint Archive, p. 381 (2021)

[Ban93] Banaszczyk, W.: New bounds in some transference theorems in the geometry of numbers. Math. Ann. **296**(1), 625–635 (1993)

[BLL+15] Bai, S., Langlois, A., Lepoint, T., Stehlé, D., Steinfeld, R.: Improved security proofs in lattice-based cryptography: using the Rényi divergence rather than the statistical distance. In: Iwata, T., Cheon, J.H. (eds.) ASIACRYPT 2015. LNCS, vol. 9452, pp. 3–24. Springer, Heidelberg (2015). https://doi.org/10.1007/978-3-662-48797-6_1

[13] For instance, when $\alpha = 1$ and $d = 4096$, the public key has size $\approx 300\,\text{KB}$.

[BLL+21] Benhamouda, F., Lepoint, T., Loss, J., Orrù, M., Raykova, M.: On the (in)security of ROS. In: Canteaut, A., Standaert, F.-X. (eds.) EUROCRYPT 2021. LNCS, vol. 12696, pp. 33–53. Springer, Cham (2021). https://doi.org/10.1007/978-3-030-77870-5_2

[BLS19] Bootle, J., Lyubashevsky, V., Seiler, G.: Algebraic techniques for short(er) exact lattice-based zero-knowledge proofs. In: Boldyreva, A., Micciancio, D. (eds.) CRYPTO 2019. LNCS, vol. 11692, pp. 176–202. Springer, Cham (2019). https://doi.org/10.1007/978-3-030-26948-7_7

[Cha82] Chaum, D.: Blind signatures for untraceable payments. In: CRYPTO, pp. 199–203. Plenum Press, New York (1982)

[DKL+18] Ducas, L., et al.: CRYSTALS-dilithium: a lattice-based digital signature scheme. IACR Trans. Cryptogr. Hardw. Embed. Syst. **2018**(1), 238–268 (2018)

[dPLS18] del Pino, R., Lyubashevsky, V., Seiler, G.: Lattice-based group signatures and zero-knowledge proofs of automorphism stability. In: ACM Conference on Computer and Communications Security, pp. 574–591. ACM (2018)

[ENS20] Esgin, M.F., Nguyen, N.K., Seiler, G.: Practical exact proofs from lattices: new techniques to exploit fully-splitting rings. In: Moriai, S., Wang, H. (eds.) ASIACRYPT 2020. LNCS, vol. 12492, pp. 259–288. Springer, Cham (2020). https://doi.org/10.1007/978-3-030-64834-3_9

[ESLL19] Esgin, M.F., Steinfeld, R., Liu, J.K., Liu, D.: Lattice-based zero-knowledge proofs: new techniques for shorter and faster constructions and applications. In: Boldyreva, A., Micciancio, D. (eds.) CRYPTO 2019. LNCS, vol. 11692, pp. 115–146. Springer, Cham (2019). https://doi.org/10.1007/978-3-030-26948-7_5

[EZS+19] Esgin, M.F., Zhao, R.K., Steinfeld, R., Liu, J.K., Liu, D.: MatRiCT: efficient, scalable and post-quantum blockchain confidential transactions protocol. In: CCS, pp. 567–584. ACM (2019)

[GK15] Groth, J., Kohlweiss, M.: One-out-of-many proofs: or how to leak a secret and spend a coin. In: Oswald, E., Fischlin, M. (eds.) EUROCRYPT 2015. LNCS, vol. 9057, pp. 253–280. Springer, Heidelberg (2015). https://doi.org/10.1007/978-3-662-46803-6_9

[GPV08] Gentry, C., Peikert, C., Vaikuntanathan, V.: Trapdoors for hard lattices and new cryptographic constructions. In: STOC, pp. 197–206 (2008)

[HKLN20] Hauck, E., Kiltz, E., Loss, J., Nguyen, N.K.: Lattice-based blind signatures, revisited. In: Micciancio, D., Ristenpart, T. (eds.) CRYPTO 2020. LNCS, vol. 12171, pp. 500–529. Springer, Cham (2020). https://doi.org/10.1007/978-3-030-56880-1_18

[LM18] Lyubashevsky, V., Micciancio, D.: Asymptotically efficient lattice-based digital signatures. J. Cryptol. **31**(3), 774–797 (2018). Preliminare version appeared in TCC 2008

[LNPS21] Lyubashevsky, V., Nguyen, N.K., Plançon, M., Seiler, G.: Shorter lattice-based group signatures via "almost free" encryption and other optimizations. In: ASIACRYPT. LNCS, vol. 13093, pp. 218–248. Springer, Cham (2021). https://doi.org/10.1007/978-3-030-92068-5_8

[LNS20] Lyubashevsky, V., Nguyen, N.K., Seiler, G.: Practical lattice-based zero-knowledge proofs for integer relations. In: CCS, pp. 1051–1070. ACM (2020)

[LNS21a] Lyubashevsky, V., Nguyen, N.K., Seiler, G.: Shorter lattice-based zero-knowledge proofs via one-time commitments. In: Garay, J.A. (ed.) PKC 2021. LNCS, vol. 12710, pp. 215–241. Springer, Cham (2021). https://doi.org/10.1007/978-3-030-75245-3_9

[LNS21b] Lyubashevsky, V., Nguyen, N.K., Seiler, G.: SMILE: set membership from ideal lattices with applications to ring signatures and confidential transactions. In: Malkin, T., Peikert, C. (eds.) CRYPTO 2021. LNCS, vol. 12826, pp. 611–640. Springer, Cham (2021). https://doi.org/10.1007/978-3-030-84245-1_21

[LS15] Langlois, A., Stehlé, D.: Worst-case to average-case reductions for module lattices. Des. Codes Crypt. **75**(3), 565–599 (2014). https://doi.org/10.1007/s10623-014-9938-4

[Lyu12] Lyubashevsky, V.: Lattice signatures without trapdoors. In: Pointcheval, D., Johansson, T. (eds.) EUROCRYPT 2012. LNCS, vol. 7237, pp. 738–755. Springer, Heidelberg (2012). https://doi.org/10.1007/978-3-642-29011-4_43

[MP12] Micciancio, D., Peikert, C.: Trapdoors for lattices: simpler, tighter, faster, smaller. In: Pointcheval, D., Johansson, T. (eds.) EUROCRYPT 2012. LNCS, vol. 7237, pp. 700–718. Springer, Heidelberg (2012). https://doi.org/10.1007/978-3-642-29011-4_41

[MR07] Micciancio, D., Regev, O.: Worst-case to average-case reductions based on Gaussian measures. SIAM J. Comput. **37**(1), 267–302 (2007)

[PFH+17] Prest, T., et al.: FALCON. Technical report, National Institute of Standards and Technology (2017). https://csrc.nist.gov/projects/post-quantum-cryptography/round-1-submissions

[PS00] Pointcheval, D., Stern, J.: Security arguments for digital signatures and blind signatures. J. Cryptol. **13**(3), 361–396 (2000)

[Rüc10] Rückert, M.: Lattice-based blind signatures. In: Abe, M. (ed.) ASIACRYPT 2010. LNCS, vol. 6477, pp. 413–430. Springer, Heidelberg (2010). https://doi.org/10.1007/978-3-642-17373-8_24

[YAZ+19] Yang, R., Au, M.H., Zhang, Z., Xu, Q., Yu, Z., Whyte, W.: Efficient lattice-based zero-knowledge arguments with standard soundness: construction and applications. In: Boldyreva, A., Micciancio, D. (eds.) CRYPTO 2019. LNCS, vol. 11692, pp. 147–175. Springer, Cham (2019). https://doi.org/10.1007/978-3-030-26948-7_6

Author Index

Printed in the United States
by Baker & Taylor Publisher Services

Printed in the United States
by Baker & Taylor Publisher Services